THE FONTANA DICTIONARY OF
MODERN THOUGHT

THE FONTANA DICTIONARY OF
MODERN THOUGHT

Edited by
Alan Bullock and Oliver Stallybrass

Collins
St. James's Place, London
1977

William Collins Sons & Co Ltd
London · Glasgow · Sydney · Auckland
Toronto · Johannesburg

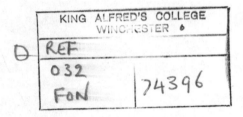
First published 1977
© Alan Bullock and Oliver Stallybrass 1977
ISBN 0 00 216149-4
Set in Times
Made and Printed in Great Britain by
William Collins Sons & Co Ltd Glasgow

Preface

The idea of a dictionary of modern thought springs from the recognition of two facts. The first is that all of us are ignorant of whole areas of modern thought. In an age of specialization this may be as true of a Nobel Laureate as it is of a college freshman – a point driven home in a letter written to one of the editors by one of the Nobel Laureate contributors to this volume, Sir Peter Medawar: 'I am looking forward immensely to the publication of the Dictionary, because there are a whole lot of things I should like to look up myself.' The second fact is that most of us never quite give up the attempt, however sporadic, to explore our areas of ignorance. But as soon as we venture outside our own territory we encounter a formidable barrier of language, of unfamiliar terms and concepts, and of unexplained allusions that puzzle and frustrate us.

Where do we go for help? An ordinary dictionary helps a little, but its definitions are necessarily brief and formal, and make no attempt to set the words defined in their intellectual, historical, or cultural context. Also, an ordinary dictionary has to be comprehensive in its coverage, and must therefore include thousands of words familiar to us all. If, on the other hand, we turn to an encyclopaedia – which for most of us will mean a visit to a library – we may need to thread our way through a vast amount of irrelevant material. The present volume steers a middle course between an ordinary dictionary and an encyclopaedia. It takes some 4,000 key terms from across the whole range of modern thought, sets them within their context, and offers short explanatory accounts (anything from ten to a thousand words) written by experts, but in language as simple as can be used without *over*-simplification or distortion. All this is done within a single pair of covers; but the reader who wishes to pursue an enquiry further is enabled to do so, not only by numerous cross-references, but by the carefully selected reading-lists which have been provided in appropriate cases.

What, in the context of this book, is meant by 'modern' and what is meant by 'thought'?

By 'modern' is meant, in broad terms, 'twentieth-century', with the emphasis on new or recent words and phrases – CYBERNETICS, STRUCTURALISM, GENERATIVE GRAMMAR, PEER GROUP, DOUBLE HELIX – and on familiar words which have acquired a special meaning: BEAT (as in *beat generation*), CREEP (in PHYSICS), GATE (in a COMPUTER), MODEL (in a wide range of contexts). (Throughout the dictionary, small capital letters indicate that there is an entry on the term in question; subsidiary terms are picked out in *italic*.) Some time-honoured terms have, however, been included, either because of their continuing importance (PHILOSOPHY supplies a number of examples) or because the subject covered by the term has acquired new ramifications. Most of us, for example, have an approximate idea of what GEOGRAPHY is; few of us would be able to distinguish clearly and succinctly between its various branches (including the new field of *perception geography*), as is done here by Professor Jean Gottmann. That class of distinction is one of the things this book is about.

If 'modern' is used in a flexible sense, so, or even more so, is 'thought'. Does a painter or a composer or a poet 'think'? T. S. Eliot's phrase 'felt thought' suggests one answer; the same author's DISSOCIATION OF SENSIBILITY suggests another. But, whether or not the artist thinks as he practises his art, he, or more probably the art critic, unquestionably does so the moment either of them starts theorizing about it. Hence the scope of this dictionary includes literature, music, and the visual arts as well as, more obviously, PHILOSOPHY, RELIGION, MATHEMATICS, PSYCHOLOGY, and the whole range of HUMANITIES, SOCIAL SCIENCES, and NATURAL SCIENCES, together with those aspects of TECHNOLOGY which are of wide general interest. Included, moreover, are terms with a wide variety of relationships to thought: not only IDEAS, CONCEPTS, schools and tools of thought, but – for example – events and phenomena which have *influenced* people's thoughts, inventions which are the *product* of thought (and may in turn affect our thinking), and even terms which might well be regarded as symptoms of *anti*- or *counter*-thought, but which are, for better or worse, part of the intellectual climate of our age.

Fields of study, movements, schools, theories, -isms and -ologies of every kind, concepts, technical terms, historical events and the places associated with them, names of organizations – all these are represented in this dictionary. Here are some examples, chosen largely at random, of the kind of question it can answer. What was the BAUHAUS and why was it important? What does an ENDOCRINOLOGIST do or study? What is STRUCTURALISM? Or ROLE THEORY? What distinguishes VERTICAL AND LATERAL THINKING? What is the difference between PSYCHIATRY and PSYCHOANALYSIS? Between SOCIAL SCIENCES, SOCIAL STUDIES, and SOCIOLOGY? SOCIAL REALISM and SOCIALIST REALISM? A SHAME CULTURE and a GUILT CULTURE? HARDWARE and SOFTWARE, LINGUISTICS and LINGUISTIC PHILOSOPHY, COLLAGE and DÉCOLLAGE? Was it Freud or Jung who distinguished between INTROVERTS and EXTROVERTS? What is CONCRETE ART (MUSIC, POETRY), CONCEPTUAL ART, KINETIC ART, TOTAL ART? Which is the smallest: ATOM, ELECTRON, MOLECULE, NUCLEUS – or is the question absurd? Who coined the term THEATRE OF THE ABSURD? MERITOCRACY? EPISTEMICS? What is meant by

ALIENATION, ATONALISM, CHARISMA, FEEDBACK, the GENETIC CODE, MARGINAL UTILITY, PSYCHEDELIC, SPRUNG RHYTHM, WELTANSCHAUUNG? These are only a few of the thousands of questions which this book attempts to answer.

Some readers may be curious to know how this dictionary came into being. It sprang, more or less fully formed, into the brain of Alan Bullock when, reading an article in the *Times Literary Supplement* while on holiday in Portugal, he encountered the word HERMENEUTICS and was uncertain what it meant. Surely there was a need for a suitable dictionary, preferably compendious enough to take with one even on holiday? He started jotting down words as they occurred to him; when he had accumulated two or three hundred he sent the list, and an outline of what he had in mind, to his agents, Curtis Brown Ltd. Here Andrew Best fastened on to the idea, persuaded him to take on a partner, and suggested Oliver Stallybrass. The three met, and by the summer of 1971 the book was under way.

We (the two editors) began, purely as a measure of convenience, by dividing 'thought' into some twenty main areas. Sharing these between us, we set about compiling lists of terms for inclusion, scouring for the purpose every existing dictionary and encyclopaedia, both general and special, that we could lay hands on. Many terms were included on several lists, either because they possessed several distinct meanings, or because of overlap between subjects. We exchanged lists, ideas, and (when we neglected the dictionary in favour of other commitments) guilt-feelings – by letter, over the telephone, or at meetings held mostly in railway buffets or the obscurer areas of august national institutions. (At a later stage, an office was set up in the Collins warehouse near King's Cross, with a secretary, a telephone, copying facilities, and an ever-growing tonnage of files; when the warehouse was sold, sanctuary was granted by Collins Liturgical Publications over Hatchard's bookshop in Piccadilly.) To a remarkable extent, our views coincided. Even more remarkably, perhaps, no disagreement has ever endangered what has steadily progressed from a working partnership to a friendship.

The next stage (in practice, of course, the stages constantly overlapped) was to send copies of our subject-lists – later, of a single consolidated list – to one or more of six consultant editors chosen for their wide range of interests and knowledge (Sir Isaiah Berlin, Sir Peter Medawar, Professors Daniel Bell, Jerome Bruner, and John Ziman, and Mr John Willett; Professors Wilfred Beckerman, Leo Labedz, and Robert Lekachman gave similar help a little later). As we had expected, some of our initial lists were roughly handled; somewhat to our surprise (and, on the whole, gratification), this seemed to happen fairly impartially as between subject-areas where we knew we were ignorant and those where we thought we knew a little.

In addition to checking and revising our lists, the consultant editors gave invaluable help in suggesting contributors. In some fields people were found who were both willing and competent to cover a wide range of topics; in others it proved necessary to break down the original lists into sub-areas and sometimes sub-sub-areas. Either way, it is safe to assert that every contributor is highly qualified, in some cases uniquely qualified, to write on his or her respective topics. (The only exceptions are that each editor, in addition to writing entries in areas where he can claim a reasonable prior degree of knowledge, has also, in order to fill last-minute gaps, written on subjects in which he makes no pretence at expertise. Such entries are very few, mostly short, and to the best of our belief accurate as far as they go.) Furthermore, every entry has been read, not only by both editors, but also by at least one of the consultant editors.

Many contributors suggested further terms for inclusion; occasionally they recommended omissions. Whether, after discussion, they agreed to take on 2 or 200 items, our procedure was the same. We allocated the contributor in question a certain number of words (within a total originally fixed at 300,000), and provided him or her with a detailed 'briefing', a batch of sample entries from those already received, and, usually, the latest version of that shifting sand-dune, the master list of headings. Within certain limits, however, the contributor was free to decide how the material could most effectively be organized; whether, for example, if he had been given 100 terms and 10,000 words, to write 100 entries of 100 words each (a most unlikely answer), or 8 entries of 1,000 words, 2 of 550, and 90 of 10 (equally improbable); or whether, perhaps, to write only 60 actual entries, of varying lengths, the other 40 terms being explained *within* these 60 entries, with appropriate cross-references. The varying solutions account for certain apparent anomalies in the space devoted to subjects of comparable scope: one entry may explain only the term which stands at its head, while another deals with half a dozen more *en passant*.

In every respect, indeed, contributors have been allowed the maximum freedom compatible with the requisite degree of uniformity and consistency in presentation. All editorial changes – mostly cuts and short cuts dictated by the need for economy in space – have been approved by the contributors; in the rare instances of a substantial editorial *addition*, the editor's initials follow those of the contributor. The juxtaposition of two or more sets of initials, with an asterisk, denotes an editorial fusion of separate contributions written, from different points of view, mainly or entirely by those indicated; in such cases, responsibility for the entry rests with the editors.

Quite the hardest task in compiling this dictionary has been that of keeping it within bounds – and hence within the purchasing power of the 'common reader' so highly regarded by that great lexicographer, Samuel Johnson. The original intention was to include full-scale entries not only on the key terms but also on the key figures of modern thought, from Darwin, Marx, and Freud down to Chomsky and Lévi-Strauss. Most reluctantly, we have had to confine ourselves to making cross-references from individual names to the various headings – including cognate terms such as DARWINISM, FREUDIAN, etc. – under which they are mentioned. Virtually all of the 2,000 or so names that occur have for completeness' sake been cross-referenced in this way; it should be emphasized that not all are of equal importance, that some may be important in areas other than those where they are mentioned, and that the preponderance of writers and artists means merely that it is harder to write about the arts than about the sciences without frequent reference to individuals.

One other restriction needs to be mentioned: for practical reasons, and because we have European and American readers principally in mind, we have limited ourselves to modern Western thought, except for a handful of entries on the major religions of the world, and on systems, such as MAOISM or ZEN, which have become part of the Western cultural scene.

Even so, the problem of selection has been formidable. We have tried very hard to exclude terms which are generally understood, or unduly specialized, or trivial, or likely to prove short-lived. All these criteria, however, are subjective ones, and no two people would make the same selection; indeed, each editor has had to make concessions to the other, and on occasions we have had to overrule our contributors and even our consultant editors. We are sure, in this first edition, to have backed some losers and failed to spot some winners; critical readers are invited to send us, care of the publishers, their comments and suggestions for subsequent editions.

This much, however, we do claim: that, if only we had managed to retain in our memories the contents – totalling nearly 400,000 words – of our dictionary, we would by now be two distinctly well-informed men. As things are, we shall be returning to it again and again.

January 1977   A.B.
                                                                        O.S.

Acknowledgements

We, the editors, wish to thank:

the consultant editors named on the left-hand titlepage, who have played so large a part in shaping this book and saved us from so many errors of judgement (any that remain being ours and not theirs);

Andrew Best of Curtis Brown Academic Ltd, who first introduced us, and who has continued to take a creative and detailed interest in the book that far exceeds the normal scope of a literary agent;

Hope Liebersohn for sub-editorial help over the psychology entries, and Diana Souhami and Sarah McPhee for similar help over the bibliographies and the entries under personal names;

Laura Harris, Lin Wells, and (for nearly three years) Sue Burton, for remaining efficient, cheerful, and interested throughout innumerable typings and retypings, countings and recountings, filings and refilings;

Christine Collins for the meticulous care with which she read proofs, working against (and at times almost round) the clock;

an army of other friends and helpers for kindnesses too numerous and varied to categorize;

our respective wives for every conceivable encouragement and support;

and, above all, the other 138 contributors listed on pages xiv–xix, who have responded with unfailing courtesy and helpfulness to our sometimes exacting demands, and whose book this is.

How to use this book

The arrangement of this book should be largely self-explanatory, and the best general rule is: follow your nose. Words and phrases should always, in the first place, be sought directly, not under some more comprehensive term; this is a dictionary rather than an encyclopaedia. The term sought *may*, of course, prove to be explained under some other heading; if so, there will always be a cross-reference. Thus, a reader wishing to learn the meaning of 'antigen' will find '**antigen,** see under IMMUNITY'.

Alphabetical arrangement. This is on the word-by-word principle – meaning, for example, that all the phrases beginning with 'art' – ART AUTRE, ART BRUT, ART MUSIC, ART NOUVEAU, ART OF THE REAL, ART SACRÉ – precede ARTIFICIAL INSEMINATION and ARTIFICIAL INTEL-LIGENCE (which on the letter-by-letter principle would come immediately before ART MUSIC). *Hyphenated words* are regarded as two words if each constituent can stand on its own (e.g. ALL-OR-NONE LAW precedes ALLELE), but as one word if the first constituent is merely a prefix (e.g. ANTI-NOVEL follows ANTINOMY). *Sets of initials* (see also below under *Full or abbreviated heading*) are treated as if they were words (e.g. ABC ART and ABM come between ABBEY THEATRE and ABNORMAL PSYCHOLOGY).

Phrases. These are mostly given under the first word of the phrase, e.g. ABSTRACT EXPRESSIONISM, AGE-AND-AREA HYPOTHESIS, NUC-LEAR PHYSICS, STREAM OF CONSCIOUSNESS, THEATRE OF THE ABSURD. In certain cases, however, the phrase has been inverted, either because the important word is not the first (e.g. GAMES, THEORY OF, *not* THEORY OF GAMES), or because a number of terms with the same second element are most easily differentiated by being grouped under that element (e.g., under WAR, *catalytic war, conventional war, limited war,* and other varieties are distinguished). Cross-references have been inserted wherever they seemed likely to be needed.

Full or abbreviated heading. Entries on *organizations* commonly known by their initials (EEC, EFTA, UNO) will be found *under these initials* (see also *Alphabetical arrangement* above) and not under the full name, which in many cases (KGB, MVD, POUM) is known only to specialists. The same applies to certain *other sets of initials* (ABM, DNA, GATT) the widespread use of which may send readers to the dictionary precisely to find out what they stand for. Where, however, few readers seem likely to need this information (e.g. that IQ stands for INTELLI-GENCE QUOTIENT), or where the use of the abbreviation without prior explanation is mostly confined to professionals addressing other pro-fessionals (ET for EDUCATIONAL TECHNOLOGY), the unabbreviated term has been preferred.

Names of people. Index-type entries are provided under, in general, the surname *as normally referred to*, e.g. GOETHE (not von Goethe), but DE GAULLE, LA FOLLETTE, LE CORBUSIER, VAN GOGH; LORCA (not the more correct García Lorca), but DAY LEWIS. Oriental names, likewise, are entered on common-sense principles rather than by rule of thumb. Names of writers best known under a pseudonym (e.g. George ORWELL) are entered under that pseudonym. In doubtful cases, cross-references are given (e.g. from CORBUSIER to LE COR-BUSIER). The word-by-word principle applies (e.g. all names begin-ning with 'de' come between DDT and DEAD SEA SCROLLS). Names containing apostrophes (e.g. D'ANNUNZIO) are treated as one word. Names beginning with 'Mac' or 'Mc' are arranged under 'Mac'.

In short, we have tried in each instance to guess where people are likely to look; those whose minds we have misread will in most cases find a signpost directing them to the chosen heading.

Cross-references. Many entries include an explicit suggestion that the reader should 'see' or 'see also' some other entry on a related topic. In addition, an *implicit* suggestion to this effect is made whenever, in the course of an entry, a word, phrase, or set of *unpunctuated* initials is picked out in SMALL CAPITALS. (By 'unpunctuated' we mean that a reference to UNO implies an entry on that subject, a reference to the U.S.A. or the U.S.S.R. does not.)

In many cases, these implied cross-references are to a slightly differ-ent form of the capitalized word or phrase. Thus, singulars and plurals are regarded as interchangeable, as are the terminations -ism and -ist: e.g., a reader following up an allusion to 'MARXIST thought' will find an entry, not on MARXIST but on MARXISM. Care has been taken, how-ever, to avoid capitalizing consecutive words which are the subjects of two or more *separate* entries; *not*, therefore ' . . . MARXIST ECONOMICS' (since there is no such heading) but ' . . . Marxist economics (see MARXISM; ECONOMICS)'. In the last example the cross-reference to ECONOMICS will only have been included if it seems genuinely relev-ant; and in general we have refrained from capitalizing if the entries in question have no relevance to the context.

For further reading. Some explanation should be given of the brief 'bibliographies' (often a single title) with which many entries conclude.

Each contributor was invited to use approximately 5 per cent of his total allowance of words in giving suggestions for further reading. How he distributed this allowance between the various entries was for him to decide. The size or importance of the subject was by no means the sole criterion. More relevant were the questions: How likely is this entry to have satisfied the reader's immediate needs? How likely is it that any suggested title will adequately meet whatever needs remain unsatisfied? How easy is it for the reader to satisfy those needs without further guidance?

If, therefore, no suggestion for further reading is given, the reason is hardly ever that no further information on the subject is available, and nearly always that no further *space* was available. Those who need further information will often find it by turning to a related heading or headings. Occasionally these headings are specified, e.g. the entry on GENERATIVE GRAMMAR ends: 'Bibl: see under CHOMSKYAN; GRAMMAR'; in other cases it is left to the reader's intelligence to tell him, for example, that further information on most of the terms relating to LINGUISTICS will probably be found in one or more of the four books listed under that heading.

Although, as mentioned, contributors were invited to make their own suggestions for further reading, we have in a number of cases ventured to fill what seemed an obvious gap, or to cut for reasons of space. As far as possible we have consulted the contributors in question; but the ultimate responsibility for the selection of titles and of editions is ours. (Our normal practice is to cite the first printing of the latest editions, both British and American, known to contain revision.)

List of Contributors

A.B.   Albert Bandura, David Starr Jordan Professor of Social Science in Psychology, Stanford University.

A.C.   Sir Alec Cairncross, F.B.A., Master of St Peter's College, Oxford.

A.F.B.   the late Alastair Buchan, Professor of International Relations, University of Oxford; formerly Director of the Institute for Strategic Studies.

A.H.   Antony Hopkins, composer, conductor, pianist, and writer and broadcaster on music; formerly Lecturer and Piano Professor, Royal College of Music.

A.K.   Alexander Knapp, Visiting Lecturer in Music, Goldsmiths' College, London.

A.K.S.   Amartya Sen, Professor of Economics, London School of Economics.

A.K.W.   Angela K. Westwater, art gallery proprietor and director; formerly Managing Editor, *Artforum*.

A.L.C.B. Alan Bullock, F.B.A., Master of St Catherine's College, Oxford.

A.Q.   Anthony Quinton, President elect of Trinity College, Oxford.

A.S.   Aaron Sloman, Lecturer in Philosophy, Cognitive Studies Programme, University of Sussex.

B.A.F.   B. A. Farrell, Reader in Mental Philosophy, University of Oxford.

B.B.S.   B. Babington Smith, consultant, management training; formerly Senior Lecturer in Experimental Psychology, University of Oxford.

B.C.   Barry Cunliffe, Professor of European Archaeology, University of Oxford.

B.F.   Brian Fender, Fellow of St Catherine's College, Oxford.

B.G.   Benny Green, author of *The Reluctant Art*, *Drums in My Ears*, etc.

B.K.   Bernard Keeffe, Professor of Conducting, Trinity College of Music, London.

B.L.B.   Barbara L. Baer, writer on dance.

B.M.   Barry MacDonald, Senior Lecturer in Evaluation, University of East Anglia.

B.M.-H.   Ben Martin-Hoogewerf, Lecturer in English, Uxbridge Technical College.

C.L.-H.   Christopher Longuet-Higgins, F.R.S., Royal Society Research Professor, University of Sussex.

C.O.   Christopher Ounsted, Medical Director, Park Hospital for Children, Oxford.

C.S.	the late Christopher Strachey, Professor of Computation, University of Oxford.
D.A.P.	D. A. Pyke, Physician, King's College Hospital, London.
D.B.	Daniel Bell, Professor of Sociology, Harvard University.
D.C.	David Crystal, Professor of Linguistic Science, University of Reading.
D.C.W.	Donald Cameron Watt, Professor of International History, University of London.
D.E.	Douglas Evans, author and lecturer.
D.E.B.	Donald Broadbent, F.R.S., external staff, Medical Research Council, University of Oxford.
D.H.	David Hartley, Lecturer in Psychology, University of Strathclyde.
D.H.G.	Dennis H. Gath, Clinical Reader in Psychiatry, University of Oxford, and Honorary Consultant Psychiatrist, the Warneford Hospital.
D.J.E.	D. J. Enright, poet, novelist, critic, editor, and publisher.
D.J.W.	D. J. Wood, Lecturer, Department of Psychology, University of Nottingham.
D.L.E.	David L. Edwards, Canon of Westminster.
D.P.	David Papineau, Lecturer in Sociology, University of Reading.
D.V.	Deryck Viney, Czechoslovak Programme Organizer, B.B.C. External Services.
E.G.	E. Grebenik, Principal, Civil Service College; Joint Editor, *Population Studies*.
E.H.	Edward Higginbottom, Research Fellow, Corpus Christi College, Cambridge.
E.H.P.B.	Sir Henry Phelps Brown, F.B.A., Professor Emeritus of Economics of Labour, University of London.
E.L.-S.	Erika Lueders-Salmon, Research Officer, Inner London Education Authority.
E.O.W.	Edward O. Wilson, Professor of Zoology, Harvard University.
E.R.L.	E. R. Laithwaite, Professor of Heavy Electrical Engineering, Imperial College of Science and Technology, London.
G.B.	George Butterworth, Lecturer in Developmental Psychology, University of Southampton.
G.B.R.	G. B. Richardson, Fellow of St John's College, Oxford, and Secretary to the Delegates of the Oxford University Press.
G.M.	Gordon Mangan, Research Officer, Department of Psychology, University of Oxford.
G.S.	G. Stuvel, University Lecturer in Economic Statistics, University of Oxford.
H.L.	Hope Liebersohn, Lecturer in Linguistics, Hatfield Polytechnic.
H.L.A.H.	H. L. A. Hart, F.B.A., Principal of Brasenose College, Oxford; formerly Professor of Jurisprudence, University of Oxford.
H. TA.	Henri Tajfel, Professor of Social Psychology, University of Bristol.
H. TH.	Howard Thomas, Director of Decision Analysis Unit, London Graduate School of Business Studies.

M.BR.	Michael Brawne, practising architect; Lecturer, Department of Architecture, University of Cambridge.
M.C.	Mary Chamot, formerly Assistant Keeper, Tate Gallery, London.
M.D.B.	Michael D. Biddiss, Lecturer in Modern History, University of Leicester.
M.E.	Maria Enzensberger, formerly Research Fellow of King's College, Cambridge.
M.E.A.B.	Marian Bowley, Emeritus Professor of Political Economy, University College London.
M.F.	the late Maurice Freedman, Professor of Social Anthropology, University of Oxford.
M.FG.S.	M.FG. Scott, Official Fellow of Nuffield College, Oxford.
M.J.C.	M. J. Crowe, Senior Lecturer, Institute of Psychiatry, University of London.
M.K.	M. Kinsbourne, Associate Professor of Pediatrics and Neurology, Duke University Medical Center.
M.L.	Mary Lambert, geography teacher, Highworth School, Ashford, Kent.
M.S.	Michael Shepherd, Professor of Epidemiological Psychiatry, Institute of Psychiatry, University of London.
M.S.BA.	M. S. Bartlett, F.R.S., Emeritus Professor of Biomathematics, University of Oxford.
M.S.BR.	Malcolm Bradbury, Professor of American Studies, University of East Anglia.
M.S.-S.	Martin Seymour-Smith, lately Visiting Professor of English, University of Wisconsin; author of *Guide to Modern World Literature*.
M.V.B.	Michael V. Berry, Lecturer in Physics, University of Bristol.
M.V.P.	Michael Posner, Fellow of Pembroke College, Cambridge.
N.T.	Niko Tinbergen, F.R.S., formerly Professor of Animal Behaviour, University of Oxford; Nobel Laureate in Physiology.
O.S.	Oliver Stallybrass, Editor, Abinger Edition of E. M. Forster.
P.B.	Peter Burke, Reader in Intellectual History, School of European Studies, University of Sussex.
P.B.M.	Peter Mandelson, St Catherine's College, Oxford.
P.C.	Patrick Conner, Keeper of Fine Art, Royal Pavilion, Museum, and Art Gallery, Brighton.
P.E.B.	Peter Bryant, University Lecturer in Psychology, University of Oxford.
P.H.	Peter Haggett, Professor of Urban and Regional Geography, University of Bristol.
P.J.	Peter Jay, British Ambassador in Washington.
P.L.H.	Paul L. Harris, Lecturer in Psychology, University of Lancaster.
P.M.	Sir Peter Medawar, C.H., F.R.S., Member of Scientific Staff, Medical Research Council; Nobel Laureate in Medicine.
P.M.O.	P. M. Oppenheimer, Student of Christ Church, Oxford.
P.S.L.	Peter S. Leuner, Head of Department of Sociology, Richmond College, Surrey.

LIST OF CONTRIBUTORS

Q.B. Quentin Bell, Emeritus Professor of Fine Art, University of Sussex.

R.A.H. R. A. Hodgkin, Lecturer in Education, University of Oxford.

R.B. Ronald Butt, Assistant Editor and political commentator, *Sunday Times*; political columnist, *The Times*.

R.C. Robert Conquest, writer; author of *The Great Terror*, etc.

R.C.O.M. R. C. O. Matthews, F.B.A., Master of Clare College, Cambridge; formerly Drummond Professor of Political Economy, University of Oxford.

R.F. Ronald Fletcher, formerly Professor and Head of Department of Sociology, University of York.

R.G. Robin Gandy, Reader in Mathematical Logic, University of Oxford.

R.H. Sir Roy Harrod, F.B.A., formerly Tutor of Christ Church, Oxford.

R.I.T. R. I. Tricker, Director, Oxford Centre for Management Studies.

R.L. Robert Lekachman, Distinguished Professor of Economics, City University of New York.

R.L.G. Richard L. Gregory, Professor of Neuropsychology and Head of the Brain and Perception Laboratory, University of Bristol.

R.M.N. R. M. Needham, Reader in Computer Systems, University of Cambridge.

R.P.-S. Renée Paton-Saltzberg, Lecturer in Psychology, Oxford Polytechnic.

R.R. Richard Rosecrance, Professor of International and Comparative Politics, Cornell University.

R.Sl. Robin Sibson, Professor of Statistics, University of Bath.

R.ST. Richard Stone, F.B.A., P.D. Leake Professor of Finance and Accounting, University of Cambridge.

R.W.S. R. W. Sharples, Lecturer in Department of Greek and Latin, University College London.

S.A. Stanislav Andreski, Professor of Sociology, Reading University.

S.BE. Stafford Beer, Visiting Professor of Cybernetics, University of Manchester; Adjunct Professor of Statistics and Operations Research, University of Pennsylvania.

S.BR. Samuel Brittan, Economics Editor, *Financial Times*; Visiting Fellow of Nuffield College, Oxford.

S.J.G. Julius Gould, Professor of Sociology, University of Nottingham.

T.C.C.M. Tom Milne, film critic and film historian.

T.M. Terence Morris, Professor of Sociology (with special reference to criminology), University of London.

T.Z.C. Thomas Z. Cassel, Faculties of Human Development, Wayne State University and the Merrill-Palmer Institute.

W.A.C.S. W. A. C. Stewart, Vice-Chancellor and formerly Professor of Education, University of Keele.

W.B. Wilfred Beckerman, Fellow of Balliol College, Oxford; formerly Professor of Political Economy, University of London, and Head of Department of Political Economy, University College London.

W.D.M.P.   W. D. M. Paton, F.R.S., Professor of Pharmacology, University of Oxford.

W.E.C.G.   W. E. C. Gillham, Lecturer in Educational Psychology, Child Development Research Unit, University of Nottingham.

W.Z.   Wendy Zerin, formerly Research Assistant, Department of Experimental Psychology, University of Oxford.

A

Aalto, Alvar (Finnish architect and furniture designer, 1898–1976), see under ROMANTICISM.

Abbaye de Créteil. An early-20th-century experiment in COMMUNITY living, called after the utopian Abbaye de Thélème imagined by Rabelais. In 1906 a group of young French writers, artists, and musicians, of whom Georges Duhamel was to become the most famous, settled in a house at Créteil, near Paris, and tried, while pursuing their artistic vocations, to support themselves by growing their own vegetables and working a printing-press. During this period Jules Romains, an associate member of the group, evolved the short-lived literary theory known as *l'unanimisme*, which tried to draw rather facile humanistic (see HUMANISM) reassurance from the fact that all the individuals in a given social group tend to be interdependent and to react on each other. The experiment ended after 14 months, because of disagreements and lack of money. In 1937 Duhamel gave a rather melancholy transposition of it in his novel *Le Désert de Bièvres.*   J.G.W.

Abbey Theatre. A Dublin theatre, after 1904 the home of the Irish National Theatre Society. Under the leadership of W. B. Yeats and Lady Gregory the Abbey presented plays in verse and prose, whose subject-matter was taken from contemporary Irish life and Celtic myth, with Yeats himself and J. M. Synge as the major dramatists of the movement. From 1923 to 1926 the Abbey again achieved international recognition with the early plays of Sean O'Casey; its refusal in 1928 to stage his play *The Silver Tassie* contributed to a decline in its stature.   M.A.
Bibl: U. Ellis-Fermor, *The Irish Dramatic Movement* (London, 2nd ed., 1954).

ABC art, see MINIMAL ART.

ABM (anti-ballistic missiles). Nuclear MISSILES designed for defensive purposes, to intercept inter-continental and intermediate-range nuclear ballistic missiles and destroy them in space, either at the apogee of their trajectory or during the descent towards their target. Should they achieve near-absolute effectiveness, the apparent invulnerability they would confer on those using them would effectively alter the balance of mutual DETERRENCE. Their development has, however, proved so costly, and the defence they provide so far from absolute, that their original possessors, the U.S.A. and Russia, have agreed to limit their production and deployment to what is necessary to protect their respective capital cities.   D.C.W.

Abnormal psychology. The branch of PSYCHOLOGY concerned with the abnormal behaviour and functioning of organisms. The organisms may be human or infra-human; but the many psychologists investigating the conditions that produce abnormalities of animal behaviour (e.g. by the use of drugs, by surgical methods, by the design of conflict-producing situations) would not naturally be described as working in the field of abnormal psychology unless their studies were also designed to throw light on the abnormalities of human functioning. The expression is further restricted to functioning that is abnormal in ways which make life difficult for the people concerned, and which may lead them to require special help. Thus, studies of men who are 6' 6" tall, or who have an INTELLIGENCE QUOTIENT of over 140, would not usually and naturally be called studies of abnormal psychology; whereas similar studies of dwarfs, or of people with I.Q.s of under 60, would be so classified (see also MENTAL RETARDATION). The expression is applied, in particular, and most importantly, to phenomena that are abnormal in that they are regarded as 'morbid' in character, i.e. as evidence that the person concerned is in an unhealthy condition. In consequence of the growth, over the last century, of a whole array of therapeutic procedures for the relief of people suffering from mental morbidities, workers in abnormal psychology have also been involved in studying the effectiveness of different methods of therapy.

Because a psychologist working in this field is characteristically concerned with people who are in difficulties or suffering from mental ill-health, he meets them (typically) as patients in a psychiatric and therefore medical context. Whereas the psychiatrist (see PSYCHIATRY) is the medical specialist concerned with the diagnosis and treatment of these patients, the psychologist is solely concerned with the scientific study of their condition, or of the therapy being given them; and he conducts his enquiries with the permission and cooperation (often very active) of the psychiatrist in charge of the patients.

In this century, work in abnormal psychology has contributed to raise standards of precision and caution in the whole field of abnormal mental functioning. It has also uncovered much that was new, e.g. about the constitutional correlates of abnormal functioning, the variables of personality involved (see PERSONALITY TYPES), the environmental conditions that adversely affect the development of personality, and the difficulties of establishing that a therapeutic method is really effective. On the other hand, it is difficult to find any general discovery claim in this field (as with psychology in general) that can stand up to sceptical scrutiny. This is not surprising, because abnormal psychology is really concerned with the malfunctioning of the machinery of the NERVOUS SYSTEM. Since we do not know yet how this machinery works, we can hardly expect the relatively crude methods of contemporary psychology to give us definitive results about what happens when our nervous machinery goes wrong. B.A.F.

Bibl: R. W. White, *The Abnormal Personality* (N.Y., 3rd ed., 1964).

Abramovich, Rafael (Russian revolutionary, 1880–1963), see under MENSHEVIKS.

abreaction. In PSYCHOTHERAPY, a term used most usefully, and perhaps most frequently, for the actual release of emotion into CONSCIOUSNESS in which the process of CATHARSIS (sense 3) culminates. It is,

however, also used synonymously with 'catharsis'. B.A.F.

absolute, the. In PHILOSOPHY, a term used by post-Kantian metaphysical idealists (see METAPHYSICS; IDEALISM) to denote the totality of what really exists, conceived as a unitary system and as the source or explanation of all the apparent variety of the world. The idea is anticipated in Spinoza's theory that the whole of reality is a single substance, called by him *Deus sive Natura* (God or Nature). For such post-Kantian idealists as Schelling and Hegel reality is spiritual in character and so their Absolute is more God than Nature, although it is a philosophical God, purged of anthropomorphic features. It is not itself a person, although it somehow contains all the persons that there are. A.Q.

absolute liability, see under STRICT LIABILITY.

absolute threshold, see under THRESHOLD.

absolute zero. The temperature of $-273.16°C$, which is the lowest possible according to the well-established theories of THERMODYNAMICS and STATISTICAL MECHANICS. At the absolute zero, the random heat motion of the constituents of matter is at a minimum, and structural order is at a maximum. This means that thermal NOISE in measuring instruments is greatly reduced at low temperatures, enabling very weak signals to be detected, e.g. faint radio emissions from distant GALAXIES and stars. Near the absolute zero, two dramatic effects of QUANTUM MECHANICS occur: SUPERCONDUCTIVITY, which is the total vanishing of electrical resistance in some metals, and superfluidity, which is the total vanishing of flow resistance in liquid helium. Temperatures within 1/1000 of a degree above absolute zero can be attained by modern CRYOGENIC techniques, but the absolute zero itself remains an unattainable limit. See also BROWNIAN MOTION; ZERO POINT ENERGY. M.V.B.

absorption cost, see under MARGINAL COSTING.

abstract. Not perceivable by the senses. Such things as numbers, ideas, and social

2

climates are said to be abstract, while things that can be perceived by the senses, e.g. buses, blankets, and bottles, are said to be concrete. Concrete things, however, may be described with a greater or lesser degree of *abstractness*, e.g. the same diagram may be described either as (*a*) a square of side half an inch drawn with black ink or (*b*) a polygon. The second description *abstracts* from some of the qualities of the square, and is therefore said to be more abstract, or more of an *abstraction*. The first description is also abstract to the extent that it does not include everything that could be said about the picture, e.g. its location and orientation. See also EQUIVALENCE RELATION.

The process of abstraction is sometimes applied also to descriptions or theories which distort in order to simplify. For instance, economists sometimes describe human beings as if they ('economic man') had a single motive, namely to get as much as possible for themselves. This may make it easier to construct theories of economic processes which are mathematically easy to understand and use, but which do not give accurate descriptions, predictions, or EXPLANATIONS of what actually happens. Similarly, if a physicist treats a gas as if it were composed of perfectly elastic, perfectly small PARTICLES, exerting no forces on one another, this makes his calculations easier, but distorts the facts. Such distortions for the sake of simplicity or elegance are sometimes called abstractions, sometimes idealizations, sometimes schematizations, and sometimes MODELS.

A.S.

abstract art. Paintings and sculpture making no identifiable reference to the visible world. Such works, which must have some claim to exist in their own right if they are to be distinguished from ornament or decoration, are often considered analogous to works of music. They have become increasingly common in Western art (and CULTURES influenced by it) since *c.* 1910, when a number of scattered experimenters influenced by SYMBOLISM and/or CUBISM began producing art with no recognizable 'subject' in the traditional sense. Among these were the German Adolf Hoelzel, the Russians Wassily Kandinsky, Kasimir Malevich, Michel Larionov, and Sonia Delaunay-Terk, the Lithuanian M. K. Čiurlionis, the Czech František Kupka, and the Dutchman Piet Mondrian. The term itself, whose use only became common after 1918, appears to derive from Wilhelm Worringer's *Abstraktion und Einfühlung* (1907), though Kandinsky's *Über das Geistige in der Kunst* (1912) is the classic exposition from a symbolist, quasi-musical point of view.

The first abstract films, by the DADA artists Hans Richter and Viking Eggeling, were shown in Germany in 1921. The first exhibition of abstract art in Paris, in 1930, led to the formation in 1931 of the Abstraction-Création group, consisting mainly of non-French artists. This became the main stream of the movement during the 1930s when abstract art was condemned in Germany and Russia for (respectively) DEGENERACY and FORMALISM. After World War II this condemnation made it seem an embodiment of Western values, particularly after the emergence in the 1950s of ABSTRACT EXPRESSIONISM in the U.S.A. Hence it has developed into an established, academically respectable form of art, with many overlapping versions, e.g. (1) such early branches as Malevich's SUPREMATISM (1915), Alexander Rodchenko's NON-OBJECTIVISM (*c.* 1920), and Theo van Doesburg's CONCRETE ART (1930); (2) general sub-categories like 'geometric' and BIOMORPHIC art (two basic divisions often adopted by critics), or, more recently, HARD-EDGE; (3) alternative names for the whole trend, such as 'non-figurative', 'non-representational', or 'non-objective'; (4) genuinely distinct recent branches like KINETIC ART and OP ART; finally (5), critics' and dealers' labels which give a deceptive air of novelty, for instance '*art autre*', MINIMAL ART, and '*réalités nouvelles*'. Other movements more or less involved with abstract art are ORPHISM, CONSTRUCTIVISM, *De* STIJL and Larionov's RAYONISM, while even SURREALISM has a link with it in the biomorphic abstractions of Joan Miró and Hans Arp.

J.W.

Bibl: Museum of Modern Art Catalogue, *Cubism and Abstract Art* (N.Y., 1936); W. Kandinsky, tr. H. Rebay, *On the Spiritual in Art* (N.Y., 1947).

abstract expressionism. A term first used in 1919, in Germany and Russia, to describe the painting of Wassily Kandinsky, and again in that context in 1929 by Alfred Barr, director of the Museum of Modern Art, New York. It was subsequently applied by the *New Yorker* critic Robert Coates in 1946 to the emerging post-World-War-II American painting, both abstract (see ABSTRACT ART) and figurative. Stylistically, the term implies loose, rapid paint-handling, indistinct shapes, large rhythms, broken colour, uneven saturation of the canvas, and pronounced brushwork, as found in the work of de Kooning, Pollock, Kline, and Gorky; it also includes more reductive painters (e.g. Barnett Newman, Mark Rothko, and Ad Reinhardt) who focus on single, centralized images expressed in terms of large areas or fields of colour – hence the term *colour field painting* subsequently applied to such painters. The term has been extended to cover several sculptors stylistically related to the painters. See also ACTION PAINTING; COBRA; NEW YORK SCHOOL.   A.K.W.

Bibl: I. Sandler, *The Triumph of American Painting* (N.Y., 1970).

abstraction, see under ABSTRACT.

absurd, theatre of the, see THEATRE OF THE ABSURD.

acceleration. The rate at which the velocity of a body is changing. Since velocity is a VECTOR involving both speed and direction of motion, a change in either of these constitutes acceleration. Thus a car starting up from rest on a straight road, and a car rounding a bend at constant speed, are both accelerating. See also NEWTONIAN MECHANICS.   M.V.B.

accelerator.
(1) In PHYSICS, a device for producing fast charged particles which are allowed to hit a target, thus providing most of the available information about interactions between ELEMENTARY PARTICLES. The acceleration is accomplished by electric FIELDS, which may either act alone, as in the VAN DE GRAAF GENERATOR and the LINEAR ACCELERATOR, or in conjunction with magnetic fields which deflect the particles into space-saving circular paths, as in the CYCLOTRON, synchroton, synchrocyclotron, and BETATRON. These machines are the largest tools of contemporary science, and the installations may occupy several square miles (they are also the costliest – see CERN). The ENERGY of the particles produced may reach several hundred thousand GeV (see ELECTRON-VOLT). In addition to investigating matter on a sub-atomic scale, the beams of high energy PARTICLES produced by accelerators are used to create new TRANSURANIC ELEMENTS, and to probe living TISSUES, e.g. in order to destroy cancer cells (see CANCER; CELL). M.V.B.

Bibl: R. R. Wilson and R. M. Littauer, *Accelerators* (London, 1962).

(2) In ECONOMICS (more formally, in this sense, the *acceleration principle*), the tendency of industrial INVESTMENT to vary with the rate of change, rather than the level, of industrial output: this relationship, first emphasized (though not originated) by J. M. Clark (1917), is the main determinant of investment in certain simplified TRADE CYCLE models (R. F. Harrod, 1936; P. A. Samuelson, 1939) and growth MODELS (Harrod, 1939; E. Domar, 1946). It is called the accelerator because it implies that an increase (decrease) in the demand for any product produces a non-sustainable increase (decrease) in demand for the machines required to make it – it is thus an example of positive FEEDBACK, and contributes to economic instability.   J.S.F.

Bibl: R. C. O. Matthews, *The Trade Cycle* (Welwyn and Cambridge, 1959); P. J. Lund, *Investment* (Edinburgh and San Francisco, 1971).

acceptability. In LINGUISTICS, the adjudged normality of linguistic data, especially of sentences. An acceptable utterance is one whose use is considered permissible or possible in some context by most, or all, native speakers. The CONCEPT is distinguished from the more specific notion of GRAMMATICALITY, which is merely one possible CRITERION of acceptability. An unacceptable (or *deviant*) sentence is generally indicated by a preceding asterisk, e.g. *A cats was asleep.*   D.C.

access time. In COMPUTING, the time that elapses between starting a reading operation on the STORE and getting back the result. Different types of store vary widely in their access times and hence in the ways in which they are used, ranging from

REGISTER (10–100ns – a nanosecond being the time light takes to travel about a foot) via SCRATCHPAD, CORE STORE, DRUM STORE, and moving-head DISC STORE to MAGNETIC TAPE (several minutes). For the last three, most of the time is the *latency* period spent waiting until the information has moved physically to the reading-head; once this has happened information can be transferred rapidly. For this reason these types of store are generally used for SERIAL ACCESS rather than RANDOM ACCESS. C.S.

accessibility. The faculty of access, as defined by physical, legal, and economic factors, to a place or resource. Human and economic GEOGRAPHY have been revolutionized by the increased accessibility to distant places resulting from recent advances in the technology of transport and communications, and problems of accessibility have become fundamental in the contemporary organization of the world. These problems, which form the subject of rapidly evolving national and international systems of regulation, now include, at selected spots, the diminished accessibility that may result from crowding (see DENSITY). J.G.

accommodation. In DEVELOPMENTAL PSYCHOLOGY, a PIAGETIAN term for the adjustment of an organized schema of action to fit new situations. More generally, the subordination of activity to the requirements of external reality, as in imitation. Along with ASSIMILATION, it is one of the main organizing concepts of Piaget's PSYCHOLOGY. P.L.H.

acculturation (U.S. term; in the U.K., *culture contact*). A kind of CULTURE change that emerges from the interaction of two or more societies or groups with different cultural traditions. Acculturation theory was slow to emerge in ANTHROPOLOGY, which was dominated, up to the 1930s, by a historical approach that concentrated on EVOLUTION and diffusion (see DIFFUSIONISM) of cultural traits. Following the efforts of Malinowski and Fortes in England, and Redfield and Linton in the U.S.A., to formulate a more consciously FUNCTIONALIST approach – which saw culture as a system rather than a collection of disparate traits – culture contact theory became more important as a means of analysing social change. The earlier contact theories tended to assume that the normal outcome of acculturation was cultural fusion or assimilation; the dominant (because of superior TECHNOLOGY or political power) culture became the melting-pot for the weaker one. Later theories have tended to be more pluralist, i.e. to show how new and creative mixtures often result from the interaction of diverse cultural traditions and groups. D.B.

achievement orientation, see under PATTERN VARIABLES.

Achleitner, Friedrich (Austrian architect and author, *b.* 1930), see under WIENER GRUPPE.

acid. A chemical substance which loses a PROTON (hydrogen ION) to a second substance known as a BASE; this definition, which stems from Bronsted and Lowrey in 1923, is the most commonly used. Strong acids such as hydrochloric acid in water (the base) lose a proton easily, but for weak acids, e.g. acetic or citric acid, the tendency to donate a proton is feeble and the acid remains largely undissociated (see DISSOCIATION). The term is sometimes used more generally as any SPECIES which accepts a pair of ELECTRONS from a donor (the base). B.F.
Bibl: R. P. Bell, *The Proton in Chemistry* (London, 1960; Cornell, 1972).

Acid Fascism. A type of eclectic violence which represents an extreme development of the widespread use of psychedelic drugs (see DRUGS; PSYCHEDELIA) such as lysergic acid diethylamide (LSD), and is exemplified by the sensational killings directed by Charles Manson in California in 1969. Manson's ideology seemed to be based equally upon OCCULTISM, MYSTICISM, and the psychedelic experience, and upon violence, authoritarian paternalism, and the desire to effect social and political changes without debate or meaningful opposition. His highly effective technique of BRAINWASHING his disciples during lsd 'trips' was also used by certain elements within less murderous millenarian cults (see CULT; MILLENARIANISM) such as *the Process,* also active in California in the late 1960s. P.S.L.
Bibl: V. Bugliosi and C. Gentry, *Helter*

Skelter (N.Y., 1974; London, as *The Manson Murders*, 1975).

Acmeism (from Greek *acme*: 'zenith, blossoming, ripening'). A movement in Russian poetry which grew out of SYMBOLISM as a reaction against its MYSTICISM and excessive allusiveness. The Acmeists wanted to restore concreteness and immediacy to poetic language, 'to admire a rose because it is beautiful, not because it is a symbol of purity'. Their refined lyrical verse combined poetic archaisms with simple everyday language.

The first Acmeist group, the 'Guild of Poets', was founded in St Petersburg in 1912 by Gumilev, the movement's main theoretician. Acmeism produced three outstanding poets: Gumilev, Anna Akhmatova, and Mandelshtam. Its main publication was *Apollon* (1909–17). It was suppressed in the early 1920s, stamped as 'decadent' and 'individualist'. Gumilev was executed in 1921 for his association with a counter-revolutionary plot, Mandelshtam perished in the purges of the 1930s (see YEZHOVSHCHINA), Akhmatova remained silent. During World War II she published patriotic poetry. In 1946 she was severely criticized (see ZHDANOVSHCHINA), but after the THAW she re-emerged on the literary scene and published several volumes of poetry. M.E.

Bibl: R. Poggioli, *The Poets of Russia* (Cambridge, Mass., 1960).

acoustics. All activities concerned with the production, transmission, reflection, dispersion, or reception of sound waves, whether in air or some other substance. It includes such things as the design and manufacture of anechoic chambers, where sound waves generated within the chamber are entirely absorbed by the walls of the chamber; acoustic RADAR (sometimes called SONAR) used for depth recording at sea and for the location of shoals of fish, submarines (in war) or sunken wrecks; and the design of lecture theatres, sound-reproducing apparatus (HI-FI, etc.), hearing aids, and MAGNETOSTRICTION oscillators. E.R.L.

acquired characteristics, see under LAMARCKISM.

acquisition, see under CORPORATE STRATEGY.

Action Française. An extremist anti-parliamentary, AUTHORITARIAN, ultra-NATIONALIST movement founded in France in 1899 during the DREYFUS CASE, and distinguished for the ANTISEMITIC, anti-Freemason, anti-Protestant views put forward by a small group of INTELLECTUALS, Charles Maurras, Jacques Bainville, and Léon Daudet. It saw itself as providing a RATIONALIST, POSITIVIST defence of France's true Graeco-Roman tradition against Teutonic MYSTICISM, and justified its nationalism by distinguishing between the true France, the *pays réal,* and the republican system, the *pays légal.* Monarchic and Catholic, its journal was put on the Index by Pope Pius XI in 1927. It played a large part in the revolt of the French RIGHT against the Third Republic, a revolt culminating in the defeat of France in 1940 and the establishment of the VICHY regime, whose demise in 1944 it did not survive. D.C.W.

Bibl: E. Weber, *Action Française* (Stanford, 1962).

action painting. A phrase coined by the critic Harold Rosenberg in 1952 to define the abstract (see ABSTRACT ART), GESTURAL painting then prevalent. Rosenberg referred particularly to Willem de Kooning, although later the phrase came to be popularly associated with the name of Jackson Pollock, and with the splashing or squirting of paint on canvas; it has also been used synonymously with ABSTRACT EXPRESSIONISM and with *tachisme,* a French term for much the same thing. According to Rosenberg, the canvas had become 'an arena in which to act', the scene of an encounter between the artist and his materials – an encounter possessing a psychological as well as a physical dimension. The term has been rejected by many artists and critics because of Rosenberg's linkage of the artist's psyche to European EXISTENTIALIST thought, and because of the FORMALIST criticism of, notably, Clement Greenberg. See also NEW YORK SCHOOL. A.K.W.

Bibl: H. Geldzahler, *New York Painting and Sculpture: 1940–1970* (N.Y., 1969).

action potential. The electrical change that accompanies the propagation of an impulse down the length of a nerve or muscle fibre. P.M.

action systems, see under PARSONIAN.

activation energy. In most CHEMICAL REACTIONS the MOLECULE or molecules involved must acquire a state of higher ENERGY before they can react. The additional energy is described as the activation energy and its requirement is the reason why some thermodynamically feasible reactions do not occur. It also accounts for the increase in the rate of chemical reaction as the temperature is raised.   B.F.

activism. Two main senses can be distinguished:

(1) In its German form *Aktivismus,* a term used at the end of World War I to signify the principle of active political engagement by INTELLECTUALS; hence a subdivision of EXPRESSIONISM, whose political wing was strong at that time. It was associated particularly with Kurt Hiller, organizer of the *Neuer Club* of early expressionist poets, and with Franz Pfemfert, whose magazine *Die Aktion,* founded in 1911, was the more politically engaged rival of *Der* STURM.   J.W.

(2) More widely, an especially vigorous attitude towards political action, an attitude resulting in particularly zestful political practice. It implies a special role for *activists* who form the active core of political parties. It is notable in REVOLUTIONARY movements and particularly important in radical party politics (see RADICALISM). In its extreme form it is held to justify DIRECT ACTION and/or the use of force for political ends. In LEFT-wing politics *militant* is sometimes used, substantively, in the same sense as *activist,* but the first refers properly to the degree of radicalism in a person's politics, the second to the degree of involvement in politics; though usually correlated, the two are clearly distinguishable. Activists of all parties are as a rule more concerned with the purity of the party's creed than are their fellow members; this is particularly true of COMMUNIST Parties, at least before they come to power, after which the role of the APPARAT becomes paramount.   L.L.

Bibl: S. M. Lipset, 'The Activists', (*The Public Interest*, Fall 1968).

Actors' Studio, see under METHOD, THE.

actuator. The mechanism for causing a particular event (usually a physical movement) to take place at a desired instant in time; e.g. an electromagnet may be supplied with current when it is required to attract an iron armature which in turn pushes an object from a moving conveyor belt at a desired position. Actuators are much used in control systems (see CONTROL ENGINEERING).
E.R.L.

Adamson, Robert (Scottish philosopher, 1852–1902), see under NEO-KANTIANISM.

adaptable theatre, see under OPEN STAGE.

adaptation.

(1) In general BIOLOGY, the process by which an organism becomes fitted to its ENVIRONMENT, or the characteristic that renders it fit.

(2) In BACTERIOLOGY, a change in a bacterial population which makes it possible, after a certain interval, for bacteria to use a new foodstuff or avoid the action of a new ANTIBIOTIC.

(3) In sensory PHYSIOLOGY, the process by which an end organ ceases to respond to some uniformly applied stimulus – e.g. the adaptation of the nose to a uniform pervasive smell. In vision, adaptations are prevented from occurring by tiny wandering or scanning movements of the eye.   P.M.

adaptive radiation. The exploitation by the members of an animal or plant group of a wide variety of different HABITATS or habits of life to each of which the organisms are appropriately adapted. Thus the higher (placental) mammals show a high degree of adaptive radiation as exemplified by terrestrial carnivores, whales, moles, bats, and chimpanzees, The marsupial mammals have undergone an adaptive radiation of their own curiously similar in many ways to that of the terrestrial higher mammals. In this context the word 'radiation' is of course figurative and refers to a fanning out of evolutionary lines; and adaptive radiation calls for no special explanations that do not apply equally to the remainder of EVOLUTION.   P.M.

additive. A chemical substance introduced in order to improve the properties of the bulk material. There are numerous examples, from the important, e.g. lead tetraethyl as an anti-KNOCK agent in petrol, to the trivial, e.g. magnesium carbonate as an aid to the free running of table salt. B.F.

Adelphi, The, see under CRITERION, THE.

Adenauer, Konrad (German statesman, 1876–1967), see under CHRISTIAN DEMOCRACY.

adequacy. A term in GENERATIVE GRAMMAR used in two distinct senses:

(1) As a CRITERION of the extent to which the goals of linguistic theory have been achieved, three *levels of adequacy*, or stages of achievement, being recognized. *Observational* adequacy is achieved when a grammar gives a correct description of a CORPUS of data, but does not make generalizations based on this. *Descriptive* adequacy is achieved to the extent that a grammar gives a correct account of a speaker's COMPETENCE, his intuitive knowledge of a language. *Explanatory* adequacy is achieved to the extent that a linguistic theory provides principles for determining which of a number of descriptively adequate grammars is the best (see EVALUATION PROCEDURE). Structural LINGUISTICS was criticized by Chomsky as being too preoccupied with observational adequacy. Very little headway has been made in the study of explanatory adequacy.

(2) As a criterion of the *capacity* of a grammar. A grammar whose rules generate a desired set of sentences, providing for each its correct structural description, is *strongly* adequate; a grammar which does not assign correct structural descriptions is *weakly* adequate. D.C.

adjustable speed, see VARIABLE SPEED.

Adler, Alfred (Austrian psychiatrist, 1870–1937), see under ADLERIAN; INDIVIDUAL PSYCHOLOGY; PSYCHOANALYSIS.

Adlerian. Adjective applied to a school of PSYCHOANALYSIS originating in the work of Alfred Adler (Vienna, 1870–1937); also a substantive, meaning a member of that school. In the course of an early, close association with Freud (see FREUDIAN), Adler began to develop his own INDI-VIDUAL PSYCHOLOGY, in which he came to reject Freud's LIBIDO theory, together with his views of infantile sexuality and of sexuality as the root source of NEUROSIS; and finally (1912) he severed relations with Freud. Adler's fundamental notion was the helplessness of the infant, with its feelings of inferiority. The infant has an urge to overcome and compensate for all this. The key conditions that determine how he achieves this compensation are the inter-personal relations in the family. The upshot is that the child acquires his own LIFE STYLE, or way of dealing with his situation. Where this fails, the person may retain an uncompensated feeling of inferiority (an INFERIORITY COMPLEX), and this can lead to a neurotic style of behaviour. Adler's influence, though to some extent indirect and unacknowledged, has been considerable, especially in the U.S.A. B.A.F.

Bibl: A. Adler, tr. P. Radin, *The Practice and Theory of Individual Psychology* (London and N.Y., 1924).

admass. Term coined by J. B. Priestley in 1955 for an entire economic, social, and cultural system dominated and saturated by the drive to consume material goods, a drive reflecting the illusory world of the advertising copy-writer's *ad* and obsessively promoted through the mass MEDIA. The fruits of such a system are a glittering CONSUMER SOCIETY which stifles creativity and individuality, and distorts real human feelings, needs, and emotions. P.S.L.

administrative law. In England, the legal rules and principles on which the courts act in controlling the exercise by public authorities of the powers of rule-making and adjudication conferred upon them by law. Administrative law is therefore an important part of constitutional law designed to secure that the wide powers and discretion conferred upon administrative bodies and regulatory agencies both to make general rules and to determine the rights of individuals are exercised fairly and within the limits expressed or implied in the law conferring such powers. In the early years of the century 'administrative law' was sometimes understood as referring to a system of special courts for deciding cases in which government officials were involved and where they might enjoy special privileges and immunities.

H.L.A.H.

Bibl: H. W. R. Wade, *Administrative Law* (Oxford and N.Y., 2nd ed., 1967); J. A. G. Griffith and H. Street, *Principles of Administrative Law* (London, 1973).

Adorno, Theodor W. (German sociologist and music critic, 1903–69), see under FRANKFURT SCHOOL; NEO-MARXISM.

adrenal gland. A composite endocrine gland (see ENDOCRINOLOGY) of dual origin and dual function.

(1) The central core (medulla) secretes *adrenalin* (= *epinephrine*) and *noradrenalin*, which have some of the effects of general sympathetic nervous stimulation: heart rate increases, the subject turns pale, and hairs prickle as their levator muscles contract. These physical signs are accompanied by the EMOTIONS of which they are usually thought to be the consequence, e.g. fright or extreme disquiet.

(2) The shell (adrenal cortex) produces the secretions which control the traffic of salts through the body and exercise a long-term effect on the activity of the lymphoid TISSUES upon which immunological responses depend (see IMMUNITY). This second function is mediated through hormones related to cortisone. The disease associated with failure of adrenal function, particularly of the cortex, is 'Addison's disease'. P.M.

adsorption. The concentration of one substance very near the surface of another (not *ab*sorption, where one substance is uniformly dispersed through the body of another). Adsorption is involved in all industrial processes relying on surface activity, such as DETERGENT production, spraying, and mineral separation. M.V.B.

adventurism, see under DEVIATIONISM.

advocacy planning. A development in urban planning, originating in the U.S.A. in the 1960s, in which the interests of different groups are represented by 'advocates' – usually professional planners. It attempts to reconcile through a DIALECTIC process conflicts between different interests (especially between the community and the municipal planning body); to increase the number involved in making decisions; and to ensure proper represen-

tation of minorities. It has proved more effective in meeting specific objections and local demands than in reconciling widely conflicting views. M.BR.

Bibl: P. Davidoff, 'Advocacy and Pluralism in Planning' (*American Institute of Planners Journal*, Nov. 1965).

aerial photography, see AIR PHOTOGRAPHY.

aerobes, see under BACTERIOLOGY.

aerodynamics. The study of the flow of gases (particularly air) past solid bodies (such as ROCKETS or aircraft), and in response to temperature and pressure variations. See also HYDRODYNAMICS. M.V.B.

aerography. A branch of AEROLOGY which seeks to measure and describe the physical and chemical properties of the atmosphere (e.g. temperature, pressure, humidity). An aerograph is any self-recording instrument carried aloft by any means to obtain such data. M.L.

aerology. Formerly a synonym for METEOROLOGY, but now that subdivision of it which deals with the free atmosphere, removed from the effect of surface conditions, through its vertical extent, as distinguished from studies confined to the atmosphere adjacent to the earth's surface. M.L.

aeronautics. All activities connected with aerial locomotion, whether powered flight, as in aircraft, or non-powered, as in gliders, or even the flight of birds. The subject embraces aeronautical engineering, i.e. the design, production, and maintenance of aircraft structures, their instruments, engines, and control. It also includes the design and control of space vehicles during their passage through the earth's atmosphere and beyond. E.R.L.

aesthetic distance. In drama and other forms of art, a critic's phrase intended to remind the spectator (reader, etc.) that a work of art is not to be confused with reality, and its conventions must be fully respected: there is little point in warning the hero that the villain is creeping up behind him with a knife. The process whereby the artist seeks to establish the aesthetic distance is known as *distancing*, or in BRECHTIAN parlance ALIENATION (*Verfremdung*). Distancing should not preclude some degree of 'identification' on the spectator's part.   D.J.E.

aestheticism. Either (1) the view that works of art should be judged by strictly aesthetic criteria (see AESTHETICS; CRITERION) and that their value has nothing to do with their moral, political, or religious UTILITY; or (2) the more extreme view that in life and action as a whole aesthetic values should take precedence over values of other kinds. Gautier's slogan 'art for art's sake' expresses the more moderate view. The theory of life expounded in the conclusion to Pater's *Renaissance* and practised by Oscar Wilde is closer to the more extreme one. It has seldom been chosen as a label by those who are held to adhere to it and has a mildly derogatory flavour.   A.Q.

aesthetics. The philosophical study of art, and also of nature to the extent that we take the same attitude to it as we do to art. The notion of an aesthetic attitude is thus of central importance. It is commonly held to be a style of PERCEPTION concerned neither with the factual information to be gained from the things perceived, nor with their practical uses, but rather with the immediate qualities of the contemplative experience itself. Works of art are human productions designed to reward this kind of attention. But it can also be given to natural objects such as scenery, flowers, human bodies. Aesthetics aims to define the CONCEPT of the aesthetic attitude and of the work of art which is its primary object. It asks to what extent works of art should be representative, and to what extent they should express the emotions of their creators. It aims to identify the characteristic value (which few would now call beauty) of aesthetically satisfying objects. It considers the problem of the nature of a work of art's existence (is it a pattern of words or sounds or patches of colour, or is it a physical thing?), and that of the relation between aesthetic and moral value.   A.Q.
Bibl: M. C. Beardsley, *Aesthetics* (N.Y., 1958); W. Charlton, *Aesthetics* (London and N.Y., 1970).

aetiology (or *etiology*), see under EPIDEMIOLOGY.

affective fallacy. Term invented by W. K. Wimsatt and Monroe C. Beardsley to describe the supposed fallacy of reading a work in terms of its 'results in the mind of its audience'. The CONCEPT is useful but limited: part of reading a work is the study of it as an independent STRUCTURE; but it would not, in practical terms, be worth study if it had no emotional effect. In fact, works have an 'effect' on Wimsatt and Beardsley, and whenever they discuss them they too are guilty of their own fallacy. Egregious though the 'affective fallacy' may be in terms of the humanity of literature, however, it has been of stimulative value.   M.S.-S.
Bibl: W. K. Wimsatt, *The Verbal Icon* (Lexington, 1954; London, 1970).

affectivity, see under PATTERN VARIABLES.

affine geometry, see under GEOMETRY.

affinity. A term widely used in early chemical literature to express the capacity of a substance for CHEMICAL REACTION. This is now seen to be related to the FREE ENERGY change.   B.F.

affluent society. Term that has become the subject of considerable discussion since being made famous by John Kenneth Galbraith with his book *The Affluent Society* (1958), in which the first and still most complete exposition of its popular meaning is given. An affluent society is one where the widespread poverty and want that have been the lot of mankind through the ages has been replaced by sufficient abundance to enable the population as a whole to enjoy conventional notions of a reasonably comfortable standard of living. In such a society the 'conventional wisdom' of economic theory, designed as it is for dealing with the problems of scarcity, is no longer a useful tool of economic analysis. For the priority traditionally given to increasing production in the PRIVATE SECTOR of the economy is no longer rational. It leads to a situation of private affluence accompanied by public squalor, for the PUBLIC SECTOR is still seen as an obstacle to the diversion of resources to expanding output of CONSUMERS' GOODS.

Hence, an affluent society produces cars but not enough roads for them, or more private wealth but not the police forces necessary to protect it, etc. This situation is aggravated by the artificial stimulation of consumer DEMAND through advertising, and the excessive expansion of consumer credit provisions. The imbalance between private and public sector output, and other effects of the conventional economic goals, mean that national product as measured may still rise although human welfare may decline.　　W.B.

Bibl: W. Beckerman, *In Defence of Economic Growth* (London, 1974).

Aflaq, Michel (Syrian social and political leader, *b*. 1910), see under BA'ATH.

after-burning.

(1) In internal combustion engines, the process whereby the burning of the fuel in the cylinder occurs, not instantaneously between the compression period and the working stroke, but partly during the latter. Despite the loss of efficiency involved, after-burning is necessary to prevent excessive (in theory infinite) pressure being created by a very rapid (in theory instantaneous) burning.

(2) In jet engines, the use of special 'after-burners' in the outlet pipe in order to minimize the escape of combustible materials and augment the power of the main jet engine.

(3) The use in exhaust pipes of catalytic or other burners in order to reduce atmospheric POLLUTION.　　E.R.L.

after-care. Term used to describe the variety of schemes devised to assist convicted offenders on their release from prison. In Britain the system was, from the early 19th century until the 1960s, predominantly in the hands of private charities, subsidized latterly by the State. Originally consisting of grants of money, vouchers, and/or clothing and tools, the system became increasingly discredited as ineffectual and socially degrading. After-care is now the responsibility of the official Probation Service, which provides throughout the sentence a wide measure of social-work assistance and advice (as distinct from financial aid) both to the

prisoner and, especially, to his dependants.　　T.M.

Bibl: K. Soothill, *The Prisoner's Release* (London, 1974).

after-image. In PERCEPTION, the visual after-effect produced by focusing on an object and then looking at a blank surface. It usually appears in a colour complementary to the original and obeys *Emmert's Law* to the effect that its apparent size varies in direct proportion to the apparent distance of the surface against which it is cast.　　J.S.B.

age-and-area hypothesis. Anthropological hypothesis that CULTURE traits tend to diffuse from single or multiple centres rather like ripples on a pond after a stone is thrown. Consequently cultures on the periphery may show traits which were characteristic of the centre in an earlier period. There is considerable dispute as to the reliability of the MODEL in reconstructing any given culture history. See also DIFFUSION, SPATIAL.　　P.H.

Bibl: M. J. Herskovits, *Cultural Anthropology* (N.Y., 1955), pp. 468 ff.

agency shop, see under CLOSED SHOP.

aggiornamento. Italian word meaning 'bringing up to date'; it usually refers to the renewal of Roman CATHOLICISM begun while John XXIII was Pope (1958–63) and in large measure authorized by VATICAN COUNCIL II. The Mass has been made a more corporate act of worship, and the use of Latin has almost ceased (see LITURGICAL MOVEMENT). More responsibility has been attributed to the laity, instead of to the clergy; and to all the bishops, instead of a Papal monopoly of power. There has been more emphasis on the Christian's involvement in the modern world (see PACEM IN TERRIS), sustained by simpler prayer. An intellectually active and free THEOLOGY, in its inspiration BIBLICAL, has begun to emerge. More acknowledgement of other Christian Churches, and more cooperation with them in the ECUMENICAL MOVEMENT, have been encouraged. Some Roman Catholics have reacted conservatively, suspecting MODERNISM. Others have felt that the officially tolerated pace of change has been too slow and have left either the

11

priesthood or the Church.   D.L.E.

Bibl: A. M. J. Kloosterman, *Contemporary Catholicism* (London, 1972); M. Trevor, *Pope John* (London and N.Y., 1967).

agglutinating (or *agglutinative*). In comparative LINGUISTICS, terms applied to a language (e.g. Turkish) in which words typically consist of long sequences of affixes and roots, each element usually having a clear identity and separate meaning. English shows little tendency to agglutinate: humorous constructs such as *antidisestablishmentarianism* are exceptional. The term is one of three used in the approach to linguistic typology proposed by August von Schlegel (1767–1845), the others being ISOLATING and INFLECTING.   D.C.

agglutination. In immunology (see IMMUNITY), the clumping together of CELLS, particularly red blood corpuscles, brought about by the action of a specific antibody. Thus SERUM from someone of BLOOD GROUP B or O will agglutinate the red blood corpuscles from someone of blood group A. The antibodies that bring this about are called *agglutinins*.   P.M.

agglutinative, see AGGLUTINATING.

aggregate demand. A central component of KEYNESIAN economic analysis, aggregate demand is the value of the total of planned expenditures in an economy. Together, aggregate SUPPLY AND DEMAND determine total output, the value of which is known as NATIONAL INCOME. Unlike the DEMAND for a single product, which is assumed to depend primarily on its own price, aggregate demand is treated as depending primarily on the total of people's incomes – national income again. In principle, if all markets cleared smoothly, there would be a set of equations relating supply and demand for each product to incomes and prices, which would determine not only the price of each product, but also the quantity, and thus the total value, of all output, i.e. national income. Keynes (1936) emphasized that the failure of certain markets, particularly the labour market, to clear continuously (a failure exemplified by involuntary UNEMPLOYMENT) made income the principal determinant of *effective* aggregate demand.   J.S.F.

Bibl: J. M. Keynes, *The General Theory of Employment Interest and Money* (London and N.Y., 1936).

aggregation.

(1) In STATISTICS, the reduction of data brought about by grouping the categories in a classification. For instance, in INPUT-OUTPUT ANALYSIS the individual branches of production may be grouped, thereby reducing the size of the table of intermediate product flows. The results obtained from grouped tables tend to be less accurate than those obtained from ungrouped tables unless either the cost structures or the sales structures of the grouped branches are very much alike. The problem of aggregation arises fairly generally in ECONOMICS, though it can also arise elsewhere.   R.ST.

(2) In BIOLOGY, a grouping or crowding together of separate organisms. The term is used also to describe the movement of tentacles and tendrils to a point which is stimulated, as for instance in sea anemones. The gregarious habit, producing aggregations of animals, is considered to be a primitive form of social behaviour. It implies a temporary grouping of individuals, usually of the same age and in the same stage of development (e.g. caterpillars on a food plant, mosquitoes over a pond). Mating may occur when aggregations exist, but the pairs usually separate soon afterwards.   K.M.

Bibl: J. L. Cloudsley-Thompson, *Animal Behaviour* (Edinburgh, 1960; N.Y., 1961).

aggression. Animal or human behaviour which is provoked by another individual and which has deterrent or aversive effects on that individual: it leads him to withdraw, either by moving away or by ceasing to dispute some object which is the occasion of the aggression. The charge of a ram in rut, the measured display of two male Siamese fighting fish, and the malicious remark made by a man about a professional colleague may all represent examples of aggression in these SPECIES.

Animal aggression is extremely widespread, and appears to evolve whenever a species needs some kind of deterrent behaviour to secure access to some commodity in short supply. Thus there may be fighting over TERRITORY, food, females, sleeping places, or nesting burrows, or for social precedence as a determinant of access to any of these. The hunting behaviour of predators shares some of the features of aggression but is essentially different in that the goal is to eat the other animal rather than simply to drive it away. It may, however, provoke aggression in the form of defensive reactions. Such reactions against predators and against prey should be distinguished from social aggression directed at members of the same species. In the latter, while there is usually the ultimate sanction of physical violence, more often the fight consists of a graduated series of escalating displays which indicate to each combatant how ready the opponent is to continue the struggle. The fight ends when one combatant either runs away or assumes some special posture of appeasement which tends to ensure safety from attack. If, however, space to flee is restricted, e.g. in captivity, the attack on the defeated animal may continue and it may be killed.

The relation between aggression in animals and in man has been much disputed, but the view outlined above suggests that the matter should be examined in the light of the life styles and needs of each species. The complexity of human society involves infinitely complex social, psychological, and biological needs, and many of these goals are achieved through aggressive behaviour, often largely verbal. Such behaviour seems to correspond to animal threat signals in that it is designed to gain access to special facilities, and if unsuccessful may lead to more violent forms of aggression. The expression of individual aggression in man can take almost any form and be associated with a great number of motivational factors, frustration of some goal-directed behaviour being a common one. In man too there is WAR, which operates as aggression at the level of society, but in which the motives of the combatants may be very different from the anger of a private dispute. J.M.C.

Bibl: K. Lorenz, tr. M. Latzke, *On Aggression* (London and N.Y., 1966); A. Storr, *Human Aggression* (London and N.Y., 1968).

Agitprop. The Department of Agitation and Propaganda, set up in September 1920 as a section of the Central Committee secretariat of the COMMUNIST Party of the Soviet Union. Through all subsequent reorganizations and changes of its full, official name, its essential function has remained the same: the control of activities concerned with the IDEOLOGICAL conditioning of the population. The scope of Agitprop's routine activities has steadily increased and its influence extended in all MEDIA of communication: press, radio, film, television, literature, and art. Anti-religious propaganda was added very early to its functions. Agitprop also promotes intermittent propaganda campaigns centred around special themes. Internally, such campaigns are often associated with new departures of the Party line. (The Chinese Communists engage regularly in such campaigns, e.g. the 'blooming and contending' campaign during the HUNDRED FLOWERS period, the subsequent 'anti-rightist' campaign, etc.) Internationally, campaigns – e.g. the 1947 Stockholm peace appeal, the campaign about the alleged bacteriological warfare in KOREA, etc. – have been conducted by Agitprop with the help of Communist FRONT ORGANIZATIONS, but the emergence of Communist POLYCENTRISM and of conflicts between different Communist Parties has deprived such campaigns of their universal scope. L.L.

Bibl: J. C. Clews, *Communist Propaganda Techniques* (London and N.Y., 1964); L. Schapiro, *The Communist Party of the Soviet Union* (rev. ed., London, 1970; N.Y., 1971).

agnosia, see under NEUROPSYCHOLOGY.

agnosticism. A word coined by T. H. Huxley (1825–95) to refer to his own conviction that knowledge (Greek *gnosis*) is impossible in many of the matters covered by religious doctrines and by philosophical speculation, so that on these matters, unless science can speak, silence is the only wisdom. A considerable degree of agnosticism about the supernatural has been a mark of almost all thinking people in the 20th century, whether or not these hold that there is TRUTH in THEISM and VALUE in THEOLOGY. In particular it has generally been agreed that religious faith does not provide factual knowledge more authoritative than NATURAL SCIENCE, and that Huxley was therefore right to defend the DARWINIAN discovery of EVOLUTION against Christians who took the biblical COSMOGONY literally. See also ATHEISM; HUMANISM; NON-THEISTIC RELIGION. D.L.E.

Bibl: W. M. Dixon, *The Human Situation* (London and N.Y., 1937).

agrarian history. The history of farming techniques and peasant customs. The term came into general use about 1950, and covers two rather different approaches:

(1) that of economic historians interested in a particular industry, agriculture; this approach is dominant in England (the 'Leicester school') and the Netherlands (the 'Wageningen school', led by B. H. Slicher van Bath);

(2) that of social historians interested in a particular social group, the peasants; this is the French approach, associated in particular with Marc Bloch and Emmanuel Le Roy Ladurie, and perhaps better described as *rural history*. P.B.

Bibl: H. P. R. Finberg (ed.), *The Agrarian History of England and Wales* (London, in progress).

agribusiness. The sum total of all operations involved in (1) the manufacture and distribution of products used for production purposes on farms; (2) production on farms; and (3) the storage, processing, and distribution of commodities produced on farms and items made from them. For the situation in most developed countries in the mid 20th century the term can be regarded as covering those activities which were carried out on family farms before draught animals were displaced by tractors and before the growth of the artificial fertilizer and specialist animal feeding-stuffs industries and the highly organized processing and distribution industries for food and natural fibres. Interest in the subject usually centres on the means of securing coordination between the various stages. K.E.H.

Bibl: J. H. Davis and R. A. Goldberg, *A Concept of Agribusiness* (Cambridge, Mass., 1957).

agrology, see SOIL SCIENCE.

agronomy. The scientific study of agricultural production processes. K.E.H.

AID, see under ARTIFICIAL INSEMINATION.

AIH, see under ARTIFICIAL INSEMINATION.

Aiken, Conrad (U.S. poet and novelist, 1889–1973), see under POETRY BOOKSHOP.

air photography. As an adjunct to ARCHAEOLOGY, the technique of photographing archaeological sites or landscapes from the air. Among the earliest archaeological air photographs were those of Stonehenge (1906). In the 1920s the method was developed by O. G. S. Crawford, Major Allen, Père Poidebard, and Col. Charles Lindberg. Its success depends on choosing the optimum conditions for registering the visibility of the buried remains. Thus in ploughed fields features may show as discolourations in the soil, while, under crop, differential growth may reflect subsoil variations. When slight relief is preserved, low sunlight will throw sharp shadows. Vertical photographs in overlapping pairs are used for stereoscopic scanning and photogrammetric planning; oblique photographs are generally used to demonstrate the buried features more clearly. Experiments with INFRA-RED photography are now under way. B.C.

Bibl: O. G. S. Crawford, *Air Survey and Archaeology* (London, 2nd ed., 1928).

Ajdukiewicz, Kazimierz (Polish logician and semanticist (1890–1963), see under PERSPECTIVISM.

Akhmatova, Anna (pseud. of Anna Gorenko, Russian poetess, 1889–1966), see under ACMEISM; ZHDANOVSHCHINA.

Aktion, Die, see under ACTIVISM; EXPRESSIONISM.

Alawites, see under BA'ATH.

al-Banna, Hasan (Egyptian founder of the Muslim Brotherhood, 1906–49), see under MUSLIM BROTHERHOOD.

Albee, Edward (U.S. dramatist, *b.* 1928), see under OFF-BROADWAY.

Albéniz, Isaac (Spanish composer, 1860–1909), see under IMPRESSIONISM.

Albers, Joseph (German-born artist, 1888–1976), see under BLACK MOUNTAIN; CONCRETE ART.

albinism. A congenital defect, of mutational origin (see MUTATION), in the pigmentary system of human beings and rodents, caused by a biochemical deficiency of pigmentary CELLS and leading to the virtually complete absence of pigmentation in the skin and the retina of the eye (which accordingly looks red). In one form of albinism the deposition of pigment is stimulated by a low skin temperature with the effect that the body generally is white but the 'points' (nose, eartips, paws) are black. This is the so-called 'Himalayan' pattern.   P.M.

Aldermaston, see under CND.

Aldington, Richard (British author, 1892–1962), see under EGOIST, THE; IMAGISM.

Aldiss, Brian Wilson (British novelist, *b*. 1925), see under SCIENCE FICTION.

aleatory (or, less commonly, *aleatoric*). An adjective (derived from Latin *alea*, a game using dice) applied to several of the arts, and indicating that the artist or writer or composer allows some element of chance to be involved.

In art, the deliberate exploitation of the workings of chance can be held to go back to the 'blot drawings' of Alexander Cozens in the late 18th century. In our own century the practice began with the 'found objects' (see OBJET TROUVÉ) of the SURREALISTS and, in the 1940s, the accidental drip technique of Jackson Pollock (see ACTION PAINTING). In KINETIC ART effects are sometimes regarded as aleatory merely in so far as they are achieved with the aid of unpredictable natural forces such as air, water, fire, magnetism, or chemical action. A more mathematical use of random selection can be seen in many forms of COMPUTER art (e.g. COMPUTER GRAPHICS) and in the permutation of symbols in some CONCRETE POETRY.

In literature, the 'cut-out' and 'fold-in' method of William Burroughs involves the random stringing together of sentences (his own and other people's) in whose combination some mystical significance is perceived; other writers (e.g. B. S. Johnson in *Trawl*) allow the reader to assemble pages *ad lib*. Michel Butor and Henri Pousseur's opera, *Votre Faust*, allows the audience to select the ending. Again, the computer is sometimes used to generate random combinations of preselected words or sentences, as by the Italian poet Nanni Balestrini or the German aesthetician (see AESTHETICS) Max Bense. The results can only be made acceptable if it is assumed that repetitiousness and boredom are legitimate elements of art.

In music, an aleatory element is introduced if, e.g., the order in which sections of a composition are performed is decided by the throwing of a dice, or if there is improvisation by the performers, usually on patterns suggested in the score. In its more extreme forms, music commonly but improperly called aleatory (since it is *indeterminate* rather than determined by chance) can be criticized as a dereliction of responsibility by the composer, as when the performer is expected to interpret symbols having no basis in any previously known form of musical notation. Yet, used imaginatively, it has proved a useful addition to the resources of the 20th-century composer.

In HAPPENINGS and other mixed-media exercises, similar random choices are common. The *I Ching* or Book of Change has had a considerable influence on some of the leading practitioners, giving an alleged deep meaningfulness to the abrogation of human choice. Other adjectives used with connotations similar to those of aleatory are *stochastic* and PERMUTATIONAL.   J.W.; P.C.; A.H.

Alechinsky, Pierre (Belgian painter, *b*. 1927), see under COBRA.

algebra. The branch of MATHEMATICS traditionally associated with performing arithmetic operations on expressions containing letters (VARIABLES) which stand for unknown or indeterminate NUMBERS. If division, except by an integer, be excluded, then every such expression is a POLYNOMIAL with rational COEFFICIENTS, e.g. $\frac{1}{2}xy^3 + \frac{1}{4}z^2 - 3x + \frac{2}{3}$. An *algebraic equation* (see also EQUATION) is the condition on the variables expressed

15

by setting such a polynomial equal to zero. If there is only one variable then there are finitely many real or COMPLEX numbers which satisfy the equation – its *roots*. An *algebraic number* is a root of some such equation. The theory of these numbers *Galois theory*, is one of the most satisfying branches of mathematics; it was founded by Évariste Galois (1811–32), who was killed in a duel at the age of 21. He showed that there can be no algebraic formula for solving equations of the 5th degree. His methods also prove that some famous geometrical problems (doubling the cube, trisecting an angle) cannot be solved by ruler and compasses. The theory of algebraic equations in more than one variable is the concern of algebraic GEOMETRY. *Abstract algebra* is concerned with general MATHEMATICAL STRUCTURES which have analogues of the arithmetical operations; see, e.g., BOOLEAN ALGEBRA; GROUPS; MATRICES; QUATERNIONS; VECTORS. Such structures may be characterized by axioms (see AXIOMATIC METHOD); of particular importance are the ASSOCIATIVE LAW and the COMMUTATIVE LAW. Algebraic methods, which reduce the solution of problems to manipulations of symbolic expressions, permeate all branches of mathematics.   R.G.

Bibl: W. W. Sawyer, *A Concrete Approach to Abstract Algebra* (London and San Francisco, 1959).

algedonic. Pertaining to REGULATION in a non-analytic mode. The word derives from the Greek words for pain and pleasure, and expresses the fact that some regulators operate within a SYSTEM from CRITERIA that exist only in a META-SYSTEM. For example, people may be trained to perform a task by explaining the system in which that task plays a part, analysing the 'why' and the 'how' of the job. But they may also be trained algedonically by a series of rewards and punishments which offer no such explanations. The metasystem making these awards constrains the system by regulating outcomes and not by direct intervention. For example, a fail-safe device switches off an entire system because some output of the system has reached a level regarded as dangerous to the whole: it may take days to discover later what actually went wrong.   S.BE.

Algol 60. A HIGH-LEVEL PROGRAMMING LANGUAGE for scientific calculations. It is more powerful than FORTRAN but less commonly available, especially in the U.S.A.   C.S.

algorithm. A procedure for performing a complicated operation by carrying out a precisely determined sequence of simpler ones – e.g. the digit-by-digit multiplication of large numbers which only uses single-digit multiplication and addition; or the direction 'First left, second right, turn right at the Red Lion, my house is the third on the left'. The same task can often be performed by different algorithms of widely varying complexity. The development of algorithms has introduced a hierarchical structure into human thought which has greatly increased its power. They form suitable subjects for computer programs (see COMPUTER; PROGRAM) since they exclude all personal judgement; and part of the importance of computers lies in the way in which they have extended the length and complexity of algorithms which can be used, and hence the range of problems which can be tackled mechanically. VALUE-JUDGEMENTS and many complicated situations are not amenable to algorithmic treatment except in the form of greatly simplified MODELS. See also PROGRAMMING.   C.S.

Ali Muhammed (*né* Cassius Clay; U.S. boxer, *b.* 1942), see under BLACK MUSLIMS.

alias transformation, see under TRANSFORMATION.

alienation. For about a century (*c.* 1840 to 1940) the term was used to denote either the transfer of ownership or title of a piece of property, or a quality of mental derangement or insanity. Then a set of new and different meanings began to appear: a sense of estrangement from society, a feeling of powerlessness to affect social change, or a depersonalization of the individual in a large and bureaucratic (see BUREAUCRACY) society. By the 1950s the new meanings had become widely established and alienation had become a central term of contemporary SOCIOLOGY.

Reasons for these developments included the evident disorientations of the Western world in the upheaval of society following World War II; the expansion of an intelligentsia (see INTELLECTUALS) which found its own ROLE and STATUS problematic; the growing influence of German sociological writers (notably Georg Simmel and Max Weber) who stressed bureaucratization and the help-lessness of the individual; the theological writings of Paul Tillich with his emphasis on the depersonalization of the individual in modern society; and – the most direct and important influence – the discovery of some early writings of Marx which had used alienation as a key CONCEPT in the analysis of CAPITALISM. (For another key concept see REIFICATION.) These were the so-called Economic and Philosophical Manuscripts written in 1844, and pub-lished only in 1932 in the abortive *Marx-Engels Gesamtausgabe.* They reflect the strong influence on Marx's thinking of Hegel, for whom alienation is the central process in the growing self-consciousness of Man. As Hegel traces the idea in his *Phenomenology of Mind,* CONSCIOUS-NESS 'divides' itself into subject and object, and alienation is the process whereby mind 'objectifies' itself in thought – a positive step in the develop-ment of self-consciousness. Marx concen-trates on the alienation of labour and emphasizes the invidious aspects. He uses three terms, all of which have confusingly been translated as 'alienation': *Vergegen-standlichung,* or objectification, whose English equivalent in the philosophical sense is REIFICATION; *Entfremdung* or estrangement (Hegel had used principally *Selbstentfremdung* – 'self-estrangement'); and *Entäusserung* or the sale of one's self as a commodity. In effect, Marx is saying that in the condition of alienation a worker loses control over the *processes* of work, over the *product* of his labour, and becomes a *thing.* Later, as Marx focused his attention on social organization and CLASS relations, this cluster of terms dis-appeared from his vocabulary, and was replaced by the specific analytical concept of *Ausbeutung* or exploitation. The resur-rection of the term 'alienation' in the late 1940s and 1950s was part of the effort of NEO-MARXISTS to reinstate a broader, more HUMANIST version of Marx's thought.

Within academic sociology, alienation was given a social-psychological emphasis (see SOCIAL PSYCHOLOGY) and, for a time, mingled with the concept of ANOMIE. Social psychologists sought to develop 'scales' of alienation to measure the degree of 'powerlessness', 'normlessness', 'meaninglessness', and 'social isolation' felt by individuals, and further efforts were made to correlate these psycho-logical states with conformity, political apathy, cynicism, suicide, and a host of similar phenomena. Most of these efforts had evaporated by the end of the 1960s. (In the modern theatre the BRECHTIAN *Verfremdungseffekt,* alienation effect, indicates 'distancing' – see AESTHETIC DISTANCE – as opposed to the direct emo-tional involvement of the spectator in the action on the stage.) Within MARXISM, an onslaught against the concept of aliena-tion as central to Marx was mounted by the French COMMUNIST philosopher Louis Althusser, who contended that Marx had discarded the earlier Hegelian influences and had come to what Althus-ser calls a STRUCTURALIST interpretation of society. For these reasons, plus the rise of a mood of revolutionary (see REVOLU-TION) ACTIVISM by students in the late 1960s, the concept of alienation had by the close of the decade begun to lose much of its resonance in LEFT-wing thinking.
D.B.

Bibl: D. Bell, 'The Debate on Aliena-tion', in L. Labedz (ed.), *Revisionism* (London and N.Y., 1962); R. Schacht, *Alienation* (N.Y., 1970); B. Ollman, *Alie-nation: Marx's Conception of Man in Capitalist Society* (London and N.Y., 1971).

alkali. A hydroxide of lithium, sodium, potassium, rubidium, or caesium; most commonly sodium hydroxide. Solutions of alkalis are strongly basic (see BASE). B.F.

alkaloid. A member of an arbitrary and ill-defined class of (pharmacologically active) plant extractives, mostly posses-sing pronounced pharmacological effects, and all tasting very bitter – the property to which they owe their name. They include atropine, morphine, and digitalis. Most of the alkaloids are BASES and form salts with ACIDS. P.M.

alkathene, see POLYTHENE.

all-or-none law. A law governing the relationships between the excitatory

17

STIMULUS acting upon a nerve fibre (whether by direct stimulation or through a sense organ) and the impulse which it excites. Nothing happens until the excitatory stimulus exceeds a certain 'threshold' value, whereupon the nerve fibre propagates an impulse at a rate which is different for different nerve fibres. As the passage of this impulse is followed by an inexcitable period known as its *absolute refractory state* it follows that the nerve fibre will perform either fully or not at all. P.M.

allele (formerly *allelomorph*). One of the hereditary factors which, in Mendelian (see MENDELISM) HEREDITY, are present in pairs, one factor from each pair deriving from each parent. When the two factors represent a choice of two from a range larger than two, the alleles are referred to as *multiple alleles*. J.M.S.

Allen, John (British theatre director and educator, *b.* 1912), see under UNITY THEATRE.

allergy. A form of exaggerated immunological reactivity (see IMMUNITY) towards foreign organic substances such as pollen grains or certain industrial chemicals. Such *allergens* are normally harmless in themselves but the reactions they sometimes excite may cause considerable physical distress. The allergies conceived in a wide sense include asthma, hayfever, urticaria, eczemas, local and systemic ANAPHYLAXIS, sensitization to industrial chemicals, and the strong reactivity towards tuberculin that is used in the Mantoux test for exposure to tubercular infection. Allergic reactivity can often be transferred from one individual to another by means of transfusions of blood SERUM containing the appropriate antibody. P.M.

allomorph, see under MORPHEME.

allophone, see under PHONEME.

allopolyploid, see under POLYPLOID.

allotrope. When an ELEMENT exists in more than one molecular or structural form, each of these is called an allotrope. There are numerous examples: molecular oxygen contains two ATOMS, ozone has three; carbon has graphite and diamond as

allotropes. The interconversion of allotropic forms is often brought about by changes in temperature and/or pressure. B.F.

allotypy. A state of affairs first described by the French immunologist (see IMMUNITY) Oudin in which the different individuals of a SPECIES possess antibody MOLECULES (immunoglobulins) belonging to one or another of a small number of distinct and well-defined chemical classes. There has since been some tendency to extend the notion to cover chemical POLYMORPHISM generally. This usage is unusual, however. P.M.

Alloway, Lawrence (British-born U.S. art critic, *b.* 1926), see under POP.

alloy. A mixture of metallic ELEMENTS, e.g. brass (copper and zinc), bronze (copper and tin), stainless steel (iron, with various other elements). B.F.

alpha particle. A very stable association of two PROTONS and two NEUTRONS, which is emitted during RADIOACTIVE decay, and which also constitutes the NUCLEUS of the helium ATOM. See also PARTICLE. M.V.B.

Alsberg, Henry Garfield (U.S. editor, 1881–1970), see under WPA.

alternation of generations. A state of affairs in which, in the ordinary course of reproduction, vegetatively and sexually reproducing organisms succeed each other alternately. Asexual reproduction by budding or equivalent processes can only give rise to genetic replicas of the parent; sexual reproduction raises the possibility of a genetic intermingling between two different kinds of GENOME, and ultimately the formation of new kinds. Alternation of generations is common in the group of animals to which hydroids and jellyfish belong, and, among plants, in bryophytes and pheridophytes. P.M.

alternative society, see under UNDERGROUND.

Althusser, Louis (French philosopher, *b.* 1918), see under ALIENATION; NEO-MARXISM.

am Ende, Hans, see ENDE, HANS AM.

amalgam. An ALLOY containing mercury. Amalgams of silver, gold, and tin are used in dentistry. B.F.

Amarú, Túpac (Peruvian Indian revolutionary, 1742(?)–81), see under TUPAMAROS.

ambiguity. The coexistence in a piece of writing of two or more meanings. William Empson introduced his *Seven Types of Ambiguity* (1930; 2nd ed., 1947) by stating: 'I propose to use the word in an extended sense, and shall think relevant to my subject any verbal nuance, however slight, which gives room for alternative reactions to the same piece of language.' This study, directly influenced by I. A. Richards and Robert Graves, was very much a product of a time excited by T. S. Eliot's poetry and criticism, by the revival of the 17th-century Metaphysical poets, and by Freud. If over-ingenious, *Seven Types of Ambiguity* is a complex and sophisticated work (Empson reminds us that 'if an ambiguity is to be unitary there must be "forces" holding its elements together'), but during the 1930s and 40s 'ambiguity' became so fashionable that many versifiers cultivated it, whether usefully or not, while critics hunted it down indiscriminately, thus denigrating those kinds of literature where they could not find it. Ambiguity is a quality of much fine writing, endowing it with richness, subtlety, or surprise, but in itself (like rhyme, onomatopoeia, figures of speech, etc.) it is neither good nor bad. See also PLURISIGNATION. D.J.E.

ambivalence. Term used originally (as *ambivalency*) in ABNORMAL PSYCHOLOGY and PSYCHIATRY, later annexed by literary criticism, to denote the situation in which someone entertains, simultaneously or in alternation, opposed attitudes or feelings or sets of values; the familiar 'love-hate relationship' may be said to exemplify reciprocal ambivalence. Whereas, in general, ambivalence is a potential source of undesirable stress (and in extreme forms is one of the four cardinal symptoms of SCHIZOPHRENIA listed by Eugen Bleuler), in a writer it is widely regarded as a source of strength and desirable TENSION, and in a fictional character as evidence of subtlety in his or her creator. O.S.; M.J.C.

Amiens, Charter of, see under SYNDICALISM.

amino acids. The molecular elements out of which PROTEINS are compounded. Proteins generally are compounded of some 20 different kinds of amino acid, some of which are essential constituents of the diet – e.g. lysine. Not all proteins contain a full representation of amino acids. Those that contain the essential amino acids are often referred to as 'complete' or 'first-class' proteins; those that lack one or more essential amino acids (e.g. gelatin) are referred to as 'second-class' proteins. P.M.

Amis, Kingsley (British poet and novelist, *b.* 1922), see under ANGRY YOUNG MAN; ANTI-HERO; MOVEMENT, THE.

Ammons, Albert (U.S. jazz musician, 1907–49), see under BOOGIE-WOOGIE.

amnesia, see under NEUROPSYCHOLOGY.

amplidyne. An electrical machine mostly used to control large quantities of power by means of very small quantities. Such devices are much in demand in CONTROL ENGINEERING and are analogous to an ELECTRONIC amplifier in that the main power comes from a reservoir of energy (such as a battery) and is controlled by a tiny electrical signal. See also METADYNE. E.R.L.

amplitude modulation (AM). A method for the radio transmission of AUDIO FREQUENCY signals, which are made to vary (or MODULATE) the strength of a RADIO FREQUENCY carrier wave. Broadcasts on short, medium, and long wavebands make use of amplitude modulation; this enables more transmissions to be crowded onto each waveband, at the price of some distortion of the signal (see also FREQUENCY MODULATION). M.V.B.

Amritsar Massacre. The breaking-up by rifle-fire of a crowd of demonstrating Indians at Amritsar in India on 15 April 1919, after widespread riots against British rule. The incident, in which 379 dead and 1,200 wounded were officially acknowledged, was intended by its instigator, the British general-in-charge, General Dyer, as a demonstration, but proved to have gone beyond the limits of what was acceptable to British domestic opinion, though welcomed by British communities in India for fear of anti-British pogroms. The Hunter Commission set up by the Government of India to investigate the incident was unable to avoid racial divisions, and this played a considerable part in the growth of the Indian NATIONALIST movement and the capture of the CONGRESS PARTY by Mahatma Gandhi from the moderates and constitutionalists. D.C.W.

anabolism, see under METABOLISM.

anaerobes, see under BACTERIOLOGY.

anal character, see under PSYCHOSEXUAL DEVELOPMENT.

analogy tests, see under MENTAL TESTING.

analogue computer, see under COMPUTER.

analogue-to-digital converter, see under DIGITAL-TO-ANALOGUE CONVERTER.

analogy. Likeness or similarity, usually with the implication that the likeness in question is systematic or structural. To argue by analogy is to infer from the fact that one thing is in some respects similar to another that the two things will also correspond in other, as yet unexamined, respects. In LOGIC, reasoning by analogy is a form of non-demonstrative (see DEMONSTRATION) argument which, unlike INDUCTION proper, draws conclusions about the nature of a *single* unknown thing from information about a known thing or things which it to some extent resembles. It is a form of reasoning that is peculiarly liable to yield false conclusions from true premises. A.Q.

analysis.
(1) In MATHEMATICS, the rigorous investigation of limiting processes (see LIMIT; CONVERGENCE). In particular it provides a firm foundation for the infinitesimal CALCULUS. Although Newton realized the importance of limits, so long as VARIABLES were thought of as things in motion it was not possible to pin down the basic CONCEPTS. In the 19th century this obstacle was overcome: the work of Bolzano, Cauchy, and Weierstrass replaced

intuitive notions by precise definitions. It became clear that *naive* intuition is a poor guide to the correct handling of limiting processes; e.g. a FUNCTION (or curve) may be continuous (see CONTINUITY) and yet nowhere have a DERIVATIVE (or tangent). The construction of such queer non-intuitive counter-examples (often described by mathematicians as *pathological*) is an essential part of analysis. Through them intuition is refined to the point where correct formulations of definitions and theorems can be found and rigorous proofs given. *Classical analysis* is concerned with functions of *real numbers* (see NUMBERS) and with COMPLEX FUNCTION THEORY. Many of its problems come from mathematical PHYSICS. In this century new branches of analysis have developed (e.g. MEASURE THEORY) and the subject has been enriched by the growth of TOPOLOGY. *Functional analysis* is concerned with operations on functions; it makes great use of (infinite-dimensional) VECTOR space and provides a mathematical foundation for QUANTUM MECHANICS (see also FOURIER ANALYSIS).

Unlike Newton, Leibniz thought in terms of *infinitesimals* – actually existing infinitely small quantities. As rigour developed these were rejected as metaphysical (see METAPHYSICS) and inconsistent. Recently, with the help of a trick from MATHEMATICAL LOGIC, it has been shown that they can be given a sound interpretation, so that vivid imagery and rigorous proof can go hand in hand in what is called *non-standard analysis*. This has already found applications in mathematical economics (see ECONOMETRICS). R.G.

Bibl: D. H. Fowler, *Introducing Real Analysis* (London, 1973); A. Robinson, *Non-Standard Analysis* (Amsterdam, 1970).

(2) In PHILOSOPHY, the discovery of verbal forms of expression for complex ideas and PROPOSITIONS which make explicit the complexity that is hidden by the more abbreviated character of their usual verbal formulation. As originally conceived by Russell and Moore, it was a kind of defining process, in which the defining terms are more elementary and unproblematic than the terms being defined. Examples are Mill's analysis of 'cause' as 'invariable unconditional antecedent' or

the analysis of 'knowledge' as 'justified true belief'. Russell's theory of *descriptions* supplied a technique of analysis that was widely adopted. It showed how sentences with problematic terms in them could be replaced by sentences equivalent in MEANING to them in which the troublesome expressions do not occur.   A.Q.

Bibl: A. J. Ayer, *Language, Truth and Logic* (London and N.Y., 1936); Bertrand Russell, *Our Knowledge of the External World* (London and N.Y., rev. ed., 1926), ch. 8.

analytic.

(1) In PHILOSOPHY, a term introduced by Kant, who defined a statement as analytic if it is either (*a*) one in which the predicate is contained, 'though covertly', in the subject (e.g. 'This square has four sides') or (*b*) one whose denial is self-contradictory. Statements that are not analytic are *synthetic*: their predicates do not repeat part or all of the MEANING of the subject and their denials are CONSISTENT and not self-contradictory (e.g. 'This square is large'). Some recent philosophers have defined analytic statements, perhaps too comprehensively, as those which are true in virtue of their meaning. A connected notion of the analytic is that of statements whose TRUTH is determined by the rules or conventions of language (see CONVENTIONALISM, sense 2). Frege's definition of analytic statements as those which can be shown to be true by laws of LOGIC and definitions alone has been widely adopted. It is universally accepted that definitional truisms are analytic (e.g. 'That bachelor is not married'). Many philosophers take the laws of logic and the PROPOSITIONS of pure MATHEMATICS to be analytic and, indeed, maintain that all necessary truths, establishable by reasoning alone, are analytic too. The distinction between analytic and synthetic has been criticized by Quine as resting on an unacceptably obscure and imprecise notion of meaning.   A.Q.

Bibl: A. Pap, *Semantics and Necessary Truth* (New Haven, 1958; London, 1966); W. V. Quine, *From a Logical Point of View* (London and Cambridge, Mass., 2nd ed., 1961), ch. 2; and see under ANALYSIS (sense 2, item 2).

(2) In comparative LINGUISTICS, adjective applied to a language (e.g. Vietnamese) in which the word forms are invariable, grammatical relations being indicated primarily by word order and the use of particles, not by inflections or compounding (as in INFLECTING and AGGLUTINATING languages respectively). An alternative term is *isolating*.   D.C.

analytic geometry, see under GEOMETRY.

analytic philosophy. The most general term for a wide variety of recent philosophical movements, largely in the English-speaking world, which (1) are sceptical of or hostile to constructive METAPHYSICAL speculation, (2) agree that there is a characteristic method of ANALYSIS with which alone philosophy can arrive at secure results, and (3), for the most part, favour the piecemeal tackling of philosophical problems. The EMPIRICISM of Locke, Hume, and Mill was analytical in tendency, seeking to show how the complex IDEAS (e.g. material object, cause, person) with which the mind thinks about the world are composed of simple ideas acquired through the senses. Analytical philosophers of this century have concentrated as a matter of principle, not on ideas in the mind, but on the language in which the mind's thinking is expressed. Bertrand Russell and G. E. Moore inaugurated analytic philosophy in the early years of the century by applying the new LOGIC, to which Russell had so greatly contributed, as an instrument of analysis. Wittgenstein, learning from and influencing Russell, made the practice systematic and emphasized the linguistic character of its proper subject-matter (see LOGICAL ATOMISM). The LOGICAL POSITIVISM of the VIENNA CIRCLE carried the work further, and the earlier suspicion of metaphysics hardened into principled hostility. Wittgenstein later came to question the adequacy of formal logic as the instrument of analysis, and his school, and that of the ordinary-language philosophers of Oxford (see LINGUISTIC PHILOSOPHY) preferred to carry out the analysis of language informally, acknowledging the multiplicity of its uses and the variety and flexibility of the rules that govern it.   A.Q.

Bibl: J. O. Urmson, *Philosophical Analysis* (Oxford, 1956); G. J. Warnock,

English Philosophy since 1900 (London, 1958).

analytic psychology, see under JUNGIAN.

analytical chemistry. The branch of CHEMISTRY concerned with the identification and estimation of ELEMENTS, RADICALS, or compounds. *Qualitative analysis* is concerned with the detection of chemical SPECIES and often makes use of CHEMICAL REACTIONS which give distinctive products (recognized by colour, solubility, etc.), but characteristic physical properties are often directly investigated. For *quantitative determinations* a wide variety of chemical and physical methods have been developed. Chemical procedures include the precipitation and weighing of an insoluble product; the determination of the oxidizing or reducing properties of a solution, and the measurement of the ACID or BASE strength of a solution. Extensive use is made of physical measurements which may be based on spectroscopic or electrical behaviour (see SPECTROSCOPY; ELECTRICITY), the use of radioactive (see RADIOACTIVITY) ISOTOPES, or MASS SPECTROMETRY. CHROMATOGRAPHIC or ION EXCHANGE methods may be employed to effect an initial separation of mixtures.   B.F.

Bibl: I. M. Kolthoff, E. B. Sandel, E. J. Meehan, and S. Bruckenstein, *Quantitative Chemical Analysis* (London and N.Y., 4th ed., 1969).

anaphylaxis. Literally, the opposite of PROPHYLAXIS. In practice its use is confined to an acute form of ALLERGY associated with the introduction of an antigen (see IMMUNITY), particularly a soluble antigen, into an organism that has already made antibodies (see IMMUNITY) directed against it. Anaphylaxis may be systemic or local.

(1) *Acute systemic anaphylaxis* occurs (notably in human beings, guineapigs, and dogs) when an antigenic substance enters the bloodstream of an organism containing specific antibodies against it. In severe cases the anaphylactic shock may be associated with rapid shallow breathing, and in extreme cases with waterlogging of the lungs and heart failure. Since the PHARMACOLOGICAL agent of anaphylactic shock is histamine, some protection can be achieved by antihistaminic drugs.

(2) *Local anaphylaxis* is brought about when an antigen, particularly a soluble antigen, is injected into the skin or other tissues of an immune animal. Human beings, guineapigs, and rabbits are specially liable to local anaphylaxis, an intense inflammation, confined to the area in which the antigen was injected, but causing in extreme cases TISSUE death.   P.M.

anarchism. A political movement advocating the abolition of the State and the replacement of all forms of governmental authority by free association and voluntary cooperation of individuals and groups. Anarchists disagree about how this society of the future is to be achieved and what specific forms of relationship (including property relationships) it is to be based on. They advocate DIRECT ACTION to achieve their aims, but their hostility towards any form of authority has inhibited the creation of effective anarchist organizations. Their precursors were divided among the followers of Proudhon (1809–65), who wanted a peaceful change, and Blanqui (1805–81), who advocated a violent seizure of power. Later Bakunin, 'the father of modern anarchism', continued the Blanqui line. His conflict with Marx in 1876 broke up the first INTERNATIONAL. The inability of the Bakuninists to achieve their aims led to a search for even more violent forms of struggle, such as the individual acts of terror ('propagation by deed') supported at first even by such idealists as Peter Kropotkin and Enrico Malatesta.

The influence of anarchist ideas did not grow except in a few instances when they proved to be ineffective, e.g. the ANARCHO-SYNDICALIST movement, Makhno and his followers during the Russian Civil War, the Spanish anarchists during the Spanish Civil War, and more recently the anarchist *gauchistes* during the 1968 'May Events' in France. But the anarchist direct-action methods continue to exert influence: both the Gandhian techniques of NON-VIOLENT protest and the violent techniques increasingly adopted by TERRORISTS in the 1970s. L.L.

Bibl: M. Nomad, *Apostles of Revolution* (N.Y., 1961); G. Woodcock, *Anarchism* (Cleveland, 1962; Harmondsworth, 1963); J. Joll, *The Anarchists* (London and N.Y., 1964).

anarcho-syndicalism. A late-19th-century cross between ANARCHISM and the trade union (French *syndicat*) movement. It originated among the followers of Bakunin in the Swiss Jura Federation of the First INTERNATIONAL. Led by James Guillaume, the Swiss disciple of Bakunin, they gave up his conspiratorial ideas and adopted trade unions as instruments of the working-class struggle and the basic institution for social transformation after the REVOLUTION. In France anarcho-syndicalism has chiefly developed out of the 'revolutionary syndicalism' propagated by Fernand Pelloutier, a former MARXIST turned anarchist. Disenchanted with the ineffectiveness of the TERRORIST strategy employed by anarchists between 1892 and 1894, he thought that the trade unions could be used not only as a weapon to improve the workers' economic conditions but also for (violent) DIRECT ACTION, ultimately leading to the abolition of CAPITALISM through a general strike. The 'revolutionary syndicalism' of Pelloutier and his followers in France was emulated elsewhere, but only in Spain had it acquired an anarchist character. It became the dominant influence in the French CGT, the American Industrial Workers of the World (I.W.W.; the 'Wobblies'), the Association of Italian Trade Unions, and the Spanish National Confederation of Labour. In Great Britain and Germany it encountered opposition from the existing trade unions, and attempts to create separate revolutionary unions ended in sectarian squabbles. Anarcho-syndicalism disappeared as a movement after World War I. However, the traditions of SYNDICALISM have persisted to some degree among the trade unionists of such countries as France and Spain.   L.L.

Bibl: P. N. Stearns, *Revolutionary Syndicalism and French Labor* (New Brunswick, N.J., 1971).

anatomy. The branch of MORPHOLOGY which deals both generally and in detail with the structure of animals – a sort of bodily geography, as the widely used and self-descriptive terms *regional anatomy* and *surface anatomy* suggest. *Comparative anatomy* is that branch of anatomy which deals with the similarities and differences between cognate structures in related animals – e.g. with the relationship between fins and limbs or the suspensory bones of the jaw on the one hand and the ossicles of the ear which in an evolutionary sense derive from them. In the latter part of the 19th century comparative anatomy played a vitally important part in establishing EVOLUTION theory.   P.M.

and-gate, see under GATE.

Anderson, Margaret (U.S. editor, 1890–1973), see under LITTLE REVIEW; POETRY (CHICAGO).

Anderson, Maxwell (U.S. dramatist, 1889–1959), see under GATE THEATRE.

Andrews, Thomas (Irish physical chemist, 1813–85), see under CRITICAL TEMPERATURE.

Andropov, Yuri Vladimirovich (Soviet politician, *b*.1914), see under KGB.

Anglicanism. The form of church life characteristic of the Anglican Communion. This consists of the Church of England (Latin *Ecclesia Anglicana*), which rejected the control of the Pope in the 16th century, and of the Churches outside England which send their bishops to the Lambeth Conference (since 1868 in London every ten years or so) under the presidency of the Archbishop of Canterbury. In some countries Anglicanism is better known as EPISCOPALIANISM; its branch in the U.S.A. is the Episcopal Church. Because it originated in England's national Church, Anglicanism tries to be comprehensive, reconciling CATHOLICISM with PROTESTANTISM, and also religious LIBERALISM with orthodoxy, in a community united in 'common prayer' and in mutual charity. This example has been an inspiration to the modern ECUMENICAL MOVEMENT. In practice, however, Anglicanism has suffered from the old-fashioned nature of the Church of England, from the declining prestige of England in the world, and from its internal controversies, e.g. those between ANGLO-CATHOLICISM and EVANGELICALISM.   D.L.E.

Bibl: S. Neill, *Anglicanism* (Harmondsworth and Baltimore, 3rd ed., 1965).

Anglo-Catholicism. A movement within

ANGOLA

ANGLICANISM, emphasizing the heritage of CATHOLICISM, in contrast with Bible-based EVANGELICALISM, as well as with modernizing LIBERALISM.   D.L.E.

Angola. A country of southern Africa, formerly a Portuguese colony. The term is frequently used to refer to the civil war that took place in Angola when Portuguese colonial rule in Africa ended after the military coup in Lisbon in April 1974. Three anti-colonial organizations (the M.P.L.A., the F.N.L.A., and Unita), which had never been able to cooperate politically in their common aim of expelling the Portuguese, fought each other for control of the country. Each organization had long-standing support from outside powers which hoped to determine the outcome of the war for various ideological, strategic, and economic reasons. Ultimately, Soviet and Cuban material and personnel aid for the M.P.L.A. was decisive in assuring victory for this organization over the other two, which received inferior assistance from the U.S.A., South Africa, and China at various times. In February 1975, the M.P.L.A. government of the People's Republic of Angola was recognized by the O.A.U. (see PAN-AFRICANISM) and EEC countries although sporadic opposition to the government continued in the country.   P.B.M.

Angry Brigade. A small LEFT-wing group which in the name of the working class mounted sporadic attacks upon various representatives of the ESTABLISHMENT. Their claimed successes included the machine-gunning of the American Embassy in London on 20 August 1967 (the first such incident) and the bombing of the Minister of Employment's home on 11 January 1971, during the time when he was preparing his controversial Industrial Relations Bill. Like their American counterparts, the WEATHERMEN, the activists of the Angry Brigade were mainly middle-class ex-students; politically, the group appeared to be more ANARCHIST than MARXIST. In 1972 its leaders were tried and imprisoned, and its bombing activities have been eclipsed by the more recent activities of the IRA in this field.   P.S.L.

angry young man. Term indiscriminately applied to a number of British writers in the mid 1950s, some of whom were remarkable for stupidity rather than anger. Writers saddled with the label have included Kingsley Amis, John Osborne, and Colin Wilson. The ARCHETYPE of the angry young man is Jimmy Porter, in Osborne's play *Look Back in Anger* (1956): confused, in the process of violently rejecting ESTABLISHMENT values, but frustrated by ignorance and the lack of alternative values to which to enslave himself. Invention of the phrase in this connection has been authoritatively attributed to the Irish writer Leslie Paul, whose autobiographical *Angry Young Man* appeared in 1951. But he was then 46; and was over 50 when he wistfully drew attention to his choice of title in a letter to the press.   M.S.-S.
  Bibl: J. R. Taylor, *Anger and After* (London, 1962; Baltimore, 1963).

Angst. A synonym for ANXIETY (sense 1).

anima. JUNGIAN term, derived from its original meaning of life force or soul, and referring to the autonomous ARCHETYPE within a man's COLLECTIVE UNCONSCIOUS which symbolizes the feminine side of his nature. In its most basic form this is an inherited collective image of woman. As with all archetypes, the *anima* is projected onto the world of experience, finding its first incarnation in one's mother; and a similar projection may govern the choice of a wife. The artist's 'muse', with its feminine and creative CONNOTATIONS, is another representation of *anima*. In his later work, Jung introduced the analogous term *animus* to refer to a woman's masculine principle, although the additional functions of *anima* for the male were never fully articulated in his presentation of the female's *animus*.   T.Z.C.

animal sonar. A faculty which enables animals to locate objects by means of the high-frequency sound waves reflected from them, and to communicate with each other by emitting such waves. Objects are located by one or both of two methods: the phase relationship between the sound impulses reflected back to each ear (whether in phase or out of phase), or the relative amplitude from sounds reaching the two ears. Animal sonar occurs in water

24

(e.g. whales, dolphins) as well as in air (e.g. bats). P.M.

animism. In ANTHROPOLOGY, a term first used by E. B. Tylor (*Primitive Culture*, 1871) for belief, based on the universal human experiences of dreams and visions, in 'spiritual beings', comprising the souls of individual creatures and other spirits. In modern anthropology, animism as a theory has little significance, other than historical, partly because it is concerned with unknowable origins of belief, partly because it fails to discriminate adequately between CONCEPTS of the soul and of spirit. But the term has carried over into some studies within PSYCHOLOGY of modes of thought among, especially, young children. See also EVOLUTION, SOCIAL AND CULTURAL; RELIGION. M.F.
Bibl: E. E. Evans-Pritchard, *Theories of Primitive Religion* (Oxford, 1965).

anion, see under ION.

***Annales* school.** A group of historians associated with the journal founded by Lucien Febvre and Marc Bloch in 1929 and now known as *Annales: économies, sociétés, civilisations*. The group stands for a particular style of history. Its members believe that the historian should place less emphasis than is customary on narrative (especially political narrative), on the chronicle of events (*histoire événementielle*), and more emphasis on analysis, on long-term STRUCTURES and trends (*la longue durée*). They also believe that economic, social, cultural, and political history should be integrated into a total history, and that, to do this, historians need to be well acquainted with the SOCIAL SCIENCES. Distinguished living members of the group include Fernand Braudel, Pierre Chaunu, Pierre Goubert, and Emmanuel Le Roy Ladurie. An outstanding example of the *Annales* approach translated into English is Fernand Braudel's *The Mediterranean and the Mediterranean World in the Age of Philip II*. See also CONJONCTURE; SERIAL HISTORY. P.B.
Bibl: P. Burke (ed.), *Economy and Society in Early Modern Europe* (London and N.Y., 1972).

annealing. The process of heating a solid metal or POLYMER to a high temperature, at which it is kept for a time, and then cooling it very slowly to its original temperature. This treatment 'dissolves' DISLOCATIONS and other crystal DEFECTS, thus relieving internal strains. When applied to glasses, annealing relieves stresses introduced during fabrication, thus reducing brittleness. When applied to metals, it has a softening effect which makes it easier to work them. M.V.B.

anode, see under ELECTRODE.

anodizing. A process designed to give a protective (and often, by the use of pigment, attractive) finish to articles made of aluminium (aluminum) or aluminium alloy. Although the surface of aluminium oxidizes rapidly in contact with air the oxide layer is often too thin to prevent CORROSION, and the process of anodizing involves the deposition of further oxide on the surface. E.R.L.

anomie. Term, resurrected from the Greek (literally, without law) by the French sociologist Émile Durkheim, to denote that condition of society which results from the disintegration of a commonly accepted NORMATIVE code. For Durkheim, industrial CLASS conflict was a symptom of anomie. More loosely, anomie was used in the 1950s and 1960s as a CONCEPT akin to ALIENATION, to describe a condition where an individual had lost his traditional moorings and was prone to disorientation or psychic disorder. D.B.
Bibl: É. Durkheim, tr. J. A. Spaulding and G. Simpson, *Suicide* (Glencoe, Ill., 1951; London, 1952).

Anouilh, Jean (French dramatist, *b.* 1910), see under BLACK COMEDY.

anthropogeography. The study of the distribution of human COMMUNITIES on the earth in relation to their ENVIRONMENT. Some geographers assume it to be synonymous with *human geography* (see GEOGRAPHY), which is the more commonly used term. M.L.

anthropological linguistics. A branch of LINGUISTICS which studies language variation and use in relation to the cultural patterns and beliefs of man, e.g. the way in which linguistic features may identify a member of a community with a social, religious, occupational, or kinship group. See also ETHNOLINGUISTICS; SOCIOLINGUISTICS. D.C.

anthropology. Although the English word is much older, the idea of a general science of man was essentially a creation of the 19th century – and it is already in some measure out of date. 19th-century anthropology, held together by a devotion to the idea of EVOLUTION, embraced the biological, prehistoric, linguistic, technological, social, and cultural origins and development of mankind. It concerned itself with PRIMITIVE forms, 'early in time' being equated, however approximately, with 'simple in stage of development'. Modern anthropology has largely retained its unity as an academic subject in the U.S.A. and some other countries (but only rarely in Britain), and is now conventionally said to comprise *physical anthropology, prehistoric archaeology, cultural/social anthropology,* and some aspects of LINGUISTICS. *Physical anthropology,* however, is increasingly looked upon as a branch of human BIOLOGY; it is concerned with the genesis of and physical differentiation within Homo sapiens (see RACE), and, through GENETICS and ETHOLOGY, with the interaction between biological endowment on the one hand and ENVIRONMENT and CULTURE on the other.

In anthropology, *culture* is that which men create for themselves and transmit to their successors by other than biological means. There is Culture and there are cultures. Culture is the common characteristic of man. Most theorists would probably say that language, tool-making, and the regulation of sex are the chief defining features of man in contradistinction to other primates. Cultures are particular historical realizations of the common human potential. *Cultural anthropology* (as it is usually called in the U.S.A.) and *social anthropology* (its British counterpart) have both historical and sociological preoccupations and connections, yet they tend to emphasize data disregarded by the historians and the sociologists. The specialization has been procured by concentrating upon 'primitive' cultures/societies, which in effect means nowadays a specialized interest in the cultures/societies of the (as yet) non-

industrialized world. Academically, the overlap between social/cultural anthropology and HISTORY is small (but see ETHNOHISTORY) and that with SOCIOLOGY large – the latter because the two disciplines base themselves upon many common ideas and because they often deal with each other's special material. Social anthropology tends to be more sociological in its interests than is cultural anthropology, the latter springing from a different intellectual tradition, and being at once more historical and more psychological in character.

See also ANTHROPOLOGICAL LINGUISTICS; DIFFUSIONISM; ETHNOGRAPHY AND ETHNOLOGY; ETHNOLINGUISTICS; EVOLUTION; EVOLUTION, SOCIAL AND CULTURAL; FIELD WORK; FUNCTIONALISM; STRUCTURALISM. M.F.

Bibl: G. A. Harrison *et al., Human Biology* (Oxford, 1964); M. Freedman, *Social and Cultural Anthropology* (Paris, forthcoming).

anthroposophy. The term (literally 'wisdom about man') adopted by Rudolf Steiner (1861–1925) to denote his teachings and to distinguish them from the THEOSOPHY whose adherents constituted his first audience. These teachings he claims to derive from 'spiritual research' based on an exact 'scientific' mode of supersensible PERCEPTION. A central thesis of anthroposophy is that the present intellectual capacities of humanity have evolved from an earlier mode of CONSCIOUSNESS which brought a direct experience of the transcendental (see TRANSCENDENCE) realities of which Steiner spoke. To carry the clarity and objectivity of the intellect now gained into new modes of spiritual perception (which he called Imagination, Inspiration, Intuition) is according to Steiner an essential future task for mankind. Such a 'resurrection' of consciousness has become possible, he held, through the deed of Christ in uniting himself with the destiny of man on earth. Steiner accordingly described one of his earliest books, *The Philosophy of Freedom*, as a 'Pauline theory of knowledge'. His work has given rise to many practical endeavours in education (see STEINER SCHOOLS), farming, medicine, the arts, etc. J.D.

Bibl: R. Steiner, tr. G. Metaxa, *Knowledge of the Higher Worlds* (London and

N.Y., 1923) and other works published in London by the Rudolf Steiner Press.

anti-art. A term used for works of the DADA movement, which used the ARTS to attack or deride all established institutions, including the very notion of 'art'. Duchamp's READYMADES were an early manifestation. The term was subsequently used by other AVANT-GARDE movements including Gruppe Zero, FLUXUS, and CONCEPTUAL ART. Other radical movements in modern art, such as POP ART and KINETIC ART, were considered to be anti-art in their initial stages but quickly became accepted as legitimate art forms. This fate has also overtaken the original Dada objects. L.M.

antibacterial. A member of a heterogeneous class of substances united by the property of being toxic or lethal to bacteria (see BACTERIOLOGY). They include:

(1) ANTISEPTICS, comprising all substances that are antibacterial through physical or chemical action;

(2) natural substances such as (*a*) LYSOZYME, an ENZYME which attacks the CELL walls of some bacterial SPECIES, (*b*) *complement* which acts in concert with antibodies (see IMMUNITY) to puncture the membranes of bacteria or red cells, and (*c*) *properdin*, a natural blood-borne antibacterial substance of unknown nature and function;

(3) ANTIBIOTICS, which presumably play some part in the ECOLOGY of the organisms that manufacture them;

(4) substances such as sulphanilamide, sulphathiazole, and sulphapyridine which exercise an antibacterial effect by metabolic means (see METABOLISM); thus sulphanilamide in effect deprives bacteria of the paraaminobenzoic acid which for most of them is an essential food factor – an early example of 'competitive inhibition'. P.M.

anti-ballistic missiles, see ABM.

antibiotic. A substance which impedes the growth or multiplication of micro-organisms. Examples are penicillin, streptomycin, terramycin. The *spectrum* of an antibiotic is the range of bacteria (see BACTERIOLOGY) over which it exercises its effect. 'Broad spectrum' antibiotics such as terramycin are particularly useful in medical practice. In general, antibiotics are ineffective against viruses (see VIROLOGY). Naturally occurring ANTIBACTERIAL substances such as INTERFERON and LYSOZYME are not normally classified as antibiotics. P.M.

antibody, see under IMMUNITY.

anti-colonialism, see under IMPERIALISM.

antigen, see under IMMUNITY.

anti-hero. In literature, a figure bearing the same relation to the conventional hero as does the ANTI-NOVEL to the conventional novel. The term was first used in this sense by W. P. Ker in 1897; but the anti-hero as type – foolish, bumbling, boorish, clumsy, immoral – is ancient. He occurs in the Greek 'new comedy', in the picaresque novel, and in the fiction from which the latter originates. The first deliberately devised anti-hero is in Honoré d'Urfé's sensationally successful *Astrée* (1607–27): this is a sentimental romance, but Hylas, with his championship of infidelity, is clearly a satirical foil to the conventional hero, Céladon. In lyrical poetry Edwin Arlington Robinson's Minniver Cheever provides an excellent example. Modern anti-heroes include Hašek's Good Soldier Švejk, Christopher Isherwood's Christopher Isherwood, Jimmy Porter in John Osborne's *Look Back in Anger*, Jim Dixon in Kingsley Amis's *Lucky Jim*, and numerous spies and go-getters in conventionally structured popular works. By way of contrast, we have the 'positive hero' of Soviet literature. M.S.-S.

anti-imperialism, see under IMPERIALISM.

anti-knock, see under KNOCKING.

anti-literature. The first, it seems, of the 'anti-arts' to be so named in English: by David Gascoyne in 1935. For other (selected) examples of arts, literary genres, etc. that stand previous conventions on their heads, or at least their shoulders, see ANTI-ART; ANTI-HERO; ANTI-NOVEL; ANTI-THEATRE. O.S.

anti-matter. Some ELEMENTARY PARTICLES are the *anti-particles* of others. For example, a POSITRON and an ELECTRON mutually annihilate one another, producing an enormous amount of ENERGY in the form of RADIATION (see MASS-ENERGY EQUATION). Matter made up of the antiparticles of ordinary matter would be *anti-matter*. None has positively been identified in nature, and its existence on a large scale is therefore hypothetical. However, it is possible that some of the intense radiation detected with RADIO TELESCOPES may be the result of collisions between GALAXIES made up of ordinary matter and anti-matter.   M.V.B.

anti-naturalism. An approach to PSYCHOLOGY and the SOCIAL SCIENCES which assumes that human beings (and perhaps intelligent animals) are so different from the subject-matter of the NATURAL SCIENCES that quite different approaches are needed for their study. Thus, in studying human beings one can communicate with them, and attempt to understand the meanings of their words and deeds, whereas a physicist cannot in the same way communicate with the physical substances and mechanisms that he studies. A related view is that human behaviour and mental processes cannot be explained in terms of the physical and chemical, or physiological, processes in the human body (see REDUCTION), and that no amount of study of the structure of the human brain and the processes that occur in it can explain the way people think, decide, act, feel, etc. The opposite view is NATURALISM (sense 3). An intermediate position is that, although human beings are physical systems, the kinds of structures and processes to be found in the human brain, or more generally in human social systems, have a kind of complexity unmatched by other physical systems, so that quite new theoretical frameworks and experimental methods are required for their study.   A.S.

Bibl: H. P. Rickman, *Understanding and the Human Studies* (London, 1967; N.Y., 1968).

antinomianism. The rejection of any element of 'law' (Greek *nomos*) in ETHICS, especially in Christian MORAL THEOLOGY, on the grounds that no detailed code of behaviour has been laid down by God. A PROTESTANT sect arising in Germany in 1535 was so named. In the 20th century, while most Christians have accepted that some rules are needed, most have put first the element usually contrasted with 'law' in this debate: love. Christians are believed to be essentially free to act as they think best in the light of love. See also SITUATION ETHICS.   D.L.E.

antinomy. A contradiction (see CONSISTENCY) between two assertions for each of which there seem to be adequate grounds. It should be distinguished from a *dilemma*, which is a form of argument designed to show that something, usually unpleasant, will follow either if a given assumption is true or if it is false, and also from a PARADOX, which is a single, unacceptable, and often self-contradictory conclusion for which there are seemingly irresistible grounds.   A.Q.

anti-novel. A compendious label for any novel that protests, explicitly or implicitly, against some other novel or novels regarded as unduly popular or influential. Although Charles Sorel described the 1633 edition of his *Le Berger extravagant* (1627), in part a satire on d'Urfé's *Astrée*, as an *anti-roman*, the first thoroughgoing anti-novel is Cervantes's *Don Quixote* (1605): devised partly as protest against popular chivalric fiction, it grew into a tragic masterpiece. It is a paradigm of the true anti-novel: it revolts against conventional form, on the grounds that the latter lulls the reader into a sense of unreality, into an avoidance of (in contemporary EXISTENTIALIST parlance) his own authenticity, and itself jerks the reader, by a series of shocks, into awareness of his own predicament. The first English anti-novel is Sterne's *Tristram Shandy* (1759), which continually confronts the reader with what he does *not* expect from fiction. The anti-novel has been revived in the 20th century (especially in France in the form of the NEW NOVEL), though not always successfully, being often either too self-consciously or too dully and philosophically expressed. The contemporary revival has been much influenced by the PHENOMENOLOGY of Husserl, if only because this is exclusively concerned with subjective experience.   M.S.-S.

Bibl: N. Sarraute, tr. M. Jolas, *Tropisms and The Age of Suspicion* (London, 1963); P. West, *The Modern Novel* (London, 1963).

anti-particles, see under ANTI-MATTER.

anti-psychiatry. A movement in therapeutic practice, initiated by R. D. Laing and others, which rejects conventional PSYCHIATRY and regards the CONCEPT of mental illness as both unscientific and stigmatizing; mental illness may, indeed, be a healthy response to a sick society. Psychiatrists and mental hospitals are regarded as agents of social repression, in league with the family and with society at large in putting pressure on non-conforming individuals; and certain procedures of psychiatry, e.g. LEUCOTOMY, ELECTRO-CONVULSIVE THERAPY, and tranquillizing drugs, as well as any authoritarian PSYCHOTHERAPY, are seen as obstructing the proper, self-directed resolution of personality disorders. The movement is represented in Britain by the *People, Not Psychiatrists* group.   H.L.
  Bibl: R. Boyers and R. Orrill (eds.), *R. D. Laing and Anti-Psychiatry* (N.Y., 1971; Harmondsworth, 1972).

antisemitism. The adherence to views or practices directed against the interests, legal rights, religious practices, or lives of Jews; a more or less constant feature of Jewish life since the Diaspora. The term was apparently coined by Ernest Renan in the 1870s, but justification has been couched in terms of the dominant structure of thought of each period, changing, as these changed, from religious to racial, from NATIONALIST to CLASS conflict theories. Since the attempt by the NAZIS in the FINAL SOLUTION physically to eliminate European Jewry, the burden of guilt and the fear of being associated in any way with the views which led to that catastrophe have been a potent force in European politics, leading in many countries to legislation against the incitement to racial hatred (see RACE) and internationally inclining the countries of Western Europe and the U.S.A. towards the side of Israel. Antisemitism is still a potent force in East European political life and, under the guise of hostility to ZIONISM, in Arab states.   D.C.W.
  Bibl: L. Poliakov, *Histoire de l'antisémitisme*, 2 vols. (Paris, 1955–61); J. H. Robb, *Working-Class Antisemite* (London, 1954).

antiseptic. A member of a class of compounds of which carbolic acid is historically the most important member, having the property of killing the organisms responsible for infectious disease, especially those responsible for wound infection (sepsis) in which bacterial proliferation is accompanied by extensive TISSUE damage and accumulation of pus. Antiseptics have a great variety of important uses in medicine and hygiene (although the attempted sterilization of wounds is no longer one of them). Thus chlorine is used to disinfect domestic water supplies, and formaldehyde vapour (very poisonous) to decontaminate rooms. Unhappily, the very properties that confer upon antiseptics their power to kill micro-organisms make them unsuitable for use in the presence of living tissues and so for attempting to secure surgical sterility; thus phenol and alcoholic solutions of iodine could only cause extensive tissue damage. (The anointment of cuts with tincture of iodine must be regarded as a RITUAL rather than a therapeutic procedure.)
  In modern surgery antiseptics have an important place as adjuncts to ASEPSIS. Thus scalpels and carbon steel instruments that would be severely damaged by high-pressure steam are sterilized as a matter of routine by immersion in strong antiseptics which are washed off before the instruments are used. By far the most effective antiseptic procedure is the exposure to steam at temperatures above 100°C and therefore, necessarily, under pressure; steam at 120°C (at a pressure of 102 pounds per square inch) is the usual method of sterilizing the drapes and gowns used in surgical operations. *Antiseptic surgery*, specially associated with the name of Joseph Lister, is the procedure in which an attempt is made to combat infection by direct use of antiseptics (e.g. by conducting an operation in a phenol spray and treating wounds with carbolic acid or other antiseptic solution). It has been wholly supplanted by asepsis.   P.M.

anti-theatre. Imprecise journalistic term generally used to denote any type of theatre that does not conform to the familiar patterns of NATURALISM. Coined in the 1950s at the same time as ANTI-NOVEL (and cf. the cult of the ANTI-HERO), it may cover anything from the plays of Ionesco and Beckett (see THEATRE OF THE ABSURD) to the wildest form of experiment.   M.BI.

antithesis, see under SYNTHESIS.

anti-trust. The name given to a body of legislation designed to protect the consumer against the exploitation of their market power by MONOPOLIES or 'trusts', as they were known in the 19th century. While there may be powerful reasons for the development of a monopoly situation in certain industries, economic theory suggests that under a monopoly prices tend to be higher and output smaller than would otherwise be the case. Thus the underlying assumption in all anti-trust legislation is that monopoly works against the public interest. In the U.S.A., Federal anti-trust legislation includes the Sherman Anti-Trust Act of 1890 and the Clayton Act of 1914, when the Federal Trade Commission was also established. British landmarks are the establishment of the Monopolies Commission (1948) and the Restrictive Trade Practices Act (1956).
                                    D.E.
Bibl: C. Edwards, *Big Business and the Policy of Competition* (Cleveland, 1956).

Antoine, André (French theatrical producer and manager, 1858–1943), see under THÉÂTRE LIBRE.

Anuszkiewicz, Richard (U.S. artist, *b.* 1930), see under OP ART.

anxiety. In ABNORMAL PSYCHOLOGY and PSYCHIATRY, a term used to refer both (1) to an emotional state (see EMOTION) and (2) to a trait of character. As (1) it is often used synonymously with 'fear', and, more specifically, to fears whose object is not known, as in the *anxiety state,* a NEUROSIS characterized by feelings of fear for which the patient can give no reason; within learning theory, it refers to the emotional state elicited by signals of impending punishment. As (2) it describes different degrees of susceptibility to fear. According to H. J. Eysenck, this trait is not unitary, but a composite of neuroticism and INTROVERSION, highly anxious people being neurotic introverts. As such, it is more prominent in women than in men, while women are also more prone to

psychiatric disturbances involving anxiety in sense (1).   J.A.G.
Bibl: I. M. Marks, *Fears and Phobias* (London and N.Y., 1969).

apartheid. Afrikaans word meaning 'apartness' or SEGREGATION, applied since 1948 by the dominant Afrikaaner Nationalist Party in South Africa to policies governing relations between white and non-white (African, Indian, or mixed-race) inhabitants of South Africa. *Apartheid* implies the total separation of races socially, economically, and in the last resort territorially, but its full realization runs contrary to the economic need for a large labouring population in white inhabited areas and the refusal of whites to perform menial duties. In practice, therefore, it requires Africans living in urban areas as aliens of temporary residence, identifiable by passes, strictly limited in freedom and virtually without rights, e.g. subject to arbitrary arrest and imprisonment. Territorial separation began with the establishment of nominally autonomous African 'homelands' or *Bantustans;* but these are not economically viable and would require considerable financial support if they were to become genuinely independent states.
                                    D.C.W.
Bibl: L. Marquand, *The Peoples and Policies of South Africa* (London and N.Y., 4th ed., 1969); E. H. Brookes, *Apartheid* (London and N.Y., 1968); F. Troup, *South Africa: an Historical Introduction* (new ed., Harmondsworth, 1975).

aphasia, see under NEUROPSYCHOLOGY.

Apocalypse, see NEW APOCALYPSE.

Apollinaire, Guillaume (French poet, 1880–1918), see under CALLIGRAMME; CONCRETE POETRY; CUBISM; FUTURISM; ORPHISM; PRIMITIVE; SURREALISM.

Apollonian and Dionysian cultures. Terms used by Ruth Benedict to distinguish two 'patterns' of CULTURE. Rooted in the school of cultural ANTHROPOLOGY of Franz Boas, she regarded cultures, especially of the simpler societies, as consistent and enduring patterns of behaviour, thought, and action; systems of INSTITUTIONS and psychological orientations with attendant PERSONALITY types. Deriving

the terms from Nietzsche (in his discussion of Greek drama) and Oswald Spengler, Benedict used Dionysian to denote a pattern of culture engendering and encouraging emotional abandonment in social responses, and Apollonian to denote one producing order and control. In the burial of the dead, for example, the Zuni Indians (Apollonian) controlled and contained their grief; the Kwakiutl Indians (Dionysian) abandoned themselves in a demonstrative orgy of wailing. Evans-Pritchard called this 'the rustling-of-the-wind-in-the-palm-trees' kind of anthropology. See also FOLK CULTURE; SUBCULTURE.   R.F.
Bibl: R. Benedict, *Patterns of Culture* (Boston and N.Y., 1934; London, 1935).

Apparat. The customary designation (anglicized as *apparatus*) for the aggregate of full-time individual functionaries (*Apparatchiki*) of the COMMUNIST Parties. The *Apparat* evolved from the body of professional revolutionaries, whose special position in the Party was Lenin's essential contribution to the structure of 'the Party of the new type'. The *Apparat* consists of a bureaucratic hierarchy (see BUREAUCRACY) which permits the effective transmission and execution of the leadership's orders. Its discipline and functioning are based on the doctrine of DEMOCRATIC CENTRALISM, which originally allowed democratic discussion before a Party decision was taken, but which in practice has been used to justify the demand for unquestioned obedience by Party members to the decisions of the Party leadership.   L.L.
Bibl: L. Schapiro, *The Communist Party of the Soviet Union* (London, rev. ed., 1970); D. Lane, *Politics and Society in the USSR* (London, 1970; N.Y., 1971).

appeasement. A term first employed in political contexts in the 1920s, when it meant the removal by mutual agreement of the grievances arising out of the 1919 peace settlement. After the appointment, on 30 January 1933, of Adolf Hitler as Chancellor in Germany, the word was applied to the (unsuccessful) policy pursued by the British and French governments of trying to avoid war with Germany by injudicious, frequently dishonourable, and inevitably unrequited concessions, weakening to those who made them and often made at the expense of third parties. The epitome of the policy of appeasement was the MUNICH agreement of 30 September 1938.   D.C.W.
Bibl: E. M. Robertson (ed.), *The Origins of the Second World War* (London, 1971).

Appel, Karel (Dutch painter, *b.* 1921), see under COBRA.

apperception. The mental state of PERCEPTION when it is self-concious, when the perceiver is aware of the fact that he is perceiving as well as of the object perceived. The term was introduced into PHILOSOPHY by Leibniz as a means for distinguishing what had hitherto been supposed inseparable: the mind's activities of perception and its awareness of those activities. Leibniz's view was that it is possible for a mind to perceive something without being aware that it is doing so. A persuasive argument he gave for this conclusion is that we can be surprised by the cessation of a noise, such as the ticking of a clock, which we had not been conscious of perceiving during the time before it stopped.   A.Q.

applied mathematics. Strictly, all those branches of MATHEMATICS developed to assist deductive reasoning in the physical and NATURAL SCIENCES. In the U.K. the term is often used in a more specialized sense to refer to the mathematical techniques useful in CLASSICAL PHYSICS.
                                    M.V.B.

applied psychology. The examination of specific practical problems of human life, using the methods and criteria of academic PSYCHOLOGY. In contrast to applied physical sciences, this area of activity can only rarely make use of generalizations which are well established by theoretical work and require merely to be related to the problem. Rather, the practical situation may often reveal new and unsuspected aspects of human nature, whose understanding is a gain to general knowledge as well as to the solution of the particular problem. Occasionally the applied psychologist may differ from the intelligent layman by knowledge of some fact, such as the likely effects of line thickness upon the visibility of illuminated signs seen at night. More usually, he differs only by the habit of seeking some specific breakdown of function behind an undesired action; e.g. multiple accidents on high-speed roads lead psychologists to suspect failures of perception of speed and distance, and of anticipation of likely delays in the driver's own response, and these failures in turn can be traced to the particular visual and other information given to the driver.

Some fields of application are now so highly developed that they are usually distinguished under their own name. Thus applications to mental health are normally termed *clinical psychology*; those to learning and adjustment at school, EDUCA-TIONAL PSYCHOLOGY; those to the wellbeing and efficiency of people engaged in industry, INDUSTRIAL PSYCHOLOGY. In most fields of application, however, there are related problems, including the construction of methods for assessing the past performance of people, whether schoolchildren, industrial managers, or some other category; the attempt to predict which people will be able to meet some situation adequately in the future, as by aircrew selection tests or clinical prognoses; and the comparison of different detailed systems of presenting information and required action, as in the EVALU-ATION of TEACHING MACHINES, of different keyboards for telephones, or of different phrasings of public notices of pension entitlement. The physical ENVIRONMENT is also a common problem, as in the effects of airport noise or school lighting; and so is the social or human environment, as in the effects of family background on school performance, or of PARTICIPATION upon the self-respect of an industrial worker.

In many of these areas the applied psychologist has had an influence, which is retrospectively seen to have been salutary, upon general attitudes to human beings. Thus the problems of assessment and prediction forced a respect for individual differences upon academic psychology; the problems of work design in complex semi-automatic systems made it clear that the mind performs highly sophisticated operations upon the STIMULI reaching it, rather than simply associating them; and the problem of the social environment, while complicating response to persuasion on food habits or RACE relations, helped to establish the importance of the cultural matrix of individual behaviour. Thus far, however, the output of applied psychology has consisted of verbal analyses and recommendations, which can be accepted or rejected like any others. More recently, tentative techniques have been explored for changing human behaviour directly: advertising, conditioning techniques of PSYCHOTHERAPY (see, for example, BEHAVIOUR THERAPY), or the participation by psychologists in GROUP sessions in a business with the aim of producing an altered organization. These techniques are likely to raise ethical questions amongst practitioners, as well as complaints of manipulation amongst those affected; but if successful they may well provide intellectual and practical gains substantially greater than those of the past. D.E.B.

apraxia, see under NEUROPSYCHOLOGY.

apriorism. In PHILOSOPHY, a more precise term for the opposite of EMPIRICISM than the more commonly used RATIONALISM. An apriorist holds either or both of the following opinions: (1) that the mind is constitutionally endowed with CONCEPTS or IDEAS which it has not derived from experience; (2) that there is knowledge which does not depend for its justification on experience and yet which is still substantially informative and not merely verbal or ANALYTIC in character. The most plausible instances of *a priori* concepts are the formal concepts of LOGIC, e.g. those of negation and implication (see under ENTAILMENT), expressed by the words 'not' and 'if'. More controversial instances are the METAPHYSICAL concepts which Kant called CATEGORIES, in particular those of SUBSTANCE and cause. The most notable alleged instances of substantial, non-analytic, *a priori* knowledge are also metaphysical, for example the PROPOSI-TIONS (called by Kant 'principles' or, more fully, 'pure principles of the understanding') that there is a fixed amount of substance in the universe (i.e. *ex nihilo nihil fit*) and that every event has a cause. More loosely, an apriorist is one who ascribes large powers for the discovery of new knowledge to pure reasoning, unassisted by experience. A.Q.

Bibl: W. H. Walsh, *Reason and Experience* Oxford, 1947); J. Hospers, *An*

Introduction to Philosophical Analysis (London and N.Y., 2nd ed., 1967).

aptitude tests, see under MENTAL TEST-ING.

aquaplaning. The action which takes place when a solid object moves on the surface of a liquid at such a speed as to create a REYNOLDS WEDGE ACTION, thereby producing a lifting force on the solid object. It is commonly used to describe the reaction between the wheel of a motor car and a wet road. At a sufficiently high speed, and if the tyre on the wheel is unable, by means of its tread, to pump the water from under the wheel sideways, the tyre may begin to slide by aquaplane action, resulting in loss of control from the steering wheel. The expression is also used in relation to certain types of water surface craft where Reynolds wedge action results from viscous effects. See also HYDROFOIL.   E.R.L.

Aquinas, Saint **Thomas** (Italian theologian, 1226–74), see under NEO-THOMISM.

Arab nationalism. The emotion of cultural and political solidarity felt by members of the Arab states in the face of non-Arab political influences and pressures, and expressed often in highly-coloured and violent language. It differs from the NATIONALISM of European nation-states in that it conflates two separate concepts: *ummaya*, loyalty to the Arab *umma* ('people', *Volk*) and *Wataniya*, loyalty to the *Watan*, the particular Arab state or region. Christian Arabs, aware that membership of the *umma* implies membership of the Islamic faith, have sought to avoid second-class STATUS in an Islamic state by giving Arab nationalism a secular element borrowed from non-Islamic models such as Western LIBERALISM, MARXISM, FASCISM, and MAOISM.   D.C.W.
  Bibl: H. B. Sharabi, *Nationalism and Revolution in the Arab World* (Princeton, 1966).

Aragon, Louis (French author, *b*.1897), see under SURREALISM.

Arbeitsrat für Kunst. German artists' and architects' council, formed after the November 1918 Revolution, with Walter Gropius emerging as chairman, and the

BRÜCKE painters as prominent members. It was important chiefly for its influence on the BAUHAUS and on German social-architectural thinking in the 1920s. In December 1919 it merged with the somewhat similar NOVEMBERGRUPPE.   J.W.
  Bibl: M. Franciscono, *Walter Gropius and the Creation of the Bauhaus in Weimar* (Urbana, Ill., 1971).

Arbenz, Jacobo (Guatemalan president, 1913–71), see under CIA.

Arbuckle, Roscoe ('Fatty'; U.S. comic actor, 1916–67), see under KEYSTONE; SLAPSTICK.

archaeology. The technique of studying man's past using material remains as a primary source. In *text-free archaeology* material remains are the sole evidence, the study being known as PREHISTORY. When texts are available the term PROTO-HISTORY is often used. Specialist branches proliferate: *classical archaeology, medieval archaeology, post-medieval archaeology,* and INDUSTRIAL ARCHAE-OLOGY are now accepted as individual disciplines, while FIELD ARCHAEOLOGY refers to an approach used by all. Recent advances, particularly in prehistory, tend to emphasize man's dynamic relationship with his ENVIRONMENT. In this way it is possible to study man through his effects on the ECOSYSTEM even when artifacts are absent. Many specialist techniques contribute to archaeology, e.g. LINGUISTICS, PALAEOBOTANY, PALAEOPATHOLOGY, PALAEOSEROLOGY, etc. HISTORY can, loosely speaking, be regarded as a technique used to augment the most recent fraction of the time span studied by the archaeologist.   B.C.
  Bibl: D. Brothwell and E. Higgs (eds.), *Science in Archaeology* (2nd ed., London, 1969; N.Y., 1970).

archaeomagnetism. The study of residual or *remanent* (in full, *thermo-remanent*) MAGNETISM, usually in an artifact or structure of baked clay. It is based on the principle that magnetite, an oxide of iron, when heated above a certain point (the *Curie point*), loses its magnetism, taking on the qualities of the earth's magnetic FIELD as it cools. These remain fossilized unless heat is again applied. Thus an *in situ* structure (e.g. a hearth or kiln) retains the magnetic characteristics of its location at the time of its use. For purposes of DAT-ING, the remanent magnetism of the sample is measured for direction (a horizontal component known as *declination* or *D*, and a vertical one known as *inclination* or *I* or *dip*) and intensity. These factors are compared with the pattern of known changes in the earth's field. The dating method is not absolute, since before *c*. 1500 A.D. calibration data must be acquired by measuring samples of known date. A wide margin of error is often encountered.   B.C.

Bibl: R. M. Cook, 'Archaeomagnetism', in D. Brothwell and E. Higgs (eds.), *Science in Archaeology* (2nd ed., London, 1969; N.Y., 1970), pp. 76–87.

archetype. A JUNGIAN term for any of a number of prototypic phenomena (e.g. the wise old man, the great mother) which form the content of the COLLECTIVE UNCONSCIOUS (and therefore of any given individual's unconscious), and which are assumed to reflect universal human thoughts found in all CULTURES.   W.Z.

Archipenko, Alexander (Russian-born sculptor, 1887–1964), see under CON-STRUCTIVISM; CUBISM.

Arden, John (British dramatist, *b*. 1930), see under ROYAL COURT THEATRE.

Ardrey, Robert (U.S. author, *b*. 1908), see under GROUP THEATRE; TERRITORIAL IMPERATIVE.

area. As used by geographers, a general, generic term for any portion of the earth's surface. An area may range in size up to the whole surface of the earth and has the dual properties of locational position and environmental content. See also AREA STUDIES; REGION.   P.H.

area studies. Educational term for inter-disciplinary, scholarly studies focusing on the peoples of a definable geographical sector. Although classical studies concerned with the culture of ancient Greece and Rome represent an early form of area studies, the term is commonly reserved for contemporary studies. In England the School of Oriental and African Studies was founded in 1916 as a language training centre but was extended after 1945 to

include cultural and social studies. The post-war period has seen rapid growth of other area-focused studies (e.g. Slavonic studies, Latin American studies, African studies) in both Europe and the U.S.A.   P.H.

Arent, Arthur (U.S. dramatist, 1904–72), see under WPA.

argument. In MATHEMATICS, a term that denotes what a FUNCTION is a function of; i.e. the independent VARIABLE(s). It is used both generically – as in 'a function of one numerical argument', and specifically – as in 'the value of the function is zero when the argument is zero'.   R.G.

Aristotle (Greek philosopher and scientist, 384–322 B.C.), see under ASSOCIATION; CATEGORY; CATHARSIS; DISTRIBUTIVE JUSTICE; INTELLIGENCE; LOGIC; MECHANISM; NEWTONIAN MECHANICS; PHILOSOPHY; SYLLOGISM.

arithmetic, higher, see NUMBER THEORY.

Arman, Armand Fernandez (French artist, *b*. 1928), see under NOUVEAU RÉALISME.

Armory Show. A landmark in the history of modern art in America, this 'International Exhibition of Modern Art' opened in February 1913 in the 69th Regimental Armory in New York and was later shown in Boston and Chicago. It contained over 1,000 works by some 300 artists, from Ingres to Marcel Duchamp. Cézanne, Gauguin, Redon, the FAUVES, and Augustus John were well represented, German EXPRESSIONISM scarcely, and FUTURISM not at all. It attracted the subsequent DADA artist Francis Picabia to the U.S.A., and thus laid the foundation of his and Duchamp's activity there.   J.W.

arms control. Restraint intentionally exercised by one or more powers upon the level, characteristics, deployment, or use of their armaments in order to promote stability, reduce the danger of war, limit its consequences, or otherwise minimize the hazards inherent in the existence or future development of modern weapons. The term is a broad one and includes measures of DISARMAMENT, inter-state agreements

on mutual restraint, and unilateral policies (normally of the great powers). The term originated in the American strategic literature in the later 1950s, and the CONCEPT derives partly from economic theory, that states, like firms, can decide to preclude activities that are mutually injurious without abandoning their general competitive or adversary stance; the term and the policy gained acceptance in the early 1960s as the need to control certain military activities (e.g. the atmospheric testing of nuclear weapons) and to limit the number of nuclear-weapon states became palpable while the prospects of negotiated multilateral disarmament remained unpromising. Recent arms control agreements include that on the non-militarization of Antarctica (1959), the Atmospheric Test Ban Treaty (1963), the Non-PROLIFERATION Treaty (1968), and the Soviet American agreements of 1972 (SALT 1) on the permanent limitation of anti-ballistic missiles (see ABM) in each country and on a five-year standstill on levels of deployed MISSILES. Measures to control the build-up of strategic nuclear weapons were discussed in the 1976 SALT 2 talks. An example of a unilateral arms control measure was the decision of the U.S.A. (and other governments) in 1969 to suspend research on biological weapons and to destroy stocks of them.   A.F.B.
Bibl: T. C. Schelling and M. H. Halperin, *Strategy and Arms Control* (N.Y., 1961); H. Bull, *The Control of the Arms Race* (London, 1961; N.Y., 2nd ed., 1965).

arms race. The continuous accretion of military power by two or more states, based upon the conviction that only by retaining an advantage in such power can they ensure their national security or supremacy. Arms races have a quantitative and a qualitative aspect; but a contemporary distinction has emerged between arms races among minor powers (e.g. Israel and the Arab states), where both aspects are of significance, and among the great (i.e. nuclear-weapon) powers where the qualitative aspect – improvements in the explosive power, accuracy, penetration, or invulnerability of long-range weapons – is the more significant. Hence the concentration of modern arms-control policy as much on the characteristics of weapons as on their numbers. See also ARMS CONTROL; SALT.
                    A.F.B.
Bibl: H. Bull, *The Control of the Arms Race* (London, 1961; N.Y., 2nd ed., 1965).

Armstrong, Daniel Louis (U.S. jazz trumpeter, 1900–71), see under CHICAGO; HOT; JAZZ; NEW ORLEANS.

Arnatt, Keith (British artist, *b.* 1930), see under CONCEPTUAL ART.

Arnold, Matthew (British poet and critic, 1822–88), see under TWO CULTURES.

Arnold, Thomas (British headmaster, 1795–1842), see under PUBLIC SCHOOLS.

Arnot, Robert Page (British Communist Party leader, *b.* 1890), see under GUILD SOCIALISM.

aromatic. Adjective applied to a vast class of cyclic organic compounds where ELECTRONS are delocalized over a closed framework of carbon ATOMS (see BENZENE RING). A number of these substances have a pleasant smell; hence the term. The sharing of electrons over several carbon atoms has a characteristic influence on chemical behaviour. Petroleum is the major source of aromatic compounds which form the basis of many POLYMERS, insecticides, DETERGENTS, dyes, etc.   B.F.

Aron, Raymond (French social and political thinker, *b.* 1905), see under IDEOLOGY; TRANSNATIONAL RELATIONS.

Arp, Jean or **Hans** (French sculptor, painter, and poet, 1887–1966), see under ABSTRACT ART; BIOMORPHIC; CONCRETE ART; DADA; MERZ; SURREALISM.

Arrabal, Fernando (Spanish-born French dramatist and novelist, *b.* 1932), see under THEATRE OF PANIC.

Arrow, Kenneth Joseph (U.S. economist, *b.* 1921), see under EQUILIBRIUM.

art autre, see under ABSTRACT ART.

art brut. The casual, often jarring, spontaneous graphic products of non-professionals, whether they be psychotics (see PSYCHOSIS), children, or graffiti-writers; or art which imitates these. *Art brut* ('raw art') was christened, adopted, and promoted by Jean Dubuffet, whose own paintings and assemblages of waste materials (see COLLAGE) owe much to the untutored scrawlings which he regards as truly creative reflections of the UN-CONSCIOUS mind.   P.C.

Bibl: *Jean Dubuffet: a Retrospective* (N.Y., Solomon R. Guggenheim Foundation, 1973).

Art-Language, see under CONCEPTUAL ART.

art music. A term used loosely to categorize a composition defined by the intention and method of its composer. He does not write primarily for money, though he usually insists on being paid, and will gladly compose to a commission. He does not despise popular success, but will not modify or simplify his style to achieve it; nor, probably, will he deny that his audience is an ÉLITE. He uses accepted methods of composition, with a high degree of technical sophistication; according to fashion, this might be academic ingenuity or controlled chaos (see ALEAT-ORY). He writes in conventional notation, unlike the composer-performer of FOLK MUSIC, whose work is perpetuated by oral tradition. Folk music is, however, always heard, whereas art music includes academic exercises doomed to eternal silence.

The passing of time and change of taste can recategorize a composition: Mozart's dance music, for example, is now regarded as art music, whereas a jazzed-up version of his 40th symphony would not be. The label 'art music' does not, in any case, imply high artistic worth, nor does the withholding of the label imply the absence of such worth. To dress up a simple expressive folk tune in the trappings of a symphony is to degrade it; and a JAZZ band may exhibit a vitality and imagination well beyond the capacity of many a composer of string quartets and symphonies. To this extent, the term 'art music' has fallen into disrepute.   B.K.

art nouveau. An artistic movement based on the use of linear flowing forms which emerged in the early 1890s in Europe and the U.S.A. and was probably strongly influenced by the introduction of Japanese art objects to the West. Named after a Paris shop, it was known in Germany as *Jugendstil* (after the satirical paper *Jugend*) and in Italy as *Stile Liberty* (after the London department store). In Austria it became associated with the Vienna SEZESSION started in 1897. The sinuous interweaving forms which became current in painting had their first major architectural application in the interior of the Auditorium Building in Chicago (1888) by Louis Sullivan and a house in Brussels (1893) by Victor Horta. These were attempts to define a new, vigorous style free of academicism and capable of unifying the arts. The notion of 'structural and dynamographic ornamentation' was developed largely by the Belgian architect Henry van de Velde, who was prominent in the WERKBUND and directed the Weimar Design School which developed into the BAUHAUS.

Art nouveau had a strong impact on the applied arts and is most visible in architecture where these meet – the furniture and decorations of the Tea Rooms in Glasgow by Charles Rennie Mackintosh, the ironwork outside his Glasgow School of Art, and that of Hector Guimard for the entrances of the Paris Métro. A full, plastic and often polychromatic expression was achieved by Antonio Gaudi in a number of buildings in Barcelona. *Art nouveau* declined soon after 1900 and remained out of favour until the late 1950s, when a search for more varied and richer forms (see, e.g., PSYCHEDELIC ART) appeared to make it relevant. See also ARTS DÉCO; GLASGOW SCHOOL; WIENER WERKSTÄT-TE.   M.BR.

Bibl: S. T. Madsen, tr. R. I. Christopherson, *Art Nouveau* (London and N.Y., 1967).

art of the real, SEE MINIMAL ART.

art sacré, F. French movement for the renewal of religious art in the light of modern painting and the example of the BEURON school in Germany. It dates from the foundation of the *ateliers d'art sacré* by the ex-NABI Maurice Denis and Georges Desvallières in 1919. In 1935 the magazine *L'Art sacré* was started, and after World War II an annual *salon d'art sacré* in Paris. From about 1950 (completion of the church of Notre-Dame at

Assy in Savoie) a number of remarkable individual or collective works were created, quite often by unbelievers, under the influence of this movement, with wide international repercussions (e.g. on the decoration of the new cathedrals at Coventry and Liverpool). In particular, Matisse at Vence and Le Corbusier at Ronchamp produced world-famous masterpieces, while outside the movement proper the ex-FAUVE Georges Rouault devoted much of his life to religious art.

J.W.

Artaud, Antonin (French actor and producer, 1896–1948), see under SUR-REALISM; TEL QUEL; THEATRE OF CRUELTY; THEATRE OF PANIC.

artificial insemination. The insemination of a female (human or animal) by other means than sexual intercourse. Semen is collected from the male – by masturbation or in the case of animals by an artificial vagina – and injected into the cervix (neck of the womb).

In animal-breeding, especially cattle-breeding, artificial insemination is now widely used. Centres exist for the collection of semen from high-quality males which is then directly injected into the females or cooled, preserved, and despatched to recipient animals anywhere. Since more semen is produced at a single ejaculation than is necessary to inseminate one female, artificial insemination has the advantage that several females can be inseminated from a semen sample of one male.

In humans a distinction is drawn between artificial insemination by the husband (A.I.H) and by a donor (A.I.D.) whose identity is usually unknown to the married couple. A.I.H. is used when because of difficulty with intercourse or, rarely, anatomical deformity natural insemination is impossible; A.I.D. is used – in an unknown but probably small number of cases – where the husband is sterile and the wife fertile. There has been controversy about A.I.D. between those who object on moral, legal, and even GENETIC grounds and those who feel that, provided certain safeguards are observed, it should be available to married couples who prefer it to adoption.   D.A.P.

ARTIFICIAL INTELLIGENCE

artificial intelligence (or *machine intelligence*). A new, COMPUTER-based science aimed partly at understanding the nature of human and animal INTELLIGENCE and specifically at creating machines capable of intelligent PROBLEM-SOLVING, by any means open to the logician and the engineer. This has proved extremely difficult, and present success is limited to specific kinds of problem, such as draughts (checkers) and chess games. ROBOTS have been built, with television camera eyes and mechanical limbs, capable of recognizing objects and assembling simple structures.

The computer may be given a DATA BASE of facts corresponding to the (sometimes artificial) world in which it operates, or it may have to learn most of these facts, sometimes from 'experience' through its 'eye' and its touch probes. It may also be fed by a human programmer with information as required, or as requested by it. The machine must generalize and compare, discover correlations, and predict probable outcomes of action. It employs inference and HEURISTIC rules, which it is generally given but may modify with 'experience'. Some critics of A.I. have suggested that computers can never be made to show true originality, or intelligence, because of the 'combinatorial explosion' resulting from considering all possibilities (see ALGORITHM). It should be realized, however, that the brain is also a finite system, but it somehow avoids the problem. If the brain can do so, how can it be *impossible* for computers? We assume that human beings avoid saturation by adopting more or less explicit rules for limiting the possibilities to be considered. When the limitation is too severe, originality may be impossible, and opinion may seem prejudiced; but *some* limitations are necessary for thinking or PERCEPTION to be possible.

At present, machines can hold their own with world draughts champions and serious amateur chess players. People with this capacity would be called intelligent; but would people with *only* this capacity be intelligent? Machines can solve mathematical problems with only limited human aid, and some can recognize printed CHARACTERS and even handwriting with a reliability up to about 99% for each character. Their ability to recognize objects, lying in any of several possible positions, and especially when there may

37

be shadows or other complications, is by human standards extremely limited. See also COMPUTER SIMULATION. R.L.G.

Bibl: M. Minsky and S. Papert, *Perceptrons* (Cambridge, Mass., 1969; B. Meltzer and D. Michie (eds.), *Machine Intelligence 7* (Edinburgh, 1972); T. Winograd, *Understanding Nature Language* (Edinburgh, London, and N.Y., 1972).

Artmann, Hans Carl (Austrian author, *b*.1921), see under WIENER GRUPPE.

arts, the. A variety of pursuits whose definition has been for centuries a stumbling-block to aestheticians and encyclopedists alike. Antithetical subdivisions have often proved useful – major/minor arts, liberal/servile, abstract/objective, decorative/industrial, upper-sense/lower-sense, and so on. These epithets offer a (not very reliable) commentary on the societies that favoured them: Bacon wrote of 'the voluptuary arts', in Reynolds's day 'the polite arts' was current, while in the 1970s 'the plastic arts' has become common.

The distinction between 'fine' and 'applied' arts remains interesting, for often in practice (e.g. the Arts Council) 'the arts' means only 'the fine arts': painting, sculpture, music, drama, and (usually) literature. (The Royal Society of Arts, however, has from the outset taken a strong interest in what is now called industrial design.) In an academic context, 'fine arts' tends to be restricted to the visual (as sometimes is the singular 'art'), and may even, in this restricted sense, be excluded from an 'arts side' which includes such subjects as ancient and modern languages, history, philosophy, and theology – i.e. which is equivalent to the HUMANITIES. P.C.

Bibl: T. Munro, *The Arts and their Interrelations* (London and Cleveland, rev. ed., 1967).

arts and crafts movement. A reaction to the Industrial Revolution and its products (especially as seen at the Great Exhibition of 1851) which was given social and intellectual definition in the writings of Ruskin and translated into practical terms by the founding by William Morris in 1861 of Morris, Marshall & Faulkner, Fine Art Workmen in Painting, Carving, Furniture and the Metals. Morris intended to foster an art restoring the dignity of the craftsman and, since 'it is not possible to dissociate art from morality, politics and religion', to establish a form of society that would combine medieval and SOCIALIST features. The movement, and its followers like Walter Crane, though backward-looking and unable to come to terms with machine production, nevertheless exerted a strong influence on the WERKBUND and hence the BAUHAUS.

The fusion of the applied arts of the movement with those in architecture can be seen in the Red House (1859), designed by Philip Webb for Morris. This later influenced Norman Shaw and C. F. Voysey, whose simple, airy houses of the 1890s proved so important to 20th-century architecture, becoming eventually almost a VERNACULAR of much suburban development. M.BR.

Bibl: N. Pevsner, *Pioneers of Modern Design* (Harmondsworth, rev. ed., 1960).

arts centre. Building or group of buildings devoted to a mixture of cultural activities, such as has been favoured by official and semi-official bodies concerned with public patronage of the ARTS in England since 1945. It may range from a specially built metropolitan complex (as on London's South Bank) to a local library staging occasional exhibitions and entertainments, but generally it involves public and/or foundation finance. The rather similar French *maisons de la culture* which started in the 1960s are more uniform, centering normally on a theatre and an exhibition space, but various other continental or North American institutions could be brought under this head. Analogous earlier centres were the Belgian *maisons du peuple*, the early Soviet Workers' Clubs, and the Italian FASCIST *dopolavoro*. J.W.

Bibl: *The Arts Enquiry: The Visual Arts* (London, 1946); A. Schouvaloff (ed.), *Place for the Arts* (Liverpool, 1970).

arts déco. Abridged name of the Exposition des Arts Décoratifs Modernes (Paris, 1925) used, then and now, for the style predominant there: a jazzy application of a second-hand visual vocabulary, derived from CUBISM, FUTURISM, FUNCTIONALISM, and other recent movements, to decorative, fashionable, and commercial ends. The architects Robert Mallet-Stevens and Michel Roux-Spitz were among those prominent in this trend, which coincided with the great period of cinema construction and still continues in, e.g., luxury bookbinding. Following a revival (exhibition at the Paris Musée des Arts Décoratifs, 1966), it has been seen by some as the natural sequel to ART NOUVEAU, whose formal inventiveness and social commitments, however, it fails to share.   J.W.

Bibl: B. Hillier, *Art Déco* (London and N.Y., 1968).

Arvatov, Boris (Russian literary theorist, 1896–1940), see under FORMALISM.

ascription, see under PATTERN VARIABLES.

asepsis (or *aseptic surgery*). The procedure by which wound infections are so far as possible prevented from occurring in the first place by the use of sterile instruments, drapes, gowns, etc., and by scrupulous attention to hygiene. Asepsis differs from *antisepsis* (or *antiseptic surgery*) in that the latter was an attempt to *kill* micro-organisms *in situ*, whereas aseptic surgery aims at *excluding* them from the operation site. Although antiseptic surgery as such is obsolete, ANTISEPTICS have an important part to play in asepsis. Thus the skin into which a surgical incision is to be made is often prepared by repeated applications of iodine in alcoholic solution or by thorough cleansing with cationic DETERGENTS.

The principal cause of wound infection used to be the surgeon himself who before the days of antisepsis or asepsis could propagate infection from one patient to another, and even today it is the micro-organisms to be found in hospitals themselves that are the major causes of wound infection – a particularly grave matter inasmuch as so many of the bacterial populations of the hospital ward are resistant to ANTIBIOTICS.   P.M.

Ashby's Law, see under VARIETY.

Ashcan School. Term applied to American painting at the beginning of the 20th century characterized by the naturalistic (see NATURALISM) depiction of scenes from everyday life, especially in the city. It has been used misleadingly as a synonym for *The Eight*, a group of independents who revolted against New York academic painting, but it more appropriately describes the painting of Robert Henri, John Sloan, George Luks, and George Bellows.   A.K.W.

Bibl: M. S. Young, *The Eight* (N.Y., 1973).

Asimov, Isaac (U.S. novelist, *b*. 1920), see under SCIENCE FICTION.

assemblage. In ARCHAEOLOGY (for its meaning in art see under COLLAGE), a group of artifacts found together in a closed CONTEXT or ASSOCIATION, e.g. in a hoard, a grave, or a single occupation level, in such a way as to imply that they were likely to have been in use at the same time. In palaeolithic studies an assemblage of tool types is usually referred to as an *industry*, while recurring assemblages can constitute a CULTURE.   B.C.

assembler. In COMPUTING, a PROGRAM which takes as input any program written in ASSEMBLY LANGUAGE and transforms (translates) it into the corresponding form of machine-code instructions. It may leave these instructions inside the machine to be obeyed immediately, in which case it may be known as an *assembler-loader* or merely a *loader*.   C.S.

assembly language. In COMPUTING, a PROGRAMMING LANGUAGE which produces, in general, one machine-code instruction for each line written in it. As a result programs written in assembly language tend to be very long and difficult to read. Despite various improvements the languages remain very close to actual machine code, so that different makes of machine require different assembly languages. See also ASSEMBLER; HIGH-LEVEL PROGRAMMING LANGUAGE.   C.S.

assimilation. In DEVELOPMENTAL PSYCHOLOGY, a PIAGETIAN term for (1) the incorporation of a new situation transformed to fit into an already organized schema of action; (2) more generally, the subordination of the external world to the activity of the self, as in fantasy and play. See also ACCOMMODATION; and for a different sense of the word, see under INTEGRATION (sense 2).   P.L.H.

ASSOCIATION

association.

(1) In COGNITIVE PSYCHOLOGY, the mental connection between two or more IDEAS or SENSE DATA (percepts) or memories, such that the presence of one tends to evoke the other(s). These are presumed to mirror the associations that exist in the external world, so that association provides a mechanism whereby the STRUCTURE of experience reflects 'reality'. The CONCEPT was central to Aristotle's doctrine of mind as well as that of the British EMPIRICISTS. w.z.

(2) In ARCHAEOLOGY, when artifacts are found together in a closed CONTEXT they are said to be in *close association*, implying contemporaneity of deposition. The term *loose association* is sometimes used in the case of contexts of broader chronological range. Characteristics may be associated on a single artifact. Juxtaposition is not necessarily association. The term is imprecise and much abused in archaeological literature. B.C.

associationism. The recurring and variously formulated view (in R. S. Woodworth's classification, one of the six main SCHOOLS OF PSYCHOLOGY) that psychological phenomena comprise elements, such as ideas, SENSATIONS, feelings, STIMULI, and responses, which have become associated (see ASSOCIATION) according to some law or laws, such as similarity or frequency of contiguity. I.M.L.H.

Bibl: E. G. Boring, *A History of Experimental Psychology* (N.Y., 2nd ed., 1950).

associative law. The law, obeyed in the multiplication of NUMBERS, which states that $a \times (b \times c) = (a \times b) \times c$. Any FUNCTION of two ARGUMENTS which satisfies a similar identity is said to be *associative*; other examples are addition and the composition of functions (since $f.(g.h)(x) = f(g(h(x))) = (f.g).h(x)$). For many MATHEMATICAL STRUCTURES (e.g. GROUPS) the law is taken as an axiom (see AXIOMATIC METHOD). R.G.

associative store (or *content-addressed store*). In a COMPUTER, a form of STORE in which the location to which access is required is indicated, not by its 'address' (or physical location) as in the usual type of store, but by a key; the location chosen will be one whose contents match the key in some way. Special arrangements are made for the cases in which there are either no locations or more than one location matching the key. An associative store appears expensive, because comparison with the key is carried out for all locations simultaneously and this involves a considerable amount of LOGIC for each location. However, as these circuits are highly repetitive, they are suitable for L.S.I. (see INTEGRATED CIRCUIT), which reduces their cost. C.S.

Astbury, William T. (British scientist, 1898–1961), see under MOLECULAR BIOLOGY.

asteroid (or *minor planet* or *planetoid*). One of several thousand masses of rock or ice, the largest about 300 miles across, which circle the sun in orbits distributed between those of Mars and Jupiter. They may be the debris of a planet ruptured by collision with another body, or by the gravitational effects (see GRAVITATION) of a close approach to Jupiter; alternatively, they may be the raw material for a planet which never consolidated. M.V.B.

asthenosphere. The analysis of earthquake waves passing through the earth has led to a simple threefold divison of the interior of the earth. The outermost solid shell, the *crust*, is of variable thickness, 30 to 75 km in continental areas but some 5 km under the oceans. The crust is succeeded inwards by the still solid and denser *mantle* which extends to a depth of 2,900 km below the surface. The very high density and mainly liquid interior of the earth is known as the *core*. In general the strength of the crust and mantle rock material increases with depth. More detailed seismic study has revealed the presence of a relatively weak plastic zone in the upper part of the mantle named the asthenosphere which extends from 100 to 400 km below the surface. The mechanical weakness of the zone is thought to be due to the presence of small quantities of interstitial liquid. The plastic asthenosphere allows the rigid lithosphere above it to move laterally over the surface of the earth (see PLATE TECTONICS). J.L.M.L.

astrology. The belief that it is possible to forecast events by observing the positions

40

of the moon, the sun, the planets, and the fixed stars. Of considerable antiquity (dating back to at least the third millennium B.C.), it has retained a hold on popular imagination despite its irreconcilability with either Christian beliefs or scientific RATIONALISM, and even despite its dubious record of reliability. D.C.W.

astronautics. The TECHNOLOGY of travel in space, involving ROCKET propulsion, TELECOMMUNICATION, CELESTIAL MECHANICS, and the design of life-support systems. M.V.B.

astronomy. The oldest exact science, in which the heavenly bodies (moon, sun, planets, stars, NEBULAE, GALAXIES, etc.) are studied. By analysing the RADIATION received from space as visible light and, more recently, X-RAYS, radio waves (see RADIO ASTRONOMY), and MICROWAVES, the following picture of the universe has been built up: the nearly-spherical earth is orbited by the moon; together they move in an ORBIT round the sun, as do the planets and their SATELLITES, and the ASTEROIDS, all the bodies so far mentioned constituting the *solar system*. The sun in turn is one star among millions, which together with nebulae and sparse interstellar debris make up the *Milky Way*, which is in turn one galaxy among millions whose mutual recession constitutes the EXPANSION OF THE UNIVERSE.

Distances in astronomy are vividly expressed in light-time, using the fact that light travels 186,000 miles per second. From the earth to the moon is 1.4 light seconds, from the earth to the sun about 8 light-minutes; the whole solar system is a few light-hours across. The nearest star is 4 light-years away, and the Milky Way is about 100,000 light-years across. The nearest galaxy is about two million light-years away. The distance at which the galaxies are receding from us with the speed of light, which on our present understanding represents the limit of the observable universe, is about ten thousand million light-years.

The study of the motion of the heavenly bodies constitutes CELESTIAL MECHANICS, the investigation of their physical nature ASTROPHYSICS. In COSMOLOGY the universe as a whole is studied, and attempts are made to account for its origin in COSMOGONY. Precise observations of the positions of heavenly bodies were used until recently to establish standards of time measurement (see ATOMIC CLOCK), while for millennia these observations have formed the basis for navigation (recently in the air and outer space as well as on the sea), as well as for ASTROLOGY. M.V.B.

Bibl: G. Abell, *Exploration of the Universe* (London and N.Y., 2nd ed., 1969); D. H. Menzel, F. L. Whipple, and G. de Vancouleurs, *Survey of the Universe* (Englewood Cliffs, N. J., 1970); F. L. Whipple, *Earth, Moon and Planets* (3rd ed., Cambridge, Mass., 1968; Harmondsworth, 1971).

astrophysics. A branch of theoretical ASTRONOMY: the study of stars, and the gases between them, in which the laws of PHYSICS established on earth are applied to the electromagnetic RADIATION and COSMIC RAYS received from space. See also BLACK HOLE; CARBON CYCLE; PULSAR; QUASAR; RADIO ASTRONOMY; RADIO TELESCOPE, SPECTROSCOPY. M.V.B.

Asturias, Miguel (Guetemalan poet and novelist, *b.* 1899), see under STREAM OF CONSCIOUSNESS.

asymptotic. A FUNCTION f is an asymptotic approximation to the function g if the percentage error $g(x) - f(x)/f(x)$ tends to zero as x tends to infinity. R.G.

atavism. The unsubstantiated belief that complete ancestral types can reappear as 'throwbacks' among an otherwise normal family. This concept of atavism, though based on a grain of truth – the fact that in Mendelian (see MENDELISM) HEREDITY grandparental or more remotely ancestral characteristics may reappear unexpectedly among offspring – belongs to the folklore of racism (see RACE); cf. the totally unwarranted name 'mongolism' for a congenital affliction (DOWN'S SYNDROME) caused by an accidental derangement of the CHROMOSOMES. P.M.

atheism. The opinion that there is no God. The chief grounds on which this is asserted are: the extent of disorder, chance, and evil in the universe as known by science and by honest experience; the impossibility of knowing anything beyond space and time, such as God (see AGNOSTICISM);

the failure of believers' (mutually conflicting) attempts to claim that God has been revealed and can be spoken about reasonably (see THEISM). The chief problems confronting atheism are man's wonder at the existence of good (see MYSTICISM), and the need which many people feel for faith and a supernatural consolation in order to endure (see RELIGION). See also HUMANISM; SECULARISM. D.L.E.

Bibl: R. Robinson, *An Atheist's Values* (Oxford, 1964); A.G.N. Flew, *God and Philosophy* (London and N.Y., 1966).

Athens Charter, see under CIAM.

atom. The smallest unit of a chemical ELEMENT. The idea that matter, which appears continuous to our gross senses, may in fact consist of tiny discrete PARTICLES which cannot be further subdivided, seems to stem from Democritus (*c.* 400 B.C.). But it was only in the late 19th century that accumulating evidence (e.g. the BROWNIAN MOTION) led to the general acceptance of the *atomic theory* among scientists. The entities which we call atoms today are only one of several 'smallest units' at the microscopic level of nature; MOLECULES are the structural units involved in chemical processes, while atoms themselves have a complicated structure (see ATOMIC PHYSICS) of which the ELEMENTARY PARTICLES represent the fundamental units. M.V.B.

atomic clock. A device for counting the vibrations of ATOMS. Because of their extreme regularity, these vibrations are used to define the standard for the measurement of time (1 second = 9,192,631,770 cycles of a certain vibration of the Caesium atom); this is expected to be consistent to about one second in a thousand years (a previous standard, based on the earth's rotation, was accurate only to about one second in one year). M.V.B.

atomic energy. ENERGY obtained from the atomic NUCLEUS during a CHAIN REACTION, which may either be controlled, as in a NUCLEAR REACTOR, or uncontrolled, as in nuclear weapons. See also FISSION; FUSION; MASS-ENERGY EQUATION. M.V.B.

atomic number (of an ELEMENT). The number of PROTONS in the atomic NUCLEUS. It is equal to the number of ELECTRONS in a neutral ATOM, and the ordinal number of the element on a scale of increasing atomic weights. No elements whose atomic number exceeds 92 (uranium) occur naturally; nuclei of the TRANSURANIC ELEMENTS are unstable because the disruptive effect of the ELECTROSTATIC repulsion between the protons outweighs the attraction due to the shorter-ranged STRONG INTERACTION. See also ISOTOPE. M.V.B.

atomic physics. The branch of PHYSICS devoted to studying the structure of ATOMS. The atom is an open structure about a ten-thousand-millionth of a metre across, consisting of a positively charged NUCLEUS about ten thousand times smaller across, whose attraction binds a number of negatively charged orbiting ELECTRONS; this number is equal to the ATOMIC NUMBER if the atom is neutral, but higher or lower if the atom is an ION. It is often helpful to compare the atom with the solar system of sun and planets, but this is not a strict analogy because electrons obey the laws of QUANTUM MECHANICS, not of NEWTONIAN MECHANICS (see WAVE-PARTICLE DUALITY; BOHR THEORY). The weakly-bound outer electrons are detached and exchanged during the CHEMICAL REACTIONS which may occur when atoms are close together. Transitions of electrons from one ORBIT to another, with a change of QUANTUM NUMBER, involves an emission or absorption of ENERGY in the form of PHOTONS, either of visible light (outer electrons) or X-RAYS (inner electrons). See also ELECTRON SHELL; ENERGY LEVEL; SPECTROSCOPY. M.V.B.

atomic pile, see NUCLEAR REACTOR.

atomic submarine, see NUCLEAR SUBMARINE.

atonal music. Music divorced from the concept of *tonality* which dominated Western musical thought for more than three centuries. Traditionally, a composer selected one of the 24 tonal families – 12 major and 12 minor – each of which is spelled out by a *scale* and known as a *key*, one note being the *tonic* towards which the others gravitate. It was common practice for the opening phrase of a work to establish the key unequivocally by stating its essential notes in melodic or harmonic terms; similarly it was virtually an unbroken rule that the final cadence (sequence of chords) should confirm the tonality. In the latter part of the 19th century, however, the increasingly free use, notably by Wagner and Liszt, of chromatic notes (those not belonging to the key of the work) led to a gradual erosion of tonality. The process was continued by Debussy (see IMPRESSIONISM; WHOLE-TONE SCALE), Scriabin, and particularly Schönberg, and culminated in *atonalism*. Atonalism is the deliberate avoidance of key; *atonality* is the term used to designate a state of atonalism.

The largest problem in atonal music is to overcome the natural tendency of certain basic intervals such as the fifth and the third to establish a tonality of sorts, however temporary. It is for this reason that atonal music is largely dissonant, since only by avoiding traditional consonances can the implications of tonality be avoided; similarly the melodic lines are harder for the average listener to absorb, since they are often characterized by angularity and wide-spaced intervals. Much, but not all, atonal music is composed according to the SERIAL principles evolved around 1920 by Schönberg.　　A.H.

attachment. In ETHOLOGY, the initial 'bonding' of mother and infant of various SPECIES, during which many crucial response mechanisms in the growing infant have been found to depend upon an adequate relationship with the mother. See also IMPRINTING.　　J.S.B.
Bibl: J. Bowlby, *Attachment and Loss* (London and N.Y., 1969).

Auden, Wystan Hugh (British -U.S. poet, 1907–73), see under CRITERION, THE; GROUP THEATRE; HORIZON; MOVEMENT, THE; NEW WRITING.

au-dessus de la mêlée ('above the battle'). An expression which became current during the 1914–18 war, as the title of an article in the *Journal de Génève* (15 September 1914), and later of a pamphlet, a collection of articles by the French writer Romain Rolland, author of *Jean-Christophe*, who had strong sympathies with German musical and literary culture. The pamphlet, a plea for peace and reasonableness, offended nationalistic sensibilities – Hermann Hesse was the only writer on either side who immediately welcomed it – and the expression came to signify reprehensible detachment or indifference.　　J.G.W.

audio frequency. A vibration frequency in the range 20–20,000 Hertz (1 Hertz = 1 complete vibration cycle per second). This is the range over which the human ear responds to sound waves, so that HI-FI consists of the faithful reproduction of audio frequencies. See also ULTRASONICS.　　M.V.B.

audio-visual aids. An aspect of EDUCATIONAL TECHNOLOGY in which material is presented for both eye and ear; examples are sound-films, film-strips with commentary, tape recordings, cassettes, and television. As the word implies, the aids are regarded as extensions of the teacher's resources, his role remaining central. Particular applications of these principles have been made in LANGUAGE LABORATORIES and in science teaching.　　W.A.C.S.

Auerbach, Erich (German–U.S. philologist, 1892–1957), see under REALISM.

Auric, Georges (French composer, *b*.1899), see under SIX, LES.

Austin, John (British jurist, 1790–1859), see under AUSTINIAN; LEGAL POSITIVISM; SOVEREIGNTY.

Austin, John Langshaw (British philosopher, 1911–60), see under LINGUISTIC PHILOSOPHY.

Austinian. Adjective formed from the name of John Austin (1790–1859). Austin's vastly influential *The Province of Jurisprudence Determined* (1832) elaborated a theory of law which insisted that the notion of a command was the key to the understanding of law, and that though there were many empirical connections between law and morals there was no necessary connection between them. Human law is therefore, according to Austin, essentially a command (expressed or tacit) of a sovereign (see SOVEREIGNTY) defined as a person or body of persons in receipt of habitual obedience from the bulk of a given society but not in any such habit of obedience to any other person or body of persons. The word 'Austinian' is most often used to refer to the imperative elements in this theory or its separation of law and morals.   H.L.A.H.

Autant-Lara, Claude (French film director, *b*. 1901), see under CINEMASCOPE.

autarky (sometimes misleadingly spelled *autarchy*, which derives from a different Greek word, and means absolute sovereignty or autocratic rule). A national policy of economic self-sufficiency, for example in food, energy, and technology. Such policies tend to be associated with controls and other interferences with free economic exchange across national frontiers and to be contrasted with such postwar ideals as FREE TRADE, convertibility and multilateralism (see BILATERALISM AND MULTILATERALISM). The high period of autarkic policies was between the two world wars, when the U.S.A. inclined to ISOLATIONISM, Britain looked to a system of IMPERIAL PREFERENCE and the STERLING AREA to assure its markets and raw materials, Japan tried to construct its GREATER EAST ASIA CO-PROSPERITY SPHERE, and Hitler's Central Bank Governor, Dr Schacht, constructed his notorious Schachtian system of controls designed to insulate Germany from the world DEPRESSION while promoting a massive armaments programme at home. In recent years the reactions of some Western countries to successive currency and energy disorders has resurrected the spectre of autarky.   P.J.

auteur. Term used analogously to its literary sense of 'author' by the French film critics whose theoretical writing precipitated the *nouvelle vague* (NEW WAVE) to distinguish between a film-maker responsible for the entire conception of his films and one who merely stages scripts written by another artist. These future film-makers believed that a true *auteur* both writes and directs his films; but since they admired above all else Hollywood directors who, like the old-guard French film-makers they were trying to displace, often worked from ready-made scripts imposed by studio chiefs, the critical debate (usually

referred to as the *politique des auteurs*) centred on the argument that great film-makers or *auteurs* (e.g. Hitchcock, Hawks) transformed the scripts given to them by imposing, visually, their own preoccupations and continuing themes. Often misunderstood, and sometimes abused to attempt to prove that a director is an *auteur* because his work reveals persistent concerns and mannerisms, or that an *auteur's* subsequent work must be good because he is an *auteur*, the argument has been adopted by English and American critics as the '*auteur* theory'.   T.C.C.M.
Bibl: A. Sarris, 'Notes on the *Auteur* Theory in 1962' (*Film Culture*, Winter 1962); P. Graham (ed.), *The New Wave* (London and Garden City, N.Y., 1968).

authoritarian personality. A PERSONALITY TYPE characterized by extreme obedience and unquestioning respect for authority. These defining characteristics are usually accompanied by rigidity, conventionality, prejudice, and intolerance of weakness or ambiguity.   w.z.
Bibl: T. W. Adorno *et al.*, *The Authoritarian Personality* (N.Y., 1964).

authoritarianism. The advocacy and justification of government based on orders which are backed by threats of punishment for disobedience. Advocates of authoritarian systems of rule believe that the rulers' authority is its own justification and that their practices should be accepted by their subjects, without consultation or persuasion, because of the authority vested in them by God, by political or social theory, or by the abstract processes of historical development.
                    D.C.W.
Bibl: J. P. Kirscht and R. C. Dillehay, *Dimensions of Authoritarianism* (Lexington, 1967).

authority, see under CHARISMA; POWER.

autism. Term derived from the Greek *autos*, self, and used to describe behavioural patterns which suggest to observers that the individual in question is absorbed exclusively in his or her own interior experiences. Early infantile autism is a SYNDROME characterized by Leo Kanner as combining 'extreme self-isolation and the obsessive insistence on the preservation of sameness'. The term is loosely used to describe any non-communicating behaviour, especially in children. c.o.

Bibl: L. Kanner, *Child Psychiatry* (Springfield, Ill., and Oxford, 3rd ed., 1957).

autochthony. Word used by K. C. Wheare in his *Constitutional Structure of the Commonwealth* (1960), and by others since, to designate a characteristic of constitutions to which some countries of the British COMMONWEALTH attached great importance when they achieved independence. They wished not only to have a constitution independent of the Parliament of the U.K., to which they had formerly been subject, but to demonstrate that the status of the new constitution as law was not derived from any legislation of the U.K., and, like the constitution of other independent sovereign states, had a 'home-grown' or autochthonous quality. H.L.A.II.

auto-destructive. A term used of any artifact designed to damage itself – though generally with a little help from outside. Celebrated examples are the Swiss sculptor Jean Tinguely's machines which dismantled themselves (e.g. 'Study no. 2 for an End of the World', detonated in the Nevada desert), and Gustav Metzger's nylon cloth which he destroyed with hydrochloric acid. Metzger described this as simultaneously 'auto-creative', on the tenuous grounds that the work of art (and not simply the artist) had a measure of 'initiative' in transforming itself. Some auto-destructive art has been intended as a reflection on the built-in obsolescence of CONSUMERS' GOODS, or on the suicidal tendencies of military powers. P.C.

Bibl: G. Metzger, 'Machine, Auto-creative and Auto-destructive Art' (*Ark, 32 (1962), pp. 7–8*).

autological, see under HETEROLOGICAL.

autolysis. Literally self-dissolution. Nearly all living CELLS contain vesicles known as *lysosomes,* which are richly charged with hydrolytic ENZYMES. When a TISSUE is deprived of its blood supply or severed from the body and kept at or near body temperature these vesicles rupture and the tissues undergo a process of self-digestion. In the normal life of the body this makes it possible for many cellular ingredients to be re-utilized and recycled. Autolysis has much to do with the process by which the 'hanging' of game makes it more tender and palatable. P.M.

automatic pilot. A CONTROL SYSTEM used in aircraft to control the altitude of the aircraft in pitch, roll, and yaw. The system can be set to keep the aircraft in straight and level flight without human intervention. The detectors in the control system usually consist of GYROSCOPES, from which error signals are derived as electrical voltages. Artificial signals may be fed into the system by a human operator to make the aircraft turn, bank, climb, or dive. As early as the 1920s automatic pilots were installed in pilotless aircraft which were used for air-gunnery target practice and these aircraft could be controlled by radio from the ground in all manoeuvres, including take-off and landing. Today's airliners are commonly set on automatic pilot immediately after take-off and remain so for the greater part of the journey. The device corrects automatically for what would otherwise be deviations from the flight path produced by storms, winds, jet streams, etc. E.R.L.

automatic (or *built-in*) **stabilizers.** Mechanisms within the economy which act counter-cyclically (i.e. against the prevailing economic cycle) without specific intervention by the authorities. An example is a progressive income-tax system, i.e. one which takes an increasing share of increasing personal incomes and a decreasing share of decreasing ones, thus acting, respectively, to restrain the growth of DEMAND or to moderate its decline. D.E.

Bibl: T. F. Dernburg and D. M. McDougall, *Macroeconomics* (N.Y., 3rd ed., 1968).

automatic translation, see MACHINE TRANSLATION.

automatic writing, see under SURREALISM.

automation. A word introduced by Delmar S. Harder in 1948 for the automatic control of the manufacture of a product through a number of successive stages. It is now generally used for the control of

AUTOMATISM

machines by machines with human intervention reduced to a minimum; examples are an automatic pilot (George), or a COMPUTER-controlled milling machine or assembly line. Automation is an emotionally charged word since it is frequently used to mean the use of machines to replace human labour. According to some, it merely continues a process of technical change (MECHANIZATION) which is at least as old as the Industrial Revolution. In industrialized societies the increase in per capita productivity during the past two centuries is largely the consequence of the increase in quantity and the improvement in quality of the machines and tools with which human workers cooperate. For the alarmists, however, automation is qualitatively different, and threatens vast technological UNEMPLOYMENT as growing numbers of skills are rendered obsolete. Thus far the gradualists have the better of the argument, but the matter is far from settled.
C.S.; R.L.

Bibl: J. N. Froomkin, 'Automation', in D. L. Sills (ed.), *International Encyclopedia of the Social Sciences* (London and N.Y., 1968), pp. 480–88.

automatism. In modern English criminal law, involuntary conduct where, owing to lack of normal control over his bodily movements, a person does an act which would, but for such lack of control, constitute an offence. The chief importance for the law of identifying such cases of automatism is that, even where an offence is one of STRICT LIABILITY, an accused person will not be criminally responsible for the consequences of his uncontrolled bodily movements unless the loss of control arose from his own failure to take reasonable precautions. The forms of uncontrolled conduct which lawyers now describe as automatism were formerly referred to as cases where there was 'no act' or 'no volition' on the part of the accused.
H.L.A.H.

automorphism. A structure-preserving PERMUTATION of the elements of a MATHEMATICAL STRUCTURE (see also ISOMORPHIC).
R.G.

autonomic nervous system, see under NERVOUS SYSTEM.

autopoiesis. In CYBERNETICS, a term coined by Humberto Maturana for a special case of HOMEOSTASIS in which the critical variable of the system that is held constant is that system's own organization.
S.BE.

autopolyploid, see under POLYPLOID.

autoradiograph. The image of a radioactive object (see RADIOACTIVITY) obtained photographically by using the RADIATION emitted during the decay process. The distribution of radioactive material is mapped directly on a photographic plate placed in close contact with the object. Autoradiography is an important technique in PHYSIOLOGY and BIOCHEMISTRY. It can be used to follow the diffusion of a radioactive TRACER and in this way has revealed details of the internal boundaries of metals and the permeability of membranes.
B.F.

autosome. A CHROMOSOME other than a SEX CHROMOSOME.
J.M.S.

auto-suggestion. A therapeutic technique whereby an individual attempts to induce a desired effect by self-instruction and self-encouragement; first made popular by Coué (*Self-Mastery through Conscious Auto-Suggestion,* London, 1922).
W.Z.

autotelic writing. An appropriately new term, in the NEW CRITICISM, for the old notion that a work of art exists for and within itself. The modern origins of this idea are found in the writings of the 18th-century Swiss critics J. J. Bodmer and J. J. Breitinger. Bodmer wrote that from the poet the reader should demand 'only poetry; in this we shall be satisfied with the probability and the reason which lies in its coherence with itself'. This led into 'art for art's sake', and declined into romantic preciosity or elegant wit (e.g. Oscar Wilde's dictum that life seeks to imitate art). The idea appears again in the 20th century in two scarcely related forms: in the work of certain poets (e.g. the 'creationism' of the Chilean Vicente Huidobro) and fiction-writers, notably Borges; and in the New Criticism, where it serves to turn attention away from irrelevancies of neo-romantic criticism and towards the text. It is not often seriously suggested that literature has no place in life, but only that it must first be studied as if it had not.　　　　　M.S.-S.

autotrophic. Term applied to organisms which can build up their body constituents from the simplest ingredients – water, mineral salts, and carbon dioxide, with sunlight as a source of energy. Organisms which have to make use of partially synthesized ingredients from other simpler organisms are described as *heterotrophic*.
　　　　　P.M.

avant-garde. French military term used before 1848 for any politically advanced republican or SOCIALIST group, later for the assumption that 'advanced' art must occupy a similar position of leadership in the fight against the BOURGEOIS, and finally in all countries after about 1910 to denote those cultural innovators, whatever their political associations, who appeared most inaccessible to public understanding. Though still able to fire the less sceptical creative artists, middlemen, and critics with a fruitful sense of minority cohesion, it is now an anachronism, since many kinds of art, music, and literature associated with it are widely accepted and officially supported.　　　　　J.W.
　　Bibl: R. Poggioli, tr. G. Fitzgerald, *The Theory of the Avant-Garde* (Cambridge, Mass., 1968); J. E. Bowlt (ed. and tr.), *Russian Art of the Avant-Garde: Theory and Criticism, 1902–1934* (N.Y., 1976).

average. Sometimes used synonymously with MEAN, but also more generally, especially in naive statistics, to mean 'typical'. See also MEASURE OF LOCATION.　R.SI.

average deviation, average variation, see MEAN DEVIATION.

aversion therapy, see under BEHAVIOUR THERAPY.

Avery, Oswald Theodore (U.S. bacteriologist, 1877–1955), see under NUCLEIC ACID.

Avogadro number. The number of ATOMS or MOLECULES whose weight in grams is equal to the atomic or molecular weight of the substance. Amedeo Avogadro (1776–1856) was the first to point out, in 1811, that equal volumes of gases should contain the same number of molecules.

Though real gases do not quite conform to this rule, recognition of the principle helped to clarify the distinction between an atom and a molecule.　　　　　B.F.

Axelrod, Pavel Borisovich (Russian Menshevik leader, 1849 or 1850 to 1928), see under MENSHEVIKS.

axiology. The philosophical theory of value in general, embracing ETHICS or the philosophical theory of morality, but extending far beyond it to include AESTHETIC, technical, prudential, hedonic, and other forms of value. Any field of human discourse in which the general value-terms 'good' and 'ought' figure falls within the range of axiology, even that of SCIENTIFIC METHOD with its principles about the degree of belief one *ought* to give to a hypothesis in the light of a given body of evidence. See also VALUE-JUDGEMENT.　　　　　A.Q.
　　Bibl: G. H. Von Wright, *The Varieties of Goodness* (London and N.Y., 1963).

axiom. For the use of axioms in MATHEMATICS see AXIOMATIC METHOD; in LOGIC see AXIOMATICS.　R.G.

axiom of choice, the (or *multiplicative axiom*). An indispensable assumption for the proof of many intuitively reasonable PROPOSITIONS concerning SETS. Let C be a collection of mutually exclusive non-empty sets (for example the parliamentary boroughs, each considered as a set of electors). The axiom asserts that there is a *choice set* for C (a parliament) which has exactly one member drawn from each of the sets in the collection. It was first formulated by Zermelo in 1904. If C is infinite, there may be no definable property or rule of selection by which one can specify the choice set; hence those who believe that mathematical objects must always be *constructed* doubt its validity. But if sets are viewed as *arbitrary* collections it is wholly plausible, and so is usually included among the AXIOMS of SET THEORY.
　　　　　A.Q.; R.G.

axiomatic method. Before the second half of the 19th century mathematicians studied MATHEMATICAL STRUCTURES which were based on practical experience. Proofs were justified, explicitly or implicitly, by an appeal to intuitions (sometimes

Though real gases do not quite conform to

quite sophisticated) abstracted from that experience. For GEOMETRY Euclid had attempted, with considerable but not complete success, to codify the intuitions in AXIOMS; the theorems should be deduced from these by purely logical arguments. By 1900 AXIOMATICS had become a flourishing industry. The investigations which led to satisfactory sets of axioms for the familiar structures (natural, real, and complex NUMBERS, Euclidean geometry) provoked interest in those seemingly counter-intuitive structures which can be characterized by modifying the familiar axioms in a more or less arbitrary way (e.g. non-Euclidean geometrics, 'number-systems' with non-commutative multiplication). Other unfamiliar structures (e.g. QUATERNIONS) had been first introduced by axioms without any obvious intuitive content. Nowadays the axiomatic method predominates. Axioms for the objects to be studied are no longer presented as codifying intuitions, but simply as rules of a game; Russell's dictum that in mathematics we do not know what we are talking about, nor care whether what we say is true, is taken literally.

The great advantages of the axiomatic method are that it liberates MATHEMATICS from the study of the traditional structures (Cantor wanted pure mathematics to be called 'free mathematics'), and that it concentrates the attention on what is essential to the proof of a particular theorem, which can then be applied to *any* objects that satisfy the axioms used in the proof (see under BOURBAKI). But it may lead to sterile ingenuity, and – as in much contemporary teaching and textbook writing – to the suppression of qualities (in particular intuition and the appreciation of significance) that are essential to good mathematics.   R.G.

Bibl: R. L. Wilder, *Introduction to the Foundations of Mathematics* (N.Y., 2nd ed., 1965).

axiomatics. The branch of logical investigation (see LOGIC) concerned with axiomatic systems, that is to say, with systems of assertions in which a handful of initial PROPOSITIONS is laid down as true (the AXIOMS) or postulated (hence the phrase *postulational method*), and further propositions (the *theorems*) are then deduced from them by means of specified rules of INFERENCE (sometimes called

transformation-rules). To be set out completely an axiom system should also contain a *vocabulary,* in which the terms of the system are enumerated, and a SYNTAX or set of *formation-rules*, determining which combinations of terms of the system constitute well-formed, or significant, assertions. The model for all later axiom-systems is Euclid's geometry (imitated in PHILOSOPHY, for example, in Spinoza's *Ethics*). The axiomatization of other branches of MATHEMATICS was carried out extensively towards the end of the 19th century. Soon techniques for the logical study of axiom systems were developed: techniques for determining the CONSISTENCY of the members of a SET of axioms with each other, their logical *independence* of each other, and the *completeness* of the set, i.e. its adequacy as a basis for the deduction of all the truths statable in the vocabulary of the system. Modern formal logic, as inaugurated by the great treatises of Frege and of Whitehead and Russell, has mostly been expounded in an axiomatic form.   A.Q.

Bibl: R. Blanché, tr. G. B. Keene, *Axiomatics* (London and N.Y., 1962).

Axis. Term invented by Mussolini in a speech of 1 November 1936 to describe the relationship between Nazi Germany and Fascist Italy, after the conclusion of Italo-German agreements (the Berchtesgaden protocols) on international policies; it has been extended to cover other bilateral relationships in which states agree to follow common policies on specific questions. In practice the appearance of joint action and support which the Axis provided was significantly belied by the realities; but it was of some advantage to its adherents so long as active involvement in crisis or war was not in question.   D.C.W.

Bibl: D. C. Watt, 'The Rome-Berlin Axis Myth or Reality, 1936–40' (*Review of Politics*, 1960); F. W. Deakin, *The Brutal Friendship* (London, 1962); E. Wiskemann, *The Rome-Berlin Axis* (London, rev. ed., 1966).

Ayer, Alfred Jules (British philosopher, *b.* 1910), see under EMOTIVISM.

Azaña y Díaz, Manuel de (Spanish statesman, 1880–1940), see under POPULAR FRONT.

B

Baader, Andreas (German revolutionary, *b.* 1943), see under NEW LEFT.

Ba'ath (Arabic for 'resurgence'). The Ba'ath Arab Socialist Party, the IDEO- LOGY of which represents an attempt to synthesize a MARXIST analysis of society with a pan-Arab (see PAN-ISLAM), NATIONALIST approach to social, economic, and political problems. Theoretically, it regards the 'regional' par- ties of the various Arab states as no more than branches of a 'national' all-Arab structure; in practice, the Syrian and Iraqi branches, which are the most active, are entirely separate and often at loggerheads with each other. Founded by Michel Aflaq in 1940–41, the Ba'ath party was instru- mental in creating the short-lived (1958–61) union of Syria and Egypt; from 1963 it formed the ruling party in Syria, although political power rested mainly with its military committee, which fully asserted its control over the regional party and created its own pan-Arab command after 1966. More recently, and especially since 1970, the party has lost prominence in Syria, where power has been increas- ingly concentrated in the hands of a minor- ity Islamic sect, the Alawites. The Iraqi Ba'ath party has been dominant since 1968 but has served as a cloak for the influence of an officers' junta with a reg- ional and familial power-base.   P.B.M.
Bibl: K. S. A. Jaber, *The Arab Ba'ath Socialist Party* (Syracuse, N.Y., 1966); I. Rabinovich, *Syria under the Ba'th, 1963–1966* (Jerusalem, 1972).

Babbitt, Milton (U.S. composer, *b.* 1916), see under COMPUTER MUSIC.

Babeuf, François (French revolutionary and journalist, 1760–97), see under EGALITARIANISM.

Babouvism, see under EGALITARIANISM.

Bachelard, Gaston (French scientist and philosopher, 1884–1962), see under TEL QUEL.

backing store, see under STORE.

Bacon, Francis (British philosopher, statesman, and essayist, 1561–1626), see under ARTS, THE; POPPERIAN.

bacteriology. The science that deals with the structure, properties, and behaviour of bacteria, particularly as disease-causing agents.
Bacteria are a highly heterogeneous group, and attempts to classify them according to the full nomenclatural hierarchy appropriate to larger organisms have not met with the general sympathy of biologists. Nevertheless a first crude divi- sion may be made on the basis of shape and habit of growth. Thus, *cocci* are spher- ical; *bacilli* are generally rod-shaped; *staphylococci* form clusters like grape- bunches; *streptococci* form chains; *vibrios* are rod-shaped with a helical twist. A taxonomic distinction of greater func- tional significance is between 'gram- positive' and 'gram-negative' bacteria. The distinction is based upon the degree of retentiveness with which the organisms bind the stain crystal violet during their preparation for microscopy. Most bacteria (the leprosy bacteria are a notable excep- tion) can be cultivated in simple media outside the body. Some bacteria ('strict or 'obligate' *aerobes*) can grow only in the presence of oxygen, others (*anaerobes*) only in its absence.
Bacteria increase their number by fission. After a so-called 'lag phase' multi- plication is characteristically of the EXPO- NENTIAL or compound-interest type, though greater or lesser departures from this norm occur as a result of changes in the growth medium produced by the bac- teria themselves, e.g. the using up of nut- rients and the accumulation of waste- products. Genetic information in bacteria resides in a nucleic acid system and the processes of coding, transcription, and translation are essentially the same in bac- teria as in higher organisms. Indeed, the study of heredity in bacteria, notably *Escherichia coli* (probably the most

deeply understood of all organisms), has thrown very great light on the processes of heredity in higher organisms.

Bacteria are highly mutable organisms, as evidenced by the readiness with which they can eventually utilize new substrates (see ENZYMES) or develop resistance towards newly devised ANTIBIOTICS. These examples of adaptation were at one time known under the comprehensive heading of 'training'. This is a misleading description, however, because it obscures the essential point that all such processes of training are strictly GENE-dependent and selective in character. Under conditions unfavourable for continued growth or even for life, many bacteria have the power to form highly resistant spores. Spores normally resist desiccation and many ordinary procedures of disinfection. Bacteria and spores are, however, killed by the use of the *autoclave* in which objects to be sterilized are exposed to steam under high pressure and at temperatures as high as 120–130°C. Bacteria are pathogenic by reason of the direct effects of their multiplication or because they contain or liberate toxic substances (*endotoxins* or *exotoxins* respectively). Bacterial infections are cured through the action of antibodies (see IMMUNITY) or of natural or artificial ANTIBACTERIALS including antibiotics. The formation of antibodies may be excited either by structural constituents of the bacteria themselves or by the toxins they liberate.

Sexual reproduction – essentially a genetic intermixture – has been described in certain bacilli. In addition a number of 'parasexual' processes may lead to genetic interchange. The most famous of these processes is the TRANSFORMATION of *pneumococci* first described in 1928 by F. Griffith. In this process a mixture of dead and living bacteria of different types leads to the acquirement by the living type of some of the properties of the dead bacteria. In Griffith's example the transforming agent was deoxyribonucleic acid (DNA). This observation was the start of all that is now known about the genetic functions of the NUCLEIC ACIDS.   P.M.

Bibl: G. S. Wilson and A. A. Miles, *Topley and Wilson's Principles of Bacteriology and Immunity* (London and Baltimore, 5th ed., 1964).

badlands. A name originally applied to an area of semi-arid climate in South Dakota which was notoriously difficult to cross; today it is a National Park with a spectacular landscape of gullies and saw-toothed ridges cut in many-coloured shales and limestones. The term is now used for any region that has been carved by rainwash, over bare ground, into an almost impassable land surface of innumerable closely spaced, steep-sided ridges and furrows. As a rule it is nearly devoid of vegetation and contrasts strongly with any remaining level plateau surfaces in the vicinity. M.L.

Baer, Karl Ernst von (German biologist, 1792–1876), see under EMBRYOLOGY; RECAPITULATION.

Bagehot, Walter (British economist and political writer, 1826–77), see under IRRATIONALISM.

Baghdad Pact, see CENTO.

Bahai. A religious movement, originating in ISLAM and stressing the spiritual unity of mankind under God. It was established by Mirza Husein Ali the *Baha-ullah* ('Glory of God') after the founder, Ali Muhammad the *Bab* ('Door'), had been executed in Persia in 1850 for alleged blasphemy. It has attracted adherents, not very numerous but widely distributed, by its support of modern idealistic movements (such as equality between the sexes), its receptivity towards scientific ideas, and its simple, personal forms of prayer.   D.L.E.

Bainville, Jacques (French political writer and historian, 1879–1936), see under ACTION FRANÇAISE.

Bakunin, Mikhail (Russian revolutionary, 1814–76), see under ANARCHISM; ANARCHO-SYNDICALISM; BOLSHEVISM; INTERNATIONAL, THE; POPULISM.

balance of nature. Term sometimes used for the relationship between the various parts of the BIOSPHERE which makes this, in the absence of human intervention, a self-renewing system. It is the well-founded fear of many ecologists (see ECOLOGY) that this balance is being upset by INDUSTRIALIZATION and the reckless exploitation of the ENVIRONMENT. P.M.

balance of payments.

(1) The difference between certain credits and debits in the accounts recording the flow of transactions in a specified period of one nation (sometimes region or group of nations) with others, usually with the rest of the world.

(2) The accounts themselves. The *balance on current account* is the difference between payments and receipts for goods and services, including interest, dividends, and profits, and (usually) transfers, i.e. unrequited transactions such as migrants' remittances or inter-governmental grants. The *balance of trade* is that part of the current balance relating to goods only. The surplus on current account so defined equals the country's net acquisition of foreign assets, and measures, in this sense, the extent to which the country is 'paying its way'. A *balance of payments crisis* need not, however, take the form of a large deficit on current account. An outflow of CAPITAL can equally threaten the exhaustion of the country's official gold and foreign exchange reserves. Consequently, attention may be focused on various other balances (e.g. *balance of monetary movements, official reserve transactions balance*). Broadly speaking, all of these attempt to measure the extent to which the country's foreign transactions are leading to an accumulation (or the reverse) of those foreign assets which are quickly and easily available to its government, or to a reduction (or the reverse) in foreign liabilities of a similar kind. A chronic *balance of payments problem* arises (and may lead to such measures as EXCHANGE CONTROL) where a country's balance of payments has a persistent tendency to go into either deficit or surplus and where the measures required to correct this have unwelcome effects, e.g. UNEMPLOYMENT OF INFLATION. M.FG.S.

Bibl: C. P. Kindleberger, *International Economics*, parts IV–V (Homewood, Ill., 5th ed., 1973).

balance of power. In international relations, the policy of organizing a combination of states to hold in check any state that might otherwise acquire a position of preponderance; traditionally, this was the policy followed by Britain against any power which threatened to exercise hegemony in Europe. A fundamental principle of international relations up to 1914, it acquired pejorative overtones after World War I, being widely held to have been responsible for its outbreak. It recovered in intellectual appeal and approval, however, at the end of the 1950s, when the breakdown of BIPOLARITY became apparent.   D.C.W.

Bibl: H. Butterfield and M. Wight, eds., *Diplomatic Investigations* (London and Cambridge, Mass., 1966), ch. 6, 7.

balance of terror. A rhetorical term describing a state of equilibrium or of mutual DETERRENCE between nuclear powers, based on the possession of weapons which allow either side to deal a mortal blow to the other. Probably coined by Lester Pearson ('the balance of terror has replaced the balance of power') in June 1955, at the 10th anniversary of the signing of the U.N. (see UNO) Charter, and based on Winston Churchill's remark 'It may well be that safety shall be the sturdy child of terror. . .'.   A.F.B.

balance of trade, see under BALANCE OF PAYMENTS.

balance theory. A view of inter-personal relations that has as its starting-point the situation where the subject's COGNITIVE view of the people he is in contact with accords with his EMOTIONS about them. If either his ideas or his feelings concerning them are altered, the balance is disturbed and stress may be introduced.   H.L.

Bibl: F. Heider, *The Psychology of Interpersonal Relations* (N.Y., 1958).

balanced budget, see under FISCAL POLICY.

Baldwin, James (U.S. novelist, dramatist, and essayist, *b*.1924), see under BLACK THEATRE.

Balestrini, Nanni (Italian poet), see under ALEATORY.

Balfour Declaration. A British Government statement in the form of a letter, dated 2 November 1917, signed by the Foreign Secretary, A. J. Balfour (1848–1930), and addressed to Lord Rothschild, expressing 'sympathy with Jewish ZIONIST aspirations' and viewing 'with favour the establishment in Palestine of a National Home for the Jewish People'. Palestine was then under Turkish occupation but became a British mandate under the LEAGUE OF NATIONS (1922). Thereafter the British Government wrestled with the intractable problem of reconciling the Balfour Declaration with the proviso, contained in the same letter, that 'nothing shall be done which may prejudice the civil and religious rights of existing non-Jewish communities in Palestine'. From this follows the chain of events leading to the breakdown of Arab-Jewish relations, the establishment of the state of Israel, and the Arab-Israeli wars. A.L.C.B.

Bibl: L. Stein: *The Balfour Declaration* (London and N.Y., 1961).

Ball, Hugo (German poet, dramatist, and actor, 1886–1927), see under DADA.

Ballard, J. G. (British novelist, *b*. 1930), see under SCIENCE FICTION.

ballistic missiles, see under MISSILES.

ballistics. The application of NEWTONIAN MECHANICS to the calculation of trajectories of MISSILES influenced by GRAVITATION and air resistance. The early development of ballistics in the 17th century marked the beginning of the application of modern science to warfare. M.V.B.

Balzac, Honoré de (French novelist, 1799–1850), see under BOURGEOIS; BUREAUCRACY; REALISM; ROMAN-FLEUVE.

bamboo curtain. Phrase coined by American publicists in the 1950s, by analogy with IRON CURTAIN, to describe the controls imposed by the Chinese COMMUNIST regime on the free movement of ideas and individuals across China's borders. D.C.W.

bancor, see under LIQUIDITY.

Bandung Conference. The first Afro-Asian conference, meeting in Bandung, Indonesia, from 18 to 24 April 1955, with representatives of 29 states of Asia and Africa (including the People's Republic of China). The main motivation of the conference was dissatisfaction with the domination of international politics by the quarrel between the American and Soviet blocs, and concern at the risk of war between the U.S.A. and China. See also NON-ALIGNMENT. D.C.W.

Bibl: P. Calvocoressi, *World Order and New States* (London and N.Y., 1962).

Bandura, Albert (U.S. psychologist, *b*. 1925), see under SOCIAL LEARNING.

Bangla Desh. Bengali phrase meaning 'Bengali Nation'. Bangla Desh was proclaimed on 26 March 1971 as a separate independent republic by the Awami League, a Pakistan political party, which in the election of December 1970 won 75% of the votes in the eastern provinces of Pakistan with a programme of autonomy for East Pakistan. The resultant civil war developed into a direct conflict (December 1971) between India and Pakistan in which Bangla Desh was recognized by India and her territory 'liberated' by Indian troops. Bengali NATIONALISM, as it developed, was racial rather than Islamic in character and expressed itself in violent persecution of the Bihari minority group. D.C.W.

Bibl: L. F. R. Williams, *The East Pakistan Tragedy* (London and N.Y., 1972).

bank rate. The rate of interest charged by a central bank on loans it makes to the banking system. Most countries have a central bank which acts as a lender of last resort, standing ready to convert illiquid assets into money, to preserve the LIQUIDITY of financial institutions. All financial institutions 'borrow short' and 'lend long' – e.g. clearing banks in England must pay holders of bank deposits on demand but cannot recall their own loans without long notice. The central bank will always provide the necessary cash, but at a price; this price is the bank rate. The equivalent in the U.S.A. is the *discount rate* of the Federal Reserve Board, and the new name for bank rate in London is the Bank of England *minimum lending rate*. Raising the bank rate is a traditional storm signal in the CITY, denoting the Government's concern to limit lending. M.V.P.

Banting, Sir **Frederick Grant** (Canadian physician, 1891–1941), see under INSULIN.

Bantustan, see under APARTHEID.

Baptist. A member of a PROTESTANT denomination which believes that Baptism should be confined to adults after a

personal confession of faith. (Other Christian Churches allow the baptism of infants, while asking that these should be the children of Christians and should also be sponsored by godparents.) The first Baptist congregation was founded in 1609; today the denomination is worldwide. Congregations maintain their independence in many matters, and Baptists vary greatly in the conservatism or radicalism of their THEOLOGY and politics. The 'Southern' Baptists in the U.S.A. (mainly in the Southern states), and also the Baptist groups in Europe including Russia, are strongly conservative. D.L.E.
Bibl: R. G. Torbet, *A History of the Baptists* (rev. ed., Valley Forge, Penn., 1963; London, 1966).

Barbaro, Umberto (Italian film director and theoretician, 1902–59), see under NEO-REALISM.

Barlach, Ernst (German sculptor, 1870–1938), see under SEZESSION.

Barmen Declaration, see under BARTHIAN.

Barr, Alfred Hamilton (U.S. art historian and museum director, *b.* 1902), see under ABSTRACT EXPRESSIONISM.

Barrault, Jean-Louis (French actor and producer, *b.* 1910), see under THEATRE OF CRUELTY; TOTAL THEATRE.

Barth, Karl (Swiss theologian, 1886–1968), see under BARTHIAN; CRISIS THEOLOGY; DOGMATICS.

Barthes, Roland (French literary critic, *b.* 1915), see under SEMIOLOGY; TEL QUEL.

Barthian. Adjective applied to a style in Christian THEOLOGY associated with Karl Barth (1886–1968), a PROTESTANT who was a professor at Bonn and Basle. Barth attempted to deduce all his doctrines from the Bible, without going so far as FUNDAMENTALISM in rejecting HIGHER CRITICISM. Disillusioned by World War I, in a commentary on St Paul's Epistle to the Romans (1919) he attacked Protestant LIBERALISM's belief that man could reach religious understanding by his own reason and develop nobly by his own

power. He stressed the corruptions of sin, as did other leaders of CRISIS THEOLOGY. But on this narrower basis he built an elaborate system of DOGMATICS marked by a joyous confidence in the TRANSCENDENCE or majestic 'otherness', and in the graciousness, of the God revealed in Jesus Christ. He extolled Jesus Christ as the 'Risen Lord' and as the one Saviour, and (unlike other CALVINISTS) maintained that God had predestined all to heaven. He took the lead in drawing up the *Barmen Declaration* (1934) against the pseudo-religious claims of NAZISM. The influence of the NEO-ORTHODOXY to which he gave eloquent expression helped many Protestants to regard the Bible as the Word of God powerfully confronting the calamities of the 1930s and 1940s. In the 1950s and 1960s his prestige among Protestant preachers was at a peak, but the influence of his theology declined because it was thought not to be sufficiently in touch with modern AGNOSTICISM. D.L.E.
Bibl: H. Hartwell, *The Theology of Karl Barth* (London and Philadelphia, 1964).

Bartók, Béla (Hungarian composer, 1881–1945), see under BITONALITY; NEO-CLASSICISM; POLYTONALITY.

Bartolozzi sounds. Term, derived from Bruno Bartolozzi's book *New Sounds for Woodwind* (1967), and frequently applied to new ways of playing woodwind (flute, oboe, clarinet, bassoon) which produce, among other things, chords from these traditionally melodic instruments. J.G.R.

Baruch, Bernard (U.S. financier, 1870–1965), see under COLD WAR.

barysphere, see BATHYSPHERE.

base.
(1) In ECONOMICS, see INDEX NUMBER.
(2) A chemical SPECIES which accepts PROTONS or donates a pair of ELECTRONS (see ACID). A compound or solution capable of acting as a base is described as *basic*. B.F.

base component, see under GENERATIVE GRAMMAR.

basic. In on-line COMPUTING, a very simple but verbose PROGRAMMING

LANGUAGE much used by beginners. It is not used by serious programmers. c.s.

basic norm, see under LAW, PURE THEORY OF.

Basie, 'Count' (U.S. musician, *b*.1904), see under BIG BAND; SWEET.

batch processing, see under COMPUTING.

Bateson, William (British biologist, 1865–1906), see under GENETICS.

Bath, B. H. Slicher van, see SLICHER VAN BATH.

bathysphere (or *barysphere* or *centrosphere* or *bathyscaphe*). A diving apparatus generally spherical in shape and capable of containing men (usually two) and instruments so that the whole can be lowered to great depths in the ocean. It is used in OCEANOGRAPHY for the study of deep-water phenomena, fauna, etc. The main feature of the apparatus is that the outer shell is capable of withstanding huge pressures such as obtain at great depth. The record depth to date is 35,082 feet (deeper than Mount Everest is high), achieved by J. Piccard and D. Walsh in 1960 in the Marianas Trench of the Pacific Ocean, 250 miles S.W. of Guam; the pressure at this depth was 16,883 lbs per square inch (over 1,200 atmospheres).
E.R.L.

Batista, Fulgencio (Cuban general and dictator, 1901–73), see under CASTROISM; CUBA.

Baty, Gaston (French dramatist and producer, 1885–1952), see under CARTEL.

Baudelaire, Charles-Pierre (French poet, 1821–67), see under IMPRESSIONISM; SYMBOLISM; SYNAESTHESIA.

Bauer, Bruno (German theologian and historian, 1809–82), see under NEO-MARXISM.

Bauhaus. A school of design, art, and architecture based on the ideas of the WERKBUND and founded as a develop-ment of the Weimar Applied Art School in 1919. It moved to Dessau in 1925 and remained there for its most fruitful years until 1932. It was dissolved by the Nazis (see NAZISM) in 1933. From 1919 to 1928 it was headed by the architect Walter Gropius, who attempted to implement the demands, voiced in his manifesto of April 1919, for a unity of all the creative arts under the primacy of architecture, and for a reconsideration of the crafts by the artist.

Many major figures of modern art and architecture – Klee, Kandinsky, Moholy-Nagy, Schlemmer, Breuer, Hannes Meyer, Mies van der Rohe – taught at the Bauhaus, though they often disagreed, especially over the relative roles of art, TECHNOLOGY, and politics. Their innovatory notions as regards form, materials, and the need for teamwork became the hallmark of the INTERNATIONAL STYLE in architecture and were evident in the extremely simple geometric forms of Bauhaus-inspired industrial design. These ideas eventually, however, hardened into another academic tradition, not least because they focused too much on a formal vocabulary derived from predilection for pure geometric shapes and too little on problems of use. Something like the Bauhaus *Vorkurs*, an introductory course aimed at creating, through practical work, an awareness of the nature of materials and of simple perceptual relationships, continued to be taught at many schools of architecture and design until well into the 1960s. See also MACHINE AESTHETIC; STIJL, DE.
M.BR.

Bibl: H. M. Wingler, tr. W. Jabs and B. Gilbert, *The Bauhaus* (Cambridge, Mass., 1969).

Bax, Arnold (British composer, 1883–1953), see under IMPRESSIONISM.

Bay of Pigs. A site on the north-east coast of CUBA where, on 17 April 1961, approximately 1,400 Cuban exiles, organized and supported clandestinely by the CIA, attempted an invasion with the purpose of overthrowing the MARXIST revolutionary regime established in 1959 by Fidel Castro. The invaders did not receive the naval and air support from American forces they had been led to expect, and were defeated. This became an occasion for much criticism, not always disinterested, of the government of President John Kennedy, who had only recently taken office (January 1961) and did not feel sufficiently confident to quash the CIA's plans. D.C.W.

Bibl: E. Abel, *The Missiles of October* (London and Philadelphia, 1966).

Bayer, Konrad (Austrian author, 1932–64), see under WIENER GRUPPE.

Bayesian statistics. A type of statistical reasoning characterized by two distinct features. First, the experimenter has a degree of belief in each hypothesis in the hypotheses open to him, and this degree of belief is represented by a number. Secondly, the experimenter uses the formula known as *Bayes's rule*, originally given by Thomas Bayes (1702–61) for inverting conditional probabilities, to modify his degree of belief in each hypothesis in the light of experiments. R.SI.

beam radio. In radio, a system for directing all the output from a transmitter along a narrow beam in order to maximize the proportion of output collected by the receiving aerial, and minimize the picking up of the signal by outside receivers. The system is analogous to the focused light beam from an electric torch, as opposed to an electric light bulb used to illuminate a whole room. E.R.L.

Beardsley, Aubrey (British book-illustrator, 1872–98), see under DECADENCE.

Beardsley, Monroe C. (U.S. literary critic, *b*. 1915), see under AFFECTIVE FALLACY; INTENTIONAL FALLACY; NEW CRITICISM.

beat. Term coined by the American novelist Jack Kerouac, in the reported phrase 'this is a beat generation', to denote a certain section of American society that emerged in the late 1940s and more particularly the 1950s. Kerouac, who saw the beats as saintly beings in a pagan world, later connected the word with 'beatific' or 'beatitude' (a related pun turned the wanderers from New York to San Francisco into *Franciscans*); but others preferred the original connotations of weariness and defeat. *Beatnik* was the slightly pejorative generic term coined by an American columnist to denote the followers and hangers-on of the Beats; in time the two words, and the phrase *beat generation*, became interchangeable. Kerouac and his friends Allen Ginsberg, Neil Cassady, Gregory Corso, and others between them exemplified, in a manner deliberately anti-literary, the various trends: rootlessness, rejection of the AFFLUENT SOCIETY and indeed of all social values, a predilection for modern JAZZ, resort to ill-assimilated oriental religions (e.g. ZEN) and to DRUGS, pseudo-relaxation ('coolness'), and free sexuality. The phenomenon represented a sudden coalescence of INTELLECTUAL or sensitive people with the *lumpen* elements that exist in all urban societies. The spiritual fathers of the beats were Walt Whitman and Henry Miller; mentors and spokesmen included Paul Goodman, Norman Mailer, and Kenneth Rexroth (who later became disillusioned). The chief *beat poets* were Ginsberg, Corso, and Lawrence Ferlinghetti; those influenced include Robert Creeley, Gary Snyder, and Michael Rumaker. Other beat or beat-influenced figures include the writers William Burroughs and Alan Watts, the painter Jackson Pollock, and the jazz musician Thelonius Monk. In so far as beat literature is intelligible at all (it set out to defy intelligibility) it represents self-indulgence as a means of self-knowledge, and a hatred of injustice that was often sincere and passionate, even if its expression was immature and over-extravagant. Politically, the Beats found expression in pacifist and anti-nuclear-bomb movements. In appearance, they were distinguished by the wearing of sandals, black roll-neck sweaters, blue jeans, and a straggly beard or pale make-up, and made the same type of sartorial impression upon the 1950s that was later made by the HIPPIES, who owe them numerous cultural and behavioural debts. P.S.L.; M.S.-S.

Bibl: J. Kerouac, *On the Road* (London and N.Y., 1958).

Beatles, The. A quartet (John Lennon, Paul McCartney, Ringo Starr, and George Harrison) of young working-class Liverpudlians whose joint musical productions enjoyed immense popularity from 1962 until their break-up in 1970. The Beatles established an indigenous ROCK style in contrast to Tin Pan Alley's crassly

commercial efforts to ape American POP music. Their impact, however, went far beyond their purely musical significance: they inspired an excessive, often hysterical, adulation ('Beatlemania') among their teenage fans; and their unconventional dress, long hair, and articulate and irreverent repartee were accepted and echoed by their contemporaries of all CLASSES. In many ways, indeed, they exemplify the quintessential flavour of the mid-60s – though an unusually daring official seal of approval (they were awarded the M.B.E. in 1965) became an embarrassment when they turned openly to experimentation with DRUGS and MYSTICISM. Their LIFE STYLE, however, continued to be endorsed by millions of young people the world over.   P.S.L.
      Bibl: H. Davies, *The Beatles* (London and N.Y., 1968).

beatnik, see under BEAT.

Beaujeu-Garnier, Jacqueline (French geographer, *b*.1917), see under SATELLITE TOWN; SUBURBANIZATION.

beaux arts. In architecture, a term used to describe a form of rigid, highly composed, and usually symmetrical design based on classical architecture and academic in character. It is associated with the teaching of the École des Beaux Arts in Paris, and hence (since that school, founded in 1671, has been in frequent opposition to contemporary trends) often used pejoratively.   M.BR.

bebop. Onomatopoeic term introduced by AVANT-GARDE jazz musicians in the U.S.A. in the early 1940s, to denote vocally the nuances of phrasing of the emergent modern JAZZ movement. The term's application rapidly broadened to include the music itself, which was characterized by irregularities of time-pulse stresses by the drums, excessive displays of double-tempo bravura by the soloists, and above all by an extension of conventerized by irregularities of time-pulse tic hinterlands. The great genius of the movement was the saxophonist Charlie Parker, its cult figure Dizzy Gillespie, its perverse eccentric Thelonius Monk. B.G.

Beccaria, Cesare, Marquis de Beccaria-Bonesana (Italian criminologist and economist, 1738–94), see under PENOLOGY.

Beck, Julian (U.S. theatre director, *b*.1925) see under LIVING THEATRE.

Beckett, Samuel (Irish-born dramatist and novelist, *b*. 1906), see under ANTI-THEATRE; THEATRE OF THE ABSURD.

Beckmann, Max (German printer and printmaker, 1884–1950), see under NEUE SACHLICHKEIT; SEZESSION.

Behan, Brendan (Irish dramatist, 1923–64), see under THEATRE WORKSHOP.

behaviour therapy. In PSYCHIATRY, the treatment of behavioural disorders by a group of procedures based mainly on learning theory. The principles derive from the experimental work of Pavlov, Watson, Hull, Skinner, and other experimental psychologists. The procedures, which are increasingly often used, include *desensitization*, an effective treatment for PHOBIAS, the principle being for the patient to re-enter the feared situation gradually and repeatedly, while ANXIETY is neutralized by relaxation; the contrasted (and less widely used) *aversion therapy*, in which an unpleasant stimulus is repeatedly coupled with an undesired behaviour in order to eliminate the latter; and OPERANT CONDITIONING. Behaviour therapy differs from traditional PSYCHOTHERAPY in not drawing on PSYCHODYNAMIC theory such as Freud's and in putting more emphasis on changing outward behaviour than on subjective factors. The two approaches are, however, not conflicting but complementary.
      The term *behaviour modification*, though used in many ways and often loosely, has two main applications. First, it is sometimes used synonymously with behaviour therapy as defined above. Second, it may be applied in a more restricted sense to B. F. Skinner's techniques of treating disorders of behaviour by operant conditioning, in which rewards are made contingent upon the subject's own behaviour. The latter methods are, for example, sometimes used to enhance the social behaviour of withdrawn schizophrenic patients (see SCHIZOPHRENIA) or the mentally handicapped (see MENTAL RETARDATION). When applied to the modification of total social

systems this approach is sometimes called SOCIAL BEHAVIOURISM. D.H.G.
Bibl: H. R. Beech, *Changing Man's Behaviour* (Harmondsworth and Baltimore, 1969).

behavioural engineering, see under SOCIAL ENGINEERING.

behavioural sciences. Those sciences which study the behaviour of men and animals, e.g. PSYCHOLOGY and the SOCIAL SCIENCES (including social ANTHROPOLOGY). Some practitioners of these sciences believe that it is unscientific to study mental processes and other phenomena which are not directly observable and measurable, and they therefore concentrate on the attempt to describe and explain *outward manifestations* of such phenomena, namely observable behaviour (like pressing buttons, eating, running through mazes, making noises) and the relations of such behaviour to external stimuli. The attempt to study men and animals on the basis that they do not have minds, but only patterns of behaviour, is called the *behavioural approach,* or sometimes BEHAVIOURISM. A.S.
Bibl: N. Chomsky, *Language and Mind* (N.Y., enl. ed., 1972); B. F. Skinner, *Verbal Behaviour* (N.Y., 1957).

behaviourism.
(1) The SCHOOL OF PSYCHOLOGY (in R. S. Woodworth's classification, one of the six main such) that studies only unambiguously observable, and preferably measurable, behaviour. It leaves out of account CONSCIOUSNESS and INTROSPECTION, and its theoretical frames of reference avoid subjective notions such as 'imaging' or 'focus of attention'. In Russia it was closely identified with PHYSIOLOGY and 'reflexes of the brain' as studied by, notably, Ivan Pavlov (see PAVLOVIAN). In America it was launched in 1913 by J. B. Watson, and was represented at its distinctive best by Clark Hull and B. F. Skinner (see also SOCIAL BEHAVIOURISM and, for an opposed view, MENTALISM). American behaviourism attracted, from the start, psychologists with certain kinds of interests, and the word *behaviouristic* came, by association, to refer to these interests, notably environmental control of behaviour under laboratory conditions which force the 'subject' into a rather passive role with limited freedom of choice; conditioned-response techniques (see CONDITIONED REFLEX); laboratory learning in animals such as rats and pigeons; elementaristic theory involving stimuli, responses, and their objective interrelations (see OPERANT CONDITIONING). This cluster of interests is typically criticized as an elegant but superficial pursuit of trivial problems couched in arid language and too artificial to have relevance for 'real life' problems of either animals or people. Behaviourists typically counter by pointing to the objectivity of their work and stressing that it is only the start of a vastly ambitious enterprise that promises to yield completely general laws of behaviour. Whatever the eventual verdict of history, the deliberate study of objective behaviour has made great strides, and even the 'behaviouristic' approach has contributed much to main-stream PSYCHOLOGY by way of factual discoveries, new ideas, and new methods of enquiry. I.M.L.H.
Bibl: J. B. Watson, *Behaviorism* (2nd ed., N.Y., 1930; London, 1931); B. F. Skinner, *Beyond Freedom and Dignity* (N.Y., 1971; London, 1972).
(2) As an application of (1) to PHILOSOPHY, the theory that takes statements about mental events and states to be equivalent in meaning to statements about the behaviour of the embodied persons in whose minds the events or states are said to occur. Many behaviourists in psychology have, in practice, seemed to make philosophical claims about what exists, rather than merely to impose methodological restrictions on what they will allow themselves to count as evidence. Thus J. B. Watson identified mental events with actual, if minimally perceptible, items of behaviour: thought, for example, with small subvocal movements of the larynx. Philosophical behaviourists, on the other hand, have generally identified mental facts with DISPOSITIONS to behaviour: for a man to be angry is for him to be disposed to hit out, swear, etc., by ANALOGY with the way in which for a rubber ball to be elastic is for it to have a disposition to bounce. Carnap and, most thoroughly and consistently, Ryle have adopted this position, which is a form of reductionism (see REDUCTION). The chief incentive to it is the problem of how one person is to know anything about the inner

experiences of another when he cannot share those experiences, but must infer them from their manifestations in behaviour. A sophisticated variant of the doctrine is expounded in the later philosophy of Wittgenstein, summarized in the slogan 'Inner processes stand in need of outward CRITERIA'.   A.Q.
   Bibl: G. Ryle, *The Concept of Mind* (London and N.Y., 1949), ch. 2.

Behrens, Peter (German architect, 1868–1940), see under NEO-CLASSICISM.

Béjart, Maurice (French dancer, choreographer, and director, *b.* 1927), see under CONCRETE MUSIC.

Bell, Clive (British art and literary critic, 1881–1964), see under BLOOMSBURY GROUP; SIGNIFICANT FORM.

Bell, Daniel (U.S. sociologist, *b.* 1919), see under IDEOLOGY; POST-INDUSTRIAL SOCIETY.

Bell, Graham (British painter, 1910–42), see under EUSTON ROAD GROUP.

Bell, John Elderkind (Canadian–U.S. psychologist, *b.* 1913), see under FAMILY THERAPY.

Bell, Vanessa (British painter, 1879–1961), see under BLOOMSBURY GROUP.

Bellows, George (U.S. painter and lithographer, 1882–1925), see under ASHCAN SCHOOL.

Bely, Andrei (pseud. of Boris Bugayev, Russian poet and novelist, 1880–1934), see under SYMBOLISM.

Benda, Julian (French philosopher and novelist, 1867–1956), see under INTELLECTUALS.

Benedict, Ruth (U.S. anthropologist, 1887–1948), see under APOLLONIAN AND DIONYSIAN CULTURES; SHAME CULTURE AND GUILT CULTURE.

Benelux. A CUSTOMS UNION between Belgium, the Netherlands, and Luxembourg conceived by the governments-in-exile of the three countries during the German occupation of their countries. The union itself was signed at The Hague on 14 March 1947. In February 1958 a more ambitious Economic Union was established providing for the free flow of CAPITAL, goods, services, and traffic, and for the free movement of people. D.C.W.

Benjamin, Walter (German essayist, 1892–1940), see under FRANKFURT SCHOOL.

Benn, Gottfried (German poet and essayist, 1886–1956), see under INTELLECTUALS.

Bennett, Arnold (British novelist, 1867–1931), see under NEW AGE.

Bense, Max (German aesthetician, *b.* 1910), see under ALEATORY; CONCRETE POETRY; TEXT, THEORY OF.

Bentham, Jeremy (British philosopher, jurist, and political writer, 1748–1832), see under DEONTOLOGY; FELICIFIC CALCULUS; LEGAL POSITIVISM; PENOLOGY; UTILITARIANISM; WELFARE.

benzene ring. The UNSATURATED six-membered ring of carbon ATOMS which is the principal unit in benzene compounds. The earliest successful ideas on its structure originated with Kekulé in 1865, but proof that the carbon atoms form a planar hexagon was not provided until the X-RAY DIFFRACTION studies of Kathleen Lonsdale in 1929. The carbon atoms are linked by BONDS which include ELECTRONS delocalized over the whole ring. In the benzene MOLECULE itself one atom of hydrogen is attached to each carbon atom, but in one or more cases the hydrogen atom may be replaced by other chemical SPECIES to generate a whole family of benzenoid compounds.   B.F.

Berg, Alban (Austrian composer, 1885–1935), see under EXPRESSIONISM; FORMALISM.

Bergson, Henri (French philosopher, 1859–1941), see under STREAM OF CONSCIOUSNESS; VITALISM.

Beria, Lavrenty Pavlovich (Soviet politician, 1899–1953), see under UNPERSON; YEZHOVSHCHINA.

Berio, Luciano (Italian composer, *b.* 1925), see under ELECTRONIC MUSIC.

Berkeley, George (Irish philosopher and bishop, 1685–1753), see under IDEA; IDEALISM; PANPSYCHISM; PERSONALISM; REALISM; SENSE-DATUM; SOCIOLOGY.

Berle, Adolf Augustus (U.S. lawyer, 1895–1971), see under MANAGERIAL REVOLUTION.

Berlin Wall. A concrete wall built by the East German Government from 12 August 1961 onwards to seal off East Berlin from the Western-occupied part of the city, and so prevent any further mass illegal emigration from East Germany to the West. Many would-be emigrés have subsequently been killed by East German frontier guards while attempting to cross. The economic revival of East Germany, and the ÖSTPOLITIK pursued by the West German Government, would, it has been argued by East German apologists, have been impossible without the Berlin Wall; but this is not a view easily accepted in the West, where the Wall continues to be regarded as a symbol of the denial of human rights by the Soviet and East European regimes.   D.C.W.

Berliner Ensemble. East German state theatre company founded in Berlin in 1949 by Bertolt Brecht and his wife Helene Weigel, noted particularly for its harshly perfectionist 'model' productions of Brecht's plays. With its insistence on clear narration, its use of projections, and its relatively cool style of acting, it could be seen as an example of BRECHTIAN (*q.v.*) EPIC THEATRE, even though Brecht's theories were not deployed there.   J.W.

Berlioz, Hector (French composer, 1803–69), see under PROGRAMME MUSIC; ROMANTICISM.

Bernadotte, Folke, Count (Swedish statesman, 1895–1948), see under STERN GANG.

Bernanos, Georges (French author, 1888–1948), see under INTELLECTUALS.

Bernard, Émile (French painter, 1868–1941), see under BEURON; PONT-AVEN; SYNTHETISM.

Berne, Eric Lennard (U.S. psychiatrist, *b.* 1910), see under TRANSACTIONAL ANALYSIS.

Bernstein, Basil (British sociologist, *b.* 1924), see under CODE; ELABORATED CODE AND RESTRICTED CODE.

Bernstein, Eduard (German socialist leader, 1850–1932), see under HISTORICAL MATERIALISM; REVISIONISM; SOCIALISM.

Bernstein, Leonard (U.S. conductor, pianist, and composer, *b.* 1918), see under RADICAL CHIC.

Berry, Brian (U.S. geographer, *b.* 1934), see under GEOGRAPHY.

Bertalanffy, Ludwig von (Austrian-Canadian biologist, *b.* 1901), see under GST.

Besant, Annie (British theosophist, 1847–1933), see under THEOSOPHY.

Best, Charles Herbert (U.S. physiologist, *b.* 1899), see under INSULIN.

beta particle. A fast ELECTRON or POSITRON emitted during the RADIOACTIVE decay of a NUCLEUS.   M.V.B.

betatron. A compact type of ACCELERATOR for ELECTRONS.   M.V.B.

béton brut, see under CONCRETE.

Beuron. Influential school of religious painting at the South German Benedictine abbey of that name. It was founded by Didier (Fr. Desiderius) Lenz with the aim of evolving an art comparable with plainsong and based on a canon of sacred measurements inspired by those of ancient Egypt. Its principal work was the decoration, 1877–1910, of the mother abbey at Monte Cassino in Italy. Through Denis and Sérusier of the NABIS, the school helped form French ART SACRÉ, while other mystically inclined artists in touch with it included Émile Bernard of PONT-AVEN, Alexei Jawlensky of the NEUE KÜNSTLER-VEREINIGUNG, and the BAUHAUS master Johannes Itten.   J.W.

Bevan, Robert (British painter, 1865–1925), see under CAMDEN TOWN GROUP.

Bevatron. A kind of ACCELERATOR for PROTONS.   M.V.B.

Biafra. Name given by the secessionist Ibo regime in East Nigeria to the state proclaimed on 30 May 1967. The name was taken from a 17th-century African kingdom, Biafara. The secessionists, who surrendered to Nigerian federal forces on 12 January 1970, for a time took, hold of Western European imaginations, partly through links, with radical Catholic INTELLECTUALS, and partly because in 1968, the year of the Soviet suppression of Dubček's regime in Czechoslovakia (see PRAGUE), and of the May riots in Paris, the Biafran cause appealed to idealist anticolonialism (see IMPERIALISM), especially in Germany and Scandinavia.   D.C.W.
Bibl: J. de Saint Jorre, *The Nigerian Civil War* (in America *The Brothers' War: Biafra and Nigeria;* London and Boston, 1972).

Bible Belt. Term coined by the American satirist H. L. Mencken, in 1925, to designate those parts of the U.S.A., mainly the rural southern and mid-western territories, where the literal accuracy of the Bible was credited and public influence correspondingly exercised in the spheres of EDUCATION and public morality by spokesmen for FUNDAMENTALIST Christian SECTS.   D.C.W.

biblical theology. The attempt of BARTHIAN and other 20th-century theologians (see THEOLOGY) to develop Christian doctrine afresh by studying the Bible instead of relying on DOGMAS. The movement has produced much enthusiasm among Roman CATHOLICS, and the decrees of VATICAN COUNCIL II appealed to the Bible more than to tradition. Biblical theology is opposed both to FUNDAMENTALISM (because it accepts the HIGHER CRITICISM of the Bible) and to religious LIBERALISM (because it denies the ability of modern man to reach religious truth without learning humbly from God's self-revelation in the events and teachings recorded in the Bible). Because of the desire to understand the Old and New Testaments without importing modern ideas, special attention is paid to the original meaning of biblical words in Hebrew or Greek.   D.L.E.
Bibl: A. Richardson (ed.), *A Theological Word Book of the Bible* (London, 1950; N.Y., 1951).

bibliography.
(1, sometimes called *enumerative*, or *systematic, bibliography*) The compilation of lists of works by or about a given author or group of authors, or about a given subject, or related to each other by the circumstances of their printing or publication; such a list (known as *a* bibliography) may be selective or comprehensive, annotated or otherwise, appended to a book or article or separately published.
(2) From the 18th century onwards, the analysis and description of books as physical objects. Bibliography in this sense originally related to the identification of first or best editions. In the later 19th century it came to include the history of printing, typography, bookcollecting, and similar topics. In the 20th century greater (and more nearly exclusive) attention has been given to the technical operation of the printing house with respect to such matters as plate corrections, concealed printings, stints of pressmen, and the like. The study of printing and the physical evidence of the books themselves is called *analytical* (or *critical*) *bibliography*; the detailed, formal description of books based on such analysis is called *descriptive bibliography*; the application of these methods and of the resulting evidence to TEXTUAL CRITICISM is called *textual bibliography* by its practitioners, though others (who consider textual criticism a wider subject) object. Bibliography has become an accepted academic discipline; a large and growing group of bibliographers have made great advances in the technical knowledge of the craft of printing and have taken over much of the responsibility for preparing scholarly editions of literary works.   J.T.
Bibl: P. Gaskell, *A New Introduction to Bibliography* (Oxford, 1972).

Biennale. A festival of modern art recurring every two years (e.g. the Venice Biennale, the São Paulo Biennale), generally with State encouragement. A *Triennale* recurs every three years.   P.C.

big band. Broad term denoting any JAZZ combination requiring prearranged musical procedures, but more specifically a generic term for the golden age of the touring orchestra in the U.S.A., a period defined by the repeal of Prohibition, 1934, and PEARL HARBOR, 1941. The archetypal big band consisted of three sections, rhythm, brass, and reeds, and was characterized by duologue between the latter two consisting of simple repeated phrases, or 'riffs'. Big-band experiments had acquired coherence as early as 1924 with the Fletcher Henderson band, but, although a few of the white big bands became world-famous, e.g. Benny Goodman, Tommy Dorsey, Artie Shaw, Glenn Miller, there is no question that artistically the Duke Ellington band was incomparably the best, or that, of the more conventional groups, Count Basie's was the most accomplished from a jazz standpoint. B.G.

big-bang hypothesis. A theory of the origin of the universe. About 10 thousand million years ago, a very dense primeval aggregate of matter at a temperature of millions of degrees is supposed to have 'exploded' into expanding matter and RADIATION which evolved into the GALAXIES, observed today to be still receding from one another. This theory is today accepted by most cosmologists. It has superseded the rival STEADY-STATE HYPOTHESIS as a result of recent evidence from RADIO ASTRONOMY concerning the distribution of distant galaxies, and the discovery of COSMIC BACKGROUND RADIATION. See also COSMOLOGY; EXPANSION OF THE UNIVERSE; PULSATING UNIVERSE. M.V.B.

Big Brother, see under ORWELLIAN.

bilateralism and **multilateralism.** Contrasted policies of negotiating agreements, especially those relating to trade or payments, between, respectively, pairs of countries and many countries. The *most favoured nation clause* in international trade agreements, which is in Article 1 of the GATT, requires that any tariff concession made by one member country to another must immediately be given to all other members, and so is essentially multilateral. Multilateralism is impossible without *convertibility* of currencies (i.e.

freedom to exchange one for another), which absolves a country from balancing its payments (see BALANCE OF PAYMENTS) with each of its trading partners; and the breakdown of convertibility was both an effect and in turn a further cause of the spread of bilateral trade and payments agreements in the 1930s and after World War II. However, since then there has been a return to multilateral trade and payments arrangements, which are now the rule, except where COMMUNIST countries are involved and even there bilateralism is in decay.

The terms are also used in connection with international aid. The distinction between *bilateral* and *multilateral aid* rests on whether it is given directly by donor to recipient governments or via an international organization, e.g. UNO or the WORLD BANK. The bulk of aid is bilateral. M.FG.S.

Bibl: J. B. Condliffe, *The Reconstruction of World Trade* (London, 1941).

Bildungsroman. German term, literally 'formation-novel', for the type of novel in which the (generally youthful) hero is seen developing through exposure to life; his story is often accompanied by an account of the forms of contemporary society. Variant terms are *Erziehunggsroman* ('education novel') and *Entwicklungsroman* ('development novel'). The genre is held to originate with Goethe's *Wilhelm Meister's Apprenticeship* (1775) and includes Novalis's *Heinrich von Ofterdingen* (1799), Gottfried Keller's *Green Henry* (1855), Hermann Hesse's *Demian* (1919), and Thomas Mann's *The Magic Mountain* (1924). The British are less given to classification but, with varying degrees of appropriateness, Fielding's *Tom Jones* (1749), Jane Austen's *Emma* (1816), Dickens's *David Copperfield* (1849–50), Samuel Butler's *The Way of All Flesh* (1903) and James Joyce's *A Portrait of the Artist as a Young Man* (1914–15) could be ascribed to this genre, though the Germans would rather consider the last-named a *Künstlerroman* ('artist-novel'). D.J.E.

Bill, Max (Swiss architect, sculptor, and painter, *b*. 1908), see under CONCRETE ART; CONCRETE POETRY.

binary scale. A method of writing numbers with base 2 (instead of the more familiar base 10). It uses only the digits 0 and 1. Examples of binary numbers (each followed by its decimal equivalent): 10 (2), 1001 (9), 10101011 (171). The binary scale is important in INFORMATION THEORY and in COMPUTERS, being the simplest scale that uses positional notation, i.e. where the value of each digit is multiplied by a power of the base depending on its position. C.S.

binary star. One of a pair of stars held together by GRAVITATION, and revolving about their common centre of gravity. Such pairs are very common: about one-third of all stars occur in binaries. M.V.B.

binary system, see under TERTIARY EDUCATION.

binding energy. The ENERGY which must be added to an atomic NUCLEUS to break the bonds between its component NUCLEONS, analogous to the energy needed to separate two pieces of wood which have previously been glued together. This energy is released during nuclear FUSION. M.V.B.

Binet, Alfred (French psychologist, 1857–1911), see under MENTAL RETARDATION; MENTAL TESTING; PSYCHOMETRICS.

biochemistry. The CHEMISTRY of living matter. The older biochemistry was largely compositional in its interests, concerned with the chemical composition of the principal ingredients of the body – PROTEINS, CARBOHYDRATES, and fats – and with the composition of the body's material input and output. The new biochemistry is above all else a chemistry of bodily processes, i.e. the chemistry of METABOLISM at both the bodily and cellular level (see CELL). See also BIOPHYSICS. P.M.

bioclimatology. The study of the relationships between the climate, life, and health of man. One of its principal objects is to determine the range of climatic conditions most favourable to human habitation and to define the areas where such climates exist. M.L.

bio-cybernetics, see under CYBERNETICS.

bio-energetics, see under REICHIAN.

bio-engineering. A scientific or para-medical discipline concerned with:
(1) the devising of mechanical substitutes for parts or organs of the body, e.g. the artificial kidney, in which the patient's blood is conducted through thin wall tubing immersed in a blood-like fluid, thus making possible a process of filtration analogous to that which occurs in the kidneys;
(2) the designing of artificial limbs and other such artificial devices;
(3) the analysis of bodily structure and function along engineering or physical lines, whether structurally (as in evaluating the mechanical properties of bone) or functionally (as in thermodynamic calculations relating to the body). See also BIONICS. P.M.

biogenesis. The law of biogenesis – *omne vivum ex vivo* – states that all living things are descended from previously existing living things, i.e. that no such phenomenon as 'spontaneous generation' occurs. Not only living CELLS, but also some of their constituents like mitochondria (see CYTOLOGY), are biogenetic in character; thus no mitochondrion is formed except from a precursor mitochondrion. Louis Pasteur's famous experiments may be said to have disproved the notion of spontaneous generation by showing that bacterial contamination of a sterilized nutrient fluid would only occur if it was re-exposed to air. Claims made for spontaneous generation are now attributed to an innocent form of self-deception, perhaps especially to the confusion created by 'myelin forms' which sometimes simulate amoeboid movement quite closely. P.M.

biogenetic. Conforming to the principle of BIOGENESIS. P.M.

biogeography. The study of the geographical distribution of plants and animals over the earth as related to present-day or recent climatic conditions. It is usually limited to land surfaces but can be extended to describe oceanic distributions. It is divided into PHYTOGEOGRAPHY and ZOOGEOGRAPHY. M.L.

biolinguistics (or *biological linguistics*). A developing branch of LINGUISTICS which studies the biological preconditions for language development and use in man. D.C.
Bibl: E. H. Lenneberg, *Biological Foundations of Language* (N.Y., 1967).

biological control. The control of pests by the deliberate introduction of their natural predators, and by other such natural means. P.M.

biological linguistics, see BIOLINGUISTICS.

biological rhythm. A periodicity of behaviour associated with a natural subdivision of time such as a day, month, or season. Biological rhythms include exactly or approximately circadian (24-hour) rhythms, oestrus and menstrual cycles, the recurrence of breeding seasons, etc. Many such rhythms are deeply grounded physiologically and are by no means totally obscured when animals are removed to an ENVIRONMENT in which the cycles conducive to rhythmic behaviour – e.g. the manifest alternation of night and day – is no longer present. P.M.

biological sciences, see BIOLOGY.

biological warfare, see under WAR.

biology. The collective name for the *biological sciences* (or, as they are increasingly called in America, *life sciences*), i.e. those NATURAL SCIENCES which deal with the CLASSIFICATION, STRUCTURE, or performance of living beings. By convention, the biological sciences include ZOOLOGY, BOTANY, ANATOMY, PHYSIOLOGY, MICROBIOLOGY, BIOSYSTEMATICS, BIOPHYSICS, BIOCHEMISTRY, and, in general, all sciences whose titles incorporate the prefix 'bio-' or the word 'biology' itself (see, for example, DEVELOPMENTAL BIOLOGY; POPULATION BIOLOGY; SOCIAL BIOLOGY). Recent convention allocates ANTHROPOLOGY and PSYCHOLOGY to the SOCIAL SCIENCES, but ETHOLOGY is distinctively a biological science. P.M.

biomathematics. MATHEMATICS applied in biological situations, including medicine and the human sciences. Mathematical reasoning may be used in relation to individual biological organisms or mechanisms (e.g. theoretical MODELS of how nerve fibres, or circulatory systems, function), or to whole animal or human populations. In the latter case especially, statistical CONCEPTS, such as population size, age distribution, sex ratio, become relevant. This leads to related terms such as *biostatistics* and BIOMETRY. M.S.BA.
Bibl: M. S. Bartlett and R. W. Hiorns (eds.), *The Mathematical Theory of the Dynamics of Biological Populations* (N.Y., 1973).

biomechanics. Short-lived doctrine of acrobatic acting preached and practised by the director Vsevolod Meyerhold at the Moscow State Higher Theatre Workshop in the 1920s under the influence of CONSTRUCTIVISM and the TIME AND MOTION researches of A. K. Gastev's Institute for the Scientific Organization of Work and the Mechanization of Man. The actors had to study the mechanics of the body, combining the movements of a skilled worker or sportsman with a dancer's rhythm and balance, performing in blue overalls with no make-up, and using gymnastic and circus apparatus on the stage. In 1922 two plays were given classic productions along these lines, in Constructivist sets: Crommelynck's *Le Cocu magnifique* and Sukhovo-Kobylin's *Tarelkin's Death* (with Eisenstein as Meyerhold's assistant). J.W.
Bibl: V. Meyerhold, ed. and tr. E. Braun, *Meyerhold on Theatre* (London and N.Y., 1969).

biometry (or *biometrics*; see also BIOMATHEMATICS). The use of mensuration, enumeration, STATISTICS, and quantitative methods generally in the study of BIOLOGY. In the post-Darwinian era many botanists and zoologists became preoccupied with qualitative descriptions of organisms which were intended to disclose their evolutionary credentials (see EVOLUTION). In reaction a number of scientists – notably Karl Pearson, W. F. R. Weldon, and D'Arcy Thompson – insisted upon the importance of measurement and numeration in the study of all biological phenomena which include an important quantitative or – as in MENDELISM – random element. Among the striking accomplishments of biometry may be mentioned

D'Arcy Thompson's and J. S. Huxley's studies of differential growth, the techniques and usages of small-sample statistics introduced by R. A. Fisher, the whole of POPULATION GENETICS, and so much of modern biology that it is hard to think of any branch in which mensuration and numeration are not extremely important. The equation of biometry with statistical analysis of numerical biological data is a degenerate usage which should be discouraged. P.M.

Bibl: J. Maynard Smith, *Mathematical Ideas in Biology* (London and N.Y., 1968).

biomorphic. Term used in ABSTRACT ART and SURREALISM for non-geometrical forms based on natural shapes, i.e. mainly curves, blobs, and bulges. It is associated primarily with the abstract paintings and sculptures of Hans Arp, who consistently used such forms from 1915 on, and secondarily with the work of such surrealists as Yves Tanguy and Joan Miró. Similar characteristics in the work of Henry Moore are sometimes termed *organic*. Before these labels had come into use, however, much the same approach was applied, with great refinement, in ART NOUVEAU and the designs of William Morris. J.W.

Bibl: K. Nierendorf (intr.), *Art Forms in Nature* (N.Y., 1967).

bionics. A portmanteau word (BIOLOGICAL electroNICS) coined by Dr Hans L. Oestreicher of Wright-Patterson Air Force Base, Ohio, and meaning the application of biological processes, especially of control, to TECHNOLOGY. It is the part of CYBERNETICS (hence sometimes called *biocybernetics*) which is concerned with taking over 'design principles' seen in biological organisms, to create novel technological devices. (Another word closely related in meaning is BIO-ENGINEERING.) Current emphasis in bionics has moved away from principles of control, to the question of how novelty or intelligence may be simulated (see SIMULATION) or produced by machines – see ARTIFICIAL INTELLIGENCE. R.L.G.

bionomics, see ECOLOGY.

biophysics. The scientific discipline concerned with the study of living things by the application of physical methods, e.g. *ultracentrifugation* (see SEDIMENTATION); filtering through ordinary plane filters of different porosities or through gels with more or less closely spaced lattice works (*gel filtration*); ELECTROPHORESIS, in which MOLECULES can be separated by reason of inequalities of electrical charge – a most important technique with such fragile and unstable molecules as those of PROTEINS. University departments of biophysics are often given the responsibility for (1) supervising the general use of physical methods in BIOLOGY, particularly the use of TRACER techniques using radioactive compounds or other ISOTOPES; (2) ULTRASONICS; and (3) therapeutic or investigative techniques turning upon irradiation. By far the most important part of biophysics is MOLECULAR BIOLOGY, the interpretation of biological structures and performances in molecular terms. P.M.

biopsy, see under HISTOPATHOLOGY.

biosphere. A word built on the model of atmosphere and HYDROSPHERE and signifying (1) the realm occupied by living things; hence (2) the living things themselves, considered collectively. P.M.

biostatistics, see under BIOMATHEMATICS.

biosynthesis. A synthetic process occurring characteristically in a living thing. PROTEINS and viruses (see VIROLOGY) are produced only by biosynthesis; they cannot yet be synthesized in the laboratory. P.M.

biosystematics. The classification of living things; also known as *taxonomy*. Biosystematics was founded by Linnaeus, who introduced the familiar binomial nomenclature in which each organism is given a generic (e.g. *Homo*) and a specific name (*Homo sapiens*). The most majestic of taxonomic distinctions is into plant and animal *kingdoms* (the subject-matters of BOTANY and ZOOLOGY respectively). Next in order of rank is the PHYLUM, the members of which are united by a basic similarity of ground plan which may only be apparent at a relatively early stage of development.

A phylum comprises a number of *classes*. Members of a class are united by a somewhat closer degree of similarity than the members of a phylum – extending to points of anatomical detail as well as to ground plan. For example, the phylum Arthropoda includes the classes Insecta and Crustacea, the Insecta being united by having three pairs of legs attached to the thoracic region of the body and respiring by means of *tracheae*; while within the Vertebrates (often accorded the rank of a sub-phylum within the phylum Chordata) fishes, reptiles, amphibians, birds, and mammals are all graded as classes.

Next below the class come successively the *order*, the *family*, and the *genus* (plural *genera*). It is not possible to specify the degree of resemblance that unites members of orders, families, or genera in a way that will apply to all animals and plants; it may be noted, however, that among mammals the whales and dolphins, the carnivores, the rodents, and the primates each form an order. Finally, below the genus comes the SPECIES; thus the great cats belong to the genus Panthera, in which *Panthera leo* (the lion) and *Panthera tigris* (the tiger) are species.

Of the larger taxonomic sub-divisions it may be said that all phyla, classes, and orders are intended to have the same 'value', i.e. to be of the same rank in the systematic hierarchy. Furthermore, each group within itself is intended to be *monophyletic*, i.e. to be such that the common ancestor of the members of the group is itself a member of the group. (There are exceptions: notoriously, the class Reptilia is polyphyletic in the sense that reptiles are subdivided into two main streams – one leading towards birds and one towards mammals – both of which evolved out of amphibian ancestors.) On the other hand, taxonomic divisions are not intended to be a dossier of evolutionary relationships (see EVOLUTION); the purpose of taxonomy is to *name* reliably and consistently. Nevertheless the fact of the evolutionary relationship imposes a certain pattern upon classification which is not to be avoided.

Taxonomic characteristics, i.e. those upon which a systematic allocation may be made, are wherever possible structural, since physiological and behavioural criteria are of little use to the museum taxonomist who normally has to handle dead specimens. Similar difficulties restrict the use of immunological criteria (see

IMMUNOLOGY) in determining blood relationships. They have, however, helped to show that whales are more nearly akin to pigs than to other mammals that have been alleged to be their relations. P.M.

Bibl: Reader's Digest Association, *The Living World of Animals* (London, 1970).

biotechnology. A term comprehending all applications of biological knowledge (see BIOLOGY) to industry. Examples are: (1) industrial fermentation (including brewing, wine-making, and in some countries the accelerated maturation of wines by the addition of ENZYMES); (2) the preparation of leather and of so-called 'biological DETERGENTS', the active ingredients of which are enzymes extracted from heat-adapted bacteria (see BACTERIOLOGY). Much of the food industry, especially as it relates to pre-prepared foods, rests on biological know-how and comes, therefore, under the heading of biotechnology. P.M.

bipartisan foreign policy. A foreign policy supported by both governing and opposition parties in a two-party system. The concept was evolved to cover Republican support of the foreign policy of the (Democratic) President of the U.S.A., Harry S. Truman, in the years 1947–8 (see TRUMAN DOCTRINE; MARSHALL PLAN), a policy in part evolved and extensively managed in Congress in consultation between the President and leading Republican senators. D.C.W.

bipolarity. An intellectual MODEL of the world powers as divided ('polarized') into two main blocs of powers each led by a 'super-power' (the U.S.A. or U.S.S.R.). As a simplified model of international relations, especially in the field of control of nuclear armaments, it seduced many American policy-advisers during the 1950s by its facile answers to some of their problems. The concept lost its attraction when it became obvious that the leadership of the 'super-powers' was never as absolute as the model required, and that this lack offered many opportunities to Soviet and Western anti-American propagandists. Compare MULTIPOLARITY. D.C.W.

Birrell, Francis (British author, journalist,

65

and bookseller, 1889–1935), see under BLOOMSBURY GROUP.

birth trauma. In PSYCHOANALYSIS, a TRAUMA postulated by Otto Rank (one of Freud's early associates), who argued that being born is a deeply disturbing experience, out of which develops the fundamental human conflict: between the wish to return to the embryonic bliss of the womb and the fear of doing so, because the womb is also associated with the fact of birth. This notion has not been widely accepted, even among psychoanalysts. B.A.F.

Bibl: O. Rank, *The Trauma of Birth* (London and N.Y., 1929).

BIS (Bank for International Settlements). 'The central bankers' central bank', set up in 1930 (in the wake of the 1929 crash) by the central banks of Britain, Belgium, Germany, Italy, Japan, and France, with the U.S.A. represented by a commercial bank, and with other European central banks, including most in Eastern Europe, taking shareholdings which they have retained to this day. Membership has since expanded; and the U.S. Federal Reserve Board is invariably represented, although the U.S.A. has never formally taken up the seat on the Board still reserved for it. The Board of Directors includes the central-bank Governors of the main Western European countries ('the Basle Club'), as well as representatives of the private business communities. The Bank acts as the agent for central banks in conducting certain operations in financial and currency markets, most notably over the last decade in the EURO-MONEY markets. Between 1958 and 1972 it also acted as the agent of first the OEEC and later the OECD in executing all operations of the *European Monetary Agreement*, a relic of the earlier post-war *European Payments Union*, whereby members cleared mutual currency claims, settling only net balances (see BALANCE OF PAYMENTS) in hard currency, chiefly dollars. In 1973 the European Monetary Cooperation Fund, set up by the EEC as a step towards full economic and monetary union, appointed the BIS as its agent, with responsibility for certain technical aspects of its operations. P.J.

Bismarck, Otto von (founder and first

Chancellor of the German Empire, 1815–98), see under REALPOLITIK; RIGHT, THE.

bit. (1) In COMPUTER SCIENCE, reputedly short for 'binary digit', a digit in the scale of 2 which will represent the result of a single yes/no decision. Most computer storage and logical elements are made of two-state devices, each of which can represent one bit. (2) In INFORMATION THEORY, the basic unit of information. A 32-bit (sense 1) unit in a computer may be used to represent anything from 0 to 32 bits of information (sense 2). R.M.N.

bitonality. In music, the mixing together of two *tonalities* (see under ATONAL MUSIC) by the simultaneous use of, e.g., two lines of melody or two blocks of harmony, each in a different key. The conflict of tonalities produces an arresting effect which is more likely to be immediately comprehensible than random dissonance, since each part in itself is based on traditional concepts of key. Bitonality was much used at the start of the century, notably by Stravinsky, Holst (in the Fugal Concerto), and Bartók, and in the 1920s by Milhaud. See also PANTONAL MUSIC; POLYTONALITY. A.H.

bivalent. Two CHROMOSOMES of maternal and paternal origin lying side by side during MEIOSIS; also used as an adjective to describe such a pair. J.M.S.

black-body radiation. Electromagnetic RADIATION in EQUILIBRIUM with matter; the radiation would be re-emitted by an ideal 'black body' which absorbs all the radiation incident on it. Black-body radiation is distributed over all wavelengths but its ENERGY is concentrated near a particular wavelength region which depends on the temperature. Examples are the INFRA-RED and visible radiation emitted by a red-hot poker, and the MICROWAVES of the COSMIC BACKGROUND RADIATION. Historically the development of the theory of black-body radiation (by Planck in 1900) was the first step leading to QUANTUM MECHANICS. M.V.B.

black-box theory. A theory that attempts to relate INPUT to output in a SYSTEM by a formal description of the *transformation rules* (see AXIOMATICS) that link the two, but without stating the nature of the process that embodies or gives realization to these rules. N. Chomsky's description of language acquisition and B. F. Skinner's theory of learning may both be considered black-box theories, since they both avoid the description of the mechanisms involved. J.S.B.

black comedy (or *dark comedy*). Drama which, although it observes many of the conventions of comedy, either presents a sombre or despairing view of the world or else includes themes traditionally excluded from the genre on account of their painful nature. The use of this style in the modern period relates to the widely held belief that tragedy is an inappropriate genre for an age which has lost religious faith and a sense of the heroic. Although the two terms are to some extent interchangeable, *dark comedy* refers rather to the tragicomic form in which laughter and despair are inextricably mingled, in the style perfected by Anton Chekhov (1860–1904), while *black comedy*, exemplified at its most extreme in the plays of Joe Orton, seeks to unsettle its audiences by laughing at pain, suffering, or serious emotion (and thus has an affinity with *sick jokes* and the THEATRE OF THE ABSURD). The term 'black comedy' (*comédie noire*) derives from Jean Anouilh, who divided his plays of the 1930s and 1940s into *pièces roses and pièces noires,* and perhaps also from *Anthologie de l'humeur noir*, the title of a volume (1940) in which André Breton illustrated the long-standing SURREALIST interest in the humorous treatment of the macabre or the shocking to indicate 'the superior rebellion of the mind'; the term 'dark comedy' was coined by the critic J. L. Styan in 1962.

M.A.; J.G.W.
Bibl: J. L. Styan, *The Dark Comedy* (London, 2nd ed., 1968).

Black Hand, see under SARAJEVO.

black hole. A hypothetical astronomical system. When a star near the end of its history contracts under GRAVITATION and becomes smaller than a certain *critical radius* (proportional to the star's mass), then, according to Einstein's theory of RELATIVITY, NO RADIATION can escape from it; as far as the rest of the universe is concerned it becomes unobservable – its

ESCAPE VELOCITY exceeds the speed of light. Such a black hole would still exert gravitational force, so that its existence could be inferred from the motion of neighbouring bodies; several black holes have been tentatively identified in this way. What happens to the matter falling into a black hole? Does it collapse to a point of infinite density, or is this prevented by QUANTUM MECHANICS, or does the matter re-explode, appearing as a 'white hole' in another universe? These are unsolved problems in theoretical PHYSICS. The sun is in no immediate danger of becoming a black hole within the next few hundred million years, because it is about half a million times larger than its critical radius, which is about 2 miles. See also HERTZSPRUNG-RUSSELL DIAGRAM. M.V.B.

Black Hundreds. Strong-arm gangs employed by RIGHT-wing organizations in Czarist Russia in the period after the Revolution of 1905 and the summoning of the first Russian parliament, to demoralize their political opponents and harass Russian Jewry. D.C.W.

Black Mountain. Black Mountain College, a PROGRESSIVE-education institution in North Carolina founded by J. A. Rice in 1933. At first the emphasis was on practical education and painting (the art-teachers included Josef Albers, formerly of the BAUHAUS), but in the early 1950s it became a centre of a new, or newly stated, American POETICS, and a place for poets: the CONNOTATION of Black Mountain is now almost exclusively literary, referring to the Black Mountain school of poets. This is one of two latter-day manifestations of an American revolt against conventional and academic poetics which began with Ezra Pound and William Carlos Williams – the other being the group of poets that crystallized round Robert Bly's Fifties/Sixties/Seventies Press.) The key to the Black Mountain poetics is to be found in American PRAGMATISM as exemplified by John Dewey, with its accompanying blind optimism. Its mentor was Charles Olson (1910–70), Rector of the College from 1951 until 1956, during which period he was joined by other Black Mountain poets (e.g. Robert Creeley, Robert Duncan), as students and as instructors. Olson's makeshift poetics (or anti-poetics) is expressed, in a mixture of baseball instructor's and jocose professional slang, in *Projective Verse* (1950), which has been widely reprinted. It is unscholarly and derivative (mostly from Williams), and raises a host of unanswered questions. But it is important as a summing-up of the attitudes of a somewhat younger generation of American poets, and as a specifically American pragmatic reaction, arising out of what has been called 'intelligent philistinism', to lifeless academicism. Olson's demands had already been fulfilled more humbly by the OBJECTIVIST minor American poets of the early 1930s, with whom Williams and Pound were briefly associated. His disciples do not really fulfil these demands; but they believe that they are doing so. The poet is to concentrate on his own breathing, on the syllable (see SYLLABICS) rather than on metre or rhyme; he is to perform on the typewriter because this spaces more precisely than writing does; syntax, in as much as it hampers the dynamic energy supplied by breath, is to go. There is much emphasis on public readings. And the prime reason for all this is that the old, 'closed' method interposed the 'poet's ego' between himself and his audience. In Black Mountain poetry, the (Deweyan) sense of *use* is not actually carried beyond the simple act of creation, and neither Olson nor his chief disciple Creeley give the least indication, outside or inside their poetry, of why they do what they do. The magazine *Origin* (1951–6), edited by Cid Corman, printed many of the Black Mountain poets. *Black Mountain Review* (1954–7), edited by Creeley, is also relevant. The claim made in one reference book that the Black Mountain poets 'have long since become a major part of 20th-century literature' is decidedly premature.

M.S.-S.

Bibl: M. L. Rosenthal, *The New Poets* (N.Y., 1967).

Black Muslims. A black nationalist separatist movement in the U.S.A., founded in 1930 as the 'Nation of Islam' by Wali Farad, on the theory that black Americans were members of an ancient Muslim tribe. Its devotees were required to adopt Muslim names, to avoid all contact with white men, and to follow exemplary lives free of allegedly white vices such

as DRUG-taking, drinking, fornication, etc. Leadership passed in 1934 to Elijah Muhammed (né Poole). After 1945 the preaching of Malcolm X (né Little), who later broke with the movement, raised membership to 100,000. Black Muslims demand a separate state for blacks and reparations for wrongs suffered at white men's hands. Cassius Clay, world heavyweight champion in the 1960s, and again in the 1970s, became the movement's best-known convert, taking the name Muhammed Ali.

D.C.W.

Bibl: J. A. Geschwender, *The Black Revolt* (Englewood Cliffs, N.J., 1971).

Black Panthers. A militant black organization in the U.S.A. preaching violence and armed self-protection of black communities, founded in California in 1968 by Huey Newton and Eldridge Cleaver, after the assassination of the moderate black leader, Martin Luther King, by hired white gunmen. The Panthers took the brunt of American police suspicions owing to their use of revolutionary rhetoric and carrying of arms. The movement, which allegedly favoured joint white–black effort in CLASS struggle, faltered with the arrest or exile of its principal leaders and, despite the acquittal of many defendants, its strength diminished as a result of internal rivalries and the policy of 'benign neglect' adopted by President Nixon towards the colour problem.

D.C.W.

Black Papers. Two issues in 1969 of the *Critical Survey,* a periodical associated with the literary *Critical Quarterly*. Their titles were *Fight for Education* and *The Crisis in Education* and the editors were C. B. Cox and A. E. Dyson, two university teachers of English literature. The contributors emphasized a deterioration, in Western Europe generally and Great Britain in particular, in standards of education and discipline ranging from children's reading to student behaviour. COMPREHENSIVE SCHOOLS, EGALITARIANISM, YOUTH CULTURES, and 'progressivism' in general (see PROGRESSIVE) came under fire on what the editors insisted were educational and not political grounds.

W.A.C.S.

black power. Term used by black ACTIVISTS in the U.S.A. from 1957

BLAST

onwards to imply black control over the CIVIL RIGHTS MOVEMENT and the employment of all resources available to black Americans, including both the organization of black voters and the use of force where force was used against them, to further the interests of the black communities. It was thus opposed to the INTEGRATIONIST and assimilationist tendencies of older civil rights organizations, and its adoption in 1967 by a national conference marked a major development in the political self-consciousness of black Americans.   D.C.W.

Bibl: R. L. Allen, *Black Awakening in Capitalist America* (N.Y., 1969; London, as *A Guide to Black Power in America*, 1970).

Black September. The clandestine TERRORIST wing of the Palestine Arab PARAMILITARY organization, AL FATAH. It took its name from the action of the Jordanian Government against the various Palestinian Arab para-military organizations in September 1970. It has engaged widely in terrorism, assassination, aircraft hi-jacking, the sabotage of West European oil installations, etc., and was responsible for the massacre of Israeli athletes at the 1972 Olympic Games in Munich. D.C.W.

black studies. Courses in various disciplines dealing with the history, culture, sociology, etc., of black Americans, introduced into a series of American colleges and universities on the demand of a minority of black students, from 1968 onwards, for courses in subjects 'relevant' to their own background and experience. Black studies, a voguish example of cultural NATIONALISM, have suffered in academic status from extremist demands that only black Americans be allowed either to teach or study them; and some students, both black and white, while sympathetic to the intention, have rejected the content as unduly restrictive. The term is sometimes widened to cover similar studies of Africa south of the Sahara.   D.C.W.

Black Theatre. A movement dedicated to the creation of a drama reflecting the consciousness of black Americans. Lorraine Hansberry's *A Raisin in the Sun* (1959) was the first major success by a black dramatist; in the 1960s, in plays by James Baldwin, Ed Bullins, and LeRoi

Jones, black drama became progressively more radical (see RADICALISM) until, influenced by the militancy of the BLACK POWER movement at the end of the decade, Black Theatre groups sought to sever their connection with the white American theatre and perform solely for black audiences. Outside the U.S.A., theatre groups in Jamaica and England (comprising West Indians and expatriate Americans) have been influenced by the Black Theatre movement; the work of West African dramatists, of whom the most powerful is the Nigerian Wole Soyinka, represents a complex fusion of indigenous and ex-colonial traditions; in the French-speaking world the plays of the Martinique-born poet and dramatist Aimé Césaire have made an important contribution to the expression of black identity (see NÉGRITUDE).   M.A.

Bibl: D. E. Abramson, *Negro Playwrights in the American Theatre, 1925–1959* (London and N.Y., 1969); *Drama Review,* Black Theatre issue, Dec. 1972, pp. 3–61; M. Banham with C. Wake, *African Theatre Today* (London, 1976).

Black Zionism, see under ETHIOPIANISM.

Blackmur, Richard Palmer (U.S. poet and critic, 1904–65), see under EXPRESSIVE FORM, FALLACY OF; NEW CRITICISM.

Blake, Peter (British painter, *b.* 1932), see under POP.

Blake, William (British poet, painter, and engraver, 1757–1827), see under MECHANIZATION; MYTHOPOEIA; SYMBOLISM.

Blanc, Louis (French utopian socialist, 1811–82), see under PROLETARIAT.

Blanqui, Auguste (French socialist and revolutionary, 1805–81), see under ANARCHISM; DICTATORSHIP OF THE PROLETARIAT; JACOBINISM.

Blast. The 'review of the Great English Vortex', published in London in two issues, June 1914 and July 1915, under the editorship of Wyndham Lewis. Preeminently a VORTICIST manifesto, presenting its attitude to the contemporary scene in a Marinetti-like display of

69

'Blesses' and 'Blasts', it was the most conspicuous expression of this post-Imagist (see IMAGISM) movement in literature and the arts. Ezra Pound was active in its compilation; there were contributions by T. S. Eliot, Ford Madox Hueffer, etc. But these typographically exciting documents are primarily fascinating as statements of an important theory about the kinetic potential of the MODERNIST arts, and as a synthetic 'projection of a world art'. M.S.BR.

blastocyst. In EMBRYOLOGY, a very early human developmental stage, after cleavage but before implantation, of the embryo, in which the CELLS into which the ZYGOTE has divided come to be arranged in the form of a sac or cyst containing fluid. The stage is thought to be somewhat analogous to the blastula – a stage which all embryos of animals on the chordate line of descent pass through. P.M.

Blau, Peter (U.S. sociologist, *b*. 1918), see under EXCHANGE MODELS; SOCIOLOGY.

Blaue Reiter, der ('the Blue Horseman'). A Munich-based almanac edited by Kandinsky and Franz Marc in 1912, whose title was used for a group of artists headed by Kandinsky who broke away from the NEUE KÜNSTLERVEREINIGUNG to hold two exhibitions in the winter of 1911–12. It included August Macke, Heinrich Campendonk, the (future ATONAL) composer Arnold Schönberg and, in the second show, Paul Klee. Though its members figured in the second Moscow KNAVE OF DIAMONDS show and in many ensuing STURM exhibitions, it ceased to exhibit as a group after 1913. It was, however, one of the main elements in EXPRESSIONISM and early ABSTRACT ART, bringing to each a SYMBOLIST, mystical, quasi-musical flavour tinged with ANTHROPOSOPHY. It later influenced the BAUHAUS, where from 1924 to 1929 Kandinsky, Klee, Lyonel Feininger, and Alexei Jawlensky formed a related group called 'the Blue Four'. J.W.

Blavatsky, Helena Petrova (Russian-born spiritualist, 1831–91), see under THEOSOPHY.

blending inheritance. Inheritance by children of characteristics which are a more or less equitable blend between those of their parents or, in respect of quantitative characteristics, midway between them. Although such a blending is a natural enough presumption the great lesson of MENDELISM is that it does not occur. If it did so, GENETIC variance would be extinguished in a few generations, whereas in point of fact genetic variance tends to be indefinitely conserved. This is because the determinants of heredity maintain their integrity generation by generation. So far from being a blend between their two parents, children display a novel and possibly a unique recombination of the genetic determinants transmitted to them by their parents. See also MENDEL'S LAWS. P.M.

Bleuler, Eugen (Swiss psychiatrist, 1857–1939), see under AMBIVALENCE; SCHIZOPHRENIA.

Bloch, Marc (French historian, 1886–1944), see under AGRARIAN HISTORY; ANNALES SCHOOL; GENETIC METHOD.

Blok, Alexander Alexandrovich (Russian poet, 1880–1921), see under SYMBOLISM.

Blomdahl, Karl-Birger (Swedish composer, 1916–68), see under SERIAL MUSIC.

blood and soil (*Blut und Boden*). A quasi-mystical NAZI catch-phrase intended to glorify the literature and emotions of the peasant as the embodiment of the two qualities from which the high quality of the German race was supposed to stem, German blood and German soil.
D.C.W.

blood groups. Many early attempts at blood transfusion from one human being to another failed because of an incompatibility between the recipient's and the donor's blood, the mechanism of which was first elucidated by Karl Landsteiner in 1900. Landsteiner found that the SERUM of some human beings caused AGGLUTINATION of the red blood corpuscles of other human beings, and that human beings could be divided into four groups,

A, B, AB, and O, whose members' serum agglutinated the corpuscles of members of other groups as follows:

a member of	agglu- tinates	is agglu- tinated by
A	B, AB	B, O
B	A, AB	A, O
AB	—	A, B, O
O	A, B, AB	—

Since the dangerous process is agglutination of the donor's corpuscles by the recipient's serum (because of the dilution effect the reverse process is of lesser significance) it follows that:

a member of	can donate to	can receive from
A	A, AB	A, O
B	B, AB	B, O
AB	AB	all groups
O	all groups	O

Inheritance of A, B, O blood groups was soon shown to follow straightforward Mendelian rules (see MENDEL'S LAWS). The A, B, O blood-group system is, however, only one among many. So many varieties of blood antigen (see IMMUNITY) are now known that a person's blood group is, if defined precisely enough, practically a personal identification mark. Among the other important blood groups are those of the Rh (Rhesus) system and the M, N, MN system. Some of these – the Rh system in particular – were discovered by indirect methods of blood typing. Thus the antibody distinguishing between Rh+ and Rh− red blood cells was formed by injecting the blood of Rhesus monkeys into rabbits. 'Natural' antibodies (see IMMUNITY) against Rh antigens do not appear, so anti-Rh immunity arises as a result of active immunization – through incompatible blood transfusions, or during the course of pregnancy when a Rh-negative mother bears a number of children by a Rh-positive man.   P.M.

Bibl: A. E. Mourant, *The Distribution of the Human Blood Groups* (Oxford and Springfield, Ill., 1954); R. R. Race and R. Sanger, *Blood Groups in Man* (Oxford and Philadelphia, 5th ed., 1968).

Bloomfield, Leonard (U.S. linguist, 1887–1949), see under BLOOMFIELDIAN; CONSTITUENT ANALYSIS.

Bloomfieldian. Characteristic of, or a follower of, the linguistic approach of Leonard Bloomfield, as exemplified in his book *Language*, published in 1933. *Bloomfieldianism* refers particularly to the school of thought which developed between the mid 1930s and 1950s, especially in America, and which was a formative influence on structural LINGUISTICS. It was especially characterized by its BEHAVIOURISTIC principles for the study of meaning, and its insistence on rigorous DISCOVERY PROCEDURES. A reaction against Bloomfieldian tenets was a powerful force in producing GENERATIVE GRAMMAR. Though Bloomfieldianism is no longer fashionable, some of its methods are still widely used in field studies.   D.C.

Bloomsbury. An area of Central London which includes the British Museum, and whose name is used (1) as a synonym for the BLOOMSBURY GROUP or one of its members ('a Bloomsbury', facetious plural 'bloomsberries'); (2) more loosely, and not currently, as a symbol of the British intelligentsia at large ('Bloomsbury INTELLECTUAL') or any section or aspect of it ('a Bloomsbury voice') towards which hostility is felt.   O.S.

Bloomsbury Group. A circle of friends without formal membership, rules, or common doctrine consisting of Lytton Strachey, Virginia and Leonard Woolf, Clive and Vanessa Bell, Maynard Keynes, Duncan Grant, Saxon Sydney-Turner, and (see also OMEGA WORKSHOPS) Roger Fry. Closely associated with this group were E. M. Forster, Gerald Shove, James and Marjorie Strachey, David Garnett, Francis Birrell, Adrian and Thoby Stephen. The group came into existence in 1905, when Thoby Stephen and his sisters, Virginia and Vanessa, then living in BLOOMSBURY, London, continued friendships begun at Cambridge. Its members were united by a belief in the importance of the arts; they were all sceptical and tolerant, particularly in sexual matters.

Beyond this it would be difficult to find any opinion or attitude shared by all. In so far as the group ever had any kind of corporate existence, it began to decline after the death of Lytton Strachey in 1931 and had ceased to exist by 1940.   Q.B.

Bibl: J. K. Johnstone, *The Bloomsbury Group* (London, 1954; N.Y., 1963); Q. Bell, *Bloomsbury* (London, 1968; N.Y., 1969); D. Gadd, *The Loving Friends: a Portrait of Bloomsbury* (London, 1974).

Blue Book. Familiar term for British Government publication of official documents presented to Parliament in sufficient number of pages to warrant being bound in a separate blue cover. They are identifiable by their 'Command numbers' and the date and year of their presentation. Those familiar with these source materials maintain that the degree of frankness observed in their publication has diminished progressively with the increase in the size of the electorate. Blue Books should be distinguished from other Command Papers known as White Papers and Green Papers. The former contain statements of Government policy and may include announcements of Government intentions and proposals on future legislation, while Green Papers are used by the Government to put forward ideas and information which are the basis of open debate and discussion rather than a commitment by the Government to a specific course of action.   D.C.W.

blue notes. Those notes in the conventional Western diatonic scale which are flattened according to the traditions of Afro-American JAZZ style, to produce a uniquely melancholic effect. The notes in question are the third and seventh of the diatonic scale, and their descent by a semitone changes them to minor third and dominant seventh respectively. With the advent of BEBOP, the fifth was treated in the same way, to become a flattened fifth. The first conventional works to popularize blue-note effects were those of George Gershwin (1898–1937).   B.G.

blue shift. A displacement towards the blue of the spectral lines of some stars. The shift arises from the DOPPLER EFFECT, and indicates that these stars are approaching us. Because of the overall EXPANSION OF THE UNIVERSE, blue shifts are rare in comparison with RED SHIFTS.   M.V.B.

blues. In JAZZ, a technical term denoting a pattern which improvisors of all styles and periods have found indispensable. The duration of the pattern is twelve bars, and its harmonic structure is formalized most strictly, although with jazz's ever-growing sophistication its harmonies have become more extravagantly ornamented, without, however, dispensing with the original structure. The blue pattern consists of four bars which end with a dominant seventh chord of the home key, then four bars pitched in the new key placed at an interval of one fourth above the home key, and finally four bars returning to the home key. In vocal blues these three sections crystallize into three lines of iambic pentameter, the second line being a repeat of the first. See also RHYTHM-AND-BLUES.   B.G.

Bibl: P. Oliver, *Blues Fell this Morning* (London, 1960; N.Y., 1961) and *The Story of the Blues* (London and Philadelphia, 1969).

Blum, Léon (French statesman, 1872–1950), see under DREYFUS CASE; POPULAR FRONT.

Bly, Robert (U.S. poet and translator, *b.* 1926), see under BLACK MOUNTAIN.

Boas, Franz (German-born anthropologist, 1858–1942), see under APOLLONIAN AND DIONYSIAN CULTURES.

Bobrowski, Johannes (German author, 1917–65), see under GRUPPE 47.

Boccioni, Umberto (Italian sculptor and painter, 1882–1916), see under FUTURISM.

Bodmer, Johann Jakob (Swiss critic, 1698–1783), see under AUTOTELIC WRITING.

body art, see under CONCEPTUAL ART.

Bogdanov, Alexander (Russian revolutionary, 1874–1939), see under PROLETKULT.

Bohr, Niels (Danish physicist, 1885–1962), see under BOHR THEORY; COMPLEMENTARITY PRINCIPLE; ORBITAL.

Bohr theory. An explanation, devised in 1913 by the physicist Niels Bohr, of the radiation emitted by atomic hydrogen. The theory is based on NEWTONIAN MECHANICS, with the addition of simple rules which appeared arbitrary at first but which were later explained by the more fundamental QUANTUM MECHANICS. See also ATOMIC PHYSICS; ENERGY LEVEL; SPECTROSCOPY.   M.V.B.

Böll, Heinrich (German author, b. 1917), see under GRUPPE 47.

Bolshevism. The IDEOLOGY of the Bolshevik Party which, under Lenin's leadership, carried out the Russian Revolution of October 1917 and established the Soviet Union. The Bolsheviks originated as a faction led by Lenin at the 1903 Brussels congress of the illegal All-Russian Soviet Democratic Workers' Party. The Congress split over the question of Party membership which reflected irreconcilable differences over the character and objectives of the Party. Lenin's faction took the name Bolsheviks (the noun in Russian means majority) from their victory over their opponents led by Martov who became known as the MENSHEVIKS (i.e. minority). In 1912 the Bolsheviks constituted themselves as a separate party. They changed their name to the All-Russian COMMUNIST Party (Bolsheviks) in 1918, to the All-Union Communist Party (Bolsheviks) in 1925, and to the Communist Party of the Soviet Union (C.P.S.U.) in 1952.

Bolshevism as a REVOLUTIONARY ideology derived from the adaptation of Western MARXISM to the Russian POPULIST tradition. After the seizure of power in 1917 it became imbued with the tradition of Russian autocracy. Its theory and practice have been codified in the canon of LENINISM. Its historical originality consists in the fact that while it retains its attachment to Marxism it has abandoned the Marxian idea that 'the emancipation of the working class will be accomplished by the workers themselves' and substituted for it the idea derived from the

Russian *Blanquist* (see ANARCHISM) Peter Tkachev, that social revolution can only be accomplished by bringing political CLASS-conciousness to the workers from outside their class by professional revolutionaries from the socialist intelligentsia (see INTELLECTUALS). The workers by themselves could not, according to Lenin, achieve more than a 'trade union consciousness', i.e. concentrate on the 'bread and butter' issues of improving their economic conditions, instead of rising to the historical level prescribed for them by Marxist theory. The concomitant idea of a tightly knit, disciplined organization led by such professional revolutionaries which was proposed by Lenin to overcome the 'backwardness of the masses' and imbue them with 'revolutionary consciousness' derived from the concepts of Ogarev, the friend of Bakunin and Herzen, and from the organizational practice of the Russian *Narodniks*. But Lenin retained (until April 1917) the classical Marxist view that socialist revolution could not be accomplished alone in as backward a country as Russia, where the economic and social preconditions for 'building SOCIALISM' did not exist.

Lenin's 'April Theses' (1917) marked the next step in modifying the original Marxist approach to this problem: they proposed the seizure of power in 'backward Russia' by the Bolshevik Party. In effect this meant the tacit acceptance by Lenin of Trotsky's theory of PERMANENT REVOLUTION, which envisaged the revolution in Russia as a precursor of socialist revolutions in the more advanced countries of Europe. The Bolshevik *coup* in October 1917 was the outcome of the transformation of Marxism into Leninism, and at the same time marked the arrival of Bolshevism on the world historical scene. The failure of the expected socialist revolutions in Europe to occur made the further evolution of Bolshevism inevitable. Lenin's party, exercising power as a DICTATORSHIP of a minority, now had to build socialism in a country where, on its own assumptions, the Marxist conditions for such a transformation were absent. The Bolsheviks set to work to create these conditions, and in the process Leninism became MARXISM-LENINISM, an ideological formula for the political practice of Stalin and his successors, continuing the Bolshevik traditions and adapting them

BOLTZMANN

to new circumstances, some unexpected and some of their own creation.   L.L.

Bibl: L. Schapiro, *The Origin of the Communist Autocracy* (London and Cambridge, Mass., 1966); A. B. Ulam, *Lenin and the Bolsheviks* (N.Y., 1965; London, 1966); T. Szamuely, 'The Birth of Russian Marxism' (*Survey*, 84, 1972).

Boltzmann, Ludwig Edward (Austrian-born physicist, 1844–1906), see under STATISTICAL MECHANICS.

Bolzano, Bernard (Austrian theologian, philosopher, and mathematician, 1781–1848), see under ANALYSIS.

Bomberg, David (British painter, 1890–1957), see under BOROUGH GROUP; VORTICISM.

Bonald, Louis Gabriel Ambroise, Vicomte de (French statesman and philosopher, 1754–1840), see under SOCIOLOGY.

bond, chemical. The forces which hold ATOMS together in a MOLECULE or solid. In some molecules, such as gaseous sodium chloride (or ionic solids), the bond arises mainly because of the electrostatic attraction between IONS of opposite charge. Bonds between atoms where the electrons are shared – covalent bonds (see COVALENCY) – are much more difficult to explain, and the modern understanding of bonding in molecules such as hydrogen, water, and benzine represents the most important success for the application of QUANTUM MECHANICS in CHEMISTRY. There are two main theoretical MODELS: the VALENCE bond model which considers interaction between individual atoms, and the now more widely used molecular orbital treatment in which the NUCLEI (or charge atomic cores) form a framework of the molecule, which is enveloped by ELECTRONS in discrete ORBITALS of definite ENERGY. Both theoretical models show how electron density builds up nuclei in the formation of a bond. The orbital picture of a molecule is conceptually attractive but it is still an approximation and, except for very simple molecules, directly calculated energies are not very accurate.   B.F.

Bond, Edward (British dramatist, *b.* 1934), see under ROYAL COURT THEATRE.

Bondi, Sir Hermann (British mathematician and cosmologist, *b.* 1919), see under STEADY-STATE HYPOTHESIS.

Bonhoeffer, Dietrich (German theologian, 1906–45), see under SECULAR CHRISTIANITY.

Bonnard, Pierre (French painter, 1867–1947), see under NABIS, LES.

boogie-woogie. A form of piano JAZZ based exclusively on the pattern of the twelve-bar BLUES, and characterized by a deliberately repetitious rolling bass pattern in the left hand analogous in some respects to the ground bass found in passacaglia and other forms of classical music. The rhythmic pulse is pervasive, but the possibilities of the style itself strictly limited. It evolved in the American mid-West in the 1920s, usually away from the main stream of jazz development, and enjoyed a brief period of hysterical popular acclaim in the later 1930s. Its most accomplished performers were Mead 'Lux' Lewis, Pete Johnson, and Albert Ammons, its most famous single work Lewis's *Honky Tonk Train Blues*.   B.G.

Boole, George (British mathematician, 1815–64), see under BOOLEAN ALGEBRA; LOGIC; MATHEMATICAL LOGIC.

Boolean algebra. A method, named after its discoverer George Boole (1815–64), of solving problems in the PROPOSITIONAL CALCULUS and in the LOGIC of *classes* by symbolic manipulations based on certain fundamental operations. For propositions these operations are disjunction, conjunction, and negation; for classes, union, intersection, and complement (see SET). In each case the operations are considered as analogues of addition, multiplication, and subtraction and, like them, satisfy various laws; see, e.g., ASSOCIATIVE LAW; COMMUTATIVE LAW. Another application of Boole's ideas is to the design of switching circuits, in particular as used in COMPUTERS (see GATE). An abstract Boolean algebra is a MATHEMATICAL STRUCTURE satisfying the above-mentioned laws (see AXIOMATIC METHOD).   R.G.

Bibl: H. G. Flegg, *Boolean Algebra and its Application* (London and N.Y., 1964).

Booth, Charles (British sociologist, 1840–1916), see under SOCIOLOGY.

Borges, Jorge Luis (Argentinian poet, story-writer, and critic, *b.* 1899), see under AUTOTELIC WRITING; ULTRAISM.

Born, Max (German physicist, 1882–1970), see under QUANTUM MECHANICS.

Borough Group. A group of artists which was formally constituted in January 1948 at the Borough Polytechnic, London. Its leader and prime influence was David Bomberg; there were nine other founder-members. This association broke up in 1950, to be replaced in 1953 by the 'Borough Bottega'. Their painting was broadly figurative, and sought emotional effect through the use of heavy *impasto* (i.e. paint so heavily applied as to stand out in lumps). P.C.
Bibl: W. Lipke, *David Bomberg* (London, 1967; N.Y., 1968).

Borstal. Shorthand term applied to the system of custodial sentence for adolescent offenders introduced in England and Wales in 1908, and taken from the name of the Kentish village where, in the old Rochester Jail, the experiment began. It is popularly regarded as the brain-child of the then Chairman of the Prison Commission, Sir Evelyn Ruggles-Brise, but penal historians consider Brise to have been influenced by the earlier Reformatory at Elmira, N.Y., which was in turn based on ideas developed by Captain MacConochie, Superintendent of the Norfolk Island Penal Colony in the 1840s. Until 1939, Borstals had high rates of success, i.e. there was little RECIDIVISM; but subsequently the special training methods characteristic of the system have become decreasingly effective as the prior criminal histories of inmates have become more extensive, and it seems likely to be merged into a common plan for the custodial treatment of this age-group. T.M.
Bibl: R. Hood, *Borstal Re-assessed* (London, 1965); A. E. Bottoms and F. H. McClintock, *Criminals Coming of Age* (London, 1973).

Bose-Einstein statistics. The QUANTUM STATISTICS that applies to PARTICLES for which the QUANTUM NUMBER describing SPIN is an integer. M.V.B.

bosons, see under QUANTUM STATISTICS.

Boudin, Eugène (French painter, 1824–98), see under IMPRESSIONISM.

boulevard comedy (*boulevard theatre,* etc.). Theatrical entertainment of a frankly commercial nature, appealing to middle-class or BOURGEOIS audiences without challenging social or artistic conventions. The term derives from the Parisian boulevards whose theatres dominated this form of entertainment in the 19th and early 20th centuries; 'Broadway' and 'Shaftesbury Avenue' carry similar CONNOTATIONS. For a contrasted type of theatre see FRINGE; OFF-BROADWAY. M.A.

Boulez, Pierre (French composer, pianist, and conductor, *b.* 1925), see under CONCRETE MUSIC; IMPRESSIONISM; SERIAL MUSIC.

bound form, see under MORPHEME.

boundary, see under TOPOLOGY.

Bourbaki, Nicolas. The pseudonym of a gradually changing group of mathematicians centred in Paris which since 1939 has been producing an encyclopaedic work on the basic MATHEMATICAL STRUCTURES (so far some 20 volumes have appeared). The work has been very influential, both as a paradigm of the AXIOMATIC METHOD, and in its insistence that every important theorem has a correct context which may be different from that in which it was first discovered. R.G.

bourgeois. In the medieval period, a member of a free city or *bourg,* being neither a peasant nor a lord; in the 17th and 18th centuries, the master or employer in relation to the journeyman or worker, or the merchant in relation to the artisan. Thus bourgeois became synonymous with the middle class.
Since the 19th century, a contradictory and paradoxical set of judgements has been applied to the bourgeoisie. Economically and politically, the bourgeoisie was regarded as open, adventurous, and revolutionary; thus Marx, in the

BOURGEOIS HEGEMONY

Communist Manifesto, writes: 'The bourgeoisie, historically, has played a most revolutionary part . . . . The bourgeoisie cannot exist without constantly revolutionizing the instruments of production . . . and with them the whole relations of society.' The political revolutions effected by the bourgeoisie, particularly the French Revolution, ended privileges based on birth, and stressed individualism and achievement as the criteria of place and position in society. Culturally, however, the bourgeoisie has been regarded, from Molière to Balzac, as mean, avaricious, tasteless, REACTION-ARY, and rapacious, having no sense of values other than the acquisition of money and objects.

The two attitudes derive from different historical perspectives. Most economic and political historians (e.g. Werner Sombart) have seen the bourgeois CLASS as tearing up the roots of traditional society and its fixed ways. Cultural historians and moralists, on the other hand, have tended to write from an aristocratic point of view and to decry the breakdown of standards when all culture becomes a commodity. (See ADMASS; MASS CULTURE.) In the late 19th and early 20th centuries a distinction was increasingly made between the *haute* or *grande* bourgeoisie, who had learned to use their wealth for purposes of refinement, and the PETITE (or petty) BOURGEOISIE who were regarded as mean-spirited and niggardly. In recent usage, 'bourgeois' has become associated less with monetary acquisitiveness than with conventional attitudes to sexual conduct.   D.B.
Bibl: W. Sombart, tr. M. Epstein, *The Quintessence of Capitalism* (London and N.Y., 1915); C. Morazé, tr. P. Wait and B. Ferryan, *The Triumph of the Middle Classes* (London and Cleveland, 1966).

bourgeois hegemony, see under HEGEMONY.

Bourguiba, Habib (Tunisian statesman, *b.* 1902), see under DESTOUR.

Bowers, Fredson Thayer (U.S. bibliographer, *b.* 1905), see under NEW CRITICISM.

Bowlby, John (British psychiatrist, *b.* 1907), see under FAMILY THERAPY.

box girder, see under STRUCTURE.

Bradley, Francis Herbert (British philosopher, 1846–1924), see under BRADLEYAN; NEO-HEGELIANISM.

Bradleyan.
(1) In Shakespearean criticism, adjective used to characterize A. C. Bradley's 'Romantic' tendency (in *Shakespearean Tragedy,* 1904) to treat Shakespeare's characters as if they were real people in real life, thus ignoring stage conventions. The best Shakespearean criticism of the 1930s was formed in reaction against Bradley, taking a cooler and more comprehensive view of the play's ingredients and of conditions in the Elizabethan theatre. Yet Bradley's 'closet' commentary, if sometimes lush, is centrally human and preferable to some later critics' REDUCTION of Shakespeare to symbol, MYTH, and pattern.   D.J.E.
Bibl: L. C. Knights, *How Many Children Had Lady Macbeth?* (Cambridge, 1933).
(2) In PHILOSOPHY, adjective applied to the ideas, style, etc. of the IDEALIST philosopher F. H. Bradley (1846–1924).
                                                A.Q.

Bragg, Sir William Henry (British physicist, 1862–1942), see under MOLECULAR BIOLOGY.

Bragg, Sir William Lawrence (British physicist, 1890–1971), see under CAVENDISH LABORATORY; MOLECULAR BIOLOGY.

Brahm, Otto (German literary critic and theatre director, 1856–1912), see under DEUTSCHES THEATER; FREIE BÜHNE; THÉÂTRE LIBRE.

brain stimulation. In NEUROPSYCHO-LOGY, a technique of direct electrical stimulation of the brain for inducing certain states or responses. It was used initially at the end of the 19th century to evoke motor patterns of a reflex nature to illustrate the organization of the motor cortex. More recently, chronically implanted ELECTRODES have been used on awake, intact animals to produce 'pleasure' (e.g. experiments by J. Olds), alertness (Donald Lindsley), various drive states (Juan Delgado). W. G. Penfield pioneered work on electric stimulation of the human brain, carried out during brain operations on patients under local anaesthetic, and showed that vivid memories could be evoked by the method. J.S.B.

Bibl: W. G. Penfield, *The Excitable Cortex in Conscious Man* (Liverpool and Springfield, Mass., 1958).

brainstorming. An American experiment in group PROBLEM-SOLVING that attempts to elicit creative thinking and new ideas through intensive discussion. The atmosphere of these sessions is non-critical, and FREE ASSOCIATION and 'thinking aloud' are encouraged. H.I..

brainwashing. A proselytizing and interrogation technique that aims at the systematic erosion and reversal of a person's habits or convictions, usually with political motive and by the use of prolonged stress. H.L.

Brando, Marlon (U.S. actor, *b*. 1924), see under METHOD, THE.

Brandt, Willy (German statesman, *b*. 1913), see under ÖSTPOLITIK.

Braque, Georges (French painter, 1882–1963), see under CUBISM; FAUVES; NEUE KÜNSTLERVEREINIGUNG.

Bratby, John (British painter, *b*. 1928), see under KITCHEN SINK DRAMA.

Braudel, Fernand (French historian, *b*. 1902), see under ANNALES SCHOOL.

brave new world. Originally a phrase used by Shakespeare's Miranda in *The Tempest*: 'O brave new world / That has such people in't'. This is ironic, as some of the people she first sees are in fact scoundrels; but it also affirms her own purity of vision. Aldous Huxley's *Brave New World* (1932) tells of a future state where utopian ideals have turned into nightmare dehumanization; and the contemporary use of the phrase alludes to this rather than to Shakespeare. M.S.-S.

Brecht, Bertolt (German poet, dramatist, and theatrical director, 1898–1956), see under BERLINER ENSEMBLE; BRECHTIAN; DEUTSCHES THEATER; EMPATHY; EPIC THEATRE; FORMALISM; GESTUS; LEHRSTÜCK; LIVING THEATRE; NEUE SACHLICHKEIT; SOCIALIST REALISM.

Brechtian. Drama critics' term for anything recalling the work of the German poet, playwright, and theatrical director Bertolt Brecht, a leading proponent of ALIENATION (see especially last paragraph) and the EPIC THEATRE, and artistic director, 1949–56, of the BERLINER ENSEMBLE. His main concern was with clear dialectical exposition, intelligible language, and the concentration of every theatrical means on putting over, with humour and elegance, a plebeian point of view, anarchic, cynical, revolutionary, or reflective. The term is, however, most commonly identified with gray colours, drab realistic costumes, brilliant lighting, slow episodic narration interrupted by projected scene titles, and the direct addressing of the audience by interpolated songs. J.W.

Bibl: J. Willett, *The Theatre of Bertolt Brecht* (3rd ed., London, 1967; N.Y., 1968); F. Ewen, *Bertolt Brecht* (N.Y., 1967; London, 1970).

breeder reactor, see under NUCLEAR REACTOR.

Breitinger, Johann Jakob (Swiss critic, 1701–76), see under AUTOTELIC WRITING.

Brentano, Franz (French philosopher, 1838–1917), see under PHENOMENOLOGY.

Breton, André (French author and editor, 1896–1966), see under BLACK COMEDY; DADA; SURREALISM.

Bretton Woods. A place in Maine, U.S.A.; in 1944 the scene of the final meetings between the Americans, British, and Canadians who set up the *International Monetary Fund* (I.M.F.) and the *International Bank for Reconstruction and Development* (popularly known as the *World Bank*). In Keynes's ironical account, 'it is very simple. The Bank is a fund; and the Fund is a bank'. Those who wish to avoid distinguishing between the twin organizations tend to refer to them and their rules as the Bretton Woods system – though this expression is more often used of the I.M.F. only. By 1973, almost all non-Communist countries belonged to both organizations; of the COMMUNIST bloc, only Yugoslavia and Romania have been willing to supply the national economic and financial data which are a condition of I.M.F. membership; they are also the only Communist-bloc members of the World Bank.

The I.M.F.'s original purpose was to provide a basis of monetary and currency stability for post-war prosperity in the form of growing world trade and expanding national economies. Members were expected to declare fixed rates of exchange which should only be changed in the event of 'fundamental disequilibrium', thus avoiding the pre-war evil of competitive DEVALUATIONS. To help countries deal with temporary BALANCE OF PAYMENTS problems without exchange-rate adjustment, the Fund was empowered to provide short- to medium-term credits to governments. Following the suspension on 15 August 1971 of the dollar's convertibility into gold, the first devaluation of the dollar in December 1971, and subsequent moves to *floating rates* (see under DEVALUATION) by a number of major currencies, the I.M.F.'s role has been much diminished. At the end of 1972 negotiations began for the comprehensive reform of world currency arrangements, as embodied in the Articles of the Fund; and it is generally agreed among major countries that these Articles will have to be amended to provide for a more flexible exchange-rate mechanism, while preserving the concept of cooperative management of the monetary system as a whole. Agreement on such reforms was reached in Jamaica in January 1976; but ratification of the resulting Proposed Second Amendment to the Fund's Articles of Agreement requires an affirmative vote by three-fifths of the number of members, having four-fifths of the voting power.

The *World Bank* was created with European reconstruction in mind, but this role was overtaken by the MARSHALL PLAN, and it became, with its affiliates the International Finance Corporation (I.F.C.) and the International Development Association (I.D.A.), the world's leading international development-lending and aid agency. Voting is weighted by CAPITAL subscription, so that the Bank is effectively controlled by the rich countries. The Bank group acquires its funds mainly by borrowing, but also from its capital and governmental subscriptions to I.D.A. It lends both on near-commercial terms, and at near-zero interest rates to very poor countries. R.H.; P.J.; I.M.D.L.

Bibl: E. S. Mason and R. E. Asher, *The World Bank since Bretton Woods* (Washington, 1973).

Breuer, Joseph (Austrian physician and physiologist, 1842–1925), see under CATHARSIS; PSYCHOANALYSIS.

Breuer, Marcel (Hungarian–U.S. architect, *b*. 1902), see under BAUHAUS.

Brezhnev, Leonid Ilich (Soviet statesman, *b*. 1906), see under BREZHNEV DOCTRINE; FORCED LABOUR.

Brezhnev doctrine. Term applied by Western commentators to the Soviet justification of their action in 1968 in suppressing the Czechoslovak government headed by Joseph Dubček (see PRAGUE) by armed intervention. This was seen in the West as constituting a new principle in the Soviet doctrine of international law. First propounded by Leonid Brezhnev, First Secretary of the Soviet COMMUNIST Party, in a speech to the Fifth Congress of the Polish Communist Party in Warsaw on 12 November 1968, this 'doctrine' asserted the right of the 'SOCIALIST community as a whole' (i.e. the Soviet Union and its allies) to intervene in the territory of any one of the members of the Socialist community whenever 'internal and external forces . . . hostile to socialism try to turn the development' of that country 'towards the restoration of a CAPITALIST regime' and thus threaten 'socialism in that country and the Socialist community as a whole'. Western commentators, and commentators in Communist China, have seen in this a doctrine limiting the full SOVEREIGNTY of states as hitherto recognized by international law, a view indignantly rebutted by Soviet commentators.
D.C.W.

Brianchon, Maurice (French painter, *b*. 1899), see under MAGIC REALISM.

Bridgman, Percy Williams (U.S. physicist, 1882–1961), see under OPERATIONALISM.

Brieux, Eugène (French dramatist, 1858–1932), see under THÉÂTRE LIBRE.

Brik, Osip (Russian editor, *b.* 1888), see under FORMALISM.

brinkmanship. A term coined by Professor T. C. Schelling of Harvard (*The Strategy of Conflict*, 1963), and based on a remark of John Foster Dulles in January 1956 about the art of going 'to the brink' of war. 'Brinkmanship is thus the deliberate creation of a recognizable risk of war, a risk that one does not completely control. It is the tactic of deliberately letting the situation get out of hand, just because its being out of hand may be intolerable to the other party and force his accommodation.' A.F.B.

British Association (for the Advancement of Science). A body formed in 1831 to provide a forum in which scientific research is publicized, and its implications discussed, at annual meetings lasting several days which are held in different cities throughout Britain. M.V.B.

British Commonwealth, see COMMONWEALTH.

Brønsted, Johannes Nicolaus (Danish physical chemist, 1879–1947), see under ACID.

Brontë, Charlotte (British novelist, 1816–55), see under FEMINISM.

Brook, Peter (British theatre producer, *b.* 1925), see under THEATRE LABORATORY; THEATRE OF CRUELTY.

Brooke, Rupert (British poet, 1887–1915), see under POETRY BOOKSHOP.

Brooke-Rose, Christine (British novelist, *b.*1923), see under NEW NOVEL.

Brooks, Cleanth (U.S. literary critic, *b.* 1906), see under COMMUNICATION, HERESY OF; NEW CRITICISM.

Brophy, John (British author, 1899–1965), see under PLR.

Brown, Kenneth (U.S. dramatist, *b.*1936), see under LIVING THEATRE.

Brownian motion. The ceaseless irregular motion of dust PARTICLES which is observed in liquids and gases (and is an example of a STOCHASTIC PROCESS). It provided the earliest evidence for the random heat motion of the underlying MOLECULES, which occurs on a much finer scale. M.V.B.

Brücke, die ('the Bridge'). Group of young painters active in Dresden, 1905–11, and Berlin, 1911–13. Influenced by the FAUVES and Edvard Munch, they were led by Erich Heckel, E. L. Kirchner, and Karl Schmidt-Rottluff, and included at various times Max Pechstein, Emil Nolde, and Otto Müller. They formed the nucleus of EXPRESSIONISM in the visual arts, giving it its dominant character of modified CUBIST distortion and great graphic virtuosity, particularly in the woodcut medium. J.W.

Bruckner, Anton (Austrian composer, 1824–96), see under ROMANTICISM.

bruitisme. The art of noise, as propounded in a manifesto of 1913 by Luigi Russolo, one of FUTURISM's two principal musicians, and featured by DADA. J.W.

Bruner, Jerome Seymour (U.S. psychologist, *b.* 1915), see under EDUCATIONAL PSYCHOLOGY.

Brunschvicg, Léon (French philosopher, 1869–1944), see under NEO-HEGELIANISM.

Brussels Treaty. Signed on 17 March 1948 by representatives of Britain, France, Belgium, the Netherlands, and Luxembourg, the Brussels Treaty set up a military alliance to resist armed attack on Western Europe, with a military command under British generalship. The initial impetus was provided by the Soviet-supported ejection of the Beneš-Masaryk government in Czechoslovakia (February 1948; see PRAGUE), and the Brussels Treaty was a first step, taken on British initiative, towards the formation of NATO. In the crisis created by the failure of the French National Assembly to ratify the treaties setting up EDC the treaty was used to provide a means for the admission of West Germany to NATO by the formation of WEU. D.C.W.

BRUT

brut, see under ART BRUT; CONCRETE.

brutalism. A movement in architecture that asserted the primacy of architectural elements – space, STRUCTURE, and materials displayed in their untrammelled form – against the visual enfeeblement of the modern movement which had occurred in the late 1940s. It inched main-stream modern from the abstract to the expressive.

Le Corbusier's Unité d'Habitation in Marseilles (1948–54), which turned the use of bare concrete patterned by its rough timber SHUTTERING into a virtuoso performance, showed the potentialities of the vivid expression of materials suggested by economic necessity. His later Maisons Jaoul at Neuilly (1956) extended the vocabulary and provided an idiom capable of imitation. The first building to be labelled 'new brutalist' was the school at Hunstanton, England, by Peter and Alison Smithson (1949). This had an exposed steel frame, unplastered brickwork, exposed floor beams and service runs, and was designed with an austerity derived from Mies van der Rohe. See also CONCRETE.   M.BR.

Bibl: R. Banham, *The New Brutalism; Ethic or Aesthetic?* (London and N.Y., 1966).

Brzezinski, Zbigniew (Polish-U.S. author, *b.* 1928), see under POST-INDUSTRIAL SOCIETY.

bubble chamber. A device invented by Glaser in 1952 and used to study NUCLEAR REACTIONS and ELEMENTARY PARTICLES. It is based on the fact that fast charged particles leave a record of their paths, in the form of a trail of bubbles, centred on IONS, when they traverse a liquid kept just above its boiling-point. See also CLOUD CHAMBER.   M.V.B.

Buber, Martin (Austrian theologian, 1878–1965), see under JUDAISM.

Bubnovy Valet, see KNAVE OF DIAMONDS.

Buchan, Alastair (British political writer, 1918–76), see under STRATEGIC STUDIES.

Buddhism. The RELIGION, covering much of Asia, which venerates Gautama the Buddha (or 'Enlightened'), who taught in

India during the 5th century B.C. Its goal is 'Nirvana' or liberation from 'becoming' things or selves; this has usually been conceived as liberation from an endless cycle of reincarnations or rebirths in different bodies. Its self-discipline is aimed at achieving detachment and an inward peace. It emphasizes compassion, but mainly in the sense of spreading such peace. It avoids the intellectualism of Christian THEOLOGY, but disagreements have grown between the *Theravada* (Little Vehicle) in Ceylon, Burma, Thailand, etc., and the *Mahayana* (Great Vehicle) in Japan, Korea, China, Tibet, and Nepal, which is more elaborately developed (and closer to Christianity, although very little influenced by it). The difference between these two types of Buddhism can amount, in Western terms, to the difference between AGNOSTICISM or PANTHEISM and THEISM based on petitionary prayer. But the attractiveness of Buddhism in the 20th century springs from the hope that its methods of meditation may fill the void left both by materialism and by the Churches. ZEN is specially respected. There is also much interest in Buddhist art. Some Westerners have become Buddhists, but many more have admired, and even envied, Buddhism as a way of life. See also TANTRA.   D.L.E.

Bibl: T. C. Humphreys, *Buddhism* (Harmondsworth, 1951).

buffer. In CHEMISTRY, a solution capable of maintaining a nearly constant hydrogen ION concentration. Normally the *pH* (*q.v.*) of a solution is very sensitive to the addition of even small amounts of strong ACID or BASE. This sensitivity can be greatly diminished in the presence of a weak acid and its anion (see ION) in comparable amounts, because the anion accepts added hydrogen ions while hydroxyl ions combine with the hydrogen atoms of the weak acid. Physiological systems are often buffered, and in blood the serum protein (see SERUM; PROTEIN) which contains both acidic and basic groups acts as a buffering agent.   B.F.

buffer state. In political geography, a small independent state lying between two or more larger and potentially hostile states and thus reducing the likelihood of border friction between them. Belgium might be thought to have served as a buf-

80

fer state in respect of France and Germany.   P.H.

bugging. A slang word for the placing of concealed microphones for the purpose of listening to or recording secret or private discussions. Modern TECHNOLOGY has made it possible to use extremely small detectors, which can be stuck underneath a table, concealed in a vase of flowers, etc., and to pick up signals from them at a sufficient distance for the receiver to remain undetected. This technique has facilitated both political and industrial espionage, and, in the case of surveillance by the police or private detective agencies, has raised the issue of whether privacy is or is not a basic human right.   E.R.L.

Bukharin, Nikolay Ivanovich (Russian revolutionary and statesman, 1888–1938), see under COMINTERN; MOSCOW TRIALS; NEP; PRAVDA; SOCIALIST REALISM.

Bullins, Ed (U.S. dramatist, b. 1935), see under BLACK THEATRE.

Bullock Report on Industrial Democracy, see under PARTICIPATION.

Bultmann, Rudolf (German theologian, b. 1884), see under DEMYTHOLOGIZE; HERMENEUTICS.

Buñuel, Luis (Spanish film director, b. 1900), see under SURREALISM.

Buonarotti, Philippe (Italian-French revolutionary, 1761–1837), see under JACOBINISM; SOCIALISM.

Bureau International de Surréalisme Révolutionnaire, see under COBRA.

bureaucracy. 'Power, influence of the heads and staff of government bureaux' (definition of *bureaucratie* in the Dictionary of the French Academy, 1789 supplement). The modern theory of bureaucracy derives largely from the German sociologist Max Weber, who saw it as the formal codification of the idea of rational organization. A bureaucracy is characterized by legal rules, a salaried administrative staff, the specialization of function the authority of the (non-hereditary) office, not the person, and the keeping of written records and documents. For Weber, the rational bureaucracy was the major element in the rationalization of the modern world.

Yet from the start popular writers have seen bureaucracy as an irrational force, dominating the lives of people, while political theorists have seen it as an independent force tending to swallow all of society in its maw. Balzac popularized the word in his 1836 novel, *Les Employés*, calling bureaucracy 'the giant power wielded by pigmies . . . a government as fussy and meddlesome . . . as a small shopkeeper's wife'. Dickens, in *Little Dorrit* (1857), summarized 'the Whole Science of Government' in his representation of the bureaucracy as 'the Circumlocution Office'. John Stuart Mill, in *On Liberty* (1859) and *Considerations on Representative Government* (1861) contrasted bureaucracy with DEMOCRACY and saw the former as a threat to representative government and to liberty. And Gaetano Mosca, in *The Ruling Class* (English edition, 1939), described the modern state as essentially a bureaucratic state ruled, inevitably, by a minority.

In contemporary theory, interest in bureaucracy focuses on two aspects. Sociological theorists tend to see bureaucracy as one modal type of organization, wherein the formal dimensions of rule and administration are paramount. Political writers have concentrated on the question whether the bureaucracy, in modern society, becomes a 'new CLASS' which takes over political rule – as, according to Milovan Djilas, has happened in the U.S.S.R. Indeed, though Marx paid little attention to this aspect of the question, it has been the central issue regarding the characterization of Soviet society. Thus Trotsky regarded bureaucracy as indicating the betrayal of the REVOLUTIONARY ideals by a new class; while SOCIALIST writers have characterized the U.S.S.R. as a new form of 'bureaucratic COLLECTIVISM'.   D.B.

Bibl: M. Weber, *Economy and Society* (N.Y., 1968), vol. 3; M. Albrow, *Bureaucracy* (London and N.Y., 1970).

Burgess, Ernest Watson (U.S. sociologist, 1886–1966), see under CHICAGO SCHOOL.

Burke, Kenneth (U.S. philosopher, critic, and poet, b. 1897), see under NEW CRITICISM.

Burliuk, David (Russian painter, 1882–1967), see under KNAVE OF DIAMONDS.

Burnet, Sir **Macfarlane** (Australian medical scientist, *b*.1899), see under VIROLOGY.

Burnham, James (U.S. political philosopher, *b*.1905), see under MANAGERIAL REVOLUTION.

Burroughs, William R. (U.S. novelist, *b*.1914), see under ALEATORY; BEAT; COLLAGE.

Burt, Sir **Cyril** (British psychologist, 1883–1971), see under MENTAL RETARDATION; PSYCHOMETRICS.

business cycles. Fluctuations in the level of general economic activity, where activity is defined chiefly with reference to the degree of utilization of productive resources; that is to say, there is more UNEMPLOYMENT or underemployment of labour and CAPITAL equipment in the *slump* (see DEPRESSION) than in the *boom*. In the context of ECONOMIC GROWTH a cyclical *recession* (downswing) may be manifested in a retardation in the rate of growth of NATIONAL INCOME, rather than in an actual contraction. Fluctuations lasting less than a year or more than about twelve years are excluded from the definition. The term (American in origin, now gradually replacing the English TRADE CYCLE) is generally used in a sense which implies that there exists some regular tendency to cycles, distinct from purely random or seasonal disturbances. Such a tendency has in fact been manifested in most countries since they became INDUSTRIALIZED or were brought into contact with industrial countries. The duration of cycles has varied considerably, however – from roughly three to twelve years – and so has their severity. There is controversy about the relative importance of real factors, especially capital investment, and of monetary factors in causing cycles. But it is generally agreed that a major element is the tendency of economic systems to *overshoot* in response to disturbances rather than adjust smoothly to EQUILIBRIUM. Since World War II deliberate government policies, generally dictated by BALANCE OF PAYMENTS considerations, have been prominent in causing or amplifying cycles in a number of countries, notably Britain. Such cycles are sometimes called STOP-GO cycles, to distinguish them from cycles that are independent of government policies or contrary to their designs.   R.C.O.M.

Bibl: M. Bronfenbrenner (ed.), *Is the Business Cycle Obsolete?* (N.Y., 1969).

business game. A MANAGEMENT training exercise in which aspects of a business, or of a competing market of businesses, are simulated (see SIMULATION), frequently with COMPUTER assistance. Teams of students make, according to the variables in the particular MODEL, a series of managerial decisions which are computed to provide the FEEDBACK results for the next cycle of the exercise.   R.I.T.

Busoni, Ferruccio (Italian composer, 1886–1924), see under MICROTONE.

bussing. American term for the transfer of children by bus from their own neighbourhood to school in another. In the U.S.A. bussing is part of the problem of DESEGREGATION and reducing the disadvantages of ghetto life. The educational issue of SEGREGATION goes back to a Supreme Court ruling of 1954, and since 1969 legislation has required such facilities to be available. Some cities, and not only in the South, have been sluggish in their provision; and determined attempts to repeal bussing legislation, or at least cause it to lapse, are being made by those who argue that the dispersal of pupils militates against the NEIGHBOURHOOD SCHOOL (an institution of importance in the U.S.A.), and that the national groupings do not in fact mix any better in their new schools, but stay with their ethnic peers. In 1975 there were severe riots in some areas over the bussing issue.   W.A.C.S.

Butler, Joseph (British philosopher, 1692–1752), see under INTUITIONISM.

Butler, Richard Austin, Baron (British politician, *b*.1902), see under CONSENSUS POLITICS.

Butor, Michel (French novelist, *b*.1926), see under ALEATORY; NEW NOVEL.

Butskellism, see under CONSENSUS POLITICS.

Butterfield, Sir **Herbert** (British historian, *b*.1900), see under WHIG INTERPRETATION OF HISTORY.

C

Cabet, Étienne (French socialist leader, 1788–1856), see under COMMUNE; PROLETARIAT; UTOPIAN IDEAL.

CAD, see COMPUTER-AIDED DESIGN.

Cage, John (U.S. composer, *b.* 1912), see under FLUXUS; HAPPENINGS; PREPARED PIANO.

Cahiers du Cinéma, see under NEW WAVE.

calcification. In GEOLOGY, the replacement of organic or inorganic material in rocks by the calcium minerals calcite and dolomite. Grains of quartz in a sandstone can be completely replaced by calcite. Fossil plant debris can be preserved by the complete calcification of the plant tissue so that the original cellular structure is retained in a hard fossil plant. Calcification in the latter example must certainly have occurred soon after deposition.   J.L.M.L.

calculus. Any system of rules for symbolic manipulations, as in LOGICAL CALCULUS and its subdivisions PREDICATE CALCULUS and PROPOSITIONAL CALCULUS. But usually, unless qualified, the term refers to the *infinitesimal calculus.* This comprises the *differential calculus,* which is concerned with calculating the DERIVATIVES (rates of change) of FUNCTIONS, and the *integral calculus,* which is concerned with INTEGRATION. The *fundamental theorem of the calculus* asserts that these are inverse operations. Calculus is concerned with the necessary manipulative rules and their application to more or less specific instances. The general theory of the processes and the investigation of the exact conditions under which the rules may be correctly applied are dignified by the title of (mathematical) ANALYSIS. For the *calculus of finite differences* see NUMERICAL ANALYSIS.   R.G.
  Bibl: L. Hogben, *Mathematics for the Million* (4th ed., London, 1967; N.Y., 1968).

calculus of finite differences, see under NUMERICAL ANALYSIS.

Calder, Alexander (U.S. sculptor, 1898–1976), see under KINETIC ART; STABILE.

Calder, Nigel (British science writer, *b.* 1931), see under TECHNOPOLIS.

Calley, Lieutenant **William** (U.S. army officer, *b.* 1943), see under MY LAI.

calligramme. A poem written, and printed, in a specific shape. The modern revival of this age-old device was pioneered under the influence of CUBISM by Guillaume Apollinaire, a volume of whose *Calligrammes* appeared in 1918. In their simplest and most light-hearted form these consist of words describing rain, or a motor-car, grouped into the shape of rain, or a motor-car. At their most difficult they seek, as a critic explained, to oblige the reader to understand 'synthetico-ideologically' instead of 'analytico-discursively'. They push experimentation as far as Apollinaire ever pushed it, and influenced CONCRETE POETRY.   M.S.-S.

calorie. A unit of heat. One calorie will raise the temperature of one gram of water by one degree centigrade. In terms of ENERGY, 857,000 calories = 1 kilowatt-hour. For nutritional and dietary purposes the 'large calorie' (also written kcalorie or Calorie), equal to 1,000 ordinary calories, is the unit commonly employed to quantify energy intake. M.V.B.

Calvinism. The Christian tradition founded by John Calvin (1509–64) in Geneva, and flourishing specially in Scotland and in New England. It has developed PROTESTANTISM by rejecting every doctrine not found in the Bible, and by finding in the Bible its own doctrines, notably the 'predestination' by God of the 'elect' to heaven and of the rest to hell. The tradition is still creative theologically (see BARTHIAN). A strict and sometimes intolerant morality is associated (see PROTESTANT ETHIC), as is the PRESBYTERIAN form of church government.　D.L.E.

Bibl: J. T. McNeill, *The History and Character of Calvinism* (London and N.Y., 1967).

Calvo, Carlos (Argentinian diplomat and jurist, 1824–1906), see under NON-INTERVENTION.

Camden Town Group. A society of artists founded in 1911; in 1913 it merged with the LONDON GROUP. Of the sixteen members those who may best be described as 'Camden Town' (a district of north London) were: Spencer Gore (President), Harold Gilman, Robert Bevan, Malcolm Drummond, and William Ratcliffe, painters who were deeply affected by the opposing influences of Walter Sickert and the POST-IMPRESSIONISTS.　Q.B.

Cameron, Sir **David Young** (British painter, 1865–1945), see under GLASGOW SCHOOL.

Camoin, Charles (French painter, 1879–1965), see under FAUVES.

Campaign for Nuclear Disarmament, see CND.

Campbell, Reginald John (British theologian, 1867–1956), see under NEW THEOLOGY.

Campendonk, Heinrich (German painter, 1889–1957), see under BLAUE REITER.

Camus, Albert (French author, 1913–60), see under HORIZON; THEATRE OF THE ABSURD.

cancer. A new growth in any TISSUE or organ that behaves as if it had escaped the surveillance of the growth-controlling processes that operate in the other tissues of the body. Cancers are described as more or less malignant in proportion as they are more or less rapidly growing and invasive. Cancer CELLS may escape from their site of origin and set up daughter colonies (*metastases*) in normal tissues elsewhere. Cancers are crudely subdivided into tumours of epithelial tissues (*carcinomas*) and tumours of cells belonging to the connective tissue and bony families (*sarcomas*).

Some industrial chemicals and food additives are known to be cancer-producing (*oncogenic*). Public-health authorities are acutely aware of these dangers, and the use of such chemicals is under very close surveillance. Many causes of cancer are known – e.g. the polycyclic hydrocarbons that are the active ingredients of coal tar, or viruses (see VIROLOGY) such as the Rous virus in chicks, polyoma virus, and Bittner's milk factor in mice. No human tumour has yet been conclusively shown to be viral in origin, though there is a strong and growing presumption that some at least are so, perhaps particularly the leukaemias (cancers of the white blood corpuscles).

The branch of medical science concerned with cancer is known as ONCOLOGY. Cancer research is devoted to the earliest possible diagnosis of malignant changes, to analysing ever more deeply the properties of the malignant cell itself and to the clinical trial of the theoretically or empirically justifiable curative procedures, notably the use of *anti-proliferative* drugs (drugs that suppress cell division, e.g. nitrogen mustards) in the leukaemias, the use of x-irradiation, and, wherever possible, the intensification of the immunological response (see IMMUNITY) which represents the body's natural defence. In addition, hormone-dependent tumours may sometimes be controlled by the artificial administration or deprivation of hormones (see ENDOCRINOLOGY). Surgery and x-irradiation nevertheless remain the bulwarks of cancer treatment throughout the world.　P.M.

Candela, Felix (Spanish architect, *b.* 1910), see under STRUCTURE.

Canova, Antonio (Italian sculptor, 1757–1822), see under NEO-CLASSICISM.

cantilever. A structural device possible with materials strong both in tension and compression which produces horizontal extensions unsupported on their forward edge. When used in either steel or reinforced concrete STRUCTURES, the cantilever has been able to suggest a series of floating planes with only non-structural, usually glass, infill between them. It was greatly used and praised by Frank Lloyd

Wright, and the characteristic view of Falling Water, the house at Bear Run, Pennsylvania (1936), is largely due to its employment. So is the corner view of the Fagus factory (Gropius and Hannes Meyer, 1910), which created the much-imitated corner glazed window apparently dissolving the solidity of the building enclosure.   M.BR.

Cantor,   Georg   (Russian-German mathematician, 1845–1918), see under AXIOMATIC METHOD; CONTINUUM; INFINITE; NUMBER; SET THEORY.

CAP. Acronym for the Common Agricultural Policy of the European Economic Community (see EEC). The theoretical aims of the policy are to increase agricultural productivity in the Community, stabilize agricultural commodity prices, and ensure that enough food is available to consumers at reasonable prices. The policy uses two principal methods to achieve these aims, 'support buying' and the levy system. 'Support buying' involves purchasing and removing from the Community market produce such as cereals, beef, sugar, and milk products when prices fall, and thus stabilizing the prices. The levy system is used to raise the prices of imported commodities to Community level if world prices are lower than those of the Community. It is also used as a tax to discourage potential Community exporters who might be attracted by the world market when world prices are higher than those prevailing in the Community. These methods have been attacked for keeping prices artificially high and for creating 'food mountains' of produce removed from the market.

For the purposes of the policy, the 'green pound' is used as an internal EEC currency exchange rate.   P.B.M.

Čapek,   Karel   (Czech   author, 1890–1938), see under ROBOT.

capital. Real or financial assets possessing a money value. The assets may be in the hands of producers (factories, machines, etc.) or consumers (houses, etc.) or belong to the community (public buildings, parks, libraries, etc.). *Real capital* (or *capital goods*) is a physical stock of productive assets; *money capital* represents the money value of assets including MONEY in

hand, STOCK EXCHANGE securities, titles to wealth, and expressions of debt. Capital may be valued at historic cost in terms of past expenditures on productive assets or at current market value in terms of the present (discounted) value of the income which it is expected to yield. Since bygones in economics are for ever bygones the significant valuation for most purposes is the second. The capital of a business is usually a combination of past expenditures at various dates and periodic adjustments reflecting the revaluation of some of the assets.   A.C.

capital gains tax. A tax specifically imposed on gains from the realization or, in certain cases, the deemed realization of CAPITAL assets. In the U.K., tax law traditionally made a clear distinction between the fruit of the tree (income), which was taxable, and the tree itself (capital), which was not. In 1962 a tax was introduced on short-term gains at full personal tax rates. Since 1965 long-term gains have also been taxed, though at a reduced rate, and in 1971 the separate short-term tax was abolished. Some argue that capital gains, especially those resulting merely from INFLATION, should not be taxed at all, whereas others suggest that capital gains ought not to be given privileged treatment compared with other forms of receipt. Taxing gains at reduced rates may reflect a practical compromise rather than a theoretically elegant solution.   J.F.C.

capitalism. In MARXIST usage, a word denoting a historical stage and connoting a VALUE-JUDGEMENT. As historical description, Marxists mean by capitalism that set of arrangements in which one CLASS, the capitalists or BOURGEOISIE, owns the factories and other tools of production, while a second class, the workers or PROLETARIANS, possesses only its labour power – its capacity to work. As value-judgement, they mean a set of transitional arrangements (terminating in SOCIALISM) which allows capitalists to exploit workers.

Non-Marxist   economists   define capitalism in terms of resource use and control, without reference to exploitation. Exploitation occurs only when monopolistic organization results in excessive prices or in wage payment below *marginal revenue product* (i.e. the sales value of the

85

additional product contributed by one more hour of labour). Most generally a capitalist society is one in which most of the instruments of production as well as objects of consumption are privately controlled. Sale occurs for profit in markets (see MARKET ECONOMY), which, while variously organized, are free in the sense that, subject to the constraints of law, entrepreneurs are at liberty to enter or depart, to expand or contract, and purchasers to buy or not to buy. Moreover, the profits from these transactions inhere, in law (and subject always to the tax demands of the State), in the owners of the enterprise. As an IDEOLOGY, capitalism contains a doctrine of social justice, an implicit assertion that inequalities of income and wealth measure, however roughly, the economic contributions of the men and women who embark their energies and resources in the productive process.

Capitalism is an exceedingly broad and somewhat vague term, covering societies as variously organized as Sweden, France, Japan, Britain, and the U.S.A., in each of which the mixture of public and private enterprise, the legal rules governing the pursuit of profit, the approved market structure, the permitted accumulation of income and wealth, differs significantly from all the others. Broadly speaking, capitalist societies are distinguished from socialist ones by the ideological preference of the former for private property and of the latter for communal ownership. Even though in practice all advanced societies have found it necessary to accept a substantial degree of state intervention, socialist societies celebrate, and capitalist ones deplore, the exigencies which have enlarged the role of the State.   R.L.

Bibl: J. A. Schumpeter, *Capitalism, Socialism and Democracy* (N.Y., 3rd ed., 1962; London, 4th · ed., 1965); J. K. Galbraith, *The New Industrial State* London and N.Y., 1967; Boston, rev. ed., 1971).

capitulationism, see under DEVIATION-ISM.

Capote, Truman (U.S. novelist, *b.* 1924), see under DOCUMENTARY.

Capuana, Luigi (Italian novelist and critic, 1839–1915), see under VERISM.

carbohydrates. An important class of naturally occurring carbon compounds, which includes cellulose and the various starches and sugars. Carbohydrates are formed in green plants by PHOTOSYN-THESIS.   B.F.

carbon cycle. In PHYSICS (for its meaning in BIOLOGY see under LIFE CYCLE), a sequence of NUCLEAR REACTIONS thought to occur inside stars, in which a mass of hydrogen NUCLEI at extremely high temperatures is converted into a smaller mass of helium nuclei in the presence of carbon nuclei; the resulting energy leaves the star as RADIATION which is observed by us as starlight or sunshine. See also BINDING ENERGY; MASS-ENERGY EQUA-TION.   M.V.B.

carbon dating, see RADIOCARBON DAT-ING.

carbon fibre. Immensely strong threads of pure graphite which may be incorporated into other materials (e.g. metals) to reinforce their strength.   M.V.B.

carcinogen (a preferable if less familiar term is *oncogen*). A substance or procedure that causes the formation of a tumour (see CANCER). Oncogenic substances and treatments include coal tar derivatives, ionizing RADIATIONS and some viruses (see VIROLOGY) or virus-like particles.   P.M.

carcinomas, see under CANCER.

cardinal (number). This measures the size of a SET and applies to both finite and INFINITE sets. Two sets are *similar,* or *equinumerous,* if it is possible to pair off each member of either set with exactly one member of the other set. This gives an EQUIVALENCE RELATION between sets; the cardinal of a set is defined as the corresponding abstract concept. The smallest infinite cardinal is the cardinal of the set $\{0, 1, 2, \ldots\}$ and is called *aleph zero.* It is smaller than the cardinal of the CON-TINUUM. Infinite cardinals are not now usually counted as NUMBERS.   R.G.

cargo cults. A variety of MILLEN-ARIANISM found in New Guinea. Its adherents believe that the valued material goods of Western civilization (the 'cargo')

ARTOGRAPHY

are about to be delivered by miraculous means, arriving with the spirits of the dead and ushering in the millennium. The cargo is clearly symbolic of a desired change in the social position of those who await it, and the cults are concerned with POWER and STATUS, not merely with the magical acquisition of material things. The term has also been applied more loosely to a number of anti-Western nativistic movements in the Melanesian region. M.F.

Bibl: K. Burridge, *New Heaven, New Earth: a Study of Millenarian Activities* (Oxford, 1969).

Carnap, Rudolf (German-U.S. philosopher, 1891–1970), see under BEHAVIOURISM; CONFIRMATION; CONNOTATION AND DENOTATION; LOGICAL EMPIRICISM; LOGICAL POSITIVISM; LOGICAL SYNTAX; PHYSICALISM; SEMANTICS; VIENNA CIRCLE.

Carné, Marcel (French film director, *b.* 1909), see under NEO-REALISM.

Carnot cycle. In THERMODYNAMICS, a particular sequence of operations involving the transfer of ENERGY to and from a system. At the end of the cycle the system has returned to its original state. The Carnot cycle is of theoretical importance, since no other cycle can convert heat into work more efficiently. Petrol and diesel engines employ cycles closely related to Carnot's. M.V.B.

Carrà, Carlo (Italian painter, 1881–1966), see under COLLAGE; METAPHYSICAL PAINTING; NEO-CLASSICISM.

Carrere, Moreno Emilio (Spanish novelist, 1881–1947), see under TREMENDISMO.

cartel. A union of sellers formed with the aim of raising the price (or other conditions of sale), and the returns to its own members, to a higher level than would prevail in a free market. To succeed, a cartel needs to control production or sales, which it does most frequently by allocating quotas to members. Without such controls, a mere price-fixing arrangement will attract new entrants who, if allowed a 'free ride', will lower the returns to all existing sellers and perhaps undermine the price structure altogether. For this reason most cartels tend eventually to decay unless bolstered by government support.

Cartels are normally regarded by economists as more harmful than the large single-firm MONOPOLY of equal restrictive effect. For, while in the latter case there may be ECONOMIES OF SCALE to offset the price-raising effect, there is no such advantage in the case of cartels, which indeed are often formed expressly to save the weaker units from destruction or damage. They are normally a product of either great weakness or great strength (real or imagined). They flourished in the interwar DEPRESSION, and attempts to organize a cartel were made by the oil-producing states in the early 1970s. Cartel-like activities can take subtle forms, e.g. unnecessarily severe entry qualifications, or limitations on the number of trainees, by highly respectable professional bodies. S.BR.

Cartel. An informal but influential alliance of the four leading independent Paris theatre directors between 1926 and World War II; known for its fresh approach to the classics, its support of such moderns as Pirandello, Chekhov, and Giraudoux, and its dislike of NATIONALISM and commercialism. It was formed to carry on the ideas of Jacques Copeau, director of the Vieux-Colombier 1913–24, and consisted of Charles Dullin (Théâtre de l'Atelier), Louis Jouvet (Comédie des Champs-Elysées, later the Athénée), Gaston Baty (Chimère and Théâtre de Montparnasse), and Georges Pitoeff (no fixed theatre). J.W.

Cartesian coordinates, see under CO-ORDINATE.

cartography. The science and art of map-making, as distinguished from the collection of material to be mapped (e.g. through survey or census-taking). The relationship of the map to the earth's surface through scale reduction was originally developed in ancient Greece though the earliest maps date back over 4,000 years. Cartography in the modern period has been strongly influenced by evolving methods of information collection (e.g. through AIR PHOTOGRAPHY and SATELLITE sensors), by changed data processing methods (e.g. COMPUTER analysis; and see

CASCADE DIFFUSION

DATA ANALYSIS), and by developments in the printing and reproduction of maps.

P.H.

Bibl: A. H. Robinson and R. D. Sale, *Elements of Cartography* (N.Y., 3rd ed., 1969).

cascade diffusion, see under DIFFUSION.

case grammar. An approach to linguistic analysis which sees the basic structure of sentences as consisting of a verb plus one or more noun phrases, which relate to it in defined ways. The syntactic MEANING RELATIONS are called *cases* (a term covering more than in TRADITIONAL GRAMMAR, where it was restricted to describing certain systems of word-endings). For example, in the sentence *John opened the door with the key, John* is 'agentive' case, *the door* 'objective', and *with the key* 'instrumental'. This approach, first formulated by Charles Fillmore in 1968, has since developed variant forms, and has exercised considerable influence in contemporary LINGUISTICS.

D.C.

Bibl: C. J. Fillmore, 'The Case for Case', in E. Bach and R. T. Harns, eds., *Universals in Linguistic Theory* (London and N.Y., 1968), pp. 1–90.

Casella, Alfredo (Italian composer and pianist, 1883–1947), see under NEO-CLASSICISM.

cash-flow, see under FUNDS-FLOW.

Casorati, Felice (Italian painter, 1883 or 1886 to 1963), see under MAGIC REALISM.

Cassandre, Adolphe (French graphic artist, stage designer, and painter, 1901–68), see under SURREALISM.

cassette, see under MAGNETIC TAPE.

Cassirer, Ernst (German-born philosopher, 1874–1945), see under NEO-KANTIANISM.

Castagnary, Jules Antoine (French art critic, 1830–88), see under NATURALISM.

caste. The name (Portuguese *casta*, RACE) for the traditional hierarchical divisions of Hindu society: (1) a hierarchy of purity, the fourfold *varna* division Brahmin-

Kshatriya-Vaisya-Sudra (priests-warriors/rulers-merchants-servants) which is assumed to embrace the whole of society except the 'scheduled castes'; and (2) the numerous *jati*, local ENDOGAMOUS groups arranged hierarchically, which compose the society of any area of the country. Beyond Hindu society caste is to be found in other societies directly influenced by Hindu culture (e.g. Sri Lanka, Bali, and among Muslims in the Indian subcontinent). The term has been extended, much more doubtfully, to such racially stratified societies as South Africa. With considerably less justification, such groups as civil servants or army officers are called castes; castes exist only as part of a system of castes. The recent vogue of the PLURAL SOCIETY has tended to push caste, in its wider sense, into the shade. See also SOCIAL STRATIFICATION.

M.F.

Bibl: O. C. Cox, *Caste, Class and Race* (N.Y., 1959); L. Dumont, tr. M. Sainsbury, *Homo Hierarchicus* (London and Chicago, 1970).

castration anxiety. In psychoanalytic theory (see PSYCHOANALYSIS), the allegedly universal fear of castration felt by boys at a certain stage of their PSYCHOSEXUAL DEVELOPMENT; its origin in the OEDIPUS COMPLEX lies in fear of retaliation by the father for the child's feelings of sexuality towards the mother and of hostility towards the competing father. Girls were also said to suffer castration anxiety originating in the ELECTRA COMPLEX; but this view has been largely abandoned.

J.S.B.

Castro, Fidel (Cuban statesman, *b*. 1927), see under BAY OF PIGS; CASTROISM; CUBA.

Castroism. A mixture of Latin American REVOLUTIONARY tradition and Communist (see COMMUNISM) IDEOLOGY created by Fidel Castro, who seized power in CUBA in 1959. The original movement, dating from 1953, did not possess any clear-cut ideology or theory but simply aimed to overthrow the corrupt rule of General Batista. The fusion of the caudillo-type GUERRILLA movement with Communism came only in 1961, when Castro decided to embrace Communism and legitimize his power in terms of MARXIST-LENINIST ideology. But Castro retained many features which gave a specific flavour to Castroism. It has remained strongly attached in Cuba to his personal CHARISMA, rather than to the impersonal mystique of the Party, and its discipline is still based on the principle of *jefatura* (personal leadership), rather than on that of DEMOCRATIC CENTRALISM.

Castroism is not a deviation from LENINISM, like MAOISM or TITOISM, but an outside growth, which joined the international Communist movement with the aspiration of providing a specific Cuban model for the revolutionary movements in Latin America. Instead of waiting for MARXIST 'objective' or Leninist 'subjective' conditions for the revolution to mature, it proposed to create them by starting guerrilla movements, which would develop from insurrectional focal points (*foci*) in the countryside and eventually conquer the whole Latin American continent. Both Castro and Che Guevara (1928–67) dispensed with Marxist and Leninist ideas on class-determined stages of revolution. As declassé scions of the middle classes, they envisaged the revolution as a protracted guerrilla struggle, bent politically on exploiting social grievances (particularly among the peasantry) and anti-*Yanqui* feelings (particularly among the intelligentsia; see INTELLECTUALS) in Latin America.

The failure of Che Guevara's Bolivian guerrilla campaign; the growing ineffectiveness of the Latin American Solidarity Organization (O.L.A.S.) and of the Afro-Asian-Latin-American Solidarity Organization (A.A.L.A.S.O.), the two organizations promoted by Cuba since the 1966 Tri-Continental Conference in Havana; the increasing economic and political dependence of Castro on the Soviet Union – all these elements diminished the general appeal of Castroism. But its emphasis on the armed struggle continues to exercise influence on the Latin American continent, particularly on the surviving extremist movements which still take their inspiration from the ideas of Che Guevara and from the second Havana Declaration of February 1962, in which Castro called for revolutionary guerrilla wars against the Latin American governments. L.L.

Bibl: B. Goldenberg, *The Cuban Revolution and Latin America* (London, 1962); T. Draper, *Castroism, Theory and Practice* (N.Y., 1965).

CAT (College of Advanced Technology), see CATS.

catabolism, see under METABOLISM.

catalysis. An alteration, usually an increase, in the rate of a CHEMICAL REACTION. The substance causing this increase is a *catalyst*. Chemical SPECIES usually require a certain amount of extra energy, the ACTIVATION ENERGY, before they react. Normally this energy is provided internally by the collision of ATOMS or MOLECULES, with the required excess ENERGY, but the number of such collisions may be small, and the rate of reaction slow. A *heterogeneous* catalyst speeds up the reactions by providing a surface on which the chemical reaction can proceed with lower activation energy. A *homogeneous* catalyst operates in the same phase and accelerates the reaction by participating in reaction intermediates. Catalysts play an important role in many industrial processes; the most effective are ENZYMES, which facilitate physiologically important reactions. B.F.

catalytic war, see under WAR.

catastrophe theory, see under TOPOLOGY.

categorical imperative. The supreme principle of morality, according to Kant, by which all such specific moral principles as 'Do not lie' and 'Do not commit suicide' are to be tested. His basic formulation of it is: So act that the maxim of your action can be willed without contradiction as a universal law. Another, loosely connected, formulation enjoins us to treat people always as ends and never merely as means. In everyday terms Kant tells us to ask of any projected action: what would happen if everyone acted like this? A.Q.

Bibl: S. Korner, *Kant* (Harmondsworth, 1955).

category. A term introduced into PHILOSOPHY by Aristotle, in very much its everyday sense of a class or kind, but restricted in its application to linguistic items, specifically to the descriptive or non-logical words or phrases which figure as the subjects and predicates of PROPOSITIONS. With his classification of terms into ten categories, Aristotle tried to systematize the restrictions on the possibilities of significant combination that exist for the different kinds of term. Thus the substance-word 'George' in 'George is heavy' can be replaced only by another term of the same category, such as 'this stone', if significance (not necessarily TRUTH) is to be preserved. Among modern philosophers, very much this idea is present in the influential theory of categories put forward by Gilbert Ryle (see also CATEGORY-MISTAKE), who regarded the tracing of the categorical properties of terms as the prime business of philosophy, but did not believe it is possible to develop a comprehensive formal theory of categories. Different, although related, is Kant's use of the term to refer to the very general and abstract CONCEPTS, such as SUBSTANCE and cause, with which philosophy has always been centrally concerned; see also APRIORISM.   A.Q.

category-mistake. A grammatically well-formed but nevertheless logically unacceptable sentence in which terms from uncombinable CATEGORIES are put together. 'The number 7 is green' is an uncontroversial example; numbers, unlike numerals, are not perceivable objects in space and cannot be significantly said to be of any colour. Ryle, who named this idea, applied it chiefly to mind-body DUALISM (see also MIND-BODY PROBLEM) which he held to be a massive category-mistake in taking mental and physical things and events to exist or occur in two different worlds.   A.Q.

Bibl: G. Ryle, *Collected Papers,* vol. 2 (London and N.Y., 1971).

category theory. A recent development in MATHEMATICS which concentrates attention not on *particular* MATHEMATICAL STRUCTURES but on the RELATIONS between them. It has had a unifying effect in ALGEBRA and TOPOLOGY. Those who like to work on particular, concrete problems refer to it as 'general abstract nonsense'.   R.G.

Bibl: S. MacLane, *Categories for the Working Mathematician* (N.Y., 1971).

catharsis (Greek word meaning 'purification', 'purgation').

(1) The 'purging' of undesirable emotions through vicarious experience, especially through seeing them represented on the stage; from its application by Aristotle

(*Poetics,* ch. 6) to the postulated effect of tragedy in removing, by the 'pity and fear' it excites, (excesses of) 'such emotions' – rather than simply stimulating them, as Plato had argued. (Aristotle seems to intend purification *from* excessive emotions rather than purification *of* them, but the latter interpretation has also been influential.)   R.W.S.

Bibl: Aristotle, ed. D. W. Lucas, *Poetics* (Oxford, 1968), Appendix II.

(2) In ABNORMAL PSYCHOLOGY, very commonly, the release of repressed emotion, irrespective of the nature of the process.   B.A.F.

(3) In FREUDIAN theory, the word has a more specific meaning. In 1882 Joseph Breuer hit upon a new method of PSYCHOTHERAPY, which he called 'cathartic'. It consisted in encouraging the patient to speak about the first occasion on which a symptom appeared; whereupon, Breuer claimed, the symptom disappeared. Freud adopted and used this method when he still believed that neurotic states (see NEUROSIS) originated in traumatic episodes (see TRAUMA). Later, however, he modified this view to allow for neurotic states that were the result of conflict; and after he developed the technique of FREE ASSOCIATION the cathartic method was seen to be only one aspect of this. In Freud's PSYCHOLOGY the mind contains charged mental elements, each of which has two aspects, the ideational and the affective (or emotional); and the charged elements are in movement towards CONSCIOUSNESS so as to discharge themselves. During treatment the patient is continually struggling to prevent the emergence of repressed emotion. When he does release it into consciousness, the element is thereby discharged. It is this whole process that is known as catharsis. See also ABREACTION.   B.A.F.

cathexis. In psychoanalytic theory (see PSYCHOANALYSIS), (1) the sexual energy (LIBIDO) which an individual 'invests' in another person or object; (2) more generally, a strong attachment to another. W.Z.

cathode, see under ELECTRODE.

cathode ray tube. A device used in television receivers and oscilloscopes to display a varying electrical signal as a moving spot on a FLUORESCENT screen. The spot

is produced by a narrow beam of ELEC-TRONS which are deflected by the signal. See also ELECTRON GUN; THERMIONICS.
M.V.B.

Catholic Action. Defined by Pope Pius XI in his ENCYCLICAL *Ubi Arcano Dei* (1922) as 'the participation of the laity in the hierarchic apostolate, for the defence of religious and moral principles, for the development of a wholesome and beneficent social order under the guidance of the ecclesiastical hierarchy, outside and above political parties, with the intention of restoring Catholic life in society and in the family'. His successor, Pius XII, applied the term not merely to specific organizations such as the Belgian *Jeunesse Ouvrière Chrétienne* and the American Young Christian Workers, the Christian Family Movement and the Young Christian Students, but to all organized movements of the Catholic laity recognized as such.
D.C.W.

Catholic commitment, see under COMMITMENT.

Catholicism. Universality, specially in the Christian Church. This is believed to be safeguarded against personal and local errors by acceptance of the Bible, the Apostles' and Nicene Creeds, the ECUMENICAL Councils, the sacraments of Baptism and Holy Communion, ordered, corporate worship, and a regularly ordained (i.e. set apart) 'ministry' of bishops, priests, and deacons. There has been much disagreement as to the exact nature of these safeguards (see DOGMA), especially about the position of the Pope as the 'vicar' or deputy of Christ entitled to jurisdiction over the whole Church. The Eastern ORTHODOX Churches, rejecting the Papal claims, have been separated from the Western Catholic Chuch since 1054. During the 16th century the Reformation split the Western Church, although the PROTESTANT Churches organized after this further revolt against the Papacy have all claimed that they remain Catholic in some sense, and ANGLO-CATHOLICISM claims it strongly. In modern usage, the word usually refers to *Roman Catholicism*, which obeys the Pope, although often in the modern spirit of AGGIORNAMENTO. See also CATHOLIC

ACTION; MODERNISM; ULTRAMONTANISM.
D.L.E.
Bibl: J. L. McKenzie, *The Roman Catholic Church* (London and N.Y., 1969).

cation, see under ION.

CATS (Colleges of Advanced Technology). Ten colleges, set up in 1956 by the British Government, and devoted exclusively to advanced work. They awarded a nationally recognized Diploma in Technology which over a period of years came to be accepted as the equivalent of a university degree. Ten years later, following the ROBBINS REPORT, they were upgraded to become universities awarding their own degrees. One of their characteristic features is the provision of SANDWICH COURSES at degree level. There are 7 in England, 2 in Scotland, and 1 in Wales.
W.A.C.S.

Cattell, James McKeen (U.S. psychologist, 1860–1944), see under MENTAL TESTING; PSYCHOMETRICS.

Cauchy, Augustin-Louis, Baron (French mathematician, 1789–1857), see under ANALYSIS.

causal explanation, see under EXPLANATION.

causality (or *causation*). The relation between two events or states of affairs in which one brings the other about or produces it. Hume took the CONCEPT to be a complex one, its components being the priority in time of cause to effect, their contiguity in space and time and what he problematically described as their *necessary connection*. Although it seems inconceivable that a cause should follow its effect, it seems possible that the two should be simultaneous. The phenomenon of GRAVITATION is an apparent exception to the requirement of contiguity; that of interaction between mind and body, if the mind is taken to be non-spatial, is another (see MIND-BODY PROBLEM). The 'necessary connection', however, seems indispensable. EMPIRICISTS follow Hume in identifying it with constant conjunction: that event is the cause of this one if events like that are regularly succeeded, in circumstances like these, by events like this.

91

It follows from this that every singular-looking causal PROPOSITION is really general, since it implies a universal law, and it can be justified only by INDUCTION, which Hume took to be unjustifiable, although natural to us. There is no one standard alternative to this view. Some take causal laws to be *a priori* truths (see APRIORISM), discoverable by reason without the aid of experience; others that we can somehow perceive or intellectually apprehend the causal relation between a pair of particular events, most plausibly, perhaps, in the case where one's will brings about a movement of one's body. We have a practical interest in knowledge of causes since we can apply it to produce or prevent occurrences through the production or prevention of other, causally related, events that are within our direct control. We have a theoretical interest too: knowledge of causes enables us to explain what has happened and predict what will happen. Many verbs (kill, lift, throw) and many words of other kinds (victim, author, father) are implicitly causal. A.Q.

Bibl: J. L. Mackie, *The Cement of the Universe: a Study of Causation* (Oxford, 1974).

Cavendish Laboratory. The department of PHYSICS at the University of Cambridge, England. Since its foundation in 1870, a series of eminent directors (including Lord Rutherford, Sir John Cockcroft, and Sir Lawrence Bragg) has stimulated the early development of many important areas of present-day science, e.g. NUCLEAR PHYSICS, CRYSTALLOGRAPHY, RADIO ASTRONOMY, and MOLECULAR BIOLOGY. M.V.B.

cavitation. In its broadest sense, the formation of cavities within a continuous material. In the case of fluids, cavities are formed behind solid objects moving through a liquid which would normally be in contact with it, e.g. behind the blades of a ship's propeller. In the case of solids, cavities are dug in hard substances by bombarding them with high-frequency sound waves (see ULTRASONICS), generated by such devices as MAGNETOSTRICTION oscillators. E.R.L.

CBW (chemical and biological warfare), see under WAR.

CDU, See under CHRISTIAN DEMOCRACY.

Cela, Camilo José (Spanish novelist, *b*. 1916), see under TREMENDISMO.

Celan, Paul (Romanian-born German poet, 1920–70), see under GRUPPE 47.

celestial mechanics. The study of the ORBITS, or trajectories, of stars, planets, spacecraft, etc. The form of the orbits arises from the force of GRAVITATION, and calculations are based on NEWTONIAN MECHANICS. Celestial mechanics is characterized by great precision (it is the original 'exact science'); the motion of the moon, for example, can be calculated to within a fraction of a second many years in advance. See also ASTRONAUTICS. M.V.B.

cell.

(1) The smallest viable functional and structural unit of a TISSUE or organ. The *cell theory*, associated with the name of Theodor Schwann (1810–82), declares that all tissues and organs including the nervous system (see NEURON) are cellular in intimate structure. The process whereby cells multiply is known as *cell division*. See also CELL BIOLOGY; CYTOLOGY. P.M.

(2) A battery, i.e. a device for converting various forms of ENERGY (usually chemical) into electricity. Types of cell include (*a*) *primary cells,* exemplified by the non-rechargeable dry battery familiar in torches, etc.; (*b*) *secondary cells*, exemplified by the lead-acid accumulator familiar in motor-cars (and recharged electrically); (*c*) the *fuel cell* currently being developed as a possible power source for electric cars (recharged by adding new fuel); (*d*) the *solar cell*, used to power instruments in spacecraft, by converting the energy of sunlight directly into electrical energy. M.V.B.

cell biology. A branch of BIOLOGY (to be distinguished from CYTOLOGY) that came to the fore after World War II, and of which the ambition is, wherever appropriate, to interpret physiological performances in terms of the behaviour of individual CELLS. Cell biology has played a specially prominent part in IMMUNOLOGY, in which every endeavour is made to interpret antibody formation and the aggressive actions of lymphocytes (one of the white blood corpuscles) in cellular terms. Indeed, that branch of immunology which deals with cell-mediated immune reactions is to quite a large extent a natural history of lymphocytes.   P.M.

Bibl: L. E. R. Picken, *The Organisation of Cells and Other Organisms* (Oxford, 1960); T. T. Puck, *The Mammalian Cell as a Microorganism* (San Francisco, 1973).

cell theory, see under CELL.

Cendrars, Blaise (Swiss poet and essayist, 1887–1961), see under CUBISM.

censorship, see under PERCEPTUAL DEFENCE.

CENTO (Central Treaty Organization). A military-political alliance on the lines of NATO and SEATO, joining Turkey, Iran, and Pakistan with Britain; its real, though not its ostensible, aim being to provide defence against the Soviet Union. Originally CENTO (under the name *Baghdad Pact*) included Iraq, the treaty setting it up being signed in Baghdad in 1955. After the Iraqi revolution of 1958, the new Iraqi government withdrew from the pact. The U.S.A. did not accede formally to the pact; but after 1958 U.S. representatives attended the meetings of its military committee. Successive British governments have confirmed support for CENTO as long as its existence is desired by the other member states, although U.S. diplomacy and power in the region have tended to make it somewhat redundant.
                                      D.C.W.

central limit theorem, see under PROBABILITY THEORY.

central nervous system, see under NERVOUS SYSTEM.

central place. A geographic term for villages, TOWNS, and cities that provide centralized wholesale, retail, service, and administrative functions for tributary REGIONS. Central-place theory specifies the relationships between SETTLEMENTS serving such central functions, with special emphasis on their number, size, spatial arrangement, and activity structure. The first formal statement of the theory is usually credited to the German geographer, Walter Christaller, who based his work on

the study of South German settlements. Modern mathematical work has been concerned with generalizing Christaller's work to accommodate a wide range of regional variations and to introduce dynamic and evolutionary dimensions to central-place theory.   P.H.

Bibl: W. Christaller, tr. C. W. Baskin, *Central Places in Southern Germany* (Englewood Cliffs, N.J., 1966).

central processing unit (CPU). The part of a COMPUTER where the data-processing is carried out. This includes the arithmetic and logical operations as well as the control of the sequence of instructions and of INPUT/OUTPUT. Though logically the most complicated part of a computer it only represents 5–10% of its cost.   C.S.

centralism, democratic, see DEMOCRATIC CENTRALISM.

centrality, see under CENTRAL PLACE.

centre, the. If there are RIGHT and LEFT wings in politics, it follows that there must be a centre between them unless the politics of the country in question is polarized between extreme positions. The centre is the name for moderate, middle-of-the-road parties and politics, scorned by the doctrinaire and idealist, and more concerned with finding compromises that will enable government to be carried on than with the pursuit of ideas to their logical conclusions.

A similar function is fulfilled by the centre group in many political parties, holding together those of more radical views (see RADICALISM) on the one hand and those with more conservative views on the other. The centre provides a convenient point on the political spectrum by which to place politicians and policies as 'left of centre' or 'right of centre'. The term 'party of the extreme centre' was coined to make the point that those who believe in moderation and the virtues of toleration and compromise may have a commitment quite as intense and quite as much based on principle as those who believe in intolerance and violence.
                                      A.L.C.B.

Centre 42. The playwright Arnold Wesker's largely unfulfilled plan for an ARTS CENTRE to be supported by the

British trades unions and labour movement. It was based on resolution no. 42 of the 1960 Trades Union Congress, by which the meeting 'recognized' the importance of the ARTS and decided to see how the movement could contribute. In 1962 six local festivals were held, not very successfully, at the invitation of various trades councils. Despite some support from the Wilson government and the acquisition of a potential centre in the Round House in London, funds were unavailable to run this as intended, let alone realize the ultimate aim of free performances.   J.W.

centres dramatiques. Theatres, sometimes with attached drama schools, set up in various French provincial towns and on the outskirts of Paris, from 1945 onwards, in an attempt to decentralize theatrical culture and bring the theatre to working-class and lower-middle-class audiences. After 1960, in some localities, the *centres dramatiques* were combined with the new *maisons de la culture* introduced by André Malraux as Minister for Cultural Affairs. Despite conflicts with local authorities (who supply part of the finance) and the upheavals of May 1968 (most of the directors belong to the LEFT), some of the *centres* have achieved notable, if temporary, success, e.g. Grenier de Toulouse, Centre Dramatique de l'Est (now Théâtre National de Strasbourg), Théâtre de la Cité (Villeurbanne) under Roger Planchon, and Comédie de Saint-Étienne under Jean Dasté.   J.G.W.

centrifuge. A device for depositing out fine PARTICLES (e.g. biological MOLECULES, organisms, etc.) suspended in a liquid contained in a tube. When the tube is whirled very rapidly about an axis, centrifugal force causes the densest particles to deposit farthest from the axis much faster than they would have settled under GRAVITATION.   M.V.B.

centrography. In GEOGRAPHY, the determination and study of the central points of spatial distributions, e.g. changes in the centre of gravity of the United States population. Centrography developed most rapidly during the 1920s and 1930s in the Soviet Union when attempts were made to define optimal centres for regional planning purposes.   P.H.

centrosphere, see BATHYSPHERE.

cephalic index. In physical ANTHROPOLOGY, the index used for recording the shape of the human skull. The index expresses the maximum width as a percentage of the maximum length measured from just above the eyebrow ridges. Where the index is below 75, the skull is described as *dolichocephalic* (long-headed); above 80 as *brachycephalic* (round-headed).
                          A.L.C.B.

ceramic. Originally a man-made refractory material based on silicates, e.g. china and porcelain. Now the term is used for any non-metallic solid made up of small crystals.   M.V.B.

cerebral dominance, see under NEUROPSYCHOLOGY.

cerebrotonia, see under PERSONALITY TYPES.

Cerenkov radiation. The cone of light or other electromagnetic RADIATION emitted by charged PARTICLES travelling through a transparent material faster than the speed of light in that material. Cerenkov radiation is impossible in empty space because according to RELATIVITY theory particles cannot travel faster than light *in vacuo.* It is analogous to the SONIC BOOM and to the water-wave pattern behind ships.   M.V.B.

CERN. European Organization for Nuclear Research (formerly Conseil Européen pour la Recherche Nucléaire). The world's largest centre, situated in Geneva, for the experimental (using ACCELERATORS) and theoretical study of ELEMENTARY PARTICLES. Set up in 1954 and currently supported by 12 nations, CERN has an annual budget of about £120 million.   M.V.B.

Cernuda, Luis (Spanish poet, 1904–63), see under ULTRAISM.

Cervantes, Miguel de (Spanish novelist, 1547–1616), see under ANTI-NOVEL.

Césaire, Aimé (Martinican poet and dramatist, *b.* 1913), see under BLACK THEATRE; NÉGRITUDE.

Cézanne, Paul (French painter, 1839–1906), see under ARMORY SHOW; CUBISM; FAUVES; IMPRESSIONISM; LONDON GROUP; POST-IMPRESSIONISM.

CGS units. A system of fundamental scientific units, based on the centimetre, gram, and second for length, MASS, and time. Now superseded by SI UNITS. M.V.B.

CGT (Confédération Générale du Travail). French trades union movement established in 1895 at Limoges, brought together with other trades union organizations in 1902 at Montpellier. It operated both on issues of wage, salary, and working conditions and on political issues; in 1906 it was captured by revolutionary SYNDICALISTS who relied on the general strike as their main weapon. The consequent collisions with state power weakened its impetus and in 1921 the revolutionary wing under COMMUNIST leadership set up a separate organization. Reunited under the slogan of the POPULAR FRONT in 1936, it was dissolved in 1940. Reconstituted in 1946, it came under Communist control, its non-Communist elements seceding in 1947 to form the Confédération Générale du Travail – Force Ouvrière. D.C.W.

Chabot, Georges (French geographer, b. 1890), see under SUBURBANIZATION.

Chabrol, Claude (French film director, b. 1930), see under NEW WAVE.

Chadwick, Sir James (British physicist, 1891–1974), see under NEUTRON.

Chagall, Marc (Russo-French painter, engraver, and designer, b. 1889), see under DONKEY'S TAIL; ÉCOLE DE PARIS.

Chaikovsky, Piotr Ilyich (Russian composer, 1840–93), see under ROMANTICISM.

Chain, Ernst Boris (German–British biochemist, b. 1906), see under LYSOZYME.

chain index, see under INDEX NUMBER.

chain reaction. Any chemical or nuclear process where each reaction produces PARTICLES which cause a chain of further similar reactions. The process may be unstable, as in explosions (conventional or nuclear), or controlled, as in NUCLEAR REACTORS. See also FISSION; FUSION; NUCLEAR REACTION. M.V.B.

chamber tomb. General term for an artificially constructed burial place designed for use on more than one occasion. Chamber tombs may be cut out of rock, MEGALITHIC, or constructed of drystone work. This type of burial place was common in Western Europe throughout the third millennium B.C., but occurs in many parts of the world at different times. B.C.

Chamberlain, Houston Steward (British political philosopher, 1855–1927), see under RACE.

Chamberlain, Joseph (British statesman, 1836–1914), see under IMPERIALISM.

Chamberlain, Neville (British statesman, 1869–1940), see under MUNICH.

Chamberlin, Thomas Chrowder (U.S. geologist, 1843–1928), see under PLANETESIMAL THEORY.

Champfleury (pseud. of Jules Husson or Fleury, French novelist and critic, 1821–89), see under FOLK ART; REALISM.

Chamson, André (French novelist, b. 1900), see under NEW WRITING.

Chandler, John (U.S. educator, b. 1923), see under DEMATERIALIZATION.

Chang Chun-chiao (Chinese politician, b. c. 1912), see under CULTURAL REVOLUTION.

channel capacity, see under INFORMATION THEORY.

Chaplin, Sir Charles (British-born film actor and director, b. 1889), see under KEYSTONE; SLAPSTICK.

character. A written sign, to indicate a sound, a meaning, or part of a word (a letter); this meaning dates from 1665. In COMPUTING, the use is extended to marks, holes in data-tape, or magnetic or other signals, 'recognized' and 'read' by machines, for information-processing or storing. Except in picture languages such as Egyptian hieroglyphics, it is now rare for a single mark or picture to stand for a meaning except in mathematical or logical notation. The numbers 1 and 2 are characters, but even here we soon get combinations, such as 12, which have a different meaning. R.L.G.

character analysis, see under REICHIAN.

characterology. A pseudo-science of diagnosing personality traits from such evidence as GRAPHOLOGY or the study of handwriting, formulated and practised by the Munich philosopher Ludwig Klages (1872–1956), and sometimes denounced (e.g. by Georg Lukács) for its contribution to the IDEOLOGY of NAZISM. It became pertinent once more after World War II with the rise of quasi-calligraphic painting and with ABSTRACT EXPRESSIONISM'S concern with GESTURAL significance. It also relates to Rorschach's system of PSYCHODIAGNOSTICS. J.W.

charisma. A term derived from New Testament Greek (meaning the gift of grace) and introduced into SOCIOLOGY by Max Weber to denote an 'extraordinary quality' possessed by persons or objects, which is thought to give them a unique, magical quality. Weber distinguished between *individual* charisma, which arises out of the personal qualities of the individual, and the charisma of *office*, which derives from the sacred nature of the position.
    Weber carried the CONCEPT over into a general theory of *authority*, in which he distinguished between three types of legitimacy – traditional, charismatic, and legal-rational – and into a rudimentary theory of social change. For, where religions or societies are hidebound, or ruled by customs sanctified by the past, the only way such authority can usually be challenged is by some *charismatic* leader whose legitimacy resides in his personal qualities. To that extent, charisma is a great revolutionary force. But once the charismatic leader has achieved his aim, he has to set about creating rational, administrative rules; secondary individuals have to be endowed with the authority of the leader, symbols replace the person, and there ensues the 'routinization of charisma'.
    Among English-speaking sociologists, the concept has been seen primarily in political terms, and has been applied to men like Nkrumah in Ghana, Sukarno in Indonesia, Nehru in India, whose personal appeals were the source of authority in these new nations. It has also been applied, by journalists and others, to all kinds of individuals and phenomena that seemed to have a special, magical ability to evoke an immediate, personal assent from the masses. D.B.

charismatic movement, see under PENTECOSTALISM.

Chaunu, Pierre (French historian, *b*. 1923), see under ANNALES SCHOOL.

chauvinism. Excessive and unreasonable NATIONALISM mingled with XENOPHOBIA. The word is derived from the name of Nicolas Chauvin, a Napoleonic soldier famous for his simple-minded devotion to Napoleon, and applied by analogy to all extreme intellectual positions held by defenders of a particular set of interests, e.g. 'male chauvinism' (see SEXISM). D.C.W.

Cheeseman, Peter (British theatre director, *b*. 1932), see under DOCUMENTARY

CHEKA, see under KGB.

Chekhov, Anton Pavlovich (Russian dramatist and story-writer, 1860–1904), see under BLACK COMEDY; CARTEL.

chelate. Term, derived from the Greek word for claw, which describes a chemical SPECIES with more than one ATOM capable of bonding (see BOND) to a central metal atom or ION. Chelating agents, more usually referred to as *polydentate ligands*, frequently form more stable complexes with a metal atom than similar monodentate groups. They find considerable use in industrial and ANALYTICAL CHEMISTRY – particularly in extraction processes. Metal ions in biological systems are often bound to chelates. B.F.

chemical and biological warfare, see under WAR.

chemical bond, see BOND, CHEMICAL.

chemical equation. A representation in symbols of a chemical reaction. Since the

19th century when Dalton restated early atomic theories in quantitative form it has been common practice to use such equations, which describe the change in atomic combinations and demonstrate that ATOMS are conserved in the process. Each atomic SPECIES is represented by an appropriate letter or letters; thus the production of water, which involves the overall reaction of two hydrogen MOLECULES with one molecule of oxygen to give two water molecules, is given as

$$2H_2 + O_2 = 2H_2O$$

The subscript figures indicate the number of atoms of that particular element in the molecule; e.g., the hydrogen molecule, H_2, is diatomic. Equations are sometimes presented in diagrammatic form so as to give an elementary description of bonding (see BOND) and STEREOCHEMISTRY. B.F.

chemical equilibrium, see under EQUILIBRIUM.

chemical physics, see under PHYSICAL CHEMISTRY.

chemical reaction. The process by which chemical compounds transform one another into different compounds. Nearly every substance has the ability to take part in a variety of chemical reactions and such reactions are a feature of normal life: the burning of oil, the discharge of a battery, the rusting of iron, the production of carbon dioxide from baking powder, etc. In addition a great many chemical reactions are involved in plant growth, the assimilation of food and oxygen by animals, and other biological activities. B.F.

chemical warfare, see under WAR.

chemistry. The scientific discipline concerned with the investigation and rationalization of the properties of the many thousands of substances which exist in nature or can be made artificially (see SYNTHETIC CHEMISTRY). Traditionally it is subdivided into PHYSICAL CHEMISTRY, which is concerned with the physical laws governing chemical behaviour and includes the specialized branches ELECTROCHEMISTRY, PHOTOCHEMISTRY, and STEREOCHEMISTRY as well as studies involving SPECTROSCOPY and THERMODYNAMICS (including THERMOCHEMISTRY); ORGANIC CHEMISTRY, which

involves the study of substances containing carbon; and INORGANIC CHEMISTRY, which deals with substances containing the remaining elements. THEORETICAL CHEMISTRY is concerned particularly with the applications of QUANTUM MECHANICS and STATISTICAL MECHANICS to chemistry. The detection and estimation of chemical SPECIES is the sphere of ANALYTICAL CHEMISTRY and (where minute amounts are involved) MICROCHEMISTRY. The distribution of elements in the earth's crust and atmosphere constitutes the study of GEOCHEMISTRY. A good deal of modern chemistry involves interdisciplinary study, especially in conjunction with PHYSICS, BIOCHEMISTRY, and METALLURGY. B.F.

Bibl: J. B. Ifft and J. E. Hearst (intr.), *General Chemistry: Readings from Scientific American* (San Francisco, 1973); G. D. Schaumberg, *Concerning Chemistry* (London and N.Y., 1974).

chemotaxis, see under TROPISM.

chemotherapy. The treatment of diseases by chemicals whose composition is known. Modern chemotherapy began in the 19th century with Paul Ehrlich's discovery of the beneficial effect of mercury on syphilis. Previously diseases, whose causes were generally unknown, were treated by a variety of non-specific remedies of varying and obscure composition. With the clearer definition of diseases in the last century, and the recognition of the microbial origin (see MICROBE) of many of them, it became possible to develop more rational treatment. The two greatest recent advances in chemotherapy have been the discovery in the 1930s of the sulphonamide group of drugs, and the introduction about 10 years later of penicillin and other ANTIBIOTICS – although, strictly speaking, penicillin treatment was not chemotherapy since penicillin, an extract from a mould, was not then a compound of known chemical composition. D.A.P.

chemotropism, see under TROPISM.

Chen Po-ta (Chinese politician, *b.* 1905), see under CULTURAL REVOLUTION.

Chesterton, Gilbert Keith (British author, 1874–1936), see under MYSTICISM.

Chiang Ching (Chinese politician, wife of Mao Tse-tung; *b.* 1914), see under CULTURAL REVOLUTION.

Chiang Kai-shek (Chinese soldier and statesman, 1887–1975), see under KUOMINTANG.

Chicago. In JAZZ, the white derivative style evolved in imitation of the New Orleans stars (e.g. Louis Armstrong) who came north. Stylistically, Chicago is a compromise between NEW ORLEANS, which concentrated on a three-man ensemble method, and the virtuosity of the SWING age, which gloried in the prowess of the individual; a Chicago performance, though beginning and ending with a New-Orleans-style ensemble chorus, would feature in the middle a succession of solos. The greatest of the Chicagoans were Benny Goodman (clarinet) and Jack Teagarden (trombone) who, perversely, was born in the South-West. Today Chicago style is essentially a historical curiosity, revived self-consciously.   B.G.

Chicago Conspiracy Trial. The trial of seven prominent LEFT-wing radicals (see RADICALISM) on charges of conspiracy arising from the riots during the Democratic Party convention in Chicago in August 1968. The defendants included two founders of Students for a Democratic Society (SDS). The trial opened in Chicago in September 1969 before Federal District Judge Julius Hoffman, who frequently entered into heated exchanges with the accused and their counsel during the course of the trial. After the jury retired, Judge Hoffman sentenced all the defendants and their counsel to terms of imprisonment for contempt of court. These sentences, amongst the longest for contempt in judicial history, and the Judge's biased conduct of the trial, were severely criticized by leading newspapers and lawyers' organizations. Five of the defendants were found guilty on one of the charges, the other two defendants were acquitted of both charges. Maximum sentences were handed down but the defendants were eventually bailed pending appeal. P.B.M.

Chicago school.
(1) In SOCIOLOGY, the first graduate department to be established in the world, and for many years the greatest. Founded

in 1892 by Albion Small (who in 1895 founded the *American Journal of Sociology*), it was centrally important in the development of sociology. Robert Park and E. W. Burgess developed basic research on 'the city' within a wide conception of sociological analysis and theory. C. H. Cooley, G. H. Mead, and W. I. Thomas developed (each with slightly different emphases) a distinctive analysis of the 'self' in 'society': perhaps the most fruitful exploration of the field of SOCIAL PSYCHOLOGY yet achieved. This 'school' in particular – now represented by 'symbolic interactionism' (see SYMBOLIC INTERACTION) and the work of Erving Goffman (see ROLE) – is referred to as the Chicago school.   R.F.
Bibl: R. C. and G. J. Hinkle, *The Development of Modern Sociology* (N.Y., 1954), pp. 28–43.
(2) An architectural movement rooted in the rapid development of Chicago following the Great Fire of 1871 and continuing up to about 1925. It had two facets: the erection of mainly commercial buildings in the business district of the Loop in the form of SKYSCRAPERS, and the development of freely planned single- or two-storey houses in the suburbs by Frank Lloyd Wright, Louis Sullivan, and their followers. It is the evolution of the skyscraper which is most frequently associated with the achievements of the Chicago school. Both aspects were neglected by historians, and it was not until the publication of Giedion's *Bauen in Frankreich* (1926) and its English-language sequel, *Space, Time and Architecture* (1941) that international interest was revived. This was reinforced by Mies van der Rohe, who had gone to Chicago in 1938 and who demonstrated the validity of its tradition; technical innovation and pure form could even in commercial buildings create architecture of a high order.   M.BR.
Bibl: C. W. Condit, *The Chicago School of Architecture* (London and Chicago, rev. ed., 1964).

Chicago Seven, see under CHICAGO CONSPIRACY TRIAL.

child-centred education. Education based on the interests, needs, and developmental growth of the child and on a knowledge of child development, as contrasted with an education that emphasizes academic features, the curriculum content, standards of achievement, and teaching methods. Originating in a psychological approach, child-centred education has acquired what is sometimes called a philosophy, and is associated with PROGRESSIVE education, and with such names as Rousseau, Froebel, Pestalozzi, Montessori, and A. S. Neill (see FROEBEL METHOD; PESTALOZZI METHODS; MONTESSORI METHOD).   W.A.C.S.

Bibl: W. B. Curry, *The School and a Changing Civilisation* (London, 1934).

child psychiatry, see under PSYCHIATRY.

child psychology, see DEVELOPMENTAL PSYCHOLOGY.

Childe, Vere Gordon (Australian prehistorian, 1892–1957), see under CULTURE; NEOLITHIC REVOLUTION; URBAN REVOLUTION.

chiliastic, see under MILLENARIANISM.

Chintreuil, Antoine (French painter, 1814–73), see under IMPRESSIONISM.

Chirico, Giorgio de (Italian painter, *b.* 1888), see under METAPHYSICAL PAINTING; NEO-CLASSICISM; SURREALISM.

chlorophyll. Any of a number of green pigments which occur in plants and a few animals and are the cause of the greenness of grass, of the leaves of trees, and of the countryside generally. Chlorophyll plays an essential part in PHOTOSYNTHESIS. These pigments have also been said to act as deodorants and have been included in toothpaste, though they are probably useless against halitosis.   K.M.

choice, axiom of, see AXIOM OF CHOICE.

Chomsky, Avram Noam (U.S. linguist, *b.* 1928), see under ADEQUACY; BLACK-BOX THEORY; CHOMSKYAN; COMPETENCE AND PERFORMANCE; DISCOVERY PROCEDURE; EVALUATION PROCEDURE; GENERATIVE GRAMMAR; LANGUE AND PAROLE; LINGUISTICS; MENTALISM; MIT SCHOOL; STRUCTURALISM; UNIVERSAL.

Chomskyan. Characteristic of, or a follower of, the linguistic principles of Avram Noam Chomsky (*b.* 1928), Professor of Modern Languages and Linguistics at the Massachusetts Institute of Technology. His book *Syntactic Structures* (The Hague, 1957) was the first to outline and justify a GENERATIVE conception of language, currently the most widely held view. Apart from his technical contributions within LINGUISTICS, he has written at length on the philosophical and psychological implications of a generative theory of language, in particular developing a view of the integral relationship between language and the human mind, and it is this which has made such an impact on disciplines outside linguistics. (See also INNATENESS HYPOTHESIS.) He has also made a powerful impression on the American and, to a lesser extent, the British public through his extensive critical writings on United States policy in VIETNAM.   D.C.

Bibl: A. N. Chomsky, *Language and Mind* (N.Y., enl. ed., 1972); J. Lyons, *Chomsky* (London, 1970).

Chopin, Frédéric or **Fryderyk** (Polish composer, 1810–49), see under ROMANTICISM.

chordate, see under ZOOLOGY.

chosism. Term imported from France ('thingism') for the occurrence, in the writers associated with the NEW NOVEL, and especially in Alain Robbe-Grillet, of obsessively detailed descriptions of trivial objects (cigar boxes, tomatoes, etc.). Some critics consider it 'arid' and ultimately pointless; others regard it as an important means of drawing attention to the tragically anthropomorphic attitude of human beings towards an indifferent ENVIRONMENT.   M.S.-S.

Chou En-lai (Chinese revolutionary and statesman, 1889–1976), see under CULTURAL REVOLUTION; PANCH SHILA.

Chrétien, Henri-Jacques (French physician and inventor, 1879–1956), see under CINEMASCOPE.

Christaller, Walter (German geographer, 1893 or 1894 to 1969), see under CENTRAL PLACE; GEOGRAPHY.

Christian democracy. Term used in relation to political parties allied with the Christian Churches, usually the Catholic Church. In the 19th century such parties were usually anti-CAPITALIST, anti-SOCIALIST, and often ANTISEMITIC. Their relations with the Vatican, not always of the happiest, turn on the Papacy of Leo XIII, when the movement began to take on a social character which betrayed some parties (as in Austria) into a COLLECTIVIST, cooperativist view, labelled CLERICO-FASCISM by their opponents. After 1945 Christian Democrat parties, breaking out of these traditions, became dominant as the major CONSERVATIVE parties in France, Italy, Austria, Belgium, the Netherlands, and West Germany, in the last of which, uniquely, the Lutheran Church played a strong part in the *Christlich-Demokratische Union* (C.D.U., Adenauer's party) which was in power from 1949 to 1968. They have also flourished in Latin America.   D.C.W.

Bibl: M. P. Fogarty, *Christian democracy in Western Europe 1820–1953* (London and Indianapolis, 1957).

Christian existentialism (or *existential theology*). A style of THEOLOGY inspired by Søren Kierkegaard (1813–55) which tests every doctrine by its derivation from human experience and by its power to illuminate human existence. It rejects metaphysical speculation about eternal ESSENCES, even when this is hallowed in traditional DOGMA, and it attempts to DEMYTHOLOGIZE the Bible. In 1950 it was condemned by Pope Pius XII's ENCYCLICAL *Humani Generis*. It is also criticized as being insufficiently concerned with nature and history, and as being too pessimistic about man's reasoning powers. But its mood of urgency and of honesty has made it a possible variety of the CRISIS THEOLOGY which has attracted many Christians in the 20th century.   D.L.E.

Bibl: D. E. Roberts, ed. R. Hazelton, *Existentialism and Religious Belief* (London and N.Y., 1957).

Christian name politics, see COMMUNITY POLITICS.

Christian Science. The name adopted by a religious body founded by Mrs Mary Baker Eddy (1821–1910), whose *Science and Health* has run into many editions in and since 1875. Its headquarters are in Boston, Mass., and it is active throughout the English-speaking world. Its principal interest is in increasing health and curing disease by a faith which denies the reality, or at least the power, of matter, suffering, and evil. Its doctrine is usually condemned both by the Churches and by AGNOSTICS, but it publishes a daily newspaper which is widely respected, the *Christian Science Monitor*.   D.L.E.

Christian socialism. Term for a variety of movements designed to combine the ethical precepts of Christianity with the COLLECTIVIST precepts of SOCIALISM. Originating in Britian and strongest in the 19th century, it has revived in the 20th in movements mainly distinguished for their general undoctrinal benevolence or for their attempts to enlist Christ in the service of socialism rather than vice versa. Such movements are to be found among Protestant Church members in France, Germany, Switzerland, Scandinavia, and the U.S.A. Its most distinguished exponents have been the German-American theologian Paul Tillich, the American social philosopher Reinhold Niebuhr, and the British social historian R. H. Tawney.   D.C.W.

Bibl: E. Heimann, *Reason and Faith in Modern Society: Liberalism, Marxism and Democracy* (Middletown, Conn., 1961; Edinburgh and London, 1962).

Christianity. The RELIGION based on the work and teaching of Jesus, who lived *c.* 4 B.C.–A.D. 30. He was regarded by his followers as the 'Anointed King' (Hebrew *Messiah*, Greek *Christos*). 'It was in Antioch that the disciples first got the name of Christians' (Acts 11:26). The life of Jesus has been much investigated and debated in the 19th and 20th centuries (see ESCHATOLOGY; MODERNISM). The main modern forms of this religion are CATHOLICISM; ORTHODOXY, EASTERN; and PROTESTANTISM. See also THEOLOGY.   D.L.E.

Christology. That part of THEOLOGY which is concerned with doctrines about the person and work of Jesus Christ. See also DOGMA.   D.L.E.

Bibl: D. M. Baillie, *God Was in Christ* (N.Y., 1948; London 2nd ed., 1956).

chromatography. A family of chemical separation techniques. The original method, described by Tsvett in 1903, referred to the separation of coloured substances (hence the name), but this is not an essential requirement. All chromatographic methods involve a stationary PHASE (a liquid or solid) and a mobile phase (liquid or gas). Separation depends on individual components of the mixture having different distributions between the two phases, so that they move at varying rates in the mobile phase. Closely similar SPECIES can be separated (e.g. ISOTOPES and ISOMERS), and the detection of very small quantities is possible. See also GAS CHROMATOGRAPHY; ION EXCHANGE; PAPER CHROMATOGRAPHY.   B.F.

chromosomes. Thread-like structures present in the NUCLEI of all CELLS; they are the carriers of the hereditary factors known as GENES. See also CROSSING OVER; GENETICS.   J.M.S.

chunking. In INFORMATION THEORY, a process of re-CODING information which reduces the number of independent symbols in a message while increasing the number of kinds of symbol. For example 011001001110110 can be recoded (by grouping the digits in threes and converting to the scale of 8: 000=0; 001=1; 010;=2; 011=3; etc.) as 31166. The octal version is easier to remember, being shorter, and the fact that there are now 8 different symbols instead of 2 does not matter. The word was first used in this sense by G. A. Miller, who suggested that an analogous process is employed by people to make the best use of the limited number (about 7) of mental or perceptual 'slots' which we seem to have for items for immediate attention.   J.S.B.

Church, Alonzo (U.S. mathematical philosopher, *b.*1903), see under RECURSIVE FUNCTION THEORY.

Churchill, Sir **Winston Spencer** (British statesman, 1874–1965), see under BALANCE OF TERROR; IRON CURTAIN; MORGENTHAU PLAN; POTSDAM; SUMMIT DIPLOMACY; TEHERAN; YALTA.

Church's thesis, see under RECURSIVE FUNCTION THEORY.

CIA (Central Intelligence Agency). The official American intelligence organization established by the National Security Act on 18 September 1947 to coordinate the total intelligence effort of the U.S.A. It has combined intelligence-gathering with active SUBVERSION and political warfare throughout the world on the one hand and sabotage and GUERRILLA-warfare-style activities against COMMUNIST countries and their allies on the other. It was believed to be involved in the overthrow of the Arben government in Guatemala and the Musadegh government in Iran in 1954, and in the BAY OF PIGS incident in 1961. In the aftermath of the WATERGATE affair, the CIA suffered a Congressional investigation of its activities, and consequent loss of power and prestige. See also ENCOUNTER.   D.C.W.
Bibl: L. B. Kirkpatrick, *The Real C.I.A.* (London and N.Y., 1968).

CIAM (*Congrès internationaux d'architecture moderne*). A series of attempts, from 1928 onwards, to solve collectively some of the dominant problems of modern architecture which were at first seen as moral rather than stylistic: CIAM's first manifesto emphasized the need to put 'architecture back on its real plane, the economic and sociological plane'. Most of the great figures of the modern movement attended its meetings and Le Corbusier dominated several of these. A number of national sub-groups were formed, that in Britain being known as M.A.R.S. (Modern Architectural Research Society). CIAM's most widely known document, the *Athens Charter*, stemmed from its 4th congress in 1933 and dealt with what were considered the four primary functions of the city: dwelling, recreation, work, and transportation. The 10th and last congress, held in Dubrovnik in 1956, saw the introduction of the notion of CLUSTER PLANNING.   M.BR.
Bibl: J. L. Sert, *Can Our Cities Survive?* (Cambridge, Mass., 1944).

cinéma vérité (sometimes known as *cinéma-direct*, from direct, as opposed to post-synchronized, sound recording). Term derived from the Russian slogan *kino-pravda* applied by Dziga Vertov to his own work in the Soviet silent cinema, and used by Jean Rouch to describe the DOCUMENTARY movement in the early

101

1960s which in part revived Dziga Vertov's kino-eye principles (the camera sees truth; the film-maker should not intervene except in his MONTAGE of what the camera records). It is associated chiefly with the work of Richard Leacock and the Maysles brothers, who attempted to present an objective record of actuality (reconstructed or otherwise), but relegated montage to a subordinate role because new technical developments (lightweight cameras and recording equipment) enabled them to film their subjects unobtrusively and uninterruptedly. Rouch himself subsequently argued that the selectivity of the film-maker's eye negated the supposed objectivity of the camera, and turned increasingly to fiction as a basis for his films, though retaining the element of fact through his approach and his use of non-actors. T.C.C.M.

Bibl: G. R. Levin (ed.), *Documentary Explorations* (Garden City, N.Y., 1971).

CinemaScope. A wide-screen process involving an anamorphic lens (*L'Hypergonar*), demonstrated by Professor Henri Chrétien in 1927 and used by Claude Autant-Lara in an experimental short film, *Construire du Feu*, in 1928, but not developed commercially until bought and copyrighted as CinemaScope by Twentieth-Century-Fox in 1952 in an attempt to combat the threat of television by producing bigger images. The first CinemaScope film was *The Robe*, 1953. The standard screen, in use since the earliest days of cinema, is a 4 × 3 rectangle; CinemaScope, using the anamorphic lens in filming to compress the image onto a standard 35 mm. frame, with a complementary lens to expand it again during projection, offered a 2.5 × 1 rectangle. Other Hollywood and foreign film companies followed suit after the success of CinemaScope with variations on this wide-screen process known as Warnerscope, Superscope, VistaVision, Dyaliscope, Tohoscope, Technirama, etc.

Analogous attempts to extend the cinema screen include *Cinerama,* a development of the triple screen used by Abel Gance in his *Napoléon* in 1927: marketed in 1952, Cinerama originally employed three separate projectors on a curved screen, but later used only one. Subsequent processes (Todd-AO, Panavision 70) dispensed with the anamorphic lens by using 70 mm film, double the width of the standard 35 mm frame. 70 mm film had been used for a few films in the early days of sound cinema, the first being *The Big Trail* and *Billy the Kid* (both 1930). T.C.C.M.

cinémathèque. French term coined (on the analogy of *bibliothèque*, library) to describe a film museum or library. The Cinémathèque de la Ville de Paris, founded in 1919, preserved only films which were considered important as historical documents or for teaching purposes. The Cinémathèque Française, founded by Henri Langlois, Georges Franju, and Jean Mitry in 1936 (three years after the British Film Institute, its sister organization in London which incorporates the National Film Archive), considers film as an end in itself rather than as a means to education: it collects, preserves, and displays not only entertainment films as well as DOCUMENTARIES, but film stills, designs, scripts, models, costumes, and optical toys. T.C.C.M.

Cinerama, see under CINEMASCOPE.

circadian rhythm. A BIOLOGICAL RHYTHM with a period of exactly or approximately 24 hours. P.M.

circulation of élites, see under ÉLITE.

citric acid cycle, see KREBS CYCLE.

City, the. The name given to the square mile of London which has traditionally housed one of the world's major financial centres. A residue of Britain's era of commercial and industrial supremacy, it has proved itself more adaptable to changing world conditions than most other parts of the British economic edifice. Among its leading financial institutions are the Stock Exchange, the money markets, the insurance institutions (including Lloyds), commercial and merchant banks, and the various commodity exchanges. It is a major source of Britain's overseas earnings and has become progressively and proportionately more important to Britain's BALANCE OF PAYMENTS. Nevertheless its channelling of British INVESTMENT overseas rather than into British industry became a contentious domestic issue in

Britain in the 1970s. As an international financial centre its only major rival is WALL STREET. D.E.
Bibl: W. M. Clarke, *The City in the World Economy* (Harmondsworth, rev. ed., 1967).

Čiurlionis, Mykolas Konstantas (Lithuanian painter, 1875–1911), see under ABSTRACT ART.

civil disobedience. A strategy adopted by the Indian National Congress at the instance of its leader, Mahatma Gandhi, in April 1930 in order to attack British imperial rule by the mass ceremonial performance of illegal actions. An essential element is the disruption of the police and judicial machinery of state by overloading their procedures to the point where they can no longer be applied, and so lose CREDIBILITY. NON-VIOLENT in intention, it requires abnormal powers of self-discipline on the part of those adopting it and a moral restraint on the use of force by those against whom it is directed; its use has been advocated as a means of resistance against external aggression by those who feel nuclear DETERRENCE is both immoral and unreliable. D.C.W.
Bibl: G. Sharp, *The Politics of Non-Violent Action* (Boston, 1974).

civil rights movement. (1) The campaign for legal enforcement of equality of status for black Americans guaranteed by the U.S. Constitution. It flourished during the 1950s and 1960s, when the main organizations were the National Association for the Advancement of the Colored Peoples (founded 1910) and the National Urban League (founded 1911). Their methods included boycotts and court action, supplemented by (at first non-violent) 'sit-ins', marches, and DEMONSTRATIONS. These efforts culminated in the 1964 Civil Rights Act, the failure of which to bring immediate improvement led from 1966 onwards to the abandonment of NON-VIOLENCE and the development of more militant BLACK POWER organizations such as BLACK PANTHERS. (2) The campaign to achieve equality of status between Catholic minority and Protestant majority in Northern Ireland, from 1967 onwards, which received under-cover support from MARXIST revolutionary groups and advocates. D.C.W.

Cizek, Franz (Austrian educationist, 1865–1947), see under FROEBEL METHOD.

cladding. The use of lightweight building materials as an enclosure where the load-bearing function of the wall is taken by some other element of the STRUCTURE. This first occurred in greenhouses, railway stations, exhibition pavilions and factories of the 19th century, and the buildings of the CHICAGO SCHOOL. A highly developed form of cladding in which MODULAR factory-made units of glazing and opaque panels are fixed to a framework held by the floor structure and referred to as a *curtain wall* has become ubiquitous and has affected the appearance of most towns. See also PREFABRICATION. M.BR.
Bibl: M. Rostron, *Light Cladding of Buildings* (London, 1964).

clairvoyance, see under ESP.

Clapham, John Howard (British economic historian, 1873–1946), see under ECONOMETRICS.

Clark, John Maurice (U.S. economist, 1884–1963), see under ACCELERATOR.

Clark, Kenneth McKenzie (Baron Clark of Saltwood; British art critic and historian, *b.* 1903), see under ZEITGEIST.

Clarke, Alan Douglas Benson (British psychologist, *b.* 1922), see under MENTAL RETARDATION.

Clarke, Arthur Charles (British novelist, *b.* 1917), see under SCIENCE FICTION.

class.
(1) In MATHEMATICS and LOGIC, a synonym for SET.
(2) In SOCIOLOGY, a CONCEPT which denotes different social strata in society. Many sociologists, such as Ralf Dahrendorf, distinguish between the 'estate' systems of feudal and pre-industrial society – in which distinctions were primarily of *rank*, resting on tradition and an intricate system of age-old, often codified rights and duties – and the true class system which emerged when CAPITALISM and the Industrial Revolution substituted for these criteria the external criterion of material possessions. In the *Communist*

CLASSICAL CONDITIONING

Manifesto Marx identified classes in relation to the means of production, and thus generalized the concept of class to all societies where such distinctions could be made. (See also SOCIAL STRATIFICATION.)

Economic class. For Marx, the criterion of class was economic. However, he never specifically defined 'economic', and at various points in his writings he laid down several quite different criteria for the identification of classes. Moreover, it is difficult to find a single unambiguous criterion, whether it be OCCUPATION or a common standing in the processes of production, that does not encounter logical difficulties in classification. (If, for example, one takes the production process as the criterion, how does one classify those who stand outside production?)

For Max Weber, class is an analytical term which identifies individuals who have similar 'life chances' in the opportunities for gaining income; market assets include skill as well as property. He sees the major historical class struggle as being between creditors and debtors, with the conflict under capitalism between employers and workers as merely a special case.

Social class. For Marx, this was determined by, and coterminous with, economic class. Other sociologists see social class as a more complex variable which includes STATUS, prestige, family lineage, and other criteria. In the U.S.A., W. Lloyd Warner and his students sought to establish a six-grade ranking system defined simply by a dichotomous division within the upper, middle, and lower classes.

Class conflict. Marx predicted, under capitalism, an increasing POLARIZATION of society, increased exploitation of the worker, and ever sharper conflict between the two classes, leading ultimately to the social REVOLUTION. Social development for the West has belied that prediction. Real wages of the working class have risen, the working class has gained increasing social and political rights, and class conflict, though not eliminated, has become regulated (i.e. subject to legal rules) and institutionally isolated (i.e. there is little carry-over from industrial conflicts into other areas of life). In many industrial societies, moreover, other forms of conflict cut across class lines and divide, say, Irish Protestant from Irish

Catholic workers rather than workers from bosses.

Class consciousness. Marx assumed that such consciousness would develop in class struggle created by the crises of the capitalist system. Lenin, however, regarded the working class, unaided, as able to develop only 'trade-union consciousness'; and to this extent the creation of 'socialist consciousness' is the task of the INTELLECTUALS. In that case the MARXIST notion that 'existence determines consciousness', and the relation between social position and IDEOLOGY, cannot easily be maintained. This is a conundrum from which Marxist theory has not yet extricated itself.   D.B.

Bibl: R. Dahrendorf, *Class and Class Conflict in Industrial Society* (London and Stanford, 1959); S. Ossowski, tr S. Patterson, *Class Structure in the Social Consciousness* (London and N.Y., 1963); T. H. Marshall, *Sociology at the Crossroads* (London, 1963; N.Y., as *Class, Citizenship and Social Development*, 1964).

classical conditioning (also known as PAVLOVIAN or *respondent* conditioning). A form of CONDITIONING that consists of the establishment of a CONDITIONED REFLEX; after an arbitrary stimulus has been repeatedly paired with the eliciting stimulus of a reflex, the previously neutral stimulus comes to elicit the reflex response even in the absence of the characteristic elicitor. The traditional example is the Russian physiologist I. P. Pavlov's experiment (1906), in which, after the ringing of a bell (the *conditioned stimulus*) had repeatedly been accompanied by the provision of meat (the *unconditioned stimulus*), it was found that the ringing of the bell caused dogs to salivate (the *conditioned response*) even if no meat was produced. Interest in the objective and precise Russian studies was a major influence on the BEHAVIOURIST revolution in America. However, many modern psychologists believe that classical conditioning is merely a special case of OPERANT CONDITIONING: since the conditioned response prepares the organism for the appearance of the unconditioned stimulus, it seems more parsimonious to view the unconditioned stimulus as an operant reinforcer than to regard classical conditioning as an independent kind of learning. Procedures developed from classical-conditioning paradigms, especially *aversion therapy* and *desensitization*, are described under BEHAVIOUR THERAPY. D.H.

classical economic theory. The system of economic theory which was included in Adam Smith's *Wealth of Nations* (1776) and developed during the period ending about 1870. It was based on the assumption that the individual was usually the best judge of his own interests. The conclusion that under a freely competitive economic system the individual pursuit of economic self-interest would result in the economic benefit of the community depended on the analysis of the functioning of the PRICE MECHANISM in allocating resources in response to the demands for goods and services. When combined with the analysis of the role of the division of labour and the investment of CAPITAL in promoting ECONOMIC GROWTH, this led to the further conclusion of the desirability of freedom in international trade and freedom of economic activity generally from government intervention. The classical economists generally accepted also the QUANTITY THEORY OF MONEY.

There were, however, numerous differences of view among writers of this school, particularly with respect to the theories of value, wages, rent, population, underconsumption (see TRADE CYCLES), banking policy, and the functions of government. One of the best-known and for a short time most influential MODELS based on classical economic theory is the *Ricardian*. This incorporated the Malthusian (see NEO-MALTHUSIANISM) theory of population, the Ricardian theory of rent based on the law of DIMINISHING RETURNS to land, and Ricardo's variant of the LABOUR THEORY OF VALUE. An important conclusion derived from this model was that ECONOMIC GROWTH was doomed to come to an end owing to the increase in the difficulty of obtaining food as population increased. M.E.A.B.

Bibl: J. Schumpeter. *History of Economic Analysis* (N.Y., 1954; London, 1955); M. Blaug, *Ricardian Economics* (New Haven, 1958); E. Whittaker, *Schools and Streams of Economic Thought* (London and Chicago, 1960); S. Hollander, *The Economics of Adam Smith* (London and Toronto, 1973).

classical physics. Those areas of PHYSICS which were formulated before the 20th-century developments of RELATIVITY and QUANTUM MECHANICS. Classical physics is built on the four great theories of NEWTONIAN MECHANICS, ELECTRO-MAGNETISM, THERMODYNAMICS, and STATISTICAL MECHANICS. Two points must be stressed: first, these theories have not been proved wrong by modern discoveries; instead they are revealed as approximately valid under fairly clearly-defined circumstances (e.g. relativity supersedes Newtonian mechanics for PARTICLES moving almost as fast as light). Second, both in the study of its conceptual foundations and in the development of its applications, classical physics remains a living, growing subject. M.V.B.

classification. In ordinary language, either the *construction* of a classification ('How do you classify architectural styles?') or the *identification* of an individual specimen ('How would you classify the architecture of Salisbury Cathedral?') In STATISTICS and DATA ANALYSIS the word is used for the former of these activities, the latter being called 'identification' or 'diagnosis'. The problems of classifying bacteria led to the development during the 1950s of numerical methods of constructing various types of classification from descriptive data about the objects to be classified, and such methods now form an important part of data analysis. See also BIOSYSTEMATICS. R.SI.

clathrate. A compound in which one molecular component (see MOLECULE) is imprisoned in the cage structure of the other. The first clathrate, a compound of hydrogen sulphide and hydroquinone, was made in 1849, and clathrates have since aroused some curiosity because their behaviour is intermediate between that of normal compounds and that of simple mixtures. B.F.

Claude, Albert (Belgian biologist, b.1899?), see under MICROSOME.

Claudel, Paul (French poet and dramatist, 1868–1955), see under TOTAL THEATRE.

cleavage, see under EMBRYOLOGY.

Cleaver, Leroy Eldridge (U. S. black

militant, *b*. 1935), see under BLACK PANTHERS.

Clemenceau, Georges (French statesman, 1841–1929), see under DREYFUS CASE.

clerico-Fascism. In the inter-war period, a pejorative phrase applied by their opponents to Catholic authoritarian political parties with PARA-MILITARY support, especially the Austrian Fatherland Front, the Slovak nationalist party led by Father Hlinka, and the Croat nationalist USTACHA, the last two of which achieved power in their own national territories during World War II.   D.C.W.

Clifford, William Kingdom (British mathematician and philosopher, 1845–1879), see under NEUTRAL MONISM.

climatology. The study of average temperature, rainfall, humidity, and sunshine in different localities over long periods of time (at least 30 years), as contrasted with METEOROLOGY, which studies short-term changes. It is hoped that long-term climatic changes such as ice ages (as revealed by, fossil vegetation, for example) may be explained by changes in the composition of the atmosphere.   M.V.B.

climax. In ECOLOGY, a final or culminating state of an undisturbed vegetational COMMUNITY. A distinction is usually drawn between an EQUILIBRIUM achieved with respect to climate (*climatic climax*) and to soil (*edaphic climax*).   P.H.

cline. A term used in neo-Firthian (see FIRTHIAN) LINGUISTICS, especially by Halliday, referring to a continuum of gradation between contrasted linguistic features, e.g. between 'emphatic intonation' and 'unemphatic intonation'.   D.C.

clinical psychology, see under APPLIED PSYCHOLOGY.

cliometrics, see under ECONOMIC HISTORY.

clock paradox. The prediction of Einstein's theory of RELATIVITY that clocks and other temporal processes run more slowly as seen by an observer moving relatively to them than similar clocks and processes in his OWN FRAME OF REFERENCE.

This effect (which is only appreciable when the moving clock travels almost as fast as light) does not violate the principle of CAUSALITY or the rules of LOGIC. Indeed it has been confirmed experimentally by the discovery that swiftly-moving MESONS in the atmosphere are observed by us to live much longer before decaying than slower-moving mesons produced in the laboratory; the meson decays according to its internal 'clock', which runs slow as seen by us.

Despite this, the clock paradox has occasioned lively controversy for over 50 years, particularly in the sharpened form of the *twin paradox*, in which a traveller is imagined to leave the earth at high speed and then, after some years, to turn round and come back; his twin, who has stayed behind, will have aged, while the traveller (whose clocks will have run slow relative to those on earth) will still be young. The paradox is this: since each twin has been moving relative to the other, might one not equally well look at the situation from the traveller's point of view, in which case the twins' roles and ageing processes will be reversed? It is resolved by the fact that the twins are not in symmetrical situations: when turning around, the traveller must accelerate, and accelerating frames of reference are not dealt with in special relativity; a full analysis requires the general theory of relativity. Einstein's position has been vindicated by the recent experiments of J. C. Hafele and R. E. Keating, who measured small differences, compatible with the predictions of relativity theory, between the times indicated by clocks that had been flown round the world and clocks that had remained in the laboratory.   M.V.B.
Bibl: L. Marder, *Time and the Space Traveller* (London, 1971).

cloisonnisme, see under SYNTHETISM.

closed class, see under WORD CLASS.

closed shop. The restriction of employment in a workplace to members of a particular union, or unions. In the *pre-entry closed shop* only those who are already union members can be engaged. In the *union shop* (U.S.A.) or *agency shop* (U.K.) non-members may be engaged, but can keep their jobs only if they become members (or alternatively, in the

U.K., contribute the amount of union dues) within a reasonable time. All forms of closed shop meet the feeling of unionists that no one working alongside them should benefit from the activity of their union without paying dues to it. The authority of the union over dissidents is greatly increased when those who leave the union or are deprived of membership are thereby deprived of their jobs too. Some employers have found the closed shop advantageous in this last respect, and many have had no alternative but to accept it; but for an employer to dismiss a satisfactory worker only because he has fallen out with the union is embarrassing, and may be actionable as unfair dismissal. To have to maintain union membership under penalty of losing his job restricts the worker's freedom. In the U.S.A. the Taft-Hartley Act, 1947, made it unlawful for employers and unions to enforce the closed shop, but not the union shop. In the U.K. Acts of 1974 and 1976 made the closed shop lawful, though the legal issues concerning enforcement remain complicated. In neither country has legal disapproval of the closed shop stopped it being maintained in practice.   E.H.P.B.

Bibl: W. E. J. McCarthy, *The Closed Shop in Britain* (Oxford and Berkeley, 1964).

closure. The completion of incomplete forms, e.g. the perception of continuity in an outline drawing which is composed of dots. In GESTALT PSYCHOLOGY, 'tendency toward closure' refers to the way in which perceiving, remembering, or thinking strive toward patterned wholes that are as coherent and stable as circumstances will allow.   I.M.L.H.

cloud chamber. A device, invented by C. T. R. Wilson in 1911, and used to study NUCLEAR REACTIONS and ELEMENTARY PARTICLES. It is based on the fact that a fast charged PARTICLE leaves a record of its path, in the form of a trail of droplets, centred on IONS, when it traverses a vapour kept just below its condensation temperature. See also BUBBLE CHAMBER.   M.V.B.

Clurman, Harold (U.S. theatre director and critic, *b*.1901), see under GROUP THEATRE.

cluster (in music), see TONE-CLUSTER.

cluster analysis. A form of FACTOR ANALYSIS in which multivariate measurements or observations on a number of individual entities are statistically analysed, usually with the aid of a COMPUTER, to try to identify internal structure, e.g. the chronological ordering of archaeological objects, or the grouping of a set of manuscripts by authorship.   M.S.BA.

cluster planning. A town-planning CONCEPT, introduced at the 10th congress of CIAM (1956), which attempts to create a complex and closely knit aggregation with a comprehensible structure; it defines an attitude rather than a specific built form. The attitude stems from a dissatisfaction both with the dispersed forms of the GARDEN CITY and with the simplistic concept of an overall organization for the whole city; the cluster suggests a way of planning by the gradual accumulation of elements, each viable, to produce a town or building complex, and is thus perhaps closer to traditional town building.   M.BR.

Bibl: A. and P. Smithson, *Urban Structuring* (London and N.Y., 1967).

CND (Campaign for Nuclear Disarmament). A British organization founded in February 1958 to mobilize mass opinion against Britain's nuclear-weapons programme and in favour of Britain's unilateral disarmament. Its method of gaining publicity was to stage notably orderly mass marches between London and the Atomic Weapons Research Establishment at *Aldermaston*. At the Labour Party conference in September 1960 CND supporters secured the passage of a resolution in favour of unilateral disarmament. The CND was split by the policy of the Committee of 100, whose members (including Bertrand Russell) favoured non-violent DIRECT ACTION; and the course of the Cuban missile crisis (see CUBA; MISSILES), the initiation of separate French and Chinese nuclear-weapon programmes, and the signature of the partial Test Ban Treaty in 1963 (see PROLIFERATION) removed much of the impetus behind the campaign. During the 1960s VIETNAM replaced nuclear disarmament as the main focus of political protest.   D.C.W.

Bibl: C. Driver, *The Disarmers* (London, 1964).

Coates, Robert Myron (U.S. art critic, 1897-1973), see under ABSTRACT EXPRESSIONISM.

Cobb, Lee J. (U.S. actor, *b*.1911), see under GROUP THEATRE.

cobol. A HIGH-LEVEL PROGRAMMING LANGUAGE for commercial data-processing (see COMPUTING).   C.S.

COBRA. A group of artists that flourished between 1948 and 1951. Its name combines the initial letters of the capital cities where the founder-members worked: Copenhagen, Brussels, Amsterdam. The association inherited the ideas (and many of the members) of three groups, the Dutch *Experimentele Groep*, the Danish *Spiralen* group, and the Belgian *Bureau International de Surréalisme Révolutionnaire*. Its leading figures were Asger Jorn, Karel Appel, Christian Dotremont, Pierre Alechinsky, Constant Nieuwenhuys, and Cornelis van Beverloo Corneille. In their exhibitions and publications they sought to express, spontaneously and/or unconsciously, profound psychic forces, and their images are often primitive, violent, and fantastic. COBRA may be seen as a European variant of ACTION PAINTING and ABSTRACT EXPRESSIONISM.   P.C.

Bibl: É. Langui, 'Expressionism since 1945 and the Cobra Movement', in J. P. Hodin *et al., Figurative Art since 1945* (London, 1971).

Cockcroft, Sir **John** (British physicist, 1897–1967), see under CAVENDISH LABORATORY.

cocktail-party phenomenon. The everyday manifestation of a phenomenon of attention in which, though one is listening to one flow of conversation and filtering out all competing conversation, the filtering is broken through by some familiar or significant stimulus such as one's name being spoken.   J.S.B.

Cocteau, Jean (French author, artist, and film director, 1889–1963), see under GATE THEATRE; SIX, LES; THEATRE OF THE ABSURD.

code. In SOCIOLINGUISTICS, a term loosely applied to the language system of a community or to a particular VARIETY within a language, e.g. Bernstein's characterization of the different linguistic capabilities of middle- and working-class children in terms of ELABORATED AND RESTRICTED CODES.   D.C.

co-determination, see under PARTICIPATION.

coding.
(1) In INFORMATION THEORY, the representation of data for transmission or storage. Coding theory concerns itself with such questions as 'Is this the shortest representation of the data?'; 'How likely is this datum to be confused with other data if the representation is corrupted?' and with the measurement of REDUNDANCY. It is the basis of the design of ENCODERS and DECODERS.   R.M.N.
(2) In COMPUTING, the final stage in preparing a problem for a COMPUTER (the others being SYSTEMS ANALYSIS and PROGRAMMING). It involves writing exhaustive instructions to make a computer carry out the tasks which have been specified in the previous stages. Typically, coders write their instructions in ASSEMBLY LANGUAGE – a very lengthy and largely mechanical process in which they are prone to error. It is difficult for anyone who has not experienced it to realize the degree of detail required in coding. This is similar to that required in a knitting pattern (English, not continental, style), and coding corresponds to constructing such a detailed pattern, given the dimensions of the garment and the basic stitch pattern. Coding can be eliminated by the use of an appropriate HIGH-LEVEL PROGRAMMING LANGUAGE.   C.S.

codomain (in MATHEMATICS), see under FUNCTION.

coefficient. In MATHEMATICS and its applications, a term more or less synonymous with PARAMETER (2), but most frequently used with reference to some specified class of FUNCTIONS. For a mathematical example see ALGEBRA; a typical example from PHYSICS is the coefficient of thermal expansion.   R.G.

coexistence, peaceful. A phrase originally coined, in a slightly different form as 'peaceful cohabitation' (*mirnoe sozhitel-*

stvo) between peoples, by Leon Trotsky on 22 November 1917, and used with varying connotations by successive Soviet leaders until December 1927 when the present term (*mirnoe sosushchestvovanie*), which has a slightly less active sense, of passive existence rather than active cohabitation, officially replaced it. Descriptive of the pacific relations between the SOCIALIST Soviet Union and its CAPITALIST rivals, the concept was designed to mobilize opinion in the latter against actively anti-Soviet policies, delaying war by 'buying off' the capitalists, in the words of Josef Stalin. In the aftermath of Stalin's death the risk of mutual destruction by nuclear weapons was felt by his successor, Khrushchev, to rule out open WAR between the Soviet and non-Soviet worlds. He nevertheless made it clear that competition between states with different social systems would continue in all other fields until COMMUNISM proved itself superior and presided over the burial of capitalism. In practice it has also become evident that avoidance of a major war between the nuclear powers does not rule out support and intervention by both sides in wars of 'national liberation'.
D.C.W.

cognition. A collective term for the psychological processes involved in the acquisition, organization, and use of knowledge. Originally, the word distinguished the rational from the emotional (see EMOTION) and impulsive aspect of mental life. It passed out of currency, to be revived with the advent of COMPUTER SIMULATION of thought processes (see ARTIFICIAL INTELLIGENCE). The term is now used in COGNITIVE PSYCHOLOGY to refer to all the information-processing activities of the brain, ranging from the analysis of immediate STIMULI to the organization of subjective experience. In contemporary terminology, cognition includes such processes and phenomena as PERCEPTION, memory, attention, PROBLEM-SOLVING, language, thinking, and imagery.
G.B.

cognitive. Adjective applied to those aspects of mental life connected with the acquisition of knowledge or the formation of beliefs (which fail, through falsehood or lack of justification, to qualify as items of knowledge). It is applied to distinguish the kind of MEANING possessed by statements, true or false, from that possessed by such utterances as commands or exclamations which, although plainly meaningful, cannot be assessed as true or false. EMOTIVISM in ETHICS maintains that the meaning of VALUE-JUDGEMENTS is either wholly ('that is wrong') or partly ('that is theft') non-cognitive.
A.Q.

cognitive consonance and **cognitive dissonance.** *Cognitive consonance* is a consistency between the knowledge, ideas, and beliefs which make up a COGNITIVE SYSTEM so that the system is harmonious and without internal contradictions; *cognitive dissonance* is the absence of such consistency. The latter term is also applied to a perceived incongruity between a person's attitudes and his behaviour. There is evidence that people tend to reduce such dissonance by making appropriate changes in their attitudes and beliefs; thus a heavy drinker rationalizes his drinking behaviour by doubting the integrity of those reporting research on the evil effects of alcohol.
A.L.C.B.; J.S.B.
Bibl: L. Festinger, *A Theory of Cognitive Dissonance* (London and Stanford, 1962).

cognitive psychology. A branch of PSYCHOLOGY defined partly by its subject-matter, i.e. COGNITION, partly by its point of view. With respect to point of view, its main PRESUPPOSITION is that any interaction between an organism and its ENVIRONMENT changes not only its overt behaviour or physiological condition, but also its knowledge of or information about the environment, and that this latter change may affect not only present response but also future orientation to the environment. E. C. Tolman, characterizing the difference between the BEHAVIOURIST theory of *stimulus* and *response* and cognitive approaches to the study of learning, applied to the former the image of a telephone switchboard in which incoming stimuli came by practice to be connected to responses, and to the latter that of a map-room where the incoming stimuli were put together into 'cognitive maps' by the use of which responses were constructed to achieve intended outcomes. Whilst the distinction is no longer so clear, thanks to the greater sophistication of the modern CONNEC-

TIONIST'S view of 'switchboards', Tolman's distinction highlights the emphasis of cognitive psychology on those mediating 'knowledge processes' that affect the complex relation between INPUT in the form of stimulation and OUTPUT in the form of response.

Perhaps the main contribution of cognitive studies to the great debates in psychology has been to redress the imbalance created by the radical behaviourism introduced in the 1920s. The new emphasis was undoubtedly given great support by new approaches to information processing in CYBERNETICS, INFORMATION THEORY, and COMPUTING.   J.S.B.

Bibl: U. Neisser, *Cognitive Psychology* (N.Y., 1967).

cognitive system. A collection of interrelated items of knowledge or belief held by an individual about a person, group, event, class of objects, or any subject, either concrete or abstract. Every human individual establishes a number of such cognitive systems. The degree to which they are interrelated varies greatly; one of the characteristics of an IDEOLOGY is the high degree of interconnection between the most important cognitive systems. For the degree of consistency *within* a cognitive system see COGNITIVE CONSONANCE AND COGNITIVE DISSONANCE.   A.L.C.B.

Cohen, Hermann (German philosopher, 1842–1918), see under NEO-KANTIANISM.

coherence. In PHYSICS (for its more general meaning see under TRUTH), a property of a beam of RADIATION, which is coherent if all its component waves have the same PHASE. A LASER emits coherent light, but an ordinary electric light (where the ATOMS vibrate independently) emits incoherent light.   M.V.B.

cohesion. The bonding together (see BOND) of ATOMS or MOLECULES in a solid.   B.F.

Cohn, Norman (British author and historian, *b*. 1915), see under REVOLUTION.

cohort analysis. In DEMOGRAPHY, a cohort is defined as a group of persons who experience a significant event (e.g.

birth or marriage) during the same period of time, normally a year or a quinquennium. Thus, all children born in the U.K. in 1970 would form the birth cohort of 1970, all women married in 1970 the female marriage cohort of 1970. Cohort analysis traces the subsequent vital history of such cohorts. It has been used particularly in the study of FERTILITY, where the number of children born to members of a cohort at different periods of their lives is a significant index. But the method may be applied in other fields, e.g. educational and morbidity studies.   E.G.

Bibl: P. K. Whelpton, *Cohort Fertility* (Princeton, 1954).

Coignet, François (French industrialist, 1814–88), see under CONCRETE.

coincidence counter. Any device for counting events which simultaneously trigger two separate detectors. For example, two GEIGER COUNTERS placed one above the other will both register a COSMIC RAY arriving vertically, whereas only one will signal the arrival of a PARTICLE from the side. The two Geiger counters constitute a coincidence counter.   M.V.B.

cold, see under HOT AND COLD.

Cold War. Phrase coined by the American financier Bernard Baruch (16 April 1947), and given wide currency by Walter Lippman. It describes a state of hostility between countries expressed in economic, political, or subversive action but stopping short of 'hot war' or a 'shooting war'. Sometimes used to describe relations between the Soviet Union and the major non-COMMUNIST powers from 1917 onwards, the term is more commonly restricted to relations, after the defeat of Nazi Germany (see NAZISM), between the Soviet Union and her former Western allies. Some would further restrict its operation to the years 1945–55; others to the period ended, in the aftermath of the Cuba missile crisis (see CUBA; MISSILES), by the 1963 Anglo-American-Russian treaty restricting the testing of nuclear weapons (see PROLIFERATION). For the American controversy on the responsibility for the Cold War, see REVISIONISM (sense 3).   D.C.W.

Bibl: L. J. Halle, *The Cold War as History* (London and N.Y., 1967); J. L.

Gaddis, *The United States and the Origins of the Cold War* (London and N.Y., 1972).

cold-worked. Metal that has been deformed at a temperature too low for ANNEALING to occur. Wire-drawing and bending, and panel-beating in motor-cars, are processes depending on cold-working.
M.V.B.

Coldstream, Sir **William** (British painter, *b*. 1908), see under EUSTON ROAD GROUP.

Coleridge, Samuel Taylor (British poet, critic, and philosopher, 1772–1834), see under EXPRESSIVE FORM, FALLACY OF; INTELLECTUALS.

collage. Internationally current French term for the sticking together of disparate elements to make a picture. The modern use of this technique, now an artistic and educational commonplace, stems from (*a*) the traditional scrapbook, (*b*) *trompe l'oeil* effects in painting, and (*c*) such housepainter's techniques as marbling and graining. In 1912 the CUBISTS began incorporating scraps of wallpaper, print, etc. in their pictures; a year later Picasso applied similar principles to the construction of three-dimensional reliefs; and thereafter such methods became adopted by FUTURISM (Soffici and Carrà), DADA (Grosz), Russian CUBOFUTURISM (Tatlin's reliefs), MERZ with its use of rubbish, and, in the mid-1920s, SURREALISM with its incongruous cutting-up of old engravings.

New terms emerged during the collage boom of the 1950s and early 1960s, which accompanied the DADA revival and the rise of POP ART: *combine-painting* (Robert Rauschenberg's use of three-dimensional components), *tableau-piège* (Daniel Spoerri's ditto) and *assemblage* (embracing both these), while DÉCOLLAGE came to signify the reverse process. Examples of collage also occurred in other arts, e.g. the 'cut-ups' of the novelist William Burroughs. The real extension of this concept, however, lay in the MONTAGE practised in the 1920s, a much wider artistic principle subsuming photomontage and all other forms of collage. J.W.

Bibl: H. Janis and R. Blesh, *Collage* (Philadelphia and N.Y., 1962).

collective choice. Choices made by, or on behalf of, a group (such as a committee, or an assembly, or a nation). Much of the theory of collective choice is concerned with rules for basing group decisions on the preferences of the members of the group, e.g. the simple majority rule. The subject includes not merely institutional decision procedures, but also systems of arguments on social policy. Any social criticism is based on some underlying theory (often implicit) on what *should have been* chosen or done in view of the preferences or interests of the members of the society (seen as individuals, or classes, or groups) and the scope of the subject is, therefore, very wide. A.K.S.

Bibl: K. J. Arrow, *Social Choice and Individual Values* (London and N.Y., 1951); A. K. Sen, *Collective Choice and Social Welfare* (San Francisco, 1970; Edinburgh, 1971).

collective consciousness. A term used by Durkheim (in *The Rules of Sociological Method*) when trying to clarify his conception of SOCIAL (or associational) FACTS. It denotes, not the mere sum total of given elements in all the individual consciousnesses in a society, but the engendering, through associative activities within the constraints of specific collective conditions, of new elements of human experience, knowledge, value, will, and behaviour. These elements are termed by Durkheim 'collective representations': distinguishable sentiments and values (e.g. the British sense of 'justice and fair play') associated with shared cultural symbols (e.g., in this instance, the perpetuated traditions of the legal profession, courts, schools, games, and patterns of education and upbringing). In their totality, these 'collective representations' make up the 'social heritage', the framework of the distinctive collective life of a community. See also CULTURE; FOLKWAYS; SOCIAL FACT; SOCIAL STRUCTURE; STRUCTURE; SUBCULTURE. R.F.

collective farm, see under COLLECTIVIZATION.

collective security. The principle of maintaining international peace by the concerted efforts of the nations, especially by the efforts of international organizations such as the LEAGUE OF NATIONS and UNO. The concept was introduced into the

Covenant of the League of Nations on British initiative and embodied the ancient Anglo-Saxon idea of a crime against civil peace being answered by the 'hue and cry' against the transgressor to which all citizens were bound to respond. During the 1930s, however, many people in the U.K. deceived themselves and others into believing that by support for the slogan of collective security (with little consideration of how it was to be enforced) they could avoid the hard choices of national foreign and defence policy. It was left to Japan, Italy, and Germany to show how little substance there was in collective security when put to the test. Great efforts were made after World War II to embody these lessons in the machinery of UNO, whose action in calling on its members to contribute forces for the KOREAN War in 1950 was the first example of collective security involving military SANCTIONS. The split between the great powers, however, has reduced UNO to a marginal role in preserving peace.

A.L.C.B.

collective unconscious. JUNGIAN term for the past experience of the human species, which has been built into the inherited brain structure, and which manifests itself in the recurrent phenomena of the ARCHETYPES. Jung argued that an individual's functioning is the product of this collective unconscious as well as of a *personal unconscious* whose contents are forgotten, repressed, subliminally perceived, thought, and felt matter of every kind, and which, therefore, is not to be equated with the UNCONSCIOUS of FREUDIAN theory.

B.A.F.

collectivisation, see COLLECTIVIZATION.

collectivism. A politico-economic theory advocating that the means of production and/or distribution should be collectively owned or controlled or both and not left to the actions of individuals pursuing their self-interest; also a system based on such collective control. SOCIALISM, COMMUNISM, and other collectivist IDEOLOGIES proclaim the desirability of such control through public ownership in the interest of the community as a whole. Forms of collective ownership range from State property to a variety of COOPERATIVE institutions, with varying degrees of

control by members over decisions affecting their lives. Collectivism has a different significance in the context of an Israeli KIBBUTZ, a Soviet *kolkhoz*, and a Chinese COMMUNE. State ownership in itself does not signify collective control. The question of who controls the State and the collective institutions existing in it has been raised by many critics of collectivism as well as by some of its advocates, who have tried to tackle such problems by advocating forms of collectivism which would provide for workers' PARTICIPATION in economic decision-making, e.g. GUILD SOCIALISM and various forms of workers' control.

L.L.

collectivity-orientation, see under PATTERN VARIABLES.

collectivization. A conversion, usually compulsory, of individually owned agricultural holdings into large collective farms; the system of agriculture which predominates in most COMMUNIST states, with the exception of Poland and Yugoslavia, and which, with certain local variations, derives from the system set up in the U.S.S.R. in the early 1930s. In the U.S.S.R. collectivization was imposed in 1930 by draconian methods which met bitter peasant resistance: millions of them starved or were arrested and deported. Collectivization in the East European Communist countries has not been so brutally enforced, and in Poland and Yugoslavia was stopped, the peasants being allowed to adhere or revert to individual farming.

In the U.S.S.R. the *kolkhoz*, the collective farm, is to be distinguished from the *sovkhoz*, the State farm, in which the peasants are employees of the State. The *kolkhozy* are, legally speaking, the joint property of their members, who receive payment in accordance with the particular farm's profits. The original 'COMMUNE' form of *kolkhoz* was early abandoned, for the most part in favour of the less rigorous *artel*, in which the peasant is permitted a small private plot and the odd cow or two. One of the reasons for this change was the decline in agricultural output: the peasants show a much higher level of productivity in cultivating their own plots. Soviet agricultural productivity still lags greatly behind that of most other comparable countries, and new types of economic incentive and forms of work are now being tried out in the U.S.S.R. in the hope of raising productivity on the collective farms.   L.L.; R.C.

Bibl: N. Jasny, *The Socialized Agriculture of the USSR* (Stanford, 1949); M. Lewin, tr. I. Nove, *Russian Peasants and Soviet Power* (London and Evanston, Ill., 1968).

colleges of advanced technology, see CATS.

colleges of education, see under TERTIARY EDUCATION.

Collingwood, Robin George (British historian and philosopher, 1889–1943), see under NEO-HEGELIANISM; PRESUPPOSITION; SITUATIONAL ANALYSIS.

collocation. In LINGUISTICS, a term, primarily FIRTHIAN, applied to the regular occurrence together of lexical items in a language, e.g. *bar* is said to collocate with such items as *steel, soap, harbour, public*. See also LEXICON.   D.C.

colloid. A dispersion of small PARTICLES of one substance (usually electrically charged) throughout the body of another. Colloids are neither true solutions (where the dispersed particles are single MOLECULES) nor suspensions (where the particles are large enough to tend to concentrate as a sediment under the action of GRAVITATION). Typical colloids are albumen and starch.   M.V.B.

colonialism, see under IMPERIALISM.

colour field painting, see under ABSTRACT EXPRESSIONISM.

combinatorial mathematics. A branch of MATHEMATICS concerned with the computation of the number of different ways certain operations can be performed. A traditional example, which shows its use in calculating probabilities (see PROBABILITY THEORY), is to compute the number of hands of a certain sort that may be dealt in a card game. It is not a unified subject, but deals with a wide range of problems and techniques. Some of these latter (e.g. GRAPH theory) have developed into distinct mathematical disciplines.   R.G.

combine-painting, see under COLLAGE.

Comecon (or CMEA; Council for Mutual Economic Assistance). A Soviet-sponsored economic organization, set up in January 1949 in reply to the successful working of the MARSHALL PLAN and embracing the Soviet satellite states in Eastern Europe. Originally only an instrument for Soviet control of the satellite economies, it was turned in the early 1960s into a means of pressing economic and industrial specialization upon the countries of Eastern Europe, pressure which on the whole was resisted. Since 1968 it has functioned more successfully as the coordinator of East European trade both within and outside the bloc. D.C.W.

Bibl: M. Kaser, *Comecon* (London and N.Y., 2nd ed., 1967).

comédie noire, see BLACK COMEDY.

comedy of menace. A dramatic style which emerged in the British theatre of the late 1950s, in which the reaction of one or more characters to some terrifying and often obscure threat to their security is treated as a subject for comedy. The term was first used by David Campton as a subtitle to his four playlets *The Lunatic View* (1957), but was soon applied more widely by critics, in particular to the early work of Harold Pinter. See also BLACK COMEDY; THEATRE OF THE ABSURD.   M.A.

Cominform. Abbreviation for the COMMUNIST Information Bureau, established on Stalin's instruction in September 1947 at a meeting in Poland. The participants included representatives of the Communist Parties of Bulgaria, Czechoslovakia, France, Hungary, Italy, Poland, Romania, the U.S.S.R., and Yugoslavia. Stressing that the world is divided into SOCIALIST and CAPITALIST camps, the Soviet delegate, Andrei Zhdanov, called for an irreconcilable hostility towards the latter. The new hard Communist line soon led to the tightening of controls in Eastern Europe and to a world-wide Communist offensive.

It was originally planned that the offices of the Cominform should be established in Belgrade, but following the Stalin-Tito break they were set up in Bucharest, and in June 1948 the Yugoslav leaders were denounced as traitors to the Communist cause. The political coordination of the Party line internationally was largely effected through the Cominform journal, *For a Lasting Peace, For People's Democracy*. The Cominform never achieved the importance of its predecessor, the COMINTERN, and after Khrushchev's attempt at reconciliation with Tito it was dissolved in April 1956.   L.L.

Comintern. Abbreviation for the Communist (see COMMUNISM) INTERNATIONAL, established in March 1919 at a meeting in Moscow. As an association of revolutionary MARXIST parties of the world rejecting REFORMISM, it was to replace the SOCIALIST International. From the outset its policies were dominated by the Russian Bolsheviks (see BOLSHEVISM), who imposed on it their own Leninist (see LENINISM) principles of organization through the *21 Conditions of Admission* (which included the subordination of the member parties to the authority of the Executive Committee of the Comintern). This meant in effect the subordination of the national sections (i.e. parties) to Soviet control of their policies.

At the 2nd Congress of the Comintern in the summer of 1920, when the Bolshevik leaders thought that Europe was on the verge of a PROLETARIAN revolution, they promoted an intransigent revolutionary strategy; they repudiated 'bourgeois democracy' (see BOURGEOIS; DEMOCRACY), and denounced both moderate and radical (see RADICALISM) socialist leaders. When Bolshevik hopes of the imminent REVOLUTION in Europe collapsed, the Comintern leaders proclaimed a 'temporary stabilization of CAPITALISM' and developed various forms of UNITED FRONT tactics.

Beginning with the 5th Congress in 1924 the Comintern reflected the internal factional struggles in the Soviet Communist Party: the elimination from it of Trotsky, Zinoviev, Bukharin, and their followers led to corresponding purges in the leadership and the national sections of the Comintern. Its 6th Congress in 1928 inaugurated the 'class against class' policy aimed at the 'radicalization of the masses'. But the disastrous result of Communist policy in Germany (where Stalin's denunciation of socialists as 'social FASCISTS' facilitated Hitler's victory in 1933) led to the adoption of POPULAR FRONT tactics at the 7th Congress of the Comintern in 1935. Soon after, most of the leaders of the Comintern, Russian and foreign, were liquidated during the Great Purge (1936–8; see YEZHOVSHCHINA).

Stalin transformed the Comintern into an obedient instrument of Soviet foreign policy. When he concluded the pact with Hitler in August 1939, Comintern propaganda which for years had inveighed against the Nazi menace was peremptorily switched to an anti-Western line. It changed again after Hitler's attack on the Soviet Union in 1941. In 1943 the Comintern was dissolved, presumably as a gesture to the Western allies. It was, however, temporarily resurrected as the COMINFORM.   L.L.

Bibl: F. Borkenau, *The Communist International* (London, 1938); J. Degras (ed.), *The Communist International, 1919–1943: Documents* vols. 1 and 2, (London and N.Y., 1956 and 1960); B. Lazitch and M. M. Drachkovitch, *Lenin and the Comintern,* vol. 1 (Stanford, 1972).

commensalism, see under SYMBIOSIS.

commercials. The breaks between or during programmes on commercial radio and television when advertisements are broadcast. On American radio, advertisers often sponsor whole programmes or series of programmes, with their financial interest ensuring control not only of the advertising material but of the content of the programmes. On television, space is bought on an *ad hoc* basis, the charges being higher during peak viewing hours. The commercials, sometimes filmed with great technical skill, considerable financial resources, and some humour, are often the work of established feature-film-makers.   T.C.C.M.

commitment. A term the widespread use of which (as of ENGAGÉ, committed) in recent years derives from the position of Jean-Paul Sartre, most succinctly presented in *L'Existentialisme est un humanisme* (1946). Sartre affirms his ATHEISM and his belief in free will; concedes that he cannot be confident in 'human goodness' or in the socially just outcome of the Russian Revolution, which he none the less admires because 'the PROLETARIAT plays a part in Russia which it has attained in no other nation'. 'Does that,' he asks, 'mean that I should abandon myself to Quietism?' The answer is: 'No . . . one need not hope in order to undertake one's work . . . people reproach us with . . . the sternness of our optimism . . . What counts is total commitment (*engagement*), and it is not by a particular case or . . . action that you are committed altogether.' 'Commitment' *tout court* is usually assumed to be LEFT-wing, usually quasi-MARXIST; other brands are usually given a specific label, e.g. *Catholic commitment* ('eternal vigilance'). M.S.-S.

commodity fetishism. Term used (with sardonic reference to FETISHISM) by Marx in *Das Kapital* in maintaining that though commodities appear to be simple *objects*, they are, in fact, bundles of social relationships, transcendentals, with a life of their own once they enter the sphere of market exchange and values. According to Marx, the apparent 'object' (a table, for example) 'abounds in metaphysical and theological niceties'. In defining the treatment of commodities in CAPITALIST production and exchange, we must therefore, he adds, 'have recourse to the mist-enveloped regions of the religious world'. R.F.
Bibl: Karl Marx, *Capital: A Critical Analysis of Capitalist Production*, part 1, ch. 1, section 4.

Common Agricultural Policy, see CAP.

Common Market, see under CUSTOMS UNION; EEC.

common sense. The source or system of those very general beliefs about the world which are universally and unquestioningly taken to be true in everyday life but with which the findings of philosophers seem frequently to conflict. Examples are the beliefs that there is a material world which exists whether I am perceiving it or not, that there exist other people besides myself, that the material world and its human inhabitants have existed for a long time and will continue to do so, that what has happened often and without exception in the past will happen again in the future. Much, perhaps most, PHILOSOPHY begins from sceptical doubts about the material world, other minds, the past, the lawfulness of nature. In the face of such conflict some philosophers, e.g. Russell, conclude

that it is so much the worse for common sense; others, e.g. Thomas Reid and G. E. Moore, regard the acceptance of common-sense beliefs almost as a criterion of sanity. In this spirit many LINGUISTIC PHILOSOPHERS have sought to unmask counter-commonsensical philosophical theses by revealing the seductive misuses of language on which they take the reasoning behind them to rest. A.Q.
Bibl: G. E. Moore, *Philosophical Papers* (London and N.Y., 1959); A. J. Ayer, *Metaphysics and Common Sense* (London, 1969).

Commonwealth (British). An organization of independent, self-governing nations which has evolved from the former British Empire, with a secretariat and conferences attended by Prime Ministers meeting almost every year since 1944. The Commonwealth takes its origin from the self-governing white Dominions set up before World War I as modified by the *Statute of Westminster* (1931). It was extended and radically altered in character as an increasing number of British colonies were given independence after 1947. Its precise character eludes analysis by political scientists, who are inclined to dismiss it as a case of the Emperor's new clothes; however, it maintains effective social and economic relationships based in part on ÉLITE links, including education, in part on aid, and has shown a capacity to survive which has surprised the sceptical. Its most important members are: the United Kingdom, Canada, Australia, New Zealand, India, Ceylon, BANGLA DESH, Malaysia, Singapore, Hong Kong, Nigeria, Ghana, Kenya, Sierra Leone, Malawi, Tanzania, Uganda, and Zambia. Former British territories which have left the Commonwealth include Burma (1947), Eire (1949), the Sudan (1956), South Africa (1961), Aden (South Yemen; 1967), and Pakistan (1972). A.L.C.B.
Bibl: N. Mansergh, *The Commonwealth Experience* (London, 1969); H. D. Hall, *Commonwealth: a History of the British Commonwealth of Nations* (London, 1971).

Commonwealth preference, see IMPERIAL PREFERENCE.

commune. The form of organization of life

COMMUNICATION

and work in a collective (see COLLECT-IVISM) in which the members hold no private property and share equally the results of their labour. In theory, communes are the highest aim of both ANARCHISM and COMMUNISM. In practice, they have invariably encountered difficulties in facing such questions as the internal inequality of its members, the economic inequality between collectives, and their relation to the wider economic and political organization of society, the market, and the State.

Early communes were founded under the influence of the utopian socialists (see UTOPIANISM; SOCIALISM) such as Robert Owen, Charles Fourier, and Étienne Cabet, but soon disintegrated. During the period of War Communism (1917–21) agricultural communes were organized in Russia. Most of them dissolved at the advent of the New Economic Policy (NEP; 1921) and the remaining ones were transformed into collective farms at the time of the COLLECTIVIZATION of Soviet agriculture. During the GREAT LEAP FORWARD in China (1958–61), large rural communes were organized. These were highly regimented; economic incentives were replaced by propaganda and political pressure for greater efforts. The experiment, presented earlier as a short cut to the full-scale communist society, ended in failure, and the communes were quietly modified (without changing their name) along more moderate lines. More recently, individual communes have been organized by dissident groups in California, where they remain a marginal and transient phenomenon, less ideologically inspired (see IDEOLOGY) than their historical predecessors.   L.L.

communication, fallacy of. Allen Tate's term for what he regards as the false belief that literature can communicate non-poetic (e.g. political) ideas. Contrast COMMITMENT.   M.S.-S.

communication, heresy of. Cleanth Brooks's term for what he regards as the mistaken belief that a poem consists of two separable components: an 'idea' and a 'form' which ornaments it.   M.S.-S.

Bibl: C. Brooks, *The Well-Wrought Urn* (N.Y., 1947; London, 1949).

communication, theories of. In SOCIO-LOGY, theories which seek to expound the origins of the meanings (especially the symbolic meanings) that constitute human CULTURE, to map the channels through which those meanings are diffused (see DIFFUSION), and to trace the consequence for social groups of their dependence upon such meanings and their capacity to create them. Most sociologists would accept as an initial assumption that communication via language is in some sense a prerequisite for 'society' – though they find a place, too, for the discussion of NON-VERBAL COMMUNICATION. The nature of communication systems is a matter for empirical study – prior to the formulation of any theories about them.   S.J.G.

Bibl: G. H. Mead, *Mind, Self and Society* (Chicago, 1934); T. Parsons, *The Social System* (Glencoe, Ill., 1951; London, 1952).

communication theory, see INFORMATION THEORY; and preceding entry.

communications. A term used in GEOGRAPHY to cover all means of transport, for example by sea, road, rail, air, canal, or mule, by which people can make contact and trade with others.   M.L.

communism. A term denoting:
(1) A set of ideas and the ideological tradition (see IDEOLOGY) connected with them. Historically the point of reference for communist ideas is the principle of communal ownership of all property. Thus primitive communism refers to non-literate societies, in which basic economic resources (such as land, boats, etc.) belong to the community as a whole and not to individuals or families. Religious groups (such as early Christians or medieval monasteries) based on communal sharing of property are referred to as examples of communist organization; so are historical societies, such as Sparta, the Münster Anabaptists, or the Jesuit Paraguay republic, as well as theoretical schemes for ideal societies, such as Plato's *Republic*, Sir Thomas More's *Utopia*, or Campanella's *City of the Sun*.

Modern communism is specifically linked with the ideas of Karl Marx and the concept of a classless society (see CLASS) based on common ownership of the means of production. Such a society should, according to Marx and his followers, emerge after the transitional period of the DICTATORSHIP OF THE PROLETARIAT and the preparatory stage of SOCIALISM. In a full communist society the State will 'wither away', differences between manual and intellectual labour and between urban and rural life will disappear, there will be no limits to the development of individual human potentialities and of productive forces, and social relations will be regulated by the principle 'from each according to his ability, to each according to his needs'.

(2) Movements, parties, and governments deriving their support and legitimation from the claim that they are implementing such ideas. See BOLSHEVISM; CASTROISM; COMINFORM; COMINTERN; LENINISM; MAOISM; MARXISM; MARXISM-LENINISM; NEO-MARXISM; POLYCENTRISM; REVISIONISM; STALINISM; TITOISM; TROTSKYISM.

(3) Distinctive methods used by such movements, parties, and governments, and institutions emerging historically as a result of their actions. See AGITPROP; APPARAT; COLLECTIVIZATION; COMMUNE; CULTURAL REVOLUTION; DEMOCRATIC CENTRALISM; FORCED LABOUR; FRONT ORGANIZATION; KGB; KULAK; LYSENKOISM; MVD; POLITBURO; POPULAR FRONT; REVOLUTION; SAMIZDAT; SHOW TRIALS; SOVIET; STAKHANOVISM; UNITED FRONT; YEZHOVSHCHINA; ZHDANOVSHCHINA.
L.L.

Bibl: R. V. Daniels, *A Documentary History of Communism* (N.Y., 1960); G. F. Hudson, *Fifty Years of Communism* (London and N.Y., 1968).

community. In ECOLOGY, a term used (e.g. 'plant community') to define a unit of vegetation or group of plants sharing the same HABITAT, having distinct recognizable features which distinguish it from others. In human GEOGRAPHY the term is also used to define a group of people living in the same village, TOWN, or suburb in a sympathetic association. M.L.

community arts. An English term, coined about 1970, for the activities of groups of (primarily visual) artists attempting to work largely with and for local authorities, schools, remedial institutions, and other communal bodies rather than for the art market. Among media commonly used are mime, costume, movement, games, live and recorded music, and the use of INFLATABLES. J.W.

community politics. A term which became fashionable in Britain, after the Liberal by-election victory at Sutton and Cheam in December 1972, as a description of Liberal tactics (not in themselves new) in subsequent by-election victories and in the General Election of February 1974. Community politics implied the concentration of candidates' attention on local issues – at the expense, so their opponents alleged, of coherent national policies. Like the allied vogue-word PARTICIPATION, it assumed that ordinary citizens were inadequately consulted about political decisions by the politicans in the two major parties, who were also insufficiently interested in the parish-pump problems which touched their constituents' lives most nearly. In its detailed attention to the problems of particular individuals in particular streets it suggests the synonym *Christian name politics*. R.B.

community psychiatry, see under PSYCHIATRY.

community schools. Schools defined in the PLOWDEN REPORT (1967) as being 'open beyond the ordinary school hours for the use of children, their parents and, exceptionally, for other members of the community'. The same principle can be seen in Henry Morris's VILLAGE COLLEGES of the 1920s and 1930s. The intention is that families should be drawn more into the school, which should in a real sense become a community centre. W.A.C.S.

commutative law. In MATHEMATICS, the law that is obeyed when the result of a binary operation (e.g. addition, multiplication) is the same regardless of the order in which the operands are taken; thus $a + b = b + a, a \times b = b \times a$. Operations that satisfy this law are called *commutative*. For abstract MATHEMATICAL STRUCTURES the law may be taken as an AXIOM. Examples of *non*-commutative operations are *exponentiation* (e.g. $2^3 \neq 3^2$) and the multiplication of QUATERNIONS and MATRICES. R.G.

commuting (or *commutation*). Term

117

referring primarily to the daily movement of employed people between their residence and work. This definition is sometimes extended to include other less regular components such as the journey to school or to shops. Since commuter movements make up over half of all vehicular movements in many modern urban areas and are usually concentrated into two peak periods each day, they contribute the major share in contemporary urban transport problems.   P.H.

comparatist. A follower of the COMPARATIVE METHOD in LINGUISTICS or literature. Comparative philology began in the 18th century; it involved the hypothetical reconstruction of parent languages (e.g. 'Indo-European'), based on a multiplicity of examples from known languages. The work of Ferdinand de Saussure (see SAUSSURIAN) in linguistics grew out of his involvement with comparative philology, as did his view of language 'as a system of mutually defining entities'. This has had a crucial influence on later developments. Comparative methods in literature embrace such things as the habit (exemplified by Sacheverell Sitwell) of comparing literary works with paintings, architecture, and music, as well as the comparison of different literatures. Comparative literature is far more widely taught in the U.S.A. than in Britain.   M.S.-S.

Bibl: R. Wellek and A. Warren, *Theory of Literature* (3rd ed., N.Y., 1956; London, 1966).

comparative education. The branch of educational theory concerned with analysing and interpreting policies and practices in different countries. Despite problems of METHODOLOGY, factors like language, SOCIAL STRUCTURE, political system, IDEOLOGY, geography (e.g. mountains or jungles producing isolated COMMUNITIES), all provide differences which can be studied comparatively, in addition to administrative structures and economic factors.   W.A.C.S.

Bibl: G. Z. F. Bereday, *Comparative Method in Education* (London and N.Y., 1964); N. A. Hans, *Comparative Education* (London, 3rd ed., 1958).

comparative history. Although the ambitious studies of Spengler and Toynbee are both comparative and historical, the term is not normally used to refer to that kind of book. It refers to more modest attempts to compare two or three societies, often neighbours but sometimes as remote from one another as France and Japan. The comparative historian is usually interested in a specific problem, such as the nature of FEUDALISM or of absolute monarchy; tends to emphasize the differences as well as the parallels between the societies he studies; and resorts to comparison not to produce general laws but to understand particular situations.   P.B.

Bibl: Marc Bloch, tr. J. E. Anderson, 'Towards a comparative history of European societies', in his *Land and Work in Medieval Europe* (London and Berkeley, 1967).

comparative law. A misleading but established name for the systematic comparison of laws of different systems. It is a method of legal study and research, and not as the name suggests a distinct branch of the law or body of legal rules. Many studies in comparative law have been inspired by various practical aims, such as the establishment of uniformity in commercial law and in private international law.   H.L.A.H.

Bibl: H. C. Gutteridge, *Comparative Law* (Cambridge, 2nd ed., 1949).

comparative linguistics, see under LINGUISTICS.

comparative method. Frequently used in the simple sense of comparing one set of facts with another (for examples see other headings beginning with COMPARATIVE), in SOCIOLOGY the term is of central importance as referring to sociology's only alternative to *controlled experiment*. It is the sociological method *par excellence* for the formulation of definitive theories, including the specification of conditions for the *crucial testing* of hypotheses. What experiment is in the NATURAL SCIENCES, the comparative method is in the SOCIAL SCIENCES. (See also SOCIAL THEORY.)

At least four distinct conceptions have been employed: (1) that of classifying societies according to some criterion (e.g. the nature of the 'social bond'), thus forming a clear framework for amassing and arranging factual information and uncovering connections between social INSTITUTIONS (Spencer, Hobhouse, etc.); (2) that of constructing a TYPOLOGY on the basis of some hypothesis (e.g. Comte's 'Law of the Three States', Spencer's 'military-industrial' polarity, Tönnies's contrast between GEMEINSCHAFT AND GESELLSCHAFT, and Marx's distinctive stages of 'productive forces') and then comparing it with actual historical societies, to see how far it illuminated them, and to test its reliability; (3) that of comparing specific sets of SOCIAL FACTS (e.g. the rate of suicide and the degree of integration within specific groups – familial, religious, etc.) in order to test theories about their 'constant concomitance'; (4) that of constructing a MODEL in order to understand one particular 'cultural configuration' (e.g. of the rise of industrial CAPITALISM in Western Europe) and comparing other similar configurations with it, in order to test the correctness and sufficiency of the interpretation (Weber).

R.F.

Bibl: H. Spencer, *The Principles of Sociology*, vol. 1 (London, 3rd ed., 1885); E. Durkheim, tr. S. A. Solovay and J. H. Mueller, *The Rules of Sociological Method* (London and N.Y., 8th ed., 1964); Max Weber, tr. A. M. Henderson and T. Parsons, *The Theory of Social and Economic Organization* (Glencoe, Ill., 1947; 2nd ed., N.Y. and London, 1964).

comparative psychology. The rapidly developing branch of PSYCHOLOGY whose focus of interest is the similarities and differences between animal SPECIES, including man, especially where these can be understood in relation to the species' BIOLOGY and way of life or to their phylogenetic relationships (see PHYLOGENY). The comparative psychologist – who often prefers to call himself a psychologist *tout court*, or an ethologist (see ETHOLOGY), or just a student of animal behaviour – may study animals because they are simpler than man in their behaviour or brain structure and therefore easier to investigate; or because they represent in some sense an earlier evolutionary stage in man's history, with the implication that the behaviour of a fish or a monkey may tell us something of the fish or monkey stage of man's EVOLUTION. It is, of course, questionable whether the behaviour of such ancestors bore much resemblance to that of the fishes and monkeys alive today; and in any case the various monkey species

today show substantial differences in behaviour, so that it is difficult to generalize about *the* monkey. Despite these difficulties it has been possible to investigate some of the animal precursors of human abilities such as INTELLIGENCE, learning skills and language.

Although comparative psychology's interest in animals is by tradition predominantly anthropocentric, problems in animals' PERCEPTION or learning or motivation or development are also studied for their own sake. Field studies of animals in their natural environments, by zoologists and psychologists, have given a great impetus to such work, and have shown how the particular psychological and behavioural characteristics of each species are often closely adapted to their everyday needs.

J.M.C.

Bibl: K. Lorenz, tr. R. Martin, *Studies in Animal and Human Behaviour*, 2 vols. (London and Cambridge, Mass., 1970–1971); W. H. Thorpe, *Animal Nature and Human Nature* (London, 1974).

comparative religion. The attempt to compare the RELIGIONS of the world objectively. The extent and variety of the faiths held by mankind were not generally known before the 19th century, and then much of the information was conveyed to the West by Christian missionaries and colonists. During the 20th century a much more sympathetic attitude has been adopted by many Westerners with a Christian background towards BUDDHISM, HINDUISM, ISLAM, JUDAISM, and other, more local, religions; indeed, each of these faiths has attracted converts from Christianity. In many universities the comparative study of religion, rather than Christian THEOLOGY, has flourished. A dialogue has begun between the leaders of the religions, although with great caution due to ignorance, prejudice, and the more reasonable fear of a syncretism that would deny the differences.

D.L.E.

Bibl: R. C. Zaehner (ed.), *The Concise Encyclopaedia of Living Faiths* (London, rev. ed., 1971); N. Smart, *The Religious Experience of Mankind* (N.Y., 1969; London, 1971).

compensatory education. A phrase used in Britain following the PLOWDEN REPORT, to denote additional educational provision in EDUCATIONAL PRIORITY AREAS

119

in order to 'compensate' socially disadvantaged children. In 1967 the SCHOOLS COUNCIL supported a research project to screen and identify children in infants' schools in need of compensatory education and to devise teaching programmes to help those whose early experience has been stunted and distorted. Educational priority areas have been set up in Liverpool, in London, and elsewhere. W.A.C.S.

Bibl: Schools Council, *Children at Risk* (Swansea, 1969).

competence (in BIOLOGY), see under ORGANIZER.

competence and **performance**. A distinction which is central to GENERATIVE GRAMMAR, and has become widely used in LINGUISTICS as a whole. Competence refers to a person's knowledge of his language, the system of rules which he has mastered so that he is able to produce and understand an indefinite number of sentences, and to recognize grammatical mistakes and ambiguities. Performance refers to specific utterances, containing features foreign to the basic rule system (e.g. hesitations, unfinished sentences). According to Chomsky, linguistics before generative grammar had been preoccupied with performance in a CORPUS, instead of with the underlying competence involved (see ADEQUACY, sense 1). The validity of the distinction has, however, been questioned (e.g. are INTONATION, STYLISTICS, DISCOURSE matters of competence or performance?) See also LANGUE.   D.C.

competition. The action of trying to gain what others are trying to gain at the same time. In economic life, competition between buyers and between sellers tends to bring the rates of profit in different trades into rough equality; at the same time, it obliges suppliers to be efficient in order not to lose custom to rivals. Thus, in private enterprise systems, it exerts a regulatory function which some economists have tried to analyse in terms of the theory of PERFECT COMPETITION.   G.B.R.

Bibl: A. Marshall, *Principles of Economics* (London and N.Y., 9th ed., 1961), book 5.

compiler. In COMPUTING, a PROGRAM which reads a program written in a HIGH-LEVEL PROGRAMMING LANGUAGE and translates it into machine code, i.e. a form suitable for a COMPUTER. This translation process can be quite elaborate, and a compiler is an expensive piece of SOFTWARE needed in the development of any computing system. *Load-go* compilers leave the machine codes inside the computer to be run immediately; other compilers output (or store) the code in a form suitable for use by an ASSEMBLER.   C.S.

complement, see under SEROLOGY.

complementarity principle. A principle in QUANTUM MECHANICS (enunciated by Niels Bohr in 1927) by which an experiment on one aspect of a system of atomic dimensions is supposed to destroy the possibility of learning about a 'complementary' aspect of the same system. See also UNCERTAINTY PRINCIPLE; WAVE-PARTICLE DUALITY.   M.V.B.

complementary distribution, see under DISTRIBUTION.

complementation. In GENETICS, the process whereby the effects of a defective GENE inherited from one parent can be masked by a functional gene from the other. If the two genes in an individual concerned with a particular function are both defective, they cannot complement one another, even if the defects are in different parts of the gene; this fact can be used to decide whether defective MUTATIONS are situated in the same functional unit.   J.M.S.

complex. In psychoanalytic theory (see PSYCHOANALYSIS), a word with no single precise meaning; most often, a nexus of repressed ideas (see REPRESSION) and related EMOTION that plays a distinct role in human development and in the genesis of neurotic disorders (see NEUROSIS). Examples are the OEDIPUS COMPLEX, the ELECTRA COMPLEX, and the INFERIORITY COMPLEX. In popular usage, the term is loosely used as a synonym for OBSESSION, also in the less technical sense.   B.A.F.

complex function theory (or simply *function theory*). The branch of MATHEMATICS dealing with those FUNCTIONS which have COMPLEX NUMBERS both as ARGUMENTS and values and which have a well-defined DERIVATIVE in a neighbourhood of each 'point' of their domain. Such a function *f* is necessarily rather smooth and well-behaved. Calculations involving such functions (in particular INTEGRATION) can often be reduced to simple algebraic manipulations. Since many of the functions which occur in mathematical PHYSICS and in NUMBER THEORY can be extended to complex functions, the theory provides a powerful and indispensable tool for their study. Further, the beauty of the subject and its connections with TOPOLOGY and algebraic GEOMETRY give it a central place in mathematics.   R.G.

complex number. An extension of the notion of real NUMBER which was made so as to ensure that every algebraic equation (see ALGEBRA) has a solution. Each complex number can be written in the form *a* + *ib* where *a* and *b* are real numbers and *i* is treated like an unknown which satisfies $i \times i = -1$; this suffices to determine the laws of addition, multiplication, and division for such numbers, e.g. $(0 + i) \times (0 + i) = (i \times i) = -1$. Formerly complex numbers were also called *imaginary* numbers; now this term is applied only when *a* (the *real* part of *a* + *ib*) is zero. Though once regarded as mysterious they now seem a relatively concrete example of an abstract MATHEMATICAL STRUCTURE. Besides their use in algebra they are important because of the power of COMPLEX FUNCTION THEORY, and because the equation $e^{i\theta} = \cos\theta + i\sin\theta$ allows problems concerning PERIODIC FUNCTIONS to be solved by simple algebraic manipulations.   R.G.

componential analysis. In SEMANTICS, a method of specifying word-meanings by establishing common components of sense, e.g. *man, woman, child, bull, cow, calf* can be distinguished semantically by setting up the components *human/animal, male/female,* and *adult/young* – the sense of *man* being a combination of the notions *human, male,* and *adult*. Theoretical discussion continues over the psychological reality of the semantic components, and over the extent to which words in different languages can be analysed into the same components.
The term has also been applied to a type of analysis in PHONOLOGY, but this use is no longer common. It should be distinguished from the general term 'compo-

nent', referring to a section of a GENERATIVE GRAMMAR.   D.C.

composition (in MATHEMATICS), see under FUNCTION.

comprehensive schools. (1) In Great Britain, term applied from 1948 onwards to SECONDARY SCHOOLS (primary schools have in this sense always been comprehensive) which cater for *all* the secondary education of *all* the children in an area, as opposed to offering *selective education* in separate grammar and secondary modern schools; for the controversy over comprehensive education, see SECONDARY SCHOOLS. (2) In America (where comprehensive schooling in the British sense has always been the norm), either (*a*) a school formed by the merging of two or more PUBLIC SCHOOLS or (*b*) a school offering a full set of curricula.
A number of variations on the 11–18 comprehensive pattern have grown up in Britain. Amongst these are the *two-tier system*, first started in Leicestershire in 1957. Pupils attend a lower school with a common programme from 11+ to 13 or 14 and an upper school with a range of choices from 13 or 14 onwards. *Sixth-form colleges*, first tried in Croydon, offer another variation by providing a common education for all up to the statutory school-leaving age (15, now 16) and then concentrating in a specially built college those who wish to continue their education voluntarily up to the age of 18.
Most comprehensive schools in Britain (unlike those in other countries) group their pupils either by STREAMING or SETTING.   W.A.C.S.; A.L.C.B.
Bibl: C. Benn and B. Simon, *Half Way There* (London, 2nd ed., 1972).

compulsion. In ABNORMAL PSYCHOLOGY and PSYCHIATRY, a force or drive or impulse within the individual to do or think or say something or other, a force which he finds difficult to resist. It is a prominent feature in obsessional disorders (see OBSESSION).   B.A.F.

computability, see under RECURSIVE FUNCTION THEORY.

computation, see COMPUTING.

computational linguistics. A branch of

LINGUISTICS which studies COMPUTER SIMULATION of human linguistic behaviour, especially such applications as MACHINE TRANSLATION and SPEECH SYNTHESIS.   D.C.

computer. A mechanical or electrical device for processing information. Originally used only for numerical calculations, computers were used secretly during the 1939–45 war for cryptography and by the 1950s for commercial data processing; by now their non-numerical uses are at least as important as their numerical ones.

In *analogue computers*, which are almost entirely confined to the numerical solution of physical problems, each physical quantity that occurs in the problem is represented by a mechanical displacement or by an electric voltage or current. The various parts of the computer are connected up in such a way that these displacements are related to one another in the same way as the corresponding quantities in the real system. The computer thus behaves as a mechanical or electrical analogue of the physical problem. The accuracy of analogue computers is limited, and the time required to set them up for a problem is usually long.

Digital computers operate arithmetically, or according to other logical rules, on strings of digits, generally on the BINARY SCALE. (There are also *hybrid computers*, which are partly analogue and partly digital.) As they work by manipulating symbols and not by direct analogues of the quantities represented, their accuracy in numerical work is limited only by the size of their STORE and the nature of the ALGORITHM used, and they are equally capable of operation on non-numerical information.

The importance of modern digital computers is their ability to carry out computations involving many steps (often over a million) at high speed and without human intervention. They do this by storing the instructions (or PROGRAM) as well as the data being manipulated. What they do *not* do is to perform those specifically human operations (thinking, proving, etc.) sometimes attributed to them by anthropomorphizers – often people who know nothing about computers, or computing enthusiasts who know little else. In the first place, computers are *aids* to thought, proof, etc., not substitutes for them. In the

second place, claims that 'computers have shown . . . ' are almost always doubly false, because they are almost always made about precisely those problems which, because they involve VALUE-JUDGEMENTS and other complicated situations (and most human problems *are* complicated by computer standards), are the least possible to represent by a completely accurate MODEL. The computer can do no more than work out the consequences of the assumptions which underlie the model, and which are therefore built into its program. If the assumptions are seriously wrong, the model will be seriously inaccurate, and its behaviour as shown on the computer will bear only a tenuous resemblance to that of the real world. See also CENTRAL PROCESSING UNIT;   INPUT/OUTPUT;   INTERFACE; LOGIC.   C.S.

Bibl: R. R. Fenichel and J. Weizenbaum (intr.), *Computers and Computation: Readings from Scientific American* (San Francisco, 1971).

computer-aided design. The use of a COMPUTER, typically associated with a VISUAL DISPLAY, in such a way that a designer can see his design immediately and the consequences of changing it, while remaining free to exercise the unprogrammable qualities of taste and judgement. This generally involves showing a perspective view of a complicated 3-dimensional object; often the point of view can be moved, giving the impression that the object is being rotated. More sophisticated systems allow for binocular vision, and the designer may even get the impression of walking about inside his proposed design. The technique is still experimental and expensive, since it makes very heavy demands on existing computers.   C.S.

computer-assisted instruction, see under PROGRAMMED INSTRUCTION.

computer graphics. Designs drawn by means of a COMPUTER. Their principal use is at present in engineering and other design work, but they have also been used for purely artistic purposes. In the latter instance the designs may be recognizable transformations of existing works of art or photographs; or the operator may supply the initial image himself (often with the aid of a mechanical plotter, or a LIGHT

PEN applied to a CATHODE RAY TUBE display); or the computer may be programmed to act unpredictably, and in many respects 'creatively'.

The term is also used, in the COMPUTING world, to cover the HARDWARE and SOFTWARE required to make it possible to present and manipulate the designs. For instance, if the screen shows a perspective view of a three-dimensional object, a PROGRAM of considerable sophistication is required to allow the viewer to change the point of view so that the object appears to rotate.   P.C.; C.S.

Bibl: J. Reichardt (ed.), *Cybernetics, Art and Ideas* (London and Greenwich, Conn., 1971).

computer music. Music composed and even performed with the aid of a COMPUTER, a resource which has provided a breakthrough into new worlds of sound. Not surprisingly, the lead has come from North America, but many university music departments in various parts of the world now have all the resources needed for computer composition and performance. They enable the composer to dispense with traditional instruments, since the sound material is entirely synthesized. With proper PROGRAMMING, any sound may be obtained. The computer stores an immense variety of sounds which can be drawn upon at will, though the technique of handling the material needs scientific and mathematical skills as well as a musician's imagination. Essentially, the computer is both instrument and performer; the composer tells it what to do by defining the sound, then specifying the moment of attack, duration, volume, etc. The sound is processed initially through a digital-to-analogue converter, then via a smoothing filter into a tape-recorder with loudspeakers. More a plaything of the scientist than of the true composer, the computer has as yet failed to produce much of artistic substance; but composers versed in ELECTRONIC MUSICAL techniques, e.g. the American Milton Babbitt, or the Greek Xenakis, may well find it an increasingly valuable aid.   A.H.

computer science, see COMPUTING SCIENCE.

computer simulation. The construction and use of a computer program (see COMPUTER; PROGRAM) to act as a MODEL for a SYSTEM in the real world and so to aid in its experimental study. Two main areas of effort can be distinguished: the *continuous* and *discrete* areas. One range of problems, including population studies, economic systems, and real-time control (see COMPUTING), covers areas where a system lends itself to expression by sets of DIFFERENTIAL EQUATIONS. These have been studied by *analogue computation*, but studies are now more often carried out by *continuous simulation* techniques on *digital computers*, using incremental INTEGRATION of the sets of equations. Another substantial range of problems, often STOCHASTIC in nature, arises in industrial MANAGEMENT or control. Where the problem is beyond the scope of LINEAR PROGRAMMING or QUEUEING THEORY one may build a computer program as a model, experiment on the model to improve its behaviour, and then transfer the results to the real thing. Such models are usually called *discrete simulations*.

The term is also used in PSYCHOLOGY and ARTIFICIAL INTELLIGENCE work to describe programs which embody hypotheses about how people play games, solve problems (see PROBLEM-SOLVING), or understand messages. A measure of 'realistic' behaviour on the part of the program may be taken as evidence for the plausibility of the hypotheses.

Simulation programs are frequently large and complex. In both the discrete and continuous areas, special-purpose HIGH-LEVEL PROGRAMMING LANGUAGES have been produced and have achieved some popularity. The importance of an adequate model needs to be stressed, as do the dangers inherent in accepting the predictions of an inadequate one. With this proviso, there are areas, e.g. heavy industry and government, in which computer simulation is important, useful, and, though expensive, cheaper than experimentation on the real world – which indeed may be impractical or even disastrous.   J.N.B.

computing (also known as *data-processing*; *electronic data-processing* or *EDP*; *information-processing*). The use of a digital COMPUTER. (The use of an analogue computer is generally called *analogue computing*.) In outline the steps required for presenting a problem to a computer are: (1) analysing the problem and preparing a suitable PROGRAM; (2) verifying or DEBUGGING the program on a computer; (3) running the program on the computer with the appropriate sets of data. The first stage is carried out entirely by people, the second partly and the third very largely by the computer. As computers grew larger and faster the time taken by individual jobs, particularly in the debugging phase, diminished until the human operators were unable to keep pace with the computer. Various modes of operation have been introduced in order to get round this mis-match of speeds; all are implemented by an OPERATING SYSTEM which largely takes the place of a human operator.

In *batch processing* the jobs are run to completion in sequence; the input (of program and data) and output (of results) takes place generally via an intermediate BACKING STORE, often MAGNETIC TAPE. The operators load the program and data onto this *off-line* – i.e. using a small auxiliary computer while the main machine is engaged in some lengthy job. When a whole batch of jobs has been loaded, the main machine will process them all in sequence, putting the output into a similar backing store or tape. When the batch is finished the results are printed off-line by the auxiliary machine. Batch processing, though relatively simple, suffers from the fact that the *turn-round time* (the time between presenting a job to the operators and receiving the printed results) is much greater than the running time in the computer, being typically from an hour to a day or more and virtually independent of the running time.

Modes of operation which get round this difficulty all involve *time-sharing*, in which the computer appears to do several jobs simultaneously; actually it works on each job for only a short time before moving on to another. In *multi-programming*, time-sharing is used to allow several batch-processing queues in the computer at the same time. By separating the large from the small jobs the turnround time for the latter can be improved. A further step is to allow *on-line computing* from a TERMINAL in place of one or more of these queues; in this mode of operation the user is in direct contact with the main computer without the intermediary of an auxiliary machine or backing store. This reduces still further the turnround for the programs from the terminal while allowing a *background job* in a batch-processing queue to use any time which would otherwise be wasted in waiting for the operator at the terminal.

An extension of this is to replace the terminal by a number of CONSOLES. The consoles, which may be hundreds of miles from the computer, are situated for the convenience of the user. A system which is principally run from consoles in this way is often called a time-sharing or *multi-console* system. Console systems can be *dedicated* – i.e. confined to a few special programs, such as airline bookings or banking – or *general-purpose*, with no foreknowledge of the programs which will be run, so that stringent precautions have to be taken to prevent one program from interfering with another, whether accidentally or by malice.

In *real-time computing* and PROCESS CONTROL there is the additional requirement that the computer complete its response to any input within a certain *critical time* which is determined by the application. This poses additional problems, particularly in situations where the computer is heavily loaded. Real-time systems are always dedicated and often need extraordinary precautions to guard against possible breakdown of the computer.   C.S.

computing science. The study of the use and sometimes construction of digital COMPUTERS. (Analogue computers are generally excluded.) It is a fashionable, interesting, difficult, and perhaps useful activity. Unfortunately, in spite of appearing to be a mathematical or physical science, it has so far a pitiably small body of generally accepted fundamental laws or principles which are likely to remain valid even for the next 20 years, and consists instead almost entirely of ephemeral 'state of the art' information. A more appropriate title at this stage of its development would probably be 'computer technology'.   C.S.

Comte, Auguste (French philosopher and sociologist, 1798–1857), see under COMPARATIVE METHOD; ECONOMETRICS; HISTORICISM; POSITIVISM; SOCIAL FACT; SOCIAL STATICS AND SOCIAL DYNAMICS; SOCIOLOGY.

concentration. In urban GEOGRAPHY, a term used in the description of the population pattern of an urban area. The *density gradient*, i.e. rate of change of density per unit distance measured from the centre to the edge, is used as a measure of the concentration of a town's population. In contrast to this, its *central density*, i.e. number of people per unit area, is used as a measure of its *congestion*. See also DENSITY.

M.L.

concentration camps. Internment centres originally employed in the Cuban rebellion of 1895 by the Spanish military and in the Boer War (1901–2) by the British military in an attempt to pacify rebels by depriving them of civilian support in their chosen areas of operation. The term is now generally used to describe the permanent camps (some 2,000 in number) which the NAZIS established in Germany and later in occupied Europe for the detention of political opponents and of racial and social 'undesirables' in conditions in which they were unlikely to survive. Such institutions are an indispensable part of any TOTALITARIAN system of government, and in the U.S.S.R. the FORCED LABOUR camps play a similar role.

After the outbreak of World War II the Nazis created a new class of 'extermination camps' or 'death camps' (e.g. Auschwitz, Treblinka) in which the mass slaughter of Jews and others was systematically organized. More than eight million people are believed to have perished in Nazi concentration camps, among them as many as five or six million Jews. A.L.C.B.

Bibl: D. Rousset, tr. R. Guthrie, *The Other Kingdom* (N.Y., 1947); tr. Y. Moyse and R. Senhouse, *A World Apart* (London, 1951); E. Kogon, tr. H. Norden, *The Theory and Practice of Hell* (N.Y., 1950).

concept. The MEANING of a term and thus the smallest unit of thought, just as a term is the smallest unit of DISCOURSE. As terms combine to form sentences, so concepts combine to form PROPOSITIONS or complete thoughts. To acquire a concept is primarily to learn, and to possess a concept is primarily to know, the meaning of some term that expresses it (only primarily, since the capacity to recognize instances of a concept sometimes precedes the possession of a word to express it). In recent times philosophers have tended to agree that a concept should not be thought of as a kind of object, such as a mental image. People can share concepts (indeed they must do so if they are to communicate), but the items of their mental furniture are distinct and proprietary to each of them. To possess a concept, then, is not to own some easily identifiable article but to be able to *do* something, specifically to recognize instances of the concept in question and to construct, and draw INFERENCES from, sentences in which some word that expresses the concept occurs. The analysis of concepts, which some would take to be the chief or even the whole business of PHILOSOPHY, is a matter of finding more perspicuous and complexity-revealing words in which to express something commonly expressed by a single term. A.Q.

conceptual art. AVANT-GARDE visual art, ABSTRACT or FIGURATIVE, which strongly emphasizes content and deliberately neglects form. It involves eccentric materials such as earth (*earth art*), cloth, and refuse; everyday media such as neon lights, maps, essays, photographs, and human bodies (*body art*), which it uses in random assemblages (see COLLAGE); installations encouraging spectator participation; systematic yet banal designs; and blunt reportage. It aims at direct communication of a CONCEPT (usually an awareness of a place or event, or a technical notion from science or PHILOSOPHY), and treats the material means of communication as unimportant – disposable, inexpressive, and unaesthetic. Paradoxically, however, these material products are claimed to be works of art. Indeed, a self-conscious preoccupation with expanding or exploding the concept of 'art' in particular is central to many conceptual works. The school evolved about 1965 out of MINIMAL ART and HAPPENINGS, which it crossed with iconoclastic strands of theory and practice stemming from Marcel Duchamp and DADA, to emerge as one of the most single-minded examples of aesthetic NIHILISM yet produced by the modern movement (see MODERNISM). It overlaps with other recent 'tendencies' such as *land art* (art which adds to or modifies landscape, often on a large scale). It is international, loose-knit, and diverse. Thus the critical label 'conceptual' is often rejected

CONCEPTUALISM

by practitioners, who include Keith Arnatt, Gilbert and George, Sol Lewitt, Richard Long, Robert Morris, and the *Art-Language* group.　　　　B.M.-H.

Bibl: L. R. Lippard, *Six Years: the Dematerialization of the Art Object from 1966 to 1972* (London and N.Y., 1973).

conceptualism.

(1) A philosophic theory of UNIVERSALS which takes them to be CONCEPTS in the minds of those who understand the general word (whether verb, adjective, or common noun) whose MEANING the universal is. To the extent that a concept is defined as the meaning common to all of a set of synonymous words, this theory is a truism, since whatever else a universal may be it is the meaning of a general word. What is controversial is the contention that a concept is something mental and proprietary to a particular mind: for if I am to understand what you say I must attach the same meaning to your words as you do. A variant form of conceptualism takes a universal or concept to be a mental image. Here the difficulty is to see how one could have an image of economic inflation or negative electric charge or the conscience. Furthermore a specific, particular image is ambiguously representative: a mental picture of a particular dog could represent retriever, dog, left-hand surface of an animal, loyalty, chestnut colour, life, or hair.　　　　A.Q.

Bibl: H. H. Price, *Thinking and Experience* (London, 2nd ed., 1969).

(2) A vice of legal reasoning, attributed to some lawyers and legal theorists, which consists in treating the general terms and CATEGORIES used in the formulation of legal rules as having an invariant and completely determinate meaning, so that their application to particular cases is regarded as a simple exercise in syllogistic reasoning. On such a view, which has been stigmatized as *mechanical jurisprudence* or the *jurisprudence of concepts,* it would be possible, simply by consulting the definition or analysis of general terms and categories, to determine whether any real or imaginary case fell within the scope of a legal rule. Legal conceptualism has been regarded as an obstacle to the judicial adaptation of the law to social change and sometimes as a cause of unreasonable or even unjust decisions.　　　H.L.A.H.

Bibl: R. Pound, *Interpretations of Legal History* (Cambridge, 1923); J. Stone, *Social Dimensions of Law and Justice* (London and Sydney, 1966).

concrete.

(1) A material used in construction either (*a*) as *mass concrete,* a mixture of cement, sand, and aggregate with water, where only compressive strength is required; or (*b*), more usually, as *reinforced concrete,* i.e. combined with steel in the form of bars or wires to create a material able to take both tensile and compressive forces. While the material is setting it is held in place, and its ultimate shape and surface texture determined, by *shuttering,* which may be timber boarding, plywood, steel sheeting, or moulded plastic; this process can occur either *in situ* or during *precasting* on special beds.

A patent for reinforced concrete was taken out by Coignet in 1855, and Hennebique showed a highly developed system of columns, beams, and floors in 1892. Reinforced concrete has since been used and highly refined by engineers such as Maillart in various spectacular bridges in Switzerland, by Nervi in exhibition halls and sports palaces, and Freyssinet in bridges and hangars, and by such architects as, e.g., Auguste Perret. A new plasticity was given to the material by Le Corbusier, who also pioneered *béton brut,* the use of unplaned timber shuttering to create a rough boarded finish often seen in BRUTALIST architecture. A method of inducing compressive forces in the concrete by stressing the reinforcement before it has to take its normal loads was developed by Freyssinet from *c.* 1926 and is now known as *prestressing.*

Many of the characteristic shapes of civil engineering (curved dams, elevated motorways) and of modern architecture (thin slab floors on columns, curved SHELLS) owe their forms to the use of reinforced concrete, commonplace in all but the smallest buildings. See also CANTILEVER; PREFABRICATION; STRUCTURES.　　　M.BR.

Bibl: S. Giedion, tr. E. Matthews, *Space, Time and Architecture* (London and Cambridge, Mass., 3rd ed., 1954); P. Collins, *Concrete* (London and N.Y., 1959).

(2) In the ARTS, a term used to emphasize materiality and specificity, i.e. concrete as opposed to what philosophers mean by ABSTRACT. See CONCRETE ART;

CONCRETE MUSIC; CONCRETE POETRY.
J.W.

concrete art. Term used in the Abstraction-Création group from c. 1930 when Hans Arp was calling his sculptures 'concretions' and Van Doesburg of De STIJL began editing the short-lived *Art Concret.* Associated above all with Max Bill, the Swiss BAUHAUS-trained artist whose strongly geometrical art is based on mathematical reasoning, it signifies the materialization of an intellectual CONCEPT. In 1944 Bill organized an International Exhibition of Concrete Art at Basel, and thereafter the movement spread to Argentina, Italy, and Brazil. The work of Joseph Albers in the U.S.A. also relates. J.W.

concrete music. A form of music, first developed by the Frenchman Pierre Schaeffer in 1948, involving sounds of all types (musical, natural, human, mechanical, etc.) which, recorded on tape, are filtered or manipulated so as to disguise their origin. The music so produced is sometimes powerful and evocative, though often needing a balletic or theatrical interpretation to make its full effect. Maurice Béjart has used *musique concrète* in a number of ballets. The composition of concrete music, though slow and laborious, has attracted composers of the stature of Boulez, Messiaen, and Sauguet in France, the Greek Xenakis, and the veteran Franco-American Varèse. See also BRUITISME; COMPUTER MUSIC; ELECTRONIC MUSIC; FUTURISM. A.H.

concrete operation. In DEVELOPMENTAL PSYCHOLOGY, a PIAGETIAN term for a mental operation involved in the classification, seriation, and enumeration of objects. The notion is applied to the mental operations governing the organization of real (concrete) objects but not the organization of imagined possibilities. Such operations are mastered by children in the middle stage of intellectual development. P.L.H.

concrete poetry. A CONCEPT formulated under the influence of Max Bill and Eugen Gomringer, and launched at the São Paulo exhibition of CONCRETE ART in 1956 by a group of Brazilian poets and designers. According to the 'Pilot Plan' in their review *Noigandres* 4 (1958), the concrete poem is an object 'in and by itself', consciously using graphic space in its structure along lines foreshadowed by Mallarmé and Guillaume Apollinaire. Subdivisions of their movement, as it spread across the world in the 1960s, were the Brazilians' *semiotic poetry* using symbols, *emergent poetry* exploiting quasi-cryptographic juggling of letters, the related KINETIC poetry with its serial methods and PERMUTATIONS, the *logograms* of the Brazilian Pedro Xisto, and *phonetic* or sound poetry. This last was not in the 'Pilot Plan' but shares its concern with what Max Bense calls 'materiality, verbal, visual, or vocal', though deriving more from the *Lautgedichte* of MERZ and the noises made by FUTURISM and DADA. With this one exception concrete poetry is essentially visual or typographic, and thus merges in a much larger (and older) confluence of the verbal, visual, and printer's arts to which LETTRISM, spatialism (see SPACE), and POP ART contribute also. J.W.
Bibl: E. Williams (ed.), *An Anthology of Concrete Poetry* (N.Y., 1967).

concrete universal.
(1) In PHILOSOPHY, a term used by absolute IDEALISTS to describe individual things of a more substantial kind (see SUBSTANCE); 'concrete' aims to emphasize the thing's individuality, 'universal' the rationally systematic coherence which such philosophers take to be the hallmark of the true individual. The only wholly genuine individual for these philosophers is the ABSOLUTE, or Spirit, or the totality of what there really is. But its preeminently substantial individuality is approximated to by finite minds or personalities and by such articulated systems of persons or persistent social groups as nations, professions, and classes. A.Q.
(2) In literature, an abstraction developed by W. K. Wimsatt in *The Verbal Icon* (1954) and much used in the NEW CRITICISM. Wimsatt seeks, on HEGELIAN lines, to erect a holistic (see HOLISM) POETICS in which the 'particulars' of a 'successful' poem would coalesce into a totality that is its 'own' universal. Another New Critic, John Crowe Ransom, accepted the term – but on condition that it should be understood in a 'Kantian' rather than in a Hegelian sense. He felt that Wimsatt left no room for Kantian 'natural beauty':

127

man needs a 'double vision', so that he may see both the rose itself, *and* (then) its 'idea'.　　　　　　　　　　　　M.S.-S.

Bibl: J. C. Ransom, *Poems and Essays* (N.Y., 1955).

conditioned reflex. The customary translation (more accurately, 'condition*al* reflex') of the Russian term for a connection established by a CLASSICAL CONDITIONING procedure between an arbitrary stimulus and a reflex response. Pavlov's work (see PAVLOVIAN) suggested to early BEHAVIOURISTS an analysis of all behaviour in terms of involuntary stimulus-response bonds, thus removing the necessity for mental CONSTRUCTS such as 'will', 'motive', and 'intention'. However, conditioned reflexes in the Pavlovian paradigm can be clearly established only in physiological systems served by the autonomic NERVOUS SYSTEM; the conditioning of voluntary behaviour seems to require reward (*reinforcement*). So, although learned emotional reactions may be analysed as conditioned reflexes, most voluntary behaviour must be conditioned by operant rather than classical procedures (see OPERANT CONDITIONING).　　　　　　　　　　　　D.H.

conditioning. The deliberate and systematic attempt to control some aspect of human or animal behaviour, either, in CLASSICAL CONDITIONING (also known as PAVLOVIAN or *respondent* conditioning), by establishing a CONDITIONED REFLEX, or, in OPERANT CONDITIONING (also known as *instrumental* conditioning), by controlling the consequences of behaviour.　　　　　　　　　　　　D.H.

confidence interval, see under INTERVAL ESTIMATION.

configuration. An English alternative to the German word GESTALT.　　I.M.L.H.

confirmation. The support given to a hypothesis by evidence: the fundamental relation between premise and conclusion in INDUCTION. The fact that every known *A* is *B* confirms the hypothesis that every *A* whatever is *B*, but does not establish it conclusively, since it is possible that some as yet undiscovered *A* is not *B*, and thus that the unrestricted generalization is false. If evidence confirms a hypothesis,

then it confers some probability on it. Some broad principles of confirmation are intuitively acceptable, i.e. those which hold it to increase with the bulk and variety of the evidence. Attempts have been made, most elaborately by Carnap, to develop comprehensive formal theories of confirmation on the basis of such principles. See also FREQUENCY THEORY. A.Q.

Bibl: R. Swinburne, *An Introduction to Confirmation Theory* (London, 1973).

conflict theory. A term loosely applied to the work of a number of recent sociological theorists who have mounted critiques of STRUCTURAL-FUNCTIONAL THEORY on the grounds that it neglects the empirical fact that conflicts of value and interest are inherent in all forms of human society; or, at best, treats conflict as a phenomenon of only secondary interest by taking the very existence of an ongoing society as in itself evidence that some fundamental consensus must prevail. Consequently, it is held, exponents of structural-functional theory underestimate the degree to which the coordination of social activities and the stability of societies derive from the direct or indirect *coercion* of less powerful by more powerful groups. Some versions of conflict theory are of a MARXIST character; others, however, reflect a political philosophy of PLURALISM.　　J.H.G.

Bibl: R. Dahrendorf, *Class and Class Conflict in Industrial Society* (London and Stanford, 1959).

confounding, see under VARIANCE, ANALYSIS OF.

confrontation. Term employed, originally by Indonesian President Sukarno in the 1960s against Malaysia, to describe a conflict in which direct attack or declaration of war is avoided, and techniques of subversion, propaganda, and GUERRILLA raids are employed as well as playing upon the fears of international conflict entertained by the allies and associates of the opposing power in order to cause them to intervene and bring diplomatic pressure to bear. More loosely, any conflict in the stage before a declaration of war or outbreak of general hostilities.　　D.C.W.

Confucianism. The main RELIGION of the Chinese, so named after Kung the Master (Chinese Kung Fu-tzu, Latin Confucius)

CONNOTATION AND DENOTATION

whose traditional dates are 551–479 B.C. The *Analects* of Confucius present a religion of self-control and duty. They advocate gentlemanly conduct and conformity to the 'way of heaven'. They neither deny THEISM nor are very keen on it. The term 'Confucianism' was invented by 19th-century Christians under the mistaken impression that such a powerful religion must, like CHRISTIANITY, have had one extraordinary founder. The enduring influence of Confucius has been thought a worthy target for a hostile campaign mounted by China's COMMUNIST rulers in the 1970s.   D.L.E.
Bibl: H. G. Creel, *Confucius* (N.Y., 1949; London, 1951).

congestion, see under CONCENTRATION.

Congrès Internationaux d'Architecture Moderne, see CIAM.

Congress of Cultural Freedom, see under ENCOUNTER.

Congress Party. The dominant political party in India, linear descendant from the Indian National Congress, founded in Bombay in 1885 by the Englishman Allan Octavian Hume to press for representative government in India, and until its alienation of the majority of Indian Moslems a professedly inter-religious embodiment of the Indian NATIONALIST movement. It was reorganized by Mahatma Gandhi during the CIVIL DISOBEDIENCE campaigns of the 1920s and 1930s, and transformed into the Congress Party after Indian independence (1947), when various regional groups and the Indian Socialist Party adopted a separate identity. In terms of numerical support and organization, it has been the most important national party in India since independence. Its dominance in parliament was used by the government of Indira Gandhi to legitimize the suspension of *habeas corpus*, imposition of censorship, and actions against opposition parties undertaken by the Government following the State of Emergency declaration in June 1975. The party therefore forms the basis of Mrs Gandhi's constitutional DICTATORSHIP.   D.C.W.
Bibl: C. H. Phillips, ed., *Politics and Society in India* (N.Y., 1962, London,

1963); R. L. Park, *India's Political System* (Englewood Cliffs, N.J., 1967).

conjoncture. (1) The French original of the economist's CONJUNCTURE. (2) A term much used by some historians of the ANNALES SCHOOL (and often misunderstood by English and American historians) to describe change, including both the short-term combination of circumstances and the medium-term trend, like the fall in population and prices in 17th-century Europe. In both cases *conjoncture* is opposed to *structure*, that which does not change or changes only very slowly.   P.B.

conjugation. In BIOLOGY, the coming together of two whole MICRO-ORGANISMS followed by the exchange of genetic material. Such a process occurs among some PROTOZOA and (see BACTERIOLOGY) some bacilli. Conjugation is thus a pregametic (see GAMETE) sexual process.   P.M.

conjuncture. A term derived from the French CONJONCTURE (German *Konjunktur*), meaning 'the state of the economy' or 'the way the economic situation is developing'. Economists making short-term economic forecasts (see FORECASTING) use the word as shorthand for 'the complex trends in employment, output, prices, the BALANCE OF PAYMENTS, and other key economic variables'. Analysis of the conjuncture is closely related to the theory of economic fluctuations and BUSINESS CYCLES.   A.C.

connectionism. Edward Thorndike's term for his analysis of psychological phenomena in terms of ASSOCIATION between, not ideas, but situations and responses. 'Learning,' he wrote in 1931, 'is connecting. The mind is man's connection system.'   I.M.L.H.
Bibl: E. L. Thorndike, *Selected Writings from a Connectionist's Psychology* (N.Y., 1949).

Connolly, Cyril (British author and editor, 1903–74), see under HORIZON.

connotation and **denotation.** Two aspects of the MEANING of expressions: the *connotation* being, roughly, the meaning proper of an expression, the *denotation*

129

the actual thing or things to which it refers or applies or of which it is true. The distinction, thus put forward by John Stuart Mill, largely corresponds to that between the *sense* and *reference* of expressions (Frege) and that between their *intension* and *extension* (Carnap); it is quite different from the distinction between the everyday senses of the words, in which denotation is what a term really means, while connotation is what is associated with or suggested by a term. Two terms with the same connotation (e.g. 'man' and 'rational animal') are synonymous; the replacement of one by the other yields a sentence that is a proper translation of the original. Two terms with the same denotation (e.g. 'man' and 'featherless biped') will not generally preserve identity of meaning under substitution, but the TRUTH-VALUE of the two statements will be the same. The distinction can be extended to cover sentences as a whole, as well as the terms of which they are composed. The connotation or sense of a sentence is a PROPOSITION; its denotation is a truth-value (Frege) or, a little less provocatively, reality if it is true, nothing if it is false. The two aspects are intimately and reciprocally related: each, in a sense, determines the other. If the connotation is determined, the things to which it refers or applies are fixed. On the other hand, we learn the meaning of some terms by being made acquainted with what they denote or, where the terms are general, with representative instances of it.   A.Q.

Bibl: C. I. Lewis, *Analysis of Knowledge and Valuation* (La Salle, Ill., 1946).

Conquest, Robert (British poet and Kremlinologist, *b.*1917), see under MOVEMENT, THE.

consciousness. The state of an individual when his faculties of seeing, hearing, feeling, thinking, etc., are functioning normally. It contrasts (1) with his state when he goes into a coma, or dead faint, or is deeply hypnotized (see HYPNOSIS), or is asleep dreamlessly; and (2) with his state when, e.g., instead of feeling a pin prick as he would normally do, he is unconscious of it – either because he has been locally anaesthetized, or because, unconsciously, he does not wish to feel it, or because AUTO-SUGGESTION has successfully enabled him to avoid feeling it, or because he

has been mildly hypnotized, or for some other reason. In these latter cases, the content of his STREAM OF CONSCIOUSNESS is somewhat restricted in character. In the case of a man blind from birth, the content is greatly and permanently restricted, since he lacks one of our normal faculties.

At present we do not know what constitutes the full set of necessary and sufficient neuro-physiological conditions (see NECESSARY AND SUFFICIENT CONDITIONS) for the normal functioning of any one of our perceptual and COGNITIVE faculties. *A fortiori* we do not know what constitutes this set of conditions for our conscious functioning in general. Moreover, although consciousness is under constant and widespread investigation under the guise, in particular, of studies in PERCEPTION and COGNITION, there are deep conceptual conflicts about the CONCEPT of consciousness embedded in our CULTURE, including the SUBCULTURE of scientists. Thus, how far down the phylogenetic scale (see PHYLOGENY) is it correct to ascribe conscious functioning? We would probably all agree to ascribe it to a monkey reaching for a banana, or a dog running to greet its master. But what about a rat learning a new maze? If we say 'yes' here, then we will also be obliged to ascribe it to an earthworm learning a maze, and we resist this ascription. If we say 'no' to the rat, our refusal and doubts at once spread upwards to embrace the dog and the monkey. Our scepticism is strengthened by current attempts in PSYCHOLOGY to explain the behaviour of the rat without postulating conscious functioning. It is all too evident, therefore, that we are really quite unclear what we are saying when we ascribe consciousness to an animal or to ourselves.

One solution has been to suggest that our conscious functioning consists in a complex and continuous process of conceptualizing input from within and without the organism. This suggestion is promising and its HEURISTIC value has not yet been fully tapped, let alone exhausted. However, it will probably turn out to have the consequence of restricting conscious functioning to ourselves and to the higher animals for parts of their daily waking lives. This, in turn, has the logical consequence that the lower animals cannot feel pain. Equally serious, this solution by itself leaves unresolved the central problem of consciousness. If we say, e.g., that, when the clamour of the church bells strikes my ears, all I do (relevantly) is to conceptualize input, then (it has been argued) we leave out of account the sensuous and phenomenal features of my auditory experience and consciousness at the time. This, in turn, suggests that there are constituents or aspects of our consciousness that cannot be brought within the order of natural events and the scope of science. So our concept of consciousness seems to commit us to a DUALISM (see also MIND-BODY PROBLEM).

There have been various attempts to remove this dualism, or make it more palatable; e.g. it has been argued that, when I hear the clamour of the bells, the bodily processes and events involved are contingently identical with those that are my hearing the bells. Though this proposal may remove the dualism of events, it leaves us with a dualism of properties, or qualities, that is just as baffling. Again, it can be argued, that, in the sense that matters, it is a mistake to claim that there is any sensuous and phenomenal manifold over and above the conceptualizing I perform in hearing the bells. This is a profound contention stemming in part from Wittgenstein. But it is also a very difficult one to grasp, and it has not been as widely appreciated as, perhaps, it deserves to be. One of the reasons for this may be that Wittgenstein's solution appears to commit us to changing our CONCEPT of consciousness (and cognate ones) in such a way that it is no longer correct and tempting for us to speak of a sensuous and phenomenal manifold over and above our conceptualizing activity. If this conceptual change were to occur, then the traditional dualism of consciousness would disappear. One of the factors helping to bring this change about is the development of science. The more psychology, and related disciplines, can show how our conscious functioning consists in conceptualizing activity, the weaker will be our resistance to the conceptual changes that will remove the problem, and so bring the phenomena of consciousness fully within the order of nature.   B.A.F.

Bibl: R. E. Ornstein, *The Psychology of Consciousness* (San Francisco, 1972).

Conseil Européen pour la Recherche Nucléaire, see CERN.

consensus politics. A term much used around 1964, in the latter days of Macmillan's Conservative Government and the earlier period of Wilson's Labour Government, to express the concept of a government (or an opposition) attempting to attract maximum support by moderate policies that do not seriously offend any important interest. Consensus politics, a natural development of *Butskellism* (so named after the moderate Conservative, R. A. Butler, and the moderate Labour politician, Hugh Gaitskell), sought to appeal to the 'middle ground' of politics – a 'middle ground' arguably represented by liberal-minded leader-writers rather than by any wide spectrum of the public. In practice, it was often an amalgam of economic and WELFARE policies designed to please the largest possible number of people without unduly offending (e.g. by taxation) any substantial minority – while in other areas of policy, notably immigration and the EEC, the consensus to which it responded was that of fashionably PROGRESSIVE opinion, and bore very little relation to the wishes and ideas of a majority of ordinary people.   R.B.

consequentialism, see TELEOLOGY.

conservation.
(1) In ECOLOGY, the use of natural RESOURCES (hence often, explicitly, *resource conservation*) in a manner such as to prevent their unnecessary waste or spoliation. Conservation implies use (as distinct from preservation), but for the benefit of mankind on a long-term rather than a short-term basis; in the words of Gifford Pinchot, first head of the U.S. Forest Service, 'conservation means the greatest good for the greatest numbers and that for the longest time'. It may be achieved by positive steps through change in TECHNOLOGY (e.g. stubble-mulching to conserve soil from wind erosion) or ownership (e.g. creation of National Parks for conserving areas of outstanding natural beauty), or by negative steps such as legislation to arrest wasteful practices (e.g. limitations on the size of fish catches). See also RECYCLING.   P.H.
(2) In DEVELOPMENTAL PSYCHOLOGY, a PIAGETIAN term for the principle that quantity does not vary across transformations in its embodiment. Thus a given number of objects remains constant

whatever their grouping, and the volume of liquid remains constant whatever the shape of the vessel in which it is contained. The child is said by Piaget to lack this principle as a conceptual formulation until approximately seven years of age. P.L.H.

conservation laws. Principles of great generality and power in PHYSICS, which state that the values of certain quantities characterizing an isolated system do not alter as the system evolves. Thus, in a power station, chemical ENERGY in coal is changed into an equal amount of electrical energy plus heat energy, and in a NUCLEAR REACTION the various colliding PARTICLES may change their electric charge but the total charge is the same before and after. Many more recondite 'conserved quantities' exist such as the PARITY of the WAVE FUNCTION in QUANTUM MECHANICS during STRONG INTERACTIONS. At a deeper level, some conservation laws follow from SYMMETRY or homogeneity principles involving space and time. Thus the deeply-rooted view that space is homogeneous – that 'one place is as good as another', so that an isolated system will behave identically in different places – leads to the conservation of MOMENTUM, and the homogeneity of time leads to energy conservation. Conserved quantities are often called *invariants*. See also MASS-ENERGY EQUATION; TRANSFORMATION. M.V.B.

conservatism. A body of political ideas and attitudes, the burden of which is a preference for the old and established in the social and political order rather than the new and untried. As such its advocates emphasize the importance of law and order, continuity, prescription, caution in innovation, tradition, variety, the imperfectibility of human nature, and the consequent ineradicability of human vices. Traditionally it embodies a degree of deference, an acceptance of a degree of inequality between men, a distrust of the purely INTELLECTUAL approach to politics, and the acceptance of property. State intervention and state subvention both for individuals and economic institutions should, in the view of the conservatives, only be employed at the margin. See also REACTIONARY; RIGHT, THE. D.C.W.

Bibl: R. Kirk, *The Conservative Mind* (London, 1954; Chicago, 3rd rev. ed., 1960); M. J. Oakeshott, *Rationalism in Politics and Other Essays* (London and N.Y., 1962).

consistency. The relationship between PROPOSITIONS which obtains if it is logically possible that they should both be true. Two propositions are inconsistent if from the truth of either it follows that the other is false: e.g. 'All men are fools' is inconsistent with 'No men are fools'. In this example, it does not follow from the falsity of either that the other is true: they cannot both be true but may be, and presumably are, both false. An inconsistency in which it *does* follow from the falsity of one that the other is true is known as a *contradiction*, e.g. 'This man is a fool' and 'This man is not a fool', one of which *must* be true. The notion of inconsistency can also be applied to groups of propositions larger than two, e.g. a triad any two of which, taken together, imply the falsity of the third. A.Q.

console. A device by which a human being can communicate directly with a COMPUTER or other machine. For a computer it consists typically of a typewriter-like keyboard and a printing device (or sometimes a VISUAL DISPLAY) controlled by the computer. Owing to the great disparity between the operating speeds of human beings and computers it is usual to attach several consoles (the figure may be as high as 500) to a single computer, which services them in rotation. See also COMPUTING. C.S.

consonance, cognitive, see under COGNITIVE CONSONANCE.

conspicuous consumption. A term heavily used by Thorstein Veblen in his *Theory of the Leisure Class* (1899) for the extravagant use of expensive goods or services in order to demonstrate STATUS (sense 2) and wealth. Such ostentatious displays of purchasing power have led in many countries to the situation where a large proportion of economic resources is allocated to the production of luxury goods and so-called CONSUMER DURABLES which need periodic replacement. Consumption patterns which are used to reinforce or emphasize one's resources and status form one of the essential features of ADMASS. P.S.L.

constancy phenomenon. In PERCEPTION, the process whereby an object maintains an apparent size, shape, or colour that conforms to its 'real' properties rather than to its retinal projection. Thus a circle held obliquely to the line of regard looks 'more circular' than warranted by its oval retinal projection shape, and white paper standing in shadow looks whiter than a piece of black coal in sunlight, though the latter is reflecting more light to the eye. When objects are isolated from their surroundings, as when viewed through a pinhole, constancy is destroyed. J.S.B.

Bibl: M. D. Vernon, *Visual Perception* (Cambridge and N.Y., 1937).

constituent analysis. In LINGUISTICS, the analysis of a sentence into its *constituents*, i.e. identifiable elements. Any complex constituent may itself be analysed into other constituents; and sentences thus come to be viewed as consisting of 'layers' of constituents. Thus the sentence *The boys are sleeping* consists of two main constituents, *The boys* and *are sleeping*; each of these has two constituents, *the* and *boys, are* and *sleeping*; and of these, two may be split further: *boy + s* (the *marker* of plurality), and *sleep + ing* (the marker of continuity). Brackets are often used to indicate constituent structure, e.g. {[The ((boy)s)] [are ((sleep)ing)]}. Such sentence analysis is generally referred to, following Bloomfield, as *immediate constituent* (IC) analysis, and the 'immediate' constituents in which the analysis results are distinguished from the residual, unanalysable *ultimate constituents* (UCs). D.C.

construct (or *logical construct*, or *logical construction*, or *hypothetical construct*). Names given to a term or CONCEPT to which it is thought that there is nothing corresponding in reality, so that it is merely a useful fiction. It may be useful for summarizing masses of detailed facts, or formulating explanatory theories. Thus, if a historian or social scientist talks about 'the mood of a nation', this is a construct summarizing, and perhaps slightly distorting, the attitudes and behaviour of millions of people. Some would argue that the theoretical terms of science (e.g. ELECTRON, GRAVITATION, FIELD, GENE, MOTIVATION, SUPEREGO) are all constructs. Others would argue that even

familiar terms of everyday language (e.g. table, tree, house) are constructs. Usually the alleged construct is contrasted with something else which 'really' exists, as opposed to being a useful fiction. However, it is very difficult to formulate and defend any precise analysis of the distinction between real existents and useful fictions. See also ABSTRACTION; ONTOLOGY; REDUCTION; SOCIAL CONSTRUCT.
A.S.

Bibl: Bertrand Russell, *The Problems of Philosophy* (London, 1911; N.Y., 1912); R. Harré, *Theories and Things* (London and N.Y., 1961).

constructivism. Internationally influential Soviet art movement of the 1920s based on the elimination of easel painting. It applied a three-dimensional CUBIST vision, inspired by the sculptor Alexander Archipenko and by Picasso's reliefs of 1912–14, first to wholly ABSTRACT non-objective 'constructions' with a KINETIC element (1914–20) and thereafter to the new social demands and industrial tasks of the time. It was thus made up of two threads: (1) the concern with space and rhythm expressed in Anton Pevsner's and Naum Gabo's *Realist Manifesto* (1920), and (2) a tussle within the Education Commissariat between such supporters of 'pure' art and a more socially-orientated group headed by Alexei Gan, Alexander Rodchenko, and his wife Varvara Stepanova who wanted this art to be absorbed in industrial production. Though all these people shared much the same constructivist vision, as did Vladimir Tatlin whose model rotating tower for the Third International was its classic realization, there was a split when Pevsner and Gabo emigrated in 1922, leaving the newly christened movement to develop on socially utilitarian lines. As the *productivist* majority went into typography, photography, industrial and theatre design (see BIOMECHANICS) it gained the support of the PROLETKULT and of the 'Left Front' of art in Vladimir Mayakovsky's magazine LEF (1923–8), becoming also a dominant influence in the modern Soviet architectural group O.S.A. Through El Lissitzky's contacts with DADA, De STIJL, MERZ, and the Hungarian László Moholy-Nagy the movement spread after 1922 to the BAUHAUS, thence to be carried everywhere as part of that school's ever widening influence in design and basic art education.

In its 'pure' form it was later assimilated in the Abstraction-Création wing of international ABSTRACT ART, making a particular impression on such English artists as Ben Nicholson, Barbara Hepworth, and, after 1950, Victor Pasmore. In Russia, meanwhile, both sides of the movement alike became identified with FORMALISM, leading to its virtual suppression between the early 1930s and the THAW of the mid-1950s, after which there was a tentative REHABILITATION of the productivist branch and its contributions to architecture and book design.   J.W.

Bibl: N. Gabo, *Constructions, Sculpture, Paintings, Drawings, Engravings* (London and Cambridge, Mass., 1957); C. Gray, *The Russian Experiment in Art, 1863–1922* (rev. ed. of *The Great Experiment*; London and N.Y., 1971).

consumer durables. CONSUMERS' GOODS that are also multiple-use assets, i.e. assets which, when used, are not used up at once but rather gradually over a period of time. Obvious examples are houses, cars, washing-machines, dish-washers, refrigerators, vacuum cleaners, furniture, clothes, etc. It is not so much the fact that they are durable instead of perishable that distinguishes consumer durables from other consumers' goods but rather their multiple-use character as against the single-use character of the other consumers' goods; e.g. tinned fish is durable and it is a consumers' good, but it is not a consumer durable. In the case of particularly long-lasting and expensive items of consumer durables it is advisable to count the services they render rather than these goods themselves as entering into consumption. This in fact is the treatment that in the national accounts is applied to owner-occupied houses.   G.S.

Bibl: G. Stuvel, 'The Production Boundary in National Accounting' (*Development and Change*, vol. 4, 1972–3, no. 2).

consumer price index.
(1) In the U.K., an INDEX comparing the current cost of all goods and services purchased by all consumers with the cost of the same commodities if they could have been bought at the prices prevailing in the base year. This current-weighted price index is implied in and can readily be obtained from national accounts estimates of consumers' expenditure at current prices and the corresponding estimates at constant (i.e. base-year) prices.
(2) In the U.S., what in the U.K. is called COST OF LIVING INDEX.   G.S.

consumer society. A society that sets an inordinate value on CONSUMERS' GOODS, which it tends to regard not merely as 'the ultimate aim of all economic activity' but as the ultimate good. See also ADMASS; CONSPICUOUS CONSUMPTION.   O.S.

consumers' goods. The ultimate aim of all economic activity is the satisfaction of human wants by means of the consumption of goods and services. It is these goods and services that are referred to as consumers' goods. All goods at earlier stages in the production process, that is before they pass into the hands of consumers, are called *producers' goods*.   G.S.

contagious diffusion, see under DIFFUSION (sense 3).

containment. In politics (for its sense in PHYSICS see under MAGNETOHYDRODYNAMICS), a policy towards the Soviet Union originally advocated by the U.S. diplomatist and head of the State Department's policy planning staff, George Kennan, writing under the pseudonym 'X' in the American quarterly magazine *Foreign Affairs,* July 1947, on 'The Sources of Soviet Conduct'. The policy assumed the current antagonism displayed by the leadership of the Soviet Union towards the Western democracies to be inherent in the internal system of power in the Soviet Union, and called for a 'long-term, patient but firm and vigilant containment of Russian expansionist tendencies'. Kennan's recommendations became thereafter the basis of American policy towards the Soviet Union, a policy aimed at accommodation, not war, and expressed in economic and technical aid to non-Communist countries as well as through diplomacy. Kennan himself, however, subsequently maintained that the policy of ringing the Soviet Union's frontiers with collective security organizations (NATO, CENTO, SEATO) and bilateral military agreements misconceived the nature of the containment for which he had called.   D.C.W.

Bibl: G. Kennan, *Memoirs 1925–1950* (Boston, 1967; London, 1968).

contemporary history. Like the serious academic study of the subject, the term goes back to about 1950. It is usually employed to refer to the history of the last 70 years or so, though in France it may refer to history since 1789. The validity of the subject is still challenged by some historians, on the grounds that it is impossible to obtain crucial documents and impossible to see recent events in perspective. It is more reasonable to regard it as a valid field of historical study with its own problems and its own methods; as one useful way, among others, of approaching the events and trends of the contemporary world. See also ORAL TRADITION.   P.B.
Bibl: G. Barraclough, *An Introduction to Contemporary History,* (London, 1964; N.Y., 1965).

content-addressed store, see ASSOCIATIVE STORE.

content analysis. The systematic, and usually COMPUTER-aided, study of speeches, newspaper reports, novels, and other writings for the purpose of producing some new description or CLASSIFICATION of the content which is both objectively testable and useful for purposes of scientific research or political decision-making. For instance, analysis of subtle changes in the style of speeches made by a politician (usually one's opponent) may reveal important changes in his attitudes or aims or expectations.   A.S.

content word, see under WORD CLASS.

context. In ARCHAEOLOGY, a term frequently employed to define the exact location of an artifact or structure. A *closed context* is one in which the ASSOCIATION of artifacts is not likely to have been disturbed. A statement of the context of an object or feature involves an assessment of the STRATIGRAPHY of the site. See also PROVENANCE.   B.C.

context-free and **context-sensitive** (or *context-dependent* or *context-restricted*). In GENERATIVE GRAMMAR, terms used to distinguish between rules which apply regardless of the grammatical context, and rules specifying grammatical conditions which limit their applicability. Grammars containing context-sensitive rules are called *context-sensitive grammars.* It is claimed that they provide more accurate and economical descriptions of sentence structure than do *context-free grammars.*   D.C.

context of situation. In LINGUISTICS, a term applied by FIRTHIAN linguists to the non-linguistic environment of utterances. Meaning is seen as a complex of relations operating between linguistic features of utterances (e.g. sounds, words) and features of the social situation in which utterances occur (e.g. the occupation of the speaker, the number of listeners present). Contexts of situation are a means of specifying and classifying those situational features that are necessary in order to understand the full meaning of utterances. Firth, and the anthropologist Malinowski, made various suggestions for the analysis of relevant contextual categories, but there have been few detailed studies. (See PHATIC LANGUAGE.)

The term is also used, with a similar meaning, outside Firthian linguistics, though *situational context,* or just *context,* is more common.   D.C.

context-sensitive, see under CONTEXT-FREE.

continental drift. A theory originally suggested in the 17th century but only comprehensively stated by A. Wegener in 1911. Wegener based his theory very largely on the remarkably similar shape of the facing coastlines of Africa and South America and on close geological similarities between the two continents. He extended this evidence to propose that the earth, until some 200 million years ago, consisted of a single huge continent, which he called Pangea, surrounded by ocean. The present distribution of the continents had resulted from the breaking up of Pangea followed by a drifting apart of the continental masses. The theory required the continental segments of the crust to move freely through the mantle and oceanic crust. However, geophysical evidence indicated that the mantle and oceanic crust were stronger than the continental crust, and since there were no known forces of sufficient magnitude to move continents the theory lost support.

Recently evidence of sea-floor spreading indicates that the continents have moved relative to one another as part of the thicker lithospheric plates. Horizontally directed convection currents in the ASTHENOSPHERE dragging mantle material against the base of the plates are a plausible driving force. See also PLATE TECTONICS.   J.L.M.L.

continentalism, see under ISOLATIONISM.

contingency.
(1) In PHILOSOPHY, the property of PROPOSITIONS or states of affairs which neither have to be true or obtain nor have to be false or not obtain. A contingent proposition may be true and may equally be false; the matter is contingent on factors external to the proposition itself. Likewise a contingent state of affairs may obtain but may equally not obtain. That there are four apples in this bowl is *contingent*; that there are four apples in a bowl containing two pairs of apples is *necessary*.   A.Q.
(2) In THEOLOGY, the state of affairs in which each and every existing person or thing might not have existed, all creation being contingent or dependent on the will of the Creator.   D.L.E.

contingency planning, see under FORECASTING.

continuity. Precise mathematical characterization of this fundamental CONCEPT is one of the initial tasks of TOPOLOGY. If one draws a line without lifting the pencil from the paper then, intuitively, the line is continuous. On the one hand this says something about the line as a *completed product* – it has no holes or gaps; this is expressed mathematically by saying that the line is a CONTINUUM, that is a topological space having certain well-defined properties. On the other hand, the drawing of the line is a *continuous process,* one which does not make sudden jumps. Mathematically, the line is a FUNCTION f from one topological 'space' (the interval of time during which it is drawn) to another (the plane of the paper). The continuity of f is defined as follows: if P is any point on the line and d is any distance, however small, then there is an interval of time during which the point of the pencil remains within distance d from P. In other words, an arbitrarily small change in the value is produced by *all* sufficiently small changes in the ARGUMENT. This gives a *general* definition applicable whenever the notions 'arbitrarily small' and 'sufficiently small' are well defined.   R.G.; A.S.

continuous assessment. A mode of replacing formal examinations at the end of a year or a course by a running check on achievement throughout the course. This cumulative testing is seen as part of the current work, a cross-check and not a ritual ordeal; thus the distorting effect of examinations is thought to be removed from the curriculum and the student relieved of much anxiety. Critics of continuous assessment point to the element of strain present in perpetual judgement, and to the lack of an incentive which a final examination provides to sum up and reflect on the course as a whole. This criticism would not apply to a combination of continuous assessment and terminal examination.   W.A.C.S.

continuous creation, see STEADY-STATE HYPOTHESIS.

continuum.
(1) In PHYSICS, the SET of values of a QUANTITY which can vary continuously. Thus, the points on a line form a one-dimensional continuum, and the points on a surface form a two-dimensional continuum. By contrast, the points on a crystal LATTICE, whose atomic positions vary discontinuously, do not form a continuum.   M.V.B.
(2) In MATHEMATICS, *the* continuum is the set of real NUMBERS; other sorts of continuum have been characterized in TOPOLOGY. Cantor's *continuum hypothesis* is that the CARDINAL of the continuum is the least cardinal greater than aleph zero. This remains an open problem of SET THEORY; it can neither be proved nor disproved from the standard axioms.   R.G.

contraction hypothesis. A long-standing theory which attempts to explain the formation of major structures of the earth, such as mountain chains, by crustal shortening. A major prop for the theory is the observation that the earth is losing heat and may therefore be cooling and contracting overall. The most rapid rate of cooling and contraction is assumed to be in a zone a few hundred kilometres below the surface. The outer crust, which is assumed not to be cooling nor contracting to any extent, has therefore crumpled and thickened to fit a smaller surface area. The simplest picture of the crust in this condition would be the skin on a dried apple. Apart from the fact that it is not known whether the earth is cooling down or heating up, crustal shortening does not explain vertical displacement of rocks nor the major lateral movements of the crust (as part of the LITHOSPHERE) implied in PLATE TECTONICS theory.   J.L.M.L.

contradiction, see under CONSISTENCY.

control engineering. The branch of ENGINEERING that deals with the adjustment of apparatus and SYSTEMS, whether or not a human operator is involved. It therefore embraces the subject of AUTOMATION and is concerned with closed-loop systems of control. The detection of an error, and the use of this information to correct the error, is often termed a FEEDBACK system. It involves the use of measuring instruments (detectors), amplifiers and power units. Control engineering, which began experimentally, developed fairly rapidly into a mathematical discipline whose theoretical aspects are closely allied to those of COMPUTING.   E.R.L.
    Bibl: R. C. Dorf, *Modern Control Systems* (Reading, Mass., 1967); O. I. Elgerd, *Control Systems Theory* (London and N.Y., 1967).

control group. In EXPERIMENTAL PSYCHOLOGY, a group of subjects matched as evenly as possible with a second group (the *experimental group*), and submitted to the same test but without prior exposure to the factor – practice, fatigue, DRUGS, or whatever – whose effects are under investigation. If the groups perform differently, the difference (the *dependent variable*) is presumed to be due to that factor (the *independent variable*). Ideally, those conducting the test and analysing the results should be unaware of which subjects are in which group.   J.S.B.

control theory, see under CONTROL ENGINEERING; CYBERNETICS.

conurbation. In GEOGRAPHY, a single, continuous urban region formed by the coalescence of two or more previously separate urban centres. A conurbation normally extends across several administrative divisions. The term was first used by Patrick Geddes and C. B. Fawcett in the first quarter of this century in describing English city regions, and officially incorporated into the British census in 1951.   P.H.

convection. The rising of hot portions of a liquid or gas, and the sinking of cold parts, which occurs because of the smaller force of GRAVITATION on the less dense hot portions. Convection is the principal agent of heat transfer in the atmosphere and oceans.   M.V.B.

conventional war, see under WAR.

conventionalism.
    (1) In philosophy of science (see SCIENCE, PHILOSOPHY OF), a doctrine advanced principally by Henri Poincaré, which holds that scientific theories are not summaries of passively received experience but are free creations of the mind for the simplest and most convenient interpretation of nature. Two degrees of conventionality in scientific theories need to be distinguished. The Newtonian formula that force is the product of MASS and ACCELERATION is a pure convention of language; it registers a decision, although not an arbitrary one, about the use of the word 'force' within PHYSICS. On the other hand, the element of convention in the choice between the Ptolemaic and Copernican accounts of the solar system is less fundamental. Both accounts agree with experience, although inconsistent with each other. Convenience dictates that Copernicus's should be preferred since it is the simpler of the two.
    (2) The theory that, since the meaning of linguistic expressions is assigned to them by convention, analytic propositions (see ANALYTIC; PROPOSITIONS) owe their TRUTH to the conventions of language.   A.Q.

convergence. Consider the infinite sequence ½, ¾, ⅞, ¹⁵⁄₁₆, . . . ; intuitively this *converges* (or *tends*) to the LIMIT 1. This is made precise by saying that however large the number k there can be found a corresponding number m such that all members of the sequence beyond the mth differ from 1 by less than $1/k$. A sequence *converges* if there is some number to which it tends. Otherwise it may *oscillate* (e.g. 1,0,1,0,1,0, . . .) or may *diverge* (tend to infinity) (e.g. 1,2,3,4, . . .). Corresponding definitions apply to infinite SERIES, the series $\frac{1}{2} + \frac{1}{4} + \frac{1}{8} + \frac{1}{16} + \ldots$, $1 - 1 + 1 - 1 + \ldots$, $1 + 1 + 1 + 1 + \ldots$ are associated in an obvious way with the above three sequences. Infinite series are a valuable tool in the CALCULUS and in the computation of mathematical tables.   R.G.

convergers and **divergers.** Two contrasted PERSONALITY TYPES postulated by Liam Hudson, who had observed two distinct patterns of intellectual style within a group of ably working children. *Convergers* are those who do better at conventional intelligence tests; *divergers* are those who do better at open-ended tests, without fixed limits or single correct responses. The distinction is a measure of bias, not of level of ability. Hudson suggests that students of the PHYSICAL SCIENCES are on the whole convergers, while students of ARTS subjects are divergers. See also INTELLIGENCE; VERTICAL AND LATERAL THINKING.   M.BE.
    Bibl: L. Hudson, *Contrary Imaginations* (London and N.Y., 1966).

conversion. In psychoanalytic theory (see PSYCHOANALYSIS), the translation of repressed material into overt symptomatic behaviour, frequently in the form of *conversion hysteria*, a nervous disorder characterized by memory lapse, hallucination, and loss of control of various sensory and motor processes.   W.Z.

converter (in COMPUTING), see under DIGITAL-TO-ANALOGUE CONVERTER.

convertibility, see under BILATERALISM AND MULTILATERALISM.

Conway, William Martin (British explorer and art critic, 1856–1937), see under IMAGINARY MUSEUM.

cool, see under HOT.

Cooley, Charles Horton (U.S. sociologist, 1864–1929), see under CHICAGO SCHOOL.

cooperatives. Voluntary associations created for mutual economic assistance and characterized by (1) being owned by their patrons (rather than by investors), (2) the annual redistribution of net earnings, and (3) being run by directors who are normally members. The cooperative movement, now widely dispersed, grew out of ideas formulated in the early 19th century by Robert Owen in Britain and Charles Fourier in France. Cooperatives have flourished in the U.S.A. where they include farming cooperatives (for marketing, processing, and purchasing); retailer-owned wholesale cooperatives; mutual insurance companies; credit and banking cooperatives; CONSUMERS' GOODS stores; and group health and medical schemes.   D.E.
    Bibl: M. Digby, *The World Cooperative Movement* (London, rev. ed., 1960).

coordinate. A mathematical device by which a geometrical or physical configuration can be represented in numerical terms. Thus the *cartesian coordinates* (x,y) of a point P in the plane are the signed parallel projections of OP onto a chosen pair of (not necessarily perpendicular) rectilinear axes OX, OY measured in terms of a chosen unit of length. The *polar* coordinates of P (with respect to the origin O and the axis OX) are the distance OP and the angle XOP. A curve can then be described by an EQUATION involving the coordinates of P which is satisfied if and only if P lies on the curve. See also TENSOR; TRANSFORMATION; VECTOR.   R.G.

co-partnership, see under PROFIT-SHARING.

Copeau, Jacques (French actor and theatre director, 1879–1949), see under CARTEL; OPEN STAGE.

Copland, Aaron (U.S. composer, *b.*1900), see under JAZZ.

Co-Prosperity Sphere, see GREATER EAST ASIA CO-PROSPERITY SPHERE.

Corbusier, see LE CORBUSIER.

core (of an economy). An allocation of goods and services to the various members of an economy is said to be in the core if there is no coalition of members of the economy who could, by isolating themselves from the rest of the economy and agreeing some distribution of what they have or can make among themselves, improve matters for themselves. This equilibrium concept is borrowed from GAMES THEORY, but it can be traced back to the economist F. Y. Edgeworth. It has interested theoretical economists because the specification is independent of any institutional framework, such as the institutions of a MARKET ECONOMY. It can be shown that in certain economies with a large number of members, no one of whom is important, any core allocation is approximately the same as a competitive EQUILIBRIUM, and this may be taken to suggest that market institutions are in some sense natural, and that any lack of such institutions requires an explanation as to why certain coalitions do not form. Among the difficulties of the concept, it should be noted that the core may be empty (i.e. not exist), and that it does not allow for many of the threats and agreements that actually occur.   J.A.M.

Bibl: K. J. Arrow and F. H. Hahn, *General Competitive Analysis* (Edinburgh and San Francisco, 1971), ch. 8.

core (of the earth), see under ASTHENOSPHERE.

core store. A form of computer STORE in which each BIT is stored separately on a small ring of ferrite. This has two states of magnetization which represent the values 0 and 1. A large COMPUTER may have several million such *cores*, each threaded by two or three wires.   C.S.

core values, see under PARSONIAN.

Corman, Cid (U.S. poet and editor, *b*. 1924), see under BLACK MOUNTAIN.

Corneille, Cornelis van Beverloo (Belgian painter, *b*. 1922), see under COBRA.

corona. A luminous halo of tenuous gas surrounding the sun. Normally it is invisible in the glare from the main body of the sun; during a total eclipse it stands out dramatically.   M.V.B.

Corot, Jean-Baptiste-Camille (French painter, 1796–1875), see under IMPRESSIONISM.

corporate state. A state based on the theory that the political community is composed of a number of diverse economic and functional groups, from which it follows that the representation of the individual citizen, or his participation in government, should be based, not on the territorial location of his home but on the functional group of which, by job or profession, he is a member. Theoretically the corporative bodies (corporations or estates) should be autonomous as were the medieval 'estates' and 'guilds' admired by the exponents of the theory of the corporate state. In practice the doctrine of the corporate state was adopted by single-party centralized FASCIST regimes, under whom the corporations remained largely powerless. Some observers profess to discover increasing elements of corporativism in the regard paid by successive British governments, in the formulation of pay, price, and public investment policies, to consultations with the T.U.C., the C.B.I., and other such bodies.   D.C.W.

Bibl: R. H. Bowen, *German Theories of the Corporative State* (London and N.Y., 1947); J. K. Galbraith, *The New Industrial State* (2nd ed., Boston, 1971; London, 1972).

corporate strategy. The process and statement of a MANAGEMENT's *long-range planning*. It involves a systematic approach to FORECASTING, the identifying of objectives, the determining of alternative strategies, evaluation, and choice, and is an important part of top management responsibility, even where there is a corporate-planning executive or department. Typically the overall corporate strategy will have several subordinate and interrelated strategies, e.g. for product and market development, for research and technical development, for finance, for management development and ORGANIZATIONAL DEVELOPMENT, and for predicting the organization's need for trained manpower (*manpower planning*). Other aspects of the corporate strategy may include *acquisition*, in which the company decides to expand by the *take-over* of other companies in contested take-over bids or by agreed *mergers*; *diversification*, which implies an intention to broaden the variety of products or services available (e.g. a clearing bank entering the credit-card business); *integration*, either *vertically* by extending the supply chain (e.g. a newspaper publisher acquiring newsagent outlets) or *horizontally* by spreading the base of related goods or services (e.g. by acquiring other companies in the same field). R.I.T.

Bibl: H. I. Ansoff, *Corporate Strategy* (N.Y., 1965).

corporation tax. A tax specifically applied to the income of companies and other corporate bodies. In the U.K. the term was first applied to the system introduced in 1965, replacing the previous income tax and profits tax applying to companies. The so-called *classical system* of corporation tax, in force in the U.K. from 1965 to 1973, imposes a tax on the company regardless of whether or not the profits are distributed and then imposes a full additional tax burden on the shareholder when the dividends are distributed. Two other systems give some relief from this double taxation of distributed profits: (1) the *imputation system* introduced in the U.K. in 1973 gives relief at the shareholder level by giving the recipient of the dividend an *imputation credit* against his personal tax liability to take partial account of the tax already borne on the profits underlying the dividend; (2) the *two-rate system* gives relief at the company level by subjecting distributed profits to a lower rate of corporation tax. The latter two systems have similar domestic, but different international, consequences. Supporters of the classical system say that it encourages companies to retain profits for INVESTMENT. Opponents say that it inhibits the functioning of the CAPITAL market, discriminates between different forms of business organization, and, at high rates, can be unfair and burdensome. J.F.C.

corpus (plural *corpora*). In LINGUISTICS, a collection of recorded spoken or written utterances, used to suggest or verify hypotheses about linguistic structure (see, e.g., ADEQUACY, sense 1). D.C.

corpuscle (in PHYSICS), see PARTICLE.

corpuscular theory. A theory in OPTICS, in which light is treated as a stream of PARTICLES. Because of the great authority of Newton, the corpuscular theory survived until 1820, even though it could not account for wave effects such as DIFFRACTION. In the present century the theory has been partially revived because of the discovery that light is emitted and absorbed in discrete PHOTONS. See also WAVE-PARTICLE DUALITY. M.V.B.

corrasion. In GEOLOGY, a process of erosion in which the principal action is abrasion. Rock particles carried along by running water, wind, or glaciers are rubbed against adjacent bedrock, and in doing so are themselves broken down into smaller particles. They are thus more easily carried away. The bed of a river is partly worn away by corrasive action, and potholes are developed in the solid rock of the bed by pebbles and boulders swirling around in eddy currents. The sea erodes the shore and cliffs of the coast in part by this process: waves pick up pebbles and sand from the beach, batter the cliffs, and wash backwards and forwards across the shore. J.L.M.L.

correlation. In STATISTICS it is common to make two or more observations simultaneously, e.g. to measure both a man's height and his weight. If neither of these observations gives any information about the other they are *independent*. If (as with height and weight) they tend to increase or decrease together, they are *positively correlated*; if the tendency is for one to decrease as the other increases, they are *negatively correlated*. If changes in one variable are proportional (whether positively or negatively) to changes in the other (as with the lengths and breadths of leaves from a tree), the correlation is *linear*; otherwise (as with the leaves' lengths and areas) it is *non-linear*. The usual type of correlation coefficient measures linear correlation, and is often misused in circumstances where the dependence is non-linear. R.SI.

correspondence, see under TRUTH.

corrosion. The chemical processes which progressively destroy a metal. Corrosion is often caused by oxygen in the air and moisture, e.g. the rusting of iron, but it may arise from the attack of other gases, ACIDS, or ALKALIS. Dissolution of the metal may occur, but OXIDATION generally takes place and the reactions are frequently ELECTROCHEMICAL, although the details of many corrosion processes are still obscure.   B.F.

Corso, Gregory (U.S. poet, *b*.1930), see under BEAT.

cosmic background radiation. On the BIG-BANG HYPOTHESIS, the first ten-thousandth of the universe's history was dominated by RADIATION. Because of the EXPANSION OF THE UNIVERSE, this primordial BLACK-BODY RADIATION should by now have cooled to a pale remnant, in the form of MICROWAVES, with a temperature a few degrees above ABSOLUTE ZERO. Its observation in 1965 by A. A. Penzias and R. W. Wilson has, more than anything else, contributed to the wide acceptance of the big-bang hypothesis among cosmologists.   M.V.B.

cosmic rays. Very fast PARTICLES (mainly PROTONS) arriving from space from largely unknown sources. Collisions between particles and ATOMS in the upper atmosphere produce cosmic ray showers made up of a variety of ELEMENTARY PARTICLES, which are detected at ground level by devices such as GEIGER COUNTERS.   M.V.B.

cosmogony. Any scientific theory, religious doctrine, or MYTH about the origins of the universe (particularly the heavenly bodies). In the West the most famous cosmogony is that presented in *Genesis* at the beginning of the Old Testament, but this is generally regarded even by religious believers as needing to be DEMYTHOLOGIZED. Currently, the BIG-BANG HYPOTHESIS, based on the discovery of the COSMIC BACKGROUND RADIATION, is widely accepted. See also COSMOLOGY; THEISM.   D.L.E.; M.V.B.

cosmology. The study of the physical universe as a whole, in which the theories of PHYSICS, especially RELATIVITY, are invoked to explain the observed distribution and motion of the stars and GALAXIES. See also BIG-BANG HYPOTHESIS; COSMIC BACKGROUND RADIATION; EXPANSION OF THE UNIVERSE; PULSATING UNIVERSE; RADIO TELESCOPE; STEADY-STATE HYPOTHESIS.   M.V.B.
Bibl: J. E. Charon, tr. P. Moore, *Cosmology – Theories of the Universe* (London, 1970); D. Sciama, *Modern Cosmology* (London, 1971).

cosmopolitanism. Soviet term first used by *Pravda* in 1949 in denigration of a few pro-Western theatre critics and extended during the Zhdanovshchina to mean any reflection of Western influences in, or application of international standards in criticism of, the Soviet arts. Regarded, like FORMALISM, as an offence against the official SOCIALIST REALIST canon, cosmopolitanism became difficult to disentangle from its overtones of ANTISEMITISM. J.W.
Bibl: H. Swayze, *Political Control of Literature in the USSR, 1949–1959* (Cambridge, Mass., 1962).

cost-benefit analysis. A way of setting out the factors which need to be taken into account in making certain economic choices. Most of the choices to which it has been applied involve INVESTMENT projects in the PUBLIC SECTOR, such as a new underground transport system, a motorway, or a new educational programme, in which SOCIAL COSTS and benefits arise. See also PPBS.   R.I.T.
Bibl: E. J. Mishan, *Cost-Benefit Analysis* (London and N.Y., 1971); R. Layard (ed.), *Cost Benefit Analysis* (Harmondsworth, 1972).

cost-of-living index (U.K. term; in the U.S.A., *consumer price index*). A price INDEX designed to show periodically, usually month by month, the percentage increase in the cost of maintaining unchanged the standard of living among working-class households in a given base period. In the U.K. the original cost-of-living index, which goes back to 1914, has been superseded by the general index of retail prices. The latter is a chain index (see INDEX NUMBER); the weights are revised annually on the basis of information derived from the Family Expenditure Surveys for the three preceding years. It is also more widely based, since it relates to the purchases of the great majority of households, excluding only the very rich and the very poor.   G.S.

cost-push, see under INFLATION.

Coubine, Othon (Czech painter, *b*. 1883), see under ÉCOLE DE PARIS.

Council for Mutual Economic Assistance, see under COMECON.

Council of Europe. An organization set up on 5 May 1949 by a statute signed by representatives of Britain, France, Belgium, the Netherlands, Luxembourg, Denmark, Eire, Italy, Norway, and Sweden. Six other states (including West Germany) joined later. The Council consists of (1) a Committee of Ministers and (2) a Consultative Assembly, with a permanent secretariat meeting at Strasbourg. To these was added a European Court of Human Rights. Opposition on the part of governments, notably the British, drastically limited the powers of the Council, but the meetings of the Assembly have provided a forum for public discussion of matters of common interest. The Council is organizationally separate from the institutions of the EEC. D.C.W.

counselling and **guidance.** The use of coordinated medical, psychological, educational, and psychiatric techniques to assist people to make a better adjustment to their social environment. Counselling covers a broad spectrum of behaviour problems, but is more usually concerned with educational difficulties, vocational guidance, and problems of personal adjustment (e.g. marriage guidance). In educational counselling, guidance consists in appraisal of the person's abilities, aptitudes, and MOTIVATION through psychological testing, and the planning of courses and careers. Personal counselling involves a psychotherapeutic relationship in which the client either receives direct help from an adviser (traditional *directive counselling*) or is given the opportunity to release negative feelings and thus promote positive growth of personality (*non-directive counselling*). See also EDUCATIONAL PSYCHOLOGY; MENTAL TESTING; PSYCHOTHERAPY. G.M.
Bibl: P. Halmos, *The Faith of the Counsellors* (London, 1965; N.Y., 1966); C. G. Wrenn, *The Counselor in a Changing World* (Washington, 1962).

countable. A SET is *countable* if it is finite or has the same CARDINAL NUMBER as the set {0,1,2,3...}. Countably infinite sets are also called *denumerable*; examples are the sets of rational and algebraic NUMBERS.

The CONTINUUM (sense 2) is not countable. R.G.

counter-culture, see under UNDERGROUND.

counterfactual (or *counterfactual statement* or *counterfactual proposition*). A statement concerned with a hypothetical event, process, or state of affairs that runs counter to the facts, i.e. has not occurred or does not exist. A *counterfactual conditional* (statement) says what would have happened if something *had been* the case, e.g. 'If the American Civil War had been averted, the South would have abolished Negro slavery in an orderly fashion within one generation'. A *counterfactual question* asks what would have happened in some state of affairs known not to exist, e.g. 'If the American Civil War had not occurred, would slavery have persisted for the rest of the century?'. There are considerable difficulties in clarifying the procedures appropriate for testing such assertions or answering such questions, especially when the counterfactual assumptions depart far from reality, or when the connection between the assumptions and the question or alleged consequent is remote, as in 'If people had wings all nations would be more prosperous'. Counterfactuals are widely employed by practitioners of econometric history (see under ECONOMIC HISTORY). Opponents of the method claim that counterfactuals are not history and cannot be verified (see VERIFICATION). Supporters reply that all historical judgements involve implicit counterfactuals and that they can be tested indirectly. A.S.; P.B.

counter-force capability, see under STRATEGIC CAPABILITY.

countervailing power. A term used to describe the forces which generally arise in MIXED ECONOMIES to counterbalance the bargaining power of large buyers and sellers. The classical example of countervailing power in the U.S. economy, for instance, is the large labour unions which, by their influence on the wages that the great corporations must pay, partially counterbalance the monopolistic power (see MONOPOLY) of big business. Similarly, the large retail chains, by their influence on purchasing policies of major manufacturing companies, partly dictate the price the manufacturer receives. Critics of the theory claim its influence on OLIGOPOLIES is marginal. D.E.

Bibl: J. K. Galbraith, *American Capitalism: the Concept of Countervailing Power* (London and Boston, 1952).

counter-value capability, see under STRATEGIC CAPABILITY.

Coup de Prague, see under PRAGUE (2).

Courbet, Gustave (French painter, 1819–77), see under IMPRESSIONISM; REALISM.

course credits. The units in a system of higher EDUCATION which divides the academic programme into a number of self-contained courses, allots credits (so many marks) to each individual course unit, and allows the student to choose whichever combination of courses he wishes. The total programme may require three or four years for completion and may be modular in kind, each unit contributing so much towards a required minimum aggregate of credits. In particular there are usually requirements within which a choice has to be made – e.g. a minimum of so many semester hours required in the arts, in social science, and in science. This elective system was found at Harvard between 1882 and 1910 and in a modified form has since spread all over the U.S.A. It is now well known in the U.K. also, e.g. through its adoption by the OPEN UNIVERSITY. W.A.C.S.

Court Theatre, see ROYAL COURT THEATRE.

covalency. Chemical bonding (see BOND) through the sharing of ELECTRONS by two ATOMS. B.F.

covering law theory. A theory about the logical character (see LOGIC) of the EXPLANATION of singular events or states of affairs. It holds that in order to explain an event (e.g. the breaking of a string) the statement reporting it must be deduced from a description of the *initial conditions* ('this string was loaded with a 10-lb weight') together with a PROPOSITION or law ('the breaking-point of this type of string is 6 lb'). Although it is widely regarded as an adequate account of explanation in the NATURAL SCIENCES, its application to HISTORY has been much contested. Its opponents argue that there are no universal historical laws, that human actions are explained by reference to motives, and that these are not causes; they insist (to use the language of the entry on EXPLANATION) that *purposive explanation* is not a special case of *deductive explanation* in the way that *causal explanation* is commonly held to be. A.Q.

Cowell, Henry (U.S. composer and pianist, 1897–1966), see under TONE CLUSTER.

Cox, Charles Brian (British literary critic, *b.* 1928), see under BLACK PAPERS.

Cox, John (British opera director), see under MUSIC THEATRE.

Cozens, Alexander (British draftsman, *c.* 1717–86), see under ALEATORY.

CPU, see CENTRAL PROCESSING UNIT.

cracking. The process by which paraffin hydrocarbons are heated under pressure to give olefins, lower-boiling-point paraffins, and hydrogen. Originally devised as a means of obtaining petrol from oils with a high boiling-point, it is now the principal method by which the chemical industry obtains the basic materials – ethylene, propylene, and butylene – for the manufacture of PLASTICS and artificial rubber products. B.F.

Crane, Hart (U.S. poet, 1899–1932), see under CRITERION, THE; LITTLE REVIEW.

Crane, Stephen (U.S. novelist and poet, 1871–1900), see under NATURALISM.

Crane, Walter (British painter and book-illustrator, 1845–1915), see under ARTS AND CRAFTS MOVEMENT.

Crawford, Cheryl (U.S. theatre director and producer, *b.* 1902), see under GROUP THEATRE; METHOD, THE.

Crawford, Osbert Guy Stanhope (British archaeologist, 1886–1957), see under AIR PHOTOGRAPHY; FIELD ARCHAEOLOGY.

CRAWHALL

Crawhall, Joseph (British painter, 1861–1913), see under GLASGOW SCHOOL.

credibility. The degree to which factors associated with an undertaking create in the minds of others the expectation that it will be carried out if the contingency to which it is addressed should arise; failure to create such an expectation is sometimes known as a *credibility gap*. The term originated in American strategic analysis in the 1950s as a component of an effective strategy of DETERRENCE vis-à-vis the U.S.S.R. and China in relation to the security of the territorial U.S.A. and to the American alliance commitments in Europe and Asia. It is accepted as having (*a*) a quantitative aspect – enough long-range nuclear weapons to inflict unacceptable damage upon a potential adversary; (*b*) a technological aspect – weapons accurate and dependable enough to achieve this purpose and invulnerable enough to prevent an adversary's first strike being a wholly disarming one; (*c*) a political and social aspect – the decision-making structure and the demonstrable national will to engage in a strategic conflict. To this was added another element as Soviet long-striking power grew in the 1950s and early 1960s, namely (*d*) local defences, especially in Europe, adequate to deter minor pressure or blackmail for which the U.S.A. (or any other guarantor power) was palpably unprepared to risk nuclear WAR.

The concept of credibility is of particular relevance to the stance of allies who do not themselves possess nuclear weapons. Hence the saying that 'it takes only 5% of American nuclear weapons to deter the Russians, and the other 95% to reassure the NATO allies'. The term is now used increasingly widely to assess political promises or undertakings of any kind.   A.F.B.

Bibl: H. Kahn, *On Thermonuclear War* (Princeton, 1960); T. C. Schelling, *Arms and Influence* (New Haven, 1966).

credit theory, see under TRADE CYCLES.

Creeley, Robert (U.S. poet and novelist, *b*. 1926), see under BEAT; BLACK MOUNTAIN.

creep. In PHYSICS, the slow 'flow' of a solid acted on by forces. Thus, stone lintels and tombstones sag under GRAVITATION after many years, metal bolts in hot parts of machines slowly stretch (requiring the nuts to be periodically re-tightened), and lead flows slowly down church roofs. It is thought that the flow takes place by the movement of DISLOCATIONS. See also RHEOLOGY.   M.V.B.

Crichton Smith, Iain (British poet, *b*. 1928), see under MOVEMENT, THE.

Crick, Francis Harry Compton (British biophysicist, *b*. 1916), see under DOUBLE HELIX; GENETICS; MOLECULAR BIOLOGY; NUCLEIC ACID.

criminology. The scientific study of criminal behaviour. Cesare Lombroso (1835–1909) is often considered the 'father' of criminology in that his theories relating criminal behaviour to the physical characteristics of criminals were the earliest systematic attempts to explain crime in other than moral or social terms. The popularity of what may be broadly termed biological theories of criminality persisted well into the present century in studies of mental defect, the relationship between personality and constitutional factors, and the genetic characteristics of offenders such as the extra CHROMOSOME. The study of criminology includes the study of *criminal statistics*, the *psychology of criminal behaviour*, and the study of offences of a particular character such as *white-collar crime* (business frauds and trust violations) and what are commonly termed *crimes without victims* (drug offences, abortion, and certain sexual offences). Contemporary criminologists have tended to emphasize approaches derived from their own disciplines, e.g. SOCIOLOGY, PSYCHOLOGY, PSYCHIATRY, STATISTICS, GENETICS, etc. The general subject-matter of criminology is also said by some to include what is more specifically defined as PENOLOGY.   T.M.

Bibl: G. B. Vold, *Theoretical Criminology* (London and N.Y., 1958); H. Mannheim, *Comparative Criminology*, 2 vols. (London and Boston, 1965).

crisis management. Phrase coined after the Cuban missile crisis (see CUBA; MISSILES) of November 1962, by Robert McNamara, then U.S. Secretary of Defence, who remarked: 'There is no

144

longer any such thing as strategy, only crisis management.' The term implies a somewhat mechanistic view of the relations between states as a system which needs to be managed by its chief members so that crises in their relations with one another may be prevented from turning into courses which could only lead to mutual destruction. D.C.W.

Bibl: C. Bell, *The Conventions of Crisis* (London and N.Y., 1971).

crisis theology. A movement arising among German and Swiss PROTESTANT theologians but also influential elsewhere, attempting to restate Christianity in response to the crises of the two world wars, the grim years between, and the aftermath of Europe's ruin in 1945. This social crisis was seen as a reminder of the perpetual crisis of sinful humanity under the judgement of God (see ESCHATOLOGY). The most famous exponent was Karl Barth (see BARTHIAN), but other theologians of the period responded to the crisis by CHRISTIAN EXISTENTIALISM. The movement was also known as *dialectical theology*, since it attempted (more strongly than EMPIRICAL THEOLOGY) to preserve the otherness of God while acknowledging that the limitations of human speech prevented DOGMAS about God from being entirely satisfactory. This term is traditional in THEOLOGY, recognizing that every statement about God involves a DIALECTIC between two others each of which is more or less unsatisfactory; e.g. to assert 'God's love' means also asserting both 'God's mercy' and 'God's holy wrath'. But the term 'dialectical' was used for these 'crisis' theologians for a wider reason: to them, every theological statement involved a dialectic between God and man. D.L.E.

Bibl: K. Barth, tr. G. Foley, *Evangelical Theology* (London and N.Y., 1963); W. Nicholls, *Systematic and Philosophical Theology* (Harmondsworth and Baltimore, 1969).

criterion.

(1) Most generally, any standard by which somebody or something is judged.

(2) More specifically, a ground for judging that something is the case which is not a logically NECESSARY AND SUFFICIENT CONDITION of the truth of the judgement but is rather a thoroughly reliable contingent indication (see CONTINGENCY) of its truth; e.g. the height of the mercury in a thermometer is a criterion of the temperature of the environment. Criterion in this sense is contrasted with the defining characteristics which are, as a matter of LOGIC, the severally necessary and jointly sufficient conditions of its presence. Thus *coherence* has been said to be a criterion, but not a definition, of TRUTH.

(3) More specifically still, in the later PHILOSOPHY of Wittgenstein, a special sense is given to the term, according to which the connection between the criterion and what it indicates is logical but nevertheless incomplete, in that its satisfaction does not ENTAIL, nor its nonsatisfaction logically preclude, the presence of what it indicates. In regarding *behaviour* as the criterion of inward feeling, Wittgenstein's interpreters take him to say that behaviour is, as a matter of logic, not-wholly-conclusive evidence for the judgement that the behaver is in a certain mental state. Wittgenstein's view is that sentences about mental events could have a publicly intelligible significance only if logically linked to what can be publicly observed. What differentiates his position from straightforward BEHAVIOURISM is that the logical linkage in question is one of CONFIRMATION, not entailment. A.Q.

Criterion, The. A quarterly – for a brief period, monthly – review of art and letters edited from London by T. S. Eliot between 1922 and 1939. Its international importance is suggested by the fact that Volume 1 contained Eliot's 'The Waste Land', cantos by Pound, Valéry Larbaud on *Ulysses*, and contributions by Virginia Woolf, Paul Valéry, W. B. Yeats, and E. M. Forster. Concerned with 'the autonomy and disinterestedness of literature', it carried such writers as Joyce, Lawrence, Proust, Gertrude Stein, Archibald MacLeish, Hart Crane, and, in the 1930s, Auden, Spender, MacNeice, Empson, Allen Tate, and Dylan Thomas. It maintained a 'classicist', and later a religious, NEO-THOMIST, position against the 'ROMANTICISM' of Middleton Murry's *Adelphi*. M.S.BR.

criterion function, see under OPTIMIZATION THEORY.

criterion-referenced, see under PSYCHO-METRICS.

critical mass. The minimum quantity of RADIOACTIVE material which will enable a CHAIN REACTION to proceed by means of nuclear FISSION. Although the critical mass for the atomic bomb is not hard to estimate, its value was one of the 'secrets' of the COLD WAR.　　　　　M.V.B.

critical path analysis. A NETWORK ANALYSIS technique whose main application is to provide optimally efficient scheduling of different phases of some complicated task. Suppose, for example, that a house is to be built by conventional methods. Certain phases – constructing foundations, building walls, fitting roof timbers, tiling – have a natural sequence, and the next cannot be started until the last is complete. Other phases – making joinery, inserting piping and wiring – fit into this scheme more flexibly, although not with complete freedom. It is usually not difficult to work out the time each phase will take, which phases must precede it, and which must follow it. Critical path analysis then provides a technique for scheduling the phases so as to complete the job as quickly as possible. When this scheduling is done it is found that some phases have the property that a small delay in them will cause changes in the schedule as a whole – these phases form the *critical path*. Other phases have a certain amount of slack, and it may be possible to take longer over them, e.g. by using a smaller work-force, without delaying completion of the job as a whole. R.SI.

critical period. In ETHOLOGY, a short period in the early life of organisms when they are susceptible to IMPRINTING or ATTACHMENT to another organism. J.S.B.

critical realism, see REALISM, CRITICAL.

critical sociology. An expression which in principle is a pleonasm, since all good SOCIOLOGY must be critical in the sense of insisting on probing and being ready to challenge current opinions. It is only because the main current of sociology had become apologetic that the justification for 'critical sociology' has arisen. In practice, however, the latter expression mostly serves as a label for denigration (rather than a discerning and original criticism) of the status quo in the West, usually inspired by uncritical MARXISM.　　　　S.A.

critical temperature. The highest temperature at which a liquid and its vapour can coexist. The critical phenomenon was first observed in 1869 by Andrews, from whose experiments it is possible to show that above the critical temperature there is no clear distinction between a liquid and its vapour. Similar critical behaviour is sometimes shown by solid or liquid solutions.　　　　　　　　　　　B.F.

critical theory, see under FRANKFURT SCHOOL.

critical time, see under COMPUTING.

Croce, Benedetto (Italian philosopher, 1866–1952), see under NEO-HEGELIANISM.

Crommelynck, Fernand (Belgian dramatist, *b.* 1888), see under BIOMECHANICS.

Crosland, Anthony (British politician, 1918–77), see under TERTIARY EDU-CATION.

Cross, Henri Edmond (French painter, 1856–1910), see under NEO-IMPRESSIONISM.

cross-cultural study. An investigation comparing performance in some psychological function (PERCEPTION, memory, INTELLIGENCE, motivation) in two or more different CULTURES in order to determine whether and in what manner it might be affected by differences between the cultures studied. The cultural differences usually investigated are patterns of child-rearing, patterns of motivation (notably achievement motivation), and differences in linguistic structure (cf. the WHORFIAN hypothesis). Earlier emphasis on the cultural RELATIVISM of mental functioning has, in recent years, been replaced by increasing evidence of certain basic universals in functioning that differ principally, between one culture and another, in emphasis and form of realization. See also ETHNOPSYCHOLOGY; PATTERN VARIABLES.　　　　J.S.B.
Bibl: P. E. Vernon, *Intelligence and Cul-*

CUBISM

tural Environment (London and N.Y., 1969); B. Lloyd, *Perception and Cognition* (Harmondsworth and Baltimore, 1972).

cross-over value, see under CROSSING OVER.

cross-section. The effective area that a target presents to an incident projectile; if the area is large, the probability is high that a collision will occur. The concept originated in NUCLEAR PHYSICS as a means of specifying the strength of interaction between colliding NUCLEI or ELEMENTARY PARTICLES.   M.V.B.

cross-sectional methods, see under LONGITUDINAL.

crossing over. The process whereby GENES on the same CHROMOSOME (i.e. linked genes; see LINKAGE) can be recombined. Crossing over is important in EVOLUTION because it increases the number of genetically different individuals that can arise in a population. It occurs during MEIOSIS, probably by a process of breakage of two chromosomes and reunion after an exchange of parts. The frequency with which two characteristics recombine, known as their *cross-over value*, is an increasing function of the physical distance between the corresponding genes on the chromosome; this fact is used in 'mapping' the genes on a chromosome.   J.M.S.

cruelty, theatre of, see THEATRE OF CRUELTY.

cryogenics. Low-temperature PHYSICS. See also ABSOLUTE ZERO; SUPERCONDUCTIVITY; THERMODYNAMICS. M.V.B.
  Bibl: K. Mendelssohn, *The Quest for Absolute Zero* (London and N.Y., 1966).

crystallography. The study of the external forms of crystals and the arrangement of ATOMS within them, using X-RAY DIFFRACTION and ELECTRON DIFFRACTION. See also LATTICE; SOLID STATE PHYSICS.   M.V.B.

CS gas. The most important tear gas. It is a derivative of benzene-chlorobenzal-malonitrile first synthesized in 1928 by the American chemists, Corson and Strough-ton. An almost colourless solid with a pungent peppery smell, it is dispersed either by thermal volatalization or as a dust. The gas has been used for civilian riot control as well as militarily. Very low levels, about 50 micrograms per cubic meter, can be detected, and the lethal dose for a human is probably about 0.2 g. B.F.

Cuba. Shorthand expression for (1) the COMMUNIST regime in Cuba established by Fidel Castro after overthrowing the repressive government of General Batista on 1 January 1959 (see CASTROISM); (2) the Cuban MISSILE crisis of 1962 in which the U.S.A. under Kennedy's leadership forced the Soviet Union to dismantle the ROCKET sites it was building in Cuba. This unsuccessful adventure is believed to have been a decisive factor in Khrushchev's fall from power.   A.L.C.B.
  Bibl: H. Thomas, *Cuba* (London and N.Y., 1971); H. S. Dinerstein, *The Making of a Missile Crisis* (Baltimore, 1976).

Cubism. An artistic movement often regarded as the most revolutionary and influential of the 20th century. Led by Picasso and Braque, the Cubists, while attempting to represent what the eye sees, aimed to render objects more essential and tangible by means of stylized forms and symbols.
  Three phases are commonly distinguished. The first may be dated from the completion early in 1907 of Picasso's *Les Demoiselles d'Avignon*, whose angular, distorted shapes reflected the growing interest in PRIMITIVE sculpture and the work of Cézanne. In the next two years Picasso and Braque depicted familiar objects by means of interlocked geometrical figures, abandoning traditional perspective and chiaroscuro.
  The second, 'analytical' phase (1910–12) is notable for the development of the techniques of presenting different facets of an object simultaneously, superimposed or side by side. Guitars, bottles, pipes, and written words appear regularly in the paintings of Picasso and Braque at this time. Other artists associated with Cubism included Gris, Léger, Delaunay, Metzinger, and Gleizes; the latter two published a theoretical work, *Du Cubisme* (1912), though their own painting tended merely to 'cubify' their subject-matter in harmonious

147

designs, without any radical restructuring.

In May 1912 Picasso included a piece of printed cloth, representing a chair seat, in a painting – a significant moment in the history of COLLAGE; in September of that year Braque incorporated strips of wallpaper in his work, and he, Picasso, and Gris soon developed the new medium of *papier collé*, which (they felt) introduced a fresh element of 'reality' into their art. This concern with textures led them to experiment with sculpture: Cubist sculpture, again pioneered by Picasso, was to reach its peak during World War I in the work of Archipenko, Laurens, and Lipchitz (forerunners of CONSTRUCTIVISM).

In the final, 'synthetic' phase (1913–14), Cubist painting tended to become more complicated and colourful, employing multiple repetitions of forms and a language of visual signs. But by this time it was less easy to discern a single Cubist school; moreover, the influence of Cubism had spread abroad, affecting EXPRESSIONISM, FUTURISM, DADA, VORTICISM, ORPHISM, SUPREMATISM, *De STIJL*, etc. The ARMORY SHOW (New York, 1913) included a Cubist contingent. The PURISTS, on the other hand, presently joined by Léger himself, reacted against Cubism in returning to undissected shapes and a severe machine-like precision.

Cubism had affinities with the new European interest in JAZZ; and in 1923 Léger designed Cubist sets for Milhaud's negro jazz ballet *La Création du Monde*. Indeed, works of art in several other fields have been called 'Cubist', either because they were directly inspired by Cubist painting (as was some of the poetry of Apollinaire and Cendrars) or because of their fragmented, multiple-image structure (Stravinsky's *Petrushka* of 1911, Satie's *Parade* of 1916, Joyce's *Ulysses* of 1922).
P.C.

Bibl: M. Raynal, *Picasso* (Paris, 1922); R. Rosenblum, *Cubism and Twentieth-Century Art* (London and N.Y., 1961); J. Golding, *Cubism* (London and Boston, 2nd ed., 1968); D. Cooper, *The Cubist Epoch* (London and N.Y., 1971).

Cubo-Futurism. Russian name for the modern poetry and art movement of *c*. 1912–18, as imported from France and Italy and identified with the early days of the BOLSHEVIK revolution. Its component elements were (*a*) the CUBISM of painters and sculptors – Kasimir Malevich, Nadezhda Udaltsova, Liubov Popova, and Ivan Puni (Jean Pougny) – who had studied in Paris; (*b*) the FUTURIST-influenced RAYONISM of Larionov and Goncharova; and (*c*) the impact, reflected most strongly in ZAUM and the poetry of Mayakovsky, of Italian Futurism, whose leader Marinetti visited Russia in 1914. It played some part in Soviet aesthetic discussions, but by then had been largely absorbed in SUPREMATISM and CONSTRUCTIVISM.
J.W.

Bibl: V. Markov, *Russian Futurism* (Berkeley, 1968; London, 1969); V. D. Barooshian, *Russian Cubo-Futurism 1910–30* (The Hague, 1975).

Cullen, Gordon (British architect and town-planner, *b*. 1914), see under TOWNSCAPE.

cult. In ANTHROPOLOGY and SOCIOLOGY, the complex of RITUAL organization, activities and beliefs surrounding a particular deity, spirit, or class of such entities in a society or number of societies. In the sociological literature the term can also mean a less organized and permanent and a more personal and private form of religious belief and worship than is conveyed by the term SECT or church. See also RELIGION.
M.F.

cultural history. Defined by one of its greatest exponents, Johan Huizinga, as the study of 'themes, symbols, concepts, ideals, styles, and sentiments', it overlaps with INTELLECTUAL HISTORY but is also concerned with material culture and with RITUAL. It is sometimes referred to as *Geistesgeschichte* by those who believe that the art and literature, science and religion of an age are all expressions of the same spirit, that an age is a whole (see HISTORICISM). For those who believe that the 'spirit of an age' (see ZEITGEIST) is an unnecessary entity, cultural history is in danger of fragmenting into such parts as art history and history of science. Cultural history is to be distinguished from *culture history*, a synonym for ETHNOHISTORY.
P.B.

Bibl: J. Huizinga, 'The task of cultural history', in his *Men and Ideas* (N.Y., 1959; London, 1960).

cultural imperialism, see under IMPERIALISM.

cultural lag. Term coined by W. F. Ogburn (*Social Change,* 1922) for 'the strain that exists between two correlated parts of CULTURE that change at unequal rates of speed' (W. F. Ogburn and M. F. Nimkoff, *A Handbook of Sociology,* 1947). An example is the disjunction that occurs when the organization of the family is considered to be lagging behind other changes in society. The term names an important fact of social life, but does not help to account for it. See also FUNCTIONALISM.   M.F.

cultural relativism, see RELATIVISM, CULTURAL.

Cultural Revolution. A political and social upheaval in China between 1966 and 1969, launched by Mao Tse-tung in his struggle against the Party BUREAUCRACY led by Liu Shao-chi. Apart from restoring to Mao the power he was losing after the failure of the GREAT LEAP FORWARD, it aimed at a fundamental change in Chinese society. For these twin purposes, Mao first used the youthful RED GUARDS against the Party cadres and then the Army to keep both under control. Many prominent Party leaders were humiliated, demoted, and dismissed. The Cultural Revolution was designed to change not only the structure of power in China, but also the motivation and behaviour of the Chinese people in an EGALITARIAN direction. It was accompanied by outbreaks of violence by the Red Guards and the building of the PERSONALITY CULT of Mao. It led eventually to the establishment of a network of Revolutionary Committees based on the 'three-in-one' combination (Army, Party, Red Guards) through which Mao tried to control the process. But the utopian vision of the Cultural Revolution, like that of the Great Leap Forward, was gradually attenuated, the Red Guards brought under control, and in 1968–9 order restored.

The Cultural Revolution had its epilogue in 1971 with the fall of the Minister of Defence, Lin Piao, Mao's designated successor. The 'ultra-leftists', headed by Chen Po-ta, had already lost ground, and the Revolutionary Committees, once dominated by the Army cadres, were gradually subordinated to the Party authority. In the process, many old Party and Army leaders dismissed during the Cultural Revolution were restored to the most important positions, the most prominent of them being Teng Hsiao-ping. Following the death of Chou En-lai in January 1976, fresh acrimony broke out within the Party leadership between factions representing 'moderate' and 'radical' elements. Teng Hsiao-ping was dismissed and replaced by Hua Kuo-feng. After the death of Mao Tse-tung in September 1976 the 'radicals' continued to stress even more the legacy of the Cultural Revolution. A month later, however, Hua Kuo-feng became the official successor to Mao, and the 'radicals', including Mao's widow Chiang Ching and the three leaders of the 'Shanghai clique', Wang Hung-wen, Chang Chun-chiao, and Yao Wen-yuan, were removed from power.   L.L.

Bibl: S. Karnow, *Mao and China* (N.Y., 1972; London, 1973); S. R. Schram (ed.), *Authority, Participation and Cultural Change in China* (London, 1973); R. MacFarquhar, *The Origins of the Cultural Revolution,* vol. 1 (London and N.Y., 1974).

culture. The subject of a book by T. S. Eliot entitled, with extreme caution, *Notes towards the Definition of Culture* (1948), of one by George Steiner entitled *In Bluebeard's Castle: Notes towards the Redefinition of Culture* (1971), and of *Culture: A Critical Review of Concepts and Definitions* (Papers of the Peabody Museum of American Archaeology and Ethnology, vol. 47, I, 1952), this elusive and emotive word ('When I hear the word culture I reach for my gun', declared the poet Heinz Johst – not Goering as is generally believed) cannot be comprehensively treated in a work such as this. The following definitions are by an archaeologist and a sociologist respectively. For an anthropologist's use of the word see ANTHROPOLOGY; for an example of its biological meaning see TISSUE CULTURE.
                                                          O.S.

In general archaeological usage, that aspect of social behaviour which can be recognized in the archaeological record. More often it is the material culture that is defined. The assumption has often been made that culture closely reflects social groupings; such a view is now treated with reserve. More precisely, culture has been defined as the consistent recurrence of an ASSEMBLAGE limited in time and space. Here again the assumption is that a culture, thus defined, reflects contemporary social distinctions. The concept was first given prominence by V. G. Childe in 1929 and was of considerable value in the simple ordering of the basic archaeological data; in recent years, however, its limitations have been recognized, and the precise definition is now rapidly declining in use. B.C.

The 'social heritage' of a community: the total body of material artifacts (tools, weapons, houses; places of work, worship, government, recreation; works of art, etc.), of collective mental and spiritual 'artifacts' (systems of symbols, ideas, beliefs, aesthetic perceptions, values, etc.), and of distinctive forms of behaviour (INSTITUTIONS, groupings, RITUALS, modes of organization, etc.) created by a people (sometimes deliberately, sometimes through unforeseen interconnections and consequences) in their ongoing activities within their particular life-conditions, and (though undergoing kinds and degrees of change) transmitted from generation to generation. See also FOLK CULTURE; SUBCULTURE. R.F.

culture area. Geographical term for a region within which a single CULTURE or similar cultures are found; originally used (*Kulturprovinz*) by the German geographer, Ratzel, in the last century and given prominence by the American anthropologist, A. L. Kroeber, in his studies of North American Indians. Thus the Great Plains formed a clearly defined geographical area associated with distinctive Plains Indian material culture, economy, and social values. P.H.

culture contact, see ACCULTURATION.

culture history, see ETHNOHISTORY.

culture shock. The TRAUMA of bewilderment and ANXIETY supposedly experienced, most often by those who, whether voluntarily (e.g. as missionaries) or involuntarily (as refugees), find themselves isolated in an alien CULTURE, but also in certain circumstances (e.g. under IMPERIALISM) by their 'hosts'. Although the phrase is perhaps used more by journalists than by anthropologists (the best of whom are doubtless largely immune), the phenomenon it describes is well attested, with symptoms ranging from overt XENOPHOBIA to (more commonly) apathy, withdrawal, and such behavioural disorders as OBSESSIONAL hand-washing. O.S.

cummings, edward esslin (U.S. poet, 1894–1962), see under HORIZON.

curtain wall, see under CLADDING.

custard pie. Term often used as a synonym for SLAPSTICK to describe the early American silent film comedies, because the throwing of custard pies, an innovation by Mack Sennett in 1913, became a popular routine. The 'custard' pies were not actually made of custard. Heroines were the favoured targets, and, to have the effects show more clearly on the screen, a mixture of blackberries, flour, and water was used for blondes, a lemon meringue base for brunettes. See also KEYSTONE. T.C.C.M.

Bibl: K. C. Lahue and T. Brewer, *Kops and Custards* (Norman, Okla., 1968).

customs union. A group of nations between whom trade is free and which apply the same duties and other regulations to trade with non-members. This second provision distinguishes the union from a *free trade area*, whose members can apply different duties and other regulations to trade with non-members. While this freedom to differ has its advantages, it may divert imports so that they enter the area through low-duty members and in this and other ways undermine the import-duty structures of the others, an undermining which can be prevented only at some administrative cost. Although they infringe the principle of non-discrimination, both systems are permitted by the GATT. There have been many attempts to form them, but outside Europe few really successful examples exist. A *common market* goes beyond a customs union in permitting free movement of labour, CAPITAL and enterprise, as well as goods. See also EEC. M.FG.S.

cut-ups, see under COLLAGE.

Cuvier, Georges, Baron (French zoologist

and statesman, 1769–1832), see under PALAEOZOOLOGY.

cybernetics. A subject which dates from 1942 and was named in 1947 by Norbert Wiener and Arturo Rosenbleuth, distinguished mathematician and physician respectively. It was then defined as 'the science of control and communication in the animal and the machine'. This definition indicated (1) that a state of 'in-control' depends upon a flow of information, and (2) that the laws governing control are universal, i.e. do not depend on the classical dichotomy between organic and inorganic systems. The name cybernetics derives from the Greek word meaning 'steersman', and was chosen to show that adaptive control is more like steersmanship than DICTATORSHIP. Today, a more general definition of cybernetics might be preferred: *the science of effective organization.*

Always an interdisciplinary subject, cybernetics was seen by its founding fathers moreover as *trans*disciplinary. This perception was followed by the original U.S. workers, and by cyberneticians in the U.K., who looked to the science as linking organizational notions in every field, and as specifying quite general principles. Elsewhere in the U.S.A., and in some other countries, notably France, early discoveries about the importance of FEEDBACK and the role of ENTROPY focused the subject on its ENGINEERING aspects, at the expense of its BIOLOGY, its ECONOMICS, its ECOLOGY, and so on. In the U.S.S.R., cybernetics was officially treated as an 'imperialist device' until the mid-1950s. At this time, Soviet work in the field, heavily dependent on MATHEMATICS, achieved such importance internationally that the Soviet authorities admitted the science officially.

There remains disagreement about its generality, especially in relation to General Systems Theory (see GST), which has objectives identical with those expressed by the founders of cybernetics. Thus, for some, cybernetics and GST are coextensive, while those could be found who regard either one as a branch of the other. In their origins, at least, they express the same intentions.

Thanks to the academic forces that will always seek to classify in a REDUCTIONIST way, one may hear of *engineering*

cybernetics (as mentioned above), of *neurocybernetics* (which deals especially with the brain), of *bio-cybernetics* (also called BIONICS), of COMPUTER cybernetics, of MANAGEMENT cybernetics, and so on. A clear perception of cybernetics must accept these distinctions by areas of application, but will not take them as undermining the transdisciplinary unity of cybernetics itself.   S.BE.

Bibl: N. Wiener, *Cybernetics* (London and N.Y., rev. ed., 1961).

cyclone, see under DEPRESSION (sense 1).

cyclotron. A type of ACCELERATOR. The PARTICLES travel in circular ORBITS under the action of a magnetic FIELD inside two hollow D-shaped ELECTRODES with their straight sides adjacent. Twice during each revolution, when the particles cross the narrow space between the D's, they are accelerated by an oscillating voltage. When the beam emerges after several thousand revolutions, its ENERGY may reach extremely high levels.   M.V.B.

cytogenetics. A term sometimes used in place of GENETICS by those who overestimate the contribution made by CYTOLOGY to our understanding of heredity. It refers especially to the cellular structures and events associated with the hereditary process.   J.M.S.

cytology. The biological science which deals with the properties that CELLS enjoy in common. It is usually contrasted with HISTOLOGY, which deals rather with the properties distinctive of each individual TISSUE and the modifications of cells associated with them, and is to be distinguished also from CELL BIOLOGY. An important branch of cytology (*karyology*) deals especially with the properties and behaviour of the cell NUCLEUS and the CHROMOSOMES contained within it. The 'generalized' animal cell as envisaged in cytology comprises a nucleus which is the seat of genetic information (see GENETIC CODE), and a greater or lesser quantity of CYTOPLASM bounded externally by a plasma membrane. In addition to the plasma membrane, the cells of plants and of bacteria have more or less structurally rigid cell walls. The cytoplasm houses a number of minute structural features known as *organelles* which serve specific

151

cellular functions, e.g. the *mitochondria* which are the seat of oxidative processes, the *ribosomes* (see NUCLEIC ACID) which are the seat of PROTEIN synthesis, the *lysosomes* (see AUTOLYSIS), and a number of adventitious fluid-filled spaces or *vacuoles*. There is evidence that mitochondria represent the contemporary evidence of some deeply ancestral SYMBIOSIS between animal cells and bacteria.   P.M.

cytoplasm. The sap of the CELL, excluding the NUCLEUS.   P.M.

cytoskeleton. A CONCEPT introduced by the biochemist R. A. Peters to account for the orderly progression of biochemical processes in the CELL and the fact that they need not be disastrously impeded by the stratification of the contents of the cell in the ultracentrifuge (see SEDIMENTATION). Although nothing corresponding to a cytoskeleton has ever been demonstrated, the important element of truth in the idea is that there is indeed a structural basis for the orderly workings of the cell – in particular in the CHROMOSOMES, mitochondria, and ribosomes (see CYTOLOGY).   P.M.

Czechoslovakia, see under PRAGUE.

D

DAC (Development Assistance Committee), see under OECD.

Dada (-ism, -ists). International movement in the arts originating in Zurich in 1916 from a sense of total disillusionment with the art-loving public, the role of the creative artist, and, finally, with art as such; famous consequently more for its spirit of artistic flippancy, BOURGEOIS-baiting, and NIHILISM than for its purely formal methods, most of which were borrowed from CUBISM and FUTURISM. Its name was 'found in a lexicon – it means nothing. This is the meaningful nothing, where nothing has any meaning'. Its founders were mainly German – the theatre director Hugo Ball, the artist Hans Arp, and the poet Richard Hülsenbeck – plus the Romanian Tristan Tzara, while its adherents at one time or another over the next few years included Georg Grosz and John Heartfield (both in Berlin), Max Ernst (Cologne), and Kurt Schwitters (Hanover; see MERZ); the Cuban Francis Picabia and the Frenchman Marcel Duchamp (both of whom had previously experimented in a comparable nihilism in New York; see READYMADES); and finally a literary group centred around André Breton's Paris review *Littérature* (1919–24).

By 1924 the various groups had either stagnated, transferred loyalties, or merged into CONSTRUCTIVISM or SUR-REALISM; after which the movement's characteristic methods – phonetic poetry (see CONCRETE POETRY), BRUITISME, COLLAGE, and nonsense dialogue, as well as its two original contributions, the PHOTOGRAM and photo-MONTAGE – were hardly again recognized as such till the publication in New York in 1951 of Robert Motherwell's *The Dada Painters and Poets*, the consequent FLUXUS revival, and the rise of POP ART. In this new context Dada, like its Futurist precursors, became relevant above all for its basic, if unformulated, conception of art as HAPPENING or manifestation, and an exercise in public relations. J.W.

Dahrendorf, Ralf (German sociologist, *b.* 1929), see under CLASS; POST-INDUSTRIAL SOCIETY.

Daladier, Édouard (French statesman, 1884–1970), see under MUNICH; POPULAR FRONT.

Dali, Salvador (Spanish painter, *b.* 1904), see under SURREALISM.

Dalton, John (British chemist and physicist, 1766–1844), see under CHEMICAL EQUATION.

Dalton Plan. An educational scheme introduced at Dalton, Mass., in 1920 by Helen Parkhurst (1887–1959) in the light of her earlier experience as the only teacher in a Wisconsin log-cabin school, with 40 pupils in 8 grades. The Plan was brought to England in the same year and used in PROGRESSIVE schools. Each pupil was given monthly assignments in each subject. The assignments, which were based on individual capacity, were divided into about 20 units, and the pupil was allowed to work at his own speed. Class lessons took place as necessary and group work was encouraged; subject rooms were called laboratories and treated as RESOURCE CENTRES. W.A.C.S.
Bibl: H. Parkhurst, *Education on the Dalton Plan* (London, 1922).

Dan, Fyodor Ilich (Russian revolutionary, 1871–1947), see under MENSHEVIKS.

D'Annunzio, Gabriele (Italian author and adventurer, 1863–1938), see under INTELLECTUALS.

Dantzig, George Bernard (U.S. mathematician, *b.* 1914), see under LINEAR PROGRAMMING.

dark comedy, see under BLACK COMEDY.

Dart, Robert Thurston (British musicologist, instrumentalist, and conductor, 1921–71), see under MUSICOLOGY.

DARWIN

Darwin, Charles Robert (British naturalist, 1809–82), see under DARWINISM; DEVELOPMENTAL PSYCHOLOGY; EMOTION; EVOLUTION; EVOLUTION, SOCIAL AND CULTURAL; GENETICS; NATURAL SELECTION; PANGENESIS; TELEOLOGY; WELTANSCHAUUNG.

Darwinism. The theory of how EVOLUTION might have come about which constitutes the great contribution to science made by Charles Darwin (1809–82). Darwin saw the evolutionary process as a series of adaptations: plants and animals differ one from another in their hereditary endowments, and those variants which equip an organism specially well to cope with the exigencies of the environment will be preserved in the 'struggle for existence' and will thus become the prevailing type. Darwin used the term NATURAL SELECTION for this process of discrimination, mainly to avoid the lengthy periphrases that would be necessary to avoid its animistic overtones (see ANIMISM), of which he was fully aware. At the turn of the century Darwinism was seriously faulted for its explanatory glibness: 'the natural selection of favourable variations' was a formula that fitted all phenomena too well. In due course Darwinism had to be reformulated in the new language of Mendelian (see MENDELISM) GENETICS, and this revised doctrine, the prevailing one today, is called *neo-Darwinism*.

Neo-Darwinism is still solidly Darwinian in principle. Inheritable variation (no other kind is relevant) is provided for by the recombinations and reassortments of GENETIC factors which Mendelian heredity allows for, and natural selection becomes now the overall name for inequalities of survival or of reproductive rate, or more generally for inequalities in the contributions made by different organisms to the ancestry of future generations. Those hereditary endowments which increase their representation generation by generation are said to confer *fitness*, and the organisms that possess them to be 'fitter' than those that do not. Thus evolution by natural selection could be represented as the *survival of the fittest*. It is to be noted that although the Mendelian process of shuffling and reshuffling GENES provides the variants upon which natural selection works, yet new genes, i.e. new genetic information (see GENETIC

CODE), can arise only by the totally random and unpredictable process of MUTATION. Critics of Darwinism regard this as a deeply objectionable and irreverent element in the process; it is, however, the case. With its emphasis on human and animal inequality and on qualities that are already present because inborn, Darwinism is naturally repugnant to LEFT-wing thought; hence the support lent by a number of British scientists and others, for purely political reasons, to the doctrine known as LYSENKOISM.   P.M.

dash-pot. Any device where motion resulting from impact is damped out by friction in a viscous fluid. Buffers on railway rolling stock provide a familiar example.   M.V.B.

Dasté, Jean (French actor, *b*. 1904), see under CENTRES DRAMATIQUES.

data analysis. The process of extracting information from complicated data. It is sometimes taken to include classical STATISTICS and sometimes to be complementary to it. The main methods of data analysis (other than statistics) include CLASSIFICATION, SCALING, the use of representative techniques such as HISTOGRAMS, FACTOR ANALYSIS, and SPLINE FUNCTIONS, and numerous techniques for transforming data so as to display more clearly the features under investigation.   R.SI.

data bank. An alternative name for a DATA BASE more generally used if the information is not held in a COMPUTER.   C.S.

data base. A large and systematically organized body of homogeneous information, often stored inside a COMPUTER. Examples are: information relating to the policies of an insurance company; the forward bookings of an airline; the fingerprints and records of criminals known to the police. Data bases are interesting technically because they nearly always have to be constructed before all the uses to which they will be put are known. Their internal structure has therefore to be designed with great care.

The layman is generally more concerned with their possible unethical uses. These dangers are often attributed to the

154

use of computers, but are in fact a consequence of the increasing centralization of society. This tendency may have been assisted by the use of computers, but certainly exists without them; and one of the most objectionable types of data base, that of credit ratings, has only recently become computer-based. C.S.

data-processing, see COMPUTING.

data retrieval, see under INFORMATION STORAGE.

dating. The establishing of dates for structures, events, and artifacts. The need for dating is paramount in such disciplines as GEOLOGY, GEOMORPHOLOGY, and ARCHAEOLOGY. In archaeology, until recently, traditional methods such as STRATIGRAPHY and TYPOLOGY were employed to provide a sequence which was then related by various means to historical dates (e.g. the Egyptian King lists). The cross-dating links were often tenuous and the resulting dated sequences were, at best, imprecise. Techniques introduced from the NATURAL SCIENCES began to be used in the 1930s, e.g. DENDRO-CHRONOLOGY and *varve dating* (the use of sediment sequences formed by melting ice). More recently the techniques of PHYSICS and CHEMISTRY have been employed to provide a wide range of dating methods including ARCHAEOMAGNETISM, THERMOLUMINESCENCE, and *obsidian dating*, which involves measurement of the rate of surface hydration. All these are *relative* methods requiring calibration. Other methods are based on measuring the rate of radioactive decay (see RADIOACTIVITY), e.g. RADIOCARBON DATING, *fission track dating*, and *potassium-argon dating*. These, theoretically, are capable of providing *absolute dates*. Frequently several techniques are brought to bear on a single problem, thus providing cross-checks. B.C.
Bibl: J. W. Michels, *Dating Methods in Archaeology* (London and N.Y., 1973).

Daudet, Léon (French journalist and novelist, 1867–1942), see under ACTION FRANÇAISE.

David, Jacques Louis (French painter, 1748–1825), see under NEO-CLASSICISM.

Davidon, William C., see under GRADIENT METHODS.

Davidovitch, Vladimir Georgievich (Russian geographer), see under SATELLITE TOWN.

Davie, Donald Alfred (British poet and critic, *b*. 1922), see under MOVEMENT, THE.

Davies, Peter Maxwell (British composer, *b*. 1934), see under MUSIC THEATRE.

Davis, Miles (U.S. jazz musician, *b*. 1927), see under HOT; JAZZ.

Davis, William Morris (U.S. geographer, geologist, and meteorologist, 1850–1934), see under GEOGRAPHY.

Davy, Sir Humphry (British chemist, 1778–1829), see under ROYAL INSTITUTION.

Day Lewis, Cecil (British poet, 1904–72), see under HORIZON.

DDT. A powerful and probably the best-known insecticide. A chlorinated hydrocarbon, dichloro-diphenyl-trichloroethane, it acts on most insects, though resistant forms may develop. It plays the major role in anti-malarial spraying but its toxicity has led to restrictions in its use. As far as is known, DDT is harmless to man; the prime case against its widespread use is that it upsets the ecological balance (see ECOLOGY; BALANCE OF NATURE) among insects. But chemical degradation is very slow so that it becomes more concentrated in successive stages of the FOOD CHAIN with, in some cases, demonstrably harmful effects on animal life. B.F.

De Amicis, Edmondo (Italian journalist and story-writer, 1846–1908), see under VERISM.

de Bono, Edward (Maltese-born physician, *b*. 1933), see under VERTICAL AND LATERAL THINKING.

de Broglie wavelength. The distance between successive crests of the wave which, according to QUANTUM MECHANICS, is associated with every moving PARTICLE. Its value is given by the EQUATION, put forward by Louis de Broglie in 1924, *wavelength* = PLANCK'S CONSTANT ÷ MOMENTUM *of particle*. The motion of the particle may be described by NEWTONIAN MECHANICS to a good approximation only if the wavelength is small in comparison with the range of the forces acting on it; this is true for all systems larger than MOLECULES. See also ELECTRON MICROSCOPE; WAVE-PARTICLE DUALITY. M.V.B.

de Gaulle, Charles (French soldier and statesman, 1890–1970), see under FLN; FRENCH COMMUNITY; GAULLISM; GRAND DESIGN; RIGHT, THE.

de Gourmont, Rémy (French literary critic, 1858–1915), see under EGOIST, THE.

de Maistre, Joseph (French author, 1753–1821), see under SOCIOLOGY.

De Morgan, Augustus (British mathematician and logician, 1806–71), see under LOGIC; MATHEMATICAL LOGIC.

de Sade, Donatien Alphonse François, Comte, known as Marquis (French novelist, 1740–1814), see under SADISM; SURREALISM; TEL QUEL.

De Santis, Giuseppe (Italian film director, *b*.1917), see under NEO-REALISM.

de Saussure, Ferdinand (French philologist, 1857–1913), see under COMPARATIST; DIACHRONIC; LANGUE AND PAROLE; LINGUISTICS; SAUSSURIAN; SEMIOLOGY.

De Sica, Vittorio (Italian film director, 1901–74), see under NEO-REALISM.

de Tocqueville, Alexis (French historian and political writer, 1805–59), see under INTELLECTUALS.

De Vries, Peter (U.S. novelist and editor, *b*.1910), see under POETRY (CHICAGO).

Dead Sea scrolls. The popular name for the manuscripts discovered in caves in and around Qumran, close to the north-west shores of the Dead Sea in Palestine, between 1947 and 1956. Some are fragments of the Old Testament. Others reflect the life of a devout community, consisting of (or connected with) the Jewish sect known as the Essenes, ending with the Roman suppression of the Jewish revolt in A.D. 70. Hidden in the wilderness, this community purified itself and prayed in preparation for the coming 'Day of the Lord'. These scrolls are, very roughly, contemporary with the Christian gospels. At some points (e.g. their sense of crisis leading to a strong ESCHATOLOGY) they resemble them; at others (e.g. this monastic community's contempt for sinful laymen and for normal daily life) they are very different. They throw more light on John the Baptist than on Jesus. D.L.E.
Bibl: M. Black (ed.), *The Scrolls and Christianity* (London, 1969).

Dean, James (U.S. actor, 1931–55), see under METHOD, THE.

death instinct. In psychoanalytic theory (see PSYCHOANALYSIS), the impulses within a person to bring about his own destruction and death. Most FREUDIANS have not accepted this CONCEPT, and when they have used it they have transformed it into innate AGGRESSION and destructiveness. The death instinct is contrasted with the LIFE INSTINCT. B.A.F.

death of God theology. A movement which flourished in the U.S.A. during the 1960s and attempted to preserve much of Christianity (especially its ETHICS and its sense of the tragedy of life) while admitting the validity of ATHEISM or at least of AGNOSTICISM. The phrase 'death of God' became famous through the *Joyous Wisdom* of Friedrich Wilhelm Nietzsche (1844–1900), whose philosophy attempted to reconstruct man's understanding of life and good on the basis of a consistent atheism. The exploration of this idea by some writers holding theological posts has been courageous, but scarcely a THEOLOGY. D.L.E.
Bibl: T. J. J. Altizer, *The Gospel of Christian Atheism* (Philadelphia, 1966; London, 1967); A. Kee, *The Way of Transcendence* (Harmondsworth, 1971).

Debray, Régis (French journalist, *b*.1940), see under GUERRILLA; REVOLUTION.

Debreu, Gerard (Franco-U.S. economist, *b*.1921), see under EQUILIBRIUM.

debugging.

(1) The final testing or commissioning of a piece of technological apparatus – an expression that arose in Britain during the 1939–45 war, when unexplained faults in Royal Air Force equipment were blamed on 'gremlins' or 'bugs'.

(2) More recently, the process of finding and removing errors from a COMPUTER PROGRAM. Detailed and sustained accuracy of the kind required to program correctly is not within the normal range of human achievement. It has therefore been necessary to work on the assumption that all programs have errors and to develop techniques for finding and correcting them. These techniques are still very imperfect, time-consuming, and costly.

(3) The removal of secret sound-detecting devices (see BUGGING).
E.R.L.; C.S.

Debussy, Claude (French composer, 1862–1918), see under ATONAL MUSIC; FORMALISM; IMPRESSIONISM; PROGRAMME MUSIC; SIX, LES; SYMBOLISM; WHOLE-TONE SCALE.

decadence. In literature, an aspect and offshoot of the 19th-century SYMBOLIST and aesthetic (Art for Art's Sake) movements. Arising from the bohemian protest against BOURGEOIS society in France from the 1840s onward, decadence took and emphasized the febrile, neurasthenic, and world-weary element in the Symbolist presumption about the poet, and also dramatized its belief in the essential amoralism of art. As in much Symbolism, it was a subject-matter and an imaginative response enacted as a LIFE STYLE. The motto of its exponents (known as *the decadents*) was Rimbaud's: 'The poet makes himself a seer by a long, intensive, and reasoned disordering of all the senses.' Intensified by a sense of cultural ANOMIE, a high-style dandyism, and a *fin de siècle* despair, it has particular associations with the 1880s and 1890s, e.g. Huysmans's *À Rebours* (1884) and in England Swinburne, Wilde, Aubrey Beardsley (artistic editor of *The Yellow Book*), Ernest Dowson, and Lionel Johnson. With the Wilde-Queensberry trial in 1895 the public display of decadence suffered a setback. However, as a poetic sensibility it has remained important in modern writing. In popular usage,

signifying a decline from established artistic and moral standards, decadence is equivalent to DEGENERACY, a CONCEPT first popularized around the same time. See also AESTHETICISM.
M.S.BR.

Bibl: Holbrook Jackson, *The Eighteen-Nineties* (London and N.Y., 1913); A. E. Carter, *The Idea of Decadence in French Literature, 1830–1900* (Toronto, 1958); E. Moers, *The Dandy* (London and N.Y., 1960).

décalage ('uncoupling, temporal displacement'). In DEVELOPMENTAL PSYCHOLOGY, a PIAGETIAN term for either (*horizontal décalage*) discrepancy in the age or level of intellectual development at which a person can deal with different versions of a problem that are identical when regarded in terms of their formal logical structure; or (*vertical décalage*) a time-gap in his mastery of problems that are different when so regarded. Vertical *décalage* is thus a logical corollary of any theory that posits STAGES OF DEVELOPMENT in the *form* of intellectual functioning, whereas horizontal *décalage* is in the nature of an anomaly.
I.M.L.H.

decentration.

(1) In PERCEPTION and thinking, successive shifts of attention which take account of various aspects of a situation and synthesize therefrom a more representative view or interpretation of it than is obtained by centering attention on one aspect only.

(2) PIAGETIAN term for the progress of the child away from an exclusively egocentric view of the world.
I.M.L.H.

decibel (db). A unit used to specify power by comparing it with a reference level. Decibels are commonly encountered in the measurement of sound intensity levels (e.g. with noise meters), and the usual reference is a barely audible sound at the threshold of hearing. The following are approximate levels: a quiet room, 20 db; light traffic, 50 db; a nearby aero engine, 120 db; the pain THRESHOLD, 130 db.
M.V.B.

decision procedure. In LOGIC, a technique for determining whether a PROPOSITION is logically true, i.e. for providing it with a proof or DEMONSTRATION. The oldest method of this kind is the axiomatic

DECISION THEORY

procedure (see AXIOMATICS) in which a proposition is deduced from others given as logically true. An attractively mechanical decision procedure is that of *truth-tables*, but it is applicable only to the PROPOSITIONAL CALCULUS and a part of the PREDICATE CALCULUS. Algebraic and diagrammatic techniques are available for some parts of logic. The method of natural deduction, in which only the validity of certain rules of INFERENCE is assumed, allows for the demonstration of logical TRUTHS as those which follow from any arbitrary assumption whatever. Demonstration proper (indirect proof by *reductio ad absurdum*) is a *prima facie* convincing decision procedure but has been rejected by mathematical INTUITIONISTS.   A.Q.

decision theory. The context in which the theory of STATISTICS is usually constructed nowadays. The experimenter is faced with a number of possible courses of action and a number of possible states of the real world; in decision theory a cost is associated with each combination of response and reality, and, loosely speaking, the decision on which course of action to adopt is taken so as to minimize the cost. Since the state of the world is usually only known in terms of relative probabilities of different states, a genuine minimal-cost policy is not usually available, and normally policies – *decision procedures* – are constructed so as to minimize the maximum possible cost or the expected cost. The type of policy sought will depend on the experimenter's trade-off between expected cost and cost VARIANCE – a classic economic problem. Most statistical reasoning, whether orthodox or BAYESIAN, can be fitted into the framework of decision theory. Decision theory is often used in the context of MANAGEMENT SCIENCE, notably in the form of RISK ANALYSIS.   R.SI.

Bibl: H. McDaniel, *An Introduction to Decision Logic Tables* (N.Y., 1968); H. Raiffa, *Decision Analysis* (London and Reading, Mass., 1968).

decision tree, see under RISK ANALYSIS.

decoder. In INFORMATION THEORY, a device or PROGRAM which takes the output of an ENCODER after transmission or storage and reconstitutes the original data. If the encoder has produced REDUNDANCY in its output, the decoder usually exploits this to correct corruptions or to detect them.   R.M.N.

décollage. A technique developed notably by the German graphic artist Wolf Vostell in the late 1950s, by which strips are torn off a COLLAGE to suggest a peeling poster. As these works often involve fragments of words and letters they bear some relation to LETTRISM, as well as to the FLUXUS movement of which Vostell formed part.   J.W.

decolonization, see under IMPERIALISM.

Dedekind, Julius Wilhelm Richard (German mathematician, 1831–1916), see under NUMBER.

deduction, see under DEMONSTRATION.

deductive explanation, see under EXPLANATION.

deductivism, see under POPPERIAN.

deep structure and **surface structure.** A central theoretical distinction in GENERATIVE GRAMMAR. The surface structure of a sentence is the string of sounds/words that we articulate and hear. Analysing the surface structure of a sentence through CONSTITUENT ANALYSIS is a universal procedure which indicates many important facts about linguistic structure; but it by no means indicates everything, e.g. it cannot explain how we recognize ambiguous sentences, or how we intuitively relate sentences which have different surface forms but the same basic meaning (e.g. *cats chase mice* and *mice are chased by cats*). For such reasons, linguists in the late 1950s postulated a deep or 'underlying' structure for sentences – a LEVEL of structural organization in which all the factors determining structural interpretation are defined and interrelated. The main current view is that a grammar operates by generating a set of abstract deep structures in its phrase-structure rules, subsequently converting these underlying representations into surface structures by applying a set of TRANSFORMATIONAL rules. This two-level conception of grammatical structure has been questioned, but is still the most widely held.   D.C.

defect (crystal). Any break in the regularity of the crystalline arrangement of ATOMS in a solid. The defect may be localized at a single point on the LATTICE, as in the case of vacancies or substituted 'foreign' atoms, or it may be centred on a line, as in the case of a DISLOCATION. The term 'defect' carries no pejorative implication. M.V.B.

defence mechanism. In psychoanalytic theory (see PSYCHOANALYSIS), a FREUDIAN term for any number of unconscious techniques or devices used by the EGO to avoid danger (which is signalled by ANXIETY). There is no single agreed list of defence mechanisms, but these techniques would usually be said to include IDENTIFICATION (sense 2), PROJECTION, RATIONALIZATION, and REGRESSION (sense 2). Most of them are unsuccessful defences, i.e. they do not succeed in getting rid of the dangerous impulse. The two best-known successful defences are the destruction of the repressed impulse in the ID, and SUBLIMATION. B.A.F.

deficiency payments. Payments from general exchequer funds to supplement market prices received by farmers with the aim of raising them to some predetermined level. Migration from farming to other occupations over a period tends to reduce the disparity in incomes with those in other sectors of the economy but not enough to prevent governments from coming under pressure to make farming more prosperous. In consequence, they have introduced a variety of measures, many of them directed towards increasing the prices for farm products above the normal market price. Some of these arrangements raise the level of prices at all stages of the distribution process, e.g. the Common Agricultural Policy (CAP) of the EEC. Others, e.g. the deficiency payments scheme, introduced first in the U.K. in the early 1930s, allow the market to operate freely. Typically, a guaranteed price is set in advance, the average actual market price is calculated, and the difference between the two paid direct to the farmer as a deficiency payment. For another method of assisting uneconomic parts of an agricultural industry see STRUCTURAL REFORM. K.E.H.
Bibl: G. Hallett, *The Economics of Agricultural Policy* (Oxford and Clifton, N.J., 1968).

deficit finance, see under FISCAL POLICY.

deficit spending, see under FISCAL POLICY.

defining, see under ESSENCE.

deflation, see under INFLATION.

Degas, Hilaire-Germain Edgar (French painter, 1834–1917), see under IMPRESSIONISM; REALISM.

degaussing. The process of neutralizing the magnetization of ferromagnetic objects (see FERROMAGNETISM) by encircling them with a coil system carrying electric current. It is commonly applied to ships in wartime, for protection against magnetic mines, and to all objects near apparatus where sensitive magnetometers are being used. E.R.L.

degeneracy. The German term *Entartung* (departure from the *Art* or 'breed'), as applied to MODERNISM in the ARTS, derives from a book (1893) of that name by Max Nordau, a doctor and a founder of ZIONISM, who argued that much of the CULTURE of his time was pathologically degenerate. Already potentially racialist (see RACE), this expression became frankly so in the 1920s with the writings of Hans Günther (*Rasse und Stil*, 1926) and the architect Paul Schultze-Naumburg (*Kunst und Rasse*, 1928), to emerge after 1933 as the principal slogan in NAZISM's campaign against modern art. During 1937 the German museums (e.g. FOLKWANG MUSEUM) were systematically purged of 'degenerate art', of which a great derisive exhibition was held in Munich; a Degenerate Music show in Düsseldorf followed in 1938. Movements condemned included CUBISM, FAUVISM, EXPRESSIONISM, DADA, CONSTRUCTIVISM, and SURREALISM, most of IMPRESSIONISM, and all but the MAGIC REALIST wing of NEUE SACHLICHKEIT (Italian FUTURISM was exempted on political grounds); and in music the twelve-note school (see SERIAL MUSIC), GEBRAUCHSMUSIK, and JAZZ. Many artists were banned from working or exhibiting; many emigrated, including all the principal teachers of the BAUHAUS. Ironically, degeneracy was largely identified with *Kunstbolschewismus* or 'Art BOLSHEVISM' though actually fulfilling much the same role as did FORMALISM in

DEHUMANIZATION

the similar purge conducted simultaneously in the U.S.S.R.　　　　　J.W.

Bibl: H. Lehmann-Haupt, *Art under a Dictatorship* (N.Y., 1954).

dehumanization. The restriction or denial of free play to those qualities, thoughts, and activities which are characteristically human. Dehumanization is self-alienation rather than ALIENATION from an external STRUCTURE or system, although Marx saw it (*Entmenschung*) as an inseparable element of the general alienation of labour in a social system where the worker is obliged to work in order to survive rather than to manifest and develop his individual personality or sensibility. Today the term is widely used in connection with those mechanical, repetitive, assembly-line tasks which reduce the performers to the level of components in a machine.
　　　　　　　　　　　　　　　P.S.L.

deism. The belief that God exists but has not revealed himself except in the normal courses of nature and history. Deists have been very cautious about describing God or offering any hope that he will save men from disaster or death. Deism flourished in England, France, and the U.S.A. in the 18th century, but more recently people so suspicious of personal RELIGION have usually described themselves as AGNOSTICS, particularly since modern studies have sharply raised the question whether God can be known in nature or history. See also THEISM.　　　　　D.L.E.

déja-vu ('already seen'). The phenomenon whereby a person feels, contrary to reason, that he has previously experienced or lived through some presently-occurring event or situation.　　　　　I.M.L.H.

Delaney, Shelagh (British dramatist, *b.* 1939), see under THEATRE WORKSHOP.

Delaunay, Robert (French painter, 1885–1941), see under CUBISM; FUTURISM; ORPHISM.

Delaunay-Terk, Sonia (Russian-French artist, *b.* 1885), see under ABSTRACT ART.

Delgado, José Manuel Rodriguez (Spanish-U.S. neurophysiologist, *b.* 1915), see under BRAIN STIMULATION.

delinquency. A fault, misdeed, or transgression (Latin *delictum*; *in flagrante delicto* = red-handed) against some written or unwritten law; also the state of being, or tendency to be, a transgressor. In the literature of CRIMINOLOGY the word, whether explicitly or implicitly qualified as *juvenile,* is used with particular reference to children and young offenders, and is almost synonymous with *juvenile crime,* although *juvenile delinquency* is perhaps more likely to imply a theory of the subject. Such theories have been derived from studies of PEER GROUPS (especially in the urban context), while psychiatrists and psychoanalysts maintain that the key to the problem lies in early childhood experiences. Whatever the causes of delinquency, there is today general agreement that juvenile delinquents are less responsible than older offenders, and require special handling in the form of juvenile courts, training institutions, etc.
　　　　　　　　　　　　　　　T.M.

Bibl: A. Platt, *The Child Savers* (London and Chicago, 1969).

Delius, Frederick (British composer, 1862–1934), see under IMPRESSIONISM.

Delphi technique, see under TECHNOLOGICAL FORECASTING.

Delvaux, Paul (Belgian painter, *b.* 1897), see under SURREALISM.

demand. In ECONOMICS, the demand for a commodity is the amount which potential purchasers would like to buy and depends on their preferences, their incomes, the price of other products, and the price of the product in question. When allowance has been made for the other three factors the dependence of demand on the product's own price is often illustrated by a *demand curve* which shows demand falling as the price rises. Together with supply, demand determines prices in competitive markets (see also SUPPLY AND DEMAND). The total of demands of different people for different products is very important in determining total (NATIONAL) INCOME. See also AGGREGATE DEMAND.　　　J.S.F.

demand-pull, see under INFLATION.

Demangeon, Albert (French geographer, 1872–1940), see under GEOGRAPHY.

dematerialization. A word used by Lucy Lippard and John Chandler in 1968 to describe a shift in interest from art as object or product to art as idea, to art based on the thinking process prior to its physical execution. Drawing on Sol Lewitt's term and articulation of CONCEPTUAL ART, they noted the rise of ' . . . an ultra-Conceptual art that emphasizes the thinking process almost exclusively' and the disintegration of traditional visual processes of art-making.   A.K.W.

Bibl: L. Lippard, *Six Years: the Dematerialization of the Art Object from 1966 to 1972* (London and N.Y., 1973).

deme. Originally denoting a township in ancient Attica, and then a COMMUNE in modern Greece, the word has also been used, though not very widely, since 1883 by some biologists to denote an assemblage or AGGREGATION particularly of single-cell organisms or even of subcellular bodies such as plastids. Occasionally the term was applied to higher plants and animals, which explains its adoption by some experimental taxonomists (see BIOSYSTEMATICS) from 1939 onwards as a root, to be used with an appropriate prefix, to denote a group of individuals belonging to a specific taxon or SPECIES, e.g. *gamodeme* (a deme of individuals which can interbreed), *ecodeme* (a deme occurring in a specified HABITAT), *topodeme* (a deme occurring in a specified area), *genodeme* (a deme differing from others genotypically; see GENOTYPE). These uses have, however, only been generally accepted by those associated with the Cambridge (England) school of experimental taxonomy.   K.M.

dementia, see under NEUROPSYCHOLOGY.

demo, see DEMONSTRATION (sense 2).

democracy.

(1) A word originating in the classical Greek city states, and meaning the rule of the *demos*, the citizen body: the right of all to decide what are matters of general concern. The size of modern nation states has meant that (apart from those which include provision for a referendum in their constitutions) democracy is no longer direct but indirect, i.e. through the election of representatives; hence the term *representative democracy*. The CRITERIA

of democracy are therefore: (*a*) whether such elections are free: i.e. whether they are held frequently and periodically, whether every citizen has the right to vote, whether candidates and parties are free to campaign in opposition to the government of the day, and whether the voter is protected against intimidation by the secrecy of the ballot; (*b*) whether such elections provide an effective choice: i.e. whether the choice of the electors is not limited to a single party, and whether a majority vote against the government in power leads to a change of government; (*c*) whether the elected body of representatives – variously known as parliament, congress, national assembly – has the right of legislation, the right to vote taxes and control the budget (deciding such matters by majority vote), and the right publicly to question, discuss, criticize, and oppose government measures without being subject to threats of interference or arrest.

Democracy is based on a belief in the value of the individual human being, and a further criterion is therefore the extent to which certain basic rights are guaranteed (in practice, not just on paper) to every citizen. These are: security against arbitrary arrest and imprisonment; freedom of speech, of the press, and of assembly (i.e. the right to hold public meetings); freedom of petition and of association (i.e. the right to form parties, trade unions, and other societies); freedom of movement; freedom of RELIGION and of teaching. As a corollary, democracy is held to require the establishment of an independent judiciary and courts to which everyone can have access.

Critics of democracy fall into two groups. The first is opposed to democracy, root and branch, on the grounds that it is the least efficient form of government and one in which the stability of the State is threatened by faction, complex issues are distorted by popular discussion, difficult decisions evaded or put off, and matters of judgement reduced to the lowest common denominator acceptable to a majority of the voters. (See TOTALITARIANISM; FASCISM.) The second, in favour of the *principles* of democracy, argues that these are inadequately realized unless carried further, e.g. by extending equal rights for all citizens from the political and legal to the economic sphere, without which (so it is argued; see SOCIALISM; COMMUNISM)

DEMOCRATIC CENTRALISM

democracy remains at best incomplete, at worst a sham (*formal democracy*) disguising the reality of CLASS rule.

A variant of this type of criticism argues that, with the growth of BUREAUCRACY and the power of governments, decisions are no longer effectively influenced by the view of the government or the elected representatives; hence the demand for greater PARTICIPATION at all levels of decision-making and the problem of how to reconcile this demand with the need for prompt and effective decision on complex and controversial issues.

(2) The same principles of representative democracy can be applied to other organizations besides the State, e.g. local government councils, trade unions, political parties, Protestant churches, etc. One of the demands of the radical movement of protest in many Western countries in the 1960s and 1970s has been for democracy to be made more effective in such organizations, as well as in government, by greater participation of the rank-and-file membership in decision-making, and for the extension of democratic procedures to other types of organization, e.g. factories (*industrial democracy*), universities (*student democracy*).

(3) Judged by the criteria set out in (1) above, no single-party Communist state, at least on the Russian pattern, can be regarded as democratic since it offers no freedom of choice and little, if any, freedom of expression to its citizens. The Communists, however, have refused to give up the appeal of the word 'democratic' and assert that they have established an alternative form with a better claim to the title – see PEOPLE'S DEMOCRACY; COMMUNISM; DEMOCRATIC CENTRALISM. See also SOCIAL DEMOCRACY.   A.L.C.B.

Bibl: S. I. Benn and R. S. Peters, *Social Principle and the Democratic State* (London, 1959); J. A. Schumpeter, *Capitalism, Socialism, and Democracy* (N.Y., 3rd ed., 1962); K. R. Popper, *The Open Society and its Enemies* (London and Princeton, 5th ed., 1966); J. P. Plamenatz, *Democracy and Illusion* (London, 1973).

democratic centralism. A basic tenet of LENINISM used as the organizational principle in all COMMUNIST parties. It is supposed to combine free political discussion in the Party and free election of its leaders with strict hierarchical discipline in the

execution of decisions reached by democratic methods (see DEMOCRACY). Historical evidence suggests that the first part of the formula has nowhere been operative for any length of time and that it has consistently been subordinated to the second. In effect, 'democratic centralism' came to signify the method of autocratic or oligarchic control of the Party through its central APPARAT. This was made clear in the *21 Conditions of Admission* to the COMINTERN, which declared that 'the Communist Party will be able to fulfil its duty only if its organization is as centralized as possible, if iron discipline prevails, and if the Party centre, upheld by the confidence of the Party membership, has strength and authority and is equipped with the most comprehensive powers'.   L.L.

Bibl: M. Fainsod, *How Russia is Ruled* (London and Boston, rev. ed., 1963); L. Schapiro, *The Communist Party of the Soviet Union* (London and N.Y., 1970).

demography. A term first used, it seems, in 1885 by the Frenchman Achille Guillard, who defined it as 'the natural and social history of the human species and the mathematical study of populations, their general movements, and their physical, civil, intellectual, and moral condition'. More recently, UNO has defined demography as 'the scientific study of human populations, primarily with respect to their size, their structure, and their development'. Formal demography deals with the properties and dynamics of human populations, the relationship between age structure and vital rates in abstraction from their association with other phenomena. Some writers would restrict demography to this field, but the term is more commonly applied to all aspects of population studies, including relationships with social and economic factors.   E.G.

Bibl: R. Pressat, tr. J. Matras, *Demographic Analysis* (London and Chicago, 1972).

demography, historical, see HISTORICAL DEMOGRAPHY.

demonstration.

(1) In LOGIC, an INFERENCE which seeks to show that its conclusion must be true. It commonly proceeds by *reductio ad absurdum*, in other words by first assum-

DENSITY

ing that the conclusion in question is false and then deducing a *contradiction* (see CONSISTENCY) from this assumption. It must be distinguished from *derivation* (or, more simply, *deduction*) in which a conclusion is validly inferred from some premises, and must be true if they are, but may not be true, and has not been shown to be true, if they are not.   A.Q.

(2) Any public action by an individual or group of individuals designed to call public attention to their interests or the cause to which their group is dedicated. Employed occasionally to overawe, by the strength of the demonstrators or the intensity of their emotions, those against whom the demonstration is directed, it can also be directed to provoking breaches of public order in the hope that those responsible for maintaining that order will either fail to do so or will use methods sufficiently violent or brutal to alienate public opinion.   D.C.W.

Demuth, Charles (British painter, 1883–1935), see under PRECISIONISM.

demythologize. To confess disbelief in the legends and mythological ideas present in the Bible, while translating the Bible's message into a religious understanding compatible with modern science and philosophy. Thus the vivid picture-language of biblical ESCHATOLOGY is held to amount to a summons to choose a more 'authentic' way of human existence relying on faith in God. The necessity of such a ruthless translation was advocated by the German Protestant theologian, Rudolf Bultmann (*b.* 1884). Controversy resulted, particularly since Bultmann preferred CHRISTIAN EXISTENTIALISM to a literal acceptance of the Bible. To BARTHIAN and other conservatives, the transcendent, living, active God as well as the time-honoured myths had been sacrificed to a passing philosophy; to AGNOSTIC critics, too much of the Bible's message about God remained. Bultmann's intention was to respond to the spiritual crisis (see CRISIS THEOLOGY) with the Christian Gospel but without causing needless offence by the use of imagery natural to the 1st century A.D. but not to the 20th. This wish is now shared by most Christian thinkers, but there is no general agreement about how much of the Bible should be demythologized.   D.L.E.

Bibl: J. Macquarrie, *The Scope of Demythologizing* (London, 1960; N.Y., 1961).

denatured, see under PROTEINS.

dendrochronology. In PALAEOBOTANY, DATING by means of counting the annual growth rings observed in a cross-section through a tree. These rings are affected by climate during the growing season, giving rise to distinctive patterns reflecting local climatic variations. By comparing the tree-ring patterns of isolated timber samples from archaeological CONTEXTS it is possible to construct a sequence in which any ring can be dated relative to any other. If the sequences can be linked to a growing tree or a sample felled at a known time, the floating chronology can be converted into an absolute chronology. The best results are obtained in areas of extreme climatic variation. The classic study was carried out by A. E. Douglass in 1929, using timbers from Pueblo villages in the south-west U.S.A. More recently, extremely long counts covering 6,500 years have been constructed, using the bristle-cone pine which grows at high altitudes in California. These sequences have proved an invaluable check to RADIOCARBON age assessments.   B.C.

Bibl: B. Bannister, 'Dendrochronology', in D. Brothwell and E. Higgs (eds.), *Science in Archaeology* (2nd ed., London, 1969; N.Y., 1970), pp. 206–14.

Denis, Maurice (French painter, 1870–1943), see under ART SACRÉ; BEURON; INTIMISM; NABIS, LES.

Dennis, Nigel (British dramatist and novelist, *b.* 1912), see under ENCOUNTER; KAFKAESQUE.

denotation, see under CONNOTATION.

density. A CONCEPT borrowed from CHEMISTRY and used to express a quantitative relationship between land and the people inhabiting it. Population density is usually expressed in numbers of persons per unit of area. Density is increasingly used to measure the CONCENTRATION of a variety of human activities (traffic, buildings, etc.).

The formation of thick densities of sedentary populations in ancient times has been held a cause of innovations such as law, government, urban society, the division of labour, and the keeping of records. High density is now considered undesirable as it leads to crowding and problems of congestion; present planning calls for the lowering of densities whenever possible, although low densities are often recognized as costly, land-consuming, and possibly inefficient. Statisticians have endeavoured to calculate 'optimum' densities for certain situations.   J.G.

denudation. A term that embraces all the processes involved in the wearing away and lowering of the land surface. *Weathering*, normally the initial stage in denudation, involves physical and chemical breakdown of the bedrock by various agents, principally ground water, but without any substantial removal of weathered material from the site. All the processes in which a transporting agent, including gravity operating on slopes, is involved are described as *erosion*. Fluvial, glacial, and wind erosion each imposes a characteristic form on a denuded landscape. See also SOIL EROSION.   J.L.M.L.

denumerable, see under COUNTABLE.

deontology. Strictly, and as the title of a book allegedly by Bentham, the branch of ETHICS which inquires into the nature of moral duty and the rightness of actions; as currently used, the particular ethical theory that takes principles of duty or obligation, those that lay down what men morally ought to do, to be self-evident or self-substantiating and neither to need, nor to be susceptible of, derivation (see DEMONSTRATION) from any supposedly more fundamental moral truths, in particular from propositions or principles about the goodness of the consequences of action. The opposed view, that the rightness or wrongness of actions is determined by the goodness or badness of their consequences (whether actual, predictable, or intended) is called TELEOLOGY or consequentialism.'Let justice be done though the heavens fall' is a deontological slogan. Kant seeks to establish deontology at the outset of his chief ethical treatise by proving that the rightness of an action is unaffected by its having, in a particular case, unfortunate consequences.   A.Q.
Bibl: B. Blanshard, *Reason and Goodness* (London and N.Y., 1961), ch. 4.

depersonalization. In ABNORMAL PSYCHOLOGY and PSYCHIATRY, a pathological state characterized by loss of the sense of reality of the physical or psychological self.   W.Z.

depression. A term whose many meanings include the following:
(1) In METEOROLOGY, an area of low atmospheric pressure with associated weather phenomena. It is formed by a system of air rotating anticlockwise in the northern hemisphere and clockwise in the southern. In the middle latitudes depressions are associated with most of the precipitation and high winds recorded in these areas. The term *cyclone* is sometimes used synonymously with mid-latitude depressions but is usually restricted to severe tropical storms or hurricanes.   P.H.
(2) In PSYCHIATRY, a state of malaise (formerly known as *melancholia*) accompanied by lowered mental and physical responsiveness to external stimuli. It may be symptomatic of a serious mental disorder (e.g. MANIC-DEPRESSIVE PSYCHOSIS), but normal depression is also known to be widespread.   W.Z.
Bibl: A. T. Beck, *Depression* (N.Y., 1967; London, 1969).
(3) In ECONOMICS, when policy was dominated by the BUSINESS CYCLE, a depression (or *slump*) was a period of falling output or of activity at low pressure, usually accompanied by high UNEMPLOYMENT. Getting rid of economic depressions meant ironing out fluctuations between boom and slump and maintaining greater steadiness in output. Now that the centre of interest has switched to growth, and cycles have become less pronounced, a depression is any period in which actual output falls perceptibly below potential output, i.e. the level of output, expanding over time, that can be sustained under conditions of FULL EMPLOYMENT.   A.C.

depth psychology. The FREUDIAN and other SCHOOLS OF PSYCHOLOGY that place major emphasis on the UNCONSCIOUS aspects of mental functioning and their effects on behaviour.   W.Z.

Derain, André (French painter, 1880–1954), see under FAUVES.

de-rehabilitation, see under REHABILITATION.

derivation, see under DEMONSTRATION (sense 1).

derivative (or *differential coefficient*). Let x be a quantity which varies smoothly with respect to some other quantity t, so that x is a FUNCTION of t; $x = f(t)$. The *derivative* of f denoted by $f'(t)$ or df/dt or dx/dt is the instantaneous rate of change of x with respect to t; it is itself a function of t. For example if t denotes time and x the distance travelled by an object moving in a straight line then $f'(t)$ is the speed at time t. The operation can be repeated to give *higher order derivatives*; in the example the second derivative $f''(t)$ or d^2x/dt^2 is the ACCELERATION at time t. Approximations to a function can be calculated in terms of its derivatives. Using first-order derivatives f can be approximated by a LINEAR function, using second-order derivatives by a quadratic function and so on. Differential CALCULUS is concerned with calculating and manipulating derivatives, ANALYSIS with the rigorous justification of these manipulations.   R.G.

desalination. The process of removing dissolved salts from water (usually sea water). The simplest method is by distillation, but this involves the supply of a large amount of heat ENERGY. Recent developments include the use of ION EXCHANGE solids (a similar process to that used in water-softeners) and a membrane process which could be described as the reverse of OSMOSIS, in which the water is squeezed through a membrane under pressure. The latter process is useful where the density of salt is of the order of 3 to 5 parts per million but difficult to apply to sea water, which has about 35 parts salt per million.   E.R.L.

Descartes, René (French mathematician and philosopher, 1596–1650), see under DUALISM; INTUITIONISM; MIND-BODY PROBLEM; RATIONALISM; REPRESENTATIONISM.

de-schooling. A view of schooling and EDUCATION associated with the names of Ivan Illich, Paul Goodman, and Paulo Freire. Illich and Freire speak from experience of the impoverished THIRD WORLD of Latin America, Goodman (who died in 1972) from urban U.S.A. All three men reject CAPITALIST, materialist society and see the school as at present a perpetuator of exploitation, and a destroyer of education, which ought to be lifelong; education must be separated from the institution of school and operate through 'educational webs', by which is meant the pupil's life experience rather than a curriculum constructed by his teachers. The de-schooling view is partly political and NEO-MARXIST, partly religious, partly ANARCHISTIC, wholly radical-reformist (see RADICALISM). See also FREE UNIVERSITY.   W.A.C.S.

Bibl: P. Goodman, *Growing Up Absurd* (N.Y., 1960; London, 1961); I. Illich, *Deschooling Society* (London and N.Y., 1971).

descriptions, see under ANALYSIS.

desegregation. The process of ending the provision of separate (i.e. inferior) facilities for recognizably distinct racial or social groups, commonly the American blacks. The term was first used in the context of legal action brought by members of the American CIVIL RIGHTS MOVEMENT to end the provision of separate schools and higher education for blacks and non-blacks in the southern states of the U.S.A., an action pronounced on by the Supreme Court in 1954. As a result orders were issued to the schools and colleges concerned to 'desegregate' and admit blacks to their classes.   D.C.W.

desensitization, see under BEHAVIOUR THERAPY.

Destour Party; neo-Destour Party. Successive Tunisian nationalist parties devoted to the emancipation of Tunisia from the French protectorate imposed in 1881. The Destour (founded 1920) appealed for the granting of a constitution in 1934. The neo-Destour, a break-away movement led by Habib Bourguiba, became the principal party in Tunisian political life before the restoration of independence in March 1956, a position confirmed by the use of the apparatus of state against its more militant opponents thereafter.   D.C.W.

Bibl: J. Berque, tr. J. Stewart, *French North Africa: the Maghrib between Two World Wars* (London and N.Y., 1967).

Destutt de Tracy, Antoine Louis Claude Graf (French politician and philosopher, 1754–1836), see under IDEOLOGY.

Desvallières, Georges (French painter, 1861–1950), see under ART SACRÉ.

détente. The reduction of tension in relations between states and consequent reduction of the possibilities of WAR. This process has featured in U.S.-Soviet relations since the end of the 1960s and is an extension of the policy of peaceful CO-EXISTENCE between nations of differing social systems which was frequently advanced by the Soviet Union after the death of Stalin in 1953. It has been accompanied and strengthened by the agreements between the U.S.A. and the U.S.S.R. on ARMS CONTROL (see SALT) and security and cooperation in Europe (see HELSINKI) and by the following of cooperative policies in many areas of the world. However, the rivalry between the two super-powers in, e.g., nuclear arms and extension of world influence has not been eliminated, and *détente* does not necessarily mean an end to ideological (see IDEOLOGY) propaganda against the different social systems.   P.B.M.

Bibl: J. Korbel, *Détente in Europe: Real or Imaginary?* (Princeton, 1972).

detention centre. A place of short-term (3 to 6 months) custody for males between 12 and 21 years introduced in England and Wales by the Criminal Justice Act, 1948. Originally intended to provide a 'short, sharp shock' through intensive drilling and discipline of the military 'glasshouse' type, the centres came under criticism from penal reformers, and the regime was modified along the lines of the more constructive borstal system. A proposed detention centre for girls was abandoned as unsuitable.   T.M.

Bibl: Advisory Council on the Penal System, *Young Adult Offenders* (London, 1974).

detergent. A chemical which removes grease. All detergents have at one end of the MOLECULE a hydrocarbon chain which penetrates oily or dirty PARTICLES, and at the other end a hydrophilic group. Ordinary soap is a hydrocarbon, or fatty acid, which has been neutralized by ALKALI, but modern detergents have a sulphate acid RADICAL which prevents their precipitation in hard water.   B.F.

determinant, see under MATRIX.

determination, see under MORPHO-GENESIS.

determinism. The theory that the world, or nature, is everywhere subject to causal law (see CAUSALITY), that every event in it has a cause. If it is true, then every event that actually happens has to happen; since it logically follows from a description of the conditions of its occurrence, together with the relevant laws of nature, that it occurs. Likewise any event that does not happen could not have happened. Sometimes the principle of determinism is taken (as by Hume and J. S. Mill) to be the most general and comprehensive of all the laws of nature, and is held to be confirmed by the way in which knowledge of causal laws so often follows the close investigation of a particular field. Sometimes, however, it is held to be a necessary TRUTH: by some because they regard it as self-evident, by others (e.g. Hobbes and Locke) because it seems easy to DEMONSTRATE, by others again (particularly Kant) because its truth is held to be a NECESSARY CONDITION of the possibility of organized and coherent experience. Its necessity would appear to be impugned by the view of the dominant school of QUANTUM physicists that the ultimate laws of nature are not causally deterministic but assert only the statistical PROBABILITY of occurrences at the SUB-ATOMIC level. If human actions are included in the deterministic system it follows that no one could ever have acted otherwise than he did, and therefore – though Hume and others have disputed this – that no one is morally responsible for his actions.   A.Q.

Bibl: S. Hook (ed.), *Determinism and Freedom in the Age of Science* (N.Y., 1958).

deterministic problems, see under DYNAMIC PROGRAMMING.

deterrence. The concept of deterrence, a word whose implications are more accurately conveyed by its French equivalent, *dissuasion,* acquired a largely strategic connotation from the 1930s onwards, by reason of the development of increasingly powerful and long-range means of mass destruction which gradually rendered obsolete older strategies of territorial or maritime defence. Though nuclear weapons are often called 'the deterrent', deterrence essentially involves all acts of State policy intended to discourage, by arousing fears of effective counter-action, hostile action by another state. It is thus applicable to general military, economic, and political as well as strategic relationships.

In its strategic context different forms of deterrence are distinguished. Thus, by a posture of *active deterrence* (British term) or *extended deterrence* (American term) a state implies that its deterrent power extends to attacks or provocative acts not only against its own territory and nationals, but against those of its allies. Conversely, a policy of *minimum* or *finite deterrence* is intended only to protect the state that exercises it (normally by having only sufficient weapons to destroy the adversary's cities, of which there are a finite number, rather than his forces and bases). By a strategy of *graduated deterrence* a state demonstrates its ability and intention to punish a whole range of hostile actions in proportion to their seriousness, while a situation of *mutual deterrence* is one in which two powers are deterred from attacking each other because of the unacceptable damage that would result from the victim's retaliation.   A.F.B.

Bibl: B. Brodie, *Strategy in the Missile Age* (London and Princeton, 1959); A. Beaufre, tr. R. H. Barry, *Deterrence and Strategy* (London and N.Y., 1965); B. Brodie, *War and Politics* (N.Y., 1973; London, 1974).

deuterium. The ISOTOPE of hydrogen whose NUCLEUS consists of a NEUTRON as well as the usual PROTON. About 0.01 % of natural hydrogen occurs as deuterium. See also HEAVY WATER.   M.V.B.

Deutsch, Otto Erich (Austrian musicologist, 1883–1967), see under MUSICOLOGY.

Deutsches Theater. Berlin theatre associated for three decades with Max Reinhardt, an eclectic perfectionist whose handling of new stage devices (e.g. spotlights, the revolving stage) and power over his actors were decisive in the history of modern theatre and film. Founded in 1893 by Adolf L'Arronge, the theatre was taken over in 1903 by Otto Brahm, whose FREIE BÜHNE society of 1889 had been constituted to perform the new NATURALIST drama, and who presented numerous plays by Ibsen, Hauptmann, Sudermann, Schnitzler, and others. In 1905 Reinhardt followed with a programme of naturalist and SYMBOLIST works (notably by Strindberg, whose chief interpreter he became) interspersed with revitalized classics, especially Shakespeare; to EXPRESSIONISM he was less sympathetic. During the 1920s, when Reinhardt increasingly left the Deutsches Theater to be managed by his aides, new staff members included the playwrights Carl Zuckmayer and, in 1924–5, Bertolt Brecht (see BRECHTIAN). In 1933 the NAZIS took it over; in 1945 it became the main theatre of the Soviet sector of Berlin, under Wolfgang Langhoff's direction, with Brecht's BERLINER ENSEMBLE as an offshoot.   J.W.

devaluation. An increase in the number of units of domestic currency required to purchase a unit of foreign currency. Devaluation raises the prices of traded goods and services in the devaluing country relative to non-traded ones and so encourages exports and discourages imports. If the resources are available, the BALANCE OF PAYMENTS on current account will generally improve after some time, and if confidence is restored short-term movements of CAPITAL will also become favourable. On the other hand, the rise in prices may be unwelcome, and tend to cancel out the effects of devaluation on the current account, and the country's prestige may be thought to suffer, so that governments have often been reluctant to devalue. An alternative to making such a traumatic decision is to have a *floating rate*, i.e. to allow the price of foreign exchange to vary without an explicit undertaking that it will be kept within narrow limits on either side of an official PARITY. The merits of this solution are gradually being appreciated.   M.FG.S.

Development Assistance Committee (DAC), see under OECD.

development economics. This in a broad sense comprises all work on the growth of incomes per head, including that of the CLASSICAL ECONOMIC THEORISTS from Smith to Mill. However, many post-

KEYNESIAN models of growth have in mind developed economies; and these models may be excluded. Development economics embraces the whole transition from poor primitive to modern industrial societies. It includes such economic theorizing as seeks to explain the co-existence of rich and poor nations; less certainly it can be held to include grand theories of historical development, or the rise and fall of civilizations, which (except for MARXIST theory in its strictly economic interpretation of history) draw their explanations of economic change predominantly from politics, PSYCHOLOGY, and SOCIOLOGY; taken perhaps too widely it can include any economic HISTORIO-GRAPHY with some theoretical content. By convention, however, development economics seems increasingly to mean simply the study of the characteristics, problems, and policies of the less developed economies as they are today: a subject in which there has been a tremendous upsurge of interest since 1945. Some economists take the view that the concepts and analytical tools developed in the West are inappropriate to this study, and have demanded a new ECONOMICS. The majority, probably, believe that the concepts are so elastic, and the tools so adaptable, that this demand makes little sense. The facts and the problems are to some extent characteristically different, and different assumptions are appropriate; but these differences give rise to special theoretical offshoots rather than to new principles.   I.M.D.L.

Bibl: G. M. Meier, *Leading Issues in Economic Development* (London and N.Y., 2nd ed., 1970).

developmental biology. The study of all aspects of the development of organisms, from the molecular events underlying the differentiation of CELLS to the patterns of multiplication, growth, and movement of masses of cells that create TISSUES and entire organisms.   E.O.W.

developmental psychology. The study of the changes in behaviour which typically take place with age, together with an analysis of their causes. Until now it has been mainly concerned with the behaviour of children as they grow older (and hence widely known as *child psychology*); recently, however, there

have been suggestions that psychologists should concern themselves with 'life-span developmental psychology', i.e. with changes in behaviour occurring in adulthood as well as in childhood. Broadly speaking, there have been three main approaches to the study of development: observational, psychometric, and experimental.

(1) The first significant studies of children's behaviour were *oberservational*; particularly notable were studies based on the observation of infants, and those by Dietrich Tiedemann, Charles Darwin, and Jean Piaget still provide some of the basic data on the emotional responses and the changes in SENSORY-MOTOR coordination which typically occur in the first few years of life. In the second quarter of this century, however, enthusiasm for the observational approach began to wane, and it remained low until comparatively recently when two events led to a notable revival. The first was the remarkable reawakening of interest in the acquisition of language (a subject well suited to observational study) which stemmed from developments in LINGUISTIC and PSYCHOLINGUISTIC theory. The second was the success of ETHOLOGY, with its observational studies of animals in their natural HABITATS.

(2) The PSYCHOMETRIC approach also had an early place in the history of developmental psychology. It provides extremely convenient measuring instruments for comparing one child's present abilities and future prospects with another's, but makes very little theoretical contribution to the understanding of development.

(3) In the *experimental* method (see also EXPERIMENTAL PSYCHOLOGY) the aim is to study different aspects of behaviour, e.g. babies' understanding of the permanence of objects which disappear from their view, or young children's understanding of the concept of number, or the extent to which children imitate AGGRESSION. This approach has proved its ability to provoke and to test some interesting hypotheses about development, such as the PIAGETIAN claim that children only gradually acquire the most basic of logical abilities, or the suggestion put forward at different times by L. S. Vigotsky and by J. S. Bruner that the acquisition of language transforms the

child's understanding of his environment. Sometimes, however, the experimental situations are so artificial that the behaviour which takes place in them may be quite unrelated to behaviour in ordinary life. The solution to this problem is perhaps to combine as far as possible observation and experiment.

See also EDUCATION; PSYCHOSEXUAL DEVELOPMENT.   P.E.B.

deviance (or *deviancy*). In SOCIOLOGY (for deviance in LINGUISTICS see under ACCEPTABILITY), social behaviour that is subjected to social sanctions, including legal sanctions. Deviant behaviour is thus defined in terms of social attitudes rather than intrinsic quality, and includes, as defined at present, not only crime but such things as HOMOSEXUALITY, mental illness, and even deviance from GROUP NORMS that may themselves be deviant from more widely accepted NORMS. The *sociology of deviance* has developed, as a discipline, partly as a reaction (especially in the U.S.A.) against traditional CRIMINOLOGY, with its emphasis on positivistic multi-causal theories of crime, and partly against consensus theories of social order.
                                                                 T.M.
   Bibl: H. S. Becker, *Outsiders* (London and N.Y., 1963); I. Taylor, P. Walton, and J. Young, *The New Criminology* (London and N.Y., 1973).

deviationism. A tendency within COMMUNIST parties to stray from the official Party line. Such tendencies are branded either as RIGHT or LEFT deviationism, depending on whether they advocate a 'harder' or 'softer' policy. In the former case, it is sometimes branded as *adventurism*; in the latter, as *capitulationism*. In doctrinal terms, deviationists are also often described as displaying *dogmatism* (i.e. sticking to the letter of MARXISM) or REVISIONISM (i.e. violating the spirit of REVOLUTIONARY theory). The adherence to one world-wide Party line was possible only as long as communism was a unitary movement. With the emergence of communist POLYCENTRISM, deviationism has remained a political offence leading to factionalism. It is therefore prohibited in accordance with the LENINIST principle of DEMOCRATIC CENTRALISM. Intra-Party polemics have gone beyond the charges of deviationism and in many cases (particu-

larly in the Sino-Soviet dispute) have produced mutual charges of the betrayal of Marxism.   L.L.

Devine, George (British actor and theatre director, 1910–65), see under ROYAL COURT THEATRE.

Dewey, John (U.S. philosopher and educationist, 1859–1952), see under BLACK MOUNTAIN; PRAGMATISM; PROJECT WORK.

diachronic. Term coined about 1913 by Ferdinand de Saussure (see SAUSSURIAN) to refer to the study of LINGUISTIC change or evolution, as opposed to *synchronic* which covers 'everything that relates to the static side of our science'. The terms were borrowed by sociologists and anthropologists to distinguish two different approaches in their own fields. Compare the distinction between 'process' and STRUCTURE made by American sociologists, and that between CONJONCTURE and *structure* made by French historians.   P.B.

dialect geography, see DIALECTOLOGY.

dialectic. A theory of the nature of LOGIC which is also a theory of the STRUCTURE and development of the world. It was devised by the post-Kantian IDEALISTS, starting with Fichte and reaching a culmination in the philosophy of Hegel. It was taken over from Hegel by Marx and put to rather different uses. Kant had distinguished two aspects within logic: (1) analytic, or the logic of understanding, which, applied to the data of sensation, yields knowledge of the natural, phenomenal world; and (2) dialectic, or the logic of reasoning, which operates independently of experience and purports, erroneously, to give knowledge of the TRANSCENDENT order of *noumena* (or 'things-in-themselves'). Hegel interpreted the dialectic operations of reason, not as concerned with the transcendent, but with reality as a whole, rather than its abstracted, mutilated parts, and thus as giving truer and deeper knowledge than the analytic understanding, which he saw as adequate for NATURAL SCIENCE and the practical concerns of everyday life but not for PHILOSOPHY. Furthermore, taking reality to be of the nature of the mind or spirit, he

DIALECTICAL MATERIALISM

supposed its activities and development to be of an essentially rational or logical kind. Standard or analytic logic, on this view, is rigid and abstract, a matter of fixed connections and exclusive oppositions. Dialectical logic sees contradictions as fruitful collisions of ideas from which a higher truth may be reached by way of SYNTHESIS. Marx took over the view that dialectical thinking is necessary if true knowledge is to be obtained, and held the process of history to be a dialectical development in which mankind progresses through the clashes of contradictory social systems.   A.Q.

Bibl: K. R. Popper, *Conjectures and Refutations* (N.Y., 2nd ed., 1968; London, 3rd ed., 1969).

dialectical materialism. A philosophical doctrine first formulated by Engels in *Anti-Dühring* (1878) and *Dialectics of Nature* (written 1873–83, published 1925). In a modified form it became the official COMMUNIST Party philosophy, providing a wider premise for HISTORICAL MATERIALISM by asserting that DIALECTIC is the underlying general law of development of nature, society, and thought. In formulating the idea of the uniform and contradictory character of the general regularities both of the external world and of human thought, it postulates 'the identity of thought and being'. It answers an epistemological question by making a metaphysical assumption about an ontological problem. (See EPISTEMOLOGY; METAPHYSICS; ONTOLOGY.) It declares that dialectic is both the way reality changes and the method of discovering its 'laws of motion'. It asserts the universal applicability of this method to all scientific disciplines.

It was Engels who thus extended the scope of dialectic; Marx applied it only to social and historical events. But Engels (who never himself used the term 'dialectical materialism') did not argue that 'historical materialism' can be deduced from it. This was done by Plekhanov, who first used the term, and by Lenin, who interpreted it in a way implying that the nature of the universe coincides with revolutionary aspirations (see REVOLUTION). Stalin modified it still further and made it into a 'political COSMOLOGY'. Plekhanov's *The Development of the Monist View of History* (1895), Lenin's *Materialism and*

Empirio-Criticism (1909), and Stalin's *Dialectical and Historical Materialism* (1939) marked the steps in this development of 'dialectical materialism' into a Party philosophy. Thus a certain view of the nature of social change was first expanded to form a general view of the nature of the universe, then reformulated to promote desirable political attitudes, and finally used to control social behaviour.   L.L.

Bibl: G. A. Wetter, tr. P. Heath, *Dialectical Materialism* (London, rev. ed., 1958); S. Hook, *From Hegel to Marx* (Ann Arbor, 1962); Z. A. Jordan, *The Evolution of Dialectical Materialism* (London and N.Y., 1967).

dialectical theatre, see EPIC THEATRE.

dialectical theology, see CRISIS THEOLOGY.

dialectology (or *dialect geography*). A branch of LINGUISTICS which studies local linguistic variation within a language. Dialects are normally defined in geographical terms (*regional* dialects), but the concept has been extended to cover socio-economic variation (CLASS dialects) and occasionally other types of linguistic VARIETY (e.g. *occupational* dialect). There is therefore some overlap with SOCIOLINGUISTICS. Within dialectology, a distinction is often made between *rural* and *urban* studies. There is also a distinction between the *traditional* dialectology of the early language atlases, with its emphasis on ISOGLOSSES, and more recent studies of systems of dialect contrast, using techniques of structural LINGUISTICS, and known as *structural* dialectology.   D.C.

dianetics. A mechanistic technique of therapy developed in 1948 by L. Ron Hubbard. It is based upon the belief that memories reach back before the moment of conception to previous lives or existences even in non-human forms or on planets elsewhere in the universe, and that if these memories can be recalled without pain or emotion an individual will be freed to develop his personality and 'beingness'. Dianetics later developed into SCIENTOLOGY.   M.BE.

170

diathermy. Local heating from high-frequency current used (1) in treatment of soft-TISSUE disorders ('muscular rheumatism'), when short-wave diathermy may bring relief of symptoms even when their cause is not fully understood; (2) for chronic deep-seated infections, when the rise of temperature is thought to accelerate healing – since the advent of ANTIBIOTICS this has become a less important method of treatment, but is still valuable, particularly in pelvic infections in women, (3) instead of ligatures, for coagulation of smaller blood vessels in surgical operations.   D.A.P.

Dicey, Albert Venn (British jurist, 1835–1922), see under RULE OF LAW.

Dick, Philip K. (U.S. novelist, *b.* 1928), see under SCIENCE FICTION.

Dickinson, Preston (U.S. painter, 1889–1930), see under PRECISIONISM.

dictatorship. Originally an office, created in times of emergency by the classical Roman republic, which conferred on a single individual complete authority over the State and the armed forces for a limited period – usually six months. By transfer, the rule of any individual other than a king who enjoys complete authority, unchecked by constitutional limits, over a state. In recent history, dictatorships can be divided into personal tyrannies, usually backed by the armed forces (e.g. in Latin American and Arab countries), and TOTALITARISM regimes, where the dictator is the charismatic leader (see CHARISMA) of a totalitarian movement.   D.C.W.

dictatorship of the proletariat. A MARXIST concept used to define the exercise of State power in the period between socialist REVOLUTION and the establishment of SOCIALIST society. Its interpretation has been subject to considerable controversy and it has undergone a significant evolution. The idea derives from Blanqui's minority 'revolutionary dictatorship', and was adapted by Marx to his own socio-historical scheme. Marx, however, never made clear the role of the revolutionary ÉLITE and the relation between the 'DICTATORSHIP of the PROLETARIAT' and the 'rule of the working class'. Nor did he explain what he meant by 'dictatorship' – which he used interchangeably with 'rule' (*Herrschaft*).

This ambiguity has become a bone of contention between his REFORMIST and revolutionary followers. The former quote Marx's opinion (in his Amsterdam address of 8 September 1872) that 'the workers may be able to attain their aims by peaceful means' in such countries as America, England, and Holland. Revolutionary Marxists, however, refer to Marx's early writings and insist on the universal necessity for a revolutionary dictatorship. Attempts to apply the Marxian formula in LENINIST practice led to the erosion of its social component and to an added significance being given to its political component. It became in effect synonymous with the dictatorship of the COMMUNIST Party. In theory, according to Engels, by taking power 'the proletariat abolishes itself as a class'; in practice, the Party rules on its behalf.

Apart from its ambiguity, an additional difficulty for Marxists in using the formula is the fact that it had to be made to fit the case of economically backward countries such as Russia and China where the 'proletariat' formed a small, or even insignificant, part of the population. Both Lenin and Mao Tse-tung (see MAOISM) developed it to suit their own purposes and so have other Communist rulers. It is, in fact, now devoid of any specific sociological meaning. Its significance is primarily political, serving as an ideological canon (see IDEOLOGY) to justify Communist rule. But some of the Communist parties (e.g. the French and the Japanese) have officially abandoned the concept, retaining instead the formula of the HEGEMONY of the working class.   L.L.

Bibl: H. Draper, 'Marx and the Dictatorship of the Proletariat', in *Études de Marxologie*, no. 6 (Paris, Sept. 1962); B. D. Wolfe, *Marxism: 100 Years in the Life of a Doctrine* (N.Y., 1965; London, 1967).

didactic play, see LEHRSTÜCK.

differential calculus, see under CALCULUS; DERIVATIVE.

differential coefficient, see DERIVATIVE.

DIFFERENTIAL EQUATION

differential equation. In MATHEMATICS, a RELATION, expressed as an EQUATION between the value of a FUNCTION f at a given ARGUMENT or arguments, the argument(s), and one or more of the DERIVATIVES. A *solution* of the equation is function which satisfies the relation for all arguments within some given interval; in general such a solution is only uniquely determined if certain *boundary conditions* on the behaviour of f at the ends of the interval are also specified. The fundamental laws of many branches of PHYSICS (e.g. DYNAMICS, ELECTROMAGNETISM, general RELATIVITY) can be concisely expressed by differential equations. R.G.

differential psychology. The branch of PSYCHOLOGY, pioneered by Francis Galton (1822–1911) and greatly developed in this century, that studies differences between the psychological characteristics of one person and another, especially by PSYCHOMETRIC techniques designed to yield quantitative measures of such differences. I.M.L.H.
  Bibl: A. Anastasi, *Differential Psychology* (London and N.Y., 3rd ed., 1958).

differential threshold, see under THRESHOLD.

differentiation. In EMBRYOLOGY, the process in the course of which the CELLS derived by MITOSIS from the fertilized egg turn into the various different cells of the body. Differentiation is always a realization of the genetic potentialities of the cells that undergo it. Its detailed mechanism is not yet known. P.M.

diffraction. In PHYSICS, the spreading of waves into the shadows behind objects or into apertures placed in their path, which occurs because of the interference between waves from different parts of the unobstructed region. In the case of sound waves, for example, diffraction enables us to hear round corners, and causes the sound from wind instruments to radiate in all directions instead of in a narrow beam directed forwards. With light, diffraction causes the pattern observed when a street lamp is viewed through the fine mesh of an umbrella. In the case of the waves associated with matter according to QUANTUM MECHANICS (see WAVE-PARTICLE DUALITY), diffraction is the

basis of Heisenberg's UNCERTAINTY PRINCIPLE. See also ELECTRON DIFFRACTION; OPTICS; X-RAY DIFFRACTION. M.V.B.

diffuseness, see under PATTERN VARIABLES.

diffusion.
  (1) In CHEMISTRY, an atomic process by which substances may mix or spread. Thus in gases the MOLECULES move almost independently and diffusive motion is hindered only by random collisions between different molecules. In a solid or liquid, diffusion can only occur when an ATOM or molecule acquires sufficient ENERGY to jump into a nearby position, and eventually these atomic movements can lead to a change in form of the solid (as in SINTERING) or to a blurring of the interface between two solids or two liquids. In liquids and even gases, mixing may be produced much more efficiently in practice by stirring or CONVECTION than by diffusion. B.F.
  (2) More generally, the spread of some aspect (whether material or non-material) of a CULTURE from its place of origin into a new area. In the early years of this century DIFFUSIONISM was taken to ludicrous extremes, particularly by W. Perry and Elliot Smith in their support for the belief that all ideas were developed in the East and diffused to the rest of the world. Before the development of RADIOCARBON DATING the validity of diffusionist thought could not easily be tested, but with the appearance of large numbers of absolute dates it is now clear that independent invention was more common in the ancient world than was hitherto thought possible. There is at present a tendency to over-react against diffusion as an explanation for culture change. B.C.
  (3) Geographers use the word (often qualified by the adjective *spatial*) in much the same sense as (2). They have shown special interest in identifying the centres of innovation, the channels of spread, and the barriers to transmission. Theoretical MODELS have been built which allow limited prediction of future patterns of spatial diffusion. Applied studies are designed to help to determine and limit unwanted spread (e.g. of an epidemic disease) and to encourage desirable innovations (e.g. adoption by farmers of

improved strains of corn). A distinction is commonly drawn between *contagious diffusion*, in which the spatial pattern of spread is continuous, and *cascade diffusion*, in which the transmission is via a network of discrete points (e.g. villages, towns, and cities).   P.H.

Bibl: T. Hägerstrand, tr. A. Pred, *Innovation Diffusion as a Spatial Process* (Chicago, 1967).

diffusionism. In ANTHROPOLOGY, the view that DIFFUSION is the chief way in which cultural similarities come about. In its extreme form it traces all CULTURE, or all forms of high culture, to a single source, and relegates independent invention to a minor role in the history of most peoples. Diffusionism, once an important part of anthropological thought, notably in German-speaking countries and in the U.S.A., has been relegated to the background by developments in evolutionary, functionalist, and structuralist anthropology (see EVOLUTION, SOCIAL AND CULTURAL; FUNCTIONALISM; STRUCTURALISM).   M.F.

Bibl: R. Heine-Geldern, 'Cultural Diffusion', in D. L. Sills (ed.), *International Encyclopaedia of the Social Sciences* N.Y., 1968), vol. 4.

digital computer, see under COMPUTER.

digital-to-analogue converter. In COMPUTING, a device which changes the representation of a numerical value from a digital ENCODING (in which it might be manipulated by a digital COMPUTER for example) to a particular value of some variable physical QUANTITY (usually an electrical potential), as used in analogue computers or to interact with other physical processes (e.g. by regulating part of an industrial plant, or driving a loudspeaker). There are *analogue-to-digital converters*, too. J.E.S.

dilemma, see under ANTINOMY.

Dilthey, Wilhelm (German philosopher, 1833–1911), see under HERMENEUTICS; SITUATIONAL ANALYSIS; VERSTEHEN.

dilution of labour. The assignment to other workers of parts of the work customarily performed only by skilled workers, or the employment on skilled work of persons who have not passed through the

course of training, usually apprenticeship, customarily required for admission to that work; more generally, the assignment to other workers of work previously reserved by custom to a particular category of workers. The issue arose in the U.K. during World War I, when the shortage of craftsmen relative to the demand in engineering and shipbuilding prompted management to concentrate the time of craftsmen on those parts of their customary work that they alone could perform, and to advance semi-skilled persons to do skilled work. In both world wars it was provided that the customary lines of demarcation should be restored after the war. It has been one of the purposes of PRODUCTIVITY BARGAINING since 1960 to economize the use of skilled labour by reallocating tasks across customary lines of demarcation.   E.H.P.B.

dimension. Roughly speaking, if a situation can be mathematically described by specifying n NUMBERS independently, then the totality of possible situations has n *dimensions* and the situation has n *degrees of freedom*. In RELATIVITY theory, for example, an 'event' is specified by 3 space COORDINATES and one time coordinate, so that SPACE-TIME is 4-dimensional. Various elaborations of the concept occur in GEOMETRY, TOPOLOGY, and the theory of VECTOR spaces.   R.G.

Bibl: G A. Gamow, *1, 2, 3, . . . ∞* (N.Y., 1955; London, 1962).

diminished responsibility. In English law, a mental condition which, since the Homicide Act of 1957, can be pleaded by any person charged with murder, and which in murder cases has largely replaced the old plea of insanity. The Act provides that a person charged with murder can be convicted only of manslaughter if he 'was suffering from such abnormality of mind as substantially impaired his mental responsibility for his acts or omissions in doing the killing'. The accused may succeed in establishing a plea of diminished responsibility, although he both knew that he had killed another person and that his act was illegal, if his capacity to act in accordance with rational judgement was substantially impaired.   H.L.A.H.

diminishing productivity (more strictly, diminishing *marginal* productivity). In ECONOMICS, the phenomenon of successive doses of any one factor yielding successively smaller increments of OUTPUT as postulated by the law of DIMINISHING RETURNS. If every successive dose of an INPUT yields less output than the preceding one, not only is the marginal product of that input falling, but also its average productivity, i.e. output per unit of the varying input. The phenomenon is important as accounting for the general tendency (other things being equal) of demand for a factor of production to fall if its price rises, since under competitive conditions (see COMPETITION) each factor is employed in such quantities that the value of its marginal product is equal to its wage or rental payment. See also MARGINAL PRODUCTIVITY THEORY OF WAGES.
J.S.F.

diminishing returns, law of (sometimes called the *law of variable proportions*). This ECONOMIC LAW, which dates back to David Ricardo (1817), expresses a presumed technical relation between INPUTS and OUTPUT: that the application of additional units of any one input (labour, land, CAPITAL) to fixed amounts of the other(s) yields successively smaller increments of output. More generally the 'law' is also deemed to hold where returns diminish only when the proportion of the variable input exceeds a certain level.
J.S.F.

Dine, Jim (U.S. painter, *b.* 1935), see under POP.

Dinge-an-sich, see NOUMENA.

Dionysian cultures, see APOLLONIAN AND DIONYSIAN CULTURES.

diophantine equations, see under NUMBER THEORY.

diploid (noun or adjective). (A CELL) containing two sets of CHROMOSOMES, one set inherited from each parent. The body cells of man and of most higher plants and animals are diploid. Contrasted on the one hand with HAPLOID, on the other with POLYPLOID.
J.M.S.

dipole. Any pair of small objects close together, some of whose properties may be described by QUANTITIES having opposite signs. Examples: (1) a MOLECULE where the positive and negative charges are separated (e.g. water); (2) a radio aerial consisting of two antennae radiating out of PHASE; (3) a HYDRODYNAMIC system made up of a source and a neighbouring 'sink' of fluid; (4) a small magnet with its north and south poles (see MAGNETISM).
M.V.B.

Dirac, Paul Adrien Maurice (British physicist, *b.* 1902), see under QUANTUM MECHANICS.

direct action. Originally an ANARCHIST idea, advocating radical action (see RADICALISM) taken outside the constitutional or parliamentary framework. One of its most common contemporary expressions is the use of industrial power (in the form of strikes) to secure political objectives. (See SYNDICALISM; ANARCHO-SYNDICALISM.)

The idea was adopted by other movements, which developed methods of direct action congruent with their own political philosophies. Gandhi expounded the idea of NON-VIOLENT direct action (*satyagraha*), such as the celebrated Salt March to the Sea. In its non-violent form it has also been used by such organizations as the British CND and the U.S. CIVIL RIGHTS campaign. More recently it has become associated with the activities of radical students who invented various new techniques (such as 'sit-downs'), and of the NEW LEFT in general.

Those who practise direct action cannot always control its consequences. They acknowledge that even in the modest form of a DEMONSTRATION it may turn into a challenge to the law and result in some form of violence. The radicalization of the New Left tended to make it move towards more extreme forms of direct action beyond the philosophy of non-violence. For some of its adherents it was only a temporary phase, from which they have turned to more conventional politics; for others it became a road towards violent forms of action, such as TERRORISM. L.L.

Bibl: A. Carter, *Direct Action and Liberal Democracy* (London, 1973).

direct-grant schools, see under SECONDARY SCHOOLS.

direct realism, see REALISM, NAIVE.

dirigisme. An inclination towards detailed State intervention in economic affairs. It can coexist with CAPITALIST, SOCIALIST, and many other systems of property ownership. *Dirigisme,* a term originally used to characterize French interventionist policy in the 17th century, has to some extent continued to guide French official economic thinking – and has strongly clashed with the German neo-liberal (see ECONOMIC LIBERALISM) post-war approach.   S.BR.

disarmament. A form of ARMS CONTROL, which may be unilateral, but which normally implies the promotion of international security by the multilateral reduction of existing military forces and weapons to some agreed minimum with provision for inspection and enforcement of the agreement. Proposals for what has become known as 'G.C.D.', i.e. disarmament that would be *general* (applying to all countries) and *comprehensive* (applying to all categories of forces and weapons) were discussed desultorily, first by the LEAGUE OF NATIONS between 1927 and 1934 and then by UNO in the decade up to 1962; neither was able to solve the problems of defining equivalence of force reductions or the subsequent issues of inspection and enforcement. Examples of *multilateral* but *partial* disarmament are the Washington Naval Treaties of 1922 and 1930. Examples of *unilateral* disarmament are the rapid demobilization of the American and other armed forces after both world wars, and the gradual reduction of the Soviet forces after the death of Stalin.   A.F.B.
    Bibl: P. Noel-Baker, *The Arms Race* (London and N.Y., 1958).

disc store. A form of computer STORE in which the information is stored on rotating magnetic discs with read/write heads on arms which can move across their surface. A disc store is a form of backing store with an enormous capacity but a relatively long ACCESS TIME.   C.S.

discontinuity. The opposite of CONTINUITY.   R.G.

discount rate, see under BANK RATE.

discounted cash flow. A method used to assist the MANAGEMENT decision-maker in the evaluation of capital investment projects (see CAPITAL; INVESTMENT). Investment opportunities involve the flow of funds: capital payments out and net receipts from the venture in return. Simple comparison between the two gives a rate of return on the investment; but the earlier the return of funds the better. The DCF method takes the timing of funds-flow into account, by calculating the discount rate that is inherent in the expected funds-flow. The *net-present-value* method also takes the timing of the funds-flow into account, but calculates a present value of expected flows, at a standard discounting rate, for assessing projects.   R.I.T.
    Bibl: A. J. Merrett and A. Sykes, *The Finance and Analysis of Capital Projects* (London and N.Y., 1963).

discourse. In LINGUISTICS, a stretch of language larger than the sentence. The term *discourse analysis* is often applied to the study of those linguistic effects – semantic, stylistic, syntactic – whose description needs to take into account sentence sequences as well as sentence structure.   D.C.

discovery procedure. In LINGUISTICS, a set of techniques which enable an investigator to derive the rules of a grammar from a CORPUS of utterances, with as little reference to INTUITION as possible. Chomsky has criticized BLOOMFIELDIAN linguistics for its preoccupation with discovery procedures at the expense of theoretical questions.   D.C.

disenagagement. A form of ARMS CONTROL, much discussed in the 1950s by European politicians and strategic writers (e.g. Anthony Eden, Hugh Gaitskell, Adam Rapacki, and the German Social Democratic Party) for reducing international tension in Europe by drawing back all non-indigenous forces or those equipped with nuclear weapons (Soviet, American, British, Canadian) from Central Europe while permitting the indigenous states of the area a controlled level of non-nuclear armament.   A.F.B.
    Bibl: E. Hinterhoff, *Disengagement* (London, 1959).

disinflation, see under INFLATION.

disinhibition theory, see under DIS-PLACEMENT ACTIVITIES.

disintegration. The breaking-up of an atomic NUCLEUS during RADIOACTIVE decay or during a NUCLEAR REACTION. M.V.B.

dislocation. A crystal DEFECT centred on a line. The two main types are the *edge dislocation,* where an extra plane of ATOMS has been inserted part-way into the crystal, and the *screw dislocation,* about which the planes of atoms are distributed like the steps of a spiral staircase. The mode of growth of crystals, and many of the mechanical properties of solids (such as CREEP), are determined by dislocations; because of this, they have been intensively studied in recent years, principally with the ELECTRON MICROSCOPE. M.V.B.

dismantling. The removal or destruction of industrial plant carried through by the occupying powers in Germany after World War II. Its purpose was to keep German industrial potential to an agreed limit sufficiently low to prevent the build-up of new armed forces and the accumulation of stocks of war materials, but cynics believed that it was also intended to benefit Germany's pre-war industrial competitors, notably Britain. Dismantling was abandoned when both sides in the COLD WAR began to build up the industrial strength of the parts of Germany they occupied. D.C.W.

displacement.
(1) In ETHOLOGY, the elicitation of an instinctive response by an inappropriate object or event or animal, consequent upon arousal of the INSTINCT to a degree that broadens the range of objects capable of releasing it (see RELEASER); see also DISPLACEMENT ACTIVITIES.
(2) In PSYCHOANALYSIS, the implication is of more 'purposeful' displacement, as when feelings of AGGRESSION are aroused by a powerful figure and expressed toward one less powerful in order to avoid retaliation – however unconscious the displacement may be. J.S.B.
Bibl: I. Eibl-Eibesfeldt, tr. E. Klinghammer, *Ethology* (London and N.Y., 1970).

displacement activities.
(1) In ETHOLOGY, a term applied to animals' movements which, to the observer who knows their primary function and causation, appear 'out of context'. Thus starlings preen their plumage under two specific and distinct sets of circumstances: (*a*) when it is wet or out of order, and (*b*) – the displacement activity – when their aggressive behaviour and withdrawal behaviour are elicited at the same time, and neither is shown in full. Displacement activities seem to occur most frequently either (*a*) when two wholly or partly incompatible behaviour systems are simultaneously elicited (as in the example of the starling), or (*b*) when a behaviour system is elicited, but is prevented from running its full course, by the absence of indispensable stimuli for the later phases or by physical prevention. Human instances of displacement activities include, in certain circumstances, scratching, lighting a cigarette, yawning, pacing up and down.
About the causation of displacement activities there are various theories, not necessarily incompatible. One, the *disinhibition theory,* is based on the fact that when one behaviour system (see INSTINCT) is strongly elicited it suppresses other systems; the theory posits that when two such systems are elicited simultaneously they suppress each other, including the suppressing effect that each normally exerts on third systems, and so allow such a system 'free rein'. Another theory, applicable to movements which belong to the rest-and-sleep systems, argues that the central NERVOUS SYSTEM compensates for the hyperexcitation caused by conflicting motivations by activating the sleep system with all its subsidiary movements. N.T.
(2) The current popular application of the term to human activities which are 'out of context' merely in the sense that they are undertaken as an escape (conscious or otherwise) from some more urgently needed activity is not quite in line with ethological usage. O.S.

displacement theory. An obsolete term for the theory of CONTINENTAL DRIFT. M.L.

disposition. The property or state of a thing in which, if certain conditions are satisfied, certain predictable results will ensue. Elasticity, solubility, inflammability are PARADIGM CASES of dispositions in natural objects. For a thing to possess a certain disposition is, minimally, for some hypothetical PROPOSITION to be true of it. Philosophical BEHAVIOURISTS, notably Ryle, have held that the mental states and events we are aware of in ourselves and other people are really dispositions to behave in certain ways.   A.Q.

Bibl: G. Ryle, *The Concept of Mind* (London, 1949; N.Y., 1950), ch. 2.

dissociation. The spontaneous break-up of a chemical compound in EQUILIBRIUM conditions of temperature and pressure, or in solution. Normally dissociation occurs with an increase in temperature, for example when a gaseous MOLECULE dissociates to give two or more molecules or FREE RADICALS, but it also describes the process by which a neutral molecule forms IONS in solution.   B.F.

dissociation of sensibility. A phrase from T. S. Eliot's essay, 'The Metaphysical Poets' (1921). Having described the unity of feeling and thought in the poetry of the Metaphysicals ('A thought to Donne was an experience; it modified his sensibility'), Eliot suggests that after the 17th century 'a dissociation of sensibility set in, from which we have never recovered'. This 'dissociation', aggravated by the powerful examples of Milton and Dryden, manifested itself in a split between 'thinking' and 'feeling' whereby poets 'thought and felt by bits, unbalanced'. The theory defines well the special achievement of the Metaphysicals in their best poems, but should not be regarded as an event as real as the Industrial Revolution and as precise in its effects as a lobotomy. The truth is that 'dissociation of sensibility' has always been with us, and that 'unification of sensibility' is a rare phenomenon, not always possible and perhaps not always called for.   D.J.E.

dissonance, cognitive, see under COGNITIVE CONSONANCE.

distancing, see under AESTHETIC DISTANCE.

distinctive feature, see under PHONEME.

distribution.

(1) In STATISTICS and PROBABILITY THEORY, the set of values taken by a RANDOM VARIABLE, together with the associated probabilities. Thus, the experiment 'toss a fair coin twice' and the random variable 'number of heads' generate a distribution in which the values 0 and 2 each have probability (chance of occurring) equal to ¼ and the value 1 has the probability equal to ½. The *distribution function* is the FUNCTION F such that if x is a value, then $F(x)$ is the probability that the random variable does not exceed x. The *probability density* is the derivative (slope) of F if this exists. Distributions arising empirically are often described roughly by a MEASURE OF LOCATION and possibly a measure of dispersion such as the VARIANCE. The *skewness* of a distribution is a measure of its asymmetry. Its *range* is the separation of its upper and lower extreme values (if meaningful) and the *mid-range* is the mid-point of this interval. The distribution given above is symmetrical about the value 1 and so has zero skewness, and its range is the interval whose endpoints are 0 and 2. Among the most important theoretical distributions are the NORMAL (*Gaussian*) and POISSON distributions. See also EXPECTATION; MODE.   R.SI.

(2) In LINGUISTICS, the range of contexts in which a linguistic unit (e.g. a WORD CLASS or PHONEME) can occur. Units which occur in the same set of contexts are said to have an *equivalent* distribution (e.g. the phonemes /h/ and /w/, which in English words occur only initially and medially); units which have no contexts in common are in *complementary* distribution (e.g. prefixes and suffixes).   D.C.

distribution map. In ARCHAEOLOGY, a map showing the spatial distribution (or DIFFUSION) of a CULTURE trait, e.g. a distinctive type of axe. It serves as a visual statement of a class of data for which an explanation is then sought. The more valuable distribution maps record both the presence and absence of the trait at every examined location. It has been said that distribution maps often reflect the distribution of field archaeologists.   B.C.

distributive justice. A specific form of justice distinguished by Aristotle, which required the burdens and benefits of social life to be distributed among individuals proportionately according to merit and the strength of other prior claims. The expression is now frequently used for standards of fair distribution (not necessarily based on merit or prior claims) which should determine the extent of individual liberties, political rights, opportunities, and ownership of property. Various alternative philosophical bases, some of which, but not all, are utilitarian, have been proposed by social theorists for the principles of distributive justice. H.L.A.H.

Bibl: N. Rescher, *Distributive Justice* (Indianapolis, 1966); J. Rawls, *A Theory of Justice* (Cambridge, Mass., 1971; London, 1972).

divergence, see under CONVERGENCE.

divergers, see under CONVERGERS.

diversification, see under CORPORATE STRATEGY.

divisionism, see under NEO-IMPRESSIONISM.

Dix, Otto (German painter and engraver, 1891–1969), see under NEUE SACHLICHKEIT.

Dixieland. A style of JAZZ. Coined with reference to the Mason-Dixon line dividing North and South in the U.S.A., the term has gradually acquired a derogatory sense. The Original Dixieland Jazz Band was a quintet of white plagiarists who first brought the new music to New York (1917) and made the first commercial jazz record. Later the term came to be synonymous with CHICAGO style, and more recently has come to symbolize the type of pseudo-Chicago jazz which that hypothetical creature, the tired American businessman, likes to hear when labouring under the illusion that he enjoys jazz. B.G.

Djilas, Milovan (Yugoslav politician and political theorist, *b*. 1911), see under BUEAUCRACY.

DNA (deoxyribonucleic acid), see under NUCLEIC ACID.

Dobb, Maurice (British economist, *b*. 1900), see under GUILD SOCIALISM.

Döblin, Alfred (German novelist and essayist, 1878–1957), see under EXPRESSIONISM.

document retrieval, see under INFORMATION STORAGE.

Documenta. A series of major art exhibitions held in Kassel, Germany, at roughly four-year intervals from 1955 on, and strongly orientated towards the latest movements. L.M.

documentary. Adjective applied to novels, plays, films, and radio and television programmes with a high factual content, especially if this takes the form of quotations from actual documents, newspapers, live camera shots of real-life material, etc. The use of documentary elements in novels is associated with literary NATURALISM and has been common since Zola's Rougon-Macquart series of novels (1871–93); other examples are John Dos Passos's *U.S.A.* (1938) and Truman Capote's self-styled 'non-fiction novel', *In Cold Blood* (1966). But the use of the term in this sense has only become widespread since the advent of the *documentary film* (or *documentary* used as a noun). First used by John Grierson in 1926 when reviewing Flaherty's *Moana* (though the concept goes back to Eisenstein and Dziga Vertov, and indeed to Lenin's idea of film), it gained currency during the early 1930s in relation to the sociologically orientated, State- or industry-sponsored work of the British documentary school headed by Grierson.

The techniques of *documentary theatre* – historical, political, or social drama incorporating authentic material in the form of quotations, projected photographs, newsreels, etc. – were developed in the work of Erwin Piscator (see EPIC THEATRE) and the LIVING NEWSPAPER tradition; in the 1960s plays by Heinar Kipphardt and Rolf Hochhuth gave wider currency to the term. In England a documentary style developed by Peter Cheeseman at the Victoria Theatre, Stoke-on-Trent, has been influenced by THEATRE WORKSHOP's *Oh What a Lovely War* and the ballad documentaries created for B.B.C. radio by Charles Parker in the 1960s. M.S.-S.; T.C.C.M.; M.A.

Bibl: F. Hardy (ed.), *Grierson on Documentary* (London, 1946); P. Rotha,

Documentary Film (London and N.Y., 3rd ed., 1963).

dodecaphonic music, see under SERIAL MUSIC.

dogma. A term in Christian THEOLOGY, meaning a doctrine claiming authority over any private opinion or hesitation in a believer's mind. It is held to be a religious truth established by divine revelation and defined by the Church. If the believer rejects it, he becomes to that extent a heretic. The term is applied specially to the decrees, mainly about CHRISTOLOGY, of the ECUMENICAL Councils of the Church (325–787). Roman Catholics accept 14 subsequent Councils. They also regard the Pope's official teaching as divinely inspired, according to a dogma defined in 1870 (see INFALLIBILITY). Protestants give greater emphasis to the authority of the Bible (see DOGMATICS). In RELIGION as in other fields, the term is today mostly used pejoratively, to mean an opinion held on grounds, and propagated by methods, which are unreasonable.   D.L.E.

dogmatics (or *systematic theology*). In Christian THEOLOGY, the systematic presentation of doctrines so as to form a coherent whole. Although the word DOGMA is usually associated with CATHOLICISM, 'dogmatics' is most familiar in connection with the BARTHIAN attempt to cover the whole theological field afresh in the light of a new understanding of the Bible. Publication of Karl Barth's major work *Die Kirchliche Dogmatik* (*Church Dogmatics*) was begun in 1932 but left incomplete on his death in 1968.   D.L.E.

dogmatism (in COMMUNIST politics), see under DEVIATIONISM.

dollar imperialism, see under IMPERIALISM.

Dolmetsch, Arnold (French-born musicologist and manufacturer of musical instruments, 1858–1940), see under MUSICOLOGY.

domain (in MATHEMATICS), see under FUNCTION.

Domar, Evsey David (Polish-U.S. economist, *b.* 1914), see under ACCELERATOR.

dominance. The behaviour pattern by which, in social animals, individuals establish the *hierarchy* of the group. In some birds, including domestic fowls, a *pecking order* develops, with one bird dominant to all the rest, and the remainder occupying more or less fixed positions in the chain. Rats and some other mammals behave similarly. Dominance is maintained by aggressive or threatening behaviour on the part of one animal, and by submission on the part of its inferior. In most cases, particularly in the wild, this aggressive behaviour becomes ritualized and ceases when the threatened individual is seen to submit, so violent combat is rare. However, some species (e.g. wild cattle, certain deer) fight to the death for the position of the leader of the group. Extrapolation from animal studies to human behaviour may be misleading, though attempts to dominate others by both men and women are made through ostentation, cunnning, and personal sartorial elegance or eccentricity of appearance. In botany, dominance in a plant community is also described (e.g. beech trees in a beech wood, heather on moorland). Here the term is applied to the species which is tallest and most obvious.   K.M.
   Bibl: N. Tinbergen, *Social Behaviour in Animals* (London and N.Y., 2nd ed., 1965); R. Ardrey, *The Territorial Imperative* (N.Y., 1966; London, 1967).

dominant, see under GENE.

domino theory. Phrase coined by President Eisenhower in 1954 for the view that neighbouring states are so interrelated that, faced with the same peril, the collapse of one will lead to the progressive consecutive collapse of its neighbours. It was applied to the war between France and North VIETNAM in 1954, and between North and South Vietnam in 1964 to justify American intervention, when it was much criticized by opponents of such intervention. The immediately consecutive collapse of the non-Communist regimes in Cambodia, South Vietnam, and Laos consequent on the North Vietnamese victory in 1975, and the swing against the U.S.A. in their foreign policy, could, however, be regarded, other things being equal, as confirming the argument. D.C.W.

Bibl: B. Brodie, *War and Politics* (London, 1974).

Donkey's Tail.
(1) Title of an art exhibition in Moscow, 1912, organized by the painter Michel Larionov. In contrast to the KNAVE OF DIAMONDS it contained works in the neo-PRIMITIVE style, influenced by Russian icons, FOLK ART, and the East. The provocative title, suggested by a prank in Paris (when brushes were tied to a donkey's tail and the resulting smear exhibited at the Salon des Indépendants), led to the removal of Goncharova's religious works by the police. Other painters taking part included Malevich, Chagall, and Tatlin.
(2) An almanack entitled *Donkey's Tail and Target* (Moscow, 1913) contained FUTURIST poetry and the manifesto of RAYONISM. M.C.
Bibl: see under KNAVE OF DIAMONDS.

Doolittle, Hilda (H.D.; U.S. poet, 1886–1961), see under EGOIST, THE; IMAGISM.

Doomwatch. A word popularized through a B.B.C. television series of the early 1970s about a semi-official watchdog agency which monitored developments in all fields of scientific research and acted whenever it felt that human values or social responsibility were being ignored or flouted. It is, therefore, a popular term for social control of the 'mad scientist'. Less sensationally, it can embrace such organizations as the Club of Rome and the Pugwash conferences which periodically extrapolate trends of growth or consumption in order to forecast scarcities of resources, and attempt to avoid potential disasters and irresponsible research. See also TECHNOPOLIS. P.S.L.

doping. The introduction of controlled and usually small amounts of a foreign ATOM to a pure compound, often in the form of a crystal, in order to modify its properties. The addition of dopants is important in determining the electrical characteristics of SEMI-CONDUCTORS and in the preparation of LASER materials. B.F.

dopolavoro, see under ARTS CENTRE.

Doppler effect (named after the Austrian physicist Christian Johann Doppler, who discovered it in 1842). The change in the perceived frequency of a wave which results when the observer moves relatively to the source. The frequency is raised when the source and observer are approaching, and lowered when they are receding. For sound waves the Doppler effect causes the drop in pitch of the whistle of a passing train, and the SONIC BOOM. For light waves, the RED SHIFT in the spectrum of distant GALAXIES is a Doppler effect (see EXPANSION OF THE UNIVERSE). Finally, police RADAR traps are based on the change in frequency of a MICROWAVE signal reflected from a moving vehicle. M.V.B.

Dorfman, Robert (U.S. economist, *b.* 1911), see under TURNPIKE THEOREM.

dormitory town. A locality where town-dwellers have come in search of cheaper housing, a few trees, and a small garden, while continuing to find employment in the neighbouring METROPOLIS. Dormitory towns are a major factor in COMMUTING. M.L.

Dorsey, Tommy (U.S. musician, 1905–56), see under BIG BAND; SWING.

Dos Passos, John (U.S. novelist, 1896–1970), see under DOCUMENTARY.

Dostoevsky, Fyodor Mikhailovich (Russian novelist, 1821–81), see under EXPRESSIONISM; NIHILISM.

Dotremont, Christian (Belgian painter, *b.* 1922), see under COBRA.

double articulation, see DUALITY OF STRUCTURE.

double entrenchment, see under ENTRENCHED CLAUSES.

double helix, the. The name given to the crystalline structure of deoxyribonucleic acid (DNA) – see NUCLEIC ACID. Also the title of a well-known book by J. D. Watson describing his discovery of this structure in 1953 in collaboration with F. H. C. Crick. P.M.

Bibl: J. Monod, *Chance and Necessity* (N.Y., 1971; London, 1972).

double-talk. The deliberately unintelligible, ambiguous, or imprecise use of words for purposes of deception: a relatively new term for what is part of the perennial exercise of POWER – of calculation, negotiation, manipulation – in human relations at all levels, from the international to the personal. Thus, says Hobbes, ' . . . words are wise men's counters, they do but reckon by them; but they are the mony of fooles, that value them by [any] authority . . . whatsoever, if but a man.'   R.F.

doublethink, see under ORWELLIAN.

double-track systems, see under RECIDIVISM.

Douglas, Major **Clifford Hugh** (British economist, 1879–1952), see under SOCIAL CREDIT.

Douglass, Andrew Ellicott (U.S. archaeologist, 1867–1962), see under DENDROCHRONOLOGY.

Doukhobors. A Russian Orthodox nonconformist sect of 18th-century origin. Its leader, Savelius Kapustin, claimed to be a reincarnation of Christ, and the bulk of its members escaped from Czarist persecution by emigrating to western Canada at the end of the 19th century. PACIFIST (though by no means always non-violent), insistent on separate schooling, sometimes practising communal landownership, and antagonistic to all taxation likely to be devoted to State purposes antipathetic to their principles, they have had frequent conflicts with the Canadian Federal and provincial authorities. Their version of Christianity denies the divinity of Christ and the doctrines of resurrection and redemption, salvation coming from personal effort.   D.C.W.
Bibl: G. Woodcock and I. Avakumović, *The Doukhobors* (London and N.Y., 1968)

doves and **hawks.** A picturesque but overworked metaphor much used by American publicists during the regimes of Presidents Kennedy and Johnson to divide those (doves) who preferred diplomacy from those (hawks) who preferred

reliance on American military strength as the answer to the problems they inherited, i.e. the defection of CUBA to the pro-Soviet ranks, the confrontation with the U.S.S.R. in Berlin, and the progressive collapse of the non-COMMUNIST regime in VIETNAM.   D.C.W.

Down's syndrome. A form of congenital idiocy first adequately described by J. L. Down (1828–96) in 1866. In this SYNDROME, as he described it, the face is flat and broad, and the eyes rather narrow and set obliquely in the face, their inner angles being abnormally far apart. Down believed quite mistakenly that his syndrome was a sign of DEGENERACY (see ATAVISM) – hence the vulgar names mongolism, Mongolian idiocy. It is in fact caused by an accidental derangement of the CHROMOSOMES. Some forms of Down's syndrome increase in frequency with the age of the mother at childbirth; others do not.   P.M.
Bibl: G. E. W. Wolstenholme and R. Porter (eds.), *Mongolism* (London, 1967).

Dowson, Ernest (British poet, 1867–1900), see under DECADENCE.

Doxiadis, Constantinos Apostolos (Greek architect and engineer, 1913–75), see under EKISTICS.

Drago, Luis Maria (Brazilian statesman, 1859–1921), see under NONINTERVENTION.

Dreyfus case. In 1894 Captain Alfred Dreyfus, a French general staff officer of Jewish origins, was condemned to life imprisonment on Devil's Island for betraying secrets to Germany. The evidence was flimsy, and a campaign, in which Clemenceau and Zola played a leading part, was launched to secure a re-trial. Fearing the effect of an acquittal on the Army's position as the embodiment of France's national will, senior officers withheld or forged evidence and secured Dreyfus's conviction at a re-trial in 1899. President Loubet immediately pardoned him. In 1906 the Court of Appeal quashed the 1894 verdict and Dreyfus was reinstated. For more than a decade *l'affaire Dreyfus* bitterly divided France and dominated French politics: it became a trial of strength between anti-clerical radicals (*Dreyfusards*, including such people as Anatole France, Marcel Proust, Daniel Halévy, and Léon Blum) on the one hand and ANTISEMITIC, Catholic, conservative defenders of the French officer corps (*anti-Dreyfusards*; see also ACTION FRANÇAISE) on the other. A.L.C.B.

Bibl: G. Chapman, *The Dreyfus Case* (London and N.Y., 1955); D. Johnson, *France and the Dreyfus Affair* (London, 1966; N.Y., 1967).

Driesch, Hans (German embryologist, 1867–1941), see under REGULATION; VITALISM.

drop-out. Literally one who drops out of, or eschews, the generally accepted behaviour patterns of the society to which he belongs. While society has always had drop-outs in the form of tramps, vagrants, hermits, etc., the typical contemporary drop-out is closely associated with DRUG-taking and the emergence of the UNDERGROUND. Dropping out in this sense involves a deliberate decision to discontinue some conventionally approved course of action (e.g. a degree course, or the use of previously acquired specialist qualifications, or even the earning of a high wage on the assembly line), and to turn elsewhere for fulfilment. Popular choices include agriculture (e.g. subsistence farming) and the development of some craft or non-technical skill, all of which can be seen as offering an element of individualism against the background MASS SOCIETY, and as a positive reaction to DEHUMANIZATION. How many of the people who followed the advice of Timothy Leary to 'turn on, tune in, and drop out' remain drop-outs today is a matter for conjecture, but dropping out is often a transient activity. See also HIPPIES.
P.S.L.

drugs.

(1) The substances which form the subject-matter of PHARMACOLOGY; see also PSYCHOPHARMACOLOGY.

(2) More narrowly, in colloquial use, those chemical substances which, when taken orally, nasally, by inhalation, hypodermically, or intravenously, alter CONSCIOUSNESS, PERCEPTION, or mood. There are four groups: (*a*) *Anaesthetics and sedatives*, such as alcohol, barbiturates, tranquillizers, and 'glues' (which are sniffed); these blunt psychic and physical pain; TOLERANCE develops, and with high doses withdrawal causes convulsions or delirium. They have the virtue of not being smoked, but barbiturate injection is particularly damaging; alcohol, fortunately, is often taken for taste or diluted with food. (*b*) *Opiates*, natural and synthetic, include morphine and heroin; these are important in medicine for relief of pain, and may produce tolerance and withdrawal symptoms. Of the latter, despite the popular literature, prolonged insomnia may be hardest to deal with. (*c*) Stimulants such as cocaine and amphetamines; cocaine, though possibly the most addictive, generates little tolerance, and only DEPRESSION on withdrawal; but an extraordinary degree of tolerance can arise to amphetamines, (*d*) *Hallucinogens* such as mescaline, LSD, and cannabis; tolerance develops rapidly to LSD, more slowly to cannabis. Cannibis is unique in its cumulative effect and the resultant slow onset of its full action and of recovery from it. Its chemical structure was only recently discovered, as also its effects on sex hormones (see ENDOCRINOLOGY) and GENETIC material, and on MEMORY and MOTIVATION.

There are probably as many reasons for taking drugs as there are individuals; recurrent themes are curiosity, PEER pressure, DEPRESSION, embarrassment, the avoidance of a problem, and boredom. Multiple drug use is now common. The great danger is *continued* use, which is why the many psychological, social, and physical factors involved in drug dependence and progression to other drugs are important. A single 'puff' or 'pill' does not cause dependence, and it occurs rarely in people who have 'come to terms' with life. The death rate for a heroin addict is about 30 times that normal for his age, largely from self-neglect or overdose. W.D.M.P.

Bibl: A. Huxley, *The Doors of Perception* (London and N.Y., 1954) and *Heaven and Hell* (London and N.Y., 1956); J. H. Willis, *Drug Dependence* (London, 2nd ed., 1974).

drum store. A form of computer STORE similar to a DISC STORE but with the information stored on the surface of a rotating magnetized drum and with stationary read/write heads. Drum stores have a smaller capacity and a shorter ACCESS TIME than disc stores. C.S.

Drummond, Malcolm (British painter, 1880–1945), see under CAMDEN TOWN GROUP.

Du Gard, Roger Martin, see MARTIN DU GARD.

Du Pont de Nemours, Pierre Samuel (French economist, 1739–1817), see under POLITICAL ECONOMY.

dualism. Any theory which holds that there is, either in the universe at large or in some significant part of it, an ultimate and irreducible distinction of nature between two different kinds of thing. Examples are (1) Plato's dualism of eternal objects (forms or UNIVERSALS), of which we can have true knowledge, and temporal objects, which are accessible to the senses, and of which we can at best have opinions; (2) Descartes's *mind-body dualism*, i.e. of mind, as conscious, and of body, as occupying space, the former always infallibly, the latter never more than fallibly, knowable (see also MIND-BODY PROB-LEM); (3) *ethical dualism*, which holds, in conformity with the doctrine of the NATURALISTIC FALLACY, that there is an irreducible difference between statements of fact and VALUE-JUDGEMENTS; (4) *explanatory dualism*, which holds that, while natural events, including mere bodily movements, have causes, human actions do not but must be explained by reference to motives or reasons; (5), sometimes called *epistemological dualism* (see also EPISTEMOLOGY), the theory that a distinction must be drawn between the immediate object of PERCEPTION (i.e. the appearance or SENSE-DATUM) and the inferred, public, material object. A.Q.
Bibl: J. A. Passmore, *Philosophical Reasoning* (N.Y., 1961; London, 2nd ed., 1970).

duality of structure (sometimes referred to as *double articulation*). In LINGUISTICS, a major defining characteristic of human language, which is seen as containing two fundamental LEVELS of structure: (1) a phonological level, at which sounds, themselves meaningless, are organized into (meaningful) combinations (see PHONETICS; PHONOLOGY); (2) a syntactic

level, at which the properties of the meaningful expression are studied (in terms of SYNTAX, LEXICON, SEMANTICS). D.C.

Dubček, Alexander (Czechoslovak statesman, *b*.1921), see under BIAFRA; BREZHNEV DOCTRINE; PRAGUE (3).

Dubuffet, Jean (French painter, *b*.1901), see under ART BRUT.

Duchamp, Marcel (French artist, 1887–1968), see under ANTI-ART; ARMORY SHOW; DADA; KINETIC ART; ORPHISM; READYMADES; SURREALISM.

Duckworth, George Eckel (U.S. classical scholar, 1903–72), see under NUMEROLOGICAL CRITICISM.

Dufy, Raoul (French painter and designer, 1877–1953), see under FAUVES.

Duhamel, Georges (French author, 1884–1966), see under ABBAYE DE CRÉTEIL; ROMAN-FLEUVE.

Dujardin, Édouard (French author, 1861–1949), see under STREAM OF CON-SCIOUSNESS.

Dulles, John Foster (U.S. statesman, 1888–1959), see under BRINKMANSHIP; MASSIVE RETALIATION.

Dullin, Charles (French actor and producer, 1885–1949), see under CARTEL.

Dumbarton Oaks. Name of the private estate in Washington, at which in August and September 1944 British, American, Soviet, and Chinese representatives met to draft a charter for the post-war international security organization to be named the United Nations (see UNO). The draft proposed four principal organs, a Security Council, a General Assembly, an International Court of Justice, and an international secretariat. D.C.W.
Bibl: R. N. Gardner, *Sterling-Dollar Diplomacy* (2nd ed., N.Y., 1969; London 1970).

dumping. Selling in a foreign market at a price below that prevailing in the exporter's home market, or below his cost of production. In comparing prices or costs in the two markets, allowance must be

DUNCAN

made for differences in terms and conditions of sale and in taxation. The conditions under which dumping is injurious or beneficial to the importing country have been long discussed. The GATT permits countries to levy anti-dumping duties if their industries are or might be injured.
M.FG.S.
Bibl: See BALANCE OF PAYMENTS.

Duncan, Robert (U.S. poet, *b*. 1919), see under BLACK MOUNTAIN.

Duranty, Louis Edmond (French art critic, 1833–80), see under REALISM.

Durey, Louis (French composer, *b*. 1888), see under SIX, LES.

D'Urfé, Honoré (French author, 1567–1625), see under ANTI-HERO; ANTI-NOVEL.

Durkheim, Émile (French sociologist, 1858–1917), see under ANOMIE; COLLECTIVE CONSCIOUSNESS; ETHNOMETHODOLOGY; INTEGRATION; KNOWLEDGE, SOCIOLOGY OF; RELIGION, SOCIOLOGY OF; SOCIAL ACTION; SOCIAL FACT; SOCIAL STRATIFICATION; SOCIOLOGY.

dust-bowl. In GEOGRAPHY, a type of man-made desert. It is a region subject to low rainfall and occasional severe drought in which arable farming is a hazardous practice. The top soil of the dust-bowl has been removed by wind erosion, usually because of excessive grazing or ploughing and cultivation of land without the necessary precautions against wind erosion, and a broad hollow is imposed on the land. The term was originally applied to areas in the western U.S.A., i.e. in western Kansas, Oklahoma, and Texas, extending into south-eastern Colorado and eastern New Mexico, and is still used mainly in this context.
M.L.

Dutt, Rajani Palme (British Communist leader, 1896–1974), see under GUILD SOCIALISM.

Dutton, Clarence Edward (U.S. geologist and seismologist, 1841–1912), see under ISOSTASY.

Duvalier, Jacques (Haitian statesman, 1907–71), see under TONTON MACOUTE.

dvizhenie. see under KINETIC ART.

Dvořák, Antonín (Czech composer, 1841–1904), see under JAZZ; ROMANTICISM.

dwarf star. A small, faint, hot star of extremely high density. It is possible that dwarf stars are what is left after the explosion of SUPERNOVAE, and therefore represent a late stage in the evolution of stars. See also BLACK HOLE; HERTZSPRUNG-RUSSELL DIAGRAM.
M.V.B.

dwarf wheat, see under GREEN REVOLUTION.

Dyer, Reginald Edward Harry (British general, 1864–1927), see under AMRITSAR MASSACRE.

Dylaby (DYnamic LABYrinth), see under ENVIRONMENT.

Dylan, Bob (U.S. singer and composer, *b*. 1941), see under GREENWICH VILLAGE.

dymaxion. A term used by the American engineer Buckminster Fuller (*b*. 1895) to describe his CONCEPT of the maximum net performance per gross ENERGY input. It has been applied by him to a factory-produced house (a hexagonal space suspended from a central mast), a bathroom, and a map projection, and is most in evidence in the construction of his *geodesic domes*. These lightweight enclosures are parts of spheres subdivided along lines following Great Circle routes across their surface. Such domes have been air-lifted by the U.S. Marine Corps, have housed RADAR equipment in arctic conditions, travelled as exhibition pavilions, and, most notably, housed the U.S. Pavilion at the Montreal Expo in 1967.
M.BR.
Bibl: J. Meller (ed.), *The Buckminster Fuller Reader* (London, 1970).

dynamic labyrinth, see under ENVIRONMENT.

dynamic programming. A technique for attacking OPTIMIZATION problems by choosing the values of the variables sequentially rather than simultaneously. It tends to be particularly appropriate for problems involving time-dependence, such as control problems. The method is expected to provide an *optimal policy*, i.e. a rule for choosing the values of the variables so as to optimize the *criterion function*. Three broad classes of dynamic-programming problems may be distinguished:

(1) In *deterministic problems* all desired information is available at all times and the criterion function can be calculated to discover the effects of any given policy. Many control problems are of this type, e.g. the problem of selecting the minimal-time or minimal-fuel flight-path for an aircraft.

(2) *Learning problems* are deterministic, but the relation between control and effect is *a priori* unknown to the optimizer, who thus has to learn about the behaviour of the criterion function while trying to optimize it. Search procedures (e.g. the classic problem of identifying the broken wire in an unlabelled multi-core cable) are usually of this type.

(3) *Stochastic problems* have the additional feature that the future behaviour of the system is not fully determined by the past and present, knowledge of which merely makes the various future possibilities more or less probable; the best that the optimizer can hope to find is a policy which will maximize the expected value of the criterion function. Among the most important problems in this last class are correction problems for systems without inherent stability, where the policy has to make the best choice between the costs of using an incorrectly set mechanism and the costs of correcting it.   R.SI.

dynamic psychology. (1) A SCHOOL OF PSYCHOLOGY that emphasizes the role of MOTIVATION. (2) More narrowly, the ideas of Freud and other psychoanalytically oriented psychologists (see FREUDIAN; PSYCHOANALYSIS) who, indeed, lay paramount stress on motivation.   I.M.L.H.

dynamics. One of the two branches of MECHANICS.   M.V.B.

dysfunctional. The opposite of one of the many meanings of *functional*. In this sense, a process or mechanism within an organism or social system is functional if it serves the interests, needs, aims, or purposes of that organism or system, dysfunctional if it interferes with them. A.S.

dysgenic. Having a tendency to promote the spread of inferior, i.e. comparatively ill-adapted, genetic constitutions. Medicine exercises a dysgenic effect when it makes possible the preservation and propagation of deleterious GENES such as those responsible for phenylketonuria or galactosaemia – 'inborn errors of METABOLISM' in Sir Archibald Garrod's phrase. Needless to say, there is no science of 'dysgenics' to promote the deterioration of the human GENOME as EUGENICS promotes its improvement.   P.M.

dyslexia. The condition of those children who experience a difficulty in learning to read which cannot be accounted for by limited ability or by emotional or extraneous factors. The term is not susceptible of precise operational definition.   A.L.C.B.

Bibl: J. Tizard, *Children with Specific Reading Difficulties* (London, 1972).

Dyson, Anthony Edward (British literary critic and editor, *b*.1928), see under BLACK PAPERS.

Dzyuba, Ivan (Ukrainian literary critic, *b*.1931), see under SAMIZDAT.

E

earth art, see under CONCEPTUAL ART.

earth sciences. An omnibus term for the group of sciences concerned with the study of the earth. The role of the earth as a planet, its origins, motions, and destiny are the concern of ASTRONOMY, its internal composition of GEOPHYSICS, its outer crust of GEOLOGY, its oceans of OCEANOGRAPHY, and its atmosphere of METEOROLOGY. Reconstruction of the origins of life on earth and its present diversity belong to PALAEONTOLOGY and BIOLOGY, while the earth's present features and resources and their relevance to human society are the concern of GEOGRAPHY. Traditional divisions between these distinctive fields have recently been lowered, and integrated earth-science courses are increasingly common in university curricula.   P.H.
   Bibl: A. N. Strahler, *The Earth Sciences* (N.Y., 2nd ed., 1971).

Eastern Orthodoxy, see ORTHODOXY, EASTERN.

Ebert, Friedrich (German statesman, 1871–1925), see under SPARTACISTS.

ECA, see under MARSHALL PLAN.

ecclesiology. That part of Christian THEOLOGY which is concerned with the Church. The modern debate about the Church's essential nature and changing tasks has been stimulated by the ECUMENICAL MOVEMENT and, in CATHOLICISM, by the AGGIORNAMENTO. Sometimes the word refers only to the architecture and furnishings of church buildings.   D.L.E.

echo sounding, see SONAR.

ecliptic. When we consider the earth as a planet, the *celestial sphere* is that imaginary sphere surrounding the earth infinitely far away on which the earth's equator and poles are projected. The plane of the earth's orbit round the sun is thus a plane passing through the centre of the celestial sphere. Its intersection with the celestial sphere will be a great circle – the ecliptic. The *plane of the ecliptic* is therefore the plane of the earth's orbit round the sun. Since it does not change, the great circle of the ecliptic on the celestial sphere will remain in a fixed position relative to other points (e.g. stars) projected on it. The earth's axis has an inclination from the vertical with respect to the plane of the ecliptic of about $23\frac{1}{2}°$ (more accurately 23° 27'). Thus the plane of the ecliptic makes the same angle with the plane of the equator.   M.L.

ecodeme, see under DEME.

École de Paris. An expression used confusingly with three overlapping meanings, all relating to the fine arts as practised in Paris during the present century:
   (1) Immediately after World War I it referred to a number of artists of non-French origin and predominantly Jewish background: notably the Russians Chagall and Soutine, the Bulgar Jules Pascin, the Czech Coubine, the Japanese Foujita, the Poles Kisling and Zak, and the Italian Modigliani. Sometimes distinguished (first, second École) according to whether they arrived in Paris before or after the war, they formed a distinctive school of FIGURATIVE, easily sentimentalized, more or less EXPRESSIONIST painting which emerged as the main new movement between CUBISM and the extension of SURREALISM to the visual arts.
   (2) Later it was extended to include Picasso, Juan Gris, and even, by association, Maurice Utrillo and his mother Suzanne Valadon.
   (3) Finally, as in the Royal Academy's exhibition in 1951 and the annual shows at the Galérie Charpentier from 1955, it was used for virtually the whole modern art movement centering on Paris.   J.W.

ecology (also known as *bionomics*). A term (Greek *oikos*, household or living-place) first used by Ernst Haeckel in 1873 for that branch of BIOLOGY which deals with the interrelationships between organisms and their ENVIRONMENT (1). During the first half of the 20th century the concept spread rapidly, and ecology became an increasingly important part of many university courses. Studies of botanical ecology generally advanced more rapidly than those involving animals, but the subject played an important part in bringing together zoologists and botanists. Within the scientific community there is some division between those who place the greatest emphasis on field observations (the 'muddy-boot ecologists') and those who are more concerned with SYSTEMS analysis, modelling (see MODEL), and COMPUTER SIMULATION of ecological processes (the 'theoretical ecologists'). Ecology is sometimes divided into various subdivisions, i.e. population ecology, evolutionary ecology, community ecology, physiological ecology, and behavioural ecology. Usually these divisions have little validity except to indicate that, possibly in some defined HABITAT, the interrelations of several species are being studied from the point of view of POPULATION DYNAMICS, EVOLUTION, and so on.

In recent years the word has been applied to any activity its users consider desirable; thus 'the ecology of litter' has meant voluntary refuse-collection. Journalists often designate as 'the ecologists' those of their colleagues most obsessed with man's harmful effects, real or imaginary, on the globe. This use accounted for statements such as Max Nicholson's that 'ecology is the study of plants and animals in relation to their environment and to one another. But it is also more than that: it is the main intellectual discipline and tool which enables us to hope that human evolution can be mutated, can be shifted on to a new course, so that man will cease to knock hell out of the environment on which his own future depends.' Because of these debased uses, however, it seems likely that scientific ecologists will, in the future, have to find some new term to describe their activities.   K.M.

Bibl: C. Elton, *Animal Ecology* (London and N.Y., 1927); A. Tansley, *The British Isles and their Vegetation* (London, 1939); E. M. Nicholson, *The Environmental Revolution* (London, 1970).

ecology, human. An extension of zoological and botanical ECOLOGY to include man. The growth of human ecology is usually associated with sociological writing in the U.S.A. in the 1920s; it has since been widely adopted in a number of other SOCIAL SCIENCES. For each discipline, the distinctive character of ecological studies is the attempt to link the structure and organization of a human community to interactions with its localized ENVIRONMENT.   P.H.

Bibl: A. H. Hawley, *Human Ecology* (N.Y., 1950).

econometric history, see under ECONOMIC HISTORY.

econometrics. Economic studies based on the combination of observations, techniques of statistical estimation, and a mathematical treatment of economic theories. The term (whose coining is usually attributed to the Norwegian economist Ragnar Frisch) should be distinguished both from economic STATISTICS, which largely consists of the aggregation and tabulation of facts relating to economic life, and from *mathematical economics,* which largely consists of the mathematical elaboration of economic propositions relating to a simple, idealized world. It has much ground in common with quantitative and applied ECONOMICS but, on the whole, it searches for knowledge which is general and enduring rather than for immediate solutions to contemporary problems.

Though many of the 'empty economic boxes' deplored by J. H. Clapham 50 years ago have now been filled, much remains to be done. First, comparable and reliable data are often lacking and can only be built up gradually. Second, these data are generated by the workings of a complex system and there is little scope for carrying out and repeating controlled experiments. Third, it is often hard to formulate a relationship in a way that is both economically acceptable and amenable to computation (though, with advances in APPLIED MATHEMATICS and COMPUTERS, this difficulty seems to be diminishing). Fourth, it seldom happens that all the determining variables on the right-hand side of any single equation are exogenous; some of them are likely to be endogenous to a system of relationships which includes the dependent variable, and this leads to the problem of IDENTIFICATION. Fifth, since an adverse economic forecast (unlike, say, an adverse meteorological forecast) will stimulate action intended to falsify it, the econometrists must be prepared to combine FORECASTING with an analysis of economic policy and control. Finally, economic systems are embedded in social systems and, while econometrists may sometimes be justified in treating social variables as constants, this procedure is not valid generally. In the end we shall have to accept Comte's plea for a unified SOCIAL SCIENCE.   R.ST.

economic determinism, see under HISTORICAL MATERIALISM.

economic growth. Increase over time in real NATIONAL INCOME or in real national income per head; usage is not uniform between these two alternatives, either in statistical or in theoretical writings, but the second is the more usual. The concept refers to growth sustained over a substantial length of time, not to movements within BUSINESS CYCLES or shorter periods. Economic growth is most usually measured in annual percentage terms. In most industrial countries the long-run rate of growth of real national income per head has been between 1 and 2% a year; but the rate has been higher than this in most industrial countries since World War II, and in some countries (notably Japan and Sweden) it has been higher than this over a long period. Economic growth at these rates is a distinctive feature of the past 150 or so years. It did not occur in earlier periods and it has not generally occurred in UNDERDEVELOPED countries. The exact definition and measurement of economic growth depends on the definition of national income and is subject to the same limitations. If the conventional definition of national income were replaced by a wider one that allowed more adequately for non-market activities, leisure time, environmental conditions, and so on, some differences would result in measured rates of growth; but it is unlikely that the broad conclusions would be altered.   R.C.O.M.

Bibl: S. Kuznets, *Modern Economic Growth* (London and New Haven, 1966).

economic history. The history of economies in the past. The history of agriculture, trade, and industry was already flourishing, especially in Germany, in the 19th century, but economic history was recognized as a separate discipline in universities only in the 20th. 'Business history' split off from it in the U.S.A. in the 1920s. Since about 1950 economic historians have made greater use of quantitative methods and taken more interest in the MODELS and theories of economists. This *new economic history* (*econometric history* and *cliometrics* are other terms often used) differs from traditional economic history in METHODOLOGY. Instead of building up generalizations gradually as a result of accumulating a large number of facts and reflecting on specific historical cases, very much as any historian might, the exponents of the new method start by framing a hypothesis, and collect data with a view to establishing its validity, very much as an applied economist would. Econometric historians also make considerable use of *counterfactual propositions* (see COUNTERFACTUAL; PROPOSITION). The new methods have made it possible to supplement traditional micro-economic history (the history of specific industries and firms) with macro-economic history (the measurement of GROSS NATIONAL PRODUCT and ECONOMIC GROWTH in the past).   P.B.

economic imperialism, see under IMPERIALISM.

economic law. A proposition in ECONOMICS supposed to be of general validity; examples are GRESHAM'S LAW, SAY'S LAW, the law of SUPPLY AND DEMAND, and the law of DIMINISHING RETURNS. Nowadays the term has a rather old-fashioned ring, and economists, more conscious perhaps of the difference between reality and their MODELS of it, tend to embody their findings in theorems rather than laws.   R.ST.

economic liberalism. The application to ECONOMICS of the doctrines of classical LIBERALISM (1), expressed as a preference for competitive markets (see MARKET ECONOMY) and for the use of the PRICE MECHANISM over more direct forms of intervention. An economic liberal is not a believer in LAISSEZ FAIRE, because he

accepts the need for government intervention (if possible through the price mechanism) to deal with EXTERNALITIES, and also to supply 'public goods' (e.g. defence or urban parks) that cannot be charged for in the market place. Many, but not all, economic liberals favour redistribution of income, preferably in the form of taxes and cash grants rather than through provision in kind or wage- or price-fixing. Where direct intervention is unavoidable, economic liberals set great store on general impersonal rules and are against discretionary decisions by politicians and officials on the supposed 'merits of the case'. They need not be committed to any particular form of property ownership; and a few even believe in *market socialism*, where the market is made up of state-owned enterprises or COOPERATIVES.   S.BR.
    Bibl: F. A. Hayek, *The Road to Serfdom* (London and Chicago, 1944); S. Brittan, *Capitalism and the Permissive Society* (London, 1973).

economic theory of imperialism, see under IMPERIALISM.

economic warfare. The disorganization of an enemy's economy so as to prevent him from carrying on war, especially by the denial to him of imports, interference with his exports, and destruction by bombing or sabotage of his industrial centres of production, storage, and distribution. In its widest sense (and in official American usage, the term includes all measures against economic activities which directly or indirectly further a belligerent's war effort. In British usage, it only covers measures against an enemy.   D.C.W.
    Bibl: W. N. Medlicott, *The Economic Blockade* (London, 1952).

economics. In Anglo-Saxon countries the definition most in vogue is some version of Lionel Robbins's statement that 'economics ... is concerned with that aspect of behaviour which arises from the scarcity of means to achieve a given end'. For Robbins, it followed that 'economics is entirely neutral between ends; that, in so far as the achievement of *any* end is dependent on scarce means, it is germane to the preoccupations of the economist. Economics is not concerned with ends as such.' The definition has the further con-

sequence of separating economics sharply from PSYCHOLOGY and ETHICS (as explanations of how ends are generated), HISTORY (as account of how ends change), and SOCIOLOGY (as interpretation of the relations between individual and group behaviour). Economists are technicians like attorneys, dentists, or accountants in the sense that they should be prepared to explain the relation of available means to any proposed end.
    Conventional economics deals with two broad categories of issue. One, the province of *price theory*, or *micro-economics*, explains how market conditions of DEMAND and SUPPLY result in a host of individual commodity prices (see PRICE MECHANISM), wage rates (see INCOMES POLICY), rental charges, and interest rates. Micro-economics includes a theory of consumer choice and another of business operation. What joins the two is a common assumption of maximizing behaviour. Consumers are said to maximize a pyschic quantity, namely satisfaction, or UTILITY; entrepreneurs a financial one, namely profit. Although the theory is particularly applicable to the more competitively organized product and labour markets, many economists argue that, even in more concentrated markets characterized by OLIGOPOLY or influenced by advertising, actual market behaviour approximates to that of competitive assumptions.
    Modern *income theory*, or *macroeconomics*, dates from John Maynard Keynes's *General Theory of Employment, Interest and Money* (1935). Until Keynes, economics assumed that, in the absence of monopolistic interferences (see MONOPOLY) on the part of business, labour, or government, economies tended towards EQUILIBRIUM at FULL EMPLOYMENT. Keynes demonstrated that equilibrium was likely in other situations also. His explanation of the economy's condition focused on the AGGREGATE DEMAND for goods and services, i.e. on the sum of consumer demand, business demand, and government expenditure. Since the cause of unemployment was inadequate aggregate demand, its cure was either encouragement of private expenditure or DEFICIT SPENDING on the part of government.
    MARXIST economists take little interest in micro-economics and deliberately ally

economics with history and sociology. The proper study of economics should be, in the words of Oskar Lange, 'the social laws governing the production and distribution of the material means of satisfying human needs'. These social laws are the product of historical evolution and of the conflict between CLASSES which is the motive force of historical change. In so far as consumers maximize, they must do so within a context circumscribed by history and by class relationships. It is far more important to explain that context than the mechanics of MAXIMIZATION.

Modern FISCAL POLICY is the application of the principles of demand management to conditions both of inadequate and excessive aggregate demand. The American tax cut of 1964 is generally taken to be the first occasion when an American President openly embraced the necessity of enlarging a public deficit in the interests of stimulating aggregate demand. By the beginning of 1971, so conservative a politician as President Nixon remarked that in economic policy he was a KEYNESIAN. The admission was widely taken to indicate the obsolescence of Keynesian doctrine.   R.L.

Bibl: L. Robbins, *The Nature and Significance of Economic Science* (2nd rev. ed., London 1935; N.Y., 1962); P. A. Samuelson, *Economics* (London and N.Y., 9th ed., 1973); J. Robinson and J. Eatwell, *An Introduction to Modern Economics* (Maidenhead, 1973).

economies of scale. Circumstances that cause the total cost of supplying a good or service to rise less than in proportion to the amount supplied. These may be associated with manufacturing processes (and often with the use of particular pieces of equipment), but they arise also at the marketing stage (both in promotion and distribution) as well as from the fact that the cost of developing a good, once incurred, is independent of the quantity subsequently produced. Scale economies may depend upon the rate at which an activity is carried out (e.g. weekly production) or its duration (so-called 'long production runs'). Industrial and commercial development has led generally to increasingly large scale economies which require for their exploitation an increase in the size of firms or in the specialization of their activities.   G.B.R.

Bibl: E. A. G. Robinson, *The Structure of Competitive Industry* (rev. ed., Welwyn, Herts., and Chicago, 1959).

ecosystem. The system formed by the interaction of all living organisms, plants, animals, bacteria, etc. with the physical and chemical factors of their ENVIRONMENT. The variety of meanings attached to the word by different ecologists (some of whom now doubt its usefulness as a precise term with a rigid definition) reflects the variety of boundaries drawn for 'the environment'. Thus foresters speak of a 'woodland ecosystem' meaning the whole tree-covered area, while an entomologist working in the same wood will restrict the term to a fallen log with its insect fauna and the fungi living on the dead material; such restricted uses have their practical value in helping scientists to define their problem. However, since an ecosystem is usually thought of as occurring within a self-contained and restricted area, and since complete isolation of most areas is impossible, it can be argued that the Earth itself is the only real ecosystem. See also ECOLOGY.   K.M.

ECSC (European Coal and Steel Community). An organization originating in a proposal (the Schuman plan, 5 May 1950) by Robert Schuman, then French Foreign Minister, for the creation of a free market in coal and steel under a supranational authority. The scheme was seen by the French as the only remaining means of preventing a nationalist revival of West German heavy industry after the establishment the previous year of the West German state. The U.K. was invited to join, but refused. Signed on 18 April 1951 by representatives of France, West Germany, Italy, the Netherlands, Belgium, and Luxembourg, the Charter of the ECSC established a 9-member High Authority with powers to set prices, draw up plans, ensure free COMPETITION, prevent MONOPOLY, and look after the welfare of employees; a common assembly as a watchdog over the Authority; a Council of Ministers and a High Court; all but the Assembly being located in Luxembourg. The ECSC served as a model for the later EEC into which it was incorporated.   D.C.W.

Bibl: W. Diebold, *The Schuman Plan* (N.Y., 1959).

ECT, see ELECTRO-CONVULSIVE THERAPY.

ectomorph, see under PERSONALITY TYPES.

ecumenical movement. 'Ecumenical' (from Greek *oikoumenikos*, 'of the inhabited world') is still sometimes used to refer to the whole of mankind. But its usual usage is Christian, and refers to the Councils of the undivided Church which laid down orthodox CHRISTOLOGY and defined other DOGMAS; to the Ecumenical Patriarch in Constantinople (see ORTHODOXY, EASTERN); or to the modern movement for Christian reunion. This movement began with the World Missionary Conference at Edinburgh in 1910. The formation of the International Missionary Council was accompanied by other world conferences on problems of 'Life and Work' and of 'Faith and Order'. These three streams united in the World Council of Churches, constituted at Amsterdam in 1948. The Roman CATHOLIC Church is the only major Christian denomination which is not a member of the W.C.C., though it participates in many of the latter's activities, and warmer relations with other Christians form an important part of this Church's AGGIORNAMENTO. Discussion about the reunion of the Churches has been active in many countries, and some mergers have been achieved. However, progress in the Churches towards unity or towards anything else has been disappointingly slow, and towards the end of the 1960s a new mood began to grow among Christians, largely ignoring the Churches' problems and hesitations, and concentrating instead on a more informal and radical witness and service in the modern world. This mood restored to the word 'ecumenical' much of its original connection with humanity.   D.L.E.

Bibl: R. Rouse and S. C. Neill (eds.), *A History of the Ecumenical Movement, 1517-1948* (London and Philadelphia, 2nd ed., 1967); H. E. Fey (ed.), *The Ecumenical Advance, 1948-1968* (London and Philadelphia, 1970).

edaphology, see under SOIL SCIENCE.

EDC (European Defence Community). A scheme originating in a proposal (24

October 1950) by the French Prime Minister, René Pleven, in reply to American proposals, inspired by the Korean war, for the participation of West German armed forces in 'an integrated force for the defence of Western Europe'. Despite Britain's refusal to participate, the proposals led to the signature in Paris of the EDC treaty of 27 May 1952. American pressure failed, however, to secure the treaty's ratification by the French National Assembly, and after its rejection (30 August 1954) the rearmament of West Germany was secured within the less restricted framework of WEU, and later of NATO.   D.C.W.

Bibl: D. Lerner and R. Aron (eds.), *France Defeats EDC* (N.Y., 1957).

Eddy, Mary Baker (founder of Christian Science, 1821-1910), see under CHRISTIAN SCIENCE.

eddy currents. Term originally applied to the irregular flow of fluids past an obstacle or series of obstacles and, as such, generally associated with a swirling motion in liquids. Since the flow of electric current is often likened to fluid flow, the term became associated with electric currents flowing in large sheets or volumes of conductor (as opposed to thin wires), especially when those currents are produced by electromagnetic induction (see INDUCTION MOTORS).   E.R.L.

Bibl: J. Lammeraner and M. Stâfl, *Eddy Currents* (London and Cleveland, 1966).

Eden, Sir **Anthony** (later Earl of Avon; British statesman, 1897-1977), see under DISENGAGEMENT.

Edgeworth, Francis Ysidro (Irish economist, 1845-1926), see under CORE.

EDP (electronic data processing), see COMPUTING.

education. A word susceptible of various definitions according to the stance of the user; e.g. (1) education is a passing on of a cultural heritage; (2) it is the initiation of the young into worthwhile ways of thinking and doing; (3) it is a fostering of the individual's growth. Many of the controversies in educational thought arise from the tension between these three attitudes. At one end of the spectrum the prime agent is seen as *the teacher*, marked with the appropriate signs of authority; at the other it is *the student*, whose unfolding gifts may perhaps be speeded up by a teacher's insight and care. In the middle ground is the view of education as a joint process, of teachers managing and arranging curriculum resources and of children acquiring the sensibilities and skills necessary to explore and to create the small world of playground and school. All three views are valid for different circumstances and are complementary.

At the infant and primary level, emphasis on feeling and 'enriched experience' predominates currently in English-speaking countries, although research findings are causing serious doubts about the *unskilled* application of open, discovery methods. At the secondary level, dissatisfaction with traditional selective systems in Britain has resulted in attempts to follow Sweden's example and use large non-selective SECONDARY SCHOOLS (see also COMPREHENSIVE SCHOOLS) as a means to social equality. Alternatively, such dissatisfaction also produces doubts about the whole purpose of compulsory secondary schooling. From this extreme reaction springs the doctrine of those who reject the notion of formal schooling altogether (see DE-SCHOOLING), or, less revolutionary, people who advocate the idea of PERMANENT EDUCATION. Workers' adult education schemes, Danish Folk High Schools, and the OPEN UNIVERSITY have all been tentative expressions of this.

Doubts about the effectiveness of secondary education also show themselves in ideas of curricular reform. Impetus for reform came first in science and technology. But it has been reinforced by changes in YOUTH CULTURE and by the teachers' own awareness of the vast increase in knowledge now being made available to children. This has led to the demand that education should be concerned more with skills of hand, eye, and brain and with the mastering of linguistic and other competence, and much less with the acquisition of examinable 'facts'. In the U.S.A. especially there has been much emphasis also on the need for vocationally relevant skills, expecially in the higher levels of secondary education (see C. E. Silberman, *Crisis in the Classroom*, N.Y., 1970).

Many of the most crucial educational

problems now cluster around the issues of maintaining and enhancing each individual's competence for coping both with life and with his inherited creative powers. At one end of the scale the psychologists are looking closely at the young child's innate capacities to make simple hypotheses, to explore and to relate (see J. S. Bruner, *Toward a Theory of Instruction*, N.Y., 1960). At the organizational end social psychologists are turning towards some of the more subtle, inter-personal aspects of school – working with small groups and analysing what actually goes on in classroom or laboratory or playground. See also CULTURE; DEVELOPMENTAL PSYCHOLOGY; EDUCATIONAL PSYCHOLOGY; INTELLIGENCE.   R.A.H.

Bibl: J. S. Bruner, *The Relevance of Education* (N.Y., 1971; London, 1972); L. Stenhouse, *An Introduction to Curriculum Research and Development* (London, 1975).

educational priority area (EPA). An appellation recommended in the PLOWDEN REPORT (1967) for certain deprived areas of Britain which should be shown 'positive discrimination' in the form of improved buildings, favourable staff/student ratios, salary bonuses, COMMUNITY SCHOOLS, and attention to the education of immigrants. The term was attacked on the grounds that it might not be appropriate to all the schools in an area so labelled, and might damage the area's reputation and morale. EPAs have been set up in Liverpool, London, and elsewhere, and in 1968–9 £3 million were voted to be spent on particular schools in 31 Local Authority Areas. See also COMPENSATORY EDUCATION.   W.A.C.S.

educational psychology. A branch of APPLIED PSYCHOLOGY concerned with several kinds of activity. The first is with studies of learning and associated forms of PROBLEM-SOLVING as these are revealed in the learning of bodies of knowledge. Closely connected are applications of DEVELOPMENTAL PSYCHOLOGY to the organization of learning and of curricula. More recently, educational psychology has also dealt with the inter-personal and social aspects of classrooms and other less formal learning situations, particularly with the manner in which these affect attitudes as well as the acquisition of knowledge; and moral education has become increasingly a matter of concern in an age of change in cultural NORMS.

A second large area of activity is in testing and EVALUATION, both of INTELLIGENCE and of special abilities such as mathematics, music, spatial capacities (i.e. ability to decipher representational pictures or diagrams of spatial arrays), etc. A principal contribution to this work (notably by Charles Spearman, L. L. Thurstone, and Sir Charles Burt) has been the partitioning of intelligence into component abilities and investigation of the extent to which these component abilities are found by FACTOR ANALYSIS to be dependent upon general intelligence – as measured by the common CORRELATION of the components.

Educational psychology has also had an active part in the organizing of school curricula, both in analysing the special problems of learning certain subject-matters, and developing theories of how subjects are learned. An example is the work of J.S. Bruner indicating that central structural CONCEPTS within a field, once learned, aid considerably in mastery of detailed information when such material is shown to be derivable from general principles. Ideas about the structuring of the curriculum have recently been embodied in PROGRAMMED INSTRUCTION.

Finally, educational psychology concerns itself with problems of the SPECIAL EDUCATION of the culturally underprivileged, the mentally retarded (see MENTAL RETARDATION), and those with physical handicaps like deafness and blindness. J.S.B.

Bibl: L. J. Cronbach, *Educational Psychology* (London and N.Y., 1963).

educational technology (ET). The use of apparatus and machines such as language laboratories, films, slides and tape-recorders, books, television, radio, video-tape, and the still camera to extend the teacher's range of effectiveness. In addition COMPUTERS have provided a powerful aid over a wide range. Critics of ET warn that, while in skilled hands it may be valuable, casual users may find the machines unexpectedly awkward to work, and that teachers must not let machines dominate their teaching responsibility. Its supporters argue that it is intended as an aid to, not a substitute for, teaching, and that in any case children are going to grow up in a technological world and should learn how to use and evaluate technological techniques. W.A.C.S.

educational tests, see under MENTAL TESTING.

educationally subnormal (ESN). Term used of children who, through limited ability (usually an INTELLIGENCE QUOTIENT of under 75) or severe but maybe temporary MENTAL RETARDATION, require SPECIAL EDUCATION. It is estimated that about 1% of the British school population require such treatment, which is given in special schools or units. These figures do not include the much larger number of 'slow learners' for whom provision is made by special teaching arrangements in ordinary schools. W.A.C.S.

Bibl: A. F. Laing (ed.), *Educating Mentally Handicapped Children* (Swansea, 1972).

Edwards, Hilton (Irish theatre director, *b*. 1903), see under GATE THEATRE.

EEC (European Economic Community). The leading example of a *common market* (see CUSTOMS UNION). Conceived by pro-Europeans as a re-launching of the EUROPEAN MOVEMENT after the failure of EDC, it originated in the Messina conference of June 1955 between the member states of ECSC, and was formally established by the Rome Treaty (March 1957), with France, West Germany, Italy, the Netherlands, Belgium, and Luxembourg ('the Six') as members. Belated British attempts to join were rebuffed by French opposition in 1963 and 1967, but in January 1972 agreement was reached that Britain, Denmark, and Eire should be admitted to membership. Movements of CAPITAL have not yet been completely freed, but in other respects the EEC goes beyond a common market in providing for common or harmonized policies in, e.g., agriculture, transport, energy, indirect taxation, MONOPOLIES, regional problems, and *macro-economic* affairs (see ECONOMICS). It thus approaches a full *economic union*, although it seems unlikely that it will complete the journey (with, e.g., a common currency) without a *political union* as well. D.C.W.

Bibl: D. Swann, *The Economics of the Common Market* (Harmondsworth, 2nd ed., 1972); U. Kitzinger, *Diplomacy and Persuasion* (London, 1973).

EEG, see ELECTROENCEPHALOGRAPH.

EFTA (European Free Trade Area). An organization originating in British proposals intended to produce an alternative to the CUSTOMS UNION and *common market* of the EEC. The supranational element of EEC was lacking; agriculture was excluded from its operations, and individual countries were left free to pursue separate tariff policies (see FREE TRADE) towards the trade of non-members. The convention establishing EFTA, signed in Stockholm on 20 November 1959 by representatives of Austria, Britain, Denmark, Norway, Portugal, Sweden, and Switzerland, envisaged the reduction by 10% annually of tariffs on manufactured goods. On the successful conclusion, in January 1972, of negotiations for the British entry into EEC the future of EFTA came to depend on the terms on which its remaining members could negotiate treaties of association with EEC.   D.C.W.

Bibl: M. Camps, *Britain and the European Community, 1955–63* (London and Princeton, 1964).

egalitarianism. A belief in the high value of EQUALITY among human beings and the desirability of removing inequalities. Such a belief forms part of many religious, political, and social movements. In the French Revolution, with its famous slogan of Liberty, Equality, and Fraternity, the second term of the revolutionary trinity took an extreme form in Babeuf's *Conspiracy of Equals* (1796), which bequeathed its legacy to a host of secret organizations in the early 19th century espousing the idea of the universal equality of incomes. 'Babouvism' provided the ground for the emergence of SOCIALIST and COMMUNIST ideas.

Marx (see MARXISM), however, stressed the paramount importance of CLASS divisions as against individual inequalities and recognized that unequal individual capacities and work will be differentially remunerated in the first stage of building communism. Stalin seized this point in his attack on the egalitarian wage structure prevailing in the U.S.S.R. until 1930 and replaced it by a system of unequal rewards to provide incentives for industrial development. In contrast, Mao Tse-tung (see MAOISM) favoured a more egalitarian economic policy.

The problems of the egalitarian distribution of goods in society have acquired a new perspective in the 20th century, because historical experience has shown that removal of one kind of inequality can be accompanied by the sharpening of other kinds. While income differences may diminish, differences in POWER within society may increase, since economic, social, and political differences do not necessarily change together. Another awkward question is raised by 'equality of opportunity'. Egalitarianism has found it difficult to accept the idea of MERITOCRACY. It also has to face the possibility that 'unequal individual endowment' may be more resilient to social change, because of GENETIC factors, than the environmentalist beliefs (see ENVIRONMENT) of earlier egalitarians allowed for. None the less egalitarianism remains one of the most powerful ideas in modern history.   L.L.

Bibl: R. H. Tawney, *Equality* (London, rev. ed., 1952); J. Rees, *Equality* (London and N.Y.,1971); J. Rawls, *A Theory of Justice* (Cambridge, Mass., 1971; Oxford, 1972).

Eggeling, Viking (Swedish-born artist, 1880–1921), see under ABSTRACT ART.

ego. In psychoanalytic theory (see PSYCHOANALYSIS), a FREUDIAN term for the part of the psychic structure that is concerned with facing up to the demands of the real world, and dealing with both the impulses from the ID and the requirements of the SUPEREGO. Outside Freudian theory, the word is apt to be used as equivalent to the self, when this is dealing with the external and internal demands on the person. See also REALITY PRINCIPLE.
   B.A.F.

Bibl: A. Freud, tr. C. Baines, *The Ego and the Mechanisms of Defence* (rev. ed., N.Y., 1967; London, 1968).

egoism.
(1) In ETHICS, the view that the foundation of morality is, or ought to be, individual self-interest;
(2) the behaviour of one who abides by this view.   W.Z.

Egoist, The. Title from 1914 until its demise in 1919 of a London fortnightly review, the exemplary 'little magazine' of this crucial period and central organ for Anglo-American MODERNISM. Originally the feminist *New Freewoman*, sponsored by Harriet Shaw Weaver, the paper changed title and content after Ezra Pound became literary editor. It included major work, creative and critical, by Pound himself, his editorial successors Richard Aldington, H. D. (Hilda Doolittle), and T. S. Eliot, and such writers as Rémy de Gourmont, James Joyce (including extracts from *Ulysses*), Ford Madox Hueffer (Ford), and F. S. Flint. In particular it introduced IMAGISM in England and was the main English outlet for new American poets, including Amy Lowell, Marianne Moore, William Carlos Williams, and Robert Frost.   M.S.BR.

Ehrenburg, Ilya (Soviet author, 1891–1967), see under THAW, THE.

Ehrlich, Paul (German chemist, 1854–1915), see under CHEMOTHERAPY.

eidetic image. A vividly clear, detailed imaging of what has previously been seen. It is lifelike, i.e. seen as located outside rather than in the head, and often contains a surprising amount of accurate detail.   I.M.L.H.

Einstein, Albert (German-U.S. physicist, 1879–1955), see under BLACK HOLE; CLOCK PARADOX; GRAVITATION; MACH'S PRINCIPLE; MASS-ENERGY EQUATION; OPERATIONALISM; PHOTOCHEMISTRY; QUANTUM MECHANICS; RELATIVITY; TENSOR.

Einstein, Alfred (German-U.S. musicologist, 1880–1952), see under MUSICOLOGY.

Einstellung ('attitude', 'set'). German term for a habitual procedure for dealing with repeatedly encountered problems of similar type. See also PROBLEM-SOLVING.   I.M.L.H.

Eisenhower, Dwight David (U.S. general and president, 1890–1969), see under DOMINO THEORY; MILITARY-INDUSTRIAL COMPLEX.

Eisenstadt, Shmuel N. (Israeli sociologist, b. 1923), see under MODERNIZATION.

Eisenstein, Sergy Mikhailovich (Russian film director, 1898–1948), see under BIOMECHANICS; DOCUMENTARY; FEX; FORMALISM; MONTAGE; PROLETKULT.

Eisler, Hanns (German composer, 1898–1962), see under LEHRSTÜCK.

ekistics. Term coined by the Greek planner, C. A. Doxiadis, for the study of human SETTLEMENTS and their problems by bringing together in an interdisciplinary and international approach experts from such subjects as ECONOMICS, GEOGRAPHY, SOCIOLOGY.   A.L.C.B.
   Bibl: C. A. Doxiadis, *Ekistics* (London and N.Y., 1968).

El Greco (Spanish painter, 1541–1614), see under EXPRESSIONISM.

elaborated code and **restricted code.** Terms arising from the linguistic work of Professor Basil Bernstein in London in the 1950s. He uses the term *restricted code* to describe language linked to immediate (context-bound) situations and possessing an incomplete grammatical, syntactic, and semantic range. The *elaborated code* is flexible and CONTEXT-FREE, and uses a varied syntax and vocabulary to express individual and abstract ideas. The working-class family, it is argued, has a traditional structure, and working-class children tend to call mainly on the restricted code. By contrast, the middle-class family has a more individualistic, personal organization, and middle-class children appear to command both codes. The task for education is to extend the working-class child's mastery of the elaborated code.   W.A.C.S.
   Bibl: B. Bernstein, 'Social Structure, Language and Learning' (*Educational Research*, June 1961); H. Rosen, *Language and Class* (Bristol, 1972).

élan vital, see under VITALISM.

elastic rebound theory. This theory explaining the origin of earthquakes was developed by H. F. Reid after he had studied the effects of the disastrous San Francisco earthquake of 1906. In essence Reid's theory postulates as the immediate cause of earthquakes the sudden movement of rocks of the crust and mantle (see LITHOSPHERE) either side of a pre-existing fracture or fault. This rapid phase is, however, only the culmination of a slow and increasing elastic distortion of the rocks over tens of years. The situation is analagous to pushing one rubber eraser over another. Both will be distorted elastically but only while the frictional resistance of their contacting surfaces is not exceeded. The rubbers 'grip' each other. When the frictional resistance is exceeded each rubber will rebound to its original shape but it will be displaced. Similarly the rocks either side of the potential fault suffer increasing distortion until the frictional resistance of the fault is exceeded. Suddenly, over a period of a few seconds the fault slips, allowing the distorted rocks to rebound to their original shape. Measured displacements along earthquake faults at the surface range from a few centimetres to several metres.   J.L.M.L.

elasticity. In ECONOMICS, a measure of the responsiveness of SUPPLY AND DEMAND to changes in price, roughly expressed as the percentage change in demand (*elasticity of demand*) or supply (*elasticity of supply*) related to a 1% difference in price. However, the apparent simplicity of this concept conceals innumerable snags. Thus, (1) elasticity may be different at different price levels. (2) If money incomes are unchanged and the price of a commodity rises, real incomes are reduced, and the consequent reduction in demand may be analysable into an *income effect* and a *substitution effect,* for each of which an elasticity can be defined. The former may even outweigh the latter to the extent of causing demand for an 'inferior good' (e.g. potatoes in Ireland in the early 19th century) to *increase* when its price rises. (3) Long-run elasticities are nearly always larger than short-run ones, as consumers and producers have more time to adjust their habits. In short, elasticities – and the demand-and-supply curves of which they are properties – are essentially static comparisons of different situations; and their use to represent time sequences is a simplification needing scrutiny.   S.BR.
Bibl: J. R. Hicks, *Value and Capital* (Oxford, 2nd ed., 1946); H. Henderson, *Supply and Demand* (London, rev. ed., 1932; N.Y., rev. ed., 1948).

elasticity of substitution, see under SUBSTITUTION.

Electra complex. In psychoanalytic theory (see PSYCHOANALYSIS), a normal emotional crisis in females resulting, at an early stage of PSYCHOSEXUAL DEVELOPMENT, from sexual impulses towards the father and jealousy of the mother. It is the female counterpart of the OEDIPUS COMPLEX.   W.Z.

electrochemistry. The oldest branch of PHYSICAL CHEMISTRY, electrochemistry is the study of solutions of ELECTROLYTES and of the processes occurring at ELECTRODES. It involves investigation of the structure of electrolytes, which are usually (but not necessarily) aqueous, the measurement and formulation of theories of ionic transport, and the kinetics of CHEMICAL REACTIONS between IONS. Electrode processes relate to the measurement of THERMODYNAMIC and KINETIC properties of reactions taking place at electrodes, to POLAROGRAPHY, and to ionic EQUILIBRIA involving membranes.   B.F.
Bibl: J. Koryta, J. Dvořák, and V. Boháčková, *Electrochemistry* (London, 1970.

electro-convulsive therapy (ECT). In PSYCHIATRY, the artificial inducement of convulsions by means of electric shock, in the treatment of specific mental and behavioural disorders such as DEPRESSION. Although the patient's observable condition often improves, little is known about why this is so or about the long-term, deleterious mental and physical side-effects.   H.L.

electrode. An emitter (*cathode*) or receiver (*anode*) of ELECTRONS, as in an ELECTRON GUN (emitter) or a THERMIONIC valve (receiver).   M.V.B.

electrodynamics. The common ground between MECHANICS and ELECTROMAGNETISM which deals with the motion of charged PARTICLES in an ELECTROMAGNETIC FIELD. Typical electrodynamic effects are VAN ALLEN BELTS and focusing in an ELECTRON MICROSCOPE. For *quantum electrodynamics* see FIELD THEORY; OPTICS.   M.V.B.

electroencephalograph (EEG). In NEUROPSYCHOLOGY, (1) an instrument used for recording electric currents originating in the brain, by means of ELECTRODES applied to the scalp or implanted within the tissues of the brain; (2) the print-out of these electric currents, i.e. records of brain waves.   W.Z.

electrolysis. A CHEMICAL REACTION occurring as the result of the passage of an electric current. Commercially important electrolytic processes include the extraction of metals from their ores, particularly aluminium, and the production of hydrogen and chlorine from brine.   B.F.

electrolyte. A substance which gives rise to IONS in solution. A strong electrolyte is a substance which is largely dissociated (see DISSOCIATION) into its ions in solution.   B.F.

electromagnetic field. The FIELD whose sources are charges, currents, and magnets. Combinations of electric and magnetic fields whose strengths vary with time constitute RADIATION; they may travel great distances from their sources. The existence of an electromagnetic field in a region is indicated by forces exerted on test charges, currents, and magnets. See also ELECTROMAGNETISM; ELECTROSTATICS; MAGNETISM.   M.V.B.

electromagnetism (or *electromagnetic theory*). One of the main branches of PHYSICS, linking the phenomena of ELECTROSTATICS, electric currents, MAGNETISM, and OPTICS into a single conceptual framework. The final form of the theory was devised by Maxwell and is one of the triumphs of 19th-century science. One of Maxwell's earliest predictions was the existence of radio waves, and his EQUATIONS are fundamental throughout modern TELECOMMUNICATIONS. See also RADAR; RADIATION.   M.V.B.

electron. The first ELEMENTARY PARTICLE to be discovered (in the late 19th century). The electron is negatively charged, stable, and about 2,000 times lighter than the hydrogen ATOM. Its importance for science as a whole stems largely from its occurrence as a relatively mobile constituent of atoms; thus it participates in the emission of light (see ATOMIC PHYSICS) and in electric conduction (see SOLIDSTATE PHYSICS).   M.V.B.

electron diffraction. The DIFFRACTION of a beam of ELECTRONS by matter in the form of a CRYSTAL LATTICE. The successful observation of electron diffraction led to the general acceptance of the WAVEPARTICLE DUALITY. See also CRYSTALLOGRAPHY.   M.V.B.

electron gun. An arrangement for producing a beam of ELECTRONS which may be focused and deflected at will, for use in, e.g., CATHODE RAY TUBES. See also ELECTRODE; THERMIONIC.   M.V.B.

electron microscope. An instrument invented in 1931 for studying small material structures, such as crystals, microorganisms, and TISSUES. It is analogous to an ordinary optical microscope with the specimen illuminated by an ELECTRON beam (accelerated by a high voltage) instead of a light beam, and focused by combined electric and magnetic FIELDS instead of glass lenses. The image is displayed on a FLUORESCENT screen instead of being viewed directly. Because of DIFFRACTION, it is impossible in any microscope to resolve objects smaller than the wavelength of the RADIATION used; the very short DE BROGLIE WAVELENGTH of high-voltage electrons (see QUANTUM MECHANICS) has enabled single ATOMS to be discerned – more than a thousand times smaller than can be resolved optically. BIOLOGY has been revolutionized by *electron microscopy*: it has opened up the ultrastructural world of CYTOLOGY and has revealed the anatomical structure of infective PARTICLES such as viruses (see VIROLOGY).   M.V.B.; P.M.

electron shell. ELECTRONS in ATOMS can be assigned to different ORBITALS so that, according to the EXCLUSION PRINCIPLE, each has a unique set of QUANTUM NUMBERS. Electrons with the same principal quantum number comprise members of a particular shell; the K shell is closest to the NUCLEUS and has 2 electrons, the next shell (L) has 8 electrons, and so on. Each atom has a characteristic shell structure, but the ENERGIES of electrons in the higher shells overlap and in these cases only electrons in the same sub-shell – i.e. with identical principal and azimuthal quantum numbers – have similar energies. The CHEMISTRY of the ELEMENTS is strongly influenced by the nature and number of electrons in the outer sub-shells. B.F.

electron spin resonance. The application of MAGNETIC RESONANCE to the SPINS of ELECTRONS. M.V.B.

electronegativity. A measure of the ability of an ATOM to attract an ELECTRON. There have been several attempts to produce a scale of electronegativity, but the concept cannot be put in a uniquely quantitative way. Pauling devised a method based on BOND energies (see ENERGY) which makes fluorine the most electronegative element, followed by oxygen, nitrogen, and chlorine. B.F.

electronic music. Music produced by electronic oscillators which can be adjusted to any desired pitch, tone-colour, or frequency. Most of the developments in electronic music have come from Cologne or Milan where leading contemporary composers such as Stockhausen, Berio, and Maderna have led the way. As with other forms of synthetic music, the main purpose is to escape from traditional musical sonorities into a new world of tonal experience. The sounds produced cover the entire range detectable by the human ear, and may be violent, horrific, tender, remote, or neutral. A recent development is to bring an element of instant transformation of sound into actual performances, during which the composer himself (e.g. Stockhausen, Smalley) or a 'technician-performer' modifies the sound by conventional instruments. A.H.

electronics. The design of electric circuits (for use in radio receivers, COMPUTERS, amplifiers, etc.) incorporating devices such as TRANSISTORS and THERMIONIC valves, whose operation depends on the behaviour of ELECTRONS. M.V.B.

electrophoresis. The movement of a charged colloidal (see COLLOID) PARTICLE under the influence of an electrical FIELD. The effect is similar to the migration of IONS in solution. Because different colloids do not have the same velocity, electrophoresis is widely used in clinical medicine to separate colloids, either as aid in preparations or prior to chemical analysis. B.F.

electrostatics. The branch of ELECTRO-MAGNETISM dealing with bodies with an excess of (positive or negative) electric charge. The operation of condensers in alternating-current circuits, and the frictional charging of clouds and aeroplanes, are electrostatic effects. M.V.B.

element. A substance which cannot be broken down into simpler constituents by chemical means, because all its ATOMS have the same ATOMIC NUMBER. The naturally-occurring elements range from hydrogen (No. 1) to uranium (No. 92), and about a dozen TRANSURANIC ELEMENTS have been produced artificially. M.V.B.

elementarism. The SCHOOL OF PSYCHOLOGY which holds that experience or behaviour is to be studied by analysing it into its component elements and then discovering how these elements associate together to produce the complex experience or behaviour. For the opposite approach see ORGANISMIC PSYCHOLOGY. I.M.L.H.

elementary particle. Any PARTICLE which contributes to structures and processes involving matter at the SUBATOMIC level. By means of observations and experiments with ACCELERATORS and COSMIC RAYS, and detectors such as CLOUD CHAMBERS and BUBBLE CHAMBERS, more than fifty elementary particles have been discovered. Of these, ELECTRONS, PROTONS, NEUTRINOS, and PHOTONS are stable, as are their antiparticles (see ANTIMATTER). The rest (see MESON; NEUTRON) are unstable. The variety of the experimental results is baffling, and as yet no comprehensive theory exists within which the masses, decay times, interaction laws, SPINS, etc. can be understood. It is not known, for instance, which particles are truly 'elementary' (i.e. not reducible to simpler constituents), and which are merely different 'states' of the same particle (see FIELD THEORY; NUCLEON; QUARK). The situation is reminiscent of optical SPECTROSCOPY before 1925, when a mass of apparently discordant data was unified by the discovery of QUANTUM MECHANICS; but it does not follow that a similar conceptual revolution is required today. Elementary-particle PHYSICS is the most hectic and expensive branch of contemporary 'big science'.   M.V.B.

Bibl: G. Wick, *Elementary Particles* (London, 1972).

eleven plus, see under SECONDARY SCHOOL.

Eliot, George (pseud. of Marian Evans, British novelist, 1819–80), see under LEAVISITE; REALISM.

Eliot, Thomas Stearns (U.S.-born poet, dramatist, and critic, 1888–1965), see under AMBIGUITY; BLAST; CRITERION, THE; CULTURE; DISSOCIATION OF SENSIBILITY; EGOIST, THE; FREE VERSE; GROUP THEATRE; IMAGISM; LEAVISITE; LITTLE REVIEW; LIVING THEATRE; MOVEMENT, THE; NEW CRITICISM; OBJECTIVE CORRELATIVE; POETRY (CHICAGO).

élite. Collective noun for those who occupy a position (or positions) of superiority within a society or group by virtue of qualities (actual, claimed, or presumed) of excellence or distinction. The term's history owes much to the use made of it by V. Pareto and the observations made by him with regard to (1) the élite as distinguished from the non-élite groups within a social order and (2) the divisions within the élite as between a governing élite and a non-governing élite. Pareto's work and that of others (such as G. Mosca and R. Michels) has generated much debate, e.g. concerning the functions and social supports of *political élites,* the types of such élites as found in different societies, their cohesiveness, and their relation to *ruling classes.* Pareto himself sought to establish the psychological basis of élite status, authority, and continuity. Within his special conceptual framework and his theory of history as 'the graveyard of aristocracies' he took shifts in that basis as explaining the *circulation of élites* – a cyclical process of élite replacement over a period of time. See also ÉLITISM; POWER ÉLITES.   S.J.G.

Bibl: V. Pareto, ed. S. E. Finer, tr. D. Mirfin, *Sociological Writings* (London and N.Y., 1966); G. Parry, *Political Élites* (N.Y., 1970).

élitism. In education, a term of abuse for the system – traditional in Britain, France and Germany, but not in the U.S.A. – whereby children of above-average ability are segregated (in, e.g., British GRAMMAR SCHOOLS or PUBLIC SCHOOLS) and educated to above-average levels; some theorists extend the term, and their disapproval, to any form of educational selection, e.g. STREAMING or university entrance requirements. The purely educational arguments for and against selection tend to be overshadowed by socio-political considerations, e.g. the tendency of the educational system to reflect and reinforce the existing SOCIAL STRATIFICATION.   W.A.C.S.

Bibl: J. Floud, A. H. Halsey, and F. M. Martin, *Social Class and Educational Opportunity* (London, 1956).

Ellington, Duke (U.S. jazz musician, 1899–1974), see under BIG BAND; JAZZ; SWEET.

Éluard, Paul (French poet, 1895–1952), see under SURREALISM.

EMA (European Monetary Agreement), see under BIS.

embryology. The branch of ZOOLOGY that deals with the history and theory of development – in particular the development that begins with a ZYGOTE. (1) In chordate animals development begins with the subdivision (*cleavage* – sometimes called *segmentation*) of the zygote into a number of separate daughter CELLS which rearrange themselves to form a hollow vesicle (*blastula*) or something equivalent to it (e.g. BLASTOCYST). (2) The next major manoeuvre is *gastrulation*, the conversion of this hollow sac into a three-layered larva – the *gastrula.* Then (3) all chordate animals go through a stage called the *neurula* – a slightly elongated embryo with a bulky head and a tapering tail with the elementary NERVOUS SYSTEM in the form of a hollow tube running from end to end, and under that the notochord or skeletal rod to which the chordates owe their name, both tube and rod being flanked on either side by *somites,* i.e. by muscle blocks arranged segmentally down the length of the body, reminding us that vertebrates are in their origin segmented animals. In chordates the principal body cavity is a *perivisceral coelom*, i.e. a cavity which holds the guts and viscera generally. The kidneys originate in all vertebrates from the narrow connections between the cavities of the segmental muscle blocks and the perivisceral coelom. The eyes of vertebrate animals are formed through the conjunction of an outgrowth from the brain which becomes the retina with a thickening of the ectoderm which becomes the lens. A transverse section through a neurula at this stage looks very much the same in all vertebrates, and only an experienced embryologist can identify the class of vertebrate animal to which a given neurula belongs. It is this fact, that the embryos of related animals resemble each other far more closely than the adults into which they develop (*von Baer's principle*), which contains the germ of truth in the doctrine of RECAPITULATION. In its simplest form this doctrine declares that in development an animal 'climbs up its own family tree'. In the heyday of recapitulation theory it was contended that the gastrula larva represents recapitulation of a very early stage in the EVOLUTION of many-celled animals, namely that stage seen today in hydroids and jellyfish, which are in essentials also simple invaginated two-layered sacs the single aperture of which serves both as mouth and anus. Embryonic development is guided by instructions contained within the DNA (see NUCLEIC ACID) of the CHROMOSOMES of the zygote. It is only in this sense that the old PREFORMATIONIST theory is true. The instructions are preformed, but their carrying out is 'epigenetic', i.e. dependent upon the right sequence of STIMULI from the ENVIRONMENT and from the cells into which the embryo itself develops.   P.M.

Bibl: L. Hamilton, *From Egg to Adolescent* (London and N.Y., 1976).

emergence. In hierarchically organized systems, especially in BIOLOGY, the appearance at some tier of the hierarchy of a novelty which is not obviously predictable or foreseeable in terms of anything that has preceded it. Thus consciousness or cerebration has been said to have 'emerged' in the EVOLUTION of higher primates. Much earnest and confused thought surrounds the notion that emergence is a kind of evolutionary stratagem which explains the appearance of novelties.   P.M.

emergent poetry, see under CONCRETE POETRY.

emergent property. A property of some complex whole which cannot be explained in terms of the properties of the parts. See also REDUCTION.   A.S.

emic and **etic.** In LINGUISTICS, terms derived from the contrast between phonemics (see PHONOLOGY) and PHONETICS, and used to characterize opposed approaches to the study of linguistic data. An *etic* approach is one where the physical patterns of language are described with a minimum of reference to their function within the language system, whereas an *emic* approach takes full account of functional relationships, setting up minimal contrastive units as the basis of a description. Thus an etic approach to INTONATION would describe an utterance's pitch movement as minutely as possible, whereas an emic approach would describe only those features of the pitch pattern which are used to signal meanings.   D.C.

Emmert's Law, see under AFTER-IMAGE.

emotion. A word used in ordinary language to refer principally to subjective experience. Such experience is of its nature outside the reach of EXPERIMENTAL PSYCHOLOGY, whose subject-matter, like that of any objective empirical science, must contain specifiable experimental operations, empirical observations, and theories formulated to account for such relationships; whereas 'emotion' refers neither to operations nor to observations, and can find a home in the language of experimental psychology only as a theory-word. However, the high tide of BEHAVIOURISM in the 1920s left psychologists reluctant to talk theory at all, preferring instead STIMULI (the psychologist's comprehensive term for experimental operations) and 'responses' (i.e. observations). None the less, the feeling persisted that the layman's term 'emotion' in some way specified a class of behaviour in a specific class of situations. To satisfy this feeling, and yet eschew the dangers of MENTALISM, the vogue arose for studying 'emotional stimuli' and 'emotional responses or behaviour'. In the absence of a theroy of emotion, however, such terms are totally undefined, so it is not surprising that they have caused much confusion. One reaction has been to say that there is *no* unitary class of behaviour which can be distinguished as 'emotional', and that the word should be dropped altogether.

A more useful reaction is to construct an explicit theory of emotion, rather than hiding behind the implicit theory embodied in the stimulus-response formulation. 'Emotion' being a layman's term, one might perhaps begin by attempting to illumine the intuitions behind our ordinary language. This, properly speaking, is the business of the philosopher of language (see LINGUISTIC PHILOSOPHY) but to date PSYCHOLOGY has not drawn much on such work. None the less, at least one current philosophic view of 'emotion' (see EMOTIVISM) – that emotion-words have to do with the appraisal as 'good' or 'bad' of the objects which give rise to emotional states – finds a satisfying echo in recent developments in the psychology of emotion. These developments spring in the main from the theory of learning; in particular, that part which concerns the way subjects (including animals; see also ETHOLOGY) respond to and learn about rewards and punishments. These (the two major forms of *reinforcement*; see OPERANT CONDITIONING) are defined operationally by the changes they produce in the behaviour on which they are contingent. A reward is a stimulus which, when made contingent upon a response, increases the latter's probability of recurrence; a punishment is a stimulus which decreases this probability.

With this in mind, we can define emotion as consisting in the set of states of the organism produced by reinforcing events or by *conditioned stimuli* (see CLASSICAL CONDITIONING) that have in the subject's previous experience been followed by reinforcing events. Put less technically, an emotional state consists in a DISPOSITION to act in particular ways, produced by exposure to stimuli which the subject wants to experience or to avoid, or by exposure to signals which predict the imminent occurrence of such stimuli. Such states are, of course, accompanied by changes in neural and hormonal processes, and these have been extensively studied. Signals of the subject's emotional state are also of biological significance for other members of the subject's SPECIES (its *conspecifics*). The study of the way in which one animal communicates to another its current emotional state, thus enabling its conspecifics to predict its likely future behaviour, was first given scientific prominence by Darwin in 1872. Recently, there have been a number of important attempts to apply to the study of emotional expression in man the techniques previously used with animals.

The MODELS proposed by psychologists for an understanding of emotion posit only a few emotional states. Yet in ordinary language there are hundreds of different names of apparently separate emotions. A simple resolution of this discrepancy is to hand. It is clear from experimental work in SOCIAL PSYCHOLOGY that, in ascribing a name to one's current emotional state, one takes into account not only its nature but also the specific circumstances that gave rise to it, and that a multiplicity of names may reflect a multiplicity, not of states but only of types of situation giving rise to a single state. For example, the tension felt by someone anticipating a specific painful experience or danger is commonly called 'fear'; the same state is often called 'ANXIETY' when the feared event is unknown or diffuse; and there is experimental evidence that it is this same state which is produced by signals of omission of reward, when one might be described as anticipating 'frustration' or 'disappointment'.   J.A.G.

Bibl: C. Darwin, *The Expression of the Emotions in Man and Animals* (London, 1872; N.Y., 1873; Chicago and London, 1965; N.Y., 1969); R. A. Hinde (ed.), *Non-Verbal Communication* (London, 1972).

emotive and referential language. A distinction between two kinds of language popularized by C. K. Ogden and I. A. Richards (*The Meaning of Meaning*, 1923); sometimes expressed as a distinction between CONNOTATION AND DENOTATION. Richards, throughout his earlier career, advocated the rights of a complex, organized emotional language – affecting attitudes – against those of the referential language of science, LOGIC, or MATHEMATICS. Poetry was 'the supreme form of emotive language'. The distinction, which crystallized with the advent of ROMANTICISM, is a necessary one; but it requires considerable refinement, if only because no serious critic could assert that there is an actual split between the emotive and the referential. The NEW CRITICISM is full of such refinements.   M.S.-S.

emotivism. In ETHICS, the theory that VALUE-JUDGEMENTS, particularly moral judgements, are expressions of the speaker's emotions about the action, person, or situation to which they refer and not, as they grammatically appear to be, statements of fact, true or false. Emotivists emphasize the distinction between utterances that *express* feeling, such as ejaculations or expletives, and utterances that *state* that a certain feeling is being experienced. It is to the former that they assimilate judgements of value. Hinted at by C. K. Ogden and I. A. Richards in the 1920s, emotivism was set out as an explicit theory by A. J. Ayer in the following decade and was developed with great detail and thoroughness in the *Ethics and Language* (1944) of C. L. Stevenson. Its immediate foundation is the apparent irresolubility of much moral disagreement. Indirectly it supplies a need created by the improved version of the doctrine of the NATURALISTIC FALLACY, which holds that value-judgements are quite different in nature from statements of fact. Emotivism's exponents tended to agree, on reflection, that the distinctive feature of value-judgements was that their acceptance by someone committed him to *acting* in a certain way, whereas the acceptance of a statement of fact committed him only to the adoption of the corresponding *belief*. If this is correct, value-judgements are more like imperatives than merely expressive utterances. As a result emotivism, notably in the influential works of R. M. Hare, has largely given way to *imperativism* or *prescriptivism*.   A.Q.

Bibl: R. M. Hare, *The Language of Morals* (Oxford, 1952; N.Y., 1964); J. O. Urmson, *The Emotive Theory of Ethics* (London, 1968).

empathy. Projection (not necessarily voluntary) of the self into the feelings of others or, anthropomorphically, into the 'being' of objects or sets of objects; it implies psychological involvement, at once Keats's pain and joy. The word itself was coined by Vernon Lee in 1904, and

then employed by the psychologist E. B. Titchener in 1909 as a translation of the German *Einfühlung* ('feeling-into'), the notion of which had been developed in Germany by R. H. Lotze in *Mikrokosmos* (1856–64; tr. 1886); it largely provoked the ALIENATION theories of Brecht in reaction to it.   M.S.-S.

empirical theology. Challenged by the general acceptance among educated people of the inductive scientific method (see INDUCTION; see also, however, POPPERIAN) as the only means of knowing anything, Christian THEOLOGY has in this century reviewed its own METHODOLOGY. Apart from DEATH OF GOD THEOLOGY, three main responses have appeared. One is the defiant reaffirmation of DOGMA. The second is the insistence in CRISIS THEOLOGY that God is not an object to be known scientifically but is nevertheless the great self-revealing reality, to be encountered and obeyed. The third is the argument that God can be known rationally or at least intuitively like any other object (or, as many would prefer, subject) in human experience, while he is also greater. D. C. Macintosh, *Theology as an Empirical Science* (1919), exemplified this effort to fit THEISM into the scientific world-view. Other LIBERAL theologians of this school included Shailer Mathews and H. N. Wieman, both of the University of Chicago. Although this mainly American movement was largely defeated by the emphasis in crisis theology on the otherness and mystery of God, the challenge which it had taken up remained, and was not entirely met by CHRISTIAN EXISTENTIALISM's derivation of doctrines from a more specifically religious experience. In the 1960s and later, Christian philosophers, mainly in England, returned to the task with a more modest programme discussing the nature and scope of religious statements, specially about God, in comparison with science and in the light of LINGUISTIC ANALYSIS. Questions asked included these: Is any religious statement necessarily nonsense? If not, what is its meaning, or at least its use? Is it verifiable, or even falsifiable, by experience – in this world or in eternity? If it is based on a disclosure of the divine presence, what sort of situation contains this disclosure, and what sort of attempt to describe it, or to draw a conclusion from it, is valid? How odd do normal words become when used in a religious context? Thus about every doctrine it is asked: what is its empirical value? D.L.E.

Bibl: K. Cauthen, *The Impact of American Religious Liberalism* (N.Y., 1962); I. T. Ramsey, *Religious Language* (London, 1957; N.Y., 1963); A. G. N. Flew and A. MacIntyre, *New Essays in Philosophical Theology* (London, 1955; N.Y., 1964); I. G. Barbour, *Issues in Science and Religion* (London and Englewood Cliffs, N.J., 1966).

empiricism. The theory (1) that all CONCEPTS are derived from experience, i.e. that a linguistic expression can be significant only if it is associated by rule with something that can be experienced, and (2) that all statements claiming to express knowledge depend for their justification on experience. The two aspects of the theory are not inseparable. Many empiricists, moreover, allow some exceptions under both heads. The formal concepts of LOGIC, e.g. those expressed by the words 'not', 'and', and 'all', are widely regarded as being purely syntactical and as having no connection with experience. As for knowledge, empiricists generally agree that there is a class of purely conceptual or analytic propositions (see ANALYTIC; PROPOSITIONS) which are necessarily true in virtue of the meanings of the words that express them, even if they stigmatize these propositions as 'trifling' (Locke) or 'merely verbal' (J. S. Mill). The opposite of empiricism is RATIONALISM or, more precisely, APRIORISM. The principle of VERIFICATION is a modern formulation of empiricism. Any statement of the empiricist theory, to be consistent (see CONSISTENCY) with itself, must be empirical or, if not, analytic. An empirical basis for the theory is provided by elementary facts about the way in which the meaning of words is learned. A.Q.

Bibl: see under CONCEPTUALISM.

Empson, William (British poet and critic, *b*. 1906), see under AMBIGUITY; CRITERION, THE; MOVEMENT, THE; NEW CRITICISM; PLURISIGNATION.

emulsion.
(1) A system where one liquid is dispersed in droplet form throughout another with which it does not mix (e.g.

mayonnaise, which consists of oil droplets in a mixture of vinegar and egg yolk).
(2) The suspension containing silver bromide which forms the light-sensitive coating on photographic plates. M.V.B.

enclaves and **exclaves.** Complementary geographical terms for a non-contiguous territory of a state embedded within the territory of another state; thus West Berlin forms an *enclave* from the viewpoint of East Germany, the state within which the outlier is located, but forms an *exclave* from the viewpoint of West Germany, the state to which the outlier belongs. Such outliers are now less common than in the past (e.g. Prussia before 1866 consisted of more than 270 disconnected segments of territory) but retain an important irritant role (e.g. Gibraltar) or economic role (e.g. Hong Kong) out of proportion to their size. P.H.

encoder. In INFORMATION THEORY, a device or PROGRAM which alters the representation of data to some desired form, usually in order to transmit the data or store them. If the transmission or storage medium is imperfect, an encoder is frequently designed to produce REDUNDANCY in its output. See also DECODER. R.M.N.

Encounter. Monthly review of 'literature, art, politics', founded in London in 1953 by Stephen Spender and Irving Kristol; among subsequent editors have been Melvin Lasky, Frank Kermode, Nigel Dennis, D. J. Enright, and Anthony Thwaite. Sponsored by the Congress of Cultural Freedom, which probably had CIA funding, the magazine was one of an international, U.S.-financed stable (*Der Monat* in Germany was another), which exchanged articles and had contributors in common; it was a symptom both of the Americanization of Europe and of the close alliance of European and American INTELLECTUALS during the COLD WAR phase. *Encounter* none the less was the main British literary-intellectual journal of the period, and pursued an independent critical line. The intellectual alliance was and remains productive; *Encounter* has published some of the most interesting figures in current intellectual life (e.g. Arthur Koestler, Michael Polanyi, Sir

ENCOUNTER GROUP

Karl Popper), as well as admirable poetry, criticism, and, to a lesser extent, fiction.

M.S.BR.

encounter group. In GROUP THERAPY, any therapeutic group in which body contact and emotional expression is encouraged rather than the traditional purely verbal interaction. The aim of encounter groups is to increase sensitivity to others, including both physical and emotional awareness. They may take many different forms, including marathon sessions (24 to 48 hours without sleep), meeting in warm baths (the *Esalen* group), and the use of special techniques such as soliloquy, ROLE-playing, PSYCHODRAMA, etc. It has been shown that encounter groups, apart from their positive effects, may also cause breakdowns in vulnerable participants.

M.J.C.

Bibl: I. D. Yalom, *The Theory and Practice of Group Psychotherapy* (N.Y., 1970).

enculturation. A term coined by M. J. Herskovits (1948) for the process by which individuals are brought up to be members of their CULTURE or society, i.e., how they are made, by EDUCATION in the broadest possible sense, to have the culture appropriate to them. The CONCEPT is thus very close to that of SOCIALIZATION, much used in SOCIOLOGY and DEVELOPMENTAL PSYCHOLOGY.

M.F.

encyclical. An official statement by a Pope, known from its opening words (in Latin), e.g. PACEM IN TERRIS, QUADRAGESIMO ANNO, RERUM NOVARUM; see also CATHOLIC ACTION. INFALLIBILITY is not claimed for encyclicals.

D.L.E.

end stage, see under OPEN STAGE.

Ende, Hans am (German painter, 1864–1918), see under WORPSWEDE.

Enders, John Franklin (U.S. microbiologist, *b*. 1897), see under VIROLOGY.

endocrinology. The branch of medical BIOLOGY that deals with the nature and manner of action of endocrine glands and their SECRETIONS. Whereas most glands in the body (*exocrine glands*) communicate through ducts with the regions of the body in which their secretions (e.g. digestive

ENZYMES) are to act, the *endocrine glands* are ductless and liberate their secretions (*hormones*) directly into the lymph vessels or the blood stream. The chief endocrine glands are: the various elements of the PITUITARY gland, the THYROID, the islet tissue of the pancreas, the thymus, the ADRENAL GLAND, and the sex glands of both sexes.

The anterior pituitary gland holds a key position in the endocrine regulation of the body, because its secretions control the activities of the adrenal cortex, the sex glands, and other endocrine organs. Its hormones belong to the PROTEIN family and are indeed *polypeptides* (see PEPTIDES; the same is true of INSULIN, secreted in the pancreas. The sex hormones and the secretions of the adrenal cortex are all STEROIDS. Many hormones can now be manufactured synthetically. P.M.

endogamy and **exogamy.** Terms invented by J. F. McLennan (*Primitive Marriage,* 1865) for rules forbidding marriage respectively outside and within a specified group. Exogamy in some form is universal, and endogamy may well exist alongside it; e.g. I must marry out of my clan or circle of relatives but within my CASTE or TRIBE. The terms are central to the theory of kinship and marriage. In DEMOGRAPHY and SOCIOLOGY the terms usually refer not to rules but to statistical norms. See also INCEST. M.F.

Bibl: R. Fox, *Kinship and Marriage* (Harmondsworth, 1967); R. Needham (ed.), *Rethinking Kinship and Marriage* (London and N.Y., 1971).

endomorph, see under PERSONALITY TYPES.

endotoxins, see under BACTERIOLOGY.

energy. The capacity of a physical system for doing mechanical work – i.e. for moving objects against forces. Energy exists in various forms, the most fundamental according to current theory being KINETIC ENERGY, matter (see MASS-ENERGY EQUATION) and the POTENTIAL ENERGIES due to GRAVITATION, ELECTROMAGNETIC FIELDS, and forces between ELEMENTARY PARTICLES (e.g. STRONG INTERACTIONS, WEAK INTERACTIONS). Other kinds of energy arise from these in complicated systems; thus, chemical energy is due to electromagnetic forces between ELEC-TRONS and NUCLEI in ATOMS, and heat energy is the total kinetic energy of random atomic motion. All these energies may be interconverted without loss because of a CONSERVATION LAW whose apparent universality makes energy one of the most important CONCEPTS in PHYSICS. The basic unit of energy is the *joule* – roughly equal to the work done when an apple is lifted through one yard. One kilowatt hour is 3.6 million joules. See also CALORIE. M.V.B.

energy level. In microscopic systems such as ATOMS the ENERGY is constrained to take only certain discrete values. The lowest level is called the *ground state* of the system, and higher levels are *excited states*. Transitions from a higher to a lower level must involve a loss of energy, which is usually emitted as PHOTONS of light or other electromagnetic RADIATION, while transitions to higher levels occur by absorption of light. These energy levels may be predicted more or less directly by QUANTUM MECHANICS whereas in the earlier BOHR THEORY they were the result of apparently arbitrary rules restricting the application of NEWTONIAN MECHANICS (in which the energy normally varies continuously). See also ATOMIC PHYSICS; SPECTROSCOPY. M.V.B.

engagé. Vogue word (like its English equivalent 'committed'; see COMMITMENT) denoting the enlistment of an individual's or group's whole sympathies, emotions, sense of morality, etc., by some cause, usually one devoted to or involved in some root-and-branch critique of existing society and in consequent struggle to amend or to destroy it. D.C.W.

Engel, Erich (German author and film critic, 1889–1971), see under NEUE SACHLICHKEIT.

Engels, Friedrich (German socialist philosopher, 1820–95), see under DIALECTICAL MATERIALISM; DICTATORSHIP OF THE PROLETARIAT; HISTORICAL MATERIALISM; MARXISM; MATERIALISM; SOCIALISM.

engineering. The utilization of (1) raw materials, (2) metals and other products from raw materials, (3) natural sources of ENERGY, and (4) the SCIENTIFIC METHOD in order to build machines and structures intended to serve a specific purpose. This purpose is most often utilitarian – transport, communication, water-supply – but may also (e.g. in the building of a RADIO TELESCOPE) subserve the ends of the NATURAL SCIENCES, i.e. enhance understanding of the physical world. It is in the use of the scientific method that engineering transcends (though it may incorporate) the traditional manufacturing crafts, and is aligned with TECHNOLOGY, of which indeed it is an important part.

Engineering has been traditionally divided into civil engineering ('civil', as in 'civil service', implying public functions such as are served by roads, bridges, harbours, waterways, etc.) and *mechanical engineering* (dealing with machines). During the 19th century, however, electrical engineering emerged as a distinct discipline demanding its own training and qualifications; the advent of aircraft brought with it aeronautical engineering; and an ever-growing list of special branches now includes municipal, electronic, radio, gas, mining, production, structural, chemical, fuel, marine, and railway engineering. E.R.L.

English Stage Company, see under ROYAL COURT THEATRE.

Enosis. Greek word for union or unification, used in various political contexts, originally by Greek nationalists intent on the realization of a Greek empire over those areas outside mainland Greece which had been under Greek rule in classical and Byzantine times and still had substantial Greek-speaking populations, a dream known as the *Megale Idea*. From 1930 the word was more particularly invoked by Cypriot Greeks in their long campaign to obtain independence from British rule, a campaign opposed bitterly by the Turkish minority on the island. The achievement of independence in 1960 led to an equally bitter conflict between the advocates of union with Greece and the Cypriot government of Archbishop Makarios. The death in January 1974 of the movement's leader, General Grivas, led to a marked if temporary decline in its activities. In July 1974, however, the military regime in Greece used its forces in Cyprus to support a coup against the Makarios government by pro-Enosis forces. Their action led to communal strife between Greek and Turkish Cypriot communities and to the invasion of Cyprus by Turkish forces. These seized part of the island, into which the Turkish community was evacuated, while Greek Cypriots took refuge in the unoccupied areas. Relations between Greece and Turkey deteriorated so badly that international mediation was unable to secure any agreement. Despite the overthrow of the military regime in Greece, the emotional support there for Enosis ran far too strong for the democratic government which succeeded it to accept the truth that the massacres of Greek and Turkish Cypriots during the period of communal strife precluded any restoration of the *status quo ante*. D.C.W.

Enright, Dennis Joseph (British poet, novelist, and critic, b.1920), see under ENCOUNTER; LEAVISITE.

Ensor, James Sydney, Baron (Belgian painter and engraver, 1860-1949), see under VINGT, LES.

entailment and **implication**. In LOGIC, *entailment* is the converse of the relation of logical consequence: for *p* to entail *q* is for *q* to follow logically from *p*. *Implication* is a more generic notion. One PROPOSITION implies another if the conditional statement that has the former as antecedent and the latter as consequent is true. 'It is cloudy' implies 'It will rain' provided that 'If it is cloudy it will rain' is true. Entailment is thus a species of implication, entailments being those implications that are guaranteed by logic or the MEANINGS of the terms involved. In modern formal logic there is a type of formula, called by Russell *material implication*, which partially corresponds, but is not strictly equivalent in meaning, to ordinary conditional statements of the form 'if *p* then *q*'. It is defined to mean the same as 'not both *p* and not-*q*' and, although statements of this form follow from the corresponding conditionals, the converse is not true. Because of this difference of sense C. I. Lewis introduced the notion of *strict implication*, defined as 'It is not possible that *p* and not-*q*', the object being a juster representation of the ordinary conditional. The systems of strict implication

are the basis of contemporary MODAL LOGIC. A.Q.
Bibl: W. V. Quine, *Methods of Logic,* part 1 (London 1952; N.Y., 3rd ed., 1972).

entelechy. (1) In Aristotelian PHILOSOPHY, the endowment that realizes or gives expression to some potential. (2) For its special use in BIOLOGY see VITALISM. P.M.

entrenched clauses. Those clauses of a constitution for the repeal or amendment of which a special legislative process is required in order to protect them from hasty or too frequent alteration. Such protection may take various forms: it may consist of a requirement that legislation amending or repealing the protected clause must be passed by a larger majority than that required for ordinary legislation, or that it must be passed by a majority of two chambers of a legislature (which normally sit separately) sitting together, or that it must be confirmed by a referendum. To give the fullest measure of protection the special procedure must be made applicable not only to the clauses of the constitution which are to be specially protected, but also, by a provision known as *double entrenchment*, to the clauses providing for such special protection. A much debated question is whether or not it is open to the British Parliament to entrench legislation (e.g. guaranteeing individual liberties) so as to preclude its repeal by the ordinary process of legislation. H.L.A.H.
Bibl: G. Marshall, *Parliamentary Sovereignty in the Commonwealth* (Oxford and N.Y., 1957).

entropy.
(1) In THERMODYNAMICS, a QUANTITY forming (along with ENERGY, temperature, pressure, etc.) part of the specification of the thermal state of a SYSTEM; a typical system is the steam in a boiler. Entropy may be calculated from the heat which must be added to the system to bring it via intermediate states to the state being considered. It is found that the entropy of any closed system never decreases. This is one formulation of the *second law of thermodynamics*, which can be explained by STATISTICAL MECHANICS, where entropy is interpreted as a measure of the *disorder* among the ATOMS making

up the system, since an initially ordered state is virtually certain to randomize as time proceeds. See also HEAT DEATH OF UNIVERSE.   M.V.B.

(2) In CYBERNETICS, entropy is generalized to measure the tendency of any closed system to move from a less to a more probable state, using the same mathematical apparatus as in (1). If, however, the system is open to information, then this tendency may be arrested. This is because, mathematically speaking, information can be defined precisely as negative entropy (or *negentropy*).   S.BE.

Entwicklungsroman   see   BILDUNGS-ROMAN.

environment.

(1) In ECOLOGY, the sum total of the biological, chemical, and physical factors in some circumscribed area, usually an area associated with a particular living organism. Essentially an environment only exists because it is inhabited by this organism. Thus a field is the environment for a cow, a cow-dung pat is the environment for a dung-beetle, and the exoskeleton of the dung-beetle is the environment of a parasitic mite. Therefore the field comprises an infinity of overlapping environments. 'Environment' is also used in the sense of HABITAT or ECOSYSTEM. K.M.

(2) In architecture, theatre, and the visual arts, the current use of this term, dating from the late 1950s, seems confined to the English language; there is no French or German equivalent. It combines three main concepts: (*a*) the notion of the all-embracing three-dimensional work of art as evolved by the American Allan Kaprow in 1958 and featured in the '*Dylaby*' (dynamic labyrinth) show (Amsterdam, 1962) by Rauschenberg, Jean Tinguely, and others, with Schwitters's Hanover MERZbau of the 1920s as its forerunner; (*b*) the HAPPENING, which developed from Kaprow's and Claes Oldenburg's work in that direction; (*c*) the use of such works and events, together with more orthodox and less autonomous aspects of visual art, to shape, enliven, embellish, and improve our surroundings. Hence such new notions as 'environmental art', 'environmental design' (covering anything from landscape gardening to the colour of bus shelters), ENVIRONMENTAL CONTROL, POLLUTION of the environ-

ment, and finally in 1970, as one of the Heath government's innovations, a Ministry of the Environment to deal with town-planning and CONSERVATION. J.W.

environmental areas, see under TRANSPORT PLANNING.

environmental control. The regulation of the air's temperature, humidity, rate of movement, and PARTICLE content within a building by mechanical means, together with the use of artificial lighting. There has been an increasing reliance on these mechanical services as building plans have become larger, and especially deeper, and external conditions in cities less and less tolerable. Services rather than STRUCTURE have as a result become one of the dominant controlling elements in architectural design.   M.BR.

Bibl: R. Banham, *The Architecture of the Well-Tempered Environment* (London and Chicago, 1969).

environmental determinism, see under ENVIRONMENTALISM.

environmental studies. Term used to cover almost all activities in schools, colleges, and universities which are aimed at making pupils more aware of, and critical of, the conditions in the world in which they live, and of the interrelationships between man, his culture, and his living and non-living surroundings. Environmental studies includes, at different levels, natural history, ECOLOGY, POLLUTION, METEOROLOGY, architecture, and much that is normally included in GEOGRAPHY. Environmental education is intended to give these topics more coherence. K.M.

environmentalism. Geographical term for the philosophical doctrine that stresses the influence of the ENVIRONMENT on man's activities. (Environment is here usually defined in terms of the physical factors, e.g. climatic conditions.) In its more extreme form it is termed *environmental determinism* or *geographical determinism*. The doctrine was enunciated by Hippocrates in the 5th century B.C. and reached its peak in the mid 19th century. Modern workers tend to acknowledge the importance of the natural environment but see it operating through a complex network of psychological, social, and economic channels which may dampen or accentuate different properties of the environment for different groups, or for the same group at different points in time.   P.H.

Enzensberger, Hans Magnus (German poet and critic, *b*.1929), see under GRUPPE 47.

enzymes. Complex organic catalysts which mediate nearly all material TRANFOR-MATIONS in the body. The substance an enzyme acts upon is known as its *substrate*, and in biochemical terminology an enzyme is named by adding the suffix -ase to the (truncated) name of the substrate; thus *proteases* are PROTEIN-splitting enzymes, etc. Compounds like proteins which are formed by the 'condensation' of their smaller structural units accompanied by the elimination of the elements of water are broken down by the opposite process of *hydrolysis*, involving the release of water. Thus most digestive enzymes are hydrolytic – among them pepsin formed in the walls of the stomach and liberated into the stomach cavity, trypsin formed in the pancreas and working in the duodenum, the carbohydrase ptyalin, a starch-splitting enzyme present in the saliva.   P.M.

EPA, see EDUCATIONAL PRIORITY AREA.

epic theatre. Originally a German expression, used in contrast to 'dramatic' theatre. 'Epic' in this sense means essentially narrative, defying the Aristotelian unities: i.e. presenting a story step-by-step (as in *Antony and Cleopatra*) rather than tying it together in a self-contained 'plot' (as in *The Tempest*). Its current use, originating in the NEUE SACHLICHKEIT phase in Berlin, is due particularly to Erwin Piscator and Bertolt Brecht.

Starting with the production of Alfons Paquet's *Fahnen* (1924), a 'dramatic novel' subtitled 'epic', Piscator developed the use of projected texts, film, the treadmill stage, and other devices, to make a new kind of DOCUMENTARY drama, revivified after his return to Berlin in 1962. Brecht took up this concept in 1926 (before coming to work with Piscator), summarized it in his *Mahagonny* notes (1930), and made it for some twenty years the keystone of his thinking. Though he also (see BRECHTIAN) saw it as an aid to

tackling new social and economic themes in the theatre, and as subsuming the new technical devices, the essential, for him, lay rather in linear narration ('each scene for itself'), stimulating the audience's reason as against its EMPATHY, and presenting the events as if quoting something already seen and heard. Though he came to call this kind of theatre 'non-Aristotelian', fusing it with his later formula of ALIENATION, he decided in the 1950s that 'epic' was too formal a concept, and thought of replacing it by the more MARXIST-sounding phrase *dialectical theatre*, meaning in effect epic theatre in a changed society.   J.W.

Bibl: B. Brecht, tr. and ed. J. Willett, *Brecht on Theatre* (London and N.Y., 1964).

epidemiology. The study of the factors influencing the frequency and spread of diseases. The subject was originally restricted to infectious diseases – e.g. those caused by MICRO-ORGANISMS, such as typhoid and smallpox – but now includes non-infectious diseases such as coronary thrombosis and high blood pressure. It has to do with the prevalence and features of a disease in a population, as distinct from an individual. Thus, the epidemiology of cholera is concerned with the time and place of outbreaks (*epidemics*) of the disease, and hence with elucidating their cause; e.g. when in 1854 Dr John Snow caused the handle to be removed from the Broad Street pump, where many Londoners drew their drinking water and then developed cholera, the outbreak stopped. Important information concerning many such modern 'epidemics' as arterial disease has come from studying their *etiology*, i.e. the factors which cause or predispose them. It was by epidemiological methods that the connection between lung CANCER and cigarette-smoking was discovered, and much information about the risks of the contraceptive pill obtained.   D.A.P.

epigenesis, see under PREFORMATION.

epigraphy. The study of inscriptions carved or otherwise written on durable material, such as stone or metal, and placed on buildings, tombs, etc. to indicate their name or purpose. Epigraphy provides one of the main sources for our knowledge of the ancient world. A.L.C.B.

epinephrine, see under ADRENAL GLAND.

epiphany. In the Christian religion the Epiphany, celebrated on 6 January, commemorates Christ's first manifestation to the Gentiles, in the form of the Magi. James Joyce was responsible for its introduction as a critical term: Stephen Hero (*Stephen Hero*, ed. 1944) is passing through Eccles Street when he overhears a colloquy: a 'triviality' that makes him 'think of collecting many such moments together in a book of epiphanies'. By epiphany he means 'sudden spiritual manifestation[s]', 'the most delicate and evanescent of such [memorable,] focusing moments'. Joyce was concerned to recapture, from the commonplace, the 'radiance', the 'whatness' – as Stephen puts it to Lynch in his conversation with him in *Portrait of the Artist as a Young Man* (1916) – the 'enchantment of the heart'. He was anticipated, e.g. by Pater's phrase 'exquisite pauses in time'.   M.S.-S.

epiphenomenalism. A theory about the nature of the causal relations between mental and bodily events (see MIND-BODY PROBLEM), where these are understood, in accordance with DUALISM, as radically different in nature. It holds that mental events are the effects of physical happenings in the organism, particularly in the brain and NERVOUS SYSTEM, but that they do not themselves exert any causal influence on the body. In T. H. Huxley's phrase epiphenomenalism conceives mental life as 'the steam above the factory'. Epiphenomenalism follows from the assumptions that mental and bodily events are, though distinct in nature, regularly correlated and that all bodily events are fully explainable as parts of the inclusive DETERMINISTIC system of physical nature, which leaves no room for causal intrusion from the domain of the mental.   A.Q.

Bibl: T. H. Huxley, *Lectures and Essays* (London and N.Y., 1903); K. Campbell, *Body and Mind* (N.Y., 1970; London, 1971).

episcopalism. The belief that episcopacy, i.e. the government of the Church by bishops (Greek *episkopos*, overseer), is best, or essential to CATHOLICISM, especially in ANGLICANISM. Those who hold this belief are *episcopalians*.   D.L.E.

episome. A GENE or group of genes which can reproduce independently of CHROMOSOME reproduction, but which can also be incorporated into and reproduced with the chromosome. Known only from bacteria (see BACTERIOLOGY). See also PLASMAGENE.   J.M.S.

epistasis. The phenomenon whereby the effects of GENES at one LOCUS are altered or masked by those at another. Thus the genes in a mouse which determine whether its hair pigment will be black or brown have no effect if the mouse is a genetic albino (see ALBINISM) because of a defect at another gene locus.   J.M.S.

epistemics. Word coined at Edinburgh University in 1969 with the foundation of the School of Epistemics. It signifies the scientific study of knowledge, as opposed to the philosophical theory of knowledge, which is known as EPISTEMOLOGY. A more extended definition of epistemics is 'the construction of formal MODELS of the processes – perceptual, intellectual, and linguistic – by which knowledge and understanding are achieved and communicated'.   C.L.-H.

epistemological realism, see under REALISM.

epistemology. The philosophical theory of knowledge, which seeks to define it, distinguish its principal varieties, identify its sources, and establish its limits. On the topic of *definition*, it has been recognized since the time of Plato that knowledge involves true belief but goes beyond it. The specification of this residual element is still a matter of controversy. One view is that what distinguishes genuine knowledge from a lucky guess is justification; another is that it is the causation of the belief by the fact that verifies it. One way of distinguishing *kinds* of knowledge is into practical knowledge-how, propositional knowledge-that, and knowledge-of (cf. French *connaître* and German *kennen*). However, the various sorts of knowledge-of seem reducible either to knowledge-how (e.g. knowing Italian) or to knowing-that (e.g. knowing the date of the battle of Waterloo). Within knowledge-that, the prime concern of epistemologists, empirical and *a priori* knowledge (see EMPIRICISM; APRIORISM) are distinguished and, within each of these realms, the basic or intuitive items of knowledge are distinguished from the derived or inferred ones. *A priori* knowledge is derived from its self-evident axiomatic bases (see AXIOMATICS) by *deduction*; empirical knowledge from uninferred observation-statements by INDUCTION. The usually acknowledged *sources* of empirical knowledge are sense-perception (see PERCEPTION; SENSE-DATUM) and INTROSPECTION, while *a priori* knowledge is said to come from reason. The determination of the *limits* of knowledge is a matter of continuing controversy, particularly about the inclusion within the realm of the knowable of morality (see ETHICS), THEOLOGY, and METAPHYSICS.   A.Q.

Bibl: A. J .Ayer, *The Problem of Knowledge* (London and N.Y., 1956).

epitrochoidal engine, see WANKEL ENGINE.

Epstein, Jacob (British sculptor, 1880–1959), see under VORTICISM.

EPU (European Payments Union), see under BIS.

equality, principle of. An assertion made most commonly in this conditional form: that in public matters all persons should be treated identically, except in contexts where sufficient reasons exist for treating particular individuals or groups differently. Such prescriptions for treating men equally (a matter as much of equity as of equality) have, however, been too readily assimilated with assertions that all men *are* equal – assertions which ignore important measurable discrepancies between individuals, e.g. in mental or physical ability. EGALITARIAN assumptions are, indeed, no more self-evidently 'natural' than inegalitarian ones; and utterances of the kind 'All men are born equal' are best viewed as moral exhortations – pleas to allow, at the very least, that by virtue of their shared humanity men should enjoy equal satisfaction of certain basic common rights and needs.

All this leaves vast room for disagreement, especially about the extent of basic rights and needs, and about the criteria for assessing whether a particular instance of differential treatment is justified. Further

difficulties arise not only over conflicts between equality and other possible social goals, such as maximal freedom of action for the individual, but even over the relationship between various kinds of equality itself: equal political rights do not necessarily imply identical shares in wealth, and equality of opportunity scarcely ends inequality of condition.

For at least 300 years much of Western political debate has focused on equality, and the drive to implement various interpretations of it has been a major force of the 20th century. Despite conceptual muddle over its positive content, the principle of equality has been negatively of great value in placing the onus of justification firmly on its opponents. M.D.B.

Bibl: J. Rees, *Equality* (London and N.Y., 1971); J. Rawls, *A Theory of Justice* (Cambridge, Mass., 1971; Oxford, 1972).

equation. An assertion that two mathematical expressions have the same value. An equation may represent a particular fact $(2 + 2 = 4)$, a general law $(x + y = y + x)$, a definition $(y^2 = y \times y)$, or a condition on the VARIABLES occurring in it $(x^2 + 2x + 1 = 0)$. For *diophantine equations* see NUMBER THEORY; see also ALGEBRA; DIFFERENTIAL EQUATION.
                                                                R.G.

equilibrium.

(1) In general, a state of affairs that has no inherent tendency to change while circumstances remain the same. The idea is used in many different sciences, e.g. PHYSICS, CHEMISTRY, ECONOMICS (see also below), PSYCHOLOGY, ECOLOGY. The equilibrium may be *static* or *dynamic*. In *static equilibrium* there is no change occurring (of interest to the science in question); e.g. the equilibrium of balanced scales. In *dynamic equilibrium* something is changing in a steady way (e.g. planets moving in a fixed orbit; a chemical reaction in a closed system proceeding as fast in one direction as the other, so that the concentrations of the reactants remain constant; or incomes rising at a fixed rate), but there are forces tending to change some aspect of the process (e.g. GRAVITATION tending to draw a planet nearer the sun, or advertisements creating increased consumption and therefore increasing wage claims), and other opposing forces

which tend to produce the opposite effect and so prevent the disturbance from occurring. Other categories of equilibrium are as follows. In *unstable equilibrium*, the slightest external disturbance will alter the state radically (e.g. a pencil balanced on its point). In *metastable equilibrium* a state may persist for a long time before changing radically (e.g. a RADIOACTIVE nucleus before its decay, or the liquid in a BUBBLE CHAMBER). In *neutral equilibrium* the state may be altered gradually by external influences (e.g. a car at rest with its brakes off on a level road). In *stable equilibrium* the system responds to small influences by returning to its original state (e.g. a cone resting on its base, or an ATOM in its lowest ENERGY LEVEL). A.S.; M.V.B.

(2) In ECONOMICS, a state of the economy in which for every commodity or service (other than free goods) total SUPPLY AND DEMAND are exactly equal. Equilibrium in this sense is never actually attained, but the movement of the economic system may often be best understood as a movement towards an equilibrium or a movement approximating to changes in the equilibrium itself as circumstances change.

The kind of economic equilibrium that has proved most amenable to analysis, and most fruitful as a starting-point for other theories, is *competitive equilibrium*; in it, no economic agent believes that the prices at which he trades vary with the amount he buys or sells, and producers are motivated by profit maximization. Léon Walras gave a clear expression to this model in his formulation of *general equilibrium theory (Théorie d'Économie Politique Pure*, 1874). Since the 1930s extensive mathematical developments have taken place, reaching definitive expression in the work of K. J. Arrow and G. Debreu. *Stability analysis*, begun by J. R. Hicks and P. A. Samuelson, studies stylized examples of disequilibrium movement. Current work concentrates on the role of expectations, the costs of operating markets, the transmission of information, and connections with the theory of GAMES. See also MARKET; MONOPOLY; PERFECT COMPETITION. J.A.M.

Bibl: A. Leijonhufvud, *On Keynesian Economics and the Economics of Keynes* (London and N.Y., 1968); E. Malinvaud, *Lectures on Microeconomic Theory* (Amsterdam and N.Y., 1973).

equity. A class of CAPITAL in a company or corporation, sometimes known as common stock, and representing the basic ownership of the company. As such it ranks after any fixed-interest capital or preferred stock issued by that company and receives its remuneration after the obligations entailed in servicing these other classes of capital have been met. Similarly if the company is wound up the equity capital is the last to be paid off. The return on equity stock is not fixed but is determined by the amount of profit available after other classes of capital have been serviced and by the dividend-paying policy of the company. Equity investment therefore involves a higher degree of risk than other forms of INVESTMENT, offering on the one hand the possibility of higher returns and on the other less protection against total loss. D.E.

Bibl: J. F. Weston and E. F. Brigham, *Essentials of Managerial Finance* (N.Y., 1966).

equivalence relation. '*A* is the same as *B*' is often used to mean not that *A* and *B* are identical, but that they are the same in all respects which are relevant in the given context. This RELATION is reflexive, symmetric, and transitive. Any relation satisfying these conditions is an *equivalence relation*. It divides objects up into non-overlapping *equivalence classes* (or SETS); all the objects in each class are the 'same' as each other, and not the same as objects in any other class. The *principle of (mathematical) abstraction* consists in associating with each class an abstract property, notion, or object (e.g. the class itself) which stands for what the things in the class have in common. Thus, in deciphering an unknown script one first decides on a relation of sameness between marks, and then associates with each mark an abstract object – the letter which the mark is an instance of. In MATHEMATICS the principle is of great importance; for examples see CARDINAL NUMBER; ORDINAL NUMBER; VECTOR. R.G.

Erastianism. The belief, named after Thomas Erastus (1524–83), that the State ought to have control over the Church even in ecclesiastical matters. D.L.E.

Erbslöh, Adolf (German painter, 1881–1947), see under NEUE KÜNSTLER-VEREINIGUNG.

ergonomics. The study of physical relationships between a man and the machine he uses, with the object of reducing strain, discomfort, and fatigue in the former. Applications include the layout of controls on a machine tool, the design of a suitable driving seat, and the positioning of dials in an aircraft.   R.I.T.

Bibl: K. F. H. Murrell, *Ergonomics* (London, 1965).

Erikson, Erik Homburger (German-U.S. psychoanalyst, *b*. 1902), see under NEO-FREUDIAN; PSYCHOHISTORY.

Ernst, Max (German painter, 1891–1976), see under DADA; SUR-REALISM.

eros, see LIFE INSTINCT.

erosion, see under DENUDATION; SOIL EROSION.

ERP (European Recovery Programme), see under MARSHALL PLAN.

error analysis. In STATISTICS, especially in REGRESSION analysis, it is often assumed that an observed value is a combination of a determinate true value together with an *error term* which is randomly distributed, e.g. has a normal DISTRIBUTION. *Error analysis* is a name often applied to simple ESTIMATION techniques which make assumptions of this type, especially in the experimental sciences.   R.SI.

Erziehungsroman, see under BIL-DUNGSROMAN.

escalation. The process whereby each side in turn increases the scope of an international crisis or the violence of an international conflict, in the hope that its adversary's self-imposed limits will be reached before its own. Escalation is thus an aspect of DETERRENCE and of CRISIS MANAGEMENT. (See also BRINKMAN-SHIP.) President Kennedy's decision in the Cuban MISSILE crisis of 1962 to impose a naval blockade on the incoming Soviet missile-carrying ships deliberately escalated the crisis to a point where any further escalation was judged, correctly, to be above the self-imposed limits of the Soviet Union. The Kennedy administration also developed an explicit doctrine of control-led escalation to give CREDIBILITY to her posture of extended deterrence in Western Europe, by making clear that a Soviet attack on the European NATO powers would incur, as it grew heavier, an increasing level of first tactical and then strategic nuclear riposte. Soviet strategic doctrine now embraces a broadly similar concept in relation to a Nato attack on the Warsaw Pact states.

Like other STRATEGIC terms, escalation is increasingly used in general political contexts, and has conceptual affinities with bargaining theory.   A.F.B.

Bibl: H. Kahn, *On Escalation* (London and N.Y., 1965).

escape velocity. The speed with which an object must be projected upwards from the surface of a heavenly body in order to escape, without further propulsion, from the GRAVITATIONAL field of the body. For the earth, the escape velocity is about 25,000 m.p.h.; for the moon, the escape velocity is only about 5,000 m.p.h., which explains the lack of any lunar atmosphere: any gas MOLECULES would tend to leak away, since their random heat motion is faster than the escape velocity.   M.V.B.

eschatology. A word coined in 1844 to cover the discussion of doctrines about the end of the world, or of this age in the world's history. The discussion has been prominent in modern Christian THEO-LOGY, for two reasons. In his review of previous German scholars' lives of Jesus (1906; *The Quest of the Historical Jesus*, 1910), Albert Schweitzer drew attention dramatically to the expectation of the imminent end of the world found in the gospels' accounts of the teaching of Jesus. Second, this consistently eschatological message, which would have seemed bizarre in more secure times, has been thought relevant, particularly to the disasters overwhelming Europe (see CRISIS THEOLOGY). Schweitzer made Jesus out to be one of the many 'Apocalyptic' visionaries of the first century who claimed that the dooms and glories of the future had been revealed to them, but later biblical scholars have stressed that the original message of Jesus, if it is recoverable from the gospels, proclaimed a 'realized' or at least an 'inaugurated' as well as a 'final' eschatology; the Kingdom of God was not only to come finally at the end of that age but was also present, already real at least in its beginnings, in the victories of Jesus himself. It has also been pointed out that Jesus disclaimed knowledge about the 'hour' or the exact manner of the final arrival of God's Kingdom. But the eschatological nature of the Christian Gospel has now generally been acknowledged, and the problem for modern theologians has been one of interpretation. Should the Christian claim that the Kingdom of God exists on earth in the Church, or is coming in the general life of society, whether through progress or revolution? Or should the message, stripped of its old images, be entirely a call to personal decision (see DEMYTHOLOGIZE)? While such questions have been debated, many FUNDAMENTALIST Christians have continued to await the 'Second Coming' or 'Advent' of Jesus, on the basis of a literal interpretation of the biblical prophecies. Others have continued to consider only the 'four last things' of traditional CATHOLICISM: death, judgement, heaven, and hell. D.L.E.

Bibl: J. Hick, *Evil and the God of Love* (London and N.Y., 1966); D. L. Edwards, *The Last Things Now* (London, 1969; Valley Forge, Pa., 1970) and *Jesus for Modern Man* (London, 1975); J. Hick, *Death and Eternal Life* (London, 1976).

ESN, see EDUCATIONALLY SUBNORMAL.

ESP (extra-sensory perception). In PARAPSYCHOLOGY, PERCEPTION or knowledge of something achieved without using sense-organs or sensory information. In *clairvoyance*, that something is an object or event; in *telepathy*, another person's thoughts; and when clairvoyance or telepathy concerns something in the future it constitutes PRECOGNITION. The main question is: does ESP exist? Anecdotal instances are open to the criticism of biased selection; e.g. premonitions of disaster are remembered when a disaster follows but forgotten when it doesn't. To avoid this bias, experiments have been done asking people to guess at an event or thought about which they could have no possible sensory information. Some experiments have seemed to validate ESP but others have been criticized on the ground of either trickery or failure to eliminate subtle but helpful clues of which neither experimenter nor 'subject' need

be consciously aware. The history of these experiments demonstrates that, at best, ESP is not robustly producible under the conditions of scientific experiment.

Another important consideration arises from the logic of scientific enquiry (see METHODOLOGY). It is held in science that a negative hypothesis can never be proved conclusively true; yet ESP is, by definition, a negative hypothesis, since it can be proved true only if all possible alternative assumptions are disproved. Thus the alleged phenomena of ESP pose both practical and logical difficulties for scientific study. At present, the conclusion is that ESP is, from a scientific viewpoint, not proven. I.M.L.H.

Bibl: C. E. M. Hansel, *ESP* (London, 1966).

Esperanto. Universalist language invented in 1887 by Louis Zamenhof with a strong basis in the Latin languages. While only one of several at its time of origin, it outstripped its rivals in the decade before World War I, just failing to achieve adoption as the universal auxiliary language by a delegation set up in 1900 by a number of international academic bodies. Although it has retained its popularity, the need it was designed to fill has largely been met by the spread of English. D.C.W.

essence. The set of properties of a thing or of instances of a kind of thing which that thing or those instances *must* possess if it is to be that particular thing or they are to be instances of that particular kind. The essence can also be said to be the *defining properties* of a thing or a kind. It is, thus, part of the essence of a ship that it is designed to float on water; but its having sails rather than an engine or carrying cargo rather than passengers is accidental or *contingent* (see CONTINGENCY). Any consistent set of properties defines an essence, but it is always a further question as to whether the kind has any instances, whether anything with just that set of properties exists. The ONTOLOGICAL proof of God's existence holds that in his case alone existence is included in essence. Critics of the proof argue that existence, not being a genuine property, cannot be part of any essence. A.Q.

essentialism. Most generally, the theory that there are ESSENCES. More specifically it is applied to the following, quite distinct, beliefs:

(1) that particular things have essences which serve to identify them as the particular things that they are;

(2) that abstract entities or UNIVERSALS exist as well as the instances or exemplifications of them that we meet with in space and time, i.e. Platonic REALISM;

(3) a thesis (sketched by Locke) in the philosophy of science (see SCIENCE, PHILOSOPHY OF) that objects have real essences which are distinct from, but capable of explaining, their observable properties, and that discovery of these real essences is the ultimate goal of scientific investigation. A.Q.

Esslin, Martin Julius (British theatre critic, *b.*1918), see under THEATRE OF THE ABSURD.

Establishment, the. A term, usually pejorative, for an ill-defined amalgam of those INSTITUTIONS, social CLASSES, and forces which represent authority, legitimacy, tradition, and the status quo. The term was popularized by Henry Fairlie in a 1955 *Spectator* article, and in Britain the phenomenon is regarded, with varying degrees of consensus and justice, as comprising the Monarchy, Parliament, the Civil Service (and the Foreign Office *par excellence*), the Church of England, the Armed Forces, the Law, the professions generally, the City, the B.B.C., certain newspapers, Oxford and Cambridge universities, the PUBLIC SCHOOLS, the landed gentry, and public opinion and individual behaviour patterns as moulded by these. (For an oft-cited element in the American 'Establishment' see WASPS.) Its precise composition, however, tends to reflect the nature and extent of the changes desired, and the sources of opposition or hostility encountered or expected, by the person using the term. It is thus likely to mean very different things on the lips of, say, a self-made millionaire, a radical (see RADICALISM) politician, a HIPPIE, and a member of the ANGRY BRIGADE. At its least precise it may merely mean everyone richer or more powerful than the speaker. O.S.

estates, see under CORPORATE STATE.

esthetics, see AESTHETICS.

estimate. In STATISTICS the experimenter may be faced with the task of using his observed data to guess the value of some PARAMETER in the MODEL he is using. Such a guess is called an estimate (or *point estimate*), and the rule for calculating the estimate from the data is called an *estimator*. The observed frequency of heads in a given number of tosses of a coin is an estimator for the probability that the coin will land heads; the actual value of this on some particular occasion is an estimate. An estimate may be good (if it is close to the true value) or bad, but since it is dependent on data whose values are random and is therefore subject to random errors it can seldom be meaningfully analysed; there is, however, an extensive theory of estimators, and much is known about how to design them so as to give consistently good estimates. See also INTERVAL ESTIMATION. R.SI.

ET, see EDUCATIONAL TECHNOLOGY.

ether. Because light is known to consist of waves, it used to be thought that an underlying, all-pervasive medium must exist to support the undulations, by analogy with air (which supports sound waves) and water (sea waves). This hypothetical medium was called the ether, and its properties provoked much speculation among 19th-century physicists. However, the MICHELSON-MORLEY EXPERIMENT (which led to the theory of RELATIVITY) showed that if the ether existed it could not be observed; furthermore, other kinds of wave (matter waves – see WAVE-PARTICLE DUALITY) are now known which do not have 'ethers' associated with them. M.V.B.

ethical neutrality, see VALUE-FREEDOM.

ethics. The branch of PHILOSOPHY that investigates morality and, in particular, the varieties of thinking by which human conduct is guided and may be appraised. Its special concern is with the MEANING and justification of utterances about the rightness and wrongness of actions, the virtue or vice of the motives which prompt them, the praiseworthiness or blameworthiness of the agents who perform them, and the goodness or badness of the consequences to which they give rise. A fundamental problem is that of whether moral utterances are really the statements of fact, true or false, that they grammatically appear to be. If they are not statements of fact, as adherents of the doctrine of the NATURALISTIC FALLACY and, in particular, EMOTIVISTS, believe, how should moral utterances be interpreted: as exclamations or commands? If they are statements of fact, are they empirical statements about such observable characteristics as conduciveness to the general happiness, as ethical NATURALISTS maintain, or are they *a priori*, the position of ethical rationalists (see APRIORISM)? A further range of problems concerns the relation of moral CONCEPTS to each other. Is the rightness of actions inferable from the goodness of their consequences? Is the virtuousness of a motive to be inferred from the rightness of the actions that it typically prompts? Next, there is the problem of distinguishing moral value from values of other kinds (see AXIOLOGY). Is the distinguishing mark the factual nature of the ends by reference to which moral injunctions are justified, such as the happiness of mankind in general, or is it the formal character of the injunctions themselves? Finally there is the problem of the conditions under which moral judgements are properly applicable to conduct. To be morally responsible, to be liable to the sanctions of blame and punishment, must an agent be free in the sense that his actions are uncaused, or is it enough that what he did was not wholly caused by factors that sanctions cannot influence? A.Q.

Bibl: J. Hospers, *Human Conduct* (N.Y., 1961; London, 1963); W. K. Frankena, *Ethics* (N.Y., 1963).

Ethiopianism. Term applied (1) to quasi-NATIONALIST movements, often of a messianic or chiliastic nature (see MESSIANISM; MILLENARIANISM), founded among American and West Indian blacks, and looking to Africa (Ethiopia being used originally as a synonym for Africa) as an entity to admire and to return to (*Black Zionism*), it being the land from which their forefathers had been exported as slaves; a notable example was the Universal Negro Improvement Association founded in Jamaica in 1914 by Marcus Moziah Garvey and active under his leadership in America 1916–1922, preaching

black self-help, pride in black history and civilization, and return to Africa; (2) to the movement to establish all-black churches among American blacks after the U.S. Civil War; (3) to the independent black African churches established partly as breakaways from established Christianity, partly in response to missionary activity from American Ethiopian churches. D.C.W.

Bibl: R. W. July, *The Origins of Modern African Thought* (London and N.Y., 1968); D. Jenkins, *Black Zion* (London and N.Y., 1975).

ethnocentrism. A word, coined by W. G. Sumner (*Folkways*, 1906) and nearly always used pejoratively, for the attitudes which uncritically presuppose the superiority of one's own group or CULTURE. Such attitudes may be found not only among the members of a TRIBE or nation who despise the other tribes or nations about them, but in the anthropologist (sociologist, etc.) himself, if he unnecessarily evaluates the culture or behaviour of members of another society by the light of his own culture. But see RELATIVISM, CULTURAL. M.F.

ethnography and **ethnology.** In some languages the word corresponding to *enthnography* is the name for social or cultural ANTHROPOLOGY. In the English-speaking countries the term is usually confined to the *descriptive* activities and results of social/cultural anthropology. But it is not to be supposed that ethnography and the non-descriptive parts of anthropology are largely separable: to describe, one needs CRITERIA of relevance; to theorize, one needs facts. *Ethnology* in the forms it takes in some languages is again a name for social or cultural anthropology, and the English form is still sometimes used in the U.S.A. in that sense. But in Britain it has come, at least since the 1930s, to mean the history of peoples, HISTORIOGRAPHY thus being contrasted with the analysis of and generalization about society. See also FIELD WORK. M.F.

ethnography of communication, see under ETHNOLINGUISTICS.

ethnohistory. A term which came into use in the 1940s to describe the history of

ETHNOLINGUISTICS

non-literate peoples, a subject which had been neglected both by anthropologists (because it was concerned with the past) and by historians (because written documents were lacking). The ethnohistorian needs to combine the skills of the archaeologist, the social anthropologist (to interpret ORAL TRADITION), and the conventional historian (to deal with documents produced by conquerors and missionaries). His results are likely to be more reliable when he reconstructs CULTURAL HISTORY and SOCIAL HISTORY than when he produces a narrative of events.

P.B.

Bibl: K. C. Wylie, 'The uses and misuses of ethnohistory' (*Journal of Interdisciplinary History*, 3, 1973, pp. 707–720).

ethnolinguistics. A branch of LINGUISTICS which studies language in relation to the investigation of ethnic types and behaviour. It often overlaps with ANTHROPOLOGICAL LINGUISTICS and SOCIOLINGUISTICS, and recently the phrase *ethnography of communication* has been applied by sociolinguists to the study of language in relation to the entire range of extra-linguistic variables. D.C.

Bibl: J. J. Gumperz and D. Hymes (eds.), *Directions in Sociolinguistics: the Ethnography of Communication* (London and N.Y., 1972).

ethnology, see under ETHNOGRAPHY.

ethnomethodology. A term coined, misleadingly (since the first element bears no relation to its usual meaning), by Harold Garfinkel for an activity which he inaugurated: the SOCIOLOGICAL study of everyday activities, however trivial, concentrating on the methods used by individuals to report their COMMON SENSE practical actions to others in acceptable rational terms. This process of imposing a *rational* scheme onto what are essentially *practical* activities is referred to in the shorthand terminology of the ethnomethodological language as 'practical reasoning'. Ethnomethodology, with its interest in how the individual experiences and makes sense of social interaction, is directly and controversially opposed to sociological theories (e.g. those of Marx, Weber, and Durkheim) that concentrate on the larger questions of SOCIAL STRUCTURE. It is therefore nearer to SOCIAL PSYCHOLOGY

than sociological theory proper, as is also true of the two previous theories from which it has derived the most – G. H. Mead's SYMBOLIC INTERACTION theory, and, more importantly, Alfred Schutz's PHENOMENOLOGY. Its critics insist that a preoccupation with trivialities is not a virtue, and that trivial exchanges like 'Hi' – 'Hi' are neither illuminated nor rendered less trivial by such pronouncements as (an actual example from the second book listed below) 'A basic rule of adjacency pair operation is: given the recognizable production of a first pair part, on its first possible completion its speaker should stop and a next speaker should start and produce a second pair part from the pair type the first is recognizably a member of'.

M.BA.

Bibl: H. Garfinkel, *Studies in Ethnomethodology* (Englewood Cliffs, N. J., 1967); R. Turner (ed.), *Ethnomethodology* (Harmondsworth, 1974).

ethnomusicology. The study of all categories of music (including FOLK MUSIC) other than Western ART MUSIC. Although the English word dates only from 1950, the subject, under its earlier name of 'comparative MUSICOLOGY', evolved at the beginning of the 20th century, in Germany, where a predominantly musicological approach was favoured, and later in the U.S.A., where anthropological methods were preferred. The two traditions were to some extent amalgamated with the foundation in 1955 of the international Society for Ethnomusicology, whose activities focus attention upon (1) the collection of data from (*a*) tangible materials (e.g. excavated instruments, early manuscripts) and (*b*) oral traditions (e.g. songs and dances); (2) transcription from tape-recordings, structural analysis (aided by mechanical and electronic devices) of *what* is performed, and detailed description of *how* it is performed; (3) collation of findings with general cultural phenomena. British universities have been conspicuously cautious in extending to the subject the recognition it has gained elsewhere. A.K.

Bibl: B. Nettl, *Theory and Method in Ethnomusicology* (London and N.Y., 1964); A. P. Merriam, *The Anthropology of Music* (Evanston, Ill., 1964).

216

ethnopsychology. The branch of PSYCHOLOGY that studies the psychological characteristics of people considered as members of cultural, social, religious, or national groups. See also CROSS-CULTURAL STUDY; RELATIVISM, CULTURAL. I.M.L.H.

ethology. The name now generally accepted for a type of behavioural study that began as a branch of ZOOLOGY, and attained prominence in the early 1930s with the work of Konrad Lorenz of Vienna. Emphasis was laid on the need to observe and describe the behaviour of as many SPECIES as possible, and there was a tendency to interpret behaviour as the result of EVOLUTION moulded by NATURAL SELECTION. Historical circumstances, e.g. the over-emphasis in PSYCHOLOGY on learning, made ethologists emphasize the non-learned aspects of animal, and even of human behaviour; much work was also concentrated (mainly under the influence of Heinroth in Germany and J. S. Huxley in Britain) on vertebrates, especially birds. Ethology was at first ignored, later severely (and in part justifiably) criticized, by psychologists and physiologists, while ecologists were on the whole receptive. Since the war ethology, psychology, and NEUROPHYSIOLOGY have come closer together, and there are signs that a more unified, more biologically oriented science of behaviour is emerging.

The importance of ethology for the understanding of human behaviour is beginning to be recognized, and the works of Lorenz and Desmond Morris have aroused worldwide interest, though many students of human behaviour (psychologists, psychopathologists, anthropologists) have found them over-assertive. There is a growing consensus that, although facts and conclusions about animal behaviour cannot be generalized and applied to human behaviour, certain methods are equally suitable to the study of either. The fact that human behaviour is the result of accumulative non-GENETIC transfer or individually acquired modifications from one generation to the next can no longer be denied. This 'cultural' or 'psychosocial' evolution, however, must not be allowed to obscure the effects of the genetic evolution which preceded it,

and which still determines the direction, and the limitations, of human behaviour. N.T.

etic, see under EMIC.

etiology (or *aetiology*), see under EPIDEMIOLOGY.

Eucharistic theology. The discussion of doctrines about the Eucharist (from the Greek for 'thanksgiving') or Holy Communion, the most ancient and important act of Christian worship. The modern LITURGICAL MOVEMENT has stimulated both rethinking and fresh agreement about the meaning of the Eucharist. D.L.E.

Bibl: E. L. Mascall, *Corpus Christi* (London, 2nd ed., 1965).

Euclid (ancient mathematician, probably Greek, *fl. c.* 365 B.C.), see under AXIOMATIC METHOD; AXIOMATICS; NUMBER; RECURSIVE FUNCTION THEORY.

Euclidean geometry, see under GEOMETRY.

eugenics. Term coined by Francis Galton, in 1883, for the attempted improvement of mankind through the adoption of GENETIC policies. A distinction is often made between 'positive' and 'negative' eugenics. An example of positive eugenics would be the adoption of fiscal or political policies to encourage child-bearing by a favoured and allegedly superior human type, e.g. the holders of university degrees or the fair-haired and blue-eyed. An example of negative eugenics would be the attempt to eradicate a harmful recessive GENE such as that which in the homozygous state is responsible for the disease known as phenylketonuria. There are grave moral, political, and genetic objections to the policies of positive eugenics. Negative eugenics also gives rise to genetic, moral, and political problems which have not yet been resolved. P.M.

eurhythmics. The art of interpreting music through body movements; specifically, the system of rhythmical gymnastics taught by the Swiss composer and educationist Émile Jacques-Dalcroze (1865–1950) in order to develop his students' physical, intellectual, and aesthetic sense of musical forms and rhythms; to increase their capacity to analyse musical structure; to give them musical 'experience' rather than musical 'knowledge'. B.L.B.

eurhythmy. An alternative to the spelling preferred by its practitioners, i.e. EURYTHMY. J.D.

Euro-money. Deposits with banks outside the country in whose currency the deposits are denominated. For example, Euro-sterling represents sterling held on deposit with banks outside the United Kingdom, including the foreign branches of British banks. These deposits are on-lent to non-bank borrowers through the inter-national money market. Much the most important form of Euro-money is the *Euro-dollar,* but there are also foreign currency deposits in sterling, francs, marks, lire, Swiss francs, and yen. The prefix Euro- is thus misleading. Euro-currencies need neither be European cur-rencies nor be deposited with European banks: there is a thriving market in Euro-yen in Singapore. A.C.

European. For organizations beginning with this word see EDC; EEC; EFTA; EMA; ERP.

eurythmics. An alternative to the spelling preferred by its practitioners, i.e. EURYTHMICS. B.L.B.

eurythmy. An art form evolved by Rudolf Steiner (1861–1925), the founder of ANTHROPOSOPHY. It aims to make visible certain qualities of movement, feeling, and character which are held to be inher-ent in the sounds of speech or music. Stage performances present interpretations of music, poetry, and prose by groups or soloists. It is also used educationally for adults and children (notably in STEINER SCHOOLS), and therapeutically, as *curative eurythmy,* under the direction of anthroposophical doctors. J.D.

Euston Road Group. A group of painters associated with The School of Drawing and Painting which was established in 1937, at first in Charlotte Street, then, from 1938 to 1939, at 314–316 Euston Road, London; more particularly, Graham Bell, William Coldstream, Law-rence Gowing, Victor Pasmore, and Claude Rogers. The work of these paint-ers was at that time marked by an insis-tence upon objective drawing, tonality, and realistic subject-matter. Q.B.

evaluation. In EDUCATION, the process of obtaining information, usually for administrators and teachers, about the effects and values of educational activi-ties. As a systematic pursuit, evaluation is typically associated with programmes of educational reform, particularly with the Anglo-American curriculum develop-ment movement (see NUFFIELD APPROACH) of the 1960s and 1970s. The initial theoretical framework (R. W. Tyler, *Constructing Achievement Tests,* 1934) stressed the PSYCHOMETRIC assessment of learning objectives, but dur-ing the 1960s the SOCIAL ENGINEERING assumptions of this MODEL were chal-lenged, and the field is currently charac-terized by a proliferation of theory. A major conventional division is that of M. Scriven (1967) between *formative* evalua-tion, designed to improve a programme, and *summative* evaluation, designed to judge its worth. B.M.

evaluation procedure. In LINGUISTICS, a set of techniques which enable a linguist to judge which of two GRAMMARS is the bet-ter account of a language. The importance of this notion was first pointed out by Chomsky, and there has since been con-siderable discussion of evaluation CRITERIA (e.g. the economy of a descrip-tion) for particular areas of language, especially PHONOLOGY. D.C.

evaluative, see under NORMATIVE.

evangelicalism. A term, mostly used in ANGLICANISM, to cover the position of Christians who emphasize the preaching and personal acceptance of the Gospel as contained in the Bible, and who attach less significance to CATHOLICISM. See also ANGLO-CATHOLICISM; EVANGELISM; PROTESTANT. D.L.E.

evangelism. The spread of any religion or opinion, usually the spread of the Christ-ian Gospel or good news (in Greek *euangelion*), whether by formal preaching (as in revivalist missions) or by personal conversations. See also EVANGELICAL-ISM. D.L.E.

Evans, Sir **Arthur John** (British archaeologist, 1851–1941), see under LINEAR A AND B.

Evans-Pritchard, Edward Evan (British anthropologist, 1902–73), see under APOLLONIAN AND DIONYSIAN CULTURES.

events, see HAPPENINGS AND EVENTS.

evolution. The theory that the existing varieties of plant and animal, so far from having existed more or less unmodified from the beginning of biological time, have come into being through a progressive diversification that has accompanied their BIOGENETIC descent from their ancestors. Although the theory had been adumbrated very many times before the publication in 1859 of Darwin's *The Origin of Species,* it was Darwin's ability to propound an acceptable theory (DARWINISM) of how evolution might have come about that brought the subject into public discussion and intensive enquiry. It is naïve to suppose that the acceptance of evolution theory depends upon the evidence of a number of so-called 'proofs'; it depends rather upon the fact that the evolutionary theory permeates and supports every branch of biological science, much as the notion of the roundness of the earth underlies all GEODESY and all cosmological theories on which the shape of the earth has a bearing. Thus anti-evolutionism is of the same stature as flat earthism. See also LAMARCKISM. P.M.

evolution, social and cultural. Although ideas of the regular development of human CULTURE and society antedate Darwin, the second half of the 19th century was the great period of evolutionary theory in the SOCIAL SCIENCES. It depended on the assumption, now abandoned, that surviving PRIMITIVE peoples represent earlier stages in the development of modern society. In one form, evolutionary theory keeps close to BIOLOGY in speaking of increasing complexity and differentiation; in another, a series of phases or stages of development is posited, although not all societies are expected to go through all of them. Evolutionary thinking is now of secondary importance in Anglo-American and Western European social and cultural ANTHROPOLOGY, but plays a central role

in countries adhering to MARXISM, although not under the name of evolution. See also DIFFUSIONISM; EVOLUTION; STRUCTURALISM. M.F.

Bibl: M. D. Sahlins and E. R. Service (eds.), *Evolution and Culture* (Ann Arbor, 1960); M. Ginsberg, *Evolution and Progress* (London, 1961).

evolutionary humanism. A sort of secular RELIGION or religion surrogate founded upon the deeply held conviction that EVOLUTION is the fundamental modality of all change in the universe, so that all agencies that provoke change and all that retard it can be described as 'good' or 'bad' respectively. Sometimes evolutionary humanism is taken for the belief that the human moral sense is itself a product of evolutionary change as opposed to a faculty indwelling in man through the mediation of some supernatural agency. In none of these forms has evolutionary humanism (though its exponents have included T. H. Huxley and Sir Julian Huxley) found for itself a significant following from moralists or theologians. P.M.

evolutionism. A doctrine especially associated with the names of Herbert Spencer (1820–1903) and Teilhard de Chardin (1881–1955) according to which evolution is the fundamental mode of change, both organic and inorganic, in the universe. Evolutionism is normally associated with a belief in the inevitability of progress. In the writings of Teilhard de Chardin (see NOOSPHERE) this assumes an extravagant metaphysical form. P.M.

exchange control. Restrictions on the right of a citizen of one country to make payment to a person not resident in his country. Before 1939, most rich Western countries had no exchange control, but today no country is free of some types of control (although both the U.S.A. and Western Germany have almost complete freedom). The main purpose of exchange control is to limit a citizen's ability to convert home assets into foreign assets (and sometimes also to resist the inflow of unwanted financial assets from foreigners). Citizens who have home assets may fear that the exchange rate between the home currency and foreign currency will become less favourable, and hence wish to 'speculate' against the home currency. Alternatively citizens (particularly companies) may wish to acquire financial or physical assets abroad, and hence wish to acquire foreign currency to make such an investment. In either case, the exchange reserve of the home countries would be depleted (see BALANCE OF PAYMENTS), and it is the aim of the authorities to prevent such depletion (or occasionally unwanted accruals) by means of exchange control.   M.V.P.

exchange energy. A stabilizing ENERGY ascribed in QUANTUM MECHANICS terms to ELECTRONS with the same SPIN in an ATOM or MOLECULE. In order not to violate the EXCLUSION PRINCIPLE the electrons must be present in different ORBITALS, and the energy can be thought of as arising from the indistinguishability of electrons with identical spin. The exchange energy is not predominant in chemical bondings (see BOND) but it has some influence on chemical reactivity (see CHEMICAL REACTION), and there are important consequences in SPECTROSCOPY and for the magnetic properties of compounds.   B.F.

exchange models. In SOCIOLOGY, MODELS, associated with George Homans and Peter Blau, that concentrate on elementary social processes in which human groups are seen as formed and held together by exchanges of rewards, satisfactions, esteem, and the creation of common sentiments. Whereas the STRUCTURAL-FUNCTIONAL THEORY deals with whole societies (*macrostructures*), exchange theory tends to concentrate on small groups (*microstructures*).   D.B.

excited states (in PHYSICS), see under ENERGY LEVEL.

exclaves, see under ENCLAVES.

excluded middle, law of the, see under INTUITIONISM.

exclusion principle (or *Pauli Principle*). A principle in QUANTUM MECHANICS, postulated in 1925 by the Austrian physicist Wolfgang Pauli, according to which no two ELECTRONS can exist in an ATOM in the same state, i.e. they cannot share the same set of QUANTUM NUMBERS. See also QUANTUM STATISTICS.   M.V.B.

existential psychology. A SCHOOL OF PSYCHOLOGY which emphasizes that each individual is constantly making choices, great and small, which cumulatively determine the kind of person he becomes. Represented by Rollo May, Abraham Maslow (associated also with HUMANISTIC PSYCHOLOGY), and Carl Rogers, it is concerned with the individual's attempts to discover a satisfying sense of his personal identity and to give meaning to his life.   I.M.L.H.

Bibl: R. May, *Love and Will* (N.Y., 1969; London, 1970).

existential theology, see CHRISTIAN EXISTENTIALISM.

existentialism. A body of philosophical doctrine that dramatically emphasizes the contrast between human existence and the kind of existence possessed by natural objects. Men, endowed with will and consciousness, find themselves in an alien world of objects which have neither. Existentialism was inaugurated by Kierkegaard in a violent reaction against the all-encompassing absolute IDEALISM of Hegel. For Hegel, God is the impersonal ABSOLUTE; finite human personalities are insubstantial fragments of this engulfing spiritual unity, and everything that happens, including human actions, can be rationally explained as a necessary element in the total scheme of things. Kierkegaard insisted on the utter distinctness of God and Man and on the inexplicability (or 'absurdity') of the relations between them, and of their actions. As developed in this century by Heidegger and Sartre, and by contrast with CHRISTIAN EXISTENTIALISM, existentialism is atheistic and draws on the PHENOMENOLOGY of Husserl as a method for investigating the peculiarities of the human situation. Man, these later existentialists contend, is a self-creating being who is not initially endowed with a character and goals but must choose them by acts of pure decision, existential 'leaps' analogous to that seen by Kierkegaard in the reason-transcending decision to believe in God. For Heidegger, man is a temporal being, conscious, through his will, of a future whose only certainty is his own death. To live authentically is to live in the light of this bleak and unrationalizable fact, in full awareness of *le* NÉANT both as one's own

ultimate destiny and as one's own nature until one has chosen a character for oneself. Sartre's particular interest is in what he sees as the paradoxical relations between one human existence and another.
A.Q.

Bibl: W. Barrett, *Irrational Man* (N.Y., 1958; London, 1961); W. Kaufmann (ed.), *Existentialism from Dostoevsky to Sartre* (N.Y. 1956; London, 1957).

exobiology. The science that deals with (1) the evidence (in practice the lack of evidence) of the existence of life or of intelligent activity on other planets or celestial objects; (2) the precautions that must be taken to prevent the contamination of celestial bodies by earth organisms and *vice versa*.
P.M.

exocrine glands, see under ENDOCRINOLOGY.

exogamy, see under ENDOGAMY.

exotoxins, see under BACTERIOLOGY.

expansion of the universe. A theory formulated by Hubble in 1923. It is observed that the light from faint (and therefore presumably distant) GALAXIES is reddened. This RED SHIFT is interpreted as a DOPPLER EFFECT, so that the galaxies are believed to be receding from us, and from each other, like spots on the surface of a balloon as it is blown up; the farther the galaxy, the greater is its speed of recession. This is measured by *Hubble's constant,* defined as the ratio *distance of galaxy ÷ speed of recession*; its value is about 10 thousand million years. The expansion of the universe is a basic phenomenon which any theory of COSMOLOGY (e.g. the BIG-BANG HYPOTHESIS or the STEADY-STATE HYPOTHESIS) must explain. Galaxies 10 thousand million light-years away are receding from us at the speed of light. More distant objects are receding faster than this so that their light can never reach us. Thus the *observable* universe accessible to ASTRONOMY seems to be finite in extent. See also COSMIC BACKGROUND RADIATION.
M.V.B.

expectation. In STATISTICS, the weighted arithmetic MEAN of the values taken in a DISTRIBUTION, the weights being the probabilities attached to the values. R.SI.

experimental group, see under CONTROL GROUP.

experimental psychology. The branch of PSYCHOLOGY that is based on the use of experimental methods. The psychologist's fundamental interest lies in the description, CLASSIFICATION, prediction, and EXPLANATION of the behaviour of living organisms. He gains access to this behaviour by a variety of techniques. Sometimes he makes his observations in the 'natural' setting, as when the animal psychologist studies the wild animal in its natural ENVIRONMENT (see ETHOLOGY) and the industrial psychologist observes 'man at work' on the factory floor (see INDUSTRIAL PSYCHOLOGY). Increasingly, however, psychological phenomena (e.g. the effect of sleep deprivation on vigilance) have been brought under scrutiny in carefully controlled experimental situations where, ideally, one is able to identify all the significant factors and uncover correlational and cause-effect relationships. The experimental approach to psychological problems was first adopted principally to investigate 'sensory' phenomena (e.g. PERCEPTION), and a whole range of elegant methods was invented to tackle such questions as just how sensitive the human being is to changes in level of sound, light, and pressure. As a result a number of principles were formulated that expressed relationships – universal under certain limited conditions – between measurable levels of stimulation and of human sensation. The use of experimental methods is continually expanding, and the 'higher mental processes' listed under COGNITIVE PSYCHOLOGY have come increasingly under experimental scrutiny.

The experimental psychologist's ideal, like that of any other experimental investigator, is to control all the factors that might affect the phenomenon under study. Usually, one or a small number of factors (the *independent variables*) is systematically varied, and aspects (the *dependent variables*) of the subject's performance in response to these variables are tabulated. These dependent variables may be relatively simple and observable responses such as a verbal reply to a question, or they may be much more complex and covert, as with many physiological responses (e.g. changes in brain-waves) to different conditions of stimulation. The ideal of complete control is seldom if ever achieved, however, because of the numerous extraneous and uncontrolled factors – the temperature of the room, time of day, the subject's idea of the experiment, etc. – that may affect the dependent variable; a familiar device for overcoming this problem is the use of a CONTROL GROUP. To assess the significance of the results of any test, the experimental psychologist also needs a sound understanding of STATISTICS. Although the experimental approach has its critics, there seems little doubt that it will continue to play an increasingly vital role in psychological enquiry.   D.J.W.

Bibl: W. G. Cochran and G. M. Cox, *Experimental Designs* (N.Y., 1950).

Experimentele Groep, see under COBRA.

explanation. The process or end-product of explaining something. The word and its meaning are, of course, perfectly familiar; less so, perhaps, are some related terms and the varieties of explanation that have been distinguished in philosophical analyses of scientific explanations. The thing to be explained is often called the *explanandum* or *conclusion*, henceforth called *C*. *C* may be a fact about some particular event, e.g. 'This apple fell from the tree', or a generalization or law, e.g. 'Unsupported apples fall'. When *C* is explained by means of a set of statements, they are said to constitute the *explanans*, or the *premises* of the explanation. Some of the statements in the explanans may themselves express laws, generalizations, or regularities, e.g. 'All bodies attract one another', and the SET of such statements will henceforth be called *L*. Other statements in the explanans, e.g. 'A wind was blowing', 'The branch was rotten', may refer to particular events or states of affairs. These are said to specify *initial conditions*, and the set of such statements will henceforth be called *I*. *I* or *L* may, in special cases, be empty, i.e. there may be no such statements. The types of explanation that can be distinguished include the following; they are illustrated with some oversimplified examples.

(1) *Deductive explanations*. In these the truth of the conclusion *C* follows logically, or deductively, from *I* and *L* together, e.g. 'The apple fell because (*I*) it was unsupported and (*L*) unsupported objects fall'. A major dispute in PHILOSOPHY concerns whether deductive (sometimes called deductive nomological) explanations are the only truly adequate scientific explanations, and whether all other kinds are really disguised versions of this kind.

(2) *Probabilistic* or *statistical explanations*. In these, the truth of the conclusion cannot be inferred logically from *I* and *L*: at most one can infer that it is more *probable* that *C* is true than that it is false, e.g. 'Tom has cancer because (*I*) Tom smokes, and (*L*) 90% of those who smoke get cancer'. Here *L* and *I* together only make Tom's having cancer *highly probable*; it does not follow logically from them that he *will* have cancer. Many explanations in PSYCHOLOGY and in SOCIAL SCIENCES have this structure.

(3) *Causal explanations*. Here *C* describes some event, and the statements in *I* describe *causes* of the event, e.g. 'The butter melted because (*I*) the temperature rose'. But what does it mean to say that one thing causes another? One answer is that there is some law (e.g. of PHYSICS, CHEMISTRY, or other branches of science) which provides a basis for inferring that, if the first thing occurs or had occurred, the second will or would have. On this analysis, causal explanations are simply a special case of deductive explanations, possibly with the relevant laws (*L*) left out, either because they are too well known, or else because it is not yet known what they are.

(4) *Functional explanations*. These – which some prefer to regard as descriptions – answer questions of the form 'What is such-and-such for?' They should not be treated as an explanation of why the such-and-such exists. Thus to say that animals have stomachs because the stomach plays a certain role in keeping the animal alive and well does not explain how it came about that animals have stomachs, unless the explanation is enlarged to include some additional hypotheses about an EVOLUTIONARY mechanism which ensures that organisms evolve what they need. Functional explanations are often confused with *purposive explanations*.

(5) *Purposive explanations*. These answer questions about why an agent (which may be a person, an animal, or a corporate body such as a committee) performed some action or took some deci-

sion, by describing the agent's intention, motive, purpose, aims, likes, fears, etc., and relating them to what the agent thought would be the consequences of the various alternatives open, e.g. 'He stole the money because he wanted to buy food'. Purposive explanations are common in everyday life and law courts, but also in some of the social sciences and psychology, though some scientists regard them as unscientific, e.g. because the explanations refer to mental events or states.

(6) *Teleological explanations*. This is simply a blanket term used to cover both functional and purposive explanations, since these are often not clearly distinguishable.

(7) *Genetic explanations*. These consist of more-or-less lengthy accounts of a sequence of events leading up to the occurrence or existence of the fact to be explained. They are common in HISTORY, GEOLOGY, BIOLOGY, and novels. The account generally mentions only a series of particular facts, so that I (the initial conditions) may be a large set of statements, whereas L may be empty, if no laws are explicitly mentioned. Often such an explanation simply amounts to a sequence of causal and purposive explanations. It is sometimes argued that a genetic explanation is always an abbreviated and sketchy version of a sequence of deductive or probabilistic explanations, where the laws are not stated explicitly because they are sufficiently well known to be taken for granted.   A.S.

Bibl: see under METHODOLOGY.

exponential. One of the most widely diffused terms in MATHEMATICS. If A, a are given, then $Aa^n(= A \times a \times a \ldots \times a)$ is an *exponential* FUNCTION of n; n is the *exponent*. This can be generalized from positive integral to real and complex ARGUMENTS. Two standard definitions are

$$e^t = 1 + t + t^2/2! + \ldots + t^m/m! + \ldots;$$
$$e^t = \lim_{m \to \infty} (1 + t/m)^m$$

where $e (= 2.718 \ldots)$ is the base of natural logarithms. If $y = Aa^t$ then $y = Ae^{bt}$, where $e^b = a$, and $dy/dt = by$, i.e. the rate of change at time t is proportional to the value at that time. Any function which satisfies this condition *grows exponentially*. The condition holds *approximately* for, e.g., the growth of CAPITAL at compound

interest or for (unchecked) population growth. It holds *exactly* if one assumes that the increase occurs continuously rather than discretely. Such a function grows faster than any power t^m of t. The exponential function is e^t. Its inverse, written $t = \log_e y$ is the *logarithmic function*; it grows more slowly than any mth root $(\sqrt[m]{y})$ of y.   R.G.

exponential smoothing. In MANAGEMENT, an adaptive method of FORECASTING that is ideally suited to COMPUTER operation. The basis of the method is that in obtaining a forecast more weight is given to the most recent information. The weights (see INDEX NUMBER) which are assigned die away exponentially; hence the name by which the method is usually known. H.TH.

Expressionism. Widely applicable term used since 1910 of all the ARTS, in three main senses:

(1) A quality of expressive emphasis or distortion, to be found in works of any period, country, or medium, e.g. in Dostoevsky's novels, Strindberg's plays, and El Greco's or van Gogh's paintings.

(2) Virtually the whole modern movement in the arts in Germany and Austro-Hungary between 1910 and about 1924, subsuming all local manifestations of FAUVISM, CUBISM, and FUTURISM, and constituting the origins of DADA and NEUE SACHLICHKEIT. Though subsequently extended backwards to cover, e.g., the paintings of the Norwegian Edvard Munch or the early work of the BRÜCKE, the formula 'Expressionism' entered Germany from France in 1910 and thereafter became used to describe the German movements first in art, then in literature, the theatre (from 1918), music, architecture, and the cinema. Its hallmarks accordingly were theirs: distortion, fragmentation, and the communication of violent or overstressed emotion.

With *Der* STURM and *Die Aktion* as its organs, it embraced (*a*) in painting, the Brücke and the BLAUE REITER; (*b*) in literature, the poetry of Georg Heym, Georg Trakl, and Franz Werfel, and the prose of Alfred Döblin and Franz Kafka; (*c*) in the theatre, the plays of Georg Kaiser and Ernst Toller; (*d*) in music, the early works of Arnold Schönberg and Alban Berg; (*e*) in architecture, Erich Mendelsohn's Einstein Tower and the utopian projects of Bruno Taut; (*f*) in the cinema, Robert Wiene's *The Cabinet of Dr Caligari* (1920).

German Expressionism's predominantly PACIFIST and SOCIALIST political aims, crystallizing in the wartime movement of ACTIVISM, were frustrated by such post-war developments as the suppression of the SPARTACISTS and the Munich SOVIET; and it was superseded by the more pragmatic NEUE SACHLICHKEIT – on which, as on the BAUHAUS, it left a distinctive mark. Though NAZISM suppressed all three movements as DEGENERATE, it was again influential in the revival of the arts in Germany after 1945.

(3) 20th-century works of art in other countries or continents which reflect the influence of German Expressionism or show similar characteristics, e.g. the Flemish Expressionism foreshadowed by Laethem-Saint-Martin, certain works of the ÉCOLE DE PARIS, and the ABSTRACT EXPRESSIONISM of such New York artists as Pollock and de Kooning in the 1950s.

J.W.

Bibl: J. Willett: *Expressionism* (London and N.Y., 1971).

expressive form, fallacy of. A prescriptive term, adopted by R. P. Blackmur from Yvor Winters, for the 'dogma that once material becomes words it is its own best form'. Winters called this the 'heresy of expressive form'. He was referring to the belief, in his view mistaken, that disintegration (of belief, of civilization) could most effectively be expressed in a chaotic form. He saw Joyce's *Ulysses* as 'disintegrated': it should have been 'disciplined'. But he was answered by critics who pointed out that *Ulysses*, or the poetry of T. S. Eliot, was not really 'chaotic': it only *looked* as though it were. Winters was attacking, essentially, Coleridge's idea of organic form. Blackmur used the notion to try to dispose of the poetry of D. H. Lawrence and Carl Sandburg, but was not dedicated to it as a theory. M.S.-S.

Bibl: S. E. Hyman, *The Armed Vision* (N.Y., 1947).

expressive movement. Meaningful action that is peculiar to the individual and can, therefore, be used in identifying individuals and differentiating one from another. Examples of such movements are gesture, posture, characteristic actions, or speech habits. See also NON-VERBAL COMMUNICATION. H.L.

Bibl: G. W. Allport and P. E. Vernon, *Studies in Expressive Movement* (London and N.Y., 1967).

extended family, see under NUCLEAR FAMILY.

extension, see under CONNOTATION.

extensionality and **intensionality.** Properties of compound PROPOSITIONS, defined by the relation between the compounds as wholes and the elementary propositions of which they are composed. A compound is *extensional* if its TRUTH or falsity is unequivocally determined by the truth or falsity of its components; it is *intensional* if it is not. Thus 'it is cold and it is wet' is extensional since it is true if both components are true and false in the other three possible cases. 'I believe that it is Thursday' is, however, intensional since the whole belief-statement can be true or false whether it is Thursday or not. The two leading kinds of intensional compound are (1) those in which the main verb refers to a 'propositional attitude' such as belief, knowledge, hope, fear, etc. and (2) modal statements of the form 'It is necessary that *p*' or 'It is possible that *p*'. Standard modern LOGIC is resolutely extensional and uses an extensional notion of material IMPLICATION which differs in MEANING from the intensional connection asserted in the conditional statements of ordinary language. LOGICAL POSITIVISTS and LOGICAL EMPIRICISTS have attempted to find ANALYSES in extensional terms of apparently intensional statements about propositional attitudes or involving modal concepts. Thus 'A believes that *p*' is analysed into 'There is some sentence "*s*" which means the same as "*p*" to which A is disposed to assent'. 'It is possible that it is raining' becomes 'The sentence "it is raining" is CONTINGENT'. A.Q.

Exter, Alexandra (Russian painter and scenographer, 1884–1949), see under KNAVE OF DIAMONDS.

externalities. In ECONOMICS, the direct effects that one consumer's or producer's actions have on other consumers and producers. In this category, economists include a great variety of phenomena, from POLLUTION to invention. The essential feature is that one man's action changes the options available to another (quite apart from any repercussions through the workings of the price and tax system). *External economies* increase, or at least improve, the range of options, as when electricity is invented, or a beautiful building erected. *External diseconomies* have the reverse effect, as when chemical products are discharged downstream, or an additional car on the road causes additional congestion. Normally people are given insufficient incentives to produce external economies, while their creation of external diseconomies is insufficiently discouraged. Economists usually argue that external economies should be subsidized and diseconomies taxed, at least when the benefits or cost can be roughly measured, but are wary of generalized claims for the encouragement – or discouragement – of industrial activity which involves unspecified and unquantified externalities.

The terms *social benefits* and *social costs* are sometimes taken to refer to externalities but may also express other respects in which the financial profits and losses of an activity fail to measure possible opinions about its value to the community. For example, one might claim that an industrial project paying most of its profits to one rich family provides too little social benefit to justify its costs (see COST-BENEFIT ANALYSIS). This latter usage has been common in the appraisal of INVESTMENT projects by economists and governments. J.A.M.

Bibl: E. J. Mishan, 'The Postwar Literature on Externalities' (*Journal of Economic Literature*, March 1971); I. M. D. Little and J. A. Mirrlees, *Project Appraisal and Planning for Developing Countries* (London and N.Y., 1974).

extinction, see under REINFORCEMENT.

extra-curricular activities. School activities which extend beyond the classroom, and in which teachers as well as pupils are expected to take part. They are more prevalent in British and American than in continental schools, and are particularly extensive in boarding schools, part of whose *raison d'être* is to provide a school life coextensive with the waking hours. Such activities extend the range of the pupils' education and help to build up informal relationships between them and their teachers. The latter are not normally paid for the additional work, which may include individual teaching (coaching), COUNSELLING and other forms of pastoral care, helping the children to organize athletic, cultural, social and hobby clubs and activities, and during the vacation taking parties camping or exploring. W.A.C.S.

extrapolation and **interpolation.** In STATISTICS (and more generally), extrapolation is the estimation of a function value outside the range in which its values are known; interpolation is the estimation of it within this range but at a point at which it is not known. Thus, censuses are carried out in England in . . ., 1931, 1941, 1951, 1961, 1971, . . . The use of population sizes recorded at these dates to estimate the population size in the year 2000 is extrapolation; their use to estimate the population size in 1956 is interpolation. *Prediction theory,* REGRESSION, and *time series analysis* are names given to deeper analytic techniques similar in spirit to simple extrapolation and interpolation. R.SI.

extra-sensory perception, see ESP.

extroversion. A term current in PSYCHOLOGY that was used by Jung (see JUNGIAN) to denote a process whereby a person who has experienced pain or conflict through being sensitive to his own feelings invests his attention and concern in others; his rapidity ('Hail, fellow, well met') in establishing inter-personal relations tends to be matched by the superficiality of such relations. This process was later reified (see REIFICATION) and generalized to refer to a PERSONALITY TYPE, the *extrovert,* much of whose life seemed to be characterized by these processes and behaviours. Although this usage makes the extrovert and the introvert seem to stand for opposed personality types, the oft-drawn contrast between extroversion and INTROVERSION is entirely superficial, their underlying causes and mechanisms being divergent but in no sense opposites. T.Z.C.

Eysenck, Hans Jurgen (British psychologist, *b.* 1916), see under ANXIETY; PERSONALITY TYPES.

Eysenck personality inventory, see under MENTAL TESTING.

F

Fabianism. An approach to the problems of implementing SOCIALIST ideas developed by the Fabian Society (established in London in 1884). Its members put their hopes in the 'permeation' of the existing INSTITUTIONS and the 'inevitability of gradualness' – hence the name, taken from the Roman general Fabius Cunctator who won his campaigns by avoiding pitched battles and instead wearing the enemy down. Fabian ideas were eclectic rather than synthetic. They concentrated on practical detailed reforms ('gas and water socialism') and shunned grandiose theoretical speculations. They rejected the doctrine of economic LAISSEZ FAIRE and stressed the need for State action to ensure greater equality (see EGALITARIANISM) and the elimination of poverty. By accepting a constitutional approach they helped to make socialist ideas respectable in Britain. Prominent members, such as Sydney and Beatrice Webb, H. G. Wells, George Bernard Shaw, and Graham Wallas are remembered through their individual achievements, rather than through their activities in the Fabian Society. Its direct influence was not very great (its membership was 640 in 1893 and under 3,000 in 1914), but it established a mode of approach to social questions, based on socialist ideas and a study of social problems, which has had a lasting impact on politics in Great Britain. L.L.

Bibl: H. M. Pelling, *The Origins of the Labour Party* (London, 1954); A. M. McBriar, *Fabian Socialism and English Politics, 1884–1918* (London, 1962).

facilitation. The establishment of a preferred reflex pathway in the central NERVOUS SYSTEM by the repetition of the stimulus that excites the reflex response. The process is no longer thought to be of paramount importance in learning. P.M.

factor analysis. The statistical analysis of a MULTIVARIATE set of observations (e.g. the scores of a group of persons in tests of various kinds) in terms of a set of hypothetical components or factors. Historically, the first such analysis was by the psychologist Charles Spearman, who claimed in 1904 to express test scores in terms of a single common factor, which was identified as general ability, and residual specific factors peculiar to each kind of test. Later, it was found necessary to employ a wider *multi-factor analysis* involving more than one common group factor (e.g. the recognition of a speed factor in test performances). It is now recognized that factor analysis can be used as a general statistical technique in other than the psychological domain (see also CLUSTER ANALYSIS). REIFICATION of any group factors emerging from such an analysis should, however, be treated with caution. M.S.BA.

factory farming. Systems of livestock production in which farm animals are kept throughout the greater part of their lives indoors under conditions in which movement is severely restricted. Pigs, laying hens, chickens for meat production ('broilers'), and calves for veal production are the animals most commonly kept under this type of intensive production. Particularly for pigs and poultry the systems are closely standardized, making possible large-scale production, with high density of animals per unit area. Many people believe, however, that such systems are unacceptable on humane grounds. K.E.H.

faculty psychology. The attempt to list classes of things done by the mind, e.g. remembering, willing. Although descriptively useful, such classifications have sometimes led to the incorrect assumption that to each faculty there must correspond one distinct mental operation. The resulting confusion is well illustrated by PHRENOLOGY. I.M.L.H.

Fairlie, Henry (British journalist), see under ESTABLISHMENT, THE.

Faisal (Saudi-Arabian king, *c.* 1906–75), see under PAN-ISLAM.

Falange. Spanish FASCIST party founded in 1933 by José Antonio Primo de Rivera, son of the former Spanish dictator, to capture the Spanish working class for an AUTHORITARIAN, socially radical NATIONALISM, and to overcome individualism and SOCIALISM as forces divisive of the nation. The Falange's failure to capture the working class confined its main strength to university students, though other RIGHT-wing forces were alarmed into supporting it by the victory of the POPULAR FRONT in the elections of February 1936. In 1937 the Spanish military leader, General Franco, took over the Falange, disciplined its leadership, and established his brother-in-law, Ramon Serrano Suñer, at its head. It was to remain firmly under Franco's control thereafter, its social RADICALISM a matter solely of rhetoric.　　　　　D.C.W.
Bibl: S. Payne, *Falange* (Stanford, 1961; London, 1962).

Falk, Robert (Russian painter, 1886–1958), see under KNAVE OF DIAMONDS.

fallacy.
(1) Any widespread false belief. (For examples of fallacies, as regarded at least by those who named them, see AFFECTIVE FALLACY; COMMUNICATION, FALLACY OF; EXPRESSIVE FORM, FALLACY OF; INTENTIONAL FALLACY; NATURALISTIC FALLACY.) Such a belief may result from:
(2) In LOGIC, an invalid pattern of argument that is frequently mistaken for a valid one. Among the most common formal fallacies are those which involve reversing the direction of an *implication* (see ENTAILMENT). Thus, to infer 'This is *B*' from 'This is *A*' and 'All *B* are *A*' is a fallacy (called 'affirming the consequent'); whereas if the second premise is reversed (becoming 'All *A* are *B*') the resulting inference is valid. Another common fallacy (that of 'denying the antecedent') is to infer 'This is not *B*' from 'This is not *A*' and 'All *A* are *B*'.　　　A.Q.
Bibl: C. L. Hamblin, *Fallacies* (London and N.Y., 1970).

Fallada, Hans (German author, 1893–1947), see under NEUE SACHLICHKEIT.

fallibilism. In EPISTEMOLOGY, the view that it is not necessary in science or in everyday life for the factual beliefs that compose the one and guide the other to be established as certain beyond the possibility of doubt. On this view it is sufficient, and perhaps all that is possible, for our beliefs to be reasonably well supported or justified. Fallibilism, of which C. S. Peirce (1839–1914) was the first thoroughgoing exponent, can be seen as a reasonable compromise between scepticism and dogmatism (or, in one of its senses, INTUITIONISM).　　　A.Q.

fallout. RADIOACTIVE material falling from the atmosphere as a result of artificial nuclear explosions or accidents in NUCLEAR REACTORS.　　　M.V.B.

falsifiability, see under POPPERIAN.

family reconstitution. A method developed by Louis Henry and used in HISTORICAL DEMOGRAPHY. Like genealogy, it consists of collecting information about the births, marriages, and deaths of all known members of a given family. Unlike the genealogist, the demographer reconstitutes families not for their own sake but as samples, using them to calculate age at first marriage, birth intervals, infant mortality, and other demographic measures (see DEMOGRAPHY). The main source for family reconstitution is the parish register. Where a long series of such registers have survived and some families have not moved out of the parish for centuries, striking results may be obtained by this method.　　　P.B.
Bibl: E. A. Wrigley, 'Family reconstitution' in E. A. Wrigley (ed.), *An Introduction to English Historical Demography* (London and N.Y., 1966), pp. 96–159.

family therapy. A form of treatment for PSYCHIATRIC or inter-personal problems arising in a family setting (e.g. behaviour disorders and NEUROSIS in children, PSYCHOSIS in the adolescent son of a depressed mother). The technique was pioneered by J. Bowlby (in England) and J. E. Bell (in the U.S.A.), and involves interviews of the whole family together. Similar conjoint interview techniques are used for couples with marital and sexual problems. Family therapists' theoretical roots are in PSYCHOANALYSIS, SYSTEMS theory, or BEHAVIOURISM, and there is a wide variation from short-term, active approaches to long-term, interpretative, and insight-giving ones. There is some evidence of efficacy, at least for the behavioural and systems-based approaches.

M.J.C.

Fanon, Frantz (Martinican psychoanalyst and social philosopher, 1925–61), see under NÉGRITUDE.

Fantin-Latour, Henri (French painter, 1836–1904), see under INTIMISM.

FAO (Food and Agriculture Organization). A SPECIALIZED AGENCY of UNO set up by an international conference meeting at Quebec in October 1945. FAO, with its headquarters at Rome, had forerunners in the international Institute of Agriculture established in Paris in 1905 and took its own origin from the American-sponsored conference held at Hot Springs, Virginia, in 1943. Its original responsibility was seen as the feeding of the population of countries whose economies had been disturbed by the war of 1939–45, but it soon passed to handling the basic problems of world distribution of food between areas of crop surplus and areas of endemic food deficiency.

D.C.W.

Farad, Wali (U.S. Black Muslim leader, *fl.* 1930–34), see under BLACK MUSLIMS.

Faraday, Michael (British physicist and chemist, 1791–1867), see under ROYAL INSTITUTION.

Fascism.

(1) Specifically, the Fascist Movement formed in 1919 which Mussolini led to power in Italy (1922–45). The Italian word, *fascismo*, is derived from the *fasces*, the bundle of rods with a projecting axe which was carried before the consuls as the insignia of state authority in ancient Rome.

(2) Generically, similar AUTHORITARIAN movements in other countries, such as NAZISM in Germany, the FALANGE in Franco's Spain, the Iron Guard in Romania, and Sir Oswald Mosley's British Union of Fascists.

(3) More particularly in the form 'Fascist', a term of political abuse much used by the COMMUNISTS both before and after World War II to discredit their opponents, whether genuinely Fascist, CONSERVATIVES, or SOCIAL DEMOCRATS, and to promote their tactics of building up anti-Fascist coalitions under Communist leadership.

Fascism was a product of the deep-seated social and economic crisis in Europe which followed World War I. It produced no coherent system of ideas, and the various Fascist movements reflected the very different national backgrounds of the countries in which they developed. None the less there were a number of common traits. All were strongly NATIONALIST, violently anti-Communist, and anti-MARXIST; all hated LIBERALISM, DEMOCRACY, and parliamentary parties, which they sought to replace by a new authoritarian state in which there would be only one party, their own, with a monopoly of power, and a single leader with charismatic qualities (see CHARISMA) and dictatorial powers; all shared a cult of violence and action, planned to *seize* power, exalted war, and with their uniforms, ranks, salutes, and rallies gave their parties a PARA-MILITARY character. In their political campaigns, they relied heavily on mass propaganda and TERRORISM; once in power, they used the power of the State to liquidate their rivals without regard for the law.

RACISM and ANTISEMITISM were strongly marked features of some Fascist movements (e.g. the German) but not all (e.g. the Italian). Fascist movements made a strong appeal to many ex-officers and N.C.O.s resentful of the results of World War I and unwilling to return to civilian life (the 'front' generation); to various groups in the middle and lower middle classes who felt their position in society threatened by INFLATION, economic DEPRESSION, the organized working-class movement, and the spectre of REVOLUTION; and to youth attracted by the cult of action and the denunciation of 'the System'. Their nationalism and anti-Marxism won them sympathy and sometimes support from the traditional parties of the RIGHT and the Army. Originally radical in many of their demands, they shed most of these when they came to power, though they represented a new ÉLITE drawn from social groups very different from the old ruling classes.

The product of World War I and the social upheaval and economic depression which followed the war, Fascism was discredited by the total defeat of the Fascist states in World War II. A number of NEO-FASCIST parties have appeared in Europe since the war (see also MSI), though without achieving any real success. Regimes with features borrowed from Fascism have appeared in other continents, e.g. PERONISM in Argentina, but in circumstances better understood in the context of their own national histories than in those of inter-war Europe. A.L.C.B.

Bibl: E. Nolte, *Three Faces of Fascism* (London and N.Y., 1965); F. L. Carsten, *The Rise of Fascism* (London and Berkeley, 1967); S. J. Woolf (ed.), *The Nature of Fascism* (London, 1968; N.Y., 1969).

Fatah, Al (Arabic for 'Victory'). A PARA-MILITARY organization of Arab Palestinians opposed to Israel, formed in 1956 in the Gaza strip, but drawing its main strength from Palestinian Arabs settled in other Arab lands or in the refugee camps in Jordan and Syria. Through its covert organization, *Jihaz al-Rasd*, the special services section of which is known as BLACK SEPTEMBER, it engages in espionage and TERRORISM with Israel, revenge action against Arab rivals, and terrorist actions against airlines and other installations of European powers regarded as too friendly towards Israel.
D.C.W.

Bibl: J. Laffin, *Fedayeen* (London and N.Y., 1973).

fatalism. The theory that every future event is already necessarily determined and inevitable. It seems to be a necessary consequence of DETERMINISM, but, in its usual form, where it asserts not merely that what will happen will happen in conformity with an all-inclusive system of laws of nature, but that what will happen will happen *whatever anybody does*, it is not. Determinism is fully compatible with the view that human action is causally effective and that in its absence events will occur which otherwise would not have occurred. But it does imply that every human action is fully determined by the laws of nature together with the conditions of its occurrence (which will include the character and desires of the agent).
A.Q.

Bibl: G. Ryle, *Dilemmas* (London and N.Y., 1954); A. J. Ayer, *Philosophical Essays* (London and N.Y., 1954).

Fauves. A loosely-knit group of French figurative painters distinguished by their use of strong, simple colour and energetic execution. In 1905 the organizer of the Salon d'Automne chose to hang the most violently coloured works in the same room: the painters concerned were Derain, Manguin, Marquet, Matisse, Puy, Valtat, and Vlaminck, whom the critic Louis Vauxcelles termed *les fauves* (the wild beasts) – referring probably to their rejection of orthodox notions of draughtsmanship, perspective, and light effects, but possibly also to Matisse's hairy overcoat. Gauguin and van Gogh were among their heroes; the IMPRESSIONISTS were not, although many of the Fauves (among whom one may also include Camoin, Rouault, and van Dongen) had themselves been through an Impressionist phase.

Typically *fauve* painting consisted of flat patterns of familiar forms, simply and freely outlined and unpredictably coloured; supposedly 'background' colours were often as vivid as 'foreground'. But by 1908 the Fauves' colour-schemes were generally more subdued. Braque, after a brief *fauve* phase, had turned to CUBISM, Friesz and Vlaminck to Cézanne, and Derain to something between the two. Dufy entered a short period of geometrical severity, and then returned to lively colouring, but in a witty, idiosyncratic style; of the leading figures, only Matisse continued to paint in a recognizably *fauve* idiom.

In Dresden the BRÜCKE painters shared with the French group an admiration for Gauguin, van Gogh, Negro sculpture, and spectacular unorthodoxy. Many Brücke canvases of 1910–12 are comparable in colouring and outline to the French *fauve* works of the preceding years. The Russian artists Kandinsky and Jawlensky also underwent *fauve* periods after visiting France. The academy organized by Matisse from 1907 to 1911 was attended by an international group of painters who spread Matisse's principles in Scandinavia, North America, Eastern Europe, and even (in the case of Matthew Smith) in England.
P.C.

Bibl: J. P. Crespelle, tr. A. Brookner, *The Fauves* (London, 1963); J. E. Muller, tr. S. E. Jones, *Fauvism* (London and N.Y., 1967).

Fawcett, Charles (British geographer, 1883–1952), see under CONURBATION.

Febvre, Lucien (French historian, 1878–1956), see under ANNALES SCHOOL; HISTORY OF MENTALITIES.

Fechner, Gustav Theodor (German experimental psychologist, 1801–78), see under PSYCHOPHYSICS.

Federal Arts Project, see under WPA.

Federal Reserve System. The Central Bank of the U.S.A., as established in 1913. There are 12 Regional Federal Reserve Banks, covering the whole of the U.S.A.; and a Board of Governors of the whole system, whose Chairman is essentially the managing director of the Central Bank. The U.S. President appoints all members of the Board of Governors. The Federal Reserve System operates in the open market through the New York Federal Reserve Bank, and controls the banking system through open-market operations, variations in its discount rates, and changes in the legal reserve ratios of the member banks. These member banks (about 6,000) are the main banking houses in the U.S.A.   M.V.P.

Federal Theater Project, see under WPA.

Federal Writers Project, see under WPA.

Fedin, Konstantin Alexandrovich (Russian novelist, *b.*1892), see under SERAPION BROTHERS.

feedback. The return of part of a SYSTEM'S output to change its INPUT. *Positive feedback* increases the input, *negative feedback* decreases it. Hence, if feedback is used (as it is in all regulatory systems) in comparing output with some standard to be approached, negative feedback is inherently stabilizing (because it decreases the error) while positive feedback is inherently destabilizing (and the error gains explosively in magnitude). The classic example of negative feedback is the Watt steam governor, in which a pair of weights attached to the engine shaft fly outward (by centrifugal force) if the engine tends to race, which movement operates a valve to reduce the supply of fuel. An example of positive feedback is a 'growth economy' in which increased profitability is ploughed back further to increase profitability, a process which indeed becomes destabilizing in the limit. The casual use of 'feedback' to mean 'response to a stimulus' is incorrect.   S.BE.

Feigl, Herbert (Austrian-U.S. philosopher of science, *b.*1902), see under VIENNA CIRCLE.

Feininger, Andreas (U.S. photographer, *b.*1906), see under BLAUE REITER.

FEKS, see FEX.

felicific calculus. A method, devised by Bentham, for the quantitative comparison of the amounts of pleasure and pain which will occur as the consequences of alternative courses of action. Some such technique is needed by any utilitarian ethical theory (see ETHICS; UTILITARIANISM) that defines the rightness and wrongness of alternative possible actions in terms of the amounts of pleasure and pain that they produce. Bentham enumerated a number of 'dimensions' of pleasure and pain: intensity, duration, certainty, propinquity, purity, fecundity, and extent. Most of these factors should be taken into account in any appraisal of the consequences of action that aims to be rational and thorough. But Bentham's idea that a fixed amount of intensity is equal in value to a fixed amount of duration rests on a false ANALOGY with spatial measurement, where an inch is the same length in every dimension.   A.Q.

fellow-traveller. Originally a Russian term (*poputchik*) coined by Trotsky to depict the vacillating INTELLECTUAL and literary supporters of the Soviet regime. When Stalin established a more monolithic rule, the term (and the social category) disappeared in Russia. But foreign sympathizers with the Soviet regime – fellow-travellers – retained the same essential characteristics. The most fundamental among these characteristics, which distinguished them from sympathizers with other causes, was their uncritical attachment to the Soviet Union while they remained outside their own national COMMUNIST parties. As a rule, they also preferred to remain at a distance. Lincoln Steffens, who once said that he saw in the Soviet Union 'the future, and it works', wrote in 1926 from the Italian Riviera: 'I am for them to the last drop, I am a patriot for Russia . . . but I don't want to live there . . . My service to it has to be outside, here.' The fellow-travellers' service usually consisted of justifying all the tergiversations of Soviet internal and foreign policy, whether it was the Moscow SHOW TRIALS, the Soviet-Nazi Pact, or charges of bacteriological warfare (see WAR) against the Americans in KOREA. The ranks of fellow-travellers were periodically shaken by defections after events or policy changes in the Soviet Union which were particularly difficult for them to accept, but the real turning-point came after Khrushchev's 'secret speech' at the 20th congress of the Soviet Communist Party in 1956. His denunciation of Stalin exposed the credulity of fellow-travellers and made an unqualified intellectual and emotional identification with 'the Soviet cause' well-nigh impossible for Western intellectuals. Many never recovered from the shock of Khrushchev's 'revelations', or the suppression of the Hungarian revolt (see HUNGARY); others transferred their attachment to Peking (see MAOISM) or Havana (see CASTROISM).   L.L.

Bibl: D. Caute, *The Fellow-Travellers* (London and N.Y., 1973).

feminism. The advocacy of the rights and equality of women in social, political, and economic spheres, and a commitment to the fundamental alteration of woman's role in society. Precursors of the formal movement range from Aristophanes' Lysistrata to 19th-century novelists such as Charlotte Brontë. Early feminist campaigners like Mrs Emmeline Pankhurst concentrated upon the political aspects of female subjugation, with female suffrage as their principal end; subsequently the emphasis shifted to economic and social equality in the form of equal pay and equal opportunity. New methods of birth-control and a changing climate of public opinion have enabled the women's movement to score some successes in the area of legislation, and a more widespread acceptance of the principle of equality in education, work, and the home. Both the aims and the image of the feminist movement have, however, altered in recent years with the advent of *Women's Liberation* as an ACTIVIST and militant wing whose more radical elements insist (e.g. books by Greer and Millett listed below) that the entire social system is pervaded by a SEXISM which structures and maintains oppression in psychological and biological terms. The type of feminism (exemplified in the last book listed below) which sees women as possessing uniquely feminine qualities and abilities and wishes to see such qualities reflected in social ROLES, is now attacked and undermined by the vanguard of Women's Liberation.   P.S.L.

Bibl: S. de Beauvoir, tr. H. M. Parshley, *The Second Sex* (London and N.Y., 1953; Harmondsworth, 1972); G. Greer, *The Female Eunuch* (London, 1970; N.Y., 1971); K. Millett, *Sexual Politics* (N.Y., 1970; London, 1972); A. Stassinopoulos, *The Female Woman* (London, 1973; N.Y., 1974).

Fénéon, Félix (French art critic, 1861–1944), see under NEO-IMPRESSIONISM.

Ferlinghetti, Lawrence (U.S. poet, b. 1920), see under BEAT.

Fermat's last theorem. This states that for $n>2$ the EQUATION $x^n + y^n = z^n$ cannot be satisfied by positive integers x,y,z. Pierre de Fermat (1601–65) claimed in an annotation to have discovered a proof 'but this margin is too small to contain it'. The result is known to hold for a great many values of n, but no proof of the general statement has yet been found, so that the 'theorem' remains a great challenge in NUMBER THEORY. Efforts to prove it in the 19th century led to the development of *algebraic number theory* (see ALGEBRA). R.G.

Fermat's principle of least time, see under LEAST-ACTION PRINCIPLE.

Fermi, Enrico (Italian-U.S. physicist, 1901–54), see under NUCLEAR REACTOR.

Fermi-Dirac statistics. The QUANTUM STATISTICS that applies to PARTICLES for which the QUANTUM NUMBER describing SPIN is a half-integer.   M.V.B.

fermions, see under QUANTUM STATISTICS.

ferrimagnetism. A relatively weak type of MAGNETISM often found in CERAMICS, in which successive elementary atomic magnets (see SPIN) point in opposite directions. The phenomenon is useful in TELECOMMUNICATIONS because most 'ferrites' are electrical insulators and make sensitive aerials for TRANSISTOR sets.   M.V.B.

ferromagnetism. The strong MAGNETISM which can be produced in the metals iron, cobalt, and nickel, where it is possible to align all the elementary atomic magnets (see SPIN) in the same direction. Ferromagnetism often occurs naturally, induced by the magnetic field of the earth. Most common horseshoe and bar magnets are ferromagnetic.   M.V.B.

fertility. A term which has acquired a specialized meaning in DEMOGRAPHY, where it is restricted to mean actual reproduction performance. Thus, a fertile woman is one who has produced at least one live-born child, a fertile man one who has begotten at least one live-born child. In medical literature and to some extent in everyday language the term is sometimes used to denote the potential capacity to reproduce, but demographers refer to this capacity as *fecundity*. A distinction is drawn between *current fertility,* measured by the births of a particular year, and period fertility or *cohort fertility,* which is measured by the total number of children born to a cohort throughout their reproductive lives.   E.G.

fetish; fetishism. E. B. Tylor (*Primitive Culture,* 1871) adopted into ANTHROPOLOGY the word *fetish,* long current in English, to mean an object in which a spirit is embodied, to which it is attached, or through which it conveys magical influence; he applied the term *fetishism* to the worship, shading into idolatry, of such an object. For an example of the non-anthropological uses of the term see COMMODITY FETISHISM.   M.F.

feudal; feudalism. Terms used since the 18th century to describe the social and military organization prevalent in Western Europe between the 9th and 16th centuries, and also other social systems with similar features in, e.g., Iran, China, and Japan – where it continued down to the 19th century. There have been many varieties of feudalism but it commonly involved a social hierarchy based on the tenure of land, jurisdiction by landlords over their tenants, and the granting of land in return for services, particularly military service, to the king or lord from whom the land was held.

More generally the word 'feudal' is used to characterize (1) any social system in which great landowners or hereditary overlords exact revenue from the land, and exercise the functions of government in their domains (e.g. the Prussian Junker class east of the Elbe); and (2) any society or social group which the writer wishes to condemn as anachronistic and based upon inequality and the privileged position of a social, political, or economic dynasty (e.g. the phrase *industrial feudalism* often used in histories of 19th-century America).   A.L.C.B.

Feuerbach, Ludwig Andreas (German philosopher and theologian, 1804–72), see under MARXISM.

FEX. The 'Factory of the Eccentric Actor', initially a theatre, then a film studio, organized in Petrograd in 1921 by the young directors Kozintsev and Trauberg ('the FEXes'). They sought to revolutionize the theatre on principles of 'eccentricity' imported from the circus and vaudeville, and to replace its obsolete methods by the more dynamic 'lower' genres: street shows, slapstick comedy, and sport. In the cinema the FEXes extolled American comedies and gangster films. Their early films tried to convey revolutionary propaganda through grotesque and fantastic imagery, shocking juxtapositions, and circus tricks. In later years their style changed considerably under the influence of Eisenstein and German EXPRESSIONIST cinema. The 'eccentric' tendency gradually gave way to more realistic themes and methods.

The Kozintsev-Trauberg collaboration ended in 1946. Their best-known films were the trilogy *The Youth of Maxim* (1935), *The Return of Maxim* (1937), and *The Vyborg Side* (1939). Kozintsev subsequently reached Western audiences with his *Hamlet* (1964) and *King Lear* (1971).   M.E.

Bibl: J. Leyda, *Kino* (London and N.Y., 2nd ed., 1973).

Fichte, Johann Gottlieb (German philosopher, 1762–1814), see under DIALECTIC; PESTALOZZI METHODS; ROMANTICISM.

Fiedler, Leslie (U.S. novelist and critic, *b.* 1917), see under MODERNISM.

field.

(1) A MATHEMATICAL STRUCTURE which admits analogues of addition, subtraction, multiplication, and division satisfying the familiar laws. Fields are important in ALGEBRA.   R.G.

(2) The systems considered in PHYSICS often consist of PARTICLES moving under the action of their mutual forces of attraction or repulsion, according to the laws of NEWTONIAN MECHANICS or QUANTUM MECHANICS. It frequently simplifies the analysis of such systems if some of the particles are considered as the sources of an influence – a *field* – which exists throughout space even when the other particles are not there to feel it. A field is thus basically a matter of conceptual convenience, the carrier of interactions between particles, avoiding the intuitively awkward notion of 'action at a distance' (but see FIELD THEORY). For example: the ELECTRONS constituting the current in the transmitting aerial of a TELECOMMUNICATIONS system produce an ELECTROMAGNETIC FIELD spreading out in space, which then exerts forces on the electrons in any receiving aerial within range; it would be needlessly complicated to consider the electron-electron interactions between the transmitter and each separate receiver.

More generally, any physical quantity varying continuously in space and time is referred to as a field (e.g. the temperature in an aircraft wing, or the pressure in a sound wave).   M.V.B.

field archaeology. That aspect of ARCHAEOLOGY which deals with the recognition and planning of ancient landscapes. The techniques used include AIR PHOTOGRAPHY, RESISTIVITY SURVEYING, surface searching ('field walking'), and survey; some archaeologists would include excavation. The importance of field archaeology was emphasized and

demonstrated by O. G. S. Crawford during his employment by the Ordnance Survey.   B.C.

Bibl: Ordnance Survey, *Field Archaeology* (London, 4th ed., 1966); J. Coles, *Field Archaeology in Britain* (London, 1972).

field painting, see under ABSTRACT EXPRESSIONISM.

field theory. The attempt to unify the basic laws of PHYSICS by deriving them from the interactions between FIELDS. These fields would become the basic entities of physics, and ELEMENTARY PARTICLES would, hopefully, appear as a result of applying the laws of QUANTUM MECHANICS. This programme is in its infancy, the most successful field theories being the general theory of RELATIVITY (incorporating GRAVITATION into MECHANICS) and *quantum electrodynamics* (incorporating ELECTROMAGNETISM into quantum mechanics).   M.V.B.

field work. In ANTHROPOLOGY (whence the term has spread to related disciplines such as industrial SOCIOLOGY), a mode of investigation consisting of sustained and first-hand observation of exotic societies; the classic instance is B. Malinowski's studies of the Trobriand Islanders during World War I. It calls for close observation, a comprehensive view of the community under study, and the use of the local language. It is not anthropology's only descriptive method (and in the long run perhaps not its most important), but it is held in particular esteem, and in the view of some anthropologists will ensure for them a distinctive role within the social sciences even when their traditional PRIMITIVE subject-matter has disappeared. See also ANTHROPOLOGY; ETHNOGRAPHY; PARTICIPANT OBSERVATION.   M.F.

Bibl: D. G. Jongmans and P. C. W. Gutkind (eds.), *Anthropologists in the Field* (Assen, 1967; N.Y., 1970); R. Naroll and R. Cohen (eds.), *A Handbook of Method in Cultural Anthropology* (N.Y., 1970).

fifth column. Phrase coined in 1936 in the Spanish Civil War during the Spanish Nationalists' advance on Madrid to denote the underground supporters who were believed ready to emerge in Madrid

itself to attack its defenders from within coincidentally with the first assault by General Mola's four columns from without. The term came to be used during World War II for any organized body working for the enemy behind the lines, on either side.   D.C.W.
    Bibl: L. de Jong, tr. C. M. Geyl, *The German Fifth Column in the Second World War* (London and Chicago 1956).

figurative. Adjective applied (as distinct from 'non-figurative' or ABSTRACT) to works of visual art involving the portrayal, however allusive or distorted, of elements of the visible world. Hence also 'figuration'.   J.W.

figure-ground phenomenon. The characteristic organization of PERCEPTION into a figure that 'stands out' against an undifferentiated background, e.g. a printed word against a background page. What is figural at any one moment depends on patterns of sensory stimulation and on the momentary interests of the perceiver. See also GESTALT.   I.M.L.H.

Fillmore, Charles J. (U.S. linguist, *b*. 1929), see under CASE GRAMMAR.

filtration, see under BIOPHYSICS.

final solution (*Endlösung*). A NAZI-German euphemism for the physical extermination of European Jewry – the final solution to 'the Jewish problem'. Implementation of such a policy was first discussed at a conference of Nazi-German ministerial representatives at Wannsee in January 1942. The means were extermination camps using mass gas chambers and mass assassination squads. In all, between four and a half and six million victims perished in what Jewish historians term the *holocaust*. At the NUREMBERG TRIALS various survivors of the Nazi regime were convicted of GENOCIDE.   D.C.W.
    Bibl: G. Reitlinger, *The Final Solution* (London and N.Y., 1953).

finite differences, calculus of, see under NUMERICAL ANALYSIS.

finite-state grammar, see under GENERATIVE GRAMMAR.

finitism, see under INTUITIONISM (3).

first-strike capability, see under STRATEGIC CAPABILITY.

Firth, John Rupert (British linguist, 1890–1960), see under CONTEXT OF SITUATION; FIRTHIAN.

Firthian. Characteristic of, or a follower of, the linguistic principles of J. R. Firth (1890–1960), Professor of General Linguistics in the University of London (1944–56), and the formative influence on the development of LINGUISTICS in Great Britain. A central notion is *polysystemicism*, an approach to linguistic analysis based on the view that language patterns cannot be accounted for in terms of a single system of analytic principles and categories (*monosystemic* linguistics), but that different systems may need to be set up at different places within a description; for other features see COLLOCATION, CONTEXT OF SITUATION, and PROSODIC FEATURE. Relatively little of Firth's teaching was published, but many of his ideas have been developed by a *neo-Firthian* group of scholars, whose main theoretician is M. A. K. Halliday, Professor of General Linguistics at University College London from 1965 to 1970 (see SCALE AND CATEGORY GRAMMAR; SYSTEMIC GRAMMAR).   D.C.
    Bibl: J. R. Firth, *Papers in Linguistics 1934–1951* (London, 1957).

fiscal drag. The deflationary impulse (see DEFLATION) generated through the budget when rising money incomes cause government revenues to expand (at unchanged rates of tax) while public expenditure lags behind. This withdrawal of purchasing power may arise because of the increase in real OUTPUT and incomes which overflows into additional tax revenue and acts as a drag on further growth unless offsetting action is taken to increase government expenditure or reduce taxation. A similar effect may be produced by INFLATION if, for example, rising money incomes are tapped by progressive taxation so that tax revenues expand faster than government expenditures.   A.C.

fiscal policy. The policy of a government in controlling its own expenditure and taxation, which together make up its budget. The term usually refers to transactions of the central government, but, depending partly on a country's political structure, may also extend to other parts of the PUBLIC SECTOR, namely state or local governments and public enterprise.

Fiscal policy has several functions. One is to regulate, together with MONETARY POLICY and *exchange rate policy*, the level of economic activity, the price level, and the BALANCE OF PAYMENTS. Another is to determine the allocation of productive resources between the public and PRIVATE SECTORS, and among the different parts of the public sector. A third is to influence the distribution of income and wealth, both through taxation and through social expenditures. The size of the public sector and the distribution of wealth are also affected by moves to extend or restrict public ownership, but this is not part of fiscal policy as such.

The government budget in a particular year is said to be in surplus, balance, or deficit according as tax receipts exceed, equal, or fall short of expenditure. Spending in excess of tax receipts is called *deficit spending*. This term is sometimes applied more narrowly to an excess of government spending on current account alone – rather than of total spending, which includes capital items – over total tax receipts. The budget position is of key importance in connection with the first of the three functions listed above, regulation of economic activity and prices. Its role here stems from the KEYNESIAN revolution. An increase in the budget deficit (or reduction in the surplus) boosts AGGREGATE DEMAND; a narrowing of the deficit restricts it. The budget position is affected not only by government decisions to alter taxation or expenditure, but also by fluctuations in economic activity itself. In the upswing, as employment and incomes rise, the budget is strengthened by accelerated tax receipts and a slow-down of social security outlays; in the downswing the movement is reversed. Since a tighter budget helps to curb the boom and an easier budget to limit the recession, the fiscal mechanism thus provides some degree of automatic stabilization to the economy.

Deficit finance is the finance for deficit spending, and is normally provided by borrowing against the issue of government

securities (bonds or Treasury bills), thus adding to the NATIONAL DEBT. Conversely, a budget surplus may be used to redeem debt. Fiscal policy and national-debt management have important implications for monetary policy. Newly issued government debt may be taken up by (*a*) the banking system, (*b*) other domestic residents, or (*c*) foreign residents. In (*a*) the quantity of MONEY expands, unless bank credit to the private sector is simultaneously reduced. In (*b*) the money stock is unchanged; a rise in interest rates may be necessary to induce the public to buy the new debt. In (*c*) the money stock again remains unchanged if the government's overseas borrowing serves to finance a BALANCE OF PAYMENTS deficit; otherwise it increases, as the central bank creates domestic currency in exchange for the foreign currency which foreigners sell in order to acquire the government debt in question.   P.M.O.

Bibl: A. R. Prest, *Public Finance* (London and Chicago, 1960); R. A. Musgrave and P. B. Musgrave, *Public Finance in Theory and Practice* (N.Y., 1973).

Fisher, Sir Ronald (British biologist, 1890–1962), see under BIOMETRY; SELECTION PRESSURE; STATISTICS.

Fisher index number, see under INDEX NUMBER.

fission. The splitting of an atomic NUCLEUS, usually by free NEUTRONS during a CHAIN REACTION. For heavy elements the total mass of the fission fragments is less than that of the original nucleus + neutrons, so that large amounts of ENERGY are released (see MASS-ENERGY EQUATION). The atomic bomb, and NUCLEAR REACTORS, derive their energy from fission. See also MODERATOR; QUANTUM MECHANICS; THERMAL NEUTRON.   M.V.B.

fission track dating, see under DATING.

fitness, see under DARWINISM.

Fitzgerald, Francis Scott (U.S. novelist, 1896–1940), see under JAZZ AGE.

fixation. In psychoanalytic theory (see PSYCHOANALYSIS), a NEUROSIS consisting of the arrestation of PSYCHOSEXUAL

DEVELOPMENT in one of its immature stages (e.g. anal, phallic). W.Z.

Flaherty, Robert (U.S. film director, 1884–1951), see under DOCUMENTARY.

Flanagan, Hallie (U.S. theatre historian and organizer, 1890–1969), see under WPA.

flash point. The temperature at which spontaneous combustion occurs. B.F.

flat characters and **round characters.** Terms coined by E. M. Forster (*Aspects of the Novel*, 1927), and used in criticism of novels, plays, and films to distinguish between, at one extreme, characters 'constructed round a single idea or quality' and, at the other, highly complex characters 'capable of surprising in a convincing way'. Flat characters, though usually 'best when they are comic', are not necessarily the product of lesser artistry than round ones: Dickens's characters, for example, are mostly flat. O.S.

Flaubert, Gustave (French novelist, 1821–80), see under REALISM.

Flaxman, John (British sculptor, 1755–1826), see under NEO-CLASSICISM.

Flechtheim, Ossip K. (German historian, *b.* 1909), see under FUTUROLOGY.

Fleming, Sir Alexander (British bacteriologist, 1881–1955), see under LYSOZYME.

Fletcher, Roger (British numerical analyst, *b.* 1939), see under GRADIENT METHODS.

flexible response. A STRATEGY based on the ability to react across the entire spectrum of possible military challenges to a state from subversion to strategic nuclear WAR. It is similar to graduated DETERRENCE and is contrasted with MASSIVE RETALIATION. In NATO planning it has acquired a more specialized meaning, namely that the alliance should maintain sufficient conventional land, sea, and air power to enable a Soviet incursion or a Nato – Warsaw Pact crisis to be contained at the lowest possible level of conflict or at least below the nuclear threshold until its size or seriousness could be accurately assessed and the process of negotiation initiated. But it could also mean the use of nuclear weapons in a controlled fashion, if conflict should ESCALATE, in order to minimize destruction and hasten negotiations. This latter meaning may have become otiose with the loss, in the later 1960s, of a marked American strategic superiority over the Soviet Union. A.F.B.
  Bibl: W. Kaufmann, *The McNamara Strategy* (N.Y., 1964); H. Kissinger, *The Troubled Partnership* (London and N.Y., 1965).

Flint, Frank Stewart (British poet, 1885–1960), see under EGOIST, THE; IMAGISM; NEW AGE.

FLN (Front de la Libéeration Nationale). An Algerian NATIONALIST organization which broke away in 1954 from the legal nationalist party in the then French colony of Algeria, in order to embark on TERRORIST action against French colonial installations and against the very substantial element in Muslim society which was part of the colonial system: rural constabulary, soldiers, policemen, presidents of tribal and village councils of elders, tax-collectors, school teachers, and other petty officials. By these means and their extension to attacks on the Europcan population in the cities, particularly in Algiers, the FLN created virtually a civil war between the French settler communities and the bulk of the Muslim population. Despite defeat in Algiers they were able to keep GUERRILLA warfare going in Algeria until de Gaulle negotiated a settlement and the evacuation of French forces and citizens by the Evian agreements of 1962. After independence, the FLN became (1963) the only recognized legal party in the Algerian state. D.C.W.
  Bibl: J. C. Duchemin, *Histoire du F.L.N.* (Paris, 1962); C. A. Julien, *L'Afrique du Nord en marche* (Paris, 3rd ed., 1972).

floating rate, see under DEVALUATION.

Flora, Francesco (Italian literary critic, 1891–1962), see under HERMETIC.

Florey, Howard Walter Florey, Baron (British biochemist, 1898–1968), see under LYSOZYME.

flotation process. The process which brings to the surface fine PARTICLES dispersed in a liquid, usually water. A SURFACTANT absorbed in the surface of the particle makes it water-repellent, thus encouraging the particle to remain at the air-water interface. Mainly used for the enrichment of ores, surfactants are used to effect a differential separation of the suspended mixture of particles.   B.F.

flow chart.
(1) In general, any sequential diagrammatic representation of the movements of materials or people.
(2) In COMPUTING, an informal method of representing an ALGORITHM or a computer PROGRAM. It is not suitable for all types of program and is most often used in commercial data-processing. It is intended for use by human beings, and the amount of detail included can vary widely. Even the most detailed flow chart has ultimately to be expressed in a formal PROGRAMMING LANGUAGE – a process known as CODING.   C.S.

fluidics. The TECHNOLOGY of small fluid devices, e.g. pipes, joints, elbows in pipes, etc., used as substitutes for ELECTRONIC circuits. Thus, a Y-shaped junction behaves as a 2-state device analogous to an electronic flip-flop circuit: the supply fluid entering by the vertical member is directed into one or other of the branches by means of a small pilot jet or vane. For some control systems (see CONTROL ENGINEERING; SYSTEMS) fluidic devices are cheaper and more robust than their electronic counterparts.   E.R.L.

fluidized bed. A bed of solid particles, e.g. sand, which is given the properties of a liquid by blowing air through the particles. The principle can be applied to the improvement of coal combustion where powdered coal is 'fluidized' by air within the combustion chamber.   E.R.L.

fluorescence. The absorption of light at one wavelength and its subsequent emission at a different wavelength, as when the coating of the tube in a fluorescent lamp absorbs ultraviolet light produced by mercury vapour in the tube, and emits visible light. See also RADIATION.   M.V.B.

fluoridation. The addition of minute quantities of fluoride IONS to drinking water to reduce the incidence of dental caries. The mechanism is obscure but the fluoride ions probably exchange with some of the hydroxyl ions in the bone mineral apatite, which forms part of the hard tissues of the teeth. The medical profession is united in recommending fluoridation as a public-health measure, but action is often blocked politically by minority groups in the name of freedom, pure water, etc. B.F.

Fluxus. Latin word for 'flux' applied by George Maciunas in 1962 to an iconoclastic group of artists, primarily American and West German, of which he was the chief spokesman and organizer. A form of DADA revival, this short-lived movement manifested itself in HAPPENINGS (beginning with a performance in Wiesbaden in 1962) and publications. Associated with Fluxus were Wolf Vostell, Allan Kaprow, and the publisher Dick Higgins, while a major influence was the composer John Cage. See also ALEATORY.   A.K.W.
Bibl: A. Kaprow, *Assemblage, Environments and Happenings* (N.Y., 1966).

FM, see FREQUENCY MODULATION.

foetalization, see under NEOTENY.

folded plates, see under STRUCTURE.

folk. An age-old and familiar word which in comparatively recent years has become the first element in an ever-growing list (see, for example, the Supplement to the *Oxford English Dictionary*) of compound nouns and phrases, a few of which are treated separately below. The common element in all these terms is that the phenomenon in question is regarded as springing from, or intimately associated with, the 'folk' in the sense of the common people, the PRIMITIVE or less educated elements of society. 'Folk' in this sense (as against POP) carries connotations of traditionalism, collective wisdom, anonymity, spontaneity, simplicity, and sincerity, and is something of a rallying cry with those people (within a wide spectrum of political views) who value such qualities, particularly in opposition to sophistication, flamboyant individualism, commercialism, MODERNISM, COSMOPOLITANISM, and DECADENCE. The adjective

folksy, on the other hand, is used mostly in a pejorative sense, by those who feel that there is a lack of discrimination, and in some cases an element of self-consciousness, among 'folk' enthusiasts.
O.S.

folk art. A category of art that acquired distinctive status (unsophisticated or PRIMITIVE art has always existed) during the latter half of the 19th century, thanks (*a*) to the development of ANTHROPOLOGY; (*b*) to the early writings on popular imagery etc. by, most notably, Champfleury, and (*c*) to the drive for popular awareness of the arts which followed the institution of compulsory education and the writings of William Morris, Tolstoy, and others. Today the concept has been somewhat tarnished by its abuse in NAZI and Soviet art policy and by its association elsewhere with nostalgia for a pre-industrial society. POP art is another matter.
J.W.

folk culture. The social heritage – the INSTITUTIONS, customs, conventions, values, skills, arts, modes of living – of a group of people feeling themselves members of a closely bound community, and sharing a deep-rooted attachment and allegiance to it. A folk culture is distinguished from more complex CULTURES in that it is predominantly *non-literate,* and so closely knit as to be transmitted from generation to generation by oral means and by RITUAL and behavioural habituation. See also SUBCULTURE.
R.F.
Bibl: R. Redfield, *Peasant Society and Culture* (Chicago, 1956).

folk literature. Term loosely applied to oral-traditional works of literary value that entertain or have entertained, and, to an (arguable) extent originate from, 'the FOLK'. The origins of folk literature (which embraces folk-song, folk-tales, ballads, riddles, proverbs, and folk-drama) are mysterious, as are those of PRIMITIVE art, and they approximate in important respects to the untrained, unsophisticated component in all literature. Thus the greatest writers – Dante, Cervantes, Shakespeare, Goethe – all incorporate much folk material in their work. Important examples of folk literature are: the early epics (the Elder Edda, the East Karelian narrative folk-songs

from which Lonnrot compiled the *Kalevala,* etc.), the ballads, the folk-songs, the folk-drama (for example, the dramatic treatment of traditional themes, usually at religious festivals, from which the ancient Greek drama developed), the earlier layers of Homeric epic, and the fairy tales.
M.S.-S.

folk music. Songs, instrumental music, and dances reflecting the everyday *mores* and inner psyche of a national group. Basic themes are domestic, social, patriotic, and religious. Melodies spun out by musical individuals are absorbed into their community's living tradition, and are communally moulded to suit the prevailing climate during the process of oral transmission from generation to generation, thus ensuring a genuine folk character. Two broad cultural categories emerge: (1) 'primitive', i.e. non-literate, societies, whose musical style includes irregular rhythmic patterns, vigorous bodily movements, and distortion of the voice; (2) 'civilized', i.e. literate, societies, whose folk music influences, and is influenced by, such features of ART MUSIC as strophic forms, sophisticated metres, modality, tonality. Though this intercourse raises the question of 'authenticity' (see ACCULTURATION), European composers have for centuries utilized common folk idioms (especially during periods of political NATIONALISM), thus preserving melodies which might otherwise have been lost through the limited powers of memory and lack of technique among untrained musicians. The serious attention paid by scholars to the traditional music of the poorer classes coincides with the increasing respect for manifestations such as JAZZ and Flamenco among the rich and educated. See also ETHNOMUSICOLOGY.
A.K.
Bibl: C. Sachs, *The Rise of Music in the Ancient World, East and West* (N.Y., 1943; London, 1944); C. M. Bowra, *Primitive Song* (London, 1962; N.Y., 1963); D. Johnson, *Music and Society in Lowland Scotland in the Eighteenth Century* (London, 1972), pp. 3–19.

folklore. A word coined by W. J. Thoms in 1846 for a central part of FOLK CULTURE: the collective 'wisdom' or 'learning' of the 'FOLK', as embodied in customs, beliefs, RITUALS, games, dances, songs,

legends, MYTHS, tales, proverbs, 'sayings', etc. (see FOLK LITERATURE; FOLK MUSIC), all passed on by word of mouth. The term, and the collection by numerous folklore societies and by scholars like Max Müller, Andrew Lang, and G. L. Gomme of stories, poems, and songs not yet committed to paper, originated in the 19th century. In current popular usage it often means merely a corpus of erroneous but widely held beliefs.　　　　R.F.
　Bibl: R. M. Dorson, *The British Folklorists* (London and Chicago, 1968).

Folkwang Museum. The world's first important museum of POST-IMPRESSIONIST art, founded in 1902 at Hagen in Westphalia by the art historian Karl Ernst Osthaus. Henri van de Velde designed the building, which by 1910 contained six Gauguins, five van Goghs, two Cézannes, and three Matisses, and had Christian Rohlfs as resident artist. In 1921 the collection was taken over by the city of Essen, whose museum thereafter bore this name. After 1933 much of it was sold off by the NAZIS as DEGENERATE.　　J.W.

folkways. Term used by W. G. Sumner for all those ways of doing things (from technical tasks to religious observances) which, within a community whose members share the same 'life-conditions', gradually come to be not only established, but also sanctioned and obligatory. Sumner believed that in every society an initial body of such folkways underlay all subsequent developments of doctrines, *mores*, law, and reflective morality. They were the distinguishing foundation of all human societies; the bedrock on which all else came to be erected.　　R.F.
　Bibl: W. G. Sumner, *Folkways* (Boston, 1907).

Fontane, Theodor (German novelist, 1819–98), see under REALISM.

food chain. A series of organisms which eat those lower in the chain, and are eaten by those higher up. A simple food chain is grass – bullock – man. Simple food chains are rare, and the term *food web* is preferable, as this recognizes that most plants are eaten by many different herbivores (e.g. caterpillars, slugs, voles, and cattle all eat grass), and that most predators consume a variety of prey. The concept of the food web also includes the breakdown, partly by bacterial decomposition, of dead animals and plants, the incorporation of the nutrients from their TISSUES into the soil, and the subsequent take-up of the same nutrients by a new generation of plants.
　A food chain usually takes the form of a pyramid. The broad base, e.g. grass, contains a great deal of material, on which a smaller mass of herbivores subsist. Higher up come the carnivores, less numerous and containing less materials. The pyramidal structure reflects the inefficiency with which the nutrient elements are used. As well as nutrients, toxic substances (e.g. DDT) pass up food chains from prey to predator, and may be retained in the greatest concentration by the organism highest in the chain.　　K.M.

force, see under POWER.

force ouvrière, see under CGT.

forced labour.
　(1) During the NAZIS' wartime domination of Europe millions of workers were forcibly deported from the defeated and occupied countries to provide forced labour for German factories and farms. In many cases they were treated as no more than slaves, and recruiting and employing forced labour was one of the WAR CRIMES with which the defendants at the NUREMBERG TRIALS were charged.
　(2) Forced labour camps were established in the U.S.S.R. as early as 1918 as penal colonies to which millions of Soviet citizens who were regarded with suspicion by the authorities were sent for 'correction', and where most of them died. During and after World War II the number of prisoners increased. The total number at any given time has never been disclosed but has been estimated as reaching a peak of 12–15 million. The huge complex of camps, estimated at the end of the Stalin era (1950) as around 200 scattered throughout Siberia, the Arctic, and the Far East, was placed under the Central Camps Administration (see GULAG), a subdivision of the KGB, which exercised an economic as well as a political function by providing forced labour for lumbering, mining, and the construction of such major projects as the White Sea – Baltic canal, particularly in areas with harsh climatic conditions.

The inhuman regime in the camps improved somewhat after 1950, but it was only after Stalin's death, when a series of strikes and revolts took place, that the government began to reduce their population. Some camps were dismantled, others were transformed into milder 'corrective labour colonies'. However, a number of labour camps with an especially harsh regime were retained. From the mid 1960s the consignment of dissenters to the forced-labour camps has again become a regular practice. The number of inmates (of which the political prisoners form only a small part) in the labour camps under Brezhnev has been estimated at over a million.

The existence of the forced-labour system under Stalin was reported in the West in the 1930s and 1940s, but these reports were met with denials by Soviet sympathizers and FELLOW-TRAVELLERS. It was only the writings of Solzhenitsyn which finally convinced the Western public of their true character and extent.
A.L.C.B.; L.L.

Bibl: (1) E. L. Homze, *Foreign Labor in Nazi Germany* (Princeton, 1967); (2) D. J. Dallin and B. I. Nicolaevsky, *Forced Labor in Soviet Russia* (New Haven, 1947; London, 1948); S. Swianiewicz, *Forced Labour and Economic Development* (London, 1965); A Solzhenitsyn, tr. T. P. Whitney, *The Gulag Archipelago* (London and N.Y., 1974–6).

Ford, Ford Madox (*b*.Hueffer; British novelist, 1873–1939), see under BLAST; EGOIST, THE; IMAGISM.

Ford, Gerald Rudolph (U.S. president, *b*.1913), see under WATERGATE.

Ford, John (U.S. film director, 1895–1973), see under WESTERN.

forecasting. In ECONOMICS (see also, however, TECHNOLOGICAL FORECASTING), the attempt to formalize the implicit estimate of the future on which decisions have to be based. It was for a long time wrongly identified by British Civil Servants with the whole of economics. Alternatives to conventional forecasting include *contingency planning* for a variety of possible outcomes; going by the present situation or recent trends (which, however, need defining); or – best of all –

devising policies which do not depend on a greater ability to foresee the future than we happen to enjoy. S.BR.

Bibl: P. Newbold, *Forecasting Methods* (London, 1973).

foreign-body reaction, see under TRAUMA.

forensic psychiatry, see under PSYCHIATRY.

form. In LINGUISTICS, a term used in a variety of technical senses, of which the most important are:
(1) any linguistic element, or combination of elements, especially when studied without reference to their syntactic FUNCTION;
(2) a variant of a linguistic element in a given context (e.g. the forms of a noun);
(3) the phonetic/phonological/grammatical characteristic of a linguistic element or unit, as opposed to its meaning (e.g. the active form of a sentence). See also MORPHEME; UNIVERSAL; WORD CLASS. D.C.

form class, see under WORD CLASS.

form criticism, see under HIGHER CRITICISM.

form word, see under WORD CLASS.

formal (in LINGUISTICS), see under NOTIONAL.

formal operation. In DEVELOPMENTAL PSYCHOLOGY, a PIAGETIAN term for a mental operation involving the manipulation of PROPOSITIONS. For example, given the statements: X is taller than Z; X is shorter than Y, the subject can infer who is the tallest. According to Piaget such INFERENCES about propositions (as opposed to concrete objects) emerge during adolescence and characterize the final stage of intellectual development. P.L.H.

formalism. Any school or doctrine that emphasizes, any emphasis on or preoccupation with, form or forms or formal elements in any sphere: of thought, conduct, religion, art, literature, drama, music, etc. Specific uses include the following. O.S.
(1) The view of MATHEMATICS, developed by Hilbert, that treats mathematical theories as pure deductive

systems, no meaning being ascribed to the expressions of the system other than that implicitly assigned to them by the *formation-rules* of the system, which regulate the possibilities of their combination in well-formed formulae (see AXIOMATICS). Russell objected that formalism takes no adequate account of the application of mathematics to the world (most elementarily in the use of arithmetic for counting), and other opponents have described it as 'a game with meaningless marks'. A.Q.

Bibl: R. L. Wilder, *Introduction to the Foundations of Mathematics* (London and N.Y., 1952).

(2) In the COMMUNIST critical vocabulary, a pejorative term deriving from the group of formalist literary analysts which flourished in the U.S.S.R. in the early days of the Revolution, studying the STYLISTIC features and formal structure of literary works. Headed by Victor Shklovsky, it included Osip Brik, an editor of *LEF*, and the leading CONSTRUCTIVIST theoretician Boris Arvatov, while Eisenstein's analytical approach to the cinema likewise reflected its influence, still visible in the 1970s in the Paris review TEL QUEL.

With the promulgation of SOCIALIST REALISM in 1934, formalism was condemned in the U.S.S.R. as a heresy, primarily for its lack of political partisanship. More significantly, the term was stretched to cover any allegedly excessive concern with the formal aspects of art at the expense of 'content', which became exclusively identified with subject-matter. Thus it applied both to those politically-minded artists who could be linked with formalism proper (e.g. the Constructivists) and to anyone who, like the founders of ABSTRACT ART, seemed self-evidently open to it. As this more easily intelligible sense gained currency, the Communist movement everywhere came to reject all development of new aesthetic forms, which were thenceforward written off as typical aberrations of late CAPITALIST society.

Most European music since Debussy and painting since the IMPRESSIONISTS were consequently rejected by the Soviet canon until the 1950s THAW, with abstract art and twelve-note music (see SERIAL MUSIC) as *bêtes noires*. Those criticized, sometimes with crushing effects, for formalism or the related offence of COSMO-POLITANISM included Shostakovitch, Eisenstein, Lissitzky, Brecht, Picasso, and Léger; Meyerhold, the founder of BIOMECHANICS, was arrested in 1939 and later shot. (Except in the early 1950s, the non-Soviet parties were much less severe.) After the Thaw there was a considerable relaxation in practice, but in principle the ban on formalism still applies throughout the Communist world. J.W.

Bibl: V. Erlich, *Russian Formalism* (The Hague, 1955).

(3) In music, the use of traditional forms such as the pavane, passacaglia, or gavotte to give formal structure to ATONAL MUSIC, as in Berg's opera *Wozzeck*. A.H.

Forrester, Jay Wright (U.S. electrical engineer and management expert, *b*.1918), see under SYSTEMS.

Forster, Edward Morgan (British novelist and essayist, 1879–1970), see under BLOOMSBURY GROUP; CRITERION, THE; FLAT CHARACTERS AND ROUND CHARACTERS; FORSTERIAN; OUTSIDER; PUBLIC SCHOOL.

Forsterian. A word desiderated in 1910 by a reviewer of *Howards End*, and subsequently adopted, to characterize the outlook (broadly speaking, LIBERAL, HUMANIST) and manner (relaxed, informal, often ironic, occasionally whimsical) of the novelist E. M. Forster (1879–1970). O.S.

Fort Knox. A U.S. Army reservation in Kentucky, since 1936 the gold bullion depository. Until the reversal in the late 1950s of the American TERMS OF TRADE, and consequently of bullion flow, Fort Knox was proverbially synonymous with the strength of the U.S. dollar as an international currency. D.C.W.

Fortes, Meyer (British anthropologist, *b*.1906), see under ACCULTURATION.

Fortran. The earliest HIGH-LEVEL PROGRAMMING LANGUAGE to achieve general acceptance, and still by far the most widely used for scientific applications. It is now technically obsolescent (at least) and survives by virtue of the intellectual capital invested in existing PROGRAMS and continued support from COMPUTER manufacturers. C.S.

Fortress America. A concept held by sections of American ISOLATIONIST opinion before the American involvement in World War II and during the years of the COLD WAR. It was based on the view that America should abstain from intervention in international politics outside the western hemisphere and should rely on the physical isolation of the American continents and a high level of armaments to deter (see DETERRENCE) or repel attacks on her from the world outside.   D.C.W.

Fortress Europe (*Festung Europa*). A NAZI propaganda symbol for enforced European unity and strength against the invasion of continental Europe by Anglo-American forces in 1943–4.   D.C.W.

Foujita, Tsugouharu Léonard (Japanese painter, *b.* 1886), see under ÉCOLE DE PARIS.

four-colour conjecture. This states that if a plane be divided into regions (countries) then it is possible to colour them with at most four colours so that no two countries with a common frontier have the same colour. A fallacious proof (by A. B. Kempe in 1879) was accepted as correct for a decade. Despite intensive research and the development of special techniques (see GRAPH) no counter-example has yet been discovered; and in July 1976 two mathematicians at Urbana, Illinois, claimed to have proved the conjecture by breaking it down into many thousands of cases and using a COMPUTER to check each one. The proof is nearly 1,000 pages long.   R.G.
    Bibl: W. W. Rouse Ball, rev. H. S. M. Coxeter, *Mathematical Recreations and Essays* (London, 11th ed., 1939).

Four Freedoms. These are 'freedom of speech and expression'; 'freedom of every person to worship God in his own way'; 'freedom from want ... [ensured by] economic understandings which will secure to every nation a healthy peacetime life for its inhabitants'; and 'freedom from fear ... [ensured by] a worldwide reduction of armaments to such a point and in such a thorough fashion that no nation will be in a position to commit an act of physical aggression against any neighbour'. They were proclaimed by President Franklin Delano Roosevelt in a speech to the U.S. Congress on 6 January 1941.   D.C.W.
    Bibl: F. R. Donovan, *Mr Roosevelt's Four Freedoms* (N.Y., 1966).

Fourier, Charles (French social theorist, 1772–1837), see under COMMUNE; COOPERATIVES; SOCIALISM; UTOPIAN IDEAL.

Fourier analysis, series. Let f be a PERIODIC FUNCTION of time t with period T. Rather weak conditions on f ensure that, for all times t, f can be expressed by its *Fourier series:*

$$f(t) = a_0 + \sum_{n=1}^{\infty} (a_n \cos(2\pi nt/T) + b_n \sin(2\pi nt/T)).$$

Thus f can be analysed as the sum of (a constant term and) a series of simple harmonic FUNCTIONS having periods $T, T/2, T/3, \ldots$ The first of these functions ($a_1 \cos(2\pi t/T) + b_1 \sin(2\pi t/T)$) is known as the *fundamental*, the subsequent ones as the *harmonics* or *overtones*. Even discontinuous functions (e.g. the 'square waves' and 'sawtooth waves' which occur in television circuitry) can be analysed in this way, and the series can then be used to calculate the effect of applying f as an INPUT to some mechanical or electronic device. If the series is replaced by an integral (see INTEGRATION), non-periodic functions can also be analysed into simple harmonic components; these constitute the *spectrum* of the function. This mathematical analysis corresponds to the physical action of a spectroscope (see SPECTROSCOPY), since an absolutely pure colour represents a single simple harmonic ELECTRO-MAGNETIC oscillation. Since the time of J. Fourier (1768–1830) many other ways of analysing a function into simpler component functions have been considered; the general theory is part of functional ANALYSIS.   R.G.
    Bibl: M. L. Boas, *Mathematical Models in the Physical Sciences* (London and N.Y., 1966).

Fourteen Points. These were contained in an address by President Woodrow Wilson to the U.S. Congress on 8 January 1918. Despite objections from Britain and France, who had not been consulted, they became the basis of the Armistice with Germany of 11 November 1918, as a result of the Germans invoking them as the basis for an armistice in a note to President Wilson of 4 October 1918. They included: (1) 'Open covenants of peace openly arrived at' instead of secret diplomacy; (2) 'absolute freedom of navigation upon the seas . . . alike in peace and war'; (3) the removal of all trade barriers; (4) general disarmament; (5) impartial settlement of all colonial claims; (6, 7, 8) evacuation and restoration of territory in Russia, Belgium, and France (including the return of Alsace-Lorraine); (9) readjustment of Italian frontiers; (10, 12) self-determination for peoples of the Habsburg and Ottoman empires; (11) restoration of territory of Romania, Montenegro, and Serbia; (13) creation of an independent Poland with access to the Baltic; (14) establishment of a LEAGUE OF NATIONS.   D.C.W.

fourth dimension. When locating an event, it is not sufficient to specify its position in ordinary three-dimensional space. The *time* at which the event occurred must also be known, and the term 'fourth dimension' emphasizes this property of time. See also SPACE-TIME.   M.V.B.

Fourth World, see under THIRD WORLD.

Fowler, Alastair (British literary critic, *b*. 1930), see under NUMEROLOGICAL CRITICISM.

Fox, George (English preacher and missionary, 1624–91), see under QUAKERS.

fractionation. The separation of chemical substances by a repetitive process. For example, boiling gives a vapour enriched in the more volatile constituent, and successive condensations and reboiling in a specially designed column can effect complete separation. Fractional distillation is widely used in laboratories and industry to separate volatile liquids, and fractional crystallization to separate compounds in solution.   B.F.

frame, see under STRUCTURE.

frame of reference. The context, viewpoint, or set of PRESUPPOSITIONS or of evaluative CRITERIA within which a person's PERCEPION and thinking seem always to occur, and which constrains selectively the course and outcome of these activities.   I.M.L.H.

France, Anatole (French author, 1844–1924), see under DREYFUS CASE.

Franciscans, see under BEAT.

Franco, Francisco (Spanish general and statesman, 1892–1975), see under FALANGE; FASCISM; POPULAR FRONT.

Franju, Georges (French film director, *b*.1912), see under CINÉMATHÈQUE.

Frank, Philipp (Austrian-U.S. physicist, 1884–1966), see under VIENNA CIRCLE.

Frankfurt School. The persons and ideas associated with the Institute for Social Research, founded and affiliated to the University of Frankfurt in 1923 under the direction of Carl Grünberg. Exiled to New York during the era of NAZISM, the Institute returned home in 1949. Leading figures have included Max Horkheimer (Director, 1931–58), Walter Benjamin, Theodor Adorno, and Herbert Marcuse. The school agreed on the necessity of providing a *critical theory* of MARXISM. This opposed all forms of POSITIVISM (especially those stressing the possibility of VALUE-FREEDOM in SOCIAL SCIENCE) and all interpretations of Marxism afflicted, like Stalin's, with crude MATERIALISM and immutable DOGMA. In the school's view, only an open-ended and continuously self-critical approach could avoid paralysis in the theory, and therefore also in the practice, of social transformation. Reinvigoration depended on greater appreciation of Marx's early writings, which became generally available only in the 1930s; they encouraged study particularly of Marxism's debt to certain features of Hegel, whose IDEALIST concern with consciousness as moulder of the world had been undervalued by the economic determinism of later orthodoxy (see HISTORICAL MATERIALISM). Consequently the school devoted more attention to areas that had been regarded as merely SUPERSTRUCTURAL and, especially through its treatment of the AESTHETICS of a MASS SOCIETY, sought to rescue Marxist cultural criticism from sterility. The school's leading contemporary figure, Jürgen Habermas, is notable particularly

FREE ASSOCIATION

for his efforts to relate the conditions of rationality to the SOCIAL STRUCTURE of language use.

Though its writings have been more invoked than read, the Frankfurt School has made an important contribution to rehabilitating the LIBERTARIAN aspect of Marx's thought. It has influenced such radical (see RADICALISM) movements as the NEW LEFT, which have been attracted by its rejection of modern technocratic society (see TECHNOCRACY) whether CAPITALIST or Soviet, and by its conviction that some satisfactory clear alternative can emerge only during the actual practice of REVOLUTION. For many opponents this latter point exemplifies most clearly an evasiveness which is deemed to reflect certain irrational inconsistencies in the school's whole approach to the CRITERIA of TRUTH.   M.D.B.

Bibl: M. Jay, *The Dialectical Imagination* (London and Boston, 1973).

free association.

(1) In PSYCHOTHERAPY, a technique which requires the patient to say at once, and to go on saying at once, whatever comes to mind. The chief idea behind free association is that, by using it in the benign and supportive situation of psychotherapy, the patient will be able slowly to approach and face the ANXIETY-producing UNCONSCIOUS material that he cannot face at the beginning, and which is at the centre of his personal difficulties.   B.A.F.

(2) In literature, a comparable process whereby one word or image derives spontaneously from another by association of ideas or sounds. The dangers of the method are suggested by L. A. G. Strong, who wrote of James Joyce's *Finnegans Wake*: 'The two processes, from association to object, from object to association, seldom harmonize, and often create serious confusion.' In art, spontaneity is no guarantee of profundity or even of interesting sense, and T. S. Eliot's remark on FREE VERSE could be adapted to read: 'No association is free for the man who wants to do a good job.'   D.J.E.

free economy, see MARKET ECONOMY.

free energy. A THERMODYNAMIC property which represents the maximum amount of work obtainable from a mechanical or chemical process. The *Helmholtz free energy* and the *Gibbs free energy* differ only in that the latter includes work done against surrounding atmosphere. The free energy is related to the internal ENERGY or heat content and the ENTROPY of the substance. Each chemical substance under particular conditions has an associated free energy, but when CHEMICAL REACTIONS occur spontaneously there is always a decrease in total free energy. For a chemical reaction in EQUILIBRIUM the driving forces associated with the changes in heat content and entropy are balanced and no change in free energy is possible.   B.F.

free enterprise, see MARKET ECONOMY.

free form, see under MORPHEME.

free radical. An uncharged RADICAL of abnormal VALENCE, which can have an independent existence. The first free radical (triphenylmethane), discovered in 1900, has trivalent instead of the usual tetravalent carbon. Since then numerous free radicals have been studied, including ATOMS of hydrogen and chlorine. Although they usually have only a transient existence free radicals play an important role in propagating CHEMICAL REACTIONS.   B.F.

free schools, see under FREE UNIVERSITY.

free trade. The absence of governmental interference in international trade. In practice, there has nearly always and everywhere been *some* interference, ranging from the banning of particular imports or exports, through quantitative restrictions, taxes on imports (i.e. *tariffs*) or exports, to health regulations. Taxes or other measures which do not discriminate against international trade as such are not usually held to infringe the freedom of trade. *Protection* results from the absence of free trade, but in ways which are often subtle and unforeseen. Restricting imports of cloth obviously helps the domestic textile industry (*positive protection*), but it harms the domestic clothing industry (*negative protection*). Economists have argued that the national objectives achieved by protection are better achieved by other means; alternatively, where protection is efficient for a nation,

244

as in improving its TERMS OF TRADE, that it only benefits that nation at the expense of others. See also GATT. M.FG.S.

Bibl: S. J. Wells, *International Economics* (London, rev. ed., 1973), chs. 5–8.

free trade area, see under CUSTOMS UNION.

free university. The CONCEPT of a university that has no entry requirements or formal curricula, and exists as part of the ALTERNATIVE SOCIETY. For reasons of preference and expense the ARTS and SOCIAL SCIENCES, not the NATURAL SCIENCES, are studied. In such examples as exist in London and San Francisco there is a primary concern with diagnosis and promotion of revolutionary change, with cooperation rather than competition, and with opposition to the MILITARY/INDUSTRIAL COMPLEX, technological/capitalist society (see CAPITALISM; TECHNOLOGY), and ÉLITIST/intellectualized education. The *free schools* at Summerhill (A. S. Neill) and in Liverpool each consist of a self-regulating community without formal timetables or curricula and share many of the assumptions of the free university. W.A.C.S.

Bibl: C. and M. Ball, *Education for a Change* (Harmondsworth, 1973); M. B. Miles (ed.), *Innovation in Education* (N.Y., 1971).

free variation. In LINGUISTICS, the relationship between linguistic units having the same DISTRIBUTION which are different in FORM (sense 3) but not thereby different in meaning, i.e. the units do not contrast. The concept is most widely used in PHONOLOGY, referring to variant pronunciations of a word; but it may be used in GRAMMAR, and also in SEMANTICS (where it is called *synonymy*). D.C.

free verse (or *vers libre*). Verse that lacks regular metre, rhyme, and other formal devices, relying in its search for 'organic form' on rhythms natural to speech which should also be 'natural' to the theme and feeling of the poem. Though by no means a modern invention, free verse became prominent with the advent of MODERNISM, and constituted a revolt against the set forms of 19th-century poetry. The easiest verse to write badly, free verse is possibly the most difficult to write well, since no external shaping aids are available. As T. S. Eliot remarked, 'no verse is free for the man who wants to do a good job' ('Reflections on *Vers Libre*', 1917). D.J.E.

Frege, Gottlob (German logician and mathematician, 1848–1925), see under ANALYTIC; AXIOMATICS; CONNOTATION AND DENOTATION; GÖDEL'S THEOREM; LOGIC; LOGICISM; MATHEMATICAL LOGIC; SET THEORY.

Freie Bühne. A play-producing organization founded in Berlin by Otto Brahm in 1889 to pioneer the new naturalistic drama (see NATURALISM). It had no permanent ensemble or theatre and played only at Sunday matinées. But it gave high-quality private performances of work banned by the German censors, including Ibsen's *Ghosts*, Zola's *Thérèse Raquin,* and Hauptmann's *Die Weber.* And although in 1894 it was affiliated to the more established DEUTSCHES THEATER it was largely responsible for introducing many key modern works into the regular German repertoire. M.BI.

Bibl: J. M. Ritchie (ed.), *Periods in German Literature* (London, 1966; Chester Springs, Pa., 1967).

Freire, Paulo (Brazilian educationist, *b.* 1921), see under DE-SCHOOLING.

French Community; French Union. The *French Union* set up in 1946 united the French Republic with its overseas territories in a union whose citizens were all citizens of France and had representation in the French National Assembly. The defection in 1954 of the various states of Indo-China, Tunisia, and Morocco and the loss of Algeria led President de Gaulle, as part of the process of substituting a Fifth Republic for the Fourth, to set up on 5 October 1958 a *French Community,* membership of which was based on self-determination by the inhabitants of the states concerned on a basis of universal suffrage. Membership of the Community was extended to the former French African colonies together with the Malagasy Republic (Guinea chose independence). It united them in a free-franc zone, largely dependent on France for trade (75% of both imports and exports), investment

FREQUENCY

(over one thousand million dollars' worth, two-thirds from official sources), enterprise, and military aid. All the members were associated with the EEC under the Yaoundé Convention of 1962.   D.C.W.

frequency, see under STATISTICAL REGULARITY.

frequency modulation (FM). A technique in radio transmission whereby AUDIO FREQUENCY signals are made to vary or modulate (see MODULATION) the frequency of a carrier wave of RADIO FREQUENCY. Broadcasts on the radio v.h.f. band employ frequency modulation, which ensures almost total freedom from interference and distortion, at the price of using a greater frequency range for each transmission.   M.V.B.

frequency theory. A system whereby the probability (see PROBABILITY THEORY) of a single event is assigned a numerical value, between 0 and 1, according to the inductively established (see INDUCTION) proportion of situations like that of the event in question in which events of that kind occur. Thus the probability that John will survive until he is 70 will be ½ if 50% of men like John have been found to do so. A problem arises about specifying the relevant situation (or *reference class*): should John be regarded as a man, as an Englishman, as an English postman, as a cigarette-smoking English postman, or what? Usually the STATISTICS will differ as between such alternatives. If all John's characteristics are taken into consideration he may turn out to be the sole instance of the class or SET, so that no statistics are available at all. The requirements of a closely fitting reference class and of copious and thus more reliable statistical evidence pull in opposite directions, and judgement has to be used in reconciling them, a judgement that can be assisted by the theory of statistical significance. It is generally held that not all probability is frequency, although the identification of the two has been attempted. The crucial point is that the statements of the statistical evidence from which frequency-judgements are derived are *inductive* and thus only *confirmed* (see CONFIRMATION) as probable, and not certified, by the grounds on which they rest.   A.Q.

Bibl: A. Pap, *An Introduction to the Philosophy of Science* (N.Y., 1962; London, 1963).

Freud, Sigmund (Austrian founder of psychoanalysis, 1856–1939), see under ADLERIAN; AMBIGUITY; BEHAVIOUR THERAPY; BIRTH TRAUMA; CATHARSIS; DYNAMIC PSYCHOLOGY; FREUDIAN; IRRATIONALISM; NEO-FREUDIAN; NEUROSIS; PENIS ENVY; PSYCHIATRY; PSYCHOANALYSIS; PSYCHOSEXUAL DEVELOPMENT; RELIGION, PSYCHOLOGY OF; SUPEREGO; TRAUMA; WELTANSCHAUUNG; WISH-FULFILMENT.

Freudian. In strict usage, an adjective referring to a tradition or school of psychoanalytic thought and practice, namely the one connected with the work of Sigmund Freud (1856–1939); the word can also be used as a substantive, meaning a member of this school. More loosely, the adjective refers to any view popularly associated with the name of Freud, especially any view that picks on the sexual origins and character of thought, motives, feelings, or conduct.

Freudian PSYCHOANALYSIS has three aspects: it is a general theory of PSYCHOLOGY, a therapy, and a method of enquiry or research. The psychology looks on the mind of the adult individual as a system of elements, each carrying a charge of energy. Any one element (e.g. Smith's love for his father) may be capable of entering CONSCIOUSNESS; but, where entry into consciousness is liable to raise the excitation of the system beyond the limits of what it can tolerate (as might happen with the element of Smith's hatred of his father), energy is redistributed in such a way that the threatening element cannot enter consciousness and remains UNCONSCIOUS. The energy of the system takes two fundamental forms. In the early version of the theory, the energy was either sexual or self-preservative in character (see LIFE INSTINCT); in the later version it took either a loving or an aggressive and destructive form (see DEATH INSTINCT).

An overriding aim, therefore, of the system is to preserve its psychic equilibrium in the face of the energy distribution, and of threats generated from within and from without. It achieves this aim, in general, by taking defensive action (see DEFENCE MECHANISM) of one sort or another; e.g.

RATIONALIZATION, SUBLIMATION, PRO-
JECTION, REGRESSION. To enable it to do
this, the mental system of the infant and
child develops an internal structure: the ID
(the source of energy supply), the EGO
(the part of the system that enables it to
face reality), and the SUPEREGO (the part
that embodies the self-controls of conscience). The child also goes through certain
stages in its development to maturity, e.g.
the Oedipal period (see OEDIPUS COM-
PLEX). If this development has been
unsatisfactory (such that energy remains
tied up, or bound, at some early stage or
STAGES OF DEVELOPMENT), then the
adult person will be disposed to exhibit
pathological conduct (see ABNORMAL
PSYCHOLOGY) and to experience difficulties of related sorts. When the defences
which were erected early in life to keep the
dangerous elements at bay break down,
then neurotic conflict ensues, and his
pathology becomes manifest (see
NEUROSIS; PSYCHOSIS).

As a therapy, Freudian psychoanalysis
is based on the rule of FREE ASSOCIATION
for the patient, and on rules for the analyst
that make him play the role of an
anonymous figure who cannot be faulted
by the patient. One important consequence of these rules is to produce a
special relationship between patient
and analyst, which encourages the rapid
growth of a subtle emotional involvement
with the analyst known as TRANSFER-
ENCE. Freudian analysis relies heavily on
this emotional involvement.

It was the use of Freudian analysis, in
particular, that has led many analysts,
psychiatrists, and others to speak of
'Freud's great discoveries'. But to speak
like this presupposes that Freudian
psychoanalysis is a valid method of
enquiry or research: one which, consequently, uncovers the truth about human
nature. This PRESUPPOSITION is so beset
by difficulties that it is hardly acceptable.

(1) It can be argued that Freudian
practice not merely 'uncovers the facts',
but helps to manufacture them, and in
ways that go to confirm the Freudian
theory used in the practice. In short, it
is to some degree a self-confirmatory procedure.

(2) When we try to pinpoint Freud's
great discoveries, it is difficult to do so in a
way that is generally acceptable, even to
analysts in the Freudian tradition.

(3) When we do look at some likely
candidate, e.g. the Freudian generalization about the stages of libidinal development (see PSYCHOSEXUAL DEVELOP-
MENT), it is far from clear what we would
have to do to falsify it. (For the principle of
falsifiability see POPPERIAN.) For LIBIDO
is a theoretical notion, whose observable
manifestations are not clear.

(4) When we examine the general
psychology that Freudian analysis has
erected upon the material produced by the
practice, it is evident that it does not
embody a 'scientific' theory, in the dominant current sense of this adjective. Its logical relations to science are uncertain, and
its whole status controversial.

Unlike Darwin, therefore, Freud's
theoretical contribution has not yet been
incorporated into science. Nevertheless,
his work has revolutionized the popular
view of human nature in the West (rather
as Marx has changed our view of society);
and it has penetrated into almost every
nook and cranny of our CULTURE. It is this
fact, perhaps, that has led many people to
rank Freud as a figure of towering genius.
Whether, however, he really turns out to
be a Darwin of the human mind, or only
someone who, like a Ptolemy or a
Mesmer, has led us up an interesting and
important dead end, is a matter which the
future of science will have to decide.

For a modification of Freudian theory
see NEO-FREUDIAN. B.A.F.

Bibl: S. Freud, tr. W. J. H. Sprott, *New
Introductory Lectures on Psychoanalysis*
(London and N.Y., 1933).

Freudian slip. In psychoanalytic theory
(see FREUDIAN; PSYCHOANALYSIS), a
momentary and transient breakdown in
the defensive position of the person, as a
result of which he gives unintended
expression in speech to repressed (see RE-
PRESSION) thoughts and feelings. W.Z.

Freyssinet, Eugène (French engineer,
1879–1962), see under CONCRETE.

Fried, Erich (Austrian writer, *b*.1921),
see under GRUPPE 47.

Friedman, Milton (U.S. economist,
b.1912), see under RIGHT, THE.

Friedman, Yona (French architect,
b.1923), see under MEGASTRUCTURE.

FRIESZ

Friesz, Othon (French painter, 1874–1949), see under FAUVES.

Fringe, the. British term (the U.S. equivalent being OFF-BROADWAY) for activities, almost exclusively theatrical – notably of SURREALIST, unconventional, unorthodox, anti-ESTABLISHMENT, obscene, AVANT-GARDE, or pseudo-*avant-garde* type – that take place away from the main popular centres of entertainment. First used in the late 1950s of events that took place on the periphery of the Edinburgh Festival, it now embraces the highly conventionalized products of the mediocre and ageing, as well as the genuinely zestful activities of students and other young artists.   M.S.-S.

fringe benefits. The elements of an employee's remuneration provided at the employer's expense under the contract of employment, other than the rate of pay per unit of time or output. They commonly comprise such items as holidays with pay, pension plans, life insurance, stock purchase plans, and payment for absence during family emergencies. They are to be distinguished from *ex gratia* payments, and from the provision of general amenities such as canteens and sports grounds. In the U.K. they are usually taken to exclude employers' statutory contributions to national insurance on the employee's behalf, but in the U.S.A., where state schemes have been relatively restricted, trade union members have obtained or supplemented many forms of social insurance by negotiation with employers, and such statutory payments as the employers also make are commonly included with fringe benefits. The extent of fringe benefits has increased as the rise in employees' real incomes has made the benefits concerned more attractive relatively to a further increase in the pay packet; though some are taxable, fringe benefits have been used to ease the pressure on executives of high marginal rates of taxation.   E.H.P.B.

Bibl: J. Backman, *Wage Determination* (Princeton, 1959); G. L. Reid and D. J. Robertson (eds.), *Fringe Benefits, Labour Costs and Social Security* (London, 1965).

Frisch, Ragnar (Norwegian economist, 1895–1973), see under ECONOMETRICS.

Froebel, Friedrich Wilhelm August (German educationist, 1782–1852), see under CHILD-CENTRED EDUCATION; FROEBEL METHOD; PROGRESSIVE.

Froebel method. An educational method associated with Friedrich Froebel (1782–1852), who sought to adapt the CHILD-CENTRED principles of Rousseau and Pestalozzi (see PESTALOZZI METHOD) to infant education in Germany. He founded the *Kindergarten* where children could grow through play, using nature work, games, toys, handicraft, music, stories, drawing, and geometrical shapes (cubes, spheres) which he called 'gifts' – the kind of approach now common in most infant schools. Froebel had an obvious influence on Montessori (see MONTESSORI METHOD), Cizek, and the whole nursery and infant school movement (see PRE-SCHOOL EDUCATION).   W.A.C.S.

Bibl: F. Froebel, ed. I. M. Lilley, *Friedrich Froebel* (London, 1967).

Fromm, Erich (German-U.S. psychoanalyst and social philosopher, *b*.1900), see under NEO-FREUDIAN; NEO-MARXISM.

front. In METEOROLOGY, a sharp boundary zone in the atmosphere between air masses of different temperatures and humidities. A *warm front* is a warmer air mass impinging on a colder one, and is characterized by a wide cloud band and rain extending well in advance of the surface position of the front. A *cold front* is colder air advancing on warmer, with associated rain showers and thunderstorms usually developing along the line of the advancing front. See also OCCLUSION.   P.H.

front organization. An organization that serves as cover for aims and activities other than its professed ones; in particular, an ostensibly non-COMMUNIST organization with liberal, religious, or other public men of goodwill as the leading figures, but in fact controlled by the Communists. Front organizations in the latter sense were devised in the 1930s by the COMINTERN'S propaganda genius, Willi Münzenberg, with aims such as supporting the Spanish Republic, justifying the MOSCOW TRIALS, and (in England in 1940) advocating peace with Germany. A more recent example is the *World Peace Council*.   R.C.

frontier. The boundary line or zone delimiting two contiguous but different countries or cultural domains. The specialists have long debated whether the frontier is a line or a zone of transition. In American usage the latter meaning predominates; the historian Frederick Jackson Turner stressed the role of the westward march of the frontier in American history, but recognized that, in the sense of the zone of transition to another civilization, the American frontier shifted after 1910 to the large cities. Metaphorical usages in which frontier means 'new opportunities' include President John F. Kennedy's characterization, in 1960–63, of his political programmes as 'the new frontier', and such phrases as 'the frontiers of science'. J.G.
Bibl: J. R. V. Prescott, *The Geography of Frontiers and Boundaries* (London and Chicago, 1965); O. Lattimore, *Studies in Frontier History* (London and N.Y., 1962).

Frost, Robert (U.S. poet, 1874–1963), see under EGOIST, THE; POETRY BOOKSHOP.

Fry, Roger Eliot (British painter and critic, 1886–1934), see under BLOOMSBURY GROUP; OMEGA WORKSHOPS; POST-IMPRESSIONISM.

Frye, Northrop (Canadian-born literary critic, *b*. 1912), see under NEW CRITICISM.

FSP (functional-sentence perspective), see under PRAGUE SCHOOL.

fuel cell. A chemical CELL in which two fuel substances (such as hydrogen and oxygen) react to produce electrical ENERGY *directly*. The process is the exact opposite to the decomposition of water by ELECTROLYSIS, for hydrogen is fed to cover one platinum ELECTRODE whilst oxygen is fed to the other. No gas escapes, water is continually produced, and an electric current can be driven through an external circuit connected to the electrodes. Invented by Grove in 1840, the fuel cell received little attention until recently; today much research is being stimulated by the possible advantages of cells which may compete with other sources of energy without polluting the atmosphere (see POLLUTION). E.R.L.

fuel element. That part of a NUCLEAR REACTOR core which contains fissionable material (see FISSION). E.R.L.

Führerprinzip. NAZI German term for the principle of leadership, i.e. the establishment of a national leader and the devolution of sovereign authority and power, by decision of the leader, to a recognized hierarchy of subordinates; the entrustment of governmental powers to such leadership rather than to decision by majority in parliament. Hitler's definition was 'unrestricted authority downwards, unrestricted responsibility upwards'. D.C.W.

full employment. Employment of a country's available MANPOWER to the fullest extent likely to be sustainable. Since it is not possible to manage the economy so that there is an exact match between job opportunities and the number of those who want jobs, full employment is consistent with some residual UNEMPLOYMENT. Published figures of unemployment are not, however, a completely reliable indicator of the margin of available manpower. They usually exclude housewives and others who would be willing to take paid employment but do not register for it. The figures may change their significance over time, e.g. because of new regulations as to unemployment benefits. There is also room for debate as to the precise level of employment that can be sustained, since the more closely full employment is approached the harder it becomes to reconcile it with other economic objectives such as the avoidance of INFLATION and a deficit in the BALANCE OF PAYMENTS. A.C.

full employment surplus. An increase in the level of economic activity adds to governmental revenues as incomes expand. It may also curtail some governmental expenditure (e.g. on unemployment benefits). These variations may cause the surplus or deficit in the budget to diverge from what was intended and forecast. The budget outcome as it would be under conditions of FULL EMPLOYMENT but with no changes in government policy (rates of taxation and provision for public expenditure) is known as the *full employment surplus* and affords a measure of any *deliberate* shift in FISCAL POLICY towards expansion or contraction of purchasing power. A.C.

Bibl: A. M. Okun and N. H. Teeters, 'The Full Employment Surplus Revisited' (*Brookings Papers on Economic Activity* 1, 1970).

full recovery cost, see under MARGINAL COSTING.

Fuller, Richard Buckminster (U.S. architect and engineer, *b*.1895), see under DYMAXION.

Fuller, Roy (British poet and critic, *b*.1912), see under SYLLABICS.

function. A fundamental CONCEPT of MATHEMATICS used whenever some quantity (the *value*) is regarded as depending on, or determined by, other quantities (the ARGUMENT(S); see also VARIABLE). A function *f* of one argument has a specified SET, say *X* (e.g. instants of time), as its *domain* and a set, say *Y* (e.g. positions in space), as its *codomain*. It assigns to each argument *x* in *X* a unique value *y* in *Y*; this is expressed by writing $y = f(x)$. Before the 19th century it was assumed that the assignment was made according to some definite mathematical or natural law (e.g. $y = x^2$). But in contemporary mathematics no such assumption is made; the assignment may be arbitrary or random. Sometimes, especially in the older literature, the term is restricted to functions whose arguments and values are real NUMBERS. The GRAPH of such a function *f* is obtained by plotting points in the plane whose COORDINATES are $(x, f(x))$. Two functions *f* and *g* may be combined by *composition* to give a new function *f.g* which is defined by $f.g(x) = f(g(x))$. All the above considerations can be extended to functions of more than one argument.

Functions in ALGEBRA and TOPOLOGY are often called *maps* or *mappings*. Functions whose arguments are themselves functions are called *functionals* or *operators*. See also ANALYSIS; COMPLEX FUNCTION THEORY. R.G.

Bibl: see under ORDERING RELATIONS.

function theory, see COMPLEX FUNCTION THEORY.

function word, see under WORD CLASS.

functional analysis, see under ANALYSIS.

functional explanation, see under EXPLANATION.

functional fixedness, see under PROBLEM-SOLVING.

functional-sentence perspective, see under PRAGUE SCHOOL.

functionalism.

(1) In ANTHROPOLOGY, a group of theories associated above all with the names of B. Malinowski (1884–1942) and A. R. Radcliffe-Brown (1881–1955), although they are perhaps more appropriately, if less agreeably, described as structural-functionalist. In one version, great store is set by the putative human needs, both biological and social, that every society must satisfy. In another (see STRUCTURAL-FUNCTIONAL THEORY), a CULTURE or society is seen as an entity all the parts of which function to maintain one another and the totality, the disruption of one part provoking readjustment among others. Many anthropologists still describe themselves as functionalists in some sense, but none would accept the common criticism that his functionalism precludes an interest in social change and the study of SYSTEMS over time. See also EVOLUTION, SOCIAL AND CULTURAL; STRUCTURALISM. M.F.

Bibl: S. F. Nadel, *The Foundations of Social Anthropology* (London and Glencoe, Ill., 1951); R. A. Manners and D. Kaplan (eds.), *Theory in Anthropology* (Chicago, 1968; London, 1969).

(2) In PSYCHOLOGY, a point of view (one of the six main SCHOOLS OF PSYCHOLOGY as classified by R. S. Woodworth) that sees mental phenomena as activities rather than as states or STRUCTURES. It assumes that function produces structure (as in ANATOMY, where the shape of an organ system reflects the demands of its function), and attempts to explain the nature of phenomena completely in terms of the uses they fulfil. In American psychology, the notion that no response occurs without implicit or explicit *reinforcement* (see OPERANT CONDITIONING) exemplifies a kind of utilitarian functionalism. Efforts to understand PERCEPTION in terms of function performed, as in E. Brunswik's

'probabilistic functionalism' where perception is given a predictive role, are still current. See also PERCEPTUAL CONSTANCY. J.S.B.

Bibl: R. S. Woodworth, *Contemporary Schools of Psychology* (N.Y., 3rd ed., 1964; London, 9th ed., 1965).

(3) In architecture, the theory embodied in Louis Sullivan's dictum 'form follows function', that the form of a building can be derived from a full knowledge of the purposes it is to serve. It derives from such 19th-century architectural writers as Viollet-le-Duc demanding the expression of each of the elements of a building and especially its structure. The theory had a further extension in the 1920s and 1930s: that the form which most closely follows function, as apparent in ships or aeroplanes, is also the most beautiful. See also INTERNATIONAL STYLE; MACHINE AESTHETIC; NEUE SACHLICHKEIT. M.BR.

fundamental particle, see ELEMENTARY PARTICLE.

fundamentalism. Belief that the Bible possesses complete INFALLIBILITY because every word in it is the Word of God. The term is derived from a series of tracts, *The Fundamentals*, published in the U.S.A. in 1909. Other doctrines defended (on the basis of this literal acceptance of passages in the Bible) include the interpretation of the death of Jesus as a 'substitutionary' sacrifice to the just wrath of God on mankind's sins; the virgin birth, physical resurrection, and 'Second Coming' of Jesus; and eternal punishment in hell. Fundamentalism is strongest among some American PROTESTANTS, and is usually accompanied by the condemnation both of the Roman CATHOLIC Church and of modern thought. D.L.E.

Bibl: J. I. Packer, *'Fundamentalism' and the Word of God* (London, 1958).

funds-flow. The movement of financial resources in an enterprise that must be planned and controlled for effective MANAGEMENT. Short-term changes in working CAPITAL are often called *cash-flow*. The net change in funds-flow through time measures the financial growth or decline of the enterprise. R.I.T.

further education, see under TERTIARY EDUCATION.

fusion. The production of an atomic NUCLEUS by the union of two lighter nuclei in a NUCLEAR REACTION. Being positively charged, the two original nuclei repel one another, and considerable KINETIC ENERGY (i.e. a high operating temperature) is necessary to get the reaction to proceed. But the amount of ENERGY released can be much greater, because the resulting nucleus is often less massive than its constituents (see MASS-ENERGY EQUATION), and a CHAIN REACTION may occur. The power of the hydrogen bomb, and the warmth and light of sunshine, are derived from fusion. M.V.B.

fusional (in LINGUISTICS), see under INFLECTING.

future shock. A phrase coined, on the analogy of CULTURE SHOCK, by Alvin Toffler to describe 'a new and profoundly upsetting psychological disease' caused in Western POST-INDUSTRIAL SOCIETY by 'a rising rate of change that makes reality seem, sometimes, like a kaleidoscope run wild . . . Change is avalanching upon our heads and most people are grotesquely unprepared to cope with it.' O.S.

Bibl: A. Toffler, *Future Shock* (London and N.Y., 1970).

Futurism. Italian movement in the arts, originating as a purely literary doctrine with F. T. Marinetti's 'Futurist Manifesto' in *Le Figaro*, Paris, 20 February 1909; subsequently extended to the other arts, then after 1922 partly assimilated in the official IDEOLOGY of FASCISM, to peter out in the mid-1930s. Its principles, asserted in a loud succession of manifestos, were dynamism, the cult of speed and the machine, rejection of the past, and the glorification of patriotism and war. Techniques put forward and practised to these ends included (1) in literature, FREE VERSE, phonetic poetry, and a telegraphic language without adjectives or adverbs or much syntax ('words in liberty'); (2) in the visual arts, NEO-IMPRESSIONISM, pictorial dynamism ('lines of force'), simultaneity, and the interpenetration of planes; (3) in music, a BRUITISME evolved by Francesco Pratella and Luigi Russolo, and based on the noises of the modern industrialized world; instruments were also to be made which would divide the octave into 50 equal MICROTONES.

These largely new methods were demonstrated and tested by, e.g., the painter-sculptor Umberto Boccioni, the painter Ardengo Soffici, and the architect Antonio Sant'Elia (notably in his 1914 series of architectural drawings, *Città Nuova*), while the movement's shows and lecture-demonstrations from 1912 to 1914 had some influence in France (on Apollinaire, Léger, and Delaunay), England (VORTICISM), and the U.S.A., making a real contribution in Russia (RAYONISM, Ego-Futurism, and CUBO-FUTURISM) and affecting German EXPRESSIONISM via *Der* STURM. Its impact on DADA from 1916 on was even more profound, not only through the new techniques, but still more by Futurism's blurring of the frontiers between different arts, and its conscious exploitation of the mass MEDIA's power to publicize any adroitly staged piece of cultural provocation. It thus paved the way both for such artistic developments as CONCRETE POETRY, CONCRETE MUSIC, and KINETIC ART, and for the concept of art as a more or less sensational event.   J.W.; A.H.

Bibl: M. W. Martin, *Futurist Art and Theory,* *1909–1915* (Oxford, 1968).

futurology. A term coined by the German historian Ossip K. Flechtheim in 1949 to designate a 'new science' of prognosis. It has been applied to various efforts, beginning in 1965, to do long-range FORECASTING in a wide range of political, sociological, economic, ecological, and other fields. Most practitioners reject the idea of a 'new science' and cavil even at the word futurology. Three terms are often distinguished: a *conjecture* or intellectually disciplined speculation; a *forecast*, which is based either on a continuing trend or on some defined probabilities of occurrences; and a *prediction*, which is a prognosis of a specific event. Most practitioners agree that one cannot formalize rules for prediction but argue that the compilation of fuller data and the use of new methods (e.g. COMPUTER SIMULATION, STOCHASTIC techniques) will allow them to do better forecasting.   D.B.

Bibl: O. K. Flechtheim, *History and Futurology* (Meisenheim am Glan, 1965); B. de Jouvenel, tr. N. Lary, *The Art of Conjecture* (London and N.Y., 1967); H. Kahn and A. J. Wiener, *The Year 2000* (N.Y., 1967; London, 1969).

G

Gabo, Naum (Russian artist, *b*. 1890), see under CONSTRUCTIVISM.

Gabor, Dennis (German-British electrical engineer, *b*.1900), see under HOLOGRAPHY.

Gaitskell, Hugh (British statesman, 1906–63), see under CONSENSUS POLITICS; DISENGAGEMENT.

galaxy. One of the collections of stars and gas into which the matter of the universe has been condensed by GRAVITATION. Galaxies , usually rotate, resulting in a discus-shaped structure with spiral arms. The earth and sun are situated about halfway out from the centre of our own galaxy, the Milky Way, which is abou 30,000 PARSECS across. See also EXPANSION OF THE UNIVERSE. M.V.B.

Galbraith, John Kenneth (U.S. economist and public servant, *b*.1908), see under AFFLUENT SOCIETY.

Gallagher, William (British Communist leader, 1881–1965), see under GUILD SOCIALISM.

Gallup poll, see under OPINION POLL; SAMPLE.

Galois theory, see under ALGEBRA.

Galsworthy, John (British novelist and dramatist, 1867–1933), see under ROMAN-FLEUVE; ROYAL COURT THEATRE.

Galton, Sir Francis (British explorer, anthropologist, and eugenicist, 1822–1911), see under DIFFERENTIAL PSYCHOLOGY; EUGENICS; PSYCHOMETRICS.

games, theory of. The general theory of the rational behaviour of two or more people in circumstances where their interests are, at least in part, conflicting. The mathematician John von Neuman first developed such a theory for two-person *zero-sum* games, i.e. for circumstances in which the gain of one participant is the loss of the other. He proposed a concept of EQUILIBRIUM, known as the *minimax* solution, in which each minimizes the maximum loss the other can impose on him; and showed that such a solution exists if the 'players' can choose *mixed strategies,* i.e. STRATEGIES in which the player chooses his action at random with probabilities assigned to the various actions available to him. In *The Theory of Games and Economic Behaviour*, Von Neumann and Morgenstern attempted to develop a theory for games, with many participants, that are not necessarily zero-sum. In these cases, since it may pay some or all of the participants to cooperate, the formation of coalitions must be considered. A number of solution CONCEPTS have been developed by subsequent authors, for games with and without coalitions, most notably the NASH EQUILIBRIUM, in which each participant maximizes his expected gain, given the strategies chosen by others, and the CORE. The study of *non-zero-sum* games has also yielded interesting examples that capture with special clarity the main features of conflict situations. For example, in the famous *prisoner's dilemma*, the only pair of strategies with the property that neither player would wish to change his own, given the behaviour of the other, is worse for both players than any other possible outcome.

At one time dismissed by most economists and other social scientists as a failed attempt to develop an abstract mathematical theory to cover too wide a range of phenomena, the theory has nevertheless contributed many fundamental concepts which have gradually changed the way in which decisions, conflicts, economies, and social systems are thought about. The theory of two-person zero-sum games has been used in the development of military strategies; many-person games have been used in ECONOMICS; and examples like the prisoner's dilemma have been used in political theory. Business firms have sometimes thought of using the theory to determine their own strategies, probably with little success.   J.A.M.

Bibl: R. D. Luce and H. Raiffa, *Games and Decisions* (N.Y., 1957; London, 1958); T. C. Schelling, *The Strategy of Conflict* (London and N.Y., 1969).

gamete (or *germ cell*). In sexual reproduction, the reproductive CELLS, comprising spermatozoa and ova, the former generally mobile, the latter stationary. Gametes are distinguished from ordinary somatic cells by having only half the adult number of CHROMOSOMES. The regular DIPLOID number is restored when the gametes unite to form a ZYGOTE. See also MEIOSIS; MENDEL'S LAWS.   P.M.

gamma rays. Electromagnetic RADIATION emitted in the form of PHOTONS during RADIOACTIVE decay. The wavelength is about the same as the size of an atomic NUCLEUS (see ATOMIC PHYSICS) or smaller.   M.V.B.

gamodeme, see under DEME.

Gan, Alexei (Soviet typographer and art theorist, 1893–1939 or 1940), see under CONSTRUCTIVISM.

Gandhi, Indira (Indian stateswoman, *b.* 1917), see under CONGRESS PARTY.

Gandhi, Mahatma (Indian statesman, 1869–1948), see under AMRITSAR MASSACRE; CIVIL DISOBEDIENCE; CONGRESS PARTY; DIRECT ACTION; HINDUISM; NON-VIOLENT RESISTANCE; POWER.

García Lorca, Federico, see LORCA.

garden cities. Towns built originally as part of a late-19th-century reformist movement derived from the UTOPIAN IDEAL in planning. They were to be places of work and residence on land of low value, and to combat the social, economic, and ENVIRONMENTAL evils of the industrial city. Though there are earlier examples at Bournville and Port Sunlight, the idea was first comprehensively outlined by Ebenezer Howard in 1898 in *Tomorrow: A Peaceful Path to Real Reform,* later renamed *Garden Cities of Tomorrow.* The first garden city designed as such was built at Letchworth, from 1903 onwards, in the form of English cottages within an arcadian setting of trees and winding roads. This visual motif – without the social and economic motivations – was later transferred to the design of garden suburbs in many parts of the world. See also SUBURBIA.   M.BR.

Bibl: W. L. Creese, *The Search for Environment* (London and New Haven, 1966).

Garfinkel, Harold (U.S. sociologist, *b.* 1917), see under ETHNOMETHODOLOGY.

Garland, Hamlin (American author, 1860–1940), see under NATURALISM.

Garnett, David (British novelist, *b.* 1892), see under BLOOMSBURY GROUP.

Garnier, Pierre (French poet, *b.* 1928), see under SPACE.

Garrod, Sir **Archibald Edward** (British physician, 1857–1936), see under DYSGENIC; PATHOLOGY.

Garvey, Marcus Moziah (Jamaican black leader, 1887–1940), see under ETHIOPIANISM.

gas bearing. A simple bearing in which a cylindrical shaft rotates in a cylindrical hole of slightly larger diameter. The space between shaft and cylinder is filled with gas at high pressure whose viscosity is such that when rotating at speed there is no metal-to-metal contact between shaft and cylinder. The frictional drag in such bearings is very much less than in, say, a ball race. See also REYNOLDS WEDGE ACTION.
E.R.L.

gas chromatography. A CHROMATOGRAPHIC method of chemical separation in which a gas or vapour is passed through a stationary PHASE, usually in a heated column, of high surface area. The technique employs either solids or more commonly a liquid phase, e.g. a high-boiling-point hydrocarbon on a solid support. Extensively used since the early 1950s, its main application is in the separation and analysis of mixtures of volatile organic compounds. Quantities less than 10^{-10} grams may often be detected.   B.F.

Gascoyne, David (British poet, *b*. 1916), see under ANTI-LITERATURE; SURREALISM.

Gaskell, Mrs **Elizabeth Cleghorn** (British novelist, 1810–65), see under REALISM.

Gastev, Alexei Kapitonovich (Russian author, 1882–1941), see under BIOMECHANICS.

gastrulation, see under EMBRYOLOGY.

gate. The basic circuit element in a COMPUTER. There are three main types of gate, each having several INPUTS and a single output. All inputs and outputs can be stable at one of two voltages representing 0 and 1. An *and-gate* gives 1 on its output only if all its inputs are 1's; an *or-gate* gives 1 on its output if any of its inputs are 1's; a *nand-gate* gives 1 on its output unless all of its inputs are 1's. A large computer can contain more than 100,000 gates in its LOGIC circuits.　　　　C.S.

Gate Theatre. (1) A London theatre devoted to the performance of new and experimental drama from 1925 until its closure in 1940. Under Peter Godfrey, later under Norman Marshall, the Gate introduced English audiences to the work of Toller, Cocteau, Eugene O'Neill, Elmer Rice, and Maxwell Anderson, evading the restrictions of censorship by operating as a club theatre; Godfrey was the first English director to be influenced by EXPRESSIONISM. In its later years the Gate became famous for a series of intimate revues. (2) A Dublin theatre founded in 1928 by Hilton Edwards and Micheál Mac Liammóir, devoted to the performance of world classics as well as contemporary Irish drama.　　　M.A.
　Bibl: (1) N. Marshall, *The Other Theatre* (London, 1947).

GATT (General Agreement on Tariffs and Trade). An international agreement, between countries accounting for over 80% of world trade, covering levels of tariffs (i.e. import duties) and a code of behaviour for governments in international trade. The GATT secretariat is in Geneva. As a result of six rounds of multilateral negotiations (see BILATERALISM AND MULTILATERALISM), starting in 1947 and ending in 1967, tariffs on manufactures imported by the developed countries have been very substantially reduced. Discussions for a further round took place in 1973. There has been less success in freeing trade in agricultural products, and various *non-tariff barriers* to trade, in general outlawed by the GATT, are attracting more attention. Developing countries (see UNDERDEVELOPMENT) are absolved from making reciprocal concessions, and many impose severe restrictions on trade.　　　M.FG.S.
　Bibl: G. Curzon, *Multilateral Commercial Diplomacy* (London, 1965; N.Y., 1966).

Gatto, Alfonso (Italian poet and journalist, 1909–76), see under HERMETIC.

Gaudi, Antonio (Spanish architect, 1852–1926), see under ART NOUVEAU.

Gaudier-Brzeska, Henri (French sculptor, 1891–1915), see under VORTICISM.

Gauguin, Paul (French painter, 1848–1903), see under ARMORY SHOW; FAUVES; IMPRESSIONISM; LONDON GROUP; NABIS, LES; PONT-AVEN; POST-IMPRESSIONISM; SYMBOLISM; SYNTHETISM.

Gaullism. (1) The French political movement devoted to the support of the policies and ideals of General, later President, de Gaulle (1890–1970). (2) The complex of ideas, prejudices, and attitudes to French history and France's place in the modern world which distinguished President de Gaulle's policy and style during his second period in office (1958–69). As the man who had rescued France from the threat of civil war and created the Fifth French Republic, de Gaulle downgraded party politics and made the presidency the dominant feature in the constitution with himself as president standing above politics, the symbol and guarantor of French sovereignty and French greatness. The administration was to be carried on by men devoted to the national, as distinct from party- or self-interest, and French policy was aimed at the leadership of a Europe from which Britain and the U.S.A. were to be excluded.　　　D.C.W.
　Bibl: A. Hartley, *Gaullism* (N.Y., 1971; London, 1972).

Gaussian distribution, see NORMAL DISTRIBUTION.

Gautier, Théophile (French author, 1811–72), see under AESTHETICISM; SYMBOLISM.

Gay Liberation Front. An organization of practising homosexuals ('gays') whose aim is to remove all laws and fight social prejudice militating against overt acceptance of their way of life. It was founded in the U.S.A., after the Stonewall Inn incident of 27 January 1969, to protest against alleged police harassment of known homosexual places of resort. The organization was spread to Britain by Americans in 1970.   D.C.W.
Bibl: D. Teal, *The Gay Militants* (N.Y., 1971).

GCD (general and comprehensive disarmament), see under DISARMAMENT.

Gebrauchs- ... (utility ...). One aspect of FUNCTIONALISM in Germany, associated particularly with the NEUE SACHLICHKEIT period, was the development of a 'utility music' and 'utility poetry', or *Gebrauchsmusik* and *Gebrauchslyrik,* on the analogy of *Gebrauchsgrafik* or commercial art, whose development in the late 1920s at the BAUHAUS and the Reimann School in Berlin stemmed from the same social-aesthetic ethos. Musical functionalism of this kind was associated particularly with Hindemith and typified in his opera *Neues vom Tage* (1929). Its poetic counterpart was christened in an article of 1928 by Kurt Tucholsky and developed most notably by Erich Kästner in light but sharply satirical rhymed verse.   J.W.

Geddes, Sir Patrick (British biologist and sociologist, 1854–1932), see under CONURBATION.

Geertz, Clifford (U.S. anthropologist, *b.* 1926), see under IDEOLOGY.

geiger counter. A device for measuring levels of RADIOACTIVITY. RADIATION from a decaying atomic NUCLEUS produces a burst of IONS in a gas. These are attracted to ELECTRODES, thus producing a pulse of electric current which can be amplified and fed into a counter.   M.V.B.

Geistesgeschichte, see CULTURAL HISTORY.

Geisteswissenschaften (literally, 'sciences of the spirit'). The disciplines that investigate man, society, and history; broadly speaking, HISTORY, PSYCHOLOGY, and the SOCIAL SCIENCES (SOCIOLOGY, ANTHROPOLOGY, POLITICAL SCIENCE, ECONOMICS). The great development of the human and social sciences in the 19th century had been speculatively reflected in Hegel's philosophy of Spirit, which treated human nature, social INSTITUTIONS, and the aspects of high CULTURE (art, RELIGION, and PHILOSOPHY) as constituting an autonomous realm, superior to, as well as distinct from, that of the material world. By the end of the century the idea was widely held that quite different methods of enquiry were appropriate to the domains of nature and spirit. Nature is to be *explained,* positivistically (see POSITIVISM), by the subsumption of its events under universal laws, inductively arrived at (see INDUCTION); spirit, the field of the *Geisteswissenschaften,* requires *understanding,* i.e. the sympathetic apprehension of the unique individuality of the persons, institutions, and events of which it is composed. The METHODOLOGICAL distinctness between the NATURAL SCIENCES and the human and social sciences is still an issue of vigorous controversy.   A.Q.
Bibl: G. H. von Wright, *Explanation and Understanding* (London and N.Y., 1971).

gel filtration, see under BIOPHYSICS.

Gelber, Jack (U.S. dramatist, *b.* 1932), see under OFF-BROADWAY.

Geller, Uri (Israeli psychist and clairvoyant, *b.* 1946), see under PSYCHOKINESIS.

Gemeinschaft and *Gesellschaft.* Two common German words ('community' and 'society') which were used by the sociologist Ferdinand Tönnies in 1887 to contrast a social relationship of solidarity between individuals based on affection, kinship, or membership of a community such as a family or group of friends (*Gemeinschaft*) with one based upon the division of labour and contractual relations between isolated individuals consulting only their own self-interest (*Gesellschaft*). Both terms are used as mental CONSTRUCTS or IDEAL TYPES which, though they do not correspond to any existing society, together provide a pair of contrasting hypotheses that can be used in investigating any system of social relationships. A.L.C.B.

Bibl: F. Tönnies, tr. and ed. C. P. Loomis, *Community and Association* (London, 1955); as *Community and Society* (N.Y., 1963); and, for a modern version, C. P. Loomis and J. A. Beagle, *Rural Sociology* (Englewood Cliffs, N. J., rev. ed., 1957).

gene. Originally (Johannsen, 1909), the atom or unit of HEREDITY, corresponding to Mendel's factors; today, the functional unit which specifies a single primary gene product, as in the hypothesis 'one gene – one ENZYME', or 'one gene – one antigen' (see IMMUNITY). For each primary function (usually, specifying a particular PROTEIN) it is typically the case that an individual receives one gene from each parent, each situated at a particular place or LOCUS on the corresponding CHROMOSOMES. The two genes at a locus may differ, in which case they are said to be different ALLELES (or *allelomorphs*). An individual with two identical genes at a locus is a *homozygote*; one with two different alleles is a *heterozygote*. In a heterozygote, it is often the case that only one of the two alleles produces an observed effect. In such cases the allele which produces an effect is said to be *dominant*, the other *recessive*. The recessive allele produces an observed effect only in a homozygote. The superior fitness (see DARWINISM) of a heterozygote to a homozygote is known as *heterosis*, and is important as a cause of variability in natural populations, and of the decline in vigour caused by inbreeding. See also GENETICS. J.M.S.

General Agreement on Tariffs and Trade, see GATT.

general equilibrium theory, see under EQUILIBRIUM (2).

general systems theory, see GST.

generative grammar. A CONCEPT, developed by Noam Chomsky in *Syntactic Structures* (The Hague, 1957), which makes it possible, by the application of a finite number of *rewrite rules*, to predict ('generate') the infinite number of sentences in a language and to specify their structure. Of several possible MODELS of generative grammar he discusses three:

(1) *Finite-state* grammars generate by working through a sentence 'from left to right'; an initial element is selected, and thereafter the possibilities of occurrence of all other elements are wholly determined by the nature of the elements preceding them; Chomsky shows how this extremely simple kind of GRAMMAR is incapable of accounting for many important processes of sentence formation.

(2) *Phrase-structure* grammars contain ordered rules which are capable not only of generating strings of linguistic elements, but also of providing a CONSTITUENT ANALYSIS of these strings, and hence more information about sentence formation.

(3) *Transformational* grammars are in Chomsky's view the most powerful of all, in that very many sentence types can be economically derived by supplementing the constituent analysis rules of phrase-structure grammars with rules for transforming one sentence into another. Thus a rule for 'passivization' would take an active sentence and re-order its elements so as to produce a passive sentence – a procedure both simpler and intuitively more satisfactory than generating active and passive sentences separately in the same grammar.

In its current outline, a transformational-generative grammar consists of (*a*) a *syntactic component*, comprising a basic set of phrase-structure rules (sometimes called the *base component*) which provide the DEEP STRUCTURE information about the sentences of a language, and a set of transformational rules for generating *surface structures;* (*b*) a *phonological component,* which provides for converting strings of syntactic elements into pronounceable utterance; and (*c*) a semantic component, which provides information about the meaning of the lexical items to be used in sentences (see LEXICON). D.C.

Bibl: see under CHOMSKYAN; GRAMMAR.

genetic assimilation. Term coined by C. H. Waddington, 1953, for a process which mimics Lamarckian inheritance (see LAMARCKISM) without involving directed MUTATION. If those members of a population which respond to an environmental STIMULUS in a particular way are selected, naturally or artificially, this will result in the accumulation of GENES which favour the response, until the response appears without the environmental stimulus. J.M.S.

genetic code. The 'dictionary' relating the sequence of nucleotides in a DNA MOLECULE (see NUCLEIC ACIDS) with the AMINO ACIDS whose nature and order of assembly into a PROTEIN they specify. An amino acid is specified not by a single nucleotide but by a triplet of nucleotides; thus uracil-uracil-uracil specifies the amino acid phenylalanine. Some triplets are either nonsensical, in the sense that they do not specify or code for any amino acid, or are 'punctuation marks' marking the beginning or the end of a certain stretch of genetic information. A consensus of scientists considers that the complex of discoveries comprising the discovery of the genetic functions of DNA, the genetic code, and the mechanism of transcription and translation constitute the greatest intellectual achievement of modern science. The central dogma of MOLECULAR BIOLOGY is that coded information can pass only from DNA to protein and never the other way about; and this irreversibility of information flow is the reason for the falsity of Lamarck's idea (see LAMARCKISM) of the inheritance of acquired characteristics. P.M.; J.M.S.
Bibl: J. D. Watson, *Molecular Biology of the Gene* (N.Y., 2nd ed., 1970).

genetic epistemology. In DEVELOPMENTAL PSYCHOLOGY, a somewhat idiosyncratic PIAGETIAN coinage which appears to serve as an umbrella term for the theoretical ideas informing his own work on the development of knowledge and understanding in the growing child – a development which he regards, to a considerable extent, as being genetically pre-programmed. C.L.-H.
Bibl: J. H. Flavell, *The Developmental Psychology of Jean Piaget* (London and Princeton 1963).

genetic explanation, see under EXPLANATION.

genetic memory. A phrase sometimes employed by nature-philosophers, e.g. Ewald Hering, for the endowment by which, for example, a frog's egg 'remembers' to grow up into a frog. There is, however, no property of genetic memory that is not explicable in terms of ordinary GENETICS and HEREDITY. Genetic memory therefore belongs to the strange philosophical museum that also contains racial memory, *élan vital* (see VITALISM), and ENTELECHY. P.M.

genetic method. Not so much a precise method as an approach, marked by interest in origins and evolution, which dominated historical studies in the 19th century. More recently historians have been turning away from the 'idol of origins' (as Marc Bloch called it), the tendency to explain recent events in terms of the remote past. The genetic approach has been most successful in biography, and most dangerous, perhaps, when applied to the history of INSTITUTIONS. See also HISTORICISM. P.B.

genetic psychology. A term used in the 1930s and 1940s to cover COMPARATIVE PSYCHOLOGY and DEVELOPMENTAL PSYCHOLOGY. It meant the phylogenetic and ontogenetic development (see PHYLOGENY; ONTOGENY) of human adult behaviour. This general approach persists and is still a valid one. The term itself, however, seems to have been dropped, probably to avoid confusion with behavioural GENETICS. P.E.B.

genetic system. (1) The reproductive and hereditary processes of a population; (2) more generally, the totality of factors that control the flow of genetic information from one generation to the next. J.M.S.

geneticism. A word coined in 1959 by P. B. Medawar on the model of EVOLUTIONISM, SCIENTISM, and HISTORICISM to refer to a scheme of thought which extravagantly overestimates the explanatory power of genetical ideas. The pretended explanation on genetic lines of every aspect of human character and every nuance of personality, and the interpretation of the rise and fall of nations along genetic lines, may all be said to belong to geneticism, which has the ill effect of bringing GENETICS into undeserved discredit. P.M.

genetics. Word coined by William Bateson in 1905 for the science of *heredity*, i.e. the tendency of like to beget like. Its methods are the study of the numbers and kinds of progeny from sexual crosses, supplemented by a microscopic and chemical study (CYTOGENETICS) of the materials actually transmitted by parents to their offspring. Modern genetics originated with the work of Mendel on peas, published in 1865. Mendel used the ratios in which different characteristics appear among the offspring of sexual crosses to develop an atomic theory of heredity. The atoms of heredity, today called GENES, are present in two complete sets in the fertilized egg or ZYGOTE, one set being derived from each parent.

Mendel's work was not appreciated at the time. With the rediscovery of his laws in 1900, it was soon recognized that genes are parts of CHROMOSOMES, which are visible at the time of division in the NUCLEI of all CELLS. The chromosome theory of heredity was in the main worked out by T. H. Morgan and his colleagues in the period 1914–28.

The original importance of genetics was that it provided a law of heredity which was the missing element in Darwin's theory of EVOLUTION by NATURAL SELECTION. (See also DARWINISM.) Today genetics can claim to be the central discipline of BIOLOGY. The discovery of the chemical constitution of genes by Watson, Crick, and Wilkins in 1952 revealed in its essentials the process whereby like begets like. This property of heredity, together with the properties of multiplication and variation, provides the necessary conditions for evolution by natural selection, and is therefore the most important property differentiating living from non-living things.

Biochemical (or *molecular*) *genetics* studies the chemical constitution of genes and their immediate products. *Physiological* (or *developmental*) *genetics* is concerned with the control of gene action and the role of genes in development. POPULATION GENETICS is concerned with the frequency of genes in populations, and the mechanism of evolution. *Behavioural genetics* is concerned with the hereditary basis of behaviour in man and in other animal species. Genetics has applications in medicine and in animal and plant breeding. J.M.S.

Bibl: L. C. Dunn, *A Short History of Genetics* (N.Y., 1965); M. Strickberge, *Genetics* (London and N.Y., 1968).

genocide. Term coined by the American scholar Raphael Lamkin for the deliberate destruction of an ethnic group, and included in the indictment presented against the principal defendants in the NUREMBERG TRIALS in relation to NAZI measures to exterminate the Jews in Europe (see FINAL SOLUTION). Genocide was classed as a crime under international law by the general assembly of UNO, when it approved the Convention on the Punishment of the Crime of Genocide (December 1948). The term has been extended to cover racial persecution that stops short of mass murder, e.g. the prevention of births within, and the mass kidnapping of children of, a particular ethnic group. D.C.W.

genodeme, see under DEME.

genome. The GENETIC apparatus of an organism considered as a whole and as characteristic of it, e.g. 'the human genome' referring to the chromosomal make-up (see CHROMOSOMES) characteristic of human beings and to the sum total of the genetic information which it embodies and imparts. P.M.

genotype. The genetic constitution of an individual, as deduced from ancestry or breeding performance, in contrast to its *phenotype*, the characteristics which are manifested in the individual. The distinction is important because it is the genotype, not the phenotype, which is reproduced and can be transmitted to future generations. J.M.S.

gentrification, see under URBAN RENEWAL.

gentry controversy. A controversy which began in 1941 when R. H. Tawney published an article on 'The Rise of the Gentry', arguing that the English Revolution of the mid 17th century resulted from the rise of a group of entrepreneur landlords between 1540 and 1640, and that political power followed economic. He was violently attacked by H. R. Trevor-Roper, who suggested that during that period the gentry were in fact in economic decline.

More historians joined in, finer distinctions were drawn, and both literary and statistical evidence received more careful scrutiny than they had first been given. In the course of this 20-year controversy, English SOCIAL HISTORY came of age. P.B.

Bibl: J. H. Hexter, 'Storm over the Gentry', in his *Reappraisals in History* (London, 1961; N.Y., 1963).

geochemistry. The description of the CHEMISTRY of the earth. Traditionally it involves the study of the abundance and distribution of ELEMENTS and their ISOTOPES, mainly in the LITHOSPHERE, but also in the seas and the earth's atmosphere. Modern geochemistry is increasingly concerned with understanding the way in which the earth and solar system have evolved by means of a combined chemical and geological (see GEOLOGY) approach. B.F.

Bibl: W. S. Fyfe, *Geochemistry* (Oxford, 1974).

geochronology. Term used in ARCHAEOLOGY to cover all DATING methods which are based on measurable changes in natural substances. They include ARCHAEOMAGNETISM, DENDROCHRONOLOGY, RADIOCARBON DATING, THERMOLUMINESCENCE, varve dating, and other techniques based on PHYSICS and CHEMISTRY. B.C.

geodesic domes, see under DYMAXION.

geodesy. The observation and measurement of the size and external shape of the earth and the variations in terrestrial gravity. Geodetic surveys based on geometric methods are only considered to be accurate for relatively small areas. Local surveys are referred to a world-wide reference surface, the *geoid*, which coincides with the mean-sea-level surface and its theoretical extension into the continental areas. The shape of the geoid, like the surface of the oceans, is determined by the gravitational attraction of the earth's mass. Since the earth is inhomogeneous, with an irregular distribution of mass (see ISOSTASY), the geoid is also an irregular surface. The precise tracking of artificial satellites has enabled this surface to be more accurately contoured. J.L.M.L.

geographical determinism, see under ENVIRONMENTALISM.

geography. The branch of knowledge which describes, classifies, and explains the distribution of material and human phenomena in the space accessible to man and man-controlled activities. It has been concerned with man's HABITAT, in the widest sense of the term, and with attempts to improve it.

Because of the extreme diversity of the globe in its physical, human, and economic features, geographical description has been mainly on a regional scale. The abundance and variety of data gathered about most of the many regions needed to be organized and interrelated to show how the local ENVIRONMENT and the local people lived and interacted within the regional unit. Such research constitutes *regional geography*, which forms a vast store of case studies about units of all sizes in the organization of space. A more ambitious task has been the search for general principles governing the spatial organization either of physical characteristics or of people and their activities. This is the field of *general* or *systematic geography*, itself subdivided into two major categories of concerns: *physical geography*, encompassing the natural phenomena of climate (see CLIMATOLOGY), GEOMORPHOLOGY (i.e. topographical forms and the processes which shape them), HYDROLOGY, OCEANOGRAPHY, soils, flora, and fauna; and *human geography*, dealing with population and settlement, resources and economic activities of all sorts (i.e. agriculture, mining, manufacturing, trade, transport, and COMMUNICATIONS), and in recent times including the distributional patterns of social, cultural, and political features and trends.

The data and problems that thus belong to geographical knowledge are so diverse, and ramify so fast, that their systematic ordering must often be recast. Meanwhile, the NATURAL SCIENCES and the SOCIAL SCIENCES which geography straddles have been subdividing into specializations and taking over some fields of research that had previously belonged to geography. For instance, most research on climatology is now done by geophysicists (see GEOPHYSICS) and meteorologists (see METEOROLOGY), and SOIL SCIENCE has become a separate, though related, discipline.

Until the 1950s geographers tended to emphasize the regional concept (see REG-

ION), elaborating the complex interplay of natural, social, and economic forces in the shaping of the region's landscapes, its functions, and its part in the world. The region, however, was always defined first by internal patterns (largely analysed by the cartographic method; see CARTO-GRAPHY) and secondly by comparison with other cases beyond its limits. The COMPARATIVE METHOD is necessary to arrive at what French geographers called the region's personality.

The individual case is basic to the ordering of data and to the elaboration of relationships; but geography could not be satisfied by the study of so many varied regions without formulating general principles about them. Each geographical location or region may be shown to be unique; such a rule of randomness is not, however, acceptable to the scientific mind, and geographic thought has owed its impetus and unity to the quest for some form of DETERMINISM amidst geographic phenomena. The oversimplified form represented by the assertion that natural features and variations of climate and topography determine the distribution of resources and the behaviour of people is now almost extinct. Rigorous determinism and interesting theoretical hypotheses have, however, been worked out and applied in physical geography, particularly (e.g. by W. M. Davis, W. Penck, and E. de Martonne) in the study of the processes of erosion and deposition shaping the forms of the relief.

In human geography, the search for general principles early resulted in outlining complex networks of relationships between forces and factors in the processes by which people shaped their environment to their use (F. Ratzel, P. Vidal de la Blache and H. J. Mackinder were the pioneers in the years 1890–1920). Geographers brought into common use such notions as the density of population (see DENSITY), landscape understood as a cultural achievement, and the classification of various types of SETTLEMENTS and cities (see URBANIZATION, METROPOLIS). Causality in human geography called at least as much on history as on local physical conditions. The historical approach has been paramount in French regional geography (Vidal de la Blache, A. Demangeon, J. Sion, and their school), and in British human geography (H. J.

Mackinder, A. J. Herbertson, P. M. Roxby).

Among the permanent general problems of geography which have recently attracted attention are LOCATION, CONCENTRATION, psychological factors, and the use of mathematical MODELS. *Location theory*, based partly on the study of CENTRAL PLACES and decision-making, has been contributed mainly by A. Lösch, W. Christaller, and W. Isard. The study of concentration, already stressed by Vidal de la Blache, who related it to the network of external relations and to technological progress, has been revived by the pace of urban growth and emphasized by Jean Gottmann. The role of psychological factors has been enhanced by growing interest in the decision-making for location and environmental management (a new field called *perception geography* is being developed), in *electoral geography* (pioneered by André Siegfried), and in the general theory of *political geography*. The fashion for mathematical models in social studies has had much impact on human geography, especially in location theory (P. Haggett and B. Berry) and the study of the DIFFUSION of innovations (T. Hägerstrand).

Geographers are increasingly employed in urban and regional planning and in the elaboration of environmental policies, often working in teams with specialists of the other human and social sciences. As advancing TECHNOLOGY and affluence make it easier to modify living conditions and the management of resources, the thinking of geographers turns towards the FORECASTING of trends and the means of solving impending problems of spatial organization.   J.G.

Bibl: R. Hartshorne, *Perspective on the Nature of Geography* (London and Chicago, 1959); P. Claval, *Essai sur l'évolution de la géographie humaine* (Paris, 1964).

geoid, see under GEODESY.

geological time chart. The chronological arrangement of the geological events which are recorded in the most complete succession of rocks exposed on the earth's surface. A purely relative chronology of geological age has been constructed and is usually presented in the form of a stratigraphic column in which the fossiliferous rocks formed since the beginning of the Cambrian period (i.e. from about 600 million years ago) are arranged in vertical succession upwards. Radiometric methods (see RADIOCARBON DATING) give a reasonably accurate DATING, usually recorded in millions of years, of rocks, so that the time chart will also indicate the duration of the periods of known geological age. This method has been applied to the metamorphic rocks of pre-Cambrian age which are almost entirely devoid of fossils. The oldest rock of the continents has been dated by this method as 3,500 million years old.　　　　　J.L.M.L.

geology. The scientific study of the earth and of other bodies in the solar system (e.g. the moon) which may provide evidence relating to its origin and evolution. The main activities of geology have been to map and classify the rocks exposed on the earth's surface and those accessible underground, and to explain their origin and distribution.　　　　　J.L.M.L.

geomagnetism, see under MAGNETISM.

geometric art, see under ABSTRACT ART.

geometry. A branch of MATHEMATICS which arose from practical problems of mensuration. Euclidean space (of 2 or 3 dimensions) is an idealization of perceived space (see SPACE PERCEPTION) which can be characterized either algebraically (see below) or axiomatically. *Euclidean geometry* is the study of those properties of figures in Euclidean space which are invariant under the following TRANSFORMATIONS: (1) parallel displacements, (2) rotations, (3) reflections, (4) uniform dilations. The least evident of the AXIOMS for Euclidean space is the *fifth postulate* or *parallel axiom*, which, in 2 dimensions, asserts: 2 lines intersect if and only if they do not have the same direction. Unlike the other axioms, it presupposes that space is infinite in extent. Efforts (mostly 1750–1830) to derive it from the other axioms, or to find a more intuitively acceptable equivalent, led to the conception of *non-Euclidean geometry*. In *hyperbolic geometry*, for example, all the lines through a point P which make angles less than θ with a line l fail to intersect l; θ depends on the distance of P from l. In elliptic geometry any two lines intersect

(and space is bounded – e.g. 'space' is the surface of a sphere and 'lines' are great circles). The transformations (1)–(4) no longer apply; in particular, uniform dilations do not exist. The historical importance of the discovery of non-Euclidean geometry is twofold: it disproved Kant's thesis that our intuitions of space are *a priori* and it encouraged the growth of the AXIOMATIC METHOD.

Projective geometry studies those properties of figures which are not only invariant under the transformations (1)–(4) but also (for 2 dimensions) under the transformation of projecting one plane from a point onto another plane; such projections were first introduced to study the conic sections. A point or line may be 'sent to infinity' by such a projection, so that the *projective plane* is got by adding a *line at infinity* to the Euclidean plane. Angles and distances are not projective concepts. *Affine geometry* is intermediate between Euclidean and projective geometry.

By introducing a system of COORDINATES, geometric objects and PROPOSITIONS may be expressed in algebraic terms. *Analytic geometry* is the study of this reduction for the particular case when the coordinates are obtained from a rectilinear system of axes. For example, in the plane, a straight line consists of all those points whose coordinates (x, y) satisfy an EQUATION of the form $ax + by + c = 0$; a, b, c are the PARAMETERS of the line. In practice 'analytic geometry' usually refers to the more elementary investigations. *Algebraic geometry* is used for the more advanced studies where the figures are given by algebraic equations (see ALGEBRA). From the algebraic point of view there is no reason to use exactly 3 coordinates; one generalizes to n dimension. Another generalization replaces real coordinates by COMPLEX NUMBERS or by elements of other appropriate MATHEMATICAL STRUCTURES. This is what recent work (since 1945) is mostly concerned with. The methods and concepts are wholly algebraic; applications are to NUMBER THEORY rather than to geometry in its original sense.

Analytic methods may be used even when a uniform system of coordinates is not available. For instance, on the surface of the earth the poles do not have a well-defined longitude. This is an example of a

manifold; one can introduce coordinates locally and define geometric notions (e.g. distance) in terms of them. *Differential geometry* studies the way in which such local geometry may vary from point to point. In particular, *Riemannian geometry* studies (*n*-dimensional) manifolds in which a metric (i.e. a notion of distance) is given at each point. According to the *general theory* of RELATIVITY space-time constitutes a 4-dimensional manifold with a metric which determines the motion (under gravity) at each point, and which is determined by the distribution of matter.
R.G.
Bibl: D. Hilbert and S. Cohn-Vossen, tr. P. Nemenyi, *Geometry and the Imagination* (N.Y., 1952).

geomorphology. The study of the nature and evolution of the surface features of the earth, particularly those landscapes produced by sub-aerial erosion. All landscapes owe their form to a balance between constructional processes, such as volcanic eruption and mountain-building, and destructional processes – erosion by the agents water, ice, and wind. Geomorphological research has made it possible to identify distinctive landforms resulting from the predominating action of one of the agents of erosion, even when it has ceased to operate. The present landscape of northern Europe and North America, for example, retains the essential features of the glaciated landscape formed during the Pleistocene epoch, even though the glaciers retreated some 15,000 years ago.
J.L.M.L.

geophysics. An interdisciplinary science where the theories and techniques of PHYSICS are applied to the atmosphere, surface, and interior of the earth. In recent decades the study of earthquake waves and rock magnetism has led to the abandonment of the notion of a rigid earth ('*terra firma*'), and its replacement by theories involving the slow flow of rocks over geological time. See also CONTINENTAL DRIFT; PLATE TECTONICS; SEISMOLOGY.
M.V.B.
Bibl: R. Fraser, *Understanding the Earth* (Harmondsworth and Baltimore, 1967); T. F. Gaskell, *Physics of the Earth* (London and N.Y., 1970); N. Calder, *Restless Earth* (London and N.Y., 1972).

geopolitics. An intellectually illegitimate offspring of political GEOGRAPHY and POLITICAL SCIENCE first conceived by the Swedish political scientist Rudolf Kjellen, developed by the British political geographer Halford Mackinder, and brought to maturity by the German Karl Haushofer. Geopolitics conceives of nations or states as supra-individual organisms engaged in a perpetual struggle for life, the key to which is control over the 'spaces' into which the earth is divided. According to geopolitics the development of these spaces is subject to 'laws' which can be derived from the study of geography and history and successfully applied in foreign policy. Haushofer's theories (he spoke of 'space-fate' and coined the catchword LEBENSRAUM) made a strong appeal to the NAZIS and German nationalists, by providing a justification for Germany's bid for political dominance in Europe.
D.C.W.
Bibl: E. M. Earle, 'Haushofer and the Geopoliticians', in his *Makers of Modern Strategy* (Princeton, 1944).

George, Stefan (German poet, 1868–1933), see under INTELLECTUALS; SYMBOLISM.

geotaxis, see under TROPISM.

geotropism, see under TROPISM.

geriatrics. The branch of medicine that deals with the special medical problems of the aged. As the diseases of youth and middle age yield to medical treatment, so the diseases of the elderly become relatively more important. Geriatrics bears the same relationship to GERONTOLOGY as PSYCHIATRY bears to PSYCHOLOGY. P.M.

germ cell, see GAMETE.

germ plasm. Term used by August Weismann (1834–1914) for the reproductive CELLS and TISSUES of the body as contrasted with the 'ordinary' parts of the body – the SOMA. Weismann's *germ plasm theory* is the theory that the cells destined to become reproductive cells are segregated very early in development and are thus untouched by influences from the ENVIRONMENT or from elsewhere in the body. This theory, even if it is not in all cases literally true, is now admitted to be effectively true, because the genetic information contained in the germ cells is indeed totally unaffected by what goes on around them in the body or in the environment. P.M.

gerontology. The branch of BIOLOGY that deals with the nature of ageing. Its central problem is whether the ageing process is an epiphenomenon of life or whether it is innate or genetically programmed in the sense that it will occur irrespective of the vicissitudes to which the organism is exposed in the course of its ordinary lifetime. There is nothing paradoxical about the idea of a genetically programmed ageing process, because the post-reproductive period of life is beyond the direct reach of the forces of NATURAL SELECTION. Among the epiphenomenal theories of ageing is Mechnikov's conjecture, now discredited, that ageing is caused by a progressive auto-intoxication through the assimilation of toxins liberated by an unsatisfactory bacterial population of the gut. Another is Orgel's theory according to which ageing is the consequence of a series of accumulated errors of transcription in the processes by which the genetic information residing in the germinal DNA (see NUCLEIC ACID) is mapped into specific structural PROTEINS or ENZYMES. Experimental evidence lends some support to the latter view. If it is true, the ageing process could not be remedied by any form of physical intervention, since it would be largely random in origin. P.M.

Gershwin, George (U.S. composer, 1898–1937), see under BLUE NOTES.

Gesamtkunstwerk (German for 'complete-art-work'). The concept, most closely associated with Richard Wagner, of a total integration of music, drama, and spectacle in which the arts involved are so interdependent that none shall dominate to the detriment of the others. Theoretically, since music, text, and theatrical concept should all emanate from the same mind, a perfect balance should be achieved; in practice, this is rarely so, since the chance of one person possessing equally imaginative gifts in three spheres is remote. After Wagner, musical landmarks in the welding of different artistic media into a synaesthetic experience (see

SYNAESTHESIA) include Schönberg's *Die Glückliche Hand* and Scriabin's *Prometheus*. In recent times, the new resources of ELECTRONIC MUSIC, coupled with immense advances in lighting techniques, back-projection, amplification, and the like, have made the concept of *Gesamtkunstwerk* more likely to be achieved, though the ultimate gain in artistic terms may be less than Wagner predicted. A.H.

Gesellschaft, see under GEMEINSCHAFT.

Gestalt. Imported German word for a configuration, pattern, or organized whole with qualities different from those of its components separately considered; e.g. a melody, since its quality does not inhere in any particular notes as such. Such whole-qualities have always been recognized and commented upon, but their explicit experimental study came into prominence in Germany when, in 1910, the self-styled *Gestalt psychologists* began studying the PHI-PHENOMENON. Here was a perceived movement corresponding neither to actual physical movement nor to elementary STIMULUS events but to several stimulus events in interaction. The founders of Gestalt psychology (in R. S. Woodworth's classification, one of the six main SCHOOLS OF PSYCHOLOGY) were Max Wertheimer, Kurt Koffka, and Wolfgang Köhler. Their key argument was that the nature of the parts is determined by, and secondary to, the whole. They saw this argument as applying to every field of PSYCHOLOGY and, indeed, of PHILOSOPHY, science, and art. They insisted that enquiry proceed from-above-down rather than from-below-up; i.e. one must not start with supposed elements and try to synthesize these into wholes, but rather examine the whole to discover what its natural parts are. The three founders, who migrated to the U.S.A. in the 1930s, applied their approach fruitfully to the concrete understanding of a wide range of phenomena in PERCEPTION, learning, and thinking processes, and inspired others to undertake Gestalt-flavoured studies of personality, SOCIAL PSYCHOLOGY, and AESTHETICS. In its early years Gestalt psychology seemed revolutionary and aroused much controversy, but by mid century it had ceased to represent a self-conscious school. While many of its fundamental problems

about organized complexities remained
unsolved, its main lessons and factual discoveries were absorbed profitably into the
mainstream of psychology.   I.M.L.H.
  Bibl: W. Köhler, *The Mentality of Apes*
(London and N.Y., 1925); K. Koffka,
Principles of Gestalt Psychology (London
and N.Y., 1935); M. Wertheimer, *Productive Thinking* (N.Y., 1959; London, enl.
ed., 1961).

Gestapo. German acronym for *Geheime
Staatspolizei*, Secret State Police. The
term was originally applied to the Prussian
plain-clothes political police force evolved
during the troubled times preceding the
appointment of Adolf Hitler as Chancellor of Germany, but was extended under
his chancellorship to the whole machinery
of terror and informants untrammelled by
any legal constraint which was used by
the NAZIS state against anyone suspected
of political deviation or opposition. It is
now freely applied as an adjective of an
opprobrious kind – 'Gestapo tactics' – to
all police operations, whether open or
covert, extra-legal or not, directed to the
restraint of illegal actions for which political motives can be adduced.   D.C.W.
  Bibl: E. Crankshaw, *Gestapo* (London
and N.Y., 1956).

gestural. In art criticism, an adjective suggesting conspicuous brushwork, and
movement of the body in the painting process. It is particularly relevant to ACTION
PAINTING.   A.K.W.

Gestus. A German term used by Lessing
in his dramatic notes of 1767 to mean
something distinct from 'gesture', and
adopted in BRECHTIAN parlance around
1930 to convey much the same as the old
English 'gest' (bearing, carriage, mien),
i.e. a mixture of gesture and gist, attitude
and point. In Brecht's view there was a
'basic gest' to any play or scene, while
everything in it was to be conveyed by a
succession of gests, each dictating its own
expression in terms of language, music,
grouping, etc. For such expression to be
'gestic' it must communicate not merely
the meaning but also the speaker's
attitude to his listeners and to what he is
saying.   J.W.

Giap, Vo Nguyen (North Vietnamese general, *b*.1912), see under GUERRILLA.

Gibbs, Willard (U.S. theoretical physicist
and chemist, 1839–1903), see under FREE
ENERGY; STATISTICAL MECHANICS.

Giddings, Franklin Henry (U.S.
sociologist, 1855–1931), see under
PLURAL SOCIETY.

Gide, André (French novelist, dramatist,
and critic, 1869–1951), see under TOTAL
THEATRE.

Giedion, Sigfried (Swiss architectural critic, 1888–1968), see under CHICAGO
SCHOOL.

gift. In anthropological usage, largely
based upon M. Mauss's pioneer study,
'Essai sur le don' (*Année Sociologique*,
1923–4), a gift is above all something
given in the expectation of reciprocation.
Gift-giving in all societies is interested: by
means of gifts people and groups create,
vary, and maintain relationships among
themselves, while, in societies lacking
markets and a system of money, gift-
giving is likely to be a chief mechanism by
which exchanges are affected.   M.F.
  Bibl: M. Mauss, tr. I. Cunnison, *The
Gift* (London and Glencoe, Ill., 1954); R.
Firth (ed.), *Themes in Economic
Anthropology* (London, 1967).

Gilbert and **George** (London-based 'living
sculptures' who conceal their surnames,
b.1942 and 1941), see under CONCEP-
TUAL ART.

Gillespie, Dizzy (U.S. musician, *b*.1917),
see under BEBOP.

Gilman, Harold (British artist,
1878–1919), see under CAMDEN TOWN
GROUP; LONDON GROUP.

Ginsberg, Allen (U.S. author, *b*.1926),
see under BEAT; GREENWICH VILLAGE.

Ginsberg, Morris (British sociologist,
1889–1970), see under IDEAL TYPES.

Giraudoux, Jean (French novelist,
essayist, and dramatist, 1882–1944), see
under CARTEL.

Giroud, Françoise (French journalist and
politician, *b*.1916), see under NEW
WAVE.

glaciology. The study of all forms of natural ice including the study of glaciers, snow, the ice cover of water and subterranean ice, and the interaction of these forms with the atmosphere, HYDROSPHERE, and LITHOSPHERE. To the geologist the principal branch of glaciology is that which deals with the behaviour of ice (principally in the form of ice-sheets and glaciers) on the earth's surface, since this provides information which can be applied to the study of ancient glaciations.

J.L.M.L.

Glaser, Donald Arthur (U.S. physicist, *b.* 1926), see under BUBBLE CHAMBER.

Glasgow School. A group of painters in watercolours and oils, active in Glasgow in the 1880s and 1890s. William MacGregor and James Paterson were its founding figures; others associated were Sir David Cameron, Joseph Crawhall, Edward Hornel, Edward Walton, and (after 1884) Arthur Melville. Influenced by French IMPRESSIONISM, they combined vigorous brushwork with decorative arrangements of form and colour.

P.C.

Gleizes, Albert (French painter and writer on art, 1881–1953), see under CUBISM; KNAVE OF DIAMONDS.

glia, see under NEURON.

glossematics. An approach to language adopted primarily by Louis Hjelmslev and associates at the Linguistic Circle of Copenhagen in the mid 1930s. The circle aimed to develop a theory applicable, not just to language, but to the humanities in general. Language, in this view, was seen as merely one kind of symbolic system, the distinctive features of which would be clarified only when it was compared with other, non-linguistic symbolic systems (e.g. LOGIC, dancing). The study of LINGUISTICS would lead on to the more general study of SEMIOTICS.

D.C.

Bibl: L. Hjelmslev, tr. F. J. Whitfield, *Prolegomena to a Theory of Language* (Madison, Wis., rev. ed., 1961).

glottochronology. In LINGUISTICS, the QUANTIFICATION of the extent to which languages have diverged from a common source. Using a technique known as *lexicostatistics*, one studies the extent

to which the hypothetically related languages share certain basic words (*cognates*) and deduces from this the distance in time since the languages separated. The theory and methods involved are not widely used, and are highly controversial.

D.C.

gnosticism. A variety of RELIGION which claims to be based on a special knowledge (Greek *gnosis*) of the spiritual world denied to the religious authorities and superior to the science of the day. Until about 300 A.D. various gnostic movements were the chief religious rivals to Catholic (see CATHOLICISM) CHRISTIANITY. In the modern world, ANTHROPOSOPHY and THEOSOPHY may be termed gnostic, and the philosophy based on JUNGIAN psychology has this tendency.

D.L.E.

Bibl: C. G. Jung, tr. R. F. C. Hull, *Answer to Job* (London, 1954; N.Y., 1960).

GNP (gross national product). An *unduplicated* measure of the total flow of output in any economy during any specified time period. 'Unduplicated' excludes *intermediate products* (i.e. goods or services used merely as INPUTS in the production of further goods or services, such as the use of steel to produce automobiles); and GNP thus corresponds to the contribution to WELFARE made by (1) the provision of *final products,* i.e. the CONSUMERS' GOODS and services which constitute the ultimate object of all productive activity, and (2) the INVESTMENT needed in order to permit consumption levels to be maintained or improved in the future. GNP may be estimated by any of three methods, with, in principle, identical results: by adding (*a*) the value of all final output (the *expenditure method*), or (*b*) the value of the net addition to output made at every stage of the productive process (the *value added method*), or (*c*) the net incomes earned at each stage of the productive process (the *income method*). The vital distinction between 'intermediate' and 'final' products is an arbitrary one, and not all countries (or economic statisticians) agree on where the boundary line should be drawn. Another vital but often arbitrary boundary is the *production boundary* between *productive activities* (whether intermediate or final) and *non-productive activities*; payments (e.g. pensions) made for the latter are known as *transfer payments*.

The 'gross' in 'gross national product' excludes the using up of CAPITAL stock by such factors as depreciation. 'National' indicates that gross national product (distinguished fom gross *domestic* product) includes income from overseas investment, and excludes profits due to foreign companies arising from production within the country in question.   W.B.

Bibl: N. and R. Ruggles, *The Design of Economic Accounts* (London and N.Y., 1970); W. Beckerman, *An Introduction to National Income Analysis* (London, 1968).

Gobineau, Arthur, Comte de (French diplomat, ethnologist, and social thinker, 1816–82), see under RACE.

Godard, Jean-Luc (French film director, *b*. 1930), see under NEW WAVE; POP.

Gödel, Kurt (Czech-U.S. mathematician and logician, *b*. 1906), see under GÖDEL'S THEOREM; VIENNA CIRCLE.

Gödel's theorem (1931) states that in any formal system which contains the arithmetic of natural NUMBERS there is a formula which, if the system is consistent, can neither be proved nor disproved, neither it nor its negation being deducible from the AXIOMS. It follows from this that it is impossible to prove the consistency of a formal system of this kind within the system itself. A generally accepted consequence of this startling discovery is that the ambition of Frege and Russell to create a unitary deductive system in which all mathematical truths could be deduced from a handful of axioms (see LOGICISM) cannot be realized. Gödel's results are comparably destructive of Hilbert's programme of demonstrating the consistency of all mathematical theories using no more than the resources of elementary LOGIC (see FORMALISM). Much more speculative is the INFERENCE of the falsity of any theory which takes the human mind to be a mechanical, deterministic system.   A.Q.

Bibl: E. Nagel and J. R. Newman, *Gödel's Proof* (N.Y., 1958; London, 1959).

Godfrey, Peter (British actor and theatre director, 1899–1970), see under GATE THEATRE.

Goebbels, Paul Joseph (German Nazi leader, 1897–1945), see under IRON CURTAIN.

Goehr, Alexander (British composer, *b*. 1932), see under MUSIC THEATRE.

Goethe, Johann Wolfgang von (German author, 1749–1832), see under BILDUNGSROMAN; MORPHOLOGY; WEIMAR REPUBLIC.

Goffman, Erving (U.S. sociologist, *b*. 1922), see under CHICAGO SCHOOL; ROLE, ROLE THEORY.

Gogol, Nikolai Vasilievich (Russian novelist and dramatist, 1809–52), see under REALISM.

Gold, Thomas (Austrian-born astronomer, *b*. 1920), see under STEADY-STATE HYPOTHESIS.

gold standard. A state of affairs in which citizens hold their money in the form of gold coins or in the form of bank deposits or notes that are convertible by their banks into gold on demand. A *gold exchange standard* is a state of affairs in which citizens cannot obtain gold on demand in exchange for their deposits etc., but can obtain on demand the currency of some other country which is on a full gold standard. The classical example of a gold standard country before 1914 was the United Kingdom; that of a gold exchange standard country was India. R.H.

Goldbach, Christian (Russian mathematician, 1690–1764), see under NUMBER THEORY.

Goll, Ivan (German-French poet and dramatist, 1891–1950), see under THEATRE OF THE ABSURD.

Gollancz, Sir Victor (British publisher, 1893–1967), see under LEFT BOOK CLUB.

Gomme, Sir George Laurence (British civil servant and writer, 1854–1916), see under FOLKLORE.

Gomringer, Eugen (German writer, *b*. 1925), see under CONCRETE POETRY.

Gomulka, Wladyslaw (Polish statesman, *b.* 1905), see under LEFT, THE; THAW.

gonads. The collective name for the male and female reproductive organs – in mammals the testes and ovaries respectively. The gonads contain two elements: a part which manufactures spermatozoa or ova, i.e. the GAMETES, and another part which is responsible for those internal secretions of the sex organs (see ENDOCRINOLOGY) upon which the development of secondary sexual characteristics depends.   P.M.

Goncharova, Natalia (Russian sculptress and painter, 1881–1962), see under CUBO-FUTURISM; DONKEY'S TAIL; KNAVE OF DIAMONDS; RAYONISM.

Goncourt, Edmond and **Jules** (French authors, 1822–96 and 1830–70), see under REALISM.

Goodman, Benny (U.S. clarinettist and band leader, *b.* 1909), see under BIG BAND; CHICAGO; SWING.

Goodman, Paul (U.S. author, 1911–72), see under BEAT; DE-SCHOOLING; POPULISM; POST-INDUSTRIAL SOCIETY.

Gore, Spencer (British painter, 1878–1914), see under CAMDEN TOWN GROUP.

Gorer, Geoffrey (British sociologist *b.* 1905), see under PORNOGRAPHY.

Gorky, Arshile (U.S. painter, 1905–48), see under ABSTRACT EXPRESSIONISM; NEW YORK SCHOOL.

Gorky, Maxim (Russian novelist and dramatist, 1868–1936), see under PROLETKULT; SOCIALIST REALISM.

Gottlieb, Adolph (U.S. painter, *b.* 1903), see under NEW YORK SCHOOL.

Gottmann, Jean (French geographer, *b.* 1915), see under GEOGRAPHY; MEGALOPOLIS; SUBURBANIZATION.

Goubert, Pierre (French historian, *b.* 1915), see under ANNALES SCHOOL.

Gourmont, Rémy de (French critic, 1858–1915), see under EGOIST, THE.

Gowing, Lawrence (British painter, *b.* 1918), see under EUSTON ROAD GROUP.

GPS (General Problem Solver), see under PROBLEM-SOLVING.

GPU, see under KGB.

gradient methods. OPTIMIZATION methods which represent the mathematical equivalent of climbing a hill by always following the steepest path up it. The simplest form of gradient method for maximizing a function causes the search process to take a step in the direction of steepest slope, then compare the direction of steepest slope at the new point with that at the old; comparison provides guidance for the choice of the next step-length. A carefully designed process of this kind works fast and efficiently except at the very last stages of the search for the optimum. More sophisticated methods allow the step-length to be chosen in the light of the rate-of-change of the gradient, and may also suggest a step-direction not exactly along the line of steepest slope; the *Newton-Raphson method* is of this type. Such methods are more laborious per step but usually need fewer steps than the more naive methods. The methods most widely used in current practice are the *variable-metric methods* developed in the 1960s and based on the work of Davidon, Fletcher, and Powell.   R.SI.

grammar. A central CONCEPT in contemporary LINGUISTICS, traditionally referring to an independent LEVEL of linguistic organization in which words, or their component parts (MORPHEMES), are brought together in the formation of sentences or DISCOURSES. (See MORPHOLOGY; SYNTAX.) In GENERATIVE GRAMMAR, however, and increasingly in other linguistic theories, the word means, more broadly, the entire system of structural relationships in a language, viewed as a set of rules for the generation of sentences. In this sense, the study of grammar subsumes PHONOLOGY and SEMANTICS, traditionally regarded as separate levels. A systematic account of a language's grammar (in either of the above senses) is known as 'a grammar'. See also CASE GRAMMAR; SCALE-AND-CATEGORY GRAMMAR; SYS-

TEMIC GRAMMAR; TAGMEMIC GRAMMAR; TRADITIONAL GRAMMAR.   D.C.
   Bibl: F. R. Palmer, *Grammar* (Harmondsworth, 1971).

grammar schools, see under SECONDARY SCHOOLS.

grammatical word, see under WORD CLASS.

grammaticality. In LINGUISTICS, the conformity of a sentence (or part of a sentence) to the rules defined by a specific GRAMMAR of a language. A preceding asterisk (see STARRED FORM) is commonly used to indicate that a sentence is ungrammatical, i.e. incapable of being generated by the rules of a grammar. See also ACCEPTABILITY.   D.C.

Gramsci, Antonio (Italian political thinker, 1891–1937), see under HEGEMONY.

Grand Design. Phrase coined by the American reporter, Joseph Kraft, in February 1962 for the policy of the Kennedy government towards Europe, a combination of trade expansion by the negotiation of large-scale reciprocal tariff concessions with the countries of the EEC together with the establishment of the same kind of 'Atlantic Community' between the European members of NATO and the U.S.A. On the military side at least the Atlantic Community was to remain under U.S. leadership. The Grand Design reached its rhetorical apogee with President Kennedy's call (4 July 1962) for a 'Declaration of Interdependence', and received its quittance at the hand of President de Gaulle of France in the press conference of 14 January 1963 in which he issued a veto on the British application for entry into the EEC.   D.C.W.
   Bibl: J. Kraft, *The Grand Design* (N.Y., 1962); D. C. Watt, 'The Defeat of the "Grand Design"', in *Survey of International Affairs* (for 1968; London and N.Y., 1970).

Grant, Duncan (British painter, *b.* 1885), see under BLOOMSBURY GROUP.

Granville-Barker, Harley (British dramatist and producer, 1877–1946), see under ROYAL COURT THEATRE.

graph. (1) A geometric representation of a FUNCTION. (2) A MATHEMATICAL STRUCTURE consisting of a set of objects (called *points*) some of which are connected to each other by *edges,* thus setting up a binary RELATION between the points. For example, a railway route map represents the relation 'is an adjacent station to'. Graph theory arose from the FOUR-COLOUR CONJECTURE and is of great use in COMBINATORIAL MATHEMATICS.   R.G.
   Bibl: A. Kaufmann, *Points and Arrows* (London, 1972).

graphic design. Design intended for printing, generally with a commercial purpose. As well as creating images and patterns, the graphic designer may be responsible for the layout, titling, scale, and colouring of magazines, books, posters, and film and television programmes. Graphic design plays an increasingly influential part in societies dominated by mass MEDIA and susceptible to skilful packaging. Pioneers of 20th-century graphic design include William Morris, El Lissitsky, and the BAUHAUS; today any of a variety of media may be employed, including relief, intaglio and surface printing, screen printing, photographic processes, and COMPUTER GRAPHICS.   P.C.

graphology. (1) The study of handwriting as a means of making inferences about the psychological characteristics of the writer. (2) A term applied by some LINGUISTS to a branch of LINGUISTICS that describes the properties of a language's orthographic system (spelling, punctuation). Graphology in this sense is analogous to PHONOLOGY in the spoken medium.
                           I.M.L.H.; D.C.

Grass, Günter (German novelist, dramatist, and poet, *b.*1927), see under GRUPPE 47.

Graves, Robert (British poet and miscellaneous writer, *b.* 1895), see under AMBIGUITY; MOVEMENT, THE.

gravitation (or *gravity*). The force of attraction between PARTICLES which arises from their MASS. Gravity is responsible for the fall of objects towards the centre of the earth, the ORBITS of the moon round the earth and the planets round the sun, and the condensation of the matter in the universe into stars and GALAXIES. The importance of gravitation diminishes as the scale of phenomena is reduced: the life of small insects is dominated by the intermolecular forces of viscosity and surface tension, while in ATOMIC PHYSICS and NUCLEAR PHYSICS gravity is completely overwhelmed by the vastly more powerful ELECTROMAGNETIC FIELDS, STRONG INTERACTIONS, and WEAK INTERACTIONS.

Gravity is in fact the weakest force known in PHYSICS, but it is also the only force which is both (1) long-range in its effects (unlike, e.g., molecular and nuclear forces, which are only appreciable very near their sources) and (2) always attractive (unlike, e.g., electric forces, which may also be repulsive, so that for large masses, where there are generally equal numbers of positive and negative charges, their effects add up to zero). Thus gravity dominates the behaviour of large systems, and is of central importance in COSMOLOGY.

In NEWTONIAN MECHANICS gravitation had the status of an ordinary force, in the same class as, say, MAGNETISM or friction, but in Einstein's general theory of RELATIVITY it is incorporated into the basic structure of MECHANICS from the start (see also MACH'S PRINCIPLE). M.V.B.

graviton. A hypothetical PARTICLE which is predicted to be associated with the FIELD of GRAVITATION in the same way as a PHOTON is associated with the ELECTROMAGNETIC FIELD. M.V.B.

gravity, see GRAVITATION.

Great Leap Forward. A policy of forced INDUSTRIALIZATION in China initiated in 1958, following a less radical 'leap forward' in 1956. It aimed at an annual rate of industrial growth of over 25%, and the Chinese economy was expected to overtake British industry within 15 years and the American in another 20 or 30 years. In contrast to the Soviet method of industrialization, the Chinese aimed at a simultaneous development of agriculture and of industry, both heavy and light, both modern and traditional. Small indigenous plants were developed all over the country in order to utilize local MANPOWER and spread industrial TECHNOLOGY; in agriculture rural labour was regimented in

very large COMMUNES. The attempt failed: in 1960–61 the economy declined, there were severe food shortages following two disastrous harvests, light industry stagnated, and exports fell. As the Great Leap Forward brought China to the brink of ruin, the policies designed to implement it were abandoned and replaced by new ones based on the priority of agricultural development. The INVESTMENT programme was reduced, modern technology was given a higher priority, birth-control was promoted, and the communes were drastically reorganized. The new policies were successful in restoring the Chinese economy. They did not, however, follow the Soviet economic model and were interrupted later by a new radical upheaval, the CULTURAL REVOLUTION. L.L.

Great Purge, see YEZHOVSHCHINA.

Greater East Asia Co-Prosperity Sphere. Name for the system of control over East and South-East Asia proposed by Japanese expansionists in the years 1941–4, a system of anti-European, inter-racial states and Japanese colonies under the general suzerainty of the Emperor. It included China, the Philippines, Indo-China, Burma, Siam, Indonesia, and Malaysia. D.C.W.

Bibl: F. C. Jones, *Japan's New Order in Asia* (London and N.Y., 1954).

Green, Frances Harriet Whipple (U.S. author and reformer, 1805–78), see under TOWN.

Green, Thomas Hill (British political theorist and philosopher, 1836–82), see under NEO-HEGELIANISM.

green belt, see under NEW TOWNS.

green pound, see under CAP.

green revolution. A dramatic change in grain crop farming in certain developing countries (e.g. Pakistan and India) resulting from the introduction of new high-yielding varieties grown by methods specifically suited to them. Wheat and rice are the crops principally concerned. New varieties, many of dwarf type, were developed during the 1960s, with the potential to produce yields nearly double those of the varieties in common use in many developing countries. To realize their potential, controlled irrigation water, heavy dressings of chemical fertilizer, and pesticides were required. In a number of countries arrangements were made for farmers to have these essential materials available as a 'package'. K.E.H.

Bibl: K. Griffin, *The Green Revolution* (Geneva, 1972).

Greenwich Village. An area of New York City whose name reflects its early origins, and which has traditionally had bohemian and literary connections. More recently it has become the backdrop to the BEAT and UNDERGROUND movements. The coffee-houses were meeting-places where creative artists, writers, and singers could present their work to a small but influential public. Henry James, Kerouac, Ginsberg, Jackson Pollock, and Bob Dylan were amongst the artists who lived and worked in the Village. In the 1960s it extended further east, to the Lower East Side which was one of the powerhouses of the Alternative Society, the East Coast equivalent to San Francisco. Today the Village suffers from a high crime rate and widespread vice and DRUG abuse. P.S.L.

Gregory, Isabella Augusta (Lady Gregory, Irish dramatist, 1852–1932), see under ABBEY THEATRE.

Grein, Jack Thomas (Dutch-British theatre manager and critic, 1862–1935), see under THÉÂTRE LIBRE.

Gresham's Law. An ECONOMIC LAW which states that 'bad money drives out good', meaning that if a coinage is debased individuals will tend to withdraw the old coins from circulation in order to realize the excess of their value as metal over their value as money. R.ST.

Grieg, Edvard (Norwegian composer, 1843–1907), see under ROMANTICISM.

Grierson, John (British film producer and director, 1898–1972), see under DOCUMENTARY.

Griffith, David Wark (U.S. film director, 1875–1948), see under KEYSTONE; MONTAGE.

Griffith, F., see under BACTERIOLOGY; NUCLEIC ACID.

Grigson, Geoffrey (British writer and editor, b.1905), see under HORIZON.

Gris, Juan (Spanish-French painter, 1887–1927), see under CUBISM; ÉCOLE DE PARIS.

Grivas, Georgios, General (Greek-Cypriot leader, 1898–1974), see under ENOSIS.

Gropius, Walter (German architect and teacher, 1883–1969), see under ARBEITSTRAT FÜR KUNST; BAUHAUS; CANTILEVER; INTERNATIONAL STYLE; OPEN STAGE; TOTAL THEATRE; WERKBUND.

Gross National Product, see GNP.

Grosz, Georg (German artist, 1893–1959), see under COLLAGE; DADA; NEUE SACHLICHKEIT.

Grotowski, Jerzy (Polish theatre director, b.1933), see under THEATRE LABORATORY.

ground state (in PHYSICS), see under ENERGY LEVEL.

group. In MATHEMATICS, a SET G of TRANSFORMATIONS forms a *transformation group* if: (1) G is closed under composition; and (2) G contains the identity transformation; and (3) G contains the inverse of each of its elements. Examples: (*a*) the 6 possible permutations of 3 objects; (*b*) the set of all rotations of a body about a fixed point; (*c*) the set of 24 rotations of a cube about its centre which leave it 'looking the same'. Example (*c*) is a *group of symmetry*. In general a situation or figure is *symmetrical* if there are transformations of it besides the identity which leave all (relevant) aspects of it unaltered. The set of all such transformations will form a group, the study of which may elucidate the nature of the symmetry. In PHYSICS, group theory is important for classification in CRYSTALLOGRAPHY, for QUANTUM MECHANICS, and in particular for the classification of the ELEMENTARY PARTICLES. In abstract mathematics the AUTOMORPHISMS of a MATHEMATICAL STRUCTURE may be viewed as its group of symmetry.

An *abstract group* is a set G of elements equipped with a binary operation (usually called 'composition' or 'multiplication') which satisfies abstract versions of (1)-(3) above and in addition the ASSOCIATIVE LAW $(xy)z = x(yz)$. (This is automatically satisfied by transformations.) G is *Abelian* if multiplication is required to satisfy the COMMUTATIVE LAW $xy = yx$. Examples: (*d*) the integers with the operation of addition; (*e*) the non-zero rational, real, or complex NUMBERS with the operation of multiplication. A group may be finite ((a), (c)), or infinite ((b), (d), (e)); the examples (*b*) and (*a*) have in addition a natural topological structure (see TOPOLOGY). Any abstract group may be *represented* in various ways as a group of transformations. R.G.

Bibl: H. Weyl, *Symmetry* (Oxford and Princeton, 1952); F. J. Budden, *The Fascination of Groups* (Cambridge, 1972).

Group, the. An attempt, in London in the late 1950s, to organize a conservative movement in poetry, by means of weekly meetings at which poets read and discussed their work. The Group, initiated by Edward Lucie-Smith, included for a time Ted Hughes and Peter Redgrove. The quality of its work may be judged by Lucie-Smith's and Philip Hobsbaum's *A Group Anthology* (1963). Later the Group, by now a spent force, became known as *Poetry Workshop*. M.S.-S.

Bibl: M. L. Rosenthal, *The New Poets* (London, 1967).

group dynamics, see under GROUP PSYCHOLOGY.

group norms. The formation of NORMS within a group of people – a phenomenon widely confirmed by observation as occurring in both natural and experimental groups. Such norms, whether they comprise agreement about mode of dress (teenage groups; see also YOUTH CULTURE), saluting (military groups), mealtimes (family groups), opinions (political groups), or perceptions (experimental groups), tend to act as a cohesive influence in the group, and to increase the number of things the group can take for granted, thus improving its efficiency in task performance. Newcomers to a group which they value may begin by merely complying with its norms, but later they may 'internalize' them. Individual members may reject the norms, either through incom-

patible external norms, through strong personality needs, through original thinking, or simply through a wish to challenge the leader. Such rejection, or DEVIANCE, is dealt with by the leader, or by more conformist group members, through frowns or other non-verbal signals, through verbal explanation ('not the done thing' etc.), or through punishment and, in the last resort, rejection. There is characteristically more conformity to group norms in public than in private acts; and particularly high degrees of conformity on the part of subjects with an AUTHORITARIAN PERSONALITY, and towards REFERENCE GROUPS with which the subject feels an important need to identify. M.J.C.

Bibl: M. Argyle, *Social Interaction* (London and N.Y., 1969).

group psychology. The branch of SOCIAL PSYCHOLOGY concerned with the behaviour of an individual when exposed to the influence of a group of which he is a member, and with the means (the *group process*) by which the group seeks to overcome any resistance to this influence. The subject is also known as *group dynamics*, though this term is more frequently used for the forces of interaction studied than for the study of them. See also GROUP NORMS. M.BE.

Bibl: D. Cartwright and A. Zander (eds.), *Group Dynamics* (London and N.Y., 1960).

Group Theatre.
(1) A proselytizing New York theatre company, lasting from 1931 to 1941, that aimed to reflect the social conditions of the time as accurately as possible and to prove that all theatrical technique has to be founded on 'life values'. Run by a fractious triumvirate of Lee Strasberg, Harold Clurman, and Cheryl Crawford, it produced some notable plays including Clifford Odets's *Waiting for Lefty* (1935), Robert Ardrey's *Thunder Rock* (1939), and William Saroyan's *My Heart's in the Highlands* (1939). It also nurtured such impressive actors as Lee J. Cobb and Franchot Tone. Ultimately it collapsed through shortage of funds and division of purpose. But it represented a major attempt to counteract the commercialism of Broadway and to provide America with the kind of ensemble spirit familiar in Europe; and its influence can still be seen

in the realistic tradition of modern American drama and in the teaching work of Lee Strasberg at the New York Actors' Studio (see METHOD, THE).

(2) A private play-producing society founded in 1932 at the Westminster Theatre, London. Its policy was never clearly defined but its chief importance lay in persuading major contemporary poets to write for it: Auden and Isherwood's *The Dog Beneath the Skin* (1936), *The Ascent of F6* (1937), and *On the Frontier* (1939), T. S. Eliot's *Sweeney Agonistes* (1935), and Stephen Spender's *Trial of a Judge* (1938) were its major productions. Its bare-stage style of presentation also gave writers a valuable geographical freedom and anticipated the scenic austerity of later years. But when it was wound up in 1953 it had long ceased to be an active or influential body.   M.BI.

Bibl: (1) H. Clurman, *The Fervent Years* (N.Y., 2nd ed., 1957); (2) N. Marshall, *The Other Theatre* (London, 1947).

group therapy. Classically, a form of PSYCHOTHERAPY in which clients, preferably strangers to each other, meet as a group with a trained therapist or therapists. Some therapists see the only advantage over individual therapy as being one of relative cheapness for the client, whereas others believe that a group process takes place which brings additional benefits. Groups can be used with hospitalized patients, although here the more disturbed patients need a more supportive kind of therapy. Recent advances in group techniques include ENCOUNTER GROUPS, PSYCHODRAMA, *sensitivity training, social competence training,* etc., with a wide variety of techniques and of training for the therapists. Some of these group techniques are also used in non-therapeutic contexts (see, e.g., ORGANIZATION THEORY).   M.J.C.

Bibl: H. Walton (ed.), *Small Group Psychotherapy* (Harmondsworth, 1971).

Groupe de Recherche d'Art Visuel, see under KINETIC ART.

Grove, Sir **William Robert** (British physicist, 1811–96), see under FUEL CELL.

Grünberg, Carl (Austrian sociologist, 1861–1940), see under FRANKFURT SCHOOL.

Gruppe 47. Informal group of mainly LEFT-wing German writers meeting annually in West Germany for readings and mutual criticism between 1947 and 1967. Their prize, awarded only when a work was felt to need publicizing, was won by (among others) Heinrich Böll in 1951, Günter Grass in 1958, and Johannes Bobrowski in 1962. Others associated with what soon became the most serious and influential movement in post-World War II German literature included Paul Celan, Uwe Johnson, H. M. Enzensberger, Erich Fried, the critics Walter Jens and Hans Mayer, and the group's founder Hans Werner Richter.   J.W.

Gruppe Zero, see under KINETIC ART.

Gruzdev, Ilya Alexandrovich (Russian author, 1892–1960), see under SERAPION BROTHERS.

GST (general systems theory). A general science of organization and wholeness. It is generally agreed to have been founded by Ludwig von Bertalanffy, who dated its inception from 1940. However, he acknowledged the same debts to precursors as did the founders of CYBERNETICS, and denied the identity of GST and cybernetics only by delimiting the definition of the latter in a way which is probably too restrictive. The objectives of the Society for General Systems Research, founded in 1954, would certainly have had the agreement of the early cyberneticians in 1942. On the other hand, they may be more general than some scientists (notably in the U.S.A. and France) would allow to cybernetics today.   S.BE.

Bibl: L. von Bertalanffy, *General System Theory* (N.Y., 1968).

Guéranger, Prosper-Louis-Pascal (French Benedictine monk, 1805–75), see under LITURGICAL MOVEMENT.

guerrilla. Spanish word for irregular warfare (see WAR) by independent or autonomous units; as used in English, a member of such a unit. Guerrilla warfare is age-old, but only in the 20th century did it come to be seen not just as an auxiliary method but as a road to the victory of REVOLUTION. Its theory was developed by its major practitioners: Mao Tse-tung (see MAOISM), the Vietnamese general Vo

Nguyen Giap (see VIETCONG), and Che
Guevara (see CASTROISM), all of whom
considered it as part of the doctrine of
'people's war'. This doctrine was an extension of LENINIST ideas about 'colonial
revolutions' and the 'anti-Imperialist
struggle' (see IMPERIALISM). COM-
MUNISTS in economically backward countries (see UNDERDEVELOPMENT) found
that their revolutionary chances depended
on the successful exploitation of local
NATIONALISM and peasant grievances.
Guerrillas could operate effectively only
in favourable surroundings (like 'fish in
water') and this provided the perspective
for the wars of 'national liberation'. In
such 'people's wars', Mao concluded, 'the
seizure of power by armed force, the
settlement of the issue by war, is the
central task and the highest form of
revolution'.

The military implications of this doctrine – and even more of the Chinese
revolutionary experience – were elaborated further by General Giap, who not
only postulated the transformation of
guerrilla warfare into a regular war, but
also introduced a psychological element
designed to shorten Mao's 'protracted
war' in a single stroke – like Dien Bien Phu
or the Tet offensive – making the enemy
lose his will and give up the struggle.
Other adherents of guerrilla revolution
went even further beyond Lenin's 'objective' conditions for a 'revolutionary situation'. Che Guevara, Régis Debray, and
Carlos Marighela addressed themselves
to the question of how to conduct guerrilla
warfare in places where Mao's 'support of
the people' was lacking. Guevara concluded that 'it is not necessary to wait until
all conditions for making revolution exist;
the insurrection can create them'. Debray
elaborated this by stressing the ideas of
foco insurrecional and of the guerrilla
force as the political vanguard, 'the Party
in embryo'. The Brazilian revolutionary
Carlos Marighella (killed in 1969) advocated guerrilla action in the cities. Latin
American *urban guerrillas* have engaged
in TERRORISM, political kidnapping, and
hijacking, but with no more success in
'arousing the masses' than ANARCHISTS in
the past with their 'propaganda by deed'.

The experience of revolutionary guerrilla struggles – rural or urban – suggests
that it is the political and not the military
side of their strategy that is paramount.

Initially they hope to elicit indiscriminate
repressions, which will 'alienate the masses' and assure their increasing support,
thus creating revolutionary conditions
which did not exist before. However, the
fulfilment or otherwise of this hope does
not depend on guerrillas alone. In Latin
America guerrilla activities have so far
only led to the proliferation of military
coups d'état.   L.L.

Bibl: R. Moss, *Urban Guerillas: the
New Face of Political Violence* (London,
1972); R. B. Asprey, *War in the Shadows:
the Guerilla in History* (N.Y., 1975;
London, 1976); W. Laqueur, *Guerilla*
(Boston, 1976; London, 1977).

Guesde, Jules (French socialist leader,
1845–1922), see under SYNDICALISM.

Guevara, Che (Cuban revolutionary,
1928–67), see under CASTROISM; GUER-
RILLA.

guidance, see under COUNSELLING.

Guild Socialism. A movement within the
British labour movement between 1906
and 1923 advocating the achievement of
SOCIALISM through the transformation of
the trade unions into monopolistic producers' guilds controlling and administering their branches of industry. A parallel
movement to SYNDICALISM in France, it
was less militant and tried to make a
synthesis of socialist and syndicalist ideas.
Guild Socialist ideas were formulated by
A. J. Penty in his *Restoration of the Guild
System* (1906), by R. A. Orage, editor of
New Age, and by S. G. Hobson, author of
National Guilds. Guild Socialists were
antagonistic both to parliamentary politics
and to the State, the proper role of which
was seen as that of an arbiter in case of
conflict rather than of an administrative
instrument. In contrast to the Fabians (see
FABIANISM), Guild Socialism was hostile
to state BUREAUCRACY.

After an unsuccessful attempt to capture the Fabian Society, Guild Socialists
established their own National Guilds
League. This split after the Bolshevik
Revolution, and many members (e.g. R
Page Arnot, R. Palme Dutt, William Gallagher, and Maurice Dobb) joined the
newly founded COMMUNIST Party o
Great Britain. In 1923 the N.G.L. broke
up and its organ, the *Guild Socialist*
ceased publication.   L.L

Bibl: S. T. Glass, *The Responsible Society: The Ideas of the English Guild Socialist* (London, 1966).

Guillard, Achille (French naturalist and demographer, 1799–1876), see under DEMOGRAPHY.

Guillaume, James (Swiss anarchist, 1844–1916), see under ANARCHO-SYNDICALISM.

Guillaumin, Armand (French painter and engraver, 1841–1927), see under IM-PRESSIONISM.

guilt culture, see under SHAME CULTURE.

Guimarães Rosa, João (Brazilian novelist, 1908–67), see under STREAM OF CON-SCIOUSNESS.

Guimard, Hector (French architect, decorator, and furniture designer, 1867–1942), see under ART NOUVEAU.

GULAG. Acronym for the Main Administration of Corrective Labour Camps – the department of the Soviet Secret Police responsible for administering the FORCED LABOUR system. Alexander Solzhenitsyn's *The Gulag Archipelago* – publication of which abroad was the immediate occasion of his expulsion in February 1974 – is a metaphorical expression for the huge scattered 'islands' of Gulag territory existing throughout the Soviet Union.   R.C.

Gumilev, Nikolai (Russian poet, 1886–1921), see under ACMEISM.

Gunn, Thom (British poet, *b.* 1929), see under MOVEMENT, THE.

Günther, Hans Friedrich (German sociologist, 1891–1968), see under DEGENERACY.

guru. A spiritual master in HINDUISM, such as every spiritually ambitious disciple is thought to need. The term is also applied to a Western teacher of the spiritual life, or even, ironically, to any mentor held in what is felt to be excessive reverence. See also SWAMI.   D.L.E.

gynandromorphism, see under INTERSEX.

gyroscope (or *gyro*). A rotating wheel so mounted on a shaft that either or both of its basic properties can be used to advantage. The first of these properties is that the wheel tends to maintain the direction of its axis of spin in space, not being influenced by the earth or by any other object in the universe, so far as is known. The second property is that if a twisting force (torque) is applied to the shaft so as to try to rotate the shaft about an axis perpendicular to the shaft, the resulting motion will be a rotation of the shaft about an axis which is at right angles both to the shaft and to the axis of the torque. Such motion is known as *precession*.

Gyroscopic properties are of great importance in the design of vehicles, including the bicycle, on account of the torques applied to the wheels during cornering. Gyroscopes are used in navigational instruments for ships, aircraft, and spacecraft; also in conjunction with a magnetic compass, for direction-finding and for the control of AUTOMATIC PILOTS. Large gyros have been used to assist the stablilization of ships in rough seas.

A gyroscope may also consist of a vibrating mass rather than a spinning wheel, and in this form it is common in living creatures such as the common crane fly ('daddy-long-legs').   E.R.L.

H

Haba, Alois (Czech composer, 1893–1972), see under MICROTONE.

Habermas, Jürgen (German social scientist, *b*. 1929), see under FRANKFURT SCHOOL.

Habimah (Hebrew for 'stage'). A theatre company founded in Moscow in 1917 to perform plays in Hebrew. Stanislavsky arranged for the actors, mostly from Polish theatres, to be trained by Yevgeny Vaktangov; the first performances were immensely successful, and the company visited America and Palestine (1928). Resident in Palestine since 1931, Habimah became Israel's official National Theatre (with a dramatic school and library) in 1953.　　　　　M.S.-S.

habitat. In GEOGRAPHY, a term used to denote the natural ENVIRONMENT of a plant or animal. It may be expressed as one of the main natural regions which are recognized in the subject, such as tropical rain forests or temperate grasslands, or as one of their subdivisions, such as chalk grassland or beech woodland.　　　M.L.

habituation. In CONDITIONING, the process of adjustment to a frequent or constant STIMULUS, whereby a minimal response is produced, or none at all. H.L.

Hadow Report, see under SECONDARY SCHOOL.

hadron. Any ELEMENTARY PARTICLE that reacts or decays with STRONG INTERACTIONS (e.g. the PROTON, the NEUTRON).　　　　　　　　M.V.B.

Haeckel, Ernst Heinrich (German biologist, 1834–1919), see under ECOLOGY; PHYLOGENY; RECAPITULATION.

Hafele, Joseph Carl (U.S. nuclear physicist, *b*. 1933), see under CLOCK PARADOX.

Hagana, see under IRGUN ZVAI LEUMI.

Hägerstrand, Torsten (Swedish geographer, *b*. 1916), see under GEOGRAPHY.

Haggett, Peter (British geographer, *b*. 1933), see under GEOGRAPHY.

Hahn, Hans (Austrian mathematician, 1879–1934), see under VIENNA CIRCLE.

Haldane, John Burdon Sanderson (British geneticist, biometrician, and physiologist, 1892–1964), see under SELECTION PRESSURE.

Halévy, Daniel (French historian, 1872–1962), see under DREYFUS CASE.

half-life. In RADIOACTIVITY, the average time which must elapse for half the NUCLEI in a large sample to decay (and which also gives the *probability* of decay in any time interval). More generally, an average time characterizing processes in any large population, e.g. the time taken to sell half the items in a given consignment of goods (the 'shelf-life').　　　　　M.V.B.

Halliday, Michael Alexander Kirkwood (British linguist, *b*. 1925), see under CLINE; FIRTHIAN; SCALE-AND-CATEGORY GRAMMAR; SYSTEMIC GRAMMAR.

Hamilton, Richard (British painter, *b*. 1922), see under POP.

Hamilton, Sir William Rowan (Irish mathematician, 1805–65), see under QUATERNION.

Hammerskjöld, Dag (Swedish statesman, 1905–61), see under UNO.

Hansberry, Lorraine (U.S. dramatist, 1930–65), see under BLACK THEATRE.

haploid (noun or adjective). (A CELL) containing only a single set of CHROMOSOMES. Contrasted with DIPLOID; POLYPLOID.　　　　　　　　　　　　　J.M.S.

happenings and events. Performances juxtaposing a variety of aural and visual material in a non-representational manner, with the aim of moving the spectator at an unconscious rather than a rational level. The genre owes its origin to the pieces combining music with other MEDIA developed by John Cage at BLACK MOUNTAIN College in the 1950s; the term 'happening' was first used by the painter Allan Kaprow (1959). In the work of Kaprow and Claes Oldenburg in New York happenings were associated with the POP ART movement of the early 1960s, particularly in the construction of ENVIRONMENTS. Throughout the 1960s the term was applied to pieces presented in Europe (see also WIENER GRUPPE) and the U.S.A. by artists (e.g. the German graphic artist Wolf Vostell) as well as theatre and dance groups, drawing eclectically upon a variety of traditions from FUTURISM and DADA to the THEATRE OF CRUELTY. In formal terms a happening contains several actions presented sequentially, while an event contains one action (which may be repeated). M.A.

Bibl: M. Kirby (ed.), *Happenings: an Illustrated Anthology* (N.Y., 1965); A. Henri, *Environments and Happenings* (London, 1974).

hard-edge. A phrase coined by the Los Angeles critic Jules Lansner in 1958 to describe the painting of several local ABSTRACT artists, including John McLaughlin, characterized by (a) flat forms rimmed by hard, clean edges presented in uniform colours, and (b) an overall unity in which colour and shape (or form) are one and the same entity. His term appeared in an introduction to the exhibition 'Four Abstract Classicists', but when in 1960 the show travelled to the Institute of Contemporary Arts in London it was re-titled 'West Coast Hard-Edge'. The term has been loosely used since to describe any art that tended towards the geometric. A.K.W.

Bibl: J. Coplans, 'John McLaughlin, Hard Edge and American Painting' (*Artforum,* Jan. 1964).

Harder, Delmar S. (U.S. engineer, b. 1892), see under AUTOMATION.

hardware. In COMPUTING, the actual COMPUTER as opposed to the PROGRAMS or SOFTWARE. C.S.

Hardy, Sir Alister (British zoologist, b. 1896), see under NEOTENY.

Hare, Richard Mervyn (British philosopher, b. 1919), see under EMOTIVISM.

Harnack, Adolf von (German theologian and historian, 1851–1930), see under LIBERALISM.

Harrison, George (British songwriter and performer, b. 1943), see under BEATLES.

Harrison, Harry (U.S. novelist, b. 1925), see under SCIENCE FICTION.

Harrod, Sir Roy Forbes (British economist, b. 1900), see under ACCELERATOR.

Hartlaub, Gustav Friedrich (German art historian, 1884–1963), see under NEUE SACHLICHKEIT.

Hašek, Jaroslav (Czech novelist, 1883–1923), see under ANTI-HERO.

Hassan, Ihab Habib (Egyptian-born U.S. literary critic, b. 1925), see under MODERNISM.

Hauptmann, Gerhart (German dramatist, novelist, and poet, 1862–1946), see under DEUTSCHES THEATER; FREIE BÜHNE; THÉÂTRE LIBRE.

Haushofer, Karl (German army officer and political geographer, 1869–1946), see under GEOPOLITICS.

Hausmann, Raoul (Austrian painter and photographer, 1886–1971), see under MONTAGE.

Hawkins, Coleman (U.S. jazz musician, 1904–69), see under HOT.

hawks, see DOVES AND HAWKS.

Hawks, Howard (U.S. film director, b. 1896), see under AUTEUR.

Hawthorne effect. In INDUSTRIAL PSYCHOLOGY, a result extrapolated from experiments conducted in the Hawthorne works of the Western Electric Company, near Chicago, between 1924 and 1936. It was found that increased productivity depended not so much on any particular incentives as on workers interpreting any change as provisional evidence of MANAGEMENT's interest and goodwill. A Hawthorne effect, then, is initial improvement in performance following a newly introduced change.　　　　H.L.

Bibl: F. J. Roethlisberger, *Management and the Worker* (Cambridge, Mass., 1939).

Hayden, Tom (U.S. radical political leader, *b*. 1940?), see under SDS.

Hayek, Friedrich August von (Austrian-British economist, *b*. 1899), see under RIGHT, THE.

Head Start Program. An American attempt (started in 1964–5 and originally known as *Operation Head Start*) to improve educational, health, and social opportunities at pre-school level for disadvantaged children and their families. Summer programmes of the kindergarten kind, now extended through the year, for children of four or five have been operating with federal grants to local and regional agencies. The aims are a class limit of 15, with a teacher and two aides per class operating 3–4 hours a day for a 15-hour week per child.　　　　W.A.C.S.

Bibl: E. D. Evans (ed.), *Contemporary Influences in Early Childhood Education* (London and N.Y., 1971), ch. 3.

Heartfield, John (German painter, designer, and journalist, 1891–1968), see under DADA; MONTAGE.

heartland. Geographical term for the central part of the Eurasian land mass. It was first used by Sir Halford Mackinder (1861–1947) to describe those parts of Eurasia not accessible from the sea and therefore presumed to be immune from attack by a maritime power.　　　　P.H.

heat death of universe. The hypothetical situation when the disordering tendency expressed by the second law of THERMO-DYNAMICS, acting over aeons of future time, results in the absence anywhere in the universe of ENERGY in a form which can be converted into work by organisms or machines of a type familiar to us. The

second law may not, however, apply to the universe as a whole, perhaps because of the long-range ordering influence of GRAVITATION. See also STATISTICAL MECHANICS.　　　　M.V.B.

heat exchanger. Apparatus for the transfer of heat to a substance which can be used directly in a piece of equipment requiring heat, from one which cannot do so for reasons inherent in the system which generated the heat. Thus, the heat energy in radioactive fluid from a NUCLEAR REACTOR can be used, after passing through a heat exchanger incorporating a RADIOACTIVE shield, to heat water in another vessel which can then be fed to a steam TURBINE.　　　　E.R.L.

heat pump. A system for pumping heat 'uphill', i.e. from a place of lower temperature to one of higher. A common example is the domestic refrigerator in which heat is ejected from the inside to the atmosphere outside. The reverse process is to be seen if a building is heated by cooling the air around it. The second law of THERMODYNAMICS demands that work is needed to perform such a task. One method in common use is to compress a gas (in the example of the refrigerator this is done *outside* the vessel). The gas liquefies, releasing in the process large quantities of heat, which is dissipated mostly by convection. The liquefied gas is then passed through a pipe system to the inside of the refrigerator where it is allowed to evaporate, i.e. to reverse the process and *take in* heat from the air inside the refrigerator. The gas is led outside again and the process repeated as many times as are necessary to maintain the required difference between internal and external temperature.　　　　E.R.L.

Heath, Edward (British statesman, *b*. 1916), see under SOCIAL COMPACT.

heavy water. Water in which one or both of the normal hydrogen atoms in each MOLECULE is replaced by DEUTERIUM. It is similar to ordinary water except for its ability to slow down NEUTRONS without reacting with them, and for this reason heavy water is used in NUCLEAR REACTORS as a MODERATOR.　　　　M.V.B.

Heckel, Erich (German painter, print-maker, and sculptor, *b*.1883), see under BRÜCKE, DIE.

hedonism. The theory that pleasure is the only thing that is intrinsically good, pain the only thing intrinsically bad. Other things, for the hedonist, are good or bad only instrumentally, to the extent that they are productive of pleasure or pain. What distinguishes hedonism as a philosophical theory from what is collo-quially understood by the same name is that it works with a much more inclusive conception of pleasure and pain. It takes pleasure to be, not just immediate bodily gratification, but the satisfaction of any desire whatever, enjoyment or grati-fication of any kind; pain, similarly, is not just bodily anguish, but any form of suffering or distress. The usual form of hedonist ETHICS, UTILITARIANISM, takes the pleasure and pain of everyone affected by it to be the CRITERION of an action's rightness, and is associated with a psychological version of hedonism which holds that human actions are motivated (see MOTIVATION) primarily by a search for pleasure and the avoidance of pain. A.Q.
Bibl: R. B. Brandt, *Ethical Theory* (Englewood Cliffs, N.J., 1959).

Hegel, Georg Wilhelm Friedrich (German philosopher, 1770–1831), see under ABSOLUTE, THE; ALIENATION; DIA-LECTIC; EXISTENTIALISM; FRANKFURT SCHOOL; GEISTESWISSENSCHAFTEN; HEGELIANISM; HISTORICISM; IDEALISM; MARXISM; METAPHYSICS; MONISM; NEO-HEGELIANISM; NEO-KANTIANISM; PANPSYCHISM; PERSONALISM; RELIG-ION; SOCIOLOGY.

Hegelianism. In PHILOSOPHY, the idealis-tic (see IDEALISM) system of G. W. F. Hegel (1770–1831) in which the method of DIALECTIC is used to systematize and complete all aspects of knowledge and experience and weld them into an inclu-sive whole. Philosophy, for Hegel, is the highest, or absolute, form of human know-ledge, and all other forms must submit to its critical modifications. Hegel concludes that reality as a whole, or the ABSOLUTE, is of the nature of a mind, and that it pre-sents itself to reflection first as a system of CONCEPTS, then as nature, and last, and most satisfactorily, as mind. A.Q.
Bibl: R. Plant, *Hegel* (London and Bloomington, 1973).

hegemony (from Greek *hegemon*, mean-ing leader or ruler).
(1) Since the 19th century it has been used especially to describe the predomi-nance of one state over others, e.g. the French hegemony over Europe in the time of Napoleon. By extension, *hegemonism* is used to describe 'great power' policies aimed at establishing such a preponder-ance, a use close to one of the meanings of IMPERIALISM.
(2) In the writings of some 20th-century MARXISTS (especially the Italian Gramsci) it is used to denote the predomi-nance of one social CLASS over others, e.g. in the term *bourgeois hegemony*. The fea-ture which this usage stresses is not only the political and economic control exer-cised by a dominant class but its success in projecting its own particular way of seeing the world, human and social relationships, so that this is accepted as 'COMMON SENSE' and part of the natural order by those who are in fact subordinated to it. From this it follows that REVOLUTION is seen not only as the transfer of political and economic POWER but as the creation of an alterna-tive hegemony through new forms of experience and consciousness. This is dif-ferent from the more familiar Marxist view that change in the economic base is what matters and that change in the SUPERSTRUCTURE is a reflection of this; instead, the struggle for hegemony is seen as a primary and even decisive factor in radical change, including change in the economic base itself. A.L.C.B.

Heidegger, Martin (German philosopher, 1889–1976), see under EXISTENTIALISM; HERMENEUTICS; PHENOMENOLOGY.

Heinroth, Oskar (German zoologist, 1871–1945), see under ETHOLOGY; IMPRINTING.

Heisenberg, Werner Karl (German physi-cist, 1901–76), see under MATRIX MECHANICS; QUANTUM MECHANICS; UNCERTAINTY PRINCIPLE.

helix, double, see DOUBLE HELIX.

HELMHOLTZ

Helmholtz, Hermann von (German scientist, 1821–94), see under FREE ENERGY; PERCEPTION.

helminthology. The branch of ZOOLOGY concerned with the *helminthes*, i.e. parasitic worms. The word is, however, now generally confined to the study of those internally parasitic flat worms (*platyhelminthes*) which include the flukes and such dangerous human parasites as *schistosoma* (or *bilharzia*). Schistosomiasis is one of the gravest and most intractable diseases of tropical Africa. The intermediate host is a water-snail, and most attempts at eradication or control are concentrated upon it.   P.M.

Helsinki. Shorthand term for the Final Act of the Conference on Security and Cooperation in Europe signed by the heads of the 35 participating states, including the U.S.A. and the U.S.S.R., in Helsinki in July 1975. The object of the Final Act was to develop better and closer relations in all fields among the participating states in an effort to make DÉTENTE a continuing process. It set out principles guiding relations between the states; measures governing aspects of security and DISARMAMENT; initiatives in economic and technological cooperation; and areas in which human contact and confidence-building might be encouraged. Important for the safeguarding of peace in Europe is the commitment of the participating states to refrain from the threat or use of force and to respect the SOVEREIGNTY and territorial integrity of states and the right of SELF-DETERMINATION of peoples. Some critics of Helsinki, such as the novelist Solzhenitsyn, argue that the Final Act provides no means of ensuring that the foregoing commitments and principles are adhered to, and that the Act, and the whole concept of détente, merely accommodate the current degree of Soviet dominance in Eastern Europe.   P.B.M.

hemispheres of the brain, see TWO HEMISPHERES.

Hendry, James Findlay (British poet, *fl.* c. 1940), see under NEW APOCALYPSE.

Hennebique, François (French engineer, 1842–1921), see under CONCRETE.

Henri, Adrian (British poet, *b.*1932), see under LIVERPOOL POETS.

Henri, Robert (U.S. painter, 1865–1929), see under ASHCAN SCHOOL.

Henry, Louis (French demographer), see under FAMILY RECONSTITUTION.

Heppenstall, Rayner (British novelist, poet, and critic, *b.*1911), see under NEW NOVEL.

Hepworth, Barbara (British sculptress, 1903–75), see under CONSTRUCTIVISM.

Herbartian psychology. The SCHOOL OF PSYCHOLOGY based on the ideas of Johann Herbart (1776–1841), German philosopher, psychologist, and educationist. He viewed mind as an organized, unitary, and dynamic interplay of ideas which actively attracted and repelled each other and struggled for a place in CONSCIOUSNESS.   I.M.L.H.

Herbertson, Andrew John (Scottish geographer, 1865–1915), see under GEOGRAPHY.

Herder, Johann Gottfried (German author, 1744–1803), see under ROMANTICISM.

heredity, see under GENETICS.

heresy. In Christian (see CHRISTIANITY) THEOLOGY, the attitude which makes a personal choice (Greek *hairesis*) rather than accepting the doctrines of CATHOLICISM. To a large extent modern thought rests on independent thinking, so that in modern times the term is seldom used pejoratively.   D.L.E.

Hering, Ewald (German physiologist and psychologist, 1834–1918), see under GENETIC MEMORY.

heritability. That part of the variability of a population which arises from GENETIC rather than environmental causes. J.M.S.

hermaphrodite, see under INTERSEX.

hermeneutics.
(1) That part of Christian THEOLOGY which is concerned with finding and inter-

preting (Greek *hermeneus,* an interpreter) the spiritual truth in the Bible, so that the Gospel is understood as addressed to each generation. Many of the issues involved were raised afresh by Rudolf Bultmann's proposal to DEMYTHOLOGIZE the New Testament.   D.L.E.

(2) More generally, the art, skill, or theory of interpretation, of understanding the significance of human actions, utterances, products, and INSTITUTIONS. In this sense the term was brought into PHILOSOPHY from theology by Dilthey in the late 19th century to refer to the fundamental discipline that is concerned with the special methods of the human studies or GEISTESWISSENSCHAFTEN, which do not merely order the raw deliverances of sensation but must seek an understanding (VERSTEHEN) of their essentially meaningful subject-matter. The term has since been more broadly applied by Heidegger to emphasize the general metaphysical purport (see METAPHYSICS) of his investigations into the nature of human existence.   A.Q.

hermetic. Adjective derived from the name of the Greek god Hermes Trismegistus (identified by the Greeks with the Egyptian Thoth, supposed author of mystical works and inventor of a magically airtight container). In literary contexts, it is applied, generally, to poetry of a Platonic, esoteric, recondite, or occult kind; or, more specifically, to a movement in contemporary Italian poetry: *poesia ermetica.* The term was coined, and its subject-matter traced, defined, and criticized, by Francesco Flora in *La poesia ermetica* (1936). The theoretical pioneer was Arturo Onofri, who carried over DECADENT and SYMBOLIST notions of 'pure poetry' from French to Italian, and who was influenced by Rudolf Steiner's ANTHROPOSOPHY. Onofri advocated (1925) a 'naked poetry', from which all logical elements would be eliminated and which would concentrate on the magic of the single word, on silences and (on the page) blankness. His programme was meanwhile being fulfilled by Giuseppe Ungaretti (1888–1970). Ungaretti sought to purge his poetry of rhetoric, and to restore the 'pristine' meanings to words by approaching them with the utmost simplicity: 'All the emphasis was on the word itself, each word, its sound, meaning,

resonance, and the space it could be made to fill.' Ungaretti's successors, Eugenio Montale and Salvatore Quasimodo, were of very different temperament; but both sought to rid poetry of rhetorical embellishment. Montale added to hermetic poetry a musicality, Quasimodo a Greek purity of diction. This simplicity of approach involved a subjectivity which some critics found excessively difficult; but *poesia ermetica* is now seen as a pioneering phase in Italian poetry. Other poets classed as hermetic include Mario Luzi, Alfonso Gatto, and Vittorio Sereni.   M.S.-S.

Bibl: C. L. Golino (ed.), *Contemporary Italian Poetry* (Berkeley and Los Angeles, 1962).

heroic materialism, see under ZEITGEIST.

Herskovits, Melville Jean (U.S. anthropologist, 1895–1963), see under ENCULTURATION; RELATIVISM, CULTURAL.

Hertzsprung-Russell diagram. An important GRAPH in ASTROPHYSICS, where the total ENERGY radiated by a star (its 'brightness') is plotted against wavelength (i.e. colour). The positions of the majority of stars on this graph lie near a diagonal line, along which, it is believed, typical 'main-sequence' stars progress in the course of their evolution from blue-bright (hot) to red-dim (cool). See also BLACK HOLE; NOVA; RED GIANT; SUPERNOVA.   M.V.B.

Herzen, Alexander Ivanovich (Russian journalist and political thinker, 1812–70), see under BOLSHEVISM; POPULISM.

Herzl, Theodor (Austrian founder of political Zionism, 1860–1904), see under ZIONISM.

Heseltine, Philip, see WARLOCK, PETER.

Hesse, Hermann (German author, 1877–1962), see under AU-DESSUS DE LA MÊLÉE.

heterokaryote, see under NUCLEUS.

heterological. In LOGIC, a term applied to a word that is not truly predicable of itself, e.g. the word 'long' (which is not long) or the word 'French' (which is not French).

Conversely, the words 'short' and 'English' are said to be *autological*. A.Q.

heterosis, see under GENE.

heterotrophic, see under AUTOTROPHIC.

heterozygote, see under GENE; MENDEL'S LAWS.

heuristic.
(1) (adjective) Concerned with ways of finding things out or solving problems; also used substantivally as a contraction of *heuristic method,* i.e. a procedure for searching out an *unknown* goal by incremental exploration, according to some *known* CRITERION (e.g. reaching the top of an unfamiliar hill in a fog by making every step an upward one). An important CONCEPT in CYBERNETICS, as is ALGORITHM. S.BE.
(2) In SOCIAL SCIENCE, the term is used especially to characterize conceptual devices such as IDEAL TYPES, MODELS, SENSITIZING CONCEPTS, and working hypotheses which are not intended to describe or explain the facts, but to suggest possible explanations or eliminate others. J.R.T.
Bibl: G. Polya, *How to Solve It* (Princeton, 2nd ed., 1971); S. Beer, *Brain of the Firm* (London and N.Y., 1972).

Heym, Georg (German poet, 1887–1912), see under EXPRESSIONISM.

Heyrovsky, Jaroslav (Czech chemist, 1890–1967), see under POLAROGRAPHY.

Hicks, George Dawes (British philosopher, 1862–1941), see under REALISM, CRITICAL.

Hicks, Sir John Richard (British economist, *b.* 1904), see under EQUILIBRIUM.

Hieatt, Allen Kent (U.S. literary critic, *b.* 1921), see under NUMEROLOGICAL CRITICISM.

hi-fi. Abbreviation of 'high fidelity', a term applied to ELECTRONIC apparatus designed to reproduce music, the human voice, or other sounds with minimal distortion. Although such reproduction requires the same high quality in the

recording microphone, the amplifiers, the transmission or storage unit, and the loudspeaker, the term is most often used colloquially to describe the output side of the apparatus, i.e. the amplifier and its loudspeaker. E.R.L.

Higgins, Dick (U.S. author and publisher, *b.* 1938), see under FLUXUS.

high culture, see under MASS CULTURE.

high-level programming language. In COMPUTING, a PROGRAMMING LANGUAGE designed with the convenience of its human users in mind rather than the peculiarities of any particular machine. Its chief merit is that it allows the programmer to leave many of the routine details of PROGRAM organization to the COMPUTER itself. It requires a COMPILER to translate the program into MACHINE CODE and typically produces 10 or more machine instructions for each statement written in it. Surprisingly, perhaps, it increases the productivity of programmers by about the same factor. A program written in a high-level language, unlike one written in an ASSEMBLY LANGUAGE, is nearly independent of the computer on which it is run. C.S.

higher arithmetic, see NUMBER THEORY.

higher criticism. The objective and exact study of the sources and methods used by the authors of the Bible. The pioneers of this scientific approach were almost all 19th-century scholars in German universities. In a book of 1881, by W. R. Smith, who was one of the British pioneers, the attempt to get behind the text to the actual history was contrasted with 'lower' criticism, i.e. with the study of manuscripts and other evidence in order to get at the text as originally written (see also TEXTUAL CRITICISM). In the 20th century, literary *source criticism* has been supplemented by *form criticism* (i.e. the attempt to discern the form taken by a story or teaching in order to make it more easily memorable, or more impressive, as it was passed on in oral tradition), and also by *redaction criticism* (i.e. the attempt to recover the theological motive of those redactors or editors who gathered these stories or teachings into the books we have). D.L.E.

Bibl: M. Black and H. H. Rowley (eds.), *Peake's Commentary on the Bible* (London, rev. ed., 1962); O. Eissfeldt, *The Old Testament: an Introduction* (Oxford, 1965); W. G. Kümmel, *The New Testament: the History of the Investigation of its Problems* (London, 1973); W. G. Kümmel, *Introduction to the New Testament* (London, rev. ed., 1975).

higher education, see under TERTIARY EDUCATION.

Hilbert, David (German mathematician, 1862–1943), see under FORMALISM; GÖDEL'S THEOREM; HILBERT SPACE; MATHEMATICAL LOGIC; META-MATHEMATICS.

Hilbert space. A CONCEPT introduced by David Hilbert (1862–1943) in his investigation of integral EQUATIONS. The characteristic feature of it and its generalizations is the application of geometric terminology and of methods which had been developed in the study of finite-dimensional (see DIMENSION) VECTOR SPACES to 'spaces' of FUNCTIONS which are infinite-dimensional (e.g. by the use of FOURIER SERIES). It is a fundamental concept of functional ANALYSIS and of QUANTUM MECHANICS.   R.G.

Hill, Christopher (British historian, *b*. 1912), see under PAST AND PRESENT.

Hiller, Kurt (German publisher, critic, and essayist, *b*. 1885), see under ACTIVISM.

Hilpert, Heinz (German actor, director, and theatre manager, 1890–1967), see under VOLKSBÜHNE.

Himmler, Heinrich (German Nazi politician, 1900–45), see under NIGHT OF THE LONG KNIVES.

Hindemith, Paul (German composer, 1895–1963), see under GEBRAUCHS-. . .; LEHRSTÜCK; NEO-CLASSICISM; NEUE SACHLICHKEIT.

Hindenburg, Paul von (German field-marshal and statesman, 1847–1934), see under NIGHT OF THE LONG KNIVES.

Hinduism. The RELIGION of most Indians. It has a rich variety, ranging from popular worship of gods in temples and homes, with petitions and celebrations, through devotional THEISM which sees these gods merely as expressions of the One God (e.g. as incarnations of Vishnu), to an austere MYSTICISM which suspects all religious images and seeks the absorption of the individual in the impersonal World-Spirit (the *Brahman*). This religion has been spread by Indians in many countries and has impressed many disillusioned or bored Christians by its tolerance, its profusion of religious emotion, its imaginative philosophy, its methods of self-mastery (specially in YOGA), and its power to give stability to a vast nation. Special admiration has been felt for the *Upanishads* (probably *c*. 800 B.C.) or ancient meditations on the position of man in a universe he did not make, and for the more warmly personal religion expressed in a later scripture, the *Bhagavad Gita* (probably *c*. 300 B.C.). The best-known Hindu of this century was Mahatma Gandhi (1869–1948), a saintly lawyer and political leader specially notable for the success of his advocacy of NON-VIOLENT RESISTANCE in ending British imperial rule. But it is difficult for those not born Indians to enter Hinduism's heritage. It is also difficult to reconcile some of its doctrines (e.g. the belief in the reincarnation of the self in successive bodies better or worse according to one's merits) with modern thought; and some of its traditional practices (e.g. the division of the population into 'castes' or strictly hereditary classes) with modern convictions about human equality. In India, which is officially a secular state (see SECULARIZATION), Hinduism is slowly adjusting itself to such challenges.   D.L.E.

Bibl: S. Radhakrishnan, *The Hindu View of Life* (London and N.Y., 1927); R. C. Zaehner, *Hinduism* (London and N.Y., 2nd ed., 1966).

hinterland. The German word *Hinterland* or 'back country' originally referred to the inland territory beyond the occupied coastal districts over which a colonial power claimed jurisdiction; thus it was applied in the late 19th century to parts of Africa. The word has been adapted by geographers to mean the land which lies behind a seaport and supplies the bulk of its exports, and in which most of its imports are distributed. In urban GEO-GRAPHY the term is also used with reference to other centres of population, e.g. market towns.   M.L.

Hippies. Term coined in California in 1966–7 to denote the mainly young people participating in the birth of the UNDERGROUND. As with their precursors the BEATS, the hippies' etymology is contentious; the most plausible derivation is from the Negro slang word 'hep' or 'hip' meaning to be knowledgeable, to have experience. Hippiedom in this first instance involved a 'philosophy' of Peace and Love together with a rejection of things material, a devotion to marijuana and lysergic acid (LSD) as instruments of enlightenment and pleasure, a propensity for communal life-styles and libertarian sexual behaviour, and a style of dress which included beads, bells, and long hair. This original conception of the hippie did not last in its pure form for longer than two years, the originators themselves staging a 'Death of Hippie' parade in San Francisco in 1968. The era of 'love-ins', 'flower-power', and 'beautiful vibes' soon degenerated, largely by over-exposure in the mass MEDIA, into commercialism, violence and widespread DRUG abuse. The term hippie is now widely, if incorrectly, used to denote any young, long-haired person suspected of unconventional standards. See also DROP-OUT.   P.S.L.

Hiroshima. The Japanese city selected as target for the first atom-bomb dropped by the U.S. Air Force, 6 August 1945. Over 78,000 were killed, a further 70,000 badly injured, and two-thirds of the city destroyed. Most of the remainder of the population suffered some long-term radiation damage. On 2 September 1945, after a further atom-bomb had been dropped on Nagasaki, the Japanese Government surrendered to the Allied forces. The decision to drop the bomb was governed by the desire to avoid the necessity of a full-scale invasion of Japan and the heavy losses this would entail.   D.C.W.

Bibl: H. Feis, *The Atomic Bomb and the End of World War II* (rev. ed., London and Princeton, 1966).

histochemistry. The branch of HISTOLOGY in which an attempt is made to use diffe-

rential colour reactions in order to identify the different chemical components of a TISSUE, e.g. PROTEINS, CARBOHYDRATES, and ENZYMES. All microscopical staining actions are in essence histochemical, e.g. the bringing of NUCLEI into prominence by staining with basic dyes such as methylene blue. Histochemistry has been most widely used in the identification of specific enzymes such as phosphatases. It is gradually being supplanted by orthodox biochemical methods of investigation which often turn upon the physical separation of the various elements of the CELL such as the nuclei, mitochondria, and cell sap (see CYTOLOGY).   P.M.

histogram. In STATISTICS, a simple representational technique for giving an idea of the shape of an empirical DISTRIBUTION. The range of values of the random variable is divided into (usually equal) intervals and a block is drawn on each interval whose area is proportional to the number of observations falling in that interval, or to the proportion of the distribution lying in it. A typical example of the use of a histogram would be to represent the distribution of heights in a SAMPLE of adult men on a centimetre-by-centimetre basis – the size of the block on the interval between, say, 175 cm and 176 cm would be proportional to the number of men of height at least 175 cm but less than 176 cm.   R.SI.

histoire événementielle, see under ANNALES SCHOOL.

histology. The branch of microscopy (i.e. investigation with the microscope) that deals with the structures and properties distinctive of individual TISSUES – e.g. nervous, muscular, glandular, or connective tissue. Histology is usually contrasted with CYTOLOGY.   P.M.

histopathology. A subject bearing the same relation to PATHOLOGY as do HISTOLOGY and CYTOLOGY to gross ANATOMY. In the interpretation of disease states it often happens that the evidence of gross pathological anatomy is not sufficiently specific or revealing, and the diseased TISSUE is therefore examined misroscopically, using the resources of HISTOLOGY and HISTOCHEMISTRY. Histopathology plays a crucially important part in the diagnosis of malignant disease (see CANCER). It may be carried out on tissues removed from the living subject (such removal and examination being known as a *biopsy*) or upon material obtained at post-mortem examination, in which case allowance must be made for the deterioration of the tissues following death. P.M.

historical demography. The statistical study of populations in the past, concerned in particular with measuring the rates of birth, marriage, and death at different periods. The subject grew up about 1950. Demographers began to study the period before 1800 (when reliable national statistics begin) and historians began to interest themselves in population movements. At first their emphasis was on the idea of a demographic 'old regime' in pre-industrial Europe, with regular crises as population pressed on the means of subsistence. More recently the stress has been on the regional variations in birth-, marriage-, and death-rates. See also FAMILY RECONSTITUTION. P.B.
Bibl: E. A. Wrigley, *Population and History* (London and N.Y., 1969).

historical materialism. A shorthand term for the MATERIALIST view of history, the cornerstone of Marx's theory of history. He expressed it most concisely in his preface to *A Contribution to the Critique of Political Economy* (1859): 'The mode of production in material life determines the general character of the social, political, and spiritual processes of life. It is not the consciousness of men that determines their existence, but on the contrary, it is their social existence which determines their consciousness. . . . In the social production which men carry on they enter into definite relations which are indispensable and independent of their will. . . . The sum total of these relations of production constitutes the economic structure of society – the real basis, on which rises a legal and political superstructure and to which correspond definite forms of social consciousness. The mode of production determines the social, political, and intellectual life processes in general.'
This theory (and the concepts used in it) have been subject to a myriad different interpretations, ranging from those which present the materialist conception of his-

tory as a monistic (see MONISM) *economic* (or technological) *determinism* to those emphasizing the interaction between the 'economic basis' and the 'political superstructure'.
Engels, like Marx, repeatedly affirmed that their theory 'explains all historical events and ideas, all politics, philosophy, and religion, from the material, economic conditions of life of the historical period in question'. But towards the end of his life he shifted the emphasis and stressed (in a letter to J. Bloch, 21 September 1890) that neither he nor Marx ever subscribed to an unqualified economic determinism which would reduce all historical development to economic causes alone. He wrote that they assert themselves historically only 'in the last resort': 'The economic situation is the basis, but the various elements of superstructure . . . also exercise their influence upon the course of the historical struggle and in many cases preponderate in determining their form. There is an interaction of all these elements. . . .'
However, as Eduard Bernstein (see REVISIONISM) noticed, once historical necessity is made dependent on economic causation only 'in the final analysis', there is no way of predicting the historical development of concrete societies, and SOCIALISM ceases to be 'scientific' in the sense attributed to it by Engels. With the MARXIST-LENINIST stress on political VOLUNTARISM, the original theoretical substance of historical materialism has fallen into disregard, and the MAOIST interpretation of it, for instance, goes so far as to include a condemnation of 'the reactionary theory of productive forces . . . [which] describes social development as a natural outcome of the development of productive forces only, especially the development of the tools of production'. L.L.
Bibl: N. I. Bukharin, *Historical Materialism* (N.Y., 1925; London, 1926); G. P. Plekhanov, *The Materialist Conception of History* (London, 1940).

historicism (or *historism*: from German *Historismus*). A word which at different times has been applied to two diametrically opposite approaches to history: (1) Originally, in the late 19th century, it meant an approach which emphasized the uniqueness of all historical phenomena and maintained that each age should be interpreted in terms of its own ideas and principles, or, negatively, that the actions of men in the past should not be explained by reference to the beliefs, motives, and valuations of the historian's own epoch. Particularly popular in Germany, this approach went with an emphasis on the function of VERSTEHEN in historical method, and with a rejection of the SOCIAL SCIENCES. (2) The term has more recently been used by K. R. Popper in an entirely different sense, which is now at least as commonly intended as the original one. To Popper historicism is the belief in large-scale laws of historical development of the kind to be found in speculative systems of history, whether linear or cyclic, such as those of Hegel, Marx, Comte, Spengler, and Toynbee. Hostile to them as being the intellectual foundations of totalitarian IDEOLOGIES, he argues that the course of history is radically affected by the growth of knowledge and that future acquisitions of knowledge cannot be predicted. Historicism, in this sense, however, is not associated exclusively with TOTALITARIANISM; most liberals (see LIBERALISM) in the 18th and 19th centuries believed in a law of inevitable progress. P.B.; A.Q.

Bibl: F. Meinecke, tr. J. E. Anderson, *Historism* (London, 1972); K. R. Popper, *The Poverty of Historicism* (London, 1957; N.Y., 1960).

historiography. The history of historical writing. At least as old as La Popelinière's *L'Histoire des histoires* (1599), historiography has become a popular subject of research only in the last twenty years. This awakening of interest in history's own past goes with an increased self-consciousness on the part of historians, and a rejection of the idea that they can produce an 'objective' description, uncontaminated by their own attitudes and values, of what actually happened. P.B.

Bibl: H. Butterfield, *Man on his Past* (London, 1955).

historism, see HISTORICISM.

history. History in the sense of writing about the past has traditionally been divided by *period* into ancient, medieval, and modern, and also into different *kinds* of history, e.g. political history, ecclesias-

tical history, art history, which hardly require explanation. This conventional subject-matter has widened enormously in the last few years. CONTEMPORARY HISTORY has been added to the list of periods. ECONOMIC HISTORY, LOCAL HISTORY, and SOCIAL HISTORY have become serious subjects of academic study and have proliferated into HISTORICAL DEMOGRAPHY, AGRARIAN HISTORY, and URBAN HISTORY. Art history has been joined by the history of science, CULTURAL HISTORY, HISTORIOGRAPHY, HISTORY OF IDEAS, and HISTORY OF MENTALITIES. These enlargements, together with the impact of the SOCIAL SCIENCES, have necessitated changes in historical method, signalled by the coining of such terms as COMPARATIVE HISTORY, ETHNOHISTORY, ICONOGRAPHY, PROSOPOGRAPHY, PSYCHOHISTORY, QUANTITATIVE HISTORY, and SERIAL HISTORY. P.B.

history of ideas. A term popularized, and a discipline founded, by Arthur Lovejoy in the U.S.A. in the 1920s. Lovejoy opposed the fragmentation of the historical study of ideas into the histories of philosophy, literature, science, etc., and suggested an interdisciplinary approach which focused on individual concepts like 'nature' and 'primitivism' and on the changes in their meaning and associations. The focus on individual ideas was a reaction against German *Geistesgeschichte* (see CULTURAL HISTORY), with its emphasis on the unity of systems of thought. Lovejoy's approach ran the risk of personifying ideas. Hence some of his successors use the term *intellectual history*, and place more emphasis on thinking men. See also HISTORY OF MENTALITIES. P.B.

Bibl: A. O. Lovejoy, *Essays in the History of Ideas* (Baltimore, 1948).

history of mentalities (*mentalités collectives*). An approach to what American scholars call the HISTORY OF IDEAS and PSYCHOHISTORY, developed in France in the 1930s, notably by Lucien Febvre and Georges Lefebvre. It is concerned with everyone's ideas, with peasants' as well as philosophers'; with sensibility as well as with concepts; and, in particular, with basic mental STRUCTURES. Thus Febvre, writing about 16th-century France, suggested that men had an imprecise sense of time and space; lacked any sense of the impossible; and perceived the world more through the ear than through the eye. His conclusions are still debated, but French historians continue to use his methods. See also ANNALES SCHOOL. P.B.

Hitchcock, Alfred (British-U.S. film director, *b*.1899), see under AUTEUR.

Hitchcock, Henry-Russell (U.S. architectural historian, *b*.1903), see under INTERNATIONAL STYLE.

Hitler, Adolf (German Nazi leader, 1889–1945), see under APPEASEMENT; COMINTERN; FÜHRERPRINZIP; GESTAPO; JULY 20TH; LOGICAL EMPIRICISM; MUNICH; NAZI, NAZISM; NIGHT OF THE LONG KNIVES; POPULAR FRONT; PRAGUE; PROLETARIAT; RIGHT, THE; SOCIAL DARWINISM; TERRORISM; WEIMAR REPUBLIC; XENOPHOBIA.

Hjelmslev, Louis (Danish linguist, 1899–1965), see under GLOSSEMATICS.

Hlinka, Andrej (Slovak Roman Catholic priest, 1864–1938), see under CLERICO-FASCISM.

Ho Chi Minh (Vietnamese statesman, 1890–1969), see under VIETMINH.

Hobbes, Thomas (British philosopher and political theorist, 1588–1679), see under DETERMINISM; DOUBLE-TALK; LEGAL POSITIVISM; NOMINALISM; SOCIAL COMPACT; SOCIAL CONTRACT.

Hobhouse, Leonard Trelawny (British sociologist and philosopher, 1864–1929), see under COMPARATIVE METHOD.

Hobsbaum, Philip (British poet, *b*.1932), see under GROUP, THE.

Hobsbawm, Eric John Ernest (British historian, *b*.1917), see under PAST AND PRESENT.

Hobson, John Atkinson (British economist and author, 1858–1940), see under IMPERIALISM.

Hobson, Samuel George (British socialist, *b*.1870), see under GUILD SOCIALISM.

Höch, Hannah (German painter, *b*.1889), see under MONTAGE.

Hochhuth, Rolf (German dramatist, *b*. 1931), see under DOCUMENTARY; VOLKSBÜHNE.

Hockett, Charles Francis (U.S. linguist, *b*.1916), see under LEXEME.

Hockney, David (British painter, etcher, and draftsman, *b*.1937), see under POP.

Hodgkin, Dorothy (British chemist, *b*.1910), see under INSULIN.

Hoelzel, Adolf (German sculptor, 1853–1934), see under ABSTRACT ART.

Hoffman, Julius J. (U.S. judge, *b*.1895), see under CHICAGO CONSPIRACY TRIAL.

Hoffmann, Ernst Theodor Amadeus (German novelist and composer, 1776–1822), see under SERAPION BROTHERS.

Hoffmann, Josef (Austrian architect, 1870–1956), see under KUNSTGEWERBESCHULE; WIENER WERKSTÄTTE.

Hofmann, Hans (German-U.S. painter, 1880–1966), see under NEW YORK SCHOOL.

Hoggart, Richard (British educationist, *b*.1918), see under MASS CULTURE.

Hohfeldian. Adjective formed from the name of the American jurist W. N. Hohfeld (1879–1918), whose study *Some Fundamental Legal Conceptions as Applied in Judicial Reasoning* (first version, 1917) represents a major clarification of the concept of a legal right. Hohfeld distinguished four basic elements for each of which the expression a 'legal right' had been loosely used by lawyers and others, sometimes without an appreciation of the difference between them. Hohfeld used in a special technical sense the four expressions: *claim-right, liberty* (or *privilege*), *power*, and *immunity* to distinguish these four elements. The distinctions drawn in this Hohfeldian analytical scheme have served to clarify not only the concept of a legal right, but also more complex notions such as that of ownership. H.L.A.H.

287

Bibl: W. N. Hohfeld, ed. W. W. Cook, Foreword by A. L. Corbin, *Fundamental Legal Conceptions as applied in Judicial Reasoning* (London and New Haven, 1974).

holism. The thesis that wholes, or some wholes, are more than the sums of their parts in the sense that the wholes in question have characteristics that cannot be explained in terms of the properties and RELATIONS to one another of their constituents. ORGANICISM is a particular version of holism, which is founded on the analogy of complex systems in general with what are literally organisms, whose parts lose their nature, function, significance, and even existence when removed from their organic interconnection with the rest of the organism. Holism is central to IDEALIST theories of the State and other social INSTITUTIONS, to many accounts of the special unity and integrity of works of art, and to the theory of science advanced by Quine, according to which science is not an assemblage of isolable bits of belief but an interconnected system which is adjusted as a whole to the deliverances of experience. Holism is hostile to the philosophical technique of ANALYSIS, which it conceives to be a falsifying mutilation of what it is applied to. See also METHODOLOGICAL INDIVIDUALISM AND METHODOLOGICAL HOLISM.   A.Q.

Bibl: E. Nagel, *The Structure of Science*, (London and N.Y., 1961).

holocaust, see under FINAL SOLUTION.

holography. A new type of photography producing three-dimensional images, which was developed by the engineer-physicist Dennis Gabor in 1947. In conventional photography based on lenses etc. only the straight-line propagation of light is utilized (see OPTICS) and wave effects constitute a nuisance. Holography, however, relies essentially on wave properties: the PHASE of the wave reflected from an object is revealed by interference resulting from the addition of a 'reference wave', the pattern produced by the combination of the two waves being recorded on an ordinary photographic film negative. When this *hologram* is illuminated by the reference wave alone, there results an image of the original object which is fully three-dimensional (i.e. it shows perspective etc.). Since the light sources must have a high degree of COHERENCE, LASERS are almost universally used.   M.V.B.

Holst, Gustav (British composer, 1874–1934), see under BITONALITY; POLYTONALITY.

Holy Rollers. A nickname given to an American group in the PENTECOSTALIST movement, because its adherents may roll on the floor in religious ecstasy. Sometimes used more widely, in order to attribute to others an enthusiasm for a primitive kind of religion (see PRIMITIVISM) combined with a lack of self-discipline, rationality, or social STATUS.   D.L.E.

Holz, Arno (German poet and dramatist, 1863–1929), see under STREAM OF CONSCIOUSNESS.

Homans, George (U.S. sociologist, *b*. 1910), see under EXCHANGE MODELS; SOCIOLOGY.

homeomorphism, see under TOPOLOGY.

homeomorphy, see under PHYLUM.

homeostasis.
(1) The widespread DISPOSITION of living beings, including people, to maintain a state of EQUILIBRIUM in the face of changing conditions, whether physical, chemical, or psychological. This disposition is often used as an explanatory principle in BIOLOGY and PSYCHOLOGY. See also ADAPTATION.   I.M.L.H.
Bibl: W. B. Cannon, *The Wisdom of the Body* (London, 1932; rev. ed., N.Y., 1939).
(2) In CYBERNETICS, this disposition is generalized mathematically to include all (not only biological) systems that maintain critical variables within limits acceptable to their own structure in the face of unexpected disturbance. See also AUTOPOIESIS; ULTRASTABILITY.   S.BE.
Bibl: W. R. Ashby, *Design for a Brain* (London and N.Y., 2nd ed., 1960).

homoerotic. Adjective often loosely equated with HOMOSEXUAL. It is used, however, to describe not so much sexual *behaviour* as the arousal of sexual *feelings* by members of the same sex, or by

PORNOGRAPHIC material involving homosexual activity. M.J.C.

homology. A CONCEPT easier to exemplify than to define. The pectoral fins of fish, the wings of birds, and the forelimbs of mammals are homologous; in spite of their differences of function and of detailed ANATOMY, they occupy morphologically equivalent positions in the body and are genetically cognate in the sense that forelimbs evolved out of fins, and wings out of forelimbs. One of the most striking achievements of MOLECULAR BIOLOGY is to have put the concept of homology upon a molecular basis. It is clear, for example, that all vertebrate haemoglobins are homologous – and that the relationship between them can now be interpreted first in terms of the nature and order of their respective AMINO ACID sequences and thus indirectly in terms of the DNA nucleotide chains (see NUCLEIC ACIDS) that specify the order of these sequences. P.M.

homology theory, see under TOPOLOGY.

homosexuality. The practise of sexual relations with members of one's own sex. Male homosexuality, condemned in Judaeo-Christian societies as the 'sin of Sodom', was condoned and even exalted in ancient Greece. Female homosexuality, or *Lesbianism* (named after the poetess Sappho, who lived on the island of Lesbos and wrote love poems to women), has never been so consistently condemned. Particularly since the liberalization of the law in England and Wales, and the foundation in America of the GAY LIBERATION FRONT, male and female homosexuals in these and many other Western countries have become less secretive about their way of life. The KINSEY REPORT of 1948–53 suggested that in both sexes exclusive homosexuals were far outnumbered by bisexuals. Some clues as to causation include the frequent concordance for homosexuality in identical twins (suggesting genetic causation), the absence of major differences in hormone balance (see ENDOCRINOLOGY) between homosexuals and heterosexuals (arguing against physical causation), and the tendency for homosexuals, both male and female, to have older, dominating mothers and passive or absent fathers

(suggesting environmental factors). Some homosexuals actually fear the opposite sex, others perhaps cannot sustain the expectations involved in fatherhood and motherhood. Treatment, where this is requested, can be by PSYCHOTHERAPY (unlikely to change sexual orientation) or by BEHAVIOUR THERAPY (likely to change sexual behaviour, but with a risk of causing DEPRESSION). M.J.C.

homotopy theory, see under TOPOLOGY.

homozygote, see under GENE.

Honegger, Arthur (Swiss composer, 1892–1955), see under PROGRAMME MUSIC; SIX, LES.

Hopkins, Gerard Manley (British poet, 1844–89), see under SPRUNG RHYTHM.

Hopper, Vincent Foster (U.S. critic, *b.* 1906), see under NUMEROLOGICAL CRITICISM.

horizon.
(1) In GEOLOGY, a distinctive stratum, assumed to have been originally horizontal, which extends over a wide area and can be used to establish a regional stratigraphy (see STRATIFICATION).
(2) In PEDOLOGY, an important morphological character exhibited by a soil when inspected in a vertical section known as the *soil profile.* The soil horizons, which occur in layers roughly parallel to the surface, can be distinguished from each other, and from parent rock material at the base of the profile, on the basis of properties such as colour, texture, and amount of organic matter. A number of processes interact to produce soil horizons: the addition and decomposition of organic material, weathering of the parent rock material, and the movement of soluble and suspended constituents by the movement of soil water. The study of the soil profile is basic to the scientific study of soil since it provides a means of identification and classification, and also data relating to soil evolution. J.L.M.L.

Horizon. A monthly review of literature and art edited by Cyril Connolly and Peter Watson from London, 1940–50, and displaying a remarkable, eclectic range of talents. Early numbers drew heavily on such writers of the 1930s as MacNeice, Day Lewis, Spender, Auden, and Geoffrey Grigson. But it also maintained close contacts with France, and in the post-war period the U.S.A., printing Malraux, Sartre, Camus, Lionel Trilling, Marianne Moore, Wallace Stevens, e. e. cummings, etc. in addition to such British writers as Evelyn Waugh (whose *Unconditional Surrender*, 1961, includes some satirical remarks about *Horizon*), George Orwell, and Angus Wilson (whom it 'discovered'). It ended in some desperation as Connolly noted a decline in the aesthetic, AVANT-GARDE impulse he favoured.　　M.S.BR.

Horkheimer, Max (German philosopher and sociologist, 1895–1973), see under FRANKFURT SCHOOL; NEO-MARXISM; REIFICATION.

hormic psychology. William McDougall's term for his form of purposive psychology (see PURPOSIVISM). Human action is governed, in this view, not by a rational search for hedonistic ends, but by primitive urges that had been largely neglected by students of man's social life.　　I.M.L.H.
　　Bibl: W. McDougall, *An Introduction to Social Psychology* (Boston, rev. ed., 1926; London, 23rd ed., 1936).

hormone, see under ENDOCRINOLOGY.

horn. In JAZZ, a word in need of clarification, since it is used by musicians to denote *any* instrument. By analogy, a pianist or guitarist may be described as 'blowing' some jazz.　　B.G.

Hornel, Edward Atkinson (Scottish painter, 1864–1933), see under GLASGOW SCHOOL.

Horney, Karen (German-U.S. psychoanalyst, 1885–1962), see under NEO-FREUDIAN.

Horniman, Annie Elizabeth Fredericka (British theatre manager and patroness, 1860–1937), see under REPERTORY.

horse opera. Affectionately derogatory term for the WESTERN, probably occasioned equally by the fact that the hero's best friend was usually his horse, and by the rise of the singing cowboy after the advent of the all-talking movie had led to a corresponding though temporary decline in the all-action western. T.C.C.M.
　　Bibl: G. N. Fenin and W. K. Everson, *The Western* (N.Y., 1962).

Horta, Victor, Baron (Belgian architect, 1861–1947), see under ART NOUVEAU.

hot. Adjective widely deployed to describe a certain kind of JAZZ, especially through to the 1930s. 'Hot' jazz has as its obvious but much later antithesis 'cool' jazz, and the main characteristics of hot music were the creation of an aura of excitement by use of a wide instrumental vibrato and a masculine, sometimes deliberately coarsened, tone. The term is best understood, however, by reference to the aural effects it implies, and the contrast between hot and cool is never more obvious than when one compares the work of the hot musician *par excellence*, Louis Armstrong, with his cool descendant, Miles Davis, or, even more marked because the two men were contemporaries, the hot tenor saxophone of Coleman Hawkins with the blander, more detached playing of Lester Young. B.G.

hot and cold. Terms drawn from JAZZ idiom (see HOT) by Marshall McLuhan (*The Gutenberg Galaxy,* 1962), in the course of establishing his thesis that the spoken word is the fullest means of human communication, since its context (intonation, facial expression, gesture, etc.) offers the most reliable means of transmitting a mental state. On this basis, hearing is 'hotter' than seeing or feeling or tasting. The television image, however, is (from a technical standpoint) poorly defined, and is therefore 'cold' (the poor definition demands – McLuhan claims – an effort from the viewer, thus *involving* him). Before the invention of printing, man was 'aural', 'hot', more 'tribal' than subsequently: his emotions lay near the surface of his personality. 'Hot' is not a precise term; Jonathan Miller's definition 'intrinsically richer' (i.e. involving more of the 'plural and voluminous' nature of human experience) is perhaps as near as it is possible to get.　　M.S.-S.

hovercraft. A vehicle whose weight is supported a short distance above the ground or above water by the pressure from an air cushion trapped by air blown around its periphery from within the vehicle itself. Hovercraft are usually propelled by one or more conventional airscrews and in this respect they represent a form of low-flying aircraft. Their ability to cross water on a foggy day when no aircraft could fly has made them especially suitable for ferry services, as well as for travelling over difficult country, e.g. swamps.

Hovercraft belong to the broader class of hovering vehicles known as 'ground effect vehicles' (G.E.V.), and include *tracked hovercraft*, which move along a predetermined route, usually a concrete beam. The clearance between the beam and the underside of the vehicle can be much smaller than that between a hovercraft and the sea or the ground, thereby reducing the loss of air and the power need per unit load lifted. Tracked hovercraft can be propelled along the track by airscrews, ROCKETS, or LINEAR MOTORS.
E.R.L.

Howard, Sir Ebenezer (British town-planner, 1850–1928), see under GARDEN CITIES.

Howard, John (British philanthropist, 1726–90), see under PENOLOGY.

Howells, William Dean (U.S. novelist and critic, 1837–1920), see under REALISM.

Hoyle, Sir Fred (British mathematician and astronomer, *b.*1915), see under STEADY-STATE HYPOTHESIS.

Hua Kuo-feng (Chinese politician), see under CULTURAL REVOLUTION.

Hubbard, LaFayette Ronald (U.S. founder of scientology, *b.*1911), see under DIANETICS; SCIENTOLOGY.

Hubble's constant, see under EXPANSION OF THE UNIVERSE.

Hudson, Liam (British educationist, *b.*1933), see under CONVERGERS AND DIVERGERS.

Hueffer, Ford Madox, see FORD, F.M.

Hughes, Ted (British poet, *b.*1930), see under GROUP, THE.

Huidobro, Vicente (Chilean poet, 1893–1948), see under AUTOTELIC WRITING; LOLITA SYNDROME.

Huizinga, Johan (Dutch historian, 1872–1945), see under CULTURAL HISTORY.

Hull, Clark Leonard (U.S. psychologist, 1884–1952), see under BEHAVIOUR THERAPY; BEHAVIOURISM.

Hulme, Thomas Ernest (British philosopher and literary critic, 1883–1917), see under IMAGISM; NEW AGE; POETRY BOOKSHOP; ROMANTICISM.

Hülsenbeck, Richard (German-U.S. poet, physician, and psychoanalyst, 1892–1974), see under DADA.

human rights. That there are human rights is a contemporary form of the doctrine of natural rights, first clearly formulated by Locke and later expressed in terms of the rights of man. Natural or human rights are those which men are conceived to have in virtue of their humanity and not in virtue of human fiat or law or convention. Such rights have therefore been frequently invoked in the criticism of laws and social arrangements. In 1948 the General Assembly of UNO adopted a Universal Declaration of Human Rights, which formulated in detail a number of rights, economic and cultural, as well as political, to form a standard of human rights. This is not a legally binding instrument, but it was followed by a number of international covenants and conventions, including the European Convention for the Protection of Human Rights and Fundamental Freedoms, which have influenced national legislation and provided some machinery for international enforcement.
H.L.A.H.

Bibl: D. D. Raphael (ed.), *Political Theory and the Rights of Man* (London and Bloomington, 1967); I. Brownlie (ed.), *Basic Documents on Human Rights* (Oxford, 1971).

humani generis, see under CHRISTIAN EXISTENTIALISM.

humanism. A term of extensively varying significance which has been generally used to indicate that a theory or doctrine is more concerned with man than with something other than man. Sometimes the contrast is with God, as in the humanism of the Renaissance which aimed to direct attention away from theoretical speculation about God to the study of the works of man as revealed in history, literature, and art, or again in the humanism proclaimed by contemporary disbelievers in God. Another contrast is with nature, as in educational emphasis on the HUMANITIES as opposed to the NATURAL SCIENCES, or again in British PRAGMATISM, which adopted as its slogan the thesis of Protagoras that man is the measure of all things, and saw beliefs, and the logical and linguistic items that enter into their composition, as human instruments for the service of conduct, not as reflections of the independent nature of things.   A.Q.

humanism, evolutionary, see EVOLUTIONARY HUMANISM.

humanistic psychology. A recent SCHOOL OF PSYCHOLOGY founded mainly by Abraham Maslow. It seeks to increase the relevance of PSYCHOLOGY to the lives of individual people, regarded from an EXISTENTIAL viewpoint. It is critical of researches that seem trivial, ahuman, and even dehumanizing because of a preoccupation with STATISTICS, elegant experimentation, white rats, COMPUTERS, and other 'side-issues' of human psychology proper.   I.M.L.H.
Bibl: F. T. Severin (ed.), *Humanistic Viewpoints in Psychology* (N.Y., 1965).

humanities. A term used in Europe and the U.S.A. to distinguish literature, languages, philosophy, history, art, theology, and music from the SOCIAL SCIENCES and the NATURAL SCIENCES. The term originated in Renaissance times, when *litterae humaniores* (a name still in use at Oxford) signified the more humane 'letters' of the revived Latin and Greek authors in contrast to the theological 'letters' of the medieval schoolmen.   W.A.C.S.
Bibl: L. Stenhouse, 'The Humanities Curriculum Project' (*Journal of Curriculum Studies,* no. 1, 1969).

Hume, Allan Octavian (British administrator in India, 1829–1912), see under CONGRESS PARTY.

Hume, David (Scottish philosopher, 1711–76), see under ANALYTIC PHILOSOPHY; CAUSALITY; DETERMINISM; IDEALISM; NEUTRAL MONISM; NOMINALISM; PSYCHOLOGISM; SENSATIONALISM; UTILITARIANISM.

Hundred Flowers. Campaign of intellectual liberalization launched in Communist China in 1956 by Mao Tse-tung, in a speech inviting intellectual criticism of the regime and calling for 'a hundred flowers to bloom' and 'a hundred schools to contend'. The campaign elicited so large-scale an indictment of the deficiencies of existing policies and their executants as to provoke a bitter anti-intellectual reaction. D.C.W.
Bibl: R. MacFarquhar (ed.), *The Hundred Flowers* (London and N.Y., 1960).

Hungary. One of two words (the other being SUEZ) used to denote the twin international crises of October and November 1956, when, following the overthrow of the STALINIST government in Poland, popular demonstrations in Budapest were fired on by Soviet occupation forces. Revolutionary councils sprang up throughout Hungary, and a national government under the moderate Communist Imre Nagy was set up. Soviet troops, withdrawn from Budapest during the first phase of the fighting, later returned in greater strength and suppressed the revolutionary forces. Over 100,000 refugees fled to the West, Nagy and others were subsequently executed after a secret trial, and the open nature of the Soviet repression led to a great drop in support for the Soviet Union outside Russia.   D.C.W.
Bibl: P. E. Zinner, *Revolution in Hungary* (London and N.Y., 1962).

Huntington, Samuel Phillips (U.S. political scientist, *b.* 1927), see under POLITICAL SOCIOLOGY.

Husák, Gustáv (Czechoslovak statesman, *b.* 1913), see under NORMALIZATION; PRAGUE (3).

Husserl, Edmund (German philosopher, 1859–1938), see under ANTI-NOVEL; EXISTENTIALISM; PHENOMENOLOGY; PSYCHOLOGISM.

Huxley, Aldous (British novelist and essayist, 1894–1963), see under BRAVE NEW WORLD; SOMA; ZEN.

Huxley, Julian Sorell (British biologist, 1887–1975), see under BIOMETRY; ETHOLOGY; EVOLUTIONARY HUMANISM.

Huxley, Thomas Henry (British scientist and humanist, 1825–95), see under AGNOSTICISM; EPIPHENOMENALISM; EVOLUTIONARY HUMANISM; TWO CULTURES.

Huysmans, Joris-Karl (French novelist, 1848–1907), see under DECADENCE; SYMBOLISM.

hydraulic civilizations. Karl Wittfogel's term for urban or rural SETTLEMENTS based on the establishment of large productive water-works for irrigation, flood control, and hydro-electric power. The type of economy on which they rely is termed by Wittfogel *hydraulic agriculture* to distinguish it from traditional rainfall farming.   M.L.
  Bibl: W. L. Thomas (ed.), *Man's Role in Changing the Face of the Earth* (Chicago, 1956).

hydraulics. The scientific study of the movement of water and other liquids through artificial channels, open or closed, and the engineering applications of hydraulic forces.   M.L.

hydrobiology, see LIMNOLOGY.

hydrodynamics. The study of the flow of liquids. Fine detail on the atomic scale (see ATOM) is ignored, so that a continuum model (see CONTINUUM; MODEL) is employed. The motion of each small volume in the liquid is analysed by NEWTONIAN MECHANICS, taking account of the pressure and viscous resistance of the surrounding liquid. Typical hydrodynamic phenomena are water waves, turbulent and streamline flow in pipes, oil lubrication, and flow in rivers. See also MAGNETOHYDRODYNAMICS.   M.V.B.

hydrofoil. A river- or sea-going craft in which the whole of the hull is maintained completely *above* the water surface. The weight of the vessel is supported by submerged foils whose action is precisely analogous to that of the aerofoil section of an aircraft wing, the only difference being that water replaces air as the medium providing the lift. The action depends

on MOMENTUM, whereas that of an AQUA-PLANE depends on viscosity.   E.R.L.

hydrogen bond. In some situations hydrogen forms BONDS with two ATOMS instead of one as predicted by classical VALENCE theory. The extra bond – the hydrogen bond – which is found with the more electronegative (see ELECTRO-NEGATIVITY) ELEMENTS (usually bound in a MOLECULE), though relatively weak, has far-reaching consequences. It is responsible for the fact that water is a liquid under normal conditions, and it determines the configuration of many biological molecules, e.g. DNA (see NUCLEIC ACID).   B.F.

hydrogenation. The incorporation of hydrogen by organic compounds either by the addition of, or reduction with, molecular (see MOLECULE) hydrogen. Alcohols and amines may be produced, but the most important commercial process is the formation of SATURATED hydrocarbons (alkanes) from UNSATURATED alkenes. A variety of catalysts (see CATALYSIS) are used.   B.F.

hydrography. The science concerned with the physical aspects of all bodies of water on the earth's surface; in particular, the preparation of navigational charts.   J.L.M.L.

hydrology. The study of continental water in its normal form as a liquid (for the study of natural ice see GLACIOLOGY), its properties, distribution, and circulation in the HYDROSPHERE and the atmosphere. In a less restricted sense hydrology is concerned with the *hydrologic cycle,* i.e. with the interchanges of water, as a vapour, liquid, or solid between the atmosphere, ocean, and land.   J.L.M.L.

hydrolysis, see under ENZYMES.

hydroponics. The cultivation of plants without soil, using instead water containing a balanced mixture of salts (see NUTRITION) and a supporting substratum such as sand or plastic granules. Very heavy crops can be produced in a small area, and the world's food production, needed to feed the growing population, might be substantially increased by the wider use of this technique. At present high costs make

HYDROSPHERE

the method unsuitable except for luxury
products such as cut flowers.   K.M.

hydrosphere. The three major realms of
the earth are the LITHOSPHERE, the
hydrosphere, and the atmosphere, respectively solid, liquid, and gaseous. The
hydrosphere includes all the surface
waters of the earth, liquid or solid, in the
oceans, and on the continents, together
with soil and ground water.   J.L.M.L.

Hyman, Herbert Hiram (U.S. sociologist,
b. 1918), see under REFERENCE GROUP.

hyperbolic   geometry,   see   under
GEOMETRY.

hypergraphy, see under LETTRISM.

hyperinflation, see under INFLATION.

hypersonic, see under MACH NUMBER.

hypnosis. The induction of a trance-like
state by one person in another. The
characteristics of the state come under
three main heads. (1) The subject suffers
a loss of initiative. He will submit to the
hypnotist's authority, and he often shows
inertia and extreme reluctance to perform
complex tasks of which he is perfectly capable. His attention is subject to redistribution, in particular to increased selectivity
resulting from the hypnotist's demands.
(2) The subject may achieve extremely
vivid recall of fantasies and past
memories, even to the point when he
believes he is actually reliving his past.
Because of the hypnotist's inducement of
calm and detachment, he is often less persistent in verifying his experience than he
would normally be, and he will accept
gross and continued distortions of reality.
In addition, post-hypnotic amnesia frequently occurs: he 'wakes' completely
forgetful of what has taken place in the
trance. The hypnotist, however, is usually
capable of restoring the subject's memory
by means of a simple command or gesture.
(3) The subject may lose his inhibitions, and lend himself enthusiastically
to the acting out of 'ROLES unusual for
him, an aspect exploited for entertainment.
    The most important factor in hypnosis is
suggestibility, and degree of suggestibility
determines the subject's suitability for

hypnosis. It is a poorly understood trait.
Post-hypnotic suggestion, the carrying out
of the hypnotist's commands after the session, has both the most promising (for
PSYCHIATRY) and the most sinister implications because it constitutes control of a
person's normal waking perceptions,
behaviour, and beliefs without his knowledge. This control, however, is not absolute even after the deepest trance, and
not even the most suggestible hypnotic
subjects will respond to post-hypnotic
suggestion that runs very strongly
counter to their beliefs and inhibitions.
     H.L.
    Bibl: E. R. Hilgard, *Hypnotic Suscepti-
bility* (N.Y., 1965).

hyponymy,   see   under   MEANING-
RELATION.

hypostatization. The attribution of real
existence to abstractions (see ABSTRACT),
i.e. to entities which have no definite, or at
least continuous, location in space and
time. Platonic REALISM, according to its
critics, hypostatizes UNIVERSALS (properties, RELATIONS, numbers). HOLISM,
likewise, is criticized for hypostatizing
social INSTITUTIONS, such as nations or
CLASSES, social movements and forces,
and large-scale historical events (e.g.
ROMANTICISM, INDUSTRIALIZATION, the
Renaissance). Resolute NOMINALISTS
regard as hypostatization all attributions
of substantial existence (see SUBSTANCE)
to things other than definitely and continuously located spatio-temporal objects,
including human beings. Philosophical
ANALYSIS is typically used to unmask
hypostatizations.   A.Q.

hypothalamus. In mammals generally the
lowermost, i.e. most ventral part of the
'between brain' or thalamus. The
hypothalamus may be thought of as the
brain of the autonomic NERVOUS SYSTEM
and it is known that the excitation of different specific areas will give rise to rage,
sleep, pleasure, hunger, or fear. Apart
from these neurological functions the
hypothalamus is also the seat of neuro-
secretory CELLS which produce many of
the hormones (see ENDOCRINOLOGY)
formerly associated with the posterior
part of the PITUITARY GLAND. It is also
now thought that the hypothalamus produces so-called 'releasing factors' which

cause the liberation of hormones from the anterior part of the pituitary gland. Such hormones include growth hormone and the GONAD-stimulating hormones. Thus the hypothalamus is in general a meeting point or overlapping area of the neurological and endocrinological controls of behaviour.   P.M.

hypothetico-deductive method, see under POPPERIAN.

hysteresis. The lag of an effect behind its cause in physical systems undergoing cyclic change. For example, an elastic solid will stretch when pulled, but it will frequently not return to quite its original length when the pulling force is reduced back to zero; similar behaviour occurs in the magnetization of FERROMAGNETS.
                              M.V.B.

hysteria, see under NEUROSIS.

I

I Ching, see under ALEATORY.

iatrogenic disease. A disorder produced by a doctor, usually as a result of medication given for another disease. Thus, DEPRESSION may be iatrogenic when caused by the drug Rauwolfia given in the treatment of high blood pressure, or anaemia may be produced by aspirin causing internal bleeding. With the recent introduction of many powerful drugs which often have toxic or side effects, iatrogenic disorders are becoming increasingly common. Their detection may be difficult, because they may be indistinguishable from other types and because the harmful effects of drugs may be delayed for months or years. The most famous iatrogenic 'disease' is the congenital absence of limb in the children of mothers who received thalidomide during pregnancy.   D.A.P.

IBM (International Business Machines). By far the largest COMPUTER manufacturer. Their almost overwhelming influence on all aspects of COMPUTING, on both the HARDWARE and the SOFTWARE sides, is not regarded by all research workers as an unmixed blessing.   C.S.

Ibsen, Henrik (Norwegian dramatist, 1828–1906), see under DEUTSCHES THEATER; FREIE BÜHNE; NATURALISM; REALISM; THÉÂTRE LIBRE.

IC (immediate constituent), see under CONSTITUENT ANALYSIS.

ICBM (inter-continental ballistic missiles), see under MISSILES.

iconography. Term used in art history for the study of the meaning of images, a visual HERMENEUTICS. An iconographical school of art historians grew up *c.* 1900 in reaction against the stress, in the art criticism of the later 19th century, on form as opposed to content. Pioneers of the new approach were Émile Mâle and Aby Warburg. Some art historians, notably Erwin

Panofsky, distinguish iconography from *iconology,* defining the latter as the study through art of 'the basic attitude of a nation, a period, a class, a religious or philosophical persuasion', i.e. the HISTORY OF MENTALITIES from visual sources. P.B.
  Bibl: E. Panofsky, *Meaning in the Visual Arts* (Garden City, N.Y., 1955; Harmondsworth, 1970), ch. 1.

id. In psychoanalytic theory (see PSYCHOANALYSIS), a FREUDIAN term for the UNCONSCIOUS system of personality that acts to reduce pain and enhance pleasure, by giving free rein to primitive impulses. Its PLEASURE PRINCIPLE is assumed to collide with the REALITY PRINCIPLE of the EGO, and with the censorious demands of the SUPEREGO, thus setting the stage for inner conflict. W.Z.

idea. The smallest unit of thought or MEANING, the elementary constituent of beliefs or assertions. In contemporary PHILOSOPHY the word CONCEPT is widely preferred because (1) in traditional EMPIRICISM 'idea' was used both in the sense given above and at the same time to mean the same as 'image', since the empiricists took thought to be a matter of operating with images; (2) Locke and Berkeley also used 'idea' to mean sense-impression or SENSE-DATUM, using it to refer to the items of immediate experience of which images are copies; (3) in the philosophy of Plato, an Idea is a UNIVERSAL, conceived, in the manner of REALISM, as existing substantially in a world of timeless ESSENCES.   A.Q.

ideal types. Term used by Max Weber to denote entities (including, e.g., types of 'action', society, or INSTITUTION) as constructed 'hypothetically' by an investigator from component elements with a view to making comparisons and to developing theoretical EXPLANATIONS; the components out of which a 'type' is constructed being empirically observable or historically recognized. Thus Max

Weber used ideal types in his studies of types of action, of religion, economy, and authority – distinguishing, for example, between ideal types of *traditional*, *rational-legal*, and *charismatic* (see CHARISMA) authority. The word 'ideal' does not carry with it any NORMATIVE load – it relates rather to what Morris Ginsberg (*On the Diversity of Morals*, London, 1956, p. 206) called 'HEURISTIC constructions . . . not definitions and averages . . .' that emphasize 'certain characteristics of a group of occurrences, and by linking up with others . . .' are 'so combined by us as to form a coherent or unitary whole'. S.J.G.

Bibl: *Max Weber on the Methodology of the Social Sciences*, tr. and ed. E. Shils and H. A. Finch (N.Y., 1949); W. G. Runciman, *A Critique of Max Weber's Philosophy of Social Science* (London, 1972).

idealism. The philosophical theory that the only things that really exist are minds or mental states or both. (The distinction between the two is rejected by those, like Hume, who take a mind to be no more than a related series of mental states and also by those, like Berkeley, who hold that a mental state is inconceivable except as part of the history of some mind.) Berkeley's philosophy is perhaps the simplest version of idealism. For him the world consists of the infinite mind of God, the finite minds that he has created, and, dependently on them, the ideas possessed or experienced by these minds. For Berkeley there are no material things that exist independently of minds: common objects are collections of ideas, in finite minds to the extent that they are observed by them, in the mind of God to the extent that they are not.

Berkeley's brand of idealism, misnamed *subjective idealism* by adherents of Hegel's *objective idealism*, is in fact as objective as the latter. It is not a form of SOLIPSISM, for it acknowledges that much exists over and above my mind and its ideas, namely the minds and ideas of other people and of God. Where Hegel's idealism differs from Berkeley's is in holding that there is only one true mind, the ABSOLUTE, or Spirit, of which finite minds are dependent fragments, not, as in Berkeley, entities created by the infinite mind with a separate existence of their own. Some idealists of Hegelian inspiration held that in this respect Hegel went too far; cf. PERSONALISM.

A third type of idealism is found in the philosophy of Plato, in which only IDEAS, in his special sense of the term, are objects of knowledge, and therefore they alone truly exist. Of the changing particulars met with in space and time we can have only opinions, and he infers that they have only a secondary brand of existence. A.Q.

ideas, history of, see HISTORY OF IDEAS.

identification.

(1) The correspondence between a MODEL of reality and the reality itself. A model consists of a set of RELATIONSHIPS connecting a number of VARIABLES, and reflects a theory of the reality which it represents. In each equation the dependent variable is related to the determining variables by PARAMETERS which in a linear EQUATION are simply coefficients; and in all equations that are not true by definition an *error term* must be included to allow for errors of observation, influences that have not been taken into account, and misspecifications of the form of the equation.

A parameter is said to be identified if it can be ESTIMATED without bias; an equation is said to be identified if all its parameters are identified; and a model is said to be identified if all its equations are identified. If these conditions hold, then the model is in a sense unique, meaning not that it is a true characterization of reality but that it is the only characterization possible within its own terms.

Identification is not simply present or absent; we may encounter *under-identification* or *over-identification*. Under-identification occurs in an equation or model whenever one or more of the parameters are unidentified. Over-identification occurs whenever two or more inconsistent estimates of a parameter can be made. There is no generally acceptable cure for under-identification since nothing can be done about it, however many observations are available, without introducing *a priori* constraints not contemplated in the formulation of the model. Over-identification, on the other hand, can be handled in a number of ways, for instance by using non-linear estimation techniques. R.ST.

(2) In SOCIAL PSYCHOLOGY, the process of associating oneself closely with

other individuals or REFERENCE GROUPS to the extent that one comes to adopt their goals and values and to share vicariously in their experiences. See also PEER GROUP.

W.Z.

identity crisis. A crisis that occurs when the integrity of a person's SELF-IMAGE is threatened, disrupted, or destroyed, usually in a conflict of loyalties or aspirations. It is said to be characteristic of adolescence and early adulthood. H.L.

Bibl: E. H. Erikson, *Childhood and Society* (N.Y., 1951).

identity theory. The view that the apparently private (see PRIVACY) mental states that each person is conscious of (see INTROSPECTION) are literally identical with certain states of the brain and NERVOUS SYSTEM that are accessible in principle to public, scientific observation. The identity in question is held to be *contingent* (see CONTINGENCY) or *empirical*, as is that of a visible flash of lightning and an electrical discharge at the same place and time, and not a matter of logical necessity, i.e. of the MEANING of the terms used to report observations of the two kinds in question. If true it provides a more satisfactory account of the mind and conscious mental life from the point of view of MATERIALISM, since it neither denies self-consciousness nor asserts an entirely implausible synonymy of mental and neural terms. A.Q.

Bibl: D. M. Armstrong, *A Materialist Theory of the Mind*, vol. 1 (London and N.Y., 1968).

ideology. A word coined by the French philosopher Destutt de Tracy (*Éléments d'idéologie*, 1801–5) to denote the 'science of ideas' which would reveal to men the source of their biases and prejudices. De Tracy believed only in trusting sense impressions and was thus akin to the impulses of English EMPIRICISM. After a period of disuse the word was revived with the publication in 1927 of Marx's previously unpublished *The German Ideology*, and in 1929 (translated 1936) of Karl Mannheim's *Ideology and Utopia*, which brought the sociology of KNOWLEDGE into contemporary concerns.

The word has been variously used to characterize IDEAS, ideals, beliefs, passions, values, WELTANSCHAUUNGEN,

religions, political philosophies, moral justifications; it is, as John Plamenatz puts it, a 'family of CONCEPTS'. (Lionel Trilling, in *The Liberal Imagination*, 1950, defined it as 'the habit or the ritual of showing respect for certain formulas to which, for various reasons having to do with emotional safety, we have very strong ties of whose meaning and consequences in actuality we have no clear understanding'.) It may be employed, as Marx employed it in *The German Ideology*, to deride the PROPOSITION that ideas are autonomous or the belief in the power of ideas to shape or determine reality; or to argue that all ideas are socially determined. Ideologies may be seen as justifications which mask some specific set of interests. Or – a widely held viewpoint – they may be regarded as 'social formulas', as belief systems which can be used to mobilize people for actions; it is in this sense that the COMMUNIST nations talk of 'ideological combat' or 'ideological competition'.

Within contemporary SOCIOLOGY, Mannheim identifies ideologies as different 'styles of thought' and distinguishes between 'particular' ideologies (the self-interests of specific groups, such as the 'ideology of the small businessman') and 'total' ideologies (*Weltanschauungen* or complete commitments to a way of life). In the 1950s and 1960s a group of sociologists, notably Raymond Aron, Edward Shils, Daniel Bell, and S. M. Lipset, applied this concept of ideology as a 'secular religion' to the judgement of an 'end of ideology', or the decline of apocalyptic beliefs in the Western industrial societies.

Talcott Parsons defines ideology as an interpretative scheme used by social groups to make the world more intelligible to themselves (see also COGNITIVE SYSTEM). Both the MARXISTS and the central sociological tradition see ideology as a 'distortion' of reality, the Marxist contrasting ideology with 'true consciousness', the sociologist with SOCIAL SCIENCE. A later group of writers, notably the anthropologist Clifford Geertz, see ideology in more neutral terms as one kind of symbol system among other cultural symbol systems such as the religious, the aesthetic, or the scientific. D.B.

Bibl: D. E. Apter (ed.), *Ideology and Discontent* (London and N.Y., 1964); G. Lichtheim, *The Concept of*

Ideology and Other Essays (N.Y., 1967); J. Plamenatz, *Ideology* (London and N.Y., 1970).

idiographic and **nomothetic.** Adjectives applied to contrasted types of study: *idiographic* to study of particular cases (e.g. persons, social groups, works of art), *nomothetic* to the search for general laws or theories which will cover whole classes of cases. Thus HISTORY and GEOGRAPHY, in so far as they are concerned with the study of particular events, persons, and places, are idiographic subjects, whereas some economists would claim that, since they formulate ECONOMIC LAWS, ECONOMICS is a nomothetic science. The word *idiographic* is not to be confused with *ideographic*, which is the adjective formed from *ideogram*. A. S.

idiolect. In LINGUISTICS, the speech habits constituting the language system of an individual. D.C.

idiotype. An antibody to an antigen which is new to the body (see IMMUNITY) is itself a PROTEIN new to the body and as such is capable of arousing an immune response. The property of the antibody that distinguishes it from antibodies to other antigens, and which confers its antigenicity upon it, is known as its idiotype. Anti-idiotype antibodies and antibodies to these antibodies in turn are now thought to play an important part in regulating the intensity and the duration of the immunological response. The theory which attributes immunological control to the action of anti-antibodies and anti-anti-antibodies is sometimes called *network theory*. P.M.

Illich, Ivan (Austrian educationist, *b*. 1926), see under DE-SCHOOLING.

illusion, argument from. The most common and persuasive argument for the conclusion, drawn by the majority of philosophers until very recent times, that material objects cannot be perceived immediately or directly but must somehow be inferred from the SENSE-DATA, or impressions, or appearances, which alone are directly perceived. The argument is that there is, or need be, no directly perceivable difference between the character of my experience when I am actually perceiving a material thing and its character

when, in a dream or hallucination, I falsely believe myself to be doing so. The ground is thus prepared for the traditional problem of PERCEPTION: how is the belief that there exists a material world, independent of my mind, to be justified if all I directly perceive is the private impressions that alone are immediately present to it? Critics see as the fatal flaw in the argument implied by this question what they take to be an equivocation in the use of the phrase 'directly perceive': in the premises of the argument it means 'acquire by perception absolutely certain knowledge of', while in the conclusion it means 'acquire, by perception and without inference, justified belief in'. The indubitable fact that our perception of material objects is *fallible* does not (such critics argue) entail that it is inferential (see INFERENCE). A.Q.

Bibl: A. J. Ayer, *The Foundations of Empirical Knowledge* (London, 1940); D. M. Armstrong, *Perception and the Physical World* (London and N.Y., 1961).

ILO (International Labour Organization). A body set up in 1919 by the Treaty of Versailles (in 1946 it became an agency of UNO) with the object of promoting social justice by associating not only the governments but also the trade unions and employers' organizations of member states in an endeavour to establish and raise common standards in the employment of labour. These standards it has embodied in conventions dealing with such matters as the limitation of child labour, the provision of social insurance, minimum wage-rates for unorganized workers, freedom of association, and equal pay. Member governments, which now number over one hundred, are invited to ratify these conventions. The annual conferences of the ILO provide a forum for the discussion of labour questions by delegates from each country's government, trade unions, and employers. The office at Geneva, besides its administrative functions, conducts many enquiries – e.g. into the MANPOWER and employment problems of developing countries – on which it issues reports. Since 1945 the ILO has developed technical assistance to the developing countries to form a major part of its work. Its continuous activity since 1919 testifies to its independence and its usefulness in the eyes of its members, especially to the developing

299

countries among them, in raising whose standards of labour law and administration it has probably made its main contribution. E.H.P.B.

imaginary museum (*musée imaginaire*; also translated 'museum without walls'). A phrase coined by André Malraux in the first volume of his *La Psychologie de l'art* (1947) to convey the vast and increasing repertoire of more or less faithful photographic reproductions which now makes it possible to discuss works of art without having been to the actual museums containing them. The implications of this were pointed out much earlier by W. Martin Conway in *The Domain of Art* (1901). J.W.

imaginary number, see under COMPLEX NUMBER.

Imagism. A brief, central episode in the development of English-language poetry that represented the latter's clearest point of transition into MODERNISM. As a movement it dates from 1912, when Ezra Pound collaborated with F. S. Flint on a manifesto and a list of poetic prescriptions printed in POETRY (CHICAGO) and reprinted in the English *New Freewoman* (later the EGOIST). In 1914 came the first Imagist anthology, *Des Imagistes*, containing H. D. (Hilda Doolittle), Richard Aldington, William Carlos Williams, Ford Madox Hueffer, James Joyce, and Amy Lowell, who was to take over the anthology side of the movement. It was Pound who enunciated the three primary principles ('direct treatment of the "thing", whether subjective or objective . . . to use absolutely no word that did not contribute to the presentation . . . as regarding rhythm, to compose in the sequence of the musical phrase') and defined the idea of the image as 'a verbal concentration generating energy'. Many of these principles were derivations, especially from the activities of a poetic group centred round T. E. Hulme which met at the Eiffel Tower Restaurant, London, around 1909. There was also a derivation from SYMBOLISM, though Imagism is distinguished by its concentration on the hard, verbally created image rather than the translucent symbol. Much subsequent poetry in England, and even more in the U.S.A., was influenced by Imagist lore and practice

(e.g. Williams, Stevens). Imagism was not merely an aesthetic, but a campaign in the politics of poetry. It transformed an entire climate and, though its concentration was on the short poem, Eliot's *Waste Land*, Pound's *Cantos*, Williams's *Paterson*, and much other modern poetry is inconceivable without it. Pound moved on from Imagism to VORTICISM, which emphasized a harder, more kinetic view of the image; Amy Lowell took over the popularization of a rather impressionist form of Imagism in the U.S.A., where it was long especially influential. M.S.BR.

Bibl: S. K. Coffman, *Imagism* (Norman, Okla., 1951); C. K. Stead, *The New Poetic* (London, 1964; N.Y., 1966); J. B. Harmer, *Victory in Limbo: Imagism 1907–1917* (London, 1975).

imago. In psychoanalytic theory (see PSYCHOANALYSIS), an idealized or fantasized figure from childhood, often a parent, whose standards the individual incorporates and uses as a model for his own behaviour in later life. W.Z.

IMF (International Monetary Fund), see under BRETTON WOODS.

immanence, see under TRANSCENDENCE.

immediate constituent, see under CONSTITUENT ANALYSIS.

immunity.

(1) In its original and narrower sense, a state of resistance or refractoriness to infection by micro-organisms that might otherwise cause infectious illness. Immunity in this sense can be acquired either 'actively' by direct exposure of the subject to an infectious organism, or 'passively' by the infusion of body fluids containing the protective substances or other agents responsible for the immune state – e.g. that of newborn mammals and chicks, which is passively acquired from the mother via the placenta or the yolk as the case may be.

(2) In the wider sense now universally adopted, any state of resistance or refractoriness caused by an adaptive reaction of the body to invasion by foreign substances including pollen grains, foreign organic matter, and grafts from different members of the same SPECIES. Examples include: ALLERGY towards pollen grains or fur; the

rejection of a foreign graft; dermatitis excited by industrial chemicals; anaphylactic shock (see ANAPHYLAXIS); hypersensitivity to drugs such as penicillin. Haemolytic disease of the newborn is an immunological disease caused by accidental leakage of *rhesus positive* (see below) blood (see BLOOD GROUPS) from an unborn child into a *rhesus negative* mother.

Substances that excite immunological reactions and thus lead to states of immunity of one sort or another are called *antigens*. The chief offending antigen in haemolytic disease of the newborn is antigen *D* of the rhesus series. The rhesus antigens owe their name to the fact that they were first discovered by injecting the blood of rhesus monkeys into rabbits, a process leading to the formation of antibodies which will react upon the red blood corpuscles of approximately 85% of human beings.

Immunity reactions are put in effect by, or mediated through, (*a*) *antibodies*, or (*b*) *lymphocytes*. (*a*) Antibodies are PROTEIN constituents of the blood, are formed in response to an antigenic stimulus, and have the power to agglutinate, precipitate, disrupt, or otherwise destroy or sequester the offending antigen or the vehicle that carries the antigen, often a living CELL. (*b*) Lymphocytes are a species of white blood corpuscle, and it is the action of sensitized lymphocytes that brings about the rejection of foreign grafts and the reactions that manifest themselves as bacterial allergies and drug allergies; see also CELL BIOLOGY.

An important and almost a defining characteristic of immunity reactions is their specificity, i.e. the very exact one-to-one matching of antigen and antibody or antigen and particular immunological response. Thus the immunological reaction excited by antigen *A* is visited upon *A* alone, and has no effect at all upon antigens *B, C,* and *D*. P.M.

Bibl: J. H. Humphrey and R. G. White, *Immunology for Students of Medicine* (Oxford and Philadelphia, 1963); W. W. C. Topley, G. S. Wilson, and A. A. Miles (eds.), *Principles of Bacteriology and Immunity* (London and Baltimore, 5th ed., 1964).

immunology. The science of IMMUNITY. P.M.

imperativism, see under EMOTIVISM.

imperfect competition. The state of affairs in which the conditions required for PERFECT COMPETITION are not fully met. In the real world, COMPETITION is in this technical sense generally imperfect but may be intense and effective nevertheless. G.B.R.

Bibl: Joan Robinson, *The Economics of Imperfect Competition* (London, 2nd ed., 1969) and 'Imperfect Competition Revisited' (*Economic Journal*, Sept. 1953).

imperial preference. The system under which lower (often zero) import duties were charged on goods imported from one member of the British Empire by another than on similar goods imported from elsewhere. The preferences were not always reciprocal, and took other forms besides tariffs. They existed in the 17th and 18th centuries, but those granted by the U.K. were abolished in the latter half of the 19th century as being incompatible with FREE TRADE. Some were introduced by the U.K. in 1919 and in the 1920s, and, most importantly, in 1932 at the Ottawa Conference. Since World War II their title has been changed to *Commonwealth preference* and their importance has gradually diminished, and should vanish as a result of Britain's accession to the EEC in 1973. Similar relations have existed in the trade between, e.g., Belgium, France, and the U.S.A. and their dependent territories. M.FG.S.

Bibl: R. S. Russell, *Imperial Preference* (London, 1947).

imperialism.

(1) In general, the extension of the power of a state through the acquisition, usually by conquest, of other territories; the subjugation of their inhabitants to an alien rule imposed on them by force, and their economic and financial exploitation by the imperial power. Imperialism in this general sense of 'empire' is as old as history.

(2) More specifically, as a development from the older term 'empire', the word 'imperialism' was adopted in England in the 1890s by the advocates of a major effort (led by Joseph Chamberlain) to develop and extend the British Empire in opposition to the policy of concentrating on home development, the supporters of

IMPERIALISM

which the imperialists contemptuously dismissed as 'Little Englanders'. The word was rapidly taken into other languages to describe the contest between rival European powers to secure colonies and spheres of influence in Africa and elsewhere, a contest which dominated international politics from the 1880s to 1914 and caused this period to be named the Age of Imperialism. Both British and continental imperialists justified their policies by claiming that they were extending the benefits of 'civilization', based upon the racial, material, and cultural superiority of the white races, to the inferior peoples of backward lands (see SOCIAL DARWINISM). After World War I their ideas were incorporated into the IDEOLOGIES of FASCISM and NAZISM.

The first systematic critique of modern imperialism was provided by the English radical J. A. Hobson whose *Imperialism* (1902) gave it a primarily economic interpretation. Taken up and developed by Lenin in *Imperialism as the Highest Stage of Capitalism* (1915), this became the *economic theory of imperialism*. According to Lenin the natural tendency of CAPITAL to accumulate leads to falling profits, and this in turn to the growth of MONOPOLIES as a self-protective device to keep the profit rate up. But this is only a palliative, and the monopoly capitalists are driven to search for profits by INVESTMENT abroad, using the control which they have acquired over government to direct foreign policy towards the acquisition of empire with a view to securing markets, raw materials, and above all opportunities for investing their surplus capital. This, however, is the last stage of CAPITALISM, for competing imperialisms lead to WAR, war brings REVOLUTION, and revolution will finally overthrow capitalism and imperialism together. Besides providing an explanation of imperialism, Lenin's theory, it will be noticed, also traced the origin of war, or at least of 'imperialist' wars, to the inexorable workings of the capitalist system.

No one today would question that economic factors played a large part in modern imperialism; but critics of the MARXIST-LENINIST theory have not found it difficult to show that it provides an over-simplified account even of the economic facts, and that it ignores a whole range of non-economic motives –

NATIONALISM, racism (see RACE), the pursuit of national power – which, as in the case of Fascism and Nazism, combine with but are not reducible to the pursuit of economic advantage. The economic interpretation of imperialism, however, as expounded by Lenin, remains one of the most important elements in contemporary MARXIST theory, with the advantage, for propaganda purposes, that by definition only non-COMMUNIST states can be accused of imperialism and Communists can always claim to be on the side of anti-imperialist and anti-colonial movements (for which see below, final paragraph).

Colonialism is a form of imperialism based on maintaining a sharp and fundamental distinction (expressed often in law as well as in fact) between the ruling nation and the subordinate (colonial) populations. Such an arrangement arises most naturally in consequence of a conquest of a remote territory with a population of a conspicuously different physique and CULTURE. These, however, are not necessary conditions – witness Nazi colonialism in Eastern Europe, bolstered up by a pseudo-racialism based on fictitious racial differences. Colonialism always entails unequal rights. The British and the Dutch empires of the last century provide the purest examples: LIBERALISM, DEMOCRACY, and the attrition of CLASS barriers in the metropolitan country, bureaucratic (see BUREAUCRACY) AUTHORITARIANISM and the colour bar in the colonies. Another fundamental feature of colonialism has been the policy of perpetuating the economic differentiation between the colonies and the METROPOLIS, with the former supplying the raw materials while the latter remains the chief source of manufactures.

Decolonization is the process whereby a metropolitan country gives up its authority over its dependent territories and grants them the status of sovereign states. It can be seen most clearly in the development following World War II of the former British Empire into the COMMONWEALTH of independent states, or the French Empire into the Communauté Française. This represented a triumph for the nationalist movements which had agitated for independence and took over power when the colonial powers withdrew. In many cases, however, the achievement of national sovereignty and admission to UNO have been followed by controversy over whether decolonization has led to real independence or only to *neo-colonialism*. This term describes a formal juridical independence accompanied by a *de facto* domination and exploitation by foreign nationals, together with the retention of many features of the traditional colonial situation, e.g. narrow economic specialization, cultural and educational inferiority.

Neo-imperialism, of which neo-colonialism is a form, describes a situation in which an independent country suffers from and resents intervention and control by a foreign government and its nationals, but not necessarily as the result of a previous colonial relationship. In some parts of the world (e.g. Latin America) the synonymous term *economic imperialism* (or, more specifically, *dollar imperialism*) is often preferred. The use of such terms is, of course, coloured by the user's political views: what is 'economic imperialism' to one man is 'aid' to another.

Cultural imperialism may be defined as the use of political and economic power to exalt and spread the values and habits of a foreign culture at the expense of a native culture. A familiar example from an earlier period is the export of American films. Although cultural imperialism may be pursued for its own sake it frequently operates as an auxiliary of economic imperialism – as when American films create a demand for American products.

Anti-colonialism and *anti-imperialism* appear to be self-explanatory. The former is rightly used to describe any movement (e.g. the various African national movements) aimed at ending the subordination of a people to colonial rule. The latter means, more broadly, opposition to any form of imperialism anywhere. Anti-imperialism, however, like anti-Fascism, is a term frequently twisted for propaganda purposes and selectively applied. If it was used with any regard for objectivity or logical consistency, opposition to the Soviet control of Eastern Europe or the Chinese conquest of Tibet or the Nigerian subjugation of BIAFRA would be called anti-imperialist. In current usage, however, the term is commonly restricted to groups hostile to the U.S.A. or the countries of Western Europe.   S.A.; A.L.C.B.

Bibl: H. Gollwitzer, tr. D. Adam and S. Baron, *Europe in the Age of Imperialism*

(London and N.Y., 1969); G. Lichtheim, *Imperialism* (London and N.Y., 1971).

implication, see under ENTAILMENT.

Impressionism.
(1) Movement in French painting originating in the 1860s and so called after the first exhibition, in 1874, of a group including Edgar Degas, Claude Monet, Berthe Morisot, Auguste Renoir, Camille Pissarro, Alfred Sisley, Paul Cézanne, and Armand Guillaumin. One of Monet's pictures there, *Impression – soleil levant* (now in the Musée Marmottan, Paris), suggested the name to the critics, though Léon Lagrange ten years earlier had already heard 'Impression roaring at the gates, with Realism joining in the chorus'. Anticipated in the work of Boudin, Chintreuil, Corot, and Turner, the movement was characterized above all by its concern with fleeting effects of light and motion, its disregard of outlines and distaste for sombre colours, its original angles of vision, and its general aura of delicate yet mundane gaiety. In its subject-matter and attitude it was at the same time a product of the REALISM of Courbet and Manet and of the open-air landscape of the Barbizon school; Degas actually conceived of its exhibitions, which continued for twelve years, as a 'realist Salon'.

Virtually every major development in 20th-century art is traceable back to the Impressionists. Thus it was at their 1880 exhibition that Gauguin began showing, in his pre-SYNTHETIST vein, while the eighth and last exhibition in 1886 saw the début of the NEO-IMPRESSIONIST Georges Seurat. Through van Gogh the movement influenced EXPRESSIONISM, through Cézanne the CUBISTS. Meanwhile Monet, whose late works were to be important for ABSTRACT EXPRESSIONISM in the 1950s, continued till his death in 1926 as the prototypical Impressionist, while the movement began to spread across the globe, affecting for instance the NEW ENGLISH ART CLUB and the Berlin SEZESSION, captivating the wealthier collectors everywhere, and selling in millions of colour reproductions.   J.W.

Bibl: J. Rewald, *The History of Impressionism* (N.Y., 1949); P. Pool, *Impressionism* (London and N.Y., 1967).

(2) In music, by analogy, a style of composition in which the composer

IMPRINTING

evokes a scene in a manner which is undramatic; hence, although there is nearly always a title, the music is descriptive rather than programmatic (see PROGRAMME MUSIC). Its greatest exponent was Debussy, whose *Prélude à l'après-midi d'un faune* (1892) first dramatically established the style. It is marked by a tendency to use sound as colour, to employ shapes of a deliberately nebulous character, to avoid clear-cut rhythm or harmony, and to eschew the dramatic dynamism shown by, e.g., Beethoven. Debussy, Ravel, Delius, Bax, Albéniz, and Respighi are typical examples. The SYMBOLIST poets Verlaine, Baudelaire, and especially Mallarmé were as potent an influence as the Impressionist painters, and that influence has extended in recent years to Boulez, making him seem in certain ways a follower of Debussy, although his music is more consciously directed by the intellect than by emotion.   A.H.

(3) In literature, impressionism means, in the most general sense, subjectivism: the work attempts to convey the author's own impression (mood, state of mind) rather than an objective description. STREAM OF CONSCIOUSNESS writing is impressionistic – provided that it avoids the deliberate distortions of Expressionism.   M.S.-S.

imprinting. In ETHOLOGY, a learning process which leads to an extremely rapid CONDITIONING, and consequent narrowing-down of the situation that elicits a response. The best-known and extreme examples are found in goslings and ducklings, which are normally led by the parents from the nest to the feeding-grounds, almost immediately after hatching and drying. When hatched in an incubator, and shown any moving object, even a matchbox or a large balloon, they will follow this, and will later continue to do so even when offered a choice between this object and their own parents. Although the phenomenon had been reported earlier by Spalding and Heinroth, it was Lorenz who first emphasized its peculiar nature, and compared it with INDUCTION (as then known) in EMBRYOLOGY. It seems likely that imprinting is an extreme case of conditioning, linked by intermediate phenomena to CLASSICAL CONDITIONING. See also ATTACHMENT; CRITICAL PERIOD.   N.T.

304

Bibl: N. Tinbergen, *The Study of Instinct* (Oxford, 1951).

in-service training. Courses to enable working schoolteachers to bring themselves up to date in the subjects they teach, or in such matters as child development, learning theory, teaching method, or EDUCATIONAL TECHNOLOGY. In Britain, the James Report and the WHITE PAPER ON EDUCATION (1972) have given in-service training a high priority. *Post-experience training* is an application of the same principles to men and women in other professions or in industry. W.A.C.S.

incest. Illicit sexual relations among persons closely related by kinship or marriage. Each society defines that range of sexually forbidden kinsmen and affines for itself, and societies differ greatly among themselves in the sanctions they apply to offenders. The 'horror of incest' is not in fact universal, although there is probably no society which would tolerate sexual relations between a woman and her son. So great are the variations from society to society that some anthropologists deny the existence of a single universal phenomenon which can be called 'incest'. Incest rules and rules of exogamy (see under ENDOGAMY) are related, not identical.   M.F.

incomes policy. Measures intended to ensure that money incomes (mainly wages, salaries, dividends, and rents) do not rise faster in the aggregate than the real output of the economy, and so set up cost INFLATION. When during World War II economists considered the possibility of maintaining FULL EMPLOYMENT afterwards, they foresaw that it would remove the constraint that UNEMPLOYMENT had been imposing on the bargaining power of trade unions, so that pay being pushed up faster than OUTPUT per man would raise costs per unit of output and the selling price of the product, unless the unions voluntarily exercised wage restraint. In 1948–50 the British Labour Government's appeal to the unions to do this, and to the employers not to raise dividends, was largely successful, but in subsequent developments of the policy governments in Great Britain and the U.S.A. have found it advisable to impose restraints by referring to investigation claims or settlements thought to be excessive, and by taking statutory powers to delay the payment of agreed rises, or reduce them in amount; and they have set up standing bodies to administer these provisions. Governments have also promulgated guidelines for non-inflationary behaviour by unions and MANAGEMENT, and extended surveillance and control to prices and property incomes. While a number of countries have applied some form of incomes policy to check surges of cost inflation, especially when these have been associated with an adverse BALANCE OF PAYMENTS, the restraints have generally been relaxed after the crisis has passed, or been broken up by accumulated pressures.   E.H.P.B.

Bibl: L. Ulman and R. J. Flanagan, *Wage Restraint: a Study of Incomes Policies in Western Europe* (Berkeley, 1971); F. Blackaby (ed.), *An Incomes Policy for Britain* (London, 1972).

incorporating (in LINGUISTICS), see POLYSYNTHETIC.

independence (in STATISTICS), see under CORRELATION.

independent assortment, see under MENDEL'S LAWS.

independent schools. Schools which do not receive money from public funds and thus depend on fees and endowments. In Great Britain they may be family or small trust concerns or limited companies, like most of the preparatory schools and a number of religious foundations; they also include the PUBLIC SCHOOLS. Nearly 500,000 boys and girls in Great Britain attend them, forming 6% of the whole school population, about 10% of all children receiving PRE-SCHOOL EDUCATION, and about 15% of those (aged 16–18) in sixth forms. All independent schools must be registered with the Department of Education and Science, but only those which have applied for and passed inspection tests by the Department are officially recognized as supplying a satisfactory education. Nearly 40% of pupils in 'recognized' schools are boarders as compared with 1% in MAINTAINED SCHOOLS.

Much the same principles govern the existence and range of independent schools in the U.S.A. They can generally be classified under three heads: privately endowed and proprietary schools, religious foundations (Catholic, Protestant, Jewish), and military schools. Some are experimental and out of the main stream both of independent and of state schools.
W.A.C.S.

Independent Theatre, see under THÉÂTRE LIBRE.

indeterminacy (in PHYSICS), see UNCERTAINTY PRINCIPLE; (in music), see ALEATORY.

indeterminism. The opposite of DETERMINISM.   A.Q.

index number (or *index*). In ECONOMICS, a device for summarizing in a single figure a comparative statistical measure of either price or quantity for a heterogeneous collection of economic objects such as goods and services. The comparison may be between different points either in time (e.g. years or months) or in space (e.g. countries or regions), the point with which comparison is made being called the *base*.

The difficulty in establishing an index number measure for, say, the price development of an aggregate such as 'food, drink, and tobacco' from one year (the base year) to another (the current year) lies in the fact that the various commodities included in the aggregate normally show rather different price developments over time. Each of these price developments can be measured by the ratio between the prices of the commodity concerned in the two years compared. These ratios are called *price relatives*. The simplest and most widely used forms of price index numbers consist of weighted AVERAGES of these price relatives. The *weights* reflect the relative importance of the various commodities included in the aggregate as measured by the share of each one of them in the total expenditure on these commodities in either the base year or the current year.

After its originator, the *base-weighted* arithmetic MEAN of the relatives concerned is called the *Laspeyres index number*, and likewise their *current-weighted* harmonic mean is called the *Paasche index number*. The best-known, but seldom used, compromise between these two alternative index-number forms is their geometric mean, which is known as the *Fisher index number*.

Index number series may have either a fixed or a moving weighting base. When each year is taken as the weighting base for the next year and the figures thus obtained are then linked together so as to have a common comparison base, i.e. year for which the index takes the value of 100, the resulting series is called a *chain index*.

G.S.

Bibl: I. Fisher, *The Making of Index Numbers* (N.Y., 3rd ed., 1927); R. Stone, *Quantity and Price Indexes in National Accounts* (Paris, 1956); R. G. D. Allen, *Index Numbers in Theory and Practice* (London, 1975).

indicator, see under SCALE.

indifference curves. In ECONOMICS, collectively, a representation of the consumer psyche as a series of contour lines surrounding a mountain of UTILITY; the consumer's object is so to arrange his purchases within the limitations of his income as to touch the highest of the contour lines on his mental map. *Isoquants* are a similar device for representing different production possibilities, the producer's object being, within the limits of his resources, to reach that contour line which represents the highest output.

R.L.

indirect rule. A system of colonial rule by delegating selected powers to indigenous institutions suitably modified and modernized. It was first put into operation by Lord Lugard in Nigeria in 1898 and widely adopted thereafter throughout the British colonial empire and to a certain extent by the French and Dutch. The system was a product of the colonial administrations' need for financial economy (in view of the unwillingness of Parliament to vote money for empire), and of their belief in the strength of indigenous institutions and leadership and in their adaptability to British ideals of good administration.

D.C.W.

Bibl: M. Perham, *Lugard* (2 vols., London, 1956–60).

individual psychology. A theory of personality originated by Alfred Adler (see ADLERIAN) whose essential principle is that human behaviour is an attempt to compensate for feelings of inferiority (see INFERIORITY COMPLEX) due to physical, psychological, or social deficiencies. It is one of the earliest theories emphasizing the importance of environmental factors in personality.

R.P.-S.

individualism, methodological, see METHODOLOGICAL INDIVIDUALISM.

individualized instruction; individualized learning. The organization of instructional materials in a form which allows each student to proceed at his own pace according to abilities and interests. Obvious examples are the DALTON PLAN and the MONTESSORI METHOD. Another area in which the principle is applied is PROGRAMMED INSTRUCTION, whether through TEACHING MACHINES or prepared books. The object is to recognize individual differences and not let them be lost among the mass of learners in a classroom.

W.A.C.S.

inductance, see under SUICIDE CONNECTION.

induction.

(1) In LOGIC, a form of reasoning that usually involves generalization, i.e. the INFERENCE from an instance or repeated instances of some conjunction of characteristics that the conjunction obtains universally. But the term is often used for any inference whose premises do not ENTAIL its conclusions, i.e. they support it but do not, if true, logically exclude the possibility that it is false. The justification of induction has been a persistent problem. It seems to presuppose an inductive principle of the form: 'For any *A* and *B,* if all known *A*s are *B*, then all *A*s whatever are *B*.' So stated, however, the principle is obviously false, as is shown by the discovery of black swans in Australia at a time when all known swans were white. A currently favoured position is to contend that the PROPOSITION 'If all known *A*s are *B*, then *probably* all *A*s whatever are *B*' is ANALYTIC, and that it implicitly defines the CONCEPT of probability in the sense of CONFIRMATION.

A.Q.

Bibl: Bertrand Russell, *The Problems of Philosophy* (London, 1912), ch. 12; P. F. Strawson, *Introduction to Logical Theory* (London and N.Y., 1952), ch. 9.

(2) In MATHEMATICS, see MATHEMATICAL INDUCTION.

(3) In classical EMBRYOLOGY, the process whereby a certain STIMULUS, such as a pin-prick or exposure to a particular chemical, initiates the formation of new TISSUES or organs from pre-existing CELLS.   E.O.W.

(4) In BIOCHEMISTRY, the process whereby the addition of a particular substance (the inducer) causes CELLS to produce the ENZYMES required to accelerate the chemical transformation of the substance. For example, when the bacterium *E. coli* encounters lactose (the inducer), it rapidly manufactures the three enzymes required to absorb the lactose into the cell and to hydrolyze it to glucose and galactose.   E.O.W.

induction motor. An electrical machine in which a circular arrangement of electromagnets (usually embedded in slots in the inner walls of a hollow laminated-steel cylinder) is fed with alternating currents so phased as to produce a rotating magnetic FIELD within the cylinder. A second (usually slotted) laminated-steel cylinder is mounted within the first cylinder and is free to spin on the output shaft. The slots of this second cylinder (*rotor*) usually contain solid copper or aluminium bars, all of which are connected together at each end of the rotor by thick conducting rings. The rotating field drives the rotor by inducing electric currents in the rotor bars. Although these are often called EDDY CURRENTS and it is true that their origins are identical, induction-motor currents are generally distinguished by being forced to flow in orderly patterns. Induction motors supply over 95% of the world's power in electric motor drives.   E.R.L.

Indus civilization. One of the major civilizations of antiquity based on the Indus valley, with twin capitals at Harappa and Mohenjo-Daro and other smaller sites extending over the Punjab, Sind, and Kathiawar, now mostly in Pakistan. The Indus civilization was brought to light in excavations by Sir John Marshall and Sir Mortimer Wheeler in the 1920s. It appears to have been fully developed *c.* 2300 B.C. (when it was in trading contact with Sumer) and to have been in decline by 1700 B.C. before its final destruction by hostile attack *c.* 1500. The buildings, which include large granaries and baths, are made of burnt brick, with an elaborate system of sewers and wells; sites show the earliest examples of gridiron town-planning. Standard weights and measures were used, and a hieroglyphic script which remains undeciphered. Apart from the archaeological remains, nothing is known of its origins or history.   A.L.C.B.

Bibl: R. E. M. Wheeler, *The Indus Civilization* (London, 3rd ed., 1968).

industrial action, see under SYNDICALISM.

industrial archaeology. The study, principally through physical remains, of industrial processes and methods in the past, especially in the period from the Industrial Revolution of the 18th and 19th centuries down to the recent past, but not excluding medieval or even earlier periods. The term is liberally interpreted to cover, for example, buildings (factories, ironworks, warehouses, industrial housing); mines machinery (power systems); transport (canals, railways, docks). Apart from its obvious debt to prehistoric ARCHAEOLOGY in the development of methods and techniques, the study owes much to the greatly increased interest in ECONOMIC HISTORY and SOCIAL HISTORY and in the history of ENGINEERING and TECHNOLOGY.   A.L.C.B.

Bibl: R. A. Buchanan, *Industrial Archaeology in Britain* (Harmondsworth, 1972); A. Raistrick, *Industrial Archaeology: an Historical Survey* (London and N.Y., 1972).

industrial democracy, see under DEMOCRACY; PARTICIPATION.

industrial dynamics, see under SYSTEMS.

industrial psychology. A branch of APPLIED PSYCHOLOGY covering applications of PSYCHOLOGY in the industrial field. Topics now classed under this title may be grouped thus: (1) fatigue, safety, accident-proneness, and mental health, all of which were originally matters of medical concern; (2) vocational guidance, selection, training, and appraisal where there are strong links to work in education; (3) personal relations, relations within groups, and relations within the structure of organizations, all of which have links with SOCIAL PSYCHOLOGY and SOCIOLOGY (industrial relations and conflict, which clearly involve psychological consideration, are, curiously enough, seldom treated in depth in works on industrial psychology); (4) interactions between human beings, machines, and the ENVIRONMENT constitute a special subject, usually called ERGONOMICS in the U.K. and *engineering psychology* in the U.S.A.; (5) in so far as matters in (3) and (4) lead to the study of control SYSTEMS they also come under the heading of CYBERNETICS.

The term 'industrial psychology' only appears after 1900, and the subject was at first concerned primarily with the efficiency and well-being of individual workers. The development of psychological techniques for testing, selection, and appraisal contributed in the 1920s to the growth of *personnel work*. Over the same period industrial psychology was affected by ideas of SCIENTIFIC MANAGEMENT and TIME AND MOTION STUDIES of work processes aimed at increasing efficiency. These had successes, but also met opposition, and increasing interest in social psychology led during the 1930s to a heightened concern with human relations. Since 1945 the scope of the subject has widened again to take into account the contributions of managers and MANAGEMENT to the well-being and effectiveness of organizations. In these developments industrial psychology overlaps sociology.

B.B.S.

Bibl: E. J. McCormick and J. Tiffin, *Industrial Psychology* (Englewood Cliffs, N.J., 6th ed., 1974).

industrialization. A broad CONCEPT, generally thought of as a massive development of CAPITALISM, as the latter came to harness the new knowledge of science by means of MECHANIZATION in new processes of factory production. It entailed new relations between owners of CAPITAL, entrepreneurs, MANAGEMENT, and wage-labourers; and new physical concentrations both of industry and of population (see URBANIZATION). After early years of uncontrolled development, with many inhumanities, subsequent efforts of reform and political policy have been to *tame* industrialization and to control it for the increase of human welfare. It has thus been regarded as ˙the central set of economic and attendant social features which first appeared with the Industrial Revolution in Britain in the late 18th and early 19th centuries, spread to other countries, and marks off 'the modern world' from all earlier periods of history. R.F.

Bibl: L. Knowles, *The Industrial and Commercial Revolutions in Great Britain during the Nineteenth Century* (London, 1926); M. Weber, tr. F. Knight, *General Economic History* (London and N.Y., 1926); M. Weber, tr. A. M. Henderson and T. Parsons, *The Theory of Social and Economic Organization* (London and N.Y., 1947).

industrialized building, see PREFABRICATION.

inertia. The ability of matter to resist ACCELERATION when acted on by forces (see NEWTONIAN MECHANICS). The measure of inertia is MASS. See also MACH'S PRINCIPLE. M.V.B.

inertial guidance. A method – based on the tendency of a MASS to move uniformly in a straight line, i.e. on its INERTIA – for continuously correcting the course of a guided MISSILE. The ACCELERATION is monitored by measuring the forces exerted on devices inside the missile (see NEWTONIAN MECHANICS); the motion thus computed is compared with a pre-programmed flight plan. M.V.B.

infallibility. The inability to err. This happy condition has been popularly ascribed to a number of politicians, scientists, etc., but is chiefly associated with the DOGMA of the Roman CATHOLIC Church (1870) that the Pope is infallible when teaching *ex cathedra* (in full official solemnity), and with the FUNDAMENTALISM of some PROTESTANTS. The number of occasions on which Popes have so taught, and the exact nature of the truth in the Bible, are matters debated even by those who accept such infallibility. D.L.E.

Bibl: H. Küng, tr. E. Quinn, *Infallible?* (London and N.Y., 1971).

inference. The process or product of reasoning or argument. In a piece of reasoning or an argument a *conclusion* is inferred or derived from a *premise* or premises; it is asserted as true, or probable, on the assumption of the truth of the premise or premises. Thus the connected sequence of assertions 'All men are mortal, Socrates is a man, so Socrates is mortal' is an inference in the sense of process of reasoning; 'Socrates is mortal' is an inference in the sense of product of reasoning. In a valid *deductive* inference the premises ENTAIL the conclusion, which thus cannot be false if they are true. In a sound *inductive* inference (see INDUCTION) the premises only *support* the conclusion, or render it probable. An inference of either kind can have both its premises and conclusions true and yet be invalid or unsound.   A.Q.

inferiority complex. (1) ADLERIAN term for a COMPLEX in which there is repressed (see REPRESSION) fear and resentment of being inferior. (2) In common parlance, any feelings of inferiority, whether conscious or UNCONSCIOUS.   W.Z.

infinite; infinity. Our imagination readily transcends the strictly finite. We can see that the sequence 0,1,2,3, ... can be continued indefinitely, without limit. But the problem of harnessing this insight to MATHEMATICS is not easy and has not been finally resolved. Throughout the history of the subject two opposed tendencies are manifest. One, akin to NOMINALISM and IDEALISM, finds its expression today in *finitism* and INTUITIONISM. ABSTRACT objects such as numbers are considered as creations of the human mind. Hence although the law describing the above sequence can be grasped, and the members up to a given point can be constructed, the sequence itself must always remain uncompleted. One says that infinity is only *potential*. Because each real NUMBER is defined by an infinite sequence or SET, this view requires a radical reworking of ANALYSIS; standard theorems are replaced by more sophisticated, less intuitive, counterparts. It is not surprising, therefore, that most mathematicians follow the other tendency, which is akin to REALISM or PLATONISM. Here it is supposed that the *completed* sequence does, in some mysterious way, exist and so can be treated as an object; the infinite is actual. If care is taken to avoid PARADOXES and inconsistencies, one can treat infinite sets rather as if they were finite. The word *transfinite* is used to indicate this extension (e.g. transfinite arithmetic). This view is given a plausible, though partial, expression in the axioms of SET THEORY.

Cantor first showed that some sets are more infinite than others (see CARDINAL). In set theory there is an infinite hierarchy of orders of infinity. Recently many new *axioms of infinity* have been contrived which extend this hierarchy. They have interesting consequences, but stretch intuition to breaking point.   R.G.

Bibl: Bertrand Russell, *Introduction to Mathematical Philosophy* (London and N.Y., 1919).

infinitesimals, see under ANALYSIS.

inflatables, see PNEUMATIC STRUCTURES.

inflation. In ECONOMICS, a term used most commonly to denote a process whereby the general price level, as measured by some broad INDEX NUMBER of prices, rises significantly and persistently for a period of several years or more; looked at the other way up, it means a persistent decline in the purchasing power of the monetary unit. Price increases which would occur in a freely operating MARKET ECONOMY may be prevented by rationing and other administrative controls; there is then *suppressed inflation*. Where inflation is not suppressed, experience has shown that the rate of price increase may vary from 3% or 4% per annum ('creeping inflation') to as much as 50% or even more. *Hyper-inflation*, such as occurred in Germany in 1923, is a special case, arising out of some radical breakdown of the monetary system and its control, and running its course in weeks or months rather than years; prices may double or treble in a single day, and the currency ends by being destroyed, losing its ability to function as a medium of exchange.

Inflation means that nominal or money incomes per head are rising faster than real OUTPUT per head. (Living standards depend on output per head; so inflation, though it causes widespread inconvenience and may hurt particular groups, does not mean that the population in general is becoming poorer.) A necessary condition for this to happen at FULL EMPLOYMENT is that there be sufficient elasticity in the monetary system to allow the NATIONAL INCOME to be circulated at ever higher price levels. This means increases either in the quantity of money or in its velocity of circulation round the system. Of these alternatives, the quantity of money depends on MONETARY POLICY and FISCAL POLICY, whereas velocity may be increased spontaneously by the economy itself, e.g. by developing extra credit channels outside the banks or by shortening the average pay period. However, the amount by which velocity changes in the short run is usually quite small, and in theory may always be offset by restricting the quantity of money.

Pre-KEYNESIAN analysis saw the cause of inflation exclusively in terms of these monetary variables. Some economists (*monetarists*) do the same today – while admitting that governments may have a variety of reasons for allowing the money stock to expand. Others make a distinction (derived ultimately from Keynes's *General Theory* and from his 1940 pamphlet on *How to Pay for the War*) between *demand-pull* and *cost-push* inflation. The former occurs when AGGREGATE DEMAND is allowed to exceed the value of the economy's maximum potential output at unchanged prices. The latter results from struggles over the distribution of the national income, especially among different groups of wage-earners, and occasionally from a rise in import prices outside the home economy's control; the monetary authorities are seen here as playing a lagging rather than a leading role in the inflationary process.

Proponents of cost-push believe that direct government influence upon the wage- and price-setting process by way of INCOMES POLICY can help to secure price stability with full employment. Monetarists and other opponents of cost-push insist that in a market economy incomes policy can have only a very short-run impact; that price stability in the long run depends on the authorities not allowing purchasing power to outgrow the economy's productive potential; and that trade unions and others will eventually adapt their wage behaviour to the monetary climate which the government sets. In the interim, however, quite serious and prolonged UNEMPLOYMENT may on this view be unavoidable – particularly if people have come (as they had by the early 1970s in most industrial countries) to expect that price increases will continue and even accelerate in the future. Such expectations are themselves a powerful price-inflationary force.

The term 'inflation' is also used with reference to increases in aggregate demand, which by implication are responsible for wage and price rises. *Disinflation* refers to policies of monetary and fiscal restraint, designed to lessen the pressure of demand. Carried further, such policies produce *deflation*. On the assumption that prices are freely flexible in both directions, inflation and deflation are symmetrical terms, the former signifying rising and the latter falling prices. Since, however, most prices are not very flexible downwards, especially in industrial economies, deflation refers more usually to a situation where there is unemployment and spare capacity in the economy. With prices being driven upwards by cost pressures and inflationary expectations, one can therefore face inflation (= rising prices) and deflation (= unemployment) simultaneously. *Reflation* denotes the expansionary policies intended to bring the system up to full employment again. In other words, disinflation and reflation describe government policy, whereas inflation and deflation are used with reference both to policy and, more commonly, to the economic situation.　　　　P.M.O.

Bibl: R. J. Ball, *Inflation and the Theory of Money* (Chicago, 1965; London, 2nd ed., 1973).

inflecting (or *fusional*). In comparative LINGUISTICS, adjectives applied to a language (e.g. Latin) in which grammatical relations are expressed primarily by means of changes within the forms of words (the *inflections*). The term *fusional* implies a characteristic, generally absent from AGGLUTINATING languages, namely that different grammatical meanings are often combined within a single affix, e.g. in Latin *bonus* the *-us* simultaneously marks nominative, masculine, and singular. D.C.

information processing, see COMPUTING.

information storage and retrieval. A generic term for activities, usually using COMPUTERS, in which data of some sort are stored in an organized way so that they may be recovered in response to enquiries. The expression is used for two quite distinct activities. In one (sometimes known as *data retrieval*) the complexity arises from the detailed structure of the data and from their bulk, all enquiries being unambiguous as are the encodings of the data. In the other (sometimes known as *document retrieval* or *reference retrieval*) the complexity arises from the impossibility of describing the content of a document, or the intent of a request, precisely or unambiguously. In the first case the difficult question is 'Where is the thing I am looking for?' and in the second 'Is this thing the one I am looking for?' R.M.N.

information theory (or *communication theory*; for another sense of that term see COMMUNICATION, THEORIES OF). In CONTROL ENGINEERING, the treatment of the problem of transmitting messages: that is, of reproducing at one point either exactly or approximately a message selected at another point. The fact that a message may have a *meaning* is irrelevant to the engineering problem, which is concerned with the ability to encode, transmit, and decode an actual message selected from a set of possible messages with which the communication SYSTEM claims to deal. Success in this depends on the quantity of information that has to be processed in a unit of time, measured against *channel capacity*, i.e. the capacity of the available channels to handle it. Mathematical tools are developed to enable such measurements to be made and compared.

The essential problem arises because of the almost universal presence of NOISE in communication systems. Noise, which may be generated by faulty components, miscoding, or outside interference, cannot by eliminated; but its corrupting effects can be diminished to an *arbitrarily* small degree by the use of REDUNDANCY. The capability of this theory to compute precise relationships between signals and noise in redundant communication is its major contribution. S.BE.

Bibl: C. E. Shannon and W. Weaver, *The Mathematical Theory of Communication* (Urbana, Ill., 1949).

infra-red. Electromagnetic RADIATION whose wavelength can range from 8 ten-millionths of a metre to about 1 millimetre, i.e. just longer than visible light, but shorter than RADIO FREQUENCY waves. Bodies less than red-hot emit infra-red radiation, so that photographic film sensitive to infra-red reveals 'hot spots' such as vehicle exhausts, even at night when there is no visible light. Infra-red radiation penetrates haze because it suffers less than visible light from DIFFRACTION by the small PARTICLES. M.V.B.

infrastructure. A term used by the French railways since the end of the 19th century to denote fixed installations such as permanent way and bridges. It came into more widespread use (and the English language) in 1952 when it was applied within the North Atlantic Treaty Organization (NATO) to distinguish 'common infrastructure' fixed installations such as airfields, TELECOMMUNICATION, pipelines, and ports, which might be used by the forces of any ally and were therefore financed by a central Nato fund, from 'national infrastructure' barracks, training establishments, etc. Since then the term has acquired a still more general meaning as the basic capital investment of a country or an enterprise, with particular reference to developing countries. A.F.B.

Inge, William Ralph (British theologian, 1860–1954), see under MODERN CHURCHMEN.

Ingres, Jean Auguste Dominique (French painter, 1780–1867), see under ARMORY SHOW; NEO-CLASSICISM.

Ingsoc, see under ORWELLIAN.

inhibition, see under PAVLOVIAN.

initial teaching alphabet, see i.t.a.

initiation. The act of introducing someone to a new STATUS (e.g. adulthood), or to membership of an association or group (e.g. a Church, the House of Commons, the Freemasons, the graduate body of a university), or to a new experience (e.g. sexual). Initiation may be of any degree of formality; at its most formal, it is accompanied by RITUAL (*initiation rites*). See also RITES OF PASSAGE. R.F.

Bibl: A. van Gennep, tr. M. B. Vizedom and G. L. Caffee, *The Rites of Passage* (Paris, 1909; London and Chicago, 1960).

innateness hypothesis. In LINGUISTICS, the view, particularly widespread in GENERATIVE GRAMMAR, that the rapid and complex development of children's grammatical COMPETENCE can be explained only on the hypothesis that they are born with an innate knowledge of at least some of the universal structural principles of human language. The hypothesis has had a considerable impact in other fields, notably PSYCHOLOGY and BIOLOGY, though it is not accepted by everyone, even within linguistics.　　D.C.

Bibl: see under CHOMSKYAN.

inner direction, see under OTHER-DIRECTION.

inorganic chemistry. The branch of CHEMISTRY concerned with the study of compounds based on ELEMENTS other than carbon. It embraces the preparation of new compounds, the elucidation of reaction mechanisms, and the measurement and rationalization of the physical and chemical properties of inorganic systems. Compounds containing carbon fall within the scope of the subject when interest is centred on another element or elements, and they are actively investigated, notably in *organometallic chemistry*. Certain areas of study interact with BIOCHEMISTRY, METALLURGY, and SOLID-STATE PHYSICS.　　B.F.

Bibl: F. A. Cotton and G. Wilkinson, *Advanced Inorganic Chemistry* (Chichester and N.Y., 3rd ed., 1972); C. S. G. Phillips and R. J. P. Williams, *Inorganic Chemistry*, 2 vols. (Oxford, 1965–6).

input/output (I/O). The parts of a COMPUTER concerned with input (i.e. the instructions and data fed to it) and output (i.e. the results it supplies in response to these). Most of the I/O (which comprises the *peripherals,* or *peripheral devices*, and their controllers) is concerned with communicating with human beings and involves the production of some visible record. Input generally starts from keystrokes (as from a typewriter) which either provide a direct input to the computer (as in a CONSOLE) or produce a machine-readable intermediate form (punched cards or paper tape, MAGNETIC TAPE); at the same time a printed copy is usually produced. In some cases (e.g. numerals printed in magnetic ink· on cheques) the two are combined. Devices for reading printed or handwritten characters (optical character-recognition) are still in a primitive state; their perfection would make a large difference to the use of computers.

Output for human consumption often comes from a *line-printer* – a device which prints a whole line at a time at rates up to about 1,000 lines per minute. Early line-printers had ugly and restricted character sets which gave the layman an unfavourable impression. More modern machines can print small and capital letters as well as a variety of other symbols. Graphical output is also possible, both in a permanent form, drawn by a computer-controlled pen, and in evanescent form on a VISUAL DISPLAY.

Some computer applications, particularly *real-time* COMPUTING and PROCESS CONTROL, use I/O which is not for human beings. Their input includes direct sensing devices for position, temperature, etc., and their output may control some machine directly.　　C.S.

input-output analysis. A method used in ECONOMICS for tracing the connections between products and the resources required to produce them. The productive system is divided into a number of branches defined in terms of their characteristic products. During any time period, each branch produces a certain quantity of *output* and in so doing uses certain quantities of *inputs*. These quantities, expressed for convenience in money values, are set out in a MATRIX called an input-output table, in which each branch is assigned a row and a column. By convention, the row entries relate to the destination of the outputs and the column entries to the provenance of the inputs: the outputs either are absorbed within the productive system (*intermediate outputs*) or flow out of it into final demand (*final outputs*); and the inputs either are supplied by the system (*intermediate inputs*) or flow into it from outside (*primary inputs*, namely land, labour, and CAPITAL). For each branch, the sum of the entries in the row (total output = total revenue) is equal to the sum of the entries in the column (total inputs = total costs).

Thus an input-output table consists of: (1) a square submatrix showing the flows of intermediate products within the system (inter-industry flows); (2) one or more additional columns showing final outputs; and (3) one or more additional rows showing primary inputs. If the intermediate inputs into a branch (the entries in a column of the inter-industry submatrix) are divided by the total output of that branch, and if this operation is repeated for all the branches, a matrix of coefficients, *A*, is obtained, usually associated with the name W. W. Leontief. The typical element, a_{jk} say, of *A* measures the amount of product *j* required directly to produce one unit of product *k*.

R.ST.

input tax, see under VALUE-ADDED TAX.

instinct. A term used in too many different senses to be of further use in the present stage of the BEHAVIOURAL SCIENCES. Derived from Latin *instinguere* (to drive or incite), it has been applied (1) to the (presumed) internal system that controls complex behaviour even in the absence of proper external stimulation; (2) to the faculty governing behaviour that is 'not learned'. Modern analysis of both the short-term control of adult behaviour and of the development of the control systems during the growth of the individual have invalidated these uses of the word by showing (*a*) that most, if not all, behaviour patterns are at any moment steered jointly by internal and external determinants, and (*b*) that they develop partly under the influence of GENETIC instructions (which limit the range of possible behaviour) and partly by complex interactions with the ENVIRONMENT.

It is also used to denote (3) a major, functionally unitary behaviour system such as feeding, sexual behaviour, etc., and (4) the mere absence of premeditation ('I braked instinctively') – a condition which has so far defied scientific analysis.

N.T.

institutions. In SOCIOLOGY, activities which are repeated or continuous within a regularized pattern that is NORMATIVELY sanctioned. Sociologists usually speak of four major complexes of institutions. *Political institutions* regulate the competition for POWER. *Economic institutions* are concerned with the production and distribution of goods and services. *Cultural institutions* deal with the religious, artistic, and expressive activities and traditions in the society. *Kinship institutions* focus on the questions of marriage and the family and the rearing of the young. Institutions are studied comparatively in order to see how different societies organize their political or religious life. Or a set of related institutions within a society may be studied as a social system in order to see how they affect each other.

D.B.

instrumental conditioning, see OPERANT CONDITIONING.

insulin. The hormone (see ENDOCRINOLOGY), secreted by the pancreas, the partial or complete lack of which results in diabetes; its discovery in 1921, by Frederick Banting and Charles Best in Toronto, has saved the lives of millions who would otherwise have died in diabetic coma. It is a *polypeptide* (see PEPTIDE) consisting of two chains, respectively of 21 and 30 AMINO ACIDS linked together by sulphur ATOMS. Its chemical formula was discovered in 1955 by F. Sanger of Cambridge, and its spatial configuration was worked out in 1970 by Dorothy Hodgkin of Oxford. It is formed in the body from a precursor, *proinsulin,* a fact discovered in 1968 by Donald Steiner of Chicago.

In medical practice insulin is given by injection; it cannot be given by mouth as it is destroyed in the stomach. If too much insulin is given, the blood sugar level falls too low, producing symptoms which if untreated can culminate in unconsciousness and convulsions; but when the dose is properly adjusted, and a satisfactory diet given, the diabetic's blood sugar can be kept near normal values, and he can lead an almost normal life.

D.A.P.

insurgency, see under WAR.

integer, see under NUMBER.

integer programming. A technique of OPTIMIZATION THEORY. Certain optimization problems lead to mathematical programming problems in which some or all of the variables can take only certain discrete values. Usually it is sufficient to consider only the case of integer values, and the resultant problems are called *integer programming problems.* Problems involving packaging objects or setting out patterns so as to waste as little space or material as possible often lead to integer programs, as do problems where processes have not only a running cost but a capital or starting cost associated with them. Integer programs are as a rule extremely laborious to solve.

R.SI.

integrated circuit. A single electronic component containing a large number of GATES and other LOGIC circuits and their interconnections. The TRANSISTORS, resistors, capacitors, and their connections are generally manufactured together and in their final positions in order to minimize the overall size of the circuit. *Medium-* and *large-scale integration* (M.S.I. and L.S.I.) are distinguished by their packing density. In L.S.I. this can amount to more than 10,000 gates on a square inch of semiconductor chip, and is approaching that of the human brain. C.S.

integrated day; integrated curriculum. A school day, or school curriculum, in which there is no detailed timetable or syllabus. Found mainly at the bottom end of the primary school (age 5–9 at most), it aims to minimize divisions between subjects because these are thought to be artificial and foreign to a child's way of learning; its methodological basis is the CHILD-CENTRED curriculum and INDIVIDUALIZED INSTRUCTION. The central problem is always whether the basic tools of learning in language (spoken, read, and written) and number (basic skills and mathematical principles) are being mastered and used. Time has also to be found in the integrated day (in some critics' view, the disintegrated day) for the opportunity to exercise expressive arts (painting, craft, drama, movement), and for physical and social activity. W.A.C.S.

Bibl: L. Hollanby, *Young Children Living and Learning* (London, 1962).

integration.

(1) Many quantities in GEOMETRY and PHYSICS are given multiplicatively: thus area = height × breadth, distance travelled = velocity × time. Integration is the process by which such a product may be evaluated when one of the factors (hereinafter 'y') is a FUNCTION f of the other: say $y = f(x)$. Intuitively the range of variation of x (say from a to b) is dissected into 'small' intervals of length, say $x_1, x_2, \ldots x_n$, in each of which the value of y (say $y_1, y_2, \ldots, y_n$) is approximately constant. The sum $y_1 x_1 + y_2 x_2 + \ldots + y_n x_n$ is then an approximation to the desired overall product; if the function f is reasonably smooth this approximation will tend to a definite LIMIT as the dissection is made finer and finer. This limit $_a\int^b y dx$, or

$_a\int^b f(x)dx$, is the *definite integral* of f between the limits a and b. If a is given, but b is considered as a VARIABLE, then the integral is a function, say $F(b)$, of b. F is an *indefinite integral* of f; conversely f is the DERIVATIVE (rate of change) of F. This fact facilitates the calculations of F. The method may be extended to quantities (e.g. volumes) which are products of more than 2 factors, by introducing *multiple integrals*. Nowadys the theory of integration is treated as part of MEASURE THEORY. R.G.

Bibl: W. W. Sawyer, *Mathematician's Delight* (N.Y., 1943; Harmondsworth, 1949).

(2) In social contexts, a term having three related, but distinguishable, meanings: (*a*) A situation of cohesion, deriving from consent rather than coercion, between the parts of a community sufficient to make it a workable whole. The conditions for this were the object of pioneering study by the French sociologist Émile Durkheim. (*b*) The process whereby any MINORITY group, especially a racial one (see RACE), adapts itself to a majority society and is accorded by the latter EQUALITY of rights and treatment. If such a process reaches the point of obliterating the minority's separate cultural identity, a preferable term is *assimilation*. (*c*) In American usage, the opposite of SEGREGATION: i.e. the process of combining into a single system any educational or other public facilities previously available only on a racially selective basis. M.D.B.

Bibl: E. J. B. Rose, *Colour and Citizenship* (London and N.Y., 1969).

integration, vertical and horizontal, see under CORPORATE STRATEGY.

intellectual history, see HISTORY OF IDEAS.

intellectuals. The word, as a noun (with which in its plural form *intelligentsia* is synonymous), emerged largely in the 19th century, first in Russia in the 1860s, to designate that section of the university-educated youth who were 'critically thinking personalities' (Pisarev's phrase) or 'nihilists' (Turgenev's term), those who questioned all traditional values in the name of reason and progress. In France it was used, pejoratively or proudly, of and by the Dreyfusards (see DREYFUS CASE).

The resultant association of the category *intellectual* with the LEFT was reinforced by such views as those of Alexis de Tocqueville and of Marx who, in the *Communist Manifesto,* described the intellectuals as a section of the BOURGEOISIE who attached themselves to the working class with the function of shaping their ideas.

Yet, if one defines intellectuals as the culture-bearers of their society, then the majority, until World War II, were not of the left, while many were on the RIGHT, e.g. Maurras, Bernanos, Mauriac; Stefan George, Jünger, Gottfried Benn; D'Annunzio, Pirandello; Wyndham Lewis, Pound, Lawrence, Yeats. And if one sees the intellectuals as the defenders of humanist values, then the majority have been of the *clerisy* (Coleridge's term), the upholders of tradition and learning against the popular passions and politics of the day; Julien Benda's *La Trahison des clercs* (1927, translated as *The Betrayal of the Intellectuals*), with its attack on the intellectuals as seeking to 'govern the world', is a major statement of that position.

In general, one can say that the intellectuals are the custodians of the tradition of creative and critical thinking about the NORMATIVE problems of their society and the effort of men to relate themselves to symbols of meaning outside their immediate self-interest and experience. In social fact, however, an intellectual is often one who simply identifies himself as an intellectual, participates with other intellectuals in discussion of questions that are deemed intellectual, and is confirmed in that STATUS by those who are recognized, informally, as the leaders of the intellectual world. Indeed, with the expansion of higher education in almost all industrial societies, and the growth of the cultural sectors (publishing, television, the ARTS), the intellectuals today constitute a distinct social CLASS. How this ROLE affects their 'historic function' (howsoever defined) is an unresolved problem. D.B.

Bibl: B. de Huszar (ed.) *The Intellectuals* (Glencoe, Ill., 1960); L. A. Coser, *Men of Ideas* (London and N.Y., 1965); E. Shils, *The Intellectuals and the Powers, and Other Essays* (London and Chicago, 1972).

intelligence. A term that came into widespread use with the rise of the MENTAL TESTING movement in the early 20th century. Intelligence was considered to be an innate general COGNITIVE ability underlying all processes of complex reasoning. In practice, it was defined operationally in terms of performances on tests of ABSTRACT reasoning. This gave rise to the statistical abstraction (see STATISTICS) of the INTELLIGENCE QUOTIENT. There is little doubt that scores on intelligence tests correlate with educational achievement and occupational STATUS. The major controversy surrounding their use lies in the NATIVIST argument that 80% of the variability in I.Q. between individuals in Western societies is attributable to GENETIC factors. On this view, intelligence is a relatively fixed attribute which sets an upper limit on individual intellectual functioning.

An alternative to the static MODEL of fixed intelligence is offered by Piaget's theory (see PIAGETIAN). Adult intelligence is conceived not as an attribute but as a complex hierarchy of information-processing skills underlying an adaptive EQUILIBRIUM between the individual and the ENVIRONMENT. Furthermore, adult forms of intellectual organization are derived from qualitatively different forms characterizing thought in infancy and childhood. Piaget's theory describes a universal sequence of stages in intellectual development culminating in the FORMAL OPERATIONS of adulthood. Since intellectual development depends on environmental factors to provide the experiential basis for change, the theory precludes any attempt to ascribe intellectual functioning to genetic or environmental factors alone.

Piaget's approach has the advantage of directing attention to the process of cognitive growth but tends to ignore the role of the CULTURE in defining what is to be considered as intelligent behaviour. A third view is that intelligence consists of skill in a culturally defined context, and that, whereas pre-literate societies depend on action-based skills taught in the context within which they will be used, technological societies (see TECHNOLOGY) require abstract reasoning skills transmitted by means of formal schooling. Consequently, what is defined as intelligence in a technological society reflects factors that make for success in school. This theory of intelligence, unlike those that stress intellectual processes alone, takes into account the contribution to skilled performance made by motivational factors. Particular emphasis is placed on the role of poverty in making the child feel he belongs to a 'culture of failure', a feeling which will tend to limit his self-imposed educational goals.

See also ARTIFICIAL INTELLIGENCE.
G.B.

Bibl: H. J. Butcher, *Human Intelligence* (London and N.Y., 1968); L. J. Kamin, *The Science and Politics of IQ* (London and N.Y., 1974).

intelligence amplifier. A mechanical or electronic aid to human INTELLIGENCE or PROBLEM-SOLVING; e.g. a slide-rule, a calculating machine, or a COMPUTER. Language, and mathematical rules and notations, might also be regarded as intelligence amplifiers, and indeed they may be crucial for giving humans a problem-solving ability so much greater than that of other animals. Whether machines will ever be able not merely to amplify human intelligence, but to *replace* it, is an open question implicitly begged by the phrase ARTIFICIAL INTELLIGENCE.   R.L.G.

intelligence quotient. The expression of an individual's INTELLIGENCE either as a ratio of his MENTAL AGE to his chronological age, with 100 representing the MEAN (the so-called 'classical I.Q.') or as a standard score, also with a mean of 100 and with a standard deviation (see under VARIANCE) conventionally of 15 or 16 I.Q. points.   W.E.C.G.

intelligentsia, see INTELLECTUALS.

intension, see under CONNOTATION ETC.

intensionality, see under EXTENSIONALITY.

intentional fallacy. Term proposed by W. K. Wimsatt and Monroe C. Beardsley (*The Verbal Icon*, 1954) to denote the converse of the AFFECTIVE FALLACY. Conceding that there is an 'intended' meaning to a literary work, Wimsatt and Beardsley none the less separate this from the 'actual' meaning – which is independent of the author (as from all the work's effects). The author's intention, on this view, may be taken as *evidence* in determining its 'actual', independent meaning;

but it should not be confused with it; such evidence is 'external'. The theory is stimulating but not easy to accept: the work's meaning *is* in one important sense inseparable from the author's whole (no doubt largely unconscious) intention; it is impossible to pretend that we read, say, Keats's work without unconscious reference to what we know about his life or to what he thought he wanted to do; and any evidence of an author's intention is nearer to the 'actual' meaning than anything else available.   M.S.-S.

interactionism, see under MIND-BODY PROBLEM.

intercontinental ballistic missiles, see under MISSILES.

interest groups and **pressure groups.** Phrases coined by American political scientists to denote organized social groups which aim to influence the behaviour of governments, members of legislatures, or administrations without seeking formal control of the government. An *interest group* defends a particular interest; a *pressure group* (or *lobby*) may promote an interest or cause and make propaganda for it, the 'pressure' lying in the application or threatened application of a SANCTION should the claim or demand advanced by the group be denied. D.C.W.

Bibl: H. W. Ehrmann (ed.), *Interest Groups in Four Continents* (Pittsburgh, 1958); S. E. Finer, *Anonymous Empire* (London, 2nd ed., 1966).

interest profiles, see under SDI.

interface. In technical contexts, the connection between two pieces of equipment. The word is mainly used, in ELECTRONICS, of equipment handling information (e.g. TELECOMMUNICATION equipment or parts of a COMPUTER); the requirement that the behaviour of the various strands in the connection should satisfy fairly complicated overall conventions makes it useful to consider the whole connection as an entity. By analogy, the word is increasingly used in other contexts, e.g. that of intercommunication between various social groups.   J.E.S.

interference (in EDUCATIONAL PSYCHOLOGY), see under TRANSFER.

interferon. The chemical agent responsible for viral interference, i.e. the process whereby the infection of a CELL by one virus (see VIROLOGY) prevents its being infected by another. The difficulties of producing interferon in very large quantities have not yet been surmounted, and it is not yet known to have clinical uses, though there is no reason to doubt that it has a function in the normal life of the body. P.M.

interior monologue, see under STREAM OF CONSCIOUSNESS.

internal relations. Those RELATIONS of a thing to other things which are essential to it, which it logically cannot cease to have without ceasing to be the thing that it is. Being the square of 4 is essential to 16, or 'being the square of' internally relates 4 to 16, since any number that was not the square of 4 could not be 16. Hegelian IDEALISTS subscribe to a general doctrine about the internality of relations, according to which the type of ABSTRACT, ANALYTIC thinking used in science and everyday life ('understanding') apprehends the relations between things, inadequately, as external, while a higher, philosophical type of thinking ('reason') apprehends all relations as internal, a thesis foreshadowed in the philosophy of Spinoza. Idealists infer from this doctrine that what appear, and are commonly taken, to be complex pluralities, such as a nation or a work of art or the multitude of finite minds, are really unanalysable wholes or systematic unities (see HOLISM). A.Q.

International, the. Term applied historically to a succession of federations of working-class SOCIALIST parties and organizations. History distinguishes: the *First International*, the international Working Men's Association, founded in London in 1864 with the support of Karl Marx, which in 1872 split into followers of Marx and those who preferred Mikhail Bakunin's brand of ANARCHISM, and in 1876 was dissolved; the *Second International*, founded in Paris in 1889 as a loose federation, which failed to survive the conflict of socialist and NATIONALIST loyalties revealed by the outbreak of World War I in 1914; the *Third International*, or COMINTERN, founded in Mos-

cow in 1919, which, it became quickly apparent, was only open to socialist parties which accepted the discipline and leadership of the Russian COMMUNIST Party, and was dissolved by Russian fiat in May 1943; the *Fourth International*, formed in 1938 by the followers of Trotsky (see TROTSKYISM); the *Labour and Socialist International*, which, recreated in 1923 from the surviving democratic socialist parties (see SOCIAL DEMOCRACY) of the Second International, ceased to function after the NAZI conquest of continental Europe; and the *Socialist International* founded in Frankfurt in 1951, with headquarters in London and a membership of 40 democratic socialist parties. D.C.W.
Bibl: G. D. H. Cole, *A History of Socialist Thought*, vols. 2–5 (London and N.Y., 1954–60).

international baccalaureate. An international university entrance examination which, ideally, can be taken in any country and is recognized by every university. It was first conceived at the International School in Geneva and taken up by the International Schools Association in 1962. By 1970 it had been recognized by all British and many American and European universities; and 22 schools in the main European countries, Nigeria, Lebanon, Iran, Chile, and Uruguay were recognized as preparing students for the examination. Candidates are examined in 6 subjects (3 at higher and 3 at subsidiary level), which include specialized and general-education elements and two languages. W.A.C.S.

International Bank for Reconstruction and Development, see under BRETTON WOODS.

International Court. The International Court of Justice is the principal judicial organ of UNO in succession to the Permanent Court of International Justice established by Article 14 of the Covenant of the LEAGUE OF NATIONS. The 15 serving judges are elected for 9 years by the Security Council and General Assembly of UNO. The Court sits in permanent session at The Hague. Only states may be parties to disputes brought before it. Since both (or all) the parties involved must agree to a dispute being submitted to the Court, in practice not many cases are brought before it. Examples are the Anglo-Norwegian fisheries dispute and that between a number of African states and the Republic of South Africa concerning the status of South-West Africa.

D.C.W.; A.L.C.B.

international liquidity, see under LIQUIDITY.

International Monetary Fund, see under BRETTON WOODS.

International Phonetic Alphabet, see IPA.

international style. The title of a book by Henry-Russell Hitchcock and Philip Johnson published in New York in 1932, and now applied to the main stream of modern architecture. The label covers the functional architecture derived from *De Stijl*, influenced by the BAUHAUS, and characterized by a simple rectangular geometry of defined planes; it was to have been a style expressive of contemporary TECHNOLOGY and social programmes. Its chief exponents during its most vital period, the second quarter of the century, were Mies van der Rohe, Walter Gropius, Le Corbusier, and other more local figures, such as G. T. Rietveld in Holland or Skidmore, Owings & Merrill in the U.S.A., who ensured the wide diffusion of the style. It continues into the 1970s, though much criticized as an oversimplified solution and easily debased when used by lesser practitioners. See also CIAM; FUNCTIONALISM; MACHINE AESTHETIC; ORGANIC. M.BR.
Bibl: J. M. Richards, *An Introduction to Modern Architecture* (Harmondsworth, 1940).

internationals, see INTERNATIONAL, THE.

interpolation, see under EXTRAPOLATION.

intersex (or *sexual intergrade*). In sexually reproducing organisms, an organism of which the secondary sexual characters are intermediate between those of the two sexes. Thus an intersex is different from a *hermaphrodite*, in which the *primary* sexual organs of both sexes are represented on a single individual. In *bilateral gynandromorphism* each side of the body is of each sex. Intersexuality may be brought about by a derangement of the SEX CHROMOSOMES, or by a dysfunction of the sex hormones (see ENDOCRINOLOGY). Hermaphroditism is common among plants and among sedentary or very slow-moving animals like snails. In hermaphrodites self-fertilization is always rare and sometimes impossible. Indeed, such a process would defeat the purpose of sexual reproduction, which is to bring about genetical commingling. P.M.

intersubjectivity, see under PHYSICALISM.

interval estimation. In STATISTICS, a way of summarizing experimental evidence about the value of a PARAMETER by calculating from the data an interval with a given fairly high probability of containing the true parameter value. The interval is a *confidence interval*. It is important to remember that the true value of the parameter is a fixed quantity and the interval is a data-dependent (and hence randomly varying) object, and not *vice versa*. The probability that the (random) interval contains the (fixed) parameter value is the degree of confidence or confidence level. One speaks, for example, of a '95% confidence interval' as a contracted form of 'confidence interval at the 95% confidence level'. A common rule-of-thumb is to take sample ±2 × sample standard deviation (see VARIANCE) as a 95% confidence interval for the true MEAN. See also ESTIMATE. R.SI.

interval scale, see under SCALE.

intimism. Term applied to the work of those late-19th-century painters who concentrated on domestic scenes, somewhat in the genre of Henri Fantin-Latour's early work, e.g. Georges Lemmen and such NABIS as Maurice Denis and Édouard Vuillard. J.W.

intonation. In PHONOLOGY, systematic variations in the pitch of the voice serving to distinguish MEANINGS. D.C.

introspection. Generally, the mind's awareness of itself; more specifically, its attentive scrutiny of its own workings as contrasted with the inattentive and unbidden consciousness which we have of our own mental states. Locke called it 'reflection' and Kant 'inner sense', thus emphasizing the ANALOGY between it and our awareness of what is external to our minds in sense-PERCEPTION. The notion raises various difficulties. One is that it seems to imply an unacceptable duality in the introspecting mind which it divides into an introspecting subject self and an introspected object self. This consequence was embraced by Kant; Ryle, with his formula 'Introspection is retrospection', took the present self to be the introspector and the immediately past self to be the introspected. (But, it may be argued, one cannot retrospect or recollect any mental event of which one was not aware at the time it occurred.) Another difficulty is the infinite regress generated by the view of Locke and many other philosophers that mental states are self-intimating in the sense that they cannot occur unless the mind whose states they are is aware of them, for the introspecting is itself a mental state, or act, which must, on this view, itself be introspected.   A.Q.

Bibl: D. M. Armstrong, *A Materialist Theory of the Mind* (London and N.Y., 1968), ch. 15.

introspective psychology. The study of states and qualities of private experiences and feelings by means of self-reports, mostly verbal descriptions given by the introspector.   I.M.L.H.

introversion. In PSYCHOLOGY, a term introduced by Jung (see JUNGIAN) to denote a process whereby an individual frustrated in his attempts to develop relationships with others withdraws his concern and LIBIDO from them and turns it towards his own fantasies. In protecting his withdrawal, the individual develops behavioural means to defend himself from the enticements to establish relations with others. This process is somewhat similar to that underlying NARCISSISM. Later the process was reified (see REIFICATION) and generalized to refer to a PERSONALITY TYPE, the *introvert,* much of whose life seemed to be characterized by these processes and behaviours. Introversion is not a true opposite of EXTROVERSION. T.Z.C.

intuition. In LINGUISTICS, the native-speaker's knowledge of or about his language, used as evidence in deciding questions of ACCEPTABILITY; also, LINGUIST's awareness of principles for evaluating analyses.   D.C.

intuitionism.

(1) In ETHICS, the theory that the fundamental moral TRUTHS are directly apprehended as true by a special faculty of moral knowledge. It takes two main forms, corresponding to two different conceptions of the nature of the fundamental moral truths. According to the first of these, which may be called particular or, less politely, unphilosophical intuitionism, my moral faculty apprehends PROPOSITIONS to the effect that something is my, or some particular person's, duty on a particular occasion, by ANALOGY with the way in which the faculty of sense-PERCEPTION apprehends particular empirical facts. This is roughly the view of Bishop Butler. According to the second, which may be called general or philosophical intuitionism, the moral faculty, here conceived as an aspect of the capacity to apprehend *a priori* truths, such as the propositions of LOGIC and MATHEMATICS, apprehends general principles of duty, for example that promises ought to be kept or that lies ought not to be told. Most ethical intuitionists are adherents of DEONTOLOGY, but some hold that moral intuition apprehends the goodness or badness of the consequences of action, either in particular cases (G. E. Moore) or in the form of general principles such as that pleasure is good (Rashdall).

(2) In EPISTEMOLOGY, any theory of knowledge which holds that there are (or must be if scepticism is to be repelled) some items of absolutely certain, self-evident, and incorrigible knowledge. Peirce criticized the epistemology of Descartes for its intuitionism and defended FALLIBILISM against it.

(3) The philosophy of MATHEMATICS, developed by L. E. J. Brouwer, which is *finitist* (see INFINITE) in that it does not assume there is a totality of NUMBERS but arrives at conclusions about all numbers by MATHEMATICAL INDUCTION, and is 'constructivist' in that it rejects indirect proofs of mathematical existence by *reductio ad absurdum* (see DEMONSTRATION) and acknowledges only such mathematical entities as can be constructed from the natural NUMBERS by intuitively acceptable procedures. In denying that the derivation of a contradiction from 'no number has the property *P*' entails that there is a number with the

property *P*, which he holds to be true only if such a number can be positively constructed, the intuitionist has to reject the universal validity of the *law of the excluded middle* (that every proposition is either true or false) and admit a third TRUTH-VALUE, possessed by a class of propositions whose members are, in default of adequate proof, undecidable.

A.Q.

Bibl: A. Heyting, *Intuitionism* (Amsterdam, 2nd ed., 1966); W. D. Hudson, *Ethical Intuitionism* (London and N.Y., 1967); A. Quinton, *The Nature of Things* (London and N.Y., 1973).

invariant, see under CONSERVATION LAWS; TRANSFORMATION.

investment. (1) The purchase of marketable securities – a process usually called 'portfolio investment' to distinguish it from (2) the creation of CAPITAL or of goods capable of producing other goods. The latter constitutes one of the two main categories of output, the other being consumption. While the level of investment plays a crucial role in determining the level of NATIONAL INCOME within an economy, it also plays an important part in determining the rate of ECONOMIC GROWTH.

D.E.

Bibl: Investment Bankers Association of America, *Fundamentals of Investment Banking* (N.Y., 1949).

investment currency. The currency resulting from the sale of foreign securities or used for their purchase when such transactions are controlled and channelled through a market separate from the market in foreign exchange.

A.C.

invincible ignorance. A term used in Roman Catholic THEOLOGY to describe the condition of those who because of their heredity, upbringing, or environment cannot see a religious or moral truth, e.g. the truth of CATHOLICISM, whatever efforts they may make, and who are therefore not to blame. The term, although apparently offensive, expresses the charitable attitude, now happily characteristic of Roman Catholics, towards both sinners and non-Catholics.

D.L.E.

invisibles. That component of a country's BALANCE OF PAYMENTS on current account which comprises receipts and payments for services (as distinct from 'visible' goods); cash gifts, legacies, and other transfers for which no service is rendered; and the two-way flow of interest, profits, and dividends between home and abroad. All these items, which may be on government or private account, make up the *invisible balance.* The phrase *invisible exports and imports,* however, is usually restricted to travel, financial, and other services such as sea transport, civil aviation, insurance, banking, merchanting, brokerage, etc. These items are also included, with visible trade, in the concept of 'exports and imports of goods and services'. Fuller definitions and figures for recent years are set out in the annual volume entitled *United Kingdom Balance of Payments.*

P.J.

I/O, see INPUT/OUTPUT.

ion. An ATOM or MOLECULE which is electrically charged because of an excess or deficiency of ELECTRONS (see ATOMIC PHYSICS); excess of electrons results in a negatively charged *anion,* deficiency in a positively charged *cation.* Ions produced by fast charged particles form the basis of several detectors used in ELEMENTARY PARTICLE physics (e.g. the BUBBLE CHAMBER, CLOUD CHAMBER, and GEIGER COUNTER). Ions of chemical salts and ACIDS in solution provide the source of current in many electrical CELLS. Because of its conceptual simplicity the ionic MODEL is a very useful way of viewing many solids and solutions, but since electrons are at least partially shared between neighbouring atoms it is at best a good approximation. See also IONOSPHERE.

M.V.B.; B.F.

ion engine. A propulsion device similar to the ROCKET, which has been proposed for SPACE PROBES. The exhaust consists of rapidly moving IONS which are propelled backwards not by the expansion due to the combustion but by ELECTROSTATIC repulsion.

M.V.B.

ion exchange. The exchange of *cations* or *anions* (see ION) between a solution and an insoluble solid. The ion exchange material consists of a chemically bonded (see BOND) framework carrying a surplus positive or negative charge which is neutralized by mobile counter-ions. The latter may leave the host framework only when replaced by ions with the same total electrical charge. Water-softeners act by exchanging calcium ions in hard water with sodium. The first synthetic ion exchangers were aluminosilicates, but today most are based on synthetic organic resins. B.F.

Ionesco, Eugène (Romanian-born French dramatist, *b.* 1912), see under ANTI-THEATRE; THEATRE OF THE ABSURD.

ionization. The production of IONS. M.V.B.

ionization potential. The ENERGY that must be supplied to an ATOM to remove an ELECTRON and thus create an ION. M.V.B.

ionosphere. The radio-reflecting layers in the atmosphere, on which over-the-horizon radio transmission depends. At heights above about 100 km, positive IONS are produced from ATOMS in the air by short-wave RADIATION from the sun; the resulting free ELECTRONS give rise to the radio reflections. See also PLASMA PHYSICS. M.V.B.

IPA (International Phonetic Alphabet). The most widely used system for transcribing the sounds of a language, originally drawn up in 1889, but subsequently modified and expanded at various times by the International Phonetics Association. See also PHONETICS. D.C.

IQ, see INTELLIGENCE QUOTIENT.

IRA. The Irish Republican Army, an anti-British para-military guerrilla force (see PARA-MILITARY; GUERRILLA) founded by Irish NATIONALISTS in 1919 to combat the British forces occupying Ireland. The IRA refused to accept the Anglo-Irish agreement of 6 December 1921 on the grounds that Ireland remained a British dominion and that Ulster had been excluded from its scope. Its rising in 1922, however, was suppressed by Irish government forces, and the IRA went underground, remaining in existence throughout the 1920–39 period, while gradually falling under extremist control. It was responsible for bomb attacks in Britain in 1938–9 and for raids into Ulster in 1957–8. In 1966, disagreement on tactics

split the IRA into two wings, the 'officials' and the 'provisionals' or 'provos'. The latter wing were largely responsible for the renewal in 1969–70 of the armed campaign against civilian, commercial, and military targets in Northern Ireland which was still being waged in 1977. The 'officials' have observed a ceasefire with the British armed forces since 1972, while continuing their political activity. Both wings have maintained a strong presence in Catholic areas of Ulster, with the toleration of the local population. Periodically, this toleration has shown signs of strain, e.g. in the second half of 1976, when a women's peace movement sought the rejection of all forms of violence by all Northern Irish communities and police bodies. D.C.W.
Bibl: C. Fitz Gibbon, *Out of the Lion's Paw: Ireland Wins her Freedom* (London and N.Y., 1969); L. de Paor, *Divided Ulster* (Harmondsworth, 2nd ed., 1972).

IRBM (intermediate-range ballistic missiles), see under MISSILES.

Irgun Zvai Leumi (Hebrew for 'National Military Organization'). An armed extremist Jewish underground organization founded in 1937 by ZIONISTS in secession from the main Palestinian Jewish self-defence organization, the *Hagana*. It engaged first in anti-Arab, then in anti-British activities, until the outbreak of war in Europe in September 1939. Remaining inactive until January 1944, it then resumed anti-British sabotage and TERRORIST activities. Irgun Zvai Leumi, acting independently of *Hagana,* was responsible for blowing up British offices in the King David Hotel, Jerusalem, in 1946 and for the massacre of Arab villagers at Deir Yasin in 1948. It was forcibly disbanded by the Israeli Government in September 1948. D.C.W.

iron curtain. A phrase used to describe the enforced isolation of areas under the political domination of the Soviet Union from the rest of the non-Soviet world. Popularized in German by the Nazi propaganda minister Goebbels in 1943, it was first used in English by Churchill on 5 August 1945 and repeated in his Fulton speech of March 1946. D.C.W.

irradiation, see under PAVLOVIAN.

irrationalism. The view either that the conduct of men *is* not or that it *should* not be guided by reason. On the whole the two views are sharply opposed, and the two parties could be called, respectively, *descriptive* and NORMATIVE irrationalists. (1) The descriptive irrationalists are, for the most part, rather disillusioned or sceptical social theorists. Mild examples are Bagehot and Graham Wallas, a more scornful one is Pareto. Marx and Freud, both themselves dedicated to rationality, can be regarded without distortion as descriptive irrationalists: Marx for his theory of the false consciousness of men in an alienating social system (see MARXISM; ALIENATION), Freud for his view that the fundamental determinants of belief and conduct are unconscious and irrational (see FREUDIAN; SUBCONSCIOUS). Any theory (like the last two, or like Mannheim's sociology of KNOWLEDGE) which implies that all human thinking is irrational has a self-refuting tendency. (2) Among normative irrationalists may be included Rousseau for his emphasis on sentiment and natural impulse and his hostility to civilized sophistication; D. H. Lawrence for his glorification of primal instinct as against BOURGEOIS prudence and calculation; Kierkegaard for his insistence on the absurdity of the human situation; and, perhaps above all, Nietzsche. Normative irrationalism began and has continued as a protest against the consequences of INDUSTRIALIZATION.   A.Q.

isallobar. Meteorological term for a line on a map connecting places with equal change in barometric pressure over a given time period.   P.H.

Isard, Walter (U.S. economist and geographer, *b.* 1919), see under GEOGRAPHY; REGIONAL SCIENCE.

Isherwood, Christopher (British-born novelist, *b.* 1904), see under ANTI-HERO; GROUP THEATRE; NEW WRITING.

Islam. The RELIGION founded by the Prophet Muhammad in Arabia in the 7th century A.D. In Arabic *Islam* means 'surrender' or 'submission', and the term expresses the complete devotion to God (Allah) of the Prophet and of all *Muslim* believers (who dislike the Western terms 'Mohammedan' and 'Mohammedanism').

Muhammad's ecstatic visions of the divine majesty, and his teachings about the divine will (at places in great detail), are recorded in the holy book of Islam, the *Quran* (or *Koran*). Mecca, which Muhammad took over in 630, is the holiest city, to which Muslims try to go on pilgrimage. Islam was soon spread by the conquests of the Arabs all over Western Asia and North Africa, and in modern times it has been spread by EVANGELISM into much of the rest of Africa. Pakistan split from India in 1945 in order to be an Islamic state. Muslims are found in considerable numbers elsewhere. Islam attracts coloured people by its freedom from racism (see RACE) and superstition, and also some whites (who, however, are seldom fully converted) by the simplicity of its worship and the strength of its moral code. Its main problem is that, although it has bred mystics (see MYSTICISM) it is essentially a practical and communal religion – and many of the regulations laid down in the *Quran* and in later Muslim law (e.g. the subjection of women and the allowance of polygamy) are now outmoded. In order to modernize, it was thought necessary to SECULARIZE Turkey dramatically in the 1920s, although the faith of the people remains strong. Christianity has made little impression on Islam.
D.L.E.

Bibl: F. Rahman, *Islam* (N.Y., 1966; London, 1967).

isobar. (1) In METEOROLOGY, a line of constant atmospheric pressure on a weather map. (2) In NUCLEAR PHYSICS, one of a pair of NUCLEI with the same number of NUCLEONS (cf. ISOTYPES).
M.V.B.

isogloss. In DIALECTOLOGY, a boundary line demarcating regions that differ in respect of a particular linguistic feature.
D.C.

isohyet. In METEOROLOGY, a line on a map connecting places with equal rainfall characteristics.   P.H.

isolating (in LINGUISTICS), see ANALYTIC (2).

isolationism. The doctrine that a nation's interests are best served by abstaining from intervention in the main issues of international politics; variously practised by Imperial China, Czarist Russia, and late Victorian Britain ('splendid isolation') but most specifically applied to grass-roots American attitudes to the world of great-power politics before 1941. The literature distinguishes between *continentalism, hemispheric isolationism* (as embodied in the MONROE DOCTRINE), and westward expansion into the Pacific – a form of isolationism which rejects involvement in European but not in Pacific politics. Isolationism has normally been coupled in America with a moralist rejection of the practices of power politics as 'un-American'. D.C.W.

Bibl: N. A. Graebner, *The New Isolationism* (N.Y., 1956); S. Adler, *The Isolationist Impulse* (London and N.Y., 1957); M. Jonas, *Isolationism in America, 1935–1941* (Ithaca, N.Y., 1966).

isomer. A chemical SPECIES, usually molecular, which differs from other MOLECULES made up of the same ATOMS. Thus ethyl alcohol and dimethyl ether each have the same chemical constitution, C_2H_6O, but they have different chemical BONDS and properties. In *stereoisomers* the bonding is similar but the atoms are arranged spatially in a different way; *optical isomers* differ only by being mirror images of each other, in their effect on polarized light, and in their chemical reactivity with optical isomers of other compounds. B.F.

isometric projection. In CARTOGRAPHY, a diagram in three dimensions, i.e. a block-diagram, usually drawn to illustrate features of GEOMORPHOLOGY, and giving the appearance of a relief model viewed obliquely. An isometric projection is not in perspective. It is true to scale in both its horizontal axes, but the scale of the vertical axis is usually exaggerated with respect to them. It can be made by using isometric graph paper or by constructing sections, using contours, along horizontal and vertical grid lines of a topographical map and projecting them onto a rhombus base. M.L.

isomorphic. Adjective applied to two or more things that have the same STRUCTURE, i.e. whose corresponding parts have similar properties and RELATIONS. Thus two chairs of identical shape are isomor-

phic even if one is made of wood and the other of metal. The 'things' may, however, be to a greater or lesser degree ABSTRACT, and the CONCEPT of *isomorphism* is important in MATHEMATICAL STRUCTURES. Consider for example the following four sequences of numbers:

(a) 2, 4, 6, 8
(b) 7, 14, 21, 28
(c) 3, 5, 7, 9
(d) 3, 6, 12, 24.

If we merely consider the number of elements in each sequence, and the fact that each element is smaller than its successor and larger than its predecessor, then they are all isomorphic. If, however, we describe them in more detail, we find that there are pairs which are isomorphic with each other but not with the rest. Thus (a) and (b) are isomorphic because in each the difference between successive elements is equal to the first element, while (a) and (c) are isomorphic because the difference between successive elements is always 2. At a still more abstract level, (a) and (d) are isomorphic because, if we let the operation of addition in (a) correspond to multiplication in (d), then in both sequences the successor of an element is got by applying the operation to the element and the number 2, i.e. in (a) the successor of n is $n + 2$, while in (d) the successor of n is $n \times 2$. Thus, whether two things are isomorphic or not depends on how they are described. It is possible to prove that almost any two things are isomorphic, if descriptions at a high enough level of abstraction are used. So talk of isomorphism without a specification of the relevant types of description is liable to be vacuous, or at least slipshod and ambiguous. A.S.

isomorphism. When two MATHEMATICAL STRUCTURES A and B are ISOMORPHIC, there must be at least one FUNCTION f which maps each element a of A into a corresponding element $b(= f(a))$ of B. Any such structure-preserving function is an *isomorphism*. R.G.

isoquants, see under INDIFFERENCE CURVES.

isorhythm. The application of a single and reiterated rhythmic pattern to differing melodic shapes. The term was originally applied by F. Ludwig in 1902 to rhythmic patterns that recur in 14th-century

motets. Recently isorhythmic patterns have been much exploited by contemporary composers, in particular Messiaen.
A.H.

isostasy. Term proposed in 1889 by C. E. Dutton for the principle that the surface features of the earth will tend towards an ideal condition of gravitational EQUILIBRIUM; the *isostatic theory* proposes that balance is achieved by sub-surface inequalities of mass and implies that there is horizontal transfer of mantle material at depth. It is known that the earth's crust is less dense than the underlying mantle (see ASTHENOSPHERE), so that the situation can be likened to blocks of wood floating on water. The bigger the block of wood, the higher it sticks out of the water, and the deeper it sinks underneath. Similarly the increasingly higher blocks of the earth's crust above sea-level are balanced by greater thicknesses of crust below sea-level. The flow of the mantle is very slow, so that the attainment of isostatic equilibrium lags behind the more rapid changes of mass caused by certain geological processes operating on the earth's surface. This is why those parts of the earth's surface that were depressed under the load of the Pleistocene ice-sheets are still rising, even though the ice melted some 15,000 years ago.
J.L.M.L.

isotherm. In METEOROLOGY, a line on a map joining places with the same temperature at a particular instant or, more usually, the same average temperature over a certain period of time. Such temperatures are usually reduced to sea level, by an addition of 1° centigrade for every 165 m altitude of a station, in order to eliminate differences due to height. In GEOGRAPHY the most commonly used isotherms are those indicating mean monthly temperatures, especially for the mid-winter and mid-summer months of January and July.
M.L.

isotopes. ATOMS of the same chemical ELEMENT, having the same ATOMIC NUMBER, but differing from each other in respect of the number of NEUTRONS in the NUCLEUS; e.g. DEUTERIUM is an isotope of hydrogen.
M.V.B.

Isou, Isidore (Romanian-French poet, *b*. 1925), see under LETTRISM.

Israel, see under JUDAISM; ZIONISM.

i.t.a. (initial teaching alphabet). An alphabet invented by Sir James Pitman and first tried in schools in 1961; the number of characters has ranged, at various times, between 42 and 44. The intention is to help children to read without dealing with the oddities of English spelling (or capital letters). Starting on i.t.a. at the age of 5, children will normally be sufficiently fluent in reading to move on to traditional orthography (t.o.) by 7. Research shows that i.t.a. classes read more quickly and with better comprehension than t.o. classes, and do not show major difficulty in the transition to t.o. However, those taught by traditional methods normally catch up by the age of 9 or 10.
W.A.C.S.
Bibl: F. W. Warburton and V. Southgate, *i.t.a.: an Independent Evaluation* (London, 1969).

Itten, Johannes (Swiss painter and sculptor, 1888–1967), see under BEURON.

Ivanov, Vyacheslav Ivanovich (Russian poet and philosopher, 1866–1949), see under SERAPION BROTHERS.

Ives, Charles (U.S. composer, 1874–1954), see under POLYRHYTHM; TONE CLUSTER.

IZL, see IRGUN ZVAI LEUMI.

Izvestia (*News*). A Soviet daily newspaper, since 1960 an evening paper, with a Sunday supplement *Nedelya (The Week)*. Established in March 1917 as the organ of the Petrograd Soviet, in 1918 it was transferred to Moscow. Like PRAVDA, it is printed in many Soviet cities, and its local editions are similarly standardized by the inclusion of material transmitted from its Moscow central editorial office. It reflects the official government point of view and only on one or two occasions in Soviet post-war history has it diverged from *Pravda*, reflecting political dissension at the top. Its estimated circulation is 8 million.
L.L.
Bibl: A. Buzek, *How the Communist Press Works* (London and N.Y., 1964).

J

j-curve. The shape of the curve said to be followed by the BALANCE OF PAYMENTS after DEVALUATION, with an initial aggravation of any deficit giving way to a steady improvement after some interval during which exporters and importers have not yet had time to make full adjustments to the new price of foreign exchange. Whether the curve is in fact of this shape depends on a number of factors such as the speed of response of exporters and importers to devaluation, the ELASTICITY OF DEMAND for exports and imports, the margin of idle capacity on which traders can draw, and the stability of domestic costs and prices. A.C.

Jack of Diamonds, see KNAVE OF DIAMONDS.

Jacob, François (French biologist, *b*.1920), see under OPERON.

Jacobinism. An extremist movement during the French Revolution associated with Robespierre and the members of the Jacobin Club, and characterized by its determination to carry through the revolution at whatever cost and not to compromise. By extension the term is used to describe similar tendencies in subsequent revolutionary movements.

Contempt for the will of the majority, DICTATORSHIP by a determined revolutionary minority, Committees of Public Safety as embryo institutions for implementing terror – these are some of the historically archetypal features of Jacobinism. Underlying it was the idea, derived from Rousseau, that the masses were insufficiently enlightened to carry out a REVOLUTION. 'How can a blind multitude, which often does not know what it wills, because it rarely knows what is good for it, carry out for itself as great and difficult an enterprise as a system of legislature?' It was therefore necessary 'to be concerned less with gathering the votes of the nation than with having the supreme authority, in the least arbitrary manner, fall into the hands of wise and strong revolutionaries' (Buonarotti). The idea was repeatedly expressed (and followed) by revolutionary extremists in the 19th and 20th centuries, from Blanqui ('the last Jacobin and the first COMMUNIST'), through Nechaev (see NIHILISM) to Lenin. The analogy between Jacobins and Bolsheviks (see BOLSHEVISM) on the one hand and Girondins and MENSHEVIKS on the other was invoked from the beginning. Lenin himself proudly characterized his followers as 'Jacobins tied up with the working class'. L.L.

Jacques-Dalcroze, Émile (Swiss composer and teacher, 1865–1950), see under EURHYTHMICS.

Jagger, Mick (British songwriter and performer, *b.* 1944), see under ROLLING STONES.

Jakobson, Roman (Russian linguist, *b*.1896), see under PRAGUE SCHOOL.

James, Henry (U.S.-born novelist, 1843–1916), see under GREENWICH VILLAGE; REALISM; SYMBOLISM.

James, William (U.S. philosopher and psychologist, 1842–1910), see under JAMES-LANGE THEORY; NEUTRAL MONISM; PRAGMATISM; STREAM OF CONSCIOUSNESS.

James Committee's Report, see under WHITE PAPER ON EDUCATION.

James-Lange theory. The theory of EMOTION proposed principally by William James (*Principles of Psychology*, 1890) and resting upon the premise that emotion is the perception of bodily changes that occur when we respond to an emotion-arousing situation. That is, we are afraid 'because' we flee rather than fleeing 'because' we are afraid. James elevated the original idea of C. G. Lange's that emotion was a change in the cardiovascular system and gave it the elaboration here noted to account for the distinctive quality of different emotions. J.S.B.

Janet, Pierre (French psychologist and neurologist, 1859–1947), see under NEUROSIS.

Jarry, Alfred (French dramatist, 1873–1907), see under THEATRE OF THE ABSURD.

Jawlensky, Alexei von (Russian painter, 1864–1941), see under BEURON; BLAUE REITER; FAUVES; NEUE KÜNSTLER-VEREINIGUNG.

jazz. Although no commentator has ever defined it to the satisfaction of any other commentator, and although in the 1960s many iron conventions of making jazz have been questioned by its AVANT-GARDE, the vast majority of the valuable jazz in existence was made by a process whereby musicians improvised on a given harmonic sequence against a background of clearly defined rhythm. The process is traceable on recordings to around 1910, but almost certainly its true history is nearer the age of a hundred.

It is a music which evolved through the clash of two antipathetic CULTURES, the West African and the American South, where the black Africans, an oppressed minority dumped in an alien environment, expressed their musical soul in a distinctive way. Even after the Emancipation which followed the American Civil War, the black man had no real access either to Conservatoire methods of training or even, very often, to legitimate instruments; hence jazz was at first very much an empirical art. It centred around the Louisiana port of NEW ORLEANS, until in 1917 with the closing down of Storyville, the city's notorious red-light district, the music began to drift north, along the line of the Mississippi, via the riverboats which employed small bands.

New Orleans's greatest son was Louis Armstrong, whose life (1900–71) spans the era between the innocent al fresco jazz of the turn of the century and the prestigious concert-hall murmurings of contemporary lions like the Modern Jazz Quartet and Miles Davis. Jazz is essentially an art of performance rather than of transcription; there are no jazz compositions, only jazz musicians who play them, although the towering figure of Duke Ellington is the contradiction which proves this rule.

The influence of jazz on music in general has been considerable. In its embryonic form it affected Dvořák during his 'New World' period; in its maturity it has influenced Stravinsky, Walton, Copland, and many lesser figures.

For some of the varieties of jazz see BEBOP; BOOGIE-WOOGIE; CHICAGO; DIXIELAND; HOT; NEW ORLEANS; RHYTHM-AND-BLUES; WEST COAST. See also BIG BAND; BLUE NOTES; BLUES; HORN; RAGTIME; SWEET; SWING. B.G.

Bibl: A. Hodeir, tr. D. Noakes, *Jazz* (London and N.Y., 1956); F. Newton, *The Jazz Scene* (London, 1959; N.Y., 1960).

jazz age. A term used, mainly with reference to the U.S.A., for the decade between the end of World War I and the Great Crash (1929). The white DIXIELAND version of negro JAZZ which formed the base of the period's characteristic dance style reflected the general atmosphere of excitement and confidence of the era, created by a popular faith in lasting peace and prosperity. Social, sexual, and cultural values were permanently altered by the social and material changes of this first period of mass-consumption, which made available silent movies, radios, cars, and other consumer goods. The flamboyance and economic confidence of the period is portrayed particularly well by Scott Fitzgerald, notably in *The Jazz Age, The Diamond as Big as the Ritz,* and *The Great Gatsby*. The jazz age was also, however, an age of hysteria over 'BOLSHEVISM' (e.g. the execution of Sacco and Vanzetti, 1927), gangster economics (e.g. the Teapot Dome scandal, 1923–4), a *prohibition* of alcohol which was everywhere defied (with pervasive attendant crime), and of intellectual anachronisms like the Scopes Monkey Trial, in which a schoolteacher was arraigned for teaching EVOLUTION. P.S.L.

jazz poetry. Poetry designed to be read with JAZZ accompaniment. In the 1960s it had a considerable vogue in Britain and parts of the U.S.A., with Christopher Logue and Kenneth Rexroth, respectively, as leading exponents. M.S.-S.

Jefferson, Thomas (U.S. president, 1743–1826), see under RADBURN LAYOUT.

Jehovah's Witnesses. A basically American religious body, also called the 'Watch Tower Bible and Tract Society'. Founded by C. T. Russell and by J. F. ('Judge') Rutherford (1869–1941), it attacks the Christian Churches and calls on its adherents to reject military service and blood transfusion. It prophesies that 144,000 Jehovah's Witnesses will form the elect in heaven at the imminent end of the world, and will rule over the 'Jonadabs' or resurrected people of good will inhabiting a new earth. The Witnesses are more active than welcome in door-to-door EVANGELISM.   D.L.E.
    Bibl: H. H. Stroup, *The Jehovah's Witnesses* (N.Y., 1945).

Jenney, William LeBaron (U.S. civil engineer and architect, 1832–1907), see under SKYSCRAPER.

Jennings, Elizabeth (British poetess, *b*.1926), see under MOVEMENT, THE.

Jennings, Paul (British humorous writer, *b*.1918), see under RESISTENTIALISM.

Jens, Walter (German novelist, *b*.1923), see under GRUPPE 47.

Jensen, Arthur (U.S. psychologist, *b*.1923), see under RACE.

jet engine. A device for propelling aircraft through the atmosphere. Air swept into the front of the engine provides the oxygen required to support the burning of fuel. The resulting heat makes the combustion gases expand through a nozzle at the rear. These gases leave the engine much faster than the air goes in at the front, so that forward motion is produced, on the ROCKET principle. See also RAM JET.   M.V.B.

Jihad ('Holy War'). A fundamental tenet of traditional ISLAM obliging the believer to fight the unbeliever until the latter embraces either Islam or the protected status accorded only to those whose religions are based on written scriptures (i.e. Jews, Christians, Sabaeans), the 'peoples of the Book'. A *Jihad* must be officially proclaimed, by a recognized spiritual leader. The status of *mujahidin* ('holy warriors') has been claimed by Algerian rebels (1954–62), Arab participants in the Six

Days War with Israel (1967), and Islamic elements in Palestine.   D.C.W.

job enrichment. Attempts to overcome job dissatisfaction and the ALIENATION that arises from repetitive, mechanistic tasks, by making non-monetary changes in working practices, providing a greater opportunity for personal achievement and satisfaction, and increasing the challenge and responsibility of work. Job enrichment can be conceived either as a pragmatic experiment in job restructuring or as a broadly based reappraisal of the SOCIAL CONTRACT in an organization.   R.I.T.
    Bibl: F. Herzberg, *Work and the Nature of Man* (Cleveland, 1966; London, 1968).

job evaluation. A systematic description of a job and its comparison with other jobs in order to establish differential rates of pay.   R.I.T.

Johannsen, Wilhelm Ludwig (Danish botanist and geneticist, 1857–1927), see under GENE.

John XXIII, Pope (1881–1963), see under AGGIORNAMENTO; PACEM IN TERRIS; VATICAN COUNCIL II.

John, Augustus (British painter, 1878–1961), see under ARMORY SHOW; NEW ENGLISH ART CLUB.

Johnson, Brian S. (British novelist, 1933–73), see under ALEATORY.

Johnson, Harry (Canadian economist, *b*.1923), see under NEO-MERCANTILISM.

Johnson, Lionel (British poet, 1867–1902), see under DECADENCE.

Johnson, Lyndon B. (U.S. president, 1908–73), see under DOVES AND HAWKS; SALT; VIETNAM.

Johnson, Pete (U.S. jazz musician, 1904–67), see under BOOGIE-WOOGIE.

Johnson, Philip (U.S. architect, *b*.1906), see under INTERNATIONAL STYLE.

Johnson, Uwe (German writer, *b*.1934), see under GRUPPE 47; NEW NOVEL.

JONES

Jones, Brian (British musician and performer, 1943–69), see under ROLLING STONES.

Jones, LeRoi (U.S. dramatist, novelist, and editor, b.1934), see under BLACK THEATRE.

Joplin, Scott (U.S. composer and pianist, 1868–1917), see under RAGTIME.

Jordan, Camille (French mathematician, 1838–1922), see under QUANTUM MECHANICS.

Jordan, Louis (U.S. jazz musician, 1908–75), see under RHYTHM-AND-BLUES.

Jorn, Asger (Danish painter, 1914–73), see under COBRA.

joule, see under ENERGY.

Jouvet, Louis (French actor and producer, 1887–1951), see under CARTEL.

Joyce, James (Irish-born novelist, 1882–1941), see under CRITERION, THE; CUBISM; EGOIST, THE; EPIPHANY; FREE ASSOCIATION; IMAGISM; JOYCEAN; LITTLE REVIEW; STREAM OF CONSCIOUSNESS; SYMBOLISM.

Joycean. Characteristic or reminiscent of the writings of James Joyce (1882–1941), particularly of *Ulysses* (1922) and whatever portion of *Finnegans Wake* (1939) the person using the word may actually have read. The characteristics alluded to include a propensity for sordid and scatological subject-matter, an immense stylistic and technical range (including the use of SYMBOLISM and the STREAM OF CONSCIOUSNESS technique), and a verbal inventiveness (with an addiction to puns and portmanteau words) that takes the English language near, and in the later work beyond, the limits of readability. O.S.

Judaism. The RELIGION of the Jews. Founded on the experiences of Israel which are recorded. in the literature known to Christians as the Old Testament, Judaism took its present shape after the destruction of the Kingdoms of Israel and Judah, the fall of the Temple, and the Jews' exile to Babylon in the 6th century

B.C. During this exile and many later wanderings and sufferings, the Jews preserved their communal identity by their devotion to the study of the Law (*Torah*), a system of morality and religious teaching originating in the Holy Scriptures and added to by generations of Rabbis; by their close adherence to dietary regulations and insistence on male circumcision; by their observance of the weekly day of rest on Saturday (*Sabbath*); through their strong family life; and through the synagogues where they gathered for prayer and education.

Jewish experiences in the 20th century have included the NAZI extermination or 'holocaust' of most of European Jewry (following centuries of Christian ANTISEMITISM), and the culmination of ZIONISM in the establishment of the state of Israel in 1948. The chief challenge to traditional Judaism, both within Israel and in the 'Diaspora' or dispersion among the 'Gentiles' (non-Jews), is SECULARIZATION. Should the old law still be observed as completely as possible, as the 'Orthodox' Rabbis teach? Or is a far more 'LIBERAL' interpretation, largely abandoning the use of Hebrew and the detailed laws about diet, etc., the best way of keeping the spirit of Judaism alive under modern conditions – as 'Reform' Judaism (originating in 19th-century Germany) advocates? In the U.S.A., 'Conservative' Judaism, a movement founded by Solomon Schechter (1847–1915), has had great influence as a compromise between the rigid and modernizing extremes. A similar attitude has been taught by Martin Buber (1878–1965). He derived a PERSONALIST and SOCIALIST philosophy and a renewed THEISM from his enthusiasm for the 'Hasidic' mystical tradition originating in the 18th century. Buber summed up his message in his little book, *I and Thou* (1923). D.L.E.
Bibl: L. Jacobs, *Principles of the Jewish Faith* (London and N.Y., 1964); J. L. Blau, *Modern Varieties of Judaism* (N.Y., 1966); H. Wouk, *This is My God: the Jewish Way of Life* (N.Y., 1970; London, rev. ed., 1973).

Jugendstil, see ART NOUVEAU.

July 20th. The date in 1944 of an abortive *coup d'état* in Nazi Germany directed at the overthrow of Hitler. Involved in the

328

conspiracy were anti-Nazi elements in the armed forces and the Prussian aristocracy, together with former diplomatists, civil servants, and trade unionists. The *putsch* failed when Hitler escaped with his life, but it achieved considerable momentary success in Paris and Vienna. The chief conspirators, whose common ground was a moral rejection of NAZISM, paid for their failure with their lives, and their courage in resisting the Nazi government has seemed more important subsequently than their failure to overthrow it. A.L.C.B.

Bibl: R. Manvell and H. Fraenkel, *The July Plot* (London, 1964).

Jung, Carl Gustav (Swiss psychologist and psychiatrist, 1875–1961), see under ANIMA; COLLECTIVE UNCONSCIOUS; JUNGIAN; PERSONALITY TYPES; PSYCHO-ANALYSIS; SUBCONSCIOUS; SYNCHRON-ICITY.

Jünger, Ernst (German novelist and essayist, *b*. 1895), see under INTELLEC-TUALS.

Jungian. Adjective applied to a theory of personality put forward by Carl Gustav Jung (1875–1961) as an alternative to the FREUDIAN view and rejecting the latter's emphasis on the centrality of sexual instincts. Jung left the psychoanalytical movement (see PSYCHOANALYSIS) in 1913 to practise *analytic psychology*, according to which man's behaviour is determined not only by the conflicts already present in his individual and racial history (the personal and COLLECTIVE UNCONSCIOUS) but also by his aims and aspirations. The character and indeed even the quality of dreams suggests the striving toward individuation; according to analytic psychology, man seeks creative development, wholeness, and completion. The individual personality contains memories, known as ARCHETYPES, of its ancestral history which can be studied through MYTHS. Jung postulated two basic PERSONALITY TYPES, characterized respectively by EXTROVERSION and INTROVERSION.   R.P.-S.

Bibl: J. Jacobi, tr. R. Mannheim, *Psychology of C. G. Jung* (London and New Haven, 6th ed., 1963).

junior college. A post-high-school institution in the U.S.A. offering a programme, usually of two years, as a terminal qualification or as a preliminary for university or further training. Usually the qualification offered is an associate-in-arts degree. These colleges began in the 1900s and there are now over 1,000; they can be run by the state, the district, a local board, or a private body. Over 90% of the colleges are of the two-year type, but some offer in addition a preliminary year or two corresponding to the last year or two of high school, or a third year corresponding to the junior year at either college or university. Some are large community colleges for students living at home and there is little campus life. Such public community colleges stress transfer, vocational, or occupational education, with entry to the state university; the private colleges tend to emphasize the two-year course as part of a liberal-arts programme.   W.A.C.S.

junior high school. In the U.S.A., a school specially for pupils from about 13 to about 16 which first appeared around 1910 in California and Ohio. It may be a separate school (sometimes called a segregated junior high school) or it may be part of an all-through junior-senior high school on the same site. There has been a continuing debate on suitable curricula. Much experimental work has been done on the content of courses in mathematics, science, and languages. But there has also been an interest in what are called 'life adjustment' courses and in the problems presented by minority groups, disadvantaged children, and low-ability pupils.   W.A.C.S.

Bibl: E. A. Krug, *The Shaping of the American High School* (2 vols., N.Y., 1964–72).

jurisprudence of concepts, see CONCEPTUALISM.

K

Kafka, Franz (Austrian novelist, 1883–1924), see under EXPRESSIONISM; KAFKAESQUE; TOTAL THEATRE.

Kafkaesque. Adjective applied to situations and atmospheres, whether real or fictional, that recall the writing of Franz Kafka (1883–1924), particularly *The Trial* and its sequel *The Castle*. The essential ingredient is a nightmarish sense of having lost one's identity, and of bewildered helplessness against a vast, sinister, impersonal BUREAUCRACY which is intuitively felt to be evil, yet which appears to have a crazy kind of transcendent logic on its side. English novelists who have approached the Kafkaesque mode include Edward Upward, Rex Warner, and Nigel Dennis.   O.S.

Kagel, Mauricio (Argentine-born composer, *b.* 1932), see under MUSIC THEATRE.

Kaiser, Georg (German dramatist, 1878–1945), see under EXPRESSIONISM.

Kamenev, Lev Borisovich (Russian revolutionary, 1883–1936), see under MOSCOW TRIALS; POLITBURO.

Kandinsky, Wassily (Russian-born painter and graphic artist, 1866–1944), see under ABSTRACT ART; ABSTRACT EXPRESSIONISM; BAUHAUS; BLAUE REITER; FAUVES; KNAVE OF DIAMONDS; NEUE KÜNSTLERVEREINIGUNG; ORPHISM; SYMBOLISM.

Kanner, Leo (U.S. psychiatrist, *b.*1894), see under AUTISM.

Kanoldt, Alexander (German painter, 1881–1939), see under MAGIC REALISM; NEUE KÜNSTLERVEREINIGUNG.

Kant, Immanuel (German philosopher, 1724–1804), see under ANALYTIC; APRIORISM; CATEGORICAL IMPERATIVE; CATEGORY; DEONTOLOGY; DETERMINISM; DIALECTIC; GEOMETRY; INTRO-SPECTION; METAPHYSICS; NEO-KANTIANISM; NOUMENA; ONTOLOGY; PRESUPPOSITION; ROMANTICISM; TELEOLOGY; TOPOLOGY; TRANSCENDENCE.

Kaprow, Allan (U.S. painter, *b.*1927), see under ENVIRONMENT; FLUXUS; HAPPENINGS.

Kapustin, Savelius (Russian founder of the Doukhobors, *d. c.* 1820), see under DOUKHOBORS.

karyology, see under CYTOLOGY.

Kästner, Erich (German writer, 1899–1974), see under GEBRAUCHS-...; NEUE SACHLICHKEIT.

Katyn. The name of some woods near Smolensk where in April 1943 the Germans announced that they had discovered several thousand bodies of Polish officers and others who, they claimed, had been murdered by the Russians in 1940. The Soviet Government at once announced that these men (captured during the Soviet invasion of Poland in 1939) had fallen into German hands in 1941 and that the Germans had murdered them. Previously it had disclaimed all knowledge about some 15,000 Polish officers not among those released after the German invasion of Russia in 1941 and allowed to go to the Middle East to form a new Polish Army. Yet the 5,000 bodies found at Katyn were in their great majority men on the lists the Poles had submitted to the Russians. (The other 10,000 have never been accounted for.)

The Germans allowed a forensic commission including prominent neutral experts to supervise part of the exhumation, which representatives of the Polish underground were permitted, and senior Allied officer prisoners compelled, to attend. All reported that the German story was clearly true; forensic, documentary, and other evidence showed that the massacre had taken place in April 1940. The facts, though accepted everywhere else, have still not been admitted by the Soviet leadership. Khrushchev is believed to have urged frankness but to have been dissuaded by the Polish COMMUNISTS. R.C.

Bibl: J. Mackiewicz, *The Katyn Wood Murders* (London, 1951); General W. Anders (intr.), *The Crime of Katyn* (London, 1965).

Kaverin, Benjamin (pseud. of Benjamin Alexandrovich Zil'ber, Russian novelist, *b*. 1902), see under SERAPION BROTHERS.

Kay-Shuttleworth, Sir James (British educationist, 1804–77), see under PESTALOZZI METHODS.

Kazan, Elia (U.S. actor and director, *b*. 1909), see under METHOD, THE.

Keating, Richard E. (U.S. physicist), see under CLOCK PARADOX.

Keaton, Buster (U.S. film actor and director, 1896–1966), see under SLAPSTICK.

Kekulé von Stradonitz, Friedrich August (German chemist, 1829–96), see under BENZENE RING.

Kelly, Ellsworth (U.S. painter and sculptor, *b*. 1923), see under MINIMAL ART.

Kelsen, Hans (Austrian-U.S. legal philosopher, 1881–1973), see under LAW, PURE THEORY OF.

Kempe, Sir Alfred Bray (British mathematician, 1849–1922), see under FOUR-COLOUR CONJECTURE.

Kendrew, John Cowdery (British biochemist, *b*. 1917), see under MOLECULAR BIOLOGY; PROTEINS.

Kennan, George (U.S. diplomat and historian, *b*. 1904), see under CONTAINMENT.

Kennedy, John Fitzgerald (U.S. president, 1917–63), see under BAY OF PIGS; CUBA; DOVES AND HAWKS; ESCALATION; FRONTIER; GRAND DESIGN; NEW FRONTIER.

Ker, William Paton (British literary critic and historian, 1855–1923), see under ANTI-HERO.

keratins, see under PROTEINS.

Kermode, John Frank (British literary critic, *b*. 1919), see under ENCOUNTER; MODERNISM.

Kerouac, Jack (U.S. poet and novelist, 1922–69), see under BEAT; GREENWICH VILLAGE.

Kerr, Clark (U.S. economist and educational reformer, *b*. 1911), see under MULTIVERSITY.

Keynes, John Maynard (British economist, 1883–1946), see under AGGREGATE DEMAND; BLOOMSBURY GROUP; BRETTON WOODS; ECONOMICS; KEYNESIAN; LIQUIDITY; SIGMOIDS.

Keynesian. Adjective applied to any of the economic theories of John Maynard Keynes (1833–1946), notably to his theory of AGGREGATE DEMAND, which he developed in the early 1930s. Keynesian economic theory is often contrasted with CLASSICAL ECONOMIC THEORY: whereas the classical economists believed that free MARKET forces could, subject to time-lags and frictions, ensure reasonably FULL EMPLOYMENT, Keynes by contrast held that a condition of UNEMPLOYMENT may continue for quite long periods, or even indefinitely, unless a government takes specific steps to remedy it.   R.H.

Bibl: J. M. Keynes, *Indian Currency and Finance* (London, 1913), *The Economic Consequences of the Peace* (London, 1919; N.Y., 1920), and *The General Theory of Employment, Interest and Money* (London and N.Y., 1936); R. F. Harrod, *The Life of John Maynard Keynes* (London and N.Y., 1951).

Keystone. Name of Mack Sennett's film studio at Edendale, California, which he made virtually synonymous with silent-film comedy. Hired as an actor by D. W. Griffith, Sennett directed his first film for the Biograph company in 1910, inadvertently discovering the comic effect gained by undercranking the camera (and thus speeding up the action on the screen), before forming his own company in 1912 and creating the style and format of the SLAPSTICK comedies. Sennett launched nearly all the great silent comedians (Chaplin, Arbuckle, Langdon, Lloyd, etc.), but his best-loved creation was probably the Keystone Kops: a hilariously inept band of policemen in handlebar moustachios and outrageously ill-fitting uniforms, for ever falling over themselves, giving futile chase, tumbling out of rattletrap cars, and careering over cliffs. See also CUSTARD PIE. T.C.C.M.

Bibl: K. C. Lahue, *Mack Sennett's Keystone* (South Brunswick, 1971).

KGB (Committee for State Security). The name, since 1953–4, of the Soviet SECRET POLICE, one of the two organizations, the other being MVD, which share, with somewhat fluctuating lines of demarcation, responsibility for order and security. Roughly speaking, the K.G.B. – like its predecessors Cheka, Vcheka, G.P.U., O.G.P.U., N.K.V.D., N.K.G.B., M.G.B., several of which have been bywords for brutality (see, especially, YEZHOVSHCHINA) – is responsible for security troops, counter-espionage, counter-subversion, loyalty supervision among the administrative, political, and military ÉLITES, and such features as the recent trials of writers and others. Its other major role is organizing the greater part of the Soviet espionage and subversion effort abroad. Its current chief, Yuri Andropov, is a full member of the POLITBURO. R.C.

Bibl: S. Wolin and R. M. Slusser, *The Soviet Secret Police* (London and N.Y., 1957).

Khlebnikov, Victor (Russian poet, 1885–1922), see under ZAUM.

Khrushchev, Nikita (Soviet statesman, 1894–1971), see under COEXISTENCE; COMINFORM; CUBA; FELLOW-TRAVELLER; KATYN; LYSENKOISM; NEW LEFT; PERSONALITY CULT; POLITBURO; STALINISM; THAW, THE.

kibbutz (plural *kibbutzim*). A form of collective settlement which has played a key role in the creation of modern Israel. The first kibbutz was founded in 1909 by a group of pioneers from Russia. By 1965 there were 230, some of them up to a thousand strong. Allowing for individual variations, the kibbutz combines three functions: (1) *economic*: cultivation of the land, often with some industrial production as well; (2) *social*: providing communities in which SOCIALIST ideals

can be put into practice, e.g. equality (see EGALITARIANISM), common property, communal living (including the rearing of children), and collective decision-making; (3) *military*: acting as watch posts, and in times of trouble as strong points with their own garrisons. In the 1960s over 80,000 Israelis were living permanently in kibbutzim. This was less than 5% of the population, but their contribution to the formation of Israel has been much greater than these figures suggest. A.L.C.B.

Bibl: S. N. Eisenstadt, *Israeli Society* (London and N.Y., 1967).

Kienholz, Edward (U.S. painter and sculptor, *b.* 1927), see under TOTAL ART.

Kierkegaard, Søren (Danish philosopher, 1813–55), see under CHRISTIAN EXISTENTIALISM; EXISTENTIALISM; IRRATIONALISM.

Kiesler, Friedrich (Austrian-U.S. architect, sculptor, and stage designer, 1892–1965), see under SPACE.

kiloton. A measure of the ENERGY released in a nuclear explosion equivalent to 1,000 tons of T.N.T. 1 kiloton equals about 100,000 kilowatt-hours. M.V.B.

kinaesthetic. Relating to those sensations produced by movements of the joints, tendons, or muscles, and those emanating from the balance organs of the inner ear. H.L.

Kindergarten, the, see under MILNER'S KINDERGARTEN.

kinematics. One of the two branches of MECHANICS. M.V.B.

kinesics, see under SEMIOTICS.

kinesthetic, see KINAESTHETIC.

kinetic art. The extension of the traditionally static arts of painting and sculpture to incorporate an element of motion (*a*) by making them mobile, (*b*) by a shifting sequence of static variations, or (*c*) by exploiting the spectator's movement around a static work so as to give it changing aspects. Though efforts in this direction have been made since the earliest times, the modern history of kineticism really starts with FUTURISM and its use of over-lapping 'simultaneous' images and 'lines of force'. Other early attempts were Tatlin's tower (1919–20) and other CONSTRUCTIVIST works, Marcel Duchamp's rotating discs (1920), and László Moholy-Nagy's 'Licht-requisit' (1930); the real breakthrough, however, came with the American Alexander Calder's invention (c. 1931–2) of the *mobile*, a balanced contraption of brightly coloured weights swinging from wires.

By the 1950s many artists (and advertising agencies) were trying their hands at mobiles, and a widespread kinetic trend set in, with Nicolas Schöffer, proponent of 'spatiodynamism' (1948) and 'luminodynamism' (1957), as its most ambitious exemplar, and the Paris *Mouvement* exhibition at the Galérie Denise René (1955) as its first collective manifestation. Sub-groups have included the German *Gruppe Zero* (from 1958), the Paris *Groupe de Recherche d'Art Visuel* (1960–68), the Italian groups 'T' and 'N', the *'programmed art'* of Bruno Munari, and the Soviet *'Dvizhenie'* collective led by Lev Nusberg.

Today virtually any practitioner of ABSTRACT ART is liable to include some element of motion or PERMUTATION in his work, the latter particularly if it is of a geometrical or OP ART kind. CONCRETE POETRY reflects a similar concern, and certain writers, mainly English and West German, have produced 'kinetic' poems where the movement consists in the calculated (or 'programmed') shifting of words and letters, line by line or page by page. There is also a quasi-cinematic or PSYCHEDELIC branch of the art in the LIGHT SHOW, which bears some relation to Moholy-Nagy's and Schöffer's researches as well as to earlier experiments in SYNAESTHESIA.   J.W.
Bibl: G. Brett, *Kinetic Art* (London and N.Y., 1968).

kinetic energy. The ENERGY of matter in motion. Because of the CONSERVATION LAW satisfied by energy, kinetic energy can only be produced at the expense of some other form of energy, e.g. chemical energy in an explosive is converted into kinetic energy of rapidly expanding bomb fragments; a stone dropped over a cliff accelerates by converting the POTENTIAL ENERGY of GRAVITATION into kinetic energy. Naturally-occurring kinetic energy can be converted into useful work, as when falling water enters a TURBINE, producing kinetic energy of rotary motion which in turn generates hydroelectric power. For a single particle in NEWTONIAN MECHANICS, kinetic energy = $\frac{1}{2} \times$ mass $\times$ (velocity)^2.   M.V.B.

King, Martin Luther (U.S. civil rights leader and Baptist minister, 1929–68), see under BLACK PANTHERS.

Kinsey Report. A questionnaire-based study of sexual attitudes and behaviour, compiled by the American zoologist Alfred Kinsey (1894–1956) and others, and published in two volumes in 1948–53. By showing that many practices (e.g. *fellatio*) commonly regarded as PERVERSIONS were actually widespread it was influential in increasing sexual PERMISSIVENESS. It also indicated CORRELATIONS of social CLASS with sexual habits. It has been criticized for faults in interviewing and SAMPLING techniques, as well as for its title, *Sexual Behaviour in the Human Male/Female*; only mid-20th-century North Americans are actually considered.   H.L.

Kipphardt, Heinar (German author, *b.* 1922), see under DOCUMENTARY; VOLKSBÜHNE.

Kirchner, Ernst Ludwig (German painter, 1880–1938), see under BRÜCKE, DIE.

Kisch, Egon Erwin (German novelist and journalist, 1885–1948), see under NEUE SACHLICHKEIT.

Kisling, Moïse (Polish-French painter and graphic artist, 1891–1953), see under ÉCOLE DE PARIS.

kitchen sink drama. Pejorative term for those English plays written from the late 1950s onwards (see ENGLISH STAGE COMPANY and THEATRE WORKSHOP) whose distinguishing feature was a portrayal of working- or lower-middle-class characters surrounded, in the view of their critics, by an undue degree of domestic squalor. 'The kitchen sink school' was a term applied first to the SOCIAL REALIST paintings of John Bratby and others showing at the Beaux Arts Gallery in London in the early 1950s, but has achieved lasting currency in relation to the theatre. M.A.

Kjellen, Rudolf (Swedish political scientist, 1864–1922), see under GEOPOLITICS.

Klages, Ludwig (German philosopher, 1872–1956), see under CHARACTERO-LOGY.

Klee, Paul (Swiss painter, 1879–1940), see under BAUHAUS; BLAUE REITER; ORPHISM; SURREALISM.

Klein, Yves (French painter, 1928–62), see under NOUVEAU RÉALISME.

Klimt, Gustav (Austrian painter, 1862–1918), see under SEZESSION.

Kline, Franz (U.S. painter, 1910–62), see under ABSTRACT EXPRESSIONISM; NEW YORK SCHOOL.

Knave (or *Jack*) **of Diamonds** (Russian *Bubnovy Valet*). Originally the title of an art exhibition organized by the painter Michel Larionov in Moscow, December 1910, including David Burliuk, Goncharova, Exter, Falk, Kandinsky, Konchalovsky, Lentulov, Malevich, Mashkov, Survage, and the French painters Gleizes, Le Fauconnier, and L.-A. Moreau. An album of 18 reproductions was published with a cover by Goncharova. She and Larionov subsequently left the group in protest against its hardening into a formal society and its French orientation; the remaining artists held a second show, with more French participation, in 1912 and continued to exist as a group till 1916. A retrospective exhibition was held at the Tretiakov Gallery in 1927. M.C.

Bibl: V. Markov, *Russian Futurism* (Berkeley, 1968; London, 1969); C. Gray, *The Russian Experiment in Art 1863–1922* (London and N.Y., 1970).

Knight, Damon (U.S. novelist, *b*. 1922), see under SCIENCE FICTION.

Knights, Lionel Charles (British literary critic, *b*. 1906), see under LEAVISITE.

knocking. Pre-ignition and detonation in an internal combustion engine. Unbranched hydrocarbons, the major constituent of normal petrol, have a pronounced knocking tendency, measured as an OCTANE RATING, in high-compression car and aero engines. *Anti-knock* agents, chiefly tetraethyl lead, are frequently employed. B.F.

knowledge, sociology of. The study of how styles of expression and the character of IDEAS or systems of thought are related to different social contexts. Thus Marx, from whom the contemporary impetus to the sociology of knowledge largely derives, sought to relate art and ideas to particular historical circumstances and the kinds of CLASS systems prevailing at the time; and Max Weber, in *The Sociology of Religion*, analysed the way in which different kinds of religions were the creation largely of specific social groups (e.g. the relation of Confucianism to the Chinese literati and BUREAUCRACY). The effort to broaden and use the sociology of knowledge as a general scheme for the analysis of all ideas is, however, associated largely with three writers: Karl Mannheim, who relativized Marx's ideas to all thought, including MARXISM itself; Max Scheler, who divided the influences on thought into 'real factors' (different at different historical moments) and 'ideal factors' (a realm of timeless ESSENCES which constituted an absolute order of TRUTH); and Émile Durkheim, who argued that the basic rhythms of social life experienced by a society – its sense of space and time – were a function of its kind of social organization. Objectors to the sociology of knowledge claim that it attaches insufficient importance to the *content* of knowledge, or to the truth or otherwise of a PROPOSITION; that a cultural SUPERSTRUCTURE, once created, retains a life of its own, and becomes part of the permanent cultural repertoire of mankind; that ideas and works of imagination are alike multivalent and it is crudely REDUCTIONIST to associate a set of ideas only with a particular political position (e.g. MATERIALISM with RADICALISM, and IDEALISM with CONSERVATISM), or to equate as 'BOURGEOIS' the contrasting work of Flaubert, Zola, Mann, Joyce, and Proust; and that art forms and ideas may unfold 'immanently', i.e. out of their inner logic and as a reflection on and extension of previous forms. See also IDEOLOGY. D.B.

Bibl: K. Mannheim, *Ideology and Utopia* (London and N.Y., 1936); W.

Stark, *The Sociology of Knowledge* (London and Glencoe, Ill., 1958); J. C. Curtis and J. W. Petras (eds.), *The Sociology of Knowledge* (London and N.Y., 1970).

Koch's postulates. The three CRITERIA, formulated by the German bacteriologist Robert Koch in 1876, which must be fulfilled if evidence of a causal connection between an illness and a bacterial infection (see BACTERIOLOGY) is to be accepted as valid. They are: (1) the bacterium is to be demonstrated in all cases of the disease; (2) its distribution in the body must correspond to the lesions, if any, associated with the disease – e.g. with ulcers, tubercles, or 'spots'; (3) the organism must be recoverable and cultivable in suitable media outside the body. Although this third criterion cannot always be applied, nevertheless, with reservations relating to the intrinsic difficulty of culturing certain organisms outside the body (e.g. the leprosy organism), Koch's postulates are still regarded as valid.   P.M.

Koestler, Arthur (Hungarian-British author, *b*.1905), see under ENCOUNTER.

Koffka, Kurt (German-U.S. psychologist, 1886–1941), see under GESTALT.

Köhler, Wolfgang (German-U.S. psychologist, 1887–1967), see under GESTALT.

Kokoschka, Oskar (Austrian painter, *b*.1886), see under KUNSTGEWERBE-SCHULE.

kolkhoz (*kollektivnoe khozyaystvo*), see under COLLECTIVIZATION.

Kolmogorov, Andrei Nikolayevich (Russian mathematician, *b*.1903), see under PROBABILITY THEORY.

Kolyma. The most notorious of Stalin's FORCED LABOUR camp areas, consisting of a large area round the valley of the River Kolyma down to the Arctic Ocean. Its main product was gold. During the period 1937–53, it is believed that up to four million prisoners died there, mainly of hunger and overwork. See also GULAG.   R.C.
   Bibl: E. S. Ginzburg, tr. P. Stevenson *et al., Into the Whirlwind* (London and N.Y., 1967).

Konchalovsky, Peter Petrovich (Russian painter, 1876–1956), see under KNAVE OF DIAMONDS.

Kooning, Willem de (Dutch-U.S. painter, *b*.1904), see under ABSTRACT EXPRESSIONISM; ACTION PAINTING; EXPRESSIONISM; NEW YORK SCHOOL.

Koprowski, Hilary (Polish-U.S. medical scientist, *b*.1916), see under VIROLOGY.

Korea. The name of one of the historic civilizations of East Asia, frequently used as a shorthand term for the Korean War of 1950–53. Having long lived under Chinese suzerainty, Korea was annexed by the Japanese in 1910 and after the Japanese defeat in 1945 was divided between a COMMUNIST state under Soviet patronage in the North and the American-supported regime of Syngman Rhee in the South. After the withdrawal of American forces in 1949, the Soviet-equipped armies of North Korea crossed the partition line and launched a full-scale invasion of the South (25 June 1950). UNO forces, largely American and under American command, came to the support of the South. When they in turn carried the war north of the partition line (the 38th parallel) they were met by Chinese Communist forces. An armistice, concluded in July 1953, redivided the country along a line close to that of the original partition. The motivation for the original North Korean attack is unclear; but suspicions that it had been instigated by the Soviet authorities played a considerable part in inspiring the collective defence of Western Europe by NATO.   A.L.C.B.
   Bibl: D. Rees, *Korea: the Limited War* (London and N.Y., 1964).

Kornilov, Lavr Georgyevich (Russian general, 1870–1918), see under SOVIETS.

Kostov, Traicho (Bulgarian Communist leader, 1897–1940), see under SHOW TRIALS.

Kozintsev, Grigori (Russian theatre and film director, 1905–1973), see under FEX.

Kraepelin, Emil (German psychiatrist, 1856–1926), see under PSYCHOSIS.

KRAFFT-EBING

Krafft-Ebing, Richard von (German neurologist and psychiatrist, 1840–1902), see under MASOCHISM; SADISM.

Kraft, Joseph (U.S. journalist, *b.*1924), see under GRAND DESIGN.

Krause, Karl Christian Friedrich (German philosopher, 1781–1832), see under PANTHEISM.

Krebs cycle (or *citric acid cycle* or *tricarboxylic acid cycle* or *TCA cycle*). The cycle, named after the biochemist Sir Hans Krebs (*b.*1900), of oxidative processes within the CELL, the structural basis of which lies in the mitochondria (see CYTOLOGY). P.M.

Kremlinology. Strictly, the study of Soviet politics at the higher levels, i.e. of the struggle for power and over policy between the leading members of the POLITBURO, who normally meet in the Kremlin in Moscow; loosely, any study of Soviet affairs. It implies deduction of what is or has been going on from such clues as emerge from behind the conventional facade of 'monolithic unity' among the leadership. R.C.
Bibl: R. Conquest, *Power and Policy in the USSR* (London and N.Y., 1961); M. Tatu, *Power in the Kremlin* (London and N.Y., 1969).

Krestinsky, Nikolai N. (Soviet diplomat, 1883–1938), see under POLITBURO.

Kretschmer, Ernst (German psychiatrist, 1888–1964), see under SCHIZOID.

Krieger, Murray (U.S. literary critic, *b.*1923), see under NEW CRITICISM.

Kristol, Irving (U.S. author and editor, *b.*1920), see under ENCOUNTER.

Kroeber, Alfred Louis (U.S. anthropologist, 1876–1960), see under CULTURE AREA.

Kronecker, Leopold (German mathematician, 1823–91), see under NUMBER.

Kropotkin, Peter (Russian revolutionary, 1842–1921), see under ANARCHISM.

Kruchenykh, Alexei Eliseyevich (Russian poet, 1886–1968), see under ZAUM.

kulak ('fist'). Originally a general Russian term for a grasping peasant, later defined as a peasant who employed labour. The COMMUNIST Party of the Soviet Union was concerned from early days to destroy this element of the peasantry, with the aid of the 'middle peasant', and the village poor. The COLLECTIVIZATION campaign of 1930–33 led to the elimination, by famine or in FORCED LABOUR camps, of about 10 million peasants defined officially as *kulaks*, though later Soviet figures show that many of them were in fact 'middle peasants'. R.C.

Kuleshov, Lev Vladimirovich (Russian film theorist and director, 1899–1970), see under MONTAGE.

Kunstgewerbeschule. Any 'School of Applied Art'; usually that at Vienna, an outstanding training-place for designers of all sorts in the opening years of this century, when the teachers included Koloman Moser and Josef Hoffmann, founder of the WIENER WERKSTÄTTE, and the students Oskar Kokoschka. J.W.

Kuomintang. Chinese nationalist revolutionary party (see NATIONALISM; REVOLUTION) established in 1905 as the Tung Men Hui ('Alliance Society') by Sun Yat-sen. Despite its eclipse after the revolution of 1912, it became the dominant party in China after its 1928 victory in the Civil War, establishing one-party 'tutelage' by the Organic Law of 4 October 1928. Under the presidency of Chiang Kai-shek, the Kuomintang waged a two-front war against both Chinese COMMUNISM and Japanese expansion, latterly with American support. In 1949 it was expelled from mainland China by the victorious Chinese Communists, and its claims (advanced from its island refuge of Formosa or Taiwan) to be the sole international representative of the Chinese people were ended in 1971 by the admission to UNO of the People's Republic of China. In its latter days the Kuomintang was a byword for AUTHORITARIANISM, incompetence, and corruption. D.C.W.
Bibl: O. E. Clubb, *20th Century China* (London, 1964; N.Y., 2nd ed., 1972).

Kupka, František (Czech-French painter, 1871–1957), see under ABSTRACT ART; ORPHISM.

L

La Follette, Robert Marion (U.S. statesman, 1855–1925), see under POPULISM; PROGRESSIVE.

La Popelinière, Lancelot Voisin, Sieur de (French historian, 1541–1608), see under HISTORIOGRAPHY.

La Rue, Danny (Irish-born female impersonator, *b.* 1928), see under TRANSVESTISM.

labour, dilution of, see DILUTION OF LABOUR.

labour, forced, see FORCED LABOUR.

Labour and Socialist International, see under INTERNATIONAL.

labour hoarding. The practice adopted by some companies, during a decline in DEMAND, of retaining their labour force intact, thus reducing the productivity of labour and raising the average variable cost per unit of output. Though widely decried, this practice has a twofold rationale: in any subsequent recovery in demand it avoids (1) problems of attracting sufficient labour back into the industry, and (2) CAPITAL costs associated with the training of a new work force.   D.E.

labour theory of value. The theory, promulgated by Adam Smith and Ricardo, and adapted by Marx, that any two products will exchange against one another in proportion to the amounts of labour necessary to make them. The theory disposes of the part played by CAPITAL in production either by assuming that the same amount of capital is used per unit of labour in making every product, or by treating capital equipment as stored-up labour, and neglecting the element of interest. The theory also neglects SCARCITY RENTS as a component of value in exchange. It is exposed to the further difficulty that it must reduce different kinds of labour to quantities of a common unit. In Western countries it has been largely superseded by forms of SUPPLY AND DEMAND analysis, but it remains basic to communist (see COMMUNISM) IDEOLOGY.   E.H.P.B.

Lacombe, Georges (French painter and sculptor, *d.* 1916), see under NABIS, LES.

Ladurie, Emmanuel Le Roy, see LE ROY LADURIE.

Lagrange, Léon (French art critic, 1828–68), see under IMPRESSIONISM.

Laing, Ronald David (British psychiatrist, *b.* 1927), see under ANTI–PSYCHIATRY.

laissez faire. A term used to describe an economy in which the activities of the government are kept down to an absolute minimum. It is an extreme form of a MARKET ECONOMY.   R.H.

Lamarckism. The conventional interpretation of the views on EVOLUTION held by the great French zoologist Jean Baptiste Pierre Antoine de Monet, le Chevalier de Lamarck (1744–1829) – the doctrine inadequately summarized as that of the 'inheritance of *acquired characteristics*'. In DARWINISM the heritable variations that are the subject of NATURAL SELECTION arise either spontaneously or not at all. Thus genetic information is self-engendered as part of the responding system. In Lamarckism the motive forces for evolutionary change are an animal's needs and the activities it undertakes in order to satisfy them. Thus, in the traditional example, a giraffe acquired the genetic specification for a long neck through generations of browsing upon the upper foliage of trees. A more sophisticated example is the ADAPTATION of microorganisms which enables them to use new sources of nutriment or to combat a new ANTIBIOTIC. Lamarckism has a great inherent plausibility, because social evolution is so obviously Lamarckian in character – we learn generation by generation and can propagate our learning to the next generation. Nevertheless, whenever Lamarckism in a purely biological context has been exposed to a critical test it has been faulted. Indeed, according to our modern notions of PROTEIN synthesis (see NUCLEIC ACID) there is no known method by which any modification brought about in a living organism during its own lifetime can be imprinted upon the genetic mechanism.

Lamarckism, like Darwinism, lends itself to political prejudices. If it were true that all human beings were born equal and that a man is what his environment and upbringing make him, then evolution could proceed only in the Lamarckian manner. It is therefore understandable that an extreme radical form of Lamarckism, bearing the same relationship to it as CALVINISM bears to Puritanism, was advocated in the Soviet Union by the agriculturalist Trofim Lysenko, after whom it has become known as LYSENKO-ISM. Lysenko's teaching became official doctrine in the COMMUNIST Party, and destroyed GENETICS in the Soviet Union as well as many of its practitioners. *Neo-Lamarckism* is the name given to an emphatic reiteration of Lamarckian beliefs by Nature-philosophers. Considered as an evolutionary procedure, Lamarckism is completely at odds with the central dogma of MOLECULAR BIOLOGY that genetic information flows only from NUCLEIC ACID towards PROTEIN or other products, and never the other way about.   P.M.

Lamb, Sydney Macdonald (U.S. linguist, *b.* 1929), see under STRATIFICATIONAL GRAMMAR.

Land, Edwin Herbert (U.S. inventor and physicist, *b.* 1909), see under POLAROID CAMERA.

land art, see under CONCEPTUAL ART.

land reform. The reform of systems of land tenure to break up large estates and distribute ownership as widely as possible, with the consolidation of small holdings. Land reform has been a necessary development where large-scale ownership has been combined with small-scale tenant farming (often on a share-cropping basis) to produce a stationary system of agricultural management. It has been much employed by reformist regimes, and also by revolutionary regimes as a necessary intermediary step towards COLLECTIVIZATION and breaking the power of the peasants.   D.C.W.
Bibl: D. Warriner, *Land Reform in Principle and Practice* (Oxford, 1969).

land use planning. Provision for the use of land in accordance with a considered policy. The term is used mainly in connection with policies for the national and regional use of land, e.g. for agricultural and non-agricultural uses and, within the latter, for housing, industrial, recreational, or other use. Provision must necessarily be made also for multi-purpose uses, e.g. for recreation and forestry. The criteria for decisions and the administrative machinery for carrying decisions into practice differ between countries and over time. K.E.H.
Bibl: J. B. Cullingworth, *Town and Country Planning in England and Wales* (London, 3rd ed., 1970; Toronto, rev. ed., 1971); D. R. Denman and S. Prodano, *Land Use* (London, 1972).

Landsteiner, Karl (Austrian immunologist and pathologist, 1868–1943), see under BLOOD GROUPS.

Lang, Andrew (British scholar and author, 1844–1912), see under FOLKLORE.

Langdon, Harry (U.S. actor, 1884–1944), see under KEYSTONE.

Lange, Carl Georg (Danish psychologist and physiologist, 1834–1900), see under JAMES-LANGE THEORY.

Lange, Friedrich Albert (German philosopher, 1828–75), see under NEO-KANTIANISM.

Lange, Oskar (Polish economist, 1904–65), see under ECONOMICS.

Langhoff, Wolfgang (German-Swiss theatre director and producer, 1901–66), see under DEUTSCHES THEATER.

Langlois, Henri (French *cinéaste*, 1914–77), see under CINÉMATHÈQUE.

language laboratory. A classroom divided into booths which are fitted with electronic equipment and connected to a master CONSOLE from which group and individual language tuition can be conducted. There is two-way communication through headphones and microphones between each pupil and the master-switchboard of the teacher. Pre-recorded tapes and prepared books are available in each booth, and the pupil can proceed at his own pace. The emphasis is, of course, on the spoken rather than the written language, though that aspect can also be covered. W.A.C.S.

langue and *parole*. Terms introduced into LINGUISTICS by Ferdinand de Saussure (see SAUSSURIAN) to distinguish between language viewed as a complete system of forms and contrasts represented in the brains of the language-users, and language viewed as the act of speaking by an individual at a given time. It is similar to Chomsky's distinction between COMPETENCE and PERFORMANCE. See also IDIOLECT. D.C.

Lansner, Jules (U.S. art critic), see under HARD-EDGE.

Laplace, Pierre Simon, Marquis de (French mathematician, astronomer, and physicist, 1749–1827), see under PROBABILITY THEORY.

Larbaud, Valéry-Nicolas (French author, 1881–1957), see under CRITERION, THE.

large numbers, laws of, see under PROBABILITY THEORY; STATISTICAL REGULARITY.

large-scale integration, see under INTEGRATED CIRCUIT.

Larionov, Mikhail Fedorovich (Russian painter and stage designer, 1881–1964), see under ABSTRACT ART; CUBO-FUTURISM; DONKEY'S TAIL; KNAVE OF DIAMONDS; RAYONISM.

Larkin, Philip (British poet, *b*. 1922), see under MOVEMENT, THE.

L'Arronge, Adolf (German dramatist and theatre director, 1838–1908), see under DEUTSCHES THEATER.

laser (Light Amplification by Stimulated Emission of Radiation). A device invented in 1960 for producing an intense beam of light with a high degree of COHERENCE, by making all the ATOMS in a material emit light in PHASE. The system is prepared by illuminating it with a flash of light which raises all the atoms into the same *excited state* (see ENERGY LEVEL). When one of the atoms falls back into its *ground state* the light emitted stimulates a small fraction of the other atoms to radiate in sympathy, their light being in phase with that from the first atom. This weak coherent pulse is not allowed to escape, but reflects back and forth between carefully spaced mirrors at each end of the specimen until all the atoms have been stimulated to radiate. One mirror is only partially reflecting, however, so that all the light eventually leaks out. The energy in the original illuminating flash (which is incoherent) has been converted into coherent light.

Laser light is used wherever coherence is necessary, e.g. in HOLOGRAPHY and METROLOGY, and wherever a highly localized source of ENERGY (obtained by focusing the beam) is required, e.g. in welding the cornea of the human eye. M.V.B.

Bibl: O. S. Heavens, *Lasers* (London, 1971).

Laski, Harold Joseph (British socialist, 1893–1950), see under LEFT BOOK CLUB.

Lasky, Melvin Jonah (U.S.-born editor, *b*. 1920), see under ENCOUNTER.

Laspeyres index number, see under INDEX NUMBER.

latency period. In psychoanalytic theory (see PSYCHOANALYSIS), the stage of PSYCHOSEXUAL DEVELOPMENT that begins at the age of about five (in the resolution of the OEDIPUS COMPLEX or ELECTRA COMPLEX) and lasts until puberty. During this time sexual tensions are repressed or sublimated (see REPRESSION; SUBLIMATION) into other less conflictive activities. Cultural RELATIVISM in the expression of this phenomenon has been sufficiently emphasized by anthropologists to bring its universality into considerable doubt. W.Z.

lateral thinking, see VERTICAL AND LATERAL THINKING.

lattice. A regular arrangement of lines or points. The ATOMS in a crystal lie approximately at points on a lattice, but the regularity is upset by (1) vibrations of the atoms about the lattice points (see SOLID-STATE PHYSICS), and (2) crystal DEFECTS such as DISLOCATIONS.   M.V.B.

Lattuada, Alberto (Italian film director, *b*. 1914), see under NEO-REALISM.

Laue, Max Theodor Felix von (German physicist, 1879–1960), see under MOLECULAR BIOLOGY.

Laugier, Marc-Antoine (French historical writer, 1713–69), see under NEO-CLASSICISM.

Laurel, Stan (British-U.S. actor, 1890–1965), see under SLAPSTICK.

Laurens, Henri (French painter and sculptor, 1885–1954), see under CUBISM.

Lautgedichte, see under CONCRETE POETRY.

Lautréamont, Comte de (pseud. of Isidore Ducasse, French poet, 1846–70), see under SURREALISM; TEL QUEL.

Laval, Pierre (French statesman, 1883–1945), see under VICHY.

Lavoisier, Antoine-Laurent (French scientist, 1743–94), see under RADICAL.

Lavrov, Peter Lavrovich (Russian political and social philosopher, 1823–1900), see under POPULISM.

law, administrative, see ADMINISTRATIVE LAW.

law, comparative, see COMPARATIVE LAW.

law, pure theory of. *Pure Theory of Law* is the title of a major contribution by Hans Kelsen to the philosophy of law and the theory of the State. First published in 1911, it presents a comprehensive account of the distinctive logical or formal structure of laws and legal systems, for the description of which it furnishes new concepts of which the most novel and important is the concept of a *basic norm*. Kelsen

called his theory 'pure' to mark its VALUE-FREE character and independence of moral or other evaluative judgement of the content of the law, and also to mark the distinction between this form of analytical study of the structure of the law and sociological studies of the law which are designed to furnish causal explanations or to establish other empirical relations between law and other phenomena.

The *basic norm* is introduced into the Pure Theory in order to explain both the systematic unity and the NORMATIVE character of law. It is not to be identified with the legal constitution of any state, or with any other form of positive law or social practice. It is, according to Kelsen, 'a juristic presumption or postulate implicit in legal thinking' prescribing that one ought to behave in the manner stipulated by the constitution and by the laws whose creation is authorized by the constitution. Kelsen believed that without such a presupposition or postulate only a sociological description and not a normative description could be given of the law and there could be nothing to unify separate laws into a single system. Hence, in Kelsen's view, the presupposition of the *basic norm* is implicit in the legal thought and the language commonly used by lawyers to describe the law.   H.L.A.H.

Bibl: H. Kelsen, tr. M. Knight, *Pure Theory of Law* (London and Berkeley, 1967); J. Raz, *The Concept of a Legal System* (Oxford, 1970).

law, the rule of. Various meanings have been given to this phrase and it has sometimes been conceived as a factual summary of the basic principles of the British Constitution and sometimes as a statement of an ideal only partly embodied in actual constitutional practices. It was used by A. V. Dicey in his *Law of the Constitution,* first published in 1885, for three principles, which he thought desirable and which in his view underlay the British Constitution. These principles require: (1) that a citizen's legal duties and his liability to punishment should be determined by the 'regular law', and not by the arbitrary fiat of officials or the exercise of wide discretionary powers; (2) that disputes between a private citizen and an official should be subject to the jurisdiction of the ordinary courts; and (3) that the fundamental rights of the citizen should not rest on a special guarantee by the Constitution but should arise from the ordinary law.

Contemporary versions of the rule of law stress the importance of two principles: (1) that the exercise of discretionary powers of rule-making and adjudication should be controlled by impartial tribunals in the light of stated general principles designed to secure that the power should be exercised fairly and within the limits prescribed by law; and (2) that as large an area of the law as possible and of the criminal law in particular should afford clear guidance to the citizen as to his rights and duties, and that he should be liable to punishment for breach of the law only if he had the capacity and a fair opportunity to conform his conduct to it.   H.L.A.H.

Bibl: A. V. Dicey, *The Study of the Law of the Constitution* (1885; London and N.Y., 3rd ed., 1889); R. F. V. Heuston, *Essays in Constitutional Law* (London, 2nd ed., 1964).

law and order. An expression used to refer to (1) social conditions in which there is general conformity to law, especially to the criminal law prohibiting such crimes as violence, theft, and disturbance of the peace, and to the firm administration of penalties imposed for breaches of the law; or (2) the conformity by law enforcement agencies themselves to the laws conferring and limiting their powers; or (3) respect for the rule of law (see LAW, RULE OF).
H.L.A.H.

Bibl: W. J. Chambliss and R. B. Seidman, *Law, Order and Power* (London and Reading, Mass., 1971).

Law Commission. A commission set up by the Law Commission Act of 1965 to consider reforms of the law and make proposals to the Government for the examination and reform of the laws. Various programmes have been laid by the Commission before the Lord Chancellor for the examination of different branches of the law, and some of these have been undertaken by the Commission itself or by other bodies. The Commission publishes informative annual reports of its activities and proposals and is also responsible for preparing legislation to provide for consolidation and revision of statute law. H.L.A.H.

Lawrence, David Herbert (British novelist, poet, and essayist, 1885–1930),

see under CRITERION, THE; INTELLECTUALS; IRRATIONALISM; LAWRENTIAN; LEAVISITE; MECHANIZATION.

Lawrentian. Adjective formed from the surname of D. H. Lawrence (1885–1930), whose novels and ideas had an enormous and liberating influence on his contemporaries and juniors. The adjective is now used in a generally non-pejorative sense (though it may occasionally refer to the crypto- or proto-FASCIST position allegedly occupied by Lawrence towards the end of his life) to refer to certain unique aspects of his writing and teaching, mostly to the latter. Qualities understood to be Lawrentian are: reliance, in human and sexual relationships, on 'blood', 'belly', 'loins', or 'bowels' (i.e. instinct) as against intellect (or, worse, 'sex in the head'); love of the particulars (birds, beasts, plants) of nature, and hatred of TECHNOLOGY; agrarianism as against urbanism; tenderness as against sophistication; sexual candour (dubiously exemplified in *Lady Chatterley's Lover*) as against prudishness or PORNOGRAPHY (Lawrence's word for what he sexually disliked). 'Lawrentian' only approximates to Lawrence's own highly complex personality, especially in the matter of sex. M.S.-S.

laws of physics, see under MODEL (2).

Le Chatelier's principle. Name given to the tendency of the environment to exert restoring forces on a system disturbed slightly away from stable static or dynamic EQUILIBRIUM.   M.V.B.

Le Corbusier, Charles-Édouard Jeanneret (Swiss-born architect and city planner, 1897–1965), see under ART SACRÉ; BRUTALISM; CIAM; CONCRETE; INTERNATIONAL STYLE; MEGASTRUCTURE; MODULE; OPEN PLAN; PEDESTRIAN SEGREGATION; POINT BLOCK; PURISM.

Le Fauconnier, Henri (French painter, 1881–1946), see under KNAVE OF DIAMONDS.

Le Guin, Ursula (U.S. novelist, *b.*1929), see under SCIENCE FICTION.

Le Parc, Julio (Argentinian artist, *b.*1938), see under OP ART.

Le Play, Pierre Guillaume Frédéric (French political economist and engineer, 1806–82), see under SOCIOLOGY.

Le Roy Ladurie, Emmanuel (French historian, *b*. 1929), see under AGRARIAN HISTORY; ANNALES SCHOOL.

Leacock, Richard (British-U.S. film director, *b*. 1921), see under CINÉMA-VÉRITÉ.

League of Nations. An international security organization created by covenant of the victors in World War I as part of the Treaty of Versailles, and established at Geneva in 1920. Its proposed method of maintaining peace was the application of economic and/or military SANCTIONS by member states against any nation committing aggression and ignoring the various procedures for the peaceful settlement of international disputes. The League's organs included a Council (with five permanent and four elected member powers) and an Assembly. The U.S.A. never joined it; Germany did not join until 1926 and withdrew in 1933; Japan withdrew in 1933; the Soviet Union joined in 1934 and was expelled in 1940.

During the 1920s the League enjoyed considerable authority and dealt successfully with a number of disputes. It also administered MANDATES and made some progress in developing various auxiliary international organizations such as the ILO and the Court of International Justice. During the 1930s, however, it failed to secure the support of the major powers in the face of Japanese, Italian, and German aggression that it was powerless to prevent, and did not survive World War II. At the end of that war it was replaced by the United Nations (see UNO).   D.C.W.

Bibl: F. P. Walters, *A History of the League of Nations* (2 vols., London and N.Y., 1952); G. Scott, *The Rise and Fall of the League of Nations* (London, 1973; N.Y., 1974).

learning problems, see under DYNAMIC PROGRAMMING.

Leary, Timothy (U.S. psychologist, *b*. 1920), see under DROP-OUT.

least-action principle. An alternative formulation of NEWTONIAN MECHANICS, which states that of all the conceivable paths along which a body may move between two points the path actually taken is such that a certain readily calculated property of the paths – the 'action' – is a minimum. A similar law in OPTICS (*Fermat's principle of least time*) governs the bending of light rays.

In the 18th century these principles were often regarded as indicating a 'desire for economy' on the part of Nature, which made objects 'choose' the minimal paths. However, this interpretation is untenable, because (1) a wide range of conceivable physical laws, including many known to be false, may be transformed mathematically into minimum principles, and (2) the action may occasionally be not a minimum but a *maximum* (when the paths or light rays have been through a focus). Least-action principles are useful in theoretical studies, such as the connection between Newtonian and QUANTUM MECHANICS.
    M.V.B.

Leavis, Frank Raymond (British literary critic, *b*. 1895), see under LEAVISITE; MASS CULTURE; TWO CULTURES.

Leavisite. Adjective or noun formed from the name of the British literary critic F. R. Leavis – and of his wife, Q. D. Leavis, whose *Fiction and the Reading Public* (1932) can perhaps be regarded as her most notable contribution to their working partnership. Since the 1930s Leavis has been, probably, the most powerful single influence on English studies: as a teacher at Cambridge University (and especially at Downing College), as founder and editor of *Scrutiny* (1932–53), and as the author of such books as *New Bearings in Poetry* (1932), *Culture and Environment* (with Denys Thompson, 1933), *Revaluation* (1936), and *The Great Tradition* (1949) – although his upward 'revaluations' (e.g. of T. S. Eliot, George Eliot, and above all D. H. Lawrence; see LAWRENTIAN) have been more generally accepted than his downward ones (e.g. of Milton, Shelley, and numerous English novelists). An outstanding exponent of the *practical criticism* (i.e. criticism based on close analysis of the text) pioneered by I. A. Richards, Leavis regards the study of English as a unique opportunity for developing a general 'critical awareness'. His own critical awareness has, however, too often led to critical and even personal acerbity, as in the TWO CULTURES controversy. The term 'Leavisite' is applied, pejoratively, not to Leavis himself nor to such former *Scrutiny* associates as L. C. Knights or D. J. Enright, but (as a noun) to his more dogmatic disciples, and (as an adjective) to the type of criticism or teaching which is concerned with the accurate 'placing' of literature (within Leavis's framework) at the expense of enjoyment.

O.S.

Bibl: E. Bentley (ed.), *The Importance of Scrutiny* (London and N.Y., 1948); G. Steiner, 'F. R. Leavis', in his *Language and Silence* (London and N.Y., 1967).

Lebensraum ('living room'). Term of biological origin meaning the area inhabited or habitable by a particular life-form (BIOSPHERE). It was introduced into political usage by German publicists after 1870 to justify Germany's territorial expansion. A central concept after 1919 in German ultra-NATIONALIST writing, including the propaganda literature of the NAZIS, it looked in particular to an expansion of Germany into eastern Europe, justifying this by the need for agricultural land to maintain the favourable balance between peasant and city-dweller on which the moral health of the German nation was supposed to rest. See also GEOPOLITICS.

D.C.W.

Lebesgue measure, see under MEASURE THEORY.

Lee, Vernon (pseud. of Violet Paget, British essayist and novelist, 1856–1935), see under EMPATHY.

Lefebvre, Georges (French historian, 1874–1959), see under HISTORY OF MENTALITIES.

Left, the. Label applied to a range of radical political views (see RADICALISM) and to those holding them. It came into being as a metaphorical extension of the seating plan of the French Estates General in 1789, where the nobility sat on the King's right and the 'Third Estate' on his left. The division of opinion crystallized in the debates on the royal veto, with the more revolutionary deputies opposing it, the conservative ones favouring it, and those in the CENTRE proposing a compromise. This perception of politics as a continuum in which the body politic is consistently divided by attitudes towards social change and social order resulted in the identification of the Left (or left wing) as the parties of change and of the RIGHT (or right wing) as the forces of the status quo. The left-right dichotomy was that of EGALITARIANISM v. inequalities, of reform (or REVOLUTION) v. tradition, of RADICALISM v. CONSERVATISM, of economic interventionism (a policy of State intervention in economic affairs) v. LAISSEZ FAIRE, of internationalism v. patriotism.

However, after World War I political attitudes no longer clustered so consistently along the old left-right division. Although the two terms continued to be used, they have undergone many shifts of meaning; and some of the old contradictory tendencies appeared in new combinations. The Left could not be defined any more by its attitude to EQUALITY *and* change: the two were sometimes divergent. The Right was no longer necessarily an epitome of conservatism and of the defence of the status quo; it could be radical, or even revolutionary like NAZISM. Nor was the Left necessarily internationalist; the emergence of national versions of COMMUNISM testified to this. Even inside the parties internal divisions were no longer always best described in terms of left and right. The Polish REVISIONISTS considered themselves to be to the left of Gomulka, whereas he denounced them as a rightist deviation (see DEVIATIONISM). The MAOIST Chinese similarly denounced Soviet 'revisionism' as a right-wing betrayal of communism, while Soviet Communists castigated the Maoists as 'leftist adventurers' *and* 'PETIT-BOURGEOIS nationalists'.

The emergence of the NEW LEFT contributed even more to the confusion and shifts in the meaning of the terms right and left. The perception of politics as a spectrum became more difficult, and a definition of 'the Left' in terms of traditional and consistent attitudes even more so. The label continues to be applied because it still helps to describe persistent divisions, but it often contributes more to the obfuscation of political realities than to the clarification of political issues. L.L.

Bibl: D. Caute, *The Left in Europe* (London and N.Y., 1966); S. Brittan,

Left or Right, the Bogus Dilemma (London, 1968).

Left Book Club. A London publishing venture, founded early in 1936, which epitomized LEFT attitudes during the POPULAR FRONT period. Its publisher was Victor Gollancz and its co-founders were John Strachey and Professor Harold Laski; its editorial director was a Communist INTELLECTUAL, John Lewis. Starting with some 10,000 members, within three years it increased five-fold. Although not all of its books were written by COMMUNISTS or FELLOW-TRAVELLERS, most of them were strongly pro-Soviet, and none was in any way critical of Stalin's Russia at the time of the Great Purge (see YEZHOVSHCHINA) and the MOSCOW TRIALS. The Club's success was interrupted by the 1939 Nazi-Soviet Pact, which was denounced by some of the Club's leaders, including Victor Gollancz. Its membership fell rapidly, and in 1948 it was dissolved.   L.L.
Bibl: V. Gollancz (ed.), *The Betrayal of the Left* (London, 1941); J. Symons, *The Thirties* (London, 1960; rev. ed., 1975).

legal positivism. A theory about the nature of law which defines it in a purely descriptive way in terms of the commands, or other *ex officio* pronouncements, of a sovereign or generally recognized authority, and without reference to moral considerations. It was first fully expounded by the 19th-century legal theorist, John Austin (see AUSTINIAN), who based his position on the ideas of Hobbes and Bentham. More recent developments of the doctrine have adjusted it to take account of the facts that not all laws are straightforwardly imperative in form and that not all constitutions contain so simply identifiable an ultimate source of law as that of Britain, whose legal system was Austin's prime example.   A.Q.
Bibl: H. L. A. Hart, *The Concept of Law* (Oxford, 1961).

legal realism. A theory about the nature of law which, like LEGAL POSITIVISM, seeks to define it without reference to moral considerations, but goes even further in interpreting statements about legal rights and duties in a straightforwardly factual way. It defines a person's legal *rights* as whatever, as a matter of fact, the courts will decide that he should be allowed to

do, his legal *duties* as whatever the courts will decide he is required to do. A common objection to this self-consciously hard-headed theory is that it can give no intelligible account of the reasoning of judges. A judge asking himself 'What are this man's legal rights?' is really, according to legal realism, asking 'What, in fact, am I going to say he should be allowed to do?'   A.Q.

Léger, Fernand (French painter, 1881–1955), see under CUBISM; FORMALISM; FUTURISM; MACHINE AESTHETIC; ORPHISM; PURISM.

legitimacy, see under POWER.

Lehmann, John (British author, editor, and publisher, *b.* 1907), see under NEW WRITING.

Lehrstück ('didactic play'). German term of the 1920s for a form of MUSIC THEATRE designed to instruct the performers rather than entertain an audience. The genre was introduced, apparently as a development of Hindemith's *Gemeinschaftsmusik* or communal music intended for amateurs, at the 1929 Baden-Baden chamber music festival, when Brecht, Hindemith, and Kurt Weill produced the *Badener Lehrstück vom Einverständnis* and the 'radio *Lehrstück*' *Flug der Lindberghs* or *Lindberghflug* (later renamed *Der Ozeanflug*). The term was virtually annexed by Brecht, whose model appears to have been the Japanese Nō drama, which henceforward became an important constituent of his EPIC THEATRE. With Weill and Hanns Eisler he wrote, in 1930–34, further didactic works, some with an expressly COMMUNIST message, for performance by children or amateurs.   J.W.
Bibl: G. Skelton, *Paul Hindemith* (London, 1975).

Leibniz, Gottfried Wilhelm (German philosopher, 1646–1716), see under ANALYSIS; APPERCEPTION; MATHEMATICAL LOGIC; MIND-BODY PROBLEM; MONAD; PANPSYCHISM; PERSONALISM; RATIONALISM; THEODICY.

Leicester school, see under AGRARIAN HISTORY.

Lemaître, Maurice (French poet, *b.* 1926), see under LETTRISM.

Lemmen, Georges (Belgian painter, 1865–1916), see under INTIMISM.

lend-lease. An Act of the U.S. Congress, signed by President Roosevelt on 11 March 1941, while the U.S.A. was still neutral, to allow the supply of arms and general supplies to Britain and subsequently to other states at war with the AXIS powers. Its basic principle was the leasing of arms and armaments in return for undertakings to return their value after war was over. The Act did not allow for any extension once hostilities had ended, and its operations were abruptly terminated in 1945 by order of President Truman.   D.C.W.

Bibl: W. F. Kimball, *The Most Unsordid Act: Lend-Lease 1939–1941* (Baltimore, 1969).

Lenin (name assumed by Vladimir Ilyich Ulyanov, Russian revolutionary, founder of the Bolshevik Party and the Soviet state, 1870–1924), see under APPARAT; BOLSHEVISM; CLASS; DIALECTICAL MATERIALISM; DICTATORSHIP OF THE PROLETARIAT; DOCUMENTARY; GUERRILLA; IMPERIALISM; JACOBINISM; LENINISM; MARXISM-LENINISM; PERMANENT REVOLUTION; POLITBURO; PROLETKULT; SPARTACISTS; STALINISM; THERMIDOR; TROTSKYISM.

Leninism. A theory based on the central beliefs of V. I. Lenin (1870–1924) on the politics, organization, and strategy of REVOLUTIONARY struggle. It provided a doctrinal underpinning of BOLSHEVISM and the first theoretical justification in MARXIST terms for revolutionary ACTIVISM in an undeveloped country. A shift from Marxist economic determinism (see HISTORICAL MATERIALISM) to Leninist political VOLUNTARISM had to be rationalized theoretically because, Lenin argued, 'there can be no revolutionary action without revolutionary theory'.

Originally, Russian followers of Marx opposed the *Narodnik* view that a historical short-cut to SOCIALISM was possible in Russia. They believed, on the basis of classical Marxist theory, that socialism can only emerge from a bourgeois-capitalist society (see BOURGEOIS; CAPITALISM), which first creates its material – economic and social – preconditions. Because Russia was still a pre-industrial, overwhelm-

ingly peasant country ruled by the Czarist autocracy, they thought that the immediate aim must be a bourgeois-democratic (see DEMOCRACY) revolution. Lenin, however, concluded that the Russian bourgeoisie was too weak and too vacillating to accomplish a 'bourgeois revolution' and that this task could be achieved only by the emerging industrial PROLETARIAT supported by the peasantry. He also thought that the workers could not develop by themselves the necessary political consciousness and that they needed an organization through which professional revolutionaries would lead them and be able to exploit a revolutionary situation when it arose (see JACOBINISM). Such a situation occurred in 1917. Lenin seized the opportunity, not to establish a democratic republic, but to overthrow one and to found a DICTATORSHIP OF THE PROLETARIAT exercised by the Bolshevik Party. The Party's paramount role in implementing revolutionary change had been made into a theoretical lynchpin of Leninism long before the Bolshevik seizure of power in October 1917. Ever since, it has become the central canon of all those Communist parties which model themselves on the Leninist idea of the revolutionary vanguard organized on the principle of DEMOCRATIC CENTRALISM.

Another important tenet of Leninism is the theory of IMPERIALISM as the last stage of a decaying 'monopoly capitalism'. This provided a justification, first for Lenin's tactics of 'revolutionary defeatism', then for the seizure of power by the Bolsheviks in the 'un-Marxist' conditions of Russia (as 'the weakest link in the chain of imperialism'), and later on in other economically backward countries (see UNDERDEVELOPMENT). It also provided the basis for the COMMUNIST perception of the world in terms of the struggle between imperialism and socialism, in which the victory of the latter is 'historically inevitable' because of the 'moribund' character of the former.

Although Lenin's own beliefs about 'bourgeois' and 'socialist' revolutions and those of his successors and followers have undergone considerable modifications since their early formulation at the beginning of the century, two essential features of Leninism have remained intact: attachment to the organizational principles of 'the Party of the new type', and the stress on its special role as a revolutionary minority, which must seize and maintain power in order to fulfil its historical mission. L.L.

Bibl: V. I. Lenin, tr. S. V. and P. Utechin, *What is to be done?* (London and N.Y., 1963); L. Schapiro and P. Reddaway (eds.), *Lenin* (London and N.Y., 1967); R. H. W. Theen, *Lenin* (Philadelphia, 1973; London, 1974).

Lennon, John (British songwriter and performer, b.1940), see under BEATLES, THE.

Lenski, Gerhard Emmanuel (U.S. sociologist, b.1924), see under STATUS.

Lentulov, Aristarkh (Russian painter, 1882–1943), see under KNAVE OF DIAMONDS.

Lenz, Didier (Fr. Desiderius; German Benedictine monk), see under BEURON.

Leo XIII, Pope (1810–1903), see under CHRISTIAN DEMOCRACY; NEO-THOMISM; RERUM NOVARUM.

Leontief, Wassily W. (Russian-U.S. economist, b.1906), see under INPUT-OUTPUT ANALYSIS.

lepton. Any ELEMENTARY PARTICLE that does not react or decay with STRONG INTERACTIONS, but instead displays only the WEAK INTERACTION or interactions via the ELECTROMAGNETIC FIELD (e.g. the ELECTRON, the NEUTRINO). M.V.B.

lesbianism, see under HOMOSEXUALITY.

Lessing, Gotthold Ephraim (German author, 1729–81), see under GESTUS.

lettrism. Parisian literary movement founded in 1946, based on a poetic and pictorial concern with letters and signs, and identified particularly with Isidore Isou and Maurice Lemaître. Its works, generally regarded as inferior to comparable exercises in CONCRETE POETRY and by allied artists of a calligraphic bent, take the form of phonetic poetry, picture-writing (*hypergraphy*), and quasi-SEMIOTIC painting. J.W.

Bibl: I. Isou, *Introduction à une nouvelle poésie* (Paris, 1947).

leucotomy (or *lobotomy*). The operation of cutting the white matter of the brain. In its most drastic form, the *prefrontal leucotomy*, a cut is made in the front part of the brain to divide connecting tracts between the frontal lobes and the thalamus.

Prefrontal leucotomy was introduced when it was noticed (and confirmed by experiments with animals) that injuries of the frontal lobes resulted in a blunting of the emotions – particularly AGGRESSION and ANXIETY. It was widely practised in the late 1940s and early 1950s, and brought undoubted relief to a number of patients with PSYCHOSIS or severe emotional disorders, but its exact value was never generally agreed, and it is now performed much less often, since better results can be achieved by treatment with drugs, which is reversible, controllable, and less drastic. D.A.P.

Bibl: W. J. Freeman and J. W. Watts, *Psychosurgery* (Oxford and Springfield, Ill., 2nd ed., 1950).

level. In LINGUISTICS, a fundamental theoretical term which is used in a number of senses, in particular (1) to denote an aspect of the structure of language regarded as susceptible of independent study; three levels (PHONETICS, SYNTAX, SEMANTICS) are generally recognized (but see also DUALITY OF STRUCTURE; FORM); (2) in GENERATIVE GRAMMAR, to characterize the distinction between DEEP STRUCTURE AND SURFACE STRUCTURE ('varying levels of depth'); (3) especially by some American linguists, in the sense of RANK. D.C.

Levin, Harry (U.S. literary critic, b.1912), see under REALISM.

Lévi-Strauss, Claude (French social anthropologist, b. 1908), see under MYTH; STRUCTURALISM; TOTEMISM.

Lewin, Kurt (Polish-U.S. psychologist, 1890–1947), see under TOPOLOGICAL PSYCHOLOGY.

Lewis, Cecil Day, see DAY LEWIS.

Lewis, Clarence Irving (U.S. logician and philosopher, 1883-1964), see under ENTAILMENT AND IMPLICATION; MODAL LOGIC.

Lewis, Gilbert Newton (U.S. chemist, 1875–1946), see under BOND, CHEMICAL.

Lewis, John (British publisher, *b*. 1889), see under LEFT BOOK CLUB.

Lewis, Meade 'Lux' (U.S. jazz musician, 1905–64), see under BOOGIE-WOOGIE.

Lewis, William Arthur (U.S. economist, *b*.1915), see under OVERPOPULATION.

Lewis, Wyndham (British painter, author, and editor, 1884–1957), see under BLAST; INTELLECTUALS; LITTLE 'REVIEW; LONDON GROUP; NEW AGE; VORTICISM.

Lewitt, Sol (U.S. sculptor and art critic, *b*. 1928), see under CONCEPTUAL ART; DEMATERIALIZATION.

lexeme. A term applied by some LINGUISTS (e.g. John Lyons) to the basic abstract lexical unit which underlies the different inflectional forms of a word, e.g. *sleep, slept, sleeps, sleeping* are variants of a single lexeme, *sleep*. Other linguists (e.g. Charles Hockett) apply the term to a type of constituent (particular MORPHEME or morpheme-sequence) which is established in a CONSTITUENT ANALYSIS. D.C.

lexical word, see under WORD CLASS.

lexicography, see under LEXICON.

lexicology, see under LEXICON.

lexicometry, see under QUANTITATIVE HISTORY.

lexicon. The dictionary component of a linguistic analysis, in which all information about the meaning and use of individual lexical items in a language is listed. It is particularly used with reference to the SEMANTIC component of a GENERATIVE GRAMMAR. The study of the properties of the lexicon is sometimes called *lexis*, sometimes *lexicology*. The latter must be distinguished from *lexicography*, the principles and practice of dictionary-making. In neo-Firthian (see FIRTHIAN) LINGUISTICS, lexis has a more restricted sense, referring only to the formal, not the semantic, characteristics of the lexicon. D.C.

lexicostatistics, see under GLOTTOCHRONOLOGY.

lexis, see under LEXICON.

Libby, Willard Frank (U.S. chemist, *b*.1908), see under RADIOCARBON DATING.

liberalism.
(1) A political philosophy which originated in the 18th century, reached the height of its influence before 1914, and was historically associated with the idea of freedom: the civil freedom of the individual; free political INSTITUTIONS; freedom of RELIGION; free enterprise and FREE TRADE in ECONOMICS. Although liberal ideas still permeate the EDUCATION, politics, and public life of the countries of Western Europe, North America, and Australasia, Liberal parties steadily lost ground after World War I, a distinction frequently expressed in the remark that there are many people who would call themselves liberal with a small 'l' but who would never think of voting Liberal with a capital 'L'. It remains to be seen whether the revival of support for Liberal parties in the 1970s (e.g. in Britain, West Germany) marks a reversal, or only an interruption, of the trend since 1914. Liberalism in its most characteristic contemporary expression emphasizes the importance of conscience and justice in politics, advocates the rights of racial and religious MINORITIES, and supports civil liberties and the right of the ordinary individual to be more effectively consulted in decisions which directly affect him. This idea of liberalism is shared by many modern American liberals who, characteristically, combine a belief in democratic CAPITALISM with a strong commitment to executive and legislative action in order to alleviate social ills. During the 1960s, American liberalism was identified with social PERMISSIVENESS; significantly, this development coincided with a broad questioning of American society in the wake of the VIETNAM war.
                                        A.L.C.B.
Bibl: K. R. Minogue, *The Liberal Mind* (London, 1963; N.Y., 1964); A. L. C. Bullock and M. Shock (eds.), *The Liberal Tradition* (London, 1965; N.Y., 1957).
(2) In RELIGION and THEOLOGY, the opinion that an individual, or a new generation, ought to have liberty to question

and reject orthodox doctrines and DOG-MAS if these seem contrary to reason or morality (see EMPIRICAL THEOLOGY), and to apply ordinary historical methods to the Bible and other sacred texts (see HIGHER CRITICISM). The greatest theologian with these attitudes was Friedrich Schleiermacher (1768–1834). Before 1914, particularly in the 'Liberal PROTESTANTISM' of Adolf von Harnack (1851–1930) and others, such an approach was often associated with an over-optimistic attitude to human progress and rationality. Hence BARTHIAN and other exponents of NEO-ORTHODOXY condemned much of it as a betrayal of the Christian Gospel.
D.L.E.

Bibl: B. M. G. Reardon (ed.), *Liberal Protestantism* (London and Stanford, 1968).

liberalism, economic, see ECONOMIC LIBERALISM.

liberation. The freeing of an individual, nation, or group from constraints imposed on them by others. Historically it referred to the 'liberation' of NAZI-dominated Europe by the British, American, French, and Soviet Russian forces in 1943–5. More recently it has been used by groups campaigning against constraints placed on their freedom of action by law, social *mores*, etc., as in GAY LIBERATION. D.C.W.

libertarianism.
(1) A theory, opposed to DETER-MINISM, about the nature of human action which holds that some human actions, those for which it is correct to hold the agent in question morally responsible, are not causally explicable, or not wholly so. Libertarians have traditionally taken free and responsible human action to be a peculiar exception to the general reign of causal law. More recently it has been argued (by Wittgenstein and Ryle, for instance) that to ask strictly causal questions about genuine human actions, as contrasted with mere bodily movements such as blinking at a bright light or falling when tripped, is logically improper.
(2) An extreme version of political LIBERALISM, hostile to all forms of social and legal discrimination between human beings and favouring the absolutely minimal constraint by society on individual freedom of action. A.Q.

libido.
(1) In early psychoanalytic theory (see PSYCHOANALYSIS), a FREUDIAN term for specifically sexual energies.
(2) Later, all psychic energies employed in the service of the LIFE INSTINCT. W.Z.

Lichtenstein, Roy (U.S. painter, *b.* 1923), see under POP.

Liebermann, Max (German painter and engraver, 1847–1935), see under SEZES-SION.

Liebknecht, Karl (German politician, 1871–1919), see under SPARTACISTS.

Liebmann, Otto (German philosopher, 1840–1912), see under NEO-KANTIANISM.

life cycle. One or other of the regenerative processes in the BIOSPHERE; examples are the *nitrogen cycle*, the *carbon cycle*, and the *oxygen cycle*. The elementary constituents of the biosphere – carbon, hydrogen, oxygen, nitrogen, phosphorus, sulphur – enter into compounds which so far from being static undergo continuous cycles of use and re-use, synthesis and degradation. Nitrogen compounds are essential for living organisms and are probably the most important limiting factor in regulating their abundance. Yet in spite of its enormous abundance (about 80% of the atmosphere) very few organisms have the power to make use of nitrogen directly. For this reason the artificial fixation of gaseous nitrogen is the most important and biologically influential technological innovation since the Industrial Revolution. The amounts of nitrogen fixed in industrial processes for the manufacture of fertilizers are of the order of tens of millions of tons per annum and are probably on the same scale as the natural fixation of atmospheric nitrogen by marine MICRO-ORGANISMS and by the micro-organisms that live in SYMBIOSIS with leguminous plants. The fixation of nitrogen has to compete with the denitrifying processes which in the latest stages of organic breakdown return nitrogen to the atmosphere, and with the wastage produced by the dissipation or misuse of sewage, which is normally rich in nitrogen compounds.

The *carbon cycle*, closely intertwined with the *oxygen cycle*, begins and ends with atmospheric carbon dioxide. Although living organisms are compounds of carbon, very much more carbon is locked up in the form of coal and other fossil fuels than in living organisms themselves. The crucial TRANSFORMATION in both the carbon cycle and the oxygen cycle is PHOTOSYNTHESIS. The chief agents fixing atmospheric carbon are terrestrial forests and marine phytoplankton. Carbon dioxide is returned to the air by respiration, by the combustion of fossil fuels, and as a terminal stage of the decomposition of organic matter. In both carbon and oxygen cycles an annual rhythm is superimposed upon a CIRCADIAN RHYTHM. P.M.

life force, see under VITALISM.

life instinct (or *Eros*). In psychoanalytic theory (see PSYCHOANALYSIS), a FREUDIAN term for the supposed source of all the impulses and drives that serve the individual in self-preservation and reproduction. It is contrasted with the DEATH INSTINCT. See also LIBIDO. W.Z.

life sciences, see BIOLOGY.

life space. In the TOPOLOGICAL PSYCHOLOGY of K. Lewin, the spatial representation of the entire psychological ENVIRONMENT as it exists for an individual person and within which he behaves according to interactions among various needs, values, obstacles, social pressures, aspirations, etc. I.M.L.H.

life style.
(1) In psychoanalytic theory (see PSYCHOANALYSIS), an ADLERIAN term for a child's method, modified continuously throughout its life, of coping with feelings of inadequacy and of attaining superiority and STATUS.
(2) In popular usage, all the observable characteristics of a person, e.g. his manner of dress, way of speaking, personal appearance, domestic habits, and choice of friends, which serve to indicate his value system and attitudes towards himself and aspects of his ENVIRONMENT. These characteristics serve as a social signal to others, who react accordingly with feelings of trust, admiration, liking, etc., or the opposite. H.L.

life table (or *table of mortality*). A statistical MODEL used in DEMOGRAPHY to illustrate the effect of mortality on a population. A *current life table* shows how many persons would survive to any given birthday out of a given initial number of births (normally 10,000 or 100,000) if the current risks of dying at each age were applied to them. A *cohort life table* (or *generation life table*) traces the survivors of an actual cohort of births, when subjected to the mortality rates of different periods of their lives. The model was first used by John Graunt in 1660, though his method of constructing tables was faulty. E.G.
Bibl: L. I. Dublin, A. J. Lotka, and M. Spiegelman, *Length of Life* (N.Y., rev. ed., 1949).

Ligeti, György (Hungarian composer, b 1923), see under MUSIC THEATRE.

light pen. A device used with a VISUAL DISPLAY to provide a graphical INPUT to a COMPUTER. It consists of a pen-like holder containing a photo-electric cell and attached to the display by a flexible lead. When this is presented to the face of the display, the computer arranges that a spot of light should appear under it. This spot follows the movement of the light pen, leaving a trail behind it, so that the light pen appears to draw a line of light on the display. C.S.

light shows, see under MEDIA.

limen, see THRESHOLD.

limit. A fundamental CONCEPT of MATHEMATICS. We give three examples of its use.
(1) Successive approximation to π may be made by calculating the perimeter p_n of a regular polygon with n sides inscribed in a circle of unit diameter. As n tends to infinity p_n tends to the limit π (see CONVERGENCE).
(2) The velocity of a body falling freely through the air tends to (but never actually reaches) a limit called the terminal velocity.
(3) A train travelling at a mile a minute tends to the first milestone as a limit as the second hand of a watch approaches the first minute, and reaches it at that time. R.G.

LIMITED WAR

limited war, see under WAR.

limnology. The science which deals with the interrelationships between the BIOLOGY, CHEMISTRY, and PHYSICS of inland water, including lakes, rivers, and marshes. The word derives from the Greek limnē (marshy lake), and some naturalists with a classical education prefer the term to be restricted to studies of muddy waters and bogs rather than clear lakes and rivers. Generally, however, it is synonymous with *hydrobiology* or *freshwater biology*.   K.M.
  Bibl: T. T. Macan and E. B. Worthington, *Life in Lakes and Rivers* (London, 1951).

Lin Piao (Chinese politician, 1907–71), see under CULTURAL REVOLUTION.

Lindbergh, Charles (U.S. aviator, 1902–74), see under AIR PHOTOGRAPHY.

Lindsay, Vachel (U.S. poet, 1879–1931), see under POETRY (CHICAGO).

Lindsley, Donald Benjamin (U.S. physiologist and psychologist, *b*.1907), see under BRAIN STIMULATION.

line and staff, see under MANAGEMENT STUDIES.

linear. Both in MATHEMATICS and in the real world the simplest non-trivial RELATION between two quantities x and y is that of proportionality. This is expressed by EQUATION (1): $y = cx$, where c is a constant. The GRAPH of y versus x is a straight line, and the relation is said to be *linear*. Even when the actual relation is less simple, equation (1) may give a serviceable approximation provided x and y are not too large. The best approximation is obtained by taking c to be the value of the DERIVATIVE of y at $x = 0$; if values of x and y are experimental data, c may be estimated statistically (see CORRELATION).
  Generalizations of this notion permeate mathematics and theoretical PHYSICS. If y be considered as a FUNCTION of x, say $y = f(x)$, then a consequence of (1) is that f satisfies (2): $f(ax + bx') = af(x) + bf(x')$. This characterization of f can be applied when x and y are non-numerical. In particular if x and y are VECTORS and f satisfies (2) then f is called a *linear map-*

ping; it can be represented by a MATRIX. If x and y are themselves functions then f is called a *linear operator*. A *linear equation* in the unknowns $x_1, x_2, \ldots, x_n$ has the form $a_1x_1 + a_2x_2 + a_nx_n = b$; the left-hand side is a *linear function* of (the vector whose components are) $x_1, \ldots, x_n$. A linear TRANSFORMATION of coordinates is one in which the old coordinates are linear functions of the new coordinates and vice versa.   R.G.

Linear A and B. Name given to two scripts used in Crete and Greece in the Bronze Age. Both are syllabic. They were first recognized on Crete by Sir Arthur Evans who proposed the name to distinguish them from the earlier hieroglyphic script. Linear B was deciphered in 1952 by Michael Ventris who showed the language used to be an early form of Greek. The subject-matter of the tablets so far translated is restricted to inventories. Linear A has not yet been deciphered.   B.C.
  Bibl: J. Chadwick, *The Decipherment of Linear B* (London, 1958; N.Y., 1963).

linear accelerator. A type of ACCELERATOR for IONS, which travel along a straight line down the common axis of hollow cylindrical ELECTRODES. The acceleration is produced in the gaps between adjacent electrodes by means of oscillating voltages.   M.V.B.

linear motor. A type of electric motor in which the parts move relative to each other along a straight line instead of rotating about an axis. Linear motors are thus well suited to the powering of sliding doors, travelling cranes, and similar devices requiring linear rather than rotary motion, and are ideally suited to high-speed transport.   M.V.B.
  Bibl: E. R. Laithwaite, *Propulsion without Wheels* (N.Y., 1968; 2nd ed., London, 1970).

linear planning. A system of structuring urban or large architectural forms about a line, usually a route of movement, with short subsidiary routes coming off this line at right angles. The principle stems from the work of the Spanish town-planner Arturo Soria y Mata, and has since been applied in a number of instances, though never on the scale of Soria's vision of a linear city from St Petersburg to Cadiz.   M.BR.

Bibl: F. Choay, *The Modern City: Planning in the 19th Century* (London and N.Y., 1969).

linear programming. A technique of OPTIMIZATION THEORY developed during World War II. Many optimization problems can be put into a form in which the *objective function* and all the constraints are linear, and all the variables are nonnegative. Such problems are *linear programs*; G. B. Dantzig's *simplex method*, developed in the 1940s, provides an efficient method of solving them.   R.SI.

linguist. In LINGUISTICS, the normal term for a student or practitioner of the subject; 'linguistician' is never used by the professional linguist about himself. Ironically, confusion sometimes arises from the earlier, and still current, sense of someone proficient in several languages.   D.C.

linguistic philosophy. A form of ANALYTIC PHILOSOPHY, the historical successor to LOGICAL ATOMISM and LOGICAL POSITIVISM, first practised by G. E. Moore in a methodologically unselfconscious way and developed as an explicit philosophical method by Wittgenstein from about 1930 and, later, by Gilbert Ryle and J. L. Austin. Like logical positivism, it is hostile to METAPHYSICS, but for a different reason: for the linguistic philosopher, the hallmark of a metaphysical PROPOSITION is its incompatibility with the COMMON SENSE view of the world, and he conceives his task to be that of unveiling the mistaken assumptions about the actual use of language on which the persuasiveness of metaphysical argumentation depends. Philosophical problems, on this view, require not solution but dissolution. Wittgenstein's style of linguistic philosophy has been reasonably described as 'therapeutic', for his concern with the rules of ordinary language extended only so far as was needed to dispel philosophical puzzlement. The Oxford philosophers of ordinary language approached it more systematically. Linguistic philosophers are generally suspicious of formal LOGIC, at least in the role of ANALYTIC instrument in which it was cast by their positivist predecessors. Sometimes the phrase 'linguistic philosophy' is applied to all varieties of analytic philosophy, but the narrower application described above is more usual among philosophers.   A.Q.

Bibl: C. W. K. Mundle, *A Critique of Linguistic Philosophy* (Oxford, 1970).

linguistics. The scientific study of language. As an academic discipline, the development of this subject has been recent and rapid, having become particularly widely known and taught in the 1960s. This reflects partly an increased popular and specialist interest in the study of language and communication in relation to human beliefs and behaviour (e.g. in THEOLOGY, PHILOSOPHY, INFORMATION THEORY, literary criticism), and the realization of the need for a separate discipline to deal adequately with the range and complexity of linguistic phenomena; partly the impact of the subject's own internal development at this time, arising largely out of the work of Chomsky (see CHOMSKYAN) and his associates, whose more sophisticated analytic techniques and more powerful theoretical claims gave linguistics an unprecedented scope and applicability.

Different branches may be distinguished according to the LINGUIST's focus and range of interest. A major distinction, introduced by Ferdinand de Saussure (see SAUSSURIAN), is between *diachronic* and *synchronic* linguistics, the former referring to the study of language change (also called *historical* linguistics, the latter to the study of the state of language at any given point in time. In so far as the subject attempts to establish general principles for the study of all languages, and to determine the characteristics of human language as a phenomenon, it may be called *general* linguistics. When it concentrates on establishing the facts of a particular language system, it is called *descriptive* linguistics. When its purpose is to focus on the differences between languages, especially in a language-teaching context, it is called *contrastive* linguistics. When its purpose is primarily to identify the common characteristics of different languages or language families, the subject goes under the heading of *comparative* (or *typological*) linguistics. (See also AGGLUTINATING; INFLECTING; ISOLATING; POLYSYNTHETIC LANGUAGE.)

When the emphasis in linguistics is wholly or largely historical, the subject is traditionally referred to as *comparative philology* (or simply *philology*), though in many parts of the world 'philologists' and 'historical linguists' are people with very different backgrounds and temperaments. The term *structural* linguistics is widely used, sometimes in an extremely specific sense, referring to the particular approaches to SYNTAX and PHONOLOGY current in the 1940s and 1950s, with their emphasis on providing DISCOVERY PROCEDURES for the analysis of a language's surface structure (see DEEP STRUCTURE); sometimes in a more general sense, referring to *any* system of linguistic analysis that attempts to establish explicit systems of relations between linguistic units in surface structure. When the emphasis in language study is on the classification of structures and units, without reference to such notions as deep structure, some linguists, particularly within GENERATIVE GRAMMAR, talk pejoratively of *taxonomic* linguistics.

The overlapping interests of linguistics and other disciplines has led to the setting up of new branches of the subject, such as ANTHROPOLOGICAL LINGUISTICS, BIOLINGUISTICS, COMPUTATIONAL LINGUISTICS, ETHNOLINGUISTICS, MATHEMATICAL LINGUISTICS, NEURO-LINGUISTICS, PSYCHOLINGUISTICS, SOCIOLINGUISTICS. When the subject's findings, methods, or theoretical principles are applied to the study of problems from other areas of experience, one talks of *applied* linguistics; but this term is often restricted to the study of the theory and methodology of foreign-language teaching.   D.C.

Bibl: J. Lyons, *Introduction to Theoretical Linguistics* (London, 1968); G. C. Lepschy, *A Survey of Structural Linguistics* (London, 1970); D. Crystal, *Linguistics* (Harmondsworth and Baltimore, 1971); R. H. Robins, *General Linguistics* (Harlow, 2nd ed., 1971).

linkage.
(1) In GENETICS, the process whereby characteristics inherited from the same parent tend to be transmitted together to the offspring, instead of being transmitted independently as they should be according to MENDEL'S LAWS. Linkage occurs because the relevant GENES are on the same CHROMOSOME. Although linked genes do not recombine randomly, they do usually show some recombination; see CROSSING OVER.   J.M.S.

(2) In SYSTEMS ANALYSIS, any recurrent sequence of behaviour which originates in one system and produces a reaction in another.   A.L.C.B.

linkage politics. A method for the analysis of international relations, based on the notion of LINKAGE (2) – in this case the interaction between international and domestic politics. Three major types of linkage politics are distinguished: (1) the *penetrative,* e.g. 'the penetration' of Western Germany and Japan by the U.S.A. after World War II; (2) the *reactive,* e.g. an increase in the defence budget of one country in reaction to increased armament in another country which is felt to be unfriendly; (3) the *emulative,* e.g. the spread of SOCIAL WELFARE measures in Western countries, or of the demand for independence in colonial countries, as a result of seeing and emulating what their neighbours are doing. It is claimed that this method of analysis has the advantage of neither denying nor exaggerating the relevance of national boundaries. A.L.C.B.

Bibl: J. N. Rosenau (ed.), *Linkage Politics* (N.Y., 1969).

Linnaeus, Carolus (Carl von Linné; Swedish botanist, 1707–78), see under BIOSYSTEMATICS.

Linton, Ralph (U.S. anthropologist, 1893–1953), see under ACCULTURATION.

Lipchitz, Jacques (Latvian-U.S. sculptor, 1891–1973), see under CUBISM.

Lippard, Lucy (U.S. art critic, b. 1937), see under DEMATERIALIZATION.

Lippman, Walter (U.S. columnist, 1889–1974), see under COLD WAR.

Lipset, Seymour Martin (U.S. sociologist and political scientist, b. 1922), see under IDEOLOGY.

liquidity. Economists' term for the possession of, or ability to realize quickly, adequate supplies of money in relation to one's commitments. An economy or sector of an economy can be said to be liquid when most people or companies in it can swiftly lay hands on plenty of cash either by drawing on their bank balance or by selling assets (sometimes called *liquid assets*) which are easily converted into money at short notice at a predictable price. *International liquidity* is the cash or near-cash available to the world's governments for settling debts between them; it is limited to the kinds of money held in the official reserves of nations, normally deposited with the central bank. Statistics of the amount and ownership of international liquidity are published monthly by the International Monetary Fund. During the post-war period the main forms of international liquidity have been gold, the reserve currencies (dollars and pounds), credit positions with the I.M.F., and – a recent addition – Special Drawing Rights (nicknamed *paper gold*). A proposal by Keynes, at the time of the BRETTON WOODS negotiations in 1944, for a new international currency (*bancor*), to be issued by a new world central bank, was rejected as too radical, and instead the I.M.F. was set up as a source of credit, but not new money, to member countries. P.J.

Lissitzky, El (Russian painter, typographer, and designer, 1890–1941), see under CONSTRUCTIVISM; FORMALISM; GRAPHIC DESIGN; MERZ; SUPREMATISM.

Lister, Joseph (British surgeon and medical scientist, 1827–1912), see under ANTISEPTIC.

Liszt, Ferencz or **Franz** (Hungarian composer, 1811–86), see under ATONAL MUSIC; PROGRAMME MUSIC; ROMANTICISM; WHOLE-TONE SCALE.

lithosphere. Prior to the theory of PLATE TECTONICS the terms lithosphere and *crust* were used synonymously for the outermost rock shell of the earth which is succeeded inwards by the mantle (see ASTHENOSPHERE). The term lithosphere is now used within the framework of plate tectonic theory for the relatively rigid outer zone of the earth, some 100 km thick, which includes the rock shell and part of the upper mantle. Thus only the term 'crust' is used for the rock shell. The boundary between the crust and the mantle is defined by an important seismological discontinuity, the *Mohorovicic discontinuity (Moho* for short). J.L.M.L.

Little Review, the. An American literary magazine, founded in Chicago by Margaret Anderson in 1914 as a rival to Harriet Monroe's POETRY (CHICAGO). It began by printing many early American radical poets and writers and importing new European ideas; after Ezra Pound took over the foreign editorship, it acquired Joyce's *Ulysses* as well as verse and prose by Eliot, Wyndham Lewis, Hart Crane, and others. After a shift to New York it moved, in 1922, to Paris and took in DADA and SURREALISM, and various French and American expatriate writers. It ended in 1929. M.S.BR.

Bibl: M. Anderson, *My Thirty Years' War* (London and N.Y., 1930).

Littlewood, Joan (British theatre director, b. 1914), see under THEATRE WORKSHOP.

Liturgical Movement. The movement to restore to the laity an active and intelligent part in the 'liturgy' (Greek *leitourgia*, people's work) or public worship of God by the Church, specially in Holy Communion. Originating in the French monastery of Solesmes under Abbot Guéranger (1805–75), this movement received the most authoritative expression and blessing in the 'Constitution of the Sacred Liturgy' of VATICAN COUNCIL II (1963), and has been the most conspicuously successful part of the AGGIORNAMENTO in the Roman CATHOLIC Church. It has also influenced other Churches, particularly ANGLICANISM. D.L.E..

Bibl: G. E. A. Dix, *The Shape of the Liturgy* (London, 2nd ed., 1945).

Liu Shao-chi (Chinese Communist leader, c. 1898–1974), see under CULTURAL REVOLUTION.

Liverpool Poets. A group of writers from that city who coalesced in the early 1960s as a product of the Anglo-American JAZZ-POETRY movement and the local POP music wave which threw up the BEATLES. Strongly impregnated with local references, yet rooted in the wider modern movement, the work of Adrian Henri, Roger McGough, and Brian Patten was designed mainly for public performance, with or without music, and appealed to a largely pop audience. It was brought to the critics' somewhat disdainful attention by Edward Lucie-Smith's anthology *The Liverpool Scene* (London, 1967) and by Penguin Modern Poets no. 10, *The Mersey Sound* (Harmondsworth, 1967). J.W.

Living Newspaper. A form of didactic political drama which uses journalistic techniques to present an account of a contemporary issue, usually in a satirical or agitational context. The Living Newspaper was developed as a form of AGIT-PROP drama by the Red Army during the Russian Revolution to reach a mass and largely illiterate audience (cf. the 'factory-wall newspaper'); in the U.S.A. the Federal Theatre Project (see WPA) established a Living Newspaper unit in 1935; in England, the UNITY THEATRE presented the first of a number of Living Newspaper productions in 1938. See also DOCUMENTARY. M.A.

Living Theatre. A radical AVANT-GARDE troupe founded by Julian Beck and his wife, Judith Malina, in New York in 1947 and disbanded in 1972. Beginning with poetic drama (Brecht, Eliot, Lorca) the group moved into improvisational realism with work like Kenneth Brown's *The Brig* (1965), set in a U.S. Marines detention cell. The Becks later moved the company to Europe where its members lived in communal poverty and became avowedly ANARCHIST. The group's aim was 'to increase conscious awareness, to stress the sacredness of life, to break down the walls'. But the calculated AGGRESSION and audience-harassment of later shows like *Paradise Now* (1968) suggested that barriers were being erected rather than broken down. Living Theatre productions were invariably exciting experiences; but the break-up of the group surprised no one. M.BI.

Bibl: J. Lahr, *Acting Out America* (Harmondsworth, 1972).

Lloyd, Harold (U.S. actor, 1893–1971), see under KEYSTONE.

loader, see under ASSEMBLER.

lobby, see under INTEREST GROUPS AND PRESSURE GROUPS.

lobotomy, see LEUCOTOMY.

local history. This includes the history of a village, a town, a county, or even a province, and can involve the study of the landscape or townscape as well as the study of documentary evidence. Long the preserve of amateurs and antiquarians, local history has been invaded in the last generation by problem-oriented professional historians for whom the regional monograph is the obvious means of testing generalizations. This new local history flourishes most in France. In England there is a group of local historians associated with the University of Leicester and concerned in particular with AGRARIAN HISTORY. P.B.

Bibl: W. G. Hoskins, *Local History in England* (Harlow, 2nd ed., 1972).

location. Geographical term used in two senses: (1) the absolute position of a place on the earth's surface, stated usually by reference to a coordinate reference system (e.g. latitude and longitude); (2) the relative location of a place in relation to other places. Studies of the changing impact of relative location on human activity have given rise to a theoretical branch of human GEOGRAPHY termed LOCATIONAL ANALYSIS. P.H.

locational analysis. In GEOGRAPHY, term for the study of the location of economic activity dealing with the broad questions 'What is where, and why there?' The where may be defined in broad *macrogeographic* terms as *regions* or in narrower *microgeographic* terms as *sites*. It is usually concerned with the relative spatial qualities of proximity, CONCENTRATION, and dispersion, and with optimization of spatial arrangements. Major branches of analysis are concerned with the location of primary (agricultural) activities, secondary (industrial) activities, and tertiary (service) activities. P.H.

Bibl: P. Haggett, *Locational Analysis in Human Geography* (London, 1965; Philadelphia, 1966).

Locke, John (English philosopher, 1632–1704), see under ANALYTICAL PHILOSOPHY; DETERMINISM; EMPIRICISM; ESSENTIALISM; HUMAN RIGHTS; IDEA; INTROSPECTION; NOMINALISM; PSYCHOLOGISM; REPRESENTATIONISM; SENSE-DATUM; SOCIAL COMPACT; SOCIAL CONTRACT.

locus (plural *loci*). Position on a CHROMOSOME occupied by one of a set of allelomorphic (see ALLELE) GENES. J.M.S.

logarithmic scale, see under SCALING.

logic.

(1) The study of INFERENCE. Logic does not simply describe the kinds or patterns of inference that are actually used; it is concerned with the rules of *valid* inference (see VALIDITY), by which those inferences whose premises really entail their conclusions (see ENTAILMENT) may be distinguished from those whose premises do not. Logicians, however, are not concerned with particular entailments except as examples, even though for each particular entailment ('This is red' entails 'This is coloured') there is a corresponding rule of valid inference (from 'This is red' infer 'This is coloured'), which can be applied on an indefinitely large number of occasions.

In the first place logic is *formal*. There are abstract patterns of inference of which an indefinite number of particular inferences, all of the same logical form, are instances (e.g., from 'No *A* is *B*' infer 'No *B* is *A*'). Logic may be said to have begun with the formulation of individual rules of this kind. Secondly, logic aims to be *systematic*. The first great logical systematizer was Aristotle, whose theory of the SYLLOGISM set out in a reasonably systematic (although not yet axiomatic – see AXIOMATICS) way all the rules for valid inference from two premises. The thoroughness of Aristotle's achievement obstructed the further development of the discipline, and its systematic elaboration caused it to be regarded as finally authoritative for more than 2,000 years and overshadowed logical discoveries in fields outside the range of his treatment. In the mid 19th century, however, Boole and De Morgan set out in mathematical form (see MATHEMATICAL LOGIC) an ALGEBRA of classes closely related to Aristotle's logic of predicative terms. De Morgan also started the logical study of *relational predicates*, traditional logic having restricted itself to *attributive predicates*; an attributive predicate is a quality, a relational predicate is a relation, or, in some people's usage, the word for a quality (e.g. an adjective) and the word for a RELATION (e.g. a transitive verb or a preposition) respectively. The major achievement of the modern period has been the mathematically rigorous system of Frege. The structurally similar, but less rigorous, system set out by Whitehead and Russell in *Principia Mathematica* (1910 onwards)

had the advantage of a simple notation, and the really fertile period in modern logic may be dated from its publication. The main ingredients of logic, as currently conceived, are (1) the logic of compound PROPOSITIONS or PROPOSITIONAL CALCULUS or TRUTH-FUNCTION theory and (2) the logic of predicates or PREDICATE CALCULUS or QUANTIFICATION theory. The logic of classes or SET THEORY is now generally viewed as the fundamental discipline of mathematics rather than as a part of logic proper. See also MATHEMATICAL LOGIC; MODAL LOGIC.   A.Q.

Bibl: W. C. and M. Kneale, *The Development of Logic* (Oxford, 1962); S. F. Barker, *The Elements of Logic* (London and N.Y., 1965); I. M. Copi, *Introduction to Logic* (London and N.Y., 3rd ed., 1968).

(2) In COMPUTERS, the digital circuits, built up largely from GATES, which form the CPU and parts of other units. Their characteristic feature is that the electrical state of each part of the circuit is stable only at a limited number of values, i.e. the output of such a circuit is the 'logical' consequence of the various INPUTS according to the rules of, say, BOOLEAN ALGEBRA. This number is most commonly two, and the logic is then BINARY. There is a continuing tendency for logic circuits to become smaller and faster, and to use less power. See also INTEGRATED CIRCUIT.   C.S.

logical atomism. A theory about the nature of the facts that constitute reality, devised by Russell (in *Philosophy of Logical Atomism*, 1918) and Wittgenstein (in *Tractatus Logico-Philosophicus*, 1922) and associated with the technique of philosophical ANALYSIS. That technique shows that some PROPOSITIONS can be analysed into others and so may be seen as theoretically dispensable abbreviations for them. The propositions in which analysis terminates reveal the actual structure of the facts which, if they obtain, make the propositions true. Wittgenstein, when a logical atomist, held that 'all propositions are TRUTH-FUNCTIONS of elementary propositions', in other words that *atomic* propositions, which are singular, affirmative, and categorical and consist of logically proper names of simple entities together with an attributive or relational predicate, directly picture their verifying facts, while *non-atomic* propositions conceal them. Analysis, then, reveals the structure of the world by exhibiting every kind of true or significant proposition as being an atomic proposition, or some assemblage of atomic propositions, in which only unanalysable words for simple individuals and properties occur. Russell's logical atomism was less thoroughgoing than Wittgenstein's, since he doubted the reducibility (see REDUCTION) to strictly atomic form of negative and universal propositions and also of apparently INTENSIONAL propositions about beliefs. The LOGICAL POSITIVISTS accepted the idea of a terminal class of propositions, constituting the part of language that is in direct contact with the world (calling them *protocol* or *basic*, rather than atomic, propositions) but saw them as direct, non-inferential reports of experience, rather than as pictures of facts.   A.Q.

Bibl: D. F. Pears, *Bertrand Russell and the British Tradition in Philosophy* (London and N.Y., 1967).

logical calculus. A systematic deductive presentation of a body of logical laws (see LOGIC) or truths of a broadly mathematical form. An ideally systematic form of presentation is that of an AXIOMATIC system. The chief logical calculi are the PROPOSITIONAL CALCULUS and the PREDICATE CALCULUS. Such calculi can be presented in non-axiomatic ways: with equal rigour and minimization of unproved assumptions by the technique of natural deduction (see DEMONSTRATION), or in a relatively informal way without the greatest possible economy of assumptions.   A.Q.

logical construction, see under REDUCTION.

logical empiricism. The philosophical school which, mainly in the U.S.A., immediately succeeded LOGICAL POSITIVISM as a result of the migration to that country, after Hitler came to power, of several leading members of the VIENNA CIRCLE, in particular Carnap. The change of name had a more than merely geographical point; it also signified some change of doctrine, most notably a remission of the anti-METAPHYSICAL fervour of the original logical positivists and a less polemical concentration on the task of articulating or reconstructing in a logically explicit and rigorous form the CONCEPTS and theories of various forms of discourse, above all MATHEMATICS and NATURAL SCIENCE.   A.Q.

Bibl: J. Jørgensen, *The Development of Logical Empiricism* (Chicago, 1951).

logical form, see under PROPOSITION, TYPES OF.

logical positivism. A body of philosophical doctrine developed from the late 1920s by the VIENNA CIRCLE under the leadership of Schlick and Carnap. It asserted the meaninglessness of METAPHYSICS, which it held to consist of all PROPOSITIONS that are neither verifiable (see VERIFICATION) by empirical observation nor demonstrable as ANALYTIC, and conceived PHILOSOPHY as consisting purely of ANALYSIS, conducted with the assistance of formal LOGIC with a view to the logical reconstruction of mathematical and scientific discourse. Most logical positivists regarded religious and moral utterances as metaphysical and thus as meaningless. There was disagreement within the school (1) as to whether the basic propositions in which philosophical analysis terminates (see LOGICAL ATOMISM) refer to immediate experience (the majority view) or to material objects (see PHYSICALISM); (2) as to whether probability should be interpreted in terms of CONFIRMATION or FREQUENCY or both; and (3) as to whether TRUTH is a relation of correspondence between propositions and extralinguistic reality or one of coherence between propositions. Logical positivism dissolved as a school at the end of the 1930s, but was continued in the U.S.A. in the slightly different form of LOGICAL EMPIRICISM.   A.Q.

Bibl: V. Kraft, *The Vienna Circle* (N.Y., 1953).

logical realism, see under REALISM.

logical syntax (or *syntactics*). The discussion of the logical properties and significance of linguistic expressions in terms that refer only to the expressions themselves and not to their relations to extralinguistic reality. Exaggerated claims on its behalf by Carnap were abandoned after the successful development of logical SEMANTICS, primarily by Tarski, in the mid 1930s.   A.Q.

Bibl: R. Carnap, *The Logical Syntax of Language* (London and N.Y., 1937).

logical types, theory of. A theory, devised by Bertrand Russell, to avoid the logical PARADOXES or ANTINOMIES which arise from *self-reference*. (For example, the statement 'This statement is false', if taken to refer to itself, is false if true and true if false. Likewise the class of classes that are not members of themselves is a member of itself if it is not and is not if it is.) The theory of types lays down that a class must always be of a higher type than its members and thus that to say of a class that it either is or is not one of its own members is meaningless. The conclusion that grammatically well-formed sentences may be neither true nor false but meaningless, that there are logical as well as grammatical restrictions on the possibilities of significant combination of words, has been widely influential. It lent force to the attack of the LOGICAL POSITIVISTS, with the VERIFICATION principle, on METAPHYSICS, and it has inspired broader, informal investigations into the possibilities of significant combination of words, investigations that have issued in modern theories of CATEGORIES. A.Q.

logicism. The school of MATHEMATICS which maintains that the fundamental CONCEPTS of mathematics can be defined in terms of the concepts, and its fundamental laws can be deduced from the laws, of LOGIC. It was the principal aim of both Frege and of Whitehead and Russell in *Principia Mathematica* to establish this point. The crucial phase of the project is the definition of NUMBER in terms of the logical notion of class. A natural number, for logicism, is the class of all classes which are 'similar' in the sense of being equinumerous. The number 2 is the class of all pairs and the statement 'There are two chairs in this room' means the same as 'The class of chairs-in-this-room is a member of the class of pairs'. GÖDEL'S THEOREM that in any system containing arithmetic there must be truths that cannot be proved within the system undermined the project of deriving all of pure mathematics from logic. A.Q.

logistics. All the activities and methods connected with supply of armed forces, including storage, transport, and distribu-tion of ammunition, petrol, food, and so on. The term is of American origin and came into general use during and after World War II by reason of the dominant position of the U.S.A. in both the wartime and post-war alliances. The word is now acquiring a more general use to connote the supply organization of non-military field operations such as mountaineering expeditions or famine relief organizations. A.F.B.

logograms, see under CONCRETE POETRY.

Logue, Christopher (British poet, *b*. 1926), see under JAZZ POETRY.

Loisy, Alfred (French linguist and theologian, 1857–1940), see under MODERNISM.

Lolita syndrome. A SYNDROME named after Vladimir Nabokov's *Lolita* (1955), whose theme is the unreasoning and self-destructive passion of a middle-aged man for a teen-age 'nymphet'. The condition is anticipated, in a psychologically more convincing manner, in the Chilean Vicente Huidobro's untranslated *Satyr, o El Poder de las palabras* (1939). M.S.-S.

Lombardo, Guy (Canadian musician, *b*. 1902), see under SWEET.

Lombroso, Cesare (Italian criminologist, 1835–1909), see under CRIMINOLOGY.

London Group. An association of British artists, founded in November 1913, incorporating the CAMDEN TOWN GROUP and certain smaller groups. Its first president was Harold Gilman; Sickert was a prime influence; the original members included Wyndham Lewis and other leading VORTICISTS. They tended to admire the POST-IMPRESSIONISTS, notably Gauguin, van Gogh, and Cézanne, but in later years their sympathies became more diverse and in many cases more conservative. The group is still extant. P.C.

Long, Richard (British artist, *b*. 1945), see under CONCEPTUAL ART.

Long March. The transfer of the Chinese COMMUNIST leadership and forces from southern China to the province of Shensi in north-west China under constant attack

from forces of the KUOMINTANG. Begun in October 1934, the Long March lasted over a year and has become one of the legendary events of modern Chinese history. During the course of it Mao Tse-tung was elected chairman of the Chinese Communist POLITBURO (January 1935), a choice which committed the party to basing the REVOLUTION on an army of revolutionary peasant GUERRILLAS operating from a rural base, not on the urban working class.   D.C.W.
Bibl: E. Snow, *Red Star over China* (N.Y., 1961; London, 1968).

long-range planning, see CORPORATE STRATEGY.

longitudinal. In PSYCHOMETRICS, adjective applied to a method or type of investigation in which selected variables are studied over time in the same sample of subjects, in contrast to *cross-sectional* methods, where similar variables are studied at different ages, but on different subjects at each age.   H.L.

Lonsdale, Dame **Kathleen** (British crystallographer, 1903–71), see under BENZENE RING.

loop gain. In CONTROL ENGINEERING, the degree of magnification of an input signal around a loop which is normally closed but which has been opened beyond the last element in order to measure such magnification.   E.R.L.

Lorca, Federico García (Spanish poet and dramatist, 1898–1936), see under LIVING THEATRE.

Lorenz, Konrad (Austrian zoologist and ethologist, *b*.1903), see under ETHOLOGY; IMPRINTING; RELEASER.

Lösch, August (German geographer, 1906–45), see under GEOGRAPHY.

Losey, Joseph (U.S.-born film director, *b*.1909), see under WPA.

Lotka, Alfred James (U.S. cyberneticist, 1880–1949), see under STABLE POPULATION.

Loubet, Émile (French statesman, 1838–1929), see under DREYFUS CASE.

Lovejoy, Arthur Oncken (U.S. philosopher, 1873–1962), see under HISTORY OF IDEAS; REALISM, CRITICAL.

Lowell, Amy (U.S. poetess, 1874–1925), see under EGOIST, THE; IMAGISM.

Lowell, Robert (U.S. poet, *b*.1917), see under MOVEMENT, THE.

Lowry, Thomas Martin (British chemist, 1874–1936), see under ACID.

LSD, see under ACID FASCISM; DRUGS; HIPPIES.

LSI (large-scale integration), see under INTEGRATED CIRCUIT.

Lubbock, Sir **John,** 1st Baron Avebury (British banker, politician, and naturalist, 1834–1913), see under THREE-AGE SYSTEM.

Lubyanka. The headquarters of the Soviet SECRET POLICE, on Dzerzhinsky Square, Moscow, containing the famous prison in which many of the leading 'State criminals' of the Soviet period have been held, and in whose basement they have been executed. It has become synonymous with the whole apparatus of interrogation, confession, and liquidation.   R.C.

Luce, Maximilien (French painter, 1858–1941), see under NEO-IMPRESSIONISM.

Lucie-Smith, Edward (British poet, *b*.1933), see under GROUP, THE; LIVERPOOL POETS.

Ludwig, Friedrich (German musicologist, 1872–1930), see under ISORHYTHM.

Lugard, Frederick John Dealtry Lugard, 1st Baron (British colonialist and explorer, 1858–1945), see under INDIRECT RULE.

Lukács, Georg or **Györg** (Hungarian philosopher and literary critic, 1885–1971), see under CHARACTEROLOGY; NEO-MARXISM; REIFICATION.

Luks, George Benjamin (U.S. painter, 1867–1933), see under ASHCAN SCHOOL.

luminodynamism, see under KINETIC ART.

Lumpenproletariat. Term coined by Karl Marx for the fluctuating antisocial elements within the poor of big cities from whom no CLASS identification or solidarity could be expected.   D.C.W.

Lunacharsky, Anatoly Vasilyevich (Russian author, publicist, and politician, 1875–1933), see under PROLETKULT.

Lunts, Lev Natanovich (Russian dramatist and essayist, 1901–24), see under SERAPION BROTHERS.

Luria, Alexander Romanovich (Russian psychologist, *b.* 1902), see under MENTAL RETARDATION.

Lutheranism. The Christian tradition begun when Martin Luther (1483–1546) inaugurated PROTESTANTISM. The Lutheran World Federation, mainly German, Scandinavian, and American, was formed in 1947. In these self-governing national or regional Churches some CATHOLIC practices, e.g. leadership by bishops, may be retained, but the dominating feature is the sermon, intended to proclaim God's grace. Luther's experience (much studied by modern scholars) convinced him that no one could become righteous before God through his own efforts; it was necessary to be 'justified' (accounted and then made righteous) by God's grace received through faith. This conviction has been at the heart of German Protestant THEOLOGY, which has thereby been liberated to embark on many intellectual adventures.   D.L.E.

Bibl: J. Pelikan, *From Luther to Kierkegaard* (St Louis, 1950); E. H. Erikson, *Young Man Luther: a Study in Psychoanalysis and History* (N.Y., 1958; London, 1959).

Luxemburg, Rosa (Polish-born revolutionary, 1870–1919), see under SPARTACISTS.

Luzi, Mario (Italian poet and essayist, *b.* 1914), see under HERMETIC.

lymph. A term improperly used to describe any free fluid contained within or expressible from the TISSUES; more properly the plasma-like fluid contained within lymphatic vessels (or *lymphatics*) which drain all the tissues into the venous system. Lymph, like plasma (see SERUM) with which it is closely in EQUILIBRIUM, is a clotting fluid which is propelled along lymphatic vessels by ordinary bodily movements. The many valves in lymphatics ensure that circulation is one way only, i.e. towards points of entry into the venous system. The characteristic cellular constituent of lymph is the *lymphocyte* which plays an important role in immunology (see IMMUNITY). All lymphatics, and therefore all lymph, pass through regional lymph nodes (in common parlance 'glands') on the way from tissues to blood system. An accumulation of lymph due to blockage of lymphatics or to prolonged inactivity is known as *lymphoedema*, of which elephantiasis is an extreme and highly abnormal example.   P.M.

Lyons, John (British linguist, *b.* 1932), see under LEXEME.

Lysenko, Trofim Denisovich (Soviet biologist and agronomist, 1898–1976), see under LAMARCKISM; LYSENKOISM.

Lysenkoism. The Soviet version of LAMARCKISM; named after Trofim Lysenko, whose views became dominant in Soviet BIOLOGY, and especially agricultural science, in the mid 1930s. Many adherents of Mendelian (see MENDELISM) GENETICS were dismissed and liquidated at this time, in particular Nikolai Vavilov, Russia's leading biologist. However, Lysenkoism only gained a complete monopoly in 1948, when the Central Committee officially decreed its correctness. Some criticisms of it were permitted during Stalin's last months, but it was reimposed under Khrushchev and it was only in 1964, and particularly after Khrushchev's fall, that it became totally discredited – though a number of Lysenkoist 'scientists' continue to hold research posts.   R.C.

Bibl: Z. A. Medvedev, *The Rise and Fall of T. D. Lysenko* (London and N.Y., 1969).

lysosomes, see under AUTOLYSIS.

lysozyme. An ENZYME present in egg white, tears, and certain other natural secretions which has the property of disrupting the CELL walls of a number of bacteria (see ANTIBACTERIAL; BACTERIOLOGY), though of none that are known to be seriously pathogenic. Lysozyme was discovered by Fleming in 1922, during his long search to find a substance having the properties now known to be possessed by penicillin. As with penicillin itself, the properties of lysozyme were investigated by Florey and Chain in the hope that the enzyme would be therapeutically usable – a hope which was unfortunately dashed. Lysozyme was the first enzyme whose molecular (see MOLECULE) structure was elucidated by the modern combination of X-RAY CRYSTALLOGRAPHY with conventional analytical techniques.

P.M.

M

Macbeth, George (British poet, *b*. 1932), see under SYLLABICS.

MacCaig, Norman (British poet, *b*. 1910), see under NEW APOCALYPSE.

McCarthy, Joseph (U.S. senator, 1908–57), see under McCARTHYISM; POPULISM.

McCarthyism. The practice, named after Senator Joseph McCarthy of Wisconsin (active during the 1950s), of accusing individuals, with little or no evidence, of membership of a group already rejected by society, thereby creating prejudice against the accused by the association of himself, his family, and his friends with such an ostracized group, and seeking to deny employment, civil rights, etc., to the individual on prejudicial grounds. In the case of McCarthy, the scapegoat group was the American COMMUNIST Party.
D.C.W.
Bibl: J. Anderson and R. W. May, *McCarthy* (N.Y., 1953).

McCartney, Paul (British songwriter and performer, *b*. 1942), see under BEATLES, THE.

McColl, Ewan (pseud. of Jimmy Miller, British actor, singer, and director), see under THEATRE WORKSHOP.

MacConochie, Captain (British penal reformer, 1787–1860), see under BORSTAL.

Macdonald, Dwight (U.S. author, *b*. 1906), see under MASS CULTURE.

Macdonald-Wright, Stanton (U.S. painter, *b*. 1890), see under ORPHISM.

McDougall, William (British psychologist, 1871–1938), see under HORMIC PSYCHOLOGY; PURPOSIVISM.

McGough, Roger (British poet, *b*. 1937), see under LIVERPOOL POETS.

McGregor, Douglas Murray (U.S. college president, 1906–64), see under ORGANIZATION THEORY.

McGregor, William York (Scottish painter, 1855–1923), see under GLASGOW SCHOOL.

Mach, Ernst (Austrian physicist and philosopher, 1838–1916), see under MACH NUMBER; MACH'S PRINCIPLE; MIND-BODY PROBLEM; NEUTRAL MONISM; SENSATIONALISM.

Mach number. The speed of a body flying through the atmosphere, divided by the local speed of sound. The Mach number (named after Ernst Mach) is less than 1 for *subsonic* speeds, greater than 1 for *supersonic* speeds, and greater than 5 for *hypersonic* speeds. Conventional aircraft fly subsonically (e.g. Mach 0.9 for the VC 10), but the Anglo-French Concorde flies at Mach 2.1. Considerable ENERGY is required to 'break the sound barrier' at Mach 1, because of the SHOCK WAVE which must be created. See also SONIC BOOM.
M.V.B.

Mach principle, see MACH'S PRINCIPLE.

machine aesthetic. A theory about the appearance of objects derived from a belief in how machine-made objects should look; the expression probably originated in Theo van Doesburg's statement: 'The new possibilities of the machine have created an aesthetic expressive of our time, that I once [in 1921] called "The Mechanical Aesthetic".' Objects were to look like machines (somewhat as in the paintings of Léger) and to look as if they were made by machines – which was taken to mean being made up from undecorated geometric solids such as the sphere, cube, cylinder, etc., even though this did not necessarily correspond with efficient machine production. See also BAUHAUS; FUNCTIONALISM.
M.BR.
Bibl: R. Banham, 'Machine Aesthetic' (*Architectural Review*, April 1955).

machine code, see under ASSEMBLY LANGUAGE.

machine intelligence, see ARTIFICIAL INTELLIGENCE.

machine translation (also called *automatic* or *mechanical translation*). The use of a COMPUTER to facilitate the production of translations between natural languages. The PROGRAM contains a set of rules for analysing the orthography, identifying the vocabulary, and parsing the syntactic structure of both source and target languages, and another set of rules which places these in formal correspondence with each other so as to establish semantic equivalences. The urgent need for rapid translation in science and TECHNOLOGY has been the main motive for work in this area, and there has been limited success; but a great deal of human sub-editing still needs to take place before translations are acceptable, and in the more aesthetic areas of language use little progress has been made. The difficulties are not so much those of INFORMATION STORAGE AND RETRIEVAL as the inadequacy of available syntactic analyses of languages. Future progress is very much dependent on advances in the appropriate branches of theoretical LINGUISTICS.   D.C.

machismo. Literally, maleness. The cult of virility in Latin America, especially Mexico, identified with a bull-like masculine aggressiveness, invulnerable and indifferent to the attacks of others, above all intransigent, withdrawn, inner-directed (see OTHER-DIRECTION), AUTHORITARIAN, absolutist; more loosely, pejorative term applied by its adversaries to the advocacy of an active, military, interventionist U.S. foreign policy (e.g. in VIETNAM).   D.C.W.
  Bibl: P. Stevens, 'Mexican Machismo: Politics and Value Orientations', in F. Moreno and B. Mitrani (eds.), *Conflict and Violence in Latin American Politics* (N.Y., 1971).

Mach's principle. The laws of NEWTONIAN MECHANICS are valid only if events are referred to certain special FRAMES OF REFERENCE. Observations show that these 'inertial frames' are those relative to which the distant matter of the universe is, on the average, not accelerating. In 1872

Mach suggested that the distant matter actually determines the inertial frames, by forces related to GRAVITATION; this principle was later given precise expression by Einstein in his general theory of RELATIVITY.   M.V.B.

Machtpolitik, see POWER POLITICS.

Macintosh, Douglas Clyde (U.S. theologian, 1877–1948), see under EMPIRICAL THEOLOGY.

Maciunas, George (U.S. artist), see under FLUXUS.

Macke, August (German painter, 1887–1914), see under BLAUE REITER.

Mackensen, Fritz (German sculptor, 1866–1953), see under WORPSWEDE.

Mackinder, Sir Halford John (British geographer, 1861–1947), see under GEOGRAPHY; GEOPOLITICS; HEARTLAND; MANPOWER.

Mackintosh, Charles Rennie (Scottish architect and designer, 1868–1928), see under ART NOUVEAU.

McLaughlin, John (U.S. painter, *b.* 1898), see under HARD-EDGE.

MacLeish, Archibald (American poet and dramatist, *b.* 1892), see under CRITERION, THE.

McLennan, John Ferguson (British lawyer and ethnologist, 1827–81), see under ENDOGAMY AND EXOGAMY.

Macleod, Ian (British politician, 1913–70), see under STAGFLATION.

Mac Liammóir, Mícheál (Irish actor and dramatist, *b.* 1899), see under GATE THEATRE.

McLuhan, Herbert Marshall (Canadian communications specialist, *b.*1911), see under HOT AND COLD; MEDIA.

Macmillan, Harold (British statesman, *b.*1894), see under CONSENSUS POLITICS.

McNamara, Robert (U.S. business executive and statesman, *b.*1916), see under CRISIS MANAGEMENT.

MacNeice, Louis (British poet, 1907–63), see under CRITERION, THE; HORIZON.

macrobiotics. The most doctrinaire of the ZEN-influenced food cults. The word itself has an illusory scientific flourish common to much neo-MYSTICISM (see also OCCULTISM; SCIENTOLOGY). First preached by Georges Ohsawa, the message of this harmless fad is that all foods are either *yin* or *yang* or both. 'Yin', the shadow, is the passive, feminine principle of life; 'yang', the sun, is the active, masculine principle. The diet, which is generally abstemious and loosely vegetarian, prescribes an equal balance of 'yin' and 'yang' components, thus ensuring that the body of the consumer is in harmony with the mystical unity of the cosmos (nothing so small as the world). Most foods contain both 'yin' and 'yang', so complicated cutting is necessary to preserve the balance: an onion is 'yin' at the top and 'yang' at the bottom; it therefore has to be cut vertically rather than horizontally. Fish are supposed to be eaten whole (so as to include their 'yang' heads and tails), and the term *whole food*, which is common to many spiritually inclined vegetarian diets, is a macrobiotic keyword, indicating the correct, equipoised balance between 'yin' and 'yang'.　　　　　　　　J.R.

macro-economics, see under ECONOMICS.

macrolinguistics, see under MICROLINGUISTICS.

macromolecule. A MOLECULE consisting of a large number (hundreds or thousands) of ATOMS. The term is generally reserved for molecules whose atoms are arranged in long chains, e.g. DNA (see NUCLEIC ACID) and related biochemicals connected with life, or the POLYMERS used in the PLASTICS industry.　　M.V.B.

macroregion, see under REGION.

macrostructure, see under EXCHANGE MODEL.

McTaggart, John Ellis (British philosopher, 1866–1925), see under NEO-HEGELIANISM; PANPSYCHISM; PERSONALISM.

Maderna, Bruno (Italian composer, *b*.1920), see under ELECTRONIC MUSIC.

Maeterlinck, Maurice (Belgian poet and dramatist, 1862–1949), see under SYMBOLISM.

Mafia. The Sicilian word for a clandestine criminal organization so deeply rooted in Sicilian rural society as to amount to a counter-government administering its own law and justice. Established among the Italian immigrant community in the U.S.A., the Mafia became the basis of various organized crime syndicates operating according to the same alternative code as in Sicily, the code of *omerta*, the Italian word for 'connivance'.　　D.C.W.
Bibl: F. A. J. Ianni and E. Reuss-Ianni, *A Family Business* (London and N.Y., 1972).

magic number. The numbers of NEUTRONS or PROTONS in an atomic (see ATOM) NUCLEUS which is highly stable against RADIOACTIVE decay. The magic numbers are 2, 8, 20, 28, 50, 82, and 126, and the stability arises from the filling of complete shells (see ELECTRON SHELL) of nuclear ENERGY LEVELS, in a similar manner to the chemical stability of the inert gases. See also PERIODIC TABLE.　　M.V.B.

magic realism. Term coined by Franz Roh in 1924 to describe certain works of the NEUE SACHLICHKEIT artists, particularly their Munich wing. The still, smoothly painted pictures of figures and objects, with their mildly disquieting SURREALISM-and-water impact, are akin to the NEO-CLASSICAL art of certain Italians (e.g. Felice Casorati) in the METAPHYSICAL wake, as well as to that of the Royal Academy. Among its practitioners were the former member of the NEUE KÜNSTLERVEREINIGUNG Alexander Kanoldt and the subsequent president of the Nazi Kunstkammer Adolf Ziegler. Though the names sound similar, the gay and decorative *Peinture de la Réalité poétique* associated with Maurice Brianchon and others is a very different affair.　　J.W.

magnetic resonance. When a system is magnetized, the ENERGY LEVELS associated with the SPINS of its ATOMS and NUCLEI split into a finely-spaced sequence. If an electromagnetic wave of RADIO FREQUENCY is applied, its ENERGY will be strongly absorbed by the system whenever the frequency is such that the wave is in RESONANCE with two energy levels. The pattern of resonances as the frequency varies is a valuable tool giving detailed information about the structure of matter. See also NUCLEAR MAGNETIC RESONANCE.   M.V.B.

magnetic storm. A period of rapid variation of the earth's MAGNETISM, which can upset long-distance radio transmissions and cause compasses to give false readings. Magnetic storms are caused by ELECTRONS and PROTONS emitted by the sun. See also VAN ALLEN BELTS. M.V.B.

magnetic tape. A thin, non-metallic tape (usually of the order of 0.01m wide), coated on one or on both sides with a very thin layer of ferromagnetic material (see FERROMAGNETISM). When such a tape is moved longitudinally at a fixed speed, very near to an electromagnet (known as a *writing-head*), magnetization is induced from place to place along the tape, varying in intensity with the variations in the electric current that is being fed to the electromagnet. When the magnetized tape is subsequently moved, again at constant speed, past a second electromagnetic device (known as a *reading-head*), the original sequence of electric currents is reproduced in the coil of the reading-head.

Magnetic tape is capable of very high accuracy of reproduction, and is used extensively for reproducing sounds (as an alternative to the gramophone record; see HI-FI) and for recording visual pictures seen by a television camera so that the tape can later be used to re-create the scenes on a television screen. Portable tape-recorders are now very popular for the enjoyment of music and other programmes that have been recorded on spools of tape specially housed in packages known as *cassettes* which can be inserted into the portable recorder and played back through a TRANSISTOR amplifier.

Magnetic tape is also used extensively in COMPUTING, as a form of backing STORE. The capacity is unlimited, but any attempt to use RANDOM ACCESS to this information tends to make the ACCESS TIME inordinately long. The consequent need to use SERIAL ACCESS makes the medium inconvenient for many applications. However, large business enterprises, postal systems, banks, etc. all depend a great deal on the tape storage system.   E.R.L.; C.S.

magnetism. The branch of ELECTRO-MAGNETISM concerned with magnetic materials and their interaction with electric currents. Magnetic FIELDS are produced by moving electric charges, e.g. the current in the windings of an electromagnet. Thus the magnetism of solid matter arises from the orbital motion and SPIN of atomic (see ATOM) ELECTRONS, while the earth's magnetism (*geomagnetism*) is thought to be due to currents in its rotating liquid core. The smallest magnetic entities are spinning ELEMENTARY PARTICLES; these are DIPOLES, and no isolated north or south poles have been found. See also ARCHAEOMAGNETISM.   M.V.B.

Bibl: E. W. Lee, *Magnetism* (N.Y., 1970).

magnetohydrodynamics. The ELECTRO-DYNAMICS of free ELECTRONS or IONS in a fluid (e.g. the IONOSPHERE). Motion of charges in the fluid can be produced by magnetic FIELDS, but it is not yet known whether a complete and stable *containment* can be achieved in this way (see PINCH EFFECT). The problem of containment is of tremendous technological importance, because, if the ENERGY of nuclear FUSION is ever to be tamed for peaceful purposes, the reacting substances must be kept together at temperatures so high that walls of any conventional material would vaporize. See also PLASMA PHYSICS.   M.V.B.

magnetostriction. A change in the dimensions of a piece of ferromagnetic material (see FERROMAGNETISM) resulting from magnetization by an externally applied field. The effect is greatest in nickel. Some materials expand in the direction of magnetization, others contract.   E.R.L.

magnitizdat, see under SAMIZDAT.

Magritte, René (Belgian painter, 1898–1967), see under SURREALISM.

Mahayana, see under BUDDHISM.

Mahler, Gustav (Austrian composer, 1860–1911), see under ROMANTICISM.

Mailer, Norman (U.S. author, *b.* 1923), see under BEAT.

Maillart, Robert (Swiss engineer, 1872–1940), see under CONCRETE; STRUCTURE.

Maillol, Aristide (French painter and sculptor, 1861–1944), see under NABIS.

main store, see under STORE.

maintained schools. In Britain, the term used to describe the schools which are 'maintained' by Local Education Authorities (L.E.A.s) from public funds and which provide education for the majority of children at both primary and secondary level. Such schools are distinguished from the INDEPENDENT SCHOOLS which receive no support from public funds and from the *direct-grant schools* (see SECONDARY SCHOOLS) which up to 1976 received a grant direct from the central Department of Education and were not under the control of L.E.A.s. Such direct grants were withdrawn by the Labour Government in 1976, and the schools which had received them were faced with the choice of becoming either maintained or independent schools.

Voluntary-aided schools represent a further category. They are voluntary in the sense that they have been founded by a voluntary religious body (most commonly, the Church of England or the Roman Catholic Church) and aided in the sense that they are supported by public funds. Running costs are met by the L.E.A., three-quarters of improvements and repairs from national funds, and the rest by the religious body. The voluntary body chooses two-thirds of the school managers, who have the right to appoint and dismiss staff and to determine the religious education given in their school.
W.A.C.S.; A.L.C.B.

maisons de la culture, see under ARTS CENTRE; CENTRES DRAMATIQUES.

maisons du peuple, see under ARTS CENTRE.

Major, Henry Dewsbury Alves (British theologian, 1871–1961), see under MODERN CHURCHMEN.

Makarios III (Greek-Cypriot archbishop and statesman, *b.* 1913), see under ENOSIS.

Makhno, Nestor (Russian anarchist, 1884–1934), see under ANARCHISM.

Malatesta, Enrico (Italian anarchist, 1850–1932), see under ANARCHISM.

Malcolm X (*né* **Little**; U.S. black leader, 1925–65), see under BLACK MUSLIMS.

Mâle, Émile (French art historian, 1862–1954), see under ICONOGRAPHY.

male chauvinism, see under SEXISM.

Malebranche, Nicolas (French theologian and philosopher, 1638–1715), see under SOCIOLOGY.

Malevich, Kasimir (Russian painter, 1878–1935), see under ABSTRACT ART; CUBO-FUTURISM; DONKEY'S TAIL; KNAVE OF DIAMONDS; MINIMAL ART; SUPREMATISM.

Malina, Judith (German-born U.S. actress, *b.* 1916), see under LIVING THEATRE.

Malinowski, Bronislaw (Polish-U.S. anthropologist, 1884–1942), see under ACCULTURATION; CONTEXT OF SITUATION; FIELD WORK; FUNCTIONALISM; MYTH; PHATIC LANGUAGE; RELIGION, SOCIOLOGY OF.

Malipiero, Gian Francesco (Italian composer, *b.* 1882), see under NEO-CLASSICISM.

Mallarmé, Stéphane (French poet, 1842–98), see under CONCRETE POETRY; IMPRESSIONISM; SYMBOLISM; TEL QUEL.

Malle, Louis (French film director, *b.* 1932), see under NEW WAVE.

Mallet-Stevens, Robert (French architect, 1886–1945), see under ARTS DÉCO.

Malraux, André (French author and politician, 1901–76), see under CENTRES DRAMATIQUES; HORIZON; IMAGINARY MUSEUM.

Malthus, Thomas Robert (British economist and demographer, 1766–1834), see under NEO-MALTHUSIANISM.

management. A term which can refer both to the group of people who manage an enterprise and to the process of managing – e.g. 'the management of Rolls Royce Ltd were questioned about the inadequate management of their finances'. In the first sense management means those senior managers whose decisions influence policy and affect the organization's relationships with its external environment. In the second sense, as a process, management is practised throughout every organization, from *top management* (concerned with CORPORATE STRATEGY for the enterprise in the longer term) through *middle management* (with functional responsibilities for production, accounting and finance, MARKETING, personnel, research and development, OPERATIONAL RESEARCH, and other services) to *operational management* (at the foreman or supervisory level).

Traditionally, management was identified with the running of business – a tough-minded, profit-orientated process – while the conduct of PUBLIC SECTOR organizations and social services was called *administration*. Today the need for effective management is recognized in government services, local government, hospitals and welfare organizations, the armed forces, educational establishments, and charitable bodies, as well as in business.

Management by exception is a type of MANAGEMENT CONTROL SYSTEM that reports to a manager only significant variations between actual performance and a predetermined plan, avoiding unnecessary detail and highlighting those situations which require attention. *Management by objectives* is a process of identifying needs and setting objectives for performance throughout an organization, with involvement and (it is hoped) commitment at all levels. See also the following entries.   R.I.T.

management control system. Procedures and methods of planning the expected performance in managers' areas of responsibility, monitoring and measuring the actual performance, and reporting discrepancies between the two for managerial action. Examples include budgetary control based on INPUT costs; profit-responsible centres treating managers as autonomous units responsible for financial OUTPUTS as well as inputs; various multiple-criteria approaches; and PPBS methods suitable for non-profit organizations. A management control system will reflect the organizational approach and the CORPORATE STRATEGY of the enterprise.   R.I.T.

management information system. The rigorous study of the information needs of MANAGEMENT at operational, tactical, and strategic levels. Although decision-makers have always needed information, such study is a recent development, concurrent with increasingly complex and interrelated decision situations, the use of a SYSTEMS approach, and the potential use of COMPUTERS. Until now, most efforts to employ computers in information systems have concentrated on information flows within the organization, i.e. on monitoring the basic resources of men, machines, materials, or money. Recently, however, COMPUTER SIMULATION and other modelling methods (see MODEL) have been used with the aim of increasing and improving information about the external environment also.   R.I.T.

management science. The body of quantitative methods that can be applied to MANAGEMENT problems; predominantly, but not exclusively, the field of OPERATIONS RESEARCH. Contrast with SCIENTIFIC MANAGEMENT.   R.I.T.

Bibl: W. J. Baumol, *Economic Theory and Operations Analysis* (London and N.Y., 2nd ed., 1965).

management studies. Studies related to MANAGEMENT. Management has, of course, been practised for as long as men have worked together to accomplish common tasks and needed to make decisions about scarce resources in uncertain situations. Only in the 20th century, however, has it been made a subject for serious study.

The measurement of work on the factory floor marked the beginning of so-called SCIENTIFIC MANAGEMENT. Then the foundations of the classical, or traditional, school of management thought were laid in the 1920s. This saw the process of managing as planning, control, coordination, organization, and leadership, quite distinguishable from the operating tasks that a manager might also undertake. Management was thought of in

MANIC-DEPRESSIVE PSYCHOSIS

hierarchical terms with responsibility and authority delegated and subsequent accountability for performance expected. Classical thinking is reflected in the *organization chart* which pictures the hierarchical chain of command. Positions may be identified as *line* or *staff,* line responsibilities being in the chain of command for decision and action, whereas staff positions are advisory. The *span of control* refers to the number of subordinates reporting directly to a manager.

Such ideas lie behind much of today's management practice and provide the conceptual underpinning of most MANAGEMENT CONTROL SYSTEMS. However, by the mid 20th century it had become apparent that management studied only as a set of functional activities was incomplete. Managers achieved their results through people. There followed a proliferation of ideas about the importance, for successful management, of understanding people, both as individuals and in groups. These viewpoints are referred to as the *behavioural approach* and classified as ORGANIZATION THEORY. Recently, an alternative set of insights into the process of management has been developed. This focuses on the use of information in decision-making, and is known as the SYSTEMS approach. Relevant concepts are also found in DECISION THEORY.   R.I.T.

managerial grid, see under ORGANIZATION THEORY.

managerial revolution. Phrase popularized by the ex-Trotskyite James Burnham in a book of that title (New York, 1941) predicting the rise of a new social CLASS, 'the managers', which would supplant the old capitalist class. Burnham saw Nazi Germany, the Soviet Union, and the NEW DEAL in the U.S.A. as variants of this new type and declared that 'the war of 1939 is the first great war of managerial society' as 'the war of 1914 was the last great war of capitalist society'. His class of managers was never precisely defined, but included production managers, administrative engineers (but not finance executives of corporations), government bureau heads, and the like. The prediction of the collapse of CAPITALISM was wrong. The 'theory' was highly simplified, and in the scope elaborated by Burnham it has been largely abandoned.

In a more restricted sense, however, the managerial revolution may be understood, in the usage of A. A. Berle and Gardiner Means (*The Modern Corporation and Private Property,* New York, 1933), as the shift *within* the modern corporation from the owner to the professional manager as the key figure in the enterprise. This is associated with a parallel change from 'ownership' to 'control' and with the decline of the importance of private property in contemporary capitalism.   D.B.

mandates system. A system by which the government of colonial territories taken from Germany and Turkey at the end of World War I was entrusted to the victorious powers Britain, France, and Italy under the supervision of a special commission of the LEAGUE OF NATIONS. The principal mandated territories were: *Class A*: the former Turkish vilayets of Iraq, Palestine, and Syria whose independence was to be provisionally recognized until they were able to stand on their own; *Class B*: the ex-German Central African colonies; *Class C*: German S.W. Africa, Samoa, New Guinea, and certain other small Pacific islands. Except in the case of *Class C* where the indigenous inhabitants were regarded as so primitive as to make this impossible, the mandates system involved a commitment to prepare the territories for self-rule. After World War II a different system of TRUSTEESHIP under UNO was adopted for the former Italian and Japanese colonies.   D.C.W.
Bibl: C. L. Upthegrove, *Empire by Mandate* (N.Y., 1954).

Mandelshtam, Osip Emilevich (Russian poet, 1891–1938), see under ACMEISM.

Manet, Édouard (French painter, 1832–83), see under IMPRESSIONISM; REALISM.

Manguin, Henri Charles (French painter, 1874–1949), see under FAUVES.

manic-depressive psychosis. A PSYCHOSIS in which an individual's behaviour alternates between extremes of mood. The manic phrase is characterized by hyperactivity and occasionally by violent outbursts; in the depressive phase feelings of inadequacy, sadness, and lack of physical coordination are manifested.   W.Z.

367

manifest function and **latent function.**
Contrasted terms applied to the purpose
served by a practice, custom, or INSTITU-
TION in a society. The two poles are not
always quite the same, and in some cases
only the context may determine whether
the intended distinction is (1) between a
manifest function of which the society's
members are aware and a latent function
of which they are not aware, or (2)
between a proclaimed (manifest) and a
real (latent) function.   A.S.

manifold, see under GEOMETRY.

Mann, Thomas (German novelist,
1875–1955), see under REALISM.

Mann, Tom (British labour leader,
1856–1941), see under SYNDICALISM.

Mannheim, Karl (German-British
sociologist, 1893–1947), see under
IDEOLOGY; IRRATIONALISM; KNOW-
LEDGE, SOCIOLOGY OF.

manpower. A term, coined by the geographer Halford J. Mackinder, for the
work force, with its quantitative and qualitative characteristics, available in a given
place or area.   J.G.

manpower planning, see under CORPO-
RATE STRATEGY.

Mansfield, Katherine (pseud. of
Katherine Mansfield Beauchamp, New-
Zealand-born story-writer, 1888–1923),
see under NEW AGE.

Manson, Charles (U.S. criminal, *b*. 1934),
see under ACID FASCISM.

Mao Tse-tung (Chinese Communist
leader, 1893–1976), see under CULTURAL
REVOLUTION; DICTATORSHIP OF THE
PROLETARIAT; EGALITARIANISM; GUER-
RILLA; HUNDRED FLOWERS; LONG
MARCH; MAOISM; RED GUARDS; RIGHT,
THE.

Maoism. In its personal aspect, 'the
thought of Mao Tse-tung'; as an IDEO-
LOGY, revolutionary strategy (see REVO-
LUTION), and political rule, the adaptation of MARXISM-LENINISM to Chinese
conditions ('Sinification of MARXISM').
The specific contribution of Mao and

the Chinese COMMUNISTS to revolutionary practice was, first, to shift the focus of
struggle from town to countryside, from
the urban workers to the peasantry.
Revolutionary action took the form of
GUERRILLA warfare which Mao skilfully
conducted until his victory in 1949, when
his peasant armies conquered the towns
after a protracted civil war (see also LONG
MARCH). In domestic policies, the characteristic traits of Maoism were reflected in
bold political and social initiatives aimed
at a radical transformation of traditional
China, its society and economy, from
agricultural reform and COLLECTIVIZA-
TION to the GREAT LEAP FORWARD and
the CULTURAL REVOLUTION. In foreign
relations, Mao reflected Chinese ETHNO-
CENTRISM. At an early stage he defied
Soviet advice on revolutionary strategy
and engaged in a struggle with a
Moscow-oriented faction. Later he presented the Chinese revolution as a model
for Asia and finally became involved in a
bitter dispute with the Soviet Union
whose leadership of the world Communist
movement he challenged.

This dispute led to the emergence of
various 'Maoist' groups abroad. Maoism,
unlike TITOISM, presented a challenge
from the LEFT and appealed to the
revolutionary elements of the NEW LEFT,
who were disenchanted with the Soviet
BUREAUCRACY and saw in Maoism an
alternative to the REVISIONISM and
REFORMISM of the SOCIAL DEMOCRATS. It
provided a guide to the PERMANENT
REVOLUTION (parallel to TROTSKYISM), to
the revolutionary war (confluent with
CASTROISM and Guevarism) and to
EGALITARIAN society (seen as being
created by Cultural Revolution). The
Maoist supporters abroad, however, presented a complex picture, some embracing
the Maoist ideological stand with enthusiasm, some with reservations. This led to
splits and factionalism within a number of
Communist Parties. Further difficulties
were caused by the shift in Chinese policy
from the Party to the State level, following
the abandonment of the Cultural Revolution. This shift has caused greater weight
to be given to China's foreign relations
than to the ideological struggle with the
Soviet 'social imperialists'; and President
Nixon's visit to Peking represented for
many Maoists abroad an ideological shock
comparable to the effect of the Nazi-

Soviet Pact on foreign Communists in 1939.　　　　　　　　　　　　L.L.

Bibl: S. R. Schram, *Mao Tse-tung* (Harmondsworth, 1966; N.Y., 1967); H. F. Schurman, *Ideology and Organization in Communist China* (Berkeley and Los Angeles, 2nd ed., 1968); S. R. Schram (ed.), *The Political Thought of Mao Tse-tung* (Harmondsworth and N.Y., rev. ed., 1969); R. H. Solomon, *Mao's Revolution and the Chinese Political Culture* (London and Berkeley, 1971).

mapping (in MATHEMATICS), see under FUNCTION; LINEAR.

maquette. French term for a scale MODEL, used in the English-speaking countries exclusively in its sense of a preliminary model for a work of sculpture.　　J.W.

Maquis. Originally the dense, almost impenetrable bush forest characteristic of the poor-soil mountainous areas of Mediterranean France. By extension, the word was applied to the bandits and outlaws for whom the Maquis provided so excellent a hiding-place, and during World War II to the armed GUERRILLA elements of the French RESISTANCE MOVEMENT against the NAZI German occupation.　　　　　　　　　D.C.W.

Marc, Franz (German painter, 1880–1916), see under BLAUE REITER; ORPHISM.

Marcuse, Herbert (German-U.S. political philosopher, *b.*1898), see under FRANKFURT SCHOOL; NEO-MARXISM; REIFICATION.

marginal costing. In MANAGEMENT, a comparison of costs based on the *marginal cost*, i.e. on the expenditure actually incurred by producing the next unit of a product or service; or, conversely, actually saved by not producing it. By contrast, *full recovery cost*, or *absorption cost*, includes both the direct expenditure incurred on the product (such as materials used and labour employed), which will vary directly with the volume produced, and an appropriate share of the overhead or fixed costs (such as staff salaries), which are constant for a period, irrespective of the level of activity or output.　　R.I.T.

Bibl: C. L. Moore and R. K. Jaedicke, *Managerial Accounting* (Dallas, 2nd ed., 1967).

marginal efficiency of capital. The productivity of the marginal, i.e. last, unit of CAPITAL employed on a given project. On the assumption that resources are used rationally this will be the contribution made to output by that unit of capital employed on the least productive task, since capital will be applied until the return no longer warrants the cost of its application. The concept of marginal efficiency is important in the theory of income distribution, since the earnings of capital, or any other factor of production, tend to be equal to its marginal efficiency.　　D.E.

Bibl: J. M. Keynes, *The General Theory of Employment, Interest and Money* (London and N.Y., 1936).

marginal principle. A verbal translation of a CONCEPT in the differential CALCULUS, used especially by economists, but applicable to the theory of rational behaviour in general. The essential point is that it is rational to extend all activities up to the point at which the *marginal gains* (or *marginal benefits* or *marginal returns*) are balanced by the *marginal costs* (some of which may be purely psychic). The applications of the marginal principle are not always obvious: thus, the long-run marginal cost of accommodating an extra tube-train passenger in the rush-hour might involve fresh INVESTMENT in equipment, and the concern might actually make a marginal loss on its peak-hour traffic, unless it adopted *marginal cost pricing*. For specific applications of the marginal principle see adjacent entries; for the view that society will benefit if prices are more closely related to marginal costs, see WELFARE ECONOMICS.　　S.BR.

marginal productivity theory of wages. The theory that the rate of pay for any group of workers tends to equal the change in OUTPUT that is associated with a variation of one unit in the size of that group. Suppose ten men are working with given equipment on a given farm: if their number were reduced to nine, all other things remaining the same, the net annual product of the farm would be reduced by a certain amount. This amount is the *marginal product* of the ten men. How big it is depends not only on the capability of the men, but on how much of the other factors, land and equipment, they are working with. If the number of workers

369

increases relatively to given amounts of those other factors, the marginal product of the workers is expected to decline: this is the law of DIMINISHING RETURNS. The theory holds that the marginal product and the wage tend to be brought into equality in two ways: if the rate of pay is fixed by negotiation or regulation, employers are taken to extend the number of workers employed up to the point at which the pay of an additional worker ceases to be offset by the increase in output associated with his employment; if what is fixed is the number of workers seeking employment, the rate of pay is taken to be adjusted by competition towards the marginal product of that number of workers. The theory has been criticized as inapplicable to the commonly found circumstances in which the number of workers per unit of equipment cannot be varied, but such variations can be made as new equipment is designed and as the relative amounts of different kinds of equipment are changed. It has also been criticized on the ground that managers do not explicitly estimate marginal productivities, but such estimation can be shown to be implicit in the minimization of cost per unit of output.   E.H.P.B.
   Bibl: J. R. Hicks, *The Theory of Wages* (London and N.Y., 2nd ed., 1963).

marginal rate of substitution, see under SUBSTITUTION.

marginal revenue product, see under CAPITALISM.

marginal utility. The UTILITY or value yielded by the marginal, i.e. last, unit of consumption. The CONCEPT is important in DEMAND theory, since under PERFECT COMPETITION the price of a product will be determined as far as demand is concerned by its marginal utility to the consumer. That is, the price which the consumer is prepared to pay for the product in general will be equal to the price which he is just prepared to pay for the last unit of that product which he consumes.   D.E.
   Bibl: G. J. Stigler, *The Theory of Price* (London and N.Y., 3rd ed., 1966).

Marighela, Carlos (Brazilian terrorist, 1904?–1969), see under GUERRILLA.

Marinetti, Filippo Tommaso (Italian poet and publicist, 1876–1944), see under CUBO-FUTURISM; FUTURISM; NEW AGE.

Maritain, Jacques (French philosopher, 1882–1973), see under NEO-THOMISM.

marker, see under CONSTITUENT ANALYSIS.

Marker, Chris (French film director, *b*. 1921), see under NEW WAVE.

market economy. A modern variant of *free economy* or *free enterprise*, all three terms describing an economy in which the greater part of the activities of production, distribution, and exchange are conducted by private individuals or companies rather than by the government, and in which intervention by the government is kept to a minimum. A market economy is characteristic of CAPITALISM in which the means of production are wholly or substantially in private hands, and incompatible with SOCIALISM in which they are (wholly or substantially) collectively owned.   R.H.

market research, see under MARKETING.

market socialism, see under ECONOMIC LIBERALISM; TITOISM.

marketing. The MANAGEMENT of the relationships between an organization and its customers and potential customers. Marketing aspects of a CORPORATE STRATEGY may include the mix and volume of products, pricing, distribution methods, guarantees and servicing, advertising and promotion, and sales force management. *Market research* seeks information on the characteristics of customers, potential customers, and competitors.   R.I.T.

Markov, Andrey Andreyevich (Russian mathematician, 1856–1922), see under PROBABILITY THEORY.

Markov process, see under STOCHASTIC PROCESS.

Markowitz, Harry Max (U.S. economist, *b*. 1927), see under PORTFOLIO SELECTION.

Marquet, Albert (French painter, 1875–1947), see under FAUVES.

MARS (Modern Architectural Research Society), see under CIAM.

Marshall, Herbert (British theatre director, 1890–1966), see under UNITY THEATRE.

Marshall, Sir John Herbert (British archaeologist, 1876–1958), see under INDUS CIVILIZATION.

Marshall, Norman (British theatrical producer, *b.* 1901), see under GATE THEATRE.

Marshall Plan. A proposal made by General Marshall, U.S. Secretary of State, in a speech at Harvard on 5 June 1947, offering American aid for European economic recovery, on condition that the European nations took the initiative in cooperative action. Under Anglo-French leadership, plans were evolved which led in 1948 to the launching of the *European Recovery Programme (ERP)* of 17 thousand million dollars and associated the American *Economic Cooperation Administration (ECA)* with the Organization for European Economic Cooperation (see OEEC) in its administration. D.C.W.

Bibl: H. B. Price, *The Marshall Plan and its Meaning* (Ithaca, N.Y., 1955).

Martenot, Maurice (French musician and inventor, *b.* 1898), see under ONDES MARTENOT.

Martin, Frank (Swiss composer, *b.* 1890), see under SERIAL MUSIC.

Martin, Karl Heinz (German theatrical director, 1888–1948), see under SPACE; VOLKSBÜHNE.

Martin du Gard, Roger (French novelist and dramatist, 1881–1958), see under ROMAN-FLEUVE.

Martonne, Emmanuel de (French geographer, 1873–1955), see under GEOGRAPHY.

Martov, Julius (Russian Menshevik leader, 1873–1923), see under BOLSHEVISM; MENSHEVIKS.

Marx, Karl (German revolutionist, sociologist, and economist, 1818–83), see under ALIENATION; ANARCHISM; ANOMIE; CLASS; COMMODITY FETISHISM; COMMUNISM; COMPARATIVE METHOD; DEHUMANIZATION; DIALECTIC; DIALECTICAL MATERIALISM; DICTATORSHIP OF THE PROLETARIAT; EGALITARIANISM; ETHNOMETHODOLOGY; FRANKFURT SCHOOL; HISTORICAL MATERIALISM; HISTORICISM; IDEOLOGY; INTELLECTUALS; INTERNATIONAL, THE; IRRATIONALISM; KNOWLEDGE, SOCIOLOGY OF; LABOUR THEORY OF VALUE; LUMPENPROLETARIAT; MARXISM; MATERIALISM; MESSIANISM; NEO-MARXISM; NEW LEFT; PERMANENT REVOLUTION; PROLETARIAT; REIFICATION; RELIGION; SOCIOLOGY; STRATIFICATION, SOCIAL; SUPERSTRUCTURE; WELTANSCHAUUNG.

Marxism. A doctrine based on the views of Karl Marx (1818–83) and Friedrich Engels (1820–95), who developed their theories under the influence of German philosophers, particularly Hegel (see DIALECTIC) and Feuerbach, of French SOCIALIST ideas emerging after the French Revolution, and of Ricardian economics (see CLASSICAL ECONOMIC THEORY) reflecting the experience of industrialization in England. All these strands of thought contributed to the Marxian view of history.

But Marx's critique of BOURGEOIS society transcended, both in its premises and in its implications, the ideas which influenced him. He visualized human history as a natural process rooted in man's material needs. This is the underlying idea of HISTORICAL MATERIALISM, which was seen by Marx and Engels as an equivalent of DARWINISM in biology. According to Engels, Marx 'laid bare' the laws of CAPITALIST development as part of general social EVOLUTION.

In this perspective the essential regularities of the historical evolution of mankind are seen to be the product of the modes and relations of production which 'in the last analysis' determine the nature of each historical epoch, the specific forms of property prevailing in it, and its CLASS structure. The struggle between classes over economic, social, and political advantages is limited by the mode of production which determines their position, but also provides an impetus for change. All history (except the stage of 'primitive COMMUNISM') is the history of class struggle.

Class antagonism is the impelling force leading to social REVOLUTION and to change in social forms of production, in property relationships, and in the distribution of goods ('the appropriation of social product').

Thus capitalism (according to Marxism) provided an unparalleled stimulus to the development of productive forces on a world scale, but is also producing conditions which hamper its further development. Through systematic impoverishment of the masses, by creating the PROLETARIAT, a class composed of exploited industrial workers selling its labour as a market commodity, it creates its own 'grave-diggers'. The proletariat, by overthrowing capitalism, will emancipate mankind as a whole. It will put an end to all class distinctions and all forms of exploitation. The ALIENATION of labour will cease with the transformation of the means of production into common property. The 'pre-history' of mankind, 'the Kingdom of Necessity' will be replaced by 'the Kingdom of Freedom'.

The Marxian vision of the future was given a 'scientific' demonstration in *Das Kapital* and other works which provide an analysis of the inner dynamics of bourgeois society. Marx and Engels believed they had discovered their system in the actual trends of 'real history'. But their expectations of revolution were disappointed in their lifetime. Nor has the industrial working class since fulfilled the revolutionary role which they attributed to it. Marxism as a doctrine has in fact proved to possess a greater appeal in countries where Marx's 'scientific' analysis did not apply, but where there was a favourable ground for revolutionary attitudes among other classes.

The working-class movement itself split into REFORMIST and revolutionary wings and this eventually led to the abandonment of the fundamental premises of classical Marxian analysis by both. SOCIAL DEMOCRATS have done so explicitly, Communists by disregarding these premises in practice while in theory elevating them to the status of a RITUAL and a DOGMA. In either case the 'scientific' part of the Marxian heritage proved irrelevant. Marxism as an IDEOLOGY became a total WELTANSCHAUUNG and a substitute for a religious attitude in a secular age. Its positivistic side (see POSITIVISM) has been

supplemented by the philosophy of DIALECTICAL MATERIALISM, which claimed to provide the key not only to history but to the universe. Yet the emergence first of socialist, then of communist REVISIONISM, and later of the NEW LEFT and of NEO-MARXISM, testified to the continuing intellectual difficulties faced in each case by those who wanted to reconcile Marxian analysis with Marxian vision, Marx's own theory with a reformist or a revolutionary practice, and Marx's prophecies with what he called 'empirical history'.

Marx's vision may not have withstood the test of history, but it has contributed powerfully to the UTOPIAN and revolutionary ideologies of our time by providing them with a 'scientific' certainty about its 'historical inevitability'. Marx (who said himself that he was 'not a Marxist') cannot be identified with all the vicissitudes of 'Marxism' as a doctrine. But his ambiguities and inconsistencies have been used by his followers for contrary interpretations. With the emergence of communist POLYCENTRISM the doctrine has splintered into more variants: Marxism in effect has been russified in LENINISM, sinified in MAOISM, latinized in CASTROISM, etc.

Marx's penetrating writings have influenced not only political movements but also the sociological perception of contemporary societies, and in this sense have contributed powerfully to the development of modern thought in general.   L.L.

Bibl: G. Lichtheim, *Marxism* (2nd ed., London, 1964; N.Y., 1965); B. D. Wolfe, *Marxism* (N.Y., 1965); D. McLellan, *Marx before Marxism* (London and N.Y., 1970).

Marxism-Leninism. A term coined during the ideological debates (see IDEOLOGY) after Lenin's death and used against Stalin's opponents in the struggle for succession. It redefined MARXISM in terms of LENINIST theory and practice as interpreted by Stalin. In the same way as the newly created Lenin cult, it served to legitimize Stalin's policies and to establish his own political and ideological authority (see STALINISM). In the post-Stalin era the concept served to legitimize successive Soviet leaderships. It has also provided an ideological basis for the condemnation of new heresies and the establishment of new orthodoxies in the polycentric (see POLYCENTRISM) COMMUNIST rivalries. In the Sino-Soviet conflict the Soviet side castigated the Chinese deviation from the ideological truth of Marxism-Leninism, while the Chinese Communists justified their stand as being based on 'Marxism-Leninism-Mao-Tse-tung-thought' (see MAOISM).

Just as Leninism modified some of the original tenets of Marxism, so Marxism-Leninism is being modified by its continuous adaptation to various local conditions and traditions, while its 'universal truth' is proclaimed by all concerned.   L.L.

Bibl: J. P. Plamenatz, *German Marxism and Russian Communism* (London and N.Y., 1954); L. Schapiro, *The Communist Party of the Soviet Union* (London and N.Y., 2nd ed., 1970).

Mascagni, Pietro (Italian composer, 1863–1945), see under VERISM.

maser (Microwave Amplification by Stimulated Emission of Radiation). A device producing high levels of power at precisely defined frequencies in the MICROWAVE region. The basic principle is that of the LASER, but the lower frequency means that the ENERGY LEVELS of MOLECULES as well as ATOMS can be used. Masers are used as oscillators in RADAR, and as amplifiers.   M.V.B.

Mashkov, Ilya (Russian painter, 1881–1944), see under KNAVE OF DIAMONDS.

Maslow, Abraham Harold (U.S. psychologist, 1908–70), see under EXISTENTIAL PSYCHOLOGY; HUMANISTIC PSYCHOLOGY; SELF-ACTUALIZATION.

masochism. A PERVERSION in which sexual pleasure is derived from being subjected to pain, either self-inflicted or inflicted by another. It was named by Krafft-Ebing after Baron Sacher-Masoch, who described it in *Venus in Furs* (tr. G. Warner, 1925).   W.Z.

mass. A fundamental QUANTITY in PHYSICS. In NEWTONIAN MECHANICS, the mass of a body is a measure of its ability to resist ACCELERATION when acted on by forces. Mass is also a measure of a body's ability to attract other bodies by GRAVITATION. The scientific unit of mass is the kilogram, and masses are measured by comparison with the standard, which is kept near Paris. Einstein's MASS-ENERGY EQUATION shows that mass is not indestructible.   M.V.B.

mass culture. A culture – known also as *popular culture*, and usually contrasted with *high culture* – which is identified with those products produced primarily for entertainment rather than intrinsic worth, for artifacts to be sold in the market in response to mass taste, rather than by patronage, and with items created by mechanical reproduction such as the printing press, gramophone records, and art illustrations. The argument about mass culture, which goes back as far as Wordsworth, was revived in the 1950s with the spread of affluence (see AFFLUENT SOCIETY) and the fear that advertising (see ADMASS) was shaping cultural tastes; but it took a very different form. Though traditionalists such as F. R. Leavis still decried the break-up of the 'organic' community, and LEFT-wing writers such as Dwight Macdonald declared that mass culture had corrupted high culture, yet other writers such as Richard Hoggart (in *The Uses of Literacy*) argued that English working-class culture had a vitality of its own, while sociologists such as Edward Shils argued that the spread of serious music recordings and art works had upgraded mass taste and brought more people 'into' society. In the 1960s the debate took another turn with the rise of POP ART. A group of critics associated with the American magazine *Partisan Review* (Susan Sontag, Richard Poirier) became advocates of 'the new sensibility' which denied the validity of any distinction between 'highbrow' and 'lowbrow' art, proclaimed film as the important art of the 20th century, and argued that the music of the BEATLES and the ROLLING STONES was as important as that of Schönberg for its evocation of popular responses. From that perspective, 'high art' is seen as ÉLITIST and artificial, and mass culture becomes a term of praise.   D.B.

Bibl: N. Jacobs (ed.), *Culture for the Millions?* (London and Princeton, 1961); J. Russell and S. Gablik (eds.), *Pop Art Redefined* (London and N.Y., 1969); S. Sontag, *Against Interpretation* (N.Y., 1966; London, 1967).

mass-energy equation. The famous EQUATION $E = mc^2$ deduced by Einstein from his theory of RELATIVITY. According to this theory matter is one of the many forms of ENERGY, and the equation predicts the amount of energy (E) that is released when a MASS (m) is annihilated (c is the speed of light in empty space). Conversion of mass takes place during NUCLEAR REACTIONS, such as FUSION and FISSION; it is responsible for the light of stars and the sun, and the power from NUCLEAR REACTORS and nuclear weapons. Only a small fraction of the mass involved disappears in these processes; if *all* the mass could be used up, the energy release would be far greater (e.g. the 'burning' of 1 kilogram every second would provide power at the rate of about 100,000 megawatts). M.V.B.

mass media, see under MEDIA.

mass society. A society in which the same tastes, habits, opinions, and activities are shared by the large majority of the population. Prerequisites for such a society include a high degree of INDUSTRIALIZATION, an extensive BUREAUCRACY, and powerful MEDIA. The negative features of mass society are the tendency to conformity, mediocrity, and ALIENATION, while positive observers point to enlarged areas of public PARTICIPATION and increased CONSENSUS over societal ends and means. See also ADMASS; MASS CULTURE. P.S.L.

mass spectrometry. A technique for separating the different masses in a beam of IONS of the same charge. The ions are sent through a vacuum chamber containing electric and magnetic FIELDS, where they are deflected in accordance with the laws of ELECTRODYNAMICS by amounts depending on their masses, and focused onto a photographic plate. The proportions of the different ISOTOPES in a sample of an ELEMENT may be measured in this way, and ATOMIC WEIGHTS may be accurately determined (see also ANALYTICAL CHEMISTRY). M.V.B.

Massachusetts Institute of Technology, see under MIT SCHOOL.

massive retaliation. A STRATEGY envisaging a strategic riposte to all identifiable provocations or attacks. The term was adapted from a phrase in a speech by John Foster Dulles on 12 January 1954 in which he said that 'the way to deter aggression is for the free communities to be willing and able to respond vigorously at places and with means of our own choosing'. This phrase was subject to contemporary misinterpretation, for American strategy never envisaged any form of automatic nuclear riposte; the message Dulles was trying to signal to the Communist powers was (*a*) that they could not hope to hide behind aggression by proxy; (*b*) that they could not expect to limit any ensuing conflict to thresholds chosen by themselves; and (*c*) that any attack on the United States would involve reprisals against their homeland. The substance of this policy was NATO doctrine from 1954 until 1966 when it was modified in favour of FLEXIBLE RESPONSE. It remains, however, official French strategic doctrine.
A.F.B.

Bibl: see under DETERRENCE.

Masson, André (French painter, *b*. 1896), see under SURREALISM.

materialism. In ONTOLOGY, the theory that everything that really exists is material in nature, by which is meant, at least, that it occupies some volume of space at any time and, usually, that it continues in existence for some period of time and is either accessible to PERCEPTION by sight and touch or is analogous in its causal properties (see CAUSALITY) to what is so accessible. This denies substantial existence (1) to minds and mental states, unless these are identified with states of the brain and NERVOUS SYSTEM, and (2), ordinarily, in the style of NOMINALISM, to abstract entities or UNIVERSALS. The first of these denials is the more crucial and controversial. It is generally agreed that statements about mental events are not equivalent in MEANING to statements about physical events in the brain. Yet the obviously close correlation between brain and mind suggests that the event that is described in mental language as experiencing a pain may be the very same event, under a non-equivalent description, as some event in the brain. EPIPHENOMENALISM is a kind of diluted materialism inspired, like the stronger form, by the intimations of complete DETERMINISM in the material world which, if true, would deprive mental events (conceived, in the manner of DUALISM, as radically non-material) of any causal efficacy.

The DIALECTICAL MATERIALISM of Marx and Engels repudiates the mechanistic account of the relations between events given by standard materialism and allows, as do other, biologically inspired forms of emergent EVOLUTIONISM, that mind, while originating in matter, is distinct in nature from it. Materialism excludes the possibility of disembodied minds, whether of God or of the dead. Materialists, from the time of Democritus to the present, have usually been NATURALISTS in ETHICS, but that does not commit them to materialism in the colloquial sense of an overriding interest in the acquisition of material goods and bodily satisfactions.   A.Q.

Bibl: F. A. Lange, tr. E. C. Thomas, *The History of Materialism* (3rd ed., London, 1925; N.Y., 1950); K. Campbell, *Body and Mind* (N.Y., 1970; London, 1971).

materialism, heroic, see under ZEITGEIST.

materialist conception of history, see HIS-TORICAL MATERIALISM.

materials science. The systematic study of matter in bulk, unifying the disciplines of METALLURGY, POLYMER science, RHEO-LOGY, and SOLID-STATE PHYSICS, and techniques such as CRYSTALLOGRAPHY, ELECTRON MICROSCOPY, and X-RAY DIF-FRACTION, in an attempt to understand matter and develop useful new materials such as CARBON FIBRES.   M.V.B.

mathematical economics, see under ECONOMETRICS.

mathematical induction (or *Peano's fifth postulate*). The assertion that if the natural NUMBER 0 has some property *P,* and if further whenever *n* has *P* then so does *n* + 1, *then* all natural numbers have *P*. It expresses the fact that the natural num-bers are precisely the things got from 0 by successive additions of 1, and is an impor-tant method of proof in NUMBER THEORY.
          R.G.

mathematical linguistics. A branch of LIN-GUISTICS which studies the mathematical properties of language, usually employ-

ing CONCEPTS of a statistical or algebraic kind (see STATISTICS; ALGEBRA).   D.C.

mathematical logic (also known as *sym-bolic logic*). A term that covers a range of interconnected disciplines. Traditional LOGIC, because of its concern with logical form (see PROPOSITION), has from the ear-liest times used symbols to replace words. Leibniz proposed that logical arguments could be reduced to algebraic manipula-tions; for traditional logic (in particular for SYLLOGISMS) this was accomplished by De Morgan and Boole in the mid 19th century (see BOOLEAN ALGEBRA). How-ever, as the work of Frege clearly showed, traditional logic does not suffice for mathematical argument. To support the thesis of LOGICISM he developed QUANTI-FICATION theory and the theory of SETS (classes) and gave them an AXIOMATIC formulation. Russell's PARADOX showed that the logic of classes needed a more mathematically sophisticated formulation (see SET THEORY). Up to this point the development of the subject-matter and the development of the symbolism for it went hand in hand, but since then the dis-tinction between the SYNTAX and the SEMANTICS of formal languages has become of crucial importance. Hilbert, in his version of FORMALISM, developed *proof theory*: through the study of formal proofs, considered simply as strings of symbols, he hoped to defend classical MATHEMATICS against the criticisms of INTUITIONISM by demonstrating that no proof would lead to a contradiction. GÖDEL'S THEOREM shows that such a demonstration must use new principles which are not formalizable in the system studied. Proof theory has thus become a recondite branch of mathematics; it is closely connected with RECURSIVE FUNC-TION THEORY. The study of the semantics of formal languages, begun by A. Tarski in 1936, has blossomed into *model theory*. Here one pushes the AXIOMATIC METHOD to its limit by studying *all* possible interpretations (MODELS) of a given for-mal language or system of AXIOMS. The results are particularly valuable for abstract ALGEBRA.   R.G.; A.Q.

Bibl: G. Boole, *The Laws of Thought* (London, 1854; London and Chicago, 1952); A. Church, *Introduction to Mathematical Logic* (Princeton, 1956);

MATHEMATICAL PSYCHOLOGY

J. N. Crossley *et al., What is Mathematical Logic?* (London, 1972).

mathematical psychology. A branch of PSYCHOLOGY concerned with devising statistical procedures (see STATISTICS) for extracting information from psychology data, and with constructing COMPUTER or mathematical MODELS that seek to simulate or represent human behaviour. See also COMPUTER SIMULATION.   J.S.B.

Bibl: G. A. Miller, *Mathematics and Psychology* (London and N.Y., 1964).

mathematical structure. Before the 19th century MATHEMATICS dealt with objects that belonged to a limited variety of well-defined species (e.g. geometric points, whole NUMBERS, real numbers) whose fundamental laws were given by intuition. Where intuition was lacking (e.g. COMPLEX NUMBERS) the 'objects' were treated with suspicion. In the 19th and 20th centuries there has been an enormous enrichment of mathematical imagination. New objects and new species were introduced, sometimes by formal postulates (e.g. non-Euclidean GEOMETRIES, QUATERNIONS), sometimes by construction (GROUPS were first introduced as sets of PERMUTATIONS), sometimes by new intuitions (e.g. the sets of Cantorian SET THEORY), often by a combination of these approaches. Gradually the AXIOMATIC METHOD emerged as the preferred way of handling the multitude of notions, each of which is seen as a particular case of the general CONCEPT (due to BOURBAKI) of mathematical structure. A *first-order structure* is defined by specifying a SET *A* of *elements* (e.g. the points of a line, the natural numbers) together with certain RELATIONS (e.g. betweenness) and/or certain FUNCTIONS (e.g. addition). For *higher-order structures* one specifies in addition certain relations of relations, functions of functions, and so on. What is significant to the pure mathematician is the pattern formed by the specified relations, functions, etc. All ISOMORPHIC structures will exhibit the same pattern; so one defines the corresponding *abstract mathematical structure* (see EQUIVALENCE RELATION). Here the elements are colourless, structureless individuals, and the specified relations etc. are defined purely extensively – by means of (possibly INFINITE) lists and tables. This means that totally arbitrary or chaotic patterns of relations etc. are counted as structures. Mathematically significant structures are singled out by imposing AXIOMS which the relations etc. are required to satisfy. The axioms may determine a unique abstract structure; more often they determine a whole family of similar structures (for examples see GROUPS and ORDERING RELATIONS). Such a family may itself be treated as a structure; see CATEGORY THEORY.   R.G.

Bibl: N. W. Gowar, *Basic Mathematical Structures* (London, 1973); R. O. Gandy, 'Structure in Mathematics', in E. D. Robey (ed.), *Structuralism* (Oxford, 1973).

mathematics. Until the mid 19th century the subject was correctly described as the science of NUMBER and QUANTITY (including the dimensional quantities of GEOMETRY). The thesis of LOGICISM and the introduction of the unifying CONCEPT of MATHEMATICAL STRUCTURE suggested a redefinition: the study of SETS and RELATIONS. The rise of the AXIOMATIC METHOD and of FORMALISM led some to describe it as the drawing of correct INFERENCES from AXIOMS. Both of these last views (which have been influential in the NEW MATHEMATICS) are disastrously misleading because they emphasize trivial facets and conceal what is important. Significant structures and difficult theorems are not discovered by playing around with relations and formal inferences. They are found by using imagination, intuition, and experience, and are often, initially, logically incoherent; logical packaging comes later. (A good mathematician once said: 'Test of good mathematician – how many bad proofs.') The standards of precision and rigour today are high, but this is not what makes 20th-century mathematics a supreme achievement of the human intellect.

Mathematics arises from trying to solve problems. The problems come from three primary directions: (1) from the external world – the source of GEOMETRY, CALCULUS, and parts of TOPOLOGY; (2) from intellectual playfulness – from this comes NUMBER THEORY, PROBABILITY THEORY, much of ALGEBRA and COMBINATORIAL MATHEMATICS (see FOUR-COLOUR CONJECTURE), some of topology (see MÖBIUS BAND); (3) from reflecting on the power and the limitations of our intellect –

see MATHEMATICAL LOGIC, INFINITY, GÖDEL'S THEOREM, RECURSIVE FUNCTION THEORY. The efforts to solve these primary problems produce not only manipulative techniques (such as ALGEBRA and the use of DIFFERENTIAL EQUATIONS, VECTORS, MATRICES, BOOLEAN ALGEBRA) but also new concepts and patterns of thought (for examples see COMPLEX FUNCTION THEORY, GEOMETRY, GROUP, SET THEORY, TOPOLOGY), which in turn produce new problems. It is these new patterns of thought, at one remove from the primary problems, which form the rich and intricate heart of mathematics. Because these patterns have been formed by *our* intellect, and so are conformable to our understanding, they modify or even revolutionize our view and knowledge of the external world. The theory of groups was invented to solve problems of pure algebra; it is now a part of the physicist's view of nature (see TRANSFORMATION; PARITY). R.G.

Bibl: E. Kasner and J. Newman, *Mathematics and the Imagination* (N.Y., 1940; London, 1949); R. Courant and H. Robbins, *What is Mathematics?* (London, 1941); L. Hogben, *Mathematics for the Million* (4th ed., London, 1967; N.Y., 1968); M. Kline (intr.), *Mathematics in the Modern World: Readings from Scientific American* (San Francisco, 1968); J. Singh, *Mathematical Ideas* (London, 1972); M. Kline, *Mathematical Thought from Ancient to Modern Times* (N.Y., 1972).

Mathews, Shailer (U.S. theologian, 1863–1941), see under EMPIRICAL THEOLOGY.

Matisse, Henri (French painter, 1869–1954), see under ART SACRÉ; FAUVES; NEO-CLASSICISM.

matrix. In MATHEMATICS an $m \times n$ matrix A is a rectangular array of objects (usually NUMBERS) which has m rows and n columns, e.g. A might give the COEFFICIENTS in a set of linear EQUATIONS, or the components of a set of VECTORS. If this was all, it would be nothing more than a handy piece of jargon. But in fact a matrix can always be considered as a linear mapping from an n-dimensional to an m-dimensional vector space. This gives rise to various operations on matrices; in particular, matrix 'multiplication' corres-

ponds to the composition of FUNCTIONS. Problems about linear functions and equations can then be described in terms of these operations, and they in turn can be described in terms of algebraic manipulations on the entries. In this connection the *determinant* of a matrix A is of great value. It is a number computed from the entries and is zero unless the matrix is square (i.e. unless $m = n$); division by A is possible if and only if the determinant is non-zero. R.G.

matrix mechanics. An alternative formulation of QUANTUM MECHANICS which does not involve a WAVE FUNCTION, devised by Heisenberg in 1925. A dynamical QUANTITY (e.g. MOMENTUM or SPIN) is represented mathematically by a MATRIX, instead of a number as in NEWTONIAN MECHANICS. These matrices form the basis of calculations aimed at predicting experimentally-measurable quantities, such as the intensities of lines in SPECTROSCOPY, the HALF-LIVES of RADIOACTIVE decay, and the ENERGY LEVELS of ATOMS. M.V.B.

matrix organization, see under ORGANIZATION THEORY.

Maturana, Humberto (Chilean biologist, *b.* 1928), see under AUTOPOIESIS.

Mauriac, François (French novelist, 1885–1970), see under INTELLECTUALS.

Maurras, Charles (French political theorist, 1868–1952), see under ACTION FRANÇAISE; INTELLECTUALS.

Maus, Octave (Belgian art critic, 1856–1919), see under VINGT, LES.

Mauss, Marcel (French sociologist and anthropologist, 1872–1950), see under GIFT.

Max-Müller, Friedrich, see MÜLLER, Friedrich Max.

Maxwell, James Clerk (Scottish physicist, 1831–79), see under ELECTROMAGNETISM; STATISTICAL MECHANICS.

Maxwell Davies, Peter, see DAVIES, Peter Maxwell

May, Rollo Reese (U.S. psychoanalyst, *b.* 1909), see under EXISTENTIAL PSYCHOLOGY.

Mayakovsky, Vladimir (Russian poet, 1893–1930), see under CONSTRUCTIVISM; CUBO-FUTURISM; SOCIALIST REALISM.

Mayer, Hans (German literary critic, *b.* 1907), see under GRUPPE 47.

Mayo, Charles and **Elizabeth** (British educationists, 1792–1846 and 1793–1865), see under PESTALOZZI METHODS.

Maysles, Al and **David** (U.S. film directors, *b.* 1926 and 1932), see under CINÉMA-VÉRITÉ.

Mazzini, Giuseppe (Italian revolutionary and political thinker, 1805–72), see under NATIONALISM.

Mead, George Herbert (Australian-U.S. psychologist, 1880–1949), see under CHICAGO SCHOOL; ETHNOMETHODOLOGY; ROLE, ROLE THEORY; SYMBOLIC INTERACTION.

mean. The mean of a SET of values is a further value calculated from them as a typical or representative value for the set; the word 'average' is sometimes used as a synonym. The most important type is the *arithmetic mean*, given by adding the values together and dividing the sum by the number n of summands. The *geometric mean* is the nth root of the product of the values, and the *harmonic mean* is the reciprocal of the arithmetic mean of the reciprocals; geometric and harmonic means are useful only when all the values involved are positive. In any technical context 'mean' (unqualified) denotes arithmetic mean: thus in STATISTICS the *sample mean* is the arithmetic mean of the observations making up the SAMPLE (see also MEASURE OF LOCATION). A *weighted arithmetic mean* is obtained by multiplying each value by some non-negative *weight* before summation and then dividing the sum of the products by the sum of the weights. R.SI.

mean deviation. In STATISTICS, the expected absolute value of the difference between the observed value of a RANDOM VARIABLE and a measure of its location (see MEASURE OF LOCATION). R.SI.

meaning. The sense, intension, or CONNOTATION of linguistic expressions, whether sentences as wholes or logically isolable parts of sentences; to be distinguished from the connected, but nevertheless different, reference, extension, or denotation of expressions. The meaning of a sentence is a function of the meaning of its constituents. The meaning of an expression is the rules which determine its use in discourse: semantic rules (see SEMANTICS) connecting it to things, properties, states of affairs, etc., and syntactical rules (see SYNTAX) governing its possibilities of combination with, and its logical RELATIONS to, other expressions. For a person to know the meaning of a word is for him to know the rules of its use; for a word to have a meaning is for there to be, among some group of speakers, a practice of using it in accordance with a set of rules. To identify the meaning of a word with the rules connecting it to objects in the world is not to say that these objects themselves are its meaning any more than the rules of a game are to be identified with the goalposts, wickets, and so forth with which the basic operations of the game are connected by the rules. Philosophical theorists of meaning, however, have an inveterate tendency to identify meanings either with the ordinary objects to which meaningful words refer or with more unusual entities specially recruited for the task. Those who take the ordinary object or objects referred to to be the meaning of a term overlook the fact that the bearer of a name is not its meaning: two names that do not mean the same can have the same bearer. Among the unordinary objects held to be the meanings of terms are such abstract entities as UNIVERSALS and CONCEPTS and such mental entities as images. A.Q.

Bibl: W. P. Alston, *Philosophy of Language* (Englewood Cliffs, N.J., 1964).

meaning-relation (also called *sense relation* or *semantic relation*). In LINGUISTICS, (1) a specific semantic association regularly interrelating sets of words in the LEXICON of a language, e.g. synonymy, antonymy (see SEMANTICS, SEMANTIC-FIELD THEORY); (2) more recently, the semantically relevant interrelationships between grammatical classes and structures, as well as between single words, e.g. the relations postulated by CASE GRAMMAR. D.C.

Means, Gardiner (U.S. economist, *b.* 1890), see under MANAGERIAL REVOLUTION.

measure of location. In STATISTICS, an empirical DISTRIBUTION is often described by giving a typical value, e.g. 'Men are about 175 cm in height'. Such a value is called a *measure of location* or *norm* (for other meanings of the latter term see NORM). Measures of location in common use include the MEAN (or EXPECTATION), *median* (see PERCENTILE), MODE, and *mid-range* (see DISTRIBUTION). R.SI.

measure theory. In MATHEMATICS, a branch of ANALYSIS (sense 1) which seeks to define notions of length, area, volume for 'figures' which are so intricate or unnatural that simple-minded definitions do not apply. The subject is closely bound up with INTEGRATION and with PROBABILITY THEORY. In particular, the introduction in 1902 of *Lebesgue measure* (and a corresponding *Lebesgue integral*) cleared up many anomalies of the traditional theory. R.G.

mechanical jurisprudence, see CONCEPTUALISM.

mechanical translation, see MACHINE TRANSLATION.

mechanics. The branch of PHYSICS dealing with the motion of matter. The subject is divided into two parts: *kinematics*, consisting of the precise geometrical description of position, velocity, ACCELERATION, ORBITS, etc.; and *dynamics*, where the causes of motion are analysed in terms of forces, interactions between objects, etc.

There are three main theories of mechanics in current use: NEWTONIAN MECHANICS is valid for systems which are large in comparison with ATOMS, moving slowly in comparison with light, and not subjected to very strong GRAVITATIONAL fields (such as those near BLACK HOLES). RELATIVITY mechanics includes Newtonian mechanics as a special case, and is

also valid near the speed of light and for objects strongly attracted by gravity; it breaks down on the atomic scale. QUANTUM MECHANICS also includes Newtonian mechanics, but remains valid for atomic and NUCLEAR systems. A completely satisfactory fusion of relativity and quantum mechanics has not yet been achieved.

Sometimes the term mechanics is used in a restricted sense, to refer to the purely Newtonian theory required for ASTRONOMY (planetary orbits etc.) and ENGINEERING (bridges, machines, vehicles, etc.). M.V.B.

Bibl: R. H. March, *Physics for Poets* (N.Y., 1970).

mechanisation, see MECHANIZATION.

mechanism. The theory that all causation is, in Aristotle's terminology, *efficient*, i.e. that for an event to be caused is for its occurrence to be deducible from the antecedent (in some cases contemporaneous) condition in which it occurs, together with the relevant universal laws of nature. The traditional opponent of mechanism is TELEOLOGY, the view that some, perhaps all, events must be explained in terms of the purposes which they serve, and thus that the present is determined by the future rather than by the past. Other views opposed to mechanism are ORGANICISM, the biological doctrines of EMERGENCE and VITALISM, and the position of the dominant school of quantum physicists (see QUANTUM MECHANICS). A.Q.

mechanization. The central technological feature of INDUSTRIALIZATION. Men have always sought to enhance their power and lighten their labour by mechanical means (levers, wheels, pulleys, etc.) and by harnessing natural energies (windmills, watermills, etc.). In the 18th century, however, technological developments, notably in METALLURGY, made it possible to harness *hidden* energies (steam, gas, electricity, nuclear energy) and thus to power machines capable of performing certain routine skills automatically and much more rapidly than was possible by hand. Over the greater part of industry, mechanization replaced the craftsman by the 'operative', thus transforming the nature of work, attitudes to work, and a wide range of human relationships. Blake, William Morris, and D. H.

Lawrence are among those writers who in different ways have emphasized the dehumanizing effects of mechanization; to their fears have been added that of massive unemployment resulting from AUTOMATION. See also MODERNIZATION. R.F.

Mechnikov, Ilya (Russian bacteriologist, 1845–1916), see under GERONTOLOGY; PHAGOCYTES.

Medawar, Sir **Peter Brian** (British zoologist, b.1915), see under GENETICISM.

media. A generic term used to indicate systems or vehicles for the transmission of information or entertainment such as radio, television, newspapers and magazines, hoardings, films, books, records, and tapes. Of these, the ubiquitous television, radio, and newspapers are generally classified as the *mass media*. Unlike the others, they form part of man's total ENVIRONMENT in MASS SOCIETY and cannot be ignored without conscious and sustained effort; far more commonly their use engenders a degree of passivity which makes them efficient for the moulding of tastes and preferences. Marshall McLuhan, however, has argued in recent years that the form of the media has a more significant effect on society and knowledge than the contents carried.
Mixed media is a recent term for the long-established CONCEPT (cf. GESAMT-KUNSTWERK) of combining more than one form or area of communication, usually for dramatic effect. Thus opera combines drama, music, and singing, while *son et lumière* presentations combine light effects, narration, drama, and music. In contemporary terms, Andy Warhol's mid-1960s 'Exploding Plastic Inevitable' was the first in a succession of mixed-media presentations in which *light shows* (projected variations of pattern and colour either on a random basis or linked with the rhythm of music), films, video playback, and music were combined. Today many forms of artistic expression such as plays, concerts, and art exhibitions utilize mixed-media techniques. P.S.L.
Bibl: M. McLuhan, *Understanding Media* (London and ·N.Y., 1964).

median, see under PERCENTILE.

Medina, Ernest L. (U.S. army officer, b.1936), see under MY LAI.

medium-scale integration, see under INTEGRATED CIRCUIT.

Megale Idea, see under ENOSIS.

megalithic. Constructed of large stones: an adjective applied to a wide range of prehistoric structures including stone circles (e.g. Stonehenge), standing stones and alignments, and many CHAMBER TOMBS. It used to be thought that megalithic structures were culturally connected, developing in the East and spreading by DIFFUSION to many parts of Europe; hence the terms 'megalithic religion' and 'megalithic saints'. More recently they have tended to be regarded rather as the outcome of a widespread constructional technique, though cultural connection between some areas adopting megalithic structures is still implied. B.C.

megalomania. In ABNORMAL PSYCHOLOGY, a pathological state in which the individual over-evaluates his own importance. W.Z.

megalopolis. Ancient Greek word for 'great city', revived since 1957 by Jean Gottmann to describe the American urban complex stretching from Boston to Washington. It has been accepted as meaning huge urban regions formed by chains of metropolitan areas. Gottmann saw in it a new pattern in the organization of inhabited space, a vast and dense concentration due to the evolution of society towards white-collar and transactional work and to the gregarious nature of people seeking opportunity. Other megalopolitan regions have been described in Japan, in north-west Europe, and along the Great Lakes. J.G.
Bibl: J. Gottmann, *Megalopolis* (N.Y., 1961); H. W. Eldredge (ed.), *Taming Megalopolis* (2 vols., N.Y., 1967).

megastructure. In architecture, a large, multi-storey framework, normally in dense urban situations, which would embrace different kinds of activities and allow different spaces to take on a variety of forms, changing while the megastructure remained. Such notions were put forward in the 1960s by the Archigram

Group in England, by Yona Friedman in France, and by the Metabolist Group in Japan. They are an enlargement and extension of Le Corbusier's original project of 1947–8 for the *Unité d'Habitation* at Marseilles where 'bottles' (dwellings) were to fit within a 'bin' (structural framework). Their enormous financial cost and likely high social cost have so far prevented any from being built. M.BR.
   Bibl: J. Dahinden, tr. G. Onn, *Urban Structures for the Future* (London and N.Y., 1972).

megaton. One thousand KILOTONS. M.V.B.

Meinhof, Ulrike (German terrorist, 1934–76), see under NEW LEFT.

meiosis. In GENETICS, two successive CELL divisions (forming a single *reduction division*) as a consequence of which the GAMETES (ova and spermatozoa) contain half the number of CHROMOSOMES present in the cells of the organism, female or male, that produces them; when fertilization occurs, this HAPLOID number is restored to the DIPLOID number. In meiosis one chromosome of each pair passes at random into one of two gametes; one of which will thus have a paternal and the other a maternal chromosome. For the genetic implications of this process see MENDEL'S LAWS. P.M.

melancholia, see DEPRESSION (2).

melanism. The occurrence of black pigmentation in organisms that are normally light-coloured – particularly in moths and in consequence of industrial processes. The black pigments in most coloured animals including human beings are *melanins* – oxidation products of the AMINO ACIDS dihydroxyphenylalanine (DOPA) or tyrosine. P.M.

Melville, Arthur (Scottish painter, 1855–1904), see under GLASGOW SCHOOL.

memory (of a COMPUTER), see STORE.

Mencken, Henry Louis (U.S. author, 1880–1956), see under BIBLE BELT.

Mendel, Gregor Johann (Austrian horticulturalist, 1822–84), see under GENE; GENETICS; MENDELISM; MENDEL'S LAWS.

Mendeleev, Dmitri Ivanovich (Russian chemist, 1834–1907), see under PERIODIC TABLE.

Mendelism. The branch of GENETICS dealing with the SEGREGATION of characters in sexual crosses of DIPLOID organisms; by extension, the theory of heredity deriving originally from the work of Gregor Mendel (1865). See also MENDEL'S LAWS. J.M.S.
   Bibl: C. Stern and E. R. Sherwood (eds.), *The Origin of Genetics* (London and San Francisco, 1966).

Mendel's laws. In GENETICS, the laws of inheritance, specifically for inheritance in DIPLOID organisms in the absence of LINKAGE. Mendel did not himself formulate his discovery (1865) in one or a series of laws, but today his findings are often summed up in two laws: of SEGREGATION, by which a hybrid or *heterozygote* transmits unchanged to each GAMETE one or other of the two factors in respect of which its parental gametes differed; and of *independent assortment*, according to which factors concerned with different characteristics are recombined at random in the gametes. Mendel's laws are now known to follow from the way in which CHROMOSOMES and therefore genetic factors are apportioned to gametes and therefore the next generation. In bisexual organisms the chromosomes are present in pairs (in man, 23 pairs); within each pair one member has derived from each parent. In the formation of gametes these pairs are separated, and each gamete contains only one chromosome from each pair (e.g. a human gamete contains 23 instead of 46 chromosomes). Since segregation is entirely random, the chromosomes in any gamete may be anything from 100% paternally derived to 100% maternally derived. The number of gametes bearing a preponderance of paternally derived chromosomes must, however, be equal to the number bearing a preponderance of maternally derived chromosomes. J.M.S.; P.M.

Mendelsohn, Erich (German architect, 1887–1953), see under EXPRESSIONISM.

Menger, Karl (Austrian mathematician, *b*.1902), see under VIENNA CIRCLE.

MENSHEVIKS

Mensheviks. Between 1903 and 1917, a political faction of the Russian Social Democratic Workers' Party; it constituted itself as a political party in August 1917. After the split between the Mensheviks and the Bolsheviks (for the origin of the names see BOLSHEVISM), a formal reunion occurred in 1906, but the struggle for the domination of the R.S.D.W.P. continued. The Mensheviks, of whom the most important were Plekhanov, Axelrod, and Martov, took the orthodox MARXIST view of Russia's development and rejected Lenin's view of the role of the Party (see LENINISM). The split was further complicated by issues such as underground versus legal forms of struggle, national defence versus revolutionary defeatism (see REVOLUTION), etc., which caused divisions among the Mensheviks themselves. Broadly speaking, however, the Mensheviks were 'softer' than the Bolsheviks and more ready to collaborate with other parties, including non-SOCIALIST ones, in the struggle for a democratic constitution (see DEMOCRACY) and against Czarist autocracy. Following the February 1917 revolution, the Mensheviks had a majority in most SOVIETS. After the Bolsheviks' seizure of power in October 1917, the Mensheviks tried to become a legal opposition, but the dissolution of the Constituent Assembly was followed by repressive measures against their Party, culminating in its suppression in 1922. In 1931 Stalin mounted a SHOW TRIAL against the Mensheviks in Moscow (only one of the accused was in fact a Menshevik). The Party maintained its existence abroad, and its leaders, such as F. I. Dan and R. A. Abramovich, continued until the late 1960s to publish commentaries on Soviet developments in the monthly *Sotsialisticheskiy Vestnik* (*Socialist Courier*).   L.L.

Bibl: L. H. Haimson, *The Russian Marxists and the Origins of Bolshevism* (Cambridge, Mass., 1955); L. H. Haimson *et al.*, *The Mensheviks from the Revolution of 1917 to the Second World War* (Chicago, 1974).

mental age. The level of mental development in a child, expressed in years and months, based on age norms for mental tests (see MENTAL TESTING) designed to measure INTELLIGENCE. See also INTELLIGENCE QUOTIENT.   H.L.

mental retardation. Variously defined, but most simply a condition attributed to those individuals placed, in respect of COGNITIVE attainments, in the bottom 2–3% of their age-group. Some 'mental retardates', however, particularly borderline cases, are so classified more on the basis of social than cognitive competence. Indeed, it has been suggested that in the British Mental Deficiency Act of 1913 (superseded in 1958) mental deficiency was defined almost exclusively in terms of social competence.

For most of the 20th century the major contribution of psychologists to the scientific study of mental retardation has been in the area of techniques of cognitive assessment, and, to a lesser extent, the assessment of social and emotional maturity. In the first decade of this century, A. Binet and T. Simon in Paris developed a MENTAL AGE scale for the more systematic appraisal of judgement and reasoning in schoolchildren. Adapted and expanded forms of this scale, notably L. M. Terman's 1916 revision (known as the *Stanford-Binet test* – a later version being known as the *Terman-Merrill revision*), allied with the CONCEPT of INTELLIGENCE and 'innate mental ability' (C. Burt, 1921), served to condemn children and adults thus 'diagnosed' to society's passive acceptance of their so-called condition. The establishment of special schools (see SPECIAL EDUCATION) and subnormality hospitals had the effect of maintaining and supporting professional and public assumptions, since the inmates not only conformed to expectations but exceeded them in that there was evidence of 'deterioration'.

In educational terms, retarded children were until recently distinguished in terms of whether they were 'educable' or merely 'trainable'. In Britain, until 1971 this was a crucial distinction, since those considered 'ineducable' were excluded from the educational system. For these children the distinction was based mainly on the results of an intelligence test (see MENTAL TESTING), the approximate borderline being an I.Q. of 50. Children in the I.Q. category of approximately 50–70 were considered EDUCATIONALLY SUBNORMAL, a term which now applies to all retarded children; in the U.S.A. a distinction is still made between 'educable' and 'trainable' mental retardates, although changes in thinking and educational practice have blurred the division.

Important changes in psychological thinking and practice with regard to mental retardation have become increasingly apparent from the early 1950s onwards – although the implications of new findings and, more importantly, new ways of thinking, have yet to be absorbed by the relevant professions, let alone society at large. In Britain, pioneer work was done by A. D. B. Clarke (1953) at the Manor Hospital in Surrey; he demonstrated the effectiveness of task analysis and training schedules in teaching adult retardates quite complex skills. In the late 1950s the theories and research findings of the Russian psychologist A. R. Luria started to become available; his thesis that retardation involved a failure to develop language as a SECOND-SIGNAL SYSTEM in the mediation of behaviour led to a reappraisal of the typical assumption implicit in Western thinking that retardates were like normals but slower in their rate of development.

Developmental studies showed that retarded children who in PIAGETIAN terms had reached the beginning of the stage of intuitive thought failed to show the rapid growth of language that characterizes normal children at the same stage of development. Defects in short-term memory often noted in retardates can also be explained in terms of inability to code and chunk (see CHUNKING) information meaningfully. The role of language has become the dominant area for psychological research in mental retardation.

More recently, the reappraisal of 'intelligence' as a useful concept has suggested approaches to the teaching of basic cognitive skills. This accompanies an emphasis in psychological thinking on the need to move away from assumptions about probable limits to attainment and towards a functional analysis of learning difficulties and 'open-ended' remediation based on the results of such analysis.　　w.e.c.g.

Bibl: A. D. B. Clarke and A. M. Clarke (eds.), *Mental Retardation and Behavioural Research* (Edinburgh, 1973).

mental testing. The measurement, by means of reliable and validated tests, of mental differences between individuals or groups, or the different responses of the same individuals on separate occasions. The tests can be used clinically, as an aid to psychological diagnosis, and vocationally to help in appropriate work placement.

Mental testing may take many forms. *Analogy tests,* which involve the form of verbal reasoning 'A is to B as C is to D', are most commonly used in the assessment of INTELLIGENCE. *Aptitude tests* are designed to measure particular skills possessed by the subject, in order to predict what he might attain with specialized training. *Educational tests* are used to assess basic skills such as reading, arithmetic, spelling, and language comprehension. *Performance tests* measure skill in arranging or otherwise manipulating material (e.g. block designs, mazes) which is visually and spatially presented. *Personality tests* may be *unstructured,* as in *story-* or *sentence-completion* (see also RORSCHACH TEST), or STRUCTURED as in the *Eysenck Personality Inventory,* in which statements about feelings and ideas are presented to the subject for sorting or ticking; his responses can be interpreted to provide insight into his emotions, and his personal and social relationships.

Mental testing began with the work of A. Binet in 1905. It has been developed by Wechsler, Spearman, Cattell, Thurstone, and many others. Today it is attacked on social and political grounds: on the one hand by those (e.g. Szasz) who fear the misuse of the *results* by an arbitrary authority (such as the State or an institution) or a malignant individual, and on the other by those, mostly EGALITARIANS, who believe that the whole CONCEPT of mental testing is contaminated with unacceptable principles (see, for example, ÉLITISM; MERITOCRACY; RACE).　　m.be.

Bibl: L. J. Cronbach, *Essentials of Psychological Testing* (N.Y., 3rd ed., 1970).

mentalism. The doctrine that mental states and processes exist independently of their manifestations in behaviour and can explain behaviour. It is thus opposed to BEHAVIOURISM and to the application of the latter known as SOCIAL BEHAVIOURISM. Its best-known proponent is A. N. Chomsky.　　a.s.

Bibl: J. A. Fodor and J. J. Katz (eds.), *The Structure of Language* (Englewood Cliffs, N.J., 1964); A. N. Chomsky, *Language and Mind* (London and N.Y., rev. ed., 1972).

mentalities, history of, see HISTORY OF MENTALITIES.

mercantilism. Term applied, historically, to the trading practices of European countries during the 16th, 17th, and 18th centuries. Employing what have been called zero-sum assumptions by GAMES theorists, mercantilists assumed that one nation's gain was another's loss. The tokens of victory were inflows of gold and silver, the tokens of defeat the reverse. This favourable balance was to be achieved by tariffs and other measures which discouraged imports, and bounties and rebates which encouraged exports. Although mercantilist doctrine is at a sharp discount among economists, mercantilist sentiment endures both among unions and businessmen whose immediate interests are threatened by foreign COMPETITION, and among public officials responsive to the plaints of their constituents.   R.L.

Bibl: E. Heckscher, tr. M. Schapiro, ed. E. F. Söderlund, *Mercantilism* (London and N.Y., rev. ed., 1956).

merger, see under CORPORATE STRATEGY.

meritocracy. A word coined by Michael Young (*The Rise of the Meritocracy*, 1958) for government by those regarded as possessing merit; merit is equated with INTELLIGENCE-plus-effort, its possessors are identified at an early age and selected for an appropriate intensive EDUCATION, and there is an obsession with QUANTIFICATION, test-scoring, and qualifications. EGALITARIANS often apply the word to any ÉLITIST system of education or government, without necessarily attributing to it the particular grisly features or ultimately self-destroying character of Young's apocalyptic vision.   O.S.

Merleau-Ponty, Maurice (French philosopher and author, 1908–61), see under NEO-MARXISM.

Merton, Robert King (U.S. sociologist, *b.* 1910), see under MIDDLE RANGE, THEORIES OF; SOCIOLOGY.

Merz. Name given by the painter, poet, and typographer Kurt Schwitters (1887–1948) to his one-man DADA splinter movement in Hanover in the 1920s. Recalling the French term *merde* and the German *ausmerzen* (to extirpate), it supposedly derived from a fragment of the word *Kommerz* (commerce) on one of his COLLAGES of 1919. Thereafter he produced *Merz* 'pictures' (assemblages of rubbish), a magazine *Merz* (1923–32) to which Lissitzky, van Doesburg, and Hans Arp all contributed, *Merz* poems, *Merz* evenings with performances of his phonetic *Lautgedichte*, three *Merzbaus* (or environmental sculptures; see ENVIRONMENT), a *Merz* stage, a new alphabet or *Systemschrift,* rubber-stamp pictures (*Stempelbilder*), and some virtually CONCRETE 'picture poems' or *Bildgedichte*. All these shared in the revival of Dada in the 1950s.   J.W.

Bibl: W. Schmalenbach, *Kurt Schwitters* (London and N.Y., 1970).

mesomorph, see under PERSONALITY TYPES.

meson. A class of ELEMENTARY PARTICLE. Mesons are exchanged during the STRONG INTERACTION of NUCLEONS, and provide the 'glue' holding the atomic NUCLEUS together against the mutual repulsion of the PROTONS in it. This behaviour resembles that of ELECTRONS whose EXCHANGE FORCES hold MOLECULES together, but mesons are unstable, and decay in less than a ten-millionth of a second into electrons, NEUTRINOS, and GAMMA-RAYS. Mesons have masses ranging from 100 to 500 times that of the electron, and may occur with positive, negative, or zero electric charge.   M.V.B.

messenger RNA, see under NUCLEIC ACID.

Messiaen, Olivier (French composer, *b.* 1908), see under CONCRETE MUSIC; ISORHYTHM; ONDES MARTENOT; POLYRHYTHM; SERIAL MUSIC.

messianism. Belief in the salvation of mankind – or, more often, of the particular group which holds the belief – through the appearance of an individual saviour or redeemer. The word is derived from the Hebrew Messiah, a king of the line of David, who was to deliver the Jewish people from bondage and restore the golden age. The adjective *messianic* is frequently used to describe thinkers who (like Marx) foretell with prophetic power that human history is predestined to lead up to an apocalyptic dénouement in which the contradictions and injustices of the present order will be swept away and Utopia, the New Jerusalem, the classless society, established. See also MILLENARIANISM; UTOPIANISM.   A.L.C.B.

Bibl: J. L. Talmon, *Political Messianism: the Romantic Phase* (London and N.Y., 1960); N. Cohn, *The Pursuit of the Millennium* (London and N.Y., rev. ed., 1970).

metabolism. Considered collectively, the processes of chemical transformation that occur in an organism, whether for the building up of bodily substances or secretions or for the liberation of energy. The predominantly synthetic or constructive elements of the processes of metabolism are known as *anabolism*; the characteristically degradative or destructive processes are known as *catabolism*.   P.M.

metadyne. A name given to a cross-FIELD electric generator that originated at the Metropolitan-Vickers Electrical Company. Like the AMPLIDYNE it is used for monitoring large currents (such as those used by London Underground trains) by means of small currents, but is not fully compensated for voltage drops on load as is the amplidyne.   E.R.L.

Bibl: C. V. Jones, *The Unified Theory of Electrical Machines* (London, 1967; N.Y., 1968).

metahistory. Another name for the *philosophy of history* which shares the ambiguity of the longer and more familiar expression. It may be understood either as critical reflection on the methods of historical reasoning, or as the attempt to construct a speculative historical system in the form of a body of laws covering the course of history as a whole (the project of HISTORICISM in Popper's sense).   A.Q.

metal fatigue. The increased liability to fail of a metal that has been subjected to repeatedly variable stress for long periods. The degree of fatigue increases (i.e. the metal is liable to break as the result of smaller and smaller stresses) with the size of the average stress and with the magnitude and frequency of the stress changes. Metal fatigue was first brought to public attention as the result of early jet-plane crashes. See also CREEP.   E.R.L.

metalanguage. In LINGUISTICS, any technical language devised to describe the properties of language.   D.C.

metalinguistics. A term used by some LINGUISTS for the study of language in relation to other aspects of cultural behaviour. It is not, as etymology might suggest, the study of METALANGUAGE.   D.C.

metallurgy. The branch of science and TECHNOLOGY which deals with metals and their alloys. Its existence as a distinct field of study (though it draws heavily on PHYSICS and CHEMISTRY) illustrates the importance of metals (particularly steel, aluminium, and copper) in everyday life. It is concerned with the extraction of metals from their ores; with the understanding of their properties in terms of ELECTRONIC and crystalline structure (see CRYSTALLOGRAPHY); with devising new alloys or new methods of treatment to meet particular needs. Metallurgy grew up as a practical, nearly empirical technology but is nowadays given academic respectability as a branch of MATERIALS SCIENCE.   B.F.

Bibl: A. C. Street and W. O. Alexander, *Metals in the Service of Man* (Harmondsworth, 6th ed., 1976); G. C. E. Olds, *Metals and Ceramics* (Edinburgh, 1968).

metamathematics. The logical investigation (see LOGIC) of the properties of axiomatically formulated mathematical systems (see AXIOMATICS), introduced by Hilbert and associated by him with a FORMALIST interpretation of the nature of MATHEMATICS. It is concerned to establish the CONSISTENCY, independence, and completeness of the AXIOMS of formalized deductive systems, that is the compatibility of the axioms with each other, the impossibility of deducing any one of them from the rest, and the deducibility from them of all the TRUTHS expressible in the vocabulary of the system. GÖDEL'S THEOREM proves the incompletability of any system that contains arithmetic. A.Q.

metamorphosis. A more or less radical rearrangement of parts that occurs in the development of those animals of which the embryonic or larval forms differ greatly from the corresponding adult forms. Examples in early EMBRYOLOGY are *gastrulation* and *neurulation*; examples from a later stage of development are the metamorphosis of the familiar tadpole into the frog and of the lepidopteran caterpillar through a pupal stage into moth or butterfly. P.M.

metaphysical painting (*pittura metafisica*). An Italian movement so named by the artists Giorgio de Chirico and Carlo Carrà at Ferrara in World War I, and later joined by Giorgio Morandi. The mysterious inhuman calmness of their pictures of empty city spaces, tailors' dummies, and banal 'ordinary things' – of which Chirico's dated largely from before the war – was influential in the development of pictorial SURREALISM, as well as having a muted echo in German MAGIC REALISM. Itself largely a reaction against FUTURISM and a re-evocation of Giotto and other Florentine masters, the movement largely petered out after about 1920, as both Chirico and Carrà became increasingly traditionalist. J.W.

metaphysics. The investigation of the world, or of what really exists, generally by means of rational argument rather than by direct or mystical intuition. It may be either *transcendent* (see TRANSCENDENCE), in that it holds that what really exists lies beyond the reach of ordinary experience (as in the picture of the world supplied by supernatural RELIGION), or *immanent*, in that it takes reality to consist exclusively of the objects of experience. Kant and the LOGICAL POSITIVISTS both denied the legitimacy of transcendent metaphysics, Kant on the ground that the *a priori* elements in thought (see APRIORISM) yield knowledge only if applied to the data of experience, the logical positivists on the ground that sentences ostensibly about the world are not even significant unless susceptible of empirical VERIFICATION. The primary component of metaphysics is ONTOLOGY, in which metaphysicians ascribe existence to, or withhold it from, three major classes of things: (1) the concrete occupants of space and time, (2) minds and their states, conceived in the manner of DUALISM as in time but not space, and (3) abstract

entities or UNIVERSALS. A further ontological issue is the number of real existences there are of the preferred kind: is there just one real SUBSTANCE, as MONISTS like Spinoza and Hegel believe, or many? Metaphysicians also propound theories about the overall structure of the world. Is it a mechanical or deterministic system or does it contain chance events or the causally inexplicable emergence of novelty? A.Q.

Bibl: W. H. Walsh, *Metaphysics* (London and N.Y., 1963).

metapsychology. Considerations about PSYCHOLOGY with regard to its definition, purposes, PRESUPPOSITIONS, METHODOLOGY, and limitations, its status as a contribution to knowledge, and its relations to other disciplines. I.M.L.H.

metastable, see under EQUILIBRIUM.

metastases, see under CANCER.

metasystem. A SYSTEM 'over and beyond' a system of lower logical order, and therefore capable of deciding PROPOSITIONS, discussing CRITERIA, or exercising REGULATION (3) for systems that are themselves logically incapable' of such decisions, such discussions, or of *self*-regulation. This is a CONCEPT used in CYBERNETICS and the SYSTEMS approach, and derives from theoretical MATHEMATICS. The emphasis is on *logical* order, not on 'seniority' in the sense of command. For example, one may observe a system in which playing-cards are dealt to a group of people who proceed to dispose of them according to a set of fixed rules which can be ascertained, and which completely determine winners and losers. Over and beyond this system is a metasystem which is expressed in entirely different terms: money. If the observer failed to understand the metasystem he would not appreciate what the game of poker is actually about. See also ALGEDONIC. S.BE.

metatheory. The set of assumptions presupposed (see PRESUPPOSITION) by any more or less formalized body of assertions, in particular the CONCEPTS implied by the vocabulary in which it is expressed and the rules of INFERENCE by means of which one assertion in the system is derived from another. The idea is a generalization of that involved in the selection of features of deductive systems for investigation that is characteristic of AXIOMATICS or METAMATHEMATICS. A.Q.

Metchnikoff, see MECHNIKOV.

meteorology. The study of short-term changes in the weather (temperature, rainfall, humidity, sunshine, etc.), as contrasted with CLIMATOLOGY, which deals with long-term changes. A picture of the state of the atmosphere is built up by observations from the ground and from SATELLITES; this forms the starting-point for COMPUTER calculations, based on AERODYNAMICS, aimed at forecasting future weather conditions.   M.V.B.
Bibl: O. G. Sutton, *Understanding Weather* (Harmondsworth, 1960).

method, the. A system of training and rehearsal for actors which bases a performance upon inner emotional experience, discovered largely through the medium of improvisation, rather than upon the teaching or transmission of technical expertise. Based on the theory and practice of Konstantin Stanislavsky (1863–1938) at the Moscow Arts Theatre, it was developed by the American director Lee Strasberg who in 1947, with Cheryl Crawford and Elia Kazan, founded the *Actors' Studio* in New York as a partial successor to the GROUP THEATRE. For some 15 years the Studio had a profound influence upon American film and theatre, in the work of actors including Marlon Brando, James Dean, and Paul Newman.   M.A.

method study, see under WORK STUDY.

Methodism. A Christian denomination active throughout the English-speaking world. Founded by John Wesley (1707–91), it was originally so nicknamed because of its claim to be methodical in observing the devotional requirements of ANGLICANISM, but was organized as a virtually independent PROTESTANT Church in Wesley's lifetime. It has stressed its warm fellowship, its strict morality, its interest in social problems, and its keen EVANGELISM. It is well organized – in the U.S.A. under bishops. Theologically it is optimistic, believing that all men can be saved, can know that they are saved, and can reach moral perfection, but it has been criticized for a lack of sophistication and of intellectual liveliness. Recently it has been much influenced by the ECUMENICAL MOVEMENT for Christian reunion.
                                          D.L.E.
Bibl: R. E. Davies, *Methodism* (Harmondsworth and Baltimore, 1963).

methodological individualism and **methodological holism.** Two contrasted approaches to the METHODOLOGY of the SOCIAL SCIENCES. They differ in their answers to such questions as the following: Is it necessary, or even relevant, to mention the beliefs, attitudes, decisions, or actions of individual people in attempting to describe and explain social, political, or economic phenomena? Is it necessary to postulate the existence of SOCIAL WHOLES which have purposes or functions or needs, or which cause events to occur, or are all mentions of such things really abbreviated references to the individual persons in the society concerned (e.g. can a nation or committee be said to have a mind of its own?)? Do SOCIAL STRUCTURES and social processes influence the attitudes, beliefs, decisions, etc. of individuals, or are all such influences to be explained simply in terms of person-to-person interaction? Is the study of society necessarily based on the study of its members, or is there some other means of observing or measuring social entities, like the will of the nation, perhaps through the study of large-scale historical processes? In answering such questions, *methodological individualists* tend to discount the importance or scientific status of social wholes, while *methodological holists* tend to discount the influence of individuals on social phenomena. It can be argued that the whole dispute is as futile as a dispute between engineers as to whether what is important in a building or mechanism is its structure or the materials or components used. Clearly both are important, but in different ways. See also HOLISM.   A.S.
Bibl: A. Ryan, *The Philosophy of the Social Sciences* (London, 1970; N.Y., 1971).

methodology. In the narrowest sense, the study or description of the methods or procedures used in some activity. The word is normally used in a wider sense to include a general investigation of the aims,

387

METROLOGY

CONCEPTS, and principles of reasoning of some discipline, and the relationships between its sub-disciplines. Thus the methodology of science includes attempts to analyse and criticize its aims, its main CONCEPTS (e.g. EXPLANATION, CAUSALITY, *experiment*, *probable*), the methods used to achieve these aims, the subdivision of science into various branches, the relations between these branches (see REDUCTION), and so on. Some scientists use the word merely as a more impressive-sounding synonym for method. A.S.
Bibl: E. Nagel, *The Structure of Science* (London and N.Y., 1961); C. G. Hempel, *Philosophy of Natural Science* (London and Englewood Cliffs, N.J., 1966); K. R. Popper, *The Logic of Scientific Discovery* (London, 3rd ed., 1968; N.Y., 2nd ed., 1968).

metrology. The precise establishment and comparison of the standard units of measurement. See also ATOMIC CLOCK; MKS UNITS; SI UNITS. M.V.B.

metropolis. A Greek word for mother-city which has long meant the main city or largest centre of activity in a region or country. With modern URBANIZATION many cities grew very big, while suburbs and SATELLITE TOWNS sprawled around them. Metropolitan regions are thus formed around many large centres. The use of the term has spread with the phenomenon. 'Metropolitan' government, police, transport, encompassing the metropolis and the region in its orbit, are common concepts, while the term *metropolitanization* has been used to describe certain trends in the U.S.A. and other countries where the majority of the population lives in metropolitan areas. The term is also used in the sense of a city recognized as a major market for a certain category of goods or services. J.G.
Bibl: S. R. Miles (ed.), *Metropolitan Problems* (London and Toronto, 1970).

Metzger, Gustav (German-British artist and critic, *b.* 1926), see under AUTO-DESTRUCTIVE.

Metzinger, Jean (French painter, 1883–1956), see under CUBISM.

Meyer, Adolph (German architect, 1881–1929), see under WERKBUND.

Meyer, Hannes (Swiss architect, 1889–1954), see under BAUHAUS; CANTILEVER.

Meyerhold, Vsevolod Yemilyevich (Russian theatre director and actor, 1874–1942), see under BIOMECHANICS; FORMALISM; OPEN STAGE.

Meynaud, Jean (French political scientist, 1914–72), see under TECHNOCRACY.

MGB, see under KGB.

MI (Military Intelligence). The gathering of information, by clandestine as well as overt means, about the intentions of enemies or potential enemies and the means at their disposal to effect their intentions. In Britain MI has become in addition a cover name for the Security Service (MI5) and the Secret Intelligence Service (MI6), both civilian forces, the one operating purely on British territory and answerable on security problems through the Home Secretary to the Prime Minister, the other operating outside British territory and therefore answerable to the Foreign Secretary. D.C.W.
Bibl: J. Bulloch, *M.I.5* (London, 1963).

Michels, Robert (German sociologist and economist, 1876–1936), see under ÉLITE.

Michelson-Morley experiment. It was believed in the late 19th century that the earth must be moving relative to the ETHER which was thought to support light waves; and that because the speed of light would be constant relative to the ether, its speed relative to the earth should vary with direction. In 1888 the American scientists Albert Michelson (1852–1931) and Edward Morley (1838–1923) tried to measure this difference in velocity for light travelling in different directions, but no effect could be detected. A large number of subsequent more accurate experiments all confirmed this result, except for that of Miller in 1924, who claimed to detect a tiny positive effect; but this was later shown to be due to an identifiable experimental error. It was concluded that the speed of light in a vacuum is independent of the relative motion of

source and observer, and this result became one of the postulates of RELATIVITY theory.   M.V.B.
Bibl: see under OPTICS; RELATIVITY.

microbe. A lay term used to describe bacteria (see BACTERIOLOGY) and also, quite wrongly, infective particles like viruses (see VIROLOGY), which are not living organisms as bacteria are.   P.M.

microbiology. The discipline concerned with bacteria and viruses in their wider aspects which grew up when it came to be realized, during the past 20 or 30 years, that BACTERIOLOGY and VIROLOGY were important not merely for their own sakes, but also because they might provide MODELS of such phenomena occurring in higher organisms as heredity (see GENETICS), development, and DIFFERENTIATION.   P.M.

microchemistry. The branch of CHEMISTRY which deals with the manipulation and estimation of chemical substances in minute quantities. Microanalytical techniques typically allow one ten-thousandth of a gram of material to be determined with an accuracy of 1% or 2%.   B.F.

microclimatology. The branch of CLIMATOLOGY concerned with small-scale atmospheric phenomena near the surface of the earth.   P.H.
Bibl: R. Geiger, tr. from 4th German ed., *The Climate near the Ground* (Cambridge, Mass., 1965).

micro-economics, see under ECONOMICS.

micro-electronics. The development of tiny TRANSISTORS, INTEGRATED CIRCUITS, and other ELECTRONIC components for use in COMPUTERS, INERTIAL GUIDANCE systems, spacecraft, etc. M.V.B.

microlinguistics. A term used by some LINGUISTS for the study of the phonological and morphological LEVELS (sense 1) of language; but also used in a general sense for any analysis or point of view which concentrates on describing the details of linguistic behaviour as against general trends or patterns (to which the term *macrolinguistics* is sometimes applied).
                                       D.C.

micronutrients, see TRACE ELEMENT.

micro-organism. A term (with much the same CONNOTATION as the layman's MICROBE) which stands generally for microscopically small organisms like bacteria, protozoa, and the mycoplasmas, and also includes viruses (see VIROLOGY) – though this is an improper use because viruses are not in any strict sense living organisms.
                                       P.M.

microregion, see under REGION.

microsome. A small cellular particle consisting mainly of ribonucleoprotein, identified in the 1930s by Albert Claude using the ultracentrifuge (see SEDIMENTATION). For a long time its real existence was in doubt, but now it is thought that microsomes represent a cellular element known as *ribosomes*. See also CYTOLOGY; NUCLEIC ACID.
                                       P.M.

microstructure, see under EXCHANGE MODEL.

microteaching. A technique in the training of teachers first used at Stanford University in 1960. A teacher takes a specially constructed lesson lasting from, say, 10 to 30 minutes with a class of about 5–10 pupils. The lesson is evaluated (under such headings as aims, content, and vocabulary) by an observer, the pupils, and the teacher; it is then reconstructed, re-presented, and re-evaluated. VIDEOTAPE is often used and the re-presentation is given to a different group of pupils.
                                     W.A.C.S.
Bibl: J. L. Olivero, *Microteaching* (Columbus, Ohio, 1970).

microtone. A fraction of a tone smaller than a semitone. Normally in Western music the octave is divided into 12 equal parts or semitones. It has been argued that a division into 24 quarter-tones would provide greater variety; in 1907, Busoni suggested 3 divisions to a semitone, making a scale of 36 chromatic notes, while the Czech composer Alois Haba experimented with 6th- and even 12th-tones. From the point of view of sheer geographical distribution, microtonal music was, indeed, for centuries the predominant idiom. Chinese, Japanese,

Indian, Polynesian, Greek, Arabic, Bulgarian, Hungarian, and Andalusian music have this common factor. Yet attempts to introduce microtones into Western concert music have so far met with limited success. It is likely, however, that the infinite variability of pitch obtainable through ELECTRONICS and the simultaneous breakaway from traditional tone-colours may hasten their acceptance. A.H.

microwaves. The shortest radio waves, with wavelengths less than about 30 cm and frequencies greater than 1,000 megahertz (1 hertz = 1 complete vibration cycle per second; 1 megaherz = 1 million hertz). Microwaves are generated by oscillating electric circuits or MASERS, and used in RADAR and TELECOMMUNICATION systems.   M.V.B.

mid-range, see under DISTRIBUTION.

middle range, theories of the. Term introduced by Robert K. Merton (1949) for theories, especially in SOCIOLOGY, which aim to integrate observed empirical regularities and specific hypotheses within a relatively limited problem-area – as opposed to either entirely *ad hoc* explanation or attempts at a quite general theory of SOCIAL ACTION or SOCIAL STRUCTURE as in, say, STRUCTURAL-FUNCTIONAL THEORY or CONFLICT THEORY.   J.H.G.
Bibl: see under REFERENCE GROUP.

middle school. (1) A term used in the PLOWDEN REPORT to denote a comprehensive-type school (see COMPREHENSIVE SCHOOLS) for children from 8 to 12 or 9 to 13. The Report proposed that there should be two stages in primary schooling, the first school from 5 to 8 or 9 and the middle school from 8 or 9 to 12 or 13; transfer from first to middle school would be made without examination. Size of school was seen as important for children, and first schools, according to the Report, should be for about 240, middle schools between 300 and 450. (2) A term used in GRAMMAR SCHOOLS to denote the 13-15 age-group.   W.A.C.S.

Middleton Murry, John, see MURRY.

Mies van der Rohe, Ludwig (German architect, 1886–1969), see under BAUHAUS; BRUTALISM; CHICAGO SCHOOL; INTERNATIONAL STYLE; NEO-CLASSICISM.

Milhaud, Darius (French composer, 1892–1974), see under BITONALITY; CUBISM; POLYTONALITY; SIX, LES.

militancy, see under ACTIVISM.

military-industrial complex. A typically inelegant coinage of President Dwight D. Eisenhower in his Farewell Address to the American electorate at the end of his second term (1956–60). The phrase, beloved of radical (see RADICALISM) and conspiratorially-minded critics of American society, denotes the combination of large-scale technologically-based industries and senior military advisers, a combination whose members are thought, *a priori*, to share a common interest in very high defence budgets, in the preservation of client relationships with small states, and in the military-strategic approach to international affairs.   D.C.W.
Bibl: C. W. Pursell (ed.), *The Military-Industrial Complex* (N.Y., 1973).

Military intelligence, see MI.

Mill, John Stuart (British philosopher and political economist, 1806–73), see under ANALYSIS; ANALYTIC PHILOSOPHY; BUREAUCRACY; CONNOTATION AND DENOTATION; DETERMINISM; EMPIRICISM; PHENOMENALISM; POPPERIAN; PSYCHOLOGISM; SENSATIONALISM; UTILITARIANISM.

millenarian (or *millennialism*). The belief and practices of those who seek, by way of a religious and/or political movement, to secure a comprehensive, salvationary solution for social, personal, and political predicaments. The term has been used by historians and social scientists as a comparative focus for the study of many movements in many parts of the world which have developed sectarian or messianic or salvationary programmes of social transformation (see, e.g., CARGO CULTS). There has been much controversy about the psychological or economic roots of such programmes, their links in specific cases with magical practices, and their utility for the diverse societies in which (or in relation to which) they have been promoted. The term originated – like the related term *chiliastic* – in the myth of Christ's return after 'a thousand years', but the idea has pre-Christian roots and is reflected in Jewish and Islamic thought.

S.J.G.

Bibl: N. Cohn, *The Pursuit of the Millennium* (London and N.Y., rev. ed., 1970); B. Wilson, *Magic and the Millennium* (London and N.Y., 1973).

Miller, Glenn (U.S. musician, 1909–44), see under BIG BAND; SWEET.

Miller, Henry (U.S. novelist, *b*. 1891), see under BEAT.

Miller, John Preston (U.S. geomorphologist, 1923–61), see under MICHELSON-MORLEY EXPERIMENT.

Miller, Jonathan Wolfe (British actor, script-writer, and theatre director, *b*. 1934), see under HOT AND COLD.

Millet, Jules (French literary critic), see under SYNAESTHESIA.

Mills, Charles Wright (U.S. sociologist, 1916–62), see under POWER ÉLITE.

Milner's kindergarten. Name given to an outstanding group of young men recruited, mainly from Oxford, by Lord Milner, the British High Commissioner for South Africa, to aid in the reconstruction of the country in the immediate aftermath of the Boer War (1899–1902). The group later became associated with the quarterly *The Round Table* which pressed for the development of the British Empire into a cooperative commonwealth of self-governing states pursuing agreed common policies on matters of foreign policy, tariffs, trade, etc.   D.C.W.

Bibl: W. Nimocks, *Milner's Young Men* (Durham, N.C., 1968; London, 1970).

mind, philosophy of. The philosophical investigation of minds and their states and our knowledge of them. Starting traditionally from the DUALIST assumption that the mental is radically distinct in nature from the physical, it was principally concerned with the apparent causal relations between mind and body: PERCEPTION in one direction and the operations of the will in the other. More recently the main problem has been that of our knowledge of the minds of others, to whose states we have no direct, INTROSPECTIVE access but which we must infer from their perceptible manifestations in speech and behaviour (see BEHAVIOURISM). A persistent problem is whether the mind is a substantial entity, distinct from the thoughts and experiences that make up its history, or whether it is simply the related totality of its experiences. A connected issue is that of personal identity. Are two experiences those of the same person by reason of association with a persisting mental substance, or with the same human body, or because of some special relation between the two, e.g. that the later contains a memory, or the possibility of a memory, of the earlier one? See also MIND-BODY PROBLEM.   A.Q.

Bibl: J. Shaffer, *Philosophy of Mind* (Englewood Cliffs, N.J., 1968).

mind-body problem. The set of issues that have emerged from the human tendency to postulate a fundamental difference between the realm of mind on the one hand and physical nature on the other. It is generally accepted that any attitude towards the dichotomy creates major, perhaps insoluble, problems of philosophical ANALYSIS. Traditionally, there have been four main attitudes: (1) *Physical monism* (see also MONISM) is probably the most widely accepted among natural scientists, assuming as it does that all phenomena of mind and of nature can be reduced to the laws of PHYSICS and BIOLOGY. (2) *Neutral monism* (or *mental monism*) holds that all is mind, and that the CONCEPT of nature is itself a CONSTRUCT of mind that can only be known through hypotheses tested by reference to experience. This view, which received its contemporary expression in the late 19th century from Ernst Mach, is today expressed as a METHODOLOGICAL principle, based on the premise that, since nature cannot be known directly but only by the mediation of a human observer, one defines nature and mind alike by the kinds of observations one makes and the nature of the INFERENCES one draws – whether these refer to a postulated 'external' system of physical nature, or to the 'internal' system called mind. (3) *Interactionism* (see also PSYCHOSOMATIC) holds that there are two interacting spheres, mind and body: a view that received its first definitive elaboration in the writings of Descartes. The issue of how the two spheres interact without each destroying the self-sufficiency of the other's body of principles remains moot. (4) The classical doctrine of *psychophysical parallelism*, usually attributed to Leibniz, is the view that physical and psychical events run a parallel course without affecting each other. For a fifth, less widespread, view see EPIPHENOMENALISM.   J.S.B.

Bibl: G. Ryle, *The Concept of Mind* (London, 1949).

mineralogy. The study of minerals, the naturally occurring solid substances which make up the earth's crust, meteorites, and lunar rocks. The use of the word 'mineral' for sand and gravel and also for plant nutrient elements derived from the soil suggests that the elasticity of the English language has been over-stretched.   J.L.M.L.

minimal art (or *ABC art, art of the real*). A term which came into use in the 1960s to describe art in which all elements of expressiveness and illusion are minimized, and which thus encroaches on the territory of what is (or was thereto) regarded as ANTI-ART. In painting, this movement has been identified with *post-painterly abstraction*, exemplified by the flat colour-fields and uncomplicated geometry of Barnett Newman and Ellsworth Kelly; forerunners include Rodchenko and Malevich. But minimalists have turned increasingly to sculpture in their quest for the inexpressive. Donald Judd, Robert Morris, and others in the later 1960s produced arrangements of large, fairly regular coloured forms, or *primary structures*, often designed to be seen in relation to a particular ENVIRONMENT. A well-publicized example is Carl André's *120 Fire-Bricks* at the Tate Gallery. Still more 'minimal' exhibits have consisted of piles of earth and photographs of simple natural features.   P.C.

Bibl: G. Battcock (ed.), *Minimal Art* (N. Y., 1968; London, 1969); Tate Gallery Catalogue, *The Art of the Real* (London, 1969).

minimax, see under GAMES, THEORY OF.

minimum lending rate, see BANK RATE.

minorities. Groups held together by common ties of descent, language, culture, or religious faith in virtue of which they feel different from the majority of the population in a country. On this consciousness of difference minorities have based political claims: for equality with the majority (e.g. against discrimination in jobs); for special treatment (e.g. education conducted in their own language); for autonomy or for separation. In many cases (e.g. the Armenians in the Ottoman Empire; the Ukrainians in Poland between the wars; the Catholics in Northern Ireland) such minorities have been subjected to discrimination and persecution. In a few cases (e.g. South Africa) the minority is in a privileged position and the majority aggrieved. 'Minority' and 'majority' in fact have become primarily political and not numerical concepts.

Before the 19th century, the only minorities to play any role in national or international politics were religious. With the growth of national consciousness (see NATIONALISM) in the 19th century, however, national minorities began to play a very large role. Thus, domestically, national minorities frequently protested their grievances and claimed better treatment (e.g. the Czechs in the Habsburg Empire), while, internationally, the existence of minorities provided grounds for one nation to claim to interfere in the affairs of another (e.g. Hitler's use of German-speaking minorities to put pressure on the Czechoslovak and Polish states).

In the U.S.A. and Western Europe there are minorities composed of immigrant ethnic groups. The U.S.A., especially, contains a large number of such groups including blacks, Puerto Ricans, and Chinese who have been attracted to that country, as others have been to countries in Europe, for economic reasons. Unequal treatment of these minorities in the fields of CIVIL RIGHTS, living conditions, and job opportunities has led to friction and, in some cases, violence between these minorities and the indigenous population. In order to alleviate the causes of this and to compensate for past discrimination, legislation on RACE relations and equal opportunities has been introduced which, in the U.S.A., has advocated positive discrimination in favour of minority groups in such areas as housing, education, and recruitment to government services.

A.L.C.B.; P.B.M.

Bibl: W. Brink and L. Harris, *The Negro Revolution in America* (N.Y., 1964); H. M. Blalock, *Toward a Theory of Minority-Group Relations* (N.Y., 1970).

Miró, Joan (French artist, *b*. 1893), see under ABSTRACT ART; BIOMORPHIC; SURREALISM.

missiles. Self-propelled projectiles employed in war and carrying explosive warheads. In *short-range missiles*, employed against tanks or low-flying aircraft, the warhead consists of ordinary explosive. In *medium-range* (M.R.B.M.), *intermediate-range* (I.R.B.M.), *intercontinental* (I.C.B.M.) and *anti-ballistic missiles* (see ABM) the warhead is NUCLEAR. The term 'ballistic' in this latter range of missiles describes the trajectory of the missile. Missiles may be ground-to-ground, ground-to-air, sea-to-air, or air-to-ground, and may be fired from ground platforms, from under the sea (see POLARIS), or from an airborne platform, although in this latter category development costs and technical problems have combined to prevent the development of all but short-range 'stand-off' missiles (i.e. missiles whose range enables them to be launched from aircraft flying out of range of conventional anti-aircraft defences). Certain ballistic missiles, including *submarine-launched ballistic missiles* (S.L.B.M.), may be equipped with *multiple, independently targetable, re-entry vehicles* (M.I.R.V.). In this case, there are a number of warheads to the missile, each of which may be targeted independently in succession, and delivered from the outer atmosphere. Mention should also be made of the 'cruise' missile, a flat-trajectory missile, comparable in speed and performance to pilotless aircraft, launchable from any kind of platform from torpedo tube to aeroplane, and adaptable to all tactical and strategical purposes. D.C.W.

MIT school. In LINGUISTICS, those scholars who, following A. N. Chomsky, Professor of Linguistics at the Massachusetts Institute of Technology, adopt a generative conception of language; see CHOMSKYAN; GENERATIVE GRAMMAR.

D.C.

mitosis. In CELL BIOLOGY, the usual process by which the NUCLEUS divides during CELL division. Each CHROMOSOME splits into two, one of the resulting duplicates passing to each of the daughter cells. The process is important in ensuring that the daughter nuclei have identical sets of chromosomes, and hence of GENES. J.M.S.

Mitry, Jean (French *cinéaste*, *b*. 1907), see under CINÉMATHÈQUE.

mixed economy. An economy in which a substantial number, though by no means all, of the activities of production, distribution, and exchange are undertaken by the Government, and there is more interference by the State than there would be in a MARKET ECONOMY. A mixed economy thus combines some of the characteristics of both CAPITALISM and SOCIALISM in a compromise which corresponds in varying degree to the actual state of affairs in many industrialized countries outside the COMMUNIST group of states, e.g. Great Britain. R.H.

mixed media, see under MEDIA.

mixed strategy, see under GAMES, THEORY OF; NASH EQUILIBRIUM.

MKS units. A set of fundamental units used in science, based on the metre, kilogram, and second for length, MASS, and time, and forming the basis of the currently employed SI UNITS. M.V.B.

mobiles, see under KINETIC ART.

mobility, social, see SOCIAL MOBILITY.

mobilization, social, see SOCIAL MOBILIZATION.

Möbius band. The one-sided surface with a single edge that is obtained by giving a strip of paper one twist and gluing the ends together. It is of interest in TOPOLOGY as being the simplest way of constructing topological spaces that have unfamiliar or unexpected properties (e.g. a cut round the band does *not* separate it into two pieces). R.G.

modal assertions, see under MODALITY.

modal logic. The part, or kind, of LOGIC concerned with INFERENCES whose constituent PROPOSITIONS embody the CONCEPTS of necessity and possibility and their opposites, CONTINGENCY and impossibility. These four concepts are interdefinable, with the aid of the concepts of negation and disjunction: thus, '*p* is possible' means the same as 'It is not necessary that not-*p*'; '*p* is impossible' as 'It is necessary that not-*p*'; and '*p* is contingent' as 'It is not necessary either that *p* or that not-*p*'. Modern modal logic was initiated by C. I. Lewis because of his dissatisfaction with the concept of IMPLICATION found in the standard propositional logic of Russell. But it has developed into an addition to, rather than an improvement upon, extensional logic (see EXTENSIONALITY) using material implication. See also MODALITY.   A.Q.

Bibl: G. E. Hughes and M. J. Cresswell, *Introductions to Modal Logic* (London and N.Y., 1968).

modality. In MODAL LOGIC, a logical property of certain PROPOSITIONS known as *modal propositions*; a modal proposition is any proposition which states of a certain fact either that it is necessary or that it is possible. The use, now common, of 'modality' as a pretentious synonym for the 'mode' or 'way' in which something happens is confusing and unnecessary.
D.P.

mode. In STATISTICS and PROBABILITY THEORY, (1) the most probable value in a DISTRIBUTION; in this sense it is sometimes used as a MEASURE OF LOCATION. (2) More generally, a value which is more probable than any *nearby* value. A distribution having more than one mode is called *bimodal* or *multimodal*, as appropriate, and often arises as the result of mixing simpler *unimodal* distributions. R.SI.

model. A representation of something else, designed for a special purpose. This representation may take many forms, depending upon the purpose in hand. A familiar purpose is to remind ourselves of something we already know about. Thus a model aeroplane, a model of Shakespeare's birthplace, or a photograph, all represent an original; they recall to our minds what that original looks like. But the purpose may be discovery. Thus a model aeroplane placed in the controlled

environment of a wind-tunnel may be used for experiments that will predict how a real aeroplane built to this design would behave in the sky. A third purpose for a model is explanation, e.g. when the solar system is proposed as a model of the ATOM. Again, the model need not necessarily 'look like' whatever it represents. A system of gravitational equations can model the behaviour of the planets as they move around the sun. Such a model is usually called a *theoretical* model.

All models have one characteristic in common, whatever their purpose. This characteristic is the *mapping* of elements in the system modelled onto the model. It is possible for every relevant element to be mapped, in which case the model is an absolute replica (e.g. a paste copy of a piece of precious jewelry). Such a model is the result of an ISOMORPHIC mapping, and the ordinary person cannot distinguish the fake from the real thing. But an expert knows the difference, because he investigates the stones at a level of abstraction (see ABSTRACT) where the mapping is no longer isomorphic. More usually, models openly lose in complexity compared with the original. But if this loss of detail is irrelevant to the purpose in hand the model is still effective. We may not need every rivet in the model aeroplane to be mapped in order either to recognize the plane, or even to experiment with it in a wind-tunnel. When complexity is deliberately sacrificed in the modelling process, according to definite scientific rules set up to govern the TRANSFORMATION, the mapping is called *homomorphic*.

The steps in building a theoretical model can be outlined as follows: (1) The variables to be used in characterizing and understanding the process must be specified. (2) The forms of the relationships connecting these variables must be specified. (3) Ignorance and the need for simplicity will ensure that all relationships other than identities are subject to error and so, for purposes of efficient statistical estimation, these *error terms* must be specified. (4) The PARAMETERS of the model must be estimated and the extent of its IDENTIFICATION ascertained; if this is inadequate, the model must be reformulated. (5) Finally, the model must be kept up to date and used, so that an impression can be formed of its robustness and reliability.

Theoretical models are of many kinds: static or dynamic; partial or complete; aggregated or disaggregated (see AGGREGATION); deterministic or STOCHASTIC; descriptive or optimizing (see OPTIMIZATION). In PHYSICS, when models are well established they are formalized as *laws of physics* and their use for prediction and design becomes a part of ENGINEERING. In ECONOMICS, although the position is rapidly changing, models have usually been static, partial, aggregated, deterministic, and descriptive. Despite the limitations of such models, this experience has enabled model-builders to walk; and it is fortunate for economics that they have consistently ignored the arguments of those who claim that if one cannot run it is pointless to be able to walk.

Nevertheless, partly because they tackle much more complicated situations, as compared with physical models, economic and social models tend to be mathematically more naïve and to lack experimental verification. In the less exact SOCIAL SCIENCES, moreover, the term 'model' is often used of the results of step (1), or at most steps (1) and (2), as numbered above, and these results may not be expressed in mathematical form. In SOCIOLOGY, especially, 'model' may be almost interchangeable with IDEAL TYPE.

In interdisciplinary studies (such as OPERATIONAL RESEARCH or CYBERNETICS) processes that are well understood in one scientific context may be used to investigate the properties of some other system altogether. This often looks as though analogies are being drawn; but a formal model involving homomorphic mapping is something more potent than an analogy. Since mappings are, strictly speaking, mathematical transformations, models are frequently expressed in mathematical notation. This accounts for the popular misconception that the models used in science are necessarily mathematical models.

The use of COMPUTERS has increased the complexity of models which can be handled, but complexity provides no guarantee of validity. Experience shows that simple and apparently reasonable rules often have remote consequences which are extravagant and that 'mid-course correction' (or FEEDBACK) is

necessary to produce an acceptable result. Unfortunately feedback of this sort is very difficult to incorporate in a model.
*S.BE.; C.S.; R.ST.; J.R.T.

model theory, see under MATHEMATICAL LOGIC.

moderator. Any material which slows down NEUTRONS without absorbing them. Moderators such as HEAVY WATER are used in NUCLEAR REACTORS, because CHAIN REACTIONS based on FISSION proceed more efficiently with slow THERMAL NEUTRONS. M.V.B.

Modern Churchmen. The name taken by a group of LIBERAL theologians within ANGLICANISM, perhaps most influential in the 1920s. Leaders included H. D. A. Major and W. R. Inge. See also MODERNISM. D.L.E.
Bibl: H. D. A. Major, *English Modernism* (Cambridge, Mass., 1927).

modernism.
(1) Although the adjective 'modern' has (cf. AVANT-GARDE and CONTEMPORARY) been applied to many different phenomena at different times, 'modernism' (or 'the modern movement') has by now acquired stability as the comprehensive term for an international tendency, arising in the poetry, fiction, drama, music, painting, architecture, and other arts of the West in the last years of the 19th century and subsequently affecting the character of most 20th-century art. The tendency is usually held to have reached its peak just before or soon after World War I, and there is some uncertainty about whether it still persists or a subsequent age of style has begun. Thus Frank Kermode has suggested 'a useful rough distinction between two phases of modernism': *palaeo-modernism* and *neo-modernism*, the former being the earlier developments, the latter being SURREALIST and post-surrealist developments. Others, especially in America (Ihab Hassan, Leslie Fiedler, etc.) have proposed a sharp distinction, a new *post-modernist* style amounting to a reaction against modernist FORMALISM, a choric, global village art, the product of a 'post-cultural' age, emphasizing developments dealt with here under ALEATORY, ANTI-ART, ANTI-

LITERATURE, AUTO-DESTRUCTIVE ART, and NEW NOVEL.

As a stylistic term, modernism contains and conceals a wide variety of different, smaller movements, usually reckoned to be those post-dating NATURALISM and characterized by the anti-positivistic (see POSITIVISM) and anti-representational leanings of many late-19th-century artists and thinkers. It would thus include the tendencies of SYMBOLISM, IMPRESSIONISM, and DECADENCE around the turn of the century; FAUVISM, CUBISM, POST-IMPRESSIONISM, FUTURISM, CONSTRUCTIVISM, IMAGISM, and VORTICISM in the period up to and over World War I; and EXPRESSIONISM, DADA, and SURREALISM during and after that war. A number of these movements contain large theoretical differences among themselves, but certain stylistic similarities. Thus ATONALISM in music, anti-representationalism in painting (see ABSTRACT ART), VERS LIBRE in poetry, fragmentation and STREAM OF CONSCIOUSNESS presentation in the novel, FUNCTIONALISM in architecture, and in general the use of spatial (see SPACE) or COLLAGE as opposed to linear or representational forms, are recurrent features; another common characteristic noted by critics is the presence of an element of, in Frank Kermode's word, 'decreation' – of technical introversion, or an often ironic self-awareness – in modernist forms. A rough cycle from the late ROMANTICISM of Symbolism and Impressionism through the 'hard', 'classical', or 'impersonal' image and then to the modern psychological romanticism of Surrealism also seems visible in literature and visual forms.

Modernism stretched across the European capitals, reaching the peak of activity and achievement in different countries at different times: in Russia in the immediately pre-Revolutionary years, in Germany in the 1890s and again just before World War I, in England in the pre-war years from about 1908, in America after 1912; in France it is a plateau rather than a peak – though sloping off after about 1939. There was great cross-fertilization between countries and also among the different arts: a complicated interaction between the merging of forms – poetry becoming like music, etc. – and intense specialized exploration within the forms ensued. Modernism had a high

aesthetic and formal constituent, and can often be seen as a movement attempting to preserve the aesthetic realm against intellectual, social, and historical forces threatening it. But it has been seen as a change larger than simply formal. Its relation to modern thought and modern PLURALISM, to the military, political, and ideological (see IDEOLOGY) dislocations of the century, is considerable. Indeed its forms, with their element of fragmentation, introversion, and crisis, have sometimes been held to register the collapse of the entire tradition of the arts in human history. They can be seen either as a last-ditch stand on behalf of the aesthetic in the face of barbarism (as in much Symbolism), or as a probe towards something new. What is clear is that, presentationally and in attitude and belief, modernism does represent a radical shift in the social STATUS and function of the artist, his art, and of form; that it is the style of a changed SPACE-TIME CONTINUUM; and that hence the modernist arts require, for their comprehension, criteria different from those appropriate to earlier art.   M.S.BR.

Bibl: S. Spender, *The Struggle of the Modern* (London and Berkeley, 1963); R. Ellmann and C. Feidelson (eds.), *The Modern Tradition* (N.Y., 1965); I. Howe (ed.), *The Idea of the Modern in Literature and the Arts* (N.Y., 1968); F. Kermode, 'Modernism', in *Modern Essays* (London, 1971); M. Bradbury and J. McFarlane (eds.), *Modernism: 1890–1930* (Harmondsworth, 1976).

(2) In THEOLOGY, the movement to modernize doctrine by taking into account the results of HIGHER CRITICISM and scientific discovery, and the conditions of modern CULTURE. In England and the U.S.A. the term has been used for the MODERN CHURCHMEN and other advocates of religious LIBERALISM, but its chief use has been as a label for the outlook of a group of Roman Catholic thinkers. This group was given both its public identity and its death sentence by the ENCYCLICAL *Pascendi* issued by Pope Pius X in 1907. Its leaders were Alfred Loisy (1857–1940) and George Tyrrell (1861–1909), priests who felt challenged by critical studies of Christianity's origins. They rejected the call of Liberal PROTESTANTISM to return to the 'pure' origins, and welcomed the development of Christianity in history. They regarded Roman Cath-

olic DOGMAS and devotions as valuable, because helpful, symbols of faith and spiritual life, but believed that a fuller CATHOLICISM was being born. The Pope condemned them as heretics, and the later Roman Catholic AGGIORNAMENTO had to take care not to be identified with them.

D.L.E.

Bibl: A. R. Vidler, *A Variety of Catholic Modernists* (London, 1970).

modernization. The term now used by, e.g., Eisenstadt and Rostow, for all those developments in modern societies which follow in the wake of INDUSTRIALIZATION and MECHANIZATION. They include the loosening of boundaries between social CLASSES and an increase in social MOBILITY; the growth of EDUCATION; new procedures of industrial negotiation; the extension of franchise; the development of social services; etc.

R.F.

Bibl: S. N. Eisenstadt, *Modernization: Protest and Change* (London and Englewood Cliffs, N.J., 1966); W. W. Rostow, *Politics and the Stages of Growth* (London and N.Y., 1971).

Modersohn, Otto (German sculptor, 1865-1943), see under WORPSWEDE.

Modersohn-Becker, Paula (German painter, 1876–1907), see under WORPSWEDE.

Modigliani, Amadeo (Italian painter, 1884–1920), see under ÉCOLE DE PARIS.

modular, see under MODULE.

modulation. In PHYSICS, any variation in the properties of a high-frequency wave (e.g. a radio wave or a LASER beam), produced by a signal of a much lower frequency. Broadcasting relies on the AMPLITUDE MODULATION or FREQUENCY MODULATION of a carrier wave.

M.V.B.

module. In architecture, a standard unit of measurement used in order to create proportional relationships between parts and the whole (as in the Classical Orders and Le Corbusier's Modulor), and to control building design, and thus the manufacture and assembly of building elements. An imaginary grid to which length and thicknesses relate is used to define the position of these elements. Buildings

planned on the basis of the module are described as *modular*. The need, common to virtually all building, for some form of dimensional coordination becomes acute in PREFABRICATION, for which the use of the modular principle is particularly appropriate.

M.BR.

Moeller van den Bruck, Arthur (German cultural critic, 1876–1925), see under NATIONAL BOLSHEVISM.

moho (Mohorovicic discontinuity), see under LITHOSPHERE.

Moholy-Nagy, László (Hungarian-U.S. painter, photographer, and art teacher, 1895–1946), see under BAUHAUS; CONSTRUCTIVISM; KINETIC ART.

Mohorovicic, Andrija (Croatian geologist, 1857–1930), see under LITHOSPHERE.

moiré effect. An illusory effect of shimmering movement, produced by superimposing one configuration of multiple lines or dots upon another very similar to it, so that the two do not quite coincide. An effect of this kind may be seen in everyday objects, such as sets of railings, or finely threaded materials (*soie moirée*, watered silk); in the 1960s moiré patterns were cultivated by OP and KINETIC artists, and employed in COMPUTER GRAPHICS.

P.C.

Bibl: J. Tovey, *The Technique of Kinetic Art* (London and N.Y., 1971).

Mola, Emilio (Spanish general, 1887–1937), see under FIFTH COLUMN.

molecular biology. A branch of BIOPHYSICS of which the purpose is to interpret biological structures and performances in explicit molecular terms. Thus much of IMMUNOLOGY and BIOCHEMISTRY is now interpretable on a molecular basis. Günther Stent distinguishes two main streams of thought in molecular biology which correspond fairly exactly to the British and the American traditions of research. The British tradition of molecular biology is predominantly structural; it may be said to have begun with W. T. Astbury's demonstration in the 1940s of an essentially crystalline and therefore molecular orderliness in the structures of, for example, hairs, feathers, and PROTEIN fibres, and to have

MOLECULE

culminated in the elucidation by Crick and Watson (1953) of the crystalline structure of NUCLEIC ACID and the interpretation by Perutz and Kendrew (1957) of the structure of myoglobin. These achievements rest upon the use of X-RAY DIFFRACTION analysis, pioneered from 1912 onwards by Laue and W. and L. Bragg. The American tradition of research has been more purely informational in character, i.e. concerned with the manner in which molecular structures may embody and transmit genetic information. The two traditions of research overlap considerably and of course converge in the elucidation of the GENETIC CODE. The elucidation of the nerve fibres' ACTION POTENTIAL is a wholly biophysical exercise that is not usually classified under molecular biology. P.M.

Bibl: G. H. Haggis *et al., Introduction to Molecular Biology* (London and N.Y., 1964).

molecule. The smallest structural unit of a material which can participate in a CHEMICAL REACTION. Molecules consist of ATOMS held together by chemical BONDS arising from EXCHANGE FORCES. See also CHEMICAL EQUATION; MACROMOLECULE. M.V.B.

Moley, Raymond (U.S. journalist, 1886–1975), see under NEW DEAL.

momentum. A measure of the ability of a moving body to resist forces acting on it. For a single PARTICLE obeying NEWTONIAN MECHANICS, MOMENTUM = MASS × velocity. This is, mathematically, a vector quantity (see VECTOR; QUANTITY) because the velocity of a body is directed along its line of motion. For a system that is isolated (i.e. not acted on by forces from outside), momentum obeys a CONSERVATION LAW which is very useful in analysing the motion of interacting parts of the system. In a NUCLEAR REACTION, for example, the total momentum before a collision (of incident particle + target) is the same as the total momentum afterwards (of all the reaction products), whatever the interactions during impact. Conservation of momentum is the basis of the motion of ROCKETS. M.V.B.

monads. According to the PHILOSOPHY of Leibniz, the ultimate substantial constituents of the world. Leibniz argued that everything complex must be made of simple and indivisible parts and that, since everything extended is divisible, the ultimate simples must be unextended and so mental or spiritual in nature. But while monads are all consciousnesses, they need not be self-conscious or endowed with APPERCEPTION, although some are. God and human souls, according to Leibniz, are monads; and everything that exists that is not a monad, such as a material object, is a collection of monads. A.Q.

Bibl: Bertrand Russell, *A Critical Exposition of the Philosophy of Leibniz* (Cambridge, 1900).

Mondrian, Piet (Dutch painter, 1872–1944), see under ABSTRACT ART; STIJL, DE.

Monet, Claude (French painter, 1840–1926), see under IMPRESSIONISM; VINGT, LES.

monetarists, see under INFLATION.

monetary policy. The policy of a government or central bank in varying the quantity of money in circulation or the cost of credit. The classical instruments used for this purpose are discount policy (changes in the central bank's lending rate) and open-market operations (purchases or sales of government paper by the central bank designed to put more or less money in circulation). Other instruments of monetary policy include government control over bank lending, directly or indirectly, and regulation of the rates of interest to be charged by banks and other financial institutions. Economists differ as to the importance of monetary policy (in comparison, for example, with FISCAL POLICY) in regulating the level of economic activity. They also differ as to the priority to be attached to the quantity of money rather than the cost of credit as the focus of monetary policy. A.C.

money. May be defined broadly as liquid purchasing power (see LIQUIDITY) or more narrowly as any means of final payment that is generally acceptable without question, such as metallic or paper currency or bank deposits transferable by cheque. There are many kinds of financial assets that approximate to money ('near-money') and rank as money under the broad definition but not under the narrow one since they cannot be used directly to make payments: for example, deposit accounts (as distinct from current accounts) with a commercial bank, cash held on deposit with a savings bank or a building society, and other kinds of liquid asset. Money as a means of payment has also to be distinguished from money as a unit of account in terms of which values are expressed and debts contracted: for example, the pound note as distinct from the pound sterling.   A.C.

mongolism (mongolian idiocy), see DOWN'S SYNDROME.

monism. In PHILOSOPHY, (1) the theory that there is only one truly substantial thing in the universe, as in Spinoza's doctrine of SUBSTANCE, also described as God-or-Nature (*deus sive natura*), and Hegel's doctrine of the *absolute idea* (see ABSOLUTE; IDEA); this kind of monism is a limiting case of HOLISM; its opposite is *pluralism*. (2) The theory that there is really only one fundamental *kind* of thing in the universe, whether it be material, as in MATERIALISM, mental as in IDEALISM, or abstract as in Platonic REALISM. The two forms of monism are variously combinable: Spinoza held that his Substance had thought and extension as attributes, as well as other unknown ones, whereas Hegel, as an idealist, was a monist in both senses. Materialists ordinarily acknowledge a plurality of individual things or substances, but Parmenides, in the 6th century B.C., did not. See also MIND-BODY PROBLEM; NEUTRAL MONISM.   A.Q.

Monk, Thelonius (U.S. pianist and composer, *b*.1920), see under BEAT; BEBOP.

monoculture. An agricultural system, such as is used for sugar cane and continuous wheat production, in which the same crop is planted successively on the same land, in contrast to systems in which a sequence of crops is planted in rotation. Some users of the term are particularly concerned to emphasize the extension of such simplified cropping over large areas of countryside, and occasionally it has been applied to all systems except those in which several crops are grown mixed together on the same fields on farms where livestock are

an integral part of the system. The simplicity of monocultural systems makes for economy in certain production costs, but they tend to break down because of the build-up of pests and diseases or the deterioration of the soil, with consequent reduction in yields.   K.E.H.

Monod, Jacques-Lucien (French biochemist, 1910–76), see under OPERON.

monopoly. The exclusive possession of the trade in some good or service. A monopolist is in a position to charge a higher price for a good than would be obtainable in competitive conditions, the extent of his power to do so being limited (if not by state control) by the presence of substitute goods to which consumers may turn. Thus salt would afford more scope for monopolistic exaction than would cellophane. A *legal monopoly* is one enjoying exclusivity conferred as a privilege by the state; a *natural monopoly* is said to exist when the ECONOMIES OF SCALE are such as would make it inefficient to have more than one supplier.   G.B.R.
  Bibl: E. A. G. Robinson, *Monopoly* (Cambridge, 1941).

monorail. A transport system for goods or passengers in which the vehicles are suspended by wheels or other means that operate along the surface of a *single* rail or beam, as opposed to the dual rail of a conventional railway. Monorails have lost favour since the early part of the 20th century as they can be shown to be more costly than an equivalent bi-rail system.   E.R.L.

monosystemic, see under FIRTHIAN.

monotheism, see under THEISM.

Monro, Harold (British poet and editor, 1879–1932), see under POETRY BOOK-SHOP.

Monroe, Harriet (U.S. editor and poet, 1860–1936), see under LITTLE REVIEW; POETRY (CHICAGO).

Monroe doctrine. A doctrine first enunciated in a message to the U.S. Congress from President James Monroe (1758–1831) on 2 December 1823. It had four elements: two aimed at restricting the activities of European powers, two those of the U.S.A. The former were: (1) the American continents are henceforth not to be considered as subjects for annexation by any European power; (2) any attempt to extend the political systems of Europe to any portion of the American hemisphere is regarded by the U.S.A. as dangerous to her peace and safety. The latter (largely inoperative since American entry into World War I in 1917) were: (1) no U.S. interference with existing European colonies etc. in the Americas; (2) no American intervention in 'the wars of the European powers in matters relating to themselves'. The doctrine is still a cardinal principle of U.S. foreign policy in so far as the restriction of inter-American conflicts to American powers and institutions is concerned (e.g. the CUBA crisis of 1962).

D.C.W.

Bibl: D. Perkins, *A History of the Monroe Doctrine* (London, rev. ed., 1960; Boston, rev. ed., 1963).

montage. French term for the assembling and erection of mechanical apparatus. Used internationally in the arts:

(1) For the technique of *photomontage* devised by the Berlin DADA group *c*. 1918 and practised mainly by Raoul Hausmann, Hannah Höch, and John Heartfield. This was an application of COLLAGE to photographic and other illustrative material, which Heartfield later adapted to political caricature. Countless designers have come to use it for large-scale display and decorative schemes.

(2) In the cinema, as the ordinary term for editing (the placing of one shot or scene next to another to make a narrative or thematic point). The early Soviet film-makers, influenced by D. W. Griffith's development of *parallel montage* (the simultaneous conduct of two or more narrative themes) in *Intolerance*, gradually developed complex intellectual theories of montage through the experiments first of Kuleshov from 1917, then of Dziga Vertov in his *Kino-Pravda* documentaries from 1922 on, until Eisenstein, elaborating his theory of the *montage of attractions* (the juxtaposition by cutting of seemingly disparate shots to produce a shock or 'attraction'), not only gave montage pride of place in the art of film-making, but raised it into what was to prove a cumbersome mystique.

(3) More loosely, for almost any type of compilation made up of disparate elements, particularly where there is a mechanical quality about the work.

J.W.; T.C.C.M.

Montale, Eugenio (Italian poet, translator, and critic, *b*. 1896), see under HERMETIC.

Monte Carlo methods. In STATISTICS and PROBABILITY THEORY, the estimation of quantities (which are perhaps too difficult to calculate analytically) by construction of a probabilistic process which is then simulated (see SIMULATION) using RANDOM NUMBERS; the Laws of Large Numbers (see STATISTICAL REGULARITY) will guarantee that after a large number of runs of the simulation the estimated PARAMETERS of the MODEL are unlikely to be far from the true values. Thus one method of finding the area inside a closed curve is to enclose it within a polygon of known area and consider the frequency with which points from a uniform DISTRIBUTION on the polygon fall inside the curve. The successful application of Monte Carlo methods depends critically on designing the simulation experiment to take maximum account of known information; design techniques of this kind are called *variance-reduction methods*. R.SI.

Montesquieu, Charles-Louis de Secondat (French political philosopher, 1689–1755), see under SOCIOLOGY.

Montessori, Maria (Italian educationist, 1870–1952), see under CHILD-CENTRED EDUCATION; FROEBEL METHOD; MONTESSORI METHOD.

Montessori method. Educational method associated with Maria Montessori (1870–1952). After qualifying, in 1894, as Italy's first woman doctor, she worked in Rome, first with feeble-minded children, later with normal children aged 3–7. Her specially designed auto-didactic apparatus and furniture provided a challenging environment which exercised the child's physical mechanisms and his discrimination of length, size, weight, texture, shape, and colour. The Montessori method and classroom were commended by progressives as both 'scientific' and sensitive, but the dominating Dottoressa was not always an acceptable champion of

MORMONS

her own doctrines. In the Anglo-Saxon world the FROEBEL METHOD has been preferred. W.A.C.S.

Bibl: M. Montessori, tr. M. J. Costelloe, *The Discovery of the Child* (Notre Dame, Ind., 1939).

MOOP, see MVD.

Moore, George (Irish-born novelist, 1852-1933), see under REALISM.

Moore, George Edward (British philosopher, 1873-1958), see under ANALYSIS; ANALYTIC PHILOSOPHY; COMMON SENSE; INTUITIONISM; LINGUISTIC PHILOSOPHY; NATURALISM; NATURALISTIC FALLACY; PARADIGM CASE.

Moore, Henry (British sculptor, *b.*1898), see under BIOMORPHIC.

Moore, Marianne (U.S. poet, 1887-1972), see under EGOIST, THE; HORIZON; POETRY (CHICAGO).

moral theology. A term, more familiar in CATHOLICISM than in PROTESTANTISM, covering the discussion of the relevance of religious, especially Christian, belief to ethical problems (see ETHICS). Most of the discussion has been about a minimum standard of conduct for Christians who do not aspire to the heights of sanctity, and has sometimes resulted in a semi-legal, even hair-splitting, code listing possible concessions to human appetites. This is pejoratively called 'casuistry', a word which can, however, have the nobler meaning of applying moral philosophy to particular cases. See also ANTINOMIANISM; SITUATION ETHICS. D.L.E.

Bibl: J. Macquarrie (ed.), *A Dictionary of Christian Ethics* (London and Philadelphia, 1967).

Morandi, Giorgio (Italian painter, 1890-1964), see under METAPHYSICAL PAINTING; NEO-CLASSICISM; PURISM.

Moréas, Jean (pseud. of Iannis Papadiamantopoulos, Greek-born French poet, 1856-1910), see under SYMBOLISM.

Moreau, Gustave (French painter, 1826-98), see under SYNTHETISM.

Moreau, Luc-Albert (French painter and engraver, 1882-1948), see under KNAVE OF DIAMONDS.

Moreno, Jacob L. (U.S. psychiatrist, 1892-1974), see under SOCIOMETRY.

Morgan, Edwin (British poet, *b.*1920), see under MOVEMENT, THE.

Morgan, Thomas Hunt (U.S. biologist, 1866-1945), see under GENETICS.

Morgenstern, Oskar (German-U.S. economist, *b.*1902) see under GAMES, THEORY OF.

Morgenthau Plan. Plan advanced at the Quebec conference of the Anglo-American war leadership of September 1944 by Henry Morgenthau (1891-1967), then U.S. Secretary of the Treasury, advocating the 'pastoralization' (i.e. total removal of all industry) from Germany. Initially accepted by Churchill and Roosevelt, the scheme was immediately disowned by the British Cabinet, which realized that a purely 'pastoral' Germany was going to need heavy foreign subsidies to keep going and would be an increased burden on European economic recovery. D.C.W.

Bibl: J. M. Blum, *From the Morgenthau Diaries: Years of War, 1941-1945* (Boston, 1967); E. L. Woodward, *British Foreign Policy in the Second World War* (London, 1962).

Morisot, Berthe (French painter, 1841-95), see under IMPRESSIONISM.

Morley, Edward Williams (U.S. chemist, 1838-1923), see under MICHELSON-MORLEY EXPERIMENT.

Mormons. A basically American religious body properly called 'The Church of Jesus Christ of the Latter-Day Saints'. Founded by Joseph Smith and Brigham Young, it attracted attention by its establishment, around Salt Lake City, of the State of Utah (1847, admitted into the U.S.A. in 1895), by the bizarre nature of its holy book (the *Book of Mormon*), and by its practice of polygamy (now abandoned). In the 20th century it has become well-known for its world-wide EVANGELISM and for its practice (based on 1 Corin-

401

thians 15) of baptising the names of the dead. It is now respected for its moral purity, if not for its THEOLOGY.　　D.L.E.

morpheme. In LINGUISTICS, the minimal unit of grammatical analysis, i.e. the smallest functioning unit out of which words are composed. Morphemes are commonly classified into *free forms* (morphemes which can occur as separate words) and *bound forms* (morphemes which cannot so occur – traditionally called *affixes*); thus *unselfish* consists of the three morphemes *un, self,* and *ish*, of which *self* is a free form, *un-* and *-ish* bound forms. Morphemes are generally regarded as abstract units; when realized in speech, they are called *morphs*. Some morphemes are represented by more than one morph according to their position in a word or sentence, such alternative morphs being called *allomorphs*. Thus the morpheme of plurality represented orthographically by the *-s* in, e.g., *cots, digs,* and *forces* has the allomorphs represented phonetically by [s], [z], and [iz] respectively; in this instance the allomorphs result from the phonetic influence of the sounds with which the singular forms of the words terminate.　　D.C.

morphogenesis. The sum of the processes by which an animal or plant develops its distinctive form. These processes are (1) *determination*, in which the fate of certain CELLS or TISSUES is determined; (2) DIFFERENTIATION, in which various cells or tissues undergo diverging courses of development; and (3) growth, in which cells enlarge, multiply, or both. See also EMBRYOLOGY.　　E.O.W.

morphology.
(1) In BIOLOGY, a term introduced by Goethe to denote a science dealing with the very essences of forms – and so distinguished from workaday descriptive sciences like ANATOMY. In Goethe's mind the word probably had a slightly mystical neo-Platonic significance.　　P.M.
(2) In GEOGRAPHY and GEOLOGY, a term used to denote the form of landscapes or elements of the natural landscape. Thus E. Raisz has defined and standardized symbols for forty 'morphologic types' such as cone volcanoes, scarplands, plains, and has added a further ten based on natural vegetation to diversify the category of plains. More recently the term *urban morphology* has been used, with reference to urban landscapes, to differentiate different parts of a town according to form and structure.　　M.L.
Bibl: E. Raisz, 'The Physiographic Method of Representing Scenery on Maps' (*Geographical Review,* 21, N.Y., 1931).
(3) A branch of LINGUISTICS, traditionally defined as the study of word structure, but now more usually as the study of the properties of MORPHEMES and their combinations.　　D.C.
Bibl: P. H. Matthews, *Inflectional Morphology* (London, 1972).

morphophonology (sometimes called *morphonology* and, especially in American linguistic work, *morphophonemics*). In LINGUISTICS, the analysis and classification of the different phonological shapes available in a language for the representation of MORPHEMES.　　D.C.

Morris, Desmond (British zoologist, *b.* 1928), see under ETHOLOGY.

Morris, Henry (British architect, 1889–1961), see under VILLAGE COLLEGE.

Morris, John (British historian, *b.* 1913), see under PAST AND PRESENT.

Morris, Robert (U.S. sculptor, *b.* 1931), see under CONCEPTUAL ART.

Morris, William (British designer, craftsman, and poet, 1834–96), see under ARTS AND CRAFTS MOVEMENT; BIOMORPHIC; FOLK ART; GRAPHIC DESIGN; MECHANIZATION; WERKBUND.

Mosca, Gaetano (Italian jurist and political theorist, 1858–1941), see under BUREAUCRACY; ÉLITE.

Moscow trials. The three great SHOW TRIALS whose leading victims were Zinoviev, Kamenev, and others (August 1936); Pyatakov, Radek, and others (January 1937); and Bukharin, Yagoda, and others (March 1938). The term is sometimes used to include earlier public trials such as the Shakhty Trial of 1928, the 'Industrial Party' Trial of 1930, the Menshevik Trial of 1931, and the 'Metro-Vickers' Trial of

1933 (when the main accused were British engineers). The principle of these rigged trials was that of public confession by the accused, though some of the earlier ones named were not wholly successful in this respect. See also YEZHOVSHCHINA.   R.C.

Moser, Koloman (Austrian painter, 1868–1918), see under KUNSTGEWERBE-SCHULE.

Moslem, see MUSLIM.

Mosley, Sir **Oswald** (British politician, b.1896), see under FASCISM.

Mössbauer effect (discovered by Rudolf Ludwig Mössbauer in 1958). The emission of GAMMA RAYS with very precisely defined frequencies by an atomic NUCLEUS in a solid. The nuclear velocities, whose DOPPLER EFFECTS broaden the range of frequencies in a gas, may be reduced virtually to zero in a solid, because the MOMENTUM due to recoil and random heat motion is absorbed by the whole crystal LATTICE.

Very small frequency shifts can be measured with these Mössbauer gamma rays; this has led to many applications of the effect in SOLID STATE PHYSICS, and to a successful test of the prediction from the theory of RELATIVITY that GRAVITATION will cause a RED SHIFT in the frequency of PHOTONS.   M.V.B.

most favoured nation clause, see under BILATERALISM.

Motherwell, Robert (U.S. painter, b.1915), see under DADA.

motivation. (1) Originally and properly, the process of motivating, i.e. of providing with a motive ('Iago's motivation in Shakespeare's part'). (2) Increasingly, a slightly pretentious synonym for motive or motives ('Iago's motivation is obscure'). (3) Most recently and loosely, any or all of the following: ambition, determination, energy, initiative, intellectual curiosity, physical stamina, moral fibre. Somebody lacking in these qualities is said to be *unmotivated* (as Lady Macbeth didn't say, 'Unmotivated! Give me the daggers').   O.S.

Moulton, Frederick Ray (U.S. astronomer and mathematician, 1872–1952), see under PLANETESIMAL THEORY.

Movement, the. Name originally given in the mid 1950s to a conservative tendency then manifesting itself in British poetry. The term is misleading in that there was never any 'movement'; Robert Conquest's *New Lines* (1956), which included poetry by Donald Davie, Kingsley Amis, Philip Larkin, John Wain, Elizabeth Jennings, Thom Gunn, and others, was programmatically retrospective, and very soon after this some British poets, including Gunn himself, Edwin Morgan, and Iain Crichton Smith, came under such very different influences as Robert Lowell's 'confessionalism' (a writing of one's own life story by way of the strictly clinical facts), EXISTENTIALISM, and the 'post-SURREALISM' of John Ashberry. The Movement's tendency – traditionalism in form, irony, 'robustness', distrust of CULTURE, an empirical approach – is most characteristically seen in Philip Larkin, arguably Britain's best post-war poet. The Movement was a reaction against the NEW APOCALYPSE and similarly loose British poetry of the 1940s, a response to the ingenuity of William Empson, and a belated, partial recognition of the achievement of Robert Graves, who in the 1930s and 1940s had been overshadowed by Auden and Eliot.   M.S.-S.

Bibl: M. L. Rosenthal, *The New Poets* (N. Y., 1967).

Moyne, Walter Edward Guinness, Lord (British politician, 1880–1944), see under STERN GANG.

Mozart, Wolfgang Amadeus (Austrian composer, 1756–91), see under POLYRHYTHM; POLYTONALITY.

MRBM (medium-range ballistic missiles), see under MISSILES.

MS. Abbreviation for (1) manuscript; (2) motor-ship; (3) MULTIPLE SCLEROSIS; (4) either Mrs or Miss: an ambiguous style of address favoured by those women, especially members of the Women's Liberation movement (see FEMINISM), who resent the implication that their marital status, unlike that of men, is an integral part of their persona.   O.S.

MSI

MSI (*Movimento Sociale Italiano*; also an abbreviation for *medium-scale integration*, for which see INTEGRATED CIRCUIT). Italian NEO-FASCIST party founded in 1946, anti-DEMOCRATIC and anti-COMMUNIST in character. Forced to work through the Italian parliamentary system, it has directed its main efforts towards attempting to draw the dominant CHRISTIAN DEMOCRAT party into a RIGHT-wing anti-Communist and anti-SOCIALIST coalition.   D.C.W.

MT, see MACHINE TRANSLATION.

Muhammed, Elijah (né Poole; U.S. Black Muslim leader, 1897–1975), see under BLACK MUSLIMS.

mujahidin, see under JIHAD.

Müller, Friedrich Max (German-British Orientalist and philologist, 1823–1900), see under FOLKLORE.

Müller, Hermann Joseph (U.S. geneticist, 1890–1967), see under RADIATION GENETICS.

Müller, Otto (Polish painter and engraver, 1874–1930), see under BRÜCKE, DIE.

multidimensional scale, see under SCALE.

multidimensional scaling, see under SCALING.

multi-factor analysis, see under FACTOR ANALYSIS; MULTIVARIATE ANALYSIS.

multilateralism, see under BILATERALISM.

multinational companies, see TRANSNATIONAL COMPANIES.

multiple-choice method. In MENTAL TESTING and other forms of examination, a method of questioning in which the answer must be selected from alternatives provided by the questioner. Such fixed-alternative questions are capable of ingenious refinements and, for some purposes, are preferable to conventional free-answer or open questions. See also CONVERGERS AND DIVERGERS.   I.M.L.H.

multiple sclerosis. A disease, usually progressive, of the central NERVOUS SYSTEM, characterized by remissions and paroxysmal increases in severity, and caused by demyelization of the white matter of the brain or spinal cord or both.   H.L.

multiples. Two- or three-dimensional art objects (other than lithographs, screen-prints, etchings, and relief prints) that are made in bulk, usually in a signed and numbered limited edition.   A.K.W.

multiplicative axiom, see AXIOM OF CHOICE.

multipolarity. An intellectual MODEL of the international political system which claims that political power is likely to become effectively concentrated and exercised by several major world powers, a process known as multipolarization. Like BIPOLARITY in the 1950s and 1960s, multipolarity is in the 1970s beginning to play an increasing role in determining U.S. foreign policy, having arisen to accommodate the resurgence of China, Japan, and Western Europe as world powers. Whereas the two 'super-powers' were set apart from the rest by the possession of nuclear capability, the determining factor in the recent evolution of several world powers has been an aggregation of economic strength.   D.E.

multi-programming, see under COMPUTING.

multivariate analysis. The statistical analysis of data involving more than one type of measurement or observation. Various subdivisions may be distinguished. Thus the CORRELATION or REGRESSION relation of a single variable (e.g. a person's weight) with several other variables (e.g. age, sex, social class) is known as a *multiple correlation* or *regression analysis*. The term multivariate analysis is often restricted to problems where more than one such dependent variable (e.g. both height and weight) are being analysed simultaneously. In some problems no external variables (such as age or sex) with which to correlate are available; and the correlation structure may be expressed in terms of an internal set of hypothetical components or *factors* (see FACTOR ANALYSIS; CLUSTER ANALYSIS).   M.S.BA.

multiversity. A word coined by Clark Kerr, former President of the University of California at Berkeley, to indicate the enormous variety of purposes in a university like California set down on about 100 campuses, many of which are universities in themselves. In a university in Newman's sense (*The Idea of a University*) the parts are those of an organism. In a multiversity, on the other hand, many parts can be added or subtracted with little effect on the whole.   W.A.C.S.
Bibl: C. Kerr, *The Uses of the University* (Cambridge, Mass., 1963).

Munari, Bruno (Italian sculptor, kinetic artist, designer, and film-maker, *b*. 1907), see under KINETIC ART.

Munch, Edvard (Norwegian painter and engraver, 1863–1944), see under BRÜCKE, DIE; EXPRESSIONISM.

Munich. The capital city of Bavaria, which became the symbol of APPEASEMENT after the 'summit' conference of 29–30 September 1938 attended by Hitler (Germany), Mussolini (Italy), Chamberlain (Britain), and Daladier (France). Acting under the German threat of war the conference (without Czech participation) awarded to Germany the fortified frontier areas of Czechoslovakia inhabited by the Sudeten-German minority. 'Munich' has since become synonymous with any ill-judged, pusillanimous, and self-defeating attempt to buy off would-be aggressors at the expense of third parties under the cloak of 'satisfying their legitimate claims'.   D.C.W.
Bibl: J. W. Wheeler-Bennett, *Munich* (London, 1948); K. Eubank, *Munich* (Norman, Okla., 1963).

Münzenberg, Willi (German Communist publicist, 1889–1940), see under FRONT ORGANIZATION.

muon. An ELEMENTARY PARTICLE in the MESON family.   M.V.B.

Murray, Henry Alexander (U.S. psychologist, *b*. 1893), see under THEMATIC APPERCEPTION TEST.

Murry, John Middleton (British literary critic, 1889–1957), see under CRITERION, THE.

Musadegh, Mohammed (Iranian statesman, 1880–1967), see under CIA.

musée imaginaire (museum without walls), see IMAGINARY MUSEUM.

music theatre. Originally, as used by the composers György Ligeti and Mauricio Kagel, a form of musical performance that takes place on a stage, with some theatrical aids such as props and costumes. In London in 1956 Alexander Goehr and John Cox formed their 'Music Theatre Ensemble' which extended this concept to cover the performance of works by Schönberg, Kurt Weill, Goehr, Maxwell Davies, and others, some of them involving a dramatically significant text. It is to be distinguished from opera, but like opera is on the whole of musical rather than theatrical interest.   J.W.

musicology. The academic study of music, with particular reference to its history and to questions of authenticity and AESTHETICS. Although musicologists often disagree about the interpretation of points of historical detail, their combined researches have opened up vast areas of music which were previously unexplored or neglected. For many years such research was treated with indifference or derision by the average concert-performer; but since about 1950 the validity of the musicological contribution to the actual performance of early music has been widely accepted. While complete authenticity is a chimera (since we cannot hear, e.g., 17th-century music with 17th-century ears and minds), the search for it is always stimulating and revealing to the performer. Notable musicologists include Arnold Dolmetsch, Albert Schweitzer, Otto Deutsch, Alfred Einstein, Oliver Strunk, Egon Wellesz, the composer Peter Warlock (Philip Heseltine), Thurston Dart, and many others.   A.H.

musique concrète, see CONCRETE MUSIC.

Muslim Brotherhood. An ultra-conservative underground political organization active mainly in Egypt and Syria in opposition to current secular regimes. Founded as an overt organization in Egypt in 1929 by Hasan al-Banna (assassinated in 1949), it was modelled on the Dervish and Sufi religious orders, al-Banna's chosen title of 'Supreme Guide' being taken from their vocabulary. In the 1940s its strength was well above 100,000; it maintained a PARA-MILITARY organization and was responsible for a good many political assassinations. It was banned by the Egyptian revolutionary regime in 1954, but its underground activities continued, its members being the target of police action in the 1960s. The Brotherhood's aim of reimposing the laws of Islam on the social and political scene and its use of assassination make it the most potent and feared source of domestic opposition to the ruling authorities in the Middle East.   D.C.W.

Mussolini, Benito (Italian statesman, 1883–1945), see under AXIS; FASCISM; MUNICH; TERRORISM.

mutant. (1) A GENE which has undergone MUTATION within the particular stock of organisms under observation; (2) an organism bearing such a gene.   J.M.S.

mutation. A change in a GENE, or in the structure or number of CHROMOSOMES. Mutation is important in the study of EVOLUTION, because it is the ultimate origin of all new inheritable variation.
    J.M.S.

Muthesius, Hermann (German architect, 1861–1927), see under WERKBUND.

MVD (Ministry of Internal Affairs). One of two Soviet organizations, the other being the KGB, which share, with somewhat fluctuating lines of demarcation, responsibility for order and security. Roughly speaking, MVD (as opposed to KGB) is devoted to the non-secret elements of police organization: the maintenance of overt order, and the regulation and, where necessary, repression (including corrective labour camps) of the ordinary population. For a time (1962-8) it was rechristened MOOP – Ministry for the Defence of Public Order.   R.C.

My Lai. Complex of villages in South VIETNAM where in 1968 U.S. troops massacred the entire population under the impression that they were supporters of the VIETCONG and that the village was a Vietcong stronghold. In 1971 Lieutenant William Calley and his immediate superior, Captain Ernest Medina, were court-martialled in the U.S.A., the former being sentenced to 20 years, the latter acquitted. The incident did much to polarize American opinion on the issue of patriotism versus justice, as it did to publicize the decline in morale and discipline of the U.S. Army in Vietnam.   D.C.W.

mycology. The study of the fungi, which include the yeasts, penicillins, and familiar fungi like mushrooms and toadstools, and are clearly enough demarcated from plants and animals to deserve the status of a kingdom of their own.   P.M.

mysticism. The direct experience of the divine as real and near, blotting out all sense of time and producing intense joy. The divine may be conceived as in PANTHEISM, so that the experience is interpreted as a glad union with all nature (as celebrated in much poetry), or it may be thought of as the bliss of ending all separate existence, as in the BUDDHIST idea of *Nirvana*. The experience may be limited to specially mysterious, sacred, or 'numinous' objects, as described in Rudolf Otto's *The Idea of the Holy* (1917), or it may simply be valued as a more intense or ecstatic awareness of the surrounding reality, an awareness which is close to the state of mind produced by psychedelic DRUGS. The possibility of such mysticism is one of the factors accounting for the popularity of COMPARATIVE RELIGION amid the modern West's materialism. But in Christianity, as in JUDAISM and ISLAM and as often in BUDDHISM and HINDUISM, the aim of mysticism has been a closer knowledge and adoration of God, leading to the 'beatific vision' of God and to eternal joy in his presence, or even in union with him (see THEISM).

Among Christians in the 20th century there has been much interest in the literature of mysticism, and also some sustained practice of the art of contemplating God in secret. In THEOLOGY, however, mysticism has often been accused of belittling the historical self-revelation of God (safeguarded by orthodoxy) and of being remote from the problems of daily life. (G.K. Chesterton wrote that mysticism begins in mist, centres in 'I', and ends in schism.) 'Mystical theology' is given a place in CATHOLICISM, but only alongside MORAL THEOLOGY and 'ascetical' theology, which deals with self-discipline and the humbler levels of prayer. D.L.E.

Bibl: W. T. Stace, *Mysticism and Philosophy* (London and Philadelphia, 1961); R. C. Zaehner, *Mysticism, Sacred and Profane* (Oxford, 1957; N.Y., 1961).

myth. A 'sacred' narrative, from which legends and fairy tales are not always clearly distinguishable. In a common tradition of analysis, myth is above all explanatory (how something came to be as it is). In the anthropological tradition best represented by B. Malinowski (1884-1942), myths are seen as justifications ('charters') of INSTITUTIONS, rights, etc. But the most recent anthropological discussions have been conducted with reference to Lévi-Strauss's thesis that the meaning of a myth lies below the narrative surface, being detectable by a close analysis of the individual incidents and items in the narrative, by their regrouping, and by their study in the context of the transformations they undergo in all versions of the myth. They then reveal an endless struggle to overcome 'contradictions'. The anthropological study of myth links with psychological, literary, and classical studies, and with POLITICAL SCIENCE and SOCIOLOGY. In the latter, myth is often no longer a 'sacred' narrative but, so to say, a whole value-bestowing area of belief. See also STRUCTURALISM. M.F.

Bibl: G. S. Kirk, *Myth, its Meaning and Functions in Ancient and Other Cultures* (London and Berkeley, 1970; E. R. Leach (ed.), *The Structural Study of Myth and Totemism* (London, 1967).

mythopoeia. Deliberate and conscious MYTH-making; a writer's return to the primitive habit of non-logical anthropomorphization and ritualization. Some artists, reacting against the sophistications of DEISM, RATIONALISM, and ATHEISM, have set out to remythologize the material of their experience, to rediscover 'belief', but in personal and diverse ways. Thus, Blake's mythopoeic system is a response to the thinking of the Enlightenment, Yeats's to the loss of Christian faith; all contemporary mythopoeic activities may be described as responses to the sense of existential disappointment (see EXISTENTIALISM) generated by godless TECHNOCRACIES. M.S.-S.

N

Nabis, les. French artists' group, formed in 1888 under the impact of Gauguin's PONT-AVEN pictures, with Pierre Bonnard, Édouard Vuillard, Maurice Denis, Paul Sérusier, and the sculptors Georges Lacombe and Aristide Maillol as leading members. Their term 'Nabi', deriving from a Hebrew word for prophet, suggests the MYSTICISM tinged with THEOSOPHY that later turned Denis and (at BEURON) Jan Verkade into religious painters. But the main feature of their work in the 15 years of the group's activity was the application of Gauguin's flat surfaces (SYNTHETISM) and bright colours to calmer, more domestic or intimate subjects. Unlike their IMPRESSIONIST precursors they also ventured into theatre design, book and magazine illustration, posters, screens, and other aspects of applied art. In painting, however, they became overshadowed by the FAUVES, who made more spectacular use of much the same pictorial language.　J.W.
Bibl: C. Chassé, tr. M. Bullock, *The Nabis and their Period* (London and N.Y., 1969).

Nabokov, Vladimir (Russian-U.S. novelist, *b.* 1899), see under LOLITA SYNDROME.

Nagy, Imre (Hungarian statesman, 1896–1958), see under HUNGARY.

Nahas Pasha, Mustafa an- (Egyptian statesman, 1876–1965), see under WAFD.

Nairn, Ian (British author and journalist, *b.* 1930), see under SUBTOPIA.

naive art, see under PRIMITIVE (2).

naive realism, see REALISM, NAIVE.

Namier, Sir Lewis Bernstein (British historian, 1888–1960), see under PROSOPOGRAPHY.

nand-gate, see under GATE.

nanosecond. 10^{-9} sec (one thousand-millionth of a second). A typical time interval in the HARDWARE of a COMPUTER, e.g. for the operation of a GATE. In PHYSICS it is the time taken for light to travel about 1 foot.　C.S.

narcissism. In psychoanalytical theory (see PSYCHOANALYSIS), extreme love of self. *Primary narcissism,* in which sexual energy is directed toward the self, is characteristic of the pre-genital stages of PSYCHOSEXUAL DEVELOPMENT, whereas *secondary narcissism* refers to feelings of pride experienced when the EGO identifies with the ideals of the SUPEREGO.　W.Z.

narcoanalysis, see under TRUTH DRUG.

Nash equilibrium. A CONCEPT in the theory of GAMES, which has been used in ECONOMICS. A number of individuals or firms, with possibly conflicting interests, are in a Nash equilibrium if each of them is following the best STRATEGY he can, given the strategies being followed by others. J. F. Nash showed in 1950 that such an EQUILIBRIUM exists rather generally if *mixed strategies* (i.e. strategies involving a random choice of action) are allowed. The concept allows no role for the formation of coalitions, or agreements to make side-payments.　J.A.M.

Nasser, Gamel Abdul (Egyptian statesman, 1918–70), see under PAN-ISLAM.

National Bolshevism. A polemical term in use in Germany between the wars to describe a policy of NATIONALIST resistance to the Treaty of Versailles and the West based on alliance with the other 'pariah power', Bolshevik Russia, against their common enemies. The idea was first started by Karl Radek in 1919: its paradoxical appeal attracted groups on both extremes of the political spectrum, nationalists on the RIGHT (like Reventlow and Moeller van den Bruck) and dissident COMMUNISTS and SOCIALISTS on the LEFT. It did not survive the NAZI capture of power.　A.L.C.B.

NATIONALIZATION

Bibl: K. von Klemperer, 'Towards a 4th Reich? The History of National Bolshevism in Germany' (*Review of Politics*, 13, 1951), pp. 191–211.

national debt (or *public debt*). The interest-bearing debt of a central government, sometimes extended to include the debt of state or local governments and public enterprises. The debt instruments may be marketable (bonds and Treasury bills) or non-marketable (deposits at savings banks and the like) and of varying maturity, from deposits withdrawable at sight to irredeemable bonds. The composition is influenced by MONETARY POLICY. The debt is accumulated through government borrowing (see FISCAL POLICY), and may be held by either home or foreign residents. Interest is paid with tax or other government receipts. Where the debt is partly held by foreign residents, interest and redemption involve debits in the BALANCE OF PAYMENTS. Except in this sense, the national debt does not constitute a burden on the economy. P.M.O.

national income. The income generated by the economic activity of a country. It corresponds to the economy's output of final consumption and INVESTMENT, since incomes included in national income – as distinct from, say, CAPITAL gains or receipts of transfer payments such as old-age pensions – are only created insofar as they arise in the provision of goods or services. More specifically, the term may be used so as to correspond either (1) to GROSS NATIONAL PRODUCT or (2) to *net* national product – i.e. national product after deduction of the amount of the economy's CAPITAL stock that has been used up in the productive process; this latter usage corresponds to the business practice of estimating profit income net of depreciation allowances or other allowances for capital consumption. W.B.

National Socialism, see NAZISM.

nationalisation, see NATIONALIZATION.

nationalism. (1) The feeling of belonging to a group united by common racial, linguistic, and historical ties, and usually identified with a particular territory. (2) A corresponding IDEOLOGY which exalts the nation state as the ideal form of political organization with an overriding claim on the loyalty of its citizens.

Developing first in Western Europe with the consolidation of nation states, nationalism brought about the reorganization of Europe in the 19th and 20th centuries (unification of Germany and Italy; break-up of the Habsburg and Ottoman empires) and has been the prime force in the political awakening of Asia and Africa. Nationalism has been a powerful source of inspiration in many of the arts and in the development of historical and language studies. This has proved to be as true of the 'new nations' of Africa and Asia as it was of 19th-century Europe where nationalism formed one of the dynamic elements in ROMANTICISM. In the first half of the 19th century nationalism was associated with DEMOCRACY, LIBERALISM, and the demand for civil and constitutional liberties; its greatest prophet, Mazzini (1805–72), gave a generous interpretation of the 'principle of nationality', seeing the individual nations as subdivisions of a larger world society which ought to live together in peace. In the later 19th century, however, nationalism assumed aggressive, intolerant forms (*integral nationalism*) identified with military and trade rivalries, national expansion at the expense of other peoples, and IMPERIALISM. In the 20th century it has been an essential element in FASCISM and other TOTALITARIAN movements, as well as a moving force in the rebellion of colonial peoples and in the resistance of nations and national MINORITIES threatened with subjugation by more powerful states. Despite the rival claims of CLASS war on the one hand and internationalism on the other, nationalism as a mass emotion has been the most powerful political force in the history of the modern world. A.L.C.B.

Bibl: H. Kohn, *Nationalism* (Princeton, 1955); E. Kamenka (ed.), *Nationalism* (London, corrected ed., 1976).

nationalization. The acquisition by the State of property previously held by private persons or companies. Such nationalization may be expropriation, when no compensation is paid; or (as widely practised in Western Europe after the end of the 1939–45 war) compensation may be paid in money or government bonds. The purpose of nationalization is sometimes explicitly political – to further the purposes of SOCIALISM or to 'acquire the commanding heights of the economy'. Sometimes, however, the aim may be more straightforwardly economic – to facilitate the imposition of certain aspects of government policy. In Western Europe since the end of World War II most countries have nationalized railways, electric power systems, sometimes the coalmines, and often the steel industry. In several countries (France and Italy in particular) motor car factories are also in the PUBLIC SECTOR.   M.V.P.

Bibl: W. A. Robson, *Problems of Nationalized Industry* (London, 1952); R. Pryke, *Public Enterprise in Practice* (London, 1971; N.Y., 1972).

nativism. In DEVELOPMENTAL PSYCHOLOGY, the theory that perceptual (see PERCEPTION) or other faculties are innate and not dependent on experiential stimuli or REINFORCEMENT for their development. See also NATURE/NURTURE. H.L.

NATO (North Atlantic Treaty Organization). An organization established on 4 April 1949 in a treaty signed by Belgium, Canada, Denmark, France, Iceland, Italy, Luxembourg, the Netherlands, Norway, Portugal, Britain, and the U.S.A.; Greece and Turkey acceded on 18 February 1952, West Germany on 9 May 1955. NATO is a permanent military alliance set up to defend Western Europe against the threat of Soviet aggression. In addition to integrated multinational commands, its organs consist of a Council, an International Secretariat, and various committees established to formulate common policies on political, social, and economic issues as well as military ones. Its founders' belief in a common Atlantic political and cultural heritage gradually dwindled with the growing European resentment of American leadership, expressed at its loudest in the withdrawal of French forces from all NATO commands in March 1966; a similar withdrawal of the Greek armed forces in August 1974 followed the renewed dispute with Turkey (also a member of NATO) over Cyprus. A number of attempts have been made – the Defence Planning Committee (1963), the Nuclear Defence Affairs Committee, the Nuclear Planning Group (1966), and the Eurogroup (1970) – to give increased Euro-pean participation in overall policy-making. Despite these tensions, NATO has provided, for nearly 30 years, the instrument by which the U.S.A. and Britain are committed to the defence of Western Europe with substantial forces stationed there even in time of peace.   D.C.W.

Bibl: E. H. van der Beugel, *From Marshall Aid to Atlantic Partnership* (Amsterdam and N.Y., 1966); P. H. Trezise, *The Atlantic Connection* (Washington, 1975).

Natorp, Paul (German philosopher, 1854–1924), see under NEO-KANTIANISM.

natural sciences. Roughly speaking, those branches of organized knowledge concerned with the material aspects of existence. But the CONCEPT of 'Nature' is so all-embracing, historically variable, and dependent upon METAPHYSICAL assumptions that it cannot be given an *a priori* definition. Traditionally, the natural world was contrasted with the 'supernatural' realm of THEOLOGY, but the modern convention is to draw a distinction between the natural sciences and the SOCIAL SCIENCES and/or. BEHAVIOURAL SCIENCES, related perhaps to the elements of CONSCIOUSNESS and choice in the sphere of human relations. The core disciplines of PHYSICS and CHEMISTRY (once called *natural philosophy*), GEOLOGY, and BIOLOGY (*natural history*) encroach on PHILOSOPHY through MATHEMATICS and spread vaguely into PSYCHOLOGY. This categorization has no practical significance, but is a convenient classification scheme for academic purposes (e.g. the Natural Sciences Tripos: an examination curriculum at Cambridge University). J.Z.

natural selection. The mechanism of evolutionary change, suggested simultaneously by Darwin and Wallace in 1858. The theory asserts that EVOLUTION occurs because those individuals of a SPECIES whose characteristics best fit them for survival are the ones which contribute most offspring to the next generation. These offspring will tend to have the characteristics by virtue of which their parents survived, and in this way the adaptation of the species to its environment will gradually be improved. It is now generally accepted that natural selection, acting on MUTA-TIONS which are in their origin non-adaptive, is the primary cause of evolution. J.M.S.

Bibl: C. Darwin, *On the Origin of Species* (1859; 6th ed., London, 1872, N.Y., 1873).

naturalism.

(1) In ETHICS, the doctrine that the CRITERION of right action is some empirical feature of the natural world such as the happiness of sentient beings or the self-preservation of an individual, group, or SPECIES. Agreeing that moral utterances are genuine PROPOSITIONS, which can be known to be true or false, it maintains that the facts that verify them (see VERIFICA-TION) are of an ordinary empirical kind and not of a supernatural character (as in MORAL THEOLOGY) or constituents of an autonomous realm of moral values, accessible only to a special moral faculty (as in INTUITIONISM). It is this doctrine, in the first instance, that G. E. Moore taxed with committing the NATURALISTIC FALLACY.

(2) More generally, any PHILOSOPHY which sees mind as dependent upon, included within, or emergent from, material nature, and not as being prior to or in some way more real than it. Its direct opposite is not *supernaturalism*, which holds that the realm of the divine is the only or primary reality, but ANTI-NATURALISM. IDEALISM is antinaturalistic but is not always supernaturalistic. A.Q.

(3) An approach to PSYCHOLOGY and SOCIAL SCIENCE which assumes that human beings are essentially physico-chemical SYSTEMS, and can be studied in exactly the same way as the rest of the physical world. For the opposite view, and for an intermediate position, see ANTI-NATURALISM. A.S.

(4) In literature and drama, a tendency – consequent on but distinguishable from REALISM – influential in Western Europe from the 1870s to the 1890s (for its Italian version see VERISM) and in the U.S.A. and Russia from the 1890s. A form of literary POSITIVISM, naturalism is basically post-Darwinian and inclined towards an environmentalist and often evolutionary explanation of life (see ENVIRONMENT; EVOLUTION); it often takes the form of close reportage and documentation and involves systematized views of connection and CAUSALITY; and it is disposed to

regard the literary act as an 'experiment' on the scientific model. This last analogy is established by Zola in the most explicit book on the subject, *Le Roman expéri-mental* (1880); his own Rougon-Macquart series of novels exemplifies classic naturalism, based on intensive research into social conditions and forces and on physiological and evolutionary principles. In the theatre the leading naturalist was Ibsen, whose influence spread massively over Europe in the last two decades of the 19th century. In America the delayed reaction to naturalism was perhaps the result of neg-lecting the vast forces for social change, and the moral and social problems, that arose in American society at its high point of INDUSTRIALIZATION; but with Frank Norris, Stephen Crane, and Hamlin Gar-land in the 1890s a tradition developed which has been remarkably persistent. By this date naturalism in Europe was giving way to a new AESTHETICISM and SYM-BOLISM: Strindberg was overtaking Ibsen, and the IMPRESSIONISTIC element in naturalism was pushing through to create the uncertain surface of much MODERNIST writing and painting. Naturalism was the transition point at the end of an era in Europe; in some countries and in some writers it has persisted significantly into the new century. M.S.BR.

Bibl: H. M. Block, *Naturalistic Triptych* (N.Y., 1970); R. N. Stromberg (ed.), *Realism, Naturalism and Symbolism* (London and N.Y., 1968); L. R. Furst and P. N. Skrine, *Naturalism* (London, 1969; N.Y., 1971).

(5) In French painting, an analogous movement which derived from mid-19th-century REALISM, and to conserva-tive eyes soon seemed a safer alternative to the IMPRESSIONISM which was spring-ing from the same roots at the same time. Its prophet was the critic Castagnary; its product the stock art of the Third Repub-lic, as exemplified by the former Musée du Luxembourg.

In senses (4) and (5), the term is used pejoratively by COMMUNIST critics, who tend to see naturalism as the dispassion-ate, more or less detailed photographic rendering of a non-tendentious scene, and compare it unfavourably with realism, and even more with SOCIALIST REALISM. The latter, however, in Western eyes, is often extremely naturalistic. J.W.

naturalistic fallacy. In ETHICS, a term coined by G. E. Moore for the alleged mistake of defining 'good' in terms of ordinary empirical expressions such as 'pleasant' or 'desired' or, indeed, of giving any ANALYSIS of 'good', that is to say any definition intended to elucidate its MEANING. Moore branded ethical NATURALISM, which involves such analyses or definitions, as fallacious, and defended ethical INTUITIONISM, taking goodness to be a characteristic of states of affairs that cannot be discerned by ordinary empirical observation but only by an autonomous moral faculty. The phrase has come to be applied to any account of ethical terms or utterances which identifies them in meaning with any terms or utterances of a factual or descriptive kind and, in particular, with any INFERENCE that purports to derive a NORMATIVE conclusion from purely factual premises, any passage in reasoning from 'is' to 'ought'. In this form it is the negative starting-point of EMOTIVISM and all other ethical theories which classify VALUE-JUDGEMENTS as some form of discourse that is not propositional (see PROPOSITION). A.Q.

Bibl: G. E. Moore, *Principia Ethica* (Cambridge, 1903), ch. 1.

nature *versus* nurture. In DEVELOPMENTAL PSYCHOLOGY, the controversy over ascribing due weight to GENETIC facts on the one hand and ENVIRONMENTAL ones on the other as factors responsible for the characteristics of an organism. See also NATIVISM. H.L.

Nazism. Term formed from the abbreviation for National Socialist German Workers' Party, a political movement founded in 1919 and taken over by Adolf Hitler (1889-1945) in the early 1920s to become the basis on which he established his twelve-year DICTATORSHIP (1933–45) in Germany. Nazism originated as a movement of protest against the surrender of 1918 and the Treaty of Versailles (and the WEIMAR REPUBLIC, which Hitler held to blame for both), but it was only in 1930, with the economic DEPRESSION and mass unemployment, that the Nazis succeeded in attracting mass support. Taken into partnership by a RIGHT-wing coalition in January 1933, Hitler rapidly disposed of his partners, liquidated the opposition

parties, and established a TOTALITARIAN regime based on a monopoly of power by the Nazi party.

Nazism shared many of the features of FASCISM in other countries. Its special characteristics were (1) its belief in the racial superiority of the 'Aryan' race and specifically of its best exemplar, the German people, a 'master race' (*Herrenvolk*) with an inalienable claim to LEBENSRAUM at the expense of other inferior races in Central and Eastern Europe; (2) a virulent ANTISEMITISM that denounced the Jews as the mortal enemies of the German people and found expression before World War II in the NUREMBERG LAWS and during the war in the FINAL SOLUTION, a plan, largely carried into effect, for the extermination of the Jewish population of Europe; (3) German ambitions, backed by German military power, to establish their hegemony over Europe; these were a principal cause of World War II; and (4) the personality, ruthlessness, and political leadership of Adolf Hitler. A.L.C.B.

Bibl: A. Bullock, *Hitler: a Study in Tyranny* (rev. ed., London and N.Y., 1964); K. D. Bracher, tr. J. Steinberg, *The German Dictatorship* (London and N.Y., 1970).

NEAC, see NEW ENGLISH ART CLUB.

Néant, le. Sartre's French equivalent of Heidegger's *Das Nichts*, both meaning the same as 'nothingness'. The notion is important to EXISTENTIALISM, where it refers variously to the object of objectless ANXIETY (i.e. to what anxiety that isn't about anything is about), to death, and to the indeterminacy of human nature until it is realized by acts of free choice. ANALYTIC PHILOSOPHERS criticize the metaphysical affirmations in which it occurs as misinterpreting a formal concept of LOGIC, that of negation, as a genuine name or *referring* expression (see CONNOTATION), as in the Lewis Carroll exchange: 'I see nobody on the road.' 'I only wish *I* had such eyes. To be able to see Nobody!' A.Q.

nebula. A GALAXY, or a cloud of incandescent gas within our own galaxy, which appears as a misty object in the heavens. M.V.B.

necessary and sufficient conditions. PROPOSITION A is a *necessary condition* of proposition B if B's truth and A's falsity are incompatible; proposition A is a *sufficient condition* of proposition B if B's falsity and A's truth are incompatible. I.M.D.L.

Nechaev, Sergei Gennadiyevich (Russian revolutionary, 1847–82), see under JACOBINISM; NIHILISM.

Needham, Joseph (British biologist and historian, *b.* 1900), see under ORGANIZER.

negative income tax. A proposal to incorporate an element of symmetry into the American system of progressive taxation by offering Treasury payments to individuals or families whose incomes fall below a certain level, while continuing to collect taxes due from the more prosperous. In conservative form the benefits are set at levels low enough to avoid competition with ill-paid jobs, or are associated with work and training requirements as in President Nixon's Family Assistance Program of welfare reform. In more generous versions, the thrust is redistributive, a deliberate attempt to shift income from the top to the bottom portions of the income distribution. R.L.

negentropy, see under ENTROPY (2).

négritude. A term coined in the 1930s, and much used since World War II, to express the sense of a common Negro inheritance and destiny among French-educated Negro INTELLECTUALS in Africa and the Caribbean. It embraces the revolt against colonialist values (see IMPERIALISM), glorification of the African past, and nostalgia for the beauty and harmony of traditional African society, which is seen as being founded on Black emotion and intuition as opposed to Hellenic reason and LOGIC. *Négritude* is, however, a universalist concept, which owes a great deal to its French, or even Parisian, intellectual origins, and it is very different from traditional African tribalism. Although it has helped the black cause, it has also been criticized by blacks themselves as resting on a doubtful belief in intrinsic cultural blackness and as neglecting contemporary political realities. The main exponents have been L.-S. Senghor

(President of Senegal) and Aimé Césaire, and the chief political critic Frantz Fanon. A useful discussion of the various issues involved is to be found in 'Orphée noir', Sartre's Introduction to Senghor's *Anthologie de la poésie nègre et malgache* (1948). J.G.W.

Nehru, Jawaharlal (Indian statesman, 1889–1964), see under PANCH SHILA.

neighbourhood. Term embodying the idea of a recognizable physical unit which is also a social unit. The idea has been highly influential in urban planning, and especially in the post-war NEW TOWNS. It stems from a view of the medieval small town as an ideal entity which requires re-creation if the anonymity of the METROPOLIS is to be avoided. Such neighbourhoods have as a rule been taken as equivalent to the catchment area of a primary school (see NEIGHBOURHOOD SCHOOL). It has, however, been argued that the real social contacts of a mobile pluralist society are not so geographically circumscribed. M.BR.

neighbourhood school. A school intended to provide education for all the children of a particular age who live within a certain distance of it. It is an administrative arrangement with an obvious social and political objective. In rural settings with strategically placed schools the area usually defines itself fairly easily. In towns several schools are sometimes within reach, and tension can arise over the desire for choice of school, e.g. in areas where new slum-clearance estates border on established housing, or where immigrant groups have settled. Religious day-schools (for example Roman Catholic schools) tend also to cut across the NEIGHBOURHOOD principle. W.A.C.S.

Neill, Alexander Sutherland (British educationist, 1883–1973), see under CHILD-CENTRED EDUCATION; FREE UNIVERSITY.

neo-classicism.
(1) In architecture, a movement between 1750 and 1850 which became the first international style, ranging from St Petersburg to Virginia, and strongly influencing the modern movement, both intellectually and visually. It was inspired

by the recent archaeological discoveries in Greece and Rome, by the rational ideas of the Enlightenment and the resulting notions of 'apparent utility' developed by Laugier, and by the rejection of baroque and rococo forms in favour of simple geometric, largely rectilinear, shapes derived from antique sources. Neo-classicism was strongest in France and Germany and its influence on such 20th-century architects as Mies van der Rohe can be traced directly back through Behrens to Schinkel (1781–1841). A perverted form was associated with TOTALITARIAN Germany, Italy, and the U.S.S.R. during the 1930s. M.BR.

Bibl: H. Honour, *Neo-Classicism* (Harmondsworth, 1968).

(2) In painting and sculpture, the evocation of the 'noble simplicity and calm grandeur' declared by Winckelmann to characterize the art of the Ancients. The style spread rapidly from the mid 18th century: Canova, David, and Flaxman, then Ingres and Thorwaldsen, were leading exponents.

More recently Picasso displayed a thoroughly neo-classical style, especially in his line-drawings of the 1920s, sometimes even taking classical subjects. The term has also been applied (though more obscurely) to various works of the same period: the Ingres-inspired paintings of Matisse, the METAPHYSICAL PAINTING of de Chirico and Carrà, and the serene still-lifes of Morandi. Just as 18th-century neo-classicism had supplanted the exuberance of baroque, so did these productions of the 1920s represent a return to passivity and restraint after the turbulent experiments of the preceding decade. P.C.

(3) In music, a 20th-century reaction against the emotional extremes of Wagner and his immediate followers, a conscious rejection of ROMANTICISM, and a harking back to 18th-century models. This postulated a certain detachment from the musical material and a suppression of personal involvement on the part of the composer. Paradoxically it was Stravinsky, whose *Rite of Spring* had revolutionized musical thought, who in turn became an anti-revolutionary, reverting to 18th-century patterns and textures in the bulk of the compositions he wrote· between about 1920 and 1950. Of these, *Pulcinella* (1919, based on music by Pergolesi, with actual quotations), the Octet for Wind

Instruments, the Piano Concerto, the Symphony in C, the ballet *Apollo,* and *The Rake's Progress* are notable examples of the neo-classical style. Hindemith, Casella, Malipiero, and to a lesser extent Bartók are other composers who tried to find a satisfactory contemporary equivalent to classical ideals. A.H.

neo-colonialism, see under IMPERIALISM.

neo-Darwinism, see under DARWINISM.

neo-Destour party, see under DESTOUR PARTY.

neo-Fascism. Movements embodying or seeming to embody a revival of the ideas and methods of pre-1945 FASCISM, especially in France and, as the MOVIMENTO SOCIALE ITALIANO, in Italy. D.C.W.

neo-Firthian, see under FIRTHIAN.

neo-Freudian. Adjective used to describe several schools of PSYCHOANALYSIS which modified the view of Freud and his followers (see FREUDIAN) that the individual is motivated by instinctual drives which control the psychic energy (the LIBIDO) behind all human action. The neo-Freudians expanded the motivating forces to include environmental factors, thereby rejecting the concept of libido with its link to the instincts. The most influential of the neo-Freudians was H. S. Sullivan (1892–1949), who created the inter-personal theory of PSYCHIATRY, according to which personality consists of the pattern of the individual's personal relationships; it exists only in the social context in which it is observed. In this view, mental illness is caused by unsatisfactory social relationships; these maladaptive patterns of relating to others are learned early in life and develop because of inadequate primary relationships between the mother and child. Other prominent neo-Freudians include Karen Horney, Erich Fromm, and Erik Erikson. R.P.-S.

neo-Hegelianism. A revival of the philosophical IDEALISM of Hegel. Prominent neo-Hegelians have been, in Britain, the school of T. H. Green (1836–82) and F. H. Bradley (1846–1924), whose most loyal (if idiosyncratic) member was J. E. McTaggart (1866–1925) and most recent R. G. Collingwood (1889–1943); in

France, Léon Brunschvicg (1869–1944); in Italy, Benedetto Croce (1891–1970).　　　A.Q.

neo-imperialism, see under IMPERIALISM.

neo-Impressionism. French school of painting deriving from IMPRESSIONISM ← but based on the more scientific approach of Georges Seurat, whose readings in SPECTROSCOPY led him to elaborate two techniques of rendering effects of light, both laborious by comparison with the Impressionist sketch: (1) *divisionism*, or the splitting of the spectrum into dabs of pure primary colour, and (2) *pointillisme*, or the reduction of those dabs to small dots. The term neo-Impressionism was coined by the critic Félix Fénéon in the Brussels magazine *L'Art moderne* on 19 September 1886, the year when Seurat's masterpiece *Un Dimanche d'été à la Grande Jatte* (now in the Art Institute of Chicago) was shown at the last Impressionist Exhibition. Among its adherents were Camille Pissarro and his son Lucien, Paul Signac, H. E. Cross, and Maximilien Luce; van Gogh too was influenced during his last few years in France. The school was ANARCHIST or SOCIALIST in its sympathies; this was sometimes reflected in the choice of subjects, especially Luce's. Outside France it embraced the Belgians Théo van Rysselberghe and Henri van de Velde (the subsequent ART NOUVEAU designer and architect), the Dutchman Jan Tooroop, the Italians Giovanni Segantini and Gaetano Previati, and through them the FUTURIST painters, who included a form of divisionism in their 'Technical Manifesto' of 1910.　　J.W.
Bibl: R. L. Herbert, *Neo-Impressionism* (N.Y., 1968).

neo-Kantianism. A school of German philosophers in the late 19th century, inaugurated by Liebmann's invocation of 1865: 'back to Kant'. In effect it was a revival of aprioristic (see APRIORISM) EPISTEMOLOGY encouraged by the failure of METAPHYSICS, as expounded by Hegel and subsequent speculative thinkers, to do justice to developments in MATHEMATICS and the NATURAL SCIENCES. Leading neo-Kantians were Lange, Cohen, Natorp, and Cassirer in Germany, Renouvier in France, Adamson in Britain.　　　A.Q.

neo-Lamarckism, see under LAMARCK-ISM.

neolithic, see under THREE-AGE SYSTEM.

neolithic revolution. Term introduced by V. G. Childe to describe the development of food-producing economies in the Middle East during the so-called New Stone Age, i.e. between 9,000 and 6,000 B.C. Childe regarded this as the first major step forward in man's development: it was followed by the URBAN REVOLUTION and the Industrial Revolution. Recent work has tended to emphasize the complexity of the processes involved and a time span greater than Childe envisaged. As a broad generalization, however, the term still has some value.　　B.C.
Bibl: S. Cole, *The Neolithic Revolution* (London, 3rd ed., 1963).

neo-Malthusianism. Malthus believed that any attempt to raise the living standards of the poorest section of the population above subsistence level was bound to be unsuccessful, because it would lead to an increase in population pressing on the means of subsistence, and this increase would restore the previous situation. The only solution he offered was 'moral restraint', i.e. postponement of marriage, coupled with pre-marital chastity, until parents were able to support a family. Later writers, while accepting his analysis, suggested that the consequences of Malthus's Principle of Population could be avoided by the adoption of birth control within marriage. This school of thought was called neo-Malthusianism.　　E.G.
Bibl: F. H. Amphlett Micklewright, 'The Rise and Decline of English Neo-Malthusianism' (*Population Studies,* July 1961).

neo-Marxism. A term first applied to the so-called FRANKFURT SCHOOL and later also to some NEW LEFT and other interpreters of Marx. With few exceptions their common tendency is to take his early writings as their starting-point, to Hegelianize (see HEGELIANISM) MARXISM, to stress its romantic and Utopian elements, to give it a more existential (see EXISTENTIALISM) than economic emphasis, to focus on ALIENATION rather than on productivity. This reversal of Marx's own evolution has its roots in such writings as *History and Class Consciousness* by Georg Lukács (1885–1971), the first systematic thinker who worked from Marx back to Hegel, substituting for Hegel's 'Spirit' (*Geist*) Marx's PROLETARIAT as a carrier of historical CONSCIOUSNESS.

The history of neo-Marxism parallels in a way the disintegration of the original Hegelian school in the 1840s. Thus the cultural pessimism of Bruno Bauer found its echo in the late writings of Horkheimer and Adorno, while the abstract UTOPIANISM of the RADICAL 'left Hegelians' found its continuity in Herbert Marcuse who provided a philosophical platform to the contemporary New Left. The intellectual dispersion of neo-Marxists parallels not only that of the young Hegelians but also the subsequent attempts to synthesize Marxism with other tendencies by giving it a special methodological or epistemological emphasis. Even before the emergence of neo-Marxism, various attempts were made to combine Marxism with POSITIVISM, PRAGMATISM, and ethical NEO-KANTIANISM. Later it came to be combined with PSYCHOANALYSIS (by Fromm), PHENOMENOLOGY (by Merleau-Ponty), EXISTENTIALISM (by Sartre), and STRUCTURALISM (by Althusser). L.L.

Bibl: G. Lichtheim, *From Marx to Hegel* (London and N.Y., 1971); M. Jay, *The Dialectical Imagination* (London and N.Y., 1973); P. Anderson, *Considerations on Western Marxism* (London, 1976).

neo-mercantilism. A term, put into circulation by the economist Harry Johnson, for modern rationalizations of policies designed to protect home producers from overseas competition, or to subsidize exporters, especially by indirect and selective methods. Old-fashioned MERCANTILISM, against which Adam Smith launched a successful onslaught in 1776, was based on the belief that a country's wealth consists of its stocks of precious metals, which should be increased by securing a favourable balance of trade. Mercantilism gained a second wind with the DEPRESSION in the 1930s, when countries tried to export their UNEMPLOYMENT by trade restrictions and competitive DEVALUATIONS. This beggar-my-neighbour approach to employment policies has not disappeared from popular political debate. But an attempt has been made to give PROTECTIONIST policies a new respectability by the cult of 'technologically advanced industries' (which very often do not pay commercially) as the key to growth, and by the argument that blocs such as the EEC must be held together by highly protectionist farm policies. S.BR.

Bibl: H. G. Johnson (ed.), *The New Mercantilism* (Oxford, 1974).

neo-modernism, see under MODERNISM.

neo-orthodoxy. A term used to describe the insistence of BARTHIAN and other PROTESTANT theologians (especially Reinhold Niebuhr in the U.S.A.), *c.* 1920–60, on the TRANSCENDENCE of God and thus on some of the central themes in 'orthodox' LUTHERANISM and CALVINISM, but with a new conviction that God's self-revelation must be interpreted afresh. See also CRISIS THEOLOGY. D.L.E.

neo-plasticism, see under STIJL, DE.

neo-Prague school, see under PRAGUE SCHOOL.

neo-realism. Term originally used by Umberto Barbaro in 1943 to define the poetic REALISM characteristic of the pre-war French cinema, in particular the Carné–Prévert films, which he held up as an object lesson to Italian film-makers at a time when Visconti's *Ossessione* (1942, a raw, uncompromisingly honest adaptation of James Cain's *The Postman Always Rings Twice*) had finally broken the stranglehold of middle-class gentility in the Fascist cinema's 'white telephone era'. The great days of Italian neo-realism began in 1945 with Rossellini's *Rome, Open City*, continued with films by Rossellini, De Sica, Visconti, Lattuada, and De Santis, and ended some five years later under opposition (financially expressed) from church and state. A product of political and social circumstances (the legacy of FASCISM and World War II), the movement was essentially a bitter outcry against widespread poverty and injustice. Though the Italian neo-realist films were disparate in approach and method, the term is now usually applied to films (of any nationality) following the guidelines laid down by Cesare Zavattini, script-writer and theorist of the movement; 'real' people, not professional actors, human situation rather than plot, humble setting (peasant, slum, outcast society), social indignation. Neo-realism is not to be confused with NOUVEAU RÉALISME. T.C.C.M.

Bibl: R. Armes, *Patterns of Realism* (London and South Brunswick, 1971); P. Leprohon, tr. R. Greaves and O. Stallybrass, *The Italian Cinema* (London and N.Y., 1972).

neoteny. An evolutionary process (see EVOLUTION) in consequence of which organisms become sexually mature and therefore in effect adult at a stage corresponding to embryonic or foetal stage of their ancestors. Neoteny has, unquestionably, been a most important evolutionary stratagem – one which makes possible what Hardy has called an 'escape from specialization'. The chordates themselves (see ZOOLOGY) probably arose neotenously from animals akin to sea-urchins. Again, the ostrich has some characteristics reminiscent of a foetal bird, and human beings have some characteristics of foetal apes – e.g. the relatively enormous size of the brain. In the latter context neoteny has been referred to as *foetalization*.   P.M.

neothermal period, see under POLLEN ANALYSIS.

neo-Thomism. The renewed appreciation in Roman CATHOLICISM of the teaching of St Thomas Aquinas (1226–74). The study of St Thomas (who was greatly indebted to Aristotle) was enjoined on all students of THEOLOGY by Pope Leo XIII in 1875, but has been made more fruitful in the 20th century (e.g. in the varied writings of Jacques Maritain, 1882–1973) by greater consideration of the issues raised in CRISIS THEOLOGY and CHRISTIAN EXISTENTIALISM. The more rigid type of Thomism is known as *scholasticism*.   D.L.E.

Bibl: E. H. Gilson, tr. L. K. Shook, *The Christian Philosophy of St Thomas Aquinas* (London and N.Y., 1957).

NEP (New Economic Policy). A policy introduced by the Soviet Government in March 1921 after the 10th Congress of the BOLSHEVIK Party. Ending the policy of 'war communism' (see COMMUNISM), it aimed at restoring the economy by concessions to private trade and industry and by abandoning the pressure on peasant smallholders. Before NEP these were forced to provide the State with compulsory deliveries of agricultural products and were considered to be the natural enemies of SOCIALISM. But although under NEP the State retained control over the 'commanding heights' of the economy – heavy industry and foreign trade – the new policy encountered opposition inside the Party from RADICAL elements, who considered it a betrayal of the workers in the interest of the peasants and of socialism for the sake of State CAPITALISM.

The economic consequences of NEP were beneficial, and the country recovered economically, reaching in 1927 the production level of 1913. Politically, NEP produced a relaxation in internal Soviet policies, but at the same time Party discipline was strengthened by the elimination of the right to factional disagreement, and the Party increased its hold over the State. By the time NEP was abandoned by Stalin in 1929 the Party was well on the way to monolithic STALINISM, with oppositionists defeated and the resistance from the Party RIGHT (led by Bukharin) to compulsory COLLECTIVIZATION and forcible industrialization neither organized nor effective. The new policies which replaced NEP after 1929 amounted in effect to a 'second revolution', this time implemented 'from above'. NEP thus proved to be an interval, a tactical retreat, perhaps shorter than Lenin envisaged when he introduced it.   L.L.

Bibl: E. H. Carr, *The Bolshevik Revolution, 1917–23*, vols. 2, 3 (London and N.Y., 1952–53).

nephanalysis. Meteorological term for the analysis of cloud patterns, e.g. in the interpretation of synoptic conditions. Its use is now generally reserved for the study of global weather by SATELLITE monitoring where nephanalysis may provide early-warning indication of hurricane centres. See also REMOTE SENSING.   P.H.

Bibl: E. C. Barrett, *Viewing Weather from Space* (London and N.Y., 1967).

Nerval, Gérard de (pseud. of Gérard Labrunie, French poet, 1808–55), see under SYMBOLISM.

Nervi, Pier Luigi (Italian engineer and architect, *b*. 1891), see under CONCRETE; STRUCTURE.

nervous system. The part of the body responsible for sensation, the excitation of muscular action, and the correlations between sensory input and motor performance that make complex behaviour possible. The nervous system is conventionally subdivided into the *central nervous system*, which is the seat of the major correlating functions of the nervous system, and the *peripheral nervous system*, which establishes the connections between on the one hand the sense organs and the central nervous system, and on the other hand the central nervous system and the muscular system. Whereas in lower vertebrates the brain is dominated by the olfactory function, and the correlation centres are relatively little developed, the higher vertebrates are distinguished by the enormous development of the *new brain* or *neopallium*, which represents as it were the hypertrophy of the correlative elements of the brain. Contrasted with the neopallium is the *ancient brain* or *archipallium*, consisting of the *brain stem*, the *midbrain*, and the *between brain* or *thalamus*. In addition to the central and peripheral nervous system, it is conventional to distinguish an *autonomic nervous system*, specially concerned with unconscious or 'automatic' functions, such as the movements of the gut, the state of dilatation of the blood vessels, etc.   P.M.

net barter terms of trade, see under TERMS OF TRADE.

net present value, see under DISCOUNTED CASH FLOW.

net reproduction rate. A statistical PARAMETER expressing a population's prevailing fertility when duly weighted by its mortality. When computed for the female part of the population only and for female births, it represents the ratio of live female births in successive generations, so that a rate higher than unity (i.e. 1 to 1) signifies a true biological increase in population numbers even allowing for mortality, while a rate less than unity indicates that the population is not biologically holding its own. At one time the net reproduction rate was regarded as a thermometer for measuring a nation's reproductive health. This use of the rate, and all other such single measures (e.g. the rate of natural increase measured by the so-called 'Malthusian parameter') are discredited, for it is realized that the net reproduction rate is very much influenced by small short-term variations in the pattern of family-building which do not necessarily have much significance for the long-term reproductive welfare of a population. P.M.

network analysis. In OPERATIONAL RESEARCH, the use of a MODEL designed to represent a SYSTEM as a concatenation of points connected together to depict a special sort of relationship between them. For a particular type of network analysis see CRITICAL PATH ANALYSIS.   S.BE.

network theory, see under IDIOTYPE.

Neue Künstlervereinigung (New Association of Artists). Munich group from which the BLAUE REITER derived. It was formed in 1909 under Kandinsky's chairmanship as a breakaway from the local SEZESSION and included the Russian Alexei Jawlensky as well as such Germans as Adolf Erbslöh and Alexander Kanoldt. Its main achievement was to introduce Germany to the work (in its 1910 exhibition) of Picasso, Braque, Rouault, and other French contemporaries.   J.W.

Neue Sachlichkeit. New Objectivity, or New Matter-of-Factness. A German term for architectural FUNCTIONALISM, used also in the other arts, where it came to stand for much of the reaction against EXPRESSIONISM during the 1920s. Thus (1) in painting it was popularized by G. F. Hartlaub, who defined it as 'the new realism bearing a socialistic flavour' and in 1925 used it as the title of an exhibition at the Mannheim Kunsthalle which featured coolly and impersonally representational pictures by Max Beckmann, Otto Dix, and the ex-DADAISTS Grosz and Schlichter, besides a group of MAGIC REALIST works. These latter apart, its main characteristics were hardness of outline, smoothness of finish, a bald but often distorted or caricatured literalism, and a choice of subjects that concentrated on modern technical apparatus and the less cheerful aspects of the big cities and their inhabitants. Differing from Soviet SOCIALIST REALISM in its debt to other modern movements, this easily merged into the 'proletarian' art (see PROLETARIAT) favoured by the German COMMUNISTS from 1928 to 1933.

(2) By extension the same label was applied in literature, where it described the socially critical fiction and documentary reportage of Ludwig Renn, Hans Fallada, and Egon Erwin Kisch, and the satirical verse of Erich Kästner and Kurt Tucholsky; again, a 'proletarian' school of writing developed from this. (3) Where the remaining arts adopted a similarly cool approach – as with the music of Hindemith and Kurt Weill, the theatre of Brecht and Erich Engel, or the typography of Jan Tschichold – the term was again often used, as was the related idea of 'utility' or GEBRAUCHS (-*musik, -lyrik, -grafik*). J.W.

Neue Sezession, see under SEZESSION.

Neumann, John von, see VON NEUMANN.

Neurath, Otto (German philosopher and sociologist, 1882–1945), see under PHYSICALISM; VIENNA CIRCLE.

neuroanatomy, see under NEURO-PSYCHOLOGY.

neurocybernetics, see under CYBERNE-TICS.

neuroglia, see under NEURON.

neurolinguistics. A new and developing branch of LINGUISTICS, sometimes called *neurological linguistics,* which studies the neurological preconditions for language development and use in man. D.C.

neurology. The branch of medicine that deals with disorders of the NERVOUS SYSTEM. Because it has to do with physical abnormalities of the brain and peripheral nervous system neurology is to be distinguished from PSYCHOLOGY and PSYCHIATRY. For the application to psychology of knowledge derived from neurology see NEUROPSYCHOLOGY. P.M.

neuron (or *neurone*). The cellular element of the NERVOUS SYSTEM. In terms of CYTOLOGY, the conducting element of the nervous system consists of neurons and a number of supporting CELLS which are known collectively as the *glia* or *neuroglia*. Although neurons do not undergo cell division they are typical cells in that they consist of a cell body (perikaryon) out of which grow long cytoplasmic extensions –

axons or dendrites, known collectively as 'nerve fibres', along the surfaces of which the nerve impulse is propagated. P.M.

neuron theory. The theory that the NEURON is the fundamental structural element of the NERVOUS SYSTEM. See also CYTOLOGY. P.M.

neuropathology. Disorders of the NERVOUS SYSTEM; also the study of such disorders. Neuropathology (in the first sense) can take one of two forms – inactivation of a neural control mechanism or its inappropriate action. It may result from flawed genetic instruction (see GENETIC CODE), mechanical damage, inflammation, deprivation of blood supply, or replacement or compression of NEURONS by tumour TISSUE. It can be investigated by clinical neurological examination (see NEUROLOGY), by electrical recording from neural tissue, by radiological techniques, and by microscopic and chemical analysis of neural tissue and surrounding fluids. Samples may be obtained during life (biopsy) or after death (autopsy). M.K.

neurophysiology, see under NEURO-PSYCHOLOGY.

neuropsychology. The study of changes in behaviour that result from alteration in the physical state of the brain. These behavioural changes are not only of scientific interest by virtue of their implications for knowledge of the way the brain is organized. They also have clinical diagnostic interest as indicators of the location of brain disease, and clinical rehabilitative interest in that they reveal the mechanism of the difficulty the patient is experiencing.

The nature of brain organization is inferred from brain-behaviour relationships. Damage to particular areas of the brain induces characteristic and recognizable changes in behaviour. It is then inferred that the affected area of brain was necessary to the integrity of the processes that normally underlie the behaviour in question. Thus damage to the most complex and evolutionarily recent area of brain, the paired cerebral hemispheres, is apt to disturb higher mental functioning, which includes PERCEPTION, memory, language, reasoning, and motor skill.

Different localized cerebral areas are implicated by damage underlying disordered perception (*agnosia*), memory (*amnesia*), language (*aphasia*), and motor skill (*apraxia*); widespread diffuse cerebral damage degrades the ability to reason (*dementia*). This localization of function within the cerebral hemispheres goes further, and each of the disorders mentioned can take a variety of specific forms according to the precise location of the damage.

The mental functions so far discussed involve the analysis of external events and the programming of specific responses. These functions tend to be represented in the left cerebral hemisphere of right-handed subjects, and are said to manifest left *cerebral dominance*. The right hemisphere also has its characteristic responsibility, namely for the ability to orient the body in space and to articulate input into an immediate and a remembered spatial framework. Thus it lends context to the precise and focused activities of the left hemisphere. In some left-handers, cerebral dominance may be less marked or even reversed. In children, delays in the development of lateralized COGNITIVE processes may be correlated with delayed language development, or in older children with delayed availability of reading skills (DYSLEXIA). Certain mental processes are represented in both hemispheres, and only suffer when damage is bilateral. Bilateral injuries may cause pathological forgetting (*amnesia*); its victim can neither remember events from the recent past nor learn new information. Still other forms of brain damage change the patient's emotional makeup, e.g. they may produce apathy and lessened motivation to act.

In animals, brain-behaviour relationships can be studied by inflicting operative damage on preselected areas of the brain and observing the behavioural results. In man, opportunities for such observations arise through naturally occurring disease and operative remedial efforts. The neuropsychologist requires expertise in relation both to behaviour and to brain structure (*neuroanatomy*) and function (*neurophysiology*) if he is to make full use of the opportunity his science offers to elucidate the organization of those processes that outstandingly characterize the human species. See also NEUROLOGY; TWO HEMISPHERES.   M.K.

neurosis (or *psychoneurosis*). In PSYCHIATRY and ABNORMAL PSYCHOLOGY in the West, a term used for one of the main classes of mental illness. Though there is no generally accepted way of defining the class (for the relationship between the neuroses and the PSYCHOSES see the latter), it is helpful to say that they are states of mental conflict, which, in different ways, represent exaggerations of our normal difficulties, and our normal impulses, feelings, etc. They include a wide range of states that have traditionally been subdivided (in part) as follows:

(1) *Anxiety states*, including PHOBIAS. The ANXIETY is beyond normal limits in intensity, and is unwarranted by the objective situation.

(2) *Obsessional states* (see OBSESSION), including *compulsive states* (see COMPULSION). In these the person develops ideas or impulses which he wishes to resist as distasteful, but from which he cannot free himself, and which often drive him into ritualistic conduct (e.g. compulsive body-washing) that can be time-consuming and exhausting.

(3) *Hysteria*. The person's functioning, in some respect or other (e.g. eyesight, digestive system, sexual functioning, motor abilities), is upset and unable to work satisfactorily. The disorder cannot be accounted for organically, and may run quite counter to what is known about the way the body works. But the symptoms enable the person to play the role of someone who is ill, and this in turn brings him certain immediate advantages in his particular situation (e.g. the battle-weary soldier who develops leg trouble).

The establishment in psychiatry of the neuroses was the outcome, in particular, of the work of the psychotherapists, e.g. Janet and Freud (see FREUDIAN). The generally recommended method of treatment is PSYCHOTHERAPY, though other methods (e.g. OPERANT CONDITIONING) have been developed. Prognosis depends on the severity of the condition, but there seem to be factors at work in these states that contribute slowly to spontaneous improvement and recovery. This fact makes it particularly difficult to establish the effectiveness of the therapy employed.
B.A.F.

Bibl: R. W. White, *The Abnormal Personality* (N.Y., 3rd ed., 1964).

neutral monism. The theory that the ultimate constituents of the world are individual momentary experiences, in themselves neither mental nor physical but of which, differently arranged, both minds and material things are composed. The ground for the theory is that such experiences are the sole direct object of empirical knowledge. It is, above all, the philosophy of Mach and his British allies, Clifford and Pearson, but was first called 'neutral monism' by William James, who took it to be the ontological consequence (see ONTOLOGY) of his 'radical EMPIRICISM'. It was adopted by Russell, largely under James's influence, around 1914. In broad terms it extends PHENOMENALISM from material objects to minds, conceiving them too, in the manner of Hume, as no more than ordered collections of experiences.   A.Q.
Bibl: Bertrand Russell, *Our Knowledge of the External World* (London and N.Y., rev. ed., 1926).

neutralism. The policy or the advocacy of neutrality, at times when international relations show symptoms of BIPOLARITY, as a means by which states can dissociate themselves from involvement in the IDEOLOGICAL conflicts which produce these symptoms. Practised before 1939 by Belgium and the Nordic states, its failure to protect many of these states from involvement in World War II did not prevent its advocacy after 1947 by the newly independent Indian state, an example followed by other Asian states, nor its becoming one of the factors which inspired the BANDUNG CONFERENCE. It was superseded by the more positive NON-ALIGNMENT.   D.C.W.
Bibl: P. H. Lyon, *Neutralism* (Leicester, 1963).

neutrality, affective, see under PATTERN VARIABLES.

neutrino. A type of stable ELEMENTARY PARTICLE emitted during the decay of NEUTRONS and MESONS. Neutrinos are difficult to detect because they have zero mass and are electrically neutral, and hardly interact at all with measuring apparatus. The original prediction of their existence was a triumph of pure reason: it was necessary to postulate 'carriers' of MOMENTUM, ENERGY, and SPIN in order

to satisfy the CONSERVATION LAWS for these QUANTITIES during neutron decay. Neutrinos differ from PHOTONS in that their QUANTUM NUMBER for spin is ½ instead of 1.   M.V.B.

neutron. An electrically neutral ELEMENTARY PARTICLE (discovered by Chadwick in 1932) which is one of the two components of an atomic NUCLEUS, the other being the PROTON. In isolation, a neutron is unstable, and undergoes RADIOACTIVE decay with a HALF-LIFE of about 12 minutes into a PROTON, an ELECTRON, and a NEUTRINO. A neutron is slightly heavier than a proton.   M.V.B.

neutron star, see under PULSAR.

Nevinson, Christopher Richard Wynne (British painter, 1889–1946), see under VORTICISM.

New Age, The. A London-based weekly review taken over in 1907 by A. R. Orage, and brilliantly edited by him until 1922, *The New Age* was a central literary, cultural, and political clearing-house of GUILD SOCIALIST political bias, carrying the work of G. B. Shaw, Arnold Bennett, H. G. Wells, F. S. Flint, Ezra Pound, T. E. Hulme, Wyndham Lewis, Katherine Mansfield, Marinetti, and other important radical (see RADICALISM) or new writers. It is a superb atmospheric record of a tempestuous period, displaying, for example, the changing response from REALIST to post-realist and POST-IMPRESSIONIST developments in literature and the general impact of European MODERNISM, strongly supporting the idea of a literary 'Risorgimento', and carrying many novel works and manifestos.   M.S.BR.

New Apocalypse. A short-lived, youthfully grandiloquent, and undisciplined movement in British poetry during World War II. The name comes from the first of three anthologies of this 'new Romantic tendency', whose most obvious elements are love, death, an adherence to myth and an awareness of war': *The New Apocalypse* (1940). This was edited by J. F. Hendry; the other two, *The White Horseman* (1941) and *The Crown and the Sickle* (1945), were edited by him and Henry Treece. Of the many poets (e.g. Vernon Watkins, G. S. Fraser, Norman

MacCaig) who contributed to the anthologies, few deserve to be described as 'new apocalyptics'. The group introduced into British poetry an awareness of contemporary American verse. M.S.-S.

New Criticism. An ill-defined term generally taken as referring to 20th-century literary criticism's self-purification: to the reaction against the view of criticism as the mere expression of personal preferences, and to the belief that precision, method, and some theory are required. When J. E. Spingarn first coined the term (1910) he used it to describe a new trend towards scholarship and the application of extra-literary, statistical, STYLOMETRIC devices. On this basis, Caroline Spurgeon's work on Shakespeare's imagery was 'old criticism' so far as her inferences were concerned; but her statistical METHODOLOGY was entirely 'new'. The names – predominantly American – of those most frequently designated 'new critics' are I. A. Richards, Allen Tate, Cleanth Brooks, John Crowe Ransom, Kenneth Burke, William Empson, R. P. Blackmur, and Yvor Winters. Ransom's *The New Criticism* (1941) found fault with Richards, T. S. Eliot, Empson, and Winters, and suggested that it was time for a new 'ontological' critic to appear. This demonstrates how little – scholarship and philosophical over-scrupulosity apart – the new critics have in common; and this variegated movement later diversified itself still further into: proponents of pure aesthetic theory (Wimsatt, Beardsley, Krieger); would-be scientific bibliographers (Fredson Bowers); and more eclectic critics who write from a particular point of view, though with due care and attention to the text. Several important critics (e.g. Lionel Trilling, Northrop Frye) were never considered as 'new' in this specific sense. M.S.-S.
Bibl: R. Wellek and A. Warren, *Theory of Literature* (London and N.Y., 1949; Harmondsworth, 3rd ed., 1963).

New Deal. Phrase coined by the American economist, Raymond Moley, in the draft of Roosevelt's speech accepting the Democratic nomination for President on 2 July 1932, and used to describe the policies and legislation of President Roosevelt's first administration (1933–7) aimed at rescuing the U.S.A. from the Great DEPRESSION by means of national measures rather than through international cooperation. The main theme of the New Deal was action by the Federal Government to reduce unemployment, to equalize wealth and opportunity, to control banking and credit, and to protect small-scale industry and agriculture, labour, and urban groups against the measures thought necessary by large-scale business for survival in a time of little economic activity. A feature of the New Deal was a series of Federal-supported public works ranging from soil CONSERVATION (e.g. the *Tennessee Valley Authority*) to the Federal Arts, Theatre, and Writers Projects (see WPA). The New Deal did not end unemployment but it helped to reduce it from 17 to 7 million unemployed. D.C.W.
Bibl: F. B. Freidel, *Franklin D. Roosevelt: the Triumph* (Boston, Mass., 1956).

new diplomacy. Phrase used by historians to describe the methods and advocacy of 'open' as opposed to 'secret' diplomacy during and after the war of 1914–18. This involved the public discussion of the aims and issues of foreign policy, the deprecation of all secret agreements, and 'open covenants, openly arrived at' in President Wilson's phrase (see FOURTEEN POINTS; in practice, however, Wilson refused all publication of his own discussions with his French, British, and Italian colleagues during the Paris Peace Conference in 1919). As used by the BOLSHEVIKS it became indistinguishable from propaganda by revelation or diplomacy by manifesto. Its underlying assumption that the peoples, unlike the governments of the powers, would be in favour of peace and international justice rather than national egotism and CHAUVINISM has not always been supported by experience. D.C.W.
Bibl: A. J. Mayer, *Political Origins of the New Diplomacy, 1917–18* (New Haven, 1959).

new economic history, see under ECONOMIC HISTORY.

New Economic Policy, see NEP.

New English Art Club (NEAC). A society of artists founded in 1885 whose members were critical of the Royal Academy and

422

the traditions which it fostered. Augustus John, Wilson Steer, and Walter Sickert were all members at some time. Many of these artists looked to France for artistic inspiration: they tempered their own work with a little mild IMPRESSIONISM. By 1910, however, the NEAC itself seemed old-fashioned to those artists who formed the CAMDEN TOWN GROUP. P.C.

Bibl: D. S. MacColl, 'The New English Art Club' (*The Studio*, March 1945).

New Frontier. Term first used by John F. Kennedy in his speech accepting the Democratic Party nomination for the Presidency of the U.S.A. on 15 June 1960. The term was intended originally to convey the speaker's view of politics as a field in which new opportunities and challenges were at hand, such as had been offered by the historical frontier of the West. Later the New Frontier came to be used for the amalgam of POLITICAL SCIENTISTS and COST-BENEFIT-conscious, statistically-minded MANAGEMENT figures which constituted Kennedy's principal addition to the usual sources of the political and bureaucratic apparatus (see BUREAU-CRACY) of a new president. D.C.W.

Bibl: A. M. Schlesinger, *A Thousand Days: John F. Kennedy in the White House* (London and Boston, 1965); T. C. Sorensen, *Kennedy* (London and N.Y., 1965).

New Left. A political tendency which emerged in the 1950s through disenchantment with the old LEFT from which it stemmed. Its idealism was more vague and utopian and it has shown a marked predilection for DIRECT ACTION. It came to embrace a broad spectrum of political tendencies which included SOCIALISM, ANARCHISM, SYNDICALISM, TROTSKYISM, MAOISM, CASTROISM, and various forms of neo-Marxist (see NEO-MARXISM) COMMUNISM.

In Britain the New Left originated in 1956 with the double TRAUMA of HUNGARY and SUEZ. Khrushchev's 'secret speech' shook some of the members of the British Communist Party who began to publish *The New Reasoner* ('A journal of socialist HUMANISM'), while at the same time a group of non-communist academic radicals (see RADICALISM) produced the *Universities and Left Review*. The merger of the two resulted in the publication of

the *New Left Review*, the first official organ of the New Left. In the U.S.A. the New Left started in the early 1960s with the CIVIL RIGHTS MOVEMENT and became more militant (see ACTIVISM) with the ESCALATION of the VIETNAM war after 1964.

The New Left was everywhere essentially a student movement, which in the U.S.A. led to the radicalization of the Students for Democratic Society (see SDS) and of the predominantly black Student NON-VIOLENT Co-ordinating Committee, to the 'campus revolution', the CHICAGO CONSPIRACY TRIAL, and the emergence of the WEATHERMEN. In France it led to the May 1968 *évènements*; in Germany to the student unrest which brought several universities to a standstill, and to the actions of the Baader-Meinhof terrorist group; in Japan to the ZENGAKUREN student politics, 'snake dance' DEMONSTRATIONS, and the TERRORISM of the RED ARMY faction.

Towards the end of the 1960s, the New Left ran out of steam. It remained a youth movement whose successes were limited, while its violent tactics had produced a middle-class and working-class reaction. In their quest for the overthrow of 'the system', its radicals turned to the tactics of the so-called 'LONG MARCH through the INSTITUTIONS', i.e. work in established political organizations and institutions. They have undergone changes: their appetite for utopia has not disappeared, but they are less occupied with rescuing Marx's CONCEPT of ALIENATION; more concerned with 'coalition politics' than with violence. They have come to cooperate with the old Left from which they are no longer so dissimilar as in the past. L.L.

Bibl: A. Cockburn and R. Blackburn (eds.), *Student Power* (Harmondsworth, 1969); L. S. Feuer, *The Conflict of Generations* (London and N.Y., 1969); M. Cranston (ed.), *The New Left* (London, 1970; N.Y., 1971); N. McInnes, *The Western Marxists* (London and N.Y., 1972).

new mathematics. Traditional schoolbooks, especially in arithmetic and ALGEBRA, seem now like Victorian cookbooks: they are full of complicated recipes for solving unappetizing problems. Contemporary mathematics, with its emphasis on the AXIOMATIC METHOD applied to a wide variety of MATHEMATICAL STRUC-TURES, is no longer very interested in such recipes – COMPUTERS can produce numerical solutions by direct methods. Rather is it concerned to uncover the fundamental ideas that lie beneath particular methods and CONCEPTS, and to use these new ideas greatly to extend and to generalize the classical results. This 'new mathematics' was born around 1880; recently parts of it have been introduced into school curricula in a number of countries. The numerical and computational are being replaced by the ABSTRACT and intuitive. SETS, BOOLEAN ALGEBRA, EQUIVALENCE RELATIONS, GROUPS, MATRICES, all occur in the syllabus of the British Schools Mathematics Project. Despite their abstractness a good teacher can bring understanding and enjoyment of such topics to children. But mathematics is more than just playing with ideas. Both for itself and for its applications it requires the patience to compute and manipulate and the determination to follow, to criticize, and to construct rigorous arguments. These qualities are fostered by the study of algebra, CALCULUS, and GEOMETRY; their reward is the ability to solve interesting problems. The new mathematics may tell one something about the TOPOLOGY of the sphere, but one requires a knowledge of traditional mathematics to calculate its volume.   R.G.

Bibl: I. Adler, *The New Mathematics* (N.Y., 1958; London, rev. ed., 1964).

new novel (*nouveau roman*). The name given to a new kind of ANTI-NOVEL, i.e. to the kind of work produced by a group of French novelists (notably Alain Robbe-Grillet, Nathalie Sarraute, and Michel Butor) who have tried deliberately to adapt the technique of novel-writing to what they consider to be the requirements of mid-20th-century sensibilities. Although they are not, and do not claim to be, a school, they all reject such features of the traditional novel as character-drawing, linear narrative, and obtrusive social or political content. Instead, they offer elaborate, and often apparently gratuitous, structures, as well as minute notation of psychological and physical detail. All are strongly avant-gardist (see AVANT-GARDE), i.e. they believe that each new generation of artists must reveal fresh aspects of reality, and they are convinced

of the inseparability of form and content. They can be seen both as following on from EXISTENTIAL PSYCHOLOGY and PHENOMENOLOGY, and as reacting against Sartre's theory of COMMITMENT, which was the prevailing literary doctrine when Robbe-Grillet, the most prominent member of the group, first emerged in the mid-1950s. Typical novels are Robbe-Grillet's *La Jalousie* (1957), Sarraute's *Les Fruits d'or* (1963) and Butor's *L'Emploi du temps* (1957), and the two major theoretical statements *Pour un nouveau roman* (1963) by Robbe-Grillet and *L'Ère du soupçon* (1956) by Sarraute. This wave of experimentalism has been important mainly in France, though there have been echoes elsewhere, e.g. Uwe Johnson in Germany, Susan Sontag in America, Christine Brooke-Rose and Rayner Heppenstall in England.   J.G.W.

Bibl: J. Sturrock, *The French New Novel* (London and N.Y., 1969).

New Orleans. The first coherent JAZZ style to evolve. It was built on the convention of a three-voice front line, clarinet, trumpet (or cornet), and trombone, which between them were able to convey the three-note triads of rudimentary harmony. It was a style tailor-made to conceal the technical deficiencies of the men playing it, but its days were numbered: eventually there would have to appear the all-powerful individual voice which would split the style at the seams. That prodigy was Louis Armstrong.   B.G.

new theology. A phrase used on two occasions to describe the ferment of ideas contained in a short book by an English writer: *The New Theology* by R. J. Campbell (1907) and *Honest to God* by John A. T. Robinson (1963). Each book emphasized the nearness, rather than the TRANS-CENDENCE, of God, and preached a radically simplified and LIBERAL Christianity.
D.L.E.

Bibl: D. L. Edwards (ed.), *The Honest to God Debate* (London and Philadelphia, 1963).

new towns. In recent years, and particularly since World War II, the growth of cities has become so rapid as to endanger the quality of life within them. Even the establishment of a *green belt* of open land around them (e.g. London) or a series of such (e.g. Copenhagen) failed to solve the problems created by large numbers of people COMMUTING to and from their work in the cities. In Britain it became Government policy to minimize commuting by the creation, beyond the green belts, of new towns in which industry and commerce were encouraged to provide employment. Under the New Towns Act of 1946, 8 new towns, starting with Stevenage, were created within a 30-mile radius of London, while 14 others (most recently Milton Keynes, 1967) relieved pressure on other overcrowded cities. In the case of the London ring the attraction and domination of London itself has proved too great, and these new towns have remained SATELLITE TOWNS. Official policy now appears to favour the expansion of small market towns (e.g. Ashford, Kent) in order to save on the cost of building town centres and providing municipal ser vices.   M.L.

new wave (*nouvelle vague*). Loose journalistic term coined by Françoise Giroud, on the analogy of 'new look' (clothing styles introduced by Christian Dior in the late 1940s) and the NEW NOVEL (*nouveau roman*), to define the sudden influx of new talent into the French cinema in 1959–60, when 67 new directors embarked on their first feature films. Spearheading the movement were the *Cahiers du Cinéma* group of critics (François Truffaut, Jean-Luc Godard, Claude Chabrol, Eric Rohmer, Jacques Rivette). The commercial and artistic success of their first films, made very quickly, cheaply, and without established stars, revolutionized production in the French film industry. But the methods characteristic of the early *nouvelle vague* films – improvisation, hand-held cameras, location shooting, minimum technical crews – were exigencies of economy rather than a matter of principle. The only real unifying principle behind the movement, which included documentarists (Alain Resnais, Chris Marker) and young film-makers from within the industry (Louis Malle, Roger Vadim), was the belief, constantly reiterated by the *Cahiers du Cinéma* critics, that a film should be the conception of one man, the AUTEUR, rather than a commercial package arbitrarily put together by a studio or a producer. In its English form, the term has subsequently been applied to

any sudden creative surge in the cinema, e.g. in Britain immediately after the French *nouvelle vague*, or in Czechoslovakia in 1966.   T.C.C.M.
Bibl: P. Graham (ed.), *The New Wave* (London and N.Y., 1968).

New Writing. A bi-annual founded in London by John Lehmann in 1936 to give voice to younger writers 'conscious of the great social, political and moral changes going on round them', rally anti-FASCIST voices, and emphasize the international dimension of this entire tendency. The venture – retitled *Folios of New Writing* (1940–41) and *New Writing and Daylight* (1942) – carried many major writers of its period: Spender, Auden, Isherwood, Edward Upward, William Sansom, Rex Warner, Orwell, Pasternak, Silone, and André Chamson, as well as a good number of working class authors. An important extension was *Penguin New Writing* (1940–50), which through the war years carried much important writing, including valuable reportage and DOCUMENTARY, and a broad interest in all the arts, to a wide audience.   M.S.BR.

New York school. A general term applied to artists working in New York City in the 1940s and 1950s, primarily in the ABSTRACT EXPRESSIONIST style. School in this case connotes no more than a sense of community, energy, and ambition among artists as diverse as Jackson Pollock, Arshile Gorky, Franz Kline, Adolph Gottlieb, Willem de Kooning, Hans Hofmann, and Barnett Newman. It is now used, analogously to ÉCOLE DE PARIS, to encompass subsequent artistic styles with an American flavour. See also ACTION PAINTING.   A.K.W.
Bibl: D. Ashton, *The New York School: A Cultural Reckoning* (N.Y., 1973).

Newell, Allen (U.S. physicist and mathematician, *b.*1927), see under PROBLEM-SOLVING.

Newman, Barnett (U.S. painter, 1905–70), see under ABSTRACT EXPRESSIONISM; MINIMAL ART; NEW YORK SCHOOL.

Newman, Ernest (British music critic, 1868–1959), see under PROGRAMME MUSIC.

NEWMAN, J. H.

Newman, John Henry (British church-man and author, 1801–90), see under MULTIVERSITY.

Newman, Paul (U.S. actor, b.1924), see under METHOD, THE.

Newsom Report (1963; a 1968 report on PUBLIC SCHOOLS is also sometimes so called). The report *Half Our Future* (London, H.M.S.O.) by the Central Advisory Council for Education (England) under the chairmanship of Sir John Newsom (1910–71) on the education in full-time courses of pupils of 'average or less than average ability' between the ages of 13 and 16. Recommendations included the raising of the school leaving age from 15 to 16 (see ROSLA); a working party to grapple with the problems of slum areas (cf. the PLOWDEN REPORT [1967] and see EDUCATIONAL PRIORITY AREAS); and experiments in the curricula, including the provision of stronger links between school and the world of work.   W.A.C.S.

Newspeak, see under ORWELLIAN.

Newton, Huey P. (U.S. Black Panther leader, b.1942), see under BLACK PAN-THERS.

Newton, Sir Isaac (English mathemati-cian, 1642–1727), see under ANALYSIS; CORPUSCULAR THEORY; NEWTONIAN MECHANICS; WELTANSCHAUUNG.

Newton-Raphson method, see under OPTIMIZATION.

Newtonian mechanics. One of the three great theories of MECHANICS. The basic principle is that the forces exerted on a material system by its interaction with other matter produce an ACCELERATION of the system – i.e. a *change* in its velocity or MOMENTUM. The precise law is: *accel-eration = force ÷ mass* (see MASS). This means that if there is no force acting on a system its acceleration is zero, and the system persists unaltered in its state of rest or motion. (By contrast, in an earlier mechanics deriving mainly from Aristotle, it was believed that force was necessary to maintain motion itself, so that a body far from all others would come to rest.)
Newtonian mechanics is prevented from being a tautology by a series of 'laws of force' which state the various ways in which systems can interact. Fortunately there appears to be only a small number of basically different forces in nature: GRAVITATION, ELECTROMAGNETISM, STRONG INTERACTIONS, and WEAK INTERACTIONS. Other forces such as fric-tion can be explained in terms of these.
When dealing with the interactions between the parts of a composite system, it is necessary to add a further postulate: the force on body A exerted by body B is equal in magnitude but opposite in direc-tion to that on body B exerted by body A (i.e. 'action and reaction are equal'). Abundant verifications of Newtonian mechanics are provided by experiments and observations ranging from the motion of the heavenly bodies (see CELESTIAL MECHANICS) to the CONTINUUM systems studied in RHEOLOGY. For systems of atomic dimensions Newtonian mechanics no longer holds, and must be replaced by QUANTUM MECHANICS, while for systems moving near the speed of light or in enormous gravitational fields it must be replaced by RELATIVITY. See also MACH'S PRINCIPLE; PHYSICS.   M.V.B.
Bibl: I. B. Cohen, *The Birth of a New Physics* (N.Y., 1960; London, 1961).

Neyman, Jerzy (Polish-U.S. statistician, b.1894), see under STATISTICAL TEST.

Nicholson, Ben (British painter, b. 1894), see under CONSTRUCTIVISM.

Nicholson, (Edward) Max (British ecologist, b.1904), see under ECOLOGY.

Niebuhr, Reinhold (U.S. theologian, 1892–1971), see under CHRISTIAN SOCIALISM; NIEBUHRIAN; SOCIAL GOSPEL MOVEMENT.

Niebuhrian. Adjective formed from the name of Reinhold Niebuhr (1892–1971), a Protestant neo-orthodox theologian (see PROTESTANTISM; NEO-ORTHODOXY; THEOLOGY) who urged and practised realism in Christian contributions to polit-ical debate. In particular he protested against UTOPIANISM.   D.L.E.
Bibl: J. R. Bingham, *Courage to Change* (N.Y., 1961).

Nietzsche, Friedrich (German philo-sopher, 1844–1900), see under APOLLO-

NIAN AND DIONYSIAN CULTURES; DEATH OF GOD THEOLOGY; IRRATIONALISM; PERSPECTIVISM.

Nieuwenhuys, Constant (Dutch painter, *b*. 1920), see under COBRA.

Night of the Long Knives. The dramatic events of the weekend of 29 June – 2 July 1934 when Hitler, with the aid of Himmler's black-shirted S.S., liquidated Ernst Roehm and the leadership of the brownshirted S.A. The S.A. stormtroopers had been an indispensable element in the NAZIS' rise to power but had become a major embarrassment in Hitler's relations with the German Army, which were the key to his succeeding the dying Hindenburg as Head of State and Commander-in-Chief as well as Chancellor. The S. A. leaders were murdered on the pretext that they were plotting a second and more radical revolution, but amongst the 83 known to have been shot were others (such as Gregor Strasser and General von Schleicher) who were the victims of private feuds. These events were the turning-point of the Nazi regime: they established Hitler's personal dictatorship, made clear the ruthless character of the Nazi state, and laid the foundations for the supremacy of the S.S. among its instruments of power.   A.L.C.B.
  Bibl: M. Gallo, tr. L. Emmet, *The Night of the Long Knives* (N.Y., 1972; London, 1973).

nihilism. An attitude or viewpoint denying all traditional values and even moral truths. The word was invented by Turgenev in his novel *Fathers and Sons* (1861) to describe that part of the radical Russian intelligentsia (see RADICALISM; INTELLECTUALS) which, disillusioned with the slow pace of reform (see REFORMISM), abandoned the LIBERAL faith of their predecessors and embraced the belief that the destruction of existing conditions in Russia justified the use of any means. The chief ideologist of revolutionary UTILITARIANISM in politics, ETHICS, and AESTHETICS was D. I. Pisarev (1840–68), who was portrayed as Bazarov in Turgenev's novel and who proudly accepted the new label. Many members of subsequent generations of the Russian intelligentsia adopted nihilistic postures, from P. G. Zaichnevsky, who summoned

his contemporaries 'to the axe', to Sergei Nechaev, author of a *Revolutionary Catechism*, who was portrayed as the unscrupulous Peter Verkhovensky in the novel by Dostoyevsky variously translated as *The Devils* or *The Possessed*. The term has subsequently been applied to various radical movements outside Russia: the NAZI victory in Germany in the 1930s was described as a 'REVOLUTION of nihilism', and in our own time some of the NEW LEFT radicals have often been labelled nihilists.   L.L.
  Bibl: M. Polanyi, 'Beyond Nihilism' (*Encounter*, March 1960); S. Hook, 'In Defense of Enlightenment', in *Pragmatism and the Tragic Sense of Life* (N.Y., 1974).

Nikitin, Nicolas (Russian author, 1897–1963), see under SERAPION BROTHERS.

Nin, Andrés (Spanish revolutionary, 1892–1937), see under POUM.

Nineteen Eighty-Four, see under ORWELLIAN.

Nisbet, Robert Alexander (U.S. sociologist, *b*. 1913), see under SOCIOLOGY.

nitrogen cycle, see under LIFE CYCLE.

Nixon, Richard (U.S. president, *b*. 1913), see under BLACK PANTHERS; ECONOMICS; MAOISM; NEGATIVE INCOME TAX; ROLE, ROLE THEORY; VIETNAM; WATERGATE.

NKGB, see under KGB.

Nkrumah, Kwame (Ghanaian political leader, 1909–72), see under CHARISMA.

NKVD, see under KGB.

noble gases (or *rare gases* or *inert gases*). The ELEMENTS helium, neon, argon, krypton, xenon, and radon, which are gaseous at room temperature. Chemically, the gases are only weakly reactive.   M.V.B.

noise. Any random disturbance superimposed on a signal. Electrical noise arises from random heat motion in circuit components, and constitutes a nuisance in TELECOMMUNICATIONS and HI-FI, where

NOLDE

much effort is devoted to producing a high 'signal-to-noise ratio'. An incoherent combination of frequencies over a wide band is termed *white noise*.   M.V.B.

Nolde, Emil (German painter, 1867–1956), see under BRÜCKE, DIE.

nomadism. Anthropological term for the LIFE STYLE in which human groups follow a wandering life. It is usually restricted to livestock-keeping groups whose movements are directly related to the search for pasture. Examples of such pastoral nomadism are increasingly rare; the Lapps of northern Scandinavia and the Kirghiz of Turkestan come nearest to the model. See also TRANSHUMANCE.   P.H.

nominalism. In PHILOSOPHY, the denial of real existence to abstract entities or UNIVERSALS. In its extreme, original form it answers the question 'What is there in common in the SET of things to which some general term is truly applicable?' by 'Nothing but the general term'. This seems to make the CLASSIFICATION of things into kinds wholly arbitrary. What is often called nominalism is the view – that of Hobbes and, in a way, of Locke and Hume – that what is common to the individuals denoted by a general term is their similarity to one another. Critics object that the similarity between the members of a set of things is as much an abstract entity as the common property which, according to REALISTS, they all exemplify.   A.Q.

nomothetic, see under IDIOGRAPHIC.

non-alignment. The refusal of states to take sides with one or other of two principal opposed groups of powers such as existed at the time of the COLD WAR. Non-alignment was less ISOLATIONIST than the NEUTRALISM which it superseded, and was associated with the CONCEPT of *positive neutrality*, i.e. of collective intervention to prevent BIPOLARITY from degenerating into open military conflict; as in the conference of non-aligned powers held at Belgrade in 1961 in which some 35 Mediterranean and Afro-Asian powers took part. The mediatory proposals there discussed won only contemptuous hearing from the leaders of the two blocs, a fate which did much to diminish subsequent enthusiasm for the concept.

See also NON-INTERVENTION.   D.C.W.
Bibl: L. Mates, *Non-Alignment: Theory and Current Policy* (Belgrade and N.Y., 1972).

non-Euclidean geometry, see under GEOMETRY.

non-figurative art, see under ABSTRACT ART.

non-intervention. The opposite view to the right of intervention maintained by the great powers of the 19th century as an accepted part of international law. According to the then accepted view, one state was within its rights in intervening (if necessary by force) in the affairs of another state, where the second state's government was unable or incompetent to exercise sovereign powers, particularly in the protection of the rights, property, and persons of nationals of the first state. This view was challenged by the Argentinian jurist, Carlos Calvo, who in 1868 maintained that all sovereign states enjoyed absolute equality. The MONROE DOCTRINE denied *European* rights to intervene in the Americas; the Calvo doctrine and that put forward by the Argentinian, Dr Louis Drago, in 1903 and embodied in part of Article I of the second Hague Convention of 1907, were directed to prevent U.S. intervention. After the BOLSHEVIK revolution the doctrine became an integral part of the treaties negotiated by the Soviet Union with its non-Soviet neighbours. In times of civil war, as in the Spanish Civil War, the major powers have adopted non-intervention as a kind of self-denying ordinance intended to avoid ESCALATION into international conflict, but usually (as in the case of Spain) with very unequal results.   D.C.W.

non-objectivism. Russian ABSTRACT ART movement led by Alexander Rodchenko during World War I.   J.W.

non-proliferation, see under PROLIFERATION.

non-representational art, see under ABSTRACT ART.

non-theistic religion. RELIGION not involving belief in God or gods. Although in the Western world religion is usually thought

428

to imply such belief (see THEISM), this is not true historically (see BUDDHISM; CONFUCIANISM; PANTHEISM). Many modern AGNOSTICS value teachings traditionally associated with religion, notably reverence for nature and for other people, self-discipline, and the spirit of service to society. See also DEATH OF GOD THEOLOGY; HUMANISM. D.L.E.

non-verbal communication. The larger inter-personal context within which all verbal communications take place. All human actions are suffused with meaning. Hence all actions communicate meanings. How I reach for, hold, and drink from, my teacup is a communicative act as well as an instrumental act. As one speaks, one's tone, speed, pause structure, gestures, facial expression, and degree of proximity to one's auditor modulate the meaning of the communication. These latter activities are the non-verbal context in which speech is embedded. Without such a context, all speech would be ambiguous. See also EXPRESSIVE MOVEMENT. T.Z.C.
Bibl: R. L. Birdwhistell, *Kinesics and Context* (Philadelphia, 1970; London, 1971); R. A. Hinde, *Non-Verbal Communication* (London, 1972).

non-violent resistance. A STRATEGY or policy of resisting an adversary's attack on an occupation of one's country by non-violent means: the appeal to world opinion, political resistance, or CIVIL DISOBEDIENCE. Recent examples are Gandhi's organization of resistance to the British Raj during its final decades, the prevailing policy of the Norwegian resistance movement in World War II, and the decision of the Czechs to offer no military resistance to the Soviet invasion of their country in August 1968, but to rely on civil disobedience and global publicity. A recent example of domestic civil disobedience is, in the U.S.A., the National Association for the Advancement of Colored Peoples' campaign for CIVIL RIGHTS. A.F.B.
Bibl: A. Roberts (ed.), *The Strategy of Civilian Defence* (London, 1967; Harrisburg, Pa., as *Civilian Resistance as a National Defense*, 1968).

non-zero-sum, see under GAMES, THEORY OF.

noosphere. A neologism introduced in an essay written in 1949 by the nature-philosopher Teilhard de Chardin on the model of BIOSPHERE and atmosphere and signifying the realm or domain in which mind is exercised. Teilhard's contention (see EVOLUTIONISM) was that in the ordinary course of the EVOLUTION of living things the biosphere is being supplanted by the noosphere. P.M.

noradrenalin, see under ADRENAL GLAND.

Nordau, Max (Hungarian physician and author, 1849–1923), see under DEGENERACY.

norm.
Two main uses need to be distinguished: (1) what is normal or usual behaviour in some community or social group (for the precise statistical sense see MEASURE OF LOCATION); and (2) an ideal or standard to which people think behaviour ought to conform, or which some legislating authority lays down. The two may coincide, but frequently they differ: thus never to drink and drive may be a norm in sense 2 but not in sense 1. The related adjectives are, for sense 1, normal (see, for example, NORMAL DISTRIBUTION) and, for sense 2, NORMATIVE. A.S.
(3) In Soviet usage, the basis of the piece-work system which long predominated in industry there, and in which the worker's pay depended on his reaching or exceeding a 'norm' of output. The 'progressive norm' method involved continual raising of the norm required for the basic wage; thus levels achieved by STAKHANOVITES tended to become obligatory for all. The norm system also prevailed among prisoners in labour camps (see FORCED LABOUR), whose bread ration was tied to their output. The past decade has seen a decline of the system, which now applies to well under half of Soviet industrial workers. R.C

norm-referenced, see under PSYCHOMETRICS.

normal distribution (or *Gaussian distribution*). In PROBABILITY THEORY and STATISTICS, a probability DISTRIBUTION on the line; the density function is a bell-shaped curve given by the formula

$f(x) = (2\pi)^{-\frac{1}{2}}\exp(-\frac{1}{2}x^2)$.

The normal distribution has MEAN 0 and VARIANCE 1; it is symmetrical about the mean. Scale change and translation along the line yield the more general normal distribution of mean µ and variance σ^2. The importance of this distribution is twofold. First, the Central Limit Theorem of probability theory states that under suitable conditions, if random variables are added together and the sum is standardized to have mean 0 and variance 1, then as the number of summands tends to infinity the distribution of the standardized sum converges to the normal distribution. For example, if a fair coin is tossed repeatedly and $+1$, -1 are scored for heads and tails respectively, then the score divided by the square root of the number of tosses converges to the normal distribution as the number of tosses increases. Second, it is found, for reasons related to the Central Limit Theorem, that empirical distributions in a wide variety of situations often conform closely to the normal distribution; it is thus common in statistics to assume that distributions encountered in such contexts are normal until the contrary is established. Many other important statistical distributions, including the chi-squared distribution and Student's t-distribution, are derived from the normal distribution.   R.SI.

normalization. Already current in the sense of (industrial) standardization, the word was used in post-1945 European contexts to signify a return to friendly relations between states, ruling parties, etc. (as after the Moscow-Belgrade breach); then specifically of Gustáv Husák's counter-reformist policy in Czechoslovakia from 1969, with restoration of complete control by pro-Soviet leaders and reintegration into the Soviet bloc in all aspects.   D.V.

Norman, Frank (British author, b. 1930), see under THEATRE WORKSHOP.

normative.
In general, concerned with rules, recommendations, or proposals, as contrasted with mere description or the statement of matters of fact. The words *evaluative* and *prescriptive* are used in much the same way, though 'normative', unlike the other two, tends to imply – cf.

NORM – that the standards or values involved are those of some social group rather than of an individual. Specific applications include the following.   A.S.
(1) In PHILOSOPHY, the label is applied to VALUE-JUDGEMENTS by EMOTIVISTS and other adherents of the doctrine of the NATURALISTIC FALLACY, who conclude that the TRUTH or falsity of value-judgements cannot be assessed. LOGIC, likewise, is sometimes called a normative science because it does not simply classify forms of INFERENCE that are actually followed but critically selects, and by implication recommends, those it regards as VALID. A valid inference, after all, is one whose conclusion *ought* to be accepted if its premises are.   A.Q.
(2) In LINGUISTICS, the adjectives *normative* and *prescriptive* are applied interchangeably to the largely outmoded view that there are absolute standards of correctness in language, and that the aim of linguistic analysis is to formulate rules of usage in conformity with them. This attitude is opposed to the aims of *descriptive* linguistics, which emphasizes the need to describe the *facts* of linguistic usage – how people actually speak (or write), not how they (or the grammarians) feel they ought to speak.   D.C.

Norris, Frank (U.S. novelist, 1870–1902), see under NATURALISM.

Norwood Report (1943), see under SECONDARY SCHOOLS.

notional and **formal.** Adjectives applied respectively to grammatical analysis which does, and does not, assume a set of undefined extralinguistic notions as its basis. 'Notional' often has a pejorative force for LINGUISTS reacting against the widespread notionalism of traditional GRAMMAR.   D.C.

noumena (or *things-in-themselves*; German *Dinge-an-sich*). Terms used by Kant to refer to the things that underlie our experience both of the physical world and of our own mental states (called by him the *phenomena* of outer and innner sense) and that are not themselves objects of possible experience.   A.Q.

nouveau réalisme. A phrase (literally, 'new realism', but bearing no relationship

to either REALISM or NEO-REALISM) coined by the French critic Pierre Restany to describe artists' work in Paris in the late 1950s and early 1960s that incorporated junk and common objects into *assemblage* and COLLAGE forms. The French artist Arman is the figure most associated with this style, which is akin to POP and *assemblage* art. Yves Klein, Jean Tinguely, Daniel Spoerri, and Martial Raysse can also be counted within this movement.   A.K.W.
Bibl: H. Martin, *Arman* (N.Y., 1973).

nouveau roman, see NEW NOVEL.

nouvelle vague, see NEW WAVE.

nova. A star whose brightness suddenly increases by up to 10,000 times through the ejection from it of incandescent gases.   M.V.B.

Novalis (pseud. of Friedrich von Hardenberg, German poet and novelist, 1772–1801), see under ROMANTICISM.

Novembergruppe. Large German cultural organization formed in Berlin in December 1918 to express the spirit of the November Revolution. Though the criterion was commitment to the new republic rather than adherence to a particular artistic school, in point of fact EXPRESSIONISM predominated. In December 1919 it absorbed the not dissimilar ARBEITSRAT FÜR KUNST. By the end of the 1920s it had virtually petered out.   J.W.

Novotný, Antonín (Czech Communist leader, 1904–75), see under PRAGUE (3).

NPV (net present value), see under DISCOUNTED CASH FLOW.

nuclear disarmament, see under CND.

nuclear family. The characteristic family unit of developed industrial societies which consists solely of husband, wife, and children, and spans only two generations. In contrast, the *extended family* of less developed societies is a numerically larger unit including and supporting three or more generations of kin. The nuclear family is more mobile socially (see SOCIAL MOBILITY) and geographically, and allows more autonomy and relative freedom. On

the other hand, it produces an observed increase in tension and stress; and rising divorce rates, increases in delinquency, and weakening of cultural transmissions have all been blamed, with some justification, on the nuclear family.   P.S.L.

nuclear fission, see under FISSION.

nuclear fusion, see under FUSION.

nuclear magnetic resonance. The application of MAGNETIC RESONANCE to the SPIN of the NUCLEUS.   M.V.B.

nuclear physics. The study of the atomic NUCLEUS and its constituent NUCLEONS, and the NUCLEAR REACTIONS between nuclei. See also QUANTUM MECHANICS.   M.V.B.

nuclear reaction. In NUCLEAR PHYSICS, any process resulting in structural changes in an atomic NUCLEUS. Generally the ATOMIC NUMBER alters so that it is possible to transmute small amounts of one ELEMENT into another, thus fulfilling the dream of the medieval alchemists; this could not be achieved in any purely CHEMICAL REACTION since only the outer ELECTRONS are involved (see ATOMIC PHYSICS). FUSION reactions are responsible for starlight and the operation of the hydrogen bomb, and FISSION reactions are involved in RADIOACTIVITY, NUCLEAR REACTORS, and the atomic bomb. See also QUANTUM MECHANICS.   M.V.B.

nuclear reactor (originally called *atomic pile*). A device (of which the prototype was completed in 1942 under the direction of Enrico Fermi) in which a controlled CHAIN REACTION is set up, based on nuclear FISSION. It contains a core of fissile materials, which when bombarded by NEUTRONS yields up a portion of its ATOMIC ENERGY as heat. This heat is then transported out of the fissile core by a variety of methods. The material undergoing fission (usually an ISOTOPE of uranium) is normally mixed with a MODERATOR to increase the efficiency of the NEUTRONS. The speed of the reaction is controlled by adjusting rods of neutron-absorbing material such as cadmium. Nuclear reactors generate (1) ENERGY, which is used to drive TURBINES, which in turn drive electric generators; and (2) RADIOACTIVITY, which is used in the production of ISOTOPES (e.g. TRACE ELEMENTS) for industry and medicine.

Nuclear reactors are classified in a variety of ways, and the types mentioned in the following sentences are selected from several classifications. A *breeder reactor* is one in which fissile material is produced in greater quantities than it is consumed, so that even if part of the final product is used in the same reactor there will still be a surplus for use elsewhere. A *fast reactor* is one in which no moderator is used, but this absence is compensated by a high concentration of core material. A *thermal reactor* is one in which the bombarding agents are THERMAL NEUTRONS. A *pressurized-water reactor* is one in which water under high pressure (of the order of 2,000 lbs per square inch) is used both as moderator and coolant. In a *boiling-water reactor* water acts as a coolant only. In a *gas-cooled reactor* (in which graphite is used to slow the neutrons) the heat is carried away by a gas (originally carbon dioxide, later helium) which can be used at very high temperatures (up to 1,000°C) and then operate directly on the blades of a gas turbine.   M.V.B.; E.R.L.

Bibl: see under QUANTUM MECHANICS.

nuclear submarine. A submarine powered by a NUCLEAR REACTOR. Refuelling is necessary only at very infrequent intervals (about once a year, though this is a lengthy process), so that the time spent under water (about one month) is limited mainly by the quantity of food etc. which can be carried and by the endurance of the crew. It cannot be detected by a heat source, and it is much less vulnerable to attack than land-based missile systems; in deep ocean, where echo-detecting systems are of little value, it is virtually invulnerable. Its limitation hitherto has been that its MISSILES have had a range of only 2,000 miles. Submarine-launched missiles now under development in the U.S.A. and the U.S.S.R. will have a truly intercontinental range.   A.F.B.

nuclear war, see under WAR.

nucleic acid. Nucleic acids are of crucial importance in all living organisms and in viruses (see VIROLOGY) as the sole vectors of genetic information. They are giant polymeric (see POLYMER) MOLECULES of which the structural unit is a *nucleotide*, a

compound built up of (1) a sugar, either ribose (in ribonucleic acid, RNA) or deoxyribose (in deoxyribonucleic acid, DNA), (2) a nitrogen-containing base, and (3) a phosphoric acid. These nucleotides are joined together linearly to form a *polynucleotide* through the combination of the phosphoric acid of one nucleotide with the sugar constituent in its neighbour and so on. In DNA the nitrogenous bases are adenine, thymine, guanine, and cytosine; in RNA uracil substitutes for thymine. Each such base defines a distinct nucleotide, and these are the symbols of the GENETIC CODE by means of which genetic information is embodied and transmitted. It was shown by Watson and Crick (1953) that DNA has a binary structure: each molecule consists of two strands aligned to each other in such a way that adenine is linked non-covalently (see COVALENCY) with thymine, and guanine with cytosine. The two strands have a helical twist – which gives them the form of the famous DOUBLE HELIX. The first crucial piece of information that nucleic acids are the vectors of genetic information came from the work of Avery and his colleagues (1944) showing that the agent responsible for bacterial TRANSFORMATIONS of the kind that had been observed by Griffith was indeed DNA itself. The flow of information from DNA into PROTEIN takes place through, first, the 'transcription' of the DNA into a single-stranded RNA, the so-called *messenger RNA*, and then the assembly of *polypeptides* (see PEPTIDES), built up of individual AMINO ACIDS through the mediation of a *transfer RNA*. Although under special circumstances transcription is reversible, there is no known mechanism by which information can flow from PROTEIN into nucleic acids, so that no structural change occurring to an organism during the course of its own lifetime can influence the genetic DNA in any specific way.   P.M.

nucleon. A generic term for either of the two types of ELEMENTARY PARTICLE, i.e. PROTONS and NUCLEONS, which form the NUCLEUS of an ATOM, and which may be regarded as different states of the same PARTICLE.   M.V.B.

nucleonics. Engineering based on NUCLEAR PHYSICS.   M.V.B.

NUMBER

nucleoprotein, see under NUCLEUS.

nucleotide, see under NUCLEIC ACID.

nucleus.
(1) In ATOMIC PHYSICS, the tiny central core (discovered by Rutherford in 1912) containing most of the mass of an ATOM. The nucleus is composed of PROTONS and NEUTRONS, held together by STRONG INTERACTIONS resulting from the exchange of MESONS. (The sole exception is hydrogen, which consists of a single proton.) Most ISOTOPES found in nature are stable, but some are unstable, and their nuclei undergo RADIOACTIVE decay. Nuclei of the TRANSURANIC ELEMENTS are all unstable because the number of protons is sufficient for their long-range ELECTROSTATIC repulsion to overcome the strong interactions. See also QUANTUM MECHANICS. M.V.B.
(2) In CYTOLOGY, the administrative centre of the CELL. The nucleus, which with rare exceptions (e.g. the red blood corpuscles of mammals) is possessed by all plant and animal cells, is separated from the main bulk of the CYTOPLASM by a membrane of its own, distinct from the outer cell membrane. It is the repository of all the cell's genetic information and of all the information, therefore, that specifies in exact detail the synthesis of the PROTEINS of the cell. Whenever the division of the nucleus is not accompanied by a divison of the cytoplasm a binucleate cell results. By special experimental methods, particularly the use of ultraviolet-inactivated Sendai virus (see VIROLOGY), two different cells can be fused in such a way that two nuclei of different origins may be housed within one cell body. Such a cell is called a *heterokaryote*, and its study can throw light upon, e.g., the properties of a CANCER cell which are responsible for its malignancy. Nuclei are composed mainly of *nucleoprotein*, which is a salt-like compound of deoxyribonucleic acid (see NUCLEIC ACID) and a basic protein such as a histone or protamine; and virtually all the DNA of the cell is housed within the nucleus. If a cell such as a ZYGOTE is deprived of its own nucleus and its place is taken by a nucleus from a cell of some other type from a later embryo, the zygote may nevertheless develop with a fair approximation to normality – an experiment which demonstrates that the GENOME of all cells in the body derived by MITOSIS from the zygote is the same. Thus DIFFERENTIATION must consist in some process by which genetic potentialities of the cell are realized in different ways in different cells. P.M.

Nuffield approach. An approach, sponsored by the Nuffield Foundation, to curriculum development in British schools. The characteristic approach has been for Project staff, often seconded from universities and schools for three or four years, to try out proposals and many kinds of apparatus in the classroom and laboratory before proceeding to publication. There have been Nuffield projects in chemistry, physics, biology, general science for junior and younger children, mathematics, English and European languages, classics, and social science. The term is also used to describe the development and practice of a particular style of science-teaching involving the use of experiments rather than lectures or demonstrations. One of the current initiatives concerns innovation in university teaching, and recently the Nuffield Foundation has interested itself in the development of RESOURCE CENTRES. W.A.C.S.

number. In MATHEMATICS, a term with several distinct meanings:
(1) The *natural numbers* {0, 1, 2, 3, . . . } (with or without 0) come first; according to Kroenecker they come from God, all else being the work of man. They may be thought of as the finite CARDINAL NUMBERS or ORDINALS, or as a MATHEMATICAL STRUCTURE satisfying axioms which were first clearly stated by Peano in 1889. The simplest, if impractical, system of *notation* is to represent the number n by n successive strokes. The Greeks and Romans used various combinations of letters, inadequate for representing arbitrary large numbers. The decimal system, derived from Babylonia, India, and the Arabs, can be generalized to an arbitrary *base b*. The choice of b is pragmatic. The decimal system ($b = 10$) seems well suited to the human brain; $b = 8$ and $b = 12$ have also been used. The BINARY SCALE is suitable for COMPUTERS or other devices whose components may be in either of two states ('on' or 'off').
(2) The *integers* $(0, \pm 1, \pm 2, . . .)$.

NUMBER THEORY

(3) The *rational numbers*: all (improper) fractions of the form p/q where p and q are integers and $q \neq 0$, with the identification $p/q \neq p/rq$ for any integer $r \neq 0$.

(4) The *real numbers*. As early as the 6th century B.C. it was known to the Pythagoreans that *incommensurable ratios*, or *irrational* numbers, exist: e.g. $\sqrt{2}$. Intuitively, once an origin and a unit of measurement have been fixed there is a one-to-one correspondence between the real numbers and the points of a straight line; for this reason the set of real numbers is called the CONTINUUM. Despite a brilliant attempt in Euclid, book 5, it was not until about 1870 that Cantor and Dedekind gave satisfactory definitions. The easiest definition to convey (though not to theorize with) is to say that every real number can be expressed as an infinite decimal: $\pm n.a_0 a_1 a_2 \ldots$ where n is a natural number and $a_0, a_1, a_2 \ldots$, is an *arbitrary* sequence of decimal digits. Observe that there is still an appeal to intuition for the understanding of 'arbitrary'; for further discussion see SET. Not all real numbers are the roots of algebraic equations (see ALGEBRA). Those which are not (e.g. e and π) are *transcendental*.

(5) The COMPLEX NUMBERS; the algebraic numbers form a subset of these.

(6) 'Number' used also to be applied to the elements of other mathematical structures occurring in algebra; but it is nowadays confined to (1)-(5) above.   R.G.

number theory (or the *higher arithmetic*). The study of the natural NUMBERS. Topics considered range from trivial conundrums to deep and difficult theorems. Areas of perennial interest include the following: (1) *Prime numbers*. The chief theorem (first proved in 1896) states that $x/\log_e x$ is an ASYMPTOTIC approximation to the number of primes less than x (more accurate estimates are now known). Famous unproved conjectures are that there are infinitely many primes p such that $p + 2$ is also prime, and Goldbach's conjecture – that every even number greater than 4 can be expressed as the sum of two primes. COMPLEX FUNCTION THEORY plays a large part in the investigations. (2) *Diophantine equations*. These are algebraic (see ALGEBRA) EQUATIONS with the stipulation that the solutions must be integers. There is a general problem of deciding whether a solution exists (see RECURSIVE FUNCTION THEORY), and there is the study of the solutions of equations having some particular form; e.g. Pell's equation $x^2 - Ay^2 = 1$ has been extensively studied. The subject merges with algebraic number theory and with algebraic GEOMETRY. The most famous unsolved problem is FERMAT'S LAST THEOREM. (3) *Additive* number theory: a typical problem is to give an ASYMPTOTIC expression for the number of ways in which a number x can be expressed as the sum of cubes.

Number theory is fascinating because it combines the particular (each number has, so to speak, a personality of its own) with the general, and because simply stated problems may require sophisticated ideas for their solution. Number theorists sometimes congratulate themselves on the lack of application of their work. The current tendency is to concentrate attention on those problems and methods which will cast light on other MATHEMATICAL STRUCTURES; practical application remains infrequent.   R.G.

Bibl: H. Davenport, *The Higher Arithmetic* (London, 4th ed., 1971).

numeracy. A word coined, on the analogy of literacy, in the Crowther Report (1959). It represents understanding of the scientific approach to study in terms of observation, measurement, assessment, experiment, and verification, and more specifically some mastery of interpretation of mathematical and statistical evidence. The Report argued that sixth forms (16–18), whatever their specialization, should continue with education in numeracy, so that an 18-year-old leaving school, whether to go to university or not, will have a facility with quantitative statements as well as verbal ones.   W.A.C.S.

Bibl: Crowther Report, *15 to 18* (London, 1959); Dainton Report, *Enquiry into the Flow of Candidates in Science and Technology into Higher Education* (London, 1968).

numerical analysis. In general, the science and art of computing approximate solutions to problems formulated in mathematical terms. In particular it must cope with the operations of the CALCULUS. For example, a DERIVATIVE will be replaced by the ratio of corresponding *finite* increments in ARGUMENT and value; the *calculus of finite differences* is the study of this process and its applications. The numerical analyst must not only use ingenuity and skill in choosing methods which will yield approximations that converge rapidly towards the true solution (see CONVERGENCE), but must also investigate with complete rigour the degree of error involved. The advent of high-speed digital COMPUTERS has greatly enhanced the importance (and the difficulty) of the subject.   R.G.

Bibl: A. Graham, *Numerical Analysis* (London, 1973).

numerical scale, see under SCALE.

numerological criticism. An ambitious attempt to apply number symbology to literary works. It owes much to Vincent Hopper's *Medieval Number Symbolism* (1938), Edgar Wind's *Pagan Mysteries in the Renaissance* (1958), and G. Duckworth's *Structural Patterns and Proportions in Vergil's Aeneid* (1962), and takes as its exemplar K. Hieatt's *Short Time's Endless Monument* (1960), a convincing examination of Spenser's *Epithalamion* in terms of the 24 hours of Midsummer's Day. Numerological criticism as now understood begins with Alastair Fowler's *Spenser and the Numbers of Time* (1964); this was followed by studies of the (alleged) numerological significance of the works of Fielding and others, and of the numerological element in medieval poetry. Numerological criticism is by no means universally recognized as valid or important.   M.S.-S.

Bibl: C. Butler, *Number Symbolism* (London, 1970).

nuptiality. The frequency of marriage in a population. A *nuptiality table* is analogous to a life table in the study of mortality, in tracing the attrition among a given group (normally 10,000 or 100,000) of never married persons of minimum marriageable age, the cause of attrition here being marriage rather than death. In a *gross nuptiality table*, death is left out of account altogether, and such a table provides a pure measure of nuptiality; a *net nuptiality table* measures the attrition caused by both marriage and death.   E.G.

Nuremberg Laws. A series of antisemitic decrees (see ANTISEMITISM) promulgated by Hitler at the Nazi Party conference in Nuremberg on 15 September 1935. These defined Jews as those with three Jewish grandparents, those practising JUDAISM, and those married to Jews. The Nuremberg Laws denied them any rights of state or local citizenship; forbade marriage, and any sexual relations, between 'Jews' and 'non-Jews'. Other decrees excluded Jews or half-Jews from public office; from owning businesses, economic enterprises, or land; and from practising as doctors, lawyers, writers, journalists, teachers in schools and universities, etc. The Nuremberg Laws, reducing the Jews to the status of second-class citizens, were the beginning of a process which led to the FINAL SOLUTION.   D.C.W.

Nuremberg Trials. The trial at the end of World War II of 24 former NAZI leaders, and the 12 subsequent trials of major war criminals from the Army, the ministries, the legal community, doctors, business, etc., on charges of crimes committed before and during the war. These included the planning and waging of aggressive war, GENOCIDE, the ill-treatment of prisoners of war and deportees, crimes against humanity, the use of FORCED LABOUR, and general breaches of the laws of war. The legal justification for such trials of the vanquished by the victors has been a matter of subsequent dispute among jurists. Of the 177 men indicted, 25 were sentenced to death, 20 to life imprisonment, and 35 acquitted.   D.C.W.

nursery class, nursery school, see under PRE-SCHOOL EDUCATION.

Nusberg, Lev (Soviet artist, *b*. 1937), see under KINETIC ART.

nutrition. The branch of PHYSIOLOGY that deals with the nature and utilization of foodstuffs. From the human standpoint the essential foodstuffs are PROTEINS, CARBOHYDRATES, and fats, together with mineral salts and VITAMINS. The energy values of foods are measured in terms of calories or kilocalories, i.e. the thermal energy released upon complete combustion in a calorimeter. In addition to mineral salts certain essential ELEMENTS must be present, notably iodine in combination because of the dependence of the THYROID upon it. P.M.

nylon. The first 'tailor-made' POLYMER (developed in the 1930s). It is useful because it can easily be formed into fibres by extrusion through small holes.

M.V.B.

O

O and M, see ORGANIZATION AND METHOD.

OAU (Organization for African Unity), see under PAN-AFRICANISM.

objective correlative. Term coined by T. S. Eliot in his essay, 'Hamlet' (1919): 'The only way of expressing emotion in the form of art is by finding an "objective correlative": in other words, a set of objects, a situation, a chain of events which shall be the formula of that *particular* emotion; such that when the external facts, which must terminate in sensory experience, are given, the emotion is immediately evoked.' Eliot maintains that Hamlet is dominated by an emotion which is 'in *excess* of the facts as they appear'. As with DISSOCIATION OF SENSIBILITY, Eliot's dictum cannot be erected into a universal law (and has been disputed in its application to Hamlet), but it provides an excellent description of the sort of immature writing where intense emotions remain inexplicable and unengaging because they lack a context which will evoke and define them. D.J.E.

objective function, see under OPTIMIZATION THEORY.

objective idealism, see under IDEALISM.

objective tests. Educational tests in which questions are so presented that there can only be one right answer and the examiner's own interpretation is eliminated from the marking process. The instructions and the length of time allowed are standardized, and usually such tests are made up of a number (or 'battery') of short sub-tests. They can be constructed in words, diagrams, symbols, or mathematical terms. Sponsoring bodies include the National Foundation for Educational Research in London, Moray House in Edinburgh, the American Council on Education, and the American Psychological Association. See also MULTIPLE-CHOICE METHOD. W.A.C.S.

Bibl: P. E. Vernon, *The Measurement of Abilities* (2nd ed., London, 1956; N.Y., 1961).

objectivism. An American poetic movement of the early 1930s, short-lived but influential. According to William Carlos Williams, whose *Collected Poems 1921–1931* was published by the Objectivist Press in 1934, 'Objectivism looks at the poem with a special eye to its structural aspect, how it has been constructed ... It arose as an aftermath of IMAGISM, which the Objectivists felt was not specific enough, and applied to any image that might be conceived.' Other poets associated with the movement were George Oppen, who founded the Objectivist Press (originally TO: The Objectivists); Louis Zukofsky, who edited *An Objectivist's Anthology*; and Charles Reznikoff. Ezra Pound gave postal encouragement. M.S.-S.

objet trouvé (found object). Any strange, romantic, or comic bit of stone, wood, or manufactured bric-à-brac which is presented by the finder as an art object. The term was much used by the SURREALISTS to whom such objects, whether found or fabricated, became from the late 1920s onwards as significant as their pictures or sculptures. J.W.

obsession. In ABNORMAL PSYCHOLOGY and PSYCHIATRY, a form of NEUROSIS marked primarily by an emotionally charged idea that may persistently impose itself in the subject's conscious awareness; in this sense, the phrase *obsessional disorder* is widely used. In popular usage, any excessive preoccupation. W.Z.

obsidian dating, see under DATING.

occlusion. In METEOROLOGY, the complex frontal structure formed when a cold FRONT overtakes a warm front. Occlusions are associated with widespread precipitation along and in advance of the surface position of the occluded front. P.H.

occultism. The occult is the mysterious that lies below the surface of things; occultism is the exercise of magical procedures to influence this, by a knowledge of it. Elements of magic, WITCHCRAFT, etc. have persisted in all civilizations; anthropologists insist that these features may be present in the RITUALS of all types of society (modern as well as PRIMITIVE), and they have not been dissipated by modern science. With the supposed 'flight from reason' during recent decades, occultism has enjoyed a popular revival. The Society for Psychical Research was founded in Britain in 1882, and in recent years a growing literature has examined telepathy, hypnotism, clairvoyance, the evidence for survival beyond death, and, in general, those supranormal faculties of man which still seem to lie beyond the range of testable knowledge.   R.F.

Bibl: Reader's Digest, *Folklore, Myths and Legends of Britain* (London, 1973).

occupation. The ways in which men obtain their livelihood are commonly divided into: (1) *primary occupations*: the production or extraction of raw materials, e.g. agriculture, fishing, hunting, lumbering, and mining; (2) *secondary occupations*: the production of man-made goods or the processing of raw materials. The growth of secondary at the expense of primary occupations is a feature of the early stages of INDUSTRIALIZATION; (3) *tertiary occupations*: the provision of services (see SERVICE INDUSTRY) rather than the production of goods. Some expansion of tertiary as well as secondary occupations takes place in the early stages of industrialization, but the marked growth of tertiary at the expense of both primary and secondary occupations is one of the distinguishing characteristics of advanced industrial societies.   A.L.C.B.

occupational therapy. In medical practice, the treatment of physical or mental disability by purposive occupation. Originally activities like farming helped to combat apathy in long-stay patients in mental hospitals. Later, handicrafts provided soothing diversions for the physically or mentally sick. Modern occupational therapy is much more actively therapeutic, aiming to foster interest and self-confidence, to overcome disability, and to develop fresh skills enabling patients to perform a useful function in the community. Activities are tailored to the needs of individual patients, and range from games to typing, domestic science, and light industrial work supervised by technical instructors. Group activities are emphasized as a means of encouraging social interaction. Occupational therapy now forms an integral part of the treatment of many illnesses, particularly chronic physical or mental handicap, whether in hospital or not.   D.H.G.

Bibl: E. M. MacDonald (ed.), *Occupational Therapy in Rehabilitation* (London, 3rd ed., 1970).

oceanography. Scientific study of the phenomena associated with the ocean waters that cover 70% of the earth's surface. The main branches are *physical oceanography* (concerned with waves, ocean currents, tides, and circulation systems); *chemical oceanography* (e.g. analyses of the constituents of ocean water); *biological oceanography* (e.g. study of marine fauna), and *geological oceanography* (e.g. study of ocean basins, MORPHOLOGY of the sea bottom, oceanic sediments). Scientific oceanography dates from the mid 19th century with growing interest in deep-sea biology, marked by the establishment of research centres such as the Stazione Zoologica in Naples, founded in 1872. The *Challenger* voyages in the 1870s are an early landmark in the development of special research exploration voyages. Current interest in oceanography is widening its scope to include broader issues of a legal, ECONOMIC, and ECOLOGICAL nature. Leading centres for oceanography include the Scripps Institution of Oceanography at La Jolla, California, the Woods Hole Oceanographic Institute in Massachusetts, and the National Institute for Oceanography at Wormley, England.   P.H.

octane rating. The measure of the KNOCKING characteristics of petrol, first introduced in 1927. On this scale iso-octane, which has low knocking tendencies, is assigned an octane rating of 100 and normal heptane zero. Particular petrols are rated in terms of the percentage by volume of the former constituent in an iso-octane-normal pentane mixture which gives equivalent knocking properties.   B.F.

Oder-Neisse line. The line formed by the river Oder and its tributary, the western Neisse, which was established by Soviet action as the boundary between East Germany and Poland in 1945. Provisionally recognized at POTSDAM, it was not formally accepted by the West German Government until 18 November 1970 – a recognition which removed the major remaining source of German-Polish tension and defied the waning political power of German refugee organizations in West Germany.   D.C.W.

Odets, Clifford (U.S. dramatist, 1906–63), see under GROUP THEATRE.

OECD (Organization for Economic Cooperation and Development). A Paris-based inter-governmental organization established under a convention of 14 December 1961 to comprise the 20 original members and associate members of OEEC, and subsequently including also Japan (1963) and Finland (1968), with special-status membership for Australia, New Zealand, and Yugoslavia. OECD extended OEEC's interests to include those of (1) longer-run economic development, including such problems as ECONOMIC GROWTH, science and education, the ENVIRONMENT, MANPOWER, social affairs, etc.; and (2) the relationships between its mainly developed member countries and the rest of the world, with a *Development Assistance Committee* (*DAC*) concerned with the level and effectiveness of aid to developing countries (see UNDERDEVELOPMENT). At the same time OECD has continued to play an important part in discussing current and longer-term international-payments problems, particularly through the Working Party No. 3 of its Economic Policy Committee.   W.B.

Oedipus complex. In psychoanalytic theory (see PSYCHOANALYSIS), the normal emotional crisis brought about, at an early stage of PSYCHOSEXUAL DEVELOPMENT, by the sexual impulses of a boy towards his mother and jealousy of his father. Resultant guilt feelings precipitate the development of the SUPEREGO (conscience). Its female counterpart is the ELECTRA COMPLEX.   W.Z.

OEEC (Organization for European Economic Cooperation). A Paris-based inter-governmental organization established under a convention of 16 April 1948 and comprising, finally, 18 European countries (Austria, Belgium, Denmark, France, Germany, Greece, Iceland, Ireland, Italy, Luxembourg, the Netherlands, Norway, Portugal, Spain, Sweden, Switzerland, Turkey, and the U.K.), plus Canada and the U.S.A. as associate members. Its primary aim was to assist in the post-war reconstruction of its members' economies on a cooperative basis, notably through the administration (1948–52) of the MARSHALL PLAN. After this American aid ended, OEEC continued to play an important role in liberalizing trade between member countries and establishing a multilateral international-payments machinery. In December 1961, after it had become clear that little further progress in eliminating restrictions on international trade, payments, and movements in labour and CAPITAL was possible within the existing framework, and that more attention should be given to the problem of UNDERDEVELOPMENT, OEEC was replaced by the more broadly based OECD.   W.B.

Oestreicher, Hans L., see under BIONICS.

Off-Broadway. A collection of some 30 theatres surrounding New York's Broadway on all sides but the west, best known for the development of new dramatists such as Edward Albee and Jack Gelber, and the revival of old masters like Eugene O'Neill. The movement and the term date back to 1915 when the PROVINCE-TOWN PLAYERS and the *Washington Square Players* established themselves in Greenwich Village. Dedicated to good productions of good plays in intimate surroundings, the movement acquired a new lease of life in 1952 with a notable revival of Tennessee Williams's Broadway failure, *Summer and Smoke.* But, despite much excellent work in the 1950s and 1960s, soaring costs and the desire for commercial success gradually turned Off-Broadway into a replica of Broadway itself. The really experimental work now takes place off Off-Broadway in coffee houses, cabarets, churches, and warehouses. For a British equivalent see FRINGE, THE.   M.BI.

Bibl: M. Gottfried, *A Theatre Divided: the Postwar American Stage* (Boston, 1969).

off-line computing, see under COMPUTING.

Ogarev, Nikolai (Russian revolutionary, 1813–77), see under BOLSHEVISM.

Ogburn, William Fielding (U.S. sociologist, 1886–1959), see under CULTURAL LAG.

Ogden, Charles Kay (British psychologist and linguist, 1889–1957), see under EMOTIVE AND REFERENTIAL LANGUAGE; EMOTIVISM; SYNAESTHESIS.

OGPU, see under KGB.

Ohsawa, Georges (pseud. of Yukikazu Sakurazawa, 1893–1966), see under MACROBIOTICS.

Okhlopkov, Nikolai Pavlovich (Russian actor and producer, 1900–67), see under OPEN STAGE; THEATRE IN THE ROUND.

Oldenburg, Claes (Swedish-U.S. sculptor, *b*. 1929), see under ENVIRONMENT; HAPPENINGS; POP.

Olds, James (U.S. neuropsychologist, *b*. 1922), see under BRAIN STIMULATION.

oligopeptide, see under PEPTIDE.

oligopoly. A state of affairs in which a commodity is sold by a number of suppliers sufficiently small for the actions of any one of them materially to affect the others. In these circumstances, which are typical of manufacturing business, firms will adopt strategies that are influenced by the way in which they expect rivals to react to what they do. As a result, a group of firms may sink their differences and jointly act as would a monopolist (see MONOPOLY). More commonly, however, competition will continue to operate even though intermittently and in limited ways; established firms are likely to find it difficult to raise prices unduly, moreover, so long as it is easy for other firms to enter their industry.   G.B.R.
Bibl: F. M. Scherer, *Industrial Market Structure and Economic Performance* (Chicago, 1970).

Olmsted, Frederick (U.S. landscape architect, 1822–1903), see under PEDESTRIAN SEGREGATION.

Olson, Charles (U.S. poet and critic, 1910–70), see under BLACK MOUNTAIN.

ombudsman. A state official entrusted by the legislature with very wide powers enabling him to intervene in the bureaucratic and administrative process in the interests of individual citizens whose complaints he investigates. The institution originated in Swedish practice as early as 1809 and has since been copied in civilian matters by Finland (1919), Israel (1950), Denmark (1953), Norway (1962), New Zealand (1962), and Britain (1967). In military matters Norway and West Germany have similar officials. The successful operation of the institution depends on the width of the official's powers and on his powers of initiative, two elements notably restricted in the British case. D.C.W.
Bibl: D. C. Rowat (ed.), *The Ombudsman* (London, 1965).

Omega Workshops. Established by Roger Fry in 1913 to provide a livelihood for young artists who undertook decorative work anonymously for a small weekly wage. Adversely affected by the war, the Omega was dissolved in 1919.   Q.B.

on-line computing, see under COMPUTING.

oncology. The branch of medical science concerned with CANCER. The prefix onco- (from a Greek word meaning 'mass' or 'bulk') denotes something to do with a tumour; thus *oncoviruses* are tumour-causing viruses (see VIROLOGY), and an *oncogen* (or CARCINOGEN) is an agent giving rise to tumours.   P.M.

ondes martenot (*ondes musicales*). An electrophonic instrument invented by Maurice Martenot in 1928 and similar to the THEREMIN, having a keyboard and capacity for glissandi. It now generally replaces the theremin and has solo roles in major works of Messiaen, notably *Turangalîla*.   J.G.R.

O'Neill, Eugene (U.S. dramatist, 1888–1953), see under GATE THEATRE; OFF-BROADWAY; PROVINCETOWN PLAYERS.

Onnes, Heike Kamerlingh (Dutch physicist, 1853–1926), see under SUPERCONDUCTIVITY.

Onofri, Arturo (Italian poet and critic, 1885–1928), see under HERMETIC.

onomastics. The study of the origins and forms of proper names, especially of people and places.   D.C.

ontogeny. The course of growth within the lifetime of a single member of a species. It is contrasted with PHYLOGENY.   J.S.B.

ontology. The theory of existence or, more narrowly, of what really exists, as opposed to that which appears to exist but does not, or to that which can properly be said to exist but only if conceived as some complex whose constituents are the things that really exist. It is the primary element in METAPHYSICS. Some ontologists have argued that many things exist that are not commonly acknowledged to do so, such as (1) abstract *entities* and (2) NOUMENA (Kant's 'things-in-themselves') inaccessible to empirical observation; others have argued that many things commonly thought to exist do not, e.g. material things, the theoretical entities of NATURAL SCIENCE, mental states conceived as something other than DISPOSITIONS to behaviour, and objective value-properties. The ontology of a theory or body of assertions is the SET of things to which that theory ascribes existence by referring to them in a way that cannot be eliminated or analysed out (see ANALYSIS) by REDUCTION.   A.Q.

op art. A scientifically-oriented ABSTRACT ART movement in the 1960s concerned with perceptual dynamics and retinal stimulation. Geometric forms, colour dissonance, and KINETIC elements were used to achieve optical effects, illusions, after-images, and MOIRÉ patterning, and to stress the act of perception as the central meaning. Artists involved in this somewhat *passé* movement were: Julio Le Parc, founder of the Groupe de Recherche d'Art Visuel in Paris in 1960; Victor Vasarely in Paris; Bridget Riley in England; and Richard Anuszkiewicz in New York. Its more romantic counterpart was PSYCHEDELIC ART.   A.K.W.
  Bibl: W. C. Seitz, *The Responsive Eye* (N.Y., 1965); F. Popper, *Origins and Development of Kinetic Art* (London, 1968; N.Y., 1969).

open-book examination. An examination in which candidates are permitted to take relevant textbooks into the examination room, or to consult reference material such as maps, mathematical tables, and dictionaries. In place of the timed test in which the candidate has to answer a set of unseen questions relying on knowledge of the subject acquired before the test, the open-book examination offers him the chance to look up material, and to exercise judgement in selecting and presenting facts and ideas, although usually a time limit is still applied.   W.A.C.S.

open class, see under WORD CLASS.

open plan. An arrangement of spaces, usually in domestic or office architecture, where the division between areas is implied by screens, columns, changes of level, or different ceiling heights, rather than defined by walls. It was largely developed by Frank Lloyd Wright in his house plans from the mid 1890s onwards and owes something to his familiarity with the traditional Japanese house. A variant, *le plan libre*, was practised by Le Corbusier, taking advantage of skeletal construction. Its acceptance is largely due to the emergence of efficient heating systems and the great reduction in the number of household servants; in the case of offices it allows the regrouping of work areas with the least disturbance.   M.BR.

open-plan schools. Schools where the architecture provides for minimal or no visual and acoustic separation between teaching-stations. Commonly between two and eight teachers and their pupils share a large teaching-space to which one or more quiet rooms or learning-bays may be connected. Teachers necessarily work in view and hearing of one another; effective teaching therefore requires them to cooperate in decisions about deployment of groups of children, scheduling, curriculum, teaching and learning problems. The focus of decision-making is typically shifted from the individual teacher to the team (see TEAM-TEACHING), and VERTICAL GROUPING is facilitated. Some pupils and teachers thrive in the atmosphere

441

of an open-plan school, but others feel lost and insecure and would be happier and better cared for in self-contained classrooms. A prime target for criticism in open-plan schools is the noise level, and adequate soundproofing is of great importance.   E.L.-S.

open prison (or *prison without bars*). An establishment with minimal or token security, and in general a less restrictive regime than that of an ordinary prison; a feature of prison systems in Britain, the U.S.A., and Scandinavia since the 1930s. Inmates are selected, for short sentences or the latter part of long ones, on the basis of their constituting negligible escape risks. There is little evidence to suggest that open prisons have more than humanitarian value.   T.M.

open society. Sir Karl Popper's (see POP-PERIAN) term for the free society, where all are able to criticize effectively those who hold authority in it. Popper quotes and approves of Pericles: 'Although only a few may originate a policy, we are all able to judge it.' This entails a forthright attack on TOTALITARIAN doctrines; on 'closed' hierarchies of social and political organization which do not allow individuals to rise according to merit; on indoctrination in education; on HISTORICIST social theories which predict the destiny of human society on the basis of 'unalterable laws' of historical development; and on totalitarian programmes for the reform of 'society as a whole' – which can easily replace one AUTHORITARIANISM by another. See also SOCIAL ENGINEERING.   R.F.

Bibl: K. R. Popper, *The Open Society and its Enemies,* 2 vols. (London and Princeton, rev. ed., 1967).

open stage. A term first used by Richard Southern (1953) to denote any form of staging in which the actor is not separated from the audience by a proscenium arch. The move towards open staging in this century is part of the reaction against NATURALISM which, in the theatre, is associated with realistic stage settings seen through the 'picture frame' or 'fourth wall' of the proscenium opening. The techniques of the open stage were developed in the first half of this century in productions by William Poel, Max Reinhardt,

Jacques Copeau, Vsevolod Meyerhold, and Nikolai Okhlopkov, and in the design of Walter Gropius's unrealized TOTAL THEATRE project for Piscator (1927). The principles of open staging have been increasingly incorporated in theatre architecture since the 1940s.

The principal forms of open stage are *thrust stage,* in which an acting area with a scenic or architectural background is surrounded on three sides by an audience; *end stage,* in which an audience faces the stage in a rectangular auditorium; *transverse stage,* in which an audience is seated on two opposite sides of a performing area; and THEATRE IN THE ROUND. An *adaptable theatre* is one designed to allow a variety of forms.   M.A.

Bibl: S. Joseph, *New Theatre Forms* (London and N.Y., 1968); S. Tidworth, *Theatres* (London and N.Y., 1973).

Open University. Originally called the *University of the Air,* the Open University (headquarters at Milton Keynes in Buckinghamshire) offers degree courses to people who have not the qualifications required for ordinary university entrance. Students, who in 1976 numbered about 49,000, register from their own homes and work for degrees on a cumulative COURSE CREDIT system, normally over at least four years. The teaching is provided through specially prepared books and book lists, weekly television and radio programmes (broadcast by the British Broadcasting Corporation), regionally organized study centres, written work on a correspondence basis, local counsellors and tutors recruited regionally, and full-time summer courses in university centres.   W.A.C.S.

operant conditioning (also known as *instrumental* conditioning). A form of CONDITIONING in which behaviour is controlled through systematic manipulation of the consequences of previous behaviour; a sophisticated branch of American BEHAVIOURIST psychology developed by B. F. Skinner (see SKINNERIAN). A central idea is that of REINFORCEMENT. Knowledge of (or control over) the delivery of reinforcements in a given situation is both a NECESSARY AND A SUFFICIENT CONDITION for the prediction (or control) of behaviour.

Although Skinner's ideas originated in

studies of rats and pigeons in restricted experimental ENVIRONMENTS (see SKINNER BOX), he has extended his conceptual analysis to human behaviour, including language. Techniques derived from operant conditioning have proved useful in PSYCHIATRY, EDUCATIONAL PSYCHOLOGY, and INDUSTRIAL PSYCHOLOGY.

D.H.

Bibl: B. F. Skinner, *The Behaviour of Organisms* (London and N.Y., 1938); *Verbal Behavior* (N.Y., 1957; London, 1959).

operating system. A PROGRAM, generally large, complicated, and expensive, which regulates the flow of work through a COMPUTER. The user is often more affected by the properties of the operating system than by those of the machine. C.S.

Operation Head Start, see HEAD START PROGRAMME.

operational research (U.K. term; in the U.S.A., *operations research*). The adoption of a numerate approach to empirical processes involving decision-taking, particularly in government and commerce. Among the many mathematical techniques used in operational research are OPTIMIZATION THEORY; DYNAMIC PROGRAMMING and control theory (see CONTROL ENGINEERING); DATA ANALYSIS, including most classical STATISTICS together with many recent nonprobabilistic techniques; and SIMULATION, usually involving both the production of a mathematical MODEL of a system and of a PROGRAM to run the model on a COMPUTER. The term was coined (and gained wide currency) during World War II to describe the increasingly scientific approach then adopted in the planning of military operations; and this is an area in which the techniques continue to be very widely used. The problems now tackled by operational research methods also include: minimal-cost adequate diet; minimal-cost distribution from supply points (depots) to demand points; optimal location of manufacture and distribution centres relative to raw-material sources and markets; effects and relative priorities of different forms of transport modernization; choice of container size for packaging mixed consignments; stock control; maintenance and inspection schedules;

analysis of marketing information; design of 'product profiles'; forward planning and needs prediction in public utilities and social services. See also CRITICAL PATH ANALYSIS. R.SI.

Bibl: S. Beer, *Decision and Control* (London and N.Y., 1966); S. Vajda, *Planning by Mathematics* (London, 1969; N.Y., 1971); P. Whittle, *Optimization under Constraints* (London and N.Y., 1971); C. H. Waddington, *OR in World War II* (London, 1973).

operationalism. A theory that defines scientific CONCEPTS in terms of the actual experimental procedures used to establish their applicability. Expounded by Bridgman in 1927, it identifies length, for example, with the set of operations by which length is measured. It is a radically EMPIRICIST doctrine and very close to that version of the VERIFICATION principle which defines the meaning of a PROPOSITION as 'the method of its verification'. Einstein's famous rejection of the concept of absolute simultaneity, on the ground that the simultaneity of events is always relative to the FRAME OF REFERENCE of the observer who is assessing it, is operationalist in spirit. A.Q.

Bibl: P. W. Bridgman, *The Logic of Modern Physics* (N.Y., 1927).

operations research, see OPERATIONAL RESEARCH.

operator. In MATHEMATICS, a synonym for FUNCTION, often used when the arguments are non-numerical or themselves functions. R.G.

operon. A group of GENES brought into action simultaneously. The concept is based on studies of gene action in bacteria (see BACTERIOLOGY) by Jacob and Monod (Nobel Prize, 1965). J.M.S.

opinion poll. The canvassing of opinions on specific issues by interviewing techniques, usually analysed by statistical methods on the basis of a sample of the group whose opinion is being polled. It is frequently used as a means of forecasting the outcome of elections (in which context it is often referred to, after one of its practitioners, as a *Gallup poll*), referenda, etc., although such forecasts have often been belied by events. See also SURVEY. D.C.W.

OPPEN

Bibl: F. F. Stephan and P. J. McCarthy, *Sampling Opinions* (N.Y., 1958); R. Hodder-Williams, *Public Opinion Polls and British Politics* (London, 1970).

Oppen, George (U.S. poet, *b*. 1908), see under OBJECTIVISM.

opportunity cost. In ECONOMICS, the cost CONCEPT consistent with the most general theory of choice: the opportunity cost of the chosen course of action is the cost of foregoing the benefits offered by the best of the rejected alternatives. This concept is independent of financial considerations, though financial costs sometimes correspond to opportunity costs: if there is a perfect market (see COMPETITION) for an INPUT the opportunity cost to a user must be its market price, for if he is buying it that is what he pays; using it for this purpose does not preclude buying more at the same price for other purposes, and if he already has some the opportunity cost of using it is the foregone selling price. Though opportunity cost is a fundamental concept to which financial costs in real (imperfect) markets can only approximate, the concept is most often given direct application in COST-BENEFIT ANALYSIS when simpler cost data are not available, e.g. in the valuation of traveller's time or of unemployed resources where the market has most obviously broken down. SHADOW PRICES are derived directly as opportunity costs. J.S.F.

optics. The branch of PHYSICS devoted to the study of light. There are four conceptual levels, appropriate to different phenomena: (1) *Geometrical optics*, where light is considered as *rays* travelling according to the laws of refraction and reflection. This is sufficient for the understanding of lenses and mirrors in cameras, telescopes, etc. (2) *Physical optics*, where the interference and DIFFRACTION effects due to the *wave* nature of light are taken into account – in order to explain, for example, the limit to the fine detail that can be discerned even with a perfect lens, or the operation of HOLOGRAPHY. (3) ELECTROMAGNETISM, where the *physical nature* of light waves as undulating ELECTROMAGNETIC FIELDS is studied. Thus light is seen in a new perspective, as just one frequency band in the spectrum of electromagnetic RADIATION. (4)

Quantum electrodynamics, where the application of QUANTUM MECHANICS to the electromagnetic field explains the parcelling of light ENERGY into discrete PHOTONS which are most easily discernible at very low levels of illumination.
M.V.B.

Bibl: A. C. S. van Heel and C. H. F. Velzel, tr. J. L. J. Rosenfeld, *What is Light?* (London and N.Y., 1968).

optimal policy, see under DYNAMIC PROGRAMMING.

optimization; optimization theory. The problem of optimization is that of making the best possible choice out of a set of alternatives; the context to which the term usually refers is the mathematically expressed version of the problem, which is the maximization or minimization of some function (the *objective function* or *criterion function*); the set of alternatives is frequently restricted by *constraints* on the values of the variables. Many of the practical applications of optimization lie in OPERATIONAL RESEARCH. Simple examples of an optimization problem include designing an electronic network to carry out specified logical operations (e.g. in a COMPUTER) using as few components as possible, and finding the most efficient transportation pattern to carry supplies of a commodity from supply points to demand points, given the amount of commodity available at each supply point and the amount needed at each demand point, and the unit cost of transporting the commodity from any of the former to any of the latter. See also DYNAMIC PROGRAMMING; GRADIENT METHODS; INTEGER PROGRAMMING; and, perhaps most importantly, LINEAR PROGRAMMING. R.SI.

OR, see OPERATIONAL RESEARCH.

or-gate, see under GATE.

oracy. A word formed by analogy with 'literacy' (the ability to read and write) and meaning mastery of the skills of speaking and listening. It was coined by Andrew Wilkinson in the 1960s to draw attention to the neglect of the oral skills in education despite the fact, confirmed by research, that the ability to communicate in speech is a necessary precondition of

---

learning to read and write and an essential stage in human development. Like NUMERACY, oracy has proved a convenient coinage that has now come into general use. A.L.C.B.

Bibl: J. Britton, *Language and Learning* (London and Coral Gables, Fla., 1970).

Orage, Alfred Richard (British editor and social thinker, 1873–1934), see under GUILD SOCIALISM; NEW AGE.

oral character, see under PSYCHOSEXUAL DEVELOPMENT.

oral history, see under ORAL TRADITION.

oral tradition. Defined by Vansina as 'oral testimony transmitted verbally from one generation to the next one or more'. Oral tradition is one of the basic sources for the study of ETHNOHISTORY. Its reliability is still controversial. The conventional wisdom of historians has been that oral tradition is valueless or that it is impossible to determine its value. This view has been challenged in the last twenty years, in particular by historians working on African societies which paid great attention to the correct transmission of their traditions.

It is convenient to reserve the term *oral history* for the study of CONTEMPORARY HISTORY through interviews, often tape-recorded, with eye-witnesses. There has been a rise of interest in oral history in Britain in the 1970s, and a journal, *Oral History*, has been founded. P.B.

Bibl: J. Vansina, tr. H. M. Wright, *Oral Tradition* (London and Chicago, 1965).

orbit. The path or trajectory along which an object travels in space according to NEWTONIAN MECHANICS. For example, the nearly circular orbit of the moon around the earth arises because the attracting force of GRAVITATION produces an inward ACCELERATION – i.e. the tangential velocity of the moon constantly changes in *direction* by bending inwards, while remaining constant in magnitude. See also BALLISTICS; CELESTIAL MECHANICS. M.V.B.

orbital. In the QUANTUM description of the ATOM, Bohr (in 1911) introduced the concept of an orbit in which the ELECTRONS followed planet-like motions around the NUCLEUS. Modern wave-mechanical treatments (see QUANTUM MECHANICS) do not allow the path of the electron to be pinpointed (see UNCERTAINTY PRINCIPLE), but there is a relation between the WAVE FUNCTION used to describe an electron in an atom or MOLECULE and its spatial distribution. The region within which there is a reasonable (say 95%) probability of finding an electron is termed an orbital. B.F.

ordering relations. In MATHEMATICS, a number of variants of the familiar RELATION 'less than'. They are characterized by AXIOMS; let '<' denote any such relation. If < is only required to be transitive and irreflexive it is called a *partial* ordering; an example is the relation of (strict) inclusion between SETS. If, in addition, it is required that for any x and y either $x < y$ or $y < x$ or $x = y$, then < is called a *linear* or *simple* ordering; this corresponds to the ordinary use of 'less than'. If, further, it is required that any (non-empty) set of elements has a least element, then < is a *well-ordering*. A familiar example is provided by the natural NUMBERS. But other *transfinite* well-orderings exist; e.g. the numbers may be arranged in a new order as follows: 0, 2, 4, . . . , 1, 3, 5, . . . Well-orderings are a useful tool in the study of INFINITE sets. R.G.

Bibl: N. W. Gowar, *Basic Mathematical Structures* (2 vols., London, 1973–4).

ordinal (number). The abstract CONCEPT defined by the EQUIVALENCE RELATION of ISOMORPHISM between well-orderings (see ORDERING RELATION). R.G.

ordinal scale, see under SCALE.

organic. In architecture (for its meaning in art see BIOMORPHIC), adjective used (1) principally by Frank Lloyd Wright (1869–1959) as a term of approval for certain buildings, including his own, which were usually asymmetrical and integrated closely with the particular features of the site; in this sense the term is opposed both to 'classical' and to the INTERNATIONAL STYLE; (2) often in its more literal sense of being abstracted from the forms of nature, especially in the case of ornaments such as the arabesque; (3) occasionally to describe buildings, or parts of buildings, organized on a direct biological analogy such as that of the human body. See also

445

FUNCTIONALISM.   M.BR.
Bibl: F. L. Wright, *The Future of Architecture* (N.Y., 1963).

organic chemistry. One of the main branches of CHEMISTRY. Originally defined as the chemistry of substances formed by living matter, but since 1828, when it was shown that organic chemicals could be produced from inanimate material, better described as the chemistry of compounds containing carbon (except for some compounds containing metal IONS). Over half a million organic compounds have been described, including petroleum products, rubber, PLASTICS, synthetic fibres, dyes, explosives, perfumes, insecticides, fertilizers, ANTIBIOTICS, VITAMINS, ALKALOIDS, hormones (see ENDOCRINOLOGY), sugars, and PROTEINS. The organic chemist is concerned with the extraction and identification of naturally occurring materials, the synthesis and study of a wide range of compounds, and the relationship between molecular structure and physiological action.   B.F.
Bibl: J. D. Roberts and M. C. Caserio, *Modern Organic Chemistry* (N.Y., 1967).

organicism. In PHILOSOPHY, the theory that some, or all, complex wholes have the kind of systematic unity characteristic of what are literally organisms. An organism is held to differ from a mere mechanism or aggregate by reason of the dependence of the nature and existence of its parts on their position in the whole. A hand is, or remains, a hand only if united to a living body. The notion has been applied to social INSTITUTIONS and to the universe at large (for example, in the philosophy of Whitehead). The organic analogy implies not only that the parts of the whole are unified by INTERNAL RELATIONS but that the whole has a characteristic LIFE CYCLE or course of development as organisms typically do.   A.Q.

organismic psychology. Any approach to PSYCHOLOGY which emphasizes that an organism, in developing from the single-CELL egg onwards, functions as a complex and many-sided but essentially unitary psychobiological whole which must be studied by proceeding from this whole to its parts rather than vice versa. For the opposite approach see ELEMENTARISM.
I.M.L.H.

Bibl: K. Goldstein, *The Organism* (N.Y., 1939).

organization and methods (O and M). The study of clerical methods and office work systems with the object of improving them.   R.I.T.
Bibl: G. E. Milward, *Organization and Methods* (London and N.Y., 1967).

organization man. Term used by William H. Whyte in *The Organization Man* (1956) to denote a character-type encountered in modern bureaucratized social systems – that of individuals who work for large-scale organizations, primarily in managerial roles within American corporate business enterprises, but also within scientific establishments; and who in various senses 'belong' to such organizations. They are dominated by a SOCIAL ETHIC rather than the PROTESTANT ETHIC. This fact or self-perception of 'belonging' or 'togetherness' affects the LIFE STYLE and wider social aspirations of such individuals – influencing, via education and IDEOLOGICAL pressures, the way in which they see themselves and their societies, and inducing a level of standardized mediocrity and conformity.   S.J.G.

organization theory. A set of theoretical insights into the behaviour of people working together, and into factors affecting the structure of an organization. Among the most important insights are the following: (1) the demonstration (by a study of worker productivity at the Hawthorne works of Western Electric Co. at Chicago in the 1920s and 1930s; see also HAWTHORNE EFFECT) of the importance of social factors such as MANAGEMENT's interest in workers' problems; (2) the concept of BUREAUCRACY, formulated by the German sociologist Max Weber (1947) and leading to modern ideas on individual attitudes, values, and goals and their effect on the structure of an organization; (3) the distinction drawn by Douglas McGregor (1960) between *theory X* managers, intent on work being performed in obedience to their commands, and *theory Y* managers, who see work as a potential source of satisfaction and self-fulfilment; (4) the recognition that the TECHNOLOGY of an enterprise, its scale and geographical spread, and the style of management adopted are important determinants of structure; (5) the concept of the *matrix organization*, which sets up transient project teams, with members drawn from various functional groups, thus mapping multi-disciplinary teams across the traditional organization chart; (6) a recent emphasis on the significance of the individual in organizations. Thus, *sensitivity training* seeks to sharpen the individual's awareness of himself; in one form of this, participants in a *T group* (training group) learn how others see them. However, while organizations can be perceived in terms of individual needs and behaviour, their structure can only be understood at the level of collective behaviour; and this is the realm of organization theory.   R.I.T.

Bibl: M. Weber, tr. A. M. Henderson and T. Parsons, *The Theory of Social and Economic Organization* (London and N.Y., 1947); D. McGregor, *The Human Side of Enterprise* (N.Y., 1960); F. Herzberg, *Work and the Nature of Man* (Cleveland, 1966); D. S. Pugh, R. Mansfield, and M. Warner, *Research in Organizational Behaviour: a British Survey* (London, 1975).

organizational development. An approach to the introduction of planned change in an organization. External social forces and other environmental factors are considered, as well as internal factors such as employees' attitudes, technical aspects, communications, and leadership. See also CORPORATE STRATEGY; ORGANIZATION THEORY.   R.I.T.

Bibl: C. Argyris, *Management and Organizational Development* (N.Y., 1971).

organizer. All animals belonging to the chordate line of descent (see ZOOLOGY) undergo, early in development, a fundamental metamorphosis known as *gastrulation* (see EMBRYOLOGY). The effect of gastrulation or of an equivalent process is to form an embryo which in addition to an outermost layer of ectoderm contains inside it an *archenteron* or rudimentary gut. The central NERVOUS SYSTEM begins as a median dorsal tubular formation in the ectoderm overlying the roof of this primitive gut. In a number of classical experiments the German embryologist Hans Spemann showed by operations on amphibian embryos that the primitive

central nervous system or nerve tube arises in response to some influence emanating from the roof of the archenteron. To this important region of the embryo he accordingly gave the name *organizer*. The nature of the influence emanating from this organization centre is not yet known. A region equivalent to the organizer of amphibian embryos is found in other vertebrate embryos. Thanks to the work of Needham and Waddington it is generally agreed that one element in the action of the organizer is a purely evocative chemical STIMULUS which realizes the potential of the overlying ectoderm to roll up into a nerve tube. The other element in its action is more strictly an organizational one, i.e. one which imposes a pattern. The ectoderm responds to the action of the organizer only when it is in a state of so-called *competence* – a condition of reactivity which is soon lost in the course of development.   P.M.

organometallic chemistry, see under INORGANIC CHEMISTRY.

Orgel, Leslie (British theoretical chemist, *d.* 1941), see under GERONTOLOGY.

origin of species, see under EVOLUTION.

orography. The branch of physical GEOGRAPHY which is concerned with mountains and mountain systems. See also TECTONICS.   M.L.

Orphism (or *Orphic Cubism*). In 1913 the paintings of Delaunay, Duchamp, Léger, and Picabia were described by Apollinaire as 'orphic', in the sense that they were more abstract (see ABSTRACT ART) and offered a more purely abstract aesthetic pleasure than did other CUBISTS; but the artist to whom this epithet has clung most firmly is Robert Delaunay, with lyrical, non-representational colour formations of 1910–14. He was joined by Sonia Terk (whom he married) and František Kupka; and his geometrical patterns influenced the work of Kandinsky, Marc, and Klee (see BLAUE REITER). The inheritors of his theories of the primacy of colour were the Americans Stanton Macdonald-Wright and Morgan Russell, who were followers of Delaunay in Paris in 1912, and who have been regarded as the initiators of the first distinctively American art movement, *synchromism*.　　　　　　　　　P.C.

Bibl: R. Delaunay, ed. P. Francastel, *Du Cubisme à l'art abstrait: documents inédits* (Paris, 1957); W. C. Agee, 'Synchromism, the First American Movement' (*Art News,* October 1965).

Ortega y Gasset, José (Spanish philosopher, 1883–1955), see under PERSPECTIVISM; REALISM.

Orthodoxy, Eastern. The faith of the ancient Christian Churches of Russia, Greece, and the Middle East, with their modern offshoots in the U.S.A. and elsewhere, all of which are in communion with the Ecumenical Patriarch of Constantinople. These Churches are self-governing and reject the Pope's claims. In general they are conservative although not uniform, and the secret of their survival despite some persecution (e.g. in Russia) is their EUCHARISTIC worship, which feeds a spiritual life that can be profound. Some smaller Eastern Churches, e.g. the Nestorians, are not 'orthodox' because they do not accept the decisions of the Ecumenical Councils about CHRISTOLOGY; but the most important causes of these continuing divisions are sociological. See also CATHOLICISM; ECUMENICAL MOVEMENT.　　　　　　　　　D.L.E.

Bibl: T. R. Ware, *The Orthodox Church* (Harmondsworth and Baltimore, 1963).

orthogenesis. When a long succession of evolutionary changes (see EVOLUTION) seems to proceed in a single direction it is sometimes said to display orthogenesis. The term is falling out of use and serves no useful purpose in evolution theory. P.M.

Orton, Joe (British dramatist, 1933–67), see under BLACK COMEDY.

Orwell, George (pseud. of Eric Arthur Blair, British author, 1903–50), see under HORIZON; NEW WRITING; ORWELLIAN; POUM.

Orwellian. Characteristic or reminiscent of the writings of George Orwell – though the word is mainly used with reference to a not particularly characteristic work: his nightmarish vision, published in 1949, of the year *Nineteen Eighty-Four*. In this novel the world is divided into three TOTALITARIAN super-states, each permanently at war with one or both of the others. Life in the state known as Oceania includes such features as *Big Brother*, whose black-moustached face gazes down from a million posters; the *Thought Police*, who make good the boast that 'Big Brother is watching you'; and the *Newspeak* language, 'designed to meet the ideological needs of *Ingsoc*, or English Socialism'. The vocabulary of Newspeak shrinks every year, the ultimate object being to make heretical thoughts (*crimethink*) 'literally unthinkable'; meanwhile *Oldspeak* (i.e. English) has borrowed from it such deliberately unlovely words as *prolefeed* ('rubbishy entertainment and fictitious news' for the submerged masses or *proles*), *doublethink* ('the power of holding two contradictory beliefs in one's mind simultaneously, and accepting both of them'), and UNPERSON. The best-known Orwellian *mot*, however, comes from his fable of Soviet COMMUNISM, *Animal Farm*: 'All animals are equal but some animals are more equal than others.'　　　　　　　O.S.

Osborne, John (British dramatist, *b.* 1929), see under ANGRY YOUNG MAN; ANTI-HERO; ROYAL COURT THEATRE.

osmosis. The process whereby, when a volume of, say, cane sugar solution is separated from a volume of pure water by a membrane which is permeable by water but not by sugar, water enters the sugar-containing compartment to dilute the solution and increase its volume. Very high *osmotic pressures* may be developed in this way. Osmosis plays a most important part in all biological transactions involving water transport or water imbibition in plants and animals. With reference to some chosen standard, solutions having an equal, higher, or lower osmotic pressure are referred to as *isotonic, hypertonic,* and *hypotonic* respectively. Osmotic pressure may sometimes be a disruptive force. Thus the red blood corpuscles soon swell up and burst in hypotonic solutions, and shrivel up and crinkle ('crenate') in hypertonic ones.　　　　　　　P.M.

ostensive. A term applied to definitions which correlate words, not to other linguistic expressions (as in the verbal definitions of a dictionary), but to actual things that are representative instances of the correct application of the word. Every verbal definition of the form '*A* means the same as *B*' has to presume that *B* is already understood if it is to explain the meaning of *A*. It is usually argued that there must therefore be some verbally undefinable, or at least undefined, terms (the colour-words are a favourite example) where meaning is explained in some non-verbal or *ostensive* way so that the process of verbal definition has a stock of already understood terms to start from. See also PARADIGM CASE.   A.Q.

Osthaus, Karl Ernst (German art historian and collector, 1874–1921), see under FOLKWANG MUSEUM.

Ostpolik ('Eastern Policy'). The policy of working for an end to the hostile relations between the Federal German Republic (West Germany) and its eastern COMMUNIST neighbours: Soviet Russia, Poland, Romania, Czechoslovakia, Hungary, and the German Democratic Republic (East Germany). Inaugurated by Willy Brandt, Foreign Minister and then Chancellor of the Federal Republic (1969–1974), it led to treaties with Poland and the U.S.S.R (ratified May 1972), and to *de facto* recognition of the ODER-NEISSE frontier with Poland and of the German Democratic Republic. This put relations between West Germany and her eastern neighbours on a more normal basis but has so far done little to reduce the basic distrust and hostility on both sides. Brandt's *Ostpolitik* was seen by its advocates as opening the way to improved relations between the Western powers (not just the Federal Republic) and the Communist bloc, and was a forerunner of the policy of DÉTENTE.   A.L.C.B.

Bibl: R. Tilford (ed.), *The Ostpolitik and Political Change in Germany* (Farnborough, Hants, and Lexington, Mass., 1975).

other-direction. A quality ascribed by David Riesman in *The Lonely Crowd* (New Haven, 1950) to persons (or their characters) predominantly influenced by a 'need for approval and direction from others'. Riesman emphasizes (1) orientation towards the individual's contemporaries ('either those known to him or those with whom he is indirectly acquainted through friends or the mass media'), and (2) a capacity for 'a superficial intimacy with and response to everyone'. Other-direction is contrasted with *tradition-direction* and *inner direction*.   S.J.G.

Otto, Rudolf (German theologian, philosopher, and historian of religion, 1869–1937), see under MYSTICISM.

Oudin, Jacques (French immunologist, *b*. 1908), see under ALLOTYPY.

output. For the precise meaning of this word in COMPUTING and ECONOMICS, see respectively INPUT/OUTPUT and INPUT-OUTPUT ANALYSIS. In more general discourse, it should be applied only to quantifiable (see QUANTIFICATION) phenomena such as a writer's output in words; to speak of, say, the 'output' of a political system is to imply (1) that this too can be quantified (which it cannot); and perhaps (2), by analogy with the output of a farm or factory, that all such 'output' is beneficial (which may not be the case).   O S

output tax, see under VALUE-ADDED TAX.

outsider. Word given currency for a few years by Colin Wilson's mish-mash of pseudo-Nietzschean and other ideas in *The Outsider* (1956). His 'outsiders' included Kierkegaard, Nietzsche, T. E. Lawrence, Kafka, and Hemingway – an oddly disparate group. In this sense the word admits of no precise definition; all that can be said is that the term as used by E. M. Forster ('the artist will tend to be an outsider') is given a 'superman' flavour: the artist should not merely stand apart from society to concentrate upon his own function within it, but should raise himself above it and become a superior being.   M.S.-S.

overheating. The inflationary consequences (see INFLATION) of excessive pressure on resources during a period of expansion in demand. So long as there are idle resources such an expansion usually leads first to increased employment and OUTPUT, and it is only at a later stage, as shortages and bottlenecks develop, that the pressure expends itself increasingly in higher prices.   A.C.

overkill. A polemic term used primarily by advocates of minimum DETERRENCE who argue that both the U.S.A. and the U.S.S.R. already possess a nuclear capability far exceeding that which is necessary for mutual destruction. It is also used in non-military contexts, e.g. of the excessive use of chemical poisons in dealing with agricultural pests.   A.F.B.
Bibl: R. Lapp, *Kill and Overkill* (N.Y., 1962; London, 1963).

overpopulation. A word whose different senses have been distinguished by W. A. Lewis as follows: (1) A country is said to be overpopulated if it could achieve a larger total output with a smaller population and a larger output per head. This assumes that the population structure in terms of age, skilled labour, and sex remains the same, whereas population change does not assume this. (2) In a more extreme sense a country is said to be overpopulated when its population is so large relative to its resources that any change would have no effect on total output; Mauritius, with very limited resources and space and a very large population, is a case in point. (3) The term sometimes means that the population is larger than can be fed without importing food; this usage can only really be justified when referring to the world population as a whole, since, however desirable self-sufficiency may be in a country, its absence can easily be rectified by trade – nor are countries which produce a surplus necessarily underpopulated. (4) The term is sometimes used to indicate that a country is using up irreplaceable resources at an excessive rate – a vague use which leads to no positive conclusions concerning the right size of population in relation to resources.
                                M.L.
Bibl: W. A. Lewis, *The Theory of Economic Growth* (London and Homewood, Ill., 1955).

OVRA (Organizzazione di Vigilanza e Repressione dell' Antifascismo: Organization for the Observation and Repression of Anti-Fascism). The Italian FAS-CIST political SECRET POLICE set up in 1927; an unpleasant organization, if somewhat less efficient than its German or Soviet equivalents (see GESTAPO; KGB).
                                D.C.W.

Owen, Robert (Welsh social reformer, 1771–1858), see under COMMUNE; COOPERATIVES; UTOPIAN IDEAL.

Owen, Wilfred (British poet, 1893–1918), see under POETRY BOOKSHOP.

oxidation. Originally regarded as the increase of oxygen associated with a given ELEMENT, oxidation is now defined more generally as any CHEMICAL REACTION which removes ELECTRONS from an ATOM. Since the total number of electrons is unchanged in a reaction, oxidation is always matched by a corresponding *reduction*. There is often scanty knowledge of the real distribution of electrons, so that atoms are assigned oxidation states by a set of simple rules. An element has zero oxidation state; for an ION, the oxidation number is equal to the electronic charge. In COVALENT compounds the electrons are assigned to the more ELECTRONEGATIVE atoms participating in a BOND, e.g. in the reaction of hydrogen and oxygen to give water each hydrogen atom is oxidized to the $+1$ state. The assignment of oxidation states in such compounds can become increasingly arbitrary, and the concept then has little or no significance.   B.F.

oxygen cycle, see under LIFE CYCLE.

Ozenfant, Amédée (French painter, 1886–1966), see under PURISM.

ozone. Oxygen whose MOLECULES consist of three ATOMS instead of the usual two (see ALLOTROPE). Ozone is a powerful oxidizing agent with deleterious effects on many organic substances (see OXIDATION). In a layer about 12 miles up in the atmosphere, ozone is a strong absorber of dangerous ultraviolet light from the sun.
                                M.V.B.

P

Paasche index number, see under INDEX NUMBER.

Pacem in Terris. An ENCYCLICAL issued by Pope John XXIII in 1963, stating the urgent problems of the peaceful development of the world and urging Catholics (see CATHOLICISM) to work for peace and justice in collaboration with others. It was a landmark in the AGGIORNAMENTO.

D.L.E.

pacifism. The belief and, consequently, conduct of those who believe that WAR and the employment of organized armed force are unjustifiable. Until the 20th century this was a view held only by such minority Christian groups as the QUAKERS and the PLYMOUTH BRETHREN. The word 'pacifism' first came into use at the beginning of the 20th century to describe movements advocating the settlement of disputes by arbitration and the reduction of armaments. Efforts to influence national policy in favour of the unilateral renunciation of war have continued (e.g. the CND, Campaign for Nuclear Disarmament), in face of the objection that a nation which adopted such a policy would be more likely to encourage than discourage aggressive action. From the time of World War I, the word has also been used to describe the refusal of individuals, on grounds of conscience, to undertake military service, whatever the consequences to themselves. States have varied a great deal in their treatment of such a refusal. In only a small number of countries has the right to conscientious objection been recognized; in the majority it is treated as a breach of the law and often harshly punished. See also NON-VIOLENT RESISTANCE.

A.L.C.B.

package. In EDUCATIONAL TECHNOLOGY, a unit of material which is worked out and presented by someone other than the teacher and which can be repeated and reproduced. Examples are the processed programmes used in TEACHING MACHINES, the tapes and books found in a LANGUAGE LABORATORY, and television programmes. These teaching resources offer advantages when there is a class of varied ability and speed of understanding, and may allow a unique experience such as an outstanding foreign film or broadcast play to be brought into the classroom. See also AUDIO-VISUAL AIDS; INDIVIDUALIZED INSTRUCTION. W.A.C.S.

Bibl: L. C. Taylor, *Resources for Learning* (Harmondsworth, 2nd ed., 1972).

palaeobotany. The study of the floral remains of the past, encompassing POLLEN ANALYSIS, DENDROCHRONOLOGY, and the identification of wood, charcoal, cultivated grain, weed seeds, and fibres. One rapidly expanding branch, *palaeoethnobotany*, is concerned with the evolution of cultivated plants. B.C.

Bibl: J. M. Renfrew, *Palaeoethnobotany* (London, 1973).

palaeoclimatology. The study of the climates of the past – a study which depends on many branches of science, mainly GEOLOGY but also CLIMATOLOGY and METEOROLOGY. The basic data have been principally geological, derived in particular from PALAEOBOTANY, whereas explanations are presented in an astronomical or meteorological framework. Evidence of climates of the past is drawn from three main sources, BIOLOGY (e.g. the restricted HABITAT of corals), LITHOLOGY (e.g. evaporites), and GEOMORPHOLOGY (e.g. glacial landforms). J.L.M.L.

palaeo-ethnobotany, see under PALAEOBOTANY.

palaeogeography. The reconstruction of the GEOGRAPHY of a given region, essentially the distribution of land and sea, at a particular time in the past. Palaeogeography is an exercise in STRATIGRAPHY, using the biological and lithological characters which are determined by the depositional ENVIRONMENT preserved in the sedimentary rocks of a particular period. It is assumed that

451

depositional environments of the past, certainly from Cambrian times (see under GEOLOGICAL TIME CHART), were similar to those of today.　　　　J.L.M.L.

palaeolithic, see under THREE-AGE SYSTEM.

palaeo-modernism, see under MODERNISM.

palaeontology. The science which deals with the fossil remains (*palaios* is the Greek word for 'ancient') of animals and plants found buried in rocks. The term, in practice, is restricted to the study of animal remains; fossil plants are dealt with by PALAEOBOTANY. Fossils are of importance to GEOLOGISTS as time-markers which help to establish the succession of strata in the earth's crust. They also throw light on the geographical conditions under which rocks were laid down and on the PALAEOGEOGRAPHY and PALAEOCLIMATOLOGY of the world as a whole. Any succession of fossil-bearing rocks shows a fossil succession which corresponds to the biological process of EVOLUTION and adds greatly to the understanding of this. Finally palaeontology is of value to ARCHAEOLOGY for the evidence fossil remains afford of the early domestication of animals and of other local environmental conditions of archaeological sites.
　　　　A.L.C.B.

palaeopathology. The use of ancient human remains for the study of disease, injury, and nutrition. Normally only skeletal material is available, but occasionally (as in the case of the Danish bog burials, the bodies preserved in permafrost conditions in the Altai Mountains, and mummified remains) hair, skin, flesh, and entrails survive for scrutiny.　　B.C.

Bibl: C. Wells, *Bones, Bodies and Disease* (London and N.Y., 1964).

palaeoserology. The study of ancient BLOOD GROUPS by testing samples of human TISSUE preserved under ideal conditions, or, more often, spongy bone tissue. The technique is not far advanced, and its limits of reliability have still to be defined.　　　　B.C.

palaeozoology. The branch of PALAEONTOLOGY which deals with fossil animals

and the historical record they embody. For most practical purposes the record begins in Cambrian times (see GEOLOGICAL TIME CHART). Until the acceptance of the theory of EVOLUTION fossil remains made very little sense – Cuvier (1769–1832), the leading zoologist of his day, could describe a fossil ichthyosaur as *homo diluvii testis* (man witness of the Flood). The fossil record is biased in as much as soft-bodied animals normally leave no fossil traces.　　　P.M.

paleface and **redskin.** Terms used (1939) by Philip Rahv to describe the 'two polar types' around which 'American writers appear to group themselves'. Thus Henry James (paleface) contrasts with Walt Whitman (redskin), Melville with Mark Twain: the 'thin, solemn, semiclerical culture of Boston and Concord' with the 'low-life world of the frontier and of the big cities'. Rahv views the polarization unfavourably, as a specifically American 'dissociation between energy and sensibility, between conduct and theories . . . between life . . . as an opportunity and life . . . as discipline', between plebeian and patrician, NATURALIST and SYMBOLIST, and so on; consequently he has since admired such bridgers of the gap as Saul Bellow and Bernard Malamud.
　　　　M.S.-S.

Bibl: P. Rahv, *Literature and the Sixth Sense* (Boston, Mass., 1969; London, 1970).

paleo . . . For words beginning thus, see PALAEO . . .

palynology. The study of pollen, especially of fossil pollen grains, for which see POLLEN ANALYSIS.　　　　K.M.

Bibl: H. Godwin, *The History of the British Flora* (Cambridge, 1956).

pan-Africanism. Less a movement for a united Africa than a quasi-NATIONALIST set of beliefs in the uniqueness and spiritual unity of black Africans, beginning among American and West Indian negroes returning to Africa from the 1850s on, and linked with the cultivation of cultural NÉGRITUDE among Black Africans from French African colonies. Pan-African conferences met in London, Paris, and New York in 1900, 1919, 1921, 1923, and 1927 and in Manchester in 1945. The first to be held in Africa met in Accra in 1958. Since the attainment of independence by most African states, pan-Africanism has expressed itself through the Organization for African Unity, in its support for 'freedom fighters' in Rhodesia, Mozambique, and Angola, and in pressure for UNO action against South Africa. D.C.W.

Bibl: C. Legum, *Pan-Africanism* (London and N.Y., 1962); J. Mayall, *Africa: the Cold War and After* (London, 1971).

pan-Arabism, see under PAN-ISLAM.

Panch Shila. 'Five Principles' publicly adhered to by Jawaharlal Nehru, Prime Minister of India, and Chou En-lai, Premier of the People's Republic of China, in 1954: non-interference in the internal affairs of other states, mutual respect for territorial integrity and sovereignty, mutual non-aggression, mutual aid, and peaceful COEXISTENCE. The same principles were adopted by the states attending the BANDUNG CONFERENCE the following year. D.C.W.

panentheism, see under PANTHEISM.

pangenesis. Now obsolete theory of heredity according to which particles travelled from all parts of the body to the GONADS, where they were incorporated into the GAMETES. It was suggested by Darwin (1868) to account for the supposed inheritance of acquired characteristics. J.M.S.

pan-Germanism. A movement aiming at the union of all German-speaking peoples into a single state, strengthened by racial theory on the one hand, HISTORICIST and GEOPOLITICAL arguments on the other. It was embodied as a political movement, the *Alldeutscher Verband*, in 1894, and was at first mainly confined to academics, INTELLECTUALS, and publicists. It captured the imagination of the German High Command during World War I and was embodied into the doctrines of the RIGHT, both parliamentary and anti-parliamentary, under the WEIMAR REPUBLIC, emerging as an essential element in NAZISM. D.C.W.

Bibl: H. C. Meyer, *Mitteleuropa in German Thought and Action, 1815-1945* (The Hague, 1955).

panic, theatre of, see THEATRE OF PANIC.

pan-Islam. Movement for the unity of the Islamic world, which originated with would-be reformers of the Ottoman Empire in the 1890s. The movement was in retreat after the Turkish dissolution of the Caliphate in 1924, but the slogan was revived (in opposition to *pan-Arabism*) by the Shah as a basis for the Sa'adabad Pact (1937) and by King Faisal of Saudi Arabia, the Shah, and the Pakistani Government in the 1950s and 1960s in opposition to Nasser's pan-Arab policy. Such a union was again proposed in 1961 by the Malaysian leader Tunku Abdul Rahman and in the late 1960s by the Indonesian Government. Following pan-Islamic conferences in Rabat, Morocco, in September 1969 and at Jiddah in March 1970, a permanent secretariat was set up at the Karachi conference (December 1970) and located in Jiddah, with anti-COMMUNISM acting as a strong motivating force. Real enthusiasm for such an organization is, however, not generally noticeable among Islamic states. D.C.W.

Bibl: World Muslim Congress, *Studies on Commonwealth of Muslim Countries* (Karachi, 1964).

Pankhurst, Emmeline (British suffragist, 1858-1928), see under FEMINISM.

Panofsky, Erwin (German-U.S. art historian, 1892-1968), see under ICONOGRAPHY.

panpsychism. The theory that everything that really exists in the world is a mind or CONSCIOUSNESS. Leibniz's theory of MONADS is, in effect, a form of panpsychism, as is Berkeley's view that the only true SUBSTANCES are minds, finite or infinite. The 'personal idealists' (see under PERSONALISM) of the late 19th century who reacted against the absorption of finite personalities into the all-engulfing ABSOLUTE of Hegel tended towards panpsychism. It was explicit in the METAPHYSICS of McTaggart, for whom reality consisted exclusively of finite selves. A.Q.

pan-Slavism. Movements for a closer union of the peoples speaking a Slav language which originated among Russian INTELLECTUALS and writers in the early

19th century, spread to the Slav peoples under the Habsburg Empire, and inspired the Russian expansionist ideas of the 1870s and 1880s. Pan-Slavism was revived as a theme of Soviet propaganda during the German-Soviet war, but has since disappeared from the repertoire of Soviet publicity. D.C.W.

Bibl: H. Kohn, *Panslavism, its History and Ideology* (N.Y., 2nd ed., 1960).

pantheism. The worship of nature (Greek *pan*, all) as divine (Greek *theos*, god). Pantheism is usually connected with MONISM, the philosophy which avoids a radical distinction between the Creator and his creation and which seeks to explain all that exists in terms of a single reality, which can be conceived of in highly spiritual terms. Its roots are close to polytheism, the worship of many gods often connected with natural phenomena such as mountains, rivers, or storms; but pantheism is different because it rejects both the TRANSCENDENCE and the personality of gods or God, and because it refines the PRIMITIVE response to nature in a sophisticated and RATIONALIST way, attempting to have RELIGION without the intellectual difficulties of THEISM. Some forms of HINDUISM are pantheistic; most notably, the 8th-century teacher Samkara denied any duality between the world and the Supreme. In the West, the word 'pantheism' was coined, by the DEIST John Toland in 1705, for an intellectual system stated by the Dutch Jewish philosopher Baruch Spinoza in his *Tractatus Theologico-politicus* (1670). In the 19th century both the poetry of William Wordsworth and Hegelian (see HEGELIANISM) PHILOSOPHY tended in this direction. For a 20th-century movement among Christians with the same tendency, see PROCESS THEOLOGY; but Christian thinkers usually prefer the term *panentheism* coined by K. C. F. Krause (1781–1832), meaning that everything exists in (Greek *en*) God. This is thought to preserve the idea of God as Creator. D.L.E.

Bibl: K. Ward, *The Concept of God* (Oxford, 1974).

pantonal music. Music whose component parts are at times identifiable in terms of various conventional 'keys', without any one key being established as predominant.

It is thus intermediate between polytonal (see POLYTONALITY) and ATONAL MUSIC, with borderlines so uncertain and subjective that Schönberg sometimes applied the adjective 'pantonal' to music that is normally called atonal. A.H.

paper chromatography. A CHROMATOGRAPHIC technique in which chemical separation is effected on an absorbent filter paper. The stationary PHASE is water supported by the cellulose MOLECULES of the paper, and the mobile phase, usually based on an organic solvent, flows by capillary action. Uses include the separation of AMINO ACIDS and PEPTIDES in the investigation of PROTEIN structures, the analysis of body fluids (e.g. for sugars), and the separation of inorganic IONS. Quantities down to 10^{-7} grams (one ten-millionth of a gram) may be detected. B.F.

paper gold, see under LIQUIDITY.

Paquet, Alfons (German author, 1881–1944), see under EPIC THEATRE.

par values, see under PARITY.

parachutists. Élite troops trained to drop by parachute from aircraft on or behind the enemy's lines and used as specialized assault forces. French army parachutists (*les paras*), employed in the Algerian conflict, acquired a reputation for particular ruthlessness, from the methods used to stamp out urban TERRORISM in Algiers. See also FLN. D.C.W.

paradigm case. A representative instance of a CONCEPT, used to provide an OSTENSIVE definition of it. In so far as some concepts must be ostensively defined for the process of verbal definition to have a starting-point, it follows that if any word is to have MEANING at all some must truly apply to actual things. This argument from paradigm cases was introduced by G. E. Moore to rebut comprehensive sceptical theories, such as that no proposition is certain or that no material object is known to exist. How, he asked, could the word 'certain' or words for material objects have meaning at all unless there are actual instances for them to be ostensively learned from? The argument assumes, questionably, that some particular words must be ostensive (a stronger claim than

PARAMETER

that there must be some ostensive words), that it is possible to establish which they are, and that 'certain' and words for material objects are among them.   A.Q.

paradigmatic, see under SYNTAGMATIC.

paradox. A statement which appears acceptable but which has unacceptable or contradictory consequences. Three kinds of paradox have proved important in the development of LOGIC and MATHEMATICS. (1) Paradoxes of the INFINITE. Zeno of Elea argued thus: space is infinitely divisible; so an arrow must pass through infinitely many points in its flight; therefore it can never reach the target. This (like many variants) is resolved by the theory of CONVERGENCE to a LIMIT: an *infinite* sequence can have a *finite* limit. (2) SEMANTIC paradoxes. Epimenides the Cretan said (and was believed by Saint Paul): 'The Cretans are always liars.' If true, the statement would have made the speaker an invariable liar, and would therefore have been false. Therefore it must be false. (For another example see HETEROLOGICAL.) (3) Paradoxes of SET THEORY. Bertrand Russell considered the class (or SET) *R* which consists of just those classes that do not belong to themselves. Then *R* belongs to itself if and only if it does not. Paradoxes of types (2) and (3) are said to involve *self-reference*. Following a suggestion of Poincaré, Russell proposed the resolution of paradoxes on the *vicious-circle principle*: an object (such as a PROPOSITION, predicate, or class) is illegitimate if its definition involves a totality to which itself belongs. Thus Epimenides' saying refers to *all* statements by Cretans, itself included, and so is not a proposition, does not express anything. The proposal was worked out in great detail as the *ramified theory of types* by Russell and Whitehead in *Principia Mathematica*; but the theory has proved unsatisfactory from almost every point of view. It is now customary to distinguish sharply between (2) and (3). The semantic paradoxes are resolved by distinguishing levels of language: Epimenides' saying is at a higher level, it is *metalinguistic* (see METALANGUAGE); the lies it refers to are those of ordinary discourse, and so it does not apply to itself and may therefore be true. The set-theoretic paradoxes are avoided in axiomatic set theory; another

solution is provided by the *simple theory of types*. In this theory, individuals are of type 0, sets (or predicates) of individuals are of type 1, sets of sets of individuals are of type 2, and so on. Sentences like 'an individual is equal to a set' or 'a set of type 2 belongs to a set of type 1' are regarded not as false but as ungrammatical, meaningless. A paradox should be distinguished from an ANTIMONY. See also CLOCK PARADOX.   R.G.
Bibl: E. P. Northrop, *Riddles in Mathematics* (London, 1945).

paradoxical sleep, see REM SLEEP.

paralanguage. In suprasegmental PHONOLOGY, a range of vocal effects (e.g. giggle, whisper; see also INTONATION) that contribute to the tones of voice a speaker may use in communicating meaning. They are at present less susceptible of systematic description than the other areas of phonology, and are considered by many linguists to be marginal to the sound-system of the language. For some scholars, the term also subsumes kinesic phenomena (see SEMIOTICS).   D.C.

parallelism, psychological, see under MIND-BODY PROBLEM.

parameter. (1) In MATHEMATICS, originally a particular auxiliary COORDINATE used in describing *conic sections*; the term is still used for an auxiliary VARIABLE in terms of which others are expressed by *parametric* equations. (2) Nowadays in mathematics and its applications, particularly ECONOMICS, a quantity which is constant in the case under consideration but which may vary from case to case. It is supposed that each case deals with changing phenomena and so will be described by certain FUNCTIONS whose ARGUMENTS and values are the variables of the situation. It is also supposed that the functions for the different cases all have the same general form, e.g. they might all have the form $y = ax + b$. The quantities (here a and b) which specify the function(s) for a particular situation are the parameters; they may have values assigned to them at the outset of the discussion (see also COEFFICIENT). (3) In STATISTICS, a summary measure such as the MEAN of a characteristic of members of a population.   R.G.; D.E.

455

PARA-MILITARY

para-military. Adjective applied to official or unofficial bodies organized on lines analogous to those of the official armed forces of the State, with ranks, chains of command, uniforms, etc., and designed to use force for political purposes. The German Freikorps, the NAZI S.A. and S.S., the Italian Fasci di Combattimenti, and Perón's People's Militia are all examples of para-military forces.　　　　D.C.W.

paranoia. In ABNORMAL PSYCHOLOGY and PSYCHIATRY, a type of PSYCHOSIS in which the individual experiences delusions, typically of persecution and/or grandeur. It is often accompanied by hallucinations.　　　　W.Z.

parapsychology (or *psychical research*). The scientific study of actual or alleged paranormal phenomena (such as ESP and PSYCHOKINESIS) which lie outside the sphere of PSYCHOLOGY.　　　　I.M.L.H.

paras, les, see under PARACHUTISTS.

Pareto, Vilfredo (Italian economist and sociologist, 1848–1923), see under ÉLITE; IRRATIONALISM; PARETO OPTIMUM.

Pareto optimum. The formal conditions, named after the great Italian sociologist and economist, under which general economic WELFARE is at maximum. The condition is said to exist either when no shift of income will make *everyone* better off or, alternatively, when those who would gain by such a shift are unable to pay large enough bribes to the losers so as at once to repair the losers' situation and enhance their own.　　　　R.L.

parity.
(1) In PHYSICS, a precise mathematical description of left-right SYMMETRY or 'handedness'. For systems of atomic size or larger, nature makes no fundamental distinction between left and right, so that an object and its mirror image are equally compatible with the laws of physics. (Left- and right-handed systems need not actually occur *equally often* in nature: by an accident of EVOLUTION, almost everybody's heart is on his left side, but the reverse occasionally occurs with no ill effects.)
A perfectly symmetrical isolated system has a value of the parity which can be calculated from the WAVE FUNCTION; as the system evolves it remains symmetrical, and the parity does not alter – it is an *invariant* (see CONSERVATION LAWS). For the WEAK INTERACTIONS between ELEMENTARY PARTICLES, however, parity is not conserved, e.g. an apparently symmetrical NEUTRON decays into components with a definite 'handedness'; on this level it appears that nature does know left from right.　　　　M.V.B.
Bibl: M. Gardner, *The Ambidextrous Universe* (N.Y., 1964; London, 1967).
(2) In ECONOMICS, the word has at least three distinct meanings:
(*a*) The exchange rate between its currency and some internationally accepted standard of value (e.g. gold) which a government declares to be the norm. Under the rules of the International Monetary Fund (see BRETTON WOODS), exchange rates should not diverge by more than 1% either way from their parities (or *par values*), nor should these be changed except in certain prescribed circumstances. Since major currencies no longer follow these rules, new rules are under consideration.
(*b*) The *purchasing power parity theory* is that the main factors determining exchange rates are price levels in different countries. In its extreme form the theory states that prices of similar goods are the same throughout the world, and is obviously false. The relative version holds that changes in exchange rates offset relative changes in the price levels (measured by INDEX NUMBERS) of the countries concerned; where the latter changes are very great, this theory is substantially true, though allowance must generally be made for other factors.
(*c*) The *parity index* is an index of prices paid by farmers in the U.S. for items used in family living and in production, and of interest on farm mortgage debt, taxes on farm real estate, and wages paid to hired farm labour; the prices reported are those for qualities currently purchased rather than for fixed specifications. The index is used to compute the *parity prices* of agricultural products on the basis of which the price support levels for these commodities are determined; the parity price of a specific commodity is defined as its base-period price times the parity index, the base period being legally fixed as 1910–14. The index is also used to com-

pute the *parity ratio* which serves as a measure of changes in the average purchasing power of farm products, and is obtained by dividing the parity index into the index of prices received by farmers. M.FG.S.; G.S.
Bibl: see under BALANCE OF PAYMENTS.

Park, Robert (U.S. sociologist, 1864–1944), see under CHICAGO SCHOOL.

Parker, Charles (British radio producer), see under DOCUMENTARY.

Parker, Charlie (U.S. jazz musician, 1920–55), see under BEBOP.

Parkhurst, Helen (U.S. educator, 1887–1959), see under DALTON PLAN.

Parkinson's Law. A principle formulated by the British political scientist C. Northcote Parkinson (*Parkinson's Law*, London, 1958) to the effect that 'work expands so as to fill the time available for its completion'. As a corollary Parkinson states that 'a perfection of planned layout is achieved only by institutions on the verge of collapse'. *Parkinson's Law* and similar popular studies such as *The Peter Principle* (which states that employees tend to be promoted above the level at which they are efficient) serve to counteract the tendency for MANAGEMENT to take itself too seriously. P.S.L.

'Parmeno' (pseud. of José López Pinillos, Spanish novelist and dramatist, 1875–1922), see under TREMENDISMO.

parole. In PENOLOGY (for its meaning in LINGUISTICS see under LANGUE), a shorthand term applied to the premature release of a convicted prisoner on expiry of part of his sentence, with provision for recall if he violates the parole terms; thus to be distinguished from *remission* which cannot be revoked once the prisoner is released. Originating in the 19th century 'ticket of leave' system for transported convicts, parole is widely used in the U.S.A., in combination with indeterminate sentences, but was introduced into Britain only by the Criminal Justice Act, 1967. The granting of parole is discretionary, following consideration by local Review Committees and the Central

Parole Board, with special arrangements for life sentences; supervision is the responsibility of the Probation and After-Care Service. T.M.
Bibl: D. Glaser, *The Effectiveness of a Prison and Parole System* (Indianapolis, 1964).

parsec (PARallax-SECond). A unit of distance in ASTRONOMY. 1 parsec = 3.26 light-years = 19 million million miles. M.V.B.

Parsonian. Derived from or resembling the sociological theories of Talcott Parsons. Parsons (*b.* 1902), professor of SOCIOLOGY at Harvard for most of his life, became the leading American sociological theorist of his generation. His approach, a type of STRUCTURAL-FUNCTIONAL THEORY, was most influential in the 1950s. Though his ideas have changed continuously, four main themes emerge. (1) Individual personalities, societies, and CULTURES can all be analysed as self-equilibrating SYSTEMS and described in terms of a common conceptual framework, that of *action systems.* (2) Action systems contain four *subsystems*, performing functions of pattern maintenance, integration, goal-attainment, and adaptation. (3) As SOCIAL ACTION systems, societies evolve towards greater functional specialization of STRUCTURE: e.g. modern political and economic INSTITUTIONS largely correspond with the analytical subsystems 'polity' and 'economy' which perform the goal-attainment and adaptation functions. (4) SOCIAL STRUCTURE is analysable into four components (values, NORMS, collectivities, ROLES), and the institutionalization of certain *core values*, through the NORMATIVE regulation of collective activities and individual role performances, primarily determines the stability and functioning of societies. Critics of Parsonian theory have asserted that it contains only verbal categorizations from which no testable PROPOSITIONS follow; or that it can (perhaps) explain stability but not change; or even that it merely expresses a conservative preference for a society devoid of significant disagreements over values. Although it has inspired much empirical research, its claim to be scientific is not yet established. J.R.T.
Bibl: W. C. Mitchell, *Sociological*

Analysis and Politics: the Theories of Talcott Parsons (London and Englewood Cliffs, N.J., 1967).

Parsons, Talcott (U.S. sociologist, *b*. 1902), see under IDEOLOGY; PARSONIAN; PATTERN VARIABLES; SOCIAL ACTION; SOCIOLOGY; STRATIFICATION, SOCIAL.

participant observation. A method of research employed by those practitioners of ANTHROPOLOGY, SOCIOLOGY, and SOCIAL PSYCHOLOGY who join a social group and to some extent engage in the same activities as its members, while observing and recording what happens, either with or without the group's knowledge. This contrasts with the use of laboratory experiments or written questionnaires or interviews conducted by detached interviewers. Disputes about the validity of the method are connected with disputes both about the aims of science and about the possibility or impossibility of understanding actions, RITUALS, or SOCIAL STRUCTURES without experiencing them from the point of view of members of the community. See also METHODOLOGY.   A.S.
Bibl: W. J. Goode and P. K. Hatt, *Methods in Social Research* (London and N.Y., 1952); H. Powdermaker, *Stranger and Friend* (N.Y., 1966; London, 1967).

participation. A slogan which came into widespread use in the 1960s to express what the EEC calls 'the democratic imperative', defined as the principle that 'those who will be substantially affected by decisions made by social and political institutions must be involved in the making of those decisions'. It is argued that the size and complexity of modern MASS SOCIETIES, the centralization of political POWER, the growth of BUREAUCRACY, and the concentration of economic power all mean that the traditional guarantees of DEMOCRACY need to be strengthened and extended in order to check the tendency for more and more decisions affecting people's lives to be made in secret by small groups which are often remote and not easily identified or called to account, since they act in the name of the State, of a local authority, or of some large, impersonal business corporation.
So far as politics is concerned, the prin-

ciple is as old as democracy itself. The problem is how to implement it – a problem likewise as old as democracy itself, but made vastly more difficult by the scale and comprehensiveness of modern government and by the need for clear-cut and rapid decisions, failure to produce which is no less a matter for protest on the part of those who demand greater participation. The new feature in the period since World War II is the proposal to extend participation to fields other than politics, e.g. to higher education, where it was the major demand of all student protests in the late 1960s and early 1970s, and, of much greater importance, to industry and business. The practice (*Mitbestimmung* or *co-determination*) by which employees take a part in MANAGEMENT decisions was introduced by the Federal Government of Germany in 1952, has spread in various forms to other countries in Western Europe, and has been adopted as an objective by the EEC. It became the subject of debate in Britain with the publication in January 1977 of the majority report of the *Bullock Report on Industrial Democracy*, proposing the appointment of employee representatives to the boards of directors of all companies employing more than 2,000 people.   A.L.C.B.

particle. A relative term, in common use throughout PHYSICS, denoting any object which may be considered as a moving point, characterized by a few simple properties such as mass and SPIN. The concept is an idealization, valid whenever the internal structure, size, and shape of the object are irrelevant to the phenomenon being considered. Thus, for instance, such a complicated system as the earth may be treated as a particle for many purposes of ASTRONOMY, and it is sufficient to treat ATOMS as particles in order to explain much of the behaviour of matter in bulk. Particles interact with one another via FIELDS. See also ATOMIC PHYSICS; ELEMENTARY PARTICLE; WAVE-PARTICLE DUALITY.   M.V.B.

particular, see under UNIVERSAL.

particularism, see under PATTERN VARIABLES.

Pascin, Jules (French painter, 1885–1930), see under ÉCOLE DE PARIS.

Pasmore, Victor (British artist, *b*.1908), see under CONSTRUCTIVISM; EUSTON ROAD GROUP.

pass laws. South African legislation requiring black Africans to obtain and carry at all times passes for all activities in areas other than those specifically reserved for the so-called Bantu people in rural areas ('Bantustans'). The pass laws are one of the principal instruments of the policy of APARTHEID. D.C.W.

Past and Present. A journal founded in 1952 by a group of young MARXIST historians (including its first editor John Morris, Christopher Hill, Eric Hobsbawm) to challenge the dominance of political history and Western European history in more orthodox periodicals. Over twenty years later it has become one of the best-known historical journals in the English-speaking world, associated with a greater variety of approaches to history than before but continuing to emphasize SOCIAL HISTORY and the history of the world outside Europe. P.B.

Pasternak, Boris (Russian poet and novelist, 1890–1960), see under NEW WRITING; SAMIZDAT; ZHDANOVSHCHINA.

Pasteur, Louis (French chemist and microbiologist, 1822–95), see under BIOGENESIS.

Pater, Walter Horatio (British critic and essayist, 1839–94), see under AESTHETICISM; EPIPHANY.

pathology. The study in all its aspects of departures from normality in respect of health and bodily function. Since all illnesses represent departures from normality it could be said, and by pathologists has been said, that pathology comprehends all medicine. Pathology is subdivided into a number of branches, notably *pathological* (gross) *anatomy* such as is laid bare on the post-mortem slab; HISTOPATHOLOGY, dealing with structural abnormalities at the TISSUE level, and nowadays *cellular pathology*, comprehending any attempt to interpret abnormalities of form or function at a cellular structural level; and *chemical pathology*, which has to do with diagnosis and interpretation of disease at a biochemical level (see BIOCHEMISTRY) –

thus it is the chemical pathology laboratory which undertakes the analysis of blood samples for evidence of impaired liver function, or tests urine samples for evidence of impaired kidney function or metabolic (see METABOLISM) abnormalities, including the 'inborn errors of metabolism' (e.g. phenylketonuria, alkaptonuria, and galactosaemia) first recognized and defined by Sir Archibald Garrod. In these disorders a defective genetical programming has the consequence that some ENZYME necessary for metabolism is missing so that intermediate metabolites, some of which may be toxic, accumulate in the body, or some biochemical function is missing altogether. The consequences of these single enzyme defects are often widespread throughout the body: thus both phenylketonuria and galactosaemia may have secondary effects on the central NERVOUS SYSTEM leading to an impairment of mental function, while galactosaemia may be associated with cataract. In many modern departments of pathology the experimental approach is supplanting the merely descriptive. P.M.

Bibl: H. W. Florey (ed.), *General Pathology* (London and Philadelphia, 4th ed., 1970).

Patten, Brian (British poet, *b*.1946), see under LIVERPOOL POETS.

pattern variables. In PARSONIAN theory, a set of paired terms specifying the ranges of variability within which persons engaging in social interaction orient themselves to one another. They were originally formulated as (1) *affectivity v. affective neutrality* (does the relationship involve EMOTION, or not?); (2) *self-orientation v. collectivity-orientation* (is the other person to be appraised in relation to my personal goals, or to those of some larger group?); (3) *universalism v. particularism* (does the other person represent a category, or something unique?); (4) *achievement v. ascription* (does the other's STATUS depend on his achievements, or on attributes beyond his control?); (5) *specificity v. diffuseness* (is the other's participation based on some specialized interest or qualification, or not?). For the most part, people assume and adjust orientations without reflection or conscious effort, because standardized expectations about behaviour in social ROLES are learned, as more or less habitual responses, in the form of NORMATIVE 'patterns'. There is only a limited number of such patterns culturally available to a society. Any pattern is in principle capable of description in terms of the five variables. This is the simplest version; in later work Parsons has modified this scheme in order to integrate it with other parts of his theory.   J.R.T.

Bibl: T. Parsons, 'Pattern Variables Revisited' (*American Sociological Review,* 25, 1960), pp. 467–85; T. Parsons and E. A. Shils (eds.), *Toward a General Theory of Action* (Cambridge, Mass., 1959).

Paul, Leslie (British author, *b*. 1905), see under ANGRY YOUNG MAN.

Pauli principle, see EXCLUSION PRINCIPLE.

Pauling, Linus Carl (U.S. chemist, *b*. 1901), see under ELECTRONEGATIVITY.

Pavelić, Ante (Croatian nationalist leader and revolutionary, 1889–1959), see under USTACHA.

Pavlov, Ivan Petrovich (Russian physiologist, 1849–1936), see under BEHAVIOUR THERAPY; BEHAVIOURISM; CLASSICAL CONDITIONING; PAVLOVIAN; SECOND-SIGNAL SYSTEM.

Pavlovian. Relating to the work or views of the Russian physiologist I. P. Pavlov (1849–1936). Pavlov maintained that the NERVOUS SYSTEM controls all physiological activity, and saw its function as being, in addition to the conduction of nervous impulses, one of setting up patterns of excitation for the control of functions and also of inhibiting impulse patterns once they had been started in the nervous system. Above all, however, he conceived of the nervous system as being involved in making connections between neural patterns so that there could be set up associations in the nervous system that mirrored associations between stimuli in the external world, as well as between incoming stimuli and responses that had been made to them in the past. The principal result of this form of connecting activity in the nervous system, known as CLASSICAL CONDITIONING, shows that the nervous system is adaptive, permitting the organism to anticipate crucial events by virtue of their being signalled by those events which precede them, thus also permitting the organism to respond in advance with an appropriate reaction. Pavlov considered the importance of the CONDITIONED REFLEX to be its role in the general organization of higher nervous systems. This organization he saw as the basis for the formation of human temperament. In his later writings, Pavlov distinguished between classical conditioning and the SECOND-SIGNAL SYSTEM.

Pavlov also emphasized the adaptive value of *inhibition*, the process by which it was possible for the organism to withhold response in the nervous system initially to protect the nervous system from firing too intensely, and which later provided a means of delay in response appropriate to the nature of the situation. He extended this notion of the adaptive function of inhibition by suggesting that sleep was itself an extension of inhibition which allowed the nervous system to recover. Pavlov was also much interested in the problem of generalization of response to an array of stimuli. This problem he attempted to solve by the doctrine of *irradiation,* a process whereby responses would be made not only to the stimuli to which they had initially been conditioned, but also to a range of similar stimuli. He extended the concept of irradiation well beyond its original meaning, and talked about the irradiation of inhibition and excitation to account for certain general response tendencies important to the development of temperament and character. Towards the end of his life Pavlov's interest moved increasingly towards PSYCHIATRY.   G.M.; J.S.B.

Bibl: I. P. Pavlov, tr. and ed. G. V. Anrep, *Conditioned Reflexes* (London, 1927); B. Simon (ed.), *Psychology in the Soviet Union* (London and Stanford, 1957); I. P. Pavlov, *Experimental Psychology and Other Essays* (N.Y., 1957; London, 1958).

Pavlovian conditioning, see CLASSICAL CONDITIONING.

peaceful coexistence, see COEXISTENCE, PEACEFUL.

Peano, Giuseppe (Italian mathematician,

1858–1932), see under MATHEMATICAL INDUCTION; NUMBER.

Pearl Harbor. Shorthand term for the attack made on the American naval base at Pearl Harbor, Hawaii, on 7 December 1941 by Japanese naval aircraft without any declaration of war, with the object of destroying American sea power in the Pacific. Hence any overwhelming *pre-emptive strike* (see STRATEGIC CAPABILITY) at the opening of hostilities between two states.   D.C.W.

Pearson, Egon Sharpe (British statistician, *b.*1895), see under STATISTICAL TEST.

Pearson, Karl (British philosopher and statistician, 1857–1936), see under BIOMETRY; NEUTRAL MONISM; PSYCHOMETRICS; STATISTICS.

Pearson, Lester Bowles (Canadian statesman, 1897–1972), see under BALANCE OF TERROR.

Pechstein, Max (German painter and engraver, 1881–1955), see under BRÜCKE, DIE.

pecking order, see under DOMINANCE.

pedestrian segregation. The separation of vehicles and pedestrians on plan or section or both so as to avoid conflict between the two; Venice is the classic prototype. Serious proposals started in the 19th century when London's horse-drawn traffic created great problems; Olmsted and Vaux's plan of about 1868 for Central Park is an early American example, and the principle was further elaborated by Le Corbusier in 1935 in *La Ville radieuse*. Most examples today consist of the closure of existing streets to vehicles, frequently to provide pedestrian shopping precincts, and the building of pedestrian decks raised above cars; in housing areas separation is often based on the RADBURN LAYOUT.   M.BR.

pedology. A component part of SOIL SCIENCE concerned with the study of soils as naturally occurring phenomena, particularly their MORPHOLOGY (see also HORIZON), CLASSIFICATION, and distribution on the land surface. The aims of pedology are to describe the properties of soils and to identify the processes which have produced particular soils. The subject has suffered from the lack of a universal system of soil classification.   J.L.M.L.

peer group. A group of people who regard themselves, or who are regarded, as of approximately equal standing in the larger society to which they belong; standing can be defined in terms of a very wide range of CRITERIA.   M.BE.

Peinture de la Realité poétique, see under MAGIC REALISM.

Peirce, Charles Sanders (U.S. scientist and philosopher, 1839–1914), see under FALLIBILISM; INTUITIONISM; PRAGMATISM.

Pelloutier, Fernand (French labour organizer and theoretician, 1867–1901), see under ANARCHO-SYNDICALISM.

Penck, Walther (Austrian geomorphologist, 1888–1923), see under GEOGRAPHY.

penetrance. In GENETICS, the frequency with which a dominant GENE (or a recessive gene in a homozygote) manifests itself in the phenotype (see GENOTYPE). The fact that penetrance is not always 100% implies that some genes require a particular environment before they are expressed.   J.M.S.

Penfield, Wilder Graves (U.S. surgeon, *b.*1891), see under BRAIN STIMULATION.

penis envy. In FREUDIAN theory, the female desire to possess male genitals: a desire arising initially out of the small girl's assumption that because she lacks a penis she must at some stage have been castrated (see CASTRATION ANXIETY). Postulated as universal by Freud, the phenomenon has been challenged on theoretical grounds by some psychologists, and on experiential grounds by some women.   W.Z.

penology. The study of the punishment and treatment of criminals. Penology originated in, and has remained closely linked with, the movement for penal reform which developed at the end of the 18th century, notably in the writings of the

461

Marquis de Beccaria (1738–94) in Italy, and of John Howard (1726–90). Jeremy Bentham (1748–1832) was concerned to develop the principles of utilitarianism as a basis for the treatment of offenders. Numerous theorists in the 19th century in Britain and the U.S.A. were influential in the introduction of new methods of treating offenders, notably within what were termed *penitentiaries*. The subject has expanded to cover all aspects of the treatment of offenders, including prisons, institutions for young offenders, and mental treatment, as well as all forms of non-custodial disposal such as probation and fines. T.M.

Bibl: L. W. Fox, *The English Prison and Borstal Systems* (London, 1952); R. J. Gerber and P. D. McAnany (eds.), *Contemporary Punishment* (London, 1972).

Pentagon. The central direction of the armed forces of the U.S.A., which is housed in a building composed of concentric pentagonal blocks of offices outside Washington. *The Pentagon Papers* was the title given by the American press to a semi-official study, based on official records, of U.S. involvement in VIETNAM. One copy of this study was purloined and very substantial sections leaked to and published by those sections of the American press, notably the *New York Times*, opposed to this involvement. D.C.W.

Bibl: S. J. Ungar, *The Papers and the papers* (N.Y., 1972).

pentecostalism. The gift of the Holy Spirit is described in the Bible (Acts 2) as having descended on the 50th day (Greek *pentekoste*) after the Jewish Passover festival, with extraordinary resultant phenomena. In the 20th century many Christians have claimed to experience the same gift (in Greek, CHARISMA) and phenomena, and are referred to as the *Charismatic Movement*. Some have remained in the historic Churches but many have organized themselves in Pentecostal Churches, specially in the U.S.A. and Latin America, with a strong emphasis on informality, confidence, and joy, and a THEOLOGY mostly FUNDAMENTALIST. The largest such Church is the 'Assemblies of God, U.S.A.' The rapidly spreading 'independent' churches in Africa, which are free from Western control and influence, have

many similar characteristics. See also QUAKERS. D.L.E.

Bibl: W. W. J. Hollenweger, tr. R. A. Wilson, *The Pentecostals* (London and Minneapolis, 1972).

Penty, Arthur J. (British architect and political thinker), see under GUILD SOCIALISM.

Penzias, Arno A. (German-U.S. physicist, *b*. 1933), see under COSMIC BACKGROUND RADIATION.

People, not Psychiatrists, see under ANTI-PSYCHIATRY.

people's democracy. A COMMUNIST euphemism for regimes which display the machinery of public participation in government while denying the electorate any real choice between political parties. Such regimes are usually distinguished by the absence of those legal and constitutional restraints on the use of the power of the State which are essential to DEMOCRACY or to any genuine PARTICIPATION by 'the people' in the processes of government. D.C.W.

Bibl: F. Fejtö, tr. D. Weissbort, *A History of the People's Democracies* (London and N.Y., 1971); F. J. Kase, *People's Democracy* (Leyden, 1968).

people's wars, see under GUERRILLA.

peptide. A relatively simple POLYMERIC MOLECULE formed by the conjunction of AMINO ACIDS. The simple or short-chain peptides are called *oligopeptides* and include many biological effectors such as hormones (see ENDOCRINOLOGY) – e.g. oxytocin and vasopressin – whereas the larger, long-chain *polypeptides* grade directly into PROTEINS which are essentially polypeptides, e.g. the trophic hormones of the anterior PITUITARY, INSULIN, etc. P.M.

percentile. In STATISTICS there is often a need to describe an empirical DISTRIBUTION roughly. One way to do this is to state a few scale values dividing the distribution in predetermined proportions. A scale value such that there is an $x\%$ chance of an observation falling to the left of it is an $x\%$ *percentile*. The 25% and 75% percentiles (with half the distribution between them and a quarter on either side) are the *quartiles* and the 50% percentile (with half the distribution on either side of it) is the *median*, which is sometimes used as a MEASURE OF LOCATION.   R.SI.

percept, see SENSE DATUM.

perception. In general, awareness or appreciation of objects or situations, usually by the senses. Specific technical meanings are related to the many theories of perception still extant in PHILOSOPHY, PSYCHOLOGY, and PHYSIOLOGY. It is a theory-laden word, and so changes its meanings and implications across rival theories. There are, in particular, two essentially different theories of perception:

(1) That perceptions are *selections of reality*: i.e. they are essentially like, and made of the same stuff as, objects of the external world. This notion has a strong appeal to philosophers wishing to accept perceptions as the unquestionable basis of empirical TRUTH. Errors of perception – illusions and hallucinations – are clearly embarrassing for such a theory; and indeed the *argument from illusion* (see ILLUSION) claims to disprove it. How can we know that a perception is true, if we have reason to believe that other perceptions appearing just as sound are illusory?

(2) That perceptions are not any kind of selection of reality; but are rather *accounts, descriptions,* or, most interesting, *hypotheses* of the object world. On this view perception is only indirectly related to reality, and there is no difficulty over illusions. But, correspondingly, it offers no guarantee that any particular perception can be relied upon as true. Thus all knowledge based on perceptions is essentially uncertain: perceptions must be checked before they can be relied upon, and even then perhaps no set of perceptions can be *completely* trusted as true. It is generally accepted that this holds also for all scientific observations, instrument-readings, or signals.

The status of perception may be very like that of scientific hypotheses. What we see is affected by what is likely; and we can be driven into error by following assumptions which are not appropriate for the available sensory data. This is a development of Hermann von Helmholtz's notion that perceptions are unconscious infer-

ences from sensory and memory data. Some illusions may be fallacies of perceptual inference.   R.L.G.

Bibl: E. G. Boring, *Sensation and Perception in the History of Experimental Psychology* (London and N.Y., 1942); M. D. Vernon (ed.), *Experiments in Visual Perception* (Harmondsworth, 1966); R. L. Gregory, *Eye and Brain* (2nd ed., London, 1972; N.Y., 1973) and *The Intelligent Eye* (London and N.Y., 1970).

perception geography, see under GEOGRAPHY.

perceptual defence. A process of unconscious 'censorship' that prevents PERCEPTION of unacceptable events, objects, words, etc., as when TABOO, words presented briefly in a *tachistoscope* are 'normalized' into an acceptable form. It is usually contrasted with *perceptual vigilance*, a state of increased sensitivity to threatening or unacceptable events.
      J.S.B.

Bibl: F. H. Allport, *Theories of Perception and the Concept of Structure* (London and N.Y., 1955).

perceptual realism, see under REALISM.

perfect competition. A hypothetical state of affairs in which a good is sold in identical form in these conditions: (1) there are many suppliers each of whom is responsible for only a very small part of total sales; (2) there is no collusion between suppliers; (3) buyers and sellers are fully informed about prices being charged throughout the market. The concept is used by some economists in their theoretical work both as a MODEL or simplified representation of the reality of competitive markets and as an ideal system which, were it to prevail universally, would ensure that all goods would be produced in the right amounts and sold at the right prices. Others have rejected the concept for both these uses, maintaining that perfect competition, even if realizable, would be unworkable, and pointing to the fact that those markets which approximate most closely to the supposed ideal (e.g. some international commodity markets) exhibit chronic and wasteful instability.
      G.B.R.

Bibl: G. J. Stigler, *The Theory of Price*

(N.Y., 3rd ed., 1966); G. B. Richardson, *Economic Theory* (London, 1964).

performance (in LINGUISTICS), see under COMPETENCE.

performance tests, see under MENTAL TESTING.

periodic functions. The FUNCTION $f(t)$ is *periodic with period T* and *frequency* $1/T$ if $f(t + T) = f(t)$ for all values of t. Mathematically and physically the simplest periodic functions are those describing *simple harmonic motion*; they have the form $f(t) = A \sin (2\pi t/T + \theta)$ or equivalently $f(t) = a \cos (2\pi t/T) + b \sin (2\pi t/T)$. Such a function has as its graph a *sine wave*; it is recognized by the ear as a pure tone, in SPECTROSCOPY as a spectral line, and is the ideal form of alternating current. Other periodic functions can be broken down into simple harmonic constituents by FOURIER ANALYSIS.   R.G.

periodic table. An arrangement of the chemical ELEMENTS into rows and columns; it was discovered by the Russian chemist Mendeleev in 1869. The ATOMIC NUMBER increases across each row and from one row to the next, while the chemical properties (e.g. VALENCY) of the elements in each column are similar (e.g. the 'inert gases' helium, neon, argon, etc. lie in the same column). The physical basis of the periodic table is explained by ATOMIC PHYSICS: elements in a given column contain the same number of ELECTRONS in the unfilled outer ELECTRON SHELL, while elements in a given row have the same number of filled shells.   M.V.B.

peripheral devices (*peripherals*), see under INPUT/OUTPUT.

peripheral nervous system, see under NERVOUS SYSTEM.

permanent education. A CONCEPT based on the belief that EDUCATION ought not to be concentrated into childhood and adolescence but should be seen as a lifelong process. The term comes from France, where advocates of *éducation permanente* lay stress on the value of a return to education in adult years for vocational or other utilitarian purposes. Alternative terms for this are IN-SERVICE TRAINING (for teachers) and *post-experience education* (for managers). But there is no reason why permanent education should be limited to vocational purposes, and in this larger sense it has much the same meaning as adult or continuing education.   W.A.C.S.

Bibl: *Adult Education* (Russell Report, London, 1973).

permanent revolution. An expression first used by Karl Marx in his *Address to the Communist League* (1850), but historically connected with Trotsky, who between 1904 and 1906 developed it into a theory postulating that Russia would become the spearhead of the world REVOLUTION. The argument rested on the idea (shared by Lenin) that it is possible to have a SOCIALIST revolution in an economically backward country. In agrarian Russia the urban BOURGEOISIE was thought by both Trotsky and Lenin to be incapable of carrying out a 'bourgeois revolution' and they envisaged a direct revolutionary confrontation between the PROLETARIAT and the autocracy. But while Lenin (see LENINISM) thought that the revolution would pass first through the 'bourgeois' and then through the 'socialist' stage in his scheme of 'uninterrupted revolution', Trotsky saw it as a single process in which the two stages were telescoped and in which the role of the peasantry and the PETITE BOURGEOISIE was subordinated to that of the proletariat which would establish its own dictatorship (see DICTATORSHIP OF THE PROLETARIAT).

In his struggle with Trotsky, Stalin (see STALINISM) opposed to the theory of 'permanent revolution' his own slogan of 'socialism in one country'. The debate was misleading, since Trotsky did not propose to abandon the 'building of socialism' in Russia, nor did Stalin cease to hope for the victory of revolution outside the Soviet Union. During the struggle Trotsky repeatedly declared (in 1925–6) that his theory was only of historical interest. He restated it, however, in exile, and it eventually came to be regarded as practically synonymous with TROTSKYISM.   L.L.

Bibl: H. Schurer, 'The Permanent Revolution', in L. Labedz (ed.), *Revisionism* (London, 1962); L. D. Trotsky, *The Permanent Revolution* (N.Y., 1969).

permissiveness. The view that the individual's pursuit of pleasure should, provided no harm is done to others, be unrestricted by external factors such as laws or by internal guilt arising from social conventions. The *permissive society*, a cliché of the late 1960s, is exemplified by the decline of stage and film censorship, by public acquiescence in the relaxation of certain moral and social conventions, and by recent legislation concerning adult consenting homosexuals, abortion, divorce, and what constitutes PORNOGRAPHY. Although legislation of this type indicates toleration rather than endorsement, there has subsequently been a public reaction which seeks a return to more rigid moral and social conventions and prescriptions.
P.S.L.

permutation. In MATHEMATICS, traditionally, any rearrangement of a finite SET *A* of objects. More abstractly it is a FUNCTION *f* which assigns to each *a* in *A* an object *b* in *A* (the new occupant of *a*'s place) such that to distinct ARGUMENTS there correspond distinct values and such that every *b* in *A* is a value of *f* for some argument. The latter definition applies equally well to INFINITE sets; it includes the identity function (*f*(*a*) = *a*). The set of all permutations of *A* form a GROUP. R.G.

permutational. Adjective applied to works of art where a prescribed set of elements, rules, or dimensions is subjected to variation, whether controlled by the artist or of an ALEATORY kind. Essential to music (especially SERIAL MUSIC), such treatment may also occur in the visual arts (notably in OP ART), in writing (as in anagrams and word-games and some kinds of CONCRETE POETRY), and in photography and film. It can also lead to the production of subtly varied MULTIPLES, particularly when guided by a COMPUTER as in COMPUTER GRAPHICS; the art then lies in the structure and sequence of the data fed to the machine. J.W.

Peronism. An IDEOLOGY associated with the name of Juan Perón (1895–1974), dictator of Argentina (1945–50), and his wife Eva. It involved: in domestic affairs, the mass demagogic organization of the Argentinian working class in labour unions and a workers' militia against the upper-middle-class ÉLITES; an organization backed by mass social-security and other redistributive methods on the one hand, and savage repression on the other; in foreign affairs, the inflammation of Argentinian national feelings against the U.S.A. and the claim that Argentina should lead Latin America. Perón proved unable to solve the economic problems facing his country and lost much support after his first wife's death in 1952; but his prestige was such that it brought him back to the Presidency by popular acclaim in 1972. On his death in 1974, the Peronist cause was briefly led by his second wife and successor as President, but perished with the revelations of incompetence and corruption that followed her overthrow by the military. D.C.W.

Bibl: J. J. Kirkpatrick, *Leader and Vanguard in Mass Society: a Study of Peronist Argentina* (Cambridge, Mass., 1971).

Perret, Auguste (French architect, 1874–1954), see under CONCRETE.

Perry, William James (British anthropologist, 1868–1949), see under DIFFUSION.

personal idealism, see under PERSONALISM.

personalism. A form of IDEALISM which holds that everything real is a person or an element in the experience of some person. Inspired more by Berkeley than by Leibniz (whose MONADS, although described as souls, are too simple to count as persons), it is generally opposed to the absolute idealism of Hegel in which all finite persons are absorbed into an ABSOLUTE which transcends personality (see TRANSCENDENCE). The *personal idealism* of such dissenters from absolute idealism as McTaggart and Rashdall around the turn of the century is perhaps the most philosophically significant form of personalism, but it has been more recently exemplified in modern French NEO-THOMISM, and there has been a continuing tradition of personalism in the U.S.A. with a strong theistic tendency (see THEISM). A.Q.

personalistic psychology. An approach to PSYCHOLOGY that takes as its FRAME OF REFERENCE the individual person as a unique, unitary being, and relates

465

fractional studies of PERCEPTION, learning, and the like to this personal frame of reference.   I.M.L.H.

Bibl: W. Stern, tr. A. Barwell, *Psychology of Early Childhood* (London and N.Y., 2nd ed., 1930).

personality cult. The formula employed by Soviet advocates of collective leadership against any of their number who seems to be accumulating too much personal power and consequent public adulation. It was first employed after Stalin's death in 1953 to discredit those who attempted to capitalize on his memory, and was one of the central themes of Khrushchev's denunciation of the STALINIST era in his 'secret speech' to the 20th congress of the Soviet Communist Party (25 February 1956). The accusation was subsequently employed to discredit Khrushchev himself after his resignation in 1964.   D.C.W.

Bibl: R. Conquest, *Power and Policy in the U.S.S.R.* (London and N.Y., 1961).

personality tests, see under MENTAL TESTING.

personality types. Idealized descriptions of personality derived either by statistical procedures (e.g. FACTOR ANALYSIS) or by theoretical postulation or by some more or less skilful combination of the two. Historically and in contemporary practice, types are based upon differences in physiological hormonal functioning (see ENDOCRINOLOGY) that reflects itself in temperament, as in the CLASSIFICATION by Galen of the *phlegmatic*, the *choleric*, the *melancholic*, and the *sanguine* that were outward manifestations of the so-called bodily humours. One of the most successful efforts to describe personality types in relation to body type is W. H. Sheldon's. By careful anthropomorphic measurement, he has been able to distinguish three basic physical types (most individual subjects appearing as a mix): the round, soft *endomorph*, the square, muscular *mesomorph*, and the long, thin *ectomorph*. By the use of personality tests (see MENTAL TESTING), Sheldon established temperamental qualities associated with these. With endomorphy goes *viscerotonia*, a certain passivity and pleasure in sensation; with mesomorphy, *somatotonia*, a pleasure in physical activi-

ty; with ectomorphy, *cerebrotonia*, a pleasure in the exercise of COGNITIVE activities. Another attempt was made by Jung, in his postulation not only of the well-known types characterized by INTROVERSION and EXTROVERSION, but also of types contrasted in terms of orientation towards the world: sensation-oriented *v.* thought-oriented, feeling-oriented *v.* instinct-oriented. The isolating of *function types* that may be mixed in any given individual is most closely associated with H. J. Eysenck. Work on *value types*, represented principally by the Allport-Vernon-Lindzey *Study of Values* (1951), is aimed at establishing dominant value orientation (i.e. political, aesthetic, social, religious, theoretical), and has achieved considerable predictive success. See also CONVERGERS AND DIVERGERS.   J.S.B.

perspectivism. In PHILOSOPHY, the theory that there are alternative systems of CONCEPTS and assumptions, not equivalent to each other, in whose terms the world may be interpreted and as between which there is no authoritative external way of making a choice. It is to be found in the philosophy of Nietzsche, for whom belief systems are instruments serving the impulse to survive and succeed and, in a less passionate and more domesticated form, in Ortega y Gasset. Broadly analogous conclusions have been reached by Ajdukiewicz and Quine (the latter under WHORFIAN inspiration). They maintain that there are, or can be, different languages which are not translatable into each other and which supply their speakers with quite different pictures of the world. Like other sceptical hypotheses of comparable generality, perspectivism invites the question: is it not itself just one perspective on thought and language among others, with no greater claim to validity than they have?   A.Q.

PERT (programme, evaluation, and review technique). A form of CRITICAL PATH ANALYSIS, in which expected timings of stages in a project are used to calculate a range of probable completion times, of varying degrees of pessimism or optimism. Many COMPUTER-assisted routines used by MANAGEMENT for project scheduling and control are derived from the PERT method, which was devised in 1958 by the U.S. Navy for the POLARIS submarine project.   R.I.T.

Bibl: A. Battersby, *Network Analysis* (London and N.Y., 3rd ed., 1970).

Perutz, Max Ferdinand (Austrian-British chemist, *b*. 1914), see under MOLECULAR BIOLOGY; PROTEINS.

perversion. Deviation from the NORMS of sexual practice; for examples see HOMOSEXUALITY; MASOCHISM; SADISM; SADO-MASOCHISM. Attitudes to such perversions or (the more neutral word) deviations have shifted, increasingly since the KINSEY REPORT (1948–53) and the Wolfenden Report (1957), from censorious condemnation to greater PERMISSIVENESS.   O.S.

Pestalozzi, Johann Heinrich (Swiss educational reformer, 1746–1827), see under CHILD-CENTRED EDUCATION; FROEBEL METHOD; PESTALOZZI METHODS; PROGRESSIVE.

Pestalozzi methods. Educational principles associated with Johann Heinrich Pestalozzi (1746–1827), a Swiss from Zurich. Pestalozzi (who at the age of 5 was left fatherless) stressed the importance of the mother and the home in the early education of a child, and the need to call on the personal sensory experience of children in helping them to develop ideas, and to use their surroundings in teaching them to synthesize experience. Pestalozzi's ideas and methods were widely influential in Prussia through the influence of Fichte and were brought to England by the Mayos and Kay-Shuttleworth.   W.A.C.S.
Bibl: K. Silber, *Pestalozzi* (London, 1960).

Pétain, Marshal **Philippe** (French soldier and statesman, 1856–1951), see under VICHY.

Peter Principle, see under PARKINSON'S LAW.

Peters, Sir **Rudolph Albert** (British biochemist, *b*. 1899), see under CYTOSKELETON.

petit bourgeois. A member of the French *petite bourgeoisie*, as opposed to the *haute bourgeoisie* (see BOURGEOIS). The *petite bourgeoisie* were men of small-scale wealth and property, owners of individual

shops, single houses, small plots of urban land, small workshops and factories, etc. The limited scale of their wealth was widely regarded as being paralleled by their limited horizons, narrow minds, and obscurantist attitude to art and culture. Hence the hyphenated adjective *petit-bourgeois* is most often used pejoratively – a connotation emphasized by the common anglicization of *petit* (or *petite*) as petty. See also POUJADISM.   D.C.W.

petrography. A division of PETROLOGY concerned with the description and CLASSIFICATION of rocks. Most rocks are aggregates of mineral grains, and an important part of the subject is the investigation of the texture of rocks, i.e. the shape and relationships of their constituent grains.   J.L.M.L.

petrology. The study of rocks, their composition (see under PETROGRAPHY), occurrence, and genesis. Three main classes of rocks are recognized, igneous, sedimentary, and metamorphic. *Igneous* rocks are those which have solidified from hot molten material called magma which is generated below the earth's crust (see LITHOSPHERE) and rises to cool on or just below the surface; *sedimentary* rocks are formed on the earth's surface, mainly on the sea floor, by the deposition of mineral matter weathered and transported from rocks on the land surface; *metamorphic* rocks are produced by the deep-seated alteration of pre-existing rocks due to the action of heat and pressure. Petrology is one of the few branches of GEOLOGY in which observation and analysis are supported by experimental work.   J.L.M.L.

Pevsner, Anton (Russo-French sculptor and painter, 1886–1962), see under CONSTRUCTIVISM.

Pfemfert, Franz (German author, 1879–1954), see under ACTIVISM.

pH. A convenient measure of the acidity or alkalinity of a solution. Defined as the logarithm of the reciprocal of the hydrogen ION concentration, pH values in aqueous solutions range from 0 to 14. Pure water has a pH of 7.   B.F.

phagocytes. CELLS which can nourish themselves by the direct entrapment and engulfment of solid particles, which are taken into the CYTOPLASM and digested by hydrolytic ENZYMES. *Phagocytosis*, the name given to this process of ingestion by cells, was discovered by the Russian zoologist Mechnikov, who may have attached undue importance to its role in bodily defences. Phagocytosis occurs in the amoeboid PROTOZOA and also among white blood corpuscles, particularly the monocytes, polymorphs, and the cells lining lymphatic sinuses. In the living organism phagocytosis of bacteria (see BACTERIOLOGY) is greatly promoted by the action of antibodies (see IMMUNITY). Thus bacteria which would not be phagocytized in their native state may come to be so if they are coated by an antibody.   P.M.

phallic character, see under PSYCHO-SEXUAL DEVELOPMENT.

pharmacology. The branch of BIOLOGY that deals with the properties and mode of action of DRUGS and other biological effectors, particularly those of external origin and thus conventionally excluding hormones, the subject-matter of ENDOCRINOLOGY. Pharmacology consists partly of a taxonomy or functional CLASSIFICATION of drugs (particularly in relation to chemical structure), partly study of their fate in the body and their metabolic transformations (see METABOLISM), and partly of an investigation of their mode of action, particularly at a cellular level; this investigation involves the identification of special drug receptors on the CELL surface and a detailed analysis of how the drug alters the cell's behaviour. It includes the study of anaesthetics, antidotes to drugs, and drug addiction. (The measuring, dispensing, and formulation of drugs is the subject-matter of *pharmacy*.) Among the biological agents that are not drugs in the conventional sense but come under the study of pharmacology are the ANTIBIOTICS. A most important branch of pharmacology is that which has to do with the standardization and testing of drugs – procedures specially necessary for those drugs which, being of biological origin, are often not chemically characterized and therefore not open to ordinary chemical methods of measurement and potency testing. Safety control is another important – sometimes vitally important – pro-

cedure associated with the preparation, marketing, and medical use of agents of biological origin such as hormones, antibodies (see IMMUNITY), and antibiotics.
                                                      P.M.

phase. (1) In PHYSICS, an angle specifying position along a wave, or the extent to which two waves are 'in register'. One complete cycle (crest + trough) corresponds to 360°. Thus waves which are a quarter wavelength out of step have a phase difference of 90°, while waves whose phase difference is 180° are half a wave out of step, and will interfere destructively if superimposed, because the crests cancel the troughs. (2) One of the chemically identical but physically different states of the same system; e.g. ice, water, and steam, or graphite and diamond (see also ALLOTROPE).   M.V.B.

phase modulation. The variation of the PHASE of a high-frequency wave in proportion to the strength of another wave of much lower frequency. Phase modulation is very similar to FREQUENCY MODULATION.   M.V.B.

phatic language. In LINGUISTICS, a term deriving from the anthropologist Malinowski's phrase *phatic communion*, and applied to language used (as in comments on the weather or enquiries about health) for establishing an atmosphere rather than for exchanging information or ideas.   D.C.

phenology. Study of the times of recurring natural phenomena. Used primarily within BIOLOGY for study of seasonal variations, e.g. in plant flowering times or bird migration.   P.H.

phenomena (in PHILOSOPHY), see under NOUMENA.

phenomenalism. The theory, propounded by J. S. Mill, that material things are 'permanent possibilities of sensation'. It has been elaborately developed by ANALYTIC PHILOSOPHERS in this century, expressed in a more linguistic idiom as the (REDUCTIONIST) theory that statements about material things are equivalent in meaning to statements about actual and possible SENSE-DATA, the sense-data that an observer would have if certain conditions were satisfied. It seems an irresistible consequence of a radically EMPIRICIST theory of meaning together with the widespread philosophical assumption, created by the *argument from illusion* (see ILLUSION), that material objects are not directly perceived (the *sense-datum theory*). But both of those premises are open to question. A.Q.

Bibl: A. J. Ayer, *The Foundations of Empirical Knowledge* (London and N.Y., 1940).

phenomenology.

(1) In PHILOSOPHY, a method of enquiry elaborated by Edmund Husserl as a development of his teacher's, Brentano's, conception of 'descriptive', as opposed to 'genetic', PSYCHOLOGY. It takes philosophy to begin from an exact, attentive inspection of one's mental, particularly intellectual, processes in which all assumptions about the causation, consequences, and wider significance of the mental process under inspection are eliminated ('bracketed'). Husserl was insistent that phenomenology is not an empirical technique. It is an *a priori* (see APRIORISM) investigation or scrutiny of ESSENCES or MEANINGS, the objective logical elements in thought that are common to different minds. The phenomenological method has been applied by others, notably Max Scheler, to less austerely intellectual subject-matter, and Husserl's pupil Heidegger used it for the investigation of the extreme states of mind in which, according to EXISTENTIALISM, the situation of man in the world is revealed. A.Q.

Bibl: H. Spiegelberg, *The Phenomenological Movement* (2 vols., The Hague, 2nd ed., 1965).

(2) In the PSYCHOLOGY of PERCEPTION, a doctrine or school which postulates that the significant role of SENSE-DATA lies in the form of the object as perceived, however erroneously or distorted, by the individual, and not in the object itself nor in material descriptions, locations, or identifications of the object that follow the rules of physical science. H.L.

Bibl: M. Merleau-Ponty, tr. C. Smith, *Phenomenology of Perception* (London and N.Y., 1962).

(3) In SOCIOLOGY, Husserl's method (see 1, above) was adapted by Alfred Schütz to investigate the assumptions involved in everyday social life. In the sociology of KNOWLEDGE, phenomenologists have concentrated on the way in which COMMON-SENSE knowledge about society feeds back, through SOCIAL ACTION, into the moulding of society itself. Other developments range from highly generalized descriptions of how people in different types of society think and feel about the world and their place in it, to analyses, in ETHNOMETHODOLOGY, of the unconscious routines by which people manage their inter-personal contacts. Critics of phenomenological sociology mistrust its aprioristic tendencies (see APRIORISM), and are impatient with its preference for description and uncontrolled hypothesis over EXPLANATION. When explanations are offered, it is claimed, they are disappointingly trite. J.R.T.

Bibl: Alfred Schütz, tr. G. Walsh and F. Lehnert, *The Phenomenology of the Social World* (Evanston, Ill., 1967).

phenotype, see under GENOTYPE.

phi-phenomenon. A type of illusory perceptual impression of movement produced when, e.g., two stationary, spatially separated lights are flashed in brief succession. 'Phi' refers specifically to an impression of pure movement dissociated from any PERCEPTION of an object. See also GESTALT. I.M.L.H.

Philipe, Gérard (French actor, 1922–59), see under THÉÂTRE NATIONAL POPULAIRE.

Phillips curve. A construction embodying the initial quantitative attempt (1958) by the British economist A. W. Phillips to measure the relationship between UNEMPLOYMENT and INFLATION. The downward-sloping curve implies that as unemployment declines the rate of change in wages and prices rises. The TERMS OF TRADE differ from one country to the next because of differences of organization in labour and product markets. Broadly speaking, the more concentrated is labour and corporate organization, the higher is the rate of unemployment at which inflation threatens, and the more expensive, in terms of further price increases, is additional reduction of unemployment. R.L.

philology, see under LINGUISTICS.

469

PHILOSOPHICAL THEOLOGY

philosophical theology. A term sometimes equivalent to PHILOSOPHY OF RELIGION, but more usually applied to the discussion of the rationality of Christian faith within the tradition of Christian THEOLOGY, e.g. by EMPIRICAL or CRISIS theologians or in CHRISTIAN EXISTENTIALISM or NEO-THOMISM.   D.L.E.

Bibl: J. Richmond, *Faith and Philosophy* (London and Philadelphia, 1966).

philosophy. A term that cannot be uncontroversially defined in a single formula, used to cover a wide variety of intellectual undertakings all of which combine a high degree of generality with more or less exclusive reliance on reasoning rather than observation and experience to justify their claims. The chief agreed constituents of philosophy are EPISTEMOLOGY, or the theory of knowledge, METAPHYSICS, and ETHICS. There is a philosophy of every major form of intellectual activity of less than wholly general scope: science (see SCIENCE, PHILOSOPHY OF), HISTORY (see METAHISTORY), RELIGION (see RELIGION, PHILOSOPHY OF), art (see AESTHETICS), and others. These departmental philosophies are either epistemologies of the type of knowledge involved or metaphysical accounts of the domain of objects which that knowledge concerns. (The distinction is often marked as that between the critical and the speculative philosophy of whatever it may be.) Until fairly recent times LOGIC was so closely associated with philosophy as, in effect, to form part of it; but today logic is as often taken to be a part, a very fundamental part, of MATHEMATICS. The philosophical theory of logic, however, that is to say SEMANTICS, in a wide sense, or the theory of MEANING, is very much part of philosophy and, to a large extent, has replaced epistemology as the fundamental philosophical discipline. In the colloquial sense of the word, philosophy is a set or system of ultimate values. This is rather the subject-matter of than identical with ethics. The rational pursuit of such a value-system must rest on a general conception of the nature of the world in which values are sought, the goal of metaphysics. Metaphysics, in its turn, presupposes a critical investigation of the various sorts of knowledge-claim and method of thinking from and by which a general picture of the

470

world (or WELTANSCHAUUNG) might be constituted, in other words epistemology. The main preoccupations of technical or academic philosophy are all to be found in the writings of Plato and Aristotle and, less comprehensively, in the work of their ancient Greek predecessors, and a continuous tradition of philosophical discussion derives from them. If a single short formula is insisted on, the least objectionable is that philosophy is *thought about thought*; this distinguishes philosophy from those various kinds of first-order thinking about particular parts or aspects of what there is (i.e. science, history, and so on) whose ideas, methods, and findings constitute the subject-matter of philosophy.   A.Q.

Bibl: J. A. Passmore, *Philosophical Reasoning* (N.Y., 1962; London, 2nd ed., 1970); A. J. Ayer, *The Central Questions of Philosophy* (London, 1973).

philosophy of history, see METAHISTORY.

philosophy of mind, see MIND, PHILOSOPHY OF.

philosophy of religion, see RELIGION, PHILOSOPHY OF.

philosophy of science, see SCIENCE, PHILOSOPHY OF.

phobia. An ANXIETY state (see also NEUROSIS) marked primarily by an intense fear out of proportion to the actual danger present in the feared situation or object. Phobias are diagnosed also by their intractibility to the effects of direct experience with the relevant situations or objects.   W.Z.

phoneme. In LINGUISTICS, the minimal unit of PHONOLOGICAL analysis, i.e. the smallest unit in the sound-system capable of indicating contrasts in meaning; thus in the word *pit* there are three phonemes, /p/, /i/, /t/, each of which differs from phonemes in other words, such as *bit, pet,* and *pin*. Phonemes are abstractions (see ABSTRACT), the particular phonetic shape they take depending on many factors, especially their position in relation to other sounds in the sentence. These variants are called allophones, e.g. the /t/ phoneme has (amongst others) both an alveolar allophone (the sound made with the tongue contacting the alveolar ridge above and behind the teeth, as in *eight*) and a dental allophone (the sound made with the tongue further forward, against the teeth, as in *eighth* because of the influence of the /th/ sound which follows).

In GENERATIVE GRAMMAR, the phoneme concept is not used: the sound features themselves (e.g. alveolar, nasal), referred to as *distinctive features*, are considered to be the most important minimal units of phonological analysis.   D.C.

phonemics, see PHONOLOGY.

phonetic poetry, see under CONCRETE POETRY.

phonetics. A branch of LINGUISTICS which studies the characteristics of human sound-making; normally divided into *articulatory* phonetics (the processes of sound articulation by the vocal organs), *acoustic* phonetics (the transmission of vocal sound through the air, often referred to as ACOUSTICS), and *auditory* phonetics (the perceptual response to human sound). The term *instrumental* phonetics is used for the study and development of mechanical aids for the analysis of any of these aspects. The name *general* phonetics is often used to indicate the aim of making phonetic principles and categories as universal as possible. See also IPA; PHONOLOGY.   D.C.

Bibl: K. L. Pike, *Phonetics* (Ann Arbor, 1943); D. Abercrombie, *Elements of General Phonetics* (Edinburgh and Chicago, 1967); J. D. O'Connor, *Phonetics* (Harmondsworth and Baltimore, 1973).

phonology. A branch of LINGUISTICS, sometimes called *phonemics*, which studies the sound-systems of languages. It is normally divided into *segmental* and *suprasegmental* (or *non-segmental*) phonology: the former analyses the properties of vowels, consonants, and syllables, the latter analyses those features of pronunciation which vary independently of the segmental structure of a sentence, e.g. INTONATION, rhythm, PARALANGUAGE. See also PROSODIC FEATURES.   D.C.

Bibl: A. C. Gimson, *An Introduction to the Pronunciation of English* (2nd ed., London, 1970; N.Y., 1971).

phonon. An elementary vibration in a crystal. Heat is conducted by an incoherent superposition of short-wave phonons (see COHERENCE), while sound in solids is a coherent superposition of phonons whose wavelength is much longer than the distance between neighbouring ATOMS in the crystal LATTICE.   M.V.B.

phosphorescence. The delayed emission of light from substances that have previously been exposed to it.   M.V.B.

photobiology. The branch of BIOLOGY that deals with the influence of light on various biological performances. It includes PHOTOSYNTHESIS, the deposition of melanin (see MELANISM) in the skin through the action of sunlight, the emission of light by such organisms as glow-worms, and the behavioural responses towards sources of light or organisms such as moths and beetles.   P.M.

photochemistry. The study of CHEMICAL REACTIONS induced by light. It was recognized early in the 19th century that only the light absorbed by a MOLECULE produces a photochemical change (the first law of photochemistry). Stark and Einstein (1912) were responsible for the second law, which states that, when a molecule is activated and caused to react, one QUANTUM of light has been absorbed. Photochemical reactions are of great importance; they include PHOTOSYNTHESIS, production of the ozone layer in the upper atmosphere, photochemical oxidation (e.g. the fading of dyes in light), photographic processes, and the chemistry of vision.   B.F.

photoelectric cell. A device for detecting the presence of light and measuring its intensity, as in a photographer's light meter. PHOTONS arriving at the surface of a suitable material (e.g. selenium) interact with ELECTRONS in it, thus producing measurable electrical effects.   M.V.B.

photogram. ABSTRACT or near-abstract photograph produced without a camera by the action of light and shade on sensitized paper. A DADAIST technique first employed by Christian Schad in Geneva in the winter of 1919–20 and subsequently by Man Ray in Paris; hence the alternative names *schadograph* or *rayograph*.   J.W.

photolysis. The decomposition of a MOLECULE by light (see PHOTO-CHEMISTRY). B.F.

photomicrograph. A photograph taken by attaching a camera to a microscope. M.V.B.

photomontage, see under MONTAGE.

photon. The ELEMENTARY PARTICLE or 'quantum' of ENERGY in which light or other electromagnetic RADIATION is emitted or absorbed when an ELECTRON, in an ATOM (see ATOMIC PHYSICS) or MOLECULE, changes its ENERGY LEVEL. The energy of a photon is equal to its frequency multiplied by PLANCK'S CONSTANT. Between emission and absorption, when the light is travelling through space, the intensity is usually so high that many photons are present, and classical OPTICS based on ELECTROMAGNETISM provides a sufficiently accurate description; this is an example of the WAVE-PARTICLE DUALITY. A burst of light containing no more than a few photons is detectable by the naked eye. M.V.B.

photosynthesis. A highly complex oxidative-reduction reaction between carbon dioxide and water which takes place in the presence of CHLOROPHYLL and involves the absorption of solar energy. The reaction results in the production of glucose and of higher CARBOHYDRATES which provide the food (and thus the energy) required by animals. In addition, the oxygen in the atmosphere is renewed by photosynthesis, so the whole LIFE CYCLE of the earth ultimately depends upon this reaction. K.M.

phototaxis, phototropism, see under TROPISM.

phrase-structure grammar, see under GENERATIVE GRAMMAR.

phrenology. A would-be science with some popularity in the 19th century but now completely discredited by the findings of NEUROPSYCHOLOGY. It supposed that mental faculties were located in distinct parts of the brain and could be investigated by feeling bumps on the outside of the head. I.M.L.H.

phylogeny. An animal's pedigree in terms of evolutionary descent (see EVOLUTION). It is contrasted with ONTOGENY, which is essentially its development (see EMBRYOLOGY). The so-called law of RECAPITULATION is sometimes, following Ernst Haeckel (1834–1919), put in the form 'Ontogeny repeats phylogeny'. See also BIOSYSTEMATICS. P.M.

phylum. A group of organisms united by basic similarity (or *homeomorphy*) of ground plan. Thus the chordates (see ZOOLOGY) form a phylum because all pass through a *neurula* stage (see EMBRYOLOGY) in which the basic layout is essentially similar throughout. P.M.

physical chemistry. A major branch of chemistry concerned with the measurement and understanding of chemical processes. It deals with chemical THERMODYNAMICS, in particular the position of chemical EQUILIBRIUM and the forces between chemical SPECIES (ATOMS, IONS, or MOLECULES) in the gaseous, liquid, and solid states. The rates of CHEMICAL REACTION and their mechanisms are a central study. Other major areas are the determination of molecular structure and the investigation of the allowed ENERGY LEVELS for chemical species in different environments. Since many of these topics might equally well be studied by physicists, there is practically no distinction, except academic convention, between physical chemistry and *chemical physics*. B.F.
Bibl: W. J. Moore, *Physical Chemistry* (London and Englewood Cliffs, N.J., 5th ed., 1972).

physicalism. The theory that all significant empirical statements can be formulated as statements referring to *publicly* observable physical objects. LOGICAL POSITIVISM, in its early stages, combined the desire to legitimize scientific statements as the PARADIGM of what is significant and knowable with a commitment to the view that the empirical basis of MEANING and knowledge is *private* sense-experience (see PRIVACY; SENSE-DATUM). Neurath held that the scientific requirement of *intersubjectivity* (i.e. of being publicly observable) must extend to its foundations and converted Carnap from his previous 'methodological SOLIPSISM'.

Neurath saw physicalism as establishing the unity of science, contending that there is no difference of method or, fundamentally, of subject-matter between the NATURAL SCIENCES and the SOCIAL SCIENCES. In its original form physicalism interpreted statements about mental events in a BEHAVIOURISTIC way as statements about the DISPOSITIONS of living human bodies to behaviour of various kinds. The doctrine has been revived by exponents of the IDENTITY THEORY of mind and body (see also MIND-BODY PROBLEM), notably Smart, for whom mental events are in fact events occurring in the brain and NERVOUS SYSTEM.   A.Q.

Bibl: J. J. C. Smart, *Philosophy and Scientific Realism* (London and N.Y., 1963).

physics. The study of the motion and interactions of matter, and the TRANSFORMATIONS between different kinds of ENERGY. On an abstract level, the subject is based on the 'six great theories' of NEWTONIAN MECHANICS, QUANTUM MECHANICS, RELATIVITY, ELECTROMAGNETISM, THERMODYNAMICS, and STATISTICAL MECHANICS. These theories make contact with the brute facts of nature via bodies of experimental data and interpretation devoted to particular kinds of system, e.g. ATOMIC PHYSICS, NUCLEAR PHYSICS, CRYOGENICS (low-temperature physics), SOLID-STATE PHYSICS, PLASMA PHYSICS, ASTRONOMY, etc. (For *chemical physics* see PHYSICAL CHEMISTRY.) However, none of the 'great theories' seems capable of explaining the interactions between ELEMENTARY PARTICLES or their origin in COSMOLOGY, and these subjects constitute the frontiers of physics today.   M.V.B.

Bibl: E. M. Rogers, *Physics for the Enquiring Mind* (London and Princeton, 1960); R. P. Feynman, *The Character of Physical Law* (Cambridge, Mass., 1965).

physiography. A term, now falling into disuse, for the purely descriptive aspect of GEOMORPHOLOGY.   J.L.M.L.

physiology. The branch of BIOLOGY that deals with function rather than structure and constitution. There are as many branches of physiology as there are distinct organ and TISSUE systems, e.g. NEUROLOGY, ENDOCRINOLOGY, etc. P.M.

phytogeography. The branch of BIO-GEOGRAPHY which studies the geographical distribution of plants. Over a limited area plant distribution depends mainly on the soil type, determined by the GEOLOGY of the underlying rock. The other main factors are climatic (see CLIMATOLOGY). Agriculture has now changed the plant cover of the whole landscape in developed countries, and man, by burning the bush for instance, has affected other, less developed areas. This means that stable natural vegetation is becoming increasingly rare, and many of the original CONCEPTS of phytogeography cannot now be easily demonstrated.   K.M.

Bibl: M. I. Newbigin, *Plant and Animal Geography* (London and N.Y., rev. ed., 1957).

phytopathology. The study of the diseases of plants; alternatively, the study of diseases caused by vegetable organisms, such as fungi. See also MYCOLOGY.   K.M.

Piaget, Jean (Swiss psychologist, *b.* 1896), see under ACCOMMODATION; ASSIMILATION; CONCRETE OPERATION; CONSERVATION; DEVELOPMENTAL PSYCHOLOGY; FORMAL OPERATION; INTELLIGENCE; PIAGETIAN; PSYCHOLOGY; STAGE OF DEVELOPMENT.

Piagetian. An adjective referring to Jean Piaget (*b.* 1896) and his theory of intellectual development. The theory is distinguished by an account of intellectual development as a universal sequence of mental stages (see STAGE OF DEVELOPMENT). The order of the stages is invariant, the later incorporating and resynthesizing the earlier. Development is divided into three broad stages: the SENSORY-MOTOR period (from birth to 18 months), in which the infant constructs a picture of a stable world divided into objects which retain their identity through space and time; the CONCRETE OPERATIONS period (from 2 to 11), in which the young child acquires classificatory principles of number, class, and quantity for organizing such objects; and the FORMAL OPERATIONS period (from 12 onwards), in which the adolescent acquires the ability systematically to coordinate his own classificatory principles.

Piaget has taken a characteristic position over various central psychological controversies. INTELLIGENCE is seen neither as a resonance to the external world (EMPIRICISM) nor as the unfolding of a predetermined system (NATIVISM), but as the progressive coordination between an organized intellectual system and the external world, beginning with the initial coordination between reflex and stimuli. Nor is intellectual development guided by cultural and social tools such as language. Instead, Piaget argues that intellectual development guides the usage of those tools.

The theory has contributed to the recent growth of COGNITIVE PSYCHOLOGY and contemporary interest in mental operations as opposed to observable behaviour (see BEHAVIOURISM). Nonetheless, even within cognitive psychology, Piaget remains distinctive. First, he adopts a developmental approach to cognition, and second, he concerns himself with epistemological categories (see EPISTEMOLOGY) and issues such as the nature of space (see SPACE PERCEPTION), quantity, and causality, rather than with psychological categories such as short-term memory, attention, and retrieval, etc. See also ACCOMMODATION; ASSIMILATION; CONSERVATION; DEVELOPMENTAL PSYCHOLOGY.   P.L.H.

Bibl: J. Piaget, tr. M. Cook, *The Origin of Intelligence in the Child* (London, 1953; N.Y., 1963); J. Piaget, tr. C. Maschler, *Structuralism* (London and N.Y., 1971); J. Piaget, tr. B. Walsh, *Biology and Knowledge* (Edinburgh and Chicago, 1971); J. Piaget, tr. W. Mays, *The Principles of Genetic Epistemology* (London, 1972).

Piatakov, Gregory Leonodovich, see PYATAKOV.

Picabia, Francis (French artist and author, 1879–1953), see under ARMORY SHOW; DADA; ORPHISM; SURREALISM.

Picasso, Pablo (Spanish painter, 1881–1973), see under COLLAGE; CONSTRUCTIVISM; CUBISM; ÉCOLE DE PARIS; FORMALISM; NEO-CLASSICISM; NEUE KÜNSTLERVEREINIGUNG; PRIMITIVE; SURREALISM.

Piccard, Jacques (Swiss scientist and explorer, b. 1922), see under BATHYSPHERE.

picture-writing, see under LETTRISM.

Pike, Kenneth Lee (U.S. linguist and anthropologist, b. 1912), see under TAGMEMIC GRAMMAR.

pinch effect. When a large electric current flows, the resulting MAGNETISM exerts a force on the moving ELECTRONS, tending to push them towards the axis of current. If the conductor is a fluid (e.g. a PLASMA or liquid metal), then a constricting effect – the pinch effect – is produced. The resulting instability is similar to the break-up of thin water jets into droplets caused by surface tension. See also MAGNETOHYDRODYNAMICS.   M.V.B.

Pinchot, Clifford (U.S. pioneer in forestry, 1865–1946), see under CONSERVATION.

Pinter, Harold (British dramatist, b. 1930), see under COMEDY OF MENACE; THEATRE OF THE ABSURD.

Pirandello, Luigi (Italian dramatist, 1867–1936), see under CARTEL; INTELLECTUALS.

Pisarev, Dmitry Ivanovich (Russian social thinker, 1840–68), see under INTELLECTUALS; NIHILISM.

Piscator, Erwin (German theatrical director, 1893–1966), see under DOCUMENTARY; EPIC THEATRE; OPEN STAGE; TOTAL THEATRE; VOLKSBÜHNE.

Pissarro, Camille (French painter, 1831–1903), see under IMPRESSIONISM; NEO-IMPRESSIONISM.

Pissarro, Lucien (French-British painter, 1863–1944), see under NEO-IMPRESSIONISM.

Pitman, Sir James (British educationist, b. 1901), see under i.t.a.

Pitoëff, Georges (Russo-French actor, producer, and dramatist, 1886–1939), see under CARTEL.

pittura metafisica, see METAPHYSICAL PAINTING.

pituitary. In ENDOCRINOLOGY, the most important endocrine gland in the body. It contains two elements of different origins and functions, on the one hand the epithelial element which began as a sort of median nose – an inpushing of the outermost layer of the skin towards the floor of the thalamic region of the brain – and on the other hand a neural element on the floor of the thalamus. The anterior pituitary derived from the epithelial element secretes *hormones* whose chief function is to control the activities of other endocrine organs, e.g. the GONADS, the THYROID, and the ADRENAL cortex. This anterior part of the pituitary is brought under the control of the brain by the action of intermediaries or 'releasing substances'. The neural element of the pituitary gland produces secretions such as oxytocin and vasopressin, the effects of which are similar to those of the autonomic NERVOUS SYSTEM. The hormones of this part of the gland are in fact manufactured in the hypothalamus and transported down the highly modified nerve CELLS to the posterior part of the pituitary, whence they are liberated into the bloodstream, as with other endocrine glands. P.M.

Pius X, Pope (1835–1914), see under MODERNISM.

Pius XI, Pope (1857–1939), see under ACTION FRANÇAISE; CATHOLIC ACTION; QUADRAGESIMO ANNO.

Pius XII, Pope (1876–1958), see under CATHOLIC ACTION; CHRISTIAN EXISTENTIALISM.

PK, see PSYCHOKINESIS.

PL/1. A HIGH-LEVEL PROGRAMMING LANGUAGE sponsored by IBM to supersede FORTRAN and COBOL. It has not yet done so. C.S.

Plamenatz, John Petrov (British political theorist, 1912–75), see under IDEOLOGY.

Planchon, Roger (French dramatist, *b.* 1931), see under CENTRES DRAMATIQUES.

Planck, Max (German physicist, 1858–1947), see under BLACK-BODY RADIATION; PLANCK'S CONSTANT.

Planck's constant. A universal constant (generally written h) first introduced by Max Planck in 1900, which relates the mechanical properties of matter to its wave properties (see WAVE-PARTICLE DUALITY). The ENERGY of a PARTICLE determines its frequency according to the EQUATION *frequency* $=$ *energy* $\div$ h, while the MOMENTUM of a particle determines its DE BROGLIE WAVELENGTH. The extreme smallness of Planck's constant makes NEWTONIAN MECHANICS an excellent approximation to QUANTUM MECHANICS in normal circumstances. M.V.B.

plane of the ecliptic, see under ECLIPTIC.

planetesimal theory. One of a number of hypotheses proposed for the origin of the solar system which have as a common starting-point the disruption of the primitive sun by an external force. T. C. Chamberlin and F. R. Moulton proposed that planetesimals, fragments which aggregated to form the planets, were derived from the break-up of the primitive sun and another star, on their close approach to each other. There are, however, serious physical and chemical objections to all theories involving disruption of the sun. Chemical evidence alone suggests that it is very unlikely that the planets were formed from the interior of the sun. J.L.M.L.

Bibl: see under EARTH SCIENCES.

planetoid, see ASTEROID.

planning. In POLITICAL ECONOMY, the mode of thinking which stresses the advantages of a central planning authority to coordinate the development of the national economy, or, more loosely, of government intervention in some form (as opposed to a LAISSEZ FAIRE approach). In the wake of the CAPITALIST chaos of the 1930s, the Soviet example of planning, and especially its emphasis on heavy industry, exercised considerable intellectual appeal. By the post-war period, not only had the Soviet Union, Eastern Europe, and China all adopted rigorous central planning, but the majority of the THIRD WORLD countries also favoured a planned approach. Meanwhile most Western industrial countries have adopted MIXED ECONOMIES of varying shades. D.E.

plasma, see under SERUM.

plasma physics. The study of fluids containing a large number of free negative and positive electric charges, e.g. the IONOSPHERE or the gases in which a FUSION reaction is occurring. Such systems are strongly affected by electric and magnetic forces, so that their complicated motions (e.g. the PINCH EFFECT) must be interpreted within MAGNETOHYDRO-DYNAMICS.   M.V.B.

plasmagene. A GENE or group of genes not incorporated into a CHROMOSOME. It once seemed that the presence in CELLS of structures such as mitochondria and chloroplasts which arise only from pre-existing structures of the same kind indicated the existence of a hereditary mechanism profoundly different from the Mendelian one (see MENDELISM). These structures are now known to contain DNA (see NUCLEIC ACID), and it seems that the difference concerns the ways in which DNA is transmitted from cell to cell rather than the process of self-replication upon which heredity depends. See also EPISOME.   J.M.S.

plastic. Any normally solid material which can flow slowly as a result of pressure or heat (see RHEOLOGY); generally the term is restricted to POLYMERS with this property.   M.V.B.

plate tectonics. A hypothesis of global TECTONICS which postulates large-scale horizontal movements of the rigid outer shell of the earth, termed the LITHOSPHERE, over a plastic layer of the upper mantle, the ASTHENOSPHERE. The theory has developed as a result of recent discoveries of patterns of remnant magnetism of the ocean floor which make it virtually certain that oceanic crust is being continually created by upwelling of mantle material along a worldwide mid-ocean fracture system. The oceanic lithosphere so created spreads laterally at a rate of a few centimetres a year, moving in opposite directions on either side of the mid-oceanic fracture system and eventually sinks down to be reabsorbed in the mantle under certain continental margins. The major zone of sinking is the circum-Pacific region from the Philippines to Chile. Six major plates of the lithosphere, five of them carrying continental crust, are moving relative to each other across the earth's surface away from the mid-ocean fracture, and in doing so they seem to determine the major tectonic features of the earth. See also CONTINENTAL DRIFT.

J.L.M.L.

Bibl: H. H. Hess, 'History of Ocean Basins', in A. E. J. Engel *et al.* (eds.), *Petrologic Studies* (N.Y., 1962).

Plato (Greek philosopher, *c.* 428 B.C. – 348/47 B.C.), see under CATHARSIS; DUALISM; EPISTEMOLOGY; IDEA; IDEALISM; PHILOSOPHY; PLATONISM; SOCIAL CONTRACT.

Platonic realism, see under REALISM.

Platonism. The theory that ABSTRACT entities or UNIVERSALS really exist, outside space and time, in an autonomous world of timeless ESSENCES. (Plato, indeed, held that such Ideas or Forms are the *only* things that really or wholly exist, on the ground that it is only of them that we have absolutely certain knowledge, namely, in MATHEMATICS.) One argument for the existence of universals is that there are statements, known to be true, which refer to them. Critics object that such references can be eliminated by ANALYSIS: 'Honesty is the best policy', with its apparent implication of the existence of honesty-in-general, is just an idiomatic abbreviation for 'Anyone who acts honestly acts prudently'. But it has been argued by Quine that any language mathematically rich enough for the needs of science must contain irreducible references to classes (see SET THEORY), and that classes are abstract entities. If *a priori* knowledge (see APRIORISM) is conceived by ANALOGY with PERCEPTION, abstract entities provide suitable objects for acts of rational insight or intellectual intuition.

A.Q.

Bibl: Bertrand Russell, *The Problems of Philosophy* (London, 1912), chs. 9, 10; W. D. Ross, *Plato's Theory of Ideas* (Oxford, 1951).

playgroups, see under PRE-SCHOOL EDUCATION.

pleasure principle. In psychoanalytic theory (see PSYCHOANALYSIS), a FREUDIAN term for the principle of mental functioning that characterizes unconscious, primitive instincts (the ID), which are driven to gratification without regard to their consequences either socially or for the individual's adaptation. It is usually contrasted with the REALITY PRINCIPLE. W.Z.

pleiotropy. The development of apparently unrelated characteristics under the influence of a single GENE. It is thought that each gene has only one primary function, and that pleiotropic effects arise because a single primary effect can have many consequences.   J.M.S.

Plekhanov, Georgy Valentinovich (Russian political theorist, 1856–1918), see under DIALECTICAL MATERIALISM; MENSHEVIKS.

Pleven, René (French statesman, b. 1901), see under EDC.

PLO (Palestine Liberation Organization). An umbrella organization for various political organizations of those Arab inhabitants of the former British MANDATE of Palestine who fled their homes after the establishment of the state of Israel. Set up by a decision of the heads of the Arab states who met in Cairo in 1964, it acquired new importance after the Israeli defeat of the Arab states in 1967 and the occupation of the whole west bank of the Jordan. The activities of various GUERRILLA groups among its component organizations (see FATAH; BLACK SEPTEMBER) were generally admired in the Arab world, although in 1970 the Jordanian Government succeeded in removing the base of these Palestinian operations from its own territory. The Organization subsequently moved its headquarters to the Lebanon, where it became a potent and independent force in Lebanese domestic politics and civil warfare. In December 1974 it was recognized as the sole and legitimate representative of the Palestinian people after it had become increasingly the focal point of a growing sense of Palestinian NATIONALISM. Its stated goal is the establishment of a secular Arab state on the territory of the former mandate, in which Jews, but not Zionists, would be welcome; this implies the dismantling of the state of Israel. The apparent willingness of its leadership to accept a piecemeal realization of this goal

led various extremist Palestinian groups to break away from it in October 1974 to form the so-called *Rejection Front*. D.C.W.

Plowden Report (1967). The two-volume report *Children and their Primary Schools* (London, H.M.S.O.) by a committee set up under the chairmanship of Lady Plowden 'to consider primary education in all its aspects and the transition to secondary education'. The report considered organization and content, staffing and resources, child development, school health and welfare services, the school management system, and the independent schools for this age range, and has had many tangible results from its 197 recommendations. See also COMMUNITY SCHOOL; EDUCATIONAL PRIORITY AREA; MIDDLE SCHOOL.
                    W.A.C.S.

PLR (Public Lending Right). The principle that authors should receive some kind of payment when their works are borrowed from public libraries. Public Lending Right may be operated in various ways; and there are different means of raising the money – e.g. by direct government grant, by a levy on the rates, etc. It exists in Denmark, Sweden, and several other countries, but not in the U.S.A. In Great Britain, where the idea was pioneered by the novelist and writer John Brophy and where it remains a controversial issue, legislation to implement it was announced in the Queen's Speeches of 1974 and 1975. British authors favour a (cheaper) scheme based on a loan-sample rather than one based on the purchase price (a once-for-all payment).   M.S.-S.

plural society. A society containing within it two or more communities which are distinct in many (predominantly cultural) respects – colour, beliefs, RITUALS, practices both institutionalized (e.g. form of marriage and family) and habitual (e.g. preferred food, dress, leisure) – and which in many areas of social behaviour remain substantially unmixed; a society whose elements acknowledge, or are constrained by, an overall political authority, but are strongly disposed to the maintenance of their own traditions and are therefore motivated towards SEPARATISM. In plural societies the problem of preserving order and freedom is especially great; a slender unity easily breaks into warring national, racial, or religious groups. All societies other than the very simplest are pluralist in possessing local, regional, and CLASS communities, but the concept has come strongly to the fore since World War II when many hitherto subjected and newly immigrant (or refugee) groups feel the right to equal STATUS, and when, with movements of population, many societies (e.g. Britain) now contain distinctive cultural groups. The plural society has created moral, legal, and political problems of a new degree of difficulty – from APARTHEID at one extreme to the all-embracing statement of EQUALITY in the constitution of the U.S.A. at the other – and has rendered any analysis of social cooperation and conflict in terms of the orthodox concepts of SOCIAL STRATIFICATION (slavery, serfdom, CASTE, estate, class) much too simple. The more detailed analysis required has been provided in discussions of the composition of a population by F. H. Giddings (in *The Elements of Sociology*, London, 1898) and of cultural communities and INTEREST GROUPS by Gustav Ratzenhofer (e.g. as expounded by Albion W. Small in *General Sociology*, Chicago, 1905). See also CULTURE. R.F.

Bibl: H. M. Kallen, *Cultural Pluralism and the American Idea* (Philadephia, 1956); M. Ginsberg, 'Cultural Pluralism in the Modern World', in R. Fletcher (ed.), *The Science of Society and the Unity of Mankind* (London and N.Y., 1974).

pluralism. In political thought (for its meaning in PHILOSOPHY see MONISM), a term with three meanings, not always clearly distinguished: (*a*) institutional arrangements for the distribution of political POWER; (*b*) the doctrine that such arrangements ought to exist; and (*c*, a somewhat slipshod usage) pluralist *analysis*, i.e. the analysis of power distributed in this way. It is frequently used to denote any situation in which no particular political, ideological, cultural, or ethnic group is dominant. Such a situation normally involves competition between *rival* ÉLITES or INTEREST GROUPS, and the PLURAL SOCIETY in which it arises is often contrasted with a society dominated by a *single* élite where such competition is not free to develop. M.BA.

Bibl: R. A. Dahl (ed.), *Political Oppositions in Western Democracies* (London

and New Haven, 1966); R. Miliband, *The State in Capitalist Society* (London and N.Y., 1969).

plurisignation. Term introduced by Philip Wheelwright, in *The Burning Fountain* (1954), as a substitute for William Empson's AMBIGUITY, which, in his view, had an irrelevantly pejorative CONNOTATION, and was over-restrictive. 'Real plurisignation differs from simply punning or wit-writing . . . Empson's use of the term "ambiguity" generally refers to the plurisignative character of poetic language; his word is inappropriate, however, since ambiguity implies an "either–or" relation, plurisignation a "both–and".' 'The plurisign, the poetic symbol, is not merely employed but enjoyed'; 'it is a part of what it means'. The term extends the Empsonian CONCEPT by relating it to the mystico-religious connotation of words. M.S.-S.

plutocracy. Word of Greek origin for the rule of the wealthy, a state in which citizenship or POWER is defined by great wealth. A strict example of such a state is difficult to find; the Venetian republic probably comes closest, while the high property franchise obtaining in France under Louis Philippe (1830–48) and the roles open to the wealthy in American politics in the last decades of the 19th century gave these societies distinctly plutocratic elements. D.C.W.

plutonium. The most important TRANSURANIC ELEMENT. Plutonium (atomic number 94) is produced artificially in a nuclear reactor from naturally occurring uranium by a succession of NUCLEAR REACTIONS which follow NEUTRON absorption. Unlike the uranium 238 ISOTOPE, which constitutes 99.3% of natural uranium, the chief isotope of plutonium (atomic weight 239) is a fissionable material and can be used in atomic bombs and to fuel NUCLEAR REACTORS. Large-scale production of plutonium and separation from uranium began towards the end of World War II, and the first plutonium-containing bomb was exploded in New Mexico in 1945. Fast breeder reactors produce excess plutonium in addition to generating power. B.F.

Plymouth Brethren. A Christian SECT, originating in 1830 in Plymouth, England, but now widely distributed and vocal, although still not large. Its doctrines are generally FUNDAMENTALIST, and one section, the 'Exclusive' Brethren, interpret biblical passages about the 'holy' people as forbidding marriage or friendship with non-members. The 'Open' Brethren are somewhat more liberal. D.L.E.

pneumatic structures. Enclosures in which a membrane is air-supported by means of the difference in pressure between the inside and outside. As a rule air is pumped into such an enclosure through fans, and this air also acts as the mechanical ventilation. To prevent its escape, the membrane is tightly sealed and entrance is through an air lock. The membrane has to be in sufficient tension to withstand wind and snow loads. Much of the technology derives from lighter-than-air balloons and dirigibles.

Pneumatic structures can be erected and dismantled quickly and have thus so far been mostly used for temporary buildings, and in HAPPENINGS, play areas, etc., where they are often called *inflatables*. Some of the most complex examples were seen at Expo '70 in Osaka. Small, totally enclosed forms have been used as furniture. M.BR.

Bibl: R. N. Dent, *Principles of Pneumatic Architecture* (London, 1971).

Poe, Edgar Allan (U.S. poet and story-writer, 1809–49), see under SYMBOLISM.

Poel, William (British actor and producer, 1852–1934), see under OPEN STAGE.

poetics. The theory and/or practice of poetry; alternatively, an exposition of such theory or practice. O.S.

Poetry (Chicago). One of the first and chief of American 'little magazines'. It began in Chicago in October 1912, edited by Harriet Monroe, with Ezra Pound as foreign correspondent, and had much to do with the modern revolution in poetry; it included work by T. S. Eliot, William Carlos Williams, Wallace Stevens, and Marianne Moore (all largely via Pound) as well as more 'native', middle-western voices like Vachel Lindsay and Carl Sand-

burg. Harriet Monroe, basically sympathetic to the latter tradition, finally lost Pound to Margaret Anderson's rival LITTLE REVIEW. Though the early years are the best, the journal's tradition continues, subsequent editors including Morton D. Zabel and Peter de Vries. M.S.BR.

Bibl: H. Monroe, *A Poet's Life* (N.Y., 1938).

Poetry Bookshop. A bookshop set up in December 1912 at 35 Devonshire Street, London, by Harold Monro (1879–1932), as an adjunct to his middle-of-the-road *Poetry Review* (succeeded by *Poetry and Drama*). His hope of bringing poetry out of the study and 'back into the street' was hardly realized; but the Poetry Bookshop, housed in a splendid 18th-century mansion, played an important part in bringing poetry to those who really wanted it. There were readings; indigent poets were offered lodgings. Most of the readings and poets were bad; but the poets included Robert Frost, Rupert Brooke, T. E. Hulme, Wilfred Owen, and Conrad Aiken. M.S.-S.

Bibl: J. Grant, *Harold Monro and the Poetry Bookshop* (London, 1967).

Poetry Workshop, see GROUP, THE.

Pohl, Frederick (U.S. novelist, *b*.1919), see under SCIENCE FICTION.

Poidebard, Père Antoine (French archaeologist and aviator, 1878–1955), see under AIR PHOTOGRAPHY.

Poincaré, Jules Henri (French mathematician and philosopher, 1854–1912), see under CONVENTIONALISM; PARADOX; THREE-BODY PROBLEM.

point block (often called *tower block*). A tall narrow block placed in a city or landscape so that its simple geometry is clearly discernible, as in Le Corbusier's plan (1922) for the centre of a city for three million people. The geometry is usually that of a rectangular block or a cylinder, and not the pyramidal form of so many SKYSCRAPERS. M.BR.

point estimate, see ESTIMATE.

point four program. A programme of aid to the economically UNDERDEVELOPED states of the world announced as the fourth point in his foreign-policy programme by President Truman in his inaugural address of January 1949. It involved the provision of technical aid and advice in the fields of agriculture, public health, and EDUCATION through bilateral treaties.

D.C.W.

pointillisme, see under NEO-IMPRESSIONISM.

Poirier, Richard (U.S. literary critic and author, *b*.1925), see under MASS CULTURE.

Poisson distribution. In STATISTICS and PROBABILITY THEORY, a DISTRIBUTION on the non-negative integers which attaches probability $\lambda^n e^{-\lambda}/n!$ to the integer n. Both the MEAN and the VARIANCE of the distribution are equal to the value of the PARAMETER λ. The distribution arises naturally in a number of ways, and is often used in applied probability as a model for the occurrence of a rare event in a large number of trials – for example, the number of misprints per page in a newspaper has approximately a Poisson distribution.

R.SI.

Polanyi, Michael (British chemist, sociologist and philosopher, *b*. 1891), see under ENCOUNTER.

Polaris. Long-range ballistic MISSILE of American manufacture, capable of being fired from a submerged submarine and hence largely invulnerable to any hostile pre-emptive strike (see STRATEGIC CAPABILITY). Now rapidly becoming obsolete, Polaris was adopted by the British Navy after the Anglo-American Nassau agreement of January 1963, an event adduced by French opponents of British entry into the EEC as evidence of Britain's dependence on the U.S.A.

D.C.W.

polarization. (1) In OPTICS, the state of affairs in which light or other radiation has different properties in different directions at right angles to the direction of propagation. (2) The process whereby, when an electric FIELD acts on mattter, positive and negative charges separate. (3) The process whereby a social or political group is divided on, for example, a political or religious issue into two diametrically opposed sub-groups, with fewer and fewer members of the group remaining indifferent or holding an intermediate position.

A.S.

polarography. A method of chemical analysis, invented by Heyrovsky around 1920, involving the measurement of current-voltage curves as mercury, which forms one ELECTRODE, drops steadily from a fine capillary through a solution. It can be used to determine dilute concentrations of any metal ION or organic SPECIES which can be reduced at the dropping electrode, as well as to investigate OXIDATION-reduction chemistry in solution.

B.F.

polaroid camera. A camera (invented by Land in 1947) producing positive contact prints a few seconds after exposure, without requiring a darkroom. A roll of positive paper covered with pods filled with developer is stored in the camera. This paper and the exposed film are brought into contact and withdrawn from the camera through pressure rollers which burst the pods. Development is complete in a few seconds, and the print can be peeled off.

M.V.B.

Polish October, the, see under THAW, THE.

Politburo. The key committee of the Russian COMMUNIST Party in charge of policy-making in the Soviet Union, and the focus of any struggle for power between different factions. It was effectively established as a subcommittee of the Party Central Committee in 1919, and consisted then of Lenin, Trotsky, Stalin, Kamenev, and Krestinsky. In 1925 the number of Politburo members was increased to nine and in 1930 to ten. Apparently, after the Great Purge of 1936–38 not all members of the Politburo attended all its meetings. As Khrushchev disclosed in his 'secret speech' of 1956, it was Stalin's practice to invite different members on different occasions. At the 19th Party Congress (in 1952) the Politburo was abolished and replaced by a greatly enlarged Presidium consisting of 25 full members and 11 candidate members. A smaller Bureau was secretly set up, but its existence was only revealed after Stalin's death, when it was abolished. At the same time the Presidium was reduced to ten members, reacquiring the policy-making functions of the old Politburo. L.L.

Bibl: M. Fainsod, *How Russia is Ruled* (Cambridge, Mass., and London, rev. ed., 1963); L. Schapiro, *The Communist Party of the Soviet Union* (London and N.Y., rev. ed., 1970).

political economy. Originally, the arrangement or management of a state as distinct from that of a household (i.e. from *domestic* economy – the original meaning of the unqualified Greek word *oikonomia*). By the end of the 18th century, however, the scope of political economy was limited by a number of writers (Du Pont in France, Verri in Italy, Sir James Steuart and Adam Smith in Great Britain) to problems connected with the *wealth* of a state. Although at this time considerations of the moral, political, and social desirability of economic policies and also the administrative problems involved were still included in treatises on political economy, during the early 19th century they were gradually excluded. Throughout that century there were discussions of the definition of political economy and of other METHODOLOGICAL issues. Attempts were made to define the relation between political economy and other SOCIAL SCIENCES, particularly SOCIOLOGY and politics. Distinctions were made between a *science* and an *art* of political economy, the former being regarded by many economists as a body of pure theory of universal validity, the latter as the application of the theory to the problems of the real world with or without the aid of other social sciences. Towards the end of the century the term political economy was being gradually superseded, in English-speaking countries, by the single word ECONOMICS, partly for convenience, partly in the hope of dissociating the conclusions of economists as scientists from the policies of the politicians they might advise. The change of name may have altered the popular image of economists slightly but it has not abolished the problems or the discussion of scope and method. M.E.A.B.

Bibl: E. Cannan, *A Review of Economic Theory* (London, 1929), ch. 2; J. Schumpeter, *History of Economic Analysis* (London, 1955), part 1, ch. 2.

political science. The study of the organization and conduct of government. This has existed since the time of Aristotle at least. But so long as reflection upon politics remained substantially inseparable from the speculations of 'moral philosophy' about society in general, it could assert no sustained claim to be a discipline in its own right. Only during the later 19th century was its independence adequately established, under British, French, and American leadership. Even then, its subject-matter remained uncomfortably ill-defined. The new discipline was distinguishable from *political philosophy*, however, in having empirical rather than NORMATIVE interests – i.e. in describing things as they are rather than as they ought to be. The comparative study of governments bulked large, and was indicative of a dominant concern with INSTITUTIONS. In the second half of this century, however, there has been a considerable shift of emphasis towards behavioural issues (see BEHAVIOURAL SCIENCES). Political scientists now devote much time to probing into the patterns of social action and behaviour which underlie the operation of political institutions and which condition such phenomena as the competition for POWER or the making and implementation of public decisions. The consequent involvement in matters of attitude and motivation, VALUE and COGNITION, suggests the extent of common ground – and the difficulties of demarcation – with, especially, POLITICAL SOCIOLOGY and SOCIAL PSYCHOLOGY. M.D.B.

Bibl: W. G. Runciman, *Social Science and Political Theory* (Cambridge, 1963); W. J. M. Mackenzie, *Politics and Social Science* (Harmondsworth, 1967).

political sociology. A field of study which came into existence to emphasize the sociological dimensions of politics. Major political issues include ÉLITES (see also POWER ÉLITE); legitimacy and effectiveness (e.g. Max Weber's analysis of three types of authority: traditional, CHARISMATIC, and legal-rational); the relation of economic to political development (e.g. Samuel P. Huntington's study of turbulence in the new states created after World War II, *Political Order in Changing Societies,* 1968); DISTRIBUTIVE JUSTICE (see also RELATIVE

DEPRIVATION); conditions of DEMOCRACY (attempts to relate effective democracy to the degrees of literacy, PARTICIPATION, the character of voluntary associations, the nature of national character, and the strength of tradition in different societies); TOTALITARIANISM; conditions of REVOLUTIONS; and the political ROLE of social groups, such as the working class or the INTELLECTUALS. Behavioural studies have concentrated in three areas: types of party systems (one-party, two-party, multi-party) and the social bases of parties and political division (e.g. CLASS, RELIGION, RACE); the comparative structure of governments (e.g. centralized and decentralized, presidential and parliamentary); and public opinion (see OPINION POLL). D.B.

Bibl: S. Keller, *Beyond the Ruling Class* (N.Y., 1963); S. M. Lipset and S. Rokkan, *Party Systems and Voter Alignments* (London and N.Y., 1967); P. Calvert, *Revolution* (London and N.Y., 1970); S. N. Eisenstadt (ed.), *Political Sociology* (London and N.Y., 1971).

pollen analysis. The recognition and counting of pollen grains preserved in a sample of soil or peat. The technique relies on the fact that the exine (outer coat) of pollen is both distinctive as between SPECIES and resistant to decay. The pollen is extracted from a suitable sample and examined under the microscope, the different species being identified and their relative commonness assessed by counting the different grains within a representative area of the microscope slide. There are two principle applications: the establishment of a general pattern of climatic change within the *neothermal period* (following the end of the Ice Age), and the study of local ENVIRONMENTS to assess the effect of man's activities on the flora. The first application has allowed the definition of a number of vegetational zones which have been calibrated by RADIOCARBON DATING methods, thus providing a sequence by means of which associated archaeological material can be dated. The second application has been extensively used to examine the initial effects of forest clearance and the introduction of a food-producing economy on a virgin area. B.C.

Bibl: K. Faegri and J. Iversen, *Textbook of Pollen Analysis* (Oxford and N.Y., 2nd ed., 1964).

Pollock, Jackson (U.S. painter, 1912–56), see under ABSTRACT EXPRESSIONISM; ACTION PAINTING; ALEATORY; BEAT; EXPRESSIONISM; GREENWICH VILLAGE; NEW YORK SCHOOL.

pollution. Until the 16th century, the verb 'to pollute' and the noun 'pollution' were used mainly in relation to morals and religion; thus pollution was defined as ceremonial impurity or defilement, or as profanation of some thing or place held to be sacred. Though these uses still continue, and PORNOGRAPHY is sometimes described as a form of literary pollution, the term is mainly used today in its later and more physical meaning, i.e. for the condition of being foul, dirty, or seriously contaminated with poisonous or unpleasant substances. ENERGY which, in the form of excessive heat from industry, damages life in rivers and lakes, is rightly called 'thermal pollution'. Excessive noise, another form of energy, is more controversial. At levels found in some places of entertainment it damages the hearing of participants and audience, so it is clearly a pollutant even if those harmed enjoy it (cf. cigarette-smokers). Non-addicts find excessive noise a serious source of environmental deterioration.

Pollution is usually related to the place or medium affected, e.g. air pollution, water pollution, pollution of the ocean. However, the word is often used very loosely to cover the presence of substances considered objectionable even when these are present in such small amounts that no recognizable harm is done to the ENVIRONMENT. Also the term pollution is used to imply the presence of chemical substances produced by man's activities, and not to the natural existence of even higher levels of the same substances. Thus, if a factory discharges lead into a river, this is thought of as polluted even if the lead is diluted down to harmless (though chemically measurable) levels, whereas lead naturally leached from rocks yielding levels which can seriously damage fish may not produce such an emotional reaction.

These loose uses of the word should be discouraged, and it should only be used when damage occurs. Thus polluted air is air which is unpleasant or dangerous to breathe, polluted water has a nasty taste or is harmful to the animals and plants living in it. Air containing the unpleasant or harmful substances at levels which are only detectable by very accurate chemical analysis, and where no discomfort or damage is suffered by man or animals breathing it, should not be considered as polluted, though it may be difficult to be completely certain that absolutely no damage is done. Thus, though gross pollution is easily recognizable, as levels fall the gradation to harmless contamination may be difficult to define. K.M.

Bibl: K. Mellanby, *Pesticides and Pollution* (London, 1969) and *The Biology of Pollution* (London, 1972); Royal Commission on Environmental Pollution (Chairmen:Lord Ashby, Sir Bryan Flowers), *Reports*, 1–5 (London, 1971-76).

Polonskaya, Elizaveta Grigorevna (Russian author, 1890–1969), see under SERAPION BROTHERS.

polycentrism. The process of splintering a unitary organization or movement into independent centres of power; also the resulting diversification. The term was first used by Togliatti to describe the developments in world COMMUNISM after the 20th Congress of the Soviet Communist Party (1956), but it refers now not just to the breakdown of what was once regarded as a political monolith under Stalin, but to the emergence of independent Communist parties in general. The process started with the Soviet-Yugoslav dispute, which produced in Yugoslavia the first Communist state no longer dominated by the ideological authority (see IDEOLOGY) of Moscow. Yugoslavia had acquired its own MARXIST ideological legitimacy in TITOISM. After Stalin's death, the number of splits between Communist parties and Communist states increased and the tendency towards national communism was reinforced, eventually leading to the establishment of independent Communist centres of power, which attempted to take greater account of local conditions in their political line. The divisions within international communism resulted not only in some Communist states (like Albania or Romania) pursuing an independent line and some parties (like the Italian or the

Dutch) insisting on their autonomy, but also in some providing a point of ideological attraction (like MAOISM or CASTROISM). The Sino-Soviet split to some extent polarized the world Communist movement, providing at the same time the opportunity for NEUTRALISM vis-à-vis the dispute. But although in some respects this extended the possibilities for the political autonomy of the national parties, in other respects it limited such possibilities by the need for support from one or other of the powerful antagonists. This need for support, however, and the demand for solidarity amongst Communist parties has not prevented the diversification of Communist ideology and the evolution of national Communist parties, as was shown in the statements made by the French, Italian, and other Communist parties at the Conference of European Communist Parties held in Berlin in 1976. These national parties stressed their independence from the Soviet Union, while, however, giving no hint of any weakening of Leninist (see LENINISM) DEMOCRATIC CENTRALISM, which constitutes a fundamental constraint on the evolution of national Communist parties. L.L.

Bibl: W. Laqueur and L. Labedz (eds.), *Polycentrism* (N.Y., 1962); L. Labedz, *International Communism after Khrushchev* (Cambridge, Mass., 1965).

polydentate ligand, see under CHELATE.

polyembryony. A state of affairs in which an animal regularly gives birth to a number of genetically identical offspring. Although the production of identical twins is the simplest example of polyembryony, the term is usually reserved for the regular production of multiplets such as those of the nine-banded armadillo. Polyembryony arises by fission of the ZYGOTE, which may occur more than once, each daughter CELL giving rise to a whole organism, or to fission of the embryo at a somewhat later stage. It must thus be distinguished from the conventional multiple births in which litter mates resemble each other no more closely than ordinary brothers and sisters (except, of course, in age). Each member of such a litter is the product of a distinct egg cell fertilized by a distinct spermatozoon. P.M.

polyethylene, see POLYTHENE.

polygene. When a single characteristic is influenced by GENES at many LOCI, its inheritance is said to be polygenic or multifactorial. The genes concerned have sometimes been called polygenes, but they probably differ from other genes only in having a small effect on the characteristic under study.   J.M.S.

Bibl: D. S. Falconer, *Introduction to Quantitative Genetics* (Edinburgh and N.Y., 1960).

polymer. Any material consisting of MACROMOLECULES formed by the linking of many similar chemical units into long chains. NYLON, POLYTHENE, and many other synthetic PLASTIC substances, as well as PROTEINS and other materials vital to life, are all polymers. Prediction *a priori* (see APRIORISM) of the properties of polymers from the fundamental laws of PHYSICS is very difficult, because of the great structural complexity of these systems. Therefore polymer science is interdisciplinary, and techniques from BIOLOGY, CHEMISTRY, and ENGINEERING are being employed to understand, e.g., the physical basis of inheritance (see DNA under NUCLEIC ACID) and the RHEOLOGY of bulk polymers such as wood.   M.V.B.

polymorphism. The presence in a single population of more than one genetically distinct type, each at a frequency too high to be explained by repeated MUTATION alone. The study of polymorphism is important for an understanding of EVOLUTION, which depends on populations being variable.   J.M.S.

polynucleotide, see under NUCLEIC ACID.

polypeptide, see under PEPTIDE.

polyploid (noun or adjective). (A CELL) containing more than two sets of CHROMOSOMES. In an *autopolyploid* the chromosomes all come from a single SPECIES; in an *allopolyploid* from two or more species. Allopolyploids arise by hybridization between species followed by a doubling of the chromosome number. They are often sexually fertile, even if the DIPLOID hybrid is not. The process has been important in the origin of wild and domestic plant varieties, including wheat and cotton, but is rare or absent in animals.   J.M.S.

polyrhythm. The mixture of markedly differing rhythms, done in such a way as to be a striking feature of the music rather than a mere incidental; in particular, the combination of rhythms based upon different pulses or metres. Dating from the Middle Ages and brought to a point of perfection by the Elizabethan madrigalists, polyrhythm became relatively unimportant in the music of the 18th and 19th centuries, though examples occur in the finale of Mozart's Oboe Quartet and the ballroom scene in *Don Giovanni*. In the 20th century composers as diverse as Charles Ives, Michael Tippett, and Olivier Messiaen have been fascinated by the exploration of polyrhythm.   A.H.

polysynthetic (or *incorporating*). In comparative LINGUISTICS, adjectives sometimes applied to a type of AGGLUTINATING language (e.g. Eskimo) which displays a very high degree of synthesis in its word forms, single words typically containing as much structural information as entire sentences in ISOLATING languages.   D.C.

polysystemicism, see under FIRTHIAN.

polytechnics, see under TERTIARY EDUCATION.

polytheism, see under PANTHEISM; THEISM.

polythene (or *polyethylene* or *alkathene*). A synthetic POLYMER whose chemical inertness and flexibility, and the ease with which it can be shaped, result in a variety of industrial and domestic applications (plastic bags, buckets, etc.).   M.V.B.

polytonality. The simultaneous combination of several tonalities, each instrumental line adhering to one key regardless of possible conflict with other lines. Used occasionally in the past for humorous purposes (e.g. Mozart's Musical Joke), it was much exploited in scores by Milhaud (e.g. the Serenade in the 3rd Symphony), Bartók, Stravinsky, Holst (e.g. the Terzetto for Flute, Oboe, and Viola), and others. Like BITONALITY, it serves to preserve some of the stability conveyed by traditional tonality, while adding harmonic bite.   A.H.

polywater. A recently-discovered dense semi-PLASTIC material formed near the surface of fine glass tubes on which water has been condensed. Polywater is probably an effect of impurities leached from the glass, rather than an ALLOTROPE of water as originally believed.　　　M.V.B.

Ponge, Francis (French poet and essayist, *b.* 1899), see under TEL QUEL.

Pant-Aven. School of French painting, centred on the small Breton town of that name, which was much frequented by artists in the late 19th century, notably Gauguin around 1886–89. With a few younger painters, including Émile Bernard and Paul Sérusier, he there established his characteristic way of painting Breton subjects, using simplified outlines, flat two-dimensional surfaces, and clear colours. This SYNTHETISM became, through Sérusier, the launching platform for the NABIS.　　　J.W.
　　Bibl: C. Chassé, *Gauguin et le groupe de Pont-Aven* (Paris, 1921).

pop. An abbreviation of 'popular' used in the arts since the 1950s to signify work employing aesthetic or symbolic elements calculated to appeal to a modern mass audience. The basis of the calculation is normally commercial, though the use made of the elements is often not. Originating in some measure as an updated and industrialized version of the FOLK concept, it differs in its overtones both from the German *volkstümlich* and from the French *populaire,* and is a purely Anglo-Saxon term which other cultures have had to import. The three main usages are:
　　(1) *Pop music.* The dominant popular musical genre developed in England and (white) America in the 1950s, it was based on the FOLK MUSIC revival, rock-and-roll dynamics (see RHYTHM-AND-BLUES), electrically amplified guitars (which allowed small groups to make a very loud noise), the portable TRANSISTOR set, and the long-playing gramophone record which took its sounds to avid young consumers all over the globe. With Elvis Presley as the prototypical pop singer, it acquired the character of a minor socio-cultural revolution with the establishment of such groups as the BEATLES and the ROLLING STONES, writing their own often original lyrics and music for skilled record executives to put together and market.
　　(2) *Pop poetry.* A type of easily intelligible poem, akin to the pop lyric and often appealing to the same age-group, which is written primarily for public reading (often in combination with JAZZ; see JAZZ POETRY) and is associated particularly with the LIVERPOOL POETS whose rise followed that of the Beatles.
　　(3) *Pop art.* A term first used in the mid-1950s by the critic Lawrence Alloway to describe such elements as flags, jukeboxes, packaging, comic strips, badges, and chromium-plated radiator grilles, then transferred to the often sophisticated, startling, ironic, or nostalgic constructions which highbrow artists began to make out of them. Based largely on the visual trappings of American industry (including the entertainment industry) and contemporary FOLKLORE (from Batman to Marilyn Monroe) much the same symbols served both British (Richard Hamilton, David Hockney, Peter Blake) and American painters (Jim Dine, Andy Warhol, Roy Lichtenstein) who throughout the 1960s used a DADA-like COLLAGE technique and the silk-screen printing process to convey their many-levelled visions. Sometimes isolating the most mundane objects – e.g. the soup-tin or the mass-produced hamburger – they were echoed by sculptors like Claes Oldenburg, who made inflated versions of these in all kinds of materials. Lettering and sign-language were further elements which sometimes became dominant. Though the term remained Anglo-American a similar imagery and approach could be found among continental artists associated with NOUVEAU RÉALISME, and it has also affected the cinema, notably certain films of Jean-Luc Godard and the Beatles' cartoon film *The Yellow Submarine.* Fashion, packaging, and GRAPHIC DESIGN quickly conformed, the whole complex sometimes being known as the *pop scene.*　　　J.W.
　　Bibl: G. Melly, *Revolt into Style* (London, 1970; N.Y., 1971).

Popova, Liubov (Russian painter, 1889–1924), see under CUBO-FUTURISM.

Popper, Sir **Karl Raimund** (Austrian-British philosopher, *b.* 1902), see under ENCOUNTER; HISTORICISM; META-HISTORY; OPEN SOCIETY; POPPERIAN;

SITUATIONAL ANALYSIS; SOCIAL ENGIN-
EERING.

Popperian. Adjective referring to Karl
Popper (b. Vienna, 1902), Professor of
Logic and Scientific Method at London
University 1949–69, and especially to his
views on (1) the nature of scientific procedure and (2) the philosophical foundations for social reform.

(1) Popper's arguments for *deductivism*, or the *hypothetico-deductive
method*, are expressed in *The Logic of Scientific Discovery* (1934; English translation 1959). He contends that a scientific
theory can never be accorded more than
provisional acceptance, and that even this
cannot properly depend upon VERIFICA-
TION of the kind made orthodox by Bacon
and Mill. Their *inductivism* (see INDUC-
TION) suggests that the scientist must
accumulate and classify particular observations and thereafter generalize the regularities which these exhibit. Popper
retorts that no number of cases of *A* being
B can establish that all *A*s are *B*. Yet he
also notes that such universal statements,
though unprovable, remain in principle
disprovable. According to this principle of
falsifiability, a theory holds until it is disproved; and falsification, not verification,
is the appropriate object of the observational and experimental procedures of
science. Enlargement of our provisional
knowledge begins with the conversion of
hunches or other imaginative insights into
hypotheses. Then, once the conditions for
their falsification have been established by
the application of deductive LOGIC, such
hypotheses must be tested through sustained search for negative instances.

(2) The same distrust of dogmatism
pervades Popper's more political writings
such as *The Open Society* (1945) and *The
Poverty of Historicism* (1957). He argues
that social theories based on mistaken
notions of certainty (e.g. 'scientific' MARX-
ISM) breed AUTHORITARIANISM and
unrealistic blueprints for total change;
they embody a 'holistic' (see HOLISM)
insistence that the individual possesses
value only in so far as he subserves the
needs of the whole. To this Popper
opposes his own brand of METHODO-
LOGICAL INDIVIDUALISM, which seeks to
understand 'all collective phenomena as
due to the actions, interactions, aims,
hopes, and thoughts of individual men,

and as due to traditions created and preserved by individual men'. Popper's preference is for programmes of 'piecemeal
SOCIAL ENGINEERING' that accord not
only with individuals' competing aspirations but also with the spirit of critical
self-scrutiny involved in the principle of
'falsification' outlined above.   M.D.B.

Bibl: B. Magee, *Popper* (London and
N.Y., 1973).

popular culture, see MASS CULTURE.

Popular Front. A COMMUNIST-inspired
policy in the 1930s, aimed at bringing
about the collaboration of the LEFT and
CENTRE parties against RIGHT-WING movements and regimes. It was launched in July
1935 at the 7th Congress of the COMIN-
TERN, after the abandonment of the policy
of attacking social democrats (see SOCIAL
DEMOCRACY) as 'social FASCISTS', which
had contributed to the victory and consolidation of power by the NAZIS in Germany. The new policy of broad Left
alliances brought Popular Front governments to power in France and Spain in
1936, and in Chile in 1938. In France the
Popular Front government of Léon Blum
(which did not include Communists,
although it was to some extent supported
by them) was replaced by that of Daladier
after the coalition broke down in April
1938. In Spain the electoral victory of the
Popular Front under President Azaña
resulted in a CONFRONTATION with the
Spanish Right and the civil war which
ended in 1939 with the victory of Franco.

Generally, the Popular Front policy
came to an end after the conclusion of the
Nazi-Soviet pact (August 1939). The new
Comintern line, radically changed, lasted
until the attack of Hitler on the Soviet
Union in June 1941. This attack once
again led the Communists to seek cooperation with other parties in an 'anti-fascist
front'.

Since World War II the policy of collaboration with SOCIALIST and 'BOURGEOIS'
parties has undergone a variety of
modifications, particularly since the
emergence of POLYCENTRISM. It was
abandoned in 1947 with the establishment
of the COMINFORM and a new tough
('Zhdanov') line, but resumed by various
Communist parties after Stalin's death,
and particularly since the Soviet
REHABILITATION of Tito (see TITOISM) in

1955. This tendency has continued. The French Communist Party has entered into an electoral pact with the Socialist Party (and other groups) under a 'common programme'; the Italian Communist Party has proposed a governmental collaboration with the Christian Democrats (see CHRISTIAN DEMOCRACY) on the basis of 'historic compromise' and entered into coalitions with the Socialists at the local-government level; the Spanish Communist Party has called for a coalition of parties ranging from monarchists to Communists to rule Spain now that Franco is dead. Although there is no longer a single directing centre or a uniform Communist strategy in different countries, coalition tactics play an increasingly important part in Communist practice. Non-communist parties have been reserved in their response to these tactics, e.g. in Italy, because of doubts concerning the Communist Party's commitment to PLURALISM and its independence from Moscow. L.L.

Bibl: D. R. Brower, *The New Jacobins: The French Communist Party and the Popular Front* (Ithaca, 1968); *Journal of Contemporary History*, special issue on *Popular Front* (no. 3, 1970).

population biology. The study of all aspects of the structure and function of populations, in so far as they can be distinguished as comprising the unit of organization between the organism and the ECOSYSTEM. The subject includes the discipline of POPULATION GENETICS; population ECOLOGY, including DEMOGRAPHY; and many aspects of SOCIOBIOLOGY. E.O.W.

population genetics. The study of genetic variation and change in populations; fundamental for an understanding of EVOLUTION, and also of animal and plant breeding. J.M.S.

Bibl: J. F. Crow and M. Kimura, *An Introduction to Population Genetics Theory* (N.Y., 1970).

populism. The promotion of political ends independently of existing parties and INSTITUTIONS by appealing to the people to exercise direct pressure on governments. As Edward Shils has pointed out, populism identifies the will of the people with morality and justice, puts this 'will' above all other social standards and mechanisms, and insists on a direct relationship between people and government. It is usually accompanied by a simple belief in the virtues of the people, which are contrasted with the corrupt character of the degenerate ruling CLASS or of any other group resented because of its dominant political or economic position or social STATUS. Populism also tends to see conspiracy and manipulation by such groups as directed against 'the people', a tendency which can be powerfully reinforced by racial or ethnic hostility.

Populism originated among the Russian radical intelligentsia (see RADICALISM; INTELLECTUALS) during the 1860s with the *Narodniks* (Populists), who believed that Russia could avoid going through the CAPITALIST stage and could establish SOCIALISM directly, on the basis of the existing peasant COMMUNES. In the 1870s the Narodnik students went to the countryside ('to the people') to propagate REVOLUTION. In the 1880s they organized the Land and Freedom Party which later split into the People's Will (*Narodnava Volva*) and the Black Distribution (*Chornyi Peredel*) organizations. The latter eventually evolved into the SOCIAL DEMOCRATIC movement.

Russian revolutionary populism was based on the ideas of Tkachev and Bakunin, liberal populism on those of Herzen and Lavrov. At first 'populism' referred to the belief that revolution must be the work of the people (which in Russia then meant peasants) and not just of the militant revolutionary minority. Towards the end of the 19th century, Russian MARXISTS began to designate the approach to revolutionary action by all their non-Marxist revolutionary rivals as 'populist' and this became the accepted usage.

The political, social, and economic ideas regarded as populist have also varied from place to place. In the U.S.A. the adjective was applied first to the Populist Party, which was formed in 1891 to defend agricultural interests, and advocated free coinage of silver and governmental control of MONOPOLIES. The tradition of early American populism passed on to Senator La Follette's Progressive Party; it manifested itself later in the NEW DEAL, in the Socialist Party of Norman Thomas, and in other similar groups. On the American RIGHT, populism could be seen after 1945 in the appeal of such figures as Senator Joseph McCarthy and Governor George Wallace. The emergence of the NEW LEFT was hailed by the late Paul Goodman as a 'global triumph of populism'.

Populism can be detected in the peasant movements of Eastern Europe before 1939, in FASCISM and NAZISM, and in the 'liberation movements' of the THIRD WORLD after 1945. It can be rural or urban, peasant or middle-class; it can be led by the intelligentsia or by frustrated PETIT-BOURGEOIS elements; it can be class-conscious or NATIONALIST, or both; and it can be LEFT or Right. But despite its vagueness and its specific political significance, it retains its HEURISTIC value as a CONCEPT, because of recognizable and important common traits.   L.L.

Bibl: F. Venturi, *Roots of Revolution* (London and N.Y., 1960); G. Ionescu and E. Gellner (eds.), *Populism* (London and N.Y., 1969).

pornography. Visual, written, or recorded communications designed primarily to arouse sexual excitement in the pornographer, an intended audience, or both. This apparently uncontentious definition proves in practice, like all definitions that hinge on motives (or incorporate such words as 'primarily'), exceedingly difficult to apply: those for whom sex is a TABOO subject tend to impute pornographic aims to all who break their taboo, while those for whom it is a rallying cry will cheerfully equate a modicum of literary or graphic skill with high aesthetic intent, or take at face value the most impudent scientific pretensions.

If pornography is defined in terms of motives, *erotica* may be defined in terms of results: X's library of erotica consists of those books which excite X, and may include items which few people would class as pornography. A further distinction is that the excitement induced by pornography is purely genital (and culminates typically in masturbation), whereas erotic art or literature may evoke also feelings of tenderness or a sense of beauty (and is more likely to lead to coitus). Not surprisingly, the consumers of commercial pornography are predominantly male; with this important qualification, and within the limits of commercial viability, it caters for every variety of sexual taste.

Attitudes to pornography reflect a society's or individual's degree of PERMISSIVENESS in sexual matters, and often of political RADICALISM also – although quasi-REICHIAN equations of pornography with REVOLUTION are perhaps little more than rhetorical flourishes, as are statements like 'War is the ultimate obscenity' and phrases like Geoffrey Gorer's 'pornography of death' (a critique of the view that death is something obscene, to be swept under the carpet). Efforts to legislate pornography out of existence have always failed, not least because of the essentially subjective nature of all attempts to define it – including, presumably, this one.   O.S.

portfolio selection. The process whereby investors, whether individuals or financial institutions, choose a range of investments in order to diversify their risks and to balance their need for income with CAPITAL appreciation. The investment set chosen might include various types and sectors of equity share, fixed-interest government bonds, property, commodity futures, or precious metals. Quantitative techniques have been applied to the problem, following pioneering work by H. Markowitz.
                                                                R.I.T.
Bibl: H. Markowitz, *Portfolio Selection* (London and N.Y., 1959).

positive neutrality, see under NON-ALIGNMENT.

positivism. The view that all true knowledge is scientific, in the sense of describing the coexistence and succession of observable phenomena. So named by Comte, it was the leading principle of his comprehensive philosophical system, which took the unsophisticated form, for the most part, of an encyclopedic CLASSIFICATION of the findings of scientific enquiry. Positivism is a scientifically oriented form of EMPIRICISM. The word is now most commonly used as an abbreviation for LOGICAL POSITIVISM. In view of its close association with PHENOMENALISM and REDUCTIONISM generally, it is sometimes opposed to REALISM, particularly in the interpretation of the nature of the unobservable theoretical entities that occur in scientific discourse.   A.Q.

positron. The positively charged anti-particle (see ANTI-MATTER) corresponding to the ELECTRON.　　　　M.V.B.

post-capitalist, post-economic, see POST-INDUSTRIAL SOCIETY.

posterior distribution, see under STATISTICS.

post-experience education, see under PERMANENT EDUCATION.

post-experience training, see under IN-SERVICE TRAINING.

Post-Impressionism. Now largely defunct English term for modern French art from IMPRESSIONISM to World War I. It derived from the Post-Impressionist Exhibitions organized by Roger Fry at the Grafton Gallery, London, in 1910 and 1912, and was used to embrace all the artists revealed there, i.e. the NEO-IMPRESSIONISTS, Gauguin and the PONT-AVEN school, Cézanne, the FAUVES, and the early CUBISTS, and also (by adoption) the work of van Gogh. Hence there is no equivalent in German or French.　　　　J.W.
Bibl: A. C. H. Bell, *Since Cézanne* (London and N.Y., 1922); C. J. Holmes, *Notes on the Post-Impressionist Painters* (London, 1910).

post-industrial society. A term coined by the American sociologist Daniel Bell to describe the new SOCIAL STRUCTURES evolving in industrial societies in the latter part of the 20th century which (he believes) point the way to the emergence of a new form of society in the U.S.A., Japan, the U.S.S.R., and Western Europe in the next century. What Bell calls the 'axial principle' of post-industrial society is 'the centrality of theoretical knowledge as the source of innovation and of policy formation for the society'. Economically, it will be marked by the change from a goods-producing to a service economy; occupationally, by the pre-eminence of the professional and technical CLASS; and in decision-making by the creation of a new 'intellectual technology'.
The same term has been used by other writers with a different emphasis on the features which they believe will mark post-industrial society, e.g. the search by

young people for a world beyond materialism (Kenneth Kenniton, Paul Goodman); or the displacement, as a result of technological change, of the working class from the role assigned to it by MARXISTS as the historic agent of change in society (various NEO-MARXISTS). Other terms which have been used to convey the same idea of the emergence of a new form of society are 'post-economic'; 'post-capitalist' (Ralf Dahrendorf); 'post-maturity' (W. W. Rostow); and 'technetronic' (Z. Brzezinski).　　　　A.L.C.B.
Bibl: D. Bell, *The Coming of Post-Industrial Society* (N.Y., 1973; London, 1974).

post-modernism, see under MODERNISM.

post-painterly abstraction, see under MINIMAL ART.

postulational method, see under AXIOMATICS.

potassium-argon dating, see under DATING.

potential. A mathematical representation of a FIELD in PHYSICS. In a field of force due to GRAVITATION, for example, the POTENTIAL ENERGY of a body at any point is obtained by multiplying its mass by the value of the potential there. Other potentials describe ELECTROMAGNETIC forces, and the velocity field in a flowing fluid.　　　　M.V.B.

potential energy. The ENERGY that a system has as a result of its position in a FIELD of force. For example, a spring which has been compressed or extended against its elastic forces, and a pair of positive electric charges pushed together against their mutual repulsion, are both systems whose potential energy has increased, because they are capable of doing work while returning to their original states. On the other hand, an apple that has fallen to the ground has lost GRAVITATIONAL potential energy, because work must be done on it to return it to its original height.　M.V.B.

Potsdam. The summer residence of the Hohenzollerns, now a town in East Germany, where Churchill, Roosevelt, and Stalin met from 17 July to 2 August 1945

after the German capitulation. This was the third and last SUMMIT conference in the series TEHERAN, YALTA, Potsdam. The main issues were again reparations and Polish control of the ODER-NEISSE territories. The conference also established machinery for the drafting of peace treaties to be concluded with the minor belligerents on the AXIS side, Bulgaria, Romania, Finland, Hungary, and Italy.
D.C.W.

Bibl: H. Feis, *Between War and Peace: the Potsdam Conference* (Princeton, 1960).

Pougny, Jean, see PUNI, IVAN.

Poujadism. A set of attitudes derived from a political movement founded by Pierre Poujade, a French small-town shopkeeper, in 1953. These embodied lower-middle-class, PETIT BOURGEOIS resentment at the increasing interference of the State by taxation, investigation of tax evasion, and other regulatory power over their economic freedom of action. Poujadism was essentially hostile to the State as anything more than the provider of LAW AND ORDER, and therefore to MODERNIZATION or any encouragement of large-scale labour or business organization. The Poujadist Association for Defence of Shopkeepers and Artisans won 50 seats and three million votes in the 1956 parliamentary elections, but disintegrated in the political crisis of 1958 with the advent of GAULLISM.   D.C.W.

Poulenc, Francis (French composer, 1899–1963), see under SIX, LES.

POUM. Acronym for *Partido Obrero de Unificacion Marxista,* a Spanish group independent of the Spanish Communist Party (see COMMUNISM; MARXISM) with considerable strength in Catalonia. Its opposition to the Popular Front government established in Spain in 1936 made it a target for the TERRORISM organized by the Russian SECRET POLICE under cover of the Spanish Communist Party. The forcible suppression of POUM in May 1937 and the murder of its leader, Andrés Nin, were immortalized by George Orwell (who fought alongside the POUM; see also ORWELLIAN) in *Homage to Catalonia* (London, 1938).   D.C.W.

Pound, Ezra (U.S. poet and editor, 1885–1972), see under BLACK MOUNTAIN; BLAST; CRITERION, THE; EGOIST, THE; IMAGISM; INTELLECTUALS; LITTLE REVIEW, THE; NEW AGE, THE; OBJECTIVISM; POETRY (CHICAGO); VORTICISM.

Pound, Roscoe (U.S. jurist, 1870–1964), see under SOCIOLOGICAL JURISPRUDENCE.

Pousseur, Henri (French composer, *b.* 1929), see under ALEATORY.

powder metallurgy. The production from a powder, without melting, of compact pieces of metal in a usable form. The process, first demonstrated by William Wollaston at the end of the 18th century, involves pressing and heating the powder in the required shape so that SINTERING causes the PARTICLES to adhere strongly. It is of value particularly for metals such as tungsten, which cannot be melted under commercial conditions. The incorporation of a second substance, e.g. graphite in bearings, may also be readily effected. B.F.

Powell, Anthony (British novelist, *b.* 1905), see under ROMAN-FLEUVE.

Powell, Enoch (British politician, *b.* 1912), see under RIGHT, THE.

Powell, Michael James David (British numerical analyst, *b.* 1936), see under GRADIENT METHODS.

power. One of the central CONCEPTS of political theory, which sociologists have sought to define by distinguishing it from *authority* on the one hand, and from *force* on the other. *Power* is the ability of its holder to exact compliance or obedience of other individuals to his *will,* on whatsoever basis. Yet, as Rousseau observed in *The Social Contract* (Book I, chapter 3), 'The strongest man is never strong enough to be always master unless he transforms his power into right and obedience into duty.'

Authority is an attribute of social organization – a family, a corporation, a university, a government – in which command inheres in the recognition of some greater competence lodged either in the person or in the office itself. Relations between states – in the absence of any com-

PRAGMATISM

mon framework of law or consensus – are usually power relations. Relations between individuals and groups, if regularized and subject to rules, traditional or legal, tend to be authority relations.

Force is a compulsion, sometimes physical (when it then becomes violence), invoked by wielders of power and authority. Force may be utilized in support of authority, as the spanking of a child or the imprisonment of a felon. And the threat of force often lies behind the use of power to enforce a power-holder's will. Yet there are examples of the use of power (i.e. will) in history without force, such as Gandhi's *satyagraha* (NON-VIOLENT RESISTANCE) to British authority.

In political theory, the State alone, among modern associations, can make legitimate use of police and military force in the exercise of its authority. In contemporary social theory, the important component in the exercise of authority is *legitimacy,* the rightful rule or exercise of power, based on some principle (e.g. consent) jointly accepted by the ruler and the ruled.   D.B.
Bibl: B. de Jouvenel, tr. J. F. Huntington, *Power* (London, rev. ed., 1952); H. D. Lasswell and A. Kaplan, *Power and Society* (New Haven, 1950; London, 1952).

power élite. A phrase coined by the American sociologist C. Wright Mills for those who stand at the heads of the major institutional hierarchies of modern society – the corporations, the military, and the State – and who, through their pooled interests, become 'an intricate set of overlapping cliques [sharing] decisions having at least national consequences'. The theory has been criticized by MARXISTS for its focus on ÉLITES, rather than on CLASSES, and by LIBERALS for preaching a conspiracy theory of POWER; for confusing *arenas* of action (e.g. the political system) with INSTITUTIONS; for loosely asserting a shared degree of interests between institutional sectors, rather than organized groups; and for failing to focus on decision-making and decisions, rather than on institutional hierarchies.   D.B.
Bibl: C. W. Mills, *The Power Elite* (London and N.Y., 1956); G. W. Domhoff and H. B. Ballard (eds.), *C. Wright Mills and the Power Elite* (Boston, 1968).

power politics. An emotive phrase applied to the employment of calculations of comparative POWER and influence made by those responsible for the major powers' conduct of foreign policy, as in the phrase 'playing power politics'. Critics of power politics wish to substitute for it the rule of ETHICS, law, and justice in international relations; others hold that, so long as the world is divided into independent sovereign states, there is no alternative to international relations being based upon considerations of power, and that it is self-deception to pretend otherwise.
      A.L.C.B.
Bibl: I. Claude, *Power and International Relations* (N.Y., 1962); M. Wight, *Power Politics* (London, 1946, rev. ed., 1977).

Pozner, Vladimir (Russian poet, *b.* 1905), see under SERAPION BROTHERS.

PPBS (programme, planning, and budgeting system; also known as *programme budgeting*). A method of determining the allocation of resources in the PUBLIC SECTOR organizations, such as EDUCATION, local authorities, and the social services, in which profit criteria are inappropriate. In contrast to the traditional budgeting of expenditure by cost item and spending department, PPBS identifies expenditures with the basic programmes of activity. Originating in the U.S. Treasury, the methods have been employed (under various names) in many organizations, including the Greater London Council. See also COST-BENEFIT ANALYSIS. R.I.T.
Bibl: D. Novick, *Program Budgeting* (London and Cambridge, Mass., 1965).

PR. Abbreviation for either PROPORTIONAL REPRESENTATION or PUBLIC RELATIONS.

practical criticism, see under LEAVISITE.

pragmatics, see under SEMANTICS.

pragmatism. In PHILOSOPHY, a version of EMPIRICISM, developed in the U.S.A. by C. S. Peirce, William James, and John Dewey, which interprets the meaning and justification of our beliefs in terms of their 'practical' effects or content. Peirce's pragmatic maxim was a theory of MEANING which identified the content of a PROPOSITION with the experiencable

491

difference between its being true and its being false. James put forward a pragmatic theory of TRUTH as that which it is ultimately satisfying to believe, either because the expectations a true belief excites are actually fulfilled or, in the less empirical case of the propositions of THEOLOGY and METAPHYSICS, because they contribute to the satisfactoriness of, and effectiveness in, the conduct of life. Dewey stressed that aspect of pragmatism which holds knowledge to be an instrument for action, rather than an object of disinterested contemplation. In general, pragmatists emphasize the conventional character of the CONCEPTS and beliefs with which we seek to understand the world as opposed to the 'intellectualism' which sees them as a passive reflection of the fixed, objective structure of things. An incentive to this view has been the idea that mutually inconsistent scientific theories can each be compatible with all the known empirical data so that only non-logical features of simplicity, convenience, and UTILITY can provide a reason for selection between them. A.Q.

Bibl: A. Rorty (ed.), *Pragmatic Philosophy* (N.Y., 1966); A. J. Ayer, *The Origins of Pragmatism* (London and San Francisco, 1968).

Prague. The capital of Czechoslovakia and the scene of three major crises of 20th-century European history, each of which is frequently named after it.

(1) Prague, 1939. In March 1939 Hitler ordered the occupation by force of the capital and the rest of Czechoslovakia, which had already been truncated by the MUNICH agreement of 1938. Apart from the consequences for the Czech people, who spent the next six years under German 'protection', this new and undisguised act of aggression ended any illusions that Hitler would be satisfied with the incorporation into the Third Reich of territories with a German-speaking population, and confronted the other powers with the choice between acquiescing in Hitler's domination of Europe or steeling themselves to fight in order to prevent it. A.L.C.B.

(2) Prague, 1948. In February 1948 the Czechoslovak COMMUNIST Party, with its adjunct the Slovak Communist Party, seized power and replaced the coalition government, in which they were already the largest single element, with a virtual single-party dictatorship. The coup was achieved by a combination of mass DEMONSTRATIONS and threats, while technically remaining within the forms of the constitution; the term *coup de Prague* has come to be used generally for any quasi-constitutional change backed by street pressures. As in the case of (1), apart from the consequences for the people of Czechoslovakia themselves, Prague 1948 ended illusions in the West that the Soviet Union would be satisfied with anything less than complete control through local Communist regimes of the countries within her sphere of influence in Eastern and Central Europe, and led to an intensification of the COLD WAR. R.C.; A.L.C.B.

(3) Prague, 1968, refers to two developments which attracted worldwide attention. The first, known as the *Prague Spring* (from an annual music festival in the capital) was the attempt by reforming elements in the Czechoslovak Communist Party, with growing public support, to liberalize domestic affairs ('SOCIALISM with a human face') and achieve some international freedom of action without abandoning overall Party control or Warsaw Pact membership. Replacement of Antonin Novotný by the more open-minded Slovak, Alexander Dubček, as Party leader in January earned the backing of Slovak autonomists for a cautious reform programme. The second development was the open intervention of the Soviet Union to suppress the reform movement, which led to the invasion of Czechoslovakia by Soviet armed forces in August 1968 and the replacement of Dubček by the conservative Gustáv Husák eight months later. The Party Congress held secretly during the invasion in Prague-Vysočany was then annulled, censorship reimposed, the ideas of the REFORMISTS abjured in favour of so-called NORMALIZATION, and their spokesmen decried as REVISIONIST or counter-revolutionary. D.V.

Bibl: (3) Z. Zeman, *Prague Spring* (Harmondsworth, 1969); G. Golan, *The Czechoslovak Reform Movement* (London, 1971).

Prague School. In LINGUISTICS, a group of LINGUISTS (notably R. Jakobson and N. Trubetskoy) working in and around Prague in the late 1920s and early 1930s.

Their primary contribution was the formulation of an influential theory of PHONOLOGY in which sounds were analysed into sets of distinctive oppositions. More recently, a neo-Prague school has concentrated on developing syntactic theory in terms of the SAUSSURIAN notion of functionally contrastive constituents of sentences (see SYNTAGMATIC AND PARADIGMATIC): this is known as *functional sentence perspective (FSP)*. D.C.

Bibl: J. Vachek (ed.), *A Prague School Reader in Linguistics* (London and Bloomington, 1966).

Prague Spring, see under PRAGUE (3).

Pratella, Francesco (Italian composer, 1880–1955), see under FUTURISM.

Pravda (Truth). A Soviet daily newspaper, the official organ of the Soviet COMMUNIST Party. It was founded in 1912 and published legally in Czarist Russia until 1914, when it was banned because of its 'revolutionary defeatism'. It reappeared after the 1917 February revolution and since October 1917 has been the leading Soviet journal. Published in Moscow since 1918, it appears seven days a week, and its editorials provide the best indication of the current Party line. Its editors have included Stalin and Bukharin; its estimated circulation is 8,300,000 – slightly higher than that of IZVESTIA. L.L.

precasting, see under CONCRETE.

precession, see under GYROSCOPE.

precisionism. A name given to American REALIST painting in the 1920s and 1930s that combined ideas and techniques of photography and CUBISM in its representation of the contemporary industrial landscape. So-called Precisionists Charles Sheeler, Charles Demuth, and Preston Dickinson painted machine forms and domestic architecture with dryness, clean detail, and sharp focus that occasionally bordered on abstraction (see ABSTRACT ART). A.K.W.

Bibl: B. Rose, *American Art Since 1900* (London and N.Y., 1967); S. Hunter, *American Art of the 20th Century* (N.Y., 1972).

precognition. The direct awareness of future events, or true prophecy, as contrasted with the rational prediction which derives beliefs about the future, which there is good reason to think true, from the present state of things together with more or less well-confirmed laws of nature. Memory, as distinct from apparent memory, implies that the event remembered really has happened. Likewise precognition implies that the event precognized really will happen. It can be argued that precognition is impossible in so far as the notion of knowledge that is logically included in it entails (see ENTAILMENT) that the state of knowing is caused by the fact known. For if there were precognition a future event would have to cause a present one and a cause can never be temporally subsequent to its effect. This, however, is a semantic point. It does not mean that people cannot have true, uninferred beliefs about the future but only that, since this cannot be causally explained, it cannot be called knowledge. A.Q.

preconscious. In psychoanalytic theory (see PSYCHOANALYSIS), a word used in two ways. (1) To refer to thoughts, which, although not actually present in CONSCIOUSNESS, are nevertheless capable of being brought into consciousness by ordinary recall and effort. By contrast, UNCONSCIOUS thoughts can be recovered only – if at all – by the aid of technical methods, such as PSYCHOTHERAPY and psychoanalysis (see also REPRESSION). (2) To refer to the part of the mental system, or apparatus, that contains these preconscious thoughts. B.A.F.

predicate calculus. One of the two chief LOGICAL CALCULI, consisting of a formal system of notation, AXIOMS, and rules for handling QUANTIFICATION. See also AXIOMATICS. R.G.

prediction theory, see under EXTRAPOLATION.

pre-emptive strike, see under STRATEGIC CAPABILITY.

prefabrication (or *industrialized building*). The manufacture of building elements for subsequent assembly at the site in an attempt to shift the major effort to the controlled conditions of the factory. The factory may be either a distant plant making complete bathroom units, for instance, or an enclosure on or near the site making CLADDING panels of precast CONCRETE.

Prefabrication in any serious sense began in the 19th century with the manufacture of cast- and wrought-iron structural members, particularly where these, together with glass, were marketed to provide complete greenhouses. After 1945 systems of industrialized building were developed in which a coordinated range of components could be assembled to provide whole schools or flats. In the U.S.S.R. and Eastern Europe the method was widely used for housing. Industrialized systems, however, have not yet shown the economic benefits claimed for them, while the visual effect has frequently been undistinguished.   M.BR.

Bibl: B. Kelly, *The Prefabrication of Houses* (London and N.Y., 1951).

preference. An international trading arrangement between two countries or more whereby one or both gives favourable treatment to the other(s) by removing or lowering its existing tariffs. Preferences run counter to an alternative principle in trading arrangements, which argues that trading arrangements should be entirely non-discriminatory, a principle enshrined in GATT. Preferences have become highly controversial as the expanding EEC makes preferential arrangements with an increasing number of countries in the Mediterranean area as well as in Africa.   D.E.

preformation and **epigenesis.** Alternative interpretations, thought in Victorian times to be mutually exclusive, of the development of animals and plants. Preformationists believed that the adult simply enlarges or unfolds from a miniature precursor, e.g. homunculus; epigenesists that development results from the evocative influences of the ENVIRONMENT shaping the germ into its adult form. The truth is now known to lie somewhere between the two: the genetic instructions which are followed in development are certainly preformed – or at all events inherited – but their working out and realization is epigenetic in pattern, i.e. depends upon an interplay between environmental STIMULI and the effects of neighbouring CELLS upon the

genetic programme built into them. See also EMBRYOLOGY.   P.M.

prefrontal leucotomy, see under LEUCOTOMY.

prehistory. The study of the past of a given region before the appearance of written records relevant to that region. See also ARCHAEOLOGY.   B.C.

prepared piano. A piano whose timbre is altered by the attachment of a variety of objects (metal, rubber, wood, glass, etc.) to the strings and hammers so as to produce intriguing and unexpected sounds. It resulted from the compositional investigations of the American John Cage (*b.* 1912). Part of the effect lies in the denial of expectation; seeing a piano, the audience has a preconceived notion of the sound it will make.   A.H.

Presbyterianism. A system of church government. In the New Testament, an 'elder' (Greek *presbuteros*) is a leader of a Christian congregation. Returning to that system as part of their Calvinist (see CALVINISM) THEOLOGY, Presbyterian churches have been established around the world, including the Church of Scotland. 'Elders' lead a local church; one of them is 'the Minister' who preaches, and representatives gather in a 'Presbytery' which supervises church life in an area. Both EPISCOPALISM and the independence of the congregation are rejected.   D.L.E.

pre-school education. Any form of organized care of children in the years before compulsory schooling. In Great Britain it takes three main forms. Pre-school *playgroups* encourage family welfare and parent participation, and, when possible, assistants qualified through the National Nursery Examinations Board are employed. The *nursery class* is attached to a primary school and is a more economical and less well equipped form of nursery school. The *nursery school* has the most complete provision in buildings, furniture, and equipment, and in fully trained, certificated teachers. In Britain less than 10% of the age group 2–5 were receiving pre-school education in 1973, but this figure is to be considerably increased when the economic situation permits. W.A.C.S.

Bibl: D. E. M. Gardner, *The Education of Young Children* (London, 1956); W. A. L. Blyth, *English Primary Education* (2 vols., London and N.Y., 1965).

prescriptive, see under NORMATIVE.

prescriptivism, see under EMOTIVISM.

présence française ('the presence of France'). Term coined in the 1950s to cover the continuing influence of French culture in its former mandates in the Middle East, Syria, and the Lebanon, an influence shown by the continuing existence of French-language schools, and in the predominance of intellectual, emotional, and cultural ties between the ÉLITES of those countries and France over any ties with other European countries. D.C.W.

present-value method, see under DISCOUNTED CASH FLOW.

Presley, Elvis (U.S. singer, *b*.1935), see under POP.

pressure group, see INTEREST GROUP.

prestressing, see under CONCRETE.

presupposition. The logically NECESSARY CONDITION of some state of affairs which must be satisfied if the state of affairs is to obtain. Thus the uniformity of nature has been held to be a presupposition of the rationality of inductive reasoning (see INDUCTION); the real existence of UNIVERSALS to be a presupposition of our ability to classify things into kinds as we do with predicative general terms; memory, less controversially, to be a presupposition of our having a CONCEPT of the past. PHILOSOPHY has sometimes been held, not unreasonably, to be a matter of the pursuit and critical examination of the presuppositions of the varieties of human thinking. Kant's theory of the synthetic *a priori* principles of the understanding (see APRIORISM) is, in effect, an account of the presuppositions of Newtonian PHYSICS, his ethical theory of the CATEGORICAL IMPERATIVE an account of the presuppositions of a particularly rigorous form of

Protestant morality. R. G. Collingwood held that in different ages men conduct their thinking within the framework of different sets of absolute presuppositions, ultimate assumptions about the nature of things which form, for their time, the limits of critical thinking. Presupposition as defined above (P. F. Strawson uses the term somewhat differently) is a species of ENTAILMENT. A.Q.

Prévert, Jacques (French poet and film-script writer, 1900–1977), see under NEO-REALISM.

Previati, Gaetano (Italian painter, 1852–1920), see under NEO-IMPRESSIONISM.

price mechanism. The way in which the responsiveness of SUPPLY AND DEMAND to prices (see ELASTICITY) can be used to bring some order and coordination into a wide range of economic activities. The term can refer either to the spontaneous adjustments of the market-place or to the deliberate governmental adjustment of prices. On either interpretation the price mechanism is at least a partial alternative to more direct intervention. In the short run it can be used to prevent shortages and surpluses; in the long run its main use is to adapt the structures of production to consumer requirements. Its successful working depends on the movement of prices *relative to each other,* whereas the containment of INFLATION is concerned with the average movement of *all* prices. Failure to appreciate this distinction is the source of much confusion. S.BR.

Bibl: F. A. Hayek, *Individualism and the Economic Order* (Chicago, 1948; London, 1949).

price relatives, see under INDEX NUMBER.

price theory, see under ECONOMICS.

Priestley, John Boynton (British novelist and dramatist, *b*.1894), see under ADMASS.

primary occupation, see under OCCUPATION.

primary structures, see under MINIMAL ART.

PRIMITIVISE

primitive. Adjective used:

(1) Traditionally, to define the subject-matter of ANTHROPOLOGY. Its use derives from the discipline's evolutionary heritage (see EVOLUTION), and it is often nowadays redefined to try to avoid evolutionary assumptions: thus primitive societies are said to be small in scale, non-literate, and based upon simple technologies; indeed, 'small-scale' (likewise 'tribal'; see TRIBE) is often used as a euphemism corresponding to 'under-developed' and 'developing' in ECONOMICS and POLITICAL SCIENCE. But it is arguable that anthropology, though it has properly eliminated 'savage', will always need 'primitive', from which it should strive to remove the last vestige of cultural and political condescension. All men are 'cultured' by definition; some CULTURES/societies are more complex (less primitive) than others.

By taking primitive forms and manifestations as the centre of its interest, anthropology deals in a special way with many of the problems studied by the various social and human sciences. For example, alongside the work done in economics, political science, and jurisprudence, there lie anthropological treatments of primitive economic organization, primitive systems of politics and government, and primitive forms of law. Again, RELIGION, MYTH, music, and visual art are all studied in their primitive manifestations by anthropologists, their special treatment sometimes being signalled by the prefix ethno- (as in ETHNO-MUSICOLOGY).   M.F.

(2) In late-19th-century art criticism, to categorize European pre-Renaissance painting, especially of the 14th and 15th centuries; thereafter it acquired a different, alternative sense with the growing appreciation of non-Western and non-academic art. After 1900 this sophisticated interest in exotic or naive work – e.g. negro sculpture and Bavarian glass paintings, with their influence respectively on CUBISM and the BLAUE REITER – combined with a new approach to child art to create a vogue for untutored contemporary 'primitives' like Henri Rousseau (1844–1910), the retired toll-collector (*douanier*) who became a spare-time or 'Sunday' painter and exhibited with the FAUVES in 1905. Leaders of this trend in France, where it affected the whole ÉCOLE

DE PARIS, included Picasso, Apollinaire, and the critic Wilhelm Uhde. More recently, with the wave of international exhibitions of naive art in the 1960s, the concept has become greatly extended, covering e.g. the art of Yugoslav peasants (in the Zagreb Museum of Primitive Art), Eskimos, Haitians, 18th- and 19th-century dilettantes, do-it-yourself architects, and extremely old ladies. Chimpanzee art, which also attracted some attention in that decade, relates more to ACTION PAINTING.   J.W.

Bibl: O. Bihalji-Merin, *Modern Primitives* (London and N.Y., 1961).

primitivism. In RELIGION (for primitivism in art see PRIMITIVE), either the desire to imitate the 'primitive' (i.e. first) Christians or, more commonly, an interest in, usually with an admiration for, the vitality of African, West Indian, etc. tribal religion, in which the supernatural and the natural, the dead and the living, the individual, the family, and the TRIBE are all bound together by a corporately accepted system of imagery, RITUAL, and behaviour. See also SHAMANISM.   D.L.E.

Bibl: J. V. Taylor, *The Primal Vision* (London, 1963); C. Lévi-Strauss, *The Savage Mind* (London and Chicago, 1966).

Primo de Rivera, José Antonio (Spanish politician, 1903–36), see under FALANGE.

prior distribution, see under STATISTICS.

prisoner's dilemma, see under GAMES, THEORY OF.

privacy. In EPISTEMOLOGY, being known to, or knowable by, only one person. It is in this sense that the thoughts and feelings of which a person is introspectively aware (see INTROSPECTION) within his STREAM OF CONSCIOUSNESS are held to be private. More precisely, a thing is private in this epistemologically important sense if it is knowable *directly* and without INFERENCE by only one person. My smile is, of course, as much mine and no one else's as my feelings are, but this makes it proprietary rather than private and is of little epistemological interest (though my smile, unlike my bicycle, cannot be mine at one time and somebody else's at another). The mental states of another are indeed private in the sense defined but that does not exclude me from having indirect, inferential knowledge of them.   A.Q.

Bibl: A. J. Ayer, *The Concept of a Person* (London and N.Y., 1963).

private sector. One of two major divisions of convenience of a national economy, the other being the PUBLIC SECTOR. The private sector embraces all private persons and industrial and commercial companies, all institutions such as insurance companies, building societies, and finance houses; and finally all private non-commercial bodies such as trade unions, charities, and churches. In sum, the private sector accounts for that part of the total economy composed of consumer expenditures for goods and services, and business expenditure for plant, equipment, and inventories.   D.E.

probabilistic explanation, see under EX-PLANATION.

probability density, see under DISTRIBU-TION.

probability theory. The mathematical theory of processes involving uncertainty; the traditional illustrative cases are those of tossing a coin, rolling a die, and drawing a card from a pack; and it was in the context of gaming odds that early probabilistic calculations were carried out from the 17th century onwards. Proper theorems (as distinct from mere calculations) including versions of the Central Limit Theorem (see below) were proved by Laplace and others, but the subject only began to be taken seriously by pure mathematicians with Kolmogorov's definitive characterization of the theory, around 1930, as a branch of the pure mathematical discipline of measure theory. Although probability theory draws heavily on analysis for its techniques, it has a strong flavour of its own in consequence of its role as a mathematical model for empirical phenomena, and probabilistic methods can on occasion feed ideas and proofs back into analysis. The major results of the theory include a class of theorems known as *Laws of Large Numbers,* which identify the probability of an event with its long-run frequency in the limit as the experiment is repeated. These theorems are enshrined in folklore as the 'law of averages', usually in a highly incor-

rect form (see STATISTICAL REGULARITY). Another major theorem is the *Central Limit Theorem,* which may be thought of as stating that suitably standardized distributions arising from the summation of large numbers of independent errors converge in the limit to the NORMAL DISTRIBUTION. The work of Markov in the early 20th century led to interest in probabilistic systems evolving through time; these are now known as STOCHASTIC PROCESSES. Probability theory forms the foundation on which STATISTICS is built, but in recent years the phrase 'applied probability' has come to mean the study of particular stochastic processes thought to be reasonable mathematical MODELS for such empirical processes as the spread of epidemics, the inheritance of GENES, the interaction of components of a biological environment, and the growth of crystals and POLYMERS.   R.SI.

Bibl: W. Feller, *An Introduction to Probability Theory and its Applications* (London and N.Y., 3rd ed., 1968).

problem-oriented language. In COMPUTING, a PROGRAMMING LANGUAGE designed with a particular class of problem in mind rather than a particular type of COMPUTER. See also ASSEMBLY LANGUAGE; HIGH-LEVEL PROGRAMMING LANGUAGE.   C.S.

problem-solving. That form of activity in which the organism is faced with a goal to be reached, a gap in the 'route' to the goal, and a set of alternative means, none of which are immediately and obviously suitable. It is studied by psychologists in a variety of forms: circumventing detours, solving puzzles and mathematical problems, finding a common basis of classification for a diverse array, solving chess problems, etc. The most widely held view of the problem-solving process in contemporary PSYCHOLOGY is some variant of what is called *means-end* analysis, illustrated best, perhaps, by the *General Problem Solver (G.P.S.)* PROGRAM of A. Newell and H. A. Simon (1957), a COMPUTER program designed to simulate a human problem-solver's procedure.

G.P.S. begins by comparing the present state of solution of the problem with the desired outcome and first determines a set of differences in terms of selected outcome attributes; thus, in the well-known 'cannibals and missionaries' example, it notes that there are too many missionaries on one side of the river. The program has available a number of *transformation-rules* (see AXIOMATICS) for altering current states in the direction of desired outcomes. The transformation highest on the list is applied; if it does not succeed, G.P.S. then tries out other means of solution, or seeks to change the situation so that other means can be applied. A rule for recognizing dead ends is included so that a stop order can be imposed, after which the next transformation on the list is tried. The 'notice order' for spotting differences between desired outcome and present state, and the order of application of transformations, are HEURISTICS or 'rules of thumb' based on knowledge of how real problem-solvers proceed. It is apparent from this account that such phenomena as *functional fixedness* (being stuck too long with an incorrect hypothesis) and other, human-like errors are committed by the program as a function of its presuppositions, and it is this feature that makes G.P.S. not a 'super-problem-solver' but a recognizably 'human' one.

Current research is concentrated on determining some of the biases inherent in programs designed in this way in order to locate more clearly the nature of the difficulties in human problem-solving.
J.S.B.

Bibl: A. Newell and H. A. Simon, *Human Problem-Solving* (Englewood Cliffs, N.J., and Hemel Hempstead, 1972).

process, the, see under ACID FASCISM.

process control. The use of an on-line COMPUTER to control a continuous process such as a chemical plant. See also COMPUTING.
C.S.

process theology. A modern form of Christian THEISM which takes account of modern science, especially the knowledge of EVOLUTION, and which teaches that God's way of working in the world is a slow process, patiently overcoming the elements of chance and evil present in the universe and including in itself all the good that is brought about. The emphasis is on God's involvement rather than his self-sufficiency, his love rather than his omnipotence. The chief philosopher in

this movement was A. N. Whitehead (1861–1947); the chief popularizer of a Christ-centred vision of the meaning of evolution was Pierre Teilhard de Chardin (1881–1955; see TEILHARDIAN). In NEO-ORTHODOXY, however, the position has been attacked as encouraging PANTHEISM.
D.L.E.

Bibl: P. Teilhard de Chardin, tr. B. Wall and others, *The Phenomenon of Man* (London and N.Y., 1959); N. Pittenger, *Process-Thought and Christian Faith* (Welwyn, Herts., 1968).

producers' goods, see under CONSUMERS' GOODS.

production boundary, see under GNP.

productivists, see under CONSTRUCTIVISM.

productivity. In LINGUISTICS, a major defining characteristic of human language, the creative capacity of language-users to produce and understand an infinite number of sentences using a finite set of grammatical rules. In this respect, human language is often contrasted with the extremely limited range of signals which constitute the communication systems of animals.
D.C.

productivity bargaining. A form of collective bargaining developed in Great Britain early in the 1960s, in which higher rates of pay are traded against employees' acceptance of changes in working practices. Traditional working practices and lines of demarcation, together with a recent growth of contrived overtime, had denied management flexibility in the deployment of labour, and led to the under-utilization of hours spent at work. An agreement at the Fawley refinery was widely noticed, and copied, because it indicated that changes in working practices could so raise output per man-hour that higher earnings and shorter hours could be attained without raising unit labour costs.
E.H.P.B.

Bibl: National Board for Prices and Incomes, Report no. 36, *Productivity Agreements* (London, 1967); and see DILUTION OF LABOUR.

profile. Metaphorically, a summary description giving the main features of some person, state of affairs, process, social group, organization, etc. In particular, if the relevant qualities can be measured, the profile may consist of a set of numbers, one for each quality. These can be expressed also as a diagram or graph, by labelling one axis with the names of the qualities and the other with the possible numerical values, making a mark at the appropriate distance above the label for each quality, and joining up the marks by means of straight lines. For *interest profiles,* see SDI. A.S.

Profintern. Red International of Labour Unions founded in Moscow in July 1921 to implement point 10 of the programme adopted by the Second Congress of the COMINTERN in 1920, and to establish a rival to the International Federation of Trades Unions. Initially (1921–8) its main tactic was the capture of national trades union movements by 'boring from within'. In 1928–35 this was replaced by the formation of competing unions, a policy abandoned in turn in 1935 for that of the POPULAR FRONT. After 1937 the Profintern was moribund. D.C.W.

profit-sharing. Term applied to a number of arrangements under which most of the employees of a firm receive a part of its profits in accordance with an agreed scheme. A common arrangement is for the balance of net profits after payment of a fixed rate of return on share capital to be divided in fixed proportions between shareholders and employees; each eligible employee participates in proportion to his earnings. The transfer to employees may be made in the form of shares. Under *co-partnership* employees hold shares and as shareholders or through consultative bodies have a voice in the conduct of the business. E.H.P.B.

program (so spelled in Britain as well as the U.S.A.). A list of statements or commands in some PROGRAMMING LANGUAGE whose purpose is to cause a COMPUTER to carry out some desired operation. The versatility of modern computers springs from the fact that a single machine can be made to do a large number of different and often complex tasks by presenting it with suitable programs. See also PROGRAMME; SYSTEMS. C.S.

programme. This spelling is used in England (but not the U.S.A.) for all meanings except the technical one in COMPUTING. A firm's computer programme is its policy for buying and using computers; its computer PROGRAMS are the detailed sets of instructions given to its COMPUTER to make it carry out particular tasks. C.S.

Programme, Evaluation, and Review Technique, see PERT.

Programme, Planning, and Budgeting System, see PPBS.

programme music. Music normally without words but directly associated with extra-musical subject-matter such as literature (e.g. Berlioz, *Roméo et Juliette*) or natural phenomena (e.g. Debussy, *La Mer*). The concept is particularly associated with 19th-century ROMANTICISM and the symphonic poem (e.g. Liszt, *Les Préludes*), but is much older; its survival in the 20th century, despite being an obvious target for anti-Romantic reaction, suggests that it is a natural form of musical expression. To its forms must now be added 'mechanical romanticism' (Honegger, *Pacific 231*). Extra-musical connotations for instrumental music are implicit even in Stravinsky's preference for *Le Sacre du Printemps* in the concert hall rather than as a ballet. Programme music may be related to the GESAMTKUNSTWERK, although the non-musical elements are usually left to the imagination. On these grounds Ernest Newman even argued that the symphonic poem should supersede the music drama. J.G.R.

programmed art, see under KINETIC ART.

programmed instruction. The technique of presenting material to be learned (*programmed learning*) in an order and form which is designed to make the learning process easy and to bring out the interconnectedness of the material, but which is altered in response to, and correction of, the learner's error patterns as shown in corrective FEEDBACK. In this last respect, it is often useful to use a COMPUTER as an aid, a technique sometimes called *computer-assisted instruction*. See also TEACHING MACHINE. J.S.B.

programming. The process of constructing the detailed set of instructions required to make a COMPUTER perform some specific task. This involves the choice (or invention) of a suitable ALGORITHM, decisions about the representation and organization of data, and consideration of the action to be taken if a machine malfunction is detected or the PROGRAM is presented with inconsistent or incorrect data. The programmer must also take account of the structure of the computer on which the program is to be run, and in particular of the nature of its STORE and OPERATING SYSTEM. He may use FLOW CHARTS (which need a further stage of CODING) or may work directly in a PROGRAMMING LANGUAGE. See also SYSTEMS.   C.S.

programming language. The medium through which computer PROGRAMS are expressed. There are by now several hundred different programming languages which can be divided roughly into ASSEMBLY LANGUAGES, each closely based on a particular type of COMPUTER, and HIGH-LEVEL PROGRAMMING LANGUAGES, which are more often PROBLEM-ORIENTED. All programming languages are *artificial*, i.e. deliberately invented; they differ from *natural* languages, which have developed gradually, by having a perfectly rigid syntax, a much smaller vocabulary, and no emotive power.   C.S.

progressive. Adjective used to characterize:

(1) Generally, believers in the possibility and desirability of progress, i.e. of a moral and social improvement in the human condition, a view which implies a certain optimism about human nature.

(2) Political parties seeking to achieve such progress by removing institutions which obstruct it and advocating measures which they believe will promote it (e.g. universal free EDUCATION). In this sense all LEFT-wing parties, LIBERALS, radicals (see RADICALISM), SOCIALISTS, and COMMUNISTS (before they come to power), can be counted as progressive. But the name Progressive has also been adopted in many countries by particular parties of a generally radical character. In the U.S.A. a Progressive Party led by the La Follette brothers and based

on Wisconsin broke away from the Republicans in 1934; Henry Wallace founded another short-lived Progressive Party in 1947. In South Africa, the Progressive Party is the only one opposed to APARTHEID.

(3) The last hundred years or so of a minority educational movement in Britain, Europe, and the U.S.A. which has developed ideas going back to Rousseau, Pestalozzi, and Froebel (see PESTALOZZI METHODS; FROEBEL METHOD). The characteristic features of *progressive education* include an interest in CHILD-CENTRED EDUCATION, a tolerant discipline, frequently a preference for coeducation, a readiness to take part in curriculum experiments, the playing down of academic and examination demands, generally liberal or LEFT politics, encouragement of the arts and crafts, manual work as an aspect of physical education, an international outlook and anti-military school organization, simplicity of living (often in boarding schools in the country), and informality of clothes.

Progressive, in marked contrast with REACTIONARY, is a term which many people like to apply to themselves, and the abbreviation 'prog', frequently used in the advertisement columns of certain periodicals, has come to denote a person with a self-conscious but not necessarily clear-headed attachment to progress in any or all of the senses distinguished above.   A.L.C.B.; W.A.C.S.

Bibl: (1) J. B. Bury, *The Idea of Progress* (London and N.Y., 1920); (3) W. A. C. Stewart, *Progressives and Radicals in English Education 1750–1970* (London, 1972).

prohibition, see under JAZZ AGE.

project work. A teaching method (in Dewey's phrase, the 'problem method') in which a topic, preferably one within the pupils' everyday experience, is approached from a number of angles. Much used in primary schools, project work cuts across traditional divisions between subjects and involves the pupils actively in the solving of problems: thus, a project on baking might incorporate elements traditionally taught as mathematics, science, history, English, and creative arts, and involve a group visit to a bakery as well as individual quests for information in the school and local public libraries. A single project may be studied by just one child, a whole class, or even an entire school. In turn, its study might be periodic (e.g. once a week for a term), or take up most of the students' time over some set period (e.g. one or two weeks, but this can also extend to a whole term).

W.A.C.S.; E.L.-S.

Bibl: G. Cowan, *Project Work in the Secondary School* (London and N.Y., 1967); G. Kent, *Projects in the Primary School* (London, 1968).

projection. In PSYCHOLOGY, the tendency to attribute to others unacceptable impulses and traits that are present in oneself. In extreme cases it may be pathological in nature, though generally it is one of the normal DEFENCE MECHANISMS. J.S.B.

projective geometry, see under GEOMETRY.

prolefeed, proles, see under ORWELLIAN.

proletariat. The word first appeared (Latin *proletarius*, from *proles*, offspring) in the Servian constitution of the sixth century B.C. in which military service and taxes were required of the landowners and other classes. Those who could not serve the State with their property did so with their offspring; hence the idea of service by labour. The term disappeared by the end of the second century of the Christian era but reappears after the enclosure movements of the 15th and 16th centuries, to designate men made landless and able to live only by selling their labour power. It was central in the *Étude sur l'économie politique* (1837) by the Swiss economist Sismondi, the founder of the underconsumption theory of economic crises (see TRADE CYCLES). It was used by Proudhon, Cabet, Louis Blanc, and other French radicals and was popularized by the German social critic Lorenz von Stein in *Der Sozialismus und Communismus des heutigen Frankreichs* (1842).

The term is, however, associated predominantly with Marx. In the *Critique of Hegel's Philosophy of Right* (1843) he talks of the proletariat as a 'CLASS in radical chains' and ends with the peroration: 'Philosophy cannot be realized without the abolition of the proletariat, the proletariat cannot abolish itself without realizing philosophy.' And the *Communist Manifesto* (1848) begins with the ringing declaration: 'The history of all human society, past and present, has been the history of class struggle. Freeman and slave, patrician and plebeian, lord and serf ... the bourgeois age ... has simplified class antagonisms ... society is splitting into two great hostile classes ... BOURGEOISIE and proletariat.' Yet it also seems likely that he used the term largely for dramatic effect. In *Das Kapital* (1867–94) it appears but infrequently; Marx uses instead the more specific (and in English more familiar) terms 'wage-labourers', 'factory hands', 'the working class'. Nonetheless it became an important concept in the COMMUNIST movement of the 1920s, not least among artists and INTELLECTUALS; and following the PROLETKULT a number of 'proletarian' cultural groupings sprang up, particularly in Germany and the U.S.S.R. They were liquidated, for differing reasons, by Hitler and Stalin respectively in the early 1930s.

D.B.; J.W.

Bibl: G. Briefs, tr. R. A. Eckhart, *The Proletariat* (London and N.Y., 1937).

Proletkult. Workers' cultural organization conceived in 1909 by the Russian SOCIALIST exiles Alexander Bogdanov, A. V. Lunacharsky, and Maxim Gorky, who saw it as a third arm of the revolutionary movement, catering for the PROLETARIAT'S spiritual life while the unions and the party looked after its economic and political interests. After holding its first conference in Petrograd in 1917 the Proletkult briefly flourished under the wing of Lunacharsky's Education Commissariat, but was distrusted by Lenin, who reduced its powers; in 1922 it lost its subsidy and thereafter petered out. Its influence, however, persisted, whether in the vocabulary of the much more aggressively 'proletarian' cultural groupings of the later 1920s or in the actual achievements of its often non-proletarian members, such as Eisenstein, whose first theatrical and film ventures (e.g. *Strike*, 1925) it sponsored. J.W.

Bibl: M. E. and C. Paul, *Proletcult* (London, 1921); B. Thomson, *The Premature Revolution* (London, 1972).

proliferation. In political contexts, an increase in the number of states possessing the technological capacity needed for independent production of and control over nuclear weapons. Thus the Treaty of 1968, by which three nuclear powers (U.S.A., U.S.S.R., and Britain) undertook not to transfer such TECHNOLOGY, and some 100 other signatory states not to develop it, is entitled the Treaty on the Non-Proliferation of Nuclear Weapons.

A.F.B.

Bibl: L. Beaton, *Must the Bomb Spread?* (Harmondsworth, 1966).

proof theory, see under MATHEMATICAL LOGIC.

prophylaxis. A preventive measure or protected state, particularly with respect to infectious diseases and achieved through a mechanism of IMMUNITY. Prophylaxis may be achieved by the prior injection of (1) a relatively innocuous organism closely related to the one against which protection is desired (e.g. against smallpox virus by cowpox virus); (2) a virulent but attenuated organism, i.e. a *vaccine* (e.g. against poliomyelitis by virus particles inactivated by treatment with, e.g., formaldehyde, Salk vaccine); or (3) heat-killed or otherwise inactivated bacteria or bacterial extracts known as *toxoids*, which retain their immunizing power but cannot cause disease (e.g. prophylaxis against diphtheria and tetanus – a procedure far superior to treatment by means of antiserum, which is fraught with dangers). See also VIROLOGY.

P.M.

proportional representation. Any system of voting in elections to a legislative body which is designed to secure that the representation in that body reflects as accurately as possible the divisions of opinion within the electorate. It is usually based on multiple-member constituencies. Modified forms are widely employed on the European mainland, usually in the form of party lists, while in Ireland and in the Commonwealth the single transferable vote is used. In the U.S.A. proportional representation is not an issue. In Britain it is suspect among the major parties because of its alleged inability to produce a government resting on a stable majority; it is correspondingly favoured by the LIBERAL Party. Much public interest in it was aroused by the results of the 1974 General Election, when over a third of those elected to Parliament were elected on a minority vote, and the Liberal Party with over 5 million votes secured only 12 seats.

D.C.W.

Bibl: S. E. Finer (ed.), *Adversary Politics and Electoral Reform* (London, 1975).

proposition, types of. In LOGIC and EPISTEMOLOGY, propositions may be distinguished in respect (1) of their *logical form*, as for example (*a*) singular, particular, or universal, (*b*) affirmative or negative, (*c*) categorical (see CATEGORY), hypothetical, or otherwise complex, (*d*) existential, attributive, or relational; (2) of their kind of TRUTH or VERIFICATION, as *a priori* (see APRIORISM) or empirical (see EMPIRICISM), necessary or contingent (see CONTINGENCY), ANALYTIC or synthetic (three distinctions that do not obviously, but may fundamentally, coincide); (3) of their subject-matter, as physical, psychological, experiential, scientific, historical, moral, philosophical, and so forth; (4) of their epistemological status as basic or intuitive on the one hand or as inferred or derivative on the other. The first of these classifications is of primary interest to logic; the other three are the concern of epistemology.

A.Q.

propositional calculus. One of the two chief LOGICAL CALCULI, consisting of a formal system of notation for representing combinations of PROPOSITIONS together with AXIOMS and rules (see AXIOMATICS) which determine the RELATIONS between them. The most frequently used *connectives* by means of which the combinations are formed are negation, conjunction, disjunction (*A* and/or *B*), and implication (if *A*, then *B*). In the *classical* propositional calculus every proposition is taken to be true or false, and the connectives correspond to TRUTH-FUNCTIONS. In INTUITIONISM (3) the connectives have different meanings and obey different rules.

R.G.

prosodic feature. In PHONOLOGY, any systematic variation in pitch, loudness, speed, or rhythm that carries a difference in meaning. See also INTONATION. In FIRTHIAN linguistics, prosodic features (or *prosodies*) are any features which can be found throughout a sequence of sounds; thus if all the sounds in a word were nasal, the nasality would be considered a prosodic feature.

D.C.

prosopography. The study of collective biography, usually but not necessarily the biography of ÉLITES such as peers or Members of Parliament. Prosopography is one of the most important types of QUANTITATIVE HISTORY. The prosopographical method has been employed regularly by historians since about 1930, in particular by political historians such as Sir Lewis Namier, and is increasing in popularity because it lends itself to computerization (see COMPUTERS). The great advantage of the method is that it gives a firm basis to some kinds of general statement about groups. It has been criticized for taking the ideas out of history, because it is easier to card-index a man's economic interests or family relationships than his fundamental values.   P.B.
Bibl: L. Stone, 'Prosopography' (*Daedalus*, 100, 1971, pp. 46–73).

prosthesis. Any artificial device which does duty for a bodily organ or member. Thus false teeth and artificial kidneys are equally prostheses.   P.M.

proteases, see under ENZYMES; PROTEINS.

protection, see under FREE TRADE.

protein synthesis, see under NUCLEIC ACID.

proteins. Giant polymeric (see POLYMER) MOLECULES, found in all living organisms, and built up of AMINO ACIDS united to each other by the so-called *peptide bond*, CO-NH. The elementary composition of a protein thus depends directly upon its constitution in terms of amino acids. Proteins contain carbon, hydrogen, oxygen, and nitrogen, and most proteins contain also sulphur and phosphorus. In skeletal structure the protein is a giant polypeptide (see PEPTIDE); the first protein of which it could be said that its structure was fully elucidated was myoglobin (by Perutz and Kendrew, 1957). The functions fulfilled by proteins are protean. ENZYMES are proteins, and so are connective TISSUE fibres including tendons and ligaments, while hairs and nails are formed by insoluble proteins of the class known as *keratins*. When proteins are altered in such a way that they lose their distinctive structures or become insoluble, they are said to be *denatured*. Heating a protein normally

causes irreversible coagulation, such as occurs in cooking an egg. The main classes of soluble protein are: albumins, globulins, and fibrous proteins such as fibrinogen out of which blood clot fibres are formed. In digestion, proteins are broken down by hydrolytic enzymes into raw peptides or individual amino acids. The enzymes that break down proteins are known as *proteases*.   P.M.

Protestant ethic. A phrase deriving from Max Weber's proposition, put forward in 1905–6, that, while CAPITALISM had existed throughout most of history, a particular *spirit* of capitalism, that of methodical accumulation and a rationalistic ethic, is found only in Western Europe and after the 16th century, in Protestant countries or among Protestant sects within Catholic countries. Though disputed by a number of writers who have argued that the spread of capitalism in Holland was due primarily to economic causes, or that the rise of capitalism was a general phenomenon whose inhibition in Catholic countries was due largely to the Counter-Reformation, Weber's thesis has been one of the most influential ideas in contemporary SOCIAL SCIENCE. Many writers still assume that the Protestant ethic undergirds contemporary capitalism; but Weber specifically argued that 'victorious capitalism', resting largely on materialist and hedonistic incentives, 'needs [the support of the Protestant ethic] no longer'. The pursuit of wealth, he maintained, had become stripped of its religious and ethical meaning.   D.B.
Bibl: M. Weber, tr. T. Parsons, *The Protestant Ethic and the Spirit of Capitalism* (London, 1930); S. N. Eisenstadt (ed.), *The Protestant Ethic and Modernization* (N.Y., 1968).

Protestantism. The RELIGION of those who make an EVANGELICAL protest against what are believed to be corruptions in CATHOLICISM, urging a return to a more purely biblical faith; so called from a *Protestatio* issued in 1529 as part of the LUTHERAN Reformation. In the 19th and 20th centuries the U.S.A. has come to share the leadership of Protestantism with Europe, but Protestantism has experienced a need to redefine its position more positively, both in its attitude to Catholicism and in its adjustment to modern thought (see MODERNISM). Where the Bible is not treated in a FUNDAMENTALIST way, the central problem for Protestantism is authority. If the only real authority is the individual's conscience, it is not clear why a Church is needed at all. D.L.E.

Bibl: M. E. Marty, *Protestantism* (London and N.Y., 1972).

protohistory. The study of the past of a given region at a time when it is referred to, but only sporadically, in written records. Protohistory follows PREHISTORY but precedes the period served by regular written sources sufficient to create a cohesive HISTORY. B.C.

proton. A positively charged ELEMENTARY PARTICLE about 2,000 times heavier than the ELECTRON. Protons are stable, and constitute one of the two structural units of the atomic NUCLEUS, the other being NEUTRONS. M.V.B.

protoplasm. An obsolescent term intended to designate the ingredient of living systems that was truly living – a sort of biological ether that permeated or lay between otherwise inert structures. With the realization that the distinctive characteristics of living things are above all else organizational, the entire conceptual background of 'protoplasm' has collapsed; nevertheless nature-philosophers, unlike practising scientists, do still confront themselves with questions like 'Are connective tissue fibres really alive?' P.M.

protozoa. A sub-kingdom of single-CELL animals comprising some 30,000 SPECIES of both free-living (e.g. amoeba) and parasitic (e.g. the malaria parasite, plasmodium; trypanosoma) forms. The protozoa also comprehend chlorophyll-bearing AUTOTROPHIC organisms intermediate between animal and plant cells – the phytomonadines. Marine planktonic protozoa with hard 'skeletons' or shells are an important element in the formation of marine geological deposits. Some protozoa produce what are in effect ANTIBIOTICS. Thus a paramecium belonging to one of the so-called 'killer' races produces an infective particle – in effect a virus which kills members of 'non-killer' races. Susceptibility to this infection (kappa) is under strict genetic control.

Because of its sexual process the genetics of paramecium is now very thoroughly understood. The protozoa generally are ubiquitous in distribution. P.M.

Bibl: D. L. Mackinnon and R. S. J. Hawes, *An Introduction to the Study of Protozoa* (Oxford, 1961).

protozoology. The branch of ZOOLOGY that deals with PROTOZOA. P.M.

Proudhon, Pierre-Joseph (French socialist, 1809–65), see under ANARCHISM; PROLETARIAT; STRATIFICATION, SOCIAL; SYNDICALISM.

Proust, Marcel (French novelist, 1871–1922), see under CRITERION, THE; DREYFUS CASE; PROUSTIAN; SYMBOLISM.

Proustian. Adjective formed from the name of Marcel Proust, the author of the outstanding French fictional work of the 20th century, *À la recherche du temps perdu* (1913–27). It may refer to Proust's method of reliving the past in the present by means of memory, and thus purporting to triumph over time; to the long, evocative sentences which constitute his normal style; to his remarkable feeling for nature, works of art, and historic buildings; or to the characteristic *belle époque* high society of aristocrats, men of fashion, and *demimondaines* that he describes. J.G.W.

provenance. The place at which something has been found, or from which it has originated. Provenance is often important in such fields as the attribution of works of art, TEXTUAL CRITICISM, and BIBLIOGRAPHY, and invariably so in ARCHAEOLOGY. In the case of archaeology it normally implies only location; it lacks the stratigraphical precision (see STRATIGRAPHY) of CONTEXT. B.C.

Provincetown Players. An American experimental theatre group founded in Provincetown, Mass., in 1915 and active in New York from 1916 to 1929. It was intimately connected with the early work of Eugene O'Neill, whose first play *Bound East for Cardiff* it presented in 1916. M.A.

Provos. (1) *Provokants*. An urban movement of Dutch radical youth of an anti-industrialist, individualist, anti-

ESTABLISHMENT kind, distinguished by its members' uniform of white socks, their preference for the bicycle (as 'non-pollutant'; see POLLUTION), and the unconventional humour of their campaigns. In the late 1960s individual provos stood for election to municipalities. (2) Abbreviation for the 'provisional' faction of the IRA. D.C.W.

proxemics, see under SEMIOTICS.

psephology. The study of elections, voting patterns, and electoral behaviour. The word is a recent coinage, being derived as an academic jest from the *psephos* (pebble) deposited in urns by voters in classical Athens. D.C.W.

pseudo-alleles. A term originally used to describe genetic units which appeared to be single entities or GENES when judged by the test of having a single primary function, but which could be split by CROSSING OVER. The term is obsolete, since it is now known that all functional units or genes can be so split. J.M.S.

pseudo-statement. Term introduced, though not formally defined, by I. A. Richards in the context of the age-old controversy, fiercely revived in this century, about whether poetry (and, by extension, literature) is COGNITIVE or emotive, or both. In *Science and Poetry* (1926) Richards presented an emotive theory of poetry; in *Poetries and Sciences* (1970), however, he puts poetry forward as a medium containing special knowledge, exclusive to itself. Philip Wheelwright's proposition of 'poetic statement' as a substitute for Richards's term has the virtues of simplicity, and of avoiding the pejorative CONNOTATIONS of 'pseudo-'. What Richards really meant, however, and what is really important is that poetic statements are different from empirical statements: they are non-verifiable, and they are not supposed to be verifiable; but they do order our impulses, and are therefore useful. 'A pseudo-statement is a form of words which is justified entirely by its effect in releasing or organizing our impulses and attitudes . . . a statement, on the other hand, is justified by its truth.' Richards has stuck to this: 'In fluid [poetic] statements a great many precise meanings may be free to dispose themselves in a multiplicity of diverse ways' (1955). M.S.-S.

psychedelic art. Art primarily concerned with sensory PERCEPTION, distortion, and hallucinations similar to those mental states produced by DRUGS such as LSD and mescaline. Such art often combines visual, aural, and KINETIC elements borrowed from TECHNOLOGY to heighten the spectator's sensory experience. Light and sound ENVIRONMENTS could be considered within this category, but psychedelic art can take so many diverse forms that its association with any one technique or medium is precluded. It has a soberer and more organized equivalent in OP ART. A.K.W.
Bibl: D. Davis, *Art and the Future* (N.Y., 1973); and see under PRECISIONISM.

psychiatry. The branch of medicine concerned with the study and treatment of mental illnesses and of other disorders, both behavioural and physical, in which psychological factors are important as causes or clinical features. A psychiatrist is a physician with advanced training in the treatment of the severe mental illnesses (PSYCHOSES) such as SCHIZOPHRENIA and MANIC-DEPRESSIVE PSYCHOSIS, the less severe NEUROSES and emotional disorders, PSYCHOSOMATIC disorders, MENTAL RETARDATION, and behavioural anomalies such as the addictions and sexual deviations.
As a branch of medicine, psychiatry has its foundations in the basic biological sciences (see BIOLOGY); it also derives fundamental CONCEPTS and methods from the BEHAVIOURAL and SOCIAL SCIENCES, particularly PSYCHOLOGY and SOCIOLOGY, and to a lesser extent ANTHROPOLOGY and ETHOLOGY. In its medical aspect, psychiatry uses modes of investigation derived from ANATOMY, PHYSIOLOGY, BIOCHEMISTRY, NEUROLOGY, and other related sciences; these methods are applicable to a range of psychiatric disorders, especially those associated with demonstrable diseases of the brain or with conditions such as epilepsy or alcoholism. In medical practice, psychiatric principles are playing a growing role in the treatment of physical illnesses, as it is increasingly recognized that psychological factors may

determine the manifestations, course, and outcome of such disorders.

The practice of modern psychiatry extends over a wide range of sub-specialities, in some of which the 'medical model' of treatment is less applicable. For example, *child psychiatry* is largely but not exclusively concerned with emotional and conduct disorders in children; *forensic psychiatry* is concerned with the behavioural deviations of delinquents and criminals (see DEVIANCE; DELIN-QUENCY; CRIMINOLOGY). PSYCHO-ANALYSIS, the FREUDIAN theoretical system and method of treatment, has been influential in the U.S.A.; most British psychiatrists, though acknowledging that Freud's contribution has been radical and stimulating, are not psychoanalysts. Sharply contrasted with the individualist approach of psychoanalysis is the recent development of *community psychiatry*, which is concerned with the provision and delivery of a coordinated programme of mental health to a specified population.

In recent years much attention has been paid to social factors as determinants of psychiatric disorders. *Psychiatric social workers* have been trained to deal with occupational, domestic, economic, and family problems. Psychiatric research has been concerned with socio-economic variables such as social isolation and SOCIAL MOBILITY, emigration, economic depriva-tion, etc. and the extent to which they are correlated with differences in the preval-ence and outcome of mental illnesses and abnormal behaviour such as suicide.

The contribution of the science of psychology should be emphasized. In psychiatry extensive use is made, for example, of PSYCHOMETRIC techniques and statistical devices applied to the measurement of COGNITIVE functions and personality. Behavioural methods derived from learning-theory principles are being increasingly used in the treatment of neuroses.

For a rejection of conventional psychiatry see ANTI-PSYCHIATRY.

D.H.G.

Bibl: A. M. Freedman and H. I. Kaplan (eds.), *Comprehensive Textbook of Psychiatry* (Baltimore, 1967); W. Mayer-Gross, E. Slater, and M. Roth, *Clinical Psychiatry* (London and Balti-more, 3rd ed., 1969); P. Hays, *New Hori-zons in Psychiatry* (Baltimore, 1964; Harmondsworth, 2nd ed., 1971).

psychic determinism, see under PSYCHOANALYSIS.

psychical research, see PARAPSYCHO-LOGY.

psychoanalysis. (1) The PSYCHOLOGY and the PSYCHOTHERAPY associated with the work of Freud and the FREUDIAN tradi-tions. (2) More broadly, the whole family of SCHOOLS OF PSYCHOLOGY, stemming from the original work of Breuer and Freud in the 1880s and 1890s. (In both senses, the word is popularly used to refer *only* to the therapy, and not to the theory on which this is based.) Themes or doc-trines common to these traditions include the following:

(*a*) The doctrine of *psychic deter-minism*. This amounts to a directive to refuse to accept an item of behaviour (e.g. a slip of the tongue, a casual remark) as a matter of chance, but to look instead for its psychological significance to the indi-vidual (see FREUDIAN SLIP).

(*b*) The doctrine of the UNCONSCIOUS. This amounts to the thesis that there are mental processes which operate outside the realm of an individual's awareness, and which play a key role in his life and in the explanation of his behaviour (whether it be a slip of the tongue or a neurotic col-lapse).

(*c*) The doctrine of *goal-directedness*. Human functioning is much more goal-directed than we ordinarily suppose. Hence this doctrine lays stress on the MOTIVATION of human thought, behaviour, etc., and prescribes that we look for the unconscious motives that, on (*b*) above, go to determine and explain our conduct.

(*d*) The doctrine of *development*. This emphasizes the importance of experience, and especially early experience, in the development of the individual towards adulthood.

(*e*) The doctrine of *treatment*. The proper form of treatment for the NEUROSES is psychotherapy. For all other non-organic disorders, psycho-analysts would confess (probably) to having a professional preference for psychotherapy, but (in general) they would not urge that it should always or even generally be adopted in these cases. For they recognize the great practical limitations of psychotherapy and the advantages to be had from using other recognized methods of PSYCHIATRY.

The main psychoanalytic schools stem from the work of Freud, Jung, and Adler, and the differences between them centre round their different psychologies (see FREUDIAN; JUNGIAN; ADLERIAN). Thus, Jung rejected Freud's view of the sexual LIBIDO and extended the notion of the individual unconscious to cover that from which the individual CONSCIOUSNESS emerges, i.e. the COLLECTIVE UNCON-SCIOUS; and he developed his own view of personality and PERSONALITY TYPES. Adler also rejected Freud's theory of libido, and emphasized the inter-personal relations in the family as a chief source of the LIFE STYLE of the person, which could be unrealistic, and so lead to neurosis. Some psychologists and psychiatrists have argued that what helped to produce these different schools in the first instance, and what helps to maintain them now, are defects in psychoanalytic method. If an analyst develops any ideas of his own about human nature, and if he feeds them into the therapeutic situation (which it is very difficult *not* to do), then he is liable to get material out of his work that goes to confirm his ideas about human nature.

All traditions of psychoanalysis report roughly the same proportion of improvement in their patients. This raises the interesting speculation that, in so far as improvement is *due* to psychoanalytic therapy, this results from the inherent nature of the psychotherapeutic situation in psychoanalysis, and not from the particular doctrines that the analyst uses in his treatment.   B.A.F.

Bibl: S. Freud, tr. W. J. H. Sprott, *New Introductory Lectures on Psycho-Analysis* (London, 1933).

psychodiagnostics. The assessment of personality characteristics and possible psychiatric disorder through interpretation of either (1) objective behavioural indices such as gait, facial expression, and GRAPHOLOGY; or (2) the way in which a person, in terms of his motivational CONSTRUCTS, responds to a series of inkblots (see RORSCHACH TEST). See also COUNSELLING; MENTAL TESTING.   G.M.

psychodrama. In PSYCHOTHERAPY, a technique in which the patient plays out a ROLE in the dramatic enactment of a particular situation, in order to help him understand his subjective and inter-personal feelings.   W.Z.

psychodynamic. An adjective, used in PSYCHIATRY and PSYCHOLOGY, for which there is no accepted definition. In one usage it is applied to theories which represent symptomatic behaviour as determined by an interplay of forces within the mind of an individual subject without involving awareness. This is exemplified by FREUDIAN psychoanalytic theory (see PSYCHOANALYSIS), which postulates intra-psychic conflicts between unconscious mental activities, such as primitive sexual and aggressive impulses, and those parts of the mind (EGO and SUPEREGO) concerned with morality. The adjective is also applied, in a wider sense, to behavioural symptoms and indicates that these are regarded as being determined by both intra-psychic and extra-psychic factors, the latter including, for example, parental influences, family conflicts, occupational and other stresses.   D.H.G.

psychohistory. A term coined in the 1960s to describe an approach to historical subjects which attempts to take into account SUBCONSCIOUS and private elements of human experience studied by psychologists, particularly of the FREUDIAN school. Although attempts have been made to apply this approach to collective experiences (e.g. WITCHCRAFT; Puritanism; MILLENARIANISM), the examples which have attracted most attention have been biographical studies, beginning with E. H. Erikson's *Young Man Luther* (1958). Other examples are biographies of Gandhi (by Erikson), Newton (by Frank Manuel), and Lyndon Johnson (by Doris Kearns).

The method has been sceptically received by most historians on the grounds that the evidence available is insufficient to produce more than conjectural conclusions. On the other hand, to write history, certainly to write biography, without assumptions about PSYCHOLOGY is impossible, and Erikson, for example, in his study of Luther faced certain crucial problems more seriously than earlier historians had been willing to do. The controversy continues.   I.S.H.; A.L.C.B.

Bibl: F. E. Manuel, 'The Use and Abuse of Psychology in History', in *Freedom from History* (N.Y., 1971; London, 1972); J. Barzun, *Clio and the Doctors* (N.Y., 1975).

psychokinesis (PK). In PARAPSYCHOLOGY, movement of physical objects caused by somebody not using physical forces; e.g. making a dice fall in a certain position merely by willing it to do so. PK is probably not involved in movements of divining rods and ouija boards since such movements can, like automatic writing, result from unconscious muscle movements. It is sometimes alleged to be responsible for poltergeist hauntings and for the performances of people, like Uri Geller, who produce movements of and in objects without using any apparent physical force. PK is the kinetic counterpart of ESP and poses the same challenges to scientific investigation.   I.M.L.H.

psycholinguistics. A branch of LINGUISTICS which studies variation in linguistic behaviour in relation to psychological notions such as memory, PERCEPTION, attention, and acquisition.   D.C.

psychological parallelism, see under MIND-BODY PROBLEM.

psychological warfare, see under WAR.

psychologism. The interpretation of philosophical problems as questions of a factual kind to be answered by PSYCHOLOGY. Locke and Hume both explicitly endorsed this conception of philosophical enquiry, although they were not wholly bound by it in practice. Their theory of MEANINGS as images causally dependent on previous sense-experiences and Hume's account of the associative mechanisms underlying the CONCEPTS of cause and identity are influential examples of psychologism. Critics have argued that psychologism treats questions of ANALYSIS and justification, which concern the correct use of words and the *right* formation of beliefs, as questions about the actual mental associates of the use of words and the psychological causation of beliefs, thus misinterpreting what is logically NORMATIVE as if it were psychologi

cally descriptive. Husserl's PHENOMENOLOGICAL theory of philosophy as the intuitive scrutiny of ESSENCES was negatively inspired by a rejection of the psychologism of Mill, particularly about MATHEMATICS. Again, the contemporary philosophy of MIND is not a very abstract and general *part* of psychology, but an examination of its PRESUPPOSITIONS.
    A.Q.

psychology. A word variously defined as the study of mind, the study of behaviour, or the study of man interacting with his social and physical ENVIRONMENT. The definition one prefers has theoretical and methodological consequences (see METHODOLOGY), since it conceptualizes what is central in one's concern about man and predisposes one to study different aspects of human experience and behaviour and their determinants. But, while its 'schools' and their theoretical debates have at times been divisive, the field has taken a fairly definite shape with respect to subject-matters studied, methods used, and professions created. At the same time, psychology has not achieved the degree of organization of its knowledge characterizing such NATURAL SCIENCES as PHYSICS or CHEMISTRY, principally because it still lacks fundamental central CONCEPTS comparable to the CONSERVATION LAWS of the physical sciences.

If one takes the ultimate aim of psychology to be the systematic description and explanation of man at the fullness of his powers, as a thinking, striving, talking, enculturated animal (see ENCULTURATION), it has often proved most advantageous to pursue that aim by comparative study. Psychology typically divides into fields of study based on the comparisons used. When, for example, one compares man with other organisms at different levels of EVOLUTION, there emerges the set of disciplines known as COMPARATIVE PSYCHOLOGY. Since its tools of analysis must be as manageable when working with animals as with man, much of the work in comparative psychology looks for its explanations in terms of the relation of brain and behaviour, of blood chemistry and the endocrine (see ENDOCRINOLOGY) system of GENETICS, and of the functional ADAPTATION of organisms to their natural environment in response to SELECTION PRESSURES. But although in theory one is looking for direct comparisons, in practice no phenomenon need be excluded, since every phenomenon has its analogue (if not its homologue) elsewhere in the animal kingdom; e.g. communication in bees or dolphins is analogous to human speech, the capacity of a chimpanzee to recognize and differentiate his own image in a mirror from that of another animal is analogous to human self-awareness.

A second comparison, that between adult and child, is the basis of DEVELOPMENTAL PSYCHOLOGY: a field including studies of growth in other species as well as in man. Developmental studies, strongly influenced by the work of Piaget, have centred increasingly in recent years on the growth of adult powers of PERCEPTION, reasoning, memory, language, and moral judgement; but analysis of the factors that may affect these (e.g. the growth and transformation of motives, the role of mother-child interaction and of the family, personality formation) has also continued. The developmental approach has also been used to explore in increasing detail the effects of different CULTURES on the growth of mental processes and motives. Since much of development is strongly affected by formal or informal schooling, the principal application of work in this field is through EDUCATIONAL PSYCHOLOGY.

A third comparison is between man operating effectively and man afflicted either by PSYCHOPATHOLOGY or NEUROPATHOLOGY, the two often being difficult to distinguish. This comparison is the basis of ABNORMAL PSYCHOLOGY, and it serves in its applied form as a field ancillary to PSYCHIATRY. A fourth comparison, of human and animal behaviour in different social settings, forms the basis of SOCIAL PSYCHOLOGY, which has recently been freed, by a marked growth in research, from an ETHNOCENTRISM often criticized by ANTHROPOLOGY. Fifth and last, there is a new and fruitful comparative study of the difference between 'natural' man functioning in his 'natural' surroundings and COMPUTER-built MODELS of man functioning in hypothesized environments, with PROGRAMS embodying assumptions about human behaviour and human environments. The assumptions are tested by direct comparison of outcomes. The study of ARTIFICIAL INTELLIGENCE is a good example.

But psychology can also be characterized in two other ways: by its choice of processes to be studied, and by its method of analysis. With respect to the processes studied, the distinctions can most easily be made in terms of an INPUT-OUTPUT metaphor. One part of psychology tends to specialize more on input processes: *sensory processing*, PERCEPTION, *short-term memory*, and HABITUATION. Generally, the object of such study is to discern the manner in which organisms transduce or transform ENERGY changes in the physical environment, converting them into sensations or percepts. It was in this enterprise that psychology was founded as an experimental science, in research that still continues rigorously in PSYCHOPHYSICS. At the other extreme psychologists are concerned with the nature of response processes, e.g. with skill, EXPRESSIVE MOVEMENT, motives and drive states, language, and various forms of social behaviour. Between the two are studies of the processes that mediate between input and output, e.g. attention, the organization of memory and learning, the formation of attitudes, and of concepts and rules whereby the organism can regulate response systematically with respect to stimulus changes, in a fashion that is systematic but not a direct reflection of the nature of the stimulation.

It is from work of these three types that psychology derives the processes used to explain the differences and similarities that emerge from its comparative studies.

With respect to methods of analysis, psychology inevitably uses a variety of approaches (EXPERIMENTAL, observational, clinical, even literary) and tools (field studies, mathematical and computer modelling). Even more striking than its growth as a university subject has been its proliferation as an applied field (see APPLIED PSYCHOLOGY) in industry (see INDUSTRIAL PSYCHOLOGY), EDUCATION, medicine, ENGINEERING, politics, and the armed forces. See also BEHAVIOURISM; COGNITIVE PSYCHOLOGY; DEPTH PSYCHOLOGY; DIFFERENTIAL PSYCHOLOGY; DYNAMIC PSYCHOLOGY; EXISTENTIAL PSYCHOLOGY; FACULTY PSYCHOLOGY; GENETIC PSYCHOLOGY; GESTALT; GROUP PSYCHOLOGY; HERBARTIAN PSYCHOLOGY; HORMIC PSYCHOLOGY; HUMANISTIC PSYCHOLOGY; INDIVIDUAL PSYCHOLOGY; INTROSPECTIVE

PSYCHOLOGY; MATHEMATICAL PSYCHO-
LOGY; ORGANISMIC PSYCHOLOGY;
PERSONALISTIC PSYCHOLOGY; PSYCHO-
LINGUISTICS; SCHOOLS OF PSYCHO-
LOGY; STRUCTURAL PSYCHOLOGY; TOPO-
LOGICAL PSYCHOLOGY.   J.S.B.

Bibl: D. Krech, R. S. Crutchfield, and
N. Livson, *Elements of Psychology* (N.Y.,
2nd ed., 1969).

psychology of religion, see RELIGION,
PSYCHOLOGY OF.

psychometrics. The techniques of quanti-
fying human mental traits, particularly the
statistical treatment of MENTAL TEST-
ING. Until recently, these techniques were
almost exclusively concerned with sorting
people into different categories, especially
for educational and vocational placement.
QUANTIFICATION is usually accomplished
by devising test items that show maximum
discrimination between individuals, and
by the use of standard test STATISTICS that
emphasize the internal consistency of the
items to one another. Such tests are
norm-referenced, i.e. individual scores are
determined by reference to the scores
achieved by a relevant group, most often a
group of the same age.

Psychometrics, and consequently the
mental testing movement, were initiated
in 1883 by the English biologist Sir Francis Galton during his investigations into
heredity (see GENETICS). His statistical
methods for the analysis of data on individual differences were developed by his
students and their associates, particularly
Karl Pearson (1892) and Charles Spearman, into a test theory which held up very
well under subsequent formal mathematical analysis. Pearson's extensive work on
CORRELATION, together with the introduction by Spearman (1904) of the CON-
CEPT of FACTOR ANALYSIS, was the breakthrough that launched the mental testing
movement, pioneered by J. McK. Cattell
(1890) and E. L. Thorndike (1904) in
America, and in Europe by A. Binet and
T. Simon (1905), who produced the first
influential measures of scholastic
aptitude. In Britain. Cyril Burt, an
associate of Spearman and devotee of
Galton, began in 1909 a lifetime's work
on the testing of INTELLIGENCE and
achievement.

The development of group testing during World War I (for classifying recruits

according to intellectual level) gave additional impetus to a movement which has
steadily expanded and proliferated.
Today, in most industrialized countries,
there are large establishments devoted to
the construction, application, and
interpretation of standardized tests which
are widely used for educational and
vocational selection, and which play an
important part in the determination of
life-chances.

In recent years, opposition to mental
testing has grown. On the one hand, it is
attacked by those who claim that its
meritocratic rhetoric masks the perpetuation of existing inequalities in the distribution of power and opportunities (see
ÉLITISM; RACISM; MERITOCRACY);
American psychometricians, for example,
have revealed the loading of most vocabulary tests in favour of whites by devising other such tests which are loaded in
favour of blacks, and in which the normal
higher white rating is reversed. On the
other hand, it is criticized for having failed
to evolve new forms to meet changing
applications, particularly in the field of
education. Here a major effort has been
made during the last decade to improve
the quality of the curriculum; but appropriate procedures for measuring the efficacy of educational treatments rather
than the performance of students have yet
to be devised.

Recently there has been a tendency
to replace norm-referenced tests by
criterion-referenced ones, whose primary
function is to compare individual
performance, not with other individual
performances, but with a specific criterion, such as how well the subject might
need to perform a specified task, or how
well he might reasonably be expected to
perform if given adequate instruction.
Since tests are traditionally validated
against how particular groups perform,
and since test STATISTICS are based on
concepts of individual differences, the
classical ways of judging tests through
'validity' and 'reliability' are not suited
to criterion-referenced tests. How to
judge their quality remains a formidable
problem.   B.M.

Bibl: R. L. Thorndike, *Educational
Measurement* (Washington, 2nd ed.,
1971).

psychoneurosis, see NEUROSIS.

psychopathology. In ABNORMAL PSYCHOLOGY and PSYCHIATRY, any disorder of mental functioning; also the study of such disorders.　　　　W.Z.

psychopharmacology. The study of the behavioural effects of DRUGS (sense 1). It is Janus-like: it may aim principally at the CLASSIFICATION of drugs according to the similarity of their effects on behaviour, or at the classification of types of behaviour according to the similarity of their susceptibility to the effects of drugs. The former aim has usually been more prominent, but the latter may eventually prove more important. With regard to the former, the existing pharmacological classifications have proved very unhelpful in predicting effects of drugs on behaviour, while it is often difficult to see any pharmacological similarity between drugs that are indistinguishable in their behavioural effects. Furthermore, drugs that have a relatively precise pharmacological action frequently turn out to have remarkably unspecific behavioural effects, while drugs that have highly specific effects on behaviour have very wide-ranging and unspecific effects on the chemistry of the brain. Thus psychopharmacology is very much a discipline in its own right and not merely an INTERFACE between its two parents, PSYCHOLOGY and PHARMACOLOGY. See also NEUROPSYCHOLOGY.　　　J.A.G.

psychophysics. The study of relations, especially quantitative, between psychological characteristics of perceived properties and physical characteristics of STIMULI, e.g. between the heard loudness and pitch of a tone and the intensity and frequency of the ACOUSTIC stimulus. Pioneered in Germany around 1850 by G. T. Fechner, psychophysics is a field in which work has continued vigorously.　　　I.M.L.H.
Bibl: see under PERCEPTION.

psychosexual development. The processes whereby human beings reach a mature expression of their sexual impulses, including attitudes and values concerning their sexuality. In Freud's view, psychosexual development included the earliest feelings of affection of the boy for his mother or the girl for her father (see OEDIPUS COMPLEX; ELECTRA COMPLEX) psychosexual development in women.

J.S.B.

Bibl: C. S. Ford and F. A. Beach, *Patterns of Sexual Behaviour* (N.Y., 1951; London, 1952).

psychosis. In PSYCHIATRY and ABNORMAL PSYCHOLOGY in the West, a term used for one of the main classes of mental illness. In the present state of psychiatric knowledge it is not possible to classify the majority of mental illnesses on the basis of causal factors, and modern systems of CLASSIFICATION go back to the work of Emil Kraepelin (1856–1926), a German psychiatrist who endeavoured to establish definite psychiatric diseases and to bring order into psychiatric taxonomy. Psychoses are usually distinguished from NEUROSES, personality disorders, PSYCHOSOMATIC disorders, and MENTAL RETARDATION, and are themselves divided into the *organic* and the so-called *functional* psychoses. In organic psychoses, such as general paralysis of the insane and delirium, there is a demonstrable physical abnormality in the brain. In functional psychoses, such as SCHIZOPHRENIA and the affective psychoses, no underlying physical disease has been discovered; but the mental and physical symptoms, together with the results of genetic research, are thought by many psychiatrists to indicate underlying morbid endocrine or biochemical changes (see ENDOCRINOLOGY; BIOCHEMISTRY).

Traditionally, much attention has been paid to the time-honoured distinction between psychoses and neuroses. Probably the origins of this distinction were mainly social and historical: psychotic (mad, insane, or lunatic) patients were those whose behaviour was so deranged that they were placed in madhouses or asylums, while neurotics were treated in physicians' consulting-rooms. There is no single characteristic by which psychoses can be defined. Psychoses have been said to be distinctively characterized by greater severity of illness; total dissolution of the personality; lack of insight into the illness; inability to distinguish between subjective experience and reality; the presence of delusions and hallucinations; the occurrence of a marked personality change which cannot be interpreted as an understandable development of the personality or reaction to psychological TRAUMA.

Exceptions are readily found to all these criteria. Nevertheless, psychiatrists of similar training can achieve a high level of agreement in classifying patients as neurotic or psychotic.

Whilst most psychiatrists agree that a system of diagnostic classification is necessary, the term psychosis is not of great value in clinical practice. Other, less inclusive diagnostic categories are more useful, and decisions as to treatment and prognosis are based on other considerations.

D.H.G.

psychosomatic. Adjective derived from the Greek words for 'soul' and 'body' and used in medical and PSYCHIATRIC contexts – it can be applied to a patient or to his disorder – to imply a relationship between mental and physical states of health; *psychosomatics* is the study of this relationship. The adjective is most commonly used in the context of physical conditions, e.g. gastric or duodenal ulcers or severe headaches, that derive from stress states. Most theories of psychosomatic illness offer inadequate EXPLANATIONS both of why some individuals 'somatize' their symptoms of stress while others do not (manifesting ANXIETY or depression instead), and of 'organ choice', i.e. why one person develops ulcers, another chronic fatigue. Contemporary research indicates that in stress there is massive involvement of the adreno-cortical system, and that this can express itself in a variety of physical symptoms by maintaining in the bloodstream high levels of circulating catecholamine which may disrupt different organ systems. See also ABNORMAL PSYCHOLOGY; MIND-BODY PROBLEM.

J.S.B.

psychotherapy. A sub-class of the methods used – either within PSYCHIATRY or outside it – for treating sufferers from mental abnormalities. The sub-class is easier to delimit by giving examples of what it *includes* (e.g. PSYCHOANALYSIS, COUNSELLING, ordinary psychiatric interviews, the non-verbal movement and body therapies) and what it *excludes* (e.g. ELECTRO-CONVULSIVE THERAPY, PSYCHOPHARMACOLOGY, surgical interference with the brain, OPERANT CONDITIONING, the *desensitization* technique of BEHAVIOUR THERAPY) than by a formal definition. But perhaps the most fruitful way of trying to distinguish between psychotherapy and other methods is in terms of the sort of situation and interaction set up in the former between patient and therapist and deliberately used for therapeutic purposes. This revolves essentially around a special relationship between patient and therapist that is produced and maintained by the rules of operation the particular therapist employs. Thus, a psychoanalyst will operate in accordance with certain rules which will generate a characteristic type of situation and relationship between patient and analyst, in which, e.g., the development of TRANSFERENCE is a key feature. In contrast, a counsellor in the tradition of Carl Rogers will operate in a different way, and this will produce a different type of situation and relationship, in which transference is minimal and the development of spontaneity in the verbal expression of feeling becomes important.

Historically, psychotherapy became an accepted part of contemporary psychiatry largely as the result of the growth and influence of psychoanalysis. Likewise, the different methods of contemporary psychotherapy are, in large measure, developments out of psychoanalytic practice. In the last three decades, however, many therapists have become increasingly dissatisfied with psychoanalytic practice because of its length and slowness, the few patients who can be reached by it, its great expense, and its rigidities, which (allegedly) restrict its effectiveness. Accordingly, many psychotherapists have struck out in novel directions in attempts to overcome the limitations of traditional psychoanalysis, e.g. by shortening the duration of therapy, and by a variety of group techniques such as GROUP THERAPY and PSYCHODRAMA. About the results of psychotherapy it is very difficult to establish any claims, whether positive or negative, because of the massive complexity of the issue, and the comparative crudities of our current techniques of investigation. At best, perhaps, it can be said that we have some grounds for thinking that psychotherapy can be of use when it is appropriately used and skilfully operated.

Despite the doubts and difficulties that surround it, psychotherapy has had an immense impact on Western culture. Thus, it has greatly affected our ways of thinking about and organizing human relations in various departments of life, e.g. educational practice, prison organization, and the selection and training of business managers. Material produced by psychotherapy has formed the evidential base for a number of theories (FREUDIAN, JUNGIAN, etc.) about human nature which are of great interest, and, if true, of enormous importance. These theories have stimulated psychologists in their efforts to uncover the hard facts about human nature, and have permeated our thought and attitudes in ways not yet adequately charted.   B.A.F.

Bibl: J. M. Hunt (ed.), *Personality and the Behavior Disorders* (2 vols., N.Y., 1944).

psychotic, see under PSYCHOSIS.

public debt, see NATIONAL DEBT.

public housing. Dwellings financed directly by governmental agencies and/or local authorities, and rented to tenants. It assumes the provision of housing as a basic social service for those groups unable to compete in the housing market, or as a service to a much wider group, depending on the political outlook of the country. In Britain the ratio between private and public housing built since 1945 has fluctuated around 40:60, with the larger share going to one or other sector according to political control. In the U.S.A. the proportion of public housing is very much smaller, in the U.S.S.R. very much greater.   M.BR.

Bibl: D. V. Donnison, *The Government of Housing* (Harmondsworth, 1967).

Public Lending Right, see PLR.

public opinion poll, see OPINION POLL.

public relations. Euphemism for the professional organization of attempts to secure public understanding and support for the activities of bodies such as governments, political parties, commercial and industrial organizations, professional bodies, etc. Public relations thus include the winning of sympathy for the public activities of one state from the peoples of other countries. It includes, but is by no means confined to, propaganda.   D.C.W.

Bibl: S. Kelley, *Professional Public Relations and Political Power* (Baltimore, 1956); D. J. G. Hennessy, *Communication and Political Power* (London, 1966).

public school. (1) In the U.S.A., any primary school or SECONDARY SCHOOL supported by public funds. (2) In Britain, a term paradoxically applied to certain private or INDEPENDENT SCHOOLS for pupils of, mostly, 13 to 18, the most famous of which, founded in the Middle Ages (e.g. Eton, Winchester) have long been the nurseries of the British governing class. Variously defined, public schools show, typically, these features: (*a*) foundation or considerable enlargement during the 19th century, in the heyday of British imperial expansion (see IMPERIALISM); (*b*) an inherited ethos which stems from Thomas Arnold's declared aim (1828) of turning out 'Christian men' and emphasizes such virtues as 'gentlemanly conduct' (Arnold's phrase), discipline, self-discipline, public service, and the 'team spirit'; (*c*) a wide range of EXTRA-CURRICULAR ACTIVITIES; (*d*) above-average academic standards and results, helped by (*e*) an above-average staffing ratio; (*f*) pupils who are predominantly or exclusively boarders, and (*g*) of one sex only (though coeducation is increasing); (*h*) very high fees. Their supporters stress (*b*), (*c*), and (*d*); opponents emphasize the unfairness of (*e*) and (*h*), the psychological effects of (*f*) ('an undeveloped heart', according to E. M. Forster), the sexual dangers inherent in (*g*), and the ÉLITISM and social divisiveness of the whole system.

In America the nearest equivalents to the British public schools, found mainly on the east coast, and today mainly coeducational, are known as *college preparatory schools*; in Britain a *preparatory school* is one that prepares pupils (from, in general, the age of about 9) for the entrance examinations of the public schools, many of whose features it shares.   O.S.

Bibl: Public Schools Commission, *First Report* (Newsom Report, London, 2 vols., 1968); *Second Report* (Dennison Report, London, 3 vols., 1970).

public sector. One of two major divisions of convenience of a national economy, the other being the PRIVATE SECTOR. The public or government sector embraces not only the official economic activity of central and local governments but also the wholly nationalized industries and any corporations that are in part publicly financed. It does not, however, embrace the economic activity represented by the consumer expenditure of government employees. In both the Soviet Union and China the public sector represents the entire spectrum of economic activity; in most MIXED ECONOMIES it represents a minimum of about one quarter of all economic activity.   D.E.

Puccini, Giacomo (Italian composer, 1858–1924), see under VERISM.

pulsar. A type of star first observed in 1967 with RADIO TELESCOPES, which emits RADIO FREQUENCY pulses separated by very regular intervals. The pulsations are almost certainly a 'lighthouse effect', produced by a jet of radiating material on a rapidly rotating *neutron star* (i.e. a star whose highly condensed matter is in the form of a 'liquid' of NEUTRONS). M.V.B.

pulsating universe. A hypothetical system in COSMOLOGY. The EXPANSION OF THE UNIVERSE resulting from the explosion postulated in the BIG-BANG HYPOTHESIS is supposed to slow down and eventually become a contraction under the mutual GRAVITATION of the GALAXIES. When all the matter is compressed into a small region of space, nuclear forces (e.g. STRONG INTERACTIONS) would result in another explosion, and the cycle would repeat itself indefinitely, with a period of about 100,000 million years. Whether the universe is in fact pulsating, or whether it will expand indefinitely, depends on the total amount of matter in it; at present the experimental evidence suggests continued expansion rather than recontraction.
M.V.B.

Puni, Ivan (Russo-French painter, 1894–1956), see under CUBO-FUTURISM.

purchasing power parity theory, see under PARITY.

pure line. A pure line of organisms is a lineage which has become virtually homozygous (see GENE), so that genetic VARIATION has been extinguished. Pure lines can be achieved in self-pollinating plants and in laboratory animals such as guinea-pigs and mice which have been bred together, parent to offspring or brother to sister, for upwards of 50 successive generations. Sex differences apart, the members of such pure lines resemble each other as closely as if they were identical twins. P.M.

pure theory of law, see LAW, PURE THEORY OF.

purism. An aesthetic movement proposed in 1918 by Amédée Ozenfant and the architect Le Corbusier (Charles-Édouard Jeanneret) in their book *Après le Cubisme* that advocated the restructuring of CUBISM. Reacting to the prettification of Cubism after 1916 by painters such as Braque, and to the NEO-CLASSICISM of Picasso, purism sought to maintain the representation of clearly identifiable objects and forms and a logical composition. No significant school developed, despite the interest of other artists such as Fernand Léger, and some analogies in the work of Giorgio Morandi and certain NEUE SACHLICHKEIT artists. A.K.W.

Bibl: A. Ozenfant, tr. E. E. Asburn, *Foundations of Modern Art* (London, 1931; N.Y., 1952); Tate Gallery Catalogue, *Léger and Purist Paris* (London, 1970); R. E. Krauss, 'Léger, Le Corbusier, and Purism' (*Artforum*, April 1972).

purposive explanation, see under EXPLANATION.

purposivism. A label for any approach to PSYCHOLOGY which asserts that man is a purposeful, striving creature who is, in large part, responsible for his own conduct and destiny, e.g., McDougall's HORMIC PSYCHOLOGY, COGNITIVE PSYCHOLOGY, EXISTENTIAL PSYCHOLOGY, HUMANISTIC PSYCHOLOGY. The opposite assertion is that man's conduct is nothing but the fully determined outcome of his heredity (see GENETICS), his past experience, and his present ENVIRONMENT. I.M.L.H.

Bibl: M. Wertheimer, *Fundamental Issues in Psychology* (London and N.Y., 1972).

Puy, Jean (French painter, 1876–1960), see under FAUVES.

Pyatakov, Gregory Leonodovich (Soviet politician, 1890–1937), see under MOSCOW TRIALS.

Q

Quadragesimo Anno. An ENCYCLICAL issued by Pope Pius XI in 1931, 40 years after RERUM NOVARUM, restating Roman CATHOLIC teaching on social problems. Both COMMUNISM and LAISSEZ-FAIRE were condemned, and a preference for GUILD SOCIALISM was implied.　D.L.E.

Quakers. Members of a religious body, so nicknamed soon after its foundation by George Fox (1624–91); its official title is the Society of Friends. Dispensing with many of the outward forms of religion such as creeds, professional clergy, and traditional words in worship, the Quakers have commended themselves by their philanthropy, their PACIFISM, and their basis in Christian (see CHRISTIANITY) MYSTICISM. Their nickname was suggested by their trembling or excitement when gripped by religious ecstasy (see PENTECOSTALISM), but nowadays in their worship calm, although spontaneous, words arise from a corporate silence.
　　　　　　　　　　　　　　D.L.E.
Bibl: H. Loukes, *The Quaker Contribution* (London and N.Y., 1965).

quantification.
(1) In general, the expression of a property or quality in numerical terms. Properties that can usefully be expressed in these terms are said to be *quantifiable*; descriptions, theories, and techniques couched in such terms are said to be *quantitative*. Despite the widespread myth that only quantitative measurements and descriptions are of use to science, many *non-quantifiable* things, i.e. things that cannot be usefully measured on numerical scales, can be given precise objective descriptions that can play a valid role in scientific theories and EXPLANATIONS. Thus LINGUISTS describe the structures of sentences, CHEMISTS describe the structures of chemical MOLECULES, and PSYCHOLOGISTS may one day be able to describe the structures of mental processes, using precise mathematical language including *non-numerical* symbols. It is arguable that much research effort has

been wasted – particularly in the SOCIAL SCIENCES, but perhaps also in the NATURAL SCIENCES, e.g. BIOLOGY – in attempting to force non-quantifiable processes into quantitative moulds, instead of searching for more relevant kinds of mathematical representation.　A.S.
(2) In LOGIC, the referring aspect of PROPOSITIONS which do not refer to a particular, designated individual but to all members or some members of a class (universally and existentially quantified propositions, respectively). In the PREDICATE CALCULUS, or logic of quantified statements, the basic, universally quantified formula 'For all *x*, if *x* is *A* then *x* is *B*' is not quite equivalent in meaning to its counterpart in ordinary language, 'All *A* are *B*'. It is entailed by it (see ENTAILMENT), but does not entail it, since the latter is not true unless there are some *A* things (i.e. unless it has 'existential import') whereas the former is, vacuously, true if there are none. The quantificational interpretation of universally and existentially general statements justifies its deviation from ordinary language by its systematic formal manipulability and by its perspicuousness. On the second point, it makes explicit the ambiguity of 'Everybody loves somebody' which it represents either as 'For any *x* there is some *y* that *x* loves' or as 'There is a *y* that every *x* loves'. Besides 'all' and 'some' and their synonyms, language contains other quantificational expressions: 'most', 'many', 'several', 'a few'.　A.Q.

quantitative history. Any serious attempt to present statistical evidence in a work of historical research. Economic historians took the lead in the 1920s with studies of price history. Political historians followed, using the methods of PROSOPOGRAPHY. More recently, quantitative methods have transformed SOCIAL HISTORY and have even made some impact on the HISTORY OF IDEAS, e.g. in the studies of *lexicometry* (the study of the frequency of theme-words in a corpus of texts) carried out for 18th-century France. Quantitative historical studies received a great boost in the 1960s, when academics began to get access to COMPUTERS for their research projects. The profession is still divided about the reliability and the significance of the results. See also ECONOMIC HISTORY; SERIAL HISTORY.

P.B.

Bibl: R. Floud, *An Introduction to Quantitative Methods for Historians* (London, 1973).

quantity theory of money. A theory relating the price level in an economy to the supply of money within that economy and the volume of goods produced: in its simplest form $MV = PT$, where M is the supply of money, V the velocity of circulation (or the number of times a unit of money changes hands within the given period), P the price level, and T the quantity of goods produced. In the alternative form

$$P = \frac{MV}{T}$$ the theory has important

implications for the control of INFLATION, since it can be shown that in the short term, when the output of goods is fixed and the velocity of circulation constant, the main determinant of the price level is the supply of money.

D.E.

Bibl: I. Fisher, *The Purchasing Power of Money* (N.Y., rev. ed., 1926).

quantum chemistry, see under THEORETICAL CHEMISTRY.

quantum electrodynamics, see under FIELD THEORY.

quantum electronics. A branch of engineering devoted to the design and construction of MICROWAVE power generators (e.g. the MASER) whose operation is based on QUANTUM MECHANICS.

M.V.B.

quantum mechanics (or *wave mechanics*; developed in the 1920s by Born, Dirac, Heisenberg, Jordan, and Schrödinger). The system of MECHANICS, based on the WAVE-PARTICLE DUALITY of matter and RADIATION, which must be used to describe systems so small that NEWTONIAN MECHANICS breaks down.

Whereas in CLASSICAL PHYSICS the state of a system is specified by a precise simultaneous determination of all relev-

ant 'dynamical variables' (position, MOMENTUM, ENERGY, etc.), the UNCERTAINTY PRINCIPLE asserts that this specification cannot be made for small-scale systems. Thus complete DETERMINISM is lost, and in quantum mechanics systems are specified by stating the *probability* of given values for position, momentum, etc. This indeterminacy can be seen very clearly whenever a single atomic event can be observed (e.g. in RADIOACTIVITY); usually, however, experiments measure an average value resulting from the cumulative effect of many atomic events (e.g. a 'line' in SPECTROSCOPY comes from the radiation of many ATOMS).

Probability enters the framework of quantum theory as the intensity of a *wave* whose frequency and wavelength are related to its energy and momentum by PLANCK'S CONSTANT; from a knowledge of the WAVE FUNCTION, all observable properties of the system may be calculated. ENERGY LEVELS, which appear *ad hoc* in BOHR THEORY, arise naturally in quantum mechanics from the interference of waves travelling round ORBITS. For example, waves describing ELECTRONS in an atom will only be in PHASE after successive circuits if a whole number of DE BROGLIE WAVELENGTHS fits into an orbit, and this only occurs at certain discrete energies; between these energies, the waves making successive circuits interfere destructively and the wave function is zero. For large systems or large QUANTUM NUMBERS, the energy levels lie too close together to be differentiated, and Newtonian mechanics affords a very accurate approximate description; this is the 'correspondence principle' between the two theories.

The INDETERMINISM in quantum mechanics (which is embodied in the COMPLEMENTARITY PRINCIPLE) has caused much controversy: Einstein wrote 'God does not play dice', while others have tried to construct theories in which 'hidden variables' operate on a very fine scale to determine, for example, the precise moment when a given atom will radiate, or a NUCLEUS decay. Despite these doubts about its conceptual foundations, quantum mechanics is supported by a great mass of experimental evidence (e.g. in ATOMIC PHYSICS and SOLID-STATE PHYSICS), and must be regarded as one of the greatest intellectual triumphs in all PHYSICS.   M.V.B.

Bibl: B. Hoffmann, *The Strange Story of the Quantum* (Harmondsworth and Gloucester, Mass., 2nd ed., 1963); J. Andrade e Silva and G. Lochak, tr. P. Moore, *Quanta* (London, 1969); G. Gamow, *Thirty Years that Shook Physics* (N.Y., 1966; London, 1972).

quantum number. A number used to label the state of a system in QUANTUM MECHANICS. For example, the ENERGY LEVELS of an ELECTRON in an ATOM have the quantum numbers 1, 2, 3, etc. (starting from the *ground state* – see ENERGY LEVEL), two further numbers label the rotational state, and a fourth (half-integral) quantum number describes the SPIN. Whenever the quantum number is an integer, it is equal to the number of oscillations of the WAVE FUNCTION.
                                                    M.V.B.

quantum statistics. The QUANTUM MECHANICS of systems of identical PARTICLES (e.g. ELEMENTARY PARTICLES). The STATISTICAL MECHANICS of such systems depends on whether or not the particles are *fermions* (e.g. ELECTRONS and NUCLEONS), which obey the EXCLUSION PRINCIPLE, or *bosons* (e.g. MESONS and PHOTONS), which do not. See also BOSE-EINSTEIN STATISTICS; FERMI-DIRAC STATISTICS; SPIN.   M.V.B.

quantum theory. A body of knowledge concerning the nature of the physical world, developed to explain a wide variety of phenomena of ATOMIC PHYSICS, NUCLEAR PHYSICS, CHEMISTRY, ASTRO-PHYSICS, etc. The central principles of this theory were originally developed as a system of QUANTUM MECHANICS, but modern developments are concerned with more fundamental problems, such as the properties of ELEMENTARY PARTICLES, which have no counterparts in classical MECHANICS.   J.Z.

quark. In PHYSICS, one of three different hypothetical PARTICLES which might be the structural units from which many of the ELEMENTARY PARTICLES are constructed. Quarks have the unusual property that their electric charges are multiples of *one-third* of the charge on the ELECTRON. Despite extensive

searches, no quarks have yet been observed.   M.V.B.

quarter-tone, see under MICROTONE.

quartile, see under PERCENTILE.

quasars (QUASI-stellAR objects; sometimes called *QSO*s). Compact sources, discovered in 1963, of RADIATION outside our GALAXY, which are observed to possess extraordinarily large RED SHIFTS of their spectra (see SPECTROSCOPY). If these red shifts arise from a DOPPLER EFFECT, then quasars must be some of the most distant objects known (see EXPANSION OF THE UNIVERSE), emitting vast amounts of ENERGY in order to produce the observed brightness. Where this energy comes from is not known; one hypothesis is that it arises from the collision of a galaxy of ordinary matter with one of ANTI-MATTER.   M.V.B.

Bibl: F. Hoyle, *Galaxies, Nuclei and Quasars* (N.Y., 1965; London, 1966).

Quasimodo, Salvatore (Italian poet and critic, 1901–68), see under HERMETIC.

quaternion. A generalization of the notion of COMPLEX NUMBER discovered by Sir W. R. Hamilton in 1843; the first example of objects whose multiplication is not COMMUTATIVE. For many purposes they have been superseded by VECTORS.
                                                    R.G.

queuing theory. Methods for determining the best ways of serving queues. For example, if a business firm's vehicles are repaired when they break down, the number arriving for repair on any day is uncertain, and it is not immediately obvious how large a repair shop the firm should run. It is not usually possible to describe the behaviour of the queue by explicit mathematical expressions, and indirect methods of computation have to be used. As a group of problems in applied PROBABILITY THEORY, the field hardly deserves the title of a 'theory'.   J.A.M.

Bibl: D. R. Cox and W. L. Smith, *Queues* (London and N.Y., 1961).

Quine, Willard Van Orman (U.S. philosopher, *b.*1908), see under ANALYTIC; HOLISM; PERSPECTIVISM; PLATONISM.

Quisling. A traitor who collaborates with his country's invading and occupying enemies, as did Major Vidkun Quisling (1887–1945), Norwegian ex-Minister of Defence, who urged and abetted the NAZI German invasion of Norway on 9 April 1940 and later headed a collaborationist government in Norway.   D.C.W.

Bibl: P. M. Hayes, *Quisling* (Newton Abbot, 1971).

Qumran, see under DEAD SEA SCROLLS.

R

Raabe, Wilhelm (German novelist, 1831–1910), see under REALISM.

race. A classificatory term, broadly equivalent to subspecies. Applied most frequently to human beings, it indicates a group characterized by closeness of common descent and usually also by some shared physical distinctiveness such as colour of skin.

Biologically, the CONCEPT has only limited value. Most scientists today recognize that all humans derive from a common stock and that groups within the SPECIES have migrated and intermarried constantly. Human populations therefore constitute a GENETIC continuum where racial distinctions are relative, not absolute. Any remaining categorization of races then relates only to gradients of frequency delineating the varying geographical incidence of particular genetical elements common to the whole species. It is also acknowledged that visible characteristics, popularly regarded as major racial pointers, are not inherited in any simple package and that they reflect only a small proportion of an individual's genetical make-up.

The educationally delicate question of correlation between race and INTELLIGENCE has remained more disputable. Since the later 1960s controversy has surrounded attempts by Arthur Jensen and others to demonstrate here a dominance of nature over nurture. But no adequate evidence has emerged to prove that some races are, for distinctively biological reasons, superior to others in intelligence or cultural potential.

Socially, race has a significance dependent not upon science but upon belief. Men depict themselves and see one another in terms of groups which, however frail their objective basis, thereby assume social importance. *Race relations* arise between groups whose interaction is conditioned by belief in the fact and relevance of their racial difference. The resulting behaviour is best studied within the wider sociological context of inter-group

relations generally. South Africa is the outstanding contemporary example of a state where domestic social and political relations are structured principally around racial criteria (see APARTHEID). *Racial prejudice*, in its usual hostile connotation, covers attitudes hastily or unreasonably formed to the detriment of those deemed racially alien. *Racialism* is preferably reserved to describe actions that discriminate, in most instances adversely, in regard to other races. But the term is tending to become interchangeable both with racial prejudice and also with *racism*.

Hitherto, however, this last label has maintained a valuably distinctive application to IDEOLOGY. There it covers particularly those systematic doctrines about the central significance of racial inequality that constituted a major, though still underestimated, theme in Western thought from at least 1850 until 1945. At first widely supported by scientists, these ideas were soon linked with SOCIAL DARWINISM. They contributed to the ethos of IMPERIALISM, and in Europe to ANTISEMITISM. Landmarks in this literature of racist DETERMINISM are A. de Gobineau's *Essay on the Inequality of the Human Races* (1853–5) and H. S. Chamberlain's *Foundations of the Nineteenth Century* (1899). The theory and practice of NAZISM marked a culmination. But even now the tradition's basic idiom of virtuous purity and vicious blending, though biologically discredited, remains embedded in much popular thinking about race.

M.D.B.

Bibl: M. Banton, *Race Relations* (London and N.Y., 1967); J. Barzun, *Race: a Study in Superstition* (London and N.Y., rev. ed., 1965).

radar (RAdio Detection And Ranging). A system whereby short pulses of MICROWAVES are sent out from an aerial, which may be on land, or on a ship or aircraft. Any objects in the path of the beam cause echoes which are received back at the source. The time delay and nature of these echoes (viewed as a display on a

CATHODE RAY TUBE) give information about the distance and nature of the reflecting object. See also SONAR. M.V.B.

Radburn layout. A form of layout separating pedestrians and traffic, developed by Clarence Stein and first applied by him at Radburn, New Jersey, in 1928. It consists of one or more *superblocks*, a superblock being an area containing a complex of houses (and/or shops, schools, offices, etc.) built around a central green or pedestrian space. Each superblock is ringed by a peripheral road off which short cul-de-sacs provide access for vehicles. For pedestrians, access is via the green areas which are linked to each other by underpasses or overpasses. The basic principle was first seen in Jefferson's plan for the University of Virginia; recent examples include housing estates, Lancaster University, and NEW TOWN shopping centres.
M.BR.
Bibl: C. S. Stein, *Toward New Towns for America* (Cambridge, Mass., 1957; Liverpool, 2nd ed., 1959).

Radcliffe-Brown, Alfred Reginald (British anthropologist, 1881–1955), see under FUNCTIONALISM.

Radek, Karl (Polish-Russian Communist leader, 1885–1939), see under MOSCOW TRIALS; NATIONAL BOLSHEVISM.

radiation. Waves or PARTICLES travelling outwards from a source; also the emission of such waves or particles. The term usually refers to electromagnetic waves (see ELECTROMAGNETIC FIELD). These cover an enormous frequency range (the 'electromagnetic spectrum') of which visible light (see OPTICS) constitutes only a very small part.
The principal kinds of electromagnetic waves, in order of increasing wavelength, are: GAMMA RAYS, X-RAYS, ULTRA-VIOLET radiation, visible light, INFRA-RED radiation, MICROWAVES, and RADIO FREQUENCY waves. Frequency and wavelength are related by the EQUATION *wavelength × frequency = speed of light in empty space,* and the speed of light is 300 million kilometres per second. See also BLACK-BODY RADIATION; QUANTUM MECHANICS; SPECTROSCOPY. M.V.B.

radiation biology (or *radiobiology*). The branch of BIOLOGY that deals with the immediate and long-term effects of RADIATIONS, particularly ionizing radiations (see IONIZATION) and the useful purposes which such radiations may be made to serve. Penetrating ionizing radiations such as X-RAYS and gamma rays have a disruptive effect on DNA (see NUCLEIC ACID) and can therefore lead to MUTATION (see RADIATION GENETICS). They also suppress CELL division – a property that is put to good use in the radiation therapy of tumours, for it is characteristic of radiation and of radiomimetic drugs (i.e. drugs whose pharmacological actions mimic those of irradiation) that they both cause cancers and also, under different conditions of administration, discourage their growth. A characteristic biological effect of radiation and radiomimetic drugs on warm-blooded animals is that of interfering with the manufacture of red blood corpuscles because of the destruction of stem cells. For a cognate reason, such radiations also diminish IMMUNITY (sense 2). In experimental animals the transplantation of bone marrow is a feasible method of repairing radiation injury in so far as it affects the manufacture of red blood corpuscles, but the genetic effects of radiation are cumulative, irreversible and, in general, harmful.
Radiobiology also includes the preparation and use of radioactively labelled ELEMENTS and compounds to serve as TRACERS in studies of METABOLISM. The use of radioactive substances (see RADIOACTIVITY) for this purpose needs to be controlled by strict regulations, and the same applies to the use of radioactive substances in painting watch dials etc. In all civilized countries legislation has been introduced to reduce to a minimum the population's exposure to radioactive substances whether produced by atomic or nuclear weapons or by atomic power plants (see ATOMIC ENERGY; NUCLEAR REACTOR). P.M.

radiation genetics. A branch both of GENETICS and of RADIATION BIOLOGY that grew up under (1) the influence of H. J. Muller's discovery that ionizing (see IONIZATION) RADIATIONS can induce MUTATION, and (2) the realization that certain industrial processes and offensive weapons may increase the dosages of radiation to which human beings are exposed. P.M.

Bibl: P. C. Koller, *Chromosomes and Genes* (Edinburgh, 1968; N.Y., 1971).

radical. In CHEMISTRY, a term used since the time of Lavoisier – though now rarely – to denote a building block in the construction of a chemical compound. A radical is often merely one ATOM, but is frequently a group of atoms which behaves as a single atom or ION. Thus ethane (C_2H_6) can be considered as the combination of two methyl (CH_3 radicals, while the ammonium ion and the sulphate ion are examples of inorganic radicals. B.F.

radical chic. A phrase coined in 1970 by Tom Wolfe, American journalist, to describe specifically a benefit concert given by Leonard Bernstein for the BLACK PANTHERS and, more generally, the current fashion of adopting radical political causes (see RADICALISM) in New York society. He likened this trendy romanticizing of primitive souls, e.g. American Indians and Chicano grape-workers, to the French 19th-century phenomenon denoted by the phrase *nostalgie de la boue* (literally, 'hankering after mud').
A.K.W.

radicalism. A tendency to press political views and actions towards an extreme. Historically, radicalism has always been associated with dissatisfaction with the status quo and an appeal for basic political and social changes. But the meaning of the word has varied in different periods and countries, ranging from the moderate CENTRE, like the *Parti Républicain Radical et Radical Socialiste* which was influential in France before 1939, but was neither radical nor SOCIALIST, to the extreme ultra-REVOLUTIONARY radicals of the post-war NEW LEFT. Although in some countries, e.g. the U.S.A., 'radicalism' is mostly used with reference to the LEFT (where radicals are clearly distinguished from LIBERALS), it can also be characteristic of the RIGHT; notable examples are FASCISM and NAZISM. The term is also used in the wider sense of a disposition to challenge established views in any field of human endeavour, e.g. in the arts or scholarship. L.L.

radio astronomy. A branch of ASTRONOMY, in which RADIO TELESCOPES are used to study electromagnetic RADIATION at RADIO FREQUENCIES emitted by sources outside the earth. Most of the radio sources are GALAXIES, but the sun and the planet Jupiter, as well as PULSARS, QUASARS, and SUPERNOVAE, all emit radio waves. Apart from visible light, radio waves (in the 1 cm to 10 metre wavelength band) constitute the only electromagnetic radiation capable of reaching the ground without being absorbed in the atmosphere or reflected by the IONOSPHERE. The revolution in COSMOLOGY in the last two decades has been stimulated largely by the discoveries of radio astronomy, especially the COSMIC BACKGROUND RADIATION. M.V.B.

Bibl: J. S. Hey, *The Radio Universe* (Oxford and N.Y. 1971).

radio frequency. A vibration frequency in the range 10,000 Hertz to 100,000 million Hertz (1 Hertz = 1 complete vibration cycle per second). Radio frequency electromagnetic RADIATION includes the relatively long waves used for broadcasting, as well as the MICROWAVES used for RADAR. M.V.B.

radio telescopes. The 'eyes' of RADIO ASTRONOMY, which receive and locate the direction of RADIO FREQUENCY electromagnetic RADIATION reaching the earth. Because the wavelength is thousands of times greater than that of visible light, radio telescopes are gigantic structures. The steerable parabolic dishes which focus the radio waves (in the same way as the mirrors of ordinary telescopes) may be hundreds of feet across, while *radio interferometers,* which locate direction by measuring the PHASE difference between the waves reaching different aerials in an array, may extend over several miles.
M.V.B.

radioactivity. The spontaneous decay of certain types of atomic NUCLEUS. Decay usually takes place by emission of an ALPHA PARTICLE or by the decay of one of the nuclear NEUTRONS and emission of the resulting BETA PARTICLE; thus radioactivity generally results in a change in ATOMIC NUMBER. It is not possible to predict the precise moment at which a given unstable nucleus will decay. However, the

HALF-LIFE can be calculated by means of QUANTUM MECHANICS.

Most naturally-occurring ISOTOPES are stable; the exceptions either have long half-lives (e.g. several thousand million years for uranium) or else are produced continuously by various processes (e.g. radium is a decay product of uranium, and radiocarbon is produced in a NUCLEAR REACTION by COSMIC RAYS – see RADIOCARBON DATING). A great number of short-lived radioisotopes can be produced artificially in NUCLEAR REACTORS (see also TRACE ELEMENT). The health hazards of radioactivity arise from the ENERGY liberated when PARTICLES collide with atomic nuclei in living matter. This causes mechanical damage to TISSUES, and affects the GENETIC structure of CELLS, often resulting in MUTATION.

M.V.B.

radiobiology, see RADIATION BIOLOGY.

radiocarbon dating. In ARCHAEOLOGY, a method of DATING pioneered by W. F. Libby, who first proposed it in 1946. It is based on the rate of decay of the radioactive (see RADIOACTIVITY) ISOTOPE C^{14} incorporated in organic matter. C^{14} is produced from nitrogen^{14} by cosmic RADIATION in the upper atmosphere and is absorbed by living matter in the form of carbon dioxide. The proportion of C^{12} to C^{14} remains constant in the atmosphere and in living plants and animals, but as soon as the organism dies, and further absorption of carbon dioxide ceases, the proportion of C^{14} to C^{12} is steadily decreased by the decay of the unstable radioactive isotope. If we know the HALF-LIFE of C^{14} and the ratio of C^{14} to C^{12} in a sample it is, in theory, possible to work out the absolute age at time of death for a substance which was once alive. The validity of the method as an absolute dating technique rests on two basic assumptions: that the half-life of C^{14} can be accurately determined, and that C^{14} has been produced at a constant rate. Early calculations used a half-life of $5,568 \pm 30$ years (the 'old half-life'), but recent recalculation suggests that 5,730 is a better approximation (the 'preferred half-life'). Comparison between radiocarbon dates and historical dates (e.g. obtained from dating Egyptian woodwork) has for some time shown a certain lack of CORRELATION.

Recent studies involving the radiocarbon dating of tree rings of known age (see under DENDROCHRONOLOGY) have confirmed the discrepancy. It is now suggested that the production of C^{14} was not constant throughout time and that it is necessary to recalibrate 'radiocarbon years' against tree-ring dates to arrive at 'real years'.

Dates are always quoted ± x years, representing the standard statistical error. 4300 ± 50 B.C. means that there is a 2:1 chance of the date lying between 4250 and 4350. Dates are often published B.P. (before the present), the present being 1950. In the wake of the confusion following the apparent need to recalibrate, some writers have adopted the procedure of quoting the date 'b.c.' meaning 'radiocarbon years' and offering a recalibrated date 'B.C.' to represent an approximation to 'real years'. Each date assessment is uniquely numbered according to international agreement. It is accepted that this laboratory number should always be quoted.

B.C.

Bibl: E. H. Willis, 'Radiocarbon Dating', in D. Brothwell and E. Higgs (eds.), *Science in Archaeology* (London, 2nd ed., 1969), pp. 46–57.

radioisotope. Any ISOTOPE of an ELEMENT which is RADIOACTIVE. Some radioisotopes occur naturally but others may be produced artificially by NEUTRON irradiation or by bombardment with helium and other light NUCLEI. They are widely used in diverse fields including medicine (e.g. for irradiation), GEOLOGY, and ARCHEOLOGY (see RADIOCARBON DATING) as well as PHYSICS, CHEMISTRY, BIOLOGY, and ENGINEERING. Radioactive TRACES provide information on the mechanism of CHEMICAL REACTIONS, diffusion processes, chemical analysis, rates of wear, etc.

B.F.

ragtime. An early variant of JAZZ about whose nature and origins debate has continued throughout the century. Although unmistakably jazz-influenced, both in its melodic patterns and in its rhythmic vitality, ragtime is unique in that alone of early jazz music it was *always* notated, so that the works of the ragtime composer-pianists have survived, whereas much early jazz music, never having been recorded or notated, has been lost.

Ragtime seems to have been among the first manifestations of the jazz muse, and certainly flourished before the start of this century. Whether it is a part of jazz or an entirely separate kind of music remains debatable; certainly it was the first form in which jazz hit Europe (*Alexander's Ragtime Band* etc.), and incidentally influenced Stravinsky and others. Its most famous pioneer practitioner – especially since the film *The Sting* – was Scott Joplin (1868–1917), his most famous compositions *Maple Leaf Rag* (1899) and *The Entertainer* (1902).   B.G.

Rahman, Tunku Abdul (Malayan statesman, *b.* 1903), see under PAN-ISLAM.

Rahv, Philip (U.S. literary critic, *b.* 1908), see under PALEFACE AND REDSKIN.

raising of the school leaving age, see ROSLA.

Raisz, Erwin Josephus (U.S. cartographer, 1893–1968), see under MORPHOLOGY.

Rajk, László (Hungarian politician, 1906–49), see under SHOW TRIALS.

Rákosi, Mátyás (Hungarian politician, 1892–1971), see under SALAMI TACTICS.

ram jet. An internal combustion engine of the simplest form, consisting of nothing more than a steel tube, a fuel inlet, and a sparking-plug. By suitable shaping of the tube the air passing through it can be subjected to the same four-stroke cycle as that in a motor-car engine. It is used in very high-speed flight. At Mach 1 (see MACH NUMBERS), the SHOCK WAVE improves the compression by decelerating the air to subsonic speeds. At higher Mach numbers, two shock waves are needed for the dual purpose of slowing down the air and raising its pressure. At Mach 3, pressure ratios as high as 36:1 are obtainable. The 'V1' 'flying bombs' of World War II were propelled in this way.   E.R.L.

ramified theory of types, see under PARADOX.

random access. A method of using a computer STORE in which no account is taken of the physical location of the information.

It is much easier to use than SERIAL ACCESS but with some forms of store, e.g. MAGNETIC TAPE, it may be several thousand times slower. See also ACCESS TIME.   C.S.

random number. To generate statistical SIMULATIONS or to ESTIMATE by MONTE CARLO METHODS, it is often convenient to program a COMPUTER to produce a sequence of random numbers – i.e. numbers which take any value in a fixed interval with equal probability. The numbers generated are actually *pseudo-random* – in fact deterministic, but with the appearance of randomness – and recently many hitherto unsuspected defects have been discovered in the conventional ways of generating such numbers.   R.SI.

random variable. Any way of obtaining a number which describes the outcome of an experiment in PROBABILITY THEORY. Thus with the experiment 'toss a coin 10 times' we might associate the random variables 'number of heads', 'length of longest sequence of heads', etc.; with the experiment 'draw a card', the random variable 'number of pips'. See also DISTRIBUTION.   R.SI.

random walk, see under STOCHASTIC PROCESS.

range (in STATISTICS), see under DISTRIBUTION.

rank. A CONCEPT in some theories of LINGUISTICS which suggests that the relationship between linguistic units and structures is best viewed taxonomically in terms of composition, a particular structure being described in terms of units which operate at a 'lower' level or rank. It is an important concept in neo-Firthian (see FIRTHIAN) linguistics, where sentence, clause, group, word, and MORPHEME are placed on a *rank scale*. See also LEVEL.   D.C.

Rank, Otto (Austrian psychoanalyst, 1884–1939), see under BIRTH TRAUMA.

rank-size relations. The distributions which result when objects in some collection are arranged by rank-size order (i.e. the largest first, the next largest second, and so on). Rank-size studies have been

Ransom, John Crowe (U.S. poet and critic, *b.* 1888), see under CONCRETE UNIVERSAL; NEW CRITICISM; TEXTURE.

Rapacki, Adam (Polish politician, 1909–70), see under DISENGAGEMENT.

rapid-eye-movement sleep, see REM SLEEP.

particularly used by biologists in the study of SPECIES abundance and by urban geographers in the analysis of city sizes by population.   P.H.
   Bibl: G. K. Zipf, *Human Behaviour and the Principle of Least Effort* (London and N.Y., 1965).

rare earth. Any ELEMENT with ATOMIC NUMBER between 57 and 71. Rare earths are all metals, closely similar in their ELECTRON SHELL structures and chemical properties.   M.V.B.

Rashdall, Hastings (British philosopher, 1858–1924), see under INTUITIONISM; PERSONALISM.

Raskolnikov, Fyodor F. (Soviet politician, 1892–1939), see under REHABILITATION.

Ratcliffe, William (British painter, 1870–1955), see under CAMDEN TOWN GROUP.

ratio scale, see under SCALE.

rational number, see under NUMBER.

rationalisation, see RATIONALIZATION.

rationalism. Either (1) APRIORISM; or (2) the opposite of IRRATIONALISM, in which sense it denies the acceptability of beliefs founded on anything but experience and reasoning, deductive (see DEMONSTRATION) or inductive (see INDUCTION); or (3), a little datedly, disbelief in the supernatural. In PHILOSOPHY the first meaning is commonest. The 'Rationalists' are the great 17th-century metaphysicians (see METAPHYSICS) Descartes, Spinoza, and Leibniz, who believed that the general nature of the world could be established by wholly non-empirical demonstrative reasoning.   A.Q.

rationalization. A DEFENCE MECHANISM whereby the individual justifies his behaviour by imposing on it a plausible rational explanation.   W.Z.

Ratzel, Friedrich (German geographer and ethnographer, 1844–1904), see under CULTURE AREA; GEOGRAPHY.

Ratzenhofer, Gustav (Austrian soldier, military jurist, and sociologist, 1842–1904), see under PLURAL SOCIETY.

Raumbühne, see under SPACE (2).

Rauschenberg, Robert (U.S. artist, *b.* 1925), see under COLLAGE; ENVIRONMENT.

Rauschenbusch, Walter (U.S. clergyman and theologian, 1861–1918), see under SOCIAL GOSPEL MOVEMENT.

Ravel, Maurice (French composer, 1875–1937), see under IMPRESSIONISM.

Ray, Man (U.S. photographer, painter, and film-maker, 1890–1976), see under PHOTOGRAM.

rayograph, see PHOTOGRAM.

rayonism. Method of painting evolved by Michel Larionov in Moscow in 1912 and expounded in his pamphlet *Luchism,* 1913 (Italian translation *Radiantismo,* 1917). Since the eye sees objects by means of rays of light, the colour relationship and intersection of these can be used in non-objective compositions. Rayonist works by Larionov and Goncharova figured in the Target (*Mishen*) exhibition in Moscow, 1913, and in Paris (1914; also a retrospective exhibition in 1948). The movement, which bears some relationship to FUTURISM and its 'lines of force', was short-lived, and few of the manifesto's other signatories made a name. In the mid 1950s Goncharova again produced some rayonist works.   M.C.
   Bibl: W. George, *Larionov* (Paris, 1966); M. Chamot, *Nathalie Gontcharova* (Paris, 1972); and see under KNAVE OF DIAMONDS.

Raysse, Martial (French painter and collage-maker, *b.* 1936), see under NOUVEAU RÉALISME.

reactionary. Adjective or noun applied to those who not merely resist change but seek to put the clock back and return to some earlier order of society which is seen as having possessed characteristics (discipline, respect for authority and privilege, a hierarchical structure, sense of duty) which the present is felt to lack. The word *reaction* was much used by 19th-century radicals (see RADICALISM) who spoke of the 'forces of reaction' (the Catholic Church, absolutist monarchies and hereditary aristocracies) blocking progress towards a more just, equal, and enlightened society. Contemporary radicals would characterize the forces of reaction differently but would have as little doubt as their predecessors that such forces exist and are still bent upon blocking change and annulling reforms already achieved.

The words 'reaction' and 'reactionary' are commonly regarded as the opposite of 'progress' and PROGRESSIVE. Few people, however, would describe themselves as reactionary, and the term is thus most frequently pejorative. It is employed mainly by the LEFT, although both the NAZIS and the FASCISTS also used it, in their case to describe the resistance of traditional INSTITUTIONS to their RIGHT-wing radicalism.   A.L.C.B.

reactor, see NUCLEAR REACTOR.

readymades. Term adopted in the U.S.A. by the painter Marcel Duchamp to describe his DADA-like use, for exhibition and similar purposes, of incongruous manufactured objects such as the porcelain urinal which he submitted to a New York jury in 1917. These continued to feature in his *oeuvre* after his return to Paris in 1919, being put forward, in an ironic-nihilistic spirit, as works of art rendered so by the arbitrary decision of the artist.   J.W.

real number, see under NUMBER.

real-time computing, see under COMPUTING.

realism. (1) In PHILOSOPHY, a term applied to two distinct theories: (*a*, as opposed to IDEALISM) the theory that there is a world of material things in space which do not depend for their existence on the fact that some mind is aware of them; and (*b*, as opposed to NOMINALISM) the theory that abstract entities or UNIVERSALS really exist in a world of their own, not in space and time, whether they have instances or not. The first view is sometimes called *perceptual realism,* or, less happily, *epistemological realism*; the second is usually called *Platonic realism* (see also PLATONISM), sometimes *logical realism. Perceptual realism* defends one of the most elementary convictions of COMMON SENSE against the consequence of the *argument from illusion* (see ILLUSION) that only private SENSE-DATA or appearances are directly perceived, doing so usually on the ground that since sense-experiences occur independently of the perceiver's will they must be attributed to a cause external to him. That conclusion is compatible with any concept of the intrinsic nature of the external cause of sense-data, including Berkeley's God, so perceptual realists go on to argue that there is some likeness, if only partial, between sense-data and their external causes, e.g. that the former at least correspond in shape, size, and relative position to the latter (see REPRESENTATIONALISM). *Platonic realism* infers (see INFERENCE) the real existence of abstract entities from the fact that there are true statements (see TRUTH) whose subject-terms are abstract nouns and (as its PRESUPPOSITION) from our ability to classify individual things together as being of various kinds and sharing various properties. The two forms of philosophic realism are, in LOGIC, entirely independent; neither implies, nor excludes, the other. They share the name because each asserts the existence of a type of problematic entity.   A.Q.

(2) In the arts, a key term used to define both a general, recurrent characteristic of nearly all art and a specific historical movement. Realism in the general sense – what Harry Levin calls the 'willed tendency of art to approximate to reality': to attempt precise imitation of external and historical experience, to make empirical observations, to follow laws of probability, to seem true – has magnetized artists as diverse as Homer, Breughel, and Defoe. During the 19th century, however, realism grew from a technique into a powerful theoretical aim: first and foremost in painting, but also in fiction and drama. Reacting against ROMANTICISM and

philosophical IDEALISM, suspicious alike of MYTH, RELIGION, and abstraction (see ABSTRACT), it concentrated heavily on the here-and-now, and developed new techniques for the detailed, accurate representation of life in all its social and domestic aspects.

In France between 1848 and 1870 it was a key aesthetic movement; it had a political component, was to some extent a child of the 1848 Revolution, and carried radical implications (see RADICALISM). Its primary theoreticians were Champfleury and Duranty; as exemplary artists they took Courbet and Degas, whose 'plebeian' realism contrasted and interacted with Flaubert's 'higher' version. A key line runs from Balzac to Flaubert to the Goncourts, and into NATURALISM. In England, Mrs Gaskell, George Eliot, and George Moore are representative; in Russia, Gogol, Turgenev, and Tolstoy; in Germany, Raabe, Fontane, and early Mann; in the U.S.A., James and Howells. The realist sensibility embraces arguments as various as George Eliot's view of Dutch genre painting as a model for the novelist; the Goncourts' demand that the novel provide the social history of the lower classes; and Flaubert's claim of 'no lyricism, no beauty, the author's personality absent'.

Both in painting, via Courbet, Manet, and Degas, and in literature, realism evolved (a) towards IMPRESSIONISM, stressing the aesthetic and perceptual technique, the new way of setting down what was seen; and (b) towards naturalism, emphasizing the scientific and evolutionary elements that help interpret the subject. Erich Auerbach in Mimesis has emphasized, however, the long historical dimension of realism, and its role in attaching art to familiar experience through numerous, sceptical techniques. Realism cannot logically be formless, nor beyond form; it is itself an aesthetic and contains certain logical structures. However, one of its triumphs is to limit complex techniques and mannerisms so that (as Ortega y Gasset puts it) art becomes 'humanized'. Thus it emphasizes character, controls fantasy and idealism, and insists on experience, fact, and the sceptical view in the spirit of W. D. Howells's 'Is it true – true to the motives, the impulses, the principles that shape the life of actual men and women?' Today it is usually

identified as a BOURGEOIS phase of style, associated with EMPIRICISM and individualism, but deep-seated concepts of realism persist in forms as varied as SOCIALIST REALISM and CHOSISM.

M.S.BR.

Bibl: E. Auerbach, tr. W. R. Trask, *Mimesis* (Princeton, 1953); G. J. Becker (ed.), *Documents of Modern Literary Realism* (Princeton, 1963); F. J. Hemmings (ed.), *The Age of Realism* (Harmondsworth, 1974); H. Levin, *The Gates of Horn* (N.Y., 1963); J. P. Stern, *On Realism* (London, 1973).

realism, critical. A theory of PERCEPTION which denies that the perceiver is ever directly aware of material objects which exist independently of him but holds that he can derive knowledge of independent material things from the appearances or SENSE-DATA which are directly present to perceptual consciousness. Dawes Hicks in Britain, Lovejoy and Santayana in the U.S.A., were the chief critical realists so to describe themselves. The word 'realism' marks a contrast with IDEALISM or PHENOMENALISM, which takes objects to be wholly constructed out of appearances or ideas; 'critical' indicates a rejection of the naive realism (see next entry) which takes our perception of material objects to be commonly immediate or direct.

A.Q.

realism, naive (or *direct realism*). The theory that in PERCEPTION we are as a rule directly and non-inferentially (see INFERENCE) aware of material objects which exist independently of us. It does not imply that we always perceive things as they really are, nor does it imply that we ever perceive more than a small selection of what is true about a material object. It rejects the consequence derived from the *argument from illusion* (see ILLUSION) that what are directly perceived are never material objects, but always private SENSE-DATA or impressions. Its adherents, disliking the derogatory epithet 'naive', often describe themselves as direct realists. A.Q.

Bibl: D. M. Armstrong, *Perception and the Physical World* (London and N.Y., 1961).

réalités nouvelles see under ABSTRACT ART.

reality principle. In psychoanalytic theory (see PSYCHOANALYSIS), a FREUDIAN term for the principle governing the functioning of the EGO. The reality principle imposes constraints on the PLEASURE PRINCIPLE by delaying gratification until the desired object or state can realistically be achieved and by causing an impulse towards such a goal to be modified into a socially acceptable form.   W.Z.

Realpolitik. Term originated by the German publicist Ludwig von Rochau in his *Grundsätze der Realpolitik* (1853), a critique of the lack of realism in the policies followed by the German Liberals during the years 1848–9. The term was particularly applied to Bismarck's policy during and after the years of German unification, and is to be distinguished from a policy of selfish self-interest or from a ruthless reliance on naked power. The phrase has been used, by American theorists of international politics opposed to the IDEOLOGICAL elements in traditional American foreign policy, to cover the integration of POWER, morality, and self-interest into a 'policy of the possible'.   D.C.W.
   Bibl: H. J. Morgenthau, *Politics among Nations* (N.Y., 4th ed., 1967).

Rebel Art Centre, see under VORTICISM.

recapitulation. The notion embodied in the familiar phrase that in development an animal 'climbs up its own family tree' – i.e., that the development of an individual animal recapitulates its ancestry. In this naive form *recapitulation theory* is associated with the name of Ernst Haeckel (1834–1919; see also PHYLOGENY) and is entirely discredited. The element of truth in it is the unquestioned fact, sometimes referred to as von Baer's principle, that the embryos of related animals resemble each other more closely than do the corresponding adults. As an animal develops from a ZYGOTE we can determine its affinities with increasing confidence: first the embryo will be recognizable as a chordate, then as a vertebrate, then as a mammal, then as a primate and finally, maybe, as a man.   P.M.

receptors. Structural or molecular groupings in, or on the surface of, a CELL which have an affinity for a pharmacological or immunological agent (see IMMUNITY;

PHARMACOLOGY). Thus in IMMUNOLOGY an *antigen* on a cell surface may be thought of as a receptor for the *antibody* whose formation it may excite if administered in a suitable way. Likewise cells which are specifically affected by them are presumed to have receptors for various drugs. The same applies to hormones, and the cells they act upon (see ENDOCRINOLOGY). Thanks to the use of ELECTRON MICROSCOPY receptor sites on cells can actually be seen.   P.M.

recessive, see under GENE.

recidivism. Literally, a 'falling back' into crime. A recidivist is strictly any offender who is convicted on more than one occasion, but for practical purposes most criminologists (see CRIMINOLOGY) are concerned to study the problem within defined time limits, e.g. percentages of offenders reconvicted in one, five, ten years. Penologists (see PENOLOGY) normally consider that recidivists merit special treatment, and many countries provide for special sentencing related to the offender's total criminal record as well as the offence of which he may be convicted. Such provisions are known variously as 'preventive detention', 'extended sentence', 'double-track systems', or arrangements made in the interests of 'social defence'. Factors explored in connection with recidivism have included age at first conviction, type of offence, the isolation of the offender in the community without family or friends, and the extent to which his criminal record increases the chances of his being further detected and convicted.   T.M.
   Bibl: W. H. Hammond and E. Chayen, *Persistent Criminals* (London, 1963); D. J. West, *The Habitual Prisoner* (London and N.Y., 1963).

recombination (in GENETICS), see CROSSING OVER.

rectifier. A device which allows an electric current to flow in one direction but not the other (e.g. a diode THERMIONIC valve, or a TRANSISTOR). If an *alternating* voltage is applied to a rectifier, a *direct* current flows.   M.V.B.

recursion (or *recursiveness*). In LINGUISTICS, the attribute of rules which may be applied an indefinite number of times in the generation of sentences, e.g. a rule which would introduce an adjective before a noun.   D.C.

recursive function theory. The study of what can and what cannot be done by an ideal COMPUTER (limitations of space and time being entirely ignored). Its importance for MATHEMATICS comes through the general acceptance of *Church's thesis*: any effective, or routine, or ALGORITHMIC process in mathematics can be performed by an (ideal) computer. The first such 'computer' considered – in 1936, before modern computers existed – was a TURING MACHINE. Let *P* be a property of natural NUMBERS or of finite sequences of symbols ('words'); *P* is *decidable* (or *computable, or solvable*) if there is a PROGRAM for an ideal computer such that when any number *n* or word *W* is given as INPUT the computer will (eventually) print 1 if *n* or *W* has the property *P* and 0 otherwise, e.g. 'being prime' is decidable. The most significant from a great range of results are: (1) '*W* is a theorem of the PREDICATE CALCULUS' is undecidable; (2) '*W* is a diophantine equation (see NUMBER THEORY) which has a solution' is undecidable. But, in contrast to (1): (3) '*W* is a correct proof in the predicate calculus' is decidable; (4) '*W* is a theorem of "elementary" Euclidean GEOMETRY' is decidable ('elementary' is a technical term; Euclid's theorems all satisfy it). The theory is closely linked with GÖDEL'S THEOREM, and with INTUITIONISM (sense 3).   R.G.

Bibl: B. A. Trakhtenbrot, tr. J. Kristian *et al., Algorithms and Automatic Computing Machines* (Boston, 1963).

recursiveness, see RECURSION.

recycling.
(1) The recovery of scrap material after use, followed by re-processing in order to permit of further use, sometimes of a different kind, as when waste paper is used in the manufacture of cardboard. The word has recently become something of a battle-cry among those concerned with the POLLUTION of the ENVIRONMENT and with the need for CONSERVATION of the earth's resources. In this context it usually refers to the decomposition of bio-degradable materials after use so as to form nutrients for fresh organic growth,

this in turn renewing the source of the original materials.

(2) In ECONOMICS, a term which came into use in the 1960s to refer to an inflow of CAPITAL that is put back into international circulation by the central bank of a recipient country, acting in agreement with other central banks. Recycling may follow a movement of privately owned funds from country A to country B which is judged to inflate the foreign exchange reserves of B and denude those of A to an undesirable extent. Foreign loans by the central bank of B will produce a recycling of funds so that they move on from B and may end up again in A, where a fresh outflow may then begin the process all over again.   A.C.

Red Army. (1) Originally, a catch-phrase for the Soviet Army. (2) Recently, a terrorist organization (*Sekigun*) of extremist if vague revolutionary views which emerged from the Japanese radical (see RADICALISM) student movement in 1969. It is distinguished from the other organizations of that movement by (*a*) its rejection of Japanese CHAUVINISM on the one hand and of NON-VIOLENT RESISTANCE on the other; (*b*) the elimination of internal disagreement by kangaroo courts ready to inflict death on convicted dissidents; (*c*) the large part played by women in its ranks; and (*d*) the transference of its activities, following drastic pressure from the Japanese police, to bases and activities in Europe and the Middle East. These include the action at Lod airport in Israel in May 1974 in which 26 were killed and 71 injured by indiscriminate machine-gunning of airport users; the hijacking of a Japanese airliner in Amsterdam in 1973; an attack on an oil refinery in Singapore in February 1974; and the seizure of the French Embassy at The Hague in September 1974.   D.C.W.

red giant. A very large relatively cool star near the end of its life (see HERTZPRUNG-RUSSELL DIAGRAM). Red giants may be hundreds of times larger than the sun in diameter, but their densities are extremely low – some are more tenuous than air.
                                M.V.B.

Red Guards. A civilian REVOLUTIONARY militia formed mainly among the young workers and students of China during the period of the CULTURAL REVOLUTION (1965–8) to implement Mao Tse-tung's efforts to maintain revolutionary fervour and initiative and to counter the increasing growth of bureaucratic and administrative centres of power in China. The Red Guards were distinguished for excess of enthusiasm and vindictiveness against their opponents and were eventually checked by the senior commanders of the Chinese People's Liberation Army after a period in which all governmental activity, including the conduct of China's relations abroad, largely came to a standstill. The name is used by analogy to describe any political organization of hot-headed idealist youth in support of a particular political party.   D.C.W.

Bibl: G. A. Bennett and R. N. Montaperto, *Red Guard* (London and N.Y., 1971); R. H. Solomon, *Mao's Revolution and the Chinese Political Culture* (London and Berkeley, 1971).

red shift. A displacement towards the red of the spectral lines of distant GALAXIES and some stars. It is usually interpreted as a DOPPLER EFFECT; this implies that the galaxies are receding, and the red shift constitutes the main evidence for the EXPANSION OF THE UNIVERSE.   M.V.B.

redaction criticism, see under HIGHER CRITICISM.

Redfield, Robert (U.S. anthropologist, 1897–1958), see under ACCULTURATION.

Redgrove, Peter (British poet, *b.* 1932), see under GROUP, THE.

Redon, Odilon (French painter and engraver, 1840–1916), see under ARMORY SHOW; SYMBOLISM; SYNTHETISM.

redskin, see under PALEFACE.

reductio ad absurdum, see under DEMONSTRATION (1).

reduction.
(1) In PHILOSOPHY and related subjects, the process whereby CONCEPTS or statements that apply to one type of entity are redefined in terms of concepts, or analysed in terms of statements, of another kind, normally one regarded as

more elementary or epistemologically (see EPISTEMOLOGY) more basic. *Reducible* is the adjective describing a type of entity that is considered susceptible of reduction; *reducibility* is the property of such a type of entity; *reductionism* is the systematic practice of reduction (also the view that reduction constitutes the business of philosophy). If entities of one kind, nations for example, are regarded as reducible to entities of another, in this case individual people, they are said to be CONSTRUCTS or *logical constructions* out of the latter.

Reduction is seldom an uncontentious activity, and to list some of the many varieties of reductionism (which may be contrasted with HOLISM) is to list a series of controversies: whether (as in PHENOMENALISM) material objects are reducible to SENSE-DATA; whether mental events and processes are reducible to physiological, physical, or chemical events and processes in human brains (see PHYSICALISM; MATERIALISM; BEHAVIOURISM; *physical monism* under MIND-BODY PROBLEM); whether SOCIAL STRUCTURES and social processes are reducible to relationships between and actions of individuals (see METHODOLOGICAL INDIVIDUALISM); whether (as denied by VITALISM) biological organisms are reducible to physical systems; whether (as in LOGICAL POSITIVISM) philosophy is reducible to ANALYSIS; whether (as in LOGICISM) MATHEMATICS is reducible to LOGIC. The reductionist sometimes justifies his activity as a principle of economy in EXPLANATION, a principle that has obviously paid off in science; the anti-reductionist argues the existence of irreducible or EMERGENT PROPERTIES.

Some of the points at issue, however, are more apparent than real, and stem largely from terminological confusion (exacerbated in some cases by plain prejudice). Thus, a *logical construction* (see above) needs to be distinguished from an aggregate or whole whose constituents are literally parts of it; e.g., the phenomenalist claims, not that a material thing is literally *composed* of sense-data, but merely that everything that can be said about material things can in principle be stated in assertions that refer only to sense-data. Some versions of reductionism, moreover, are purely METHODOLOGICAL, involving only the claim that the study of phenomena of type *A* has to be restricted to the study of evidence provided by class *B*; thus a methodological behaviourist might argue that, although mental events and processes exist, they can only be studied in terms of the behaviour they produce.

A.Q.; A.S.; J.S.B.

Bibl: A. J. Ayer, *Language, Truth and Logic* (London, rev. ed., 1946), ch. 2; E. Nagel, *The Structure of Science* (London, 1961), chs. 11, 14; A. Koestler and J. R. Smythies (eds.), *Beyond Reductionism* (London, 1969; N.Y., 1970).

(2) In CHEMISTRY, the addition, to an ATOM or MOLECULE, of ELECTRONS or electropositive groups such as hydrogen IONS, or the removal of electrons or electronegative groups such as oxygen ions. The opposite of OXIDATION. M.V.B.

reduction division, see under MEIOSIS.

redundancy.

(1) In INFORMATION THEORY, the representation of data by longer strings of symbols than are necessary to distinguish between all the possible different data items in a context. Redundancy is a bad thing if it leads to unnecessary expense in storage or transmission of representations of data, but a good thing if it permits reconstitution of data whose representation has been accidentally corrupted. Compare 19F3 with nineteen sebenty three; each has one character wrong.

R.M.N.

(2) In CYBERNETICS, usage (1) is familiar, but the term is also applied to extra channels in a network that are intended to guard a whole system against the failure of an entire channel. It is possible to calculate mathematically how much redundancy is required to reduce the risk of a mistake (getting the message wrong in (1), or failure of the system in (2)) to an *arbitrarily* small degree. S.BE.

Bibl: C. E. Shannon and J. McCarthy (eds.), *Automata Studies* (Princeton, 1956).

re-entry. In ASTRONAUTICS, the return of a space vehicle through the earth's atmosphere. It is during re-entry that the vehicle is subjected to the highest temperature, great heat being generated by the friction and pressure between air and vehicle. Radio contact with the vehicle is lost for most of the re-entry period. E.R.L.

reference. In LINGUISTICS, the relationship between linguistic forms and the objects, events, etc. *(referents)* in non-linguistic experience to which these forms refer. Most LINGUISTS are careful to distinguish reference from *sense*, which is a purely intra-linguistic property arising from the MEANING RELATIONS between words. D.C.

reference class, see under FREQUENCY THEORY.

reference group. Term introduced by Herbert H. Hyman (in *Archives of Psychology,* 1942) for a social collectivity, real or imagined, in relation to which an individual regularly evaluates his own situation or conduct. A *comparative* reference group is one which serves as a standard against which the individual appraises his achievements, social circumstances, life-chances, rewards, etc., and which thus influences the level of his expectations and, in turn, his degree of relative satisfaction or deprivation; thus the structure of comparative reference groups among members of different occupations has been shown to be important in determining the extent to which wage differentials are regarded as legitimate and the level at which wage claims are made. A NORMATIVE reference group is one which the individual perceives as a source of values and GROUP NORMS of which he approves, and with whose members he would wish to identify himself; thus a socially aspiring individual may take the ÉLITE of his local community as a normative reference group, and seek to emulate their LIFE STYLE, manners, tastes, opinions, etc. in the hope of being himself accepted into the élite. J.H.G.

Bibl: R. K. Merton, *Social Theory and Social Structure* (N.Y., 2nd ed., 1957), chs. 8, 9.

reference retrieval, see under INFORMATION STORAGE.

referential language, see EMOTIVE AND REFERENTIAL LANGUAGE.

reflation, see under INFLATION.

reflex, conditioned, see CONDITIONED REFLEX.

reformism. A policy of social and economic reform by gradual stages rather than by REVOLUTIONARY change. The term has been applied in particular to a tendency in the SOCIALIST movement to abandon the idea of revolutionary violence and to rely instead on the slow transformation of social INSTITUTIONS through democratic means. It found its expression in British FABIANISM, French *réformisme*, German REVISIONISM, Russian 'economism', etc., but it was only in countries with a parliamentary suffrage that the constitutional framework favoured such a gradualist approach. It eventually became the hallmark of the Socialist INTERNATIONAL. The establishment of the COMMUNIST International reflected the split in the labour movement between the evolutionary and the revolutionary attitudes, a split resting upon fundamental differences of attitude towards DEMOCRACY and MARXISM.

Some socialist parties, like the British Labour Party, never embraced Marxism; some, like the German Social Democrats (see SOCIAL DEMOCRACY) abandoned it later. The further evolution of the socialist movement has produced a growing differentiation between moderate and radical elements (see RADICALISM). The latter have tended to prefer the socialist, the former a social-democratic label. In some countries, like Italy and Japan, this division has led to the establishment of separate socialist and social-democratic parties. In others it tends to create a growing gap between the moderate and LEFT-wing groups in labour and socialist movements.

L.L.

Bibl: J. Joll, *The Second International* (London, 1955; N.Y., 1966); W. E. Paterson and I. Campbell, *Social Democracy in Post-War Europe* (London and N.Y., 1974).

region. Geographical term for a homogeneous area of the earth's surface with characteristics which make it distinct from the areas that surround it. The distinction may be based on natural or man-made characteristics or a combination of both. Scale distinctions are made between large-scale regions of continental proportions *(macroregions)* down to very small structures *(microregions)*; similarly, regions with common region-wide characteristics *(uniform regions)* are distin-

guished from those in which the characteristic is most strongly discernible at or near the centre of the region and least strongly at the boundaries *(focal regions)*.

P.H.

Bibl: D. S. Whittlesey, 'The Regional Concept and the Regional Method', in P. E. James and C. F. Jones (eds.), *American Geography: Inventory and Prospect* (Syracuse, N.Y., 1954).

regional planning. A term applied usually to planned intervention by central government so as to adjust regional inequalities within a state. It is also used to describe intervention by two or more governments to meet the conjoint problems of a shared natural REGION (e.g. a river basin).

P.H.

Bibl: J. Friedmann and W. Alonso (eds.), *Regional Development and Planning* (Cambridge, Mass., 1964).

regional science. An interdisciplinary field within the SOCIAL SCIENCES that focuses on the integrated study of economic and social phenomena in a regional setting. The term is particularly associated with W. Isard's research group at the University of Pennsylvania which draws heavily on mathematical MODELS to frame regional-science theories. See also REGION.

P.H.

Bibl: W. Isard, *Methods of Regional Analysis* (Cambridge, Mass., 1960).

regionalism. Geographical term for socio-political movements which seek (1) to foster or protect an indigenous culture in particular regions, or (2) to decentralize central government to an intermediate level between that of the State and the traditional units of local government. The movement has been traditionally strong in France and Spain, and has become of increasing importance in Great Britain with the establishment in the 1960s of Regional Economic Planning Councils.

P.H.

register. (1) In neo-Firthian (see FIRTHIAN) *linguistics*, a regular, situationally-conditioned, and distinctive range in language use, e.g. 'scientific', 'upper-class', 'formal' registers. (2) In COMPUTING, the fastest type of computer store.

D.C.; C.S.

regression.

(1) In STATISTICS, it is common to attempt to explain the variation in some observed quantity as a combination of some simple kind of dependence on values set by the experimenter, together with an error term (see ERROR ANALYSIS). Such a representation is called a *regression*. It is found, for example, that the rate at which a cicada chirps is linearly related to the difference between the ambient temperatures, but any particular observation may as a result of random error fail to lie exactly on this regression line: this example is of *linear regression*. The design of experiments to obtain good ESTIMATES of regression coefficients is an important statistical problem.   R.SI.

(2) In PSYCHOLOGY, a DEFENCE MECHANISM whereby an individual responds to stresses such as fear, frustration, isolation, etc. by reverting to behaviour characteristic of a less complex, more primitive and impulsive stage of development. In psychoanalytic theory (see PSYCHOANALYSIS) the regression is either to an earlier state of libidinal interest and sexual organization (see LIBIDO; PSYCHOSEXUAL DEVELOPMENT) or to an earlier stage of EGO development. In the former, the person regresses from adult genitality to earlier (pre-genital) oral or anal sexual interests. In the latter, the person deals with the danger threatening him by behaving in a more childlike and generally primitive way. W.Z ; B.A.F.

regression analysis, see under MULTI-VARIATE ANALYSIS.

regulation.

(1) In EMBRYOLOGY, the process of CELL reorganization or readjustment that occurs in the restoration of an organic defect or incompleteness; more especially, the phenomenon whereby, if a sea urchin's or starfish's embryo at the two-cell stage is divided into the two separate cells, each one will grow up into a whole organism. This phenomenon was made the basis of very far-reaching philosophical speculations by Hans Driesch (1867–1941).   P.M.

(2) In ENGINEERING, a QUANTITY that expresses – unexpectedly, in view of the normal meaning of the word – the degree of imperfection of a device or SYSTEM. Familiar examples are electrical transformers and electrical transmission systems, where the regulation is the amount by which the voltage falls when the appliance or load is connected, and driving motors, where it is the amount by which the speed of the motor falls when its load is coupled to the motor. Both voltage and speed regulation are usually expressed as a percentage of their respective values when no load is connected. See also VARIABLE SPEED.   E.R.L.

(3) In CYBERNETICS, any systematic behaviour within a system that tends to restrict fluctuations of any variable. This systematic behaviour will be embodied in a set of physical connections, which will need some form of ENERGY to operate them. However, the critical commodity used by any regulator is *information*. All regulators detect discrepancies from some expectation (which may be not a fixed value, but the varying output of some other part of the system) and FEEDBACK information to make adjustments that reduce the discrepancy.   S.BE.

rehabilitation. Term used particularly of the posthumous acquittal and restoration to Party favour of Communists executed during the purges in Russia and in Eastern Europe in the Stalin epoch. In Russia, it is applied largely to political leaders executed in secret, to Army leaders, and to certain writers. Of those accused in the public MOSCOW TRIALS only half a dozen have been publicly rehabilitated, though statements have been made which are incompatible with the guilt of any of the others. Rehabilitation on criminal charges does not always imply complete political rehabilitation as well. A further process, sometimes known as *de-rehabilitation*, has also been noted, by which certain Party officials (e.g. F. Raskolnikov) restored to Party favour in the early 1960s have been denounced as traitors once again.   R.C.

Reichian. Relating to the beliefs or the followers of Wilhelm Reich (born in Austria in 1897, died in the U.S.A. in 1958). Reich's career began in orthodox PSYCHOANALYSIS, but he quickly developed original theories, relating NEUROSIS to sexual frustration and failure to achieve complete orgasm. This led to a complex therapeutic approach called *character analysis* or *bio-energetics*. Reich's interest in sexual energy led to his

REICHENBACH

'discovery' of the *orgone*, a 'life force' (for Bergson's earlier version of this see VITALISM) which he found to be blue in colour, and to be present in living and inorganic matter throughout nature and interstellar space. His commitment to the 'Orgone Energy Accumulator' (a metal box which, he claimed, concentrated orgone energy and cured illness) led to his imprisonment in 1955 for selling medical equipment prohibited by the U.S. Food and Drug Laws. The technique of 'bio-energetics' as a therapy for neurosis is again popular (along with other GROUP THERAPY techniques), and the film *Mysteries of the Organism* has helped to keep Reich's views in the public gaze. It is still not clear whether he was a charlatan or a genius; the truth doubtless lies somewhere between the two.   M.J.C.

Bibl: M. Gardner, *Fads and Fallacies in the Name of Science* (N.Y., 1957).

Reichenbach, Hans (German-U.S. philosopher, 1891–1953), see under VIENNA CIRCLE.

Reid, Harry Fielding (U.S. seismologist and glaciologist, 1859–1944), see under ELASTIC REBOUND THEORY.

Reid, Thomas (Scottish philosopher, 1710–96), see under COMMON SENSE.

reification. The act of regarding an abstraction (see ABSTRACT) as a material thing.

An analysis of any RELATIONSHIP in a complex world involves a process of simplification through a set of abstractions in which certain aspects of a given phenomenon are selected and stressed for HEURISTIC purposes. These abstracted elements of reality may be reduced to an IDEAL TYPE or a conceptual MODEL. If they are taken as a complete description of the real phenomenon and the resulting abstractions endowed with a material existence of their own, the process exemplifies what A. N. Whitehead called in his *Science and the Modern World* (1926) 'the fallacy of misplaced concreteness', which is in effect a special case of the fallacy of reification. (See also *reductionism*, under REDUCTION.)

Reification as a CONCEPT with a special meaning was used with particular emphasis by Karl Marx (see MARXISM).

For him, reification (*Versachlichung, Verdinglichung*) meant that the 'social relation between men ... assumes for them the fantastic form of a RELATION between things'. In CAPITALIST society, he saw it as the result of ALIENATION (*Entäusserung*) or the estrangement (*Entfremdung*) of labour, a separation of the worker from the product of his work. Marx wrote that 'the general social form of labour appears as the property of a thing' and is 'reified' through the 'FETISHISM of commodities'. This is a social situation which is determined by 'the action of objects which rule the producers instead of being ruled by them'.

Marx's concepts of reification and alienation have been used as key terms by the NEW LEFT. In their popular form alienation was taken to mean the estrangement of man from an oppressive society, reification the treatment of men as objects of manipulation, as things rather than as human beings. In the theoretical writings of the Marxist forerunners of the New Left, such as Lukács and the philosophers of the FRANKFURT SCHOOL, the concept of reification has been applied to all pre-REVOLUTIONARY activities and INSTITUTIONS, including science (which for Horkheimer is a 'reified IDEOLOGY'), TECHNOLOGY (which for Marcuse is a 'vehicle for reification'), and general intellectual concepts (which for Lukács are instances of reification).   L.L.

reinforcement. In the context of OPERANT CONDITIONING, the supplying of a consequence for certain behaviour which will *strengthen* that behaviour, i.e. make it more likely to recur in the same situation. In *positive reinforcement*, the behaviour is strengthened by the contingent presentation of a reward (e.g. food); in *negative reinforcement*, the behaviour is strengthened by the contingent removal of an aversive stimulus (e.g. electric shock, loud noise). Sometimes, *negative reinforcement* is extended to include the case where behaviour is made *less* likely to recur as the result of contingent presentation of an aversive stimulus, an operation properly termed *punishment*. The behaviour may be abolished (*extinguished*) if reinforcement no longer follows it; the abolition procedure is known as *extinction*. The rules that specify when and under what circumstances an operant

534

response should be reinforced are known as *schedules of reinforcement*; such schedules may require, e.g., a minimum time interval between responses, or the occurrence of a set number of unreinforced responses between successive reinforced ones.   D.H.

Bibl: C. B. Ferster and B. F. Skinner, *Schedules of Reinforcement* (N.Y., 1957).

Reinhardt, Ad (U.S. painter, 1913–67), see under ABSTRACT EXPRESSIONISM.

Reinhardt, Max (Austrian-U.S. theatrical producer, 1873–1943), see under DEUTSCHES THEATER; OPEN STAGE.

Rejection Front, see under PLO.

relations. What is ascribed to groups of two or more individual things by the predicates of sentences in which there is separate mention of two or more things. Logicians distinguish various formal properties of relations. (1) A relation is *symmetrical* if *A*'s standing in it to *B* entails (see ENTAILMENT) that *B* stands in it to *A* (e.g. '*A* is married to *B*'), *asymmetrical* if *A*'s standing in it to *B* entails that *B* does *not* stand in it to *A* (e.g. '*A* is older than *B*'), *non-symmetrical* if it possesses neither of these properties (e.g. '*A* loves *B*'). (2) a relation is *transitive* if *A*'s standing in it to *B* and *B*'s standing in it to *C* entails that *A* stands in it to *C* (e.g. 'is the same age as'), *intransitive* if the two conditions just mentioned entail that *A* does *not* stand in it to *C*, (e.g. 'is one year older than'), otherwise *non-transitive* (e.g. 'loves'). (3) a relation is *reflexive* if everything must have it to itself (e.g. 'is as tall as'), *irreflexive* if nothing can have it to itself (e.g. 'is older than'), otherwise *non-reflexive* (e.g. 'loves'). Relations that involve the CONCEPT of sameness or identity (EQUIVALENCE RELATIONS) are ordinarily transitive and symmetrical (and therefore reflexive); relations that involve that of more or less are ordinarily transitive and asymmetrical. See also INTERNAL RELATIONS; ORDERING RELATIONS.   A.Q.

relative deprivation. A CONCEPT introduced by the American sociologist S. A. Stouffer in 1949 and based upon the proposition that people's attitudes, aspirations, and grievances depend largely upon the FRAME OF REFERENCE in which they are conceived. Thus, when one community observes another comparable community or REFERENCE GROUP to be relatively prosperous, a feeling of deprivation arises which, prior to comparison, did not exist. The concept is a useful reminder of human envy, but fails to establish criteria for determining the point at which deprivation becomes absolute as well as relative.   P.S.L.

Bibl: W. G. Runciman, *Relative Deprivation and Social Justice* (London and Berkeley, 1966).

relativism. The view that beliefs and principles, particularly evaluative ones, have no universal or timeless validity but are valid only for the age in which, or the social group or individual person by which, they are held. It is most inviting as a reaction to the differences of moral belief as between different societies. But many of these differences can be reconciled if it is recognized that both the actual and the expected consequences of an action can differ from one society to another as a result of their differences in knowledge and circumstances. It is a common but not inevitable associate of HISTORICISM, in the original sense of that word. It is implicitly present in the ethical speculations of the ancient Greek Sophists and, encouraged by the findings of ANTHROPOLOGY (see RELATIVISM, CULTURAL), was revived in the 19th century.   A.Q.

Bibl: E. Westermarck, *Ethical Relativity* (London and Westport, 1932).

relativism, cultural. Cultures (see ANTHROPOLOGY) are relative in the trivial sense that what is right and good in one society may not be in another. 'Cultural relativism' is usually restricted, however, to an anthropological doctrine most forcefully expounded by Melville J. Herskovits (1895–1963), according to which the values and institutions of any culture must be taken to be self-validating. In so far as this doctrine entails a stance of moral RELATIVISM, it is subject to the criticism (among others) that we are often obliged to judge the actions of members of other societies by standards which are not theirs. See also ETHNOCENTRISM.   M.F.

Bibl: M. J. Herskovits, *Man and His Works* (N.Y., 1948); D. Bidney, *Theoretical Anthropology* (London and N.Y.,

RELATIVITY

1953); M. Ginsberg, *On the Diversity of Morals* (London, 1956; N.Y., 1957).

relativity.

A system of MECHANICS developed by Einstein early in this century, based on the principle that it must be possible to express the physical laws governing the motion of a body in a manner which is independent of the motion of any observer who may be studying the body. In other words, no absolute FRAME OF REFERENCE exists. Relativity is divided into two parts:

(1) In the *special (or restricted) theory* (1905), only frames of reference moving relatively to one another with constant velocity are considered. In addition, the status of a basic postulate is given to the result of the MICHELSON-MORLEY EXPERIMENT, i.e. that the speed of light in a vacuum is the same for all observers (a result inconsistent with NEWTONIAN MECHANICS). The principal deductions are: (*a*) The TRANSFORMATIONS between the position and time of an event as viewed by differently moving observers imply that the separate CONCEPTS of absolute space and absolute time must be replaced by the four-dimensional CONTINUUM of SPACE-TIME. In particular this leads to many surprising predictions such as the CLOCK PARADOX. (*b*) The MASS of a body increases with its speed, becoming infinite at the speed of light (see REST MASS); thus an INFINITE force would be necessary to 'cross the light barrier', and the speed of light is a natural upper limit in mechanics (but see TACHYON). (*c*) Matter is a form of ENERGY (see MASS-ENERGY EQUATION). These deductions have all been abundantly verified for ELEMENTARY PARTICLES moving near the speed of light in experiments with ACCELERATORS and in NUCLEAR REACTORS.

(2) The *general theory* (1916) goes on to consider transformations between *any* frame of reference which may have a mutual ACCELERATION. In addition, the fact that GRAVITATION attracts bodies so that they all fall with the same acceleration (which appears as a coincidence in Newtonian mechanics) is built into the basic structure of the theory. The space-time continuum is not 'flat' (i.e. *Euclidean*) as in the special theory, but 'curved' (i.e. *Riemannian*; for these terms see GEO-

METRY). The curvature is produced by matter (see MACH'S PRINCIPLE), and PARTICLES move along 'straight lines', or GEODESICS, in this curved space – analogous to the 'great circles' connecting points on the two-dimensional continuum of points on the earth's surface; thus gravitation is explained as geometry.

On the comparatively small scale of the solar system, general relativity predicts that the motion of planets and light rays will differ slightly from that expected in Newtonian mechanics, and these effects have been confirmed – although not as precisely as the predictions of special relativity. The difference between Newtonian mechanics and general relativity is, however, much greater near BLACK HOLES and on the vast scales contemplated in COSMOLOGY.   M.V.B.

Bibl: H. Bondi, *Relativity and Common Sense* (N.Y., 1964; London, 1965); C. Lanczos, *Albert Einstein and the Cosmic World Order* (London and N.Y., 1965).

relaxation. A general term used in PHYSICS to denote the process whereby a system attains EQUILIBRIUM by neutralizing a disturbing force. For example, when a solid is suddenly stretched, large elastic forces are set up, which gradually relax to zero as CREEP occurs. Electric conduction in metals is a relaxation effect: the ELECTRONS neutralize an applied voltage by adjusting the rate at which they collide with IONS.   M.V.B.

relaxation time. The time taken for RELAXATION to occur. In RHEOLOGY, solids are characterized by long relaxation times (e.g. about a year for glass), fluids by short relaxation times (e.g. one thousandth of a second for water), while visco-elastic materials occupy an intermediate position (e.g. 'potty putty', whose relaxation time is several seconds, bounces elastically under the sudden force of impact, but flows slowly under the more persistent force of GRAVITATION). M.V.B.

releaser. (1) In ETHOLOGY, a translation of German *Auslöser*, a term coined by Lorenz in 1935 to denote those structures, movements, sounds, scents, etc. which act as social signals. Releasers in this narrow sense are intricately adapted, as far as is compatible with other requirements, to their dual function of conspicuousness and unambiguity. The majority are intraspecific, i.e. they serve to ensure cooperation between members of one SPECIES; examples are the breeding colours of many animals, the songs of songbirds, and other mating-calls. Other releasers are used in inter-species relationships, such as SYMBIOSIS on the one hand, and repulsion of predators on the other. Releasers are often structures or behaviour patterns that have originally had another function and have evolved their special signalling properties as a secondary ADAPTATION *(ritualization)* to the need for effective communication.

(2) By extension, the word is often misleadingly applied to *any* external STIMULUS complex that 'releases' or elicits behaviour. Thus the silvery colour of many pelagic fish may 'release' hunting behaviour in predatory fish such as the pike, even though the function to which it is adapted is the opposite one of concealment.   N.T.

religion. An attitude of awe towards God, or gods, or the supernatural, or the mystery of life, accompanied by beliefs and affecting basic patterns of individual and group behaviour. In Latin *religare* means 'to bind', and religion is traditionally what most deeply binds a society, but the 20th century has been, more than any previous age, an age of SECULARIZATION. Paradoxically, the many challenges to inherited patterns of belief and behaviour in religion have made this a fertile age in THEOLOGY, at least so far as CHRISTIANITY is concerned, and one of the reasons for the success of COMMUNISM has been its ability to bind a society with new ideals and hopes when the traditional religion of that society no longer seems sufficiently plausible or vital. Not for nothing was Karl Marx descended from a a long line of Jewish rabbis and deeply influenced by the semi-Christian philosopher, Hegel. NATIONALISM has also been a religion in a loose sense.   D.L.E.

religion, philosophy of. The logical study of religious language and ideas. The main stimulus in 20th-century study has come from LINGUISTIC ANALYSIS of traditional THEOLOGY and devotion, and from EXISTENTIALIST challenges to religious statements not rooted in experience. See also EMPIRICAL THEOLOGY; PHILOSOPHICAL THEOLOGY.   D.L.E.

Bibl: H. D. Lewis, *Philosophy of Religion* (London, 1965).

religion, psychology of. The analysis of religious experience (both MYSTICISM and more everyday phenomena), not necessarily admitting or denying its validity but relating it to the rest of PSYCHOLOGY. The main challenge has come from Sigmund Freud's (see FREUDIAN) treatment of all religious belief as an unhealthy illusion. In contrast, the JUNGIAN approach has been to stress the universality and life-interpreting functions of the basic symbols used in religion, although this need not mean that the symbols correspond with eternal realities. In addition to these great attempts to make sense (or nonsense) of the whole of religion, there have been many less judgemental case-studies, largely with an American background, of the functions of religious beliefs and customs in personal existence.   D.L.E.

Bibl: W. James, *The Varieties of Religious Experience* (London and Cambridge, Mass., 1902); G. W. Allport, *The Individual and his Religion* (London and N.Y., 1951); R. H. Thouless, *An Introduction to the Psychology of Religion* (London, 3rd ed., 1972).

religion, sociology of. The dispassionate study of the behaviour of groups influenced by religious beliefs. This can involve surveys of the adherents of a religious body in a given area, or may extend to the discussion, inevitably more speculative, of the interaction of social and emotional pressures in the beliefs of a whole society, e.g. the PROTESTANT ETHIC in its relations to the values of CAPITALISM. It may even embrace a general theory of the origins and functions of RELIGION in the life of mankind. The pioneers in these FUNCTIONALIST enquiries were Max Weber (1864–1920), who stressed religion's role as giving 'meaning' to social life; Émile Durkheim (1858–1917), who believed that through religious RITUAL the social group periodically reaffirms its identity and values; and Bronislaw Malinowski (1884–1942), who analysed religion as escape from the stress of powerlessness, e.g. in the face of death. There has been special interest in the role of religious SECTS in protesting against the

REM SLEEP

social order of the day, and in the role of the more 'respectable' churches in maintaining it, as in Ernst Troeltsch, *The Social Teaching of the Christian Churches* (1912). There is disagreement among sociologists about whether, in view of the central role of religion in the past, society can ever be thoroughly SECULAR. D.L.E.

Bibl: B. Wilson, *Religion in Secular Society* (London, 1966); P. L. Berger, *The Social Reality of Religion* (London, 1969).

REM sleep (rapid-eye-movement sleep; also known as *paradoxical sleep*). A normal sleep pattern in which most dreaming takes place. It is characterized by the sudden occurrence of ELECTRO-ENCEPHALOGRAPH arousal, the slowing of physiological functions such as the heart rate, and rapid eye movements. It is a 'deeper' sleep, and harder to arouse the sleeper from, than *slow-wave sleep*, with which it alternates. H.L.

Bibl: G. Luce and J. Segal, *Sleep* (N.Y., 1966; London, 1967).

remedial education. Special forms of teaching given to pupils who have failed to reach a level expected of them. Such teaching (to be distinguished from the more fundamental SPECIAL EDUCATION) is short-term and looks for measurable improvement in specific fields such as reading. Much depends on the teacher's ability to restore the pupil's confidence and by encouragement to instil a sense of purpose and, by degrees, achievement. W.A.C.S.

remission, see under PAROLE.

remote sensing. Surveying the earth's surface from aircraft or SATELLITES using instruments to record different parts of the electromagnetic spectrum. Conventional photographic techniques using the visible light-band have been greatly extended over the last two decades to include the INFRA-RED and RADAR bands of the spectrum. Monitoring of the earth's surface by remote sensing from orbiting satellites has permitted major advances in the understanding of its surface, geological structure, mineral-resource potential, ocean circulation, and atmospheric phenomena. See also NEPHANALYSIS. P.H.

Renan, Ernest (French philosopher, his-

torian, and essayist, 1823–92), see under ANTISEMITISM.

Renn, Ludwig (pseud. of Arnold Friedrich Vieth von Golssenau, German novelist, b. 1889), see under NEUE SACHLICHKEIT.

Renoir, Pierre-Auguste (French painter, 1841–1919), see under IMPRESSIONISM; VINGT, LES.

Renouvier, Charles-Bernard (French philosopher, 1815–1903), see under NEO-KANTIANISM.

repertory. (1) The collection of plays in active production at a theatre in one season, each play taking its turn in a constantly changing programme. Long established on the Continent, the system of playing 'in repertory' is still not widespread in Britain: only the National Theatre, the Royal Shakespeare Company, and a handful of regional theatres have adopted the practice. (2) A British theatrical movement in which plays are mounted by a permanent company for limited runs of anything from one to four weeks (the very opposite of Continental repertory). Initiated by Miss A. E. F. Horniman at the Gaiety Theatre, Manchester, in 1907, the movement has provided an excellent training-ground for actors and directors. With help from the Arts Council, the British repertory movement is now in a flourishing condition, comprising some 60 subventioned theatres scattered throughout the land.

In the U.S.A. the nearest equivalent is *summer stock* (short seasons of interesting plays taking place outside the big cities and often graced by visiting stars), but in New York successive attempts to set up a permanent company have come to grief. Only OFF-BROADWAY's Negro Theatre Ensemble is currently permanent and flourishing. M.BI.

Bibl: J. Elsom, *Theatre outside London* (London, 1971).

Repin, Ilya Yefimovich (Russian painter, 1844–1930), see under SOCIALIST REALISM.

replacement theory. In MANAGEMENT, a theory concerned with working out the most economical policy for replacing equipment: it does so by comparing the

538

discounted costs likely to be incurred under different arrangements. One type of problem relates to the choice between equipment which is of equal performance but differs in other respects (e.g. expected lifetime, initial cost), and which deteriorates with age. Another relates to the cheapest way of replacing equipment which, without deteriorating, is liable to failure. Here there is a choice between individual and group replacement. If a productive unit is dependent on a single component, that component must be replaced at once; but if this is not the case it may prove cheaper to replace all components of a certain class at stated intervals, regardless of their condition. R.ST.

representationism. In PHILOSOPHY, the theory that our knowledge of material objects is gained through our direct PERCEPTION of the private impressions or SENSE-DATA which they cause us to experience and which, in some way or other, they resemble. In Descartes and Locke the resemblance is held to extend only to the 'primary qualities', i.e. the mathematically measurable, spatial qualities with which PHYSICS is principally concerned. On this view the secondary qualities of colour, texture, sound, smell, and taste are subjective, at least to the extent that there is no similar property in the material objects that cause us to perceive them. The crucial difficulty for the theory is the justification of the thesis that there is a resemblance between objects and our impressions of them, when the first term of the relation is not accessible for purposes of comparison with its perceived effects. The aim of representationism is to show that the sense-datum theory does not imply SOLIPSISM. A.Q.

repression. In psychoanalytic theory (see PSYCHOANALYSIS), a FREUDIAN term which is used largely to refer to two distinct processes. (1) *Primal repression*. An infant or child defends itself against the threat of excessive tension by attaching energy to some object or activity – which energy functions antithetically, or counter, to the threatening tension. (2) *Actual repression*, or *repression proper*. When an adult is threatened by the excessive tension that might arise if some UNCONSCIOUS wish, or impulse, moved into CONSCIOUSNESS, this danger is signalled by ANXIETY, and is met in various ways, e.g. by withdrawing energy from the idea of the threatening impulse, so that it cannot move into consciousness but remains unconscious. Repression proper is a function of the EGO, and is unconscious in its operation. See also DEFENCE MECHANISM. B.A.F.

repressor. In GENETICS, a substance, produced by a *repressor gene*, which inactivates another GENE or group of genes (OPERON). J.M.S.

reproduction rate. A measure which indicates the extent to which a population is replacing itself. The *gross reproduction rate* is the number of daughters a woman would produce if throughout her lifetime she were subjected to current age-specific FERTILITY rates; the *net reproduction rate* is the number of daughters that she would have if she were subjected to current age-specific fertility and mortality rates. A net reproduction rate of less than unity (i.e. one) means that in the long run a continuation of current rates would mean a population decline, a value greater than unity an increase, and a value equal to unity a stationary population. These rates, however, are complex and must be interpreted with caution. E.G.

Bibl: G. W. Barclay, *Techniques of Population Analysis* (N.Y., 1958).

***Rerum Novarum*.** An ENCYCLICAL issued by Pope Leo XIII in 1891, applying some of the key ideas of Roman Catholic (see CATHOLICISM) MORAL THEOLOGY to the conditions created by the Industrial Revolution. The Pope taught that workers should be paid a 'just wage', i.e. enough to support a family in frugal comfort, and should be allowed to combine, e.g. in trade unions, to achieve this. D.L.E.

resistance movements. (1) Loose organizations of resistance to foreign occupation (especially to German and Italian occupation of other European territory, 1939–45) engaging in sabotage, espionage, propaganda, and eventually military risings against the occupying forces and their indigenous collaborators, with or without aid from states hostile to their occupiers (see MAQUIS; SOE). (2) By transference, German or Italian organizations sufficiently opposed to NAZI or FASCIST rule to contemplate and plan the use of force against them by *coup d'état* or otherwise (see JULY 20). D.C.W.

Bibl: H. Michel, tr. R. Barry, *The Shadow War: Resistance in Europe 1939–45* (London, 1972); M. R. D. Foot, *Resistance* (London, 1976).

resistentialism. A fictitious philosophical school invented by Paul Jennings in 1948. Foreshadowed by the 19th-century thinkers Freidegg and Heidansiecker, the school has as its leading luminary Pierre-Marie Ventre. Ventre 'reversed the traditional mechanism of philosophy, which until then had been the consensus of what men think about Things: Resistentialism is concerned with what Things think about men. Briefly, they are Against us *(Les choses sont contre nous)*.' Resistentialism crystallizes definitively ideas which have long been in circulation: one's shoelaces are always impossibly tangled into knots when one is in a particular hurry, the better the carpet the more often the toast falls butter-side-down, and so on. Harassment of the animate by the inanimate is seen not as the just punishment for hubris, but as an inevitable consequence of the animate/inanimate dichotomy. The absence of any physical basis for resistentialism is more than counterbalanced by its appeal as a psychological theory.

R.SI.

resistivity surveying. In ARCHAEOLOGY, a technique for discovering buried features by measuring differences in the resistance of the subsoil. It is based on the principle that man-made disturbances such as a buried ditch or wall retain water in differing degrees as compared with the undisturbed soil. Since resistance depends on water content, where an area containing buried features is surveyed with a resistivity meter disturbances will appear as anomalous readings. Recent improvements include continuous recording on punched tape and COMPUTER plotting.

B.C.

Resnais, Alain (French film director, *b*. 1922), see under NEW WAVE.

resonance. The sympathetic vibrations of a system subjected to an oscillating force whose frequency is close to one of the

'natural frequencies' of the system. Examples: (1) a child on a swing raises it by 'pumping' ENERGY into it at its natural frequency; (2) the tuning of radio receivers is based on 'resonant circuits' which oscillate only when stimulated by electromagnetic RADIATION of the correct RADIO FREQUENCY; (3) a PHOTON can be absorbed by an ATOM only if its frequency corresponds to an energy equal to the difference between two ENERGY LEVELS of the atom. See also MAGNETIC RESONANCE. M.V.B.

resource centres. Storage centres, in schools, for educational materials such as books, press cuttings, film strips, charts, maps, models, periodicals, and children's work. In PROJECT WORK these materials are available to pupils as well as teachers. Resource centres are an attempt to facilitate efficient and economic use of costly apparatus and materials. They are frequently found in conjunction with TEAM TEACHING and similar methods. While including books, they represent a more comprehensive and flexible provision of educational materials than the books in a library. W.A.C.S.

Bibl: N. W. Beswick, *School Resource Centres* (London, 1972).

resources, natural. That part of the material components of the ENVIRONMENT, including both MASS and ENERGY, physical and biological, that can be used by man. As such, resources are bounded by concepts of UTILITY, and resource estimates change with changing technological and socio-economic conditions. A distinction is conventionally drawn between *non-renewable resources* (sometimes termed *stock resources*), like coal deposits, and *renewable resources* (sometimes termed *flow resources*), like tidal power. See also CONSERVATION. P.H.

Bibl: H. J. Barnett and C. Morse, *Scarcity and Growth* (Baltimore, 1963).

Respighi, Ottorino (Italian composer, 1879–1936), see under IMPRESSIONISM.

respondent conditioning, see CLASSICAL CONDITIONING.

rest mass. The MASS of a system as measured by an observer at rest relative to it. According to the special theory of

REVISIONISM

RELATIVITY, the mass of a body moving relative to the observer is greater; the difference is appreciable only near the speed of light. M.V.B.

Restany, Pierre (French art critic), see under NOUVEAU RÉALISME.

restricted code, see under ELABORATED CODE.

restrictive practices. Industrial and commercial agreements or arrangements which operate in restraint of free COMPETITION even though they may be valid under the ordinary law of tort or contract. Since the enactment in 1948 of the MONOPOLIES and Restrictive Practices Act, they have been subjected to various forms of legal control, notably the Restrictive Practices Act of 1956, which created a new judicial tribunal, the Restrictive Practices Court, to investigate agreements or arrangements designed to restrict in various ways the supply of goods and to declare them void if they are found to operate contrary to the public interest. Examples of such restrictive practices are agreements regulating the prices to be charged for goods supplied to customers, or the quantities to be supplied, or the conditions of supply. H.L.A.H.
Bibl: R. B. Stevens and B. S. Yamey, *The Restrictive Practices Court* (London, 1965).

retaliation, massive, see MASSIVE RETALIATION.

retardation, mental, see MENTAL RETARDATION.

retro-rocket. A small ROCKET whose thrust is directed forwards to slow down a SPACE PROBE, e.g. when making a soft landing on the moon or planets. M.V.B.

returns to scale. Phrase embodying a generalization which, as distinguished from the law of DIMINISHING RETURNS, applies to situations when all the inputs (see INPUT-OUTPUT ANALYSIS) are variable. Although with considerably less certainty than they hold to the law of diminishing returns, economists believe that the general characteristics of business organization are such that past a certain size ECONOMIES OF SCALE cease to oper-

ate and *dis*economies of scale begin to exert themselves, in consequence of the increasing bureaucratic difficulty of maintaining efficient control and rapid response to market exigencies. The success of enormous organizations like General Motors and I.B.M. casts an empirical shadow over the hypothesis. So also does the increasing power of sophisticated COMPUTERS rapidly to process masses of data and spew out usable results. In the case of so-called natural MONOPOLIES – telephone service, electric power distribution, and rail transportation – the rule, if it holds at all, does so for a scale tantamount to the entire market to be served. R.L.

Reventlow, Ernst zu Count (German politician, 1869–1943), see under NATIONAL BOLSHEVISM.

revisionism.
(1) A CONCEPT denoting a critical reinterpretation of MARXIST theories and/or a doctrinal deviation (see DEVIATIONISM) from the official ideological position (see IDEOLOGY) among COMMUNIST factions, parties, and states. In Communist polemics, the relationship of revisionism to orthodoxy appears to be a secular counterpart to that of heresy to religious DOGMA. The term dates from the 1890s, when the German Social Democrat (see SOCIAL DEMOCRACY) Eduard Bernstein attempted to modify Marxist ideas in the light of historical experience. In the Communist movement it became a term of opprobrium for any attempt to revise official interpretations of the Marxist canon. It has been invoked particularly since the emergence of Communist POLYCENTRISM. After the 20th Congress of the Soviet Communist Party (1956), which undermined Party infallibility by admitting Stalin's errors, revisionism became a label frequently used to denounce the ideas, policies, and general ideological positions of the opposing Communist parties, Soviet and Chinese, Yugoslav and Albanian, all of which claimed to be orthodox. Their own doctrinal innovations they described not as revisions but as 'a creative development of MARXISM-LENINISM' or its application to local conditions.
(2) A term applied before World War II to the claims of such countries as Germany, Hungary, and Bulgaria to the

541

territories which they had lost in World War I.   L.L.

(3) A tendency in American HIS-TORIOGRAPHY in the 1960s and early 1970s to rewrite the history of the COLD WAR and shift the blame for it onto the U.S.A. This trend was strongly reinforced by the faults and failure of U.S. policy in VIETNAM, which revisionist historians argued were not a divergence from but a consequence and illustration of an IMPERIALIST foreign and economic policy followed by the U.S.A. from the end of World War II. The revisionists' attack on the orthodox version of U.S. post-war policy represents the second stage in the historiography of the Cold War. This in turn has been succeeded by a third stage which offers a more balanced appreciation of the complexities of the situation in the 1940s and represents a synthesis of the first two.
                                                        A.L.C.B.

Bibl: (1) L. Labedz (ed.), *Revisionism* (London, 1962); (3) R. J. Maddox (ed.), *The New Left and the Origins of the Cold War* (London and Princeton, 1973); R. Aron, tr. F. Jellinek, *The Imperial Republic: the United States and the World, 1945–1973* (Englewood Cliffs, N.J., 1974; London, 1975).

revolution. A term (meaning rotation or turn) which was applied by Copernicus to the movement of celestial bodies in his treatise *De Revolutionibus Orbium Coelestium* and which in the 17th century, after the astronomical revolution, began to be applied metaphorically to political and social upheavals. From this it has developed to mean any fundamental or complete change in the mode of production (the Industrial Revolution, technological revolution, etc.), in the political and social system (the French Revolution, the Russian Revolution, etc.), or in some aspect of social, intellectual, or cultural life (scientific revolution, CULTURAL REVOLUTION, etc.). But it is sudden radical changes in the political, social, and economic structure of society that form the subject of revolutionary theories and of the theories of revolution. These are concerned not with mere changes of rulers ('palace revolutions'), but with changes of ruling CLASSES, of the methods of rule, and of social INSTITUTIONS, with the revolutionary passions and actions which

lead to these changes, and with their consequences.

Revolutionary theories, like MARXISM or LENINISM, not only advocate revolution; they also try to explain how it comes about. The classical Marxist approach looked for the 'causes' of revolution in the development of 'the forces of production' which, by clashing with 'the conditions of production', engender industrial class-struggle to the point of explosion. Leninism shifted the emphasis from 'objective' to 'subjective' conditions for revolution, stressing the role of the revolutionary organization, the Party.

Most contemporary sociological theories (see SOCIOLOGY) focus on the need for MODERNIZATION as a 'root' cause of modern revolutions; they point to the confluence of the aspirations of the 'advanced intelligentsia' (see INTELLECTUALS) and the miseries of the 'backward peasantry'. However, the theories of revolution concentrating on UNDER-DEVELOPMENT fail to explain the absence of revolutionary developments in some backward countries and their presence in some industrial ones. On the other hand, the experience of the 20th century points to the abandonment of Marxian *Gesetz-mässigheit,* i.e. of the belief that the stages of social development leading to revolution conform to a system of regular (and predictable) 'laws'. Such a belief cannot survive 'revolutions of underdevelopment' and the decoupling of the NEW LEFT theoreticians of the 'subjective' from the 'objective' conditions for revolution, a separation that goes beyond Leninist VOLUNTARISM (as in the early theories of Régis Debray) and renders the old Marxist debate about the relation between BOURGEOIS and SOCIALIST revolutions obsolete.

Some contemporary analysts of the revolutionary phenomenon go beyond the relation between revolution and economic development (Marx), underdevelopment (Lenin), and 'over-development' (the New Left), or even the question of 'modernization'. Their view of revolution transcends purely economic causation or even sociological DETERMINISM. They emphasize the recurrence of utopian and MILLENARIAN motives in history, and look for chiliastic elements in contemporary secular movements (Norman Cohn, Eric Voegelin). In this perspective, the history of the revolutionary idea may throw more light on the phenomenon of revolution than do either the existing revolutionary theories or the existing theories of revolution. See also PERMANENT REVOLUTION. L.L.

Bibl: C. J. Friedrich (ed.), *Revolution* (N.Y., 1966); Chalmers Johnson, *Revolutionary Change* (Boston, 1966; London, 1968); E. Voegelin, *From Enlightenment to Revolution* (Durham, N.C., 1975); M. J. Lasky, *Utopia and Revolution* (London and Chicago, 1977).

revolving stage. A turntable stage whose earliest recorded use was in Roman theatres in the 1st century B.C. The first such device installed as permanent equipment was used in Japanese Kabuki theatre around 1760; its first recorded use in modern Europe was at Munich in 1896. Difficulties in fitting three or more sets into one circle led to the invention of sliding stages, rising and falling stages. The most elaborate of these were installed in cabaret theatres such as the Pigalle in Paris in the 1920s. But the basic turntable stage is now a standard feature of most large theatres, greatly facilitating changes of scene. M.BI.

Bibl: A. M. Nagler, *A Source Book in Theatrical History* (N.Y., 1959).

rewrite rules, see GENERATIVE GRAMMAR.

Reynolds, Sir Joshua (British painter, 1723–92), see under ARTS, THE.

Rexroth, Kenneth (U.S. poet, critic, and translator, *b*. 1905), see under BEAT; JAZZ AGE.

Reynolds wedge action. A HYDRODYNAMIC effect which is the operating principle of lubricating devices such as ball and roller bearings. The frictional resistance to relative motion of two adjacent metal surfaces is greatly diminished if the surfaces can be inclined at a slight angle to one another, because the force necessary to squeeze the lubricant (oil or – for very rapidly moving surfaces – air) through the wedge-shaped space between them prevents the surfaces from coming into contact and thus possibly 'seizing up'. M.V.B.

Reznikoff, Charles (U.S. poet, *b*. 1894), see under OBJECTIVISM.

RF, see RADIO FREQUENCY.

Rhee, Syngman (Korean statesman, 1875–1965), see under KOREA.

rheology. The branch of NEWTONIAN MECHANICS dealing with the deformation and flow of materials which are neither solid nor completely liquid, such as nondrip paint, bread dough, modelling clay, glacier ice, and lead on roofs. See also RELAXATION; RELAXATION TIME. M.V.B.

rhesus factor, see under IMMUNITY.

Rhodesia. Originally the British colony of Southern Rhodesia, which had been self-governing on the basis of a white electorate since 1922, and became isolated by the break-up of the Central African Federation and the grant of independence by Britain to Northern Rhodesia (Zambia) and Nyasaland (Malawi) in 1964, with electoral franchises conferring power on black African leadership. Rather than admit the African majority to a wider share in the franchise, the RIGHT-wing Rhodesian Front, under the leadership of Ian Smith, made a *unilateral declaration of independence* (U.D.I.) in 1965. Britain ruled out the use of force in order to restore its authority in the colony, and instead attempted on successive occasions to negotiate a settlement based on provision for ultimate black African majority rule. The illegal regime was able to withstand this diplomatic pressure, and the effect of economic SANCTIONS imposed with the backing of UNO, through the support given to it by South Africa until 1976. In that year the growing strength of militant black nationalist forces supported by neighbouring African states, and concern over a possible repetition of events that took place in ANGOLA a year before, led South Africa to withdraw its support of the illegal regime and join the U.S.A. in insisting on moves towards majority rule. A conference at Geneva under British chairmanship, however, failed to produce an acceptable scheme of transition, and it remains an open question whether the transfer of power in an independent Zimbabwe (the African name) will take place peacefully or by force. D.C.W.

Bibl: O. N. Ransford, *The Rulers of Rhodesia: from Earliest Times to the Referendum* (London, 1968); R. C. Good,

U.D.I.: the International Politics of the Rhodesian Rebellion (London, 1973).

rhythm-and-blues. A style of American, small-group black JAZZ which flourished (before an almost exclusively black audience) in the 1920s and 1930s. The style, which concentrated almost exclusively on the traditional twelve-bar BLUES formula, tended to stress the rhythmic strength rather than the harmonic colours of the form, and may perhaps be defined as the urban amendment to the old rural blues of the American Deep South. (The centre of the rhythm-and-blues industry in the 1920s was Chicago.) From time to time authentic rhythm-and-blues musicians have enjoyed a wider popularity, the success during World War II of Louis Jordan and his Tympany Five being a good example. In the last 20 years, however, rhythm-and-blues has been vulgarized in its new, more broadly popular form of *rock music,* which has retained little of the original riches of the blues apart from a heavy rhythmic offbeat.   B.G.

ribbon development. In GEOGRAPHY, the extension of a town or village in the cheapest possible way, i.e. next to its main services and thus alongside its main roads. Many industrial towns of Britain, e.g. those of south-west Lancashire, were linked in this way. Post-war development has tended to infill such areas so that building has taken place between the ribbons. In contrast, the Rhondda valley mining villages in Wales, confined from the start by topography, the position of coal seams, and the practices of the coal-mining industry, are linear in shape but not, strictly speaking, examples of ribbon development since their shape was unavoidable.   M.L.

ribosome, see under NUCLEIC ACID.

Ricardian, see under CLASSICAL ECONOMIC THEORY.

Ricardo, David (British economist, 1772–1823), see under CLASSICAL ECONOMIC THEORY; DIMINISHING RETURNS, LAW OF; LABOUR THEORY OF VALUE.

Rice, Elmer (U.S. dramatist, 1892–1967), see under GATE THEATRE.

Rice, John Andrew (U.S. author and educator, 1888–1968), see under BLACK MOUNTAIN.

Richards, Ivor Armstrong (British critic and poet, *b.* 1893), see under AMBIGUITY; EMOTIVE AND REFERENTIAL LANGUAGE; EMOTIVISM; LEAVISITE; NEW CRITICISM; PSEUDO-STATEMENT; STOCK RESPONSE; SYNAESTHESIS.

Richardson, Dorothy (British novelist, 1873–1957), see under STREAM OF CONSCIOUSNESS.

Richardson, Henry Hobson (U.S. architect, 1838–86), see under ROMANTICISM.

Richter, Hans (German-U.S. painter and film-maker, *b.* 1888), see under ABSTRACT ART.

Richter, Hans Werner (German writer, *b.* 1908), see under GRUPPE 47.

Rickert, Heinrich (German philosopher, 1863–1936), see under VERSTEHEN.

Riemannian geometry, see under GEOMETRY.

Riesman, David (U.S. sociologist, *b.* 1909), see under OTHER-DIRECTION.

Rietveld, Gerrit Thomas (Dutch architect, 1888–1964), see under INTERNATIONAL STYLE.

Right, the. Label applied to a range of political views at the other end of the political spectrum from the LEFT (*q.v.* for the origin of both terms), and to those holding such views. Originally, the Right comprised those who defended the monarchical INSTITUTIONS attacked by the French Revolution. During the 19th century the term was associated with authority, patriotism, tradition, strong government, property, the Church, and the Army. In France it remained monarchist even after the establishment of the Third Republic, but it was everywhere evolving from its aristocratic affinities towards the protection of CAPITALIST interests against the threat of SOCIALISM. It was now opposed not only to EGALITARIANISM, but also to State intervention in the economy, which the ultra-right French Legitimists and Bismarck had strongly favoured.

But the new Right was concerned not just with economic policies. It became increasingly influenced by the attitudes and ideas of romantic NATIONALISM. After World War I a new radical (see RADICALISM) Right emerged which was sharply different from the traditional conservative Right (see CONSERVATISM). It was no longer preoccupied simply with the defence of the established order, but often hostile to the interests of the upper classes; its most extreme form was Hitler's National Socialism (see NAZISM). In line with its mystique of the nation and the State, it was hostile to economic LAISSEZ FAIRE and in favour of strong economic controls for its TOTALITARIAN and military aims.

After World War II the terms Right and Left began to be applied in a still different way. Some of the Right's traditional values clashed and new political mixtures emerged which again transcended the previous right-left divisions. Now conservatives advocating the monetarist policies (see INFLATION) of Milton Friedman and the anti-interventionism of F. A. Hayek were regarded as being to the right of conservatives favouring the KEYNESIAN approach; similar labels were attributed to political attitudes towards educational policy, whether the issues were COMPREHENSIVE SCHOOLS in Great Britain or BUSSING and educational 'quotas' in the U.S.A.

In general, after World War II, the right-wing label became more of a term of opprobrium than the left-wing label (although 'Leftie', like 'Commie', is offensive by intention). This applied both in the West, where conservative politicians avoided it, and in the East, where the COMMUNIST leaders abhorred it. But the demarcation lines had become increasingly blurred. In the West, the nationalist Right, from de Gaulle to Enoch Powell, combined with the radical Left against European unification. In the East, it was the 'right-wing' dissidents who were against the status quo in the Soviet Union, and in China it was the 'left-wing' radicals who supported Mao's CULTURAL REVOLUTION. More and more the labels have to be qualified by specific references if they are to help understanding.　L.L.
Bibl: D. Bell (ed.), *The Radical Right:*

the New American Right (Garden City, N.Y., 1963); H. Rogger and E. Webber (eds.), *The European Right* (London and Berkeley, 1965); S. M. Lipset and E. Raab, *The Politics of Unreason* (N.Y., 1970; London, 1971).

Riley, Bridget (British painter, *b.* 1931), see under OP ART.

Rilke, Rainer Maria (Austrian poet, 1875–1926), see under SYMBOLISM; WORPSWEDE.

Rimbaud, Arthur (French poet, 1854–91), see under DECADENCE; SURREALISM; SYMBOLISM.

Rio Treaty. The Inter-American Treaty of Reciprocal Assistance signed by representatives of 18 Latin American countries and of the U.S.A. at Rio de Janeiro in August 1947, as a mutual defence alliance against armed aggression and other situations threatening the peace of the American continents. Regular meetings of foreign ministers of the signatories provide a consultative organ. The Treaty became a model for other regional security pacts such as NATO and SEATO.
　　　　　　　　　　　　　　　　D.C.W.
Bibl: G. C. Smith, *The Inter-American System* (London and N.Y., 1966).

risk analysis. An application to MANAGEMENT SCIENCE of DECISION THEORY whereby SIMULATION techniques are used to form *probability density functions* (see DISTRIBUTION; FUNCTION) of the outcomes corresponding to the various alternative actions. The object is to give a clear picture of the relative risks and the probable odds of occurrence of each outcome. It has been extended recently to cover sequential decision problems (i.e. problems with several decision points over a planning horizon); this version of the procedure uses a *decision tree* and is known as *stochastic decision tree analysis*. Risk analysis is widely applied in organizations, particularly in the context of strategic decision-making.　　　　　　　　H.TH.

rites of passage. Term invented by the French ethnographer Arnold van Gennep (*Les Rites de passage,* 1909) to describe the ceremonies which celebrate an individual's or a group's transition from one

STATUS to another within his or her society, e.g. the ceremonies associated with birth, puberty, marriage, and death. Van Gennep maintained that analysis of such RITUAL observances showed, in most cases, a threefold sequence: *separation* of the individuals (or the group) from their previous condition; *transition* or limen (French *marge*), when the individuals (or the group) are in a state of suspension, in limbo; and *incorporation* (French *agrégation*) or integration into their new status. Interest in the study of rites of passage was renewed in the 1950s and 1960s.

A.L.C.B.

Bibl: A. van Gennep, tr. M. B. Vizedom and G. L. Caffee, *The Rites of Passage* (London and Chicago, 1960); M. Gluckman (ed.), *Essays on the Ritual of Social Relations* (Manchester, 1962).

ritual. (1) All formal actions that are primarily symbolic; (2) more narrowly, symbolic actions associated with RELIGION. Difficulties with (1) are that it includes such trivialities as crooking the little finger when holding a teacup, and that it presupposes a clear distinction in all cases between the symbolic and the utilitarian or technological. A drawback to (2) is its assumption that we have a clear notion of religion. Further difficulties arise from uses of the term in PSYCHOLOGY (referring sometimes to routine actions devised for themselves by individuals, as in NEUROSIS) and in the study of animals (where ritualized behaviour is that which, having evolved by NATURAL SELECTION, is a signal in the form of exaggerated behaviour).

M.F.

Bibl: J. S. Huxley (ed.), 'Ritualization of Behaviour in Animals and Man' (*Philosophical Transactions of the Royal Society*, 251, 1966).

ritualization, see under RELEASER.

Rivette, Jacques (French film director, *b.* 1928), see under NEW WAVE.

RNA (ribonucleic acid), see under NUCLEIC ACID.

Robbe-Grillet, Alain (French novelist, *b.* 1922), see under CHOSISM; NEW NOVEL.

Robbins, Jerome (U.S. choreographer, *b.* 1918), see under THEATRE LABORATORY.

Robbins, Lionel (Baron Robbins of Clare Market; British economist, *b.* 1898), see under ECONOMICS; ROBBINS REPORT.

Robbins Report (1963). The report on *Higher Education* (London, H.M.S.O.; Cmnd 2154) by a committee set up under the chairmanship of Lord Robbins, to review the pattern of full-time higher education in Great Britain, patterns of long-term development, and likely new types of institution. Its importance lay in making clear the much larger scale on which higher education would be required in the future. It suggested that higher education should be available for all suitably qualified applicants, and forecast a tripling of the intake by 1982. A Council for National Academic Awards was proposed for the validation of degree and diploma awards outside the university in the newly constituted polytechnics. Teacher-training colleges were to be brought into closer association with the universities through schools of education, and B. Ed. degrees made available to their students. Colleges of Advanced Technology (CATS) were to become universities. W.A.C.S.

Roberts, William (British painter, *b.* 1895), *see under* VORTICISM.

Robespierre, Maximilien de (French Jacobin leader, 1758–94), see under JACOBINISM; THERMIDOR.

Robinson, Edwin Arlington (U.S. poet, 1869–1935), see under ANTI-HERO.

Robinson, John Arthur Thomas (British churchman and theologian, *b.* 1919), see under NEW THEOLOGY.

robot. A term deriving from the Czech *robota*, work, and introduced into English via Karel Čapek's play *R.U.R.* (Rossum's Universal Robots; 1920, translated 1923) to describe a machine built to resemble a human in appearance and functioning. While such machines can be, and have been, manufactured with varying degrees of verisimilitude, the word is now applied more generally to any piece of apparatus which does the work normally performed by a human operator, e.g. traffic lights which do the job of a policeman on point duty were called 'robots' when they were first introduced. E.R.L.

Rochau, Ludwig von (German publicist and politician, 1810–73), see under REALPOLITIK.

rock music, see under RHYTHM-AND-BLUES.

rocket. A propulsion device for SPACE PROBES, MISSILES, etc., in which fuel is burned and the combustion gases emitted backwards at high speed. The *total* MOMENTUM of rocket + fuel does not change (see CONSERVATION LAWS), so that the increasing backward momentum of all the hot gases can only be produced by a compensating forward ACCELERATION of the rocket. Unlike the JET ENGINE, therefore, the rocket does not require an atmosphere; indeed, air friction slows it down. M.V.B.

Rodchenko, Alexander (Russian painter, 1891–1956), see under ABSTRACT ART; CONSTRUCTIVISM; MINIMAL ART; NON-OBJECTIVISM; SUPREMATISM.

Roehm, Ernst (German army officer, 1887–1934), see under NIGHT OF THE LONG KNIVES.

Rogers, Carl (U.S. psychologist, *b.* 1902), see under COUNSELLING; EXISTENTIAL PSYCHOLOGY; PSYCHOTHERAPY.

Rogers, Claude (British painter, *b.* 1907), see under EUSTON ROAD GROUP.

Roh, Franz (German art historian, 1890–1965), see under MAGIC REALISM.

Rohlfs, Christian (German painter, 1849–1938), see under FOLKWANG MUSEUM.

Rohmer, Eric (French film director, *b.* 1920), see under NEW WAVE.

role, role theory. In SOCIAL PSYCHOLOGY, 'role' connotes the bundle of formal and predictable attributes associated with a particular social position, as distinct from the personal characteristics of the individual who occupies that position. The waiter or the doctor, for instance, is called

upon to perform a professional role expected of him by his public audience which may be quite at variance with his own inclinations of the moment. Roles as official and publicly recognized as these are frequently supported by uniforms and strict linguistic codes. But most social 'roles' are so inexactly defined that they are barely more than intuitively felt guidelines to the correct behaviour for a particular social situation.

The earliest systematic uses of the term were in G. H. Mead's social psychology (see SYMBOLIC INTERACTION), which emphasized the importance of 'taking the role of the other', and the role-playing therapy invented by J. L. Moreno (see SOCIOMETRY; PSYCHODRAMA). Later it became current in social ANTHROPOLOGY, where it lent itself especially to describing the rights and duties associated with positions in kinship systems. Sociological theorists often adopted it, together with STATUS, as a suitable term for the basic elements from which SOCIAL STRUCTURES are built up, and various attempts have been made to use it as an interdisciplinary CONCEPT, bridging the gap between, on the one hand, the treatment of social systems and INSTITUTIONS by sociologists and political scientists and, on the other hand, the experimental study of personality, motivation, and group processes by social psychologists. The STRUCTURAL-FUNCTIONAL and NORMATIVE emphasis given to 'role' in PARSONIAN theory was not accepted by all students of standardized behaviour, and prompted a rediscovery of the original dramaturgical metaphor, which had suggested a degree of conscious theatre in everyday social life, and which had been largely forgotten when the term became part of a technical vocabulary.

It was in this sense that Erving Goffman expanded the term in *The Presentation of Self in Everyday Life* (1956), where he elaborated two key CONCEPTS: *role distance* (the extent to which the individual may free himself from the demands of mere adequacy in a given role, and exploit the possibilities of play and improvisation above and beyond the necessities of 'correct' behaviour); and *role conflict* (what happens when the individual finds himself in the position of playing two or more roles at once – when, for example, the doctor has to minister to a member of his own family, thereby confusing his professional and fatherly roles). Armed with these more subtle and modified terms, Goffman presented a most influential analysis of social behaviour as an elaborately mounted drama, in which virtually no area of human activity, public or private, was excluded from the essentially histrionic demands and conditions of the 'presented' self.

During the 1960s, the term became part of the commonplace idiom of social workers and political journalists. *Role*, along with other dramaturgical vogue words (notably, *scenario*) was used to describe any kind of staged or impersonated performance, especially those in public life. A newspaper describes a recorded conference between Nixon and his aides over the WATERGATE affair as 'a role-playing session'; a projected course of events is referred to as 'a scenario'. In both examples there is an implication of dishonest artifice, a hint that public men are simply 'acting out' a deviously prepared script. Role theory has provided a convenient vocabulary for the kind of cynically knowing journalism which likes to present the public world as a continuing charade; and Goffman himself has been attacked by his academic colleagues on much the same grounds. The main problem with the concept of 'role' is its lack of constraint; it is a tearaway word which tends to carry all of human behaviour indiscriminately away with it.   J.R.; J.R.T.

Bibl: J. A. Jackson (ed.), *Role* (London, 1972).

Rolland, Romain (French novelist, dramatist, and essayist, 1866–1944), see under AU-DESSUS DE LA MÊLÉE; ROMAN-FLEUVE.

Rolling Stones, the. A London-based group centering on Mick Jagger which emerged in the early 1960s featuring a strong 'white' version of RHYTHM-AND-BLUES. Their songs, and their attitude to their elders and interlocutors, reflect a harsher, less sentimental, more defiant outlook than the BEATLES': it would be inconceivable to consider them as candidates for public honours. such as the M.B.E. Their notoriety reached a peak when they received a heavy (in *The Times*'s view vindictive) sentence for possession of cannabis. The group has enjoyed a long life by pop standards, despite occasional changes in personnel since Brian Jones died. Its members remain slightly *outré*, Jagger having at one stage adopted a TRANSVESTITE style.
                                                    P.S.L.

Romains, Jules (French novelist, 1885–1972), see under ABBAYE DE CRÉTEIL; ROMAN-FLEUVE.

Roman Catholicism, see under CATHOLICISM.

roman-fleuve ('river-novel'). French term, used originally perhaps with ironical intent, for the multi-volume novel which attempts to cover a large area of society or to follow the fortunes of a family through more than one generation. (The term *fleuve* has no specific connection with the concept of the STREAM OF CONSCIOUSNESS.) Balzac's *La Comédie humaine* and Zola's *Les Rougon-Macquart* can be classed retrospectively as *romans-fleuves,* but the term appears to have been first used with reference to Romain Rolland's *Jean Christophe* (1906–12). More recent French examples are *Les Thibault* by Roger Martin du Gard, *La Chrònique des Pasquier* by Georges Duhamel, and *Les Hommes de bonne volonté* by Jules Romains. English and American examples include Galsworthy's *Forsyte Saga*, Anthony Powell's *The Music of Time,* and Upton Sinclair's Lanny Budd series.
                                                    J.G.W.

Romanticism.

(1) In the ARTS generally and in PHILOSOPHY, an overwhelming international tendency which swept across Western Europe and Russia at the end of the 18th and beginning of the 19th century, in reaction against earlier NEO-CLASSICISM, MECHANISM, and RATIONALISM. Arising in an age of social and internal revolutions, involving a new model of being, Romanticism has much that relationship to the 19th century that MODERNISM has to the 20th. More than simply a return to nature, to the UNCONSCIOUS, the realm of imagination or feeling, it was a synthesizing temper that transformed the entire character of thought, sensibility, and art; many of its preoccupations and notions remain central to the modern mind, including interest in the psychological and

the expressive, in the childlike, the revolutionary, the nihilistic, the PLEASURE PRINCIPLE. It was a specific revolt against formality and containment in art, ideas, and notions of man, an assertion of the primacy of the perceiver in the world he perceives; hence theories of the imagination as such are central to it. In central Romantic thought, the organic relation of man and nature, of the interior and the transcendent imagination, is proposed; but much Romanticism is about loss of contact and 'dejection', and can lead to the hallucinatory or fantastic as a mode of perceptual redemption. Hence its relation to the tradition of 'romance', and its disposition toward fantasy, MYTH, the picturesque, the Gothic, the Faustian and Promethean. Romanticism takes different forms in different national strands (despite its internationality and its primary interest in the foreign and strange, it contains deep NATIONALISTIC and POPULIST assumptions), ranges from strongly individualistic to revolutionary-collective concerns, and extends from IDEALISM and neo-PLATONISM to an agonized NIHILISM. Hence definitions of it vary widely. In fact, it is as much an international sensibility as a style or a philosophy; and its writing, painting, music, architecture, and thought, some of it intensely subjective and solipsistic (see SOLIPSISM), some of it strongly marked by distancing and fantasy, amount to an eclectic new world-view or WELT-ANSCHAUUNG which shifts the prevailing idea and function of the artist and of man himself and his role in the world.

Romanticism is usually held to have originated in French (especially Rousseau) and German (notably Herder, Kant, Fichte, Schelling) thought; to have strong roots in German *Sturm und Drang* writing of the 1770s; to have spread to England and then America, returned to France somewhat later, and to have shaped and affected all Europe in varying degrees at different times. Clearly related to dislocations in thought and SOCIAL STRUCTURE consequent on three revolutions – the American, the French, and the industrial – and to the new, self-conscious isolation of the artist or INTELLECTUAL in a post-patronage era, it dominates perhaps three literary generations, from the 1790s to the 1840s. It then splinters, on the one hand towards REALISM, which philosophically

amends it, on the other towards latter-day versions like SYMBOLISM and AESTHETICISM. There is now much argument whether we still live in a Romantic age of style and sensibility; one strand in MODERNISM assaults Romanticism's 'split religion' (T. E. Hulme's phrase) but another (e.g. Symbolism, EXPRESSIONISM) seeks to restore it. Certainly its REVOLUTIONARY and pre-FREUDIAN overtones affect much modern art and thought. M.S.BR.

Bibl: M. H. Abrams, *The Mirror and the Lamp: Romantic Theory and the Critical Tradition* (London and N.Y., 1953); N. Frye (ed.), *Romanticism Reconsidered* (N.Y., 1963); J. B. Halsted (ed.), *Romanticism* (Boston, 1965).

(2) In architecture, a tendency that largely derives from the Picturesque movement of the 18th century, especially as embodied in English landscape practice. In modern architecture it manifests itself not so much as a return to an earlier period as in an emphasis on natural materials and forms. In America it is exemplified by the ORGANIC architecture of Frank Lloyd Wright, which evolved from the work of H. H. Richardson and Louis Sullivan. In Europe, where it was influenced by ART NOUVEAU, it is an alternative tradition to that of the INTERNATIONAL STYLE. The most notable examples come from Alvar Aalto, who dominated Finnish architecture from the 1930s until his death in 1976. His freely and flowingly arranged forms, whether in buildings, furniture, or light fittings, have that appearance of being naturally composed which the tenets of the Romantic movement require. M.BR.

Bibl: V. J. Scully, *Modern Architecture* (London and N.Y., 1961).

(3) In music, a movement belonging largely to the first half of the 19th century, and exhibited notably in the works of Beethoven, Weber, Schubert, Schumann, Chopin, Berlioz, Liszt, Verdi, and Wagner. It received its stimulus partly from German literature of the late 18th century (A. W. Schlegel, Tieck, Novalis), and partly from the ideals associated with the French Revolution. It is characterized by a tendency among composers to view music as an expression as much of their psyche as of their craft; through the power of association they sought to embody their own ideals and passions in their music; in

so doing they cultivated an extremely personalized and sometimes exaggerated style. Reflected in their music is a series of opposing forces: between the individual and society; between intimacy and bombast; between the fusion of poetry and music and the pronounced self-sufficiency of instrumental music. Constant is the belief in music's power to translate human experience and to express human ideals. The term is often extended to include late-19th-century NATIONALIST composers (Dvořák, Chaikovsky, Grieg), and the 'late Romantics' Bruckner, Mahler, and Richard Strauss. For reactions against Romanticism see IMPRESSIONISM; NEO-CLASSICISM.   E.H.
   Bibl: A. Einstein, *Music in the Romantic Era* (London and N.Y., 1947).

Ronconi, Luca (Italian theatre director), see under TOTAL THEATRE.

Roosevelt, Franklin Delano (U.S. president, 1882–1945), see under FOUR FREEDOMS; LEND-LEASE; MORGENTHAU PLAN; NEW DEAL; POTSDAM; TEHERAN; WPA; YALTA.

Rorschach, Hermann (Swiss psychiatrist, 1884–1922), see under CHARACTEROLOGY; RORSCHACH TEST.

Rorschach test. A projective test (see PROJECTION; MENTAL TESTING) designed by the Swiss psychiatrist Hermann Rorschach, and consisting of ten bilaterally symmetrical inkblots the interpretation of whose meaning by a subject is presumed to indicate general personality characteristics and unresolved personal conflicts. It is generally included in a test battery used in the diagnosis of mental illness. After telling what each inkblot looks like to him, the subject is questioned about them in a non-directive manner. Responses are interpreted according to their content, their commonness or uncommonness, and the proportion and particular features (colour, shading, etc.) of the inkblot responded to. Although no single category of response is regarded as significant by itself, the whole test is designed to be diagnostic of integrative capacity, impulsiveness, etc.   R.P.-S.
   Bibl: H. Rorschach, tr. P. Lemkau and B. Kronenberg, ed. W. Morgenthaler, *Psychodiagnostics* (Berne, 3rd ed., 1942).

Rosa, João Guimarães, see GUIMARÃES ROSA.

Rosenberg, Harold (U.S. author, *b.* 1906), see under ACTION PAINTING.

Rosenbleuth, Arturo (Mexican neurophysiologist, 1900–1970), see under CYBERNETICS.

Rosenthal effect. In EDUCATIONAL PSYCHOLOGY, a form of self-fulfilling prophecy, named after the American psychologist Robert Rosenthal, who demonstrated that high expectations of pupils' aptitude, on the part of teachers, even when these expectations were based on fictitious test scores, produced an improvement in the pupils' subsequent performance.   W.Z.
   Bibl: R. Rosenthal and J. Jacobson, *Pygmalion in the Classroom* (London and N.Y., 1968).

ROSLA (or RSLA). Abbreviation for the *raising of the school leaving age* in Great Britain (i.e. the age at which compulsory schooling ends) from 15 to 16. This was proposed in the NEWSOM REPORT (1963) and finally put into effect in 1973. In preparation for the change, much effort was put into curriculum reform (e.g. by the SCHOOLS COUNCIL), into the improvement and extension of COUNSELLING services, and into developing closer links between schools and local industry.
                                          W.A.C.S.

Rossellini, Roberto (Italian film director, *b.* 1906), see under NEO-REALISM.

Rostow, Walt Whitman (U.S. economist, *b.* 1916), see under MODERNIZATION.

Rothko, Mark (U.S. painter, 1903–70), see under ABSTRACT EXPRESSIONISM.

Rothschild, Lionel Walter, Baron (British zoologist, 1868–1937), see under BALFOUR DECLARATION.

Rouault, Georges (French painter, 1871–1958), see under ART SACRÉ; NEUE KÜNSTLERVEREINIGUNG.

Rouch, Jean (French film director, *b.* 1917), see under CINÉMA-VÉRITÉ.

round characters, see under FLAT CHARACTERS.

Rousseau, Henri (French painter, 1844–1910), see under PRIMITIVE.

Rousseau, Jean-Jacques (French philosopher and political theorist, 1712–1778), see under CHILD-CENTRED EDUCATION; FROEBEL METHOD; IRRATIONALISM; JACOBINISM; POWER; PROGRESSIVE; ROMANTICISM; SOCIAL COMPACT; SOCIAL CONTRACT; SOCIAL STRATIFICATION; SOCIOLOGY.

Roussel, Raymond (French novelist and dramatist, 1877–1933), see under TEL QUEL.

Roux-Spitz, Michel (French architect, 1888–1957), see under ARTS DÉCO.

Roxby, Percy Maude (British geographer, 1880–1947), see under GEOGRAPHY.

Royal Court Theatre. A London theatre twice associated, since its opening in 1871, with important movements in the English theatre. From 1904 to 1907, under the management of J. E. Vedrenne and Harley Granville-Barker, it presented new plays by Shaw, Galsworthy, and Granville-Barker himself. In 1956 it became the home of the *English Stage Company* under the management of George Devine (1910–66): John Osborne, John Arden, Arnold Wesker, and Edward Bond are among the dramatists whose work was first presented by the Company.   M.A.
    Bibl: G. Rowell, *The Victorian Theatre* (Oxford, 1967); T. Browne, *Playwright's Theatre* (London, 1975).

Royal Institution. A body formed in 1799 to perform and publicize scientific research; its most famous directors were Humphry Davy and Michael Faraday. Although evening meetings are held throughout the year, the Institution is best known for its Christmas lectures delivered in London by eminent scientists before an audience of schoolchildren.   M.V.B.

Royal Society of London. One of the oldest scientific societies, founded in 1662. As well as organizing discussion meetings and administering various funds for the support of scientific research, the Society publishes its *Proceedings* and *Philosophical Transactions,* which rank among the world's leading scientific journals. To be elected one of the few hundred Fellows of the Royal Society is one of the highest honours that can be bestowed on a British scientist by his peers.   M.V.B.

RSLA, see ROSLA.

Rudd, Mark (U.S. revolutionary, *b.* 1947), see under SDS.

Ruggles-Brise, Sir Evelyn (British penal reformer, 1857–1935), see under BORSTAL.

Ruhm, Gerhard (Austrian author, *b.* 1930), see under WIENER GRUPPE.

rule, work to, see WORK TO RULE.

rule of law, see LAW, RULE OF.

Rulfo, Juan (Mexican novelist, *b.* 1918), see under STREAM OF CONSCIOUSNESS.

Rumaker, Michael (U.S. story-writer, *b.* 1932), see under BEAT.

rural history, see under AGRARIAN HISTORY.

Ruskin, John (British author, 1819–1900), see under ARTS AND CRAFTS MOVEMENT; STIJL, DE.

Russell, Bertrand Arthur William, 3rd Earl (British mathematician and philosopher, 1872–1970), see under ANALYSIS; ANALYTIC PHILOSOPHY; AXIOMATIC METHOD; AXIOMATICS; CND; COMMON SENSE; ENTAILMENT AND IMPLICATION; FORMALISM; GÖDEL'S THEOREM; LOGIC; LOGICAL ATOMISM; LOGICAL TYPES, THEORY OF; LOGICISM; MATHEMATICAL LOGIC; MODAL LOGIC; NEUTRAL MONISM; PARADOX; SET THEORY; SYNDICALISM.

Russell, Charles Taze (U.S. religious leader, 1852–1916), see under JEHOVAH'S WITNESSES.

Russolo, Luigi (Italian artist and musical theorist, 1885–1947), see under BRUITISME; FUTURISM.

Rutherford, Ernest, 1st Baron (British chemist, 1871–1937), see under CAVENDISH LABORATORY; NUCLEUS.

Rutherford, Joseph Franklin (U.S. religious leader, 1869–1941), see under JEHOVAH'S WITNESSES.

Ryle, Gilbert (British philosopher, 1900–1976), see under BEHAVIOURISM; CATEGORY; CATEGORY-MISTAKE; DISPOSITION; INTROSPECTION; LIBERTARIANISM; LINGUISTIC PHILOSOPHY; VOLITION.

S

Sabin, Albert B. (U.S. medical scientist, *b.* 1906), see under VIROLOGY.

Sacco, Nicola (Italian-born U.S. anarchist, 1891–1927), see under JAZZ AGE.

Sacher-Masoch, Baron **Leopold von** (1836–95), see under MASOCHISM.

Sade, Marquis de, see under DE SADE.

sadism. A PERVERSION in which sexual pleasure is derived from inflicting pain on others. It was named by Krafft-Ebing after the Marquis de Sade, who described its practice in *Justine* (1791) and other works. The word is often used loosely to denote cruelty of any kind.   W.Z.

sado-masochism. The coexistence in the same person of both SADISM and MASOCHISM, or their alliance as the complementary halves of a two-person relationship. However, the adjective *sadomasochistic* is usually reserved for fantasies of destruction or being destroyed, causing pain or receiving pain, which are thought by psychoanalysts to relate back to the anal stage of development – specifically, the anal-sadistic phase (age 2½ to 4 years; see PSYCHOSEXUAL DEVELOPMENT). Such fantasies are much more common in conditions such as PARANOIA and SCHIZOPHRENIA than in DEPRESSION, but can occur in obsessional (see OBSESSION) NEUROSIS and certain PHOBIAS. They occur in the majority of children as a developmental phenomenon.   M.J.C.

Saint-Simon, Claude Henri de (French socialist thinker, 1760–1825), see under SOCIALISM; STRATIFICATION, SOCIAL; TECHNOCRACY.

Sakharov, Andrei Dmitrievich (Russian physicist, *b.* 1921), see under SAMIZDAT.

salami tactics. The technique whereby one element in a governmental coalition achieves a monopoly of POWER by destroying its allied parties section by section; in particular as employed in Eastern Europe after 1945. The phrase derives from a frank account by the Hungarian COMMUNIST leader Mátyás Rákosi of how the majority Smallholders Party and the SOCIAL DEMOCRATIC Party had each in turn been bullied into 'slicing off' first their RIGHT wing, then their CENTRIST members, until only close collaborators of the Communists remained.   R.C.

Salinas, Pedro (Spanish poet, dramatist, and critic, 1891–1951), see under ULTRAISM.

Salk, Jonas Edward (U.S. virologist, *b.* 1914), see under VIROLOGY.

SALT (Strategic Arms Limitation Talks). Talks undertaken by the U.S.A. and the U.S.S.R. in November 1969 and still continuing in 1976. The talks were originally suggested by U.S. President Johnson in January 1967 as an attempt to limit the ARMS RACE and have been justified for their contribution to DÉTENTE. The first round of talks (SALT I) were concluded in May 1972 with the signing by the two powers of the Treaty on the Limitation of Defensive ABM (anti-ballistic missile) Systems and the Interim Agreement on Certain Measures with respect to the Limitation of Strategic Arms. The latter pact was to remain in force for up to five years, during which time SALT II was to produce more complete measures limiting strategic offensive arms. SALT II, however, has made slow progress and has been frequently deadlocked. At the Vladivostok summit meeting in November 1974 it was agreed that the final treaty would limit each side to specified numbers of vehicles and MISSILES of various types. Once these ceilings have been worked out in detail under SALT II it is expected that talks will be resumed after a ten-year period. It is not expected, however, that the current talks will result in a substantial curtailment of the build-up of strategic nuclear weapons.   P.B.M.

553

Bibl: J. Newhouse, *Cold Dawn: the Story of SALT* (N.Y., 1973).

samizdat ('self-publication'). A Russian coinage, in general use since about 1966, for the circulation in typescript (including carbons) of literary and political books and articles refused by, or not submitted to, regular publishers. The format is designed to evade legal restrictions on printing and duplicating – though (as many cases have shown) people may afterwards be charged with the possession or circulation of 'anti-Soviet material'. The large and striking literature in *samizdat* ranges from such novels as Solzhenitsyn's *The First Circle* to political analyses such as Academician Andrei Sakharov's *Progress, Coexistence and Intellectual Freedom* and Ivan Dzyuba's *Internationalism or Russification*, together with much poetry and various periodical publications, notably the *Chronicle of Current Events*. The analogous *tamizdat* ('published there') consists of work in Russian published in the West and reaching the U.S.S.R. more or less clandestinely, as have copies of Pasternak's *Dr Zhivago*. *Magnitizdat* refers to such material as dissident songs and poetry (or foreign broadcasts) recorded on tapes which circulate unofficially in the U.S.S.R.   R.C.
Bibl: P. Reddaway (ed.), *Uncensored Russia* (London and N.Y., 1972).

sample, sampling. In STATISTICS, the data themselves, or the random selection from which they are obtained, are often called the sample; sampling is the process of collecting such data. Thus an experiment to determine the height distribution of adult males in Britain might involve the selection of a random sample of, say, 5,000, from a total population of around 20 million. The problem of sampling is to ensure that the sample is in some sense a fair representation of the underlying population; a sample which is not is sometimes said to be *biased*. Ideally selection procedures should be such that every individual has an equal chance of being chosen, but in a population which is known to be divided into sub-populations it may be advantageous to sample from each sub-population in the correct proportions. A *Gallup Poll* is a SURVEY of voting intentions carried out in this manner.   R.SI.

Samuelson, Paul Anthony (U.S. economist, *b.* 1915), see under ACCELERATOR; EQUILIBRIUM; TURNPIKE THEOREM.

sanctions. Coercive measures taken to secure fulfilment of international obligations. Such measures may be deterrent or – e.g. the French occupation of the Ruhr in 1923 when Germany failed to pay reparations – punitive in nature. Article 16 of the LEAGUE OF NATIONS Covenant envisaged the application of economic and military sanctions against states in breach of the Covenant; economic sanctions involve the severance of economic and financial relations with the offending state, military sanctions involve acts of war. Experience, especially during the Italo-Abyssinian conflict of 1935–6, and in the British attempts to bring pressure on the Southern RHODESIAN regime which declared its independence in 1965, has shown economic sanctions to be a somewhat ineffective weapon.   D.C.W.

Sandburg, Carl (U.S. poet, 1878–1967), see under POETRY (CHICAGO).

sandwich course. A course in a college, polytechnic, or technological university organized to allow a period of college-based study to alternate with a period in industry planned as an integral part of the work. A 'thick' sandwich consists of two years in university, one year in industry, and a final year in university, and is the norm in high-level programmes. A 'thin' sandwich, usually consisting of six-month layers, is found in lower-level diploma and certificate programmes.   W.A.C.S.
Bibl: L. Cantor and I. F. Roberts, *Further Education in England and Wales* (London, 1969; N.Y., 1970).

Sanger, Frederick (British biochemist, *b.* 1918), see under INSULIN.

Sansom, William (British novelist, 1912–76), see under NEW WRITING.

Santayana, George (Spanish-U.S. philosopher, 1863–1952), see under REALISM, CRITICAL.

Sant'Elia, Antonio (Italian architect, 1888–1916), see under FUTURISM.

Sapir, Edward (U.S. linguist, 1884–1939), see under WHORFIAN.

Sarajevo. Capital of the then Austrian, now Yugoslav, province of Bosnia-Herzogovina, where on 28 June 1914 the Archduke Franz Ferdinand, heir to the throne of the Habsburg Empire, and his morganatic wife, Sophie, were assassinated by a young Bosnian student, Gavrilo Princip, at the instance of the *Black Hand*, a Serbian TERRORIST organization. The murder was taken as an occasion to settle Austrian scores with Serbia, which claimed Russian protection. Efforts to limit and contain the conflict failed, Russian mobilization leading to a rapid ESCALATION of the conflict until Germany, Austro-Hungary, and Turkey were embroiled with Britain, France, Serbia, and Czarist Russia in World War I. The name of the town has become identified with the murder as the immediate occasion of the war.   D.C.W.

Bibl: V. Dedijer, *The Road to Sarajevo* (N.Y., 1966); J. Remak, *Sarajevo* (London, 1959).

sarcomas, see under CANCER.

Saroyan, William (U.S. dramatist and fiction writer, *b.* 1908), see under GROUP THEATRE.

Sarraute, Nathalie (French novelist, *b.* 1902), see under NEW NOVEL; TROPISM.

Sartre, Jean-Paul (French author and philosopher, *b.* 1905), see under COMMITMENT; EXISTENTIALISM; HORIZON; NÉANT, LE; NÉGRITUDE; NEO-MARXISM; NEW NOVEL; TEL QUEL.

satellite. Any body constrained by GRAVITATION to revolve in a circular ORBIT around a much more massive body. For example, the planets are satellites of the sun, while the moon and all the artificial communications satellites are satellites of the earth.   M.V.B.

satellite town. In expanding, a town causes the formation of industrial or residential centres which depend upon it, which are separate from it, and without which its activities cannot be considered. Such a centre is often called a satellite town.

V. G. Davidovich has defined a satellite by three characteristics, all of which require that communications between a central town (which may rank as a METROPOLIS) and its satellites are easy and frequent: (1) people living in a satellite town come to work in the central town; (2) the central town guarantees a certain number of services, notably cultural services, for its satellites; (3) the satellites accommodate the town's population for relaxation, e.g. in parks, sports centres, and public houses. J. Beaujeu-Garnier has distinguished between a *consumer satellite* (i.e. a DORMITORY TOWN) and a *production satellite*, for which the term satellite town should be reserved. Under this classification, the satellite town is one in which some provision is made for the industrial and commercial employment of its inhabitants independently from employment provided by the metropolis, e.g. the NEW TOWNS developed since World War II as a means of decongesting London.   M.L.

Bibl: V. G. Davidovich and B. S. Khorev (eds.), *Satellite Towns* (Washington, 1962); J. Beaujeu-Garnier and G. Chabot, tr. G. M. Yglesias and S. H. Beaver, *Urban Geography* (London and N.Y., 1967).

Satie, Erik (French composer, 1866–1925), see under CUBISM; SIX, LES.

satori, see under ZEN.

saturated. In ORGANIC CHEMISTRY, term used to describe a compound which will not react by adding other chemical SPECIES. In such compounds each carbon ATOM is singly bonded (see BOND) to four neighbouring atoms as in methane, and ethyl alcohol. See also UNSATURATED.
B.F.

Sauguet, Henri (pseud. of Jean Pierre Poupard, French composer, *b.* 1901), see under CONCRETE MUSIC.

Saussurian. Characteristic of, or a follower of, the principles of Ferdinand de Saussure (1857–1913), especially as outlined in his posthumous *Cours de linguistique générale* (Paris, 1916), translated by W. Baskin as *Course in General Linguistics* (New York, 1959). His conception of language as a system of mutually defining entities underlies much of contemporary

SAVARY

structural LINGUISTICS. See also the
distinctions between synchronic and
DIACHRONIC, LANGUE AND PAROLE,
SYNTAGMATIC AND PARADIGMATIC;
see also COMPARATIST; SEMIOLOGY. D.C.

Savary, Jerome (French theatre director),
see under THEATRE OF PANIC.

Say's Law. An ECONOMIC LAW which
states that 'SUPPLY creates its own
DEMAND'. From an accounting point of
view this is a truism: since accounts must
balance, the incomes accruing to the factors of production from an increase in
output will be matched in the national
accounts by an equal increase in final
expenditure. However, the increase in
'expenditure' may not in fact reflect an
increase in demand but simply represent
the value at cost of unsold stocks. Unless
these stocks find buyers, the increase in
output, far from being maintained, will be
reversed.   R.ST.

scalar, see under VECTOR.

scale. In the sense of an objective basis for
measuring, comparing, or classifying
things, a scale may belong to one or more
of several identifiable types. A scale that
makes it possible to describe things in
terms of some numerical quantity, e.g.
length in miles, weight in tons, or voltage,
is called a *numerical scale*. The simplest
type of scale assumes merely that objects
can be arranged in a definite order, and
then assigns numbers or labels to positions
in that order, as when social CLASSES are
ranked as 'upper', 'upper middle', 'lower
middle', or 'working', or when objects are
assigned one of the numbers from 1 to 7
according to their hardness as measured in
a standard test; this is called an *ordinal
scale*. In such scales, only the order is usually significant, and differences between
positions carry no usable information;
e.g., if the INTELLIGENCE QUOTIENTS of
four persons are 96, 101, 146, and 156,
then although the difference between the
first two numbers is half the difference
between the second two it is not possible
to deduce that half as much teaching is
required to bring the first person to the
level of the second as is required to bring
the third to the level of the fourth. When
the differences or intervals *are* significant,
as with measurement of temperature (the

difference between 96°C and 101°C being
physically related to the difference between 146°C and 156°C), the scale is
called an *interval scale*. However, *ratios*
between numbers on this scale are
meaningless: something with a temperature of 80°C is not twice as hot as something with a temperature of 40°C, but
merely twice as far from an arbitrary zero
point, i.e. one that does not correspond to
zero amount of anything. When the zero
point of a scale is *not* arbitrary, as with
measurement of lengths or weights, the
scale is called a *ratio scale*.
    Some phenomena cannot be measured
along any single scale, but can be decom-
posed into constituent parts that are
measureable on several different scales.
Thus it can be argued that there is no
single measure of the wealth of a nation.
If, however, it is possible to agree on a way
of assigning numbers to the separate
aspects of wealth – e.g. the amount of food
consumed per head, the average quality of
housing, the standard of EDUCATION and
medical care provided, the variety of
entertainments available – then the wealth
of the nation can be measured by giving a
set of numbers, one for each type. This is
called a *multidimensional scale*, each
component being an *indicator* of the
nation's wealth. See also QUANTIFICA-
TION (1); SCALING.   A.S.

scale, economies of, see ECONOMIES OF
SCALE.

scale, returns to, see RETURNS TO SCALE.

scale-and-category grammar. A theory of
GRAMMAR developed by Halliday and
other neo-FIRTHIAN scholars in the early
1960s, and so named because it analyses
grammatical patterns into a small number
of theoretical *categories*, interrelating
these through the use of *scales* (see, e.g.,
RANK). The grammatical analysis presupposes a general MODEL of language
which distinguishes three basic LEVELS of
substance, form, and *context*.   D.C.
    Bibl: M. A. K. Halliday, 'Categories of
the Theory of Grammar' (*Word,* 17,
1961, pp. 241–92).

scaling. The activity carried out by a statistician when he selects one out of several
possible SCALES of measurement, e.g.
when he decides whether to measure

556

seeds by length or volume or weight. For biometric data (see also BIOMETRY) there are often good reasons for working with the logarithm of the observed quantity; this is called a *logarithmic scale*. Sometimes scaling problems can involve variation in more than one dimension; the resolution of such *multidimensional scaling* problems involves lengthy and complicated computation (see COMPUTING), but the techniques involved are very powerful weapons of DATA ANALYSIS for a wide variety of problems.   R.SI.

scanning. The systematic traversal of a region by a narrow beam, e.g. the 'flying spot' of ELECTRONS which builds up a television picture by varying in brightness while scanning the screen of a CATHODE RAY TUBE in a total of 625 lines traversed too quickly for the eye to follow. M.V.B.

scarcity rents. Payments made in respect of any of the factors of production (land, labour, equipment) which are permanently or temporarily in short supply. The classical case is land: the supply of this is fixed irrespective of the level of rents, but, because the supply is not big enough to satisfy all potential users, landowners are able to charge rents that reduce the quantity demanded to the quantity available. Equally, however, the supply of some equipment, or of some labour, may be fixed, at least for a time, irrespective of the amount paid for it, which thus resembles a rent.   E.H.P.B.

scenario, see under ROLE; TECHNOLOGICAL FORECASTING.

Schacht, Hjalmar (German financier and politician, 1877–1970), see under AUTARKY.

Schad, Christian (German painter and photographer, *b.* 1894), see under PHOTOGRAM.

Schadenfreude. German term for pleasure derived from the misfortunes of others. In English it tends to be used, more or less jokingly, to describe satisfaction at what is felt to be a just retribution. Its occasional occurrence is thus a perfectly normal feeling; excessive proneness to it indicates an unkind or malicious nature, but is quite distinct from SADISM.   O.S.

schadograph, see PHOTOGRAM.

Schaeffer, Pierre (French composer, *b.* 1910), see under CONCRETE MUSIC.

Schechter, Solomon (Romanian-born Judaic scholar, 1847–1915), see under JUDAISM.

scheduled territories, see under STERLING AREA.

schedules of reinforcement, see under REINFORCEMENT.

Scheler, Max (German philosopher, 1874–1928), see under KNOWLEDGE, SOCIOLOGY OF; PHENOMENOLOGY.

Schelling, Friedrich Wilhelm Joseph von (German philosopher, 1775–1854), see under ABSOLUTE, THE; ROMANTICISM.

Schelling, Thomas Crombie (U.S. writer on strategic topics, *b.* 1921), see under BRINKMANSHIP.

Schinkel, Karl Friedrich (German architect, 1771–1841), see under NEO-CLASSICISM.

schizoid. In PSYCHIATRY, a term associated with the name of Kretschmer, who believed that the whole population fell along a normal curve of distribution (see NORMAL DISTRIBUTION) from MANIC-DEPRESSIVES at one end to schizophrenics (see SCHIZOPHRENIA) at the other. The group which was closest to the schizophrenic end of the curve, but not psychotic (see PSYCHOSIS) and therefore not abnormal, was the group he called schizoid.

Today the word is characteristically applied, independently of Kretschmer's theory, to a PERSONALITY TYPE whose main features are shyness, extreme sensitivity, and a tendency to suppress the outward show of emotion. This usage is imprecise and apt to vary from one clinical worker to another, while the CONCEPT which it reflects is based on the impressionistic judgements of clinicians, and has not yet been satisfactorily validated by objective methods. Some workers, nevertheless, find it useful.   B.A.F.

SCHLEGEL

schizophrenia. In PSYCHIATRY and ABNORMAL PSYCHOLOGY, a term introduced by Eugen Bleuler in 1911 to denote forms of mental illness characterized by a lack of connection (splitting of the mind) between mental functions, which seem to the observer incongruous with one another and not understandable. Schizophrenia is traditionally classed as a PSYCHOSIS, and the wide range of symptoms subsumed under it includes disorders of thought, such as delusions; sense deceptions, such as hallucinations; abnormalities of mood, such as unresponsiveness or incongruous reactions to situations; and behavioural disturbances such as loss of drive and social withdrawal.

The causal factors are probably multiple: GENETIC factors undoubtedly play a part, though how much is disputed; BIOCHEMICAL disorders in the brain may be influential but are as yet unproven; disturbances of early parent-child relationships have been suggested but without convincing evidence. Although causation remains obscure, in the past 20 years the course of schizophrenia has been improved by two developments. First, symptoms are frequently alleviated by drugs (phenothiazines), particularly in the acute stage. Second, active social and psychological treatment measures may greatly reduce long-term handicaps resulting from social withdrawal and from lack of suitable occupation and stimulation.

D.H.G.

Schlegel, August Wilhelm von (German critic, poet, and translator, 1767–1845), see under AGGLUTINATING; ROMANTICISM.

Schleicher, Kurt von (German general and politician, 1882–1934), see under NIGHT OF THE LONG KNIVES.

Schleiermacher, Friedrich (German philosopher and theologian, 1768–1834), see under LIBERALISM.

Schlemmer, Oskar (German painter and theatrical designer, 1888–1943), see under BAUHAUS.

Schlichter, Rudolf (German painter, 1890–1955), see under NEUE SACHLICHKEIT.

Schlick, Moritz (Austrian philosopher, 1882–1936), see under LOGICAL POSITIVISM; VIENNA CIRCLE.

Schmidt-Rottluff, Karl (German painter and engraver, 1884–1976), see under BRÜCKE, DIE.

Schnitzler, Arthur (Austrian dramatist and novelist, 1862–1931), see under DEUTSCHES THEATER.

Schoenberg, Arnold, see SCHÖNBERG.

Schöffer, Nicolas (French artist, b. 1912), see under KINETIC ART; SPACE.

scholasticism, see under NEO-THOMISM.

Schönberg, Arnold (Austrian-born composer, 1874–1951), see under ATONAL MUSIC; BLAUE REITER; EXPRESSIONISM; GESAMTKUNSTWERK; MUSIC THEATRE; PANTONAL MUSIC; SERIAL MUSIC; SYMBOLISM.

Schools Council for Curriculum and Examinations. A national body set up in London in 1964 to keep under review the development of the curriculum in primary and secondary education, together with teaching and examining methods in so far as these influence the curriculum. The constitution of the Council provides for representation of teachers, research bodies, administrators, Local Education Authorities, universities, teacher-training colleges, and the Department of Education and Science. Steering committees cover the full school age range from 2 to 16 and over; other committees include a Welsh committee, an examinations committee, and at least ten subject committees. The Council has sponsored major projects on curriculum reform in the sciences, humanities, social sciences, mathematics, and technology, together with work for the disadvantaged and handicapped and for school-leavers. In 1976 the Council undertook the difficult task of rationalizing school examinations at 16, 17, and 18 into a common system with sufficient flexibility to test adequately pupils of widely differing abilities.

W.A.C.S.

schools of psychology. Psychological issues, being many-sided and complexly interrelated, can be regarded from many viewpoints which, although different, are not necessarily contradictory, and which vary according to the psychological aspect being studied, the method of study, and the theoretical FRAME OF REFERENCE within which the study is set. These diverse approaches can themselves be classified in different ways and are sometimes grouped into so-called schools so as to highlight theoretical similarities and divergences. There is no agreed repertoire of schools but the phrase 'schools of psychology' most often refers to certain groupings that dominated theoretical PSYCHOLOGY, particularly in America, during roughly the first half of this century, when psychology was asserting its independence from other disciplines.

According to R. S. Woodworth (*Contemporary Schools of Psychology,* 1931, revised 1948 and 1964), whose historical interpretation is widely accepted in America, there were six main schools. STRUCTURALISM sought by systematic introspection to discover the elementary contents of CONSCIOUSNESS, while FUNCTIONALISM was concerned with the activities by which the mind worked (see also COGNITIVE PSYCHOLOGY). ASSOCIATIONISM wanted to study isolated psychological elements in their interconnection, while GESTALT psychology asserted the priority of whole-characteristics and resisted segmentation into elements. BEHAVIOURISM insisted that only objective behaviour, and not subjective experience, be studied. PSYCHOANALYSIS attempted in a distinctive way to understand the motivational forces governing conscious and unconscious phenomena. Of these six, only behaviourism and psychoanalysis survived the mid-century as distinctive schools separated from the eclectic, middle-of-the-road orientation of most psychologists who bow to the breadth and diversity of their subject-matter by accepting that no one theory or method or field of specialization has proper monopoly and that complex problems are profitably approached, even simultaneously, from different viewpoints.   I.M.L.H.

Schopenhauer, Arthur (German philosopher, 1788–1860), see under VOLUNTARISM.

Schreyer, Lothar (German author, 1886–1966), see under STURM, DER.

Schrödinger, Erwin (Austrian-German physicist, 1897–1961), see under QUANTUM MECHANICS; SCHRÖDINGER WAVE EQUATION.

Schrödinger wave equation. An EQUATION formulated in 1926 by Erwin Schrödinger, and having as its solution the WAVE FUNCTON of QUANTUM MECHANICS.   M.V.B.

Schubert, Franz (Austrian composer, 1797–1828), see under ROMANTICISM.

Schultze-Naumburg, Paul (German architect and author, 1869–1949), see under DEGENERACY.

Schuman, Robert (French statesman, 1886–1963), see under ECSC; THIRD FORCE.

Schuman Plan, see under ECSC.

Schumann, Robert (German composer, 1810–56), see under ROMANTICISM.

Schütz, Alfred (Austrian-U.S. philosopher and sociologist, 1899–1959), see under ETHNOMETHODOLOGY; PHENOMENOLOGY.

Schwann, Theodor (German anatomist, 1810–82), see under CELL.

Schweitzer, Albert (German theologist, musicologist, and medical missionary, 1875–1965), see under ESCHATOLOGY; MUSICOLOGY.

Schwitters, Kurt (German poet and painter, 1887–1948), see under DADA; ENVIRONMENT; MERZ; STURM, DER; TOTAL ART.

science, philosophy of. The study of the inner LOGIC of scientific theories, and the relations between experiment and theory, i.e. of SCIENTIFIC METHOD. There are two main problems: (1) How are the quantities and constructs in scientific theories (e.g. a 'characteristic' in GENETICS or MOMENTUM in NEWTONIAN MECHANICS) related to events in the natural world outside our minds? (2) How can it be said that a theory or SCIENTIFIC LAW is 'true', on the basis of INDUCTION from a limited number of experiments? See also POP-PERIAN.   M.V.B.

Bibl: E. Nagel, *The Structure of Science* (London and N.Y., 1961); J. T. Davies, *The Scientific Approach* (London and N.Y., 1965).

science, sociology of. The study of the social relations and INSTITUTIONS of the scientific community. Typical problems are: (1) How efficiently is scientific knowledge communicated by journals, conferences, etc.? (2) How can the SCIENTIFIC METHOD persist virtually unchanged, when scientists come from countries differing radically in their political IDEOLOGIES?   M.V.B.

Bibl: A. M. Weinberg, *Reflections on Big Science* (Oxford and Worcester, Mass., 1967); J. M. Ziman, *Public Knowledge* (London, 1968).

science fiction. Unsatisfactory but firmly established term for an Anglo-American literary genre that shows average human beings confronted by some novelty, usually daunting: an invasion from another planet, a plague, space-travel, time-travel, a non-human civilization, a society ruled by machines, etc. There are anticipations in tales of wonder from the 17th century onwards and notably in the works of Jules Verne, but the first and still the greatest true exponent was H. G. Wells in *The Time Machine* (1895), *The War of the Worlds* (1898), etc. Until about 1940 most stories involved gadgetry, simple menace, or fantastic adventure. The next 25 years widened the range to include political, economic, technological, and psychological speculation. In the later 1960s the so-called New Wave imitated the stylistic and presentational trickery of the ANTI-NOVEL, but this has passed and the genre has returned to its traditional themes, though with an added emphasis on the potentialities of the· mind and on philosophical questions. Often ostensibly concerned with the future, science fiction at its best throws a fresh light on today. Leading writers include Brian W. Aldiss, Isaac Asimov, J. G. Ballard, Arthur C. Clarke, Philip K. Dick, Harry Harrison, Damon Knight, Ursula Le Guin, Frederik Pohl, and Robert Silverberg. The abbreviations SF and sf are approved by practitioners and connoisseurs; sci-fic and sci-fi are not.   K.A.

Bibl: B. W. Aldiss, *Billion-Year Spree* (London and N.Y., 1973).

scientific law. A general statement of fact, methodically established by INDUCTION, on the basis of observation and experiment, and usually, though not necessarily, expressed in mathematical form. In so far as it is empirical, a scientific law is not a necessary, demonstrable (see DEMON-STRATION) truth; in so far as it is methodically derived from intentionally acquired evidence, however, it differs from everyday commonsensical generalization. Ideally, scientific laws are strictly universal or deterministic (see DETER-MINISM) in form, asserting something about all members of a certain class of things, but they may also be 'probabilistic' or statistical and assert something about a methodically estimated proportion of the class of things in question. There is a problem about the distinction of laws from 'accidental' generalizations, statements that just happen to be true about all the things there are of the kind to which they relate. This distinction is marked, but not explained, by the fact that laws do, but accidental generalizations do not, imply COUNTERFACTUAL conditionals. Only if 'All *A* are *B*' is a law does it imply that if this thing, which is actually not *A*, had been *A*, it would have been *B*. This logical peculiarity lends some support to the view that scientific laws do not just describe universally pervasive regularities but assert some necessary connection between the kinds or properties mentioned in them.
                                                              A.Q.

scientific management. Term coined by Frederick Winslow Taylor in 1911 to describe the techniques he adopted to increase the output of workers. Controversial at the time (it was the subject of a Congressional Hearing in 1912), the approach is today seen as mechanistic and anachronistic. Contrast with MANAGE-MENT SCIENCE.   R.I.T.

Bibl: F. W. Taylor, *The Principles of Scientific Management* (London and N.Y., 1911).

scientific method. The procedure by which, as a matter of definition, SCIEN-TIFIC LAWS, as contrasted with other

kinds of general statement, are established. The orthodox view is that this procedure is inductive (see INDUCTION), but several philosophers of science have criticized *inductivism* (see POPPERIAN) as misrepresenting the actual procedure of scientists. Two phases of scientific activity need to be distinguished: the initial formulation of hypotheses, which seems mainly, as the anti-inductivists maintain, to be a business of inspired guessing that cannot be mechanized, and the CONFIRMATION of hypotheses thus formulated, which does appear to be a comparatively pedestrian and rule-governed undertaking.   A.Q.
    Bibl: K. R. Popper, *The Logic of Scientific Discovery* (London and N.Y., 1959).

scientism. The view that the characteristic inductive methods (see INDUCTION) of the NATURAL SCIENCES are the only source of genuine factual knowledge and, in particular, that they alone can yield true knowledge about man and society. This stands in contrast with the explanatory version of DUALISM which insists that the human and social subject-matter of history and the SOCIAL SCIENCES (the GEISTESWISSENSCHAFTEN) can be fruitfully investigated only by a method, involving sympathetic intuition of human states of mind, that is proprietary to these disciplines.   A.Q.

scientology. An organization of a quasi-religious character founded in the U.S.A. in 1952 by L. Ron Hubbard and purporting to bring its members complete mental health. It has been widely accused of authoritarian attitudes and of indoctrinating, hypnotizing, and BRAINWASHING its members so as to destroy their social links with non-members, including even close relatives. Several Australian states, New Zealand, Canada, and Great Britain have held official enquiries into its practices, and measures aimed at adversely publicizing its activities or drastically reducing their scope have been adopted in a number of them.   D.C.W.
    Bibl: J. G. Foster, *Enquiry into the Practice and Effects of Scientology* (London, 1971).

Scott, Howard (U.S. economist, *b.* 1890), see under TECHNOCRACY.

scratchpad. A form of computer store (see COMPUTER; STORE).   C.S.

Scriabin, Alexander Nikolayevich (Russian composer, 1872–1915), see under ATONALISM; GESAMTKUNSTWERK; SYMBOLISM.

Scriven, Michael (British-U.S. philosopher of science, *b.* 1928), see under EVALUATION.

Scrutiny, see under LEAVISITE.

SDI (selective dissemination of information). A name used for systems, usually using COMPUTERS, which attempt to distribute copies or notices of publications to recipients on the basis of their own statements of what they are interested in. These statements are often called *interest profiles,* and the essence of an SDI system is that from time to time, e.g. weekly or monthly, descriptions of all new documents are matched against all available interest profiles.   R.M.N.

SDS (Students for a Democratic Society). A radical (see RADICALISM) American student organization founded at Columbia University in New York by Mark Rudd and Tom Hayden which played a major part in disrupting university activities in Columbia in spring 1968 and in the demonstrations which accompanied the Democratic Party conference in Chicago that summer. The organization spread rapidly to other American universities, over two hundred of which suffered disruption of varying degrees of violence in the years 1968–9. SDS was an offshoot of the movement against American involvement in VIETNAM which had little positive to offer beyond a rather romanticized concept of REVOLUTION and fell victim to sectarian factionalism in 1969, one extremist faction developing into the WEATHERMEN. Two members of SDS were among those tried in Chicago on conspiracy charges in 1969 in the sensational CHICAGO CONSPIRACY TRIAL, in which their disruptive tactics were answered with exceptional judicial severity. D.C.W.

Searle, Humphrey (British composer, *b.* 1915), see under SERIAL MUSIC.

SEATO (South-East Asia Treaty Organization). An organization established at Manila on 8 September 1954 in a treaty signed by Australia, Britain, France, New Zealand, Pakistan, the Philippines, Thailand, and the United States. Its purpose was to provide a defensive alliance on the model of NATO for the protection of the South-East Asia and South-West Pacific areas including, by an agreed protocol, Laos, Cambodia, and South VIETNAM. Seato, however, lacked the long-term commitment of members' forces that was a feature of Nato; French and British commitments were always marginal, and Pakistan withdrew after the Indo-Pakistani war of 1971. In September 1975 it decided to phase itself out of existence.

D.C.W.

Bibl: G. A. Modelski (ed.), *SEATO* (Melbourne, 1962); P. H. Lyon, *War and Peace in South-East Asia* (London and N.Y., 1969).

second-order theorizing. Making theories about theories. The term has no unique field of application, but two typical kinds of second-order theorizing can be broadly distinguished: (1) epistemological, logical, mathematical, etc. theories about the formal properties of other theories, e.g. demonstrating their structural similarity, justifying their claims to validity, or explicating their assumptions (see METATHEORY); (2) sociological, psychological, historical, etc. theories about how theories come into being, persist, or change. The first-order theories which compose the subject-matter of second-order theorizing are perhaps most commonly those of the NATURAL SCIENCES and SOCIAL SCIENCES. J.R.T.

Bibl: T. S. Kuhn, *The Structure of Scientific Revolutions* (Chicago, 2nd ed., 1970); K. R. Popper, *Objective Knowledge* (Oxford, 1972).

second-signal system. In PSYCHOLOGY, a PAVLOVIAN term used to differentiate a physical stimulus that was directly conditioned and linked to a response (see CONDITIONED REFLEX) from one that has been categorized in language and can thus be associated by meaning with a range of other similarly coded STIMULI. Pavlov aimed to distinguish CONDITIONING in animals from learning in man, in which the ordinary laws of conditioning were superseded by linguistic association.

J.S.B.

second-strike capability, see under STRATEGIC CAPABILITY.

secondary occupation, see under OCCUPATION.

secondary schools. In Great Britain, MAINTAINED (or *state*) SCHOOLS, in which the majority of children receive their education, fall into two categories: primary schools for the age-range from five to eleven and a half, and secondary schools from eleven and a half onwards. Compulsory secondary schooling now ends at 16 (see ROSLA), but an increasing number of pupils continue their education voluntarily up to the age of 18. The break at 11+ was recommended by the *Hadow Report* in 1926; there are variations (e.g. a three-tier system with breaks at 9 and 13) but this is the standard pattern.

The oldest type of secondary school in Britain is the *grammar school*; this is a confusing term since it refers both to historic foundations dating from earlier centuries, supported by fees and endowments, and to the secondary grammar schools which Local Education Authorities (L.E.A.s; established by the Education Act of 1902) were empowered to create. The Education Act of 1944 made secondary education available for all and abolished fees in the maintained schools. Since then the age for compulsory attendance at school has been successively extended from 14 to 16. The *pattern* of secondary education, however, has become a matter of bitter educational and political controversy in Britain.

After the 1944 Act and largely following the recommendations of the *Norwood Report* (1943), the pattern generally adopted provided secondary grammar schools for the academically abler children, or occasionally *technical high schools* for able children with practical rather than academic talent; and secondary modern schools for the academically less gifted majority. This pattern was, however, complicated not only by the existence of independent schools but by the fact that many of the historic grammar schools of England and Wales also retained their independence of the L.E.A.s, continuing to be financed partly by fees and endowments, partly from a grant per pupil provided direct from the Department of Education. The list of such *direct-grant schools* was limited to some 175, most of which were noted for their high academic standard. In return for this public support they were required to provide not less than 25% and not more than 50% of places for pupils whose fees were paid by the L.E.A. but who had to satisfy the schools' entry requirements.

At the end of the primary-education stage an examination (known from the age at which it was taken as the *Eleven Plus*) selected (1) those who were to go on to secondary grammar schools (or, when available, to the more prestigious direct-grant schools), with their *sixth forms* leading to a university and other forms of higher education, and (2) those (the majority) who were to receive their education in secondary modern schools where everyone was expected to leave as soon as the age for compulsory schooling had been reached, or (occasionally) in technical high schools. This selection process, however, came under increasing criticism, on the grounds that far too much in the way of later educational advantages and career opportunities was made to depend upon what were often said to be highly fallible decisions at too early an age. More fundamental is the criticism that, even if it were possible to devise a fair method of selection, any selective pattern of secondary education perpetuates class divisions and social inequality (see ÉLITISM) and may well be psychologically damaging to those children who see themselves labelled as failures through their inability to secure a place in the academically and socially superior grammar school.

An alternative pattern of secondary education is the COMPREHENSIVE SCHOOL which provides for *all* the secondary education of *all* the children within a given area and which, beginning in Anglesey (Holyhead School, opened in 1949) was adopted by an increasing number of L.E.A.s in the 1960s. The decision to 'go comprehensive' is a local one, but there has been increasing pressure from successive Labour Governments committed to abolishing selection at 11+ and with it the separate grammar school in favour of a common school. A recent ruling (1976) by the courts has left one L.E.A. (Thameside, near Manchester) with the option of maintaining at least two of its grammar schools, together with the selection process necessary to support them.

Supporters of the comprehensive principle argue that common schools reduce the CLASS divisions from which, in their view, Britain notoriously suffers; opponents see comprehensive education and the abolition of the grammar schools as leading to a general debasement of educational standards. The battle has been extended by the decision of the Labour Government to withdraw grants from the direct-grant schools, thereby forcing them to conform with the comprehensive nonselective pattern which is being made universal in the State system of education or to become INDEPENDENT SCHOOLS, free to follow a selective pattern but only at the price of charging high fees and excluding all but the minority able to pay them. The Conservative Party has announced its intention, if returned to power, of reversing this decision and restoring the direct-grant schools.　　　W.A.C.S.; A.L.C.B.

Bibl: D. Ayerst, *Understanding Schools* (Harmondsworth, 1967); T. Burgess, *A Guide to English Schools* (Harmondsworth, rev. ed., 1969).

secret police. A special police force employed in clandestine, and often extra-legal, operations of surveillance, investigation, and suppression of 'enemies of the State'. It is an institution of which DEMOCRATIC regimes, save in time of IDEOLOGICAL conflict, feel little need, but which is the more needed, the less tolerant a regime feels it can afford to be of political opposition. The secret police is one of the essential institutions in all TOTALITARIAN one-party states: the best known examples in this century are the German GESTAPO and the Russian KGB.　　　D.C.W.

secretion. The synthetic product of an organ or gland, whether liberated externally (e.g. sweat, tears) into a body space (e.g. digestive juices) or directly into the blood stream, as with a ductless gland (see ENDOCRINOLOGY).　　　P.M.

sect. By contrast with a church, which is all-embracing and 'universal', a sect begins as a movement breaking away from a church and then maintains itself in distinction. Membership of a church is typically automatic, that of a sect voluntary. The scale and nature of sects assure a more intense religious and social interaction among their members than is found in other organizational forms of RELIGION. This usage can be traced back to the work of Ernst Troeltsch (1865–1923) on Christianity.   M.F.

Bibl: B. Wilson, *Religious Sects: a Sociological Study* (London and N.Y., 1970).

secular Christianity. The attempt to restate Christianity in sympathetic response to SECULARIZATION. The movement has been stimulated by the thought of Dietrich Bonhoeffer (1906–45), particularly by his *Letters and Papers from Prison,* sent to friends before he was hanged by the NAZIS. The emphasis is on this world rather than the supernatural, behaviour rather than belief, freedom rather than obedience, and a bold maturity rather than conservatism; but the ATHEISM which runs through the DEATH OF GOD THEOLOGY is usually avoided, notably by the devout Bonhoeffer.   D.L.E.

Bibl: P. van Buren, *The Secular Meaning of the Gospel* (London and N.Y., 1963); E. Bethge, tr. E. Mosbacher *et al., Dietrich Bonhoeffer* (London and N.Y., 1970).

secularism. The rejection of RELIGION after SECULARIZATION. See also ATHEISM; HUMANISM.   D.L.E.

Bibl: C. D. Campbell, *Toward a Sociology of Irreligion* (London and Valley Forge, Pa., 1971).

secularization. The decline of RELIGION. This has been more marked in the 20th century than in any previous period of recorded history, and the concentration on this age (Latin *saeculum*) instead of on the divine has become the real orthodoxy of the modern ESTABLISHMENT. At its minimum, secularization means the decline of the prestige and power of religious teachers. It involves the ending of State support for religious bodies; of religious teaching in the national schools; of religious tests for public office or civil rights; of legislative protection for religious doctrines (e.g. the prohibition of contraception); and of the censorship or control of literature, science, and other intellectual activities in order to safeguard religion. Individuals are then free to deviate openly from religious DOGMAS and ETHICS. In all or most of these senses, secularization now seems desirable to many religious believers as well as to all AGNOSTICS (see SECULAR CHRISTIANITY). In the U.S.A., for example, Church and State are strictly separate, although most Americans are personally attached to one or other of the Christian churches; and the Republic of India is officially 'secular', although most Indians are devout Hindus (see HINDUISM).

The term can, however, also mean the decline of widespread interest in religious traditions, so that the religious bodies no longer attract many practising supporters or enjoy popular respect. Most industrial workers suspect religion of being 'opium for the people' to keep them quiet under injustice, while the influence of religion has also been blamed for the stagnation of rural life. INTELLECTUALS tend to resent religion's record of interference with freedom of opinion and behaviour, preferring HUMANISM. In COMMUNIST countries such as Russia and China there have been systematic, official attempts to suppress religion as antisocial. At its maximum, secularization would mean the end of all interest in religious questions and attitudes, including MYSTICISM. There is, however, little evidence that the 20th century has reached this last stage. On the contrary, both communism and the worldwide YOUTH CULTURE seem to owe some of their popularity to the inclusion (in secular form) of religious features such as idealism, uniformity of dogma, and hero-worship. See also RELIGION, SOCIOLOGY OF.   D.L.E.

Bibl: D. L. Edwards, *Religion and Change* (London, 1969); V. Pratt, *Religion and Secularisation* (London and N.Y., 1970).

sedimentation. The slow natural settling of substances under the influence of gravity (see GRAVITATION) – especially the formation of sedimentary rocks, such as chalk, slate, and shales, by the compacted calciferous or siliceous skeletons of myriads of minute sea animals, especially PROTOZOA. The term normally refers to the settling out of particulate matter (see PARTICLE). It can also, however, be extended to the sedimentation of

MOLECULES – a process normally impeded by BROWNIAN MOTION.

Sedimentation is enormously speeded up by increasing gravitational forces – achieved in laboratories by the use of the CENTRIFUGE, an apparatus which enables most precipitates formed in chemical reactions to be thrown down as a sediment in a matter of minutes where otherwise they might take hours to undergo natural sedimentation. By this means, blood is separated into red blood CELLS (the lowest stratum), white blood cells (the next above), and plasma. Svedberg's *ultracentrifuge* is widely used to separate particulate suspensions in suspending media differing from them only very slightly in density. In this apparatus centrifugal forces up to 100,000 times that of gravity can be achieved as a matter of routine. Large molecules, particularly of the larger PROTEINS, can also be thrown down by such strong centrifugal forces.
P.M.

Segantini, Giovanni (Italian painter, 1858–99), see under NEO-IMPRESSIONISM.

segmentation, see under EMBRYOLOGY.

segregation.
(1) In GENETICS, the apportioning out of CHROMOSOMES to GAMETES, and thereby of genetic factors to the next generation; see MENDEL'S LAWS. P.M.
(2) The establishment by law or custom of separate (and inferior) facilities for social or (the most usual sense) ethnic groups as in the 'Jim Crow' legislation of the Southern states of the U.S.A. providing separate educational, recreational, and other facilities for whites and blacks. Segregation inevitably results in discrimination in favour of one group over the other or others. The word has been extended to cover a whole range of discriminatory practices including the denial of employment and voting rights and prohibition against intermarriage. In South Africa the term APARTHEID is used; see also DESEGREGATION.
(3) In SOCIOLOGY, the ecological process by which individuals and groups settle in those areas of a community already occupied by people of similar social characteristics or activities. D.C.W.

segregation, pedestrian, see PEDESTRIAN SEGREGATION.

seismology. A subject which began as the study of earthquakes but has widened its field to cover all the movements of the solid earth. The types of earth movement range from fast vibrations due to earthquake bodywaves, with a period of one second, to diurnal earth tides caused by the attraction of the sun and moon. The bulk of our knowledge about the interior of the earth has depended on seismic studies. J.L.M.L.
Bibl: R. H. Tucker *et al., Global Geophysics* (London and N.Y., 1970).

Sekigun, see RED ARMY (2).

selection pressure. A figurative expression of the magnitude of the force of NATURAL SELECTION. One of the conundrums of pre-Mendelian DARWINISM was to devise some means of measuring this force. The problem was solved independently and in slightly different ways by J. B. S. Haldane (1892–1964) and R. A. Fisher (1890–1962). Common to both is the principle that selection pressure is measured by the rate at which one ALLELE replaces another in the course of EVOLUTION. Fisher's system is modelled closely on demographic practice (see DEMOGRAPHY) and amounts to allocating a NET REPRODUCTION RATE to the possessors of a particular GENE or GENOTYPE. P.M.

selective dissemination of information, see SDI.

selective education, see under COMPREHENSIVE SCHOOL.

self-actualization. In EXISTENTIAL PSYCHOLOGY, a term used by Abraham Maslow for the processes whereby an individual comes to understand himself and thereby develops his talents and capacities with acceptance of his limitations. W.Z.

self-determination. Originally the right of the subjects of a state to choose their own government or form of government (a concept embodied both in the American Declaration of Independence of 1776 and in the French revolutionary Declaration of the Rights of Man of 1793). From this, by way of the nationalist assumption that the state must reflect the national group, self-determination came to encompass additionally the idea of national groups seceding from multinational states and empires in order to set up their own national state. (See NATIONALISM; SEPARATISM.) As such it played an important part in Allied propaganda during World Wars I and II (e.g. in the FOURTEEN POINTS), was embodied at various points in the Charter of UNO, and became the main basis for ANTI-IMPERIALISM.

D.C.W.

Bibl: A. Cobban, *National Self-Determination* (London and N.Y., 1945).

self-image. The impression an individual has of himself, which may differ greatly from the impression he gives others. w.z.

self-orientation, see under PATTERN VARIABLES.

semantic-field theory. In LINGUISTICS, the view that the vocabulary of a language is not simply a listing of independent items (as the headwords in a dictionary would suggest), but is organized into areas, or *fields,* within which words interrelate and define each other in various ways. The words denoting colour are often cited as an example of a semantic field: the precise meaning of a colour word can only be understood by placing it in relation to the other terms which occur with it in demarcating the colour spectrum. D.C.

semantic relation, see MEANING-RELATION.

semantics.
(1) The branch of LINGUISTICS that studies MEANING in language (and sometimes in other symbolic systems of communication). Much neglected by early linguists, it is now the central focus of theoretical interest, though no adequate semantic theory has yet been developed. One influential approach is that of *structural* semantics, the application of the principles of structural linguistics to the study of meaning through the notion of MEANING RELATIONS. See also COMPONENTIAL ANALYSIS. D.C.

Bibl: F. R. Palmer, *Semantics* (London, 1976).
(2) In PHILOSOPHY and LOGIC, (*a*) the

study of the RELATIONS between linguistic expressions and the objects in the world to which they refer or which it is their function to describe. This discipline was inaugurated by the Polish logician Alfred Tarski in the 1930s as the field in which lay his own influential investigations into the CONCEPT of TRUTH, in opposition to the view that all logical and philosophical problems about the meaning of linguistic expressions could and should be treated within (logical) SYNTAX, namely the study of the relations of linguistic expressions to each other; (*b*) more generally, the philosophical theory of meaning as a whole, in which to semantics narrowly conceived as in sense (*a*) are added both syntax and *pragmatics,* the study of the dependence of the meaning of linguistic expressions on their users, and on the circumstances in which and the purposes for which they are used. Carnap employed the word SEMIOTICS in this sense to bring these three disciplines together, but in this sense it has not caught on. A.Q.

Bibl: C. Morris, *Foundations of the Theory of Signs* (Chicago, 1938).

semeiology, see SEMIOLOGY.

semiconductor. A material which is normally an electrical insulator but becomes a conductor either when the temperature is raised ('intrinsic semiconductor') or when 'doped' with a small number of 'impurity' ATOMS of another ELEMENT ('extrinsic semiconductor'; see also SOLID-STATE PHYSICS.

The ease with which their electrical characteristics can be adjusted accounts for the importance of semiconductors in TECHNOLOGY, the principal application being the TRANSISTOR. The elements germanium and silicon are commonly-used intrinsic semiconductors; almost any atoms may be used as impurities, provided their VALENCE differs from that of the bulk. M.V.B.

semiology (or *semeiology*). The general (if tentative) science of signs: systems of signification, means by which human beings – individually or in groups – communicate or attempt to communicate by signal: gestures, advertisements, language itself, food, objects, clothes, music, and the many other things that qualify. The subject was proposed by the LINGUIST Ferdinand de Saussure (see SAUSSURIAN), but influentially developed by the French writer Roland Barthes. Barthes's complex Gallic METHODOLOGY has seemed over-recondite or obscure to some Anglo-Saxons; but the value of many of his insights, if not of his system, is undisputed.

M.S.-S.

Bibl: R. Barthes, tr. A. Lavers and C. Smith, *Elements of Semiology* (London and N.Y., 1968).

semiotic poetry, see under CONCRETE POETRY.

semiotics. The study of patterned human behaviour in communication in all its modes. The most important mode is the auditory/vocal, which constitutes the primary subject of LINGUISTICS. The study of the visual mode – of systematic facial expressions and body gestures – is generally referred to as *kinesics*. The study of the tactile mode – e.g. inter-personal movement and touch activity – is some-times called *proxemics*. Semiotics can also mean the study of sign and symbol systems in general; for which an alternative term is SEMIOLOGY. A similar approach to animal communication is called *zoosemiotics*.

D.C.

Bibl: T. A. Sebeok, A. S. Hayes, and M. C. Bateson (eds.), *Approaches to Semio-tics* (The Hague, 1964).

Senghor, Léopold Sédor (French West African poet and statesman, *b.* 1906), see under NÉGRITUDE.

Sennett, Mack (U.S. film producer, 1880–1960), see under CUSTARD PIE; KEYSTONE.

sensationalism. In PHILOSOPHY, the theory that the only things which ulti-mately and irreducibly exist, and to which everything else that exists is reducible are sensations. It has close affinities with NEUTRAL MONISM and differs from it only in describing the elements of reality as mental rather than as neither mental nor physical. Mach was a sen-sationalist, as, with some qualifications, were Hume and J. S. Mill. If all factual knowledge comes from PERCEPTION and, as the SENSE-DATUM theory maintains, only sensations or sense-impressions are perceived, it seems to follow that we can

know nothing to exist apart from sensa-tions (and what can be constructed from them).

A.Q.

sense-datum. The private impression or appearance which, if the *argument from illusion* (see ILLUSION) is correct, is the direct and immediate object of PERCEP-TION. The *sense-datum theory* is the belief that this is so. Sense-data have also been called sensations, sensa, presentations, representations, percepts, and (by Locke and Berkeley) IDEAS. A visual sense-datum is commonly taken to be a colour-patch or array of colour-patches in, or constituting, the visual field; a tactual sense-datum is a felt, textured, resistant surface. The sense-datum theory is pre-supposed by REPRESENTATIONISM and PHENOMENALISM which seek to avoid SOLIPSISM by explaining how belief in an external world can be rationally grounded in direct knowledge confined to sense-data.

A.Q.

Bibl: A. J. Ayer, *The Foundations of Empirical Knowledge* (London, 1940), chs. 1, 2.

sense-relation, see MEANING-RELATION.

sensitivity training, see under ORGANIZA-TION THEORY.

sensorium. Biological term for the sensory system of the body considered in its entirety. It includes the entire NERVOUS SYSTEM as well as the grey matter of the brain and spinal cord.

M.BE.

sensory deprivation. The condition pro-duced by cutting off all patterned stimula-tion from the visual, auditory, tactual, and other sensory systems (including those activated from within the organism) by such devices as diffusing goggles, *white noise* (see NOISE), padded gloves and clo-thing, and flotation in a liquid medium. Its effect is to produce feelings of unreality and loss of identity, together with a marked decline in such intellectual opera-tions as reasoning, comparison, and learn-ing. Beyond a certain duration, subjects may report quasi-psychotic symptoms (see PSYCHOSIS). The work on this phenomenon has underlined the necessity of continuous sensory activity for the maintenance of effective functioning. Sen-sory deprivation is not to be confused with

BRAINWASHING, with which it is sometimes associated in science fiction. See also KINAESTHETIC; NEUROPSYCHOLOGY; SENSATION.   J.S.B.

Bibl: P. Solomon et al. (eds.), Sensory Deprivation (Cambridge, Mass., 1961).

sensory-motor. In DEVELOPMENTAL PSYCHOLOGY, adjective applied to the period of early infancy (from birth to 18 months) when many coordinations of PERCEPTION and action emerge. See also PIAGETIAN.   P.L.H.

sensum, see SENSE-DATUM.

separatism. The demand of a particular group or area to separate from the territorial and political sovereignty of the state of which it forms a part, e.g. the desire of Catalans or Basques in Spain for an independent Catalan or Basque state, or the demand of French-speaking nationalists in Quebec for their own state. See also NATIONALISM; SELF-DETERMINATION.
                              D.C.W.

Serapion Brothers. A Russian literary group named after E. T. A. Hoffmann's hero. It was formed in Petrograd in 1921 by the young writers Fedin, Kaverin, Lunts, Ivanov, Zoshchenko, Nikitin, Slonimsky, Gruzdev, Tikhonov, Elizaveta Polonskaya, and Pozner, most of whom were to become leading Soviet writers and literary critics. Their literary work was initially guided by Zamyatin and the novelist, literary critic, and leading FORMALIST theoretician Victor Shklovsky.

The Serapions stood for creative freedom, and in their writings shunned any form of political partisanship or UTILITARIANISM. They had no formal organization and no common aesthetic platform or literary tradition, being united mainly by their concern for literary craftsmanship. Along with other writers of moderate political outlook who wrote about the Revolution and Civil War, the Serapions were dubbed by Trotsky FELLOW-TRAVELLERS of the Revolution.
                              M.E.

Bibl: M. Slonim, Soviet Russian Literature (N.Y., 1964).

Sereni, Vittorio (Italian poet, b. 1913), see under HERMETIC.

serial access. A method of using a COMPUTER store in which the information is used in a sequence determined by its physical location in the STORE. This is much more difficult to use than RANDOM ACCESS and for some problems proves impossible. The need to use serial access exerts an overwhelming and often disastrous influence on the choice of ALGORITHM. See also ACCESS TIME.   C.S.

serial history (l'histoire sérielle). Term current in France from about 1960 among the ANNALES SCHOOL for attempts to study long-term trends rigorously as continuities and discontinuities within a series. What is needed for this approach to be fruitful is a long sequence of relatively homogeneous data. Wheat prices, births, and Easter communicants have all been studied in this way. As these examples suggest, 'serial history' is a new term for an older practice: it is one kind of QUANTITATIVE HISTORY.   P.B.

Bibl: P. Chaunu, 'L'histoire sérielle' (Revue Historique, 243, 1970, pp. 297-320).

serial music. Music organized according to a system devised by Schönberg and later extended by Webern, Boulez, Stockhausen, and others. Around 1910 disillusionment with the lines of development established in the last two decades of the 19th century seems to have set in, and Stravinsky with Le Sacre du Printemps and Schönberg with Pierrot Lunaire broke completely new ground. Stravinsky, however, was not to turn to serialism until after 1950; it was Schönberg who consciously grasped the problems raised by the break-up of tonality (see ATONAL MUSIC) and who, between 1910 and 1920, devised the serial method of composing. Serial music is not, however, necessarily atonal; certain composers, e.g. Alban Berg (notably in his Violin Concerto), Frank Martin, Humphrey Searle, and Karl Blomdahl, have employed serial techniques within a recognizably tonal framework.

Serialism is a PERMUTATIONAL method rather than a style. Every serial composition is based on the concept of a tone-row, a sequence that uses, normally but not invariably, all twelve notes of the chromatic (semitone) scale in an order which is chosen for the purpose, and which varies from work to work. (The term *twelve-note* (or *dodecaphonic*) applies only to works which follow this norm, not to works – e.g. Stravinsky's *In Memoriam Dylan Thomas,* based entirely on a 5-note row – where the series is of more or fewer than 12 notes.) Normally no more may reappear in the row after its initial appearance, lest it should assume the characteristics of a tonal centre, and establish a sense of traditional key. Initially, the row is conceived in 4 guises: (*a*) the row itself; (*b*) its *inversion* (i.e. with falling intervals replacing rising ones and *vice versa*); (*c*) its back-to-front or *retrograde* form; and (*d*) the inversion thereof. To add to his resources, the composer may also transpose the whole series so that it begins on any one of the 12 semitones. There are thus 48 possible PERMUTATIONS of the original row.

Serial method is a discipline that concerns the composer alone, and not his audience. In no sense is it a complex extension of a traditional form such as fugue. It is simply a new grammar and syntax for handling a new concept of musical language. A later development, around 1950 and associated with Messiaen, Boulez, and Stockhausen, was *total serialization,* i.e. the strict organization of rhythm, silences, and even dynamics (gradations of volume and timbre). It was doubtless in reaction against this that the drift towards ALEATORY music began. A.H.

serial order effect. The well-established tendency for the beginnings and the ends of lists to be memorized more easily than the middle, and for the middle to be forgotten more quickly. J.S.B.

seriation. The arrangement of different types of artifact in a series, either simple or complex, taking into account TYPOLOGY, ASSOCIATION, and DATING. B.C.
Bibl: G. L. Cowgill, 'Models, Methods, and Techniques for Seriation', in D. L. Clark (ed.), *Models in Archaeology* (London and N.Y., 1972), pp. 381–424.

series. In MATHEMATICS, the sum of a sequence of terms. For infinite series see CONVERGENCE. R.G.

serology. The branch of IMMUNOLOGY that deals with antibodies and other effector agents, e.g. *complement,* which are found in and carried by SERUM. P.M.

Serrano Suñer, Ramon (Spanish politician, *b.* 1901), see under FALANGE.

serum. The fluid part of the blood after blood has clotted, as distinguished from *plasma,* which is the fluid part of the blood in its native state. Serum, like plasma, is a yellow PROTEIN-containing fluid, but serum is normally free from CELLS because red and white blood corpuscles and blood platelets are caught in the fibres of the clot when blood clots. After a meal, particularly a fatty meal, very large numbers of fat droplets in an emulsified state may be present. P.M.

Sérusier, Paul (French painter, 1863–1927), see under BEURON; NABIS, LES; PONT-AVEN.

service industry. An industry which provides customers with services rather than tangible objects. Service industries range from coach tours and retailing to the banking facilities of the CITY of London and teaching or broadcasting. The view that they are unproductive is sheer superstition, although the productivity of some service industries is inherently much more difficult to measure than that of, say, CONSUMER DURABLES. (What is the productivity of a teacher, and is it reduced if the numbers in his class go down?) See also OCCUPATION; QUANTIFICATION. S.BR.

servomechanism. In CONTROL ENGINEERING, an automatically operating control device actuated by the difference between the actual and desired value of some variable determining the behaviour of a SYSTEM, and using some external source of power to drive the actual value towards the desired. See also FEEDBACK. S.BE.

set. In MATHEMATICS and LOGIC, a collection of objects, itself considered as a single abstract object. Except in *axiomatic set theory* (see AXIOMATIC METHOD; SET THEORY), 'set' and 'class' are synonymous. Two sets are identical if they have the same members. (It is convenient also to admit a unique *empty set*: unique, because the set of unicorns and the set of centaurs each have, in their negative way, the same members.) Sets are to be distinguished (1) from the predicates signifying the properties that define them (the predicates 'featherless biped' and 'man' differ in meaning but define the same class); (2) from mere assemblages. Thus, the United Nations is a set whose 180-odd members are nations; each nation can in turn be considered as a set of people, but these individuals are not members of the U.N. Similarly, to each object A (e.g. a person) there corresponds its *unit class* whose only member is A and which is distinct from A (it is a set, not a person). As with FUNCTIONS, mathematicians no longer think that a set must be defined by an expressly stated property; it is determined by its members and these can be chosen at random. (In fact functions can be defined in terms of sets, and sets in terms of functions, so that it is a matter of convenience which notion is taken as primary.)

Some useful notions concerning sets are now familiar to every schoolchild who learns the NEW MATHEMATICS, so it is appropriate to give them here. A *subset A* of a set B is a set which is included in B; every member of A is a member of B. Conventionally the empty set and B itself are counted as subsets of B. If A and B are sets, then the *union* of A and B consists of the members of either, the *intersection* of A and B consists of members of both (it is empty if A and B are *disjoint*) and the *complement* of A in B consists of those members of B which are not members of A. Under these operations the subsets of a given set form a BOOLEAN ALGEBRA.

R.G.; A.Q.

Bibl: R. L. Wilder, *Introduction to the Foundations of Mathematics* (N.Y., 2nd ed., 1965).

set of numbers, see under SCALE.

set theory. SETS (or classes) occur naturally in MATHEMATICS, but their importance was only appreciated after G. Cantor (1845–1918) had developed the theory of INFINITE sets. His ideas formed the basis for the LOGICISM of Frege and Russell. The discovery of various PARADOXES showed that the naive theory of classes is contradictory. Cantor himself made a distinction between collections (such as the totality of *all* abstract objects) which are too all-embracing to be treated as wholes and smaller totalities (such as the set of all real NUMBERS) which can be regarded as single objects; nowadays the former are called *proper classes,* the latter are called *sets.* On this basis modern *axiomatic set theories* (see AXIOMATIC METHOD) have been erected. They provide a foundation for contemporary mathematics and are apparently free from contradiction. The various theories differ in strength; e.g., the AXIOM OF CHOICE may be included or rejected. All of them are incomplete; that is, there are important questions concerning infinite sets which cannot be decided on the basis of the AXIOMS (e.g. the CONTINUUM hypothesis). This reflects an inadequacy of contemporary intuition. Opinions differ as to how far this inadequacy may eventually be overcome.

R.G.

Bibl: A. Fraenkel and Y. Bar-Hillel, *Foundations of Set Theory* (Amsterdam, 1958); W. S. Hatcher, *Foundations of Mathematics* (London and Philadelphia, 1968).

setting. A form of internal school organization by which children are grouped in 'sets' which can vary in membership from subject to subject, instead of in forms or classes which remain together for all subjects (STREAMING). Since all the children in any set are of comparable ability in that subject, group teaching is facilitated and the pupil can go at his own pace. W.A.C.S.

settlement. The forms and processes of population distribution over the land. Settlement may be classified as urban, rural, suburban, or pioneer. Settlement policies, redistributing people within a territory, are needed in case of migration or rapid population change. Such problems as overpopulation, resettlement, decentralization, and planning of new towns, have usually been controversial. See also DENSITY; EKISTICS; URBANIZATION.

J.G.

Seurat, Georges (French painter, 1859–91), see under IMPRESSIONISM; NEO-IMPRESSIONISM.

sex chromosomes. CHROMOSOMES which differ in number or structure between the sexes. The commonest pattern is that found in man and other mammals, in which females have two large chromosomes, the X chromosomes, and males have one X chromosome and a smaller Y chromosome. Spermatozoa bearing X and

Y chromosomes are produced in approximately equal numbers, and the sex of the new individual is determined at the time of fertilization by the type of sperm fertilizing the X-bearing egg.

Characteristics determined by GENES on the X chromosome are inherited differently from those determined by other genes. Such characteristics are said to show SEX LINKAGE. Examples in man are haemophilia and red-green colour blindness. There are few or no genes on the human Y chromosome other than those determining maleness.   J.M.S.

sex linkage. A form of LINKAGE that arises when more than one genetic determinant is present on a SEX CHROMOSOME, particularly the X CHROMOSOME. With a sex-linked recessive (see GENE) disease such as haemophilia (at least in one of its forms) the condition can be inherited only through females. On the average, half the sons of a maternal carrier of the haemophilia gene will be afflicted and half her daughters will be carriers like herself.   P.M.

sex ratio. The ratio of males to females at birth or at any other age. We may take it that the norm for bisexual organisms is unity (1 to 1) over the reproductive period, but in large industrial populations and wherever there is adequate provision for antenatal, maternal, and infant welfare the ratio exceeds unity and in England is about 1.06 (106 male births to 100 female births). Later in life the ratio falls below unity because females have a better life expectancy at all ages and women therefore preponderate in the most senior age groups. It has been repeatedly observed that the sex ratio rises at or towards the end of major wars. The exact causes of this are not known but it is not helpful to describe it as 'nature's way of making good' the disproportionate loss of male lives.   P.M.

sexism. A word coined, on the analogy of racism (see RACE), for a deep-rooted, often unconscious system of beliefs, attitudes, and INSTITUTIONS in which distinctions between people's intrinsic worth are made on the grounds of their sex and sexual roles. Whether consciously or not, the sexist sees woman (or man) as inferior, and behaves accordingly. As with racism,

the term – though not the phenomenon – tends in practice to be restricted to one-way attitudes only, i.e. to male sexism. In the aggressive form of sexism known as *male chauvinism* the paradigm is one of an assumed innate male supremacy in all the most important areas of social activity (with the possible exception of child-rearing), accompanied by a predisposition to treat women as anonymous objects for male sexual pleasure. For a female response to male sexism see FEMINISM.
    P.S.L.

sexual intergrade, see INTERSEX.

Sezession. Name given in the German-speaking countries to a number of art organizations seceding from the official academies around 1900, to start their own annual exhibitions. The first was that in Munich (1892), the most important that in Vienna (1897), which gave the name 'Sezession' to the Austrian ART NOUVEAU style and is associated particularly with the paintings of Gustav Klimt, its president from 1898 to 1903. In 1900 a Berlin Sezession was formed, with the IMPRESSIONIST Max Liebermann as its first president and Ernst Barlach and Max Beckmann among the early exhibitors. A *Neue Sezession* which split off in 1910, with the BRÜCKE painters and others, lasted only two years.   J.W.

SF, see SCIENCE FICTION.

shadow prices. In ECONOMICS, prices emerging from an exercise in OPTIMIZATION or maximization rather than being taken as given by the decision-maker. They originally appeared in the context of LINEAR PROGRAMMING which deals with the problem of maximizing an objective function subject to linear constraints. A typical constraint is on the availability of some resource for alternative uses. The shadow price of the resource is the amount by which the maximum attainable level of the objective function could be increased if an extra unit of the resource were available. Shadow prices are thus OPPORTUNITY COSTS. In COST-BENEFIT ANALYSIS prices calculated as shadow prices (e.g. in exercises involving the maximization of OUTPUT subject to the availability of labour and other constraints) are often used instead of observable market prices (e.g. the wage rate, especially in developing countries).   J.S.F.

Bibl: R. Dorfman, P. A. Samuelson, and R. M. Solow, *Linear Programming and Economic Analysis* (N.Y., 1958); I. M. D. Little and J. A. Mirrlees, *Project Appraisal and Planning for Developing Countries* (London, 1974).

Shaffer, Peter (British dramatist, *b.* 1926), see under BLACK COMEDY.

shamanism. A variety of RELIGION which reveres the ability of the tribal priest-doctor (Russian *shaman*) to influence the good and evil spirits controlling life. It is found among various peoples of northern Asia, and also among the American Indians, specially in the north-west. See also PRIMITIVISM.   D.L.E.

Bibl: M. Eliade, tr. W. R. Trask, *Shamanism* (London and N.Y., 1964).

shame culture and **guilt culture.** Terms apparently introduced into ANTHROPOLOGY by Ruth Benedict in *The Chrysanthemum and the Sword* (1946) to distinguish between cultures which rely, respectively, 'on external sanctions for good behaviour' and 'on an internalized conviction of sin'. Societies differ, no doubt, in the extent to which individuals are expected to consult their own consciences and monitor their own behaviour; but no society could dispense either with the internalization of norms (how otherwise could men influence one another?) or with the systematic surveillance of an individual's conduct by his fellows. The terms spring from a phase in the development of psychological anthropology and now have little currency.   M.F.

Bibl: M. E. Spiro, 'Social Systems, Personality and Functional Analysis', in B. Kaplan (ed.), *Studying Personality Cross-Culturally* (N.Y. and Evanston, Ill., 1961).

Sharpeville. A town in South Africa where on 21 March 1960 the South African police fired on African demonstrators against the PASS LAWS, killing 67 and wounding 186, including 48 women and children. The catch-phrase 'Remember Sharpeville' has been much used by advocates of international action to force the South African Government to grant full

rights to its coloured and black African populations (see APARTHEID).   D.C.W.

Shavian. Characteristic or reminiscent of the writings of George Bernard Shaw (1856–1950). Nouns to which the adjective is frequently applied are wit, irreverence, paradox, ebullience, insouciance.   O.S.

Shaw, Artie (U.S. musician, *b.* 1910), see under BIG BAND; SWING.

Shaw, George Bernard (Irish-born dramatist and miscellaneous writer, 1856–1950), see under FABIANISM; NEW AGE; ROYAL COURT THEATRE; SHAVIAN; VITALISM.

Shaw, Norman (British architect, 1831–1912), see under ARTS AND CRAFTS MOVEMENT.

Sheeler, Charles (U.S. painter and photographer, 1883–1965), see under PRECISIONISM.

Sheldon, William Herbert (U.S. psychologist, *b.* 1898), see under PERSONALITY TYPES.

shell structure of atoms and nuclei, see under ELECTRON SHELL; MAGIC NUMBER.

Shelley, Percy Bysshe (British poet, 1792–1822), see under SYMBOLISM.

Shils, Edward Benjamin (U.S. sociologist, *b.* 1915), see under IDEOLOGY; MASS CULTURE; POPULISM.

Shinto. The official RELIGION of the Japanese. This 'way of the gods' (Chinese *shin tao*) was defined in the 6th century, in a patriotic response to the introduction of Mayahana BUDDHISM, and its chief scriptures date from the 8th century. Essentially a way of purification and of respectful communion with the divinities and spirits of the Japanese tradition, Shintoism also became identified with the honours accorded to the Emperor (Japanese *Mikado*) as a descendant of the sun-goddess. When the Americans occupied Japan in 1945, Shintoism was therefore subjected to one of the many reforms it has received.   D.L.E.

Bibl: J. M. Kitagawa, *Religion in*

Japanese History (London and N.Y., 1966).

Shklovsky, Victor Borisovich (Russian author, *b.* 1893), see under FORMALISM; SERAPION BROTHERS.

shock wave. A sound wave in which the air pressure, temperature, and density vary suddenly instead of in the usual oscillatory manner. Shock waves arise whenever ENERGY travels at supersonic speeds, as in explosions and SONIC BOOMS.   M.V.B.

Shostakovitch, Dmitry (Russian composer, 1906–75), see under FORMALISM; PROGRAMME MUSIC.

Shove, Gerald (British economist, 1887–1947), see under BLOOMSBURY GROUP.

show trials. Trials run on the principles of the MOSCOW TRIALS, e.g. in Eastern Europe in the 1940s and 1950s: the trials of László Rajk and others in Hungary (1949), of Traicho Kostov and others in Bulgaria (1949), and of Rudolf Slánsky and others in Czechoslovakia (1952). R.C.

shuttering, see under CONCRETE.

SI units (Système Internationale d'Unités). The system of units used at present for scientific work. SI units are built on the MKS system, extended to include electric current, temperature, luminosity, and molecular weight.   M.V.B.

sick jokes, see under BLACK COMEDY.

Sickert, Walter Richard (British painter, 1860–1942), see under CAMDEN TOWN GROUP; LONDON GROUP; NEW ENGLISH ART CLUB.

Siegfried, André (French sociologist and geographer, 1875–1959), see under GEOGRAPHY; THIRD FORCE.

sigmoids. Bounded relationships in which the dependent variable moves away from a lower bound and towards an upper bound (or *vice versa*) as each independent variable increases. They are much used in BIOLOGY, since there are limits to the growth of individuals, and in DEMOGRAPHY, since there are limits to the

growth of populations, especially those living in a confined space. They are rarely used in ECONOMICS, where growth trends are commonly assumed to be EXPONENTIAL. However, the recent realization that there are limits to what man can with impunity do to nature may in time wean economists from their excessive preoccupation with the short run and their slavery to Keynes's aphorism 'In the long run we are all dead'.   R.ST.

Signac, Paul (French painter, 1863–1935), see under NEO-IMPRESSIONISM.

significance (in STATISTICS), see under STATISTICAL TEST.

significant form. A term coined by Clive Bell in 1913 to describe the essential quality of a work of art, that which (he believed) evoked a special 'aesthetic emotion'. It was supposed to consist of certain forms and relations of forms, including colour. The theory of significant form was briefly influential in English AESTHETICS, especially as it coincided with the rise of the POST-IMPRESSIONISTS.   P.C.
   Bibl: A. C. H. Bell, *Art* (London and N.Y., 1914).

silicones. A group of synthetic silicon-containing compounds in which the silicon ATOMS are held together by BONDS to oxygen atoms acting as 'bridges'. Each silicon atom is attached to at least one organic RADICAL. Apart from simple compounds (strictly called *siloxanes*), silicon and oxygen can be linked in branched or unbranched chains to generate oils and POLYMERS which find use as water-repellents, lubricants, and rubbers. They are more resistant to heat than carbon-linked polymers, and the viscosity of the oils changes little over a wide temperature range.   B.F.

Silone, Ignazio (pseud. of Secondo Tranquilli, Italian author, *b.* 1900), see under NEW WRITING.

Silverberg, Robert (U.S. novelist), see under SCIENCE FICTION.

Simmel, Georg (German sociologist and philosopher, 1858–1918), see under ALIENATION.

SIMON

Simon, Herbert Alexander (U.S. social scientist, *b.* 1916), see under PROBLEM-SOLVING.

Simon, Théodore (French psychologist, 1873–1961), see under MENTAL RETARDATION; PSYCHOMETRICS.

simplex method, see under LINEAR PROGRAMMING.

Simpson, Norman Frederick (British dramatist, *b.* 1919), see under THEATRE OF THE ABSURD.

simulation. A technique of applied PROBABILITY THEORY (and hence of OPERATIONS RESEARCH) used to compare a STOCHASTIC model with reality by actually generating particular random results from the MODEL. RANDOM NUMBERS are usually used to produce the simulation, commonly on a COMPUTER. R.SI.

Sinclair, Upton (U.S. novelist, 1878–1968), see under ROMAN-FLEUVE.

singularity. In many branches of MATHEMATICS one makes use of FUNCTIONS which are for the most part well-behaved, but behave badly at certain ARGUMENTS, e.g. they are undefined, or become INFINITE (e.g. $1/x$ at $x = 0$) or are discontinuous or fail to have a DERIVATIVE. These arguments are the *singularities* of the function in question. R.G.

Sinn Fein ('Ourselves Alone'). An Irish political party, founded in 1900 with a programme of Irish independence. In the British general election of December 1918 it captured every seat previously held by the parliamentary NATIONALISTS, and seceded to form a separate assembly which in turn proclaimed Irish independence in January 1919. Sinn Fein refused to accept the Anglo-Irish settlement of 6 December 1921, in particular the partition of Ireland and the separate status of Ulster. It has remained the political wing of the IRA, operating as an overt political party in Irish politics, though never enjoying more than a limited degree of electoral support. D.C.W.

sintering. The process by which an agglomerate of fine PARTICLES binds together on heating. DIFFUSION of ATOMS in a solid leads in stages to a smoothing of particles, shrinkage of the agglomerate as necks between adjacent particles form and widen, and a final densification in which individual particles grow and pores are eliminated. Sintering is important in POWDER METALLURGY and the manufacture of CERAMICS. B.F.

Sion, Jules (French geographer, 1879–1940), see under GEOGRAPHY.

Sisley, Alfred (French painter, 1839–99), see under IMPRESSIONISM.

Sismondi, Jean Charles Léonard Simonde de (Swiss author, 1773–1842), see under PROLETARIAT.

site catchment analysis. The study of the interrelationship between a COMMUNITY and the territory which it exploits. The occupants of each SETTLEMENT utilize a tract of land and in doing so create changes within the natural ENVIRONMENT. In site catchment analysis the territory upon which the settlement or community is dependent is defined in terms of the total material needs of the community, and explanations are sought for the processes by which the environment is utilized. The CONCEPT has recently been introduced into ARCHAEOLOGY from GEOGRAPHY. It is of particular value in the early prehistoric period (see PREHISTORY), but its usefulness in periods of complex social organization needs to be demonstrated. B.C.
Bibl: M. Chisholm, *Rural Settlement and Land Use: an Essay in Location* (London, 2nd ed., 1966; N.Y., 1970).

Sitte, Camillo (Austrian town-planner and architect, 1843–1903), see under TOWNSCAPE.

situation ethics. The insistence, against the legalism characteristic of much conventional morality and MORAL THEOLOGY, that the right solution of any moral problem depends much more on the situation itself than on any general, external code; and that the key to the solution is always love. This position is criticized as leading to ANTINOMIANISM. D.L.E.
Bibl: J. Fletcher, *Situation Ethics* (London and Philadelphia, 1966).

situational analysis; situational logic (terms introduced by Karl Popper, 1945). An approach to the explanation of SOCIAL ACTION in which a detailed reconstruction of the circumstances of action (including both objective conditions and the participants' aims, knowledge, beliefs, values, and subjective 'definitions' of the situation) is taken as a basis for hypothesizing rational courses of action for the individuals involved, through which their observed behaviour may be rendered intelligible; i.e. through which its subjective logic in relating means to ends under given constraints may be appreciated. The approach has a close affinity with that of VERSTEHEN as advocated by Max Weber, but rejects any reliance on intuition as in the HERMENEUTICS of Dilthey or Collingwood.   J.H.G.

Bibl: I. C. Jarvie, *Concepts and Society* (London and N.Y., 1972); K. R. Popper, *Objective Knowledge* (Oxford, 1972).

Sitwell, Sacheverell (British poet and essayist, *b.* 1897), see under COM-PARATIST.

Six, les. A group of six composers, five of them French, brought together by Jean Cocteau in 1917. Although said to be influenced by and disciples of the French composer Erik Satie, no common aesthetic identity can really be observed except for an occasional and fashionable cynicism. Auric, Milhaud, Poulenc, and Germaine Tailleferre were each to develop their own musical styles; Durey's talent soon faded, while the Swiss Honegger felt no particular admiration for Satie. As a significant artistic force their influence proved negligible, their collective name being little more than a convenient label attached by critics to a certain aspect of French 20th-century music that moved in a different direction from the IMPRESSIONISM of Debussy.   A.H.

sixth-form colleges, see under COM-PREHENSIVE SCHOOLS.

sixth forms, see under SECONDARY SCHOOLS.

skeuomorph. An object made in a form similar to that which it would have had if it had been made in another material. *Skeuomorphism* – the close copying of form and function in a substitute material – is often well demonstrated by pottery types; e.g. in southern Britain in the 6th century B.C. a small bowl was produced with a sharply angled shoulder, furrowed decoration, an indented (or omphalos) base, and a surface covering of hematite to give a glossy red-brown appearance. Many of these characteristics are alien to a ceramic technique but are evidently adopted to give the pot the appearance of contemporary bronze vessels. A modern plastic bucket still retains skeuomorphic features, reflecting its galvanized iron ancestry.   B.C.

skewness, see under DISTRIBUTION.

Skinner, Burrhus Frederic (U.S. psychologist, *b.* 1904), see under BEHAVIOUR THERAPY; BEHAVIOURISM; BLACK-BOX THEORY; OPERANT CONDITIONING; SKINNER BOX; SKINNERIAN; SOCIAL BEHAVIOURISM; SOCIAL ENGINEERING.

Skinner box. A device developed by B. F. Skinner (see SKINNERIAN) for training animals to learn appropriate responses. The animal is placed in an isolating box provided with little more than one or more buttons or levers to press. Correct responses produce escape, food, water, etc. Using techniques of AUTOMATION, the investigator can register a cumulative record of response to different conditions of *reinforcement* (see OPERANT CONDITIONING), etc.   W.Z.

Skinnerian. In PSYCHOLOGY, adjective applied to a type of experiment (see also SKINNER BOX) and a type of EXPLANATION associated with the American BEHAVIOURIST B. F. Skinner. The typical experiment involves an *operant response* (see OPERANT CONDITIONING), like pressing a button or lever, followed immediately by a REINFORCEMENT that increases the probability of the operant response being repeated. At a theoretical level, the term applies to explanations that eschew any reference to internal mediating or mental processes.   J.S.B.

Bibl: B. F. Skinner, *The Behaviour of Organisms* (London and N.Y., 1938).

skyscraper. Term applied since the 1880s, particularly in America, to tall multi-storey buildings; their actual height has progressively increased from W. Le B. Jenney's 10-storey Home Insurance Company, Chicago (1883–5) to the 102-storey Empire State Building, New York (1931) and even higher recent buildings in both cities. Their evolution stemmed from high land values and was made possible by the development of the skeleton frame, the lift, the water closet, and central heating. See also CHICAGO SCHOOL; POINT BLOCK; STRUCTURES. M.BR.

Bibl: H. R. Hitchcock, *Architecture: Nineteenth and Twentieth Centuries* (Harmondsworth and Baltimore, 1958).

Slánsky, Rudolf (Czechoslovak politician, 1901–52), see under SHOW TRIALS.

slapstick. Term deriving from the flanged stick carried by Harlequin in *Commedia dell'Arte* pantomimes as a weapon with which to belabour his adversaries. The slapstick survived in the pantomimic comedy routines featured in English music-hall and American burlesque theatres. Hence, since nearly all the great silent comedians (e.g. Chaplin, Keaton, Laurel, Arbuckle) were trained in either music-hall or burlesque, its use as a generic term in the cinema to describe the knockabout falls and chases, often filmed in speeded-up motion, which were the mainstay of the early silent comedies from 1912 onwards. The term is still used to describe nonverbal low-comedy routines in films. See also CUSTARD PIE; KEYSTONE. T.C.C.M.

Bibl: K. C. Lahue, *World of Laughter* (Norman, Okla., 1966).

SLBM (submarine-launched ballistic missiles), see under MISSILES.

slice of life. A term originally applied (*tranche de vie*) to fiction of the French NATURALISTS, particularly Zola, one of whose conscious aims was to present a cross-section of society (usually lower-class) in its actual, unselected, totality. M.S.-S.

Slicher van Bath, Bernhard Hendrik (Dutch historian, *b.* 1910), see under AGRARIAN HISTORY.

Sloan, John (U.S. painter, 1871–1951), see under ASHCAN SCHOOL.

Slonimsky, Milkhail Leonidovich (Russian author, 1897–1972), see under SERAPION BROTHERS.

slump, see DEPRESSION.

Smailes, Arthur Eltringham (British geographer, *b.* 1911), see under TOWN.

Small, Albion Woodbury (U.S. sociologist, 1854–1926), see under CHICAGO SCHOOL; PLURAL SOCIETY.

Smalley, John Roger (British composer, *b.* 1943), see under ELECTRONIC MUSIC.

Smart, John Jamieson Carswell (British-Australian philosopher, *b.* 1920), see under PHYSICALISM.

Smith, Adam (Scottish political economist, 1723–90), see under CLASSICAL ECONOMIC THEORY; LABOUR THEORY OF VALUE; NEO-MERCANTILISM; POLITICAL ECONOMY.

Smith, Grafton Elliot (Australian anatomist and ethnologist, 1871–1937), see under DIFFUSION.

Smith, Iain Crichton, see CRICHTON SMITH.

Smith, Ian Douglas (Rhodesian political leader, *b.* 1919), see under RHODESIA.

Smith, Joseph (U.S. religious leader, 1805–44), see under MORMONS.

Smith, Sir Matthew (British painter, 1879–1959), see under FAUVES.

Smith, William Robertson (Scottish theologian and orientalist, 1846–94), see under HIGHER CRITICISM.

Smithson, Peter and **Alison** (British architects, *b.* 1923 and 1928), see under BRUTALISM.

Smyth, William Henry (British-U.S. engineer, 1855–1940), see under TECHNOCRACY.

SNCC (Student Non-Violent Co-ordinating Committee), see under NEW LEFT.

Snow, Charles Percy (Baron Snow of Leicester; British novelist and scientist, 1905–72), see under TWO CULTURES.

Snow, John (British anaesthetist and epidemiologist, 1813–58), see under EPIDEMIOLOGY.

Snyder, Gary (U.S. poet, *b.* 1930), see under BEAT.

soap opera. Derogatory term for films, or television and radio programmes, which prolong the melodramatic agony for as long as possible before the inevitable happy ending. The term derives from the prevalence of soap manufacturers among the commercial sponsors of American radio serials in the early 1930s. Then at the height of their popularity, these serials usually featured the romantic tribulations of a starry eyed girl, or the domestic trials of a fond mother.   T.C.C.M.
Bibl: R. W. Stedman, *The Serials* (Norman, Okla., 1971).

social, see under SOCIETAL.

social action. In politics, activity by an interested group aimed at securing some particular reform, or support for a cause. In SOCIOLOGY, the most general term used for the subject-matter of the science: human activity regarded from the point of view of its social context. Theorists have disagreed as to where and how the boundary should be drawn. Some (e.g. Weber) have distinguished sharply between, on the one hand, natural events and the scientific procedures appropriate to studying them, and, on the other hand, human actions, which can only be identified through the ideas and purposes of conscious agents and which therefore call for different methods of study. Others (e.g. Durkheim) have minimized this difference and aimed to study human actions naturalistically, as SOCIAL FACTS. A further difference is between theorists who regard social action as synonymous with human action (e.g. because it involves conceptual thinking and hence language, a social product) and others who define social action as a sub-class of human actions, involving direct interaction between persons, or a conscious reference to the expectations of others. Talcott Parsons's (see PARSONIAN) synthesis of Weber's and Durkheim's approaches located social action within social systems, treating CULTURE and personality as other types of action system. This synthesis stressed purposive interaction, but proposed a naturalistic and functional analysis in terms of the SYSTEMIC properties of its results. The vogue of Parsonian FUNCTIONALISM has, of late, provoked a reaction in favour of a neo-Weberian 'action approach'. Where functionalists preferred EXPLANATIONS in terms of adaptive responses to social expectations by 'actors' who are presumed to have learned and accepted the NORMS pertaining to their ROLES, action theorists emphasize the agent's own 'definition of the situation', his power of rational choice, and his ability to negotiate interaction or manipulate expected role performances. This approach shares common ground with the theory of SYMBOLIC INTERACTION and with PHENOMENOLOGY.
                                                            J.R.T.
Bibl: T. Parsons, *The Structure of Social Action* (London and N.Y., 1937); P. Winch, *The Idea of a Social Science* (London and N.Y., 1958); M. Weber, tr. A. M. Henderson and T. Parsons, *The Theory of Social and Economic Organization* (London and N.Y., 1964), ch. 1; J. Rex, *Key Problems of Sociological Theory* (London, 1961), ch.5.

social anthropology, see under ANTHROPOLOGY.

social behaviourism. An approach, linked with the name of B. F. Skinner, to the analysis and modification of social systems within the framework of BEHAVIOURISM (1). It turns directly to the relationship between behaviour and the ENVIRONMENT, and neglects supposed mediating states of mind. It is based upon the idea that behaviour is shaped and maintained by the consequence of previous behaviour, and also that the environment can be manipulated so that preferred responses are rewarded and so reinforced (see OPERANT CONDITIONING). The claim that if properly used it would solve the problems of mankind has been criticized because the direction of the changes in behaviour cannot be derived from the theory. It raises the question of which basic values are to be chosen and inculcated, and by whom.   M.BE.

Bibl: B. F. Skinner, *Beyond Freedom and Dignity* (N.Y., 1971; London, 1972).

social benefits, see under EXTERNALITIES.

social biology. The study of the application of BIOLOGY to social problems, from food production, POLLUTION, overpopulation, etc., to the long-range goals of social and ecological (see ECOLOGY) planning. To be distinguished from SOCIOBIOLOGY. E.O.W.

social compact. An expression coined by the British Labour Party in Opposition between 1970 and 1974 as an escape route from the impasse of an incomes policy, whether voluntary or statutory, which had been abandoned by the Labour Party under trade-union pressure, and which brought Edward Heath's Conservative administration into open conflict with the trade unions. The Social Compact – a phrase conveniently confusable with the SOCIAL CONTRACT of Hobbes, Locke, and Rousseau, by which term indeed it was rapidly ousted – denoted the bargain proposed to the trade unions by the 1974 Labour Government in an effort to achieve their support for wage restraint. The terms of the bargain were a Government undertaking to introduce specific social policies (including price subsidies, price restraint, dividend restraint, etc.) demanded by the unions in return for a general but unspecified indication that the unions would moderate their wage demands. The essential difference between the Social Compact and the Social Contract as historically developed is that, whereas the latter was envisaged as between Government and nation, the former was between Government and a section of the nation. The question whether, and in what form, the unions would be free to abandon their allegiance to the Government (analogously to the right of unsatisfied subjects to break the Social Contract) was left unexplored. R.B.

social construct. A CONSTRUCT devised to aid in the analysis and understanding of social phenomena. It is a deliberate abstraction (see ABSTRACT) from reality which focuses on particular aspects and ignores others in order to open up new lines of thought and new areas of investigation. Its function is HEURISTIC, not descriptive. Examples are the CONCEPTS of STATUS and ROLE. A.L.C.B.

social contract. The unwritten agreement between the members of a society to behave with reciprocal responsibility in their relationships under the governance of the 'State' which, in *social contract theory* (or *contract theory*) is presupposed by the existence of that society. The idea is of ancient origin (cf. Plato, Lucretius, etc.) but it was chiefly used as a tool for criticizing established, traditional authority when the modern nation states were breaking away from Christendom, and seeking both autonomy and just internal constitutions. Its chief exponents were Hobbes, who argued that the social contract *created* mutual obligations which did not exist prior to the constituted State; Locke, who argued that moral principles and obligations existed before the creation of the State, so that men could change the State if it failed to uphold these principles; and Rousseau, who devoted a famous work to the subject. For a new twist to the term see SOCIAL COMPACT. R.F.

Bibl: J. W. Gough, *The Social Contract* (Oxford, 1936).

social costs, see under EXTERNALITIES.

social credit. A theory of economic and social development, largely discredited, which rests on the proposition that modern economies suffer from a deficiency of purchasing power. The remedy for this situation, according to Major C. H. Douglas, who first propounded the theory in the inter-war years, was to increase purchasing power by controlling prices and creating 'social credit' which would be distributed to consumers by discounts paid to retailers, and also by 'dividends' paid to citizens for the heritage of earlier generations. Social Credit came to power in Alberta, Canada, in 1935 on a programme of issuing social credits based on the real worth of the land, but never implemented its theory while in office. D.E.

Bibl: C. H. Douglas, *Social Credit* (London and N.Y., 3rd ed., 1933).

social Darwinism. The application of the concept of EVOLUTION to the historical development of human societies which lays particular emphasis on 'the struggle for existence' and 'the survival of the fittest'. Though not rooted in DARWINISM (the idea preceded publication of the *Origin of Species*) such theories had a great popular vogue in the late 19th and early 20th centuries, when they were applied to the rivalries of the Great Powers and provided a pseudo-biological justification for POWER POLITICS, IMPERIALISM, and war. Hitler picked up these ideas in Vienna before 1914 and made them a feature of NAZISM.

R.F.; A.L.C.B.

Bibl: L. T. Hobhouse, *Development and Purpose* (London, rev. ed., 1927) and *Morals in Evolution* (London, 7th ed., 1951); M. D. Sahlins and E. R. Service (eds.), *Evolution and Culture* (Ann Arbor, 1960).

social democracy. That part of the SOCIALIST and labour movement which accepts the democratic structure of the State and postulates social changes by means of reforms (see REFORMISM) rather than REVOLUTION.

Historically, social democracy emerged after the collapse of the First INTERNATIONAL, when the various socialist parties which formed the Second International became almost everywhere integrated into the political life of their respective countries. In Russia political conditions were not favourable for the social-democratic approach. Elsewhere, however, the social democrats attracted significant support from the workers, and the socialist parties abandoned revolutionary politics, first in practice and then in theory; the transition to parliamentary gradualism, though subject to ebb and flow, was a corollary of the economic and social gains of the workers and the increase in the strength of the social-democratic parties and of the trade unions before World War I. The split in the socialist movement caused by the BOLSHEVIK victory in Russia resulted in a clear-cut division between reformist social democracy and revolutionary COMMUNISM.

After World War II, social democrats recovered their influence in Western Europe, but were suppressed in Eastern Europe. The policies of the ruling social-democratic parties in Western countries appeared to many as not sufficiently militant; hence the continuing tension between their LEFT and RIGHT wings or even splits resulting in separate socialist and social-democratic parties (as in Italy where both belong to the same Socialist International). The disenchantment with IDEOLOGIES in general made the moderate social democrats somewhat sceptical and exhausted their socialist fervour, while it was precisely the utopian element in socialism which appealed to the younger generation. This was manifested in the emergence of the NEW LEFT and its hostility to social democracy. The post-war experience and the growing economic difficulties in the West made the social-democratic idea of 'planning in freedom' less convincing than in the immediate aftermath of war. The prospects for social democracy are connected with the prospects for DEMOCRACY in general and its continuing political vitality in facing the problems of social and economic change.

L.L.

Bibl: J. Vaizey, *Social Democracy* (London, 1971; N.Y., 1972).

social dynamics, see under SOCIAL STATICS.

social engineering. The planning of social changes according to a blueprint instead of allowing social INSTITUTIONS to develop in a haphazard manner. Related terms are *social technology*; *social intervention*; *behavioural engineering*, which is associated with the psychologist B. F. Skinner and explores the possibilities of altering individual behaviour through manipulation of the ENVIRONMENT; and EUGENICS, which raises in an acute form the ethical problems inherent in any approach to social reform that sees it as a technological problem of product specification and design. The approach has been criticized, notably by educationists, for applying a mechanistic analysis to an organic structure, and for failing to recognize the plurality of values involved; for a criticism implied by Sir Karl Popper's preference for *'piecemeal social engineering'* see POPPERIAN.

*M.BA.; B.M.

Bibl: K. R. Popper, *The Poverty of Historicism* (London, 1957); B. F. Skinner, *Walden Two* (N.Y., 1948).

social ethic. Term used by W. H. Whyte in *The Organization Man* (1956) to denote 'that contemporary body of thought which makes morally legitimate the pressures of society against the individual. Its major propositions are three: a belief in the group as the source of creativity; a belief in "belongingness" as the ultimate need of the individual; and a belief in the application of science to achieve the belongingness'. Whyte stresses the paradox that though 'practical' in its use within modern corporate INSTITUTIONS it is, in essence, a 'utopian faith'. See also OTHER-DIRECTED.   S.J.G.

social fact. The term used, especially by Émile Durkheim, to make clear the distinctive subject-matter of SOCIOLOGY and to emphasize the psychological creativity of human society. It is not the case, Durkheim argues, that human association is 'sterile' – a mere AGGREGATION of a number of individuals whose mental characteristics already exist, in given, permanent form, before association takes place. On the contrary, association is a *creative* process, producing new experiences, and new levels of experience; without it, indeed, the human 'person' could not come to exist. Social facts are therefore a qualitatively distinct *level* of facts in nature, requiring careful analysis and investigation at this level, and therefore a new and appropriate science – sociology. This, of course, was the essential, initial statement of Comte, which Durkheim reiterated and emphasized. See also COLLECTIVE CONSCIOUSNESS; CULTURE; FOLKWAYS; SOCIAL STRUCTURE; STRUCTURE; SUBCULTURE.   R.F.
Bibl: E. Durkheim, tr. S. A. Solovay and J. H. Mueller, ed. G. E. G. Catlin, *The Rules of Sociological Method* (Chicago, 1938), ch. 1.

social gospel movement. The attempt of many influential liberal Protestants (see LIBERALISM; PROTESTANTISM), specially in the U.S.A. from *c.* 1880 to 1930, to bring 'the Kingdom of God' closer by working for the improvement of society, usually along SOCIALIST and PACIFIST lines. The most influential theologian was Walter Rauschenbusch (1861–1918). The evolutionary optimism involved was later attacked by NEO-ORTHODOX thinkers such as Reinhold Niebuhr (see NIEBUHRIAN). But this was not the end of the passionate concern of American Christ-

ians to improve and perfect society. D.L.E.
Bibl: R. T. Handy (ed.), *The Social Gospel in America* (N.Y., 1966).

social history. A subject traditionally left to amateur historians, defined as the history of everyday life, and studied mainly from literary sources. Since about 1950, however, the subject has undergone a revolution. It has become the history of social groups or CLASSES, and of changes in the SOCIAL STRUCTURE, carried out by professional historians or sociologists, using the methods of QUANTITATIVE HISTORY. This revolution has made the traditional term an embarrassment to some, but the alternatives suggested, 'sociological history', 'the history of society', 'societal history', and 'social structural history', have not become generally accepted. See also GENTRY CONTROVERSY; PAST AND PRESENT.   P.B.
Bibl: E. J. Hobsbawm, 'From Social History to the History of Society' (*Daedalus,* 100, 1971, pp. 20–43).

social intervention, see under SOCIAL ENGINEERING.

social learning. Term used by the American psychologist A. Bandura as the basis of a psychological theory that emphasizes the role of COGNITIVE, vicarious, and self-regulatory factors in human behaviour. While recognizing that people learn by direct experience, social learning theory stresses that they also learn, with fewer attendant hazards and burdens, by observing the example of others. Theories that portray behaviour as the product of external rewards and punishments alone are criticized as ignoring the part played by self-evaluation. Social learning theory acknowledges three ways in which REINFORCEMENT operates: people regulate their actions on the basis of consequences they experience directly, of those they see happening to others, and of those they create for themselves. Transitory experiences are coded into imaginal, verbal, and other symbols for memory representation, and thus have lasting effects, since these internal representations of behaviour patterns and their probable consequences serve as guides for action on later occasions. Social learning theory stresses the reciprocal influence between people and the environment: behaviour is influenced by environmental contingencies, but the contingencies are partly of people's own making. A.B.

Bibl: A. Bandura, *Social Learning Theory* (Englewood Cliffs, N. J., 1977).

social medicine. In one sense, the interface between SOCIOLOGY and medicine; in a more practical sense, the practice of medicine considered as a social service. It thus comprehends (1) analysis of mortality or sickness by geographical regions or by OCCUPATION – analyses of the kind that led to the recognition of a CORRELATION between smoking and the incidence of lung CANCER, and one between the degree of hardness of water and the incidence of cardiovascular disease; (2) investigation of FERTILITY and the means that must be taken to promote it or, where necessary, to reduce it; (3) investigation of the actual or possible contributions of the disabled to society and the means which may be taken to restore them to ordinary life; (4) a large part of hygiene and sanitary engineering, especially that part which deals with the elimination or containment of infectious organisms; (5) devising and promoting the legislation and other activities that safeguard the nation's health, e.g. the institution of vaccination or quarantine programmes; (6 – of especial importance in an epoch of increasing longevity) medical care of the aged and the steps that must be taken to secure their position in society (see GERIATRICS). Social medicine is thus very closely bound up with the legislative and administrative provisions that are necessary if its findings are to be translated into practical use. In the U.K. the Department of Health has for some time been also the Department of Social Service. P.M.

social mobility. The movement of individuals, families, or groups from one social position to another which is usually designated higher or lower on some socially evaluative scale (see SOCIAL STRATIFICATION; STATUS). The idea that each person in a society should have an equal chance to rise, or gain a place commensurate with his talents, is a fruit, largely, of the modern EGALITARIAN idea. In modern industrial society, social mobility is largely occupational mobility, and education is the chief means of access to a higher (i.e. more skilled) position –

though family background and cultural advantages give the children of the upper and middle classes a better start than children of the working class. The major change in modern society, however, is the status change upward in the entire slope of the occupational structure as the number of unskilled jobs decline under AUTOMATION and the number and proportion of white-collar and office employments expand in the POST-INDUSTRIAL phase of society. D.B.

social mobilization. The movement of individuals, families, or social groups to political consciousness within society, leading them either to greater influence and participation or to apathy and ALIENATION. Social mobilization is fostered by a movement of populations from rural to urban settings, from illiteracy to literacy, from barter to MARKET ECONOMIES, from traditional to modern social organizations (see MODERNIZATION). New political demands result. Depending upon governmental response, social mobilization reinforces either NATIONALISM and social solidarity (as occurred after the French Revolution) or distrust of political INSTITUTIONS. After 1945 the social mobilization of Asian, African, and Latin American societies undermined traditional polities and also the IMPERIAL ties on which they rested. The process also offers challenges to developed states; an example is the remobilization of ethnic populations in Western Europe and the British Isles. R.R.

Bibl: K. Deutsch, *Nationalism and Social Communication* (Cambridge, Mass., and N. Y., 1953); K. Deutsch, 'Social Mobilization and Political Development' (*American Political Science Review*, Sept. 1961).

social overheads. The costs imposed on the public purse by private agents, costs for which they do not necessarily have to pay unless the tax burden is suitably adjusted. The stock examples are the schools, roads, sewage facilities, etc. associated with urban and industrial development. S.BR.

social precedence, see under AGGRESSION.

social psychology. A branch of PSYCHOLOGY, usually defined as the scientific study of human social behaviour. In order to test its theories and hypotheses, social psychology endeavours to use methods of laboratory experimentation and of controlled research in 'natural' surroundings. Its theories often attempt to explain and systematize the complexities of human social behaviour in terms of wide-ranging generalizations about the individual psychological roots of various aspects of social interaction such as competition, cooperation, conformity, the functioning of small groups, the exercise of social influence, the development of social motives in the individual, relations between human groups, etc. Most of this work has been done in the context of Western societies, but efforts at cross-cultural validation (see CROSS-CULTURAL STUDY) have also been made.

The need to formulate and empirically test its theories has often led social psychology to look for its data to the study of individual reactions rather than to characterizing the properties or reactions of larger social aggregates. Typical is its emphasis on the study of individual attitudes, their formation and change. Much has been gained in precision by this approach, but there is increasing dissatisfaction with some of its constraints. Social psychology is today in process of change, characterized by a continuous search for new CONCEPTS and methods capable of bringing present individualistic concepts of man in society nearer to the social complexities of human life and to a more adequate analysis of man as both a creature and a creator of his society. In research methods, this is reflected in the growing influence of ETHOLOGY, and of other attempts to study behaviour in 'natural' settings. In the development of theory, there is much preoccupation with the study of human social communication and with the manner in which social behaviour is determined or affected by the conceptions about his society that each individual assimilates from the CULTURE. There is also increasing suspicion of the value of premature and often disappointing attempts to reduce the complexities of human social behaviour and experience to 'simpler' or 'elementary' laws of functioning.

Nowadays a social psychologist is someone who functions simultaneously as a 'man from Mars' and as a social anthropologist (see ANTHROPOLOGY), the former because he needs to achieve detachment from his material, and be aware of the social origins of his theoretical assumptions, the latter because he cannot hope to study human social conduct unless he relates it to the context of values, NORMS, and social expectations by which social action is powerfully affected.

Social psychology's subject-matter lies in the area between the biological (see BIOLOGY) and the SOCIAL SCIENCES. Evolutionary, genetic, and physiological perspectives (see EVOLUTION; GENETICS; PHYSIOLOGY) contribute to the understanding of how and why man became the kind of social animal he is; they also define his limitations, particularly in relation to the laws governing his development, both as a SPECIES and as an individual. But, in order to adapt, man has also created much of his ENVIRONMENT, not only social but also physical. He survived as a species because of his flexible ability to construct new modes of existence for himself. The understanding of these modes of adaptation requires a level of analysis that transcends the biological. Obviously, the range of social choices and actions open to individuals is dependent also upon individual psychological processes. In order to study the actual content of human social behaviour, therefore, social psychologists must look at the manner in which individuals perceive and conceptualize social and physical events, and at their motives, values, and norms developed in reaction to these idiosyncratic views of the world.

While social psychology is one of the oldest of human preoccupations, its importance for our understanding of the human condition remains to be proved. It is at present widely used in application to studies of consumer habits, voting behaviour (see PSEPHOLOGY), worker morale, and RACE prejudice, and is an established part of many industrial, political, and military organizations.   H.TA.

Bibl: R. W. Brown, *Social Psychology* (London and N.Y., 1965); P. Kelvin, *The Bases of Social Behaviour* (London and N.Y., 1970).

social realism. Socially concerned yet objectively presented works of REALIST art or literature of several different formal schools. To be distinguished from SOCIALIST REALISM.   J.W.

social sciences. Those disciplines that attempt, in a more or less systematic and objective manner, to study social systems, SOCIAL STRUCTURES, political and economic processes, and interactions between different groups or different individuals, with a view to establishing knowledge capable of being tested. Examples are ANTHROPOLOGY, ECONOMICS, POLITICAL SCIENCE, SOCIAL PSYCHOLOGY, SOCIOLOGY and some aspects of LINGUISTICS.

Social sciences are sometimes contrasted with NATURAL SCIENCES (e.g. PHYSICS, CHEMISTRY, GEOLOGY) on the grounds that there are essential differences between 'natural' physical systems and situations involving human beings (see ANTI-NATURALISM). One way of classifying social scientists (not social sciences) is by their attitudes to this issue. At one extreme are those who write like would-be physicists, using much mathematical and technical jargon, and scorning evidence not collected by elaborate formalized procedures; at the other extreme are those who sound more like novelists, literary critics, preachers, or philosophers. Though fashions change, economists tend to fall in the former category, anthropologists in the latter. The first group of social scientists see the natural and social sciences as having common aims (i.e. EXPLANATION, prediction, and increased control over happenings in the world) and requiring common methods, e.g. the use of numerical SCALES of measurement, the use of experiments and statistical techniques (see STATISTICS) to search for CORRELATIONS between variables, and the construction of mathematical MODELS to represent STRUCTURES and processes under investigation. The second group sees the social sciences, like the HUMANITIES, as aiming to enhance self-understanding, rather as art criticism helps one to understand a painting, or PSYCHOANALYSIS helps a patient to understand himself. This is sometimes called a HERMENEUTIC approach.

Parallel to the above contrast is a division of social scientists into those who adopt the BEHAVIOURAL approach and those who are MENTALISTS. A third contrast concerns the scale of the system studied; see METHODOLOGICAL INDIVIDUALISM AND METHODOLOGICAL HOLISM. For an attempt to cut across some of the distinctions and controversies and form a new synthesis see STRUCTURALISM; for a new discipline in which rapid progress is being made in developing and testing suitable conceptual tools see ARTIFICIAL INTELLIGENCE.   A.S.

Bibl: E. Nagel, *The Structure of Science* (London and N.Y., 1961); H. P. Rickman, *Understanding and the Human Studies* (London, 1967); S. Andreski, *Social Sciences as Sorcery* (London, 1972).

social statics and social dynamics. The application to SOCIOLOGY of a distinction, valid for all sciences, which Auguste Comte made between two types of *method*: *statics*, which analyses the distinctive nature of the subject-matter (in the case of sociology, the distinctive nature of social systems or societies), and *dynamics*, which applies this analysis to establishing testable knowledge about the varieties of the subject actually existing in the continuing processes of nature and history. A common fallacy is the belief that social statics (and certain schools of theory, such as FUNCTIONALISM) regard society in a static way, studying it at one particular point of time, whereas social dynamics studies societies 'on the move'. Neither Comte nor anyone else held that a human society could ever be *static*; indeed, Comte insisted that one of the distinctive features of societies was their essentially changing, cumulative, historical nature.   R.F.

Bibl: A. Comte, tr. J. H. Bridges *et al.*, *System of Positive Polity*, vols. 2 and 3 (London, 1875–7).

social stratification. The process that occurs when individual inequalities – of physique, strength, wealth, power, etc. – become systematic, are given positive and negative evaluation, and organized into patterns that are recognized, if not accepted, by most members of a society. There are two general theories of stratification: the FUNCTIONALIST theory, derived from the work of Émile Durkheim and Talcott Parsons, in which every society necessarily grades its activities because some functions are valued more than others; and a contrary theory, derived from Rousseau, Proudhon, and Marx, which argues that POWER, not functional necessity, is the basis of stratification. Max Weber accepted, in part, the MARXIST notion that stratification is a manifestation

583

of unequal power in society, but argued that stratification exists along three different dimensions, economic, social, and political. Some writers, deriving from the Saint-Simonian tradition, have argued that stratification may exist as a functional necessity, and create levels of command in a society based on technical competence, but these need not be converted into material advantage and into exploitative or power relations; this is the foundation for a theory of a MERITOCRACY. See also CLASS; SOCIAL MOBILITY.   D.B.

Bibl: F. Parkin, *Class Inequality and Political Order* (London and N.Y., 1971).

social structure. The discernible framework, form, shape, pattern, of the interrelationships of men in a society. It is always an outcome both of deliberate purpose in specific activities and of the manifold unforeseen consequences of all activities, and it can be analysed into its major elements, e.g. its political, legal, military, religious, educational, and family organization. All these, however, are interconnected both by INSTITUTIONS (e.g. marriage, which links the family, religion, law, property relations, political authority, etc.) and by groups, within many of which the same individuals have varying functions, ROLES, and STATUS. In any society, therefore, the total social structure can be broken down into the specific roles, and sets of roles, which individual persons have to fulfil. See also STRUCTURE; SUPERSTRUCTURE.   R.F.

Bibl: R. M. MacIver and C. H. Page, *Society* (London, 1949).

social studies. The wide variety of studies which concern themselves with urgent social problems (e.g. RACE, DRUGS, poverty), or with areas of social life (e.g. the development of transport, home-making, leisure activities, the mass MEDIA). Though supposedly resting on the foundations of the SOCIAL SCIENCES, social studies frequently fail to exercise scientific stringency. Indeed, they may even not attempt to do so, being concerned merely to make people aware of problems, of ways of investigating and discussing them, and of political policies which might be designed to solve them. In schools and colleges they may simply be elementary studies introducing children and young people to methods of analysing their own

experience and the world in which they live.

Social studies also enter into courses for the training of social workers. This has led to a conflict of standards between them and the social sciences; but social workers are increasingly turning to social sciences for a more systematic study of the problems with which they are concerned. R.F.

Bibl: R. Richardson and J. Chapman, *Frontiers of Enquiry* (London, 1971).

social technology, see under SOCIAL ENGINEERING.

social theory. Used loosely, this term connotes all those areas of thought that concern men and women as social beings. Its more precise, modern use denotes what would more accurately be termed 'sociological theory'. In this usage social theory is to be distinguished (1) from SOCIAL SCIENCE, i.e. speculative and analytic ideas are distinguished from those statements that claim scientific, falsifiable status (see POPPERIAN); (2) from the social INSTITUTIONS or practices it seeks to explain; (3) from economic, political, or psychological theory (see ECONOMICS; POLITICAL SCIENCE; PSYCHOLOGY).
          M.BA.

Bibl: P. Cohen, *Modern Social Theory* (London and N.Y., 1968).

social welfare. A measure, based on NORMATIVE criteria, of the WELFARE of a given society as a whole. In the 1930s a respectful misunderstanding of the philosophical distinction between facts and values made economists unusually suspicious of the notion of social welfare, and in trying to keep economics 'scientific' and VALUE-FREE they departed from the earlier traditions of POLITICAL ECONOMY. More recently, however, economists have been concerned with the systematic use of normative criteria in judging economic progress (e.g. in the analysis of NATIONAL INCOME, or in evaluating ECONOMIC GROWTH) as well as in providing a framework for choosing between alternative social policies (e.g. in COST-BENEFIT ANALYSIS). Ultimately, evaluation of social welfare relates to choice between alternative policies and even between alternative social systems.   A.K.S.

Bibl: I. M. D. Little, *A Critique of Welfare Economics* (Oxford, 2nd ed. 1957);

M. H. Dobb, *Welfare Economics and the Economics of Socialism* (London, 1969).

social whole. Generally, the larger social context within which a particular SOCIAL FACT requires to be seen before it can be sufficiently explained or understood. In sociological analysis, the CONCEPT operates at different levels. Thus, the full significance of a particular form of marriage can only be understood within its wider context of the family and kinship system; but this in turn can only be understood within the wider context of the property relations, the religious doctrines and RITUAL, the political authority and welfare provisions, of the society as a whole. This 'whole society', again, may only be fully understood as part of a wider CULTURE AREA, or as having been fragmented from, or having separated itself from, a wider civilization (e.g. the European nations from medieval Christendom). See also SOCIAL STRUCTURE.   R.F.

socialisation, see SOCIALIZATION.

socialism. A CONCEPT with many meanings, but generally understood as a social system based on common ownership of the means of production and distribution. In COMMUNIST theory, it is the first stage on the road to full communism. In socialist writings, it differs from communism by an attachment to ethical and democratic values (see ETHICS; DEMOCRACY), as well as by an emphasis on the distinction between common and State ownership.

In the 1830s, when the term began to be used, socialism was the intellectual heir of the Enlightenment, having been propagated by radical thinkers (see RADICALISM) spanning the period between the French Revolution and the emergence of industrialism, between Buonarotti and Saint-Simon. The distinctly utopian characteristics shown by its followers and its early theoreticians (e.g. Fourier) appeared as a secular counterpart of salvationist attitudes in religious ages. Later on, Engels claimed that MARXIST theory had shifted socialism from a utopian to a scientific basis. But it is revolutionary (see REVOLUTION) communism which retained the utopian tradition; the socialist movement, while not discarding it altogether, came in practice to neglect it ideologically (see IDEOLOGY).

This may be the root of the difference between two political movements stemming from the same intellectual tradition, for salvationist utopianism has always been connected with intolerance and has therefore tended to express itself in tyrannical political practice.

As a historical phenomenon, the socialist movement has been essentially confined to the European LEFT. In European countries, it has successfully pressed for the extension of universal suffrage, social reforms, improved social conditions, and a greater economic role for the State in controlling the MARKET mechanism. After World War II, socialist parties were suppressed in Eastern European countries. In the THIRD WORLD, the European type of socialist labour movement has failed to strike root: socialism became associated with single-party rule, and the Asian or African concept of economic development appeared as more akin to communist than to socialist ideas. In the West, the historical experience of the communist countries made the socialist vision of public ownership less attractive, and raised the question whether political monopoly is not an inevitable concomitant of economic MONOPOLY.

More recently, the idea of ECONOMIC GROWTH, traditionally connected with socialist thought, has had to confront the general realization of the global scarcity of natural resources and the prospect of demographic explosion. The decline of the idea of progress has weakened the utopian impulse underlying the socialist vision of an egalitarian and libertarian society, forcing many to ask how far EGALITARIANISM and LIBERTARIANISM are compatible. Thus the 20th-century historical experience has confronted socialists with the necessity not just of REVISIONISM – as with Bernstein's revision of Marxist doctrines – but of reassessing the very premises of socialist thought. Such a reappraisal poses the question whether socialism can preserve its separate identity while retaining those values which have been historically associated with it.   L.L.

Bibl: G. Lichtheim, *The Origins of Socialism* (London and N.Y., 1969) and *A Short History of Socialism* (London and N.Y., 1970); L. Kolakowski and S. Hampshire (eds.), *The Socialist Idea* (London,

1974); R. N. Berki, *Socialism* (London, 1975).

Socialist Courier, see under MENSHEVIKS.

Socialist International, see INTERNATIONAL.

socialist realism. The Soviet official formula for the COMMUNIST Party's demands of the creative artist, whatever his medium. First proclaimed by Maxim Gorky and the politicians N. Bukharin and A. A. Zhdanov at the Soviet Writers' Congress of 1934, this recipe has never been precisely defined, though its essence has proved to consist in the harnessing of late-19th-century REALIST techniques of art (Repin), fiction (Turgenev), and theatre (Stanislavsky) to the portrayal of exemplary Soviet characters (the 'positive hero') and a rosy future (the 'positive conclusion'). Socialist realism has, however, been regarded as incompatible not only with any kind of pessimism but also with FORMALISM, COSMOPOLITANISM, and other forms of DEGENERACY. While its practical application has been modified since the heyday of STALINISM, so that formerly unacceptable innovators like Mayakovsky and Brecht could be posthumously covered by it, this doctrine remains a serious obstacle to the development of the Soviet arts, not least because of the vagueness of its relevance to music and architecture, where for many years it seemed to signify the use (respectively) of FOLK tunes and mock-classical ornamentation, as favoured by the party leaders. Outside the U.S.S.R. it has been a great embarrassment to many Communist parties, particularly the French, so that its interpretation and practical implementation now vary widely from country to country. Socialist realism is to be distinguished from SOCIAL REALISM.   J.W.

Bibl: L. Aragon, *Pour un réalisme socialiste* (Paris, 1935); A. Zhdanov *et al., Problems of Soviet Literature* (London, 1935).

socialization. In DEVELOPMENTAL PSYCHOLOGY, the early stages of induction of an infant or child into a CULTURE's values, rules, and ways of operating. It is one of the major topics of CROSS-CULTURAL STUDIES. In the early work on socialization, major emphasis was placed on the control of motivation by systems of reward and punishment (see OPERANT CONDITIONING), with special reference to critical stress points in development: early bowel-training, control of AGGRESSION, the transition into adolescent sexuality (an emphasis attributable to FREUDIAN theory). More recent studies have been more concerned with the process whereby children learn underlying rules and properties of the culture, an approach partly influenced by the emergence in ANTHROPOLOGY of STRUCTURALISM, with its insistence upon the connected role patterns characterizing cultures. See also PSYCHOSEXUAL DEVELOPMENT.   J.S.B.

Bibl: P. H. Mussen (ed.), *Carmichael's Manual of Child Psychology* (N.Y., 3rd ed., 1970).

societal. A term which in current usage functions mostly as a pseudo-scientific and pompous variant of 'social'. Nevertheless, a case for retaining it can be made in view of the exceedingly wide range of meaning of 'social' as in 'social work', 'social event', 'social inadequacy', and 'social revolution'. 'Societal' could be defined as a term which refers to the attributes of society as a whole: its STRUCTURE or the changes therein. 'Social' would remain a wider term which not only includes 'societal' but can also be applied to inter-personal relations as well as to attributes or acts of an individual which affect other human beings.   S.A.

societal history, see under SOCIAL HISTORY.

sociobiology. The study of all aspects of social behaviour up to and including the evolution of social behaviour in man (see EVOLUTION, SOCIAL). It consists of five major topics: group size, age composition, mode of organization including the forms of communication, division of labour, and time budgets of both the group and its members. A theory of sociobiology which will unify all this information is one of the great but manageable tasks of BIOLOGY in the next two to three decades; it is likely to be formulated on the basis of the first principles of population ECOLOGY and POPULATION GENETICS. Sociobiology is to be distinguished from SOCIAL BIOLOGY.   E.O.W.

Bibl: J. H. Crook (ed.), *Social Behaviour in Birds and Mammals* (London and N.Y., 1970); J. F. Eisenberg and W. S. Dillon (eds.), *Man and Beast: Comparative Social Behaviour* (Washington, 1971); E. O. Wilson, *The Insect Societies* (Cambridge, Mass., 1971) and *Sociobiology: the New Synthesis* (Cambridge, Mass., 1975).

sociogram. A presentation in diagrammatic form of the relations among members of a social group. Although originating in the eclectic body of doctrine known as SOCIOMETRY, it is frequently employed without reference to the tenets of that creed. The credibility and informativeness of a sociogram greatly depend on the skill of its author.   K.H.
Bibl: M. L. Northway, *A Primer of Sociometry* (Toronto, 2nd ed., 1967).

sociolinguistics. A branch of LINGUISTICS which studies the relationship between language and society, e.g. the linguistic identity of social groups, the patterns of national language use. There is some overlap in subject-matter between this branch and ANTHROPOLOGICAL LINGUISTICS. See also DIALECTOLOGY.   D.C.
Bibl: D. Hymes (ed.), *Language in Culture and Society* (N.Y., 1964); P. Trudgill, *Sociolinguistics* (Harmondsworth and Baltimore, 1973).

sociological history, see under SOCIAL HISTORY.

sociological jurisprudence. An approach to the study of the law which starts from the conviction that no statutes or codes, however detailed, can relieve the courts of the task of choosing between conflicting social interests and considering the weight of different values recognized by the community. Jurists impressed by these facts, e.g. the American jurist Roscoe Pound, have urged the need for a sociological jurisprudence drawing upon all the SOCIAL SCIENCES to provide the courts with an analysis and classification of the various interests which they are called upon to adjust and of the different values which influence the law's development, and a realistic account of the legal system, including the judicial process itself.   H.L.A.H.

Bibl: E. W. Patterson, *Jurisprudence* (Brooklyn, 1953); R. Pound, *Jurisprudence* (St Paul, Minn., 1959).

sociology. The study of societies: both the observation and description of social phenomena, and the articulation and application to these phenomena of a coherent conceptual scheme. In so far as there are several competing schemes, sociology is less fully a discipline than, say, ECONOMICS (with its general EQUILIBRIUM theory), and needs to be considered historically, by reference to the three different streams which one can identify in the rise of modern sociology:
(1) Curiosity about how a society hangs together. The major impulse here is NEWTONIAN MECHANICS, which inspired many efforts (e.g. Malebranche, Berkeley) to create an analogous 'social physics' that would account for, say, the distribution of human populations on the basis of some single principle, or (Montesquieu) explain the variations between societies and peoples by reference to climate, soil, numbers, or some combination of these physical attributes. Rousseau contrasted the 'state of nature' with society, and postulated a SOCIAL CONTRACT in which the wills of all are fused into a single personality, the community. Finally, the French Revolution suggested to de Maistre and Bonald the role of common faiths or MYTHS in holding a society together.
(2) A theory of social EVOLUTION which derives either from the Enlightenment belief in progress as developed by Auguste Comte, from the immanent development of consciousness or man's material powers (Hegel and Marx), or from SOCIAL DARWINISM (Herbert Spencer). These three independent skeins of thought together gave a powerful impetus to the idea of SOCIETAL change and a progressive direction of history.
(3) A curiosity about the actual facts of social life that became translated into systematic empirical enquiry. Notable examples are Frédéric Le Play's *Les Ouvriers européens* (2nd ed., 6 vols., 1877–99), the famous 'blue books' which Marx and Engels used to document their statements about the English working class, and Booth's *Labour and Life of the People in London* (9 vols., 1892–7) with its quantitative data and case studies.

Most of the concerns and problems of contemporary sociology, if not the conceptual structures as well, derive in large measure from four men:

(1) For Karl Marx (1818–83), all SOCIAL STRUCTURE was CLASS structure, and the history of all societies was the history of class struggles. In his fundamental METHODOLOGY, Marx argued that social existence determines CONSCIOUSNESS, and that IDEOLOGY is merely a SUPERSTRUCTURE, economic relations being the substructure. (See MARXISM; BOURGEOIS; PROLETARIAT.)

(2) Herbert Spencer (1820–1903) saw society in organismic terms and aimed to construct a social MORPHOLOGY of societies in terms of their structure and function. Sociology's fields were the family, political organization, ecclesiastical structures, the system of restraints (i.e. social control), and industry or work; its task was 'to give an account of [how] successive generations of units are produced, reared, and fitted for cooperation'.

(3) For Émile Durkheim (1858–1917), the major focus of sociology was social solidarity, or social cohesion: society consisted of a 'collective conscience', a moral force, at the centre of which is a core of values or beliefs that is considered sacred. (Society is thus the source of RELIGION.) Durkheim saw social change in terms of the breakdown of 'segmentation', i.e. the replacement of isolated social structures by complex and interdependent modern society, with its competition, specialization, and structural differentiation.

(4) For Max Weber (1864–1920) the focus of sociology was on types of action, of which economics and law were the MODELS of rational action, and religion of non-rational action. His encyclopedic work, based on the COMPARATIVE METHOD, covered the great religious systems of the world, the studies of large bureaucratic systems, and the interrelations of economics, law, and society. Much of it is definitional, and Weber was concerned to identify the different kinds of authority (traditional, CHARISMATIC, and rational), the different kinds of POWER (*Macht* or force and *Herrschaft* or coordinated domination), the evolution of BUREAUCRACY (patriarchal, patrimonial, and legal-rational), and the different kinds of rational conduct. He also aimed

to unfold the complex process by which rationality, in its various forms, developed in the West rather than other CULTURES. Modern CAPITALISM was defined on the basis of a rationalizing spirit and the creation of large rationalized organizations, and capitalism and SOCIALISM were two variants of a larger, more inclusive entity, bureaucratic society.

Spencer, Durkheim, Weber, and also Ferdinand Tönnies (1855–1936) all conceptualized social change in terms of contrasting modal types of societies (roughly speaking, traditional and modern), with sufficient overlap to allow for an assimilation of the terms to one another. In the one kind of society, relations were personal, communal, primary, with strong similarity of attitudes, and in orientation to the past. In the other, relations are impersonal, bureaucratic, differentiated, open, and mobile, and men look to the future. Whereas Marx placed his sequence of societies – feudal, capitalist, and socialist – completely within a historical frame, the implicit intention of the other four was to use these historical types as building blocks for the ahistorical analysis of different kinds of social relations in any society.

The most comprehensive effort to use sociological concepts purely as analytical elements, outside historical frameworks, has been made by the American sociologist Talcott Parsons (see PARSONIAN; PATTERN VARIABLES). In the period after World War II Parsons was the dominant figure in American and indeed Western sociology; in the last decade there has been a reaction against his schemes as being too abstract and a return to historical categories and problems of social change and social conflict.

Among the key *unit-ideas* of sociology Robert Nisbet listed COMMUNITY, authority, STATUS, the sacred, and ALIENATION. To the extent, however, that sociology becomes a discipline, it has to achieve this status through the articulation of a coherent set of interrelated CONCEPTS which can be applied to phenomena and codified as theories, or through the construction of simplifying MODELS which facilitate EXPLANATION. Unlike economics, sociology has no systematic theories which are formalized in mathematical terms. There are, instead, a number of different kinds of models:

the *structure-function* model (see STRUCTURAL-FUNCTIONAL THEORY), associated with the work of Talcott Parsons and Robert Merton; EXCHANGE MODELS, associated with George Homans and Peter Blau; *conflict models* (see CONFLICT THEORY); *evolutionary models* (see EVOLUTION; TECHNOLOGY); *ecological models* (see ECOLOGY); and a growing number of *mathematical models*, which seek to formalize the RELATIONS or VARIABLES which are stated in the other models. Finally, one can look at sociology not as a scientific discipline, defined by its concepts and methods, but, in a view derived from the humanities, as a mode of consciousness, as a way of observing the subtle and complex ways in which men interact with one another, and of reporting these interactions in their complexity rather than simplifying them as a science necessarily does.

A survey, necessarily brief, cannot take into account the thousands of detailed empirical studies which seek to relate social phenomena (e.g. social class to occupation, crime to migration, family roles to value changes) in systematic enquiry.   D.B.

Bibl: H. S. Hughes, *Consciousness and Society* (N.Y., 1958); R. K. Merton, L. Broom and L. S. Cottrell (eds.), *Sociology Today* (N.Y., 1959); R. Aron, tr. R. Howard and H. Weaver, *Main Currents in Sociological Thought* (London and N.Y., 1965); G. D. Mitchell, *A Hundred Years of Sociology* (London and N.Y., 1968), R. W. Friedrichs, *A Sociology of Sociology* (N.Y., 1970); L. A. Coser, *Masters of Sociological Thought* (N.Y., 1971).

sociology of knowledge, see KNOWLEDGE, SOCIOLOGY OF.

sociology of religion, see RELIGION, SOCIOLOGY OF.

sociology of science, see SCIENCE, SOCIOLOGY OF.

sociometry. The attempt to analyse interpersonal relations in such a way that the results can be plotted in diagrammatic form, on a SOCIOGRAM. Replies to a questionnaire about individual friendship and leadership choices are plotted by means of connecting lines to indicate which members of a particular social group are the effective leaders, the isolates, or the popular 'stars'. This approach to small-group social relations formed part of the idiosyncratic approach to social life adopted by its founder, J. L. Moreno. Although Moreno hoped that his technique would have very wide applicability, it is now seen as merely one of the available methods of obtaining popularity or leadership ratings from members of a social group.   M.BA.

Bibl: J. L. Moreno, *Who Shall Survive?* (N.Y., 1953).

SOE (Special Operations Executive). An independent British secret service set up in January 1940 to conduct subversive warfare and sabotage in enemy-occupied territory either in isolation or in cooperation with native RESISTANCE MOVEMENTS. See also MAQUIS.   D.C.W.

Bibl: M. R. D. Foot, *S.O.E. in France* (London, 1966) and *Resistance* (London, 1976).

Soffici, Ardengo (Italian painter, 1879–1964), see under COLLAGE; FUTURISM.

software. In COMPUTING, the PROGRAMS as opposed to the HARDWARE. Although properly applied to all programs, the term is often reserved for the large and complex programs which are needed to assist all users whatever their particular application. These programs, which include the OPERATING SYSTEM, COMPILERS, ASSEMBLERS, and INPUT/OUTPUT controls, are generally written by the COMPUTER manufacturer and supplied with the machine; their cost has become a serious embarrassment.   C.S.

soie moirée, see under MOIRÉ EFFECT.

soil erosion. The partial or complete removal of the soil of farmland by the action of running water or wind. Rain collecting as surface water can flow down sloping land as a sheet removing the fertile top soil, or it can concentrate in channels to cut deep gullies. In regions of low rainfall soils are liable to dry to an incohesive state. Strong winds which sweep the coarse soil particles along the surface are capable of carrying the finest dust up into the atmosphere to be deposited hundreds of miles away (see DUST BOWL).

The basic cause of soil erosion is the

unavoidable removal, during harvesting, of much of the vegetative cover, and the consequent exposure of bare soil; over-grazing of grassland by stock can also reduce the plant cover to a point where soil erosion is inevitable. Vegetation protects the soil from the impact of raindrops which break down soil aggregates into smaller and therefore more easily removable individual particles. It also combats wind erosion by reducing wind velocity and by trapping moving soil. J.L.M.L.

soil science (or *agrology*). The study of the soil, embracing PEDOLOGY and also *edaphology*, i.e. the study of the soil as the natural medium in which plants grow. The object of soil science is the UTILITARIAN one of improving plant production through a better understanding of plant/soil relationships. The science is concerned therefore with investigating the reasons for the varying fertility of soils so as to conserve and improve the productivity of land. J.L.M.L.

solar cell, see under CELL (2).

solid-state device. In ELECTRONIC circuits, a unit consisting principally of a piece of semiconducting material connected to ELECTRODES so that the element may be used to control the flow of current. Such devices include TRANSISTORS and THYRISTORS. Among their advantages over electronic and THERMIONIC valves is that they require no heating element. See also SEMICONDUCTOR; SOLID-STATE PHYSICS. E.R.L.

solid-state physics. A branch of PHYSICS, whose intense development in recent decades has been stimulated by the demands of TECHNOLOGY and by the understanding of solids made possible by QUANTUM MECHANICS. There are two main parts to the subject:
(1) The study of the crystal LATTICE on which the ATOMS are arranged: DEFECTS in the regularity of this lattice (especially DISLOCATIONS) are responsible for the brittleness, ductility, hardness, etc. of solids, while the random vibrations of atoms about the lattice positions (see PHONON) determine how well solids conduct heat or electricity.
(2) The study of the ELECTRONS in solids: instead of the ENERGY LEVELS charac-

teristic of ATOMIC PHYSICS, the electron states are grouped into 'energy bands', separated by 'energy gaps'. Solids whose most energetic electrons lie at the top of a band are *insulators,* except when the next energy gap is very narrow, in which case the solid is a SEMICONDUCTOR. If the electrons only half fill a band, the solid is a *metal* which conducts electricity to a degree determined by lattice vibrations (see also SUPERCONDUCTIVITY.)
In the HI-FI industry, the phrase 'solid state' is used honorifically to denote any apparatus containing TRANSISTORS. M.V.B.
Bibl: A. Holden, *The Nature of Solids* (N.Y., 1965).

solipsism. The theory that nothing really exists but me and my mental states. Not surprisingly, philosophers are more frequently accused of being solipsists than ready to admit to being of that opinion. If the ultimate source of all factual knowledge is taken to be INTROSPECTION or self-awareness, and if immediate experience is held to be the only thing that is directly known, solipsism is a consequence hard to avoid. The usual recourse for doing so, among philosophers committed to some version of the SENSE-DATUM theory, is the causal argument from the involuntary character of sense-experience proper, as contrasted with images. A taint of solipsism, even if it is dismissed as 'methodological', attaches to the alternative, PHENOMENALIST, way of reconciling the existence of an external world with the sense-datum theory. A.Q.

Sollers, Philippe (French novelist and critic, *b.* 1936), see under TEL QUEL.

Solow, Robert Merton (U.S. economist, *b.* 1924), see under TURNPIKE THEOREM.

Solzhenitsyn, Alexander (Russian novelist, *b.* 1918), see under FORCED LABOUR; GULAG; HELSINKI; SAMIZDAT.

soma. Name used (1) by August Weismann (1834–1914) for the 'ordinary' parts of the body in contrast to the GERM PLASM; (2) by Aldous Huxley for a harmless but generally elevating DRUG much used by the inhabitants of his BRAVE NEW WORLD (1932). P.M.

somatotonia, see under PERSONALITY TYPES.

Sombart, Werner (German sociologist, 1863–1941), see under BOURGEOIS.

son et lumière, see under MEDIA.

sonar (SOund NAvigation Ranging; also called *echo sounding*). A technique whereby short pulses of ULTRASOUND are emitted under water, and the time delay and nature of any echoes are interpreted to yield information about the presence and location of shoals of fish, submarines, the sea bed, etc. Sonar was developed because radio waves cannot be transmitted through water, so that RADAR cannot be used. See also ANIMAL SONAR. M.V.B.

sonic boom. The sound caused by the passage of a SHOCK WAVE from a supersonic aircraft. The shock takes the form of a cone whose tip is pulled along by the aircraft as it continually overtakes the sound waves it produces, in an extreme form of the DOPPLER EFFECT. The boom, which sounds more like a crack, is heard by an observer on the ground as the cone passes through him; this may occur many seconds after the aircraft has passed overhead. Sometimes two booms are heard, one from the nose and one from the tail. M.V.B.

Sontag, Susan (U.S. novelist and critic, *b.* 1933), see under MASS CULTURE; NEW NOVEL.

sorcery, see under WITCHCRAFT.

Sorel, Charles (French author, 1602–74), see under ANTI-NOVEL.

Sorel, Georges (French philosopher, 1847–1922), see under SYNDICALISM.

Soria y Mata, Arturo (Spanish architect and town-planner, 1844–1920), see under LINEAR PLANNING.

sound-law. In PHILOLOGY, a term referring to a hypothetical phonetic principle governing regular changes in sounds at different periods in a language's history. Such a hypothetical principle is derived from the analysis of uniform sets of correspondences operating between the sounds at these different periods. D.C.

Soupault, Philippe (French author, *b.* 1897), see under SURREALISM.

source criticism, see under HIGHER CRITICISM.

South Bank religion. The attempt of some English Christians in 1960 to modernize RELIGION in an urban social setting; so called because some of them were then working in the ANGLICAN diocese of Southwark, south of the river Thames. See also NEW THEOLOGY; SECULAR CHRISTIANITY. D.L.E.

Southern, Richard (British theatre historian, *b.* 1903), see under OPEN STAGE.

Soutine, Chaïm (French painter, 1894–1943), see under ÉCOLE DE PARIS.

sovereignty. A term used in much political and legal theory, sometimes at the cost of confusion, to characterize both (1) a modern nation-state and (2) a supreme legislature within a state. The sovereignty of a state is that area of conduct in which according to international law it is autonomous and not subject to legal control by other states or to obligations of international law. On the other hand a legislature within a state is said to be sovereign if there are no legal limits on its legislative competence. According to conventional legal theory the U.K. Parliament is such a sovereign legislature, whereas the U.S. Congress is not, since its legislative powers are legally limited by the Constitution. John Austin (see AUSTINIAN) attempted unsuccessfully to show that every legal system must, by the very definition of 'law', include a legislative sovereign, and that in countries where the ordinary supreme legislature is, as in the U.S.A., legally limited the sovereign is to be identified with those who have the power to change the constitution. H.L.A.H.

Soviets. Originally workers' councils which first emerged in Russia during the 1905 revolution. In 1917 they appeared again as Soviets of Workers' and Soldiers' Deputies. After General Kornilov's attempt to halt the Revolution (September 1917), many important Soviets switched allegiance and transformed a MENSHEVIK into a BOLSHEVIK majority. The Petrograd Soviet, led by Trotsky, established a Military Revolutionary Committee which became an instrument for the Bolshevik seizure of power under the slogan 'All Power to the Soviets'. Since then they have lost their autonomy, becoming the COMMUNIST Party's 'transmission belts to the masses' and eventually the principal INSTITUTIONS in the formal structure of power.

The Supreme Soviet, constitutionally the highest organ of state in the U.S.S.R., consists of two chambers: the Soviet of the Union and the Soviet of Nationalities. Its deputies are elected for five years (virtually unanimously, in one-candidate constituencies). All their decisions are also passed unanimously (by a show of hands).

L.L.

Bibl: M. Fainsod, *How Russia is Ruled* (London and Cambridge, Mass., rev. ed., 1963).

sovkhoz,, see under COLLECTIVIZATION.

Soyinka, Wole (Nigerian dramatist and poet, *b.* 1934), see under BLACK THEATRE.

space.
(1) In METEOROLOGY and ASTRONOMY, space is considered to be the region lying beyond the limit of the earth's atmosphere. M.L.
(2) In the arts, space has become an increasingly important concept with the development of ABSTRACT ART, notably as rationalized by the CONSTRUCTIVISTS. Among the terms' uses and abuses are (*a*) the space-stage, or *Raumbühne*, of Friedrich Kiesler and Karl Heinz Martin in the 1920s; (*b*) the 'spatio-dynamism' of Nicolas Schöffer's KINETIC works; (*c*) the 'spazialismo' manifesto of the Movimento Spaziale (Milan, 1954); (*d*) the French 'Espace' movement of 1951; and (*e*) the poetic 'spatialism' of Pierre Garnier, a freer form of CONCRETE POETRY. J.W.

space frames, see under STRUCTURE.

space perception. The process in vision whereby we locate the positions, sizes, and distances of objects in external space. Problems arise because any size of image in an eye – a retinal image – may be given by a small near object or by a corresponding larger and more distant object. So the size of retinal images is not sufficient to determine how large or how distant an object is, or appears. The two eyes work together to give *stereoscopic* depth; but this does not function for distant objects, because the 'base line' given by the eye separation is too short, only 2½ inches. The visual world seems to be scaled for size and distance by acceptance of typical features, such as perspective convergence and texture gradients, present in the retinal image as 'clues' to size and distance. This implies that the brain must carry out quite complicated computations to estimate scale. When the available 'clues' are not typical they may mislead PERCEPTION, to produce distortions of visual space, such as some of the well-known visual illusions in perspective drawings. See also GESTALT; VISUAL CLIFF. R.L.G.

space probe. A ROCKET equipped with instruments, which is sent into space to study RADIATION, COSMIC RAYS, etc. M.V.B.

space-stage, see under SPACE (2).

space-time. A mathematical CONSTRUCT, representing the arena of events. In NEWTONIAN MECHANICS, the three dimensions of space and the FOURTH DIMENSION of time can be clearly separated; this means that the distance separating two events, and the time interval between them, are independent of the motion of the FRAME OF REFERENCE from which they are studied.

But according to RELATIVITY this absolute separation between space and time cannot be made; *both* the time and the distance between events will vary with the motion of the observer. The only 'absolute' quantity, which can truly be said to belong to the events themselves independently of any observer, is the so-called 'interval', a mathematical analogue of distance in four-dimensional space-time. M.V.B.

Spalding, Douglas A. (U.S. zoologist), see under IMPRINTING.

span of control, see under MANAGEMENT STUDIES.

Spartacists. Anglicization of the *Spartakusbund*, a LEFT-wing REVOLUTIONARY splinter group (named after the leader of the Roman slaves' revolt of 73–71 B.C.), which broke away from the German SOCIAL DEMOCRATIC movement in 1917 under the leadership of Rosa Luxemburg and Karl Liebknecht. The Spartacists attacked the continuation of the war, supported the BOLSHEVIK revolution in Russia, and called for the overthrow of the government by direct action and a SOCIALIST revolution in Germany to be carried out by setting up workers' and soldiers' SOVIETS. In the period of revolutionary disorder that followed the abdication of the Kaiser (9 November 1918) the Spartacists (who reconstituted themselves as the Communist Party of Germany on 30 December) led a series of mass demonstrations against the compromise policy of Ebert's republican government and in January 1919 occupied a number of public buildings and newspaper offices in Berlin. They were driven out by force and their two leaders shot by army officers. The murder of Liebknecht and Rosa Luxemburg ensured them a place in COMMUNIST hagiography which criticism of Lenin's tactics and their dislike of large-scale organization and party discipline would certainly have denied them had they lived. Since 1971 the name has been revived by the Communist student organizations in West Germany and California.

D.C.W.

Bibl: J. P. Nettl, *Rosa Luxemburg* (2 vols., London and N.Y., 1966).

spatial diffusion, see under DIFFUSION (3).

spatialism, see under SPACE(2).

spatiodynamism, see under KINETIC ART.

Spearman, Charles Edward (British psychologist, 1863–1945), see under FACTOR ANALYSIS; MENTAL TESTING; PSYCHOMETRICS.

special education. As defined in Great Britain, EDUCATION provided to meet the special needs of pupils with marked disabilities of body or mind. Such provision is made under the 1944 Education Act and subsequent regulations, the children (from the age of two and upwards) being classified as blind, partially sighted, deaf, partially hearing, delicate (including diabetics, asthmatics, heart cases), educationally sub-normal (ESN), epileptic, maladjusted, physically handicapped, or speech-defective. Special education is provided in many forms: particular arrangements in ordinary schools, special classes, boarding-houses or hostels, hospitals, guidance clinics of many kinds (see COUNSELLING), special schools, and home-visiting. Training in the teaching of handicapped children is widely offered in colleges and Institutes of Education, usually in the form of one-year courses for teachers already possessing normal qualifications and school experience.

In the U.S.A. the classifications of special educational need are similar to those in Great Britain, although under the heading of the education of exceptional children the intellectually gifted are also included. Special education is administered at Federal, State, and local levels, funds for training and research coming from Federal sources, direct services to children from State and local ones.

W.A.C.S.

Bibl: S. Jackson, *Special Education in England and Wales* (London, 2nd ed., 1969); S. A. Kirk, *Educating Exceptional Children* (Boston, 2nd ed., 1971).

specialized agency. An international organization, normally part of UNO, charged with developing international action in a particular field where technical expertise is felt to be desirable. Examples are FAO, WHO, ILO, and the International Maritime Consultative Organization.

D.C.W.

species.

(1) The terminal element in the taxonomic hierarchy of BIOSYSTEMATICS. This, however, is a description rather than a definition. Definitions range from the ruthlessly pragmatic view that a species is anything regarded as such by a competent systematist, to the assertion that a species is essentially a 'point-cluster in n-dimensional character space'; both definitions are equally unhelpful. In any event the CONCEPT of species has been profoundly modified by POPULATION GENETICS. It is now universally agreed, however, that no species consists of identical individuals, so that no one individual

593

and no one genetic formula is representative of a species as a whole. A species is an actually or potentially inter-fertile assemblage of unlike individuals of which the genetically defining characteristics can only be represented by a 'GENE pool', the elements of which are variously recombined and reassorted in the process of sexual reproduction. In EVOLUTION a new species may arise by genetic transformation of an existing species leading to the establishment of a new and distinctive 'gene pool'; or, under unequal selective pressures, a single species may divide into two. The practical problem in systematics at a species level is that of actually attaching a particular name to a particular plant, animal, or museum specimen. Yet if the genetical view is correct the exact typological characterization of species in this way cannot be possible, though an attribution may be made of such a high degree of likelihood that it is virtually a certain one. The element of personal judgement in such decisions is only to be deplored when experts disagree. It follows from the genetic conception of species that some measure of reproductive isolation, whether by geographical or other means, is a necessary precondition for speciation, for otherwise the gene pool would not maintain its integrity.   P.M.

(2) In CHEMISTRY, a general term which may be used to describe an ELEMENT, MOLECULE, RADICAL, or ION. B.F.

specificity, see under PATTERN VARIABLES.

spectrographic analysis. A method of quantitative analysis involving a study of the light emitted when a substance vapourizes. It is based upon the fact that the light produced by each element, when split by a prism, yields a characteristic pattern of black lines crossing its spectrum. In practice a small sample of the substance to be analysed is caused to vapourize between graphite ELECTRODES, the light emitted being recorded, usually on a photographic plate. Since the method requires relatively small quantities of material it is particularly useful in ARCHAEOLOGY for analysing artifacts such as bronze implements and weapons. B.C.

spectrometry, mass, see MASS SPECTROMETRY.

spectroscopy. The analysis of electromagnetic RADIATION emitted by matter. By means of a spectroscope (simply a glass prism in the case of visible light) the different frequencies or colours in the radiation are spread out into a spectrum. Each frequency has been emitted as the result of transitions of ELECTRONS in the source from one ENERGY LEVEL to another. The distribution of energy levels is different for all substances and all states of temperature, pressure, etc., so that the intensities with which the various frequencies occur in the spectrum provide a precise and powerful method for determining the nature of the source. The spectra of the sun and stars consist of continuous coloured bands emitted by the dense hot core, crossed by thousands of sharp dark lines caused by absorption by ATOMS in the tenuous relatively cool atmosphere (see also ASTROPHYSICS).
    M.V.B.

speech synthesis. The simulation of human speech by artificial means. Early attempts used mechanical MODELS of the human vocal tract, air being pumped through while the model was manipulated in accordance with the hypothesized processes of articulation. More recently, electronically generated noise has been modified so as to simulate the resonances of the different parts of the vocal tract. It is now possible, using COMPUTERS, to produce synthesized speech which sounds extremely natural; but the process is laborious and expensive, and the possibilities of producing general-purpose artificial talking devices are still very distant. The main importance of speech synthesis is as a technique in experimental PHONETICS for evaluating hypotheses about the perceptual analysis of speech: if a particular acoustic feature is believed to be a significant determinant of a sound's recognizability, this can be tested by synthesizing the sound with the feature present in varying degrees, and rating the products for intelligibility and naturalness.   D.C.

speleology. The exploration and study of caves, especially the interconnected caverns formed by the dissolving action of ground water percolating through limestone strata. Understandably, perhaps, a rather neglected field of GEOLOGY.

J.L.M.L.

Spemann, Hans (German anatomist and cell physiologist, 1869–1941), see under ORGANIZER.

Spencer, Herbert (British philosopher and sociologist, 1820–1903), see under COMPARATIVE METHOD; EVOLUTIONISM; SOCIOLOGY.

Spender, Stephen (British poet, critic, and editor, *b*. 1909), see under CRITERION, THE; ENCOUNTER; GROUP THEATRE; HORIZON; NEW WRITING.

Spengler, Oswald (German author, 1880–1936), see under APOLLONIAN AND DIONYSIAN CULTURES; HISTORICISM.

Sperry, Roger Wolcott (U.S. neurobiologist, *b*. 1913), see under TWO HEMISPHERES.

sphere of influence. Geographical term denoting a territory over which a state is acknowledged to have preferential rights of a political or economic kind but over which it exercises little or no effective government. Spheres of influence may be declared unilaterally as in the MONROE DOCTRINE (1823), in which the U.S.A. stated its special interest in the Western hemisphere, or multilaterally as in the agreement over African territory between France, Germany, and Britain in the last quarter of the 19th century. One of the classic cases of bilateral agreement was the Anglo-Russian 1907 agreement dividing Persia into a northern Russian sphere, a southern British sphere, and a neutral sphere between.

P.H.

Bibl: N. J. G. Pounds, *Political Geography* (N.Y., 1963).

spin. Rotation of a body about an axis. Within PHYSICS the term usually refers to SUBATOMIC PARTICLES, in which case the magnitude and direction of spin are restricted by QUANTUM MECHANICS. The spin QUANTUM NUMBER may be either half-integral (in which case the particles are *fermions,* e.g. the ELECTRON with spin $\frac{1}{2}$) or integral (in which case they are *bosons,* e.g. the PHOTON with spin 1). See also QUANTUM STATISTICS.

M.V.B.

spin-off. A useful, usually unplanned, by-product of some activity. For instance, spin-off from the space exploration programme includes the improvement of domestic electronic equipment such as radios and television sets.

A.S.

Spingarn, Joe Elias (U.S. literary critic, 1875–1939), see under NEW CRITICISM.

Spinoza, Benedictus de (Dutch philosopher and theologian, 1632–77), see under ABSOLUTE, THE; AXIOMATICS; INTERNAL RELATIONS; METAPHYSICS; MONISM; PANTHEISM; RATIONALISM.

Spiralen Group, see under COBRA.

spline functions. Mathematical FUNCTIONS obtained by fitting together polynomials at junction-points called knots. They are used in ENGINEERING, and also in DATA ANALYSIS.

R.SI.

split-brain. In NEUROPSYCHOLOGY, a separation of the right and left lobes of the cerebral cortex effected by sectioning the great commissure (*corpus callosum*). In man, when such an operation is performed, the result is that the left cortex appears to be dominant and superior in processing information received in linguistic form, the right for dealing with SENSORY-MOTOR messages.

J.S.B.

Bibl: M. S. Gazzaniga, *The Bisected Brain* (N.Y., 1970).

Spoerri, Daniel (Swiss sculptor, *b*. 1930), see under COLLAGE; NOUVEAU RÉALISME.

sprawl. In GEOGRAPHY, a term usually applied to an irregularly spread or scattered group of buildings, whether similar or different in kind. *Urban sprawl* is a spread of residential areas, shopping centres, and small industries without any apparent plan.

M.L.

sprung rhythm. A term coined by Gerard Manley Hopkins (1844–89): 'One stress makes one foot, no matter how many or how few the syllables', and 'the feet are assumed to be equally long or strong and their seeming inequality is made up by pause or stressing'. Hopkins added, 'it is natural in Sprung Rhythm for the lines to be *rove over,* that is for the scanning of each line immediately to take up that of the one before', so that the stanza is to be scanned as a whole, from beginning to end, and for its full effect the verse should be read aloud. Thus, from 'The Wreck of the Deutschland' (1876):

Thou hast bóund bónes and véins in me, fástened me flésh,
And áfter it álmost únmade, whát with dréad,
   Thy dóing: and dóst thou tóuch me afrésh?

Hopkins noted that Sprung Rhythm can be found at times in old English alliterative verse, the Psalms, Elizabethan plays, and nursery rhymes, and 'it is the rhythm of common speech and of written prose, when rhythm is perceived in them'. It does much to account for the dramatic expressiveness of his own poetry.   D.J.E.

Spurgeon, Caroline (British literary critic, 1869–1942), see under NEW CRITICISM.

stabile. Term coined by the American sculptor Alexander Calder for his static, non-'mobile' works (see KINETIC ART). But a *teatro stabile* is the Italian version of a REPERTORY theatre (sense 2).   J.W.

stability analysis, see under EQUILIBRIUM (2).

stabilizers, see AUTOMATIC STABILIZERS.

stable population. If, in a given population and over a period of time, there is no change in the chance either of dying at a given age or of a woman giving birth at a given age, A. J. Lotka has shown that such a population will ultimately reach a state in which it will grow, or decline, at a fixed annual rate, and where the proportion of the population at each age will remain constant. Such a population is called a stable population. If the annual rate of growth were zero the population would be called a *stationary population*. Stable-population MODELS play an important part in the analysis of demographic data.   E.G.

   Bibl: G. W. Barclay, *Techniques of Population Analysis* (London and N.Y., 1958).

stage of development. In DEVELOPMENTAL PSYCHOLOGY, each of successive developmental periods, especially of INTELLIGENCE. Each stage is assumed to be characterized by a relatively stable structure. In PIAGETIAN theory, the sequence of stages is invariant, later stages incorporating and resynthesizing the structures of earlier stages. See also EDUCATION.   P.L.H.

stagflation. A term introduced by Ian MacLeod to mean a combination of INFLATION and industrial stagnation. If measures are taken to restrict demand while wages and other costs keep rising, inflation may continue unchecked while OUTPUT ceases to expand.   A.C.

Stakhanovism. A movement associated with the name of Alexei Stakhanov, a miner in the Ukraine who in 1935 devised a system of increasing his OUTPUT by the skilled organization of a group of subordinate workers. Others followed him in other industries, and the Stakhanovites became the official heroes of Soviet labour. They were, moreover, paid according to an incentive scheme which put them into the richest section of the community. For this and other reasons they tended to be unpopular with rank-and-file workers. The word has been applied, by extension, to anyone putting in particularly effective and energetic work in any field.   R.C.

Stalin, Josef Vissarionovich (name adopted by J. V. Dzugashvili, Soviet statesman, 1879–1953), see under BOLSHEVISM; COEXISTENCE, PEACEFUL; COMINFORM; COMINTERN; DÉTENTE; DIALECTICAL MATERIALISM; DISARMAMENT; EGALITARIANISM; FELLOW-TRAVELLER; FRANKFURT SCHOOL; KOLYMA; LEFT BOOK CLUB; LYSENKOISM; MARXISM-LENINISM; MENSHEVIKS; NEP; PAN-SLAVISM; PERMANENT REVOLUTION; PERSONALITY CULT; POLITBURO; POLYCENTRISM; POPULAR FRONT; POTSDAM; PRAVDA; PROLETARIAT; REVISIONISM; STALINISM; TEHERAN; THAW, THE; THERMIDOR; TITOISM; TROTSKYISM; UNPERSON; XENOPHOBIA; YALTA; YEZHOVSHCHINA.

Stalinism. The policies and methods associated with the rule of Joseph Stalin (1879–1953) and his followers in the Soviet Union. They included bureaucratic (see BUREAUCRACY) TERRORISM and the propagation for obligatory acceptance, both in Russia and in Eastern Europe, of fictions which were accepted as DOGMAS in the COMMUNIST movement while Stalin was alive.

Stalinism emerged when Stalin began to consolidate power during and after his struggle to succeed Lenin (d. January 1924). His policy of 'SOCIALISM in one country' meant in effect the enforced COLLECTIVIZATION of agriculture and forcible INDUSTRIALIZATION in the Soviet Union. In implementing these aims, Stalin expanded police controls over the population, using harsher and more ruthless means to achieve his ends. Purges (see YEZHOVSHCHINA), FORCED LABOUR camps, the use of SECRET POLICE (see KGB; MVD), and other TOTALITARIAN methods were combined with the PERSONALITY CULT of Stalin to enforce conformity and present a picture of a benevolent ruler protecting with infinite wisdom his happy and prosperous people from the hostile 'CAPITALIST encirclement'. All the resources of state propaganda, the monopoly of information, SOCIALIST REALISM in literature, the rewriting of history, etc., were used to inculcate this vision of reality internally and to propagate it externally. The victory of the Soviet Union in World War II and its post-war expansion were used to indicate the historical inevitability of its world-wide triumph.

The process of 'de-Stalinization' which began with Khrushchev's 'secret speech' to the 20th Party Congress in 1956 and the repudiation of 'the errors of the personality cult' weakened the Soviet Union's authority in the international Communist movement, strengthened the POLYCENTRIC tendencies in it, and raised the question of Stalinism's role in Soviet history. The attempts to dissociate Stalinism from MARXISM-LENINISM as the basis of ideological (see IDEOLOGY) legitimacy, both internally and externally, during the de-Stalinization period were minimized after the fall of Khrushchev. Later developments in the U.S.S.R. have underlined the durability of the Stalinist legacy and the continuous impact of his rule on Soviet INSTITUTIONS and on Communist orthodoxy.   L.L.

Bibl: B. Franklin (ed.), *The Essential Stalin* (Garden City, N.Y., 1972; London, 1973); A. Ulam, *Stalin* (N.Y., 1973; London, 1974); A. Solzhenitsyn, tr. T. P. Whitney, *The Gulag Archipelago* (London and N.Y., 1974–6); R. Hingley, *Joseph Stalin* (London, 1974).

standard deviation, see under VARIANCE.

standard of living. A CONCEPT often identified – wrongly – with the level of economic OUTPUT or income enjoyed by an individual or society. But the standard of living is a wider and vaguer concept and is more correctly defined to include items that add to WELFARE but do not enter into normal economic transactions. Such items could include the conditions of work, the home and external ENVIRONMENT, the amount of leisure time available, health, and so on. Since it would be difficult to obtain a wide measure of agreement on the items to be included, and impossible in the present state of knowledge to find objective means of *weighting* (see INDEX NUMBER) these items together according to the relative importance that society would attach to them, no objective overall index of the standard of living can be constructed. See also GNP.   W.B.

Stanford-Binet test, see under MENTAL RETARDATION.

Stanislavsky, Konstantin Sergeivich (Russian actor and producer, 1863–1938), see under HABIMAH; METHOD, THE; SOCIALIST REALISM.

Stark, Johannes (German physicist, 1874–1957), see under PHOTOCHEMISTRY.

Starr, Ringo (British musician, *b.* 1940), see under BEATLES, THE.

starred forms. In LINGUISTICS, a linguistic FORM (sense 1) preceded by an asterisk to indicate that it is either a historical reconstruction or a deviant utterance (see ACCEPTABILITY) in a language or IDIOLECT.   D.C.

states rights. In the U.S.A., the political doctrine that the several states of the Union should enjoy the exclusive exercise of powers not specifically granted to the Federal Government. The advocates of states rights oppose the steady extension of federal jurisdiction as undesirable and unconstitutional. In 1815 this was the cry of the New England states; but since the 1850s and the Civil War (which ended the claim that states could secede), the argument of states' rights has been characteristic of the southern states, especially since the CIVIL RIGHTS MOVEMENT secured the support of the law and of federal law enforcement agencies for DESEGREGATION by appeal to the Supreme Court in 1954.   D.C.W.

Bibl: C. J. Bloch, *States' Rights* (Atlanta, Georgia, 1958); W. Brooke Graves, *American Intergovernmental Relations* (N.Y., 1964).

statistical explanation, see under EXPLANATION.

statistical mechanics. A basic theory of PHYSICS developed in the 19th century by Boltzmann, Maxwell, and Willard Gibbs, in which the behaviour of matter in bulk is explained in terms of forces and collisions between vast numbers of constituent ATOMS and MOLECULES interacting according to the laws of MECHANICS. It would be impossibly complicated to compute the trajectories of all the atoms, and in any case their initial positions and velocities cannot be measured with sufficient precision. Therefore, the laws of mechanics are supplemented by the methods of PROBABILITY THEORY, in order to calculate AVERAGE values of dynamical QUANTITIES. For example, air pressure is calculated from the average MOMENTUM of air molecules continually striking solid surfaces, while temperature is calculated from the average KINETIC ENERGY of random molecular heat motion.

The behaviour of bulk matter is *irreversible* – it is easier to demolish a house than to build one – so that the future can always be distinguished from the past; this 'arrow of time' is expressed by the second law of THERMODYNAMICS, according to which ENTROPY always increases. But the laws of mechanics are *reversible* (see SYMMETRY), and any closed system must eventually return approximately to its original state, no matter how highly ordered this was. This apparent contradiction is resolved by statistical mechanics, within which the laws of thermodynamics can be shown to hold with overwhelming probability

rather than certainty. The chances of observing a spontaneous return to order are remote, because the average time between such returns far exceeds the age of the universe as at present estimated from COSMOLOGY. The implication that the direction of time is defined only for large-scale systems has caused considerable controversy, still not completely resolved.

Despite a century of intensive development, only relatively simple phenomena can be accurately described by statistical mechanics. A proper statistical theory of melting and boiling is still lacking, as is a detailed atomic explanation of the RHEOLOGY of bulk matter. M.V.B.

statistical regularity, or the 'law of averages' in PROBABILITY THEORY and STATISTICS, is correctly viewed as the *laws of large numbers* and other limit theorems in practical operation; if an event of probability p is observed repeatedly and the repetitions are independent, then the observed *frequency* – the number of times the event actually occurs divided by the number of times the experiment is repeated – becomes close to p as the number of repetitions becomes large. There is a common misconception that some form of mysterious compensatory mechanism involving memory is required to bring this convergence about; this sort of mistake is enshrined in the advice to air travellers always to carry a bomb – because the chance that there are *two* bombs on a plane is so small as to be negligible. (Such reasoning is perhaps an illegitimate extension of the doctrines of RESISTENTIALISM.) The gambler's run of good or bad luck is of a similar nature; there is no reason to believe that such runs occur with other than the frequency which probability theory predicts.   R.SI.

statistical test. A rule for deciding from the data whether to retain the initial (*null*) *hypothesis* or whether to reject it in favour of a specified *alternative hypothesis*. For example, if a coin were tossed 100 times and landed heads 93 times, most experimenters would regard this as good evidence for rejecting the null hypothesis that the coin was fair in favour of the alternative hypothesis that it was biased towards heads. The test in this case might take the form 'reject the null hypothesis if the number of heads is N or more, otherwise retain it', where N is fixed in advance by the experimenter. A large value of N would lead to a small probability of wrongly rejecting the null hypothesis but a large probability of wrongly retaining it; these are called *errors* of the *first* and *second kinds* respectively. Similarly a small value of N would give a small probability of an error of the second kind at the cost of a large probability of an error of the first kind. The probability of an error of the first kind is the *size* or *significance level* of the test, and 1 minus the probability of an error of the second kind is the *power* of the test. Usually the significance level is chosen in advance, typically as 5%, and a test is designed to give the largest possible power at that significance level – there is an extensive theory of the design of such tests, based on the work of Neyman and E. S. Pearson.   R.SI.

statistics. A word with different meanings for different people, and with different meanings in the singular and plural. To the layman a statistic is a piece of numerical information, often of a singularly useless variety; statistics are a multiplicity of these, often assembled with the intention of baffling or confusing him, or concealing something underhand – witness the familiar slander 'lies, damned lies, and statistics'. To the statistician such information is 'data', which he tends to view in the same jaundiced light as does the layman: statistics is the analysis of such data, usually with a probabilistic MODEL as a background (*classical statistics*; but see DATA ANALYSIS); 'statistic' is a technical term for a function of the data; and a statistician is a man who is prepared to estimate the probability that the sun will rise tomorrow in the light of its past performance. Early attempts at statistical reasoning can be traced back to classical antiquity, but it was the work of Karl Pearson and R. A. Fisher around the early years of the 20th century which first gave the subject coherence. Statistical theory has always been noted for deep and acrimonious divisions between various schools of thought, particularly for that between orthodox and BAYESIAN statisticians. In recent years DECISION THEORY has tended to unify the subject again by revealing that some of the differences are more apparent than real.

The basic idea of statistics is to regard some repeatable empirical phenomenon (the experiment; say, tossing a coin) as being governed by a probabilistic model not all of whose PARAMETERS are known (the probability of landing 'heads' is the unknown parameter in the coin-tossing experiment). The object of statistical analysis is to use the data obtained from repeated experimentation to provide information about the parameter values. This may take the form of hypothesis testing (STATISTICAL TEST) – failing to reject a null hypothesis (coin fair) or rejecting it in favour of an alternative hypothesis (coin biased); or of *point estimation* – giving a good guess (ESTIMATE) for the values of the parameters (say, probability of heads is 0.65); or of INTERVAL ESTIMATION – giving an interval for each parameter (confidence interval) (or a region for the set of parameters) in which the value of the parameter is likely to lie (say, $0.55 \leqslant$ probability of heads $\leqslant 0.75$); or – the Bayesian approach – of altering the weights (*prior distribution*) attached to the parameter values as degrees of belief so as to obtain a new system of weights (*posterior distribution*). Sometimes a statistic is used simply to summarize information about the data – for example the *sample mean* (see MEAN) of a set of observations may be used as a MEASURE OF LOCATION of the distribution, or a HISTOGRAM may be plotted to show it in more detail.   R.SI.

Bibl: D. Huff, *How to Lie with Statistics* (London, 1954); M. G. Kendall and A. Stuart, *The Advanced Theory of Statistics* (3 vols., London and N.Y., 1958–66); T. S. Ferguson, *Mathematical Statistics* (London and N.Y., 1967).

status. In SOCIOLOGY, a term used (1) neutrally, to designate a *position* in the SOCIAL STRUCTURE, such as the status of a father, or of a legislator (cf. ROLE, which defines the expectations of conduct assigned to a status); (2) to describe different social *evaluations* – in the form of rank, prestige, etc. – of a person or group. In pre-capitalist society, status was often fixed and recognized by distinctive dress; in modern society, status distinctions are marked by different LIFE STYLES. In pre-modern societies status was often accorded on the basis of birth; in contemporary industrial society prestige is usually associated with the rankings of OCCUPATIONS.

Status as a dimension of SOCIAL STRATIFICATION, rather than a motive, is a feature of the analytical sociology of Max Weber. Weber contrasted status with CLASS on the one hand and POWER on the other, and used the term *status groups* to designate certain segregated groups, e.g. CASTES or ethnic groups, who are marked off by distinct CRITERIA from other social groups in the society. Lenski has used the term *status inconsistency* to deal with the common phenomenon of individuals (e.g. blacks with high occupations) being ranked differently on different scales; and the theory of status inconsistency has been applied to discrepancies in political behaviour and RACE and class contact. The opposite of status inconsistency, *status consistency*, is sometimes called *status crystallization*. D.B.

Bibl: G. Lenski, *Power and Privilege* (London and N.Y., 1966); J. A. Jackson (ed.), *Social Stratification* (London, 1968).

status symbol. Any visible sign of a person's social STATUS (sense 2). It may indicate either affluence, as with a Rolls Royce car or lavish entertaining (see also CONSPICUOUS CONSUMPTION), or non-financial standing, as with the aristocrat's coat of arms, the don's gown, or the barrister's wig. Evidence from ANTHROPOLOGY refutes the widely held misconception that the status symbol is a product of modern CONSUMER SOCIETY. M.BA.

statutory instruments. In modern English ADMINISTRATIVE LAW, all those regulations and orders of a legislative character which are made by government departments and which, under the Statutory Instruments Act of 1946, must be published and laid before both Houses of Parliament before they come into operation. In some cases statutory instruments require for validity an affirmative resolution of one or both Houses; in other cases, they are valid unless annulled by an adverse resolution of either House. H.L.A.H.

Bibl: J. E. Kersell, *Parliamentary Supervision of Delegated Legislation* (London, 1960); C. K. Allen, *Law and Orders* (London, 3rd ed., 1965).

steady-state hypothesis. A theory proposed by Hoyle, Bondi, and Gold in 1948, in which the observed EXPANSION OF THE UNIVERSE is compensated by a continuous creation of matter throughout space, at a rate which need not exceed 10^{-43} kilograms per cubic metre per second – too low to be directly observable. The theory had the attractive feature of requiring neither an initial moment of creation nor a limit to extension of space; nevertheless, it has now been superseded by the rival BIG-BANG HYPOTHESIS, both as a result of the latest evidence from RADIO ASTRONOMY, which suggests that the distribution of GALAXIES is evolving rather than being in a steady state, and also because of the discovery of the COSMIC BACKGROUND RADIATION. See also COSMOLOGY. M.V.B.

Steer, Wilson (British painter, 1860–1942), see under NEW ENGLISH ART CLUB.

Steffens, Lincoln (U.S. journalist, 1866–1936), see under FELLOW-TRAVELLER.

Stein, Clarence (U.S. architect and town-planner, *b.* 1882), see under RADBURN LAYOUT.

Stein, Gertrude (U.S. novelist and poet, 1874–1946), see under CRITERION, THE; SYMBOLISM.

Stein, Lorenz von (German social critic, 1815–90), see under PROLETARIAT.

Steiner, Donald Frederick (U.S. biochemist and physician, *b.* 1930), see under INSULIN.

Steiner, Rudolf (German educationist and founder of anthroposophy, 1861–1925), see under ANTHROPOSOPHY; EURYTHMY; HERMETIC; STEINER SCHOOLS; THEOSOPHY.

Steiner schools. Schools based on the principles of Rudolf Steiner, the founder of ANTHROPOSOPHY. The first such school was founded by Steiner himself in 1919, in a cigarette factory in Stuttgart; it was closed by the Nazis and reopened in 1946. There are now over 70 Steiner schools throughout the world and about 120 special schools for handicapped children, who are understood and treated against a background of belief in *karma* or reincarnation. Children in Steiner schools do not learn reading or number work until after 7 years of age, and much emphasis is given to art, drama, EURYTHMY, and music. There is no STREAMING, and entry to a class is determined by chronological age.

W.A.C.S.

Bibl: L. F. Edmunds, *Rudolf Steiner Education* (London, rev. ed., 1962).

stenothermous, see under ZOOGEO-GRAPHY.

Stent, Günther Siegmund (German-U.S. molecular biologist, *b*. 1924), see under MOLECULAR BIOLOGY.

Stepanova, Varvara (Russian painter, 1894–1958), see under CONSTRUC-TIVISM.

stereo. In sound reproduction, a system whereby a programme is recorded simultaneously, on what are effectively two separate channels, by means of two microphones (A and B) forming with the sound source S an angle ASB, equal to the angle XLY formed, when the recording is played back, by the listener (L) and the two loudspeakers (X and Y) that are transmitting the recordings of microphones A and B respectively. In the gramophone-record type of storage it is usual to record both channels within the same groove in the surface by using two different 'walls' of the groove for the different recordings. A recent development (known as *four-way stereo* or *quadriphonic sound*) makes use of four microphone-recorders and plays back through four loudspeakers placed, for example, in the four corners of a room with the listener in the centre. The 'three-dimensional' effect of these types of reproduction adds greatly to the 'realism' experienced by the listener.

E.R.L.

stereochemistry. The study of shapes of MOLECULES or complex ionic SPECIES. Stereochemistry is particularly concerned with the immediate atomic environment of an ATOM or ION and is thus intimately connected with descriptions of chemical bonding (see BOND).

B.F.

stereoisomer, see under ISOMER.

stereoscopy. Term, deriving from the invention of the stereoscope by Sir Charles Wheatstone in 1838, for the artificially induced illusion of relief in visual PERCEPTION.

(1) In photography, two separate photographs, taken from slightly different points of view corresponding to the position of two human eyes, are mounted side by side on a card. When viewed through the angled prisms of the stereoscope, the two views blend into one, giving the appearance of depth or solidity. The process is very important in aerial photography (both for military and for survey purposes), and in medical photography.

(2) In the cinema, experimental stereoscopic processes have been demonstrated since the early 1930s, most successfully during the Festival of Britain in 1951, but were not developed commercially until 1952 when (for the same reason as the introduction of CINEMA-SCOPE) the first '3-D' feature film, *Bwana Devil,* was launched in a process called Natural Vision. Combining the use of polaroid glasses and twin projection of superimposed images, the process had a certain success as a novelty, but proved too cumbersome for general commercial dissemination, though it is still occasionally used. In Russia, a process involving a grille of copper wires (later, optical lenses) to split the images thrown by two projectors – thus dispensing with the need for special glasses – has been developed.

T.C.C.M.

Bibl: N. A. Valyus, tr. H. Asher, *Stereoscopy* (London and N.Y., 1966).

stereotype. An over-simplified mental image of (usually) some category of person, INSTITUTION, or event which is shared, in essential features, by large numbers of people. The categories may be broad (Jews, gentiles, white men, black men) or narrow (women's libbers, Daughters of the American Revolution), and a category may be the subject of two or more quite different stereotypes. Stereotypes are commonly, but not necessarily, accompanied by prejudice, i.e. by a favourable or unfavourable predisposition towards any member of the category in question.

O.S.

Sterling Area. A term long applied to a group of countries which have used sterling as a reserve currency, and as a trading currency for a substantial part of their transactions. From World War II onwards the grouping became a more formal one for EXCHANGE CONTROL purposes and was known as the *Scheduled Territories.* Since sterling *floated* (see under DEVALUATION) on 22 June 1972, only the U.K., the Channel Islands, the Isle of Man, the Republic of Ireland, and Gibraltar remain within this definition. The other countries are listed as the *Overseas Sterling Area,* to which exchange control rules different from the Scheduled Territories and other *non-scheduled territories* apply.

The special COMMONWEALTH trading relationships, which originally provided part of the purpose of the Sterling Area (although Sterling Area and Commonwealth were never coterminous), have been overtaken by the progressive liberalization and internationalization of world trade. Other privileges enjoyed by Sterling Area members, such as access to borrowing in the London CAPITAL market, have become less important as international capital transactions have moved increasingly into the Euro-dollar market (see EURO-MONEY). P.J.

Stern gang. A militant ZIONIST underground organization named after its founder Abraham Stern, which broke away from IRGUN ZVAI LEUMI after the latter's declaration in September 1939 of a truce vis-à-vis the British occupation of Palestine. The Stern gang was responsible for the assassination of the British Minister of State in the Middle East, Lord Moyne, in Cairo in 1944 and of the United Nations mediator, Count Folke Bernadotte, in Jerusalem in 1948. The gang was disbanded after Israeli police action in 1948. Stern himself had died in British captivity in 1942. D.C.W.

Sterne, Laurence (British novelist, 1713–68), see under ANTI-NOVEL; STREAM OF CONSCIOUSNESS.

steroids. A class of organic compounds which contain a characteristic group of four carbon rings (a hydrogenated cyclopentanophenanthrene carbon skeleton). A number of steroids are physiologically important, including cholesterol, cortisone, testosterone (male sex hormone), estrone (human estrogenic hormone), and progesterone (human pregnancy hormone). Oral contraceptives are steroids. B.F.

Steuart, Sir **James** (Scottish economist, 1712–80), see under POLITICAL ECONOMY.

Stevens, Wallace (U.S. poet, 1879–1955), see under HORIZON; IMAGISM; POETRY (CHICAGO).

Stevenson, Charles Leslie (U.S. philosopher, *b.* 1908), see under EMOTIVISM.

Stijl, De The name (1) of a Dutch magazine first published in June 1917; (2) of the group which founded it; (3) eventually, of a whole movement. The aim of the magazine was 'to make modern man aware of new ideas that have sprung up in the plastic arts', i.e. of a pure form of abstraction (see ABSTRACT ART) which was to be 'the direct expression of the universal' and which they simply labelled 'the style'. It found its clearest expression in the paintings of Piet Mondrian, who called his attempts to paint without reference to any objective reality *neo-plasticism,* and whose rectangular primary-coloured paintings had direct counterparts in the architecture and furniture of Gerrit Rietveld. The group's intellectual leader was Theo van Doesburg, architect, painter, poet, and critic, who visited the Weimar BAUHAUS and ensured the introduction there of *De Stijl* ideas. Shortly after his death, the influence of the movement began to decline. This Dutch contribution to modern art left, however, an international legacy of a purity and vividness in abstraction which has been paralleled but hardly equalled. See also INTERNATIONAL STYLE. M.BR.
Bibl: H. L. C. Jaffe, *De Stijl, 1917–1931* (London and Amsterdam, 1956).

stimulus. An event which excites a nerve impulse, either by direct action upon the sensory nerve fibre or, more usually, through a TRANSDUCER such as a sense organ. A uniform stimulus of unvarying intensity soon ceases to excite an impulse (see ADAPTATION). See also ALL-OR-NONE LAW; SUMMATION. P.M.

stochastic, see under ALEATORY.

stochastic decision tree analysis, see under RISK ANALYSIS.

stochastic problems, see under DYNAMIC PROGRAMMING.

stochastic process. In PROBABILITY THEORY, a system involving time-dependence. For example, suppose that a 'drunkard's walk' is defined by repeated tosses of a coin: when the coin lands heads, the drunkard takes a step forwards; when tails, backwards. This is a stochastic process of a particularly simple kind, in that its future behaviour depends only on its present state and not on the route by which that state was reached – the process has no memory; such a process is called a *Markov process.* The progress of an epidemic, the behaviour of the economy or an ECOSYSTEM, BROWNIAN MOTION, the flow of traffic, and the serving of a queue all represent complicated empirical phenomena for which stochastic processes provide MODELS. R.SI.

stock response. The reader's ready expectation that, for example, in verse 'June' will be followed by 'moon', 'dove' by 'love', and his predictable reaction to well-worn themes or situations. The term is used in connection with undemanding art which presents conventional subject-matter or appeals to fixed attitudes. 'Against these stock responses the artist's internal and external conflicts are fought, and with them the popular writer's triumphs are made' (I. A. Richards, *Principles of Literary Criticism,* 1924). Though seemingly a permanent phenomenon, stock responses are affected by fashion: the unhappy ending is now as conventional and looked-for as the happy ending, the ANTI-HERO as the hero. D.J.E.

Stockhausen, Karlheinz (German composer, *b.* 1928), see under ELECTRONIC MUSIC; SERIAL MUSIC.

stop-go. An alternation of government measures involving the periodic restriction and subsequent expansion of purchasing power and a consequent suspension and resumption of the growth of industrial output. The term came into current use in Britain about 1960 after a succession of BALANCE OF PAYMENTS crises and accompanying 'packages' of restrictive measures. 'Stop-go' is essentially a caricature of the vacillations of short-term demand management in implied contrast to an ideal policy of planned long-term expansion. A.C.

store. The most expensive part of a COMPUTER, where the information (both PROGRAM and data) is kept. The neutral term *store* is to be preferred to *memory* to avoid the danger of anthropomorphizing computers. There are many forms of store which differ widely in their cost and ACCESS TIME, and in the attempt to reconcile the requirements of speed, a large store, and tolerable cost, computers are generally made with several forms of store. These may include, in decreasing order of speed, (1) a few *registers* (store built from LOGIC units); (2) a few hundred WORDS of fast *working store* (sometimes called a *scratchpad store*) which may include some ASSOCIATIVE STORE; (3) a *main store,* generally on CORES; and (4) a *backing store* generally on DRUM, DISC, or MAGNETIC TAPE. Using these different levels of store to best advantage is one of the most difficult parts of PROGRAMMING. C.S.

Stouffer, Samuel Andrew (U.S. sociologist, 1900–1960), see under RELATIVE DEPRIVATION.

Strachey, James Beaumont (British psychiatrist, 1887–1967), see under BLOOMSBURY GROUP.

Strachey, John (British politician and author, 1901–63), see under LEFT BOOK CLUB.

Strachey, Lytton (British biographer and essayist, 1880–1932), see under BLOOMSBURY GROUP.

Stradonitz, see KEKULÉ VON STRADONITZ.

Stramm, August (German poet and dramatist, 1874–1915), see under STURM, DER.

strangeness. A property of some of the more exotic ELEMENTARY PARTICLES whose lifetime before decay is millions of times greater than expected. This must arise from some characteristic of their internal structure, corresponding to a 'strangeness QUANTUM NUMBER' which is zero for ordinary particles.   M.V.B.

Strasberg, Lee (Austrian-born U.S. theatre director, *b.* 1901), see under GROUP THEATRE; METHOD, THE.

Strasser, Gregor (German politician, 1892–1934), see under NIGHT OF THE LONG KNIVES.

Strategic Arms Limitation Talks, see SALT.

strategic capability. The war-making or reprisal capability of those states that possess long-range aircraft or MISSILES has become differentiated according to its technical characteristics. Thus *first-strike capability* characterizes a force which is sufficiently vulnerable (e.g. bombers on airfields) to be destroyed by an enemy strike and which therefore must be employed first in a *pre-emptive strike* if the possessor state is not to be disarmed; an example is the attack on Egyptian airfields by the Israeli Air Force on 5 June 1967. *Second-strike capability* characterizes a force capable, through a combination of RADAR early warning systems and missiles in underground silos or in submarines, of surviving a first strike in sufficient strength to inflict unacceptable damage on the adversary. *Counter-force capability* characterizes a strategic force capable of crippling the adversary's strategic military installations and troop concentrations while leaving a reserve for the destruction of his cities and industries; the U.S.A. is thought to have possessed such a capability in relation to the U.S.S.R. in the early 1960s, and both probably still possess it in relation to China. Its antithesis, *counter-value capability,* characterizes a force sufficient only to destroy or damage an adversary's cities and industries; the British and French nuclear forces are of this kind. See minimum DETERRENCE.   A.F.B.
Bibl: H. Kahn, *Thinking about the Unthinkable* (London and N.Y., 1962).

strategic studies. A widely used term first proposed in 1958 to the founders of the

Institute of that name in London by its first Director, Alastair Buchan, to connote the scholarly analysis of the role of military and PARA-MILITARY force in international relations. The field of strategic studies is considerably wider and more political in character than military or war studies and embraces not merely problems like defence and DETERRENCE but also ARMS CONTROL and the economic and social consequences of armaments, ARMS RACES, and DISARMAMENT. Though the central focus of the field is the reinforcement of international security or peace, 'security' has so many meanings (social security, internal security, national security, personal security, commercial securities, etc.) as to make it valueless as a descriptive term, while 'peace' or 'conflict' studies and research, as evolved in Scandinavia and elsewhere, are either based on behavioural rather than political assumptions or else largely concerned with one aspect of the field, namely disarmament.   A.F.B.
Bibl: H. Bull, 'Strategic Studies and its Critics' (*World Politics,* July 1968).

strategy. A term which, though often used (in contradistinction to 'tactics') to refer to the long-run objectives and plans of parties to military, political, and other conflicts, has been given a precise and distinct meaning in DECISION THEORY and the theory of GAMES, where it describes a whole set of plans to cover all contingencies, such as complete instructions for playing a game, or rules for deciding when to terminate a scientific experiment. A strategy may be thought of as the precise and detailed description of a method. An *optimal strategy* is one that maximizes an explicit mathematical FUNCTION. When several individuals act independently, the question arises whether they can pursue mutually consistent strategies (see NASH EQUILIBRIUM).   J.A.M.

stratification. The most obvious characteristic of sedimentary rocks is that they invariably occur as layers known as beds or strata. Each bed, which may be anything from less than a centimetre to over a metre thick, is of broadly uniform composition and represents a period of uniform conditions in the depositional ENVIRONMENT. The upper and lower surfaces of beds are known as *bedding* or *stratification* *planes.* The study of stratified rocks is termed STRATIGRAPHY. Bedding is a pervasive structure of sedimentary rocks which persists after deformation of the rock body. It is therefore a fundamental reference plane in TECTONICS.   J.L.M.L.

stratification, social, see SOCIAL STRATIFICATION.

stratificational grammar. A theory of GRAMMAR developed by S. M. Lamb in the 1960s, the name reflecting his choice of the term STRATUM to refer to the various interrelated LEVELS of linguistic structure recognized by the theory.   D.C.
   Bibl: S. M. Lamb, *Outline of Stratificational Grammar* (Washington, 1966).

stratigraphy. The principle used in GEOLOGY and ARCHAEOLOGY which states that a layer must be earlier than the one which *seals* it (i.e. which can be physically demonstrated to lie above it). Stratigraphy is the basis of all modern archaeological excavations. Most sites occupied for any period of time show a superimposition of layers, the careful observation of which provides the raw material for constructing a sequence. Particular attention is paid to the recognition of the surface from which any feature, e.g. a wall footing, post-hole, or pit, is cut, since depth alone is not a criterion by which the stratigraphic position of an artifact can be assessed. The position of an artifact or structure in a stratified sequence is referred to as its CONTEXT. A well-stratified site provides a relative chronology which can be calibrated by means of dated artifacts or absolute dating methods (e.g. RADIOCARBON). *Horizontal stratigraphy* is the linear development of a site whose focus gradually shifts. It is particularly appropriate to the study of cemeteries.   B.C.
   Bibl: C. O. Dunbar and J. Rodgers, *Principles of Stratigraphy* (N.Y., 1957).

stratosphere. Meteorological term for the upper layer of the earth's atmosphere lying immediately above the TROPOSPHERE. Its lower boundary varies from 7 or 8 km high above the poles to about 16 km at the equator, and it extends upward to a height of around 60 km above the ground. Despite its great thickness the stratosphere contains only one quarter of

the mass of the atmosphere, and about 10% of its water vapour. Very few clouds occur in the stratosphere but a major feature is the *mid-latitude jet streams,* very strong and highly localized westerly winds.   P.H.

Strauss, Richard (German composer, 1864–1949), see under PROGRAMME MUSIC; ROMANTICISM.

Stravinsky, Igor (Russian-born composer, 1882–1971), see under BITONALITY; CUBISM; JAZZ; NEO-CLASSICISM; POLYTONALITY; PROGRAMME MUSIC; SERIAL MUSIC.

Strawson, Peter Frederick (British philosopher, *b.* 1919), see under PRESUPPOSITION.

stream of consciousness. Phrase coined by William James in his *Principles of Psychology* (1890) to describe the ceaseless, chaotic, multi-levelled flow that characterizes human mental activity: 'let us call it the stream of thought, of CONSCIOUSNESS, or of subjective life.' Bergson's account of the mind (1889) is also much concerned with this, and was highly influential in the development of stream-of-consciousness fiction, which attempts, often by means of *interior monologue,* to capture the exact nature of this flow. Pre-Jamesian examples include Sterne's *Tristram Shandy* (1767) and Édouard Dujardin's *Les Lauriers sont coupés* (1887); modern exponents include James Joyce (Molly Bloom's interior monologue in *Ulysses*), Virginia Woolf, and the less intrinsically important Dorothy Richardson (*Pilgrimage,* 1916–57). Originally, as in Dujardin, the stream-of-consciousness technique was an extension of REALISM; it has since taken two forms. In one the author – e.g. Dorothy Richardson – merely attempts to mime or imitate mental activity (the extreme example is the German Arno Holz's *'Sekundenstil',* which tries to represent the passing of seconds). In its other, more fruitful form the author is aware that he can only *simulate* mental activity: he deliberately abandons realistic, descriptive techniques (though of course aiming at a deeper realism) in order to achieve his artful – and artistic – purpose. This form is fundamentally EXPRESSIONIST, although, as in Joyce, it may give the appearance of realism. Virginia Woolf hovers uncertainly between the two forms. Four main techniques of stream-of-consciousness fiction have been noted: soliloquy, omniscient narration of mental processes, and both indirect and direct interior monologue. The most sophisticated and revealing forms of stream-of-consciousness fiction are at present to be found in the works of Latin-Americans: João Guimarães Rosa, Miguel Asturias, Juan Rulfo, and others. M.S.-S.

Bibl: R. Humphrey, *Stream of Consciousness in the Modern Novel* (Berkeley, 1954); W. H. Sokel, *The Writer in Extremis* (Stanford, 1959).

streaming. British term (the U.S. equivalent being *tracking*) for a form of internal school organization in which children are grouped for teaching across the whole curriculum by some criterion such as age, ability, aptitude, intelligence, or a combination of two or more of these. Streaming, based principally on achievement in reading and arithmetic, starts in primary schools and, following the Hadow reports of 1926 and 1931 and the Norwood Report of 1943, extends into selective secondary education (see SECONDARY SCHOOLS). In the 1950s and 1960s the alternative pattern of classes of mixed abilities was widely recommended for primary schools and COMPREHENSIVE SCHOOLS in order to build up community sense and eliminate feelings of failure; the PLOWDEN REPORT (1967) also recommends 'unstreaming'. Research on the comparative merits of streaming and unstreaming is inconclusive, and much depends on the teacher. See also CHILD-CENTRED EDUCATION; SETTING. W.A.C.S.

Bibl: M. L. Goldberg, A. H. Passow, and J. Justman, *The Effects of Ability Grouping* (N.Y., 1966).

street furniture, see under TOWNSCAPE.

strict (or *absolute*) **liability.** In English law, as in that of most civilized countries, a person accused of a crime is generally not liable to conviction if he did not intend to do what the law forbids or know that he was doing it, and took reasonable care to avoid doing it. In · the case of some offences, however, e.g. breaches of law regarding adulteration of food or drugs and driving offences, most but not all of which carry minor penalties, a man may be liable to conviction without proof of such knowledge, intention, or lack of reasonable care. Such offences are known as offences of strict liability. H.L.A.H.

Bibl: G. L. Williams, *Criminal Law* (London, 2nd ed., 1961); A. R. N. Cross and P. A. Jones, *Introduction to Criminal Law* (London, 6th ed., 1968).

Strindberg, August (Swedish dramatist, 1849–1912), see under DEUTSCHES THEATER; EXPRESSIONISM; NATURALISM; SYMBOLISM; THÉÂTRE LIBRE.

Strong, Leonard Alfred George (British novelist, 1896–1958), see under FREE ASSOCIATION.

strong interaction. The strongest force known, which is an attraction acting over extremely short distances between NUCLEONS, and thus enabling the atomic NUCLEUS to resist the ELECTROSTATIC mutual repulsion of its PROTONS. Strong interactions are caused by the exchange of MESONS, and are about a million million times stronger than WEAK INTERACTIONS. M.V.B.

structural-functional theory (also known as *structural-functionalism*; to be distinguished from STRUCTURALISM). A mode of theorizing in SOCIOLOGY (developed from FUNCTIONALISM in social ANTHROPOLOGY) in which societies, or smaller units such as communities or organizations, are conceptualized as SYSTEMS, and the attempt is then made to explain particular features of their SOCIAL STRUCTURE in terms of their contribution – i.e. the function they fulfil – in maintaining the system as a viable entity. Thus RITUAL and ceremonial practices may be explained as serving to reinforce shared beliefs and values and to maintain solidarity among different groups within a society – even though this function may be quite unrecognized in the purposes of those engaging in ritual and ceremony. Structural-functional theory is thus able to treat SOCIAL ACTION from the standpoint of unintended as well as intended consequences. A major problem which it faces is that of specifying precise criteria for the viability of social systems, whether in the sense of their 'survival' or of their 'efficiency'. Structural-functional theory has also been criticized by exponents of CONFLICT THEORY for its neglect of the part played by *coercion* in organizing social activities and preserving social stability. See also PARSONIAN.   J.H.G.

Bibl: A. R. Radcliffe-Brown, *Structure and Function in Primitive Society* (London, 1952); N. J. Demerath and R. A. Peterson (eds.), *System, Change, and Conflict* (London and N.Y., 1967).

structural linguistics, see under LINGUISTICS.

structural psychology. A SCHOOL OF PSYCHOLOGY concerned with the systematic, experimental, elementaristic (see ELEMENTARISM) study of conscious experience. By analogy with CHEMISTRY's periodic table, the aim is to isolate and classify the elementary constituents of CONSCIOUSNESS without regard to their function.   I.M.L.H.

structural reform. The process of assisting parts of an agricultural industry which are uneconomic (because farms are small or badly laid out or suffer from other deficiencies) to become capable of providing acceptable living conditions. Among the reasons why farm incomes may be low compared with those in other sectors of the economy, or even in other parts of a country's agricultural industry, are the small size of farms, the farmers' lack of business and technical skills, and poor access roads and other elements of the INFRASTRUCTURE. Since they had too little to sell, measures to improve prices of farm products (see DEFICIENCY PAYMENTS) could not solve the problems of these farmers. Consequently various countries, including those in the EEC, have introduced measures designed to encourage the early retirement of farmers and the amalgamation and consolidation of farms.   K.E.H.

Bibl: Organization for Economic Cooperation and Development, *Structural Reform Measures in Agriculture* (Paris, 1972).

structural semantics, see under SEMANTICS.

structural unemployment, see under UNEMPLOYMENT.

structuralism.

(1) In LINGUISTICS, any approach to the analysis of language that pays explicit attention to the way in which linguistic features can be described in terms of STRUCTURES and systems. In the general, SAUSSURIAN sense, structuralist ideas enter into every school of linguistics. Structuralism does, however, have a more restricted definition, referring to the BLOOMFIELDIAN emphasis on the processes of segmenting and classifying the physical features of utterance (i.e. on what Chomsky later called SURFACE STRUCTURES), with little reference to the abstract, underlying structures (Chomsky's DEEP STRUCTURES) of language or their meaning. It is this emphasis which the CHOMSKYAN approach to language strongly attacked; for GENERATIVE linguists, accordingly, the term is often pejorative.   D.C.

(2) In the (other) SOCIAL SCIENCES (but see also SCHOOLS OF PSYCHOLOGY), a movement characterized by a preoccupation not simply with structures but with such structures as can be held to underlie and generate the phenomena that come under observation, or, to use the Chomskyan distinction mentioned in (1), with deep structures rather than with surface structures. The outstanding contributor in the social sciences is Claude Lévi-Strauss. For him a social structure is not a web of social relationships that may quickly be abstracted from concrete behaviour, but a MODEL. Further, any set of relationships making up a structure must be transformable by systematic change in the relationships. In his first major structuralist work, *Les Structures élémentaires de la parenté* (1949), Lévi-Strauss strove to demonstrate that the wide variety of kinship behaviour and INSTITUTIONS rests ultimately upon a principle of communication that is the driving force behind INCEST prohibitions and the exchange of women in marriage. In that study modes of action and modes of thought were treated together, but his later work on TOTEMISM and MYTH has concentrated upon modes of thought. Structures have, of course, to be devised for each body of material selected for study, but in the last analysis they are all referable to basic characteristics of the mind (apparently considered to operate on a binary principle); and it is perhaps this feature of structuralism that

STRUCTURE

distinguishes it most sharply from other movements in contemporary ANTHROPOLOGY. Like them, it starts from cultural variety, but unlike them it busies itself with the ultimate basis from which the variety is generated. See also EVOLUTION, SOCIAL AND CULTURAL; EXOGAMY; FUNCTIONALISM.   M.F.

Bibl: C. Lévi-Strauss, tr. C. Jacobson and B. G. Schoepf, *Structural Anthropology* (London and N.Y., 1963); J. Ehrmann (ed.), *Structuralism* (London and N.Y., 1970); R. Boudon, tr. M. Vaughan, *The Uses of Structuralism* (London, 1971); J. Piaget, tr. C. Maschler, *Structuralism* (N.Y., 1970; London, 1971).

structure.

(1) A word with a wide range of familiar meanings which has perhaps been overworked and even misused (as has *structured,* meaning often no more than 'organized') since the advent of STRUCTURALISM. Literally it is the basic framework, form, or outline of a material artifact: a building (see below), a vehicle, ship, aeroplane, chair, dress, etc.; objects with the same structure are said to be ISOMORPHIC. But it is also applied, by extension, to works of art and literature (a play, novel, symphony) and to elements of social organization (a political constitution or INSTITUTION, a system of EDUCATION). In nature all the distinctive forms of life, and in societies all the distinctive forms of association, have discernible structures which permit analysis in terms of their elements and the ways in which these operate together in the living whole. Whether in human artifacts, or in emergent natural and social forms, elements of structure are clearly and closely associated with their *functions*; hence the significance of STRUCTURAL-FUNCTIONAL THEORY in the NATURAL SCIENCES and SOCIAL SCIENCES. See also DIACHRONIC; MATHEMATICAL STRUCTURE; SOCIAL STRUCTURE; SUPERSTRUCTURE.   R.F.

Bibl: A. R. Radcliffe-Brown, *Structure and Function in Primitive Societies* (London, 1952).

(2) Specifically, in architecture, that part of a building which carries loads and resists stresses such as those caused by wind or ground movement. The exploitation of structure, and especially of its ability to span large spaces, to CANTILEVER, and to create expressive roof shapes, has been a major feature of 19th- and 20th-century architecture. Innovations have taken a number of specific forms.

The *frame,* characteristic of the CHICAGO SCHOOL, had a great liberating effect by separating the properties of enclosure and load-bearing previously assumed by a masonry wall. Steel or CONCRETE columns were able to support floors containing much lighter walls that served merely to separate spaces and act as weather barriers. Planning was also freed from the necessity to superimpose walls on each other.

Extremely thin, light roof construction became possible through the use of *curved concrete* forms, often curved in two dimensions, as in an eggshell. The best-known examples are by Maillart, Nervi, and Felix Candela in Mexico.

Folded plates are in a sense planar *shells* in which strength is achieved by the folding of surfaces. A familiar example is a corrugated roofing sheet. A complex form can be seen in the conference hall of the Unesco (see UNO) building in Paris (1953–7), designed by Nervi.

Space frames are created by joining a large number of struts to produce a lattice work in three dimensions. These lightweight roof or floor structures can span in two directions, and can be supported by irregularly spaced columns at wide intervals.

Tensile structures that do not have to resist buckling can be made smaller in cross-sectional area and thus lighter. Attempts have therefore been made to create roof membranes carried by cables in tension. Several such structures were built in Munich for the 1972 Olympic Games.

The tensile strength of steel has also been used in bridge construction to achieve wide spans in suspension structures as well as the strength that can be attained by a tube with intervening membranes, as in a bamboo stem, and which when rectangular in cross-section becomes a *box girder*. See also DYMAXION; PNEUMATIC STRUCTURES.   M.BR.

Bibl: E. Torroja, tr. J. J. and M. Polivka, *Philosophy of Structure* (Berkeley, 1958); F. Otto (ed.), tr. D. Ben-Yaakov and D. Pelz, *Tensile Structures* (3 vols., Cambridge, Mass., 1967–71).

Strunk, Oliver (U.S. musicologist, *b.* 1901), see under MUSICOLOGY.

Student Non-Violent Co-ordinating Committee, see under NEW LEFT.

Sturm, Der. A complex of Berlin cultural enterprises founded by Herwarth Walden around his magazine of that name (1910–32), which was the chief organ of German EXPRESSIONISM before 1914 and did much to introduce the ideas of the FUTURISTS, CUBISTS, and other innovators into Germany. There was a *Sturm* gallery (from 1912), *Sturm* readings featuring the near-phonetic poetry (see CONCRETE POETRY) of August Stramm, a *Sturm* theatre under Lothar Schreyer (later of the BAUHAUS), and even a *Sturm* march composed by the founder. After World War I the *Sturm* lost ground, its one important new recruit being Kurt Schwitters, whose energies went rather into MERZ.   J.W.

Styan, John Louis (British theatre critic, *b.* 1923), see under BLACK COMEDY.

stylistics. A branch of LINGUISTICS which studies the characteristics of situationally-distinctive uses of language (see REGISTER), with particular reference to literary language, and tries to establish principles capable of accounting for the particular choices made by individuals and social groups in their use of language. D.C.
Bibl: D. Crystal and D. Davy, *Investigating English Style* (London, 1969; Bloomington, 1970).

stylometry. A specialized branch of STYLISTICS: the methodical study of an author's chronology or development by analysing the proportions of parts of speech to one another in a particular work, his shifting preoccupations of thought or imagery, and other such factors. Such analyses are best made with the aid of COMPUTERS.   M.S.-S.

subatomic particle. Any PARTICLE smaller than an ATOM, i.e. the atomic NUCLEUS and the ELEMENTARY PARTICLES. M.V.B.

subconscious. A term of popular PSYCHOLOGY used to refer to those mental items and processes that are outside the range of an individual's awareness. Though frequently used as a synonym for unconscious, it is not equivalent to UNCONSCIOUS in FREUDIAN theory, primarily because it blurs the distinction between unconscious and PRECONSCIOUS. Moreover, though apt to be associated rather with the psychology of Jung (see JUNGIAN), it is not equivalent, either, to Jung's CONCEPT of the personal unconscious, since, in his theory, it is used to refer to the part, or aspect, of the personal unconscious which is closer to the COLLECTIVE UNCONSCIOUS, and not to those parts which are closer to CONSCIOUSNESS.
                   B.A.F.

subculture. A body of attitudes, values, beliefs, and behavioural habits, shared by the members of a particular group or stratum within a society, which has significant determining effects upon them as individuals, and is distinguishable from the commonly accepted CULTURE (or majority culture) held to be characteristic of the society as a whole. The slum-dwellers of a large city, for example, may have a subculture of their own, distinct from that held to be the governing culture of the whole city. Similarly, ethnic, regional, linguistic, and other groups may each have their distinctive subculture. With a common shared citizenship this raises difficult questions of responsibility, especially in the field of crime and punishment, and remains a concept much in debate. See also FOLK CULTURE; PLURALISM.   R.F.
Bibl: M. M. Gordon, 'The Concept of the Sub-Culture and its Application' (*Social Forces*, 26, 1947); J. Floud, 'Sociology and the Theory of Responsibility', in R. Fletcher (ed.), *The Science of Society and the Unity of Mankind* (London and N.Y., 1974).

subjective idealism, see under IDEALISM.

subjectivism. In ETHICS, the theory which holds that impersonally formulated VALUE-JUDGEMENTS, such as 'This is good' and 'That ought to be done', are in reality only statements about the likes and dislikes, desires and aversions of the speaker. More generally, any ethical theory which denies the ultimate resolubility in principle of disagreements about questions of value. More generally again, but on a somewhat different tack, any

609

theory which takes private experience to be the sole foundation of factual knowledge is subjectivist, even if it admits that objective knowledge can be derived from this subjective basis.   A.Q.

sublimation. In psychoanalytic theory (see PSYCHOANALYSIS), a FREUDIAN term for the gratification of instinctual impulses, usually sexual or aggressive in nature, through the substitution of socially acceptable behaviour for prohibited drives. See also DEFENCE MECHANISM; REPRESSION; SUPEREGO.   W.Z.

subliminal. Adjective applied to stimulation operating below the THRESHOLD (*limen*) of PERCEPTION. There is much concern that subliminally presented messages can alter attitudes, but this has not been borne out by research.   H.L.

submarine-launched ballistic missiles, see under MISSILES.

subnormal, see EDUCATIONALLY SUBNORMAL.

sub-optimization, see under SYSTEMS.

subsistence agriculture. Farming intended primarily to supply the food and clothing needs of the farmer and his dependants. Subsistence agriculture accounts for a substantial part of the agricultural industries of many low-income countries. The term is occasionally used in high-income countries to refer to the activities of those who run small farms, which would be uneconomic as business enterprises, largely for the satisfaction of having home-grown foodstuffs and the amenities of country life, while earning their living in other ways.   K.E.H.
Bibl: C. Clark and M. R. Haswell, *The Economics of Subsistence Agriculture* (N.Y., 3rd ed., 1968; London, 4th ed., 1970).

subsonic, see under MACH NUMBER.

substance. In PHILOSOPHY, either (1) a concrete individual thing, to which existence can be attributed in an unqualified way (everything else that exists being reducible to it; see REDUCTION), or (2, sometimes called *substratum*), that which, as distinct from the properties which a concrete thing may share with other things, confers its individuality on it. Substance in the first, Aristotelian, sense is a complex, composed of properties together with an individuating substratum or substance in the second sense. Many philosophers have held that there are no individuating substrata, and thus that a thing is no more than the collection of its properties. Mental substance, the soul or self, is often conceived as the substratum of the series of mental states that make up the biography of a person.   A.Q.
Bibl: see under INTUITIONISM.

substitution. It is a major theme of ECONOMICS that different goods and services can in varying degrees be substituted for one another. For example, a consumer may willingly substitute raspberries for strawberries in his weekly consumption. His *marginal rate of substitution* is the number of raspberries he will have to be given, per strawberry, if he is to be just willing to make the substitution; and a rational consumer will equate his marginal rate of substitution to the ratio of the market prices.
Two commodities that can very easily substitute for one another in consumption, or in production, are said to have a high *elasticity of substitution*. (See also ELASTICITY.) Typical propositions are that a shortage of oil will not seriously harm a country if oil has a high elasticity of substitution with other INPUTS (such as CAPITAL); or that capital accumulation will increase the share of wages and salaries in NATIONAL INCOME (as compared with property income) if capital equipment has low elasticity of substitution with labour. Neither proposition can be accepted without qualification. In any case, estimation of degrees of substitutability present serious statistical problems.   J.A.M.

substrate, see under ENZYMES.

substratum, see SUBSTANCE.

sub-system, see under SYSTEMS.

subtopia. A term first used by Ian Nairn in the *Architectural Review* to denote certain areas beyond or within suburbs, areas which were 'the world of universal low-density mess' and included such things as

'abandoned aerodromes, fake rusticity, wire fences, traffic roundabouts, gratuitous notice boards, car parks and Things in Fields'. Nairn's campaign aimed to emphasize the distinction between town and country and to preserve the characteristics of each. In its more extreme forms, however, it became an attack on any low-density building in SUBURBIA.
M.BR.
Bibl: I. Nairn, *Outrage* (London, 1955).

suburbanization. The development of the suburbs, outskirts, or urban fringe of a TOWN rather than the concentrated growth of the centre. J. Beaujeu-Garnier and G. Chabot have defined the French *banlieue* or urban fringe as the space under the jurisdiction of a town proclaimed by the 'ban' in the Middle Ages. For a long time these suburbs were limited to the immediate neighbourhood of the town, but the growth of towns and the development of COMMUNICATIONS in modern times has given a greater complexity to such a suburb, so that it is better described as an aureole round the town. Suburban life tends to become concentrated at points where communications are easiest. Such growth centres often use neighbouring villages and small towns as support. Jean Gottmann has defined such a suburbanized zone as that area round a town centre where less than 25% of the active population works on agriculture.
M.L.
Bibl: J. Beaujeu-Garnier and G. Chabot, tr. G. M. Yglesias and S. H. Beaver, *Urban Geography* (London and N.Y., 1967).

suburbia. At first a realization by the 19th-century middle class of the arcadian idyll through which the industrial city need only be used for work and shopping (see also GARDEN CITIES). Successive waves of SUBURBANIZATION dealt with progressively lower socio-economic groups and resulted in lower space standards, and thus the end of the idyll. Suburbs tended to be one-class communities, remote from places of work, and dedicated largely to the supposed interests of children. Their spread in continuous rings around all great cities was made possible by a new mobility but resulted in prolonged journeys to work (see COMMUTING), until recent relocation of offices and

factories in suburban localities has tried to reverse the trend.
M.BR.
Bibl: L. Mumford, *The City in History* (Harmondsworth and Baltimore, 1966).

subversion. The act of attempting to overthrow a state, government, or other political INSTITUTION by covert methods designed to destroy its internal cohesion, corrupt the loyalties of a significant section of its members, destroy confidence in its leaders' integrity, exploit internal dissensions, set one section against another, etc. Such activity is popularly associated with the under-cover work of COMMUNIST and ANARCHIST movements of the LEFT but the term is equally applicable to FIFTH-COLUMN actions on behalf of any type of political movement.
D.C.W.

Sudermann, Hermann (German dramatist and novelist, 1857–1928), see under DEUTSCHES THEATER.

Suez. Term used to denote the international crisis of October and November 1956 (see also HUNGARY) that followed the nationalization by Egypt of the Suez Canal and the other assets of the Suez Canal Company, the main part of whose shares were owned by the British Government and by French private shareholders. The British and French governments took advantage of an Israeli attack on Egypt, of which they had foreknowledge, to attempt a forcible occupation of the Canal zone. Their action attracted universal condemnation and was abandoned, in the face of a collapse of international confidence in sterling. The episode is taken to mark the last, unsuccessful, attempt by Britain and France to assert great-power STATUS independently of the two 'super-powers', the U.S.A. and the U.S.S.R.
D.C.W.
Bibl: H. Thomas, *The Suez Affair* (London and N.Y., 1967).

sufficient condition, see NECESSARY AND SUFFICIENT CONDITIONS.

suicide connection. Name given to a technique employed for the rapid reversal of the motion of very large electric motors; e.g., a 15,000-horsepower motor may be reversed from full speed forward to full speed reverse in three seconds. The problem is to neutralize very rapidly the

ENERGY stored in the magnetic FIELD within the motor, and to overcome the field's *inductance,* i.e. reluctance to have its value changed. It is solved by reconnecting the motor's field and armature circuits so that the motor becomes a *generator* and the whole of the vast KINETIC ENERGY of the rotating armature becomes converted to electrical energy which is fed to the field coils to cancel their stored magnetic energy. Thus the motor, as it were, turns the knife on itself and kills its own magnetic field. The technique is used chiefly in rolling mills, where repeated passage of the *billet* (bar of metal) through the rolls calls for very rapid reversal of the drive.   E.R.L.

Sukarno (Indonesian national leader, 1902–70), see under CHARISMA; CONFRONTATION.

Sukhovo-Kobylin, Alexander (Russian dramatist, 1817–1903), see under BIOMECHANICS.

Sullivan, Harry Stack (U.S. psychiatrist, 1892–1949), see under NEO-FREUDIAN.

Sullivan, Louis (U.S. architect, 1850–1924), see under ART NOUVEAU; CHICAGO SCHOOL; FUNCTIONALISM; ROMANTICISM.

summation. A STIMULUS below a certain THRESHOLD of intensity does not excite a NERVE IMPULSE. The repetition of subthreshold stimuli may, however, eventually end in the discharge of an impulse. The property to which repeated subthreshold stimuli owe their efficacy is known as *summation.* See also ALL-OR-NONE LAW.   P.M.

summer stock, see under REPERTORY.

summit diplomacy. Personal negotiations held face to face between heads of state or government of the major powers in the hope of resolving their mutual conflicts. The term originated with Winston Churchill's call for a 'parley at the summit' in his election speech of 15 February 1950. Originally it carried connotations of hostility to traditional diplomatic methods of negotiation as tending to enhance rather than reduce those failures in communication held by liberal idealists to be the point of origin of most international conflicts. After the failure of the Paris summit conference of May 1960, the device fell into disrepute in the West, and the term (sometimes in the form *summitry*) has been downgraded to describe any special meeting between heads of state or government of any power, however small or undistinguished.   D.C.W.

Bibl: K. Eubank, *The Summit Conferences, 1919–1960* (Norman, Oklahoma, 1966); D. C. Watt, 'Summits and Summitry Reconsidered' (*International Relations,* vol. 2, no. 8, 1963).

Sumner, William Graham (U.S. sociologist, 1840–1910), see under ETHNOCENTRISM; FOLKWAYS.

Sun Yat-sen (Chinese revolutionary leader, 1866–1925), see under KUOMINTANG.

Suñer, Ramon Serrano, see SERRANO SUÑER.

superblock, see under RADBURN LAYOUT.

superconductivity. The complete disappearance of electrical resistance observed (first by Onnes in 1911) when certain materials are cooled below a certain *transition temperature* (generally a few degrees above ABSOLUTE ZERO). An electric current set up in a superconducting circuit will persist undiminished for years without requiring a CELL to drive it around. These 'persistent currents' may be employed as memory elements in COMPUTERS, while on a much larger scale their magnetic FIELDS may power rapid-transit vehicles between cities, levitated above superconducting track. The transition to and from the normally-conducting state is sudden, and easily induced by changes of temperature or magnetic field; this has led to 'superconducting switches', applicable to large complex systems like computers where economy of space is important. In these technological applications, promise has so far outstripped performance.   M.V.B.

Bibl: see under CRYOGENICS.

superego. In psychoanalytic theory (see PSYCHOANALYSIS), a FREUDIAN term for that part of the structure of the mind which is concerned with controlling exci-

SUPREMATISM

tation from the ID and the activity of the EGO. This control is largely UNCONSCIOUS, but manifests itself in CONSCIOUSNESS in the pronouncements of conscience and feelings such as guilt and shame. The superego is developed in the child through subtle and complex identifications with the parents, and by introjecting them as controlling or guiding models, with their corresponding moral attitudes. B.A.F.

supernova. An exploding star, which may be millions of times brighter than the sun. It is thought that the contraction of a RED GIANT due to the GRAVITATION of its MASS may cause nuclear FUSION reactions which accelerate the contraction, thus producing a catastrophic collapse and the emission of vast amounts of ENERGY. With the naked eye only two supernovae have been observed in the past thousand years, but with the aid of telescopes many have been seen in other GALAXIES. See also DWARF STAR. M.V.B.

supersonic, see under MACH NUMBER.

superstructure. According to Marx and Engels's theory of HISTORICAL MATERIALISM, the primary reality in the world is matter and its quantitative combinations; the qualitative characteristics of differing natural forms are secondary, emerging from the nature and changes of such combinations. In history, the material STRUCTURE (basis) of any society (its economic system; its productive forces – including its socio-economic CLASSES) is the primary reality, and on this rests a qualitative *superstructure* of INSTITUTIONS. This superstructure has two sides, or perhaps layers. First, there are the legal and institutional forms of the social system, the State, the machinery of law, government, and official power; second, there is the IDEOLOGY of the system, the body of ideas and beliefs – moral, political, religious, and philosophical – which serve to ratify the society's institutional arrangements, particularly its property system or mode of distributing the fruits of the productive process. Marx's view is that the predominant direction of causal influence is from base to superstructure: major historical change begins in the economic base and leads to a more or less revolutionary transformation of the superstructure.
R.F.; A.Q.

Bibl: K. Marx, Preface to *A Contribution to the Critique of Political Economy,* in *Karl Marx: Selected Works* (London and N.Y., 1968).

supply and demand. The usual term for the MARKET forces governing prices in the absence of administrative control and, through prices, OUTPUT and the distribution of income. These forces make themselves felt through the price mechanism as responses in the quantities offered for sale (supply) or the quantities that consumers are prepared to buy (demand) when the market price changes. Normally the responses are equilibrating since a rise in price tends to enlarge the supply and reduce the demand, and *vice versa* (the ECONOMIC LAW of supply and demand); but they may at times be disequilibrating (for example, if the change in price excites expectations of a further change in the same direction). Emphasis on supply and demand (as a kind of 'hidden hand') implies, not that there should be no interference with the price mechanism, but that control dampens market reactions and risks perpetuating a shortage or surplus. The more any form of economic organization relies on market forces, the more freedom it must allow to supply and demand to respond to changes in price.
A.C.

suprematism. A form of more or less geometric ABSTRACT ART propounded by the Russian ex-CUBIST Kasimir Malevich (1878–1935) in a manifesto of 1915 and exemplified in his classic painting of a white square on a white background (now in the Museum of Modern Art, New York). Though it influenced Lissitzky, Rodchenko, and other CONSTRUCTIVISTS, his movement was virtually stifled by their campaign against pure art and easel painting, only to be revived at the BAUHAUS (which published his book *The Non-Objective World*) and again in the 1960s, when there were exhibitions of his work at Stockholm and Amsterdam. In his own country it is still held to be FORMALISM, and accordingly unacceptable. J.W.
Bibl: K. S. Malevich, tr. X. Glowacki-Prus and A. McMillin, ed. T. Andersen, *Essays on Art* (London and Chester Springs, Pa., 1969).

surface structure, see under DEEP STRUC-
TURE.

surfactant (or *surface-active agent*). A
substance (e.g. a DETERGENT) which
accumulates at a surface and makes it
easier for the surface to spread. This
lowering of the surface tension is used
to encourage the 'wetting' of a material,
and surfactants are also used to assist
FLOTATION PROCESSES.   B.F.

Surrealism. French literary movement
evolving from the Paris wing of DADA during 1920–23, thereafter establishing itself
also in the visual arts, theatre, and cinema,
to become the last (to date) of this century's great international modern currents. Though the name had been coined
in 1917 by Guillaume Apollinaire, the
true spiritual ancestors of the movement
were Rimbaud, the newly rediscovered
poet Lautréamont, the German and other
late-18th-century ROMANTICS (including
de Sade), and the SYMBOLISTS. Its
animator was the poet André Breton, who
in 1919 founded the review *Littérature*
with his friends Louis Aragon and
Philippe Soupault, joined later that year
by Paul Éluard, and there published his
first experiments in *automatic writing*: a
random stream of words coming from that
SUBCONSCIOUS which the movement now
deliberately set out to explore. Already
aware of the manifestoes and activities of
Zurich Dada, as well as Tzara's poems, in
the winter of 1919–20 Breton joined
forces with Picabia and Tzara himself to
create a comparable succession of Parisian
shocks and scandals, whose aggressive,
continually newsworthy tactics thenceforward became an integral part of his
movement. In 1924, with Dada outside
France effectively dead and his new allies
discarded, Breton and his friends formally
constituted the Surrealist group. Its
manifesto, proclaiming the inferiority of
REALISM to 'psychic automatism' and
'previously neglected forms of association' of a magical, irrational, hallucinatory
sort, appeared that October; its new,
politically-tinged review *La Révolution
Surréaliste* two months later.

Though visual art was neglected in the
manifesto and its place at first far from
clear, a distinctive Surrealist art gradually
developed. Its main model was the
METAPHYSICAL PAINTING of de Chirico,

with its disquietening perspectives and
poeticizing of the banal, but the more
Dadaist work of Arp, Ernst, Duchamp,
and Picabia also contributed and some
attempt was made to annex Picasso and
Paul Klee. In 1923 André Masson began
to make 'automatic drawings' (or largely
random doodles), influencing the light-
hearted BIOMORPHIC art of Joan Miró
who, with Arp, represented the more
ABSTRACT wing of the movement. But the
surreal poetry of de Chirico's pictures –
a blend of strikingly dead subject-matter,
at once familiar and improbable, with a
smoothly academic technique – was not
developed further until the emergence,
during the second half of the 1920s, of
such artists as Yves Tanguy, the Belgians
René Magritte and Paul Delvaux, and
finally the Spaniard Salvador Dali, who
settled in Paris at the end of 1929. Basing
himself on a 'paranoiac-critical method'
(delirium tempered by a Meissonier-like
meticulousness), Dali depicted soft
watches, decomposing human limbs, and
other glutinously biomorphic props lost in
endless arid landscapes. By a mixture of
technical skill and brilliant self-projection
he became, for the public of the next two
decades, the quintessential surrealist.

As a literary movement, Surrealism
spread mainly to those areas where
French cultural influence was strong, e.g.
Latin America, the Middle East, Spain,
and Eastern Europe, though it had its followers (such as David Gascoyne) in England, while there was an important group
in pre-1939 Czechoslovakia. As a political
force, dedicated to a concept of REVOLU-
TION that became increasingly TROTSKY-
IST, it was always negligible, its pretensions, which were largely those of Breton
himself, leading only to disagreements
(hence the secession of Aragon and
Éluard in 1932 and 1938 respectively)
and mystification. In the visual field, however, as also in Antonin Artaud's
THEATRE OF CRUELTY and Luis Buñuel's
films, it had a world-wide impact, particularly as a result of the London Surrealist
Exhibition of June 1936, of Dali's
window-dressing and HAPPENINGS in New
York of 1939, of the posters of A. M. Cassandre and other epigones, and finally of
the arrival in the U.S.A. of Breton, Ernst,
Masson, Tanguy, and other refugees from
German-occupied France. Gimmicks

apart – and certainly it had these – Surrealism acted throughout the second quarter of this century as a universally intelligible plea for a revival of the imagination, based on the UNCONSCIOUS as revealed by PSYCHOANALYSIS, together with a new emphasis on magic, accident, irrationality, symbols, and dreams. Not the least of its achievements was that it led to a major revaluation of comparable romantic movements in the past.   J.W.

Bibl: *Minotaure* (Paris, 1933–9); A. Breton, tr. D. Gascoyne, *What Is Surrealism?* (London, 1936); M. Nadeau, tr. R. Howard, *The History of Surrealism* (N.Y., 1965; London, 1968); W. S. Rubin, *Dada, Surrealism and their Heritage* (N.Y., 1968).

surtax. A tax additional to income tax imposed prior to April 1973 in the U.K. on those with personal incomes in excess of a certain figure. Income tax and surtax have now been replaced by UNIFIED TAX.
                                                     J.F.C.

Survage, Leopold (Russian-French painter, 1879–1968), see under KNAVE OF DIAMONDS.

survey. A method for estimating characteristics of a population by analysis of a SAMPLE, whose members are so selected that the techniques of STATISTICS may be employed to assess the accuracy with which inferences may be made from sample to population. Its aim is not perfect precision but the control and estimation of random error (see ERROR ANALYSIS). Its preferred techniques of investigation are interviewing, the postal questionnaire, and observation. It contrasts with other methods of empirical social enquiry such as PARTICIPANT OBSERVATION and the case study in that it typically uses more rigidly standardized procedures for eliciting information, and seeks to minimize the exercise of judgement in the recording of responses. A survey is distinguished from an enumeration or registration by the fact that a respondent or interviewee participates in a representative capacity. The method is at its best in eliciting information by questions which the informant regards as significant but not intrusive, but it can be misleading when it involves assessment of matters remote from his present concerns.

Survey analysis is regarded with suspicion by some because its complex techniques are often unsustained by adequate data, because analyses may be undertaken to give scientific legitimation to a preformed policy or IDEOLOGY, and because the mass MEDIA have low standards of reporting both the technical details and the institutional affiliations of survey enquiries. Nevertheless it remains an indispensable means for investigating the degree of VARIANCE of a characteristic, and the extent to which characteristics co-vary. A non-trivial general proposition about a population can, in strict logic, be established or refuted only by analysis of data which represent that population to a known degree of approximation.   K.H.

Bibl: C. A. Moser and G. Kalton, *Survey Methods in Social Investigation* (London and N.Y., 2nd ed., 1971).

survival of the fittest, see under DARWINISM.

survival value. The degree to which any qualification contributes to an organism's survival and the perpetuation of its kind.
                                                     P.M.

Svedberg, Theodor (Swedish chemist, 1884–1971), see under SEDIMENTATION.

swami. In HINDUISM, a formal title given to a specially honoured spiritual teacher. GURU is a more informal term.   D.L.E.

Swedenborg, Emanuel (Swedish mystic and visionary, 1688–1752), see under SYMBOLISM.

sweet. In JAZZ, a more or less derogatory term used to point the contrast between authentic jazz orchestras like those of Duke Ellington and Count Basie, and the frankly commercial or 'sweet' dance-bands which catered for massed ranks of customers. The epitome of the sweet orchestra was Guy Lombardo and his Royal Canadians, who displayed consummate technical skill in producing saccharine effects. The most popular orchestra which leant heavily on sweet effects was Glenn Miller's.   B.G.

Swinburne, Algernon Charles (British poet, 1837–1909), see under DECADENCE.

swing. In musical contexts, a term used in three quite different ways, as verb, noun, and adjective, the noun being unconnected with the other two. To swing means to play with that degree of rhythmic subtlety and animation which renders the performance vital and exciting; hence to say that somebody swings is the highest praise. Similarly, 'swing music' is music played by a musician with the talent to bring his music alive.

But 'swing', as a noun, means the type of music which became popular in the middle and later 1930s, and is therefore a term with very definite historical and stylistic CONNOTATIONS. Swing was the name given to the phenomenon of the period between 1934 and 1942 (see BIG BAND) when large orchestras played across the American ballroom circuits to hysterical acclaim. To differentiate this type of music from the tougher, more direct small-group music which preceded it, and has always been called JAZZ, people gave the 'swing' label to music like that of Tommy Dorsey and Artie Shaw. The archetypal swing figure was the clarinettist Benny Goodman, who graduated from the CHICAGO small group to become the 'King of Swing'.   B.G.

Bibl: A. Shaw, *The Trouble with Cinderella* (N.Y., 1952; London, 1955); B. Goodman and I. Kolodin, *The Kingdom of Swing* (N.Y., 1961).

Sydney-Turner, Saxon (British civil servant, 1880–1962), see under BLOOMS-BURY GROUP.

syllabics (or *syllabic verse*). Names given to a type of verse, written in the late 1950s and early 1960s, which was based simply on syllable-count (the number of syllables in a line, irrespective of their duration or accentual value). The verses in question (by, for example, George Macbeth) were mostly crude or flat or both; but serious experimentation may well prove fruitful. A fairly cogent if incomplete recent discussion, by a practising poet, occurs in Roy Fuller's *Owls and Artificers*. M.S.-S.

syllogism. In LOGIC, a deductive argument in which a *conclusion* is derived from two *premises* and in which each of the three PROPOSITIONS asserts or denies that all or some things of a certain kind are also of another kind. Each of the terms, or kinds,

mentioned in the conclusion occurs in only one premise, together with a term (the *middle term*) which occurs in both premises but not in the conclusion. Thus in the syllogism 'All men are mortal, all Greeks are men, so all Greeks are mortal', 'men' is the middle term; 'mortal', the second term in the conclusion, is the *major term,* and the premise in which it occurs the *major premise*; and 'Greeks', the first term of the conclusion, is the *minor term,* and its premise the *minor premise.* The order of terms in the premises can be reversed, jointly or severally. This yields four patterns of term-arrangement or 'figures'. Each of the three propositions may be of any of the four recognized logical forms: all A are B, no A are B, some A are B, some A are not B. There are thus 256 possible syllogistic forms: 64 possible form-combinations multiplied by the four figures. Of these only 19 are valid. The theory of the syllogism was developed to a high degree of systematic completeness by Aristotle.   A.Q.

symbiosis.
(1) The original meaning: in BIOLOGY, the state of affairs in which two often very dissimilar organisms live together in mutual dependence and for mutual benefit, each making up for the other's shortcomings. Thus a lichen is a symbiotic union of fungus and single-celled green alga. The compound organism, unlike a fungus, is AUTOTROPHIC. Symbiosis may have played an important part in EVOLUTION. Thus mitochondria (see CYTOLOGY) may have originated as symbiotic bacteria (see BACTERIOLOGY), and chloroplasts may have originated in the same way by union of non-CHLOROPHYLL-containing CELLS with single-celled green algae. A phenomenon which may be regarded as a step on the road towards full symbiosis is *commensalism,* in which two organisms 'dine at the same table': thus a sea anemone may grow on the shell which houses a hermit crab, and various little crustacea live within the giant respiratory chambers of, for example, sea squirt. The field of study dealing with symbiosis is sometimes known as *symbiotics*.   P.M.
(2) In SOCIOLOGY, relations of mutual dependence between different groups within a community are described as *symbiotic* when the groups are unlike and the relations complementary; as *commensal*

when they are like and the relations are supplementary. A.L.C.B.

symbolic interaction. The aspect of human behaviour on which G. H. Mead based his ROLE THEORY. Mead argued that what distinguishes man from the other animals is the enormous number of symbolic or conventional meanings which his highly complex NERVOUS SYSTEM and the faculty of language enable him to store in his memory and to express by particular words and actions. These agreed meanings are learned through the process of symbolic interaction, i.e. of seeing yourself as you are seen by others, which is a necessary condition of playing roles; thus as a child you learn the role of bus-passenger-at-a-request-stop by taking the role of the driver, i.e. by imagining him seeing your raised hand, realizing you are trying to attract his attention, and stopping. This account of the learning process is extremely vulnerable to criticism from a SKINNERIAN or BEHAVIOURIST standpoint; while Mead's insistence that the self is merely the sum of the social roles an individual plays can be taxed with failing to take into account GENETIC or PERSONALITY factors. See also CHICAGO SCHOOL (1). M.BA.
Bibl: A. Strauss (ed.), *The Social Psychology of G. H. Mead* (London and Chicago, rev. ed., 1964).

symbolic logic, see MATHEMATICAL LOGIC.

Symbolism. A general literary term and technique; but, specifically, the name of a central late-19th-century movement in the arts which marks the turn from ROMANTICISM to MODERNISM. Historically there are many Symbolist movements and tendencies, but Romanticism opened new possibilities by attaching special value to the imagination, the seer-poet, and the poetic path toward a transcendent world (Blake, Shelley, Poe). France, the 1850s, and Baudelaire form the starting-point for fresh developments: the matching of the Swedenborg-type theory of 'correspondences' (connections within the visible, or between the visible and invisible, worlds), with a prime role for the hyper-aesthetic imagination of the poet, who digests the 'storehouse of images and signs' in the visible world and relates them to create 'a new world, the sensation of newness'. Language itself had a transcendent content: thus Baudelaire's sonnet on the vowels. In 1886, Jean Moréas held that Symbolism had replaced all prior movements, and asserted the TRANSCENDENCE of art. In Rimbaud, Verlaine, Gautier, Nerval, Mallarmé, and Valéry, these ideas evolve into complex interplays of a subjective, magical poetic vision and the idea of a timeless, epiphanic image (see EPIPHANY) which art pursues and releases by its rhythmic, metaphoric, or linguistic action. As in Romanticism, the poet risks his own senses and experience for occult discovery through the imagination; Valéry emphasizes his special 'psychophysiology', Yeats his 'visions'. However, Symbolism emphasized much more than Romanticism the need to *create* form; a high premium is set on the fictionalizing act itself; linguistic mechanisms are stressed; technique becomes an end in itself; the idea of the 'supreme fiction' emerges. The world is seen less as an imaginative power than as a bundle of fragments; when the notion of cultural, historical, and linguistic crisis is added, this leads the way to much 20th-century modernist thought.
Hence the 'Symbolist movement' was particularly concentrated in the transitional 1890s: in Paris, with the Mallarmé circle, Huysmans, and Valéry; in Britain, with Yeats, Wilde, Symons; not much later in Germany (Stefan George), Austria (Rilke), and Russia (Bely, Blok, etc.). Though strongly focused on the SYNAESTHESIA of poetry, it stressed the relation of all art-forms. It is evident in fiction (late James, Joyce, Proust), drama (Strindberg, Maeterlinck), music (Debussy, Scriabin), painting (Redon, Gauguin), and dance. Edmund Wilson rightly sees Symbolism coming through into familiar modernism; much early EXPRESSIONISM is really Symbolism (Trakl, Schönberg, Kandinsky). Gradually the transcendent element in Symbolism, its devotion to penetrating the veil beyond time, fades: IMAGISM and SURREALISM are distinguishable from it because the neo-Platonic bias goes. However, much modernist writing is Symbolist in spirit, because of the high value it places on form, holistically conceived (see HOLISM), as against materialistic, realistic, historical, or DOCUMENTARY presentation. See also

SYMMETRY

AESTHETICISM; DECADENCE.   M.S.BR.
Bibl: Arthur Symons, *The Symbolist Movement in Literature* (London, 1899); Edmund Wilson, *Axel's Castle* (London and N.Y., 1931); C. M. Bowra, *The Heritage of Symbolism* (London, 1943; N.Y., 1954); A. G. Lehmann, *The Symbolist Aesthetic in France, 1885–1895* (Oxford, 2nd ed., 1968).

symmetry. The property possessed by any system which remains essentially unaltered after various operations have been performed on it. Examples: (1) the image of a stocking in a mirror is indistinguishable from the original; thus stockings, unlike shoes, possess *left-right symmetry* (see also PARITY). (2) Patterned wallpaper and crystal LATTICES are unaltered after being moved through a distance equal to the spacing between two of their elementary units; these systems have *translational symmetry*. (3) If the velocities of all the PARTICLES of a system are reversed, the system will pass successively through its former states; thus the laws of MECHANICS have *time-reversal symmetry* (see also GROUP; STATISTICAL MECHANICS; TRANSFORMATION.)   M.V.B.

symmetry, group of, see under GROUP.

Symons, Arthur (British poet and critic, 1865–1945), see under SYMBOLISM.

synaesthesia. The experience, whether real or hallucinatory, in which a stimulus applied to one sense elicits a response from one or more others; also, the literary device that corresponds to this experience, as in 'silvery trumpet-note', 'scarlet stench', 'loud, stinking colour'. First used in this latter sense by Jules Millet in 1892, synaesthesia (*synesthésie*) occurs in all poetry, but was especially popular among the ROMANTIC and SYMBOLIST poets (as in Baudelaire's sonnet 'Correspondances') of the 19th century – mainly because mentally disturbed or drugged people claim to have experienced it. The CONCEPT enjoyed some facile revival in the DRUG-dominated 1960s, as 'sense-overload' and other such journalistic notions. The PSYCHEDELIC light-show (see MEDIA) was a practical manifestation.   M.S.-S.

synaesthesis. Term coined by James Wood, I. A. Richards, and C. K. Ogden in *The Foundations of Aesthetics* (1922) to describe the harmony allegedly achieved by a work of art, which is said to raise the receptor to an awareness of beauty by its equilibrium: its capacity to balance strong emotions.   M.S.-S.

synapse. The special interface between neighbouring NEURONS which according to the CELL theory are the cellular basis of the NERVOUS SYSTEM. Nerve impulses can travel in either direction along a nerve fibre from a point of stimulation in the middle. The impulses are polarized at the synapse, across which they travel in one direction only. Transmission across the synapse is chemically mediated rather than simply electronic in character.   P.M.

synapsis, see under MEIOSIS.

synchromism, see under ORPHISM.

synchronic, see under DIACHRONIC; LINGUISTICS.

synchronicity. JUNGIAN term for an acausal connecting principle that would give meaning to series of coincidences (e.g. the frequent recurrence of a particular numeral over a short period of time) not explicable through notions of simple causality, as well as to the experiences labelled DÉJÀ VU and PRECOGNITION. In this CONCEPT, Jung argued against the classical elementaristic view of experience, in favour of a view of events as participants within a structured whole (see STRUCTURALISM). Hence, on this view, the meaning of events is to be found in terms of their structural relationships, as well as their causal antecedents. Jung's structuralism entails a form of experiential harmony – harmony among events, and a harmony between the structure of our understanding and the event structure.
                                          T.Z.C.

synchronism. In ARCHAEOLOGY, to establish a synchronism means to demonstrate, usually by means of TYPOLOGY, the contemporaneity of CULTURES, artifacts, or structures. Thus the synchronism of two disparate settlements might be argued on the basis of both containing like ASSEMBLAGES of distinctive tool types. Synchronisms over larger areas may be constructed with reference to the occur-

618

rence of characteristic types extensively traded. Until the advent of RADIOCARBON DATING this was one of the few methods available for correlating prehistoric cultures. B.C.

synchronous orbit. The path in space of an artificial SATELLITE which always remains directly above a fixed point on the equator. It is necessary for the ORBIT to be a circle about 22,500 miles above the earth; this figure is calculated from NEWTONIAN MECHANICS, using the MASS and radius of the earth and the fact that the orbit must be traversed in exactly one day. Synchronous satellites are used for intercontinental TELECOMMUNICATIONS.
M.V.B.

syncopation. The transference of musical accents onto the subsidiary pulses of a musical measure. Normally, music has a regular pulse or time, of which 3-beat (waltz) and 4-beat (march) are the commonest. The natural accentuation falls on the first beat of 3, and on the first and (to a lesser degree) third beats of 4. In a syncopated rhythm the accent is shifted, although the main pulse continues in the background, even if only by implication. Examples of syncopation can be found as early as the 14th century; it has been a marked feature of much 20th-century music, and in JAZZ is all-pervasive. A.H.

syncretism. Fusion, in PERCEPTION or thought (including dreams), of incompatible elements; e.g. an inchoate dream image of someone who is at once mother and brother, or man and horse. I.M.L.H.

syndicalism. A militant trade union movement which started in France (*syndicat* is the French word for trade union) in the 1890s, and aimed at transferring the control and ownership of the means of production, not to the State, but to the unions themselves. The movement derived partly from the anti-parliamentary ideas of Proudhon and partly from the reaction of the workers against both the 'parliamentarism' of the SOCIALIST Party and the exclusive emphasis placed on politics by such MARXIST leaders as Jules Guesde. The syndicalists rejected politics, regarding CLASS struggle in the form of *industrial action* as more effective; the fight on the shop floor

was eventually to lead to a 'general strike' (which Georges Sorel later made into the cornerstone of his theory of DIRECT ACTION). Socialist INTELLECTUALS were regarded with suspicion, and the need for workers' solidarity as a precondition of the success of any industrial and trade-union action was stressed in the *Charter of Amiens* (1906) and other texts of the Confédération Générale du Travail, in the pronouncements of the famous British leader of 'industrial unionism', Tom Mann, and in those of the organizers of the American Industrial Workers of the World (the *'Wobblies'*).

Another factor permeating the syndicalist movement was the Bakuninist ANARCHIST tradition, particularly in France, Switzerland, Italy, and Spain, countries where in its early phase syndicalism appeared in its REVOLUTIONARY form of ANARCHO-SYNDICALISM. In other countries, syndicalism as a reaction to a still decentralized economy was seen, in Bertrand Russell's words, as 'the anarchism of the market place'. As an IDEOLOGY legitimizing direct industrial action by the workers, syndicalism has left a strong legacy in their trade-union organizations, but as a political current it disappeared from the scene as an effective force before World War I. L.L.
Bibl: G. Sorel, tr. T. E. Hulme, *Reflections on Violence* (N.Y., 1914; London, 1916); F. F. Ridley, *Revolutionary Syndicalism in France* (London, 1970).

syndrome. (1) In medicine, the specific combination of symptoms distinguishing a particular disease, e.g. DOWN'S SYNDROME stemming from John Down (1828–96) who studied it. (2) By extension, distinguishable conditions of mind (and even social-psychological conditions) regarded as pathological, e.g. SCHIZOPHRENIA. (3) In popular current usage, a specific characteristic, set of characteristics, or behaviour pattern that has come to be symbolized by or associated with one person (real or fictitious) or group; e.g. the LOLITA SYNDROME.
R.F.
Bibl: R. D. Laing, *The Politics of the Family* (London and N.Y., 1971).

synergism. In BIOLOGY, the relationship between agents whereby their combined effect is greater than the sum of the effect

SYNERGY

of each one considered individually. Thus, considered as narcotics, barbituric acid derivatives and alcohol have a greater depressant effect than the sum of the two acting separately. The more general term SYNERGY can also bear this specific meaning. P.M.

synergy. The additional benefit accruing to a number of SYSTEMS should they coalesce to form a larger system. This CONCEPT reflects the classical opinion that 'the whole is greater than the sum of the parts'. In practice, synergy may turn out to be negative, because the totality is ill-conceived or ineffectively organized. Synergy is formally studied as a property of systems by CYBERNETICS. In MANAGEMENT, synergy is the subject of measurement by OPERATIONAL RESEARCH, especially where business mergers are concerned; but the word is also frequently used in a much looser way in discussions of CORPORATE STRATEGY, simply to indicate general expectations of collaborative benefit. More generally still, the term is applied to the generation of unplanned social benefits among people who unconsciously cooperate in pursuit of their own interests and goals. The term derives from BIOLOGY, where it is an alternative term for SYNERGISM. *R.I.T.; S.BE.

Synge, John Millington (Irish dramatist, 1871–1909), see under ABBEY THEATRE.

synonymy, see under FREE VARIATION.

syntactics, see LOGICAL SYNTAX.

syntagmatic and **paradigmatic.** In LINGUISTICS, adjectives applied to two kinds of relationship into which all linguistic elements enter. Syntagmatic refers to the linear relationship operating at a given LEVEL between the elements in a sentence; paradigmatic refers to the relationship between an element at a given point within a sentence and an element with which, syntactically, it is interchangeable. For example, in the sentence *He is coming,* the relationship between *He, is, com-* and *-ing* is syntagmatic (at the level of MORPHOLOGY); the relationship between *He* and *She, is* and *will be,* etc. is paradigmatic. D.C.

syntax. In LINGUISTICS, a traditional term

for the study of the rules governing the way words are combined to form sentences in a language. An alternative definition (avoiding the concept of *word*) is the study of the interrelationships between elements of sentence structure, and of the rules governing the arrangement of sentences in sequences (see DISCOURSE). See also CONSTITUENT ANALYSIS; DEEP STRUCTURE AND SURFACE STRUCTURE; GRAMMAR. D.C.

synthesis. The final stage, succeeding thesis and antithesis, in a DIALECTIC triad, a phase of the dialectic process. (See also DIALECTICAL MATERIALISM.) First some thought is affirmed; the *thesis.* On reflection this reveals itself as unsatisfactory, incomplete, or contradictory, and prompts the affirmation of its opposite: the *antithesis.* But further reflection shows that this too is inadequate and so it, in turn, is contradicted by the *synthesis.* This, however, does not, as in classical LOGIC, where double negation is identical with affirmation, simply reinstate the original thesis. The synthesis is held to embrace or reconcile the more rational and acceptable elements in the conflicting and now superseded thesis and antithesis from which it emerges in a 'higher unity'. A.Q.

synthesizer. Apparatus for producing ELECTRONIC MUSIC. Synthesized music on tape differs from CONCRETE MUSIC in that the sounds electronically transformed are also electronically created. An almost limitless range of pitch, timbre, and volume can be obtained. Small synthesizers, with or without keyboards, are used for live electronic music; for the composition of music onto tape, very complex equipment may be required, making use of COMPUTER memory. J.G.R.

synthetic, see under ANALYTIC.

synthetic chemistry. The laboratory or industrial preparation of chemical substances from simpler starting materials. Synthetic methods may be routine or directed to the preparation of new compounds. B.F.

synthetic foods. Strictly, synthetic foods limited to certain VITAMINS and AMINO ACIDS, e.g. methionine, which can be synthesized on a commercial scale; in general usage (for which *unconventional foods* is perhaps a preferable term), foods derived from other than traditional sources of farm and fishery produce. PROTEIN foods which are essential for body growth have been a particular concern at a time of pressure on world food supplies. Unconventional sources include protein derived directly from leaves by mechanical and chemical processes (leaf protein), and from unicellular organisms grown on residues from the mineral oil industry, or on molasses or other CARBOHYDRATE materials. Conventional sources of protein such as soya bean, which in their normal form are not very palatable, may by suitable processing be converted to a form which tastes like meat and is acceptable as a substitute.   K.E.H.

Bibl: N. W. Pirie, *Food Resources, Conventional and Novel* (Harmondsworth and Baltimore, rev. ed., 1976).

synthetism. One wing of the SYMBOLIST movement in painting, developed mainly by Gauguin and the young Émile Bernard, whose *Pots de grès et pommes* of 1887 was inscribed 'premier essai de synthétisme et de simplification'. With its use of clearly defined flat areas of colour (sometimes called *cloisonnisme* because of its dependence on *cloisons* or partitions), synthetism was quite different from the more atmospheric, SURREAL symbolism of Odilon Redon and Gustave Moreau. Its adherents, who showed as a group at the Café Volpini in Paris in 1889, were drawn mainly from the PONT-AVEN school. J.W.

Bibl: H. R. Rookmaaker, *Synthetist Art Theories* (Amsterdam, 1959).

system, see SYSTEMS.

system dynamics, see under SYSTEMS.

systematic theology, see DOGMATICS.

systematics, see under BIOSYSTEMATICS.

Système Internationale d'Unités, see SI UNITS.

systemic. Of or pertaining to a SYSTEM. In the SOCIAL SCIENCES, it is mainly used to qualify terms such as 'change', 'equilibrium', 'function', or 'contradiction' when they designate properties of social or political systems, as in various theoretical perspectives, e.g. general systems theory (GST), PARSONIAN theory, MARXISM.
                                        J.R.T.

systemic grammar. A theory of GRAMMAR which Halliday developed from his earlier SCALE-AND-CATEGORY GRAMMAR, the new name reflecting his view of language as an organization of *system networks* of contrasts.   D.C.

systems; systems approach; systems analysis.
(1) A *system* is a group of related elements organized for a purpose. The nature of systems is studied by the science of CYBERNETICS and by *general systems theory* (see GST). A *systems approach* (or *systems analysis,* though this phrase also bears the narrower meaning defined in (2) below) is an approach to the study of physical and social systems which enables complex and dynamic situations to be understood in broad outline. It is a conceptual tool, the user of which may also receive scientific assistance from OPERATIONAL RESEARCH. The approach is valid whether the topic is a heating system, a postal system, a health or education system, a firm, an economy, or a government.

To identify a system it is necessary to distinguish its boundaries, to be aware of its purposes (whether these are a blueprint for its design or inferred from its behaviour), and to define the level of abstraction (see ABSTRACT) at which it is to be treated. Systems may turn out to contain recognizable *sub-systems,* sub-sub-systems, and so on. These arrangements are sometimes investigated as hierarchies; but because the arrangement often involves a nesting (in the manner of Chinese boxes) of systems within each other they may also be defined by RECURSION. One of the discoveries made by the systems approach is the extent to which attempts to improve the performance of a sub-system by its own criteria (*sub-optimization*) may act to the detriment of the total system and even to the defeat of its objectives.

In MANAGEMENT contexts, the systems approach concerns itself with growth and stability in the system under a range of possible futures, unpredictable perturbations, and alternative policies. The classic tool for studying these matters is a systems MODEL which is used for purposes of

SIMULATION, and whose implications can be explored by means of a digital COMPUTER. *System dynamics* is a term coined by Jay Forrester for a style of model-building in which large structures are built which make little use of empirical evidence or previous knowledge of the subject. Forrester has shown how policies, decisions, STRUCTURE, and delayed responses are interrelated to influence growth and stability. First applied to industrial systems, his METHODOLOGY has subsequently been used to study urban and world ecological systems where the vision of an all-embracing model and its striking conclusions have gained a wide audience. The systems approach to a problem can alert scientists to interactions whose importance they have failed to recognize. However, systems analysis has also been applied to a number of disciplines where its contributions have yet to achieve significant influence.

See also MANAGEMENT INFORMATION SYSTEM; METASYSTEM.

*S.BE.; R.I.T.; J.A.M.; M.A.H.D.

(2) More narrowly, *systems analysis* is the first stage in presenting any large task to a computer (the other stages being PROGRAMMING and CODING). It is performed by a *systems analyst* and consists of analysing the whole task in its setting and deciding in outline how to arrange it for the computer; estimating how much work is involved and hence how powerful a computer will be needed; dividing the process into a number of relatively independent parts; and finally specifying each of these, together with their interconnections, in sufficient detail for a programmer to take over. C.S.

Bibl: J. W. Forrester, *Industrial Dynamics* (London and Cambridge, Mass., 1961), *Urban Dynamics* (Cambridge, Mass., 1969), and World *Dynamics* (Cambridge, Mass., 1971); C. W. Churchman, *The Systems Approach* (N.Y., 1968); E. Laszlo, *The Systems View of the World* (N.Y., 1972); G. J. Klir (ed.), *Trends in General Systems Theory* (N.Y., 1972).

systems engineering, see CONTROL ENGINEERING; CYBERNETICS; SYSTEMS.

Szasz, Thomas Stephen (U.S. psychiatrist, *b.* 1920), see under MENTAL TESTING.

T

T groups, see under ORGANIZATION THEORY.

table of mortality, see LIFE TABLE.

tableau-piège, see under COLLAGE.

taboo. A linguistic legacy to Europe from Polynesia, through Captain Cook. In its homelands the word seemed to mean both that which was holy and that which was prohibited. It is the latter sense upon which English has for the most part seized, and taboo (or tabu) is now, as noun, verb, and adjective, employed loosely to mean prohibition/prohibit/prohibited in the vast field of behaviour ranging from etiquette to RELIGION (but usually excluding law). In the SOCIAL SCIENCES, however, the term has taken on technical senses, some of which incorporate the apparent duality of its Polynesian origins. For many anthropologists, taboo means a RITUAL prohibition that may express either the sacredness (holiness) or uncleanness of what is set apart. The thing tabooed is in some fashion dangerous. The duality is preserved in a different manner in FREUDIAN psychoanalytic theory (see PSYCHOANALYSIS), where taboo prevents people from doing what their unconscious desires impel them towards. INCEST and food taboos are among the commonest of those discussed in the literature.   M.F.
Bibl: F. Steiner, *Taboo* (London and N.Y., 1956); M. Douglas, *Purity and Danger* (London and N.Y., 1966).

tachisme, see under ACTION PAINTING.

tachyon. A hypothetical PARTICLE travelling faster than light. Because of the 'light barrier' of RELATIVITY theory, tachyons could not be produced by the ACCELERATION of ordinary particles. Tachyons would generate a special kind of electromagnetic RADIATION, but this has not been detected.   M.V.B.

tagmemic grammar. A theory of GRAMMAR developed by K. L. Pike in the early 1950s. The name reflects the use the theory makes of the CONCEPT of the *tagmeme,* a device for conveying simultaneously formal and functional information about a particular linguistic unit. Thus, in the sentence *The cat sat on the mat,* the formal information that *the cat* is a noun phrase and the functional information that it is the subject of the sentence are combined in a single tagmemic statement, written S:NP. Many of the principles underlying Pike's linguistic theory have since been applied to the analysis of non-linguistic phenomena (see also EMIC), of particular note being his *Language in Relation to a Unified Theory of Human Behaviour* (The Hague, 2nd ed., 1967).   D.C.

Tailleferre, Germaine (French composer, *b.* 1892), see under SIX, LES.

take-off point. A phrase derived from W. W. Rostow's *Stages of Economic Growth* (1960). The essential idea is that there is a recognizable stage in a country's history, lasting for perhaps 20–30 years, during which the required conditions for sustained and fairly rapid growth are consolidated, and beyond which such growth is more or less assured. The idea is pooh-poohed by most ECONOMIC HISTORIANS, but the phrase has nevertheless become a part of the language of economic development.   I.M.D.L.

take-over, see under CORPORATE STRATEGY.

tamizdat, see under SAMIZDAT.

Tanguy, Yves (French painter, 1900–1955), see under BIOMORPHIC; SURREALISM.

Tantra. A discourse imparting doctrines in the tradition of Mayahana BUDDHISM, usually said to have been spoken by a mythical Buddha. Thousands of Tantras have been written from *c.* 500 A.D. onwards, and some have received a new

attention as a result of the worldwide interest in Buddhism in the 19th and 20th centuries; most notably the *Tibetan Book of the Dead,* written probably in the 8th century to give guidance to dying persons.
D.L.E.

Taoism. A RELIGION of the Chinese. Less official than CONFUCIANISM, it has been essentially a way (Chinese *Tao*) of life through virtue to prosperity, longevity, and immortality. Virtue has been seen as conformity to nature without and within man. This way has included both meditation in temples of great beauty and tranquillity, and a more popular traffic in charms and magical formulae, often linked with secret societies. Although the China Taoist Association was formed in 1957 with government permission, on the whole the COMMUNIST rulers of China since 1949 have suppressed Taoism.
D.L.E.
Bibl: W. Chan, *Religious Trends in Modern China* (N.Y., 1953).

Tarski, Alfred (Polish-U.S. mathematical logician, *b.* 1902), see under LOGICAL SYNTAX; MATHEMATICAL LOGIC; SEMANTICS.

TAT, see THEMATIC APPERCEPTION TEST.

Tate, Allen (U.S. poet and critic, *b.* 1899), see under COMMUNICATION, FALLACY OF; CRITERION, THE; NEW CRITICISM; TENSION.

Tatlin, Vladimir (Russian painter and sculptor, 1885–1953), see under COLLAGE; CONSTRUCTIVISM; DONKEY'S TAIL; KINETIC ART.

Taut, Bruno (German architect, 1880–1938), see under EXPRESSIONISM.

Tawney, Richard Henry (British historian and social critic, 1880–1962), see under CHRISTIAN SOCIALISM; GENTRY CONTROVERSY.

tax credit. (1) A credit for foreign tax given for the purpose of relieving international double taxation. In the U.K., the U.S.A., and certain other countries income of a resident individual or company is (with exceptions) subject to tax regardless of source. Where the income

has borne tax in its country of source, the gross amount is assessed to tax, but a 'tax credit' is given for the foreign tax paid or borne. (2) A synonym (the French *avoir fiscal* is another) for the *imputation credit* described under CORPORATION TAX. (3) A tax credit system was proposed by the U.K. Government in a Green Paper dated October 1972. These proposals are, in substance, similar to those referred to in the U.S.A. as NEGATIVE INCOME TAX.
J.F.C.

taxis, see under TROPISM.

taxonomic linguistics, see under LINGUISTICS.

taxonomy, see under BIOSYSTEMATICS.

Taylor, Frederick Winslow (U.S. engineer, 1856–1915), see under SCIENTIFIC MANAGEMENT.

TCA cycle, see KREBS CYCLE.

Tch . . . For Russian names sometimes transliterated thus, see CH . . .

teaching machine. Any device which facilitates learning, from pebbles to film strip projectors. In current use the term refers usually to individually operated machines in which programmed material (see PACKAGES) can be exposed. The theory of INDIVIDUALIZED INSTRUCTION on which many such machines are based was realized in the 1950s and 1960s in programmes offering at first a linear sequence and later a branching programme which enabled better students to jump phases. The next, more sophisticated phase will be to incorporate COMPUTER-assisted sound, colour, and multi-media systems. See also EDUCATIONAL TECHNOLOGY; PROGRAMMED INSTRUCTION.
W.A.C.S.
Bibl: J. Carmichael, *Educational Revolution* (London, 1969; N.Y., 1970).

Teagarden, Jack (U.S. jazz musician, 1905–64), see under CHICAGO.

team teaching. Teaching performed by a team of teachers responsible for a group or groups of pupils – either for all their activities (mainly in primary schools) or for certain subject-matters (mainly in

SECONDARY SCHOOLS). A team may be *hierarchical* (with a leader bearing overall responsibility) or *collegial* (with members of equal STATUS deciding collectively how to share the workload). Team teaching is particularly appropriate in OPEN-PLAN SCHOOLS (to optimize use of space and avoid conflict between classes) and for curricula centred on PROJECT WORK (when teachers can take responsibility for groups of various sizes, enabling a wider range of instructional methods to be used). Some teachers feel that their creativity and spontaneity in dealing with pupils is restricted by the novel need to accept group decisions (and in open-plan schools by the visual and acoustical proximity to colleagues). E.L.-S.
Bibl: J. T. Shaplin and H. F. Olds (eds.), *Team Teaching* (N.Y., 1964).

technetronic society, see under POST-INDUSTRIAL SOCIETY.

technical high schools, see under SECONDARY SCHOOLS.

technocracy. Term coined in 1919 in California by an engineer, William Henry Smyth, for his proposed 'rule by technicians'. In 1933–4 it was taken over and popularized by Howard Scott, a former associate of Thorstein Veblen (whose book *The Engineers and the Price System*, 1921, was taken as a bible for the idea), and technocracy as a social movement had a brief vogue in the U.S.A. during the early depression years. During the 1960s the term gained wider currency in France, where it was identified with the theories of Saint-Simon (who predicted a society ruled by scientists and engineers) and used by writers such as Jean Meynaud to argue that 'real power' has shifted from the elected representatives to the technical experts and that there now 'begins a new type of government, neither DEMOCRACY nor BUREAUCRACY but a technocracy'. The power of the technocrats is identified with the rise of economic PLANNING, strategic thinking in defence matters, and the expansion of science and research. Most social analysts agree that in advanced industrial society the role of the expert has been enlarged but doubt that rule by technicians can supplant the political order. D.B.
Bibl: W. H. G. Armytage, *The Rise*

of the Technocrats (London, 1965); J. Meynaud, tr. P. Barnes, *Technocracy* (London, 1968; N.Y., 1969).

technological forecasting. A range of techniques used, in formulating CORPORATE STRATEGY, to predict potential technological developments. The principal methods are intuitive ones based on individual expectations; the *Delphi technique* (developed by the Rand Corporation), in which experts work together in a laboratory situation to crystallize their reasoning and reach a consensus on likely developments; the EXTRAPOLATION of trends; CORRELATION analysis; and imaginative statements (often called *scenarios*) of possible events and their likely outcomes. R.I.T.
Bibl: J. R. Bright (ed.), *Technological Forecasting for Industry and Government* (Englewood Cliffs, N.J., 1968).

technological unemployment, see under UNEMPLOYMENT.

technology. The systematic study of techniques employed in industry, agriculture, etc. More generally, the term is used for any application of the discoveries of science, or the SCIENTIFIC METHOD, to the problems of man and his environment in peace and war. See also ENGINEERING; ENVIRONMENTAL CONTROL; METALLURGY. M.V.B.
Bibl: J. D. Bernal, *Science in History,* 4 vols. (3rd ed., London, 1969; Cambridge, Mass., 1971).

technopolis. A term popularized in 1969 by Nigel Calder to describe a society which is moulded and continuously and drastically altered by scientific and technical innovation; scientific *policy* being either non-existent or concerned with such peripheral issues as efficiency per pound invested, or speed of results, rather than with ultimate direction or moral considerations. P.S.L.
Bibl: N. Calder, *Technopolis* (London and N.Y., 1969).

tectonics. The study of the deformation of rocks, with the principal aim of establishing the extent and exact nature of the deformation and when it occurred. It may be possible to infer from the deformation the orientation of the stresses involved and the mechanism which produced them. Tectonics can be studied on all scales from microscopic distortions of single crystals to the displacement of whole continents (see PLATE TECTONICS). J.L.M.L.

Teheran. The capital of Iran, and scene (28 November – 2 December 1943) of the first war-time SUMMIT conference between Churchill, Roosevelt, and Stalin. Although mainly concerned with military matters, the conference also saw exchanges of views on the future treatment of Germany, the post-war colonial settlement, the post-war frontiers of Poland, and the organization of international security. It was mainly distinguished by President Roosevelt's efforts to achieve recognition of China as one of the post-war Big Four, and to win the confidence of Stalin, efforts carried to such lengths as to isolate Britain and enable Russia to take advantage of Anglo-American differences. D.C.W.

Bibl: H. Feis, *Churchill, Roosevelt, Stalin* (London and Princeton, 1957); E. L. Woodward, *British Foreign Policy in the Second World War,* vol. 2 (London, 1973).

Teilhard de Chardin, Pierre (French palaeontologist, theologian, and philosopher, 1881–1955), see under EVOLUTIONISM; NOOSPHERE; PROCESS THEOLOGY; TEILHARDIAN.

Teilhardian. Adjective derived from the name of Pierre Teilhard de Chardin (1881–1955), a Jesuit who was also a palaeontologist and who wrote visionary books, widely popular when published after his death, about the Christian meaning of EVOLUTION. See also NOOSPHERE; PROCESS THEOLOGY. D.L.E.

Bibl: R. Speaight, *Teilhard de Chardin* (London, 1967).

Tel Quel. An influential French literary magazine, founded in 1960 by the novelist and critic Philippe Sollers (*b.* 1936). Its aims and objects are usefully stated in Sollers's *Logiques* (1968). Influences on the *Tel Quel* school include Bachelard, Ponge, Roussel, Barthes (see also SEMIOLOGY), and the quasi-MARXIST EXISTENTIALISM of Sartre. The position of *Tel Quel* was originally aesthetic; but over its first decade this evolved into a complex

ACTIVISM. Briefly, the *Tel Quel* school believes that certain writings (e.g. of de Sade, Lautréamont, Mallarmé, Artaud) could transform society for the better, but are ignored by society in various subtle ways. *Tel Quel* aims to restore to language its 'original revolutionary power', and proposes literature as the prime means of doing this because 'literature is a language made with language'. M.S.-S.

telecommunication. Communication over long distances, based on ELECTROMAGNETISM. In telephony and telegraphy signals are transmitted as electric impulses travelling along wires, while in radio and television the signals are transmitted through space as MODULATIONS of carrier waves of electromagnetic RADIATION. M.V.B.

teleological explanation, see under EXPLANATION.

teleology (or *consequentialism*). Literally, the study of ends, goals, or purposes; more specifically, the theory that events can only be explained, and that evaluation of anything (objects, states of affairs, acts, agents) can only be justified, by consideration of the ends towards which they are directed. Teleologists contend that minds or living organisms can only be explained in a forward-looking way and that MECHANISTIC explanation in terms of efficient causes is inadequate. As an ethical doctrine (see ETHICS) teleology argues, in opposition to DEONTOLOGY, that rightness is not an intrinsic property of actions but is dependent on the goodness or badness of the consequences, whether actual, predictable, or expected, to which they give rise. There are, undoubtedly, teleological systems, i.e. complexes of events (e.g. a stock exchange or a cat stalking a bird) which take on a significant order only if seen as all directed towards some outlying purpose. The controversial issue is whether the teleology of the whole can be reduced (see REDUCTION) to the mechanically explicable behaviour of its parts (e.g. by taking the desires of the stockbrokers to buy and sell, or of the cat to kill the bird, as efficient causes). The invention of SERVOMECHANISMS such as thermostats and self-correcting gun-aiming devices encourages the view that such reduction is possible in principle. Darwin's theory of NATURAL SELECTION supplied a mechanistic account of the EVOLUTIONARY process; the discovery of DNA (see NUCLEIC ACID) did much the same for the special properties of living matter. Kant reasonably described the argument from the evidences of design in the natural world to a supernatural designing intelligence as the teleological proof of God's existence.   A.Q.

telepathy, see under ESP.

Teng Hsiao-ping (Chinese politician, *b.* 1904), see under CULTURAL REVOLUTION.

Tennessee Valley Authority, see under NEW DEAL.

tension. In the NEW CRITICISM, a term defined by Allen Tate (who derives it from the logical terms *ex*tension and *in*tension – see CONNOTATION AND DENOTATION) as the sum total of meaning in a poem. The poem has a literal MEANING (extension) and a metaphorical one (intension); the simultaneity of these meanings results in tension. New Critics tend to judge poetry by its ability to achieve such tension.
                                M.S.-S.
Bibl: J. O. A. Tate, *Reason in Madness* (N.Y., 1941).

tensor. A generalization of the notion of VECTOR which can be used to represent RELATIONS between vectors. For example the elasticity tensor relates the deformation at each point of an elastic body to the applied stress. The *tensor calculus* was first developed in connection with differential GEOMETRY and was the fundamental tool used by Einstein in formulating the general theory of RELATIVITY.   R.G.

Terk, Sonia, see DELAUNAY-TERK.

Terman, Lewis Madison (U.S. psychologist, 1877–1956), see under MENTAL RETARDATION.

Terman-Merrill revision, see under MENTAL RETARDATION.

terminal. A station, usually removed from the main machine, whence a COMPUTER can be used. A terminal is often only a CONSOLE, but sometimes more powerful devices (e.g. line-printers and card-readers) are used. In the latter case, a small *satellite* computer may be used at the terminal to allow certain simple jobs to be carried out locally by the terminal; such a terminal is sometimes called *intelligent*.
                                C.S.

terms of trade. The quantity of purchases for which a given quantity of sales will exchange. An INDEX NUMBER measuring changes in the terms of trade is obtained by dividing an index number of prices of sales by one of prices of purchases, a rise indicating an improvement. The concept may be applied to transactions within a country (e.g. between farmers and the rest of the economy), or between one type of product and another (e.g. between raw materials and manufactures), but is mostly applied to the imports and exports of a nation. Economists call these the *net barter terms of trade,* and have invented other concepts (e.g. 'gross barter', 'income', 'single', and 'double factorial' terms of trade) which have attracted less general interest.   M.FG.S.
Bibl: C. P. Kindleberger, *The Terms of Trade* (London and N.Y., 1956).

territorial imperative. Phrase coined by the American scientific popularizer, Robert Ardrey, for the theory that man is a creature whose behaviour in relation to the ownership, protection, and expansion of the territory he regards as his or his group's exclusive preserve is analogous to the territorial behaviour of animals (see TERRITORY) and is acquired genetically in the same way. In accordance with the principles of territorial behaviour, mutual antagonism grows as natural hazards diminish.   D.C.W.
Bibl: R. Ardrey, *The Territorial Imperative* (N.Y.,1966; London, 1967).

territory.
(1) The portion of geographical space under the jurisdiction of a recognized authority. Territorial claims have often been at the root of political tensions and conflicts; recently these claims have been related more to the resources available within the territory than to its function as shelter. Territorial SOVEREIGNTY extends over adjacent maritime and air spaces,

and maritime powers are now widening the breadth of their territorial seas and claiming control over the contiguous continental shelf. See also ACCESSIBILITY. J.G.

Bibl: R. Y. Jennings, *The Acquisition of Territory* (Manchester and N.Y., 1963); J. Gottmann, *The Significance of Territory* (Charlottesville, 1973).

(2) In ETHOLOGY, an area in which an organism or a group of individuals is dominant – e.g. the territory within which a male bird will allow no intrusion and towards which he acts in a way distinctly analogous to that of a human being (in most societies) towards his private property, or the 'group territories' of lions, hyenas, and some other mammals and birds, which likewise evoke behaviour analogous to human behaviour. This pattern of behaviour is known as *territoriality*. See also TERRITORIAL IMPERATIVE. P.M.

Bibl: H. Kruuk, *The Spotted Hyena* (London and Chicago, 1972); G. B. Schaller, *The Serengeti Lion* (London and Chicago, 1972).

terrorism. The policy or activity of using terror to break the spirit of resistance to a particular political movement by inculcating the fear of death, mutilation, and torture, or of similar action against resisters' families and dependants. As a policy it lacks reality until sufficient examples have been provided for the terror to become effective. Terrorism can be both official and counter-revolutionary (e.g. Hitler's and Mussolini's use of it) as well as revolutionary. In opposition it is essentially the weapon of a minority which sees no chance of success by persuasion. If revolutionary terror is to be successful it must first impose its will on those whom it wishes to lead into battle. A term with strong pejorative overtones, it figures much, and usually with some reason, in official propaganda against insurgents. D.C.W.

Bibl: R. Gaucher, tr. P. Spurlin, *The Terrorists* (London, 1968).

tertiary education. A term used in Britain to describe full- or part-time education for those who have completed their education at the secondary level (see SECONDARY SCHOOLS). Tertiary education includes *higher education* (i.e. the universities) and *further education* (i.e. technical, commercial, and art colleges maintained by Local Education Authorities). This division, which dates from the Education Act of 1944, is now blurred, however, by the changing position of the *polytechnics* and *colleges of education.*

In the late 1960s, thirty leading further-education institutions were selected to become *polytechnics,* with courses over a wide range of social sciences as well as technology and science, and with full- and part-time students able to take degrees and other qualifications of the Council for National Academic Awards (C.N.A.A.). The polytechnics (numbers in which might grow to 335,000 in 1981, roughly the equivalent of university numbers) thus have links with both higher and further education.

In an effort to make the position clearer, Anthony Crosland (Secretary of State for Education in the Labour Government) outlined, in a speech at Woolwich Polytechnic in 1965, a *binary system* of government and finance for higher education: (1) The universities constitute the so-called *autonomous sector*: these are self-governing, award their own degrees, and derive their main financial support from a single central source, the University Grants Committee (see UGC). (2) The polytechnics, which were originally based on Local Authority regional colleges, constitute the so-called *public sector*: the Local Authorities are responsible for major decisions of policy and finance, and degrees and diplomas are awarded by the C.N.A.A., a non-university body.

The fact is that the pattern of tertiary education is in constant process of development and the *colleges of education* (formerly teacher training colleges) are now passing through an equally confusing period of transition following the publication of the James Report and the WHITE PAPER ON EDUCATION. In these circumstances, tertiary education has obvious advantages as a term to describe the whole spectrum of post-secondary education within which the academic and organizational lines of division (with the universities at one end and local colleges of further education at the other) are continually shifting. See also CATS.

W.A.C.S; A.L.C.B.

tertiary occupation, see under OCCUPATION.

tetrahedral theory. An extension of the CONTRACTION HYPOTHESIS to explain the distribution of the continents and oceans. If the earth was cooling and contracting, its shape would tend to become tetrahedral, since the tetrahedron is the regular figure with the smallest volume. Though the distribution of continents and oceans is roughly tetrahedral, with the oceans corresponding to the faces, the theory presents a picture which is inconsistent with ISOSTASY and it has therefore been abandoned. J.L.M.L.

Bibl: A. Holmes, *Principles of Physical Geology* (London and N.Y., 2nd ed., 1969).

text, theory of. Term used by the German critic Max Bense and others to convey the 'scientific' analysis of 'text' – chosen as a word free from the VALUE-JUDGEMENTS implicit in terms like 'literature' or 'poetry' – by largely quantitative methods such as STYLOMETRY. J.W.

textual criticism. The part of editing a literary work which deals with the establishment of the text. The need for textual criticism is occasioned by the fact that all texts of every kind tend to become *corrupt* (i.e. falsified) in the normal course of transmission. In many cases different witnesses offer variant readings at particular points, and often there are radically different versions of a work. It is now fairly generally agreed that the ideal of textual criticism is to present the text which the author intended.

Textual criticism was the principal form of literary study, by professionals and amateurs alike, from the time of classical antiquity until the 19th century. The main subjects were the New Testament and the Greek and Latin classical writers; the chief method was *emendation* of words or passages on aesthetic grounds, either by logic or by reference to the readings of other witnesses. The formalization of analysis (with the construction of *stemmata*, i.e. of family trees of witnesses) and the emergence of BIBLIOGRAPHY (as the detailed and systematic study of the printed book) at the end of the 19th century caused the practice of textual criticism to be confined to specialists, who have now brought editing to a laborious, sophisticated, and time-consuming level.

The textual critic needs a sound aesthetic (see AESTHETICS), a thorough knowledge of the text under consideration, and access to any authorial or other relevant statements about the text. The five major steps to textual criticism are *collecting* the *texts* (i.e. the various appearances of the *text*); *analysing* the differences between the texts; *selecting* the *copy-text* (i.e. the version regarded as most authoritative and therefore used as a basis); *perfecting* the copy-text (i.e. replacing passages known or thought to be corrupt by the introduction, from other sources, of readings known or thought to be authorial); and *explaining* and justifying the editor's procedures and decisions. J.T.

Bibl: J. Thorpe, *Principles of Textual Criticism* (San Marino, 1972).

texture. In the NEW CRITICISM, the particular aspect of a poem as distinct from its abstract or universal aspect; just as the smooth or rough texture of a vase may be distinguished from its general design. John Crowe Ransom has elaborated this: the general design of a poem, its argument, is its STRUCTURE, while its texture consists of all its 'local' detail, its personal or unique qualities. In poetry, Ransom argues, texture clashes with and modifies structure. Compare TENSION. M.S.-S.

Bibl: J. C. Ransom, *The World's Body* (London and N.Y., 1938).

thaw. Term deriving from Ilya Ehrenburg's *The Thaw* (Part 1 of which appeared in 1953), and used to describe (1) periods of relaxation of Communist Party control over literature, and to a certain degree over the citizen's life in general, in the U.S.S.R., notably 1953–4, 1956–7, 1961–2 and 1963–4; (2) more generally (and by a natural extension from COLD WAR), periods of international *détente* between the U.S.S.R. and the West – the term being most often applied to the first such period, that between Stalin's death in March 1953 and the onset of the second Berlin crisis in November 1958; (3) the relaxation in Soviet methods of control over the East European satellites which culminated in the overthrow of the STALINIST regime in Poland in October 1956 by local nationally inspired Communists (see NATIONALISM; COMMUNISM) led by W. Gomulka (the *Polish October*), but ended with Soviet suppression of the Hungarian revolution (see HUNGARY) in November of the same year.   R.C.; D.C.W.

Bibl: M. D. Shulman, *Beyond the Cold War* (London and New Haven, 1966); R. C. Tucker, *The Soviet Political Mind* (N.Y., rev. ed., 1971).

theatre in the round. Any form of staging in which the acting area is surrounded on all sides by the audience, minimizing the scenic element and concentrating attention upon the figure of the actor. The use of this form is attested for some medieval and primitive drama; in the 20th century its attraction has lain in the sharp contrast it presents to 'picture-frame' NATURALISM (see OPEN STAGE). The first important central stage production of modern times was by Okhlopkov in Moscow (*The Mother,* 1933); the first permanent theatre in this form was the Penthouse Theater, University of Washington, Seattle (1940). The form has been used for large-scale, circus-like productions with spectacular effects achieved by movement, costume, and mobile stage properties and units, and for small-cast plays where a sense of intimate involvement between actor and audience is required. Few directors, however, have been willing to confine their work exclusively to this form.   M.A.

Bibl: S. Joseph, *Theatre in the Round* (London, 1967); see also OPEN STAGE.

Theatre Laboratory. An itinerant and highly influential experimental Polish theatre company directed by Jerzy Grotowski (*b.* 1933). In Grotowski's theatre the actor is paramount and must make use of all the physical and mental powers at his disposal; the emphasis is on austerity, poverty, and simplicity, in reaction against the 'wealth' of contemporary theatre; and the texts are mainly Grotowski's own radical adaptations of classic Polish works. The company was founded in 1959, gave its first performance outside Poland in 1966, and has since had a major influence on figures as diverse as the director Peter Brook and the choreographer Jerome Robbins. Also Grotowski's notion of a company as a monastic, self-contained troupe has become gospel for many of the AVANT-GARDE, e.g. notably the LIVING THEATRE.   M.BI.

Bibl: J. Grotowski, *Towards a Poor Theatre* (London, 1969; N.Y., 1970).

Théâtre Libre. An experimental Parisian theatre club founded in 1887 by André Antoine that had a profound influence on French play-writing, acting, and design. It became a showplace for naturalistic writers like Eugène Brieux dedicated to a theatre aimed at the cure of social evils; but it also staged controversial works by the great European dramatists such as Ibsen, Strindberg, Hauptmann, and Verga and the kind of *comédies rosses* ('cynical comedies') popular in the closing years of the century. At the same time it helped to liberate French acting from sentimental rhetoric and scenic design from artificial prettiness. It also inspired the creation of similar theatres such as Otto Brahm's FREIE BÜHNE in Berlin and J. T. Grein's *Independent Theatre* in London. It closed in April 1897, largely for economic reasons, but its influence in Europe and beyond was incalculable.   M.BI.

Théâtre National Populaire (TNP). A state-financed theatre, established in 1951 in the Palais de Chaillot, under the direction of Jean Vilar, with the express purpose of appealing to a wide popular audience and creating an atmosphere different from that of the commercial BOURGEOIS theatre. The TNP enjoyed a period of exceptional prestige when Gérard Philipe was its resident star, and it has done much to familiarize schoolchildren and factory-workers with the drama, both French and foreign. In 1963 Vilar was succeeded as director by Georges Wilson, who carries on the same tradition of serious, eclectic theatre.   J.G.W.

theatre of cruelty. A form of theatre which seeks to communicate to its audience a sense of pain, suffering, and the presence of evil, primarily through non-verbal means. The term was first used by the SURREALIST actor Antonin Artaud in his essay 'Le Théâtre de la cruauté' (1932). He developed his ideas further in a series of essays, letters, and manifestos published as *Le Théâtre et son double* (1938). Artaud rejected the Western tradition of theatre, whose emphasis upon REALISM and psychological character-study he considered trivial, and hoped to re-create theatre at the more universal level which he found in primitive RITUAL and oriental drama. Artaud's writing is visionary rather than practical, and no complete body of theory exists behind it. Outside France, where he had a strong influence upon the director Jean-Louis Barrault, Artaud was little known before the first English translation of his book in 1958. In the 1960s his ideas were widely discussed, and the concept of the theatre of cruelty was explored and developed, most notably in productions by Jerzy Grotowski (see THEATRE LABORATORY), Peter Brook, and the LIVING THEATRE. See also THEATRE OF THE ABSURD.   M.A.

Bibl: A. Artaud, *The Theatre and its Double* (tr. M. C. Richards, N.Y., 1958; tr. V. Corti, London, 1970); E. Sellin, *The Dramatic Concepts of Antonin Artaud* (Chicago, 1968).

theatre of panic. Term (*théâtre panique*) coined by the Spanish-born French dramatist, Fernando Arrabal, in 1962 to describe the kind of ceremonial theatre he favours. The reference is to the god Pan, a deity combining the attributes of rustic vitality, grotesque fun, and holy terror; and Arrabal's concept is a blend of tragedy and a Punch-and-Judy show, of bad taste and refinement, of sacrilege and the sacred. Heavily influenced by the theories of Antonin Artaud, Arrabal has put his ideas into practice in a number of ritualistic plays including *The Architect and the Emperor of Assyria* (1967) and *And They Handcuffed the Flowers* (1969). Similar ideas are apparent among French AVANT-GARDE companies, most notably Jerome Savory's rowdily picturesque and widely travelled Grand Magic Circus.   M.BI.

theatre of the absurd. Term coined in 1961 by the critic Martin Esslin to define a form of theatre which, rejecting NATURALISM as the basis for its presentation of character and action, uses a variety of dramatic techniques defying rational analysis and explanation to express, by implication rather than direct statement, the 'absurdity' of the human condition; Esslin adopts and expands the concept of the absurd employed by the EXISTEN-TIALIST Albert Camus in *Le Mythe de Sisyphe* (1942). The absurd is not so much a single, identifiable theatrical tradition as

a common denominator to be found in the work of a number of 20th-century dramatists, who are individually indebted to a variety of independent traditions from DADA and SURREALISM to the routines of vaudeville and the circus. Some elements of the absurd may be traced back to Alfred Jarry's *Ubu Roi* (1896), and found in plays by Cocteau and Ivan Goll written in the 1920s; but the term is usually associated with writers active after World War II, notably Samuel Beckett, Eugene Ionesco, N. F. Simpson, and Harold Pinter. In its rejection of rational, analytical processes, the genre has some affinities with THEATRE OF CRUELTY.   M.A.

Bibl: M. Esslin, *The Theatre of the Absurd* (rev. ed., Harmondsworth, 1968; N.Y., 1969).

Théâtre Populaire. A less successful predecessor, in the 1930s, of the THÉÂTRE NATIONAL POPULAIRE.   J.G.W.

Theatre Workshop. A theatre company founded, with a policy of COMMITMENT to the LEFT, by Joan Littlewood and Ewan McColl in 1945, and housed since 1953 in the Theatre Royal, Stratford, East London. In the second half of the 1950s it presented work by new dramatists including Brendan Behan, Shelagh Delaney, and Frank Norman, all infused with a theatrical vigour that was indebted equally to the writers' working-class backgrounds and to Joan Littlewood's directorial style. In 1963 her production of *Oh What A Lovely War!* helped to inspire a distinctively English form of DOCUMENTARY theatre.   M.A.

Bibl: J. R. Taylor, *Anger and After* (Baltimore, rev. ed., 1963; London, 2nd ed., 1969).

theism. Belief in at least one God (Greek *theos*) as the Creator of the universe and the Saviour and Ruler of human life, and as TRANSCENDENT because eternal and infinite (i.e. free from the limitations of time and space) as well as *immanent* (i.e. present and active in time and space). This belief produces the desire to understand any divine self-revelations and to enter, through prayer and corporate worship, into a humble relationship with God pictured as a person, specially as a Father, or with the gods. (DEISM, by contrast, denies the possibility of divine self-revelation.)

Polytheism is the belief in many gods, and is generally regarded as more primitive than *monotheism,* the belief in One God who is in some sense 'Almighty' or sovereign. All this has been shaken by scientific EXPLANATIONS of previously mysterious phenomena and by the disintegration of the stable societies where RELIGION was at home. Modern theologians have tried to reconcile the monotheism inherited from past ages of faith with the NATURAL SCIENCES' explanations of the EVOLUTIONARY emergence of matter, life, and man (see PROCESS THEOLOGY) and with the general process of MODERNIZATION. They have emphasized God's Being (more than mere existence) as the source, ground, and goal of all that exists or is possible, rather than God's miraculous interventions in the processes of nature. They have also stressed that much, if not all, talk of God (e.g. as being personal or 'above' us) is symbolic and may need a radical revision to be meaningful in our CULTURE. The most important Protestant theologian with such modern emphases was Paul Tillich (1886–1965, a German philosopher who acquired a wide influence in the U.S.A.).

For a sophisticated recent attempt to restate Christian belief while frankly abandoning the whole of theism, see DEATH OF GOD THEOLOGY. For its antecedents, see NON-THEISTIC RELIGION. For attempts to restate Christian theism, see DIALECTICAL THEOLOGY, EMPIRICAL THEOLOGY, and NEO-THOMISM. For the older identification of God with the universe, which still has some influence, see PANTHEISM. For the personal experience which is held to be a basis of theism, see MYSTICISM. Theism is professed by all Christians, Jews (see JUDAISM), and adherents of ISLAM, HINDUISM, and tribal religions. Many adherents of BUDDHISM also worship a divine Saviour. Under the pressure of SECULARIZATION, however, many nominal adherents of these religions live and think without much (if any) reference to theism. Their conception of religion is chiefly ethical (see ETHICS), and intellectually is marked by a cautious AGNOSTICISM. The more complete scepticism of ATHEISM rejects theism as an illusion and THEOLOGY as nonsense. On the whole, theism has declined as an intellectual force during the 20th century, together with the practices of prayer and corporate worship, although few people outside COMMUNIST countries admit to being convinced and consistent atheists.   D.L.E.

Bibl: H. D. Lewis, *Our Experience of God* (London and N.Y., 1959); D. W. D. Shaw, *Who Is God?* (London, 1968); H. Zahrnt, tr. R. A. Wilson, *The Question of God* (London, 1969; N.Y., 1970).

thematic apperception test (TAT). A projective test (see PROJECTION; MENTAL TESTING) developed by Henry Murray, in which the subject is asked to describe what is happening in a series of standard pictures that are sufficiently vague to permit a variety of interpretations. Interpretations are assumed to reflect *themas* (i.e. themes) that play a major role in the subject's own life.   W.Z.

theodicy. In THEOLOGY, a theory that asserts God's justice (Greek *dike*) in creating the world. The need for such a theory is rendered acute by the problem of evil. There is evil in the world: either God could not prevent it (but he is by definition omnipotent), or he did not choose to do so (but he is by definition benevolent). The word was coined in 1710 by Leibniz, who argued that even if there were no specific evils in the created world it would still be imperfect, just because created and not the source of its own existence, as God, the most perfect being, is alleged to be. One attempted method of solving the problem of evil is to argue that evil is merely negative, an absence of good, and so not truly real. Another method, less elusive, is to attribute the world's defects to the free will with which God endowed the minds, human and possibly diabolic, which he created, a free spirit being more perfect, because more like God, than one that is not free.   A.Q.

Bibl: J. H. Hick, *Evil and the God of Love* (London and N.Y., 1966).

theology. The attempt to talk rationally about the divine (see THEISM). Every RELIGION produces some theology, but Christianity has been intellectually active to a unique, perhaps excessive, extent. The term is therefore mostly used in a Christian context. It may cover the historical study of Christian scripture, history, and thought on the largely tacit and unexamined assumption that these subjects are important because the Christian faith is correct; or it may refer to an explicit, systematic, and often-renewed attempt to work out doctrines in the light of this faith (see CRISIS THEOLOGY; DOGMATICS; EMPIRICAL THEOLOGY; PHILOSOPHICAL THEOLOGY). This acceptance of Christianity may be contrasted with the wider and more neutral approach of 'religious studies', which emphasize COMPARATIVE RELIGION. D.L.E.

Bibl: J. Macquarrie, *Principles of Christian Theology* (London and N.Y., 1966); A. Richardson (ed.), *A Dictionary of Christian Theology* (London, 1969).

theoretical chemistry. An academic discipline in which theoretical PHYSICS is applied to chemical phenomena, such as BONDING, reaction rates (see CHEMICAL REACTION, CATALYSIS, COHESION, etc.). Much effort is devoted to mathematical calculations of the properties of theoretical MODELS, using QUANTUM MECHANICS (hence the near-synonym QUANTUM CHEMISTRY) and STATISTICAL MECHANICS. B.F.

Bibl: P.W. Atkins, *Molecular Quantum Mechanics* (Oxford, 1970); R. P. H. Gasser, *Entropy and Energy Levels* (Oxford, 1974).

theory X and **theory Y**, see under ORGANIZATION THEORY.

theosophy. A religious movement founded by Madame H. P. Blavatsky and Annie Besant in India towards the end of the 19th century and subsequently gaining adherents in many countries, specially in Germany, where in turn it gave rise to the ANTHROPOSOPHY taught by Rudolf Steiner. These terms come from the Greek, meaning respectively 'wisdom about God' and 'wisdom about Man', but the movement's mixture of Eastern and Western ideas appeals to few of those usually reckoned to be wise. D.L.E.

Theravada, see under BUDDHISM.

theremin. An ELECTRONIC musical instrument invented *c.* 1924 by a Russian scientist of that name. Tone is generated by the proximity of the player's hand to a short antenna attached to two oscillators, one operating at a fixed frequency, the other at a variable frequency. The difference between the two frequencies causes a 'beat' effect which is the third 'audio' frequency. The player controls pitch with one hand, volume with the other. A.H.

thermal neutron. A slow NEUTRON, whose KINETIC ENERGY is roughly equal to that of the random heat motion in the material through which it is passing. Thermal neutrons produce most of the FISSION reactions in a NUCLEAR REACTOR (see also MODERATOR). M.V.B.

thermal reactor, see under NUCLEAR REACTOR.

Thermidor. In the history of the French Revolution the Jacobin 'terror' (see JACOBINISM) was ended by the *coup d'état* of 9th Thermidor (27 July 1794), followed by a very marked BOURGEOIS reaction against both Robespierre's revolutionary concepts and the Parisian working class. The term was first applied in 20th-century revolutionary thought by Trotsky (see TROTSKYISM) in 1903 when he maintained that Lenin's imposition of strong central control on the revolutionary Russian Democratic Party was preparing the ground for the 'Thermidorians of socialist opportunism'. A main theme in the struggle for the Russian leadership after Lenin's death was the danger, alleged by Trotsky and his allies, of a new 'Thermidor', that is, a betrayal of the Russian Revolution and the Russian working class by the new state and party BUREAUCRACY. After his defeat Trotsky later claimed to perceive the Soviet Thermidor already in the suppression of the so-called 'left opposition' in 1923; but the course of Stalin's own rule, the COLLECTIVIZATION of agriculture, the first Five Year Plan and the great purges make such an analogy difficult to draw, the rise of a 'new class' and the end of the Soviet mass terror failing to coincide with what happened in Revolutionary France. D.C.W.

Bibl: L. Trotsky, tr. M. Eastman, *The Revolution Betrayed* (London and N.Y., 1937).

thermionics. The design of ELECTRONIC devices whose operation depends on the emission of ELECTRONS from the surface of a hot metal cathode (see ELECTRODE), e.g. the ELECTRON GUN in a CATHODE RAY TUBE, and the thermionic valve used in radio receivers and COMPUTERS before the advent of the TRANSISTOR.　M.V.B.

thermistor. A substance whose resistance changes rapidly with temperature. This property enables thermistors to be used for making devices in control systems (see CONTROL ENGINEERING). The active element is a SEMICONDUCTOR such as a mixture of nickel and manganese oxides with finely divided copper.　E.R.L.

thermochemistry. The part of THERMODYNAMICS concerned with the accurate measurement of the heat given out or absorbed during CHEMICAL REACTIONS.　B.F.

thermodynamics. A branch of PHYSICS developed in the 19th century, dealing with heat and temperature. The subject is based on three laws:
(1) The *first law* connects thermodynamics with MECHANICS by the statement: 'Heat is a form of ENERGY.' This implies that no engine can produce work indefinitely without a permanent source of heat, so that 'perpetual motion machines' cannot be made.
(2) The famous *second law* expresses the irreversibility of processes: 'It is impossible to produce work by transferring heat from a cold body to a hot body in any self-sustaining process.' It is of course possible to use the reverse process – heat transfer from hot to cold – to produce work, and this is the basis of the internal combustion engine, the steam engine, and nuclear and conventional power stations. A mathematically equivalent form of the second law is: 'ENTROPY always increases in any closed system not in EQUILIBRIUM, and remains constant for a system which is in equilibrium.'
(3) The *third law* states: 'It is impossible to cool a system right down to the ABSOLUTE ZERO of temperature.'
In addition to their importance in the theory of heat engines and CRYOGENICS, these three laws provide relations between the thermal properties of materials (e.g. the amount of heat necessary to produce a given rise in temperature) and their mechanical properties (e.g. the pressure necessary to produce a given decrease in size). They involve no mention of the underlying atomic structure of matter; the more powerful methods of STATISTICAL

MECHANICS enable the laws to be derived, and their significance understood, in terms of atomic motions.　M.V.B.

thermoluminescence. In ARCHAEOLOGY, a DATING technique based on the principle that, if a clay body is heated, ALPHA PARTICLES, trapped in the crystal LATTICE, will be released as light ENERGY which can be measured. The light is therefore proportional to the number of trapped alpha particles which in turn are directly related to the degree of flawing of the lattice, the intensity of the RADIOACTIVE environment in which the object was buried, and the length of exposure. The first variable can be determined by re-exposing the sample to a source of known strength and measuring the light emitted on reheating; the second can be measured directly. It is thus possible to estimate the length of the exposure, which in terms of baked clay means the time between the last ancient firing (usually the date of manufacture) and the date of testing. The method has value as a means of absolute date assessment. It is also widely used to test the authenticity of artifacts out of CONTEXT.　B.C.

thermonuclear reaction. A CHAIN REACTION based on nuclear FUSION.　M.V.B.

thermonuclear war, see under WAR.

thermoplastic. A POLYMER (PLASTIC) which becomes soft and relatively fluid on heating but hardens on cooling. Such plastics, like polyvinylchloride, typically have long polymer chains with few chemical BONDS between the chains, and when hot are easily moulded, extruded, or rolled into sheets. Thermosetting plastics are originally semi-fluid polymers with quite short polymer chains which on heating react to give a rigid three-dimensional cross-linked network.　B.F.

thesis, see under SYNTHESIS.

things-in-themselves, see NOUMENA.

third force. Name adopted in France by a grouping of SOCIALIST and Catholic M.R.P. (Mouvement Républicain Populaire) deputies, who held a central position between the RIGHT wing and the COMMUNISTS in the National Assembly. Many of the governments of France in the years 1946–51 came from this alliance. The term was adapted in 1949 by André Siegfried to cover proposals for the development of European cooperation by states sharing the political traditions of Europe and hoping to escape 'the Communist embrace, if possible without putting themselves under too close protection by the United States'. The concept inspired the Schuman plan out of which grew the ECSC, but was later submerged under GAULLISM.　　　　　　　　D.C.W.

Third World. (1) Collective term of French origin (*le Tiers-monde*), taken up by American writers, for those states not regarded or regarding themselves as members of either the developed CAPITALIST or the developed COMMUNIST 'worlds': they are thus classified by their state of economic development as 'underdeveloped', 'less developed', or 'developing' states (see UNDERDEVELOPMENT). The Third World includes most of the countries of Latin America and the recently independent states of Asia and Africa. Many of these share a colonial past and strong resentment against IMPERIALISM; they are poor and, thanks largely to the population explosion, are growing poorer by comparison with the industrialized nations; in foreign policy, following the Indian example, many of them have favoured NEUTRALISM. The Third World accounts for about one-third of the membership of UNO and is strongly represented in UNCTAD.

(2) More recently, some writers have begun to distinguish between the *Third World*, which they confine to those developing countries with rich natural resources such as the oil-producing states of the Middle East, and the *Fourth World*, in which are counted all the other underdeveloped countries which have no such resources and little if any prospect of development.　　　　　　　　A.L.C.B.

Thomas, Dylan (Welsh-born poet, 1914–53), see under CRITERION, THE.

Thomas, Norman M. (U.S. socialist, 1884–1968), see under POPULISM.

Thomas, William Isaac (U.S. sociologist, 1863–1947), see under CHICAGO SCHOOL.

Thompson, Sir D'Arcy Wentworth (Scottish zoologist, 1860–1948), see under BIOMETRY; TRANSFORMATION.

Thompson, Denys (British educationist, *b.* 1907), see under LEAVISITE.

Thoms, William John (British antiquary, 1803–85), see under FOLKLORE.

Thomsen, Christian Jürgensen (Danish prehistorian, 1788–1865), see under THREE-AGE SYSTEM.

Thorndike, Edward Lee (U.S. psychologist, 1874–1949), see under CONNECTIONISM; PSYCHOMETRICS.

Thorwaldsen, Bertel (Danish sculptor, 1768 or 1770 to 1844), see under NEO-CLASSICISM.

thought police, see under ORWELLIAN.

three-age system. A simple technological MODEL used to order the past. It was introduced in Denmark in 1816–19 by C. Thomsen, who proposed that the prehistoric period (see PREHISTORY) could be divided into an Age of Stone, an Age of Bronze, and an Age of Iron. His theoretical scheme was soon shown by excavation to be largely valid. With numerous elaborations and subdivisions, including the subdivision of the Stone Age into *palaeolothic* ('Old Stone Age') and *neolithic* ('New Stone Age') periods by Sir John Lubbock in 1865, it was widely adopted in the Old World but the development of American and African ARCHAEOLOGY showed that it was not universally applicable. It is now regarded as a gross over-simplification of little further value, although its basic terminology is still used as a convenient shorthand.　　　　　　　　B.C.
Bibl: G. Daniel, *The Three Ages* (Cambridge, 1943) and *The Origins and Growth of Archaeology* (Harmondsworth, 1967; N.Y., 1971).

three-body problem. A variety of questions arising from the fact that in the (Newtonian) theory of GRAVITATION one cannot solve completely the DIFFERENTIAL EQUATIONS which govern the motion of three or more bodies. One can compute approximate solutions, but these will only be valid for *limited* periods of time; they cannot tell one, for example, whether the earth and moon will *eventually* spiral away from the sun. Work on such qualitative problems was initiated by H. Poincaré (1854–1912) who developed and applied the methods of algebraic TOPOLOGY for this purpose.   R.G.

threshold (or *limen*). In the measurement of sensation, the statistical point at which (1) two STIMULI resemble each other so closely as to be confusable (the *differential threshold*) or (2) a stimulus is so weak that its presence cannot be detected except by chance (the *absolute threshold*).   H.L.

throwback, see under ATAVISM.

thrust stage, see under OPEN STAGE.

Thurstone, Louis Leon (U.S. psychologist, 1887–1955), see under MENTAL TESTING.

Thwaite, Anthony (British author and editor, *b.* 1930), see under ENCOUNTER.

thyristor. A SOLID-STATE DEVICE employing SEMICONDUCTORS and having some of the properties of an electrical switch, e.g. it can initiate a flow of current. However, it can only stop the flow if the voltage across the thyristor is reversed, and in this respect it behaves in much the same way as a gas-filled ELECTRONIC valve. The fact that thyristors have replaced such valves in virtually all applications is due to their advantages in size (a whole order of magnitude smaller than their valve counterparts), efficiency, robustness, and reliability, and to the fact that they require no separate heater circuit, as does the valve. The development of thyristors has extended the use of semiconductors into the 'power' field of electrical engineering in a similar way to that in which the TRANSISTOR has replaced the electronic valve. A single thyristor can regulate electric power supplies of the order of many kilowatts.   E.R.L.
    Bibl: A. W. J. Griffin and R. S. Ramshaw, *The Thyristor and its Application* (London, 1965).

thyroid gland. An important endocrine gland (see ENDOCRINOLOGY) under the control of the PITUITARY and responsible for the control of basal metabolic rate.

Anatomically the gland is a system of vesicles containing a secretory product of which a principal ingredient is thyroglobulin. Active thyroid hormones are thyroxin and triiodothyronine. Both contain iodine, and the working of the thyroid is dependent upon its being in adequate supply. Iodides are added to table salt in areas where iodine would otherwise be lacking.   P.M.

Tieck, Ludwig (German poet, novelist, and dramatist, 1773–1853), see under ROMANTICISM.

Tiedemann, Dietrich (German philosopher, 1748–1803), see under DEVELOPMENTAL PSYCHOLOGY.

Tikhonov, Nikolai (Russian author, *b.* 1896), see under SERAPION BROTHERS.

Tillich, Paul (German-U.S. theologian, 1886–1965), see under ALIENATION; CHRISTIAN SOCIALISM; THEISM.

time and motion study, see under WORK STUDY.

time error. In PSYCHOPHYSICS, the tendency for the second of two stimuli – visual, auditory, or tactual – of equal magnitude to be judged as greater by virtue of the fact that the later is being judged against the earlier's diminished magnitude in immediate memory.   J.S.B.

time series analysis, see under EXTRAPOLATION.

time-sharing, see under COMPUTING.

Tinguely, Jean (Swiss sculptor, *b.* 1925), see under AUTO-DESTRUCTIVE; ENVIRONMENT; NOUVEAU RÉALISME.

Tippett, Sir **Michael** (British composer, *b.* 1905), see under POLYRHYTHM.

tissue. A system of CELLS which fulfils a definite physiological or structural function – e.g. connective tissue, bone, cartilage, or nervous tissue.   P.M.

tissue culture. A system by which living CELLS in a normal or cancerous TISSUE can be cultivated and propagated for many generations of cell division outside the body in suitable nutrient media. Both connective tissue cells (fibroblasts) and epithelial cells have been cultivated in this way. It was at one time thought that tissue cultures lived indeterminately, and that a famous strain of fibroblasts derived from the heart of an embryonic chicken had been maintained for 10 or 20 years in the Rockefeller Institute. Newer evidence shows that this is not the case. Tissue cultures that remain DIPLOID in CHROMOSOME make-up have a determinate lifespan which varies in length in inverse proportion to the age of the organism from which the tissues were taken for cultivation. In the older forms of tissue culture the growth medium was a semi-solid one, being composed of a mixture of chicken's plasma (see SERUM) with a watery extract of chicken embryos which contains the full range of nutrient substances required for continued growth. Today, however, systems of fluid culture have become almost universally adopted. Long-cultivated tissues sometimes undergo a TRANSFORMATION associated with the acquisition of cancerous or malignant properties. Malignant strains have an indeterminate lifespan. Tissue cultures are widely used for the cultivation of viruses (see VIROLOGY) – e.g. polio virus – for the preparation of vaccines.　　　　P.M.

Titchener, Edward Bradford (U.S. psychologist, 1867–1927), see under EMPATHY.

Tito, Josip Broz (Jugoslav statesman, b. 1892), see under COMINFORM; POPULAR FRONT; TITOISM; USTACHA.

Titoism. A term invented to characterize the specific political evolution of Yugoslav domestic and foreign policies after Tito's break with Stalin in 1948; it has also been applied to the policies of other Communist parties displaying similar tendencies towards doctrinal REVISIONISM and national COMMUNISM. Internally, Titoism was marked by some attenuation of the Party's administrative (though not its political) role and of the power exercised by the political police. It permitted a far greater contact with other countries by liberalizing travel, allowing emigration, and developing the tourist industry. It reversed the harsh COLLECTIVIZATION drive in favour of individual small-scale

farming. Its most novel policy, which it claims as its doctrinal trade-mark and the most distinctive characteristic of Yugoslav SOCIALISM, was that of introducing 'workers' self-government' through 'workers' councils', together with the industrial 'self-management' of enterprises in a *market socialism*. Political decentralization led to demands for autonomy in federal states on ethnic and economic grounds and this produced a certain reversal of Tito's policies, a clamp-down on 'anarcho-liberal' tendencies and on Croat and other local NATIONALISMS.

Externally, Tito's foreign policy since 1948 has become completely independent of the Soviet Union. It has achieved this by taking advantage of the balance of power in Europe and by developing special relationships with the THIRD WORLD countries on the basis of NON-ALIGNMENT. The resumption of closer relations with the Soviet Union on the Party level did not impair Tito's jealously guarded independence, which was expressed not only in foreign policy, but also in his cordial relations with those Communist parties (e.g. the Romanian, Italian and Spanish) which opposed the Soviet Union's attempts to re-establish its doctrinal and political leadership in the Communist movement, and to exclude China from it.

The dangers to Titoism are (1) the risk that the European balance may be upset by the increasing power of the Soviet Union and (2) uncertainty about the internal stability of Yugoslavia after Tito, particularly the threat of Slovenian and Croatian separatism, an instability which could be exploited by the Soviet Union to re-establish its domination in the Balkans.　　　　L.L.

Bibl: M. Zaninovich, *The Development of Socialist Yugoslavia* (Baltimore, 1968); H. M. Christman (ed.), *The Essential Tito* (N.Y., 1970; Newton Abbot, 1971); D. Rusinow, *The Yugoslav Experiment, 1948–74* (London, 1977).

Tkachev, Peter (Russian revolutionary, 1844–86), see under BOLSHEVISM; POPULISM.

TNP, see THÉÂTRE NATIONAL POPULAIRE.

Tocqueville, Alexis de, see DE TOCQUEVILLE.

Toffler, Alvin (U.S. author, *b.* 1928), see under FUTURE SHOCK.

Togliatti, Palmiro (Italian Communist leader, 1893–1964), see under POLY-CENTRISM.

Toland, John (Irish-born philosopher, 1670–1722), see under PANTHEISM.

tolerance. In IMMUNOLOGY, a state of specific non-reactivity towards a substance that would normally excite active IMMUNITY. The institution of specific tolerance is the goal to which all research in TISSUE and organ transplantation is directed. Many means of producing tolerance are in use, but its precise mechanism is not known.   P.M.

Toller, Ernst (German dramatist, 1893–1939), see under EXPRESSIONISM; GATE THEATRE.

Tolman, Edward Chase (U.S. psychologist, 1886–1959), see under COGNITIVE PSYCHOLOGY.

Tolstoy, Count Lev Nikolayevich (Russian novelist and social thinker, 1828–1910), see under FOLK ART; REALISM.

tonality, see under ATONAL MUSIC.

Tone, Franchot (U.S. actor, 1906–68), see under GROUP THEATRE.

tone-cluster (or *cluster*). A group of adjacent notes, usually played on a keyboard instrument, and not susceptible of conventional harmonic analysis. Tone-clusters may be played with the palm of the hand, the forearm, or a piece of wood or other material of a specified length. First appearing in the music of American AVANT-GARDE composers such as Charles Ives and Henry Cowell, they have now become a routine device and part of the normal vocabulary of music.   A.H.

tone-row, see under SERIAL MUSIC.

Tönnies, Ferdinand (German sociologist and philosopher, 1855–1936), see under COMPARATIVE METHOD; GEMEINSCHAFT AND GESELLSCHAFT; SOCIOLOGY.

Tonton Macoute. In Haitian Creole literally: Uncle bagmen. A 10,000-strong PARA-MILITARY storm-troop organization, personally recruited from 1959 onwards by Jacques Duvallier, dictator of Haiti, to terrorize (see TERRORISM) political opponents and critics of the regime. Officially entitled *Volontaires de la Sec-urité Nationale,* and untouched by any legal restraint, its members acquired a name for violence, extortion, torture, and brutality, especially during the reign of terror from 1960 to 1965.   D.C.W.
  Bibl: R. I. Rotberg, *Haiti: the Politics of Squalor* (Boston, 1971).

Toorop, Jan (Dutch artist, 1858–1928), see under NEO-IMPRESSIONISM.

topodeme, see under DEME.

topological psychology. A form of PSYCHOLOGY associated with Kurt Lewin who, much influenced by GESTALT psychology, used topological GEOMETRY (i.e. non-metric spatial relations; see TOPOLOGY) to represent and theorize about the field of interacting psychological forces (the LIFE SPACE) within which a person lives and acts.   I.M.L.H.
  Bibl: C. Lewin, tr. F. and G. M. Heider, *Principles of Topological Psychology,* (London and N.Y., 1936).

topology. A branch of MATHEMATICS often picturesquely but inaccurately described as the study of those properties of figures in space which persist under all continuous deformations. Thus interlocking is a topological property of closed curves in 3 dimensions: one cannot separate two interlocked rubber bands without cutting one of them (a *dis*continuous deformation). But intuitively, as Kant emphasized, the above description is too narrow: intrinsically a (lined) left-hand glove does not differ from a right-hand one, but one cannot be continuously deformed into the other in 3 dimensions. Further, there is no reason to limit investigations to 3-dimensional space, or even to spaces which can be said to have a DIMENSION. All that is required of a general *topological space* is that there should be a notion of closeness (or *neighbour-hood*) associated with it. *Continuous* FUNCTIONS, or *maps* from one space into another, are required to preserve the notion of closeness; an invertible (two-way) map is called a *homeomorphism*. Topology, then, is the study of those properties of topological spaces which are preserved by homeomorphisms. (And there *is* a homeomorphism of 3-dimensional space onto itself which turns a right-hand glove into a left-hand one.)

General topology is concerned with the properties of 'figures' (which are often arbitrary collections of points) in general or only slightly specialized topological spaces. Among the CONCEPTS it studies are the notions of LIMIT and of *connectedness*. Its theorems do not go deep, but they have a very wide range of application.

The most powerful and beautiful theorems of topology, however, concern more restricted 'figures' in spaces which are more specialized and which may carry additional structure. This makes it possible to represent the situation (in *combinatorial topology*) or to approximate to it (in *algebraic topology*) by a 'framework', or *complex* (e.g. a covering of a space by a network of triangles) to which numerical and algebraic methods can be applied. As in *analytic* GEOMETRY, feats of geometric insight can be replaced by more or less routine computations. (Perversely, *analytic topology* seeks to obtain results without resort to algebra.)

Homology theory is concerned with the notion of *boundary*; e.g. the boundary of a sphere in 3 dimensions is its 2-dimensional surface, which in turn has zero boundary. The formal properties of the boundary OPERATOR also recur in purely algebraic contexts; this is the prime ingredient of *homological* ALGEBRA. *Homotopy theory* is concerned with the properties of figures and of maps which persist under continuous deformation.

Various specific topological problems (e.g. the classification of the topological types of 2-dimensional surfaces) were solved in the 19th century. In the first half of this century the foundations of algebraic topology were developed. Many of the most powerful techniques and results belong to the last 25 years. But some classic problems (e.g. the classification of 3-dimensional manifolds) remain unsolved.

Apart from its intrinsic interest, topology is important because it can give significant qualitative results about continuous phenomena without requiring a knowledge of detail (see THREE-BODY PROBLEM). Applications to the theory of DIFFERENTIAL EQUATIONS have been particularly fruitful. Recently *catastrophe theory* has used topology to classify the different ways in which a dynamical system can pass through a point of instability; qualitative applications have been made to ECONOMICS, SOCIOLOGY, and MORPHOGENESIS.   R.G.

Bibl: R. Courant and H. Robbins, *What is Mathematics?* (London and N.Y., 1941); S. Barr, *Experiments in Topology* (N.Y., 1964; London, 1965).

Torre, Guillermo de (Spanish-Argentinian author, 1900–1971), see under ULTRAISM.

total art. The creation of 'total environments' – walls, rooms, large spaces – usually involving various media, so as to disturb or in some way interest the spectator (or explorer). Examples are the houses, interiors, and accumulations (MERZ structures) built by Kurt Schwitters, and more recently the tableaux of Ed Kienholz. In its attempt to free the concept of art from its associations with collectors' pieces, and to break down the traditional barriers between 'art' and 'life', total art has roots in CONSTRUCTIVISM, SURREALISM, and DADA.
                                                        P.C.
Bibl: A. Henri, *Environments and Happenings* (London and N.Y., 1974).

total serialization, see under SERIAL MUSIC.

total theatre. Theatre regarded as primarily a director's medium using the text as only a minor part of an overall theatrical experience of lights, music, movement of all sorts, sets, and costumes. The term was first used in the mid-1920s: an abortive *Totaltheater* planned by Walter Gropius for Erwin Piscator in Berlin; but the concept was first effectively executed by Jean-Louis Barrault in works like Claudel's *Christophe Colombe* (production of 1953) and Barrault's adaptation (with André Gide) of Kafka's *The Trial* (1947). Subsequently it was taken much further by other directors: especially the Italian, Luca Ronconi, in his travelling version of Ariosto's *Orlando Furioso* (1970), in which the peripatetic spectators were constantly engulfed by the action.

M.BI.

Bibl: J. L. Barrault, tr. B. Wall, *Reflections on the Theatre* (London, 1951).

totalitarianism. A theoretical view of NAZISM, FASCISM, and Soviet COMMUNISM which sees them as examples of a political system dominated by a single party and IDEOLOGY in which all political, economic, and social activities are absorbed and subsumed and all dissidence suppressed by police TERRORISM. Total monopoly of the ordinary flow of information and public argument is essential to such a system. This view was much current in the 1930s–1950s period among dissident MARXIST intellectual commentators on the *Gleichschaltung* (Nazification) of parties, trade unions, universities, professional associations, etc. in Nazi Germany and on the degree of central control exercised by the STALINIST dictatorship in the U.S.S.R. It owes much to organic theories of the State. Later writers have tended to emphasize the degree to which rivalries for the leadership, factionalism, and the development, in industry, applied science, or the armed forces, of separate centres of POWER and influence and of hierarchies parallel to the party but essential to the State, preserve an element of PLURALISM and modify the earlier monolithic image of the totalitarian State.

D.C.W.

Bibl: F. Neumann, *Behemoth: the Structure and Practice of National Socialism* (London, 1942); K. A. Wittfogel, *Oriental Despotism* (New Haven, 1957); H. Arendt, *The Origins of Totalitarianism* (London, 2nd ed., 1961; N.Y., new ed., 1966).

totemism. For long regarded as a large and heterogeneous set of religious practices in PRIMITIVE societies in which groups of people associated themselves, usually as descent groups, with natural objects. In the early 1960s Claude Lévi-Strauss revived interest in the subject by radically changing our vision of it. He argued that what had hitherto been treated under that head was a mode of thought and a classification of nature in relation to men. The argument sought to strip away both the religious and utilitarian elements that had accumulated in the theoretical writings since the last century. See also STRUCTURALISM.

M.F.

Bibl: C. Lévi-Strauss, tr. R. Needham, *Totemism* (Boston, 1963; London, 1964); E. R. Leach (ed.), *The Structural Study of Myth and Totemism* (London, 1967).

tower block, see POINT BLOCK.

town. A geographical term not easy to define. In Britain a clear-cut dichotomy between town and country, or rural and urban SETTLEMENT, does not exist at the present time either physically or socially. Instead there is an urban-rural continuum within which towns may be distinguished as foci where central services tend to concentrate. A. E. Smailes and F. H. W. Green have been responsible for investigating and identifying such foci of central services. In England, Scotland, and Wales they found that the best criterion for deciding what is or is not a town is afforded by the presence or absence of a bus station.

M.L.

townscape. The visual effect created by urban forms and usually considered analogous to the picturesque effects found in landscape. The idea stems from Camillo Sitte's *City Planning according to Artistic Principles* (Vienna, 1899), which was based largely on an analysis of the compositional elements of European urban squares. The term was given wide currency by the *Architectural Review* in the 1950s. Through the drawings of Gordon Cullen, it was directed towards an emphasis on ground surfaces, *street furniture* (lamp-posts, seats, bollards, etc.), and such qualities as spatial surprise and the visual effects of a mixture of urban activities.

M.BR.

Bibl: G. Cullen, *The Concise Townscape* (N.Y., 1971; London, 1972).

toxicology. The science of poisons – identification, mode of action, and antidotes. *Toxins* and *venoms* are poisons of biological origin. In general they are *antigens* and their remedies are *antibodies* (see IMMUNITY). Snake venoms are very often ENZYMES which have profound effects on blood-clotting processes, and for that reason may be used therapeutically, e.g. in haemophilia. The belief that very low doses of poisonous substances – e.g. strychnine – have a stimulatory and thus salutary effect is altogether without foundation. Toxins deprived of their poisonous but not their antigenic properties are described as *toxoids* – e.g. diphtheria or tetanus toxoid. Toxoids excite active immunity, and their use is greatly preferable to that of *antisera,* e.g. anti-tetanus SERUM. Vast numbers of industrial chemicals are now known to be poisonous substances: thus coal tar and its derivatives are CARCINOGENS, and organic solvents like carbon tetrachloride (used in the dry-cleaning industry) are known to cause grave liver damage.   P.M.

toxoids, see under PROPHYLAXIS.

Toynbee, Arnold Joseph (British historian, *b.* 1889), see under HISTORICISM.

trace element. Biologically important substances, also called *micronutrients,* and found, usually in minute amounts, in the soil and in food. Those needed for healthy plant growth are iron, molybdenum, boron, magnesium, copper, chlorine, and cobalt. For animals micronutrients include copper, iron, manganese, cobalt, zinc, molybdenum, iodine, and selenium. Certain animals and plants require specific elements which do not seem essential to most others, e.g. tunicates require vanadium, some plants need barium and strontium. Although needing only small amounts, living organisms concentrate trace elements in their tissues, sometimes having levels many thousand times higher than those found in soil or food. Trace elements are probably important as part of ENZYMES rather than as general tissue constituents. However, there is no rigid division in all animals between major nutrients and micronutrients.

Some soils are naturally deficient in trace elements (e.g. copper in South Australia), and until they are added farming is impossible. Micronutrients are also added to the diet of farm animals, particularly those reared intensively. But care must be taken to avoid overdosing, as trace elements may be very poisonous in excessive quantities. Thus copper in small amounts is needed by plants, but in higher concentrations is used as a fungicide and a weedkiller; and even man is harmed by water containing 10 parts per million. K.M.

Bibl: G. W. Cooke, *The Control of Soil Fertility* (London, 1967).

tracer. A distinguishable variant of some common ELEMENT which, being handled by the body in exactly the same way as its normal form, can be used to follow the course of a metabolic reaction (see METABOLISM), in the body as a whole or in CELLS in a test-tube or other artificial environment. Tracer elements are distinguished from their normal counterparts by RADIOACTIVITY or by differences of mass. Tracer techniques represent the most important advance in biochemical methodology in the present century, and it is no exaggeration to say that the whole of modern BIOCHEMISTRY and much of immunology (see IMMUNITY) is founded upon their use. An example in medicine is the use of radioactive iodine to examine the functions of the THYROID. Tracer technology is combined with microscopy in the technique known as *autoradiography,* in which a histological section containing radioactive tracers is made, in effect, to take a photograph of itself by applying it to a photographic emulsion; see AUTORADIOGRAPH.   P.M.

tracked hovercraft, see under HOVERCRAFT.

tracking, see STREAMING.

Tracy, A. L. C. G. Destutt de, see DESTUTT DE TRACY.

trade cycles. Successions of alternating booms and DEPRESSIONS. Though trade cycles have been proceeding for centuries, there are still differences of opinion about their fundamental causes. (1) The *credit theory* attributes them to fluctuations in the willingness of banks to make advances to their customers. (2) The *underconsumption theory* holds that as people get richer they tend to save a rising proportion of their incomes (i.e. consume a smaller proportion). At the same time, the rate of increase of requirements for CAPITAL expenditure will rise at the same rate as that of the rise of consumption. Consequently the demand constituted by the fraction of income spent on consumption and that caused by INVESTMENT requirements tend to fall below the productive potential of the economy and a depression occurs. The use of the word 'underconsumption' implies that it is desirable for income receivers to continue to spend a constant fraction of their income on consumption. If they did this, so the theory holds, then depressions caused by the inadequacy of consumption and investment taken together would not occur. R.H.

tradition-direction, see under OTHER-DIRECTION.

traditional grammar. A summarizing (and often pejorative) term in LINGUISTICS, referring to the set of opinions, facts, and principles which characterize grammatical analysis not carried out within the perspective of modern linguistics; e.g. the NORMATIVE emphasis of traditional grammar contrasts with the descriptive emphasis within linguistics. D.C.

trahison des clercs, see under INTELLECTUALS.

Trakl, Georg (Austrian poet, 1887–1914), see under EXPRESSIONISM; SYMBOLISM.

transactional analysis. In PSYCHOTHERAPY, a theoretical and practical approach developed by Eric Berne, and popularized in his book *Games People Play* (New York, 1964; London, 1966). It postulates three positions from which people can communicate (child, adult, and parent) and six possible classes of transaction (e.g. work, pastimes, intimacy), of which games are most frequently the focus of transactional analysis. In a typical game, one player pretends to be having an adult-adult relationship with another, but is actually trying to manipulate the other into being a 'parent' to his 'child', and thereby to achieve a goal such as avoiding responsibility for his own actions. The analyst, usually working with a group (see GROUP THERAPY), exposes such games, and encourages more constructive ways of interacting. M.J.C.

transcendence. The state of being beyond the reach or apprehension of experience; its opposite is *immanence.* The THEIST'S God, conceived as a creator external to the perceivable world he creates, is *transcendent;* whereas the PANTHEIST'S God, who is identified with the perceivable world, or some part of it, is *immanent.* Kant held that the metaphysical (see METAPHYSICS) CONCEPT of the soul, as an unobservable SUBSTANCE underlying the particular mental states that are accessible to INTROSPECTION, is transcendent, as is the conception of nature as a unity or complete whole. There is an important distinction in the philosophy of Kant between the transcendent and the *transcendental.* The former is unknowable by our minds, dependent as they are on the senses for raw material (see SENSE-DATA). What is transcendental is the logical apparatus of concepts and principles, common to all rational minds, that organizes experience and is thus logically prior to it. The transcendental aspect of the mind's operations can be elicited by a critical philosophy that works out the PRESUPPOSITIONS of our knowledge. A.Q.

transducer. A device for transforming one type of wave, motion, signal, excitation, or oscillation into another; the transformation is called *transduction.* For example, the crystal cartridge in a record-player is a transducer producing a varying electric signal from the oscillations of the stylus as it traverses the grooves of a gramophone record; a loudspeaker is a transducer producing sound waves from a varying electric signal; and a sense organ such as the eye is a transducer which converts information contained in light ENERGY into nervous impulses. M.V.B.; P.M.

transduction. (1) In PHYSICS, see under TRANSDUCER. (2) In BIOLOGY, see under TRANSFORMATION, sense 2(a).

transfer. In EDUCATIONAL PSYCHOLOGY, the improvement of one type of mental or motor activity by training in another, related one. Identical response elements may be transferred, when the new task has some of the same components as the old one; e.g. learning tennis after learning squash. Or rules may transfer, e.g. from one branch of MATHEMATICS to another. Or transfer may take place when the learning of a specific skill results in a non-specific faculty being trained; e.g. the general logical discipline supposedly gained from chess-playing or learning Latin. Transfer may be positive (helpful) or negative (hindering). Negative transfer results either from *proactive interference* between moderately similar response patterns, each partially learned, where earlier learning of one affects later learning of another, or from *retroactive interference* with mastery of a previously learned skill by the learning of a new one.   H.L.

transfer payments, see under GNP.

transfer RNA, see under NUCLEIC ACID.

transference. In PSYCHOANALYSIS, the patient develops strong positive or negative feelings towards the analyst. Positive transference facilitates treatment by creating an artificial NEUROSIS, in which the patient's symptoms acquire a new focus, the therapeutic relationship itself, which can then be worked on more directly in therapy. W.Z.

transfinite, see under INFINITE.

transformation.
(1) In MATHEMATICS and PHYSICS the objects studied are often referred to by using *labels* (usually numerical). Examples: (*A*) the diagrams in a book are referred to by number; (*B*) the points in a plane are described by their COORDINATES; (*C*) VECTORS are described by their components. A systematic relabelling is called an *alias transformation* (or a *transformation of coordinates*). It can be specified by, and it is often identified with, a FUNCTION *f* given by (1) *a'* = f(*a*), where *a'* is the new label of the object whose old label is *a*; *f* is a PERMUTATION of the labels. Note that in example (*B*) *f* consists of two real-valued functions, one for each coordinate. The result of successive transformations is obtained by composition: if *a"* = *g* (*a'*), then *a"* = *g*(*f*(*a*)) = *g.f*(*a*). Equation (1) may be interpreted in another way: one regards *a'* as the (old) label of a different object, into which the object with label *a* has been sent by the transformation *f*; *f* is then called an *alibi transformation*. It represents a movement of the objects.

Any RELATION between, or function of, objects can be expressed in terms of their labels. In general this expression will change with relabelling. If it remains identically the same under a transformation *f*, or under all the transformations belonging to some set *S*, then the corresponding relation or function is said to be an *invariant* of *f* or *S*. If *f* is considered as an alibi transformation, then an invariant represents an unchanging feature of the situation; e.g. the distance between two points of a rigid body is invariant under any rotation of it.

There are two classic problems: (1) given certain relations and functions to find the set (actually a GROUP) of all transformations (here called AUTOMORPHISMS) under which they are invariant; (2) given a group *G* of transformations, to find all (or, better, methods for constructing all) the invariants of *G*. Both problems are of great significance for physics. In the special theory of RELATIVITY it is postulated that light rays (as relations between points of SPACE-TIME) are invariants; the corresponding group is the Lorentz transformations. Knowledge of the invariants of this group (and others) plays an essential role in the theory of the fundamental PARTICLES. See also PARITY. R.G.
Bibl: J. Singh, *Mathematical Ideas* (London and N.Y., 1972).
(2) In BIOLOGY, (*a*) a change in the genetic make-up of a MICRO-ORGANISM, particularly a bacterium (see BACTERIOLOGY), brought about by a quasi-infective action of a NUCLEIC ACID. If the nucleic acid is introduced by a vector of some kind, e.g. a VIRUS, the process is spoken of as TRANSDUCTION. (*b*) D'Arcy Thompson's 'method of transformations' was a scheme for showing up similarities and differences between outline drawings of related plants or animals by inscribing them within COORDINATE systems by which one can be shown to be a regular geometric transformation of the other. (*c*) A change that occurs in some CELLS under long-term TISSUE CULTURE as a consequence of which they change their appearance and habit of growth and acquire malignant properties. P.M.

transformation-rules, see under AXIOMATICS.

transformational grammar, see under GENERATIVE GRAMMAR.

transhumance. In GEOGRAPHY, regular seasonal cycles of livestock movement, e.g. the Turkana system of cattle movement between mountains and plains or the use of summer Alp pastures in central Europe. The basis of the movement is regular seasonal changes in pasture availability related to seasonal thermal and moisture cycles. Transhumance is more restricted in usage than pastoral NOMADISM, which describes irregular and non-seasonal herding movements. P.H.

TRANSISTOR

transistor. A SOLID-STATE DEVICE, (invented 1948), based on the action of junctions between SEMICONDUCTORS with different electrical characteristics, which can be used as an amplifier or RECTIFIER for electrical signals. Because of their small size, robustness, and safeness (since they operate at low voltages) transistors have virtually superseded THERMIONIC valves as the principal ELECTRONIC components in HI-FI, radio, television, and COMPUTERS. They have also rendered practicable medical and surgical apparatus which could not otherwise have existed.   M.V.B.

transition element. Any ELEMENT with an unfilled inner ELECTRON SHELL. There are several groups of transition elements in the PERIODIC TABLE; elements within each group have closely similar physical and chemical properties.   M.V.B.

translocation. In GENETICS, a MUTATIONAL event by which part of one CHROMOSOME becomes attached to or intercalated into another chromosome. Translocations almost invariably have important genetic effects.   P.M.

transmutation of elements, see under NUCLEAR REACTOR.

transnational (or *multinational*) **companies.** Business corporations which are registered, and which operate, in several countries at once. By providing a 'package' of resources in the shape of INVESTMENT funds combined with managerial, technical, and entrepreneurial skills, the transnational companies have contributed substantially to the growth not only of world visible trade (which in the 1960s grew appreciably faster than world output) but also of invisible trade, i.e. increased income flows in profits, interest, and dividends. This mobility of CAPITAL constitutes their greatest asset in its flexibility of response to national conditions, while exposing them to the criticism that they have no enforceable loyalty to any national government in such sensitive areas as taxation (which they can readily avoid by moving their funds around). The need to regulate transnational companies by some international agency or code is widely recognized.   D.E.

Bibl: C. Tugendhat, *The Multinationals* (London, 1971; N.Y., 1972).

transnational relations; transnational society. Terms coined by Raymond Aron (*Paix et guerre entre les nations*, Paris, 1962) to describe the variety of relationships, activities, and organizations which operate across national frontiers and which include, for example, the Roman Catholic Church; TRANSNATIONAL COMPANIES; trade unions; professional, scientific, and sporting organizations; REVOLUTIONARY movements. Aron suggested that when such activities flourished, as in Europe before 1914, the freedom of exchange, of movement, and of COMMUNICATION, the strength of common beliefs, and the number of nonnational organizations created a transnational society. He contrasted this with the period 1946–53 when the COLD WAR was at its height and communication between Western and Soviet Europe reduced to a minimum and conducted solely through governmental channels. A.L.C.B.

Bibl: R. O. Keohane and J. S. Nye (eds.), *Transnational Relations and World Politics* (Cambridge, Mass., 1972); *International Affairs,* July 1976 issue.

transport planning. The organization of movement systems, both public and private, within an urban or regional area, in order to relate the range of urban activities. Too often it has been restricted to *traffic* planning, i.e. to facilitating the movement of cars in towns, by means of road construction or management. Construction has included such systems as *ringways*, i.e. circular or tangential roads intended to deflect traffic from inner urban areas; the separation of intersecting roads by means of *fly-overs* or *underpasses*; and the linking of two major multi-lane roads by means of a *clover-leaf* intersection. Management methods include the designation of certain existing roads as *clearways* or *throughways* on which parking is prohibited at all times or during critical periods; one-way systems; and parking restrictions. The relation between traffic planning and general urban planning, and especially the notion of differentiating between different types of vehicular movement in order to create *environmental areas* (zones with no extraneous traffic), has been studied and is having some effect on practice. It has also been recognized that the preservation or revival of public transport is essential to the survival of cities. See also PEDESTRIAN SEGREGATION; RADBURN LAYOUT. M.BR.

Bibl: R. B. Mitchell and C. Rapkin, *Urban Traffic* (London and N.Y., 1954); *Traffic in Towns:* Reports of the Steering Group and Working Group of the Ministry of Transport (London, 1963).

transuranic element. Any artificially produced ELEMENT whose ATOMIC NUMBER exceeds 92. The atomic NUCLEUS of these elements is unstable and undergoes RADIOACTIVE decay or FISSION. About a dozen transuranic elements have been produced (usually in very small quantities) in NUCLEAR REACTORS. M.V.B.

transverse stage, see under OPEN STAGE.

transvestism. The wearing of clothes usually associated with the opposite sex. The practice is immemorial and, despite the part played by conventions such as the male portrayal of female roles on the Elizabethan stage, usually sexual in its implications. These may range from the overt expression of homosexuality to the widespread latent bisexuality implied by the recent growth of 'unisex' fashion in the late 1960s and the adoption of this style by contemporary rock culture (see RHYTHM-AND-BLUES). It has been popularly accepted as an entertainment form for some time and manifests itself in the 'drag' acts which have been enthusiastically received in British public houses over the past few years. Andy Warhol's coterie and Danny La Rue illustrate different aspects of the phenomenon today. P.S.L.

Trauberg, Ilya (Russian theatre and film director, 1905–48), see under FEX.

trauma (Greek word for 'wound'). A physical injury or emotional shock such as may lead to TRAUMATIC NEUROSIS. In early FREUDIAN terminology the trauma is usually emotional (e.g. BIRTH TRAUMA) and can be specifically sexual (e.g. seduction by a parent). The trauma is supposed to break through the individual's defences, and in the absence of normal ABREACTION to cause a *foreign-body reaction* – the mental equivalent of the process whereby the TISSUES of the body wall off a

foreign body lodged in them. Subsequent emotional arousal may reawaken early traumatic experience, resulting in an attack on DEFENCE MECHANISMS from inside and outside simultaneously. In Freud's later writings the concept of trauma assumes much less importance. M.J.C.

traumatic neurosis. A NEUROSIS precipitated by extreme shock or TRAUMA, which upsets the previous stability of the person, and leads him (typically) to exhibit uncontrollable EMOTION, or to experience disturbances of sleep with ANXIETY dreams in which the trauma is relived. The precipitating trauma may be primarily emotional (e.g. seduction in childhood or terrifying experiences in battle) or purely physical (e.g. severe concussion leading to the post-concussional SYNDROME, in which neurotic complaints such as blurred vision or lack of concentration are experienced). B.A.F.; M.J.C.

Treasury, the. The government department which in both the U.S.A. and Britain, by its influence over government expenditure, FISCAL POLICY, and MONETARY POLICY, has a major role in formulating and executing government policy as a whole. The U.S. Treasury has two primary responsibilities: (1) to act as chief fiscal adviser to the President (supported by the Council of Economic Advisers and the Office of Management and Budget); (2) revenue collection, the manufacture of the currency, and various law-enforcement duties. The British Treasury's duties include not only the preparation of the budget and the coordination of overall economic policy but also, by tradition, a high degree of control over the expenditure of all government departments. D.E.

Treece, Henry (British poet, 1911–66), see under NEW APOCALYPSE.

tremendismo. A Spanish word not yet naturalized as 'tremendism'. The word *tremendista* was first applied to Camilo José Cela's novel *La Familia de Pascual Duarte (The Family of Pascal Duarte,* 1942), because the reader's shock and horror at what is revealed can only be described as 'tremendous'. Cela's Spanish precursors were 'Parmeno' and Emilio

Carrere; but fundamentally *tremendismo* is a late, intensive, specifically Spanish development of NATURALISM arising from the horrors of the Civil War, the victory of the RIGHT, and Spain's consequent social backwardness. The savage vein, if not the term itself, continues in Spanish fiction.
M.S.-S.

Trevor-Roper, Hugh Redwald (British historian, *b.* 1914), see under GENTRY CONTROVERSY.

tribe. In ANTHROPOLOGY, a term too vaguely used for political entities, territorially defined, of differing scale. It is applied sometimes to (relatively) independent political entities, in which case it becomes analogous to 'nation' in more complex societies (though a tribe is not necessarily centralized and hierarchical in its organization); sometimes to divisions of such larger entities. A tribe is usually assumed to be culturally and linguistically homogeneous, and when people from different tribal backgrounds congregate in towns, those of one such background are sometimes referred to as a tribe, despite their lack of political organization. In urban conditions of this kind tribal associations may be formed. The adjective *tribal* has among some anthropologists the more general sense of pre-modern, non-literate, PRIMITIVE; tribal society then becomes the chief subject-matter of anthropology. M.F.
Bibl: L. Mair, *Primitive Government* (Harmondsworth and Baltimore, 1970).

tribology. The science and design of interacting surfaces in relative motion, including the study of such topics as friction and wear and the study and manufacture of bearing metals and lubricants.
E.R.L.

tricarboxylic acid cycle, see KREBS CYCLE.

Triennale, see under BIENNALE.

Trilling, Lionel (U.S. critic and novelist, 1905–75), see under HORIZON; IDEOLOGY; NEW CRITICISM.

Troeltsch, Ernst (German theologian and philosopher, 1865–1923), see under RELIGION, SOCIOLOGY OF; SECT.

tropism.
(1) In BIOLOGY, an involuntary directional movement determined by the pattern of incidence of an external STIMULUS. For most ordinary purposes tropism and *taxis* can be regarded as synonymous. Orientations towards light, gravity, and sources of chemical stimuli are known as *photo-*, *geo-* and *chemo-taxis* or *-tropism* respectively. P.M.
(2) In literary criticism, the word has been popularized by the French novelist Nathalie Sarraute (see NEW NOVEL), who sees mental life as being made up of myriads of infinitesimal responses to stimuli. The problem of REALISM is to translate these movements into words before they have been falsified by the grid of conventional language embodying ossified attitudes and beliefs. J.G.W.

troposphere. In METEOROLOGY, the lowest layer of the earth's atmosphere. The thickness of the troposphere varies from about 7 or 8 km near the poles to about 16 km at the equator. It contains about three quarters of the mass of the atmosphere, and about 90% of its water vapour, so that almost all 'weather activity' directly relevant to man occurs in the lower layers of the troposphere. The upper boundary of the troposphere is termed the *tropopause.* See also STRATOSPHERE. P.H.

Trotsky, Leon (Russian revolutionary leader, 1879–1940), see under BOLSHEVISM; BUREAUCRACY; COEXISTENCE; COMINTERN; FELLOW-TRAVELLER; PERMANENT REVOLUTION; POLITBURO; SERAPION BROTHERS; SOVIETS; THERMIDOR; TROTSKYISM.

Trotskyism. The version of COMMUNISM associated with Leon Trotsky (1879–1940), Stalin's unsuccessful rival in the struggle for power in the U.S.S.R. after Lenin's death. Trotsky argued for using the Communist base in Russia for the achievement of world REVOLUTION. Stalin rejected Trotsky's thesis of PERMANENT REVOLUTION and called for the building of 'SOCIALISM in one country' as an impregnable stronghold against counter-revolution.
After Trotsky's defeat and expulsion from the Soviet Union (1929) he continued to criticize Stalin's politics, charg-

ing him with the betrayal of the revolution and with being a representative of the 'Bonapartist BUREAUCRACY'. In 1938 Trotsky and his followers founded the 4th INTERNATIONAL, but their hopes that World War II would create a revolutionary situation which they could exploit, as Lenin had during World War I, proved illusory. Trotsky was murdered in 1940; the Trotskyites became a political force in only one country, Ceylon; and the international revolutionary movement named after him has remained divided by sectarian disputes, although all the groups claiming to be Trotskyist are inspired by a revolutionary fundamentalism.   L.L.

Bibl: J. Rabaut, *Tout est possible* (Paris, 1974); C. Slaughter, *Trotskyism versus Revisionism* (4 vols., London, 1974); H. Romerstein, *Trotskyite Terrorist International* (Washington, 1975).

Trubetskoy, Nikolay (Russian linguist and philosopher, 1890–1938), see under PRAGUE SCHOOL.

Truffaut, François (French film director, *b*. 1932), see under NEW WAVE.

Truman, Harry S. (U.S. president, 1884–1972), see under BIPARTISAN FOREIGN POLICY; LEND-LEASE; POINT FOUR PROGRAMME; TRUMAN DOCTRINE.

Truman Doctrine. An important declaration of U.S. foreign policy by President Truman in an address to Congress on 12 March 1947. At a time of growing tension between the Soviet Union and the Western world, Truman went on record as saying that 'it must be the policy of the U.S.A. to support free people who are resisting subjection by armed minorities or outside pressures'. At the request of the President, Congress voted $400 million to help Greece and Turkey, and three months later the U.S. Secretary of State made the offer to Europe which became known as the MARSHALL PLAN. The Truman Doctrine is taken by historians to mark an important stage in the COLD WAR, a break with the U.S.A.'s traditional policy of no commitments in peace-time, and the first of many subsequent U.S. economic- and military-aid programmes.   A.L.C.B.

Bibl: J. M. Jones, *The Fifteen Weeks* (N.Y., 1955); J. L. Gaddis, *The United States and the Origins of the Cold War* (N.Y., 1972).

trusteeship. A method provided after World War II by Article 75 of the Charter of UNO for administering certain non-self-governing territories. Trusteeship developed from the MANDATES SYSTEM of the LEAGUE OF NATIONS which provided for colonial territories wrested from the defeated powers of 1914–18 to be administered by one of the victorious powers under international supervision. Reports on trust territories are submitted to the Trusteeship Council of the General Assembly of UNO. As a result of decolonization (see IMPERIALISM) it now has under its jurisdiction only certain U.S.-administered Pacific islands (Marshall, Mariana, and Caroline Islands, with a total population of 75,000).   A.L.C.B.

Bibl: E. J. Sady, *The United Nations and Dependent Peoples* (Washington, 1957).

truth. (1) The property implicitly ascribed to a PROPOSITION by belief in or assertion of it; the property implicitly ascribed to a proposition by disbelief in or negation of it is *falsity*. There have been many theories of the nature of truth. The most common sees it as a *correspondence* between a proposition and the fact, situation, or state of affairs that verifies it (see VERIFICATION). To explain the MEANING of a sentence is to teach someone its truth-conditions, the circumstances under which it is correct to assert it; and, in the simplest cases, this is done by uttering it, in an exemplary way, in circumstances in which it is true. Thus, for someone to have learned the meaning of 'It is raining' is for him to have been trained to believe or be ready to assert it when it is, in fact, raining. The correspondence may, but need not, be regarded as some sort of natural *similarity* or *resemblance* between proposition and fact. (2) Some philosophers, holding that all awareness of facts is itself propositional, i.e. that it necessarily involves the assertion of some proposition, maintain that truth is a relation of *coherence* between propositions. (3) PRAGMATISTS define truth in terms of the *satisfactoriness of belief*, the empirically verifying fulfilment of expectations being only one form of this. (4) Occasionally truth has been taken to be a *quality* rather than a relation, a view which has some plausibility in connection with ANALYTIC propositions whose truth depends not on something external to them but on the meaning that is intrinsic to them. A.Q.

truth drug. A popular but misleading term for any chemical compound administered to an individual in order to obtain information which has been withheld, either consciously or not. In this sense the term was originally applied to scopolamine in 1932, but the evidence obtained since then argues against the validity of the original claims. In the diagnosis and treatment of some abnormal states, however, it may be useful to administer centrally-acting drugs which loosen the subject's inhibitions and so facilitate discussion. The term *narcoanalysis* is sometimes given to this procedure, for which the drugs most commonly used are the barbiturates and methedrine. There is no medico-legal justification for the use of such substances in judicial processes, since even if consent is given false statements can be made under their influence. M.S.

truth-function. A compound PROPOSITION whose TRUTH or falsity is unequivocally determined by the truth or falsity of its components for all possible cases. Thus '*p* or *q*' is a truth-function of *p* and *q* since it is false if they are both false, but true if *p* is true or if *q* is true or if they both are. The principle of EXTENSIONALITY states that *all* compound propositions are reducible (see REDUCTION) to truth-functions of their ultimate components. Some compound propositions, however, do not appear to be truth-functional at first glance: '*p* because *q*' cannot be true unless both *p* and *q* are true, but if they are it may be either true or false. See also PROPOSITIONAL CALCULUS. A.Q.

truth-value. In standard or classical 'two-valued' LOGIC, TRUTH *or* falsity. Some logicians, however, have devised systems with more than two truth-values. INTUITIONISTS (sense 3) have contended that there is a third class of undecidable PROPOSITIONS which are neither true nor false, and the formal properties of systems of logic with three or more truth-values have been investigated. A.Q.

Tschichold, Jan (German-Swiss book-designer and calligrapher, *b*.1902), see under NEUE SACHLICHKEIT.

Tsvett, Mikhail Semenovich (Russian botanist, 1872–1919), see under CHROMATOGRAPHY.

Tucholsky, Kurt (German satirist, 1840–1935), see under GEBRAUCHS- . . . ; NEUE SACHLICHKEIT.

Tukhachevsky, Mikhail (Soviet marshal, 1893–1937), see under YEZHOVSHCHINA.

Tungku Abdul Rahman, see RAHMAN.

Tupamaros. A band of Uruguayan urban GUERRILLAS, LEFT-WING REVOLUTIONARIES, notorious for their practice of kidnapping prominent foreigners and holding them to ransom. Their name derives from that of the 18th-century Inca leader, Túpac Amarú. The Tupamaros achieved prominence in 1969 but by the end of 1974 had been crushed out of existence. Tactics similar to those employed by the Tupamaros, however, have been used by guerrilla groups in other Latin American countries, notably Argentina, where a large number of assassinations of political figures have been undertaken by RIGHT-wing as well as left-wing groups. D.C.W.

turbine. An engine in which a fluid is forced past a series of vanes or blades that are mounted on a shaft and so shaped and positioned that the passage of fluid through the blades causes the shaft to rotate. Turbines are quick-starting, freer from vibration than reciprocating engines, and relatively light and compact – notably in the case of the *air turbine* used by dentists to propel dental drills at very high speeds. A *gas turbine* propels the gas through the blades by burning the gas, thus creating a pressure. Gas turbines are cheap to run on low-grade fuel, and are used to propel aircraft and high-powered railway locomotives. In the case of aircraft a propulsion jet is also incorporated, making a *turbo-jet* engine. The RAM-JET, although it has features in common with the turbo-jet, contains no turbine but operates more in the manner of an internal combustion engine, i.e. on a four-stroke cycle. *Steam turbines* are used extensively in power stations to drive alternators for the production of electric power. E.R.L.

turbo-jet, see under TURBINE.

Turgenev, Ivan (Russian novelist, 1818–83), see under INTELLECTUALS; NIHILISM; SOCIALIST REALISM.

Turing machine. An ABSTRACT, mathematically defined 'machine' introduced by A. M. Turing in 1936 to make the idea of mechanical computability precise – by reducing it to the properties of a universal Turing machine. Turing machines form a very simple type of COMPUTER. In consequence of this simplicity, the resulting PROGRAMS are inordinately long. For this reason practical computers are not much like Turing machines. C.S.

turn-round time, see under COMPUTING.

Turner, Frederick Jackson (U.S. historian, 1861–1932), see under FRONTIER.

Turner, Joseph Mallord William (British painter, 1775–1851), see under IMPRESSIONISM.

turnpike theorem. A PROPOSITION about the way in which an economy can reach some objective in minimum time. Given a number of simplifying assumptions, it can be shown that the economy would have to spend much of its time close to a structure of production which would, if maintained, make possible maximum growth at a constant rate for ever. The economy does not actually grow at a constant rate; but the production structure appropriate to steady growth at a maximum rate (first studied by the mathematician John Von Neumann) provides the fastest route, though not the most direct. Although the theorem is not immediately applicable to real-world growth policies, a number of authors following the discoverers, Dorfman, Samuelson, and Solow, have obtained similar results relating optimal growth paths to 'turnpike' paths in which the economy grows at a constant rate. The constant-growth path is generally much easier to analyse than the theoretically optimal path, and policies for long-run economic growth are likely to be guided by some conception of a 'turnpike'. J.A.M.
Bibl: R. Dorfman, P. A. Samuelson, and R. M. Solow, *Linear Programming and Economic Analysis* (N.Y., 1958).

TVA (Tennessee Valley Authority), see under NEW DEAL.

twelve-note music, see under SERIAL MUSIC.

twin paradox, see under CLOCK PARADOX.

two cultures, the. Term introduced in *The Two Cultures and the Scientific Revolution* (1959) by C. P. Snow (Lord Snow) in reviving an old controversy, that of science versus literature and/or religion. This was the Rede Lecture at Cambridge, and it was answered by F. R. Leavis (see LEAVISITE) in the Richmond Lecture at Downing College, Cambridge, in 1962. Snow diagnosed society's INTELLECTUALS as divided, unable to speak to each other, having no common language. Each group he called a 'CULTURE'; he maintained that scientists can't read and that 'humanists' can't understand even simple scientific CONCEPTS such as the second law of THERMODYNAMICS. Leavis's answer was perhaps no more ill-mannered and shot with sour irrelevancies than Snow's original lecture, brashly in favour of scientific culture in the interests of human survival, was ill-argued. The kernel of the dispute may be found, in a civilized form, in T. H. Huxley, *A Liberal Education and Where to Find It* (1868) and *Science and Culture* (1881), and in Matthew Arnold's answer, *Literature and Science* (1882). A. N. Whitehead's *Science and the Modern World* (1927) is a brilliant and reconciliatory essay by a truly distinguished mind. M.S.-S.
Bibl: L. Trilling, *Beyond Culture* (N.Y., 1965; London, 1966).

two hemispheres, the. Studies of brain damage have suggested that the two halves (hemispheres) of the human brain may perform differing but complementary functions; and Roger Sperry has shown experimentally that, in cases where the hemispheres had been surgically separated, patients were being controlled by two distinct brains, neither of which 'knew' the recent experiences of the other half. Further investigation confirmed that the left hemisphere, which controls the right-hand side, is largely concerned with logical, sequential, and digital processes such as language, whereas the right hemisphere is much more concerned with spatial, musical, and pictorial functions. Non-human primates appear not to share this specialization of cerebral function, and it has been suggested that this development in human EVOLUTION was linked with tool use and the emergence of language. The educational and cultural implications of these findings are likely to be great. See also NEUROPSYCHOLOGY.

R.A.H.

Bibl: R. E. Ornstein, *The Psychology of Consciousness* (San Francisco, 1972; London, 1975); S. J. Dimond and J. G. Beaumont (eds.), *Hemisphere Function in the Human Brain* (London, 1974).

two-tier system, see under COMPREHENSIVE SCHOOLS.

Tyler, Ralph Winfred (U.S. educationist, *b*. 1902), see under EVALUATION.

Tylor, Sir **Edward Burnett** (British anthropologist, 1832–1917), see under ANIMISM; FETISH.

types, ideal, see IDEAL TYPES.

typology.

(1) Any system for classifying things, people, social groups, languages, etc., by types. Typology has long been a mainstay of ARCHAEOLOGY. The grouping of a series of artifacts according to type, and the arrangement of like types in the form of a type series illustrating change, have in the past been the major preoccupation of some archaeologists, and the basis for detailed chronologies. Many of these are of value, particularly those supported by independent chronological evidence. However, with the advent of absolute DATING methods, the need to construct elaborate typologies has decreased. B.C.

(2) In THEOLOGY and Christian art, the joining of ideas or images in the Old Testament with ideas or images in the New.

D.L.E.

Tyrrell, George (Irish theologian, 1861–1909), see under MODERNISM.

Tzara, Tristan (Romanian-born French poet, 1896–1963), see under DADA; SURREALISM.

U

UC (ultimate constituent), see CON-STITUENT ANALYSIS.

Udaltsova, Nadezhda (Russian painter, 1886–1961), see under CUBO-FUTURISM.

UDI (Unilateral Declaration of Independence), see under RHODESIA.

UGC (University Grants Committee). A committee set up in Great Britain in 1919 to allocate government money to universities individually. A recurrent grant was until recently given in 5-year allocations, and capital grants in yearly or two-yearly sums, the grants being based on consideration of individual university estimates and submissions. The full Committee now has a full-time chairman, about 21 part-time members (over half being academics, who usually serve for 5 years), and a permanent secretariat of about 120. It is expected to offer confidential advice to the government as well as to represent university interests on university matters, including academic as well as financial planning. While the UGC has not escaped criticism, universities prefer working with and through it to having direct negotiations with the Department of Education and Science or the Treasury.   W.A.C.S.

Uhde, Wilhelm (German art critic and historian, 1874–1947), see under PRIMITIVE.

ultimate constituent, see CONSTITUENT ANALYSIS.

ultracentrifuge, see under SEDIMENTATION.

ultraism. In general, extremism; specifically, a Spanish literary movement (*ultraismo*) that flourished around 1919–23 and is best characterized as Spanish EXPRESSIONISM. The chief theoretician and coiner of the term was Guillermo de Torre; other more important writers (Borges, Lorca, Cernuda, Salinas) were influenced by it. The ultraists' programme involved the purga-tion of all rhetorical, romantic, and anthropomorphic elements from poetic language. Partly SURREALIST, partly HERMETIC, ultraism reflected the peculiarly Spanish awareness of MODERNISM. Borges took ultraism back with him to Argentina, but soon abandoned it. M.S.-S.

ultramontism (from Latin *ultra montes*, 'beyond the mountains', i.e. the Alps viewed from France). The emphasizing of the doctrinal INFALLIBILITY and practical authority of the Pope, at the expense of the looser and more national organization of the CATHOLIC Church as advocated by the French 'Gallicans'. See also VATICAN COUNCIL II.   D.L.E.

ultrasonics. The study of waves of the same physical nature as sound, i.e. longitudinal undulations of pressure and density, but whose frequency is so high that the waves are not heard by the human ear. Ultrasonic waves are usually generated by applying electrical oscillations to a quartz crystal TRANSDUCER, or by a MAGNETOSTRICTION oscillator. In the latter case a rod of ferromagnetic material is alternately magnetized and demagnetized by means of a coil around it which carries alternating current. This current causes the rod to expand and contract at the same frequency as that of the current. The length of the rod is chosen to 'tune' at the frequency required to obtain increased amplitude of vibration. When one end of the rod is clamped, the acoustic waves are sent out from the opposite end.

Ultrasonic waves are used for non-destructive testing of metal castings which may contain cracks. Medical examination of unborn babies is carried out with ultrasound, and the short wavelength (centimetres or millimetres) enables fine detail to be detected. Very high intensity waves can, however, be destructive and are used for the scaling of boilers and in dentists' drills. In such circumstances the generator is placed near to the surface to be attacked. The action by which the sound waves rip off the surface layer is known as CAVITATION. High-ENERGY waves are being tested medically for brain surgery without opening the skull, for waves of given frequency can be made to produce cuts at a given depth of penetration in a given position. At lower intensities the waves can shake loose the MOLECULES of air nearest to a surface and not normally movable by CONVECTION. This effect is used to improve the heat transfer across a surface, as in boilers.

Many animals (e.g. dogs, bats, dolphins) and insects (mosquitoes, moths) are capable of hearing and in some cases emitting ultrasound below about 100,000 Hz. They use it for sexual communication, 'seeing' in total darkness, and for the detection and evasion of enemies.

M.V.B.; E.R.L.

ultrastability. In CYBERNETICS, the capacity of a system in HOMEOSTASIS to return to an equilibrial state after perturbation by unknown or unanalysed forces (against the intervention of which the system was not explicitly designed). S.BE.

ultra-violet. Electromagnetic RADIATION whose wavelengths are shorter than visible light but longer than X-RAYS. M.V.B.

unanimisme, see under ABBAYE DE CRÉTEIL.

uncertainty principle (or *indeterminacy principle*). A consequence of QUANTUM MECHANICS, discovered by Heisenberg in 1927, which states that it is impossible to measure the position and MOMENTUM of a PARTICLE simultaneously with more than strictly limited precision. In fact, the uncertainty in position, multiplied by the uncertainty in momentum, must always exceed PLANCK'S CONSTANT. This result arises from the WAVE-PARTICLE DUALITY: any attempt to fix the position of, say, a beam of ELECTRONS, by interposing a narrow slit in its path, will produce DIFFRACTION, i.e. a sideways spreading of the beam, which renders its direction, and hence its momentum, uncertain. The uncertainty principle is a special case of the COMPLEMENTARITY PRINCIPLE.

M.V.B.

unconscious. A familiar word with, in psychoanalytic theory, two meanings: (1) as an adjective applied to thoughts which cannot be brought to CONSCIOUSNESS by ordinary means, but only, if at all, by technical methods such as PSYCHOTHERAPY and PSYCHOANALYSIS (see also PRECONSCIOUS; REPRESSION); (2) as a noun in the expression 'the unconscious', i.e. the part of the mental system or apparatus which contains these unconscious thoughts. To be distinguished from SUBCONSCIOUS.

B.A.F.

UNCTAD (United Nations Conference on Trade and Development). An organ of the United Nations General Assembly, set up by a resolution of December 1964, which meets irregularly to discuss the promotion of international trade and the acceleration of economic development. It has become the principal organ by which the views of the developing countries can be organized and brought to the attention of the major industrial and trading nations on such issues as participation in discussions on multilateral tariff negotiations, international monetary reform, commodity prices, preferences, etc. UNCTAD's main executive organ, the Trade and Development Board, meets annually. Its headquarters are in Geneva. D.C.W.

underconsumption theory, see under TRADE CYCLES.

underdevelopment. The state of those countries which have successively and with increasing euphemism been termed backward, underdeveloped, lessdeveloped, and developing (see also THIRD WORLD), and which are enumerated by UNO, for policy purposes connected with aid and trade. They comprise the majority of independent countries in Central and South America, Africa, and Asia, the main exclusions being South Africa, mainland China, and Taiwan. There is also an OECD enumeration which includes Turkey and the poorer countries of Southern Europe. Or the word may be used without reference to either of these lists, and without precise meaning. The original meaning, indicating that resources exist which have not been exploited, seems to have vanished. Although the word is now close in meaning to 'poverty', a few 'underdeveloped' countries, especially those with much oil and few people, are very rich in income per head. They may still be regarded as underdeveloped where the quality of institutions, the skills, educational attainments, and health of the people are well below those of countries of longer-standing wealth.   I.M.D.L.

Underground. The name (recalling the RESISTANCE MOVEMENTS of World War II) under which in the mid 1960s an emergent movement of HIPPIES and kindred spirits expressed its corporate identity and sense of community in the face of opposition and even organized attack by the ESTABLISHMENT. The phenomenon first occurred in the U.S.A., but also emerged in other highly developed urban-industrial societies. Its LIFE STYLE, which was reminiscent of the BEATS, involved, typically, a tendency towards MYSTICISM, a taste for rock (see RHYTHM-AND-BLUES), the use of DRUGS, ideas of Universal Love expressed partly in terms of sexual PERMISSIVENESS, and a willingness to adopt communal forms of living without great regard for traditional standards. The movement, whose character is anti-technological, anti-materialist, experimental, and individualist, and is therefore opposed to the tenets, customs, and values of MASS SOCIETY, has its own newspapers, films, plays, music, and art, and its own outlets for disseminating them – facts which lend some plausibility to the Underground's claim to be regarded as a *counter-culture* or an *alternative society*.

In order to survive and proselytize, the Underground required some relatively formal STRUCTURES, and these developed mainly through pressure from indigenous political elements; the earliest was the underground press, which described the new forms of life style, discussed the problems involved, and debated the STRATEGIES to be devised. Generally, however, the Alternative Society has limited its corporate activities to the establishment of self-help organizations which advise and assist DROP-OUTS, those in trouble over drugs, and those with medical, travel, or basic survival problems. Alternative living structures have emerged, such as COMMUNES, non-profit shops and entertainment facilities, and, for a brief period, alternative schools. For the majority of the population, however, a real alternative society in terms of parallel structures has yet to emerge.   P.S.L.
Bibl: R. Neville, *Play Power* (London

and N.Y., 1970); T. Roszak, *The Making of a Counter-Culture* (Garden City, N.Y., 1969; London, 1970).

underlying structure, see DEEP STRUCTURE.

unemployment. Inability to find a paid job at the going rate of wages. Involuntary unemployment of this kind may arise either because of a general deficiency of demand (see SUPPLY AND DEMAND) and a widespread absence of job opportunities or because of some more specific and local mismatch between jobs and men. The first kind of unemployment, which has usually been the more important, can be cured by expanding demand, while the second cannot. War-time experience showed that even when the demand for labour is intense, some frictional unemployment continues because of seasonal fluctuations, erratic changes in work load, bad organization, labour turnover, and so on. From time to time emphasis is also put on *structural* and *technological unemployment* associated with rapid industrial change, as if these would continue independently of the pressure of demand. It is, of course, true that, as industries contract or change in organization or location, jobs are extinguished, often in localities where fresh jobs do not spring up and structural unemployment results. Technical change, such as AUTOMATION involves, may also make labour redundant and leave a residue of technological unemployment. But if demand is maintained unemployment of this type rarely assumes major proportions.

Changes in unemployment usually go with larger changes in employment, because as more jobs become available workers postpone retirement or re-enter the labour market alongside those taken off the unemployment register.   A.C.

Ungaretti, Giuseppe (Italian poet, 1888–1970), see under HERMETIC.

unified tax. In Great Britain, a tax on individual incomes, introduced in 1973 in place of income tax and surtax, which were separately assessed and subject to different rules. Unified tax is imposed at a 'basic rate'. Those with assessable incomes in excess of a certain figure pay 'taxes at higher rates' in accordance with a scale. Certain income may also be subject to an investment income surcharge. Previously income tax had been subject to a reduction for earned income. This was not always understood and the country suffered the disincentive effect of the assumed *marginal rate* (the extra tax on an extra pound of earnings) while only collecting revenue at the lower actual rate. The reduction of the nominal rate to the earned income rate with the imposition of a surcharge on investment income has made the system much more comprehensible to the ordinary taxpayer.　　J.F.C.

unilateral declaration of independence, see under RHODESIA.

Unitarian. A believer in God and in Jesus Christ's supreme goodness who rejects the doctrine of the Trinity, i.e. that God is 'Son' and 'Holy Spirit' as well as 'Father'. Unitarian congregations were first constituted in Europe in the 16th and 17th centuries, but have flourished chiefly in New England and elsewhere in the U.S.A. in the 19th and 20th centuries. Some Unitarians accept the authority of the Bible, but others are guided only by reason and conscience.　　D.L.E.

Bibl: H. McLachlan, *The Unitarian Movement* (London, 1934).

united front. An alliance between the COMMUNIST Party and other parties; distinguished from POPULAR FRONT by the fact that all parties in the former are regarded as working-class parties. In effect, the phrase is usually employed for cooperation between the Communist and SOCIAL DEMOCRATIC parties. In Communist tactical parlance a distinction is made between a 'United Front from above' (involving agreement between the two parties as such) and 'United Front from below' (implying united action by Communists and local Social Democratic members or branches against the Social Democratic leadership).　　R.C.

Unity Theatre. A LEFT-wing, amateur theatre group established in London in 1935 with the object of presenting SOCIALIST and COMMUNIST plays and encouraging working-class dramatists. As well as presenting American, Russian, and British plays under the direction of André van Gyseghem, John Allen, Her-bert Marshall, and others, it successfully pioneered the LIVING NEWSPAPER in England and produced a series of satirical pantomimes. Unity Theatre groups, most of them short-lived, were founded in a number of cities, and in 1946 it briefly established professional companies in London and Glasgow.　　M.A.

universal.

(1) In PHILOSOPHY, a term contrasted with *particular*: universals are abstract properties and RELATIONS, particulars the concrete things that exemplify them. Redness and fatherhood are universals; an individual tomato is a particular exemplifying the former, the pair of individuals composed of a man and his child are two particulars which, as a pair, exemplify the latter. Particulars are concrete in the sense that they are individuals or objects of reference with a position in time and also, ordinarily, in space. Universals are referred to by abstract nouns derived from verbs (e.g.'suspicion'), from adjectives (e.g. 'roundness'), from prepositions (e.g. 'betweenness') and from common nouns (e.g. 'motherhood'). They either have no location in space and time or are indefinitely scattered throughout them (redness, one could say, is all over the place) and, if so, are frequently superimposed within them (a particular lemon, for example, has a multitude of properties at the same place at the same time). Particulars are ordinarily continuous in time and in space, and each excludes all other particulars, except its parts and the wholes it is a part of, from the spatio-temporal region it occupies. Logical, or Platonic, REALISM ascribes real existence to universals; NOMINALISM denies it to them. Those who deny that there is more to an individual thing than the set of its properties would seem committed to the view that particulars are reducible (see REDUCTION) to universals.　　A.Q.

(2) In LINGUISTICS, (*a*) a linguistic feature claimed as an obligatory characteristic of all languages; (*b*) a type of linguistic rule which is essential for the analysis of any language. Chomsky called the former *substantive* universals, the latter *formal* universals. The establishment of linguistic universals is of considerable contemporary interest, particularly in relation to the question of how children learn a language. See also INNATENESS HYPOTHESIS.　　D.C.

universalism, see under PATTERN VARI-ABLES.

universe of discourse. The field or range of entities to the members of which a particular discussion makes reference. Thus the universe of discourse of PHYSICS contains material bodies and physical forces; it does not contain mental images, political parties, or prime numbers. The notion of universe of discourse is convenient for the interpretation of statements about fictional or imaginary entities. 'There was no such person as Mr Pickwick' is true of the universe of discourse of actual men, but false of the universe of Dickensian characters. 'There was no such person as Mrs Pickwick' is true of both universes of discourse. A.Q.

University of the Air, see OPEN UNIVERSITY.

UNO (United Nations Organization). An international body established by charter on 26 June 1945 as world security organization with the following organs: Security Council, General Assembly, Secretariat-General, Economic and Social Council, Trusteeship Council, INTERNATIONAL COURT of Justice; to which various SPECIALIZED AGENCIES such as WHO, FAO, UNCTAD, etc. were added. Any of the five permanent members of the Security Council – Britain, China, France, the U.S.S.R., the U.S.A. – can veto proposals for action; hence, despite the obligation in the charter to maintain peace and security, the peace-keeping role passed in 1950 from the Security Council to the General Assembly. Intervention by arms against presumed aggression, as in KOREA in 1950–54, gave way to intervention, aimed merely at separating combatants, by military observers or U.N. emergency forces. From the mid 1950s onwards, with the creation of new states, the number of members grew very considerably, establishing a permanent majority of the new membership uncommitted either to Soviet or U.S. leadership, and absorbed after 1960 in activities critical of the residual colonial position of the leading European powers. Since the death (1962) of the second Secretary-General, Dag Hammerskjold, in the course of U.N. intervention in the Congo, the U.N. has played a diminished role in the resolution of conflicts (e.g. VIETNAM, India-Pakistan, Arab-Israeli, Malaysia-Indonesia). D.C.W.

Bibl: H. G. Nicholas, *The U.N. as a Political Institution* (London and N.Y., 4th ed., 1971).

unperson. ORWELLIAN term (from *1984*) for those individuals with the memory of whose existence the TOTALITARIAN state has decided to dispense. Orwell doubtless had in mind the Soviet Russian practice of removing the names of Stalin's rivals, sentenced in the MOSCOW TRIALS of 1936–8, from all works of history, all works of biographical reference, etc., as though they had never lived. The replacement of the entry in the Soviet Encyclopaedia for the head of the MVD, Lavrenty Beria, by one dealing with the Behring Sea, after Beria's fall and execution in December 1953, is a classic case in point. D.C.W.

unsaturated. Term used from the early days of ORGANIC CHEMISTRY to signify a compound which can react (see CHEMICAL REACTION) by the addition of other chemical SPECIES. Unsaturated compounds contain at least one carbon ATOM with a double or triple BOND to its neighbour. Common examples include ethylene, acetylene, and allyl alcohol. Addition reactions to give SATURATED compounds usually occur rather readily, so that unsaturated compounds are important intermediates in the synthesis of organic compounds. B.F.

Upward, Edward (British novelist, *b*. 1903), see under KAFKAESQUE; NEW WRITING.

urban guerrilla, see under GUERRILLA.

urban history. The history of towns is a traditional branch of LOCAL HISTORY, but the term 'urban history' or 'the new urban history' came into use in the 1960s to refer to a new approach, practised most of all in the U.S.A. This new urban history is problem-oriented, concerned in particular with ECOLOGY, immigration, and social MOBILITY. It draws heavily on urban SOCIOLOGY for its concepts and makes considerable use of quantitative methods. P.B.

Bibl: H. J. Dyos (ed.), *The Study of Urban History* (London and N.Y., 1968);

S. Thornstrom, 'Reflections on the New Urban History' (*Daedalus*, 100, 1971, pp. 359–75).

urban renewal. The rebuilding and/or rehabilitation of decaying urban areas through planning policies and, frequently, the provision of governmental and/or municipal finance. It tends to reduce the continually shrinking stock of inexpensive, and usually well-liked, buildings, and has often resulted in the displacement of the urban poor (a process sometimes known as *gentrification*) and of small but essential shops and workshops. Though often defended on the grounds that the needs of the motor car make such changes inevitable, heavy criticism, particularly in the U.S.A., has made urban renewal a highly suspect operation.　M.BR.

Bibl: J. Jacobs, *The Death and Life of Great American Cities* (N.Y., 1961; London, 1962).

urban revolution. Term used to describe the emergence of urban centres in the Middle East. The phrase was introduced into ARCHAEOLOGY by V. G. Childe as part of a broad scheme in which he suggested that man had passed through three great periods of change, the NEOLITHIC REVOLUTION, the urban revolution, and the Industrial Revolution. During the first he learned to produce food and acquired a static form of existence which paved the way for the second, the development of organized city life. Childe believed that cities developed rapidly in the valleys of the Tigris and Euphrates. Recent discoveries in Palestine and Turkey, however, have shown that the phenomenon was more widespread in time and space. The CONCEPT is now little used among archaeologists, although geographers still seem to find some value in it.　B.C.

Bibl: V. G. Childe, *New Light on the Most Ancient East* (London and N.Y., 1958) and *What Happened in History* (Harmondsworth and N.Y., 1942).

urban sprawl, see under SPRAWL.

urbanisation, see URBANIZATION.

urbanism. (1) An alternative term for URBANIZATION; (2) In America (and cf. French *urbanisme*), an alternative term for town-planning; (3) the urban charac-

ter or typical condition of the town. The functions of the town should be largely divorced from the rural society surrounding it for this term to be applicable.　M.L.

urbanization. The process and effects of gathering people in cities and TOWNS. The concept covers urban expansion in area and population, the resulting changes in land use, ways of life, landscapes, geographical and occupational distribution of people, and their economic activities. The unprecedented scale and speed of urbanization in the 20th century – the majority of mankind will soon be living in urban places – has brought a host of urgent needs, from more housing to government reform and REGIONAL PLANNING, and has made it a major concern of our time. See also METROPOLIS; MEGALOPOLIS.　J.G.

Bibl: A. Toynbee, *Cities on the Move* (London and N.Y., 1970); C. A. Doxiadis, *Ecumenopolis* (in English; Athens, 1974).

Ustacha. A Fascist-style TERRORIST organization of Croat NATIONALISTS organized in the early 1930s by Ante Pavelić with clandestine support from Italy and Hungary, both of which were interested in weakening the Yugoslav state. After the German invasion of Yugoslavia in 1941 and the creation of an independent Croatian state, the Ustacha committed massacres of Serbs in Croatia and Bosnia Herzogovina. After Tito's victory the Ustacha degenerated into bands operating in the Yugoslav mountains. Pavelić himself succeeded in evading a widespread hunt to capture and bring him to trial.　D.C.W.

Bibl: W. R. Roberts, *Tito, Mihailović and the Allies 1941–1945* (New Brunswick, N.J., 1973).

utilitarianism. In ETHICS, the theory that takes the ultimate good to be the greatest happiness of the greatest number and defines the rightness of actions in terms of their contribution to the general happiness. It follows that no specific moral principle is absolutely certain and necessary, since the RELATION between actions and their happy or unhappy consequences varies with the circumstances. Sketched by earlier philosophers, notably David Hume (1711–76), utilitarianism was made fully explicit by Jeremy Bentham (1748–1832)

and, in a qualified way, by John Stuart
Mill. It was widely rejected in their time
for its unedifying HEDONISM (which was
nevertheless altruistic). In this century it
has been criticized for its commission of
the supposed NATURALISTIC FALLACY. Its
chief opponents are the kind of ethical
INTUITIONISM that takes values to be
quite distinct in nature from matters of
empirical fact, and the DEONTOLOGY
(often associated with that view) that
holds certain kinds of conduct to be right
or wrong intrinsically and quite independently of any consequences they may
have.   A.Q.
   Bibl: J. S. Mill, *Utilitarianism* (London,
1863); A. Quinton, *Utilitarian Ethics*
(London, 1973).

utility (or *value*). The capacity to satisfy
human wants. This capacity may be found
in goods or services, and the worth of such
goods and services to the consumer is
determined by the degree to which they
are capable of satisfying his wants. While
this degree cannot be objectively measured it is reflected in the price which the
consumer is prepared to pay. And in
economic theory the theory of value is
often equated with the theory of prices.
                                         D.E.

utility theory. In studying the behaviour of
a consumer we can proceed either empirically, postulating a given form of the
DEMAND functions which connect the
quantities demanded with prices and
income, or theoretically, attempting to
derive the form of these FUNCTIONS from
the capacity of goods and services to
satisfy his wants, i.e. from their UTILITY to
him. So utility theory is concerned with
the formulation of a utility function
describing the consumer's system of pre-

ferences and with the maximization of this
function within the limit of what he can
spend in a period. The form of the utility
function determines the form of the
demand functions and, if these are
mathematically manageable, their implications can be examined for plausibility
and they can be fitted to aggregated data
(see AGGREGATION).   R.ST.

utopian ideal. An important strand in the
development of planning and architecture
based on the ideas of English, French, and
American utopian reformers such as
Robert Owen (1771–1858), Charles
Fourier (1772–1837), and Étienne Cabet
(1788–1858). Each of these tried to exe-
cute social experiments in which the physical disposition of buildings would correct
the obvious evils of the industrial city and
allow man to flourish fully as a rational
and emotionally fulfilled being. Owen's
cooperative at New Lanark in Scotland,
Fourier's projected Phalanstery, and
Cabet's Icarian settlements in the U.S.A.
were all attempts to create an early form
of SOCIALISM and give it visible expression. Each placed his ideal community in a
rural setting but tried to provide it with
urban facilities. This combination had a
marked impact on the GARDEN CITY
movement and, through its insistence on
the relation of social wellbeing and buildings, on the whole modern movement in
architecture.   M.BR.
   Bibl: L. Benevolo, tr. J. Landry, *The
Origins of Modern Town Planning* (London and Cambridge, Mass., 1967).

utopianism, see under SOCIALISM.

Utrillo, Maurice (French painter,
1883–1955), see under ÉCOLE DE PARIS.

V

vaccine, see under PROPHYLAXIS.

Vadim, Roger (French film director, *b*.1928), see under NEW WAVE.

Vaktangov, Yevgeny (Russian actor and director, 1883–1922), see under HABIMA.

Valadon, Suzanne (French painter, 1869–1938), see under ÉCOLE DE PARIS.

valence (or *valency*). A NUMBER characteristic of a particular ELEMENT describing the number of BONDS that it makes with other ATOMS in a MOLECULE. Thus, in methane (CH_4) carbon forms four bonds with hydrogen, and is therefore four valent (or quadrivalent), while hydrogen is univalent. The same element may, however, have different valencies in different compounds – e.g. phosphorus trichloride (PCl_3) and phosphorus pentachloride (PCl_5). The explanation of valency in terms of the sharing of ELECTRONS between adjacent atoms (COVALENCY) is one of the major achievements of QUANTUM THEORY. B.F.
Bibl: C. A. Coulson, *Valence* (London and N.Y., 2nd ed., 1961).

Valéry, Paul (French poet, 1871–1945), see under SYMBOLISM.

validity. The characteristic of an INFERENCE whose conclusion must be true if its premises are (see SYLLOGISM). An inference can be valid and yet have a false conclusion, but only if not all of its premises are true. Equally, an inference can be invalid even though both its premises and its conclusion are true, for example, *some men are Catholics, some Catholics are pipe-smokers,* therefore *some men are pipe-smokers.* (The invalidity of the inference becomes clear if 'women' is substituted for 'pipe-smokers'.) A.Q.

Valtat, Louis (French painter, 1869–1952) see under FAUVES.

value, see UTILITY.

value-added tax. A system for taxing final consumption of goods and services by which tax is collected from all registered businesses. A tax at the appropriate percentage rate must be collected on all deliveries of goods or rendering of services and accounted for to the collecting authority which, in the U.K., is the Customs and Excise. This is *output tax*. However, the business can, in paying this, deduct any *input tax* it has itself borne on its purchases. Any excess of input tax over output tax can, in general, be reclaimed. The tax is passed forward to and borne by the ultimate consumer. The same general form of V.A.T. has been adopted in all EEC countries, but with differences of rates and coverages.
Certain businesses and certain categories of output are exempted from V.A.T. Although no tax is charged on the supply, the supplier himself cannot recover input tax. Other categories of output are 'zero rated', which means that the tax is formally imposed, but at a rate of zero. The business can then recover any input tax collected at earlier stages. In the EEC form of the tax, exports are zero rated whereas imports are taxable. This results in the tax being effectively a tax at the appropriate rate on final consumption, collected by the country in which consumption takes place and regardless of the country of origin of the goods or services. J.F.C.

value analysis. The study of a manufactured product in order to identify opportunities for reducing the cost by improving style, shape, function, materials, or method of manufacture. R.I.T.
Bibl: L. D. Miles, *Techniques of Value Analysis and Engineering* (N.Y., 1961).

value-freedom (translation of the German *Wertfreiheit*). The exclusion of value-words and VALUE-JUDGEMENTS from the discussion of human and social affairs. Its adoption in the SOCIAL SCIENCES as a METHODOLOGICAL ideal (recommended by Max Weber) does not imply that the valuations of the men being studied cannot be discussed, or that the selection of the problem in hand for investigation does not reflect a value-judgement about its interestingness, or that logical evaluations about the strength of evidence and the VALIDITY of INFERENCES will not figure in it. What is excluded is the making by the social scientist of moral and political value-judgements about the people in his field of study. The aim is to minimize possibilities of disagreement by eliminating from scientific work controversial and disputable matter. It reflects a methodological value-judgement that to count as scientific a body of assertions must contain only what can be established objectively as true or reasonable by SCIENTIFIC METHODS. Though there is no inconsistency in that, it is an ideal that is hard to realize in practice. Synonyms for *value-free* are *value-neutral* and *ethically neutral*; its opposite is *value-loaded, evaluative,* or NORMATIVE. A.Q.

value-judgement. An utterance which asserts or implies that some thing, person, or situation is good or bad, some action ought or ought not to be done. Value-judgements need not explicitly contain the pure value-words: good, bad, right, wrong, ought, and their obvious synonyms and cognates. 'That is stealing' is a value-judgement, since 'steal' means the same as 'take wrongly'. On the other hand, the presence of a pure value-word is not an infallible mark of a value-judgement. 'The train ought to have arrived by now', said at a distance from the station and in ignorance of the actual facts, is only vestigially evaluative, meaning simply that it is reasonable to believe that the train has arrived. A.Q.

value theory, see AXIOLOGY.

Van Allen belts. Two groups of charged PARTICLES (discovered by the American physicist J. A. Van Allen in 1958) whose ORBITS lie just outside the earth. It is thought that the particles come from COSMIC RAYS and from the sun; their motion is influenced by the earth's MAGNETISM rather than by GRAVITATION. M.V.B.

van Beverloo Corneille, Cornelis, see CORNEILLE.

van de Graaf generator. A machine for producing the high voltages needed to accelerate SUBATOMIC PARTICLES (see ACCELERATOR). Electric charge is 'sprayed' onto a moving belt which transfers it to a large hollow metal sphere whose potential may eventually reach millions of volts. M.V.B.

van de Velde, Henry (Belgian architect and designer, 1863–1959), see under FOLKWANG MUSEUM; NEO-IMPRESSIONISM.

van der Waals force. Attraction (named after the Dutch physicist J. D. van der Waals, 1837–1923) between ATOMS and MOLECULES resulting from interaction between the fluctuating DIPOLES induced in each as a result of POLARIZATION by the electromagnetic (see ELECTROMAGNETISM) FIELDS of the ELECTRONS and NUCLEUS of the other. M.V.B.

van Doesburg, Theo (Dutch painter, decorator, poet, and art theorist, 1883–1931), see under ABSTRACT ART; CONCRETE ART; MACHINE AESTHETIC; MERZ; STIJL, DE.

van Dongen, Kees (Dutch-French painter, 1877–1968), see under FAUVES.

van Gennep, Arnold (French ethnographer, 1873–1957) see under RITES OF PASSAGE.

van Gogh, Vincent (Dutch painter, 1853–90), see under EXPRESSIONISM; FAUVES; IMPRESSIONISM; LONDON GROUP; NEO-IMPRESSIONISM; POST-IMPRESSIONISM.

van Gyseghem, André (British actor and director, *b.*1906), see under UNITY THEATRE.

van Rysselberghe, Théo (Belgian painter, 1862-1926), see under NEO-IMPRESSIONISM; VINGT, LES.

Vansina, Jan Maria Jozef (Belgian-U.S. anthropologist and historian, *b.*1929), see under ORAL TRADITION.

Vanzetti, Bartolomeo (Italian-born U.S. anarchist, 1888–1927), see under JAZZ AGE.

VARÈSE

Varèse, Edgar (French-U.S. composer, 1885–1965), see under CONCRETE MUSIC.

variable. A symbolic device essential in MATHEMATICS; the name, which is misleading, arose in connection with the CALCULUS. The fundamental use of variables is to express FUNCTIONS (e.g. $f(u, v) = u^2 + v^2 + 1$). The letters used for the ARGUMENT(s) of the function are the *independent* variables; if a letter is used to denote the value of the function it is called the *dependent* variable. Particular values of the function can be computed after assigning values to the variables which occur in its expression (its arguments). If an expression or statement depends on *all* the values of the function, as in '$\int f(x)dx$' or '$f(u, v)$ is positive for all u, v', then the (argument-denoting) variables are said to be *bound* and it makes no sense to substitute values for them. Otherwise they are *free*. Variables may be restricted by implicit or explicit hypotheses or conditions. If the problem is to find values for them which satisfy the conditions they are called *unknowns*. Symbols for constants (e.g. π) and for PARAMETERS can be thought of as variables which are restricted by more or less permanent hypotheses. When letters are used for purely manipulative purposes, without thought of assigning meaning to them, they are often called *indeterminates*. R.G.

variable-metric methods, see under GRADIENT METHODS.

variable proportions, law of, see DIMINISHING RETURNS, LAW OF.

variable speed. Confusion arises from the different meanings of this term, notably as between engineers in Europe and their counterparts in America. In the latter the term applies to a motor whose speed varies as the result of an applied load – normally an undesirable property. In Britain it applies to a motor whose speed can be varied at will by the human operator – often a desirable property. Americans describe such a machine, more accurately, as an *adjustable* speed motor. E.R.L.

variance. In STATISTICS, the variance of a DISTRIBUTION is a measure of how scattered it is – a measure of dispersion. The variance is the expected squared differ-

ence between the expected value of a RANDOM VARIABLE and its actual value – in mathematical terms it is $\mathbf{E}((X - \bar{X})^2)$ where $\bar{X} = \mathbf{E}(X)$ is the expected value of X. The variance is often denoted by σ^2, and its square root σ is called the *standard deviation*; it is a root mean square error. For the NORMAL DISTRIBUTION of mean 0 and variance 1 the probability of the interval $[-1.96, +1.96]$ is 0.95 – hence the rule of thumb that for a bell-shaped density function 95% of the probability lies within 2 standard deviations of the mean. R.SI.

variance, analysis of. In STATISTICS, a procedure for allocating the variability found in a population to different sources, as in attempting to determine crop yield as a function of fertilizer used, chemical composition of soil, amount of rainfall, etc. It requires a design for analysis that keeps the variables isolated. (Failure in this respect is known as *confounding* – as when a study of the effect of social CLASS on the rate of bodily growth ignores differences in the nutrition enjoyed by the different classes.) Its basic ·logic is the comparison of the total variability in a population with the variability contributed by each of the sources of variance studied, and its typical test for 'significance' of a source of variability is the ratio of the variance left after all known sources have been extracted. J.S.B.

variance-reduction methods, see under MONTE CARLO METHODS.

variation. In BIOLOGY, the process that leads to differentiation between the members of a single SPECIES. We may distinguish between (1) *heritable variation*, which is the consequence of GENETIC differences and may therefore be propagated to the next generation, and (2) *phenotypic variation*, the consequence of differences of ENVIRONMENT or upbringing. Phenotypic variation is not heritable and therefore makes no direct contribution to evolutionary change. See also POLYMORPHISM. P.M.

variety. In CYBERNETICS, the total number of possible states of a system, or of an element of a system. The *Law of Requisite Variety (Ashby's Law)* expresses the fact that 'only variety can absorb variety': a regulating system must be able to generate as many states as can the system regulated.   S.BE.

Bibl: W. R. Ashby, *An Introduction to Cybernetics* (London and N.Y., 1956).

varve dating, see under DATING.

Vasarely, Victor (French painter, *b.* 1908), see under OP ART.

vasectomy. Division of the spermatic cords which convey spermatozoa from the testes to the urethra and thence to the exterior. When both cords are cut no sperm can pass and the man is thus rendered sterile. The operation is almost invariably successful, although sterility is not normally achieved for several weeks or even months until all living spermatozoa are finally lost; most doctors recommend the continued use of contraceptives until two semen specimens have been shown to contain no spermatozoa. Vasectomy can sometimes be reversed by reconnecting the cut ends of the cord, but is best confined to men who want to be made permanently sterile.   D.A.P.

Vatican Council II. The ECUMENICAL Council (1962–4) opened by Pope John XXIII to renew Roman CATHOLICISM. Whereas the First Vatican Council (1869–70) had seen the triumph of ULTRAMONTANISM, this Council did much to authorize a more BIBLICAL THEOLOGY and the aspirations of the AGGIORNAMENTO.   D.L.E.

Bibl: W. M. Abbott (ed.), *The Documents of Vatican II* (London and N.Y., 1966).

Vaux, Calvert (U.S. landscape architect, 1824–95), see under PEDESTRIAN SEGREGATION.

Vauxcelles, Louis (French art critic, *b.* 1870), see under FAUVES.

Vavilov, Nikolay Ivanovich (Russian geneticist, 1885–1942), see under LYSENKOISM.

Vcheka, see under KGB.

VDU, see VISUAL DISPLAY UNIT.

Veblen, Thorstein (U.S. sociologist and economist, 1857–1929), see under CONSPICUOUS CONSUMPTION; TECHNOCRACY.

vector. Many notions in GEOMETRY and PHYSICS (e.g. the instantaneous velocity of a PARTICLE, a force, a rotation of a body about a fixed point) are completely specified by giving a definite direction together with a (positive) numerical magnitude. Any such vector x can be represented geometrically by a line OP from O to P with the appropriate direction and with the distance OP equal to the magnitude of x. If QR is equal and parallel to OP, then QR represents the same vector. The components of the vector with respect to a given system of rectilinear axes Ox, Oy, Oz are then just the COORDINATES (x, y, z) of P. (1) The *sum* $x + x'$ of two vectors is defined as the vector whose components are $(x + x', y + y', z + z')$, or equivalently as the vector represented by the diagonal of the parallelogram with sides OP, OP'. (2) If a is a number (in this context also called a *scalar*) then the vector ax is defined as having components (ax, ay, az). The use of these (and certain other) notations allows geometric and physical facts to be described more succinctly and transparently than does the exclusive use of components. In studying continuous phenomena one is often concerned with a *vector field*, i.e. a FUNCTION which assigns a vector (as value) to each point of a region of space.

From a more abstract point of view, the above definitions, in particular (1) and (2), do not depend on there being precisely 3 components. A *vector space* (over the real numbers) is a MATHEMATICAL STRUCTURE for which the operations (1) and (2), obeying certain natural AXIOMS, are defined. Vector spaces are closely connected with the notion of LINEARITY and have application wherever that notion occurs.   R.G.

Bibl: J. Singh, *Mathematical Ideas* (London and N.Y., 1972).

Vedanta. A system of beliefs developed by many Indian thinkers (most notably Samkara in the 8th century A.D.) and based on four of the ancient scriptures of HINDUISM, all having the Sanskrit *veda*, knowledge, in their titles. The emphasis is on the unity of the ultimate *Brahman*, and on the unreality of the world in comparison.   D.L.E.

Bibl: C. Isherwood (ed.), *Vedanta for the Western World* (Hollywood, 1945; London, 1948).

Vedrenne, John E. (British theatre manager, 1867–1930), see under ROYAL COURT THEATRE.

Ventris, Michael (British architect, 1922–56), see under LINEAR A AND B.

Verdi, Giuseppe (Italian composer, 1813–1901), see under ROMANTICISM.

Verfremdungseffekt, see under ALIENATION.

Verga, Giovanni (Italian dramatist and novelist, 1840–1928), see under THÉÂTRE LIBRE; VERISM.

verification. The establishment of a belief OT PROPOSITION as true. The chief philosophical employment of the notion is in the verification principle of the LOGICAL POSITIVISTS which requires a proposition, if it is to be significant, to be verifiable by sense-experience (see SENSE-DATUM), or by attention to the MEANING of the words that express it, or, indirectly, by INFERENCE from propositions that are directly verifiable in either of these two ways, i.e. by INDUCTION or DEMONSTRATION. Formulation of the principle gave much difficulty. Whose experience is relevant? If, as seems reasonable, it is that of the speaker, are propositions about the past or other minds therefore meaningless? Must meaningful propositions be conclusively verifiable? Can the verification principle itself be verified? A.Q.

verism. In art and literature, an alternative name for NATURALISM (senses 4, 5). In its Italian form, *verismo*, the term was applied particularly to the violent, melodramatic operas, around 1900, of Puccini, Mascagni, and others, But the tendency began earlier in literature: in Edmondo De Amicis, and then – more certainly and deliberately – in Luigi Capuana and, particularly, in Giovanni Verga. The emphasis was ostensibly on truth-at-allcosts; but really on low life, gloom, dirt, poverty, violence, despair. The roots of verism are, for perhaps obvious reasons, Sicilian. M.S.-S.

Verkade, Jan (Dutch painter, 1868–1946), see under NABIS, LES.

Verlaine, Paul (French poet, 1844–96), see under IMPRESSIONISM; SYMBOLISM.

vernacular. In architecture, adjective applied to an indigenous style of building that is largely untutored, but thought to be of considerable virtue and to some extent associated with a golden past. It is the architecture of the Cotswold village or the Mediterranean hillside town or the adobe settlement of the American Indian. Modern architects have often claimed as one of their aims the establishment of a new vernacular. M.BR.
Bibl: B. Rudofsky, *Architecture without Architects* (N.Y., 1964).

Verne, Jules (French novelist, 1828–1905), see under SCIENCE FICTION.

Verri, Pietro, Count (Italian economist, 1728–97), see under POLITICAL ECONOMY.

vers libre, see under FREE VERSE.

Ver stehen. Term used in Germany from the late 19th century to denote understanding from within, by means of EMPATHY, intuition, or imagination, as opposed to knowledge from without, by means of observation or calculation. The term was employed in particular by the sociologist Max Weber and by philosophers of the NEO-KANTIAN school such as Dilthey and Rickert. *Verstehen* was thought by some to be characteristic of the SOCIAL SCIENCES as opposed to the NATURAL SCIENCES; by others, to be characteristic of history and literature, as opposed to the social sciences. Today, the value of *Verstehen* is most debated by sociologists. See also HERMENEUTICS; HISTORICISM. P.B.
Bibl: W. Outhwaite, *Understanding Social Life* (London, 1975).

vertical and lateral thinking. Terms coined by Edward de Bono for two contrasted but complementary modes of thinking. In PROBLEM-SOLVING, vertical thinking elaborates methods for overcoming obstacles in the chosen line of approach, while lateral thinking tries to bypass them by switching to a radically

different approach involving a distinct reformulation of the problem. The two modes of thinking are characteristic of, respectively, CONVERGERS AND DI-VERGERS.   I.M.L.H.
Bibl: E. de Bono, *Lateral Thinking* (London and N.Y., 1970).

vertical grouping. An arrangement whereby children admitted to an infants' school do not enter a single class with other new entrants (the *reception class*), but are distributed among small groups each ranging in age between 5 and 7. In this 'family' setting older children can teach younger ones, a process said to confer social and educational benefits as well as enabling new techniques of teaching to be developed. Vertical grouping corresponds to SETTING at an older age, while the reception class corresponds to STREAMING.   W.A.C.S.

vertical integration. Control by one management of two or more steps in the process of production and distribution of a product, as when a book publisher acquires a printing press or a bookshop, or a firm which slaughters and packs broiler chickens for distribution obtains management control of the production process on farms through agreements with farmers.   K.E.H.

Vertov, Dziga (Russian film director, 1896–1954), see under CINÉMA-VÉRITÉ; DOCUMENTARY; MONTAGE.

vestigial organ. An organ which has been superseded or has become functionally redundant in the course of EVOLUTION. Such an organ often dwindles in size and loses its distinctive characteristics. The human vermiform appendix is a classical example – but possibly an erroneous one, because immunology (see IMMUNITY) warns us that such an important lymphoid organ should not too easily be dismissed as functionless. A better example is the pineal organ in the brain, the evolutionary remnant of what was at one time a functional median dorsal eye – a function still possessed by the pineal of the lampreys.   P.M.

Vichy. An inland spa in southern France, the seat of government of the capitulationist French regime headed by Marshal Pétain in July 1940, following France's defeat by the Germans. From 1940 to 1942 Pétain's government (the leading figure in which was Pierre Laval) administered the southern, unoccupied half of France, and Vichy, an authoritarian regime with support from French FASCIST organizations, became a byword for military defeatism and the willingness of the wealthy to accept national defeat and humiliation rather than REVOLU-TION. After the occupation of the whole of France by the Germans (November 1942), Vichy became openly collaborationist and its leaders were tried and convicted of treason after the defeat of Germany.   A.L.C.B.
Bibl: R. Aron, tr. H. Hare, *The Vichy Regime, 1940–1944* (London and N.Y., 1958); R. O. Paxton, *Vichy France* (N.Y., 1972; London, 1973).

Vidal de la Blache, Pierre (French geographer, 1845–1918), see under GEO-GRAPHY.

videofrequency. A vibration frequency in the RADIO FREQUENCY region used to transmit television pictures.   M.V.B.

videotape. A kind of MAGNETIC TAPE used to store information which can be reconstructed into pictures; television programmes are stored on videotape. M.V.B.

Vienna Circle (*Wiener Kreis*). A group of philosophers, mathematicians, and scientists who came together under the leadership of Moritz Schlick in the late 1920s to inaugurate the school of LOGICAL POSITIVISM. Leading members were Rudolf Carnap, Friedrich Waismann, Otto Neurath, Herbert Feigl, Hans Hahn, Philipp Frank, Karl Menger, and Kurt Gödel. It was associated with a like-minded group in Berlin, led by Hans Reichenbach, and the two groups jointly published the journal *Erkenntnis*. Schlick's death in 1936 and Hitler's occupation of Austria in 1938 brought the Vienna Circle to an end as an organized group, but its ideas were developed, under the name of LOGICAL EMPIRICISM, by various members who emigrated to the U.S.A. and elsewhere.   A.Q.
Bibl: V. Kraft, *The Vienna Circle* (N.Y., 1969).

Vietcong. Term coined by the government of South VIETNAM to describe the COMMUNIST elements in the 'National Liberation Front' forces, the successors of the VIETMINH GUERRILLAS which had operated in South Vietnam before 1954. In action from 1958 onwards and coming increasingly under control of the Communist cadres from North Vietnam, the Vietcong by 1965 were wholly dependent on North Vietnam for any chance of gaining control in the South.   D.C.W.

Bibl: D. Pike, *Viet Cong* (London and Cambridge, Mass., 1967).

Vietminh. Abbreviation of the VIETNAM Duc Lap Dong Minh (Vietnamese Independence League), founded among pro-COMMUNIST Vietnamese emigrés in China in 1941 by Ho Chi Minh, representative of the COMINTERN, as a FRONT ORGANIZATION for the Indo-Chinese Communist Party. Suppressed by the Chinese Nationalists, it was revived in 1943–4 and developed into the main cover for the Indo-Chinese Communist Party after the Japanese surrender in 1945.   D.C.W.

Vietnam. A country of South-East Asia under French colonial rule until 1954; from 1960 to 1975 the scene of civil war between the COMMUNIST government of North Vietnam (capital Hanoi) and the non-Communist government in the South (capital Saigon). The term is frequently used to refer to United States support for the South. Growing military pressure by the North and increasing Communist strength in surrounding states (Laos and Cambodia) caused the U.S.A. to commit combat aircraft and personnel to the area and to carry out large-scale bombing of North Vietnam from 1965 to 1972. This did not, however, discourage the North from continuing to supply the VIETCONG operating in South Vietnam.

American actions in Vietnam deeply polarized U.S. society and discredited the U.S. internationally. The anti-war movement dominated U.S. politics, causing widespread domestic dissension and demonstrations and bringing about the premature retirement of President Johnson. The bombing of North Vietnam was continued, while attempts were made by President Nixon's administration to secure the best possible circumstances in which to carry out a U.S. withdrawal. This withdrawal, completed in 1975, led to the fall of non-Communist regimes in South Vietnam, Laos, and Cambodia and represented a serious defeat for U.S. foreign policy. Subsequently, popular opinion in the U.S.A. has been opposed to U.S. combat involvement in Asia and Africa.   P.B.M.

Bibl: R. Gallucci, *Neither Peace nor Honor* (Baltimore, 1975); B. Andrews, *Public Constraint and American Policy in Vietnam* (London, 1977).

Vieux-Colombier, see under CARTEL (2).

vigilantes. Self-appointed law-enforcement groups appearing spontaneously when the established authorities seem unable or unwilling to cope with lawlessness and disorder. They first made their appearance under this name on the American frontier, especially during and after the Californian gold rush. Other classic vigilante groups were found in Montana in 1864 and in New Orleans in 1868, and in the anti-MAFIA riots of 1890. Their activities are often indistinguishable from mob-rule or lynch-law.   D.C.W.

Vigotsky, Lev Semenovich (Russian psychologist, 1896–1934), see under DEVELOPMENTAL PSYCHOLOGY.

Vilar, Jean (French actor and producer, 1912–71), see under THÉÂTRE NATIONAL POPULAIRE.

Village, the, see GREENWICH VILLAGE.

village college. A type of institution proposed in Cambridgeshire in 1924 by the county's then Secretary for Education, Henry Morris, in which all forms of education in a village or group of villages were to be coordinated under one roof. Each college was to include nursery, primary, and SECONDARY SCHOOLS, space for adult classes, a branch of the county library, and a village hall, with facilities for indoor and outdoor recreation. The first such college, Sawston, opened in 1930 and there are at present 12, although not all the provisions can be offered even now. These colleges were copied in Leicestershire, Cumberland, and elsewhere and were a valuable stimulus in rural life. See also COMMUNITY SCHOOL.   W.A.C.S.

Vingt, les. Brussels artists' exhibiting society founded by Octave Maus, internationally significant for its support of the SYMBOLISTS and NEO-IMPRESSIONISTS. Among the artists featured in its first Salon (1884) were Renoir, Monet, Whistler, and the Belgians James Ensor and Théo van Rysselberghe.   J.W.

Viollet-le-Duc, Eugène (French architect, 1814–79), see under FUNCTIONALISM.

virology. The science that deals with the structure, properties, and behaviour of the sub-microscopic infective particles known as viruses, especially as agents of disease.

Viruses were at one time thought to be rudimentary living organisms, as if they were sub-microscopic bacteria using the CELL sap as a culture medium such as that in which bacteria grow (see BACTERIOLOGY). This description is now known to be misleading. Viruses do not grow in the conventional sense, and are not self-reproducing: they subvert the synthetic machinery of the cells which they infect in such a way as to produce more copies of themselves, and have no existence apart from the cells they infect. Thus viruses cannot like bacteria be cultivated in fairly simple media outside the body, but must be propagated either in TISSUE CULTURES or in embryonated hens' eggs (the discovery of Sir Macfarlane Burnet). All viruses contain NUCLEIC ACID (DNA or RNA). It is this that transforms the metabolism of the affected cell to make it produce more virus copies, usually at the cell's expense. Viruses that produce visible changes in the cells they infect are referred to as *cytopathogenic*. It is conceivable, though, that many other viruses exist which are not recognizable as viruses because they produce no such effects. Thanks to ELECTRON MICROSCOPY and orthodox chemical analysis the structure and composition of several viruses are now well known (e.g. human adenovirus 12 and tobacco mosaic virus). Viruses have a core of nucleic acid and an outer shell of PROTEINS. Because of their small size (of the order of millimicrons) they pass through filters fine enough to retain bacteria, and heat is the only reliable method of destroying them.

Diseases caused by viruses include smallpox (variola), cowpox (vaccinia), poliomyelitis, common colds (for which one or more of upwards of forty 'rhinoviruses' may be responsible), influenza, and some forms of hepatitis. In addition viruses are now known to cause malignant growths in experimental animals, and it is thought likely that they cause certain human tumours, particularly leukaemias, though conclusive evidence is still to seek. ANTIBIOTICS do not act upon viruses, but a naturally occurring agent, INTERFERON, may protect uninfected cells against infection by virus. Recovery or protection from a viral infection depends upon the action of antibodies (see IMMUNITY), and this also makes the basis of preventive methods.

Poliomyelitis vaccines are of two main kinds: (1) Salk vaccine (1954), an inactivated virus administered by injection, the preparation of which was made possible by the discovery of J. F. Enders and his colleagues that polio virus can be propagated in tissue cultures; and (2) an attenuated virus strain (1955), particularly associated with the names of H. Koprowski and A. Sabin, that can be taken by mouth. The result of these public-health procedures is that poliomyelitis like smallpox is a disappearing disease, and the genetic information coded in the respective virus nucleic acids will be lost.   P.M.

viscerotonia, see under PERSONALITY TYPES.

Visconti, Luchino (Italian film director, 1906–76), see under NEO-REALISM.

visual cliff. A device for testing young animals' PERCEPTION of depth. It consists of two identically patterned horizontal surfaces, one well below the other, the upper being extended over the lower by means of a sheet of transparent glass. An animal unwilling to move off the upper surface onto the transparent glass that projects over the lower surface is said to possess *depth perception*. Many SPECIES have been found to possess it at birth.
                                                      J.S.B.

visual display unit (VDU). A device by which the output of a COMPUTER is represented as a visual image on the screen of a CATHODE RAY TUBE. It can be used (with a character generator) to display text or diagrams. It has the advantages of being rapid and silent, but cannot produce hard

VITALISM

copy easily. With the aid of a device known as a LIGHT PEN it can also be used as an input device. See also COMPUTER-AIDED DESIGN; INPUT/OUTPUT.   C.S.

vitalism. A miscellany of beliefs united by the contention that living processes are not to be explained in terms of the material composition and physico-chemical performances of living bodies. Woodger distinguishes several varieties of vitalism, one of which is *dogmatic vitalism*, such as we find in the writings of Hans Driesch (1867–1941) and Henri Bergson (1859–1941), according to which living things are animated by a vital principle such as an ENTELECHY (Driesch's term) or an *élan vital* or *life force* (Bergson's, popularized in England by G. B. Shaw). Dogmatic vitalism is contrasted with MECHANISM, the system of beliefs or lack of beliefs to which modern BIOLOGY and medicine owe all their great triumphs, and which consists, methodologically, of behaving *as if* all vital activities could be adequately explained in terms of material composition and physico-chemical performance.   P.M.

vitamin. An essential dietary ingredient which cannot be synthesized by the body and has therefore to be supplied in ready-synthesized form. What is a vitamin for one animal need not be a vitamin for another, e.g. men and guineapigs need vitamin C but mice can do without it. Vitamins are of necessity fairly widespread and abundant, for otherwise the animals that need them would not have survived. Vitamin deficiency diseases are often well-defined clinical SYNDROMES associated with lack of inadequacy of a specific vitamin. Thus the vitamin-C deficiency syndrome is known as 'scurvy' and the vitamin-D deficiency syndrome as 'rickets'. Most vitamins have now been chemically characterized and synthesized, whereupon they are known by their chemical names: thus vitamin C = ascorbic acid, vitamin B = aneurin. The growth of welfare and medical knowledge has relegated vitamin deficiency diseases to a comparatively minor place in medicine today.   P.M.

Vlaminck, Maurice (French painter, 1876–1958), see under FAUVES.

666

Voegelin, Eric (German political scientist, *b.* 1901), see under REVOLUTION.

Vogeler, Johann Heinrich (German painter, 1872–1942), see under WORPSWEDE.

voiceprint. A visual representation of certain acoustic characteristics of the human voice, which it is claimed will uniquely identify an individual. The claims have been strongly attacked, particularly when voiceprinting was used as evidence in American courts of law in the mid 1960s, and there is as yet no general agreement as to its reliability.   D.C.

volition. An act of will or decision, conceived as a mental event immediately antecedent to voluntary bodily movement or action proper, as contrasted with purely reflex or automatic behaviour. Ryle, wishing to deny the existence of inner mental states in the interests of his version of BEHAVIOURISM, declared the concept of volition to be empty or mythical. Certainly not all voluntary action seems to be preceded by introspectible mental preliminaries (see INTROSPECTION), but some does. Against the view that the occurrence of volition is a CRITERION of freedom and responsibility in action Ryle argued that volitions are themselves represented as a species of, admittedly inward, actions about which the question of intention or voluntariness can again be raised, thus generating an infinite regress.   A.Q.
   Bibl: A. J. Kenny, *Action, Emotion and Will* (London and N.Y., 1963).

Volksbühne (The People's Stage). A German theatre association founded by Bruno Wille in 1890, which remains the most successful and longest-lived product of the European 'people's theatre' movement around that time. Starting with no theatre of its own, it split on the issue of alignment with the SOCIALIST Party, then reunited 70,000 strong to open its own Berlin theatre in 1914. Here Erwin Piscator (1893–1966), a pioneer of the EPIC and DOCUMENTARY theatres, became the chief director in 1924, leaving in 1927 to set up his own company with the support of the COMMUNIST section of the membership. Subsequent directors before the NAZI take-over included Karl Heinz Martin and Heinz Hilpert. Suppressed under the Nazis, it was reactivated after World War II but soon fell into two halves, one in East Berlin, the other in West. In 1962 the latter was again taken over by Piscator, who introduced the new documentary dramas of Rolf Hochhuth, Peter Weiss, and Heinar Kipphardt. Its new West Berlin theatre was opened in 1963.   J.W.

Bibl: H. F. Garten, *Modern German Drama* (N.Y., 1962; London, 2nd ed., 1964).

voluntarism.
(1) Any theory that emphasizes the role of the will in mental life, especially thinking and the pursuit of knowledge, or, again, in decisions about conduct. PRAGMATISM is voluntaristic in its conception of knowledge as subservient to action and of our CONCEPTS or beliefs as instruments devised by us for the satisfaction of our desires. The philosophy of Schopenhauer is a highly generalized form of voluntarism, in which ultimate reality is taken to be of the nature of will.   A.Q.
(2) In historical, political, and social theories about the behaviour of man voluntarism emphasizes the individual choice in decision-making, which it considers as not entirely determined by external conditions. It stands in contrast to the deterministic (see DETERMINISM) MODEL of human behaviour which excludes will and voluntary action as causative factors in individual experience and in society. L.L.

voluntary-aided schools, see under MAINTAINED SCHOOLS.

von Baer's principle, see under EMBRYOLOGY.

Von Neumann, John (Hungarian – U.S. mathematician (1903–57), see under GAMES, THEORY OF; TURNPIKE THEOREM.

Vorticism. One of the very few English modern-form movements in the arts, and the one most contemporary with international developments in all the visual arts. Related to CUBISM and FUTURISM in painting, and partly emerging from IMAGISM in literature, it was a unique

compound of new theories of energy and form, rare in England, in that it brought painters (e.g. William Roberts) and writers (especially Ezra Pound) together in the 'Great English Vortex'. Wyndham Lewis, its prime founder, was both: he saw the movement visually as 'a mental emotive impulse . . . let loose on a lot of blocks and lines', verbally as a hard, unromantic, external presentation of kinetic forces. Pound, in parallel, dropped the neoSYMBOLIST bias of IMAGISM, with which he was disillusioned, and emphasized the hard energy-centre in poetry. The movement, anti-representational, brutalist, an 'arrangement of surfaces', came out of the *Rebel Art Centre,* founded by Lewis, Edward Wadsworth, Christopher Nevinson, and others in 1913; associated painters and sculptors included Bomberg, Gaudier-Brzeska, and Epstein. A Vorticist exhibition was held at the Doré Gallery in March 1915; the main document of the movement was the visual-verbal manifesto-magazine BLAST.
M.S.BR.
Bibl: R. G. Cork, *Vorticism and Abstract Art in the First Machine Age* (vol. 1, London, 1976).

Vostell, Wolf (German graphic artist, *b.* 1932), see under DÉCOLLAGE; FLUXUS; HAPPENINGS.

Voysey, Charles Francis Annesley (British architect and designer, 1857–1941), see under ARTS AND CRAFTS MOVEMENT.

Vuillard, Édouard (French painter, 1868–1940), see under INTIMISM; NABIS, LES.

vulcanology. The study of volcanoes, their life-history, and their lava, gas, and fragmentary constituents. Vulcanology is concerned with the study of all volcanoes, active, dormant, and extinct, and their distribution in space and time. The monitoring of active volcanoes is an important social aspect of the subject but one in which long-term predictions of eruptions, though demanded, cannot be produced with any degree of certainty.   J.L.M.L.

W

Waddington, Conrad Hal (British biologist, 1905–75), see under GENETIC ASSIMILATION; ORGANIZER.

Wadsworth, Edward (British painter, *b.* 1889), see under VORTICISM.

Wafd. Shortened version of *al-Wafd al-Misri* ('the Egyptian delegation'), an Egyptian NATIONALIST party founded in 1919 by Said Zaghlul as the basis for Egyptian representation at the Paris Peace Conference when it was hoped to negotiate Egyptian independence with Britain. Overwhelmingly the largest Egyptian political party in the 1920s, it became involved in a three-way conflict with the British occupying authorities and the Egyptian court, and grew increasingly authoritarian and corrupt, with a Blue Shirt PARA-MILITARY organization. During World War II, under the leadership of Nahas Pasha, the Wafd became so compromised in Egyptian eyes by its association with the British as to lose any chance of maintaining power, and it finally disappeared after the military coup of 1952.
D.C.W.
Bibl: P. J. Vatikiotis, *The Modern History of Egypt* (London and N.Y., 1969).

wage restraint, see under INCOMES POLICY.

Wageningen school, see under AGRARIAN HISTORY.

wages policy, see INCOMES POLICY.

Wagner, Richard (German composer, 1813–83), see under ATONAL MUSIC; GESAMTKUNSTWERK; NEO-CLASSICISM; ROMANTICISM.

Wain, John (British poet, novelist, and critic, *b.* 1925), see under MOVEMENT, THE.

Waismann, Friedrich (Austrian-British philosopher, 1896–1959), see under VIENNA CIRCLE.

Walden, Herwarth (pseud. of Georg Lewin, German musician, author, and art critic, 1878–?), see under STURM, DER.

Wall, the, see BERLIN WALL.

Wall Street. The name given to the lower end of Manhattan Island, New York, where the world's most important financial centre – comprising banks, trust companies, insurance companies, exchanges, etc. – is situated, and which also houses the headquarters of most of America's largest business corporations. Among its best-known exchanges are the New York Stock Exchange, the American Stock Exchange, the New York Cotton Exchange, and the Maritime Exchange. As a popular term Wall Street, or 'the Street', has become increasingly synonymous with the interests of American CAPITALISM and embraces businesses far removed physically from the area to which it properly refers. D.E.

Wallace, Alfred Russel (British naturalist, 1823–1913), see under NATURAL SELECTION.

Wallace, George Corley (U.S. politician, *b.* 1919), see under POPULISM.

Wallace, Henry (U.S. politician, 1888–1965), see under PROGRESSIVE.

Wallas, Graham (British socialist, 1858–1932), see under FABIANISM; IRRATIONALISM.

Walras, Léon (French economist, 1834–1910), see under EQUILIBRIUM.

Walsh, Don (U.S. oceanographer, *b.* 1931), see under BATHYSPHERE.

Walton, Edward (Scottish painter, 1860–1922), see under GLASGOW SCHOOL.

Walton, Sir William (British composer, *b.* 1902), see under JAZZ.

Wang Hung-wen (Chinese politician, *b*. 1937), see under CULTURAL REVOLUTION.

Wankel engine (or *epitrochoidal engine*). A rotary internal combustion engine with no reciprocating parts. The rotating part is shaped like an equilateral triangle with slightly curved convex sides. The casting in which it rotates is so shaped that, when the rotor revolves eccentrically through the use of an epicyclic gear, the 3 spaces between the sides of the 'triangle' and the walls of the casing each go through the sequence: intake, compression, power stroke, exhaust, as is usual in conventional internal combustion engines. The tips of the triangular rotor make seals with the casing to separate the 3 chambers and enable the action to take place.   E.R.L.

war (or *warfare*). Developments in technological means of destruction in political organization, in the international system, and in analysis of the subject have led to the classification of different kinds of war. Thus *catalytic war* is conflict between two states brought about by the deliberate actions of a third. COLD WAR is a state of international conflict wherein all measures short of organized military violence are used to achieve national objectives. *Conventional war* is armed conflict between states in which nuclear weapons are not used; *nuclear war* (under which is subsumed *thermonuclear war*) is conflict in which they are. *Chemical warfare* involves the use of incendiary, asphyxiating, or otherwise noxious chemicals, *biological warfare* the use of living organisms such as disease germs; the two are often bracketed together as 'C.B.W.' (chemical and biological *weapons*), although the employment or intended employment of (particularly) the biological component is more often asserted than proved. GUERRILLA war or *insurgency* is conflict conducted by irregular forces within a state and aimed at alienating the mass of the population from the authority of the established government with a view to its final overthrow. *Limited war* is military conflict limited either by terrain, the weapons used, or the objectives pursued. *Psychological warfare* involves the use of propaganda (by radio, agents, etc.) to weaken the morale of an adversary population or army, and to discredit the motives and diminish the authority of an adversary government.   A.F.B.
Bibl: A. F. Buchan, *War in Modern Society* (London, 1968).

war crimes. (1) Acts of provoking war which are crimes according to the *jus contra bellum*, the law against war; and (2) violations of the laws and customs of war and of the laws of humanity, the *jus in bello*. Trials for war crimes are, however, a feature almost entirely confined to the 20th century, apart from those which represent the exercise of martial law by a military authority against civilians. International tribunals for the trial of alleged war criminals were proposed after 1918 but came to nothing. After 1945 international tribunals sat in Nuremberg and Tokyo. The victorious powers claimed the right to speak and act for the international community in judging the leaders of the defeated states on charges of both kinds. Their legal justification remains a subject of controversy. The Nuremberg and Tokyo verdicts, however, were reflected in a revision of manuals of military law even by the victorious powers.   D.C.W.

Warburg, Aby (German art historian, 1866–1929), see under ICONOGRAPHY.

warfare, see WAR.

Warhol, Andy (U.S. pop artist, *b. c.* 1930), see under MEDIA; POP; TRANSVESTISM.

Warlock, Peter (pseud. of Philip Heseltine, British composer and musicologist, 1894–1930), see under MUSICOLOGY.

Warner, Rex (British novelist, *b*. 1905), see under KAFKAESQUE; NEW WRITING.

Warner, William Lloyd (U.S. anthropologist and sociologist, 1899–1970), see under CLASS.

Washington Square Players, see under OFF-BROADWAY.

Wasps. American slang acronym for White Anglo-Saxon Protestants. Wasps are alleged to be the largest ethnoreligious group in the U.S.A., to be predominant in the supply of political, economic, and social ÉLITES, and to discriminate against Roman Catholics, Jews, other European ethnic groups, Blacks and Latin Americans.   D.C.W.

Watergate. An apartment block in Washington, D.C., at which the Democratic Party's National Committee maintained its campaign headquarters for the 1972 Presidential election. In June of that year employees of the rival Republican Party's Committee to Re-elect the President were caught red-handed breaking into the apartment block and removing electronic spying devices. The subsequent scandal named from the apartment block was contained by the cover-up activities of various members of President Nixon's personal White House staff until after his re-election. The subsequent revelations in the American press and before a Senate investigation committee revealed the President either as himself personally involved in the cover-up, or as one singularly ill-advised in the selection of his personal staff, and, on either view, isolated from and suspicious of the outside world to a degree which suggested abnormality, and did much to discredit his leadership. After the Supreme Court had forced the release to investigative officers of the tape recordings, made at President Nixon's order, of all conversations held in his office at the White House, the President was forced to confess his involvement in the cover-up. He thereupon resigned, being the first U.S. President to do so; measures to bring about his removal from office by impeachment already lay before Congress. His successor, President Ford, gave him a blanket pardon, which did not, however, extend to the accomplices who had acted under his orders.   D.C.W.
   Bibl: B. Woodward and C. Bernstein, *All the President's Men* (London and N.Y., 1974); T. H. White, *Breach of Faith* (London and N.Y., 1975).

Watkins, Vernon (British poet, 1907–69), see under NEW APOCALYPSE.

Watson, James Dewey (U.S. biochemist, *b*.1928), see under DOUBLE HELIX; GENETICS; MOLECULAR BIOLOGY; NUCLEIC ACID.

Watson, John Broadus (U.S. psychologist, 1878–1958), see under BEHAVIOUR THERAPY; BEHAVIOURISM.

Watson, Peter (British art patron, *d*.1956), see under HORIZON.

Watts, Alan (U.S. author and philosopher, *b*. 1915), see under BEAT.

Waugh, Evelyn (British novelist, 1903–66), see under HORIZON.

wave function. The mathematical representation of the strength of the waves associated with matter according to the WAVE-PARTICLE DUALITY. Each state in QUANTUM MECHANICS is fully described by a wave function which varies from point to point in space. The intensity of this wave at a given point gives the probability that a particle will be found there. For example, the wave function of an ELECTRON in an ENERGY LEVEL of an ATOM is characterized by oscillations in the region where an ORBIT of the same ENERGY would exist if the electron obeyed NEWTONIAN MECHANICS; outside this region, the wave function falls smoothly to zero, so that there is a high probability that the electron will be found somewhere near its Newtonian orbit.   M.V.B.

wave guide. A metal tube used to transmit MICROWAVES for use in RADAR; the electromagnetic equivalent of the old-fashioned 'speaking tube' for sound waves.   M.V.B.

wave mechanics, see QUANTUM MECHANICS.

wave-particle duality. The manifestation in matter (which usually behaves as if made of PARTICLES) of interference and DIFFRACTION behaviour characteristic of wave motion, and the manifestation in light (which usually behaves as waves of electromagnetic RADIATION) of collision, absorption, and emission in the form of discrete ENERGY packets resembling particles. This duality provides the experimental foundation of QUANTUM MECHANICS (see ELECTRON DIFFRACTION) and is an instance of the COMPLEMENTARITY PRINCIPLE.
   The QUANTITY that undulates in 'matter waves' is the probability of finding a particle (see WAVE FUNCTION), so that their physical nature is completely different from other wave motions (e.g. light or sound), although their mathematical form

is similar. Likewise, PHOTONS, or 'particles' of light, have a REST MASS of zero, and so differ physically from particles of matter.   M.V.B.

weak interaction. The force which causes the unstable ELEMENTARY PARTICLES (e.g. NEUTRONS) to decay. PARITY is not conserved during weak interactions, which are about a million million times weaker than the STRONG INTERACTIONS that bind NUCLEONS together.   M.V.B.

Weathermen. A NIHILIST faction of the American radical (see RADICALISM) fringe group, SDS (Students for a Democratic Society), devoted to the spreading of its political ideas by bomb explosions, apparently in the belief that the creation of chaos would automatically be followed by a new Brotherhood of Man. In 1969-70 over 4,330 bomb incidents took place in the U.S.A. In July 1970, 12 members of the Weathermen were indicted on charges of conspiracy to commit bombing. Those arrested were eventually freed in 1974 on a motion by the U.S. Government, the Supreme Court having precluded the use of wire-tap evidence on which the Federal prosecutor based much of his case. D.C.W.

Weaver, Harriet Shaw (British patron of the arts, 1876–1961), see under EGOIST, THE.

Webb, Beatrice (British sociologist and socialist, 1857–1943), see under FABIANISM.

Webb, Philip (British architect, 1831–1915), see under ARTS AND CRAFTS MOVEMENT.

Webb, Sidney (British sociologist and socialist, 1858-1947), see under FABIANISM.

Weber, Carl Maria Friedrich Ernst von (German composer, 1786–1826), see under ROMANTICISM.

Weber, Max (German sociologist, 1864–1920), see under ALIENATION; BUREAUCRACY; CHARISMA; CLASS; COMPARATIVE METHOD; ETHNOMETHODOLOGY; IDEAL TYPES; KNOWLEDGE, SOCIOLOGY OF; ORGANIZATION THEORY; POLITICAL SOCIOLOGY; PROTESTANT ETHIC; RELIGION, SOCIOLOGY OF; SITUATIONAL ANALYSIS; SOCIAL ACTION; SOCIAL STRATIFICATION; SOCIOLOGY; STATUS; VALUE-FREEDOM; VERSTEHEN.

Webern, Anton von (Austrian composer, 1883–1945), see under SERIAL MUSIC.

Wechsler, David (U.S. psychologist, b. 1896), see under MENTAL TESTING.

Wegener, Alfred (German meteorologist, 1880–1931), see under CONTINENTAL DRIFT.

Weierstrass, Karl (German mathematician, 1815–97), see under ANALYSIS.

Weigel, Helene (Austrian-German actress, 1900–1971), see under BERLINER ENSEMBLE.

weightlessness. The state experienced by an astronaut in a spacecraft whose ROCKETS are not firing, or during 'free fall' from an aircraft before a parachute opens. The force of GRAVITATION continues to act in these cases, so that the 'weight' is unaltered and the term 'weightlessness' is misleading. All the peculiar 'floating' effects arise from the absence of the usual *upward* force produced by contact with the ATOMS in the solid ground which opposes gravity and prevents us from falling further towards the centre of the earth.   M.V.B.

weights and weighting, see under INDEX NUMBER; MEAN.

Weill, Kurt (German-U.S. composer, 1900-1950), see under LEHRSTÜCK; MUSIC THEATRE; NEUE SACHLICHKEIT.

Weimar Republic. The first German parliamentary democratic republic established on the abdication of Kaiser Wilhelm II on 9 November 1918, the constitution of which (promulgated 11 August 1919) was drawn up at Weimar, the Thuringian city associated with the memory of Goethe. Burdened by the resentments of the supporters of monarchism and by all the other resentments directed from the RIGHT against the terms of the Treaty of Versailles, challenged by a series of unsuccessful revolutionary outbursts on the LEFT, and under great external pressure from France, the Republic never captured the loyalties of a sufficient proportion of the German people. Its parliamentary government collapsed in 1930, after the onset of the world economic crisis, to be followed by a series of minority governments, acting under the reserve powers of the Presidency, until on 30 January 1933 Adolf Hitler, leader of the NAZI party, was established as Chancellor. The record of the Weimar Republic was taken by many as fundamental evidence of the German lack of capacity for DEMOCRACY or a democratic tradition, a view now increasingly difficult to maintain. In contrast to its political vicissitudes, the period of the Weimar Republic was marked by a remarkable flowering of the experimental attitude in the arts, a view which has been confirmed in retrospect.

D.C.W.

Bibl: E. Eyck, tr. H. P. Hanson and R. G. L. Waite, *A History of the Weimar Republic* (2 vols., N.Y., 1967); P. Gay, *Weimar Culture* (N.Y., 1968; London, 1969); W. Laqueur, *Weimar* (London, 1974; N.Y., 1975).

Weismann, August (German biologist, 1834–1914), see under GERM PLASM; SOMA.

Weiss, Peter (German-born Swedish novelist, dramatist, painter, and film producer, *b*. 1916), see under VOLKSBÜHNE.

Weizmann, Chaim (biochemist, Zionist leader, and Israeli president, 1874–1952), see under ZIONISM.

Weldon, Walter Frank Raphael (British zoologist, 1860–1906), see under BIOMETRY.

welfare; welfare economics.
(1) The word 'welfare' in *welfare legislation* or the *welfare state* refers generally to government support for the poor, and particularly to the free or subsidized supply of certain goods or services, e.g. health and education.
(2) The word has a very different meaning in the theory of welfare economics, which investigates the conditions under which SOCIAL WELFARE functions can be maximized, subject to the economic constraints of scarce resources; increasing notice is· also being taken of political or administrative constraints.

The maximand mostly used, deriving from Bentham, is the aggregate UTILITY of everyone for all of the future, where more utility for an individual means a preferred state of affairs. In the absence of policy constraints, which may give rise to unsolved problems, NECESSARY CONDITIONS but not sufficient conditions, concerning the proper production and exchange of goods, can be derived without weighting individual utilities. If these conditions, typified by the rule that production must be such that *marginal cost* (see MARGINAL COSTING; MARGINAL PRINCIPLE) equals price, and known as the PARETO-OPTIMUM conditions, are not all fulfilled, then it must be possible to increase someone's utility without diminishing that of anyone else; but fulfilling the conditions does not imply that no one loses, merely that the gainers could if required more than compensate the losers. Any taut categorical statement requires individual weights. Few believe in any objective basis for such weights, although they are implicit in many decisions of any governing body. In the absence of individual weights, *applied welfare economics* can at best arrive at loose, though valuable, statements such as 'The gains resulting from this policy would, in money terms, probably exceed the losses, and those likely to lose are few, or would lose little, or may be thought unworthy'. Welfare economics as described above necessarily embraces all policy-oriented economics except in so far as social ends can be expressed in more objective forms, e.g. more employment – but even then the question arises as to whether such ends are not really means. It is thus a very large part of ECONOMICS.

I.M.D.L.

Bibl: I. M. D. Little, *A Critique of Welfare Economics* (Oxford, 2nd ed., 1957); A. K. Sen, *Collective Choice and Social Welfare* (San Francisco, 1970).

welfare state. A political system assuming State responsibility for the protection and promotion of the social security and welfare of its citizens by universal medical care, insurance against sickness and unemployment, old age pensions, family allowances, public housing, etc., on a 'cradle to grave' basis. Social insurance was introduced in Germany in the 1880s and in Britain before 1914, but a comprehensive scheme (and the term 'welfare state') was first adopted by the British Labour Government of 1945–50. Similar provision is made by the State in many other countries, e.g. in Western Europe, Scandinavia, New Zealand. Critics of the welfare state assert that its beneficiaries become less industrious and self-reliant, and that the element of personal choice is so restricted and of State control so enhanced as to create a modern version of serfdom. D.C.W.

Bibl: R. M. Titmuss, *Essays on 'The Welfare State'* (London, 1958); F. A. von Hayek, *The Constitution of Liberty* (London and Chicago, 1960).

Wellesz, Egon (Austrian-British composer and musicologist, 1885–1974), see under MUSICOLOGY.

Wells, Herbert George (British novelist and miscellaneous writer, 1866–1946), see under FABIANISM; NEW AGE; SCIENCE FICTION; WELLSIAN.

Wellsian. Characteristic or reminiscent of the writings of H.G. Wells (1866–1946). The label is applied more to his numerous works of SCIENCE FICTION than to the comedies of, particularly, the shabby-genteel world (e.g. *Kipps, Tono-Bungay, The History of Mr Polly*) which are likely to prove his most enduring work.

O.S.

Weltanschauung (German for *world-outlook*). General conception of the nature of the world, particularly as containing or implying a system of value-principles. Any total philosophical system may be so styled which derives practical consequences from its theoretical component. It is common for important but comparatively local scientific discoveries or conjectures to be generalized into total systems of this kind, for example, those of Newton, Darwin, Marx, and Freud.

A.Q.

Weltschmerz. German word ('world-pain') for a feeling of the overwhelming oppressiveness of existence that may colour an individual's entire WELT-ANSCHAUUNG. W.Z.

Werfel, Franz (Austrian poet, novelist, and dramatist, 1890–1945), see under EXPRESSIONISM.

Werkbund. The *Deutscher Werkbund* was founded in 1907 by the architect and then Superintendent of the Prussian Board of Trade for Schools of Arts and Crafts, Hermann Muthesius, who had been influenced by William Morris and the ARTS AND CRAFTS MOVEMENT. The *Werkbund* attempted to harness the artist to machine production in order to ensure a place for Germany in the growing industrial export market. Its stated aim was to achieve quality through 'not only excellent durable work and the use of flawless, genuine materials, but also the attainment of an organic whole rendered functional, noble and, if you will, artistic by such means'. The idea had considerable diffusion: an Austrian *Werkbund* was started in 1910, a Swiss in 1913; the Design and Industries Association was founded in England in 1915 and a similar Swedish institution by 1917. An important *Werkbund* Exhibition was held at Cologne in 1914 at which Walter Gropius and Adolf Meyer designed a model factory. In 1919 Gropius went to head the BAUHAUS, which continued the ideals shaped by Muthesius. M.BR.

Bibl: N. Pevsner, *Pioneers of Modern Design* (London and N.Y., rev. ed., 1960).

Wertfreiheit, see VALUE-FREEDOM.

Wertheimer, Max (German psychologist, 1886–1943), see under GESTALT.

Wesker, Arnold (British dramatist, *b.* 1932), see under CENTRE 42; ROYAL COURT THEATRE.

Wesley, John (British evangelist, 1709–91), see under METHODISM.

western. A perennially popular genre in the American cinema since 1903, when *The Great Train Robbery* charted its main ingredients: the masked raiders, the hold-up, the chase, the gunfight. Its most frequently recurring theme is reflected in the equally perennial childhood game of cowboys and Indians. At its best, the western has an epic sweep and excitement matched by no other genre, and its greatest practitioner, John Ford, painted through his films an astonishingly detailed canvas portraying America's pioneer past. In the 1960s the genre suffered a surprising transplant to Italy, resulting in a sudden surge of 'spaghetti westerns'. See also HORSE OPERA.

T.C.C.M.

Bibl: P. French, *Westerns* (London, 1973).

Westminster, Statute of, see under COMMONWEALTH.

WEU (Western European Union). A now largely defunct organization set up (5 May 1955) on a British proposal to enable the rearmament of West Germany to take place inside an international organization which could control and supervise it, after the French National Assembly had rejected EDC. The Union revived the organization established by the BRUSSELS TREATY of 1948, with Italian and West German membership, bound West Germany not to manufacture nuclear, biological, or chemical weapons (see WAR), pledged Britain to keep a permanent military force on the European mainland, and established a Council of Ministers and an Assembly. In the 1960s it enjoyed a brief period of political importance as the sole organization uniting Britain with the member states of the EEC but suffered an eclipse with the development of the 'Eurogroup' of nations within NATO after 1970.

D.C.W.

Wheare, Sir **Kenneth Clinton** (British political scientist, *b.* 1907), see under AUTOCHTHONY.

Wheatstone, Sir **Charles** (British scientist and inventor, 1802–75), see under STEREOSCOPY.

Wheeler, Sir **Robert Eric Mortimer** (British archaeologist, 1890–1976), see under INDUS CIVILIZATION.

Wheelwright, Philip Ellis (U.S. literary critic, *b.* 1901), see under PLURI-SIGNATION.

Whig interpretation of history. Defined by Herbert Butterfield, who coined this somewhat ethnocentric term in 1931, as the tendency of historians to see the past as the story of the conflict between PRO-GRESSIVES and REACTIONARIES, in which the progressives, or Whigs, win and so bring about the modern world. He suggested that this was to overestimate the

likenesses between present and past and to assume, fallaciously, that men always intend the consequences of their actions, whereas no one in the past actually willed the present.

P.B.

Bibl: H. Butterfield, *The Whig Interpretation of History* (London, 1931; N.Y., 1951).

Whistler, James Abbott McNeill (U.S. painter, engraver, and wit, 1834–1903), see under VINGT, LES.

white noise, see under NOISE.

White Paper on Education. A White Paper published by the British Government in December 1972 (*Education: a Framework for Expansion*) which gave, for the first time, a comprehensive view of the development of the whole educational system, from nursery school to university, during the 1970s. Among its most important proposals were: availability of free nursery education for children under 5; a radical reform of the training of teachers following the James Committee's Report (*Teacher Education and Training*, 1972); and a rapid expansion of the polytechnics and other non-university colleges (together with a considerable expansion of the university sector) to help meet the demand for higher education.

A.L.C.B.

Whitehead, Alfred North (British-U.S. mathematician and philosopher, 1861–1947), see under AXIOMATICS; LOGIC; LOGICISM; ORGANICISM; PARADOX; PROCESS THEOLOGY; REIFICATION; TWO CULTURES.

Whitman, Walt (U.S. poet, 1819–92), see under BEAT.

WHO (World Health Organization). A SPECIALIZED AGENCY of UNO, whose forerunners were the International Office of Public Health set up in Paris in 1909 and the Health Office of the LEAGUE OF NATIONS (1923). Its activities include the encouragement of research, the control of epidemic and endemic diseases (e.g. malaria), and aid to strengthen the national programmes of member states in the field of public health. Its headquarters are in Geneva.

D.C.W.

whole food, see under MACROBIOTICS.

whole-tone scale. A musical scale in which the 12 semitones of the octave are divided into two sets of 6 equal tones, thus producing, e.g., the scale A, B, C sharp, D sharp, F, G, A. It appears a number of times in compositions by Liszt; but it was Debussy who exploited it to the full. Music based on the whole-tone scale gives a curiously nebulous effect, seeming to lack the positive character given by normal tonality (see under ATONAL MUSIC). This is partly because there are only two possible 'scales', each employing 6 of the 12 semitones. The equality of interval precludes the possibility of any other PERMUTATION, nor does any note in the 'scale' give the feeling of being a root or 'tonic'.
A.H.

Whorfian. In LINGUISTICS, characteristic of, or a follower of, the views of Benjamin Lee Whorf (1897–1941), particularly the 'Sapir-Whorf hypothesis' (also propounded by Edward Sapir) that our conceptual categorization of the world is partly determined by the structure of our native language. The strong form of this hypothesis, that our conceptualization is largely or wholly determined in this way, has been rejected by most LINGUISTS.
D.C.
Bibl: B. L. Whorf, ed. J. B. Carroll, *Language, Thought and Reality: Selected Writings* (London and N.Y., 1956).

Whyte, William Hollingsworth (U.S. sociologist, *b.* 1917), see under ORGANIZATION MAN; SOCIAL ETHIC.

Wieman, Henry Nelson (U.S. theologian, *b.* 1884), see under EMPIRICAL THEOLOGY.

Wiene, Robert (German film director, 1881–1938), see under EXPRESSIONISM.

Wiener, Norbert (U.S. mathematician, 1894–1964), see under CYBERNETICS.

Wiener, Oswald (Austrian jazz musician, *b.* 1935), see under WIENER GRUPPE.

Wiener Gruppe (Vienna Group, not to be confused with the VIENNA CIRCLE). Five young writer-performers who collaborated in that city between 1952 and about 1960 in occasional readings, cabaret sketches, and early HAPPENINGS, often in

a spirit akin to that of DADAISM. They were Hans Carl Artmann, writer and linguist, Friedrich Achleitner, originally an architect, the CONCRETE POET Gerhard Ruhm, the JAZZ musician Oswald Wiener, and the short-lived experimental prose writer Konrad Bayer.
J.W.

Wiener Kreis, see VIENNA CIRCLE.

Wiener Werkstätte (Vienna Workshops). A manufacturing association of Austrian craftsmen and designers formed in 1903 by the architect Josef Hoffman and colleagues from the KUNSTGEWERBESCHULE and the Vienna SEZESSION. Notable for its fine modern furniture, jewellery, and cutlery.
J.W.

Wilde, Oscar (Irish-born dramatist and poet, 1854–1900), see under AESTHETICISM; AUTOTELIC WRITING; DECADENCE; SYMBOLISM.

Wilhelm II (German emperor, 1859–1942), see under WEIMAR REPUBLIC.

Wilkins, Maurice Hugh Frederick (British biochemist, *b.* 1916), see under GENETICS.

Wilkinson, Andrew (British educationist), see under ORACY.

Wille, Bruno (German author, 1860–1928), see under VOLKSBÜHNE.

Williams, Tennessee (U.S. dramatist, *b.* 1914), see under OFF-BROADWAY.

Williams, William Carlos (U.S. poet and novelist, 1883–1963), see under BLACK MOUNTAIN; EGOIST, THE; IMAGISM; OBJECTIVISM; POETRY (CHICAGO).

Wilson, Angus (British novelist and critic, *b.* 1913), see under HORIZON.

Wilson, Charles Thomson Rees (Scottish physicist, 1869–1959), see under CLOUD CHAMBER.

Wilson, Colin (British author, *b.* 1931), see under ANGRY YOUNG MAN; OUTSIDER.

Wilson, Edmund (U.S. author, 1895–1972), see under SYMBOLISM.

Wilson, Georges (French theatre director, *b*. 1921) see under THÉÂTRE NATIONAL POPULAIRE.

Wilson, Sir Harold (British statesman, *b*. 1916), see under CONSENSUS POLITICS.

Wilson, Robert Woodrow (U.S. astronomer, *b*. 1936), see under COSMIC BACKGROUND RADIATION.

Wilson, Thomas Woodrow (U.S. president, 1856–1919), see under FOURTEEN POINTS; NEW DIPLOMACY.

Wimsatt, William Kurty (U.S. critic and scholar, *b*. 1907), see under AFFECTIVE FALLACY; CONCRETE UNIVERSAL; INTENTIONAL FALLACY; NEW CRITICISM.

Winckelmann, Johann Joachim (German art historian, 1717–68), see under NEO-CLASSICISM.

Wind, Edgar (British art historian, 1900–1971), see under NUMEROLOGICAL CRITICISM.

Winters, Yvor (U.S. poet and critic, 1900–1968), see under EXPRESSIVE FORM, FALLACY OF; NEW CRITICISM.

wish-fulfilment. FREUDIAN term for seemingly fortuitous actions, mispercep-tions, fantasies, and dreams that represent fulfilments of a conscious or UNCON-SCIOUS wish. Freud claimed that such wish-fulfilment constituted the essence of dreams.   I.M.L.H.

wishful thinking. A type of thinking, akin to fantasy and hallucination, that is so dominated by some goal or wish that the relevant realities are ignored, contra-dicted, or distorted. 'It is especially preval-ent in young children, in certain abnormal conditions (e.g. AUTISM), and in people gripped by strong prejudice.   I.M.L.H.

witchcraft. In ANTHROPOLOGY, a term usually restricted to mean causing harm to other people and their possessions by the involuntary exercise of extraordinary, mystical powers, and distinguished from *sorcery*, which is the intentional practice of rites for this purpose. Unlike sorcery, witchcraft can be known only after its alleged occurrence and by its alleged

results. What anthropologists study, therefore, is *accusations* of witchcraft. These accusations are often closely examined in relation to the structure of the society (e.g. to see whether there is a tendency for particular classes of person to be accused, such as women married into patrilineally constituted domestic groups); and ideas of witchcraft are studied in relation to the total system of ideas about moral responsibility, right conduct, and causation.   M.F.
    Bibl: M. Douglas (ed.), *Witchcraft Con-fessions and Accusations* (London and N.Y., 1970); L. Mair, *Witchcraft* (London and N.Y., 1969).

Wittfogel, Karl (German-U.S. historian, *b*. 1896), see under HYDRAULIC CIVILI-ZATION.

Wittgenstein, Ludwig (Austrian philo-sopher, 1889–1951), see under ANALYTIC PHILOSOPHY; BEHAVIOURISM; CRITER-ION; LIBERTARIANISM; LINGUISTIC PHILOSOPHY; LOGICAL ATOMISM.

'Wobblies', the (American Industrial Workers of the World), see under SYN-DICALISM.

Wolfe, Tom (U.S. journalist and author, *b*. 1931), see under RADICAL CHIC.

Wollaston, William Hyde (British chemist, 1766–1828), see under POWDER METAL-LURGY.

women's liberation, see under FEMINISM.

Wood, James (British psychologist), see under SYNAESTHESIS.

Woodger, Joseph Henry (British biologist, *b*. 1894), see under VITALISM.

Woodworth, Robert Sessions (U.S. psychologist, 1869–1962), see under SCHOOLS OF PSYCHOLOGY.

Woolf, Leonard (British historian, critic, and publisher, 1880–1969), see under BLOOMSBURY GROUP.

Woolf, Virginia (British novelist and cri-tic, 1882–1941), see under BLOOMSBURY GROUP; CRITERION, THE; STREAM OF CONSCIOUSNESS.

word. In COMPUTING, the unit of information which is dealt with at one time. Its size (known as the word-length) varies with the COMPUTER, common values being 12, 16, 24, 32, 40, 48, and 64 BITS.   C.S.

word class. In LINGUISTICS, a class of words which are similar in their formal behaviour (e.g. noun, adjective). Such CLASSIFICATIONS are made to facilitate the economic statement of grammatical rules, and many different detailed systems have been proposed, the most familiar being the system of *parts of speech*, which uses notional as well as formal criteria (see FORM). Various general classifications have also been used, e.g. the dichotomy between *form* (or *function*, or *grammatical*) *words*, whose primary role is to indicate grammatical relationships, and *content* (or *lexical*) *words*, whose primary role is to provide referential meaning (see REFERENCE); or the distinction between *open classes* of words (i.e. classes whose membership is capable of indefinite extension, e.g. nouns) and *closed classes* (or *systems*) of words (classes containing a small, fixed number of words, e.g. conjunctions). A classification of linguistic forms not restricted to the notion of words is a *form class*.   D.C.

Wordsworth, William (British poet, 1770–1850), see under PANTHEISM.

Work Projects Administration, see WPA.

work study. A set of MANAGEMENT TECHNIQUES, covering *method study* and *work measurement*, which are used to ensure efficient employment of people and other resources in carrying out specific tasks. Method study involves the systematic examination of ways of doing work and making improvements. Work measurement establishes the time needed for a qualified worker to carry out a specified job to a defined standard of performance. The older phrase *time and motion study* is seldom used professionally.   R.I.T.
Bibl: International Labour Office, Geneva, *Introduction to Work Study* (Geneva, rev. ed., 1969).

work to rule. A form of strike without withdrawal of labour, in which OUTPUT is reduced by the workers taking the time needed to comply to the fullest extent with requirements of working rules drawn up by management – for example, the rule that a driver shall satisfy himself that his vehicle is in serviceable condition before he takes it out. Those working to rule are able to place pressure on management, and intensify it at will without losing the pay due for hours worked. The employer has no remedy short of locking the workers out.   E.H.P.B.

working store, see under STORE.

World Bank, see under BRETTON WOODS.

World Peace Council, see under FRONT ORGANIZATION.

Worpswede. North German village near Bremen, centre of an artists' colony (*c.* 1890–1914) whose outstanding figure was the short-lived Paula Modersohn-Becker (*d.* 1907), a forerunner of EXPRESSIONISM. Other members included Fritz Mackensen, Otto Modersohn, Heinrich Vogeler, and Hans am Ende. An account of the colony was given by Rilke in his *Worpswede* (1902).   J.W.

WPA (Work Projects Administration; later Work Progress Administration). A NEW DEAL organization, set up by President Roosevelt in 1935, with an initial appropriation of $4,880 million, to counter some of the effects of the post-1929 DEPRESSION. WPA, which included the Federal Arts, Theater, and Writers Projects (and, until 1939, the National Youth Administration), was killed by Congress long before its official death in 1943. *The Federal Arts Project* was mainly concerned with the rebuilding, redesigning, and mural decoration of public offices. *The Federal Theater Project* was the most remarkable in its results, since it implemented its intention to give dramatists and actors a livelihood without inhibiting their creative freedom. The guiding spirit and director was Hallie Flanagan, who inaugurated an experimental LIVING NEWSPAPER (which was edited by Arthur Arent, and from which emerged Joseph Losey and others), put on DOCUMENTARY and original plays, and staged important revivals. The Theater Project was effectually shut down in 1939, soon after Christopher Marlowe, author

WRIGHT

of one of these revived plays, had been indicted as a COMMUNIST. The *Federal Writers Project* was run by Henry G. Alsberg. Its most notable achievement was the production of the American Guide Series, a state-by-state portrait of the American people (which, in the main, they resented). M.S.-S.

Bibl: H. F. Flanagan, *Arena* (N.Y., 1940); E. M. Gagey, *Revolution in American Drama* (N.Y., 1947).

Wright, Frank Lloyd (U.S. architect, 1869–1959), see under CANTILEVER; CHICAGO SCHOOL; OPEN PLAN; ORGANIC; ROMANTICISM.

X

X chromosomes, see under SEX CHROMO-SOMES.

X-ray diffraction. The DIFFRACTION of X-RAYS by the ATOMS in a crystal LATTICE, which occurs because the wavelength of the X-rays is comparable with the interatomic spacing. X-ray diffraction is a principal tool in CRYSTALLOGRAPHY and BIOCHEMISTRY, where it has made possible the structural analysis of DNA (see NUCLEIC ACID) and other MACRO-MOLECULES associated with life.   M.V.B.

X-rays. Electromagnetic RADIATION (discovered by Röntgen in 1895) whose wavelength is about 1,000 times smaller than that of visible light, and which is emitted during transitions of the innermost ELECTRONS in an ATOM between low-lying ENERGY LEVELS. X-rays are produced by bombarding a metal target with fast electrons from an ELECTRON GUN. The medical usefulness of X-rays in forming shadow images of bones arises because the absorption of X-rays in a material increases rapidly with its density and ATOMIC NUMBER, and because X-rays can form an image on an ordinary photographic plate. See also X-RAY DIFFRAC-TION.   M.V.B.

Xenakis, Iannis (Greek-French composer, *b.* 1922), see under COMPUTER MUSIC; CONCRETE MUSIC.

xenophobia. The condition of disliking individuals or groups thought of as foreign. The 'groups' may range in size from an entire continent (as with anti-American or anti-European feeling) to a neighbouring family of immigrants (or even of migrants from another part of the country if regarded as intrusive); and the dislike can range in intensity from a normally controlled awareness of preferences to an abnormal state of pathological fear and ANXIETY. It commonly takes an ethnic form (see RACE; ANTISEMITISM), and in its most extreme and widespread forms of expression may reflect the paranoid, psychotic state (see PARANOIA; PSYCHOSIS) of those in power, as it did with Hitler and Stalin.   M.BE.

xerography. A photographic copying process for documents and line drawings with a high degree of contrast. An image of the original document is focused onto a type of photoelectric surface which converts light into electric charge. This ELECTRO-STATIC image attracts charged ink powder, which is in turn attracted to charged paper; here it forms a visible image – the copy – which is permanently fixed by heating.   M.V.B.

Xisto, Pedro (Brazilian poet), see under CONCRETE POETRY.

Y

Y chromosomes, see under SEX CHROMO-
SOMES.

Yagoda, Genrikh Grigorevich (Soviet
police chief, 1891–1938), see under MOS-
COW TRIALS.

Yalta. A town in the Crimea, the scene
(4–11 February 1945) of the second war-
time SUMMIT conference between Churchill, Roosevelt, and Stalin. Even more
than at TEHERAN the conference was
marked by President Roosevelt's determination to subordinate every other consideration to winning Soviet good will and,
a new development, to securing early
Soviet participation in the war against
Japan. Britain, much more concerned
than the U.S.A. with the post-war settlement in Europe, secured a postponement
(in practice, abandonment) of plans to
dismember Germany, and a vote for
France in the occupation and control of
Germany. On all other issues, notably the
post-war frontiers of Poland, the Soviet
view was accepted. In the 1950s, Yalta
became a point of attack for American
RIGHT-wing critics of Roosevelt, who
accused him of betraying America's long-
term interests to the enemy of American
democracy.   D.C.W.
Bibl: H. Feis, *Churchill, Roosevelt, Stalin* (London and Princeton, 1957); E. L.
Woodward, *British Foreign Policy in the
Second World War,* vol. 2 (London,
1973).

yang, see under MACROBIOTICS.

Yao Wen-yuan (Chinese politician,
b. 1924), see under CULTURAL REVOLU-
TION.

Yeats, William Butler (Irish poet and
dramatist, 1865–1939), see under ABBEY
THEATRE; CRITERION, THE; INTELLEC-
TUALS; MYTHOPOEIA; SYMBOLISM.

Yezhovshchina ('the Yezhov time'). The
period of the most intense terror in Russia
under Stalin, namely ·from September
1936 to December 1938, when Nikolai
Yezhov (1894–1939) was People's Com-
missar for Internal Affairs, i.e. head of the
SECRET POLICE. It included the second
and third great MOSCOW TRIALS, and the
trial and execution of Marshal
Tukhachevsky and other leading officers
in June 1937. Soviet estimates published
later imply that during this period at least
seven million people were arrested, 90%
of whom – including half the Party membership, three-quarters of the Central
Committee, about half of the corps of
officers, and several hundred writers,
artists, and scientists – perished in FORCED
LABOUR camps or by execution. After
Yezhov's dismissal, he was himself shot.
He was succeeded by Lavrenty Beria. R.C.
Bibl: R. Conquest, *The Great Terror*
(London and N.Y., 1968).

yin, see under MACROBIOTICS.

Yippies. The Youth International Party, a
fringe organization of radical (see
RADICALISM) educated youth in the
U.S.A., distinguished mainly by their
rejection of American society and their
addiction to free love and DRUGS. The
Yippies enjoyed a brief period of notoriety during the public disorders which
accompanied the Democratic convention
of June 1968, in which they were one of
the more obvious targets of the Chicago
police force.   D.C.W.

yoga. The spiritual discipline of the higher
forms of HINDUISM, including a carefully
planned course of fasting with physical
and mental exercises in order to concentrate the mind. In its narrower sense the
term refers to a Hindu movement which
produced the *Yoga Sutras,* scriptures
describing union (Sanskrit *yoga*) with the
supreme Spirit after such self-sacrifice. As
used in the West, the phrase may refer
more loosely to exercises for mental and
physical fitness, adapted from Indian
sources.   D.L.E.

Young, Brigham (U.S. Mormon leader, 1801–77), see under MORMONS.

Young, Lester Willis (U.S. jazz musician, 1909–59), see under HOT.

Young, Michael (British sociologist, *b.* 1915), see under MERITOCRACY.

youth culture. A loosely used label, often mistakenly employed as a synonym for *counter-culture* or *alternative society* (for both of which see UNDERGROUND). In most advanced industrial societies, and more frequently from a diffuse youthful energy than from conscious hostility to accepted adult values, adolescent and young adult communities have developed their own transient NORMS and values, their LIFE STYLE symbolized by specific modes of dress, language, music, and consumption patterns. Such characteristics are but loosely correlated, not all young people subscribe to the culture named after them, and the age limits of its adherents have never been adequately defined.

P.S.L.

Z

Zabel, Morton Dauwen (U.S. editor, 1901–64), see under POETRY (CHICAGO).

Zaghlul, Said (Egyptian nationalist, 1857–1927), see under WAFD.

Zaichnevsky, Peter (Russian revolutionary, 1842–96), see under NIHILISM.

Zak, Eugène (Polish painter, 1884–1926), see under ÉCOLE DE PARIS.

Zamenhov, Ludwig Lazarus (Polish linguist, 1859–1917), see under ESPERANTO.

Zamyatin, Yevgeny Ivanovich (Russian novelist and dramatist, 1884–1937), see under SERAPION BROTHERS.

Zaum. The Russian word for trans-sense (transrational) language – the arbitrary combination of sounds, or the play with the morphological components of a familiar word practised by Russian FUTURIST poets, notably Kruchenykh and Khlebnikov. Zaum stemmed from the Futurists' belief that the word, as the material of poetry, should be emancipated from its 'traditional subservience to meaning' and become a self-sufficient entity, interesting for its outward form, i.e. its graphic and phonic characteristics. It led to the creation of poetic neologisms, or completely non-referential words.　　　　　M.E.

Zavattini, Cesare (Italian filmscript-writer, b. 1902), see under NEO-REALISM.

Zeitgeist German word meaning literally 'the Spirit of the Time (or Age)'. It is associated with attempts to epitomize the mode of thought or feeling deemed fundamentally characteristic of a particular period, e.g. to interpret the 19th century as an age of 'heroic materialism' (Kenneth Clark). The term was first regularly employed by the German Romantics (see ROMANTICISM). Tempted always to reduce the past to essences, they often treated the Zeitgeist less as a conceptual instrument than as a grandiose historical character in

its own right. Most historians handle the term with caution on the grounds that the characteristics of any historical period are more complex than a formulation of a Zeitgeist can suggest. See also CULTURAL HISTORY.　　　　　M.D.B.

Bibl: G. W. F. Hegel, tr. H. B. Nisbet, *Lectures on the Philosophy of World History* (Cambridge, 1975).

Zen. The Japanese version of the Ch'an sect of BUDDHISM in China, noted for its simple austerity, its MYSTICISM leading to personal tranquillity, and its encouragement of EDUCATION and art. Some of its scriptures and paintings have become widely known and admired in the West; and Aldous Huxley and others in California led something of a cult of Zen, which in the 1960s began appealing to students as a way of having religious experience without DOGMAS or religious INSTITUTIONS. The trouble is, however, that the reality experienced after ecstasy (*satori*) is hard to describe, and the approach to it hard to reconcile with reason. Many of the statements encouraged by the masters of Zen seem deliberately nonsensical – e.g. the idea of a single hand clapping – although they are intended to open the doors of PERCEPTION into a world of wonder.　　D.L.E.

Bibl: A. Watts, *The Way of Zen* (London and N.Y., 1957).

Zengakuren ('Mainstream Faction'). A LEFT-wing organization of Japanese university students (the All-Japan Federation of Student Self-Government Associations) formed in 1948, and claiming to represent 300,000 students, 40% of them in the Tokyo area. It was divided into four factions – the *Chikaku* (perhaps best translated as 'hard-core'), the *Hantei* (anti-imperialist), the *Kakamura* (revolutionary MARXIST) and the COMMUNIST Party faction – and its extremely violent methods culminated in the six-month occupation of Tokyo University, broken finally by quasi-military police action in January 1969. Since that date the extremists have tended to organize their activities through

small splinter groups, and the main student organization has been comparatively quiescent.   D.C.W.
   Bibl: H. D. Smith, *Japan's First Student Radicals* (Cambridge, Mass., 1972).

Zermelo, Ernst Friedrich Ferdinand (German mathematician, 1871–1953), see under AXIOM OF CHOICE.

Zero, Gruppe, see under KINETIC ART.

zero point energy. The ENERGY of the motion remaining in a body at ABSOLUTE ZERO of temperature. The body is then in its *ground state* (see ENERGY LEVEL), which according to the UNCERTAINTY PRINCIPLE of QUANTUM MECHANICS cannot correspond to the complete absence of motion.
                                    M.V.B.

zero-sum, see under GAMES, THEORY OF.

Zhdanov, Andrei A. (Soviet politician, 1896–1948), see under COMINFORM; POPULAR FRONT; SOCIALIST REALISM; ZHDANOVSHCHINA.

Zhdanovshchina ('the Zhdanov time'). The period 1946 8, in which heavy Party pressure was brought to bear in the Soviet cultural field, under the aegis of Andrei Zhdanov, Secretary of the Central Committee in charge of IDEOLOGY. It was marked by attacks on many leading Soviet writers, notably Mikhail Zoshchenko, Anna Akhmatova, and Boris Pasternak.
                                    R.C.
   Bibl: H. Swayze, *Political Control of Literature in the USSR, 1946-1959* (Cambridge, Mass, 1962).

Ziegler, Adolf (German painter, *b.* 1892), see under MAGIC REALISM.

Zinoviev, Gregory Evseyevich (Russian revolutionary, 1883–1936), see under COMINTERN; MOSCOW TRIALS.

Zionism. The Jewish national movement to re-establish the Jewish nation in Palestine. Zionism was a secularist and NATIONALISTIC transformation of an aspiration basic to orthodox JUDAISM, in reaction to the Czarist persecution of Russian and Polish Jewry and to other outbursts of ANTISEMITISM, e.g. during the DREYFUS CASE. Theodor Herzl, the

founder of modern Zionism (who reported the Dreyfus trials for an Austrian paper), argued in his book, *Der Judenstaat*, that the only alternative to continued persecution was to found a Jewish state, and in 1897 he called the first World Zionist Congress in Basle. It was Chaim Weizmann (1874–1952) who insisted that a Jewish nation could only be re-created in Palestine, a course which became practicable with the BALFOUR DECLARATION of 1917. Since the foundation of the state of Israel in more or less permanent conflict with her Arab neighbours, Zionism has come to refer mainly (1) to the organized sympathies of non-Israeli Jews in the West for Israel; (2) to efforts by Soviet Jewry to emigrate to Israel.   A.L.C.B.
   Bibl: I. Cohen, *The Zionist Movement* (London, 1912; rev. ed., N.Y., 1946); W. Laqueur, *History of Zionism* (London, 1972).

Zola, Émile (French novelist, 1840–1902), see under DOCUMENTARY; DREYFUS CASE; FREIE BÜHNE; NATURALISM; ROMAN-FLEUVE; SLICE OF LIFE.

zoning. In Britain, an expedient whereby zones or catchment areas are allocated to schools in order to prevent overcrowding in some schools and under-use of others. Zoning, which may occur in both urban and rural areas, is regarded as a temporary measure which should not remain in force longer than is necessary or affect children already in the schools. See also BUSSING; NEIGHBOURHOOD SCHOOLS.   W.A.C.S.

zoogeography. The branch of BIOGEOGRAPHY which studies the geographical distribution of animals. In any region this is determined by the nature of the vegetation on which the herbivorous animals (the vast majority) depend. Thus forest-inhabiting animals only occur after trees have grown up. On the world scale, climate and EVOLUTION are important. Many species are *stenothermous*, i.e. they exist only over a narrow range of temperature. Isolated areas, e.g. Australia, have seen the evolution and establishment of SPECIES (e.g. kangaroos and other large marsupials) which have been protected from competition with the 'higher' forms dominant elsewhere.   K.M.

ZOOLOGY

Bibl: P. J. Darlington, *Zoogeography* (N.Y., 1957).

zoology. The science that deals with the classification (see BIOSYSTEMATICS), structure, and functions of animals, including by convention those chlorophyll-containing PROTOZOA which could equally well be classified as plants. The old-fashioned distinction between vertebrates and invertebrates is not taxonomically useful and makes no kind of sense in terms of PHYLOGENY. There is a tendency nowadays therefore to distinguish two main lines of descent among animals:

(1) a *chordate* line of descent including the chordates themselves (animals distinguished by the possession at some stage of their life history of a notochord, and a central NERVOUS SYSTEM in the form of a median dorsal hollow nerve tube), and certain other PHYLA related to the chordates by fundamental similarities of early development; these include those phyla of which typical members are sea-urchins, sea-cucumbers, and starfish (echinodermata), together with sea-squirts (tunicata), all forming together the chordate line of descent; and

(2) a miscellany of *non-chordate* phyla including the worms strictly so-called (annelida) and – wrongly so-called – the flatworms (platyhelminthes) and roundworms (nematodes) and one or two other groups of lesser importance. P.M.

zoosemiotics, see under SEMIOTICS.

Zoshchenko, Mikhail Mikhailovich (Russian humorous writer, 1895–1958), see under SERAPION BROTHERS; ZHDANOVSHCHINA.

Zuckmayer, Carl (German dramatist and poet, 1896–1977), see under DEUTSCHES THEATER.

Zukofsky, Louis (U.S. poet, *b*. 1904), see under OBJECTIVISM.

zygote. The single CELL that is the product of the fusion between an egg cell and a spermatozoon from which all vertebrate development proceeds. As a result of this fusion, a zygote contains the normal double complement (DIPLOID number) of CHROMOSOMES. P.M.

KING ALFRED'S COLLEGE LIBRARY
684